Special Edition

Using

Using

MICROSOFT®

Office 97

Professional, Best Seller Edition

Special Edition

Using

Using

MICROSOFT®

Office 97

Professional, Best Seller Edition

Jim Boyce, et al.

Special Edition Using Microsoft Office 97 Professional, Best Sellers Edition

Library of Congress Catalog No.: 97-68761

ISBN: 0-7897-1396-9

99   7

Interpretation of the printing code: the rightmost double-digit number is the year of the book's printing; the rightmost single-digit number, the number of the book's printing. For example, a printing code of 97-1 shows that the first printing of the book occurred in 1997.

Screen reproductions in this book were created using Collage Plus from Inner Media, Inc., Hollis, NH.

Contents at a Glance

Table of Contents

II | Word: Beyond the Basics

3 Word Quick Start Guide   45

III | Excel: Beyond the Basics

12 Excel Quick Start Guide 237

13 Workbooks, Worksheets, and Ranges 251

IV | PowerPoint: Beyond the Basics

VII | Internet and Intranet Integration

45 Integrating with the Internet   885

VIII | Using Office 97 Tools

52 Using Drawing Features   1035

53 Charts and Equations   1059

Appendixes

Credits

PRESIDENT
Roland Elgey

SENIOR VICE PRESIDENT/PUBLISHING
Don Fowley

PUBLISHER
Joseph B. Wikert

PUBLISHING DIRECTOR
Karen Reinisch

MANAGER OF PUBLISHING OPERATIONS
Linda H. Buehler

GENERAL MANAGER
Joe Muldoon

DIRECTOR OF EDITORIAL SERVICES
Carla Hall

MANAGING EDITOR
Thomas F. Hayes

DIRECTOR OF ACQUISITIONS
Cheryl D. Willoughby

ACQUISITIONS EDITOR
Don Essig

SENIOR PRODUCT DIRECTOR
Lisa D. Wagner

PRODUCT DIRECTORS
Dana S. Coe
Rick Kughen

PRODUCTION EDITOR
Julie A. McNamee

PRODUCT MARKETING MANAGER
Kourtnaye Sturgeon

ASSISTANT PRODUCT MARKETING MANAGER
Gretchen Schlesinger

EDITORS
Lisa M. Gebken
Jean Jameson
Sydney Jones
Jeanne Lemen
Kathy Simpson
Tonya Maddox

TECHNICAL EDITORS
Kyle Bryant
David Garratt
Stan Spink
Verley & Nelson
Brad Lindaas
Ron Ellenbecker, MCSE

MEDIA DEVELOPMENT SPECIALIST
David Garratt

ACQUISITIONS COORDINATOR
Tracy M. Williams

SOFTWARE RELATIONS COORDINATOR
Susan D. Gallagher

EDITORIAL ASSISTANTS
Jeff Chandler
Virginia Stoller

BOOK DESIGNER
Ruth Harvey
Kim Scott

COVER DESIGNER
Sandra Schroeder

PRODUCTION TEAM
Jenny Earhart
Bryan Flores
Nicole Ruessler
Heather Stephenson

INDEXERS
Ginny Bess
Cheryl A. Jackson

Composed in *Century Old Style* and *ITC Franklin Gothic* by Que Corporation.

About the Authors

Jim Boyce, the lead author for *Windows NT Installation and Configuration Handbook*, is a contributing editor and columnist for *WINDOWS* Magazine and a regular contributor to other computer publications. He has been involved with computers since the late seventies and has worked with computers as a user, programmer, and systems manager in a variety of capacities. He has a wide range of experience in the DOS, Windows, and UNIX environments. Jim has authored and co-authored over two dozen books on computers and software.

Scott Fuller is President of IDEAS and a former employee of (EDS) Electronic Data Systems. IDEAS is a nationwide computer solutions firm that consults on a variety of MIS-related issues.

Mr. Fuller has extensive experience in computer systems operation, networking, software engineering, and end-user education. He is the co-author of numerous computer books, including *Learn Timeslips for Windows in a Day, Inside Windows 95, Windows 95 for Network Administrators, Learn CompuServe in a Day, Learn Windows 95 in a Day,* and *Intranet Firewalls.* You can reach Mr. Fuller via e-mail at **ScottFuller@msn.com.**

Read Gilgen is Director of Learning Support Services at the University of Wisconsin, Madison. He holds a Ph.D. in Latin American Literature. His professional interests include support of higher education, especially foreign language education. He has taught and written extensively on DOS, Windows, and WordPerfect since the early 1980s. He is author of Que's *WordPerfect for Windows Hot Tips,* contributing author to Que's *Special Edition Using WordPerfect for Windows,* and a frequent contributor to *WordPerfect for Windows* Magazine.

John Green lives and works in Sydney, Australia. He has 30 years of computing experience, a Chemical Engineering degree, and an MBA and specializes in financial planning and modeling using spreadsheets. He is an MVP on the MS Excel CompuServe forum where his ID is **100236,1562**. He can also be contacted as **jgreen@enternet.com.au** on Internet.

He established his company, Execuplan Consulting, in 1980, which develops computer bases planning applications and carries out PC training. He has lectured extensively on spreadsheets and operating systems both in Australia and overseas.

Joe Habraken is a freelance writer and has served as an author, editor, curriculum designer, and software instructor during his career as a computer technology professional. Joe earned his MA in Communications from American University in Washington, D.C. Most recently he has written the *Complete Idiot's Guide to Access 97* and *The Big Basics Book of the Internet, 2nd Edition.*

Joe Kraynak has been writing and editing successful training manuals and computer books for over ten years. His long list of computer books include *The Complete Idiot's Guide to PCs, The Complete Idiot's Guide to Netscape Communicator, Microsoft Internet Explorer 3 Unleashed,* and *Windows 95 Cheat Sheet.* Joe has a Master's degree in English from Purdue University and a computer degree from the college of hard knocks.

George Lynch is a Microsoft Certified Professional and has written six computer books, among them two *Word For Windows For Dummies Quick Reference Guides*. George, Jesse Cassill and Steve Ryan are partners in RTFM Consulting, Inc., a Microsoft Solution Provider company based in New York City that specializes in application development, training, and documentation.

Keith MacKay is Director of Desktop Application Development for Village Software. Keith holds a B.S. in Brain and Cognitive Science from the Massachusetts Institute of Technology.

Keith has programmed everything from Apples to the Sinclair ZX81 (including both CRAYS and VCRs). Prior to his work at Village Software, Keith served as a computer consultant for organizations including Coopers & Lybrand, MIT, Tufts University, and USC. He also worked for the U.S. Government for several years on a system for Nuclear Test-Ban Treaty Verification.

Keith has often been a featured speaker regarding VBA in both live and online events. He lives with his fiancee in the greater Boston area, and can be reached via e-mail at **keithm@villagesoft.com**.

Village Software (**http//www.villagesoft.com**) provides pre-built and custom solutions to Fortune 1000 companies and small businesses, and wrote all the Spreadsheet Solutions included in Microsoft Office 95 and 97, as well as solutions included in Lotus 1-2-3 version 5, Lotus Smartsuite95 and 97, and Corel PerfectOffice 97.

Kevin Marlowe is a systems analyst with Computer Sciences Corporation at NASA's Langley Research Center in Hampton, Virginia. A graduate of the University of Virginia and Old Dominion University with more than ten years' experience in information systems, his current work focuses on the management of scientific data with Access databases and the application of computing technology to scientific problems. In his spare time, he serves as an officer in the U.S. Navy Reserve and consults on office automation solutions. His interests include user interface design, the use of PCs in the technical community, gardening, and fathering. His wife and favorite computer user, Jill, is a NASA aerospace engineer. They live with their two children, future rocket scientists, in Yorktown, Virginia.

John Purdum is very experienced with Applications and Internet Technology, including: Office 97, Windows 95, Netscape Navigator, Internet Explorer, and Microsoft Exchange. He is skilled in PC setup, software installation, hardware maintenance, HTML programming, and Java. John is currently working toward a Computer Science degree at Butler University.

Patrice-Anne Rutledge is a computer consultant and author based in the San Francisco area. She writes frequently on a variety of topics including technology, business, and travel and is the author or contributing author of 12 computer books on topics such as Microsoft Office and Microsoft FrontPage. As both an independent consultant and member of the IS team for leading international technology firms, Patrice has been involved in many aspects of computing including software development, systems analysis, and technical communications. Patrice discovered computers while pursuing her original career as a technical translator and was quickly hooked. She holds a degree in French Linguistics from the University of California and has been working with Excel for more than seven years.

Liz Tasker currently works as a Senior User Interface Designer at Hyperion Software Corporation, a company that specializes in developing client-server software applications. Her career includes twelve years in technical writing, nine years in software development, and five years in user interface design. She earned a Master of Arts degree in professional writing from Carnegie-Mellon University in 1990, and has received several awards in technical writing, including the Society of Technical Communication's International Award of Excellence in Technical Publication in 1992.

Nancy Warner is a private consultant in the computer and publishing arenas. She has written and contributed to numerous computer books including: *Special Edition Using Microsoft Office 97 Best Seller Edition, Platinum Edition Using Microsoft Office 97, How to Use Access 97, How to Use Outlook 97, How to Use Netscape Communicator, Easy Windows NT Workstation 4.0, 10 Minute Guide to Microsoft Exchange 5.0, Delphi By Example, Special Edition Using SQL Server,* and *Special Edition Using PowerBuilder.* She graduated from Purdue University in Computer Information Systems, worked in computer and publishing positions, and is currently living in Arizona.

We'd Like to Hear From You!

Que Corporation has a long-standing reputation for high-quality books and products. To ensure your continued satisfaction, we also understand the importance of customer service and support.

Tech Support

If you need assistance with the information in this book or with a CD/disk accompanying the book, please access Macmillan Computer Publishing's online Knowledge Base at **http://www.superlibrary.com/general/support**. If you do not find the answer to your questions on our Web site, you may contact Macmillan Technical Support by phone at **317/581-3833** or via e-mail at **support@mcp.com**.

Also be sure to visit Que's Web resource center for all the latest information, enhancements, errata, downloads, and more. It's located at **http://www.quecorp.com/**.

Orders, Catalogs, and Customer Service

To order other Que or Macmillan Computer Publishing books, catalogs, or products, please contact our Customer Service Department at **800/428-5331** or fax us at **800/835-3202** (International Fax: 317/228-4400). Or visit our online bookstore at **http://www.quecorp.com/**.

Comments and Suggestions

We want you to let us know what you like or dislike most about this book or other Que products. Your comments will help us to continue publishing the best books available on computer topics in today's market.

Rick Kughen
Product Director
Que Corporation
201 West 103rd Street, 4B
Indianapolis, Indiana 46290 USA
Fax: 317/581-4663 E-mail: **rKughen@que.mcp.com**

Please be sure to include the book's title and author as well as your name and phone or fax number. We will carefully review your comments and share them with the author. Please note that due to the high volume of mail we receive, we may not be able to reply to every message.

Thank you for choosing Que!

Introduction

by Jim Boyce

Microsoft's Office application suite has for quite some time held a lion's share of the productivity application market. That hold on the market shows no signs of weakening, and you can expect Office to continue to be the most popular application suite for at least the foreseeable future.

Now, having chosen such a popular suite of applications, you no doubt are expecting to get the best possible performance and usefulness from it. Many people use only a fraction of Office's features, and some don't use specific applications in the suite at all. For example, you might spend 90 percent of your time with Word and 10 percent with Excel (or vice-versa) but never touch Access, PowerPoint, or Outlook.

Often, the reason you use only a portion of Office's features is that you never need them. If your job doesn't involve making presentations, for example, you probably have no use for PowerPoint. But sometimes the reason for not taking advantage of some of the more powerful features in Office is less clear-cut. Maybe you just don't have a complete picture of what you can accomplish with the applications in Office 97. That is exactly the focus of *Special Edition Using Office 97 Professional, Best Sellers Edition.* ■

Why You Should Use This Book

It isn't our intention to explain the basics of writing a letter or entering numbers in spreadsheet cells. Instead, *Special Edition Using Office 97 Professional* will show you how to automate tasks, use advanced productivity features, integrate Office and the Internet, and tie together your Office applications and documents to produce better documents in less time. For example, we won't teach you how to type a letter, but we will show you how to merge a contact database in Access with your Word document to create a mass mailing for your entire customer or contact base. In effect, we'll familiarize you with all those advanced productivity features you never knew you had or never had the time to figure out on your own.

Even though this isn't meant to be a beginner's guide to Office, we do offer Quick Start chapters for each application to bring you up to speed quickly. So, if you've never used PowerPoint or Access, for example, the Quick Start chapters will have you creating presentations and building databases in almost no time at all. Once you get your feet wet, you might quickly realize that those applications you never used before are as indispensable as the ones you have used every day.

How This Book Is Organized

Special Edition Using Office 97 Professional contains eleven parts, each dedicated to a specific application in the Office suite or to special features that are common to all Office applications. The following list presents an overview of the contents of *Special Edition Using Office 97*:

Part I, "Introducing Office 97," starts with an overview of Office 97 as an integrated suite and also details the Office 97 features that are common to the individual suite components. Part II, "Word: Beyond the Basics," starts with a Quick Start guide to Word to show you how to navigate in Word and create documents. Then, Chapter 4, "Simplifying and Automating Tasks," will help you begin to automate many of the tasks you now perform manually in Word and will point out to you features that will make creating and working with multiple documents much easier. In the remaining chapters in Part II, you'll learn how to use such features as outlines, templates, and styles. You also will learn how to integrate graphics into your documents, add background textures to documents, create watermarks, and even create your own 3D objects for Word.

Formatting is another important topic covered in Part II. You'll learn to use columns, bullets and numbers, field codes, and items that change dynamically in the document, and even how to create forms. Tables, mail merge, and customization make up the remaining chapters, with macros and Visual Basic for Applications (VBA) rounding out the material

Part III, "Excel: Beyond the Basics," will help you become an Excel expert. After the Quick Start chapter brings you up to speed on navigating in and using Excel, you begin to learn about using multiple worksheets, advanced selection methods, and other topics that simplify the creation of complex spreadsheets. Then, it's on to formulas and functions to begin creating spreadsheets that do much more than simply add columns or rows of numbers.

You also will read in Part III about creating forms in Excel, protecting spreadsheets, and creating dialog boxes for data entry in Excel. Then you'll learn about the many features in Excel that enable it to act much like a database, keeping track of and sorting information in nonlinear ways. You'll find an extensive chapter on PivotTables, one of Excel's most powerful features for analyzing data. Other chapters in Part III cover Excel's other analysis tools in considerable detail. Finally, you'll learn how to automate tasks and integrate Office applications with Excel using macros and VBA.

Part IV, "PowerPoint: Beyond the Basics," will help you begin to create your own appealing presentations, complete with great graphics and dynamic multimedia. After the Quick Start chapter helps you get your feet wet, you'll learn about the features in PowerPoint that help you lay out and create presentations automatically. Next, you'll begin to add advanced features such as animation, transitions, and speaker notes. Part IV also covers integration with other Office applications, teaching you to import data from Word and Excel. Then you'll learn how to take your show on the road to actually make the presentation through hard copy or directly from your PC. Part IV finishes with a look at VBA and how you can put it to work for you in PowerPoint.

Part V, "Access: Beyond the Basics," is where you turn to begin building and using databases and integrating them into your other documents. Part V explains how to set up databases manually and through the wizards supplied with Access. You'll find excellent tips on how to plan and implement a database design in addition to actually creating the database. Because a database is nothing but a collection of data, you need to know how to sort and manage that data Part V places an emphasis on the many ways you can sort, filter, and analyze an Access database.

Forms play a big role in Access, both for data entry and output. So, Part V offers an in-depth look at form creation and reporting. You'll also learn to work with multiple data tables, use the add-on utilities included with Access, repair databases, and create macros. A look at VBA and Access rounds out Part V.

Part VI, "Outlook: Beyond the Basics," provides comprehensive coverage of the integrated e-mail, fax, personal information manager (PIM), and scheduler in Microsoft Office. Outlook is one of the features in Office you'll either love or hate, and learning to love it means understanding its capabilities and faults. Part VI not only will show you how to use Outlook to send and receive e-mail and fax messages, but also how to configure user profiles and add other message services such as CompuServe Mail and Internet Mail to Outlook.

Part VI also examines the many advanced messaging features in Outlook including message filtering and rules, using signatures and autoresponders, working with public folders, using recipient groups, and much more. Part VI also provides an in-depth look at using Outlook to maintain contact lists, manage your personal task list, work with forms, and use journals and notes to keep track of the jobs on which you work.

Part VII, "Internet and Intranet Integration," shows you how to access the Internet from Office applications, publish documents to the Web from Office, and create forms for use on the Internet. Part VII also explains how to take advantage of ActiveX controls in Office 97. You'll learn how to use binders to bring together documents from the different Office applications into a single logical document for management and printing. Part VII also explores the creation of compound documents, which are individual documents that contain data from multiple sources. For example, a Word document that contains a link to an Excel spreadsheet is a compound document. Integrating Access databases into Word, Excel, and PowerPoint rounds out part VII.

Part VIII, "Using Office 97 Tools," expands on the integration theme of *Special Edition Using Office 97 Professional* to cover the application-independent utilities included with Office that let you create content for use in all of the Office applications. You'll learn to use the drawing and image editing features included in Office 97, create 3D text objects, and build dynamic maps into your documents. Part IX also shows you how to make the most of the Microsoft Chart, Equation Editor, and Organization Chart add-ons.

Part IX, "Applying Office 97 in a Network or Workgroup," will help you extend Office 97's capabilities across your local area network (LAN) and workgroup. In addition to learning about sharing resources across the network, you'll also find tips for securing your data. Part X also explains how to collaborate with other users to create compound documents and track revisions as multiple people contribute to a document.

Part IX also includes a look at file compatibility issues and shows you how to move your data between different versions of Office, other applications, and even different hardware platforms.

Part X, "Introduction to Developing Office Applications," rounds out *Special Edition Using Office 97* and further expands on the integration theme to give you an overview of how to create your own custom applications using Office 97 and VBA. You'll learn how to add automation through VBScript. You'll also learn more about VBA and how to create your own program interface with it.

And finally, no book is complete without a few appendixes. The appendixes in *Special Edition Using Office 97 Professional* explore the CD included with this book, and business sites on the Web which lists other sources of information available to you online and through printed media.

Conventions Used in This Book

Special conventions are used in *Special Edition Using Office 97 Professional* to help you get the most from the book and Office itself. The following sections explain these conventions.

Special Typefaces and Representations

Various typefaces in this book identify terms and other special objects. These special typefaces include the following:

Type	Meaning
Italics	New terms or phrases when initially defined; functions and Visual Basic syntax variables
<u>Underline</u>	Menu and dialog box options that appear underlined on-screen, indicating hotkeys
Boldface	Information you type
`Special type`	Information that appears on-screen or in figures; VBA code

You'll find some text in all uppercase. Typically, these are used to indicate Excel objects such as functions and cell references. File names are initial-capped only as they generally appear in Windows 95 and Windows NT.

Key combinations are represented using either a plus or minus sign, depending on the way you should press the keys. If you press two or more keys at the same time, the keys appear together with a plus sign. For example, to bring up the Close Program dialog box in Windows 95, you press Ctrl+Alt+Del. That is, press the Control, Alt, and Delete keys on the keyboard at the same time. Keys that you press in succession are separated by commas. To display the file dialog box in a program, for example, you press Alt,F,O. That is, press and release Alt, press and release F, then press and release O. In most cases, we assume you will be using the mouse to control Windows 95 and Office features.

N O T E Notes such as this one offer additional information about the current topic and serve to supplement the material in the main body of the section.

 T I P Tips suggest alternate methods for accomplishing a task or additional information that will help you get the most out of a feature in Office or Windows 95.

CAUTION

A Caution like this one points out actions that might have undesired consequences. If we suggested you invoke the Fdisk program from a command prompt, for example, you can be sure we'd include a caution that it could wipe out all the data on your hard disk if you didn't know what you were doing.

Scattered throughout the book you'll find references to Internet Web sites that supplement the material discussed in the chapter.

 ON THE WEB

Update for home users:

http://www.microsoft.com/windows95

Other Special Components

Scattered throughout each chapter you'll find cross-references to other sections of the same chapter or to sections in other chapters. These cross-references point you to information elsewhere in the book that is related to or supplements the topic being discussed. The cross-reference contains the name of the section, page number, and chapter number where the information appears.

▶ **See** "Hacking into Secure Government Systems," **p. 237**

You also will find troubleshooting sections scattered throughout the book. These troubleshooting sections, which appear in most chapters, discuss common problems you are likely to encounter and their solutions.

Part I: Introducing Office 97

CHAPTER 1

Overview of Office 97

by Jim Boyce

Microsoft Office 97 is the most popular productivity suite selling today. Part of the popularity of the suite is due to its source: Microsoft. Office 97 ensures its popularity by offering a solid range of applications and features that make it a solid choice for almost any business or individual.

This chapter provides an overview of Office 97. The chapter also offers a brief look at the features that are new in Office 97. ■

Overview of Office 97 applications

Office 97 includes applications for word processing, spreadsheets, databases, presentations, messaging, and contact management.

Office 97's new features

Microsoft has added many features to the Office application suite to provide better ease of use, stronger Internet integration, and greater flexibility in application and customization.

The Office 97 Application Suite

In the early days of personal computing, applications stood alone. You typically bought a word processing program from one company, a spreadsheet program from another, and a database from a third. Little chance existed that the applications' interfaces looked or functioned the same, which made learning to use a new program more difficult, because you had to learn a completely new menu system.

Part of the reason why the applications stood alone was the operating system on which they ran: MS-DOS. Because the original 8086/8088 CPUs were not designed to support multitasking, DOS could run only one program at a time.

The introduction of later processors and the Windows operating environment changed the way we use PCs by introducing the capability to multitask applications, a capability offered prior to that time by UNIX, Macintosh, and other platforms. Today's processors and operating systems offer true multitasking capability, providing an environment in which two or more applications can function at the same time, sharing the CPU and the computer's other resources.

An Integrated Approach

With multitasking came *application suites*, which essentially are stand-alone programs that are designed to look and function in much the same way. Today's application suites, including Microsoft Office, further integrate the applications by using common program code and objects within the different applications. More than 50 percent of Office 97's program code, for example, is shared across all the applications in the suite. Shared code means a quicker development cycle for the suite (shorter time to program updates and enhancements) and a leaner, more efficient set of applications.

This integrated approach also lends itself to a consistent interface, and that is exactly what Office 97 provides across its applications. Although interface components such as toolbars naturally change to some degree from one program to another, many of the toolbars are the same, as is the menu structure. In addition, you customize the toolbars, menus, and keyboard shortcuts by using the same method in each application.

The integration among applications in the Office 97 suite also means that you can easily move information among the various applications. You can use an Access database or your Outlook contact address list to easily create mailing labels in Word, for example. You also can use Visual Basic for Applications (VBA) to create custom programs that integrate the various Office applications to perform various tasks for you.

Although integration is the theme behind Office 97, the applications within the suite can stand alone as individual applications. If you don't need a presentation program or database, for example, you simply don't install PowerPoint or Access; you can continue to use Word, Excel, Outlook, and the other features of Office 97. In addition, each application is different enough from the others that it warrants examination as a separate program. Therefore, the following sections provide an overview of each of the applications in the Office 97 suite, to give you an idea of the capabilities of Office 97 and its individual applications.

Word

Microsoft Word 97 is a word processing application. You can use Word to create letters, reports, memos, invoices, newsletters, brochures, short stories, novels, and any other type of written document. Figure 1.1 shows the Word program interface with a sample of the type of document that you can create with Word.

▶ **See** "Understanding What Word Can Do," **p. 46**

FIG. 1.1

Use Word to create professional-looking letters, reports, and other documents, such as this invoice form.

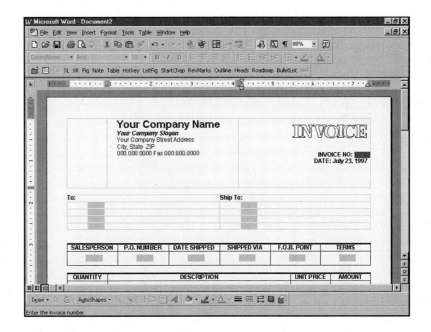

The documents that you create with Word can contain text; graphics; and other objects, such as sound and video clips. Word makes it a simple matter to apply character formatting—typeface, bold, underline, and so on—to text in the document. You also have extensive control of paragraph properties, such as margins, line spacing, and space before and after the paragraph. The integrated spelling and grammar checkers not only check your document after you finish it, but even check the document as you go along, pointing out possible misspelled words or grammatical mistakes so that you can correct them right away.

Word offers several key features that make it an outstanding choice for creating written documents. In addition to offering several features for controlling paragraph and text formatting and appearance, Word includes built-in features for integrating graphics into your documents. You can use WordArt and OfficeArt to create special 3-D text effects and draw a wide variety of shapes in a document. Word's new support for background images enables you to create visually appealing documents for display on-screen or the Internet. And, Word's support for HTML makes it a good tool for the casual or beginning Web page designer to create Web pages for an intranet or the Internet.

In short, Word is the tool that you should use to create any type of written document. Word also is an excellent tool for creating forms for use either on-screen or in a printed version.

Excel

An electronic spreadsheet such as Excel (see Figure 1.2) is much like an electronic ledger that you use to track and analyze financial and other numeric information. An Excel document consists of *cells* in which you enter numbers, formulas, and labels to define the spreadsheet. Excel calculates the spreadsheet, determining the results of the formulas and showing the results in the cell in place of the formula. So the formula acts behind the scenes to generate the results that you see in the spreadsheet.

▶ **See** "Understanding What Excel 97 Can Do," **p. 238**

FIG. 1.2

Excel is a spreadsheet program that functions as an electronic ledger for data tracking and analysis.

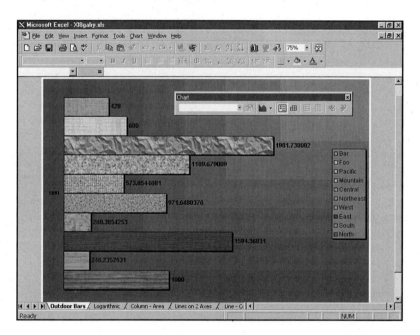

Although Excel's forte is crunching numbers, it also can manage lists of data, much like a database. The program supports extensive charting capability, making it easy to create two-dimensional or three-dimensional charts from the data in the spreadsheet. In addition, you can incorporate graphics and text into an Excel spreadsheet from other applications in the Office 97 suite, such as Word and PowerPoint.

PowerPoint

You can use PowerPoint to create presentations for sales meetings, seminars, the classroom, or any other situation in which you want to present information to a group of people by using graphics, text, and charts. In effect, PowerPoint acts as an electronic slide-show program, but the "slides" can be paper handouts, transparencies, or images viewed on-screen by projecting your computer's display through an overhead projection system or to a large monitor. You can even output your slides to real photographic slides for a true slide show on a slide projector. Figure 1.3 shows PowerPoint with a sample presentation being developed.

▶ **See** "Understanding What PowerPoint Can Do," **p. 476**

FIG. 1.3
PowerPoint allows you to create professional-quality presentations with a mixture of graphics, text, and even sound.

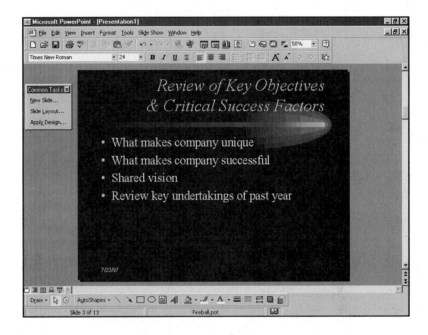

PowerPoint presentations are not limited to static text and graphics, however. For presentations that you make through your computer, you can include animation effects, sound, CD audio, narration, and other multimedia effects. PowerPoint's capability to send its output to two monitors enables the presenter to view his or her notes along with the presentation on one display while the audience sees only the slides.

Access

Microsoft Access 97 is a powerful database program that you can use to store, sort, and manage almost any type of data. Examples include product inventories, names and addresses, information about suppliers or vendors, and even your favorite recipes. Figure 1.4 shows Access with a sample database loaded.

▶ **See** "Exploring Access 97," **p. 586**

FIG. 1.4

You can use Access to maintain, sort, and analyze almost any type of data.

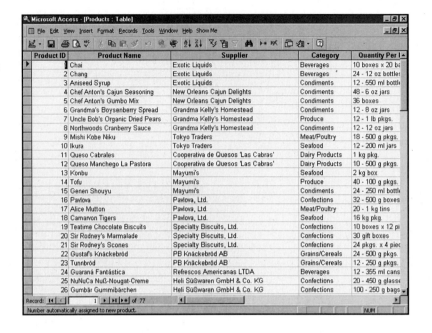

Access is a relational database manager. A *relational database* is one in which the database records can be compared and analyzed against one another and other data sources to create a dynamic data source. The database can change based on the results or sorts, queries, or other data operations.

Although Access is a powerful program, it is simple to use. You define a database simply by specifying the data fields that it is to contain (name, address, and ZIP Code, for example). You can easily create data forms that help you or others enter data into the database without having any other knowledge of database programs or of Access itself. In addition, Access' integration with Visual Basic and VBA means that you can build powerful front-end programs for entering and manipulating data, as well as exporting data to other applications, including those in the Office 97 suite.

Outlook

Microsoft Outlook 97 is a combination e-mail program and Personal Information Manager (PIM). Outlook relies on the core messaging components provided by Microsoft Exchange and Windows 95. Outlook supports multiple *messaging service providers*, which are add-on modules that enable Outlook to process different types of messages and work with different messaging servers. Outlook supports Microsoft Mail, Internet Mail, the Microsoft Network (MSN), and CompuServe Mail with separate providers. These additional service providers mean that your e-mail from CompuServe and the Internet can be integrated in a single Inbox and that you can compose, read, and manage messages through a single interface: Outlook (see Figure 1.5).

▶ **See** "Understanding What Outlook Can Do," **p. 728**

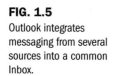

FIG. 1.5
Outlook integrates
messaging from several
sources into a common
Inbox.

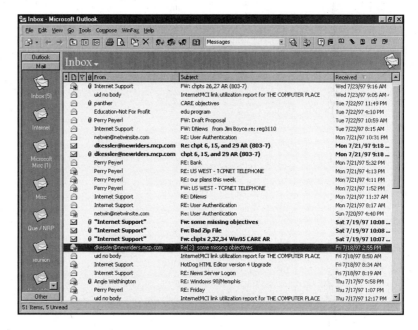

In addition to supporting electronic mail, Outlook supports sending and receiving faxes through the Microsoft Fax service provider, as well as Delrina WinFax. These fax service providers enable you to use Outlook to send and receive faxes if your computer system includes a fax/modem.

Outlook does more than just provide e-mail and fax capability, however. The program's PIM features also offer a means for you to manage contact addresses and phone numbers, schedule meetings, plan and manage tasks, associate notes with tasks and meetings, and much more. Outlook is an important part of the Office 97 suite because it can support such a wide range of tasks. Best of all, you can easily integrate into the other Office 97 applications the information that you maintain with Outlook. Using your Outlook address book to create mailing labels or form letters in Word, for example, is a simple matter.

What's New in Office 97

If you have used a previous version of Microsoft Office, you probably are familiar with much of what Office can do to simplify and automate your everyday tasks. The following sections provide a brief overview of the new features offered by Microsoft Office 97.

The Office Assistant

Help has always been available in the Office applications by pressing F1. In previous versions, Help was provided through the standard Windows Help engine, which essentially provided an electronic book of information about each program (see Figure 1.6).

FIG. 1.6

The standard Help engine in Windows presents helpful information about programs in electronic-book format.

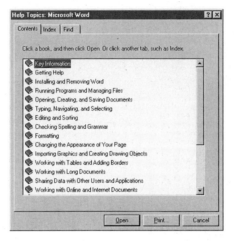

The Office Assistant, a new feature in Office 97, makes Help much more intuitive than before. In fact, the Office Assistant can even offer help when you don't realize that you need it! If you start to write a letter in Word, for example, the Office Assistant recognizes that you are writing a letter and asks whether you want help creating and formatting the letter. The Office Assistant offers tips and suggestions in all the Office applications to help you get the most use possible from Office 97.

The Office Assistant allows you to ask a question by using a normal sentence. The Office Assistant pulls apart the sentence, looking for keywords to help it determine what you want to accomplish; then it displays a menu of items matching the topics that contain words or phrases that you provided. If you want to create a form letter, for example, you simply ask the Office Assistant, "How do I write a form letter?" (see Figure 1.7).

Command Bars and Tear-Off Menus

In previous versions of Office, a program's menu was static and belonged only to that program. Each program used its own menu with the resource memory and hard-disk space associated with each menu. Each application's toolbars also were unique to the application, taking up further disk space and memory.

▶ **See** "Working with Toolbars," **p. 26**

Office 97 integrates menus and toolbar buttons into a new interface component called a *command bar*. Although a program's menu still appears at the top of the application window by default, you can tear off the menu and place it anywhere on the display, including outside the application window. The menu appears as a self-contained menu toolbar, or floating menu (see Figure 1.8). You can even dock the menu bar at the bottom or sides of the document window.

▶ **See** "Customizing Office 97," **p. 39**

FIG. 1.7
You can pose questions to the Office Assistant by using your own words.

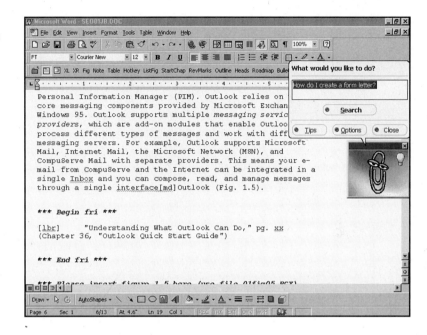

FIG. 1.8
You can tear off an Office application menu and place it anywhere on the display.

The Office 97 application toolbars also act as tear-off objects, and you can place them in any location on the display.

Menus and toolbars are much easier to create and customize in Office 97 as well. To add a command to a menu or toolbar, for example, you simply right-click the menu or toolbar and then choose Customize from the context menu. You then can use the resulting Customize property sheet (see Figure 1.9) to drag and drop new commands into the menu or toolbar. You also can use shortcut menus, which enable you to limit the number of items that appear in a menu but that include scroll buttons at the top and bottom of the menu to allow you to scroll additional menu selections.

Microsoft IntelliMouse Support

Microsoft recently introduced a new pointing device called the Microsoft IntelliMouse. The IntelliMouse includes a thumbwheel between the two mouse buttons that you can use to scroll and zoom the display. The thumbwheel simplifies scrolling in a document, because you don't have to worry about the position of the mouse pointer in the scroll bars.

FIG. 1.9

Customizing a command bar in Office 97 applications is a simple drag-and-drop operation when you use the Customize dialog box.

OfficeArt

Office 97 adds new drawing capabilities through OfficeArt, which provides many drawing tools that formerly were available only in PowerPoint. OfficeArt includes more than 100 adjustable shapes, such as polygons, cubes, and arrows. OfficeArt also enables you to draw Bezier (compound, point-defined) curves to create nonlinear shapes. The program's 3-D effects enable you to quickly create three-dimensional shapes and then apply various light source and shading options to those shapes. Also included are a variety of shadow and perspective effects to add depth and realism to images.

▶ **See** "Using OfficeArt," **p. 1044**

OfficeArt includes several types of connectors that you can use to connect objects in a drawing. These connectors include straight, angled, and curved lines, as well as various types of arrows with a selection of terminators. Several features are included to allow you to align and accurately position objects in a drawing.

Another important aspect of OfficeArt is WordArt. In previous versions of Office, WordArt enabled you to create special text effects, such as curved, stretched, and slanted text. WordArt in Office 97 is enhanced to enable you to create 3-D text with textures and other special effects (see Figure 1.10).

▶ **See** "Using WordArt," **p. 1048**

FIG. 1.10

Use WordArt to create special effects for text.

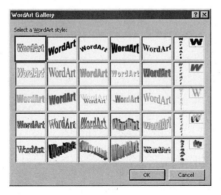

Another handy feature in OfficeArt is the capability to apply a transparent background to bitmaps. This capability enables the bitmap to appear as part of the document, rather than something inserted into a box.

Internet Explorer Integration

Office 97 provides a considerable degree of integration between Internet Explorer and the Office applications. A user who clicks a link in Internet Explorer to an Office document views the document right in Explorer, rather than in the Office application in which the document was created. Viewing the document in Internet Explorer helps eliminate the need for the user to have multiple application windows open at one time. In effect, this new feature makes Internet Explorer a viewer for any Office document.

FindFast Web Query

The FindFast Web Query feature in Office 97 simplifies searching for information contained on your local-area network (LAN). This new Office 97 feature offers the same search techniques that a user might employ on the Internet to locate information, but it applies those search techniques to Office documents on the LAN. FindFast Web Query offers several options that enable you to customize its performance and optimize a search.

Hyperlinks

You can add to your Office 97 documents hyperlinks that, when clicked, take you to other Office documents, Internet Web addresses, and other common Internet-style links. These links can include HTML files (Web page), Office documents, e-mail addresses, FTP sites, Universal Naming Convention (UNC) path names to network disk resources, text, graphics, OLE objects, and many other objects.

Hyperlinks are useful for building dynamic hypertext documents. You can create an outline of a long document in Word, for example, and then link each chapter heading to the document files that contain each chapter. A person reading the outline can simply click a chapter heading to open the chapter file.

Web Toolbar

In Office 97, Word, Excel, Access, and PowerPoint use a common Web toolbar that simplifies navigating hyperlinks in documents. The Web Toolbar allows you not only to navigate Office documents that contain hyperlinks, but also to enter any URL or file location and jump to that resource quickly, even when those resources are located on the Internet.

Save As HTML

The Office 97 applications support HTML (Hypertext Markup Language) as a recognized file format. You can open HTML files from the Internet or from an intranet server or FTP site. The Office applications also enable you to save files in HTML format. Support for HTML format means that you can use these applications to create Web pages for publishing on the Internet or a company intranet.

VBA Development Environment

All the Office 97 applications support Visual Basic for Applications (VBA), which enables you to write powerful programs comprising Visual Basic syntax, methods, and properties. By supporting VBA across the application suite, Microsoft enables users to integrate the Office applications to create custom applications. You can create a custom VBA application, for example, that uses Word to generate monthly invoices or statements from data in an Access database or Excel spreadsheet.

▶ **See** "Creating Your Own Applications with VBA" **p. 1143**

Microsoft Forms

In Office 97, creating forms for use on-screen, on paper, or on the World Wide Web is fairly simple. You can use Word, for example, to create an employee information form that employees use to sign up for insurance benefits and other company programs. You also can use Office applications to create forms for use on the Internet. Office 97's inclusion of ActiveX controls enables you to place such components as drop-down lists, check boxes, and option buttons in your forms.

Developer Edition

The Microsoft Office 97 Developer Edition includes all the features of Office 97 Professional, as well as features and components that simplify the creation of custom Office applications. The Developer Edition includes tools for distributing custom applications, software tools, sample code, documentation, and developer licensing.

Free Online Extras

Microsoft maintains a Web site specifically for Microsoft Office 97; this site offers support information, tips, and access to free add-ons for the Office applications. You can find such utilities as the PowerPoint Animation Player, additional templates for Word (use them to create such items as invoices, additional clip art, and graphics), and many other resources. A few hours browsing and downloading from the Office Web site yields a wealth of handy add-ons that you can use to tailor Office to your needs.

 ON THE WEB

Microsoft Office 97 Web Site **http://www.microsoft.com/msoffice**

CHAPTER 2

Using Common Office 97 Features

by Nancy Warner

Microsoft Office is a suite of applications. In other words, many applications bundled together make up Microsoft Office. Each application has its own strengths and weaknesses, but all the applications are controlled in a similar fashion. Just as most Windows applications have a title bar and a Control menu, Office applications share menus, toolbars, and dialog boxes.

The similarities among the Office applications enable you to learn to use all the applications quickly. If you learn to use the printing feature in one Office application, you know how to print from all the Office applications. Although not all features are exactly alike, many are at least similar.

These features are commonly used and are similar among all the Office applications, but they are not necessarily the same. Learn the basics of these features and apply them to the different Office applications as needed. ■

Use shortcut menus

Use shortcut menus to quickly perform actions on objects in an Office document.

Customize toolbars

Arrange and size toolbars so that you can work faster in Office applications.

Navigate documents

Learn to move around quickly in Office documents by using either the mouse or the keyboard.

Select objects

All Office documents are made up of objects. Learn how to select and work with these objects.

Find Help

Help is available in many forms. Learn several methods for using Office help files and how to get help on the Internet.

Working with Menus

Menus are used to perform actions. Different types of menus are available; some are accessed through the menu bar, and others are accessed directly from the objects that they affect. The two types of menus can contain identical commands. When both menus contain the same command, you can choose to use the menu that is best for you.

 T I P   Some elements are common to all Windows applications. One such element is the *ellipsis* (...). When an ellipsis appears in a menu or on a button, choosing that command or clicking that button opens a dialog box that allows you to determine how the command is carried out.

Using Menus

Menus are used mainly through the menu bar. The menu bar normally is located directly below the title bar of the application. Some menus contain submenus, which are indicated by an arrow to the right of the menu item. Choosing a submenu opens another menu at the location of the arrow.

> **N O T E**   Submenus can also contain submenus. In fact, the number of submenus that can be used is virtually unlimited, but applications rarely use more than two or three continuous submenus. ▓

You can open menus by using the mouse or the keyboard. Regardless of which method you use, commands issued by means of a menu are carried out the same way. To open the Help menu with your keyboard, for example, follow these steps:

1. Start any of the Office applications.
2. Press the Alt key and the H key simultaneously to open the <u>H</u>elp menu.

   The letter H is the hot key for the Help menu. That is why the Help menu opens when the H key is pressed in conjunction with the Alt key. To open the <u>F</u>ile menu, for example, you press the Alt key and the F key.

 T I P   When a menu is open, pressing the left-arrow or right-arrow key closes the current menu and opens the menu to the immediate left or right.

3. Press the W key to open the Microsoft on the <u>W</u>eb submenu.

   You could also use down and right arrow keys to move to and open this menu.
4. Press the Enter key to choose a menu option (which will close the menu) or press the Esc key to close the currently selected menu or submenu. Figure 2.1 shows the Microsoft on the Web submenu.

You can operate other menus by using their hot keys and the arrow keys. To use the mouse, click a menu to open it. After clicking a menu, you can hold the mouse button down or release it. If you hold the mouse button down, choose the option that you want by placing the mouse pointer on that option; then release the mouse button. Otherwise, click the option that you want to use.

FIG. 2.1

Hot keys can make using the keyboard faster than using the mouse to choose menu commands.

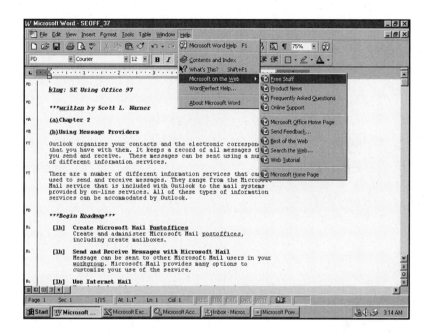

Part

I

Ch

2

Using Shortcut Menus

Shortcut menus are like all other menus except for the way that they are opened. Instead of using the menu bar, you select an object and right-click to open its shortcut menu. See "Selecting and Working with Objects" later in this chapter for more information on working with objects in Office applications.

Shortcut menus are specific to the selected objects, meaning that a shortcut menu for an Access table contains different commands from those contained in a shortcut menu for an element in a PowerPoint presentation. To use shortcut menus in any of the Office applications, follow these steps:

1. Start any Office 97 application.

2. Right-click any object.

   For this example, use an Excel spreadsheet. As shown in Figure 2.2, the shortcut menu for a cell opens directly below the mouse pointer.

3. Choose an option to perform that action or press the Esc key to close the menu.

   You can also click another cell to close the menu.

FIG. 2.2

Shortcut menus offer context-sensitive options, meaning that available commands apply to the task at hand.

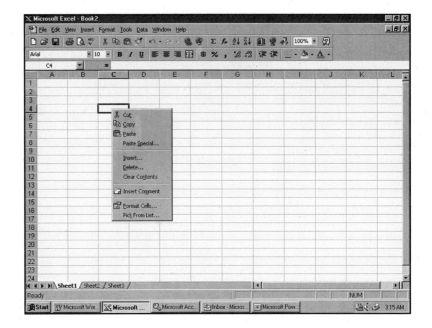

 TIP Windows 95-compatible keyboards have a key that opens the shortcut menu of the currently selected object. This key is located next to the Ctrl key on the right side of the keyboard and usually is labeled with a Windows icon.

4. Right-click one of the sheet tabs at the bottom of the page.

The menu choices change, as shown in Figure 2.3. Different actions are performed in sheet tabs than in cells, with the shortcut menu presenting options that are possible for the selected object. In this case, the sheet tab is the selected object.

Using Tear-Off Menus

Another unique menu type is the tear-off menu. As its name suggests, a tear-off menu can be torn from its location in a menu bar or submenu; then it becomes a toolbar (discussed in the next section, "Working with Toolbars"). A *move handle*, which is a thin solid strip at the top of a menu, identifies tear-off menus. To use a tear-off menu, follow these steps:

1. Start any Office application.

For this example, use Word.

2. Choose Insert, AutoText and the AutoText submenu will appear.

3. Click the mouse pointer on the move handle of the AutoText tear-off menu.

N O T E When selected, the move handle changes to a darker color just like a selected menu option.

FIG. 2.3

Each type of object has a shortcut menu defined for it.

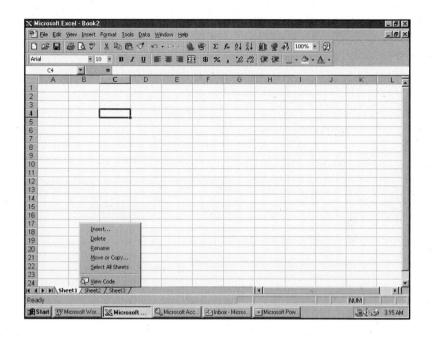

Part

I

Ch

2

4. Drag the tear-off menu's toolbar to the desired location. Figure 2.4 shows the outline of the toolbar before it is created.

FIG. 2.4

Tear-off menus become floating toolbars for quicker access.

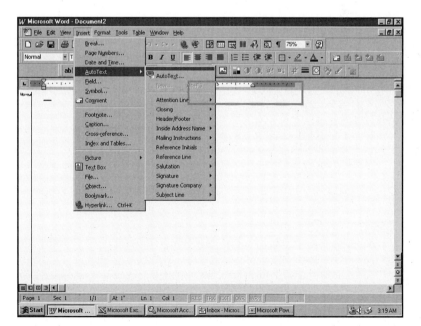

After a tear-off menu becomes a toolbar, it has some new features that are unique to toolbars, which are discussed in the next section.

Working with Toolbars

Toolbars organize commands in groups, so that you can find and use them quickly. You use toolbars by clicking the toolbar button that represents the command that you want to use. Toolbar buttons represent commands that can also be issued through a menu, but they eliminate the need to identify the menu or submenu that contains the command.

 TIP To find out what a button does, rest the mouse pointer on that button. After a few seconds, a ScreenTip appears at the base of the mouse pointer, telling you what the button does.

Toolbar buttons are graphical representations of commands and are marked with unique icons. A menu command and its toolbar counterpart are marked with the same icon.

N O T E   In addition to buttons, toolbars can contain menus—including tear-off menus.

You can use several methods to display and hide toolbars. When displayed, toolbars can take either of two different forms, each of which can be customized. These forms will be covered in the sections that follow.

Using the Toolbar Menu

Each of the Office applications contain a variety of toolbars. A standard toolbar contains the most frequently used commands. Specialized toolbars focus on a certain function, such as formatting or reviewing. In addition to the default Office toolbars, you can create custom toolbars that contain your most-often-used commands. For more information on customizing Office 97, see "Customizing Office 97" later in this chapter.

You cannot display all the available toolbars at the same time. Usually, you display the one or two toolbars that you use the most. Word displays the Standard and Formatting toolbars by default, for example.

N O T E   The menu bar is also a toolbar, although it is a specialized toolbar.

You can control which toolbars are displayed. To display the Web toolbar, for example, choose View, Toolbars, Web. Figure 2.5 shows the Toolbars submenu for Word. For more information on how toolbars are displayed, see "Using Docked Toolbars" and "Using Floating Toolbars" later in this chapter.

 TIP You can also open the Toolbars menu by right-clicking any toolbar.

FIG. 2.5

You can display
additional toolbars by
choosing View, Toolbars.

The last choice in the Toolbars menu is Customize, which opens the Customize dialog box, shown in Figure 2.6. The Toolbars page of the Customize dialog box contains a list of the available toolbars. Currently displayed toolbars are identified with a check mark. Click any of the check boxes to display or hide the corresponding toolbar.

FIG. 2.6

Use this dialog box to
hide or display toolbars
in any Office 97
application.

Using Docked Toolbars

The default toolbars are displayed in a docked position. *Docked toolbars* are attached to one of the sides of the application's window. Docked toolbars can be stacked or displayed side by side, depending on how big they are and how much space is available in the window.

Figure 2.7 shows the menu bar and the Standard, Formatting, Forms, Picture, and Reviewing toolbars displayed in Word.

The window shown in the figure has been arranged to illustrate several features that are common to docked toolbars:

- Move handles, which are used to move docked toolbars, indicate the beginning of a toolbar.
- Buttons allow users to perform commands through the toolbar.
- Separators group the buttons in a toolbar.
- More indicators (arrows at the end of the toolbar) show that not all of a toolbar is displayed.

FIG. 2.7

Toolbars can be arranged for your convenience.

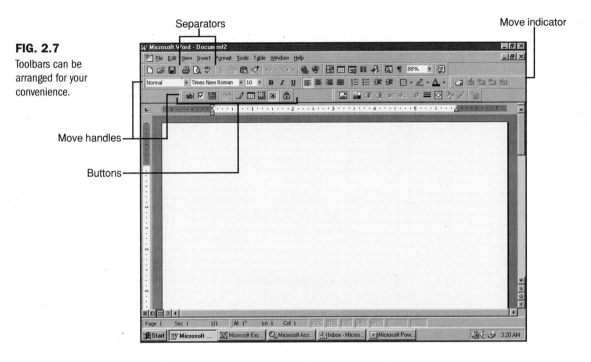

Separators

Move indicator

Move handles

Buttons

Docked toolbars can be moved from one side of a window to another or moved above or below other toolbars. To move a docked toolbar in any Office application, follow these steps:

1. Start any Office application.

   For this example, use Word.

2. Click the move handle of any docked toolbar and drag the toolbar to the bottom of the window.

N O T E You can also drag a docked toolbar by clicking any area that doesn't contain a button or other control. ■

3. When the outline of the toolbar changes to a long thin shape at the bottom of the screen, release the mouse button to drop the toolbar.

   Figure 2.8 shows Word with the Formatting toolbar at the bottom of the window.

In addition to docking toolbars at the top and bottom of a window, you can dock toolbars on the right and left sides of a window. If you drop a toolbar in an area in which it cannot be docked, it becomes a floating toolbar, as discussed in the next section.

 T I P To place a toolbar between two other toolbars, drop it directly between the other two toolbars. Drop a toolbar directly on top of another toolbar to take the place of that toolbar, sliding the first toolbar to the right of its original position.

FIG. 2.8

Toolbars can be docked on any side of a window.

Part

I

Ch

2

Using Floating Toolbars

Toolbars that are not docked are referred to as *floating toolbars*. These toolbars can be anywhere inside and outside an application window. In addition to having a different location, floating toolbars have several features that are different from those of docked toolbars. Figure 2.9 shows Word's Reviewing toolbar and points out the common features of floating toolbars:

- Title bars, which identify floating toolbars, are used to move them around.
- The Close button is used to hide the toolbar.
- Buttons allow users to perform commands through the toolbar.
- Separators group the buttons in a toolbar.

N O T E The close button in a floating toolbar hides the toolbar. It is the same as choosing to hide the toolbar by using the Toolbars menu or the Customize dialog box. ▪

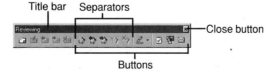

FIG. 2.9

The elements of a floating toolbar.

Floating toolbars can be moved to any location in a window. If a toolbar is moved to a position that allows it to be docked, however, it becomes a docked toolbar. To move and reshape a floating toolbar in any Office application, follow these steps:

1. Start any Office application.

   For this example, use Word.

2. Display the Reviewing toolbar.

   If the toolbar is not a floating toolbar, drag it to the middle of the window to make it a floating toolbar.

3. Click the title bar of the Reviewing toolbar and drag it to a new location.

T I P Double-clicking the title bar of a toolbar docks the toolbar; clicking the close button hides the toolbar.

4. Release the mouse button. The toolbar is displayed in its new location.

5. Place the mouse pointer on one side of the toolbar. The mouse pointer becomes a double-sided arrow, indicating you are going to alter the shape.

6. Drag the side of the toolbar to change its shape. The new shape is indicated by the outline displayed.

7. Release the mouse button when you have the shape that you want.

Toolbars are intended to help you complete your work faster. Use the type of toolbar that helps you the most, and be sure to customize that toolbar for your work habits.

N O T E Office applications remember which toolbars you used last, including their position. A toolbar appears in the same location, with the same properties, each time you display the toolbar until you change its properties manually. ■

Working with Dialog Boxes

Dialog boxes are used to collect information from you. That information is then used to perform an action. For example, a dialog box might ask you if you want to save a document before exiting an Office application. The complexity of dialog boxes range from the very simple yes or no type described in the previous example to elaborate ones that require many different types of input. In the following three sections, different types of dialog boxes are discussed.

Using Dialog Boxes

A simple dialog box is a window with a variety of controls in it. These controls always include at least one button, the Close button. You use this button to close the dialog box after reading the message it displays or making the choices that it requires. Figure 2.10 shows the Print dialog box, which contains most of the controls that appear in a dialog box.

The Print dialog box is displayed when you choose File, Print. The dialog box allows you to make changes in the print settings for the document before it is printed. You click the OK button to apply your changes—or accept the current configuration—or click the Cancel button to abort.

FIG. 2.10
The Print dialog box contains every control except the list box.

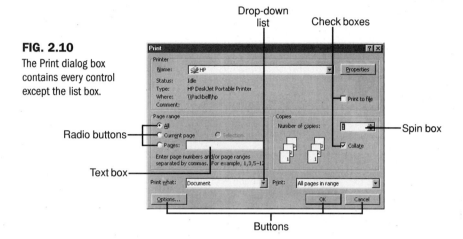

Drop-down list

Check boxes

Radio buttons

Spin box

Text box

Buttons

CAUTION

Some dialog boxes have an Apply button. Clicking the Apply button immediately applies any changes that you make in a dialog box. Clicking the Cancel button after clicking the Apply button does not reverse any changes that you made.

In a dialog box, a Yes button may be used for the same purpose as an OK button, but a No button doesn't always perform the same task as a Cancel button. If you close an Office application without saving the current document, for example, the application opens a dialog box that asks whether you want to save the document. The dialog box has Yes, No, and Cancel buttons. Clicking the Yes button saves the document; clicking the No button does not. The application still closes if the Yes or No button is clicked, but if the Cancel button is clicked, the close command is canceled.

 Pressing the Esc key on your keyboard is the equivalent of clicking the Cancel button, and pressing the Enter key usually is the same as clicking the OK or Yes button. Pressing the Enter key while editing a value may place a carriage return in the text.

Dialog boxes can serve many functions and can be broken into parts because of the number of functions that they serve. Tabs are used to group the controls by function and make using the dialog box easier. Figure 2.11 shows the Options dialog box for Word. You click a tab to display that tab's controls.

 You can navigate the pages of a tabbed dialog box by pressing the Tab key until the active tab is selected. The tab has an outline around its title when it is selected. After selecting the current tab, press one of the arrow keys to move to a different page.

Part

I

Ch

2

FIG. 2.11

Tabs group controls by function.

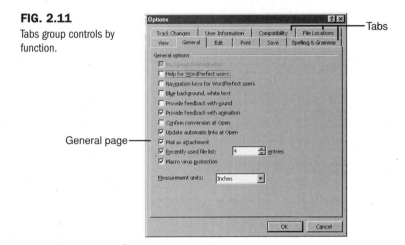

General page

Tabs

Using Wizard Dialog Boxes

W*izards* are groups of dialog boxes that help you complete complex tasks. Each wizard dialog box either asks for some information or explains the process that is taking place—and usually, it does both. Each Office application has wizards to help you with complex tasks. Figure 2.12 shows the first dialog box of Excel's Lookup Wizard.

FIG. 2.12

An explanation and an example make completing complex tasks easier.

Explanation of wizard

Example

Wizard dialog boxes have some common features. Some of these features are not always available:

- The Cancel button closes the wizard without performing an action.
- The Back button closes the current dialog box and opens the preceding one.
- The Next button accepts the values selected in the current dialog box and opens the next one.
- The Finish button uses the information that has been collected and performs the task that the wizard is stepping through.

N O T E   You can click the Finish button on any step in the wizard to perform the task at hand. The wizard will use the information collected to that point. For example, if you are on step three of a five-step wizard, you can choose to not complete steps four and five, by choosing the Finish button at that point. Everything you have entered in steps one, two, and three will be performed by the wizard. ■

▶ **See** "Using Wizards and the Office Assistant," **p. 75**

Navigating Office Documents

Part
I
Ch
2

Office documents can be viewed in many ways. Some of these views limit the amount of a document that can be displayed. Display all of a large document may be impossible. Several tools are available for navigating Office documents.

Using Scroll Buttons

Scroll buttons are a kind of hybrid scroll bar. Instead of changing the general area of a document that is being viewed, scroll buttons have a specific way of changing the view. Scroll buttons may change the worksheet that is being viewed in an Excel workbook, for example, or move from one graphic to the next in Word.

Using Scroll Buttons in Word   The scroll buttons in Word are located at the bottom of the vertical scroll bar. These two buttons have double arrows: one set pointing up and one pointing down. Between the two scroll buttons is the Select Browse Object button. Click the Select Browse Object button to choose which type of object the scroll button moves you to. Figure 2.13 shows the choices of the Browse Object button. For example, if you choose the Browse by Heading option, then every time you click the double arrows (up or down) you will immediately be moved to the next Heading in a document.

▶ **See** "Viewing a Document," **p. 60**

▶ **See** "Using the Document Map," **p. 74**

FIG. 2.13
Use the scroll buttons to quickly find graphics or other types of objects in a Word document.

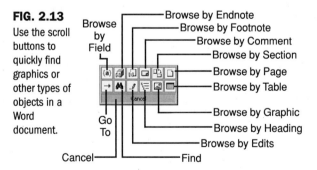

Browse by Field

Browse by Endnote
Browse by Footnote
Browse by Comment
Browse by Section
Browse by Page
Browse by Table
Browse by Graphic
Browse by Heading
Browse by Edits

Go To
Cancel
Find

Using Scroll Buttons in Excel   The scroll buttons in Excel are located next to the worksheet tabs. This location is appropriate, because these scroll buttons are used to switch between worksheets. Figure 2.14 shows the buttons and their uses.

FIG. 2.14

Scroll buttons can make changing worksheets in a large workbook easier.

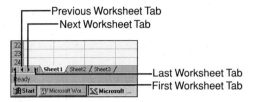

▶ **See** "Working with Excel Documents," **p. 241**

▶ **See** "Working with Multiple Workbooks and Worksheets," **p. 252**

Using Scroll Buttons in PowerPoint   Just like in Word, the scroll buttons in PowerPoint are at the bottom of the vertical scroll bar. These scroll buttons have a single use. The top button moves to the preceding slide, and the bottom button moves to the following slide.

▶ **See** "Working with the PowerPoint Interface," **p. 477**

▶ **See** "Working with PowerPoint Documents," **p. 480**

Using Scroll Buttons in Access   Access has the most unique scroll buttons of all the Office 97 applications, because they are used to navigate the records of a database. The scroll buttons are at the bottom of table and query windows. The options of current record and the total number of records are shown along with the scroll buttons, in addition to the moving to other records option. Figure 2.15 shows the scroll buttons for Access.

▶ **See** "Exploring Access 97," **p. 586**

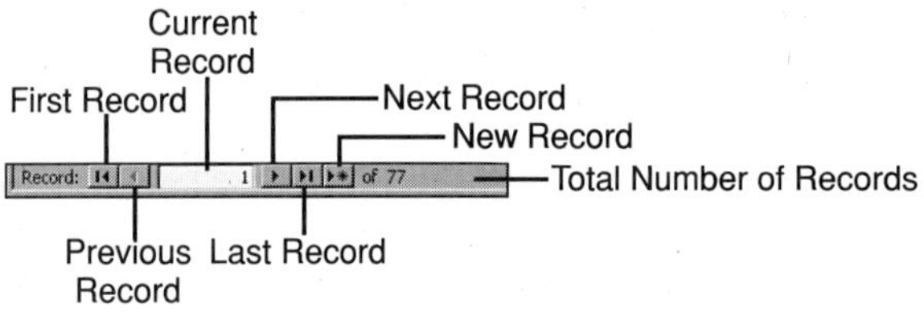

FIG. 2.15

The Access scroll buttons are unique among the Office applications.

Using Split Windows

Word and Excel use a feature called a split window. *A split window* allows you to view two parts of a document at the same time. You may want to view the introduction of a document at the same time that you are working on a page in the middle of a large document, for example. Using a split window eliminates the need to continually scroll back and forth. To use a split window, follow these steps:

1. Start Word or Excel.

2. Place the mouse pointer on the split-window handle, which is the thin gray bar at the top of the vertical scroll bar. The mouse pointer should take the form of two horizontal lines with an arrow pointing away from each line.

3. Drag the split-window pointer downward until the desired amount of space is shown in both windows.

Figure 2.16 shows an Excel document viewed with a split window.

FIG. 2.16

Split windows allow users to view different sections of Word or Excel files simultaneously.

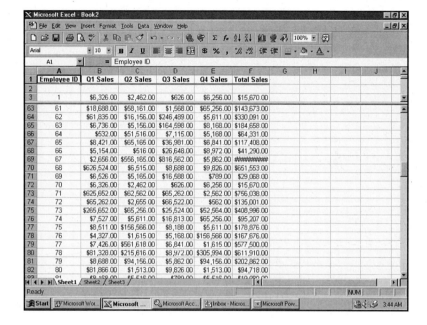

N O T E Double-click the split-window handle to open or close a split-window view.

4. Drag the split-window divider back to the top of the screen to close the split-window view.

 T I P Use the split-window view to view the column headers of a spreadsheet that contains many rows. That way, when you are viewing rows at the bottom of a spreadsheet, you know what information is displayed in the columns. Figure 2.16 shows an example.

Selecting and Working with Objects

Office documents contain many types of objects, ranging from text to documents from other applications. To work with these objects, you must select them. After you select objects, you can manipulate (format or edit) or delete them.

Working with Text

Text is the most common object used in Word documents. You may want to select text to format it, copy it, or delete it.

N O T E   You can select text by using the arrow keys in combination with the Shift key. To select a
word, place the insertion at the beginning of the word and hold down the Shift key. Holding
the Shift key down, press the right-arrow key to move the selection to the end of the word. ▨

You can use the mouse to select text in several ways:

- Select any amount of text by placing the mouse pointer at the beginning of the text to be selected and clicking the mouse button. Then move the mouse pointer to the end of the text to be selected and release the mouse button.

- Double-click any word to select that word.

- Move the mouse pointer to the left side of the document until it points to the right, and click to select the line of text that the mouse pointer is pointing at.

- Move the mouse pointer to the left side of the document until it points to the right, and double-click to select the paragraph of text that the mouse pointer is pointing at.

- Move the mouse pointer to the left side of the document until it points to the right, and click three times to select the entire document.

 T I P   When you select text by clicking the left side of the document, clicking again causes the next level of
text to be selected. After clicking three times and selecting the entire document, for example, clicking a
fourth time causes only the paragraph to be selected. Clicking again causes only the line to be
selected; another click causes the paragraph to be selected again. This is because one click is for a
line (level one), two clicks are for a paragraph (level two), three clicks are for the document (level
three), and anything more than that works the level back down (level two).

When text is selected, you can work with it by using commands available in the Edit, Format, Tools, and Shortcut menus.

- ▶ **See** "Creating and Using Styles," **p. 98**
- ▶ **See** "Using and Formatting Sections," **p. 111**

Working with Graphics

Graphics can be created in one of the Office applications, imported from another application, or downloaded from the Web. Regardless of how a graphic is obtained, it adds to the appeal of documents created in Office applications. To select a graphic, click it.

 T I P   In Word, double-click a graphic to edit it. Right-click a graphic in any Office application to open a
shortcut menu listing the actions that you can perform on the graphic.

When a graphic is selected, it can be moved or resized. Place the mouse pointer on the graphic, and when the mouse pointer changes to a four-headed arrow, and drag the graphic to a new location to move it. Place the mouse pointer on one of the boxes around a graphic's border, and when the mouse pointer changes to a double-headed arrow, drag the border to the desired length or width to resize a graphic.

▶ **See** "Integrating Graphics," **p. 124**

▶ **See** "Advanced Techniques and Graphics," **p. 517**

Opening and Saving Documents

Two actions that are common to almost all Windows applications are opening and saving files. These actions should be familiar to you from other work that you've done in Windows. To open a document, follow these steps:

Part
I
Ch
2

1. Start the Office application that you want to use.

2. Choose File, Open or click the Open button in the Standard toolbar.

   The Open dialog box appears, as shown in Figure 2.17.

FIG. 2.17
The Open dialog box shows only the documents of the type selected in the Files of Type drop-down list.

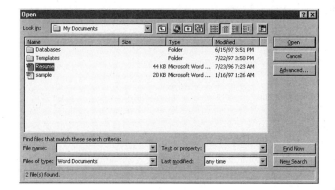

N O T E When you start Access and PowerPoint, these programs ask whether you want to open an existing file or create a new one. You can choose one of the options or click the Cancel button and then use the method described in this section to open a document. ▪

3. Select the file that you want to open.

   You can change the folder to search in by changing the Look In drop-down list, and you can change the type of files (Word documents, text files, and so on) being displayed by changing the Files of Type drop-down list.

4. Click the Open button to open the selected document.

 The File menu contains a list of recently used files. Choose one of these files from the File menu to open it without using the Open dialog box.

You save documents by using a dialog box that is similar to the Open dialog box. To save a document, follow these steps:

1. Choose File, Save or File, Save As, or click the Save button. The Save dialog box opens, as shown in Figure 2.18.

FIG. 2.18
The Save As dialog box
allows you to select
options for saving a
document.

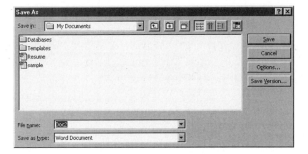

CAUTION

Unless a document is being saved for the first time, choosing File, Save or clicking the Save button saves the
document under its original name. This type of save means that the original document is now available only
with the changes that you just made. To avoid saving over a document, choose File, Save As and give the
document a new name.

2. Specify where to save the document by making a choice from the Look In drop-down list.

3. Specify the format in which you want the file to be saved by making a choice from the
    Save as Type drop-down list.

4. Click the Save button to save the document.

 If you have to share documents with users who don't have the same version of Office as you or who
use a different application, change the Save as Type setting in the Save dialog box to match the
application or version of Office that those users have.

▶ **See** "Sharing Office Documents," **p. 1088**

▶ **See** "Using Import/Export Filters," **p. 1123**

▶ **See** "Understanding Backward Compatibility Issues in Office 97," **p. 1132**

Printing

Another feature in all the Office applications is the capability to print. Choose File, Print to print
the current document. The Print dialog box opens enabling you to choose exactly what is
printed and how it is printed. Click the OK button to print with the choices you make in the
Print dialog box.

 You can print properties of the document by making a choice from the Print What drop-down list.

Clicking the Print button in the Standard toolbar does not open the Print dialog box. Instead,
clicking the button immediately prints the current document, using the options that were last
chosen in the Print dialog box for that document.

Customizing Office 97

Office 97 applications have many features that can be customized. Generally, these features fall into two categories: tools and views. Tools are such things as printing and file locations. Views are used to display documents in different ways.

Using Options

To change the options for Office 97 tools, choose Tools, Options. The Options dialog box opens (see Figure 2.19). Click the tabs to change different types of options, and click the OK button to save any changes that you make.

FIG. 2.19

Each Office application has options that can be changed.

Changes made in the Options dialog box may affect how a document is saved or whether the scroll bars are displayed.

Using Views

The View menu changes the way that documents are displayed. To change the view, choose a different one from the View menu. You can choose Slide Sorter view in PowerPoint to view all of the slides at the same time, as shown in Figure 2.20.

 T I P Word and PowerPoint have view buttons in the bottom-left sides of their windows. By clicking one of the view buttons, you can change the way that documents are displayed without using the View menu.

Getting Help

Each of the Office applications comes with a help file that contains information to help you complete your tasks. You can access the information contained in the help file in several ways. Choose Help, Contents and Index to open the Help Topics window for an Office application.

FIG. 2.20
Views display documents in different ways.

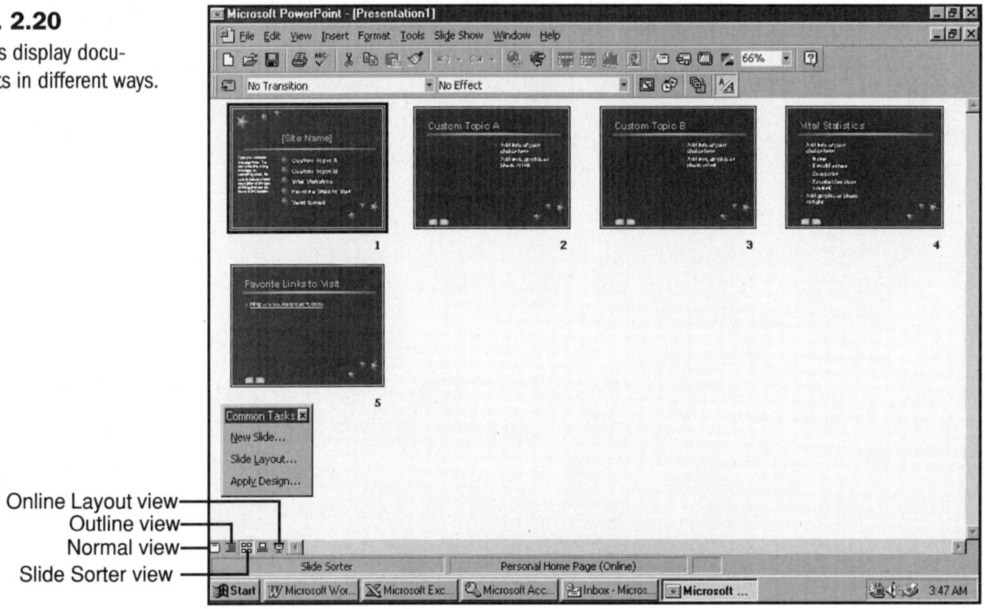

Online Layout view
Outline view
Normal view
Slide Sorter view

The following list describes the tabs in the Help Topics window:

■ The Contents page, shown in Figure 2.21, organizes information by topic or category.

FIG. 2.21
The Contents page arranges topics as though they are chapters in a book.

■ The Index page, shown in Figure 2.22, organizes information by means of an index that the authors of the help file created.

■ The Find page, shown in Figure 2.23, allows you to search the entire file for topics that contain words that you supply.

FIG. 2.22

The Index page allows you to search for topics as though you were using a book's index.

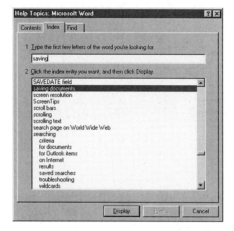

FIG. 2.23

The Find page gives you the most powerful search tool, because it searches the entire help file.

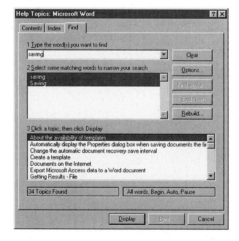

When you find the help topic that you're looking for in the Help Topics window, double-click the topic to open it and view the information from the help file. You can also obtain help by pressing the F1 key, which opens the Office Assistant, an interactive tool that you cab question. Using the question, the Office Assistant offers help topics that may help you.

N O T E   When you open the Office Assistant, it offers help topics dealing with the type or part of an Office document that is currently active. Check these help topics to see whether one of them can answer your question. ■

▶ **See** "Using Wizards and the Office Assistant," **p. 75**

In addition to the help files that come with the Office applications, Microsoft provides updated help files on its Web site. You can reach these files by choosing Help, Microsoft on the Web. ●

Part
I
Ch
2

Part II: Word: Beyond the Basics

CHAPTER 3

Word Quick Start Guide

by Jim Boyce

Microsoft Office 97 contains five applications, each designed for specific tasks. One of the applications in Office 97, Microsoft Word 97, is designed for creating written documents such as letters, reports, and the occasional great American novel. But any type of document containing text and graphics is a candidate for creation with Word. ■

Understanding what Word 97 can do

Discover Word 97's primary focus and additional capabilities for creating a variety of documents.

Using the Word interface

Learn how to navigate through Word's commands and features and understand how Word differs from other Windows 95 programs in its interface.

Composing documents

Run through a quick lesson on how to compose a document in Word.

Formatting text and paragraphs

Learn to use different typefaces, font sizes, paragraph spacing, and other formatting characteristics.

Using cut and paste

Discover how to reuse parts of your documents in the same or other documents, as well as move material around within a document.

Saving and printing documents

Examine aspects of saving and printing documents that are unique to Word.

Understanding What Word Can Do

Microsoft Word 97 is a word processing application, generically called a *word processor*. Word's primary focus is to help you create what have traditionally been known as written documents. These types of documents include letters, reports, newsletters, brochures, and even so-called niche documents like screenplays and novels.

Word isn't limited to just processing text. The documents you create with Word can contain graphics, tables from Microsoft Excel, charts, drawings, and almost any other type of data you create with any of your Windows applications (see Figure 3.1). Word documents can even contain multimedia clips—you can embed sounds in a Word document that play when the reader double-clicks the sound's icon.

FIG. 3.1

Word 97 documents can contain many types of data other than just text.

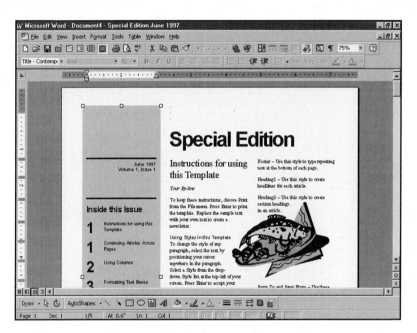

The following list describes the primary advantages of using a word processor such as Word to create documents:

- *Document appearance.* You can use different typefaces and fonts, paragraph styles, and other formatting to create professional-looking documents.
- *Easy editing.* Because your documents are stored on disk, you can open a document and quickly change it, then print another hard copy if you need one.
- *Reusing documents.* You can use one document to create another and make use of templates (a special type of document) to quickly create specific types of documents.
- *Spelling and grammar.* Word's built-in spelling and grammar checkers scan your document for spelling and grammatical errors.

■ *Integrate many data types.* Your Word documents can contain a wide variety of data other than text, including charts and graphs, graphics, sounds, video clips, and much more.

Now that you have a basic understanding of what Word can do, the next step in becoming comfortable using Word is to learn your way around the Word interface.

Using the Word Interface

The Microsoft Word interface is much like any other Windows program, so if you are familiar with other programs, you should have no problem using Word. As you can see in Figure 3.2, the default Word window contains a standard Windows application menu above two toolbars. Below the toolbars are the ruler and the document area in which you enter text and graphics to compose the document.

Part
II

Ch
3

FIG. 3.2
The Word interface follows the design of most Windows applications.

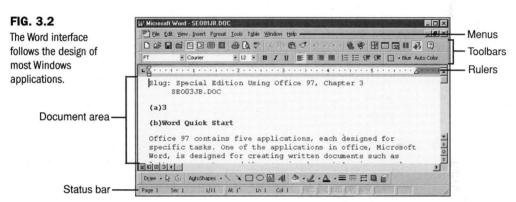

The following list describes the main components of the Word interface:

■ *Menu.* Word's menu bar contains menus such as File, Edit, View, Window, and Help that are common to all Windows programs. The menu bar also contains Office/Word-specific menus. You use the menus to perform most tasks other than typing.

▶ **See** "Working with Menus," **p. 22**

■ *Toolbars.* The toolbars give you quick access to many Word features. By default, only the Standard and Formatting toolbars appear, but you can configure Word to show any combination of its other predefined toolbars, as well as create your own. Holding the cursor motionless over a toolbar button displays a *ToolTip* that describes the button's function. Just click a toolbar button to use the feature assigned to it.

▶ **See** "Working with Toolbars," **p. 26**

The Office 97 toolbars, including those in Word, are *tear-off* toolbars. You can drag the toolbar from the top of the window and dock it at the bottom or side of the Word window if you prefer. Or, you can drag them over the document area and let them float on the document or desktop. To drag a toolbar, just click any blank area of the toolbar, hold down the mouse button, and drag the toolbar to the desired location. You can even drag the menu bar to a different location! The best place to grab a menu or toolbar to move it is on the handle (double bars) at the very left of the toolbar / menu. Note that when the toolbar / menu is attached to the side of the window, the handle is at the top.

- ▪ *Ruler.* The ruler shows paragraph indents, tab stops, page margins, and column widths. You also can use the ruler to set these document properties.

- ▪ *Document Area.* The document area contains the body of your document, including all text, graphics, and other objects in the document. You can view the document in different ways, including Page Layout, which shows the document as it will appear when printed. Outline view is another useful way to view the document in the document area.

  ▶ **See** "Creating and Using Outlines," **p. 86**

- ▪ *Status bar.* The status bar displays status information about the document, including the current location of the cursor, number of pages, and other status information. You can double-click items in the status bar to change the associated document option or characteristic.

- ▪ *Scroll bars.* The scroll bars appear at the bottom and right sides of the document area. You use the scroll bars to scroll through the document by line or page. The horizontal scroll bar also lets you select different document views such as Normal, Outline, and so on.

The interface components described in the previous list are not the only ones with which you'll work in Word, but they are the most common. You'll learn about other Word features and interface components in upcoming chapters.

Entering Text

When you start Word, it opens with a new document window in which you can immediately begin entering text. In many cases, that's all you need to do—just start typing. The cursor is already located in the document area, and as you type, the text appears in the document. You can format the text and paragraphs after you have typed them, or you can format the document as you go along. The section "Formatting the Document" later in this chapter explains how to begin applying page, paragraph, and text formatting. This section concentrates on explaining how to enter text in the document.

 To start Word without a blank document automatically being created, add the **/N** switch to the Word command line. To do so, locate the shortcut you use to start Word (by default located in \Windows\ Start Menu\Programs). Right-click the Word program's shortcut icon and choose Properties from the context menu. Click the Shortcut tab, then add a space and **/N** to the end of the text in the Target text box.

▶ **See** "Using Word Startup Switches," **p. 216**

As you type, Word places the text in the document area. You can choose text and paragraph formatting options before you begin typing a selection of text, or after.

Moving Around in the Document

The *insertion point* is the place in the document at which data is inserted in the document, either when you type or use the various insert and paste commands. The cursor is represented by a flashing vertical bar. To insert text or other objects at a specific place in the document, first move the cursor to that location. If you want to insert a few words at a specific place in a sentence, for example, move the cursor to the point in the sentence where you want the text inserted, then just type the new text.

Normally, text that follows the insertion point moves to the right as you type new text. However, you can turn on *overtype mode* to cause the new text to overwrite the existing text to its right. Double-click the OVR indicator on the status bar to toggle on and off overtype mode. Or, choose <u>T</u>ools, <u>O</u>ptions, Edit and place a check in the Overtype Mode check box.

 The speed at which the cursor flashes is controlled through the Keyboard icon in the Windows 95 Control Panel.

You can move the insertion point in the document with the arrow keys on the keyboard. Or, you can click in the document with the mouse I-beam pointer to locate or position the insertion point.

 Hold down the Ctrl key while pressing the arrow keys to move one word (left/right arrow keys) or one paragraph (up/down arrow keys) at a time.

The scroll bars at the bottom and right edge of the document area let you scroll through the document. Click the single arrows to move one line at a time, or click in the lighter colored area above or beneath the arrows to move one page at a time. The double arrows on the vertical scroll bar are *browse selectors*. By default they are set to browse through the document by previous page and next page, respectively. Click the button between the two double arrow buttons to specify a different browse method. Chapter 4, "Simplifying and Automating Tasks," explains the navigation tools in more detail.

N O T E Scrolling with the Page Up/Page Down keys moves the insertion point, but scrolling with the scroll bar does not. You can use the Page Up / Page Down keys to scroll through the document one page at a time, moving the insertion point as you do. ▪

▶ **See** "Using the Navigation Tools," **p. 79**

To go to a specific point in the document, follow these steps:

1. Press Ctrl+G or choose Edit, Go To to open the Go To page of the Find and Replace dialog box (see Figure 3.3).

2. Choose from the Go To What list the type of item you want to go to, then further define your jump request by entering the necessary information, such as page number, in the associated text box or field name as shown in the figure.

3. Click Next or Previous to jump to the next or previous occurrence, respectively.

FIG. 3.3

Use the Go To page to jump to a specific location in the document.

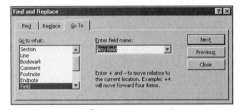

Selecting Text

You typically must select text before moving, copying, deleting, or formatting text. Selecting text is also called *highlighting* the text, although the term also applies to formatting text with a colored background, much like using a highlighter marker on a paper document.

To select text, use any of the following methods:

- Click and drag the mouse pointer over the text.
- Position the insertion point at the beginning of the text, hold down the Shift key, and select text with the arrow keys. Also hold down the Ctrl key if you want to select by words or paragraphs.
- Double-click a word to select the word.
- Triple-click a word to select its paragraph.
- Move the mouse pointer to the left edge of a line. When the pointer changes from an I-beam to an arrow, click to select the line.

Undoing an Action (Oops)

Occasionally you will change your mind after performing an edit on a document, or you might accidentally press the wrong button or choose the wrong command. To undo the last edit, just choose;command Edit, Undo or press Ctrl+Z. Word supports multiple levels of undo, which means you can undo several actions by repeatedly pressing Crtl+Z.

The opposite of Undo is Redo, which also appears on the Edit menu. If you undo an action and then realize you didn't want to undo it, just choose Edit, Redo.

Working with the Status Bar

The status bar shows the current page, section number, and total number of pages in the document. The status bar also shows the current location of the insertion point. The following five areas also appear on the status bar and indicate status as well as serve as shortcuts you can use to perform actions:

- *REC.* This area indicates when a macro is being recorded. Double-click it to begin recording a macro.

- *TRK.* This area toggles on and off revision marks. When it is dimmed, revision marks are turned off.

- *EXT.* This area turns on and off extended selection. Double-click it, then move the arrow keys to select text.

- *OVR.* This area toggles on and off overtype, or insert mode. When overtype mode is turned on, text that you type replaces the existing text ahead of it.

- *WPH.* This area opens the WordPerfect Help dialog box.

 T I P   You'll also see an icon of an open book in the status bar. Double-click this icon to check spelling, or right-click it and choose Options to set spelling check and grammar check options.

Working with Word Documents

Word offers considerable flexibility for formatting the page, paragraphs, characters, and other aspects of a document. The following sections provide a brief introduction to formatting documents in Word.

Setting Page Properties

Page properties for a document in Word include margins, paper size, paper source, and overall layout. To set page properties, choose File, Page Setup to display the Page Setup property sheet (see Figure 3.4).

FIG. 3.4
Use the Page Setup property sheet to set global document formatting and page definition information.

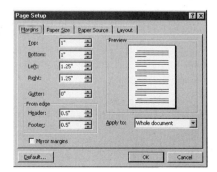

Part

II

Ch

3

The options in the Page Setup property sheet are generally self-explanatory. Section formatting is explained in more detail in Chapter 6, "Advanced Formatting and Graphics."

▶ **See** "Using and Formatting Sections," **p. 111**

Applying Paragraph Formatting

Word gives you extensive control over paragraph formatting such as line spacing, indents, alignment, space before and after the paragraph, and more. To set paragraph formatting options, right-click the paragraph and choose Paragraph from the shortcut menu. Or, click the paragraph and choose Format, Paragraph. Either action opens the Paragraph property sheet shown in Figure 3.5.

FIG. 3.5

Use the Paragraph property sheet to set paragraph, line, and page break options.

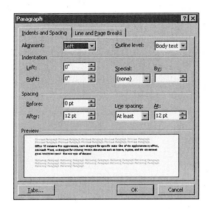

 TIP You can set paragraph alignment by clicking the desired alignment button (Left, Center, Right, or Justify) on the Formatting toolbar. The Formatting Toolbar is the one with the Style, Typeface, and Font Size drop-down lists at the left. To turn on the Formatting toolbar, choose View, Toolbars, Formatting.

Most of the formatting options in the Paragraph property sheet are described in Chapter 6.

Applying Character Formatting

You can apply various types of character formatting to text in a Word document. For example, you might want to use multiple typefaces (generally called *fonts*), different character sizes (font size), bold, italics, underline, and other character formatting. Word uses whatever font settings are in place at the time you are typing the text. So, you can set formatting options and have Word use them as you type. For example, once you set the current font, Word uses that font until you change it. The same is true with bold, italic, and other character formatting—once you turn on those characteristics, the text you type takes on those characteristics.

N O T E The default font is defined by the document's template. Templates are discussed in Chapter
5, "Using Outlines, Templates, and Styles." Choose Format, Font and click the Default
button to change the default font. ▨

To set font properties, position the insertion point where you want to begin using a specific
font. Right-click and choose Font from the shortcut menu. Choose the typeface, font style, size,
and other characteristics from the Font property sheet (see Figure 3.6). Use the Character
Spacing page to set character width and height options. Use the Animation page to apply special animated formatting to the text. Then, choose OK to apply the font.

FIG. 3.6
Use the Font property
sheet to set typeface
and font characteristics.

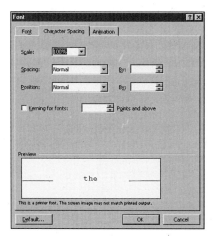

Part
II

Ch
3

You also can format text after you type it. To do so, just select the text you want to change, then
right-click the text and choose Font. Or, choose Format, Font to open the Font property page.
Choose the desired font options and click OK.

Copying and Reusing Data

If you are familiar with Windows programs, you know that you can use the Clipboard to move
data from one place to another in a document as well as between documents and applications.
To delete text, just select the text to be deleted and press Del on the keyboard or press the
Backspace key. Or, place the insertion point at the end of the text you want to remove and
press the Backspace key to remove text.

To copy text or other data on the Clipboard for use elsewhere in the document or a different
document, select the text and press Ctrl+C or choose Edit, Copy. To cut the text from the document, select the text and press Ctrl+X or choose Edit, Cut. To paste the text in the document,
position the insertion point where you want the text inserted and press Ctrl+V or choose Edit,
Paste.

You also can move text around in the document using drag and drop. Just select the text to be moved, then drag the text to a new location to move it. Hold down the Ctrl key while dragging the text to copy instead of move it.

 T I P   Text and other data that you place on the Clipboard remains there until you cut or copy something else to the Clipboard.

Printing from Word

Printing from Word is as easy as printing from any other Windows application. This section offers a few tips on printing topics that are specific to Word.

In Word you can print an entire document, specific pages, or a selection of the document. First, choose File, Print to open the Print dialog box (Figure 3.7). You also can press Ctrl+P to open the Print dialog box.

FIG. 3.7

Use the Print dialog box to control printing options and print the document.

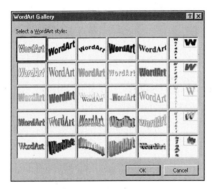

Choose the All option from the Page Range group to print the entire document. Choose the Current Page option to print the page in which the insertion point is currently located. To print a selection of the document, first select with the cursor the part of the document to be printed, then open the Print dialog box and choose the Selection option.

To print a selection of pages, choose the Pages option from the Page Range group, then specify in the associated text box the pages to print. You can enter a range of page numbers by specifying the first and last pages in the range separated by a dash, as in **3-22**. This example would print pages 3 through 22. Separate individual pages and ranges of pages with commas. For example, use **1-4,8-12** to print pages 1 through 4 and 8 through 12.

The Print What drop-down list in the Print dialog box lets you choose from the following items to print:

- *Document.* Choose this option to print the contents of the document.
- *Document Properties.* Use this option to print only the document's properties, such as author, title, file size, and so on.

■ *Comments*. Choose this option to print only the embedded comments in the document.

■ *Styles*. This option lets you print the style definitions defined in the document.

■ *Autotext Entries*. Choose this option to print the Autotext entries stored in the document.

■ *Key Assignments*. Use this option to print a list of shortcut key assignments stored in the document.

To further control printing options, choose the Options button on the Print dialog box to display the Print dialog box shown in Figure 3.8.

FIG. 3.8

Use this Print dialog box to control options for printing.

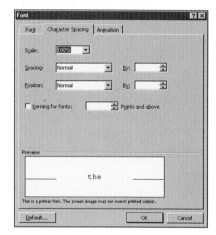

The options on the Print dialog box are generally self-explanatory or will become apparent as you read about other features in upcoming chapters. ●

CHAPTER 4

Simplifying and Automating Tasks

by Jim Boyce

The primary purpose for computers is to simplify, automate, and speed up tasks we would normally perform manually. Word does a great job of simplifying and automating (and therefore speeding up) many tasks associated with document creation. This chapter explores the many features in Word that help you create documents more quickly and easily. We'll start with a quick overview of the new automation features in Word. ■

Overview of new Word features

New features include automating tasks and new capabilities for creating online and Internet-based documents.

Using AutoCorrect, AutoComplete, and AutoSummarize

Word can correct your spelling and typing errors as you type. Word also enables you to quickly create a summary of a document.

Using the Document Map

The Document Map enables you to quickly navigate through many types of documents.

Using wizards and the Office Assistant

The Office Assistant and several wizards help you automate common tasks such as generating invoices, memos, and letters.

Using navigation tools

Navigate quickly through a document by page, keywords, sections, or other elements.

Creating simple macros and using shortcut keys

Macros enable you to automate frequently performed tasks. Word also lets you assign shortcut keys to commands.

Overview of New Features

Microsoft added several new features to Word in Office 97 to improve automation and ease of use. Some features are completely new, while others are enhancements to existing features. This section provides a quick overview of these features. New features that relate to other areas of Word are covered in other chapters in Part II.

Letter Wizard

The Letter Wizard in Office 97 (see Figure 4.1) has been enhanced to offer many more options for creating a letter than in the Office 95 version. The Letter Wizard can pull address information from Outlook, eliminating the need for you to enter address information manually or maintain address information in more than one location. Other options in the Letter Wizard further simplify letter creation. For example, you can choose from multiple letter types, specify mailing instructions, and define other options that determine the appearance and content of the letter.

FIG. 4.1

The Letter Wizard provides several options to help you automatically create various types of letters.

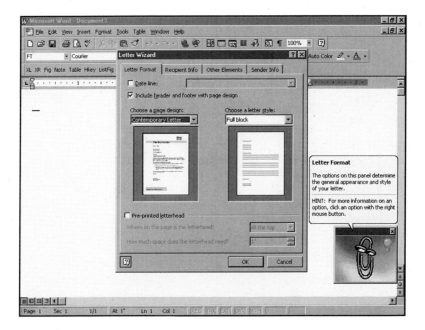

AutoSummarize

The new AutoSummarize feature in Word 97 analyzes a document to determine the key sentences and automatically creates a summary based on that analysis. AutoSummarize is helpful if you need to create an executive summary for a lengthy document. You can modify the summary as needed after Word creates it.

AutoComplete

AutoComplete is another new feature in Word. AutoComplete automatically completes text as you type. For example, if you begin to type the name of a month, Word opens a tip box near the cursor to suggest a completion for the text. Entering "Octo," for example, would cause AutoComplete to suggest the text "October." When AutoComplete displays its suggestion, just press Enter to accept the suggestion and have AutoComplete type it for you.

AutoCorrect

AutoCorrect has been enhanced in Word 97 to replace multiple words, fix common grammatical mistakes, and let you add words to the AutoCorrect dictionary with a right-click of the mouse. For example, common word pairs that are spelled correctly but are grammatically incorrect are replaced by AutoCorrect. Type "their are," for example, and AutoCorrect automatically changes it to "there are." In addition, misspelled words that are found by automatic spelling check can be easily added to AutoCorrect with a right-click of the mouse.

AutoFormat

AutoFormat has been enhanced to automatically apply a lead-in emphasis to text in bulleted lists. If the first few words in the first bullet are bold, AutoFormat will automatically apply the same formatting to subsequent lists. AutoFormat also now converts URLs (Uniform Resource Locators), e-mail addresses, and UNC (Universal Naming Convention) names to live hyperlinks.

Part
II

Ch
4

Style Preview

The Style drop-down list is enhanced to show a sample of the style's formatting, font size, and justification (see Figure 4.2). This makes it easier to choose the style you want when you are not quite sure of its name.

Automatic Style Definition and Updating

Another new feature in Word 97 is Automatic Style Definition. This new feature automatically creates styles based on paragraphs as you type. If you enter a one-line paragraph, center it, and apply bold to the font, for example, Word assumes you are creating a title and automatically creates a new Title style.

Automatic style updating has been enhanced from the previous version of Word to allow you to change a style in one location and have that change applied throughout the document.

AutoText

AutoText, which lets you add text to a document without typing it, has been enhanced to offer context-sensitive entries. This enables you to categorize AutoText entries and select from a list of entries that are relevant to the current situation.

FIG. 4.2
Style Preview shows an example of each style in the Style drop-down list.

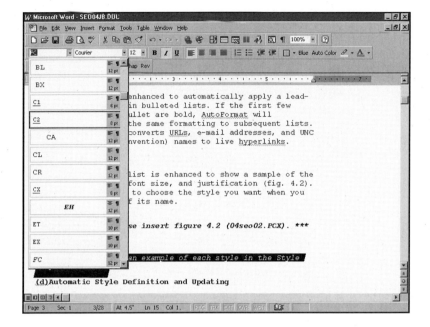

Bullets and Numbering

Bullets and Numbering has been enhanced in several ways. Numbered lists can contain tables, nonindented paragraphs, and page breaks between numbered elements. Multilevel lists, bullets, and numbering are all integrated within a single dialog box. And, Word 97 adds a new field code called NumList, which can be inserted anywhere within the text of a paragraph and used to automatically number items in the text.

Wizards

All of the wizards in Word that help you automatically create documents and document elements have been improved to better show the process and status of the wizard. In addition, the Office Assistant offers additional levels of help after a wizard finishes.

Viewing a Document

Word provides several modes for viewing the contents of the document. These view modes make it possible for you to use different working views as you edit a document. These different types of views can make it easier to navigate in the document or see how the document will look when printed. These view modes include the following:

■ *Normal*. This mode applies character and paragraph formatting but does not show the extent of the margins or how the document will appear on paper.

■ *Online Layout*. This new mode improves readability by using larger fonts and shorter line lengths, and by changing page length to match your monitor size.

- *Page Layout.* This mode shows the document by page, as it will appear when printed.
- *Outline.* Outline mode provides an expandable/collapsible outline view of the document based on the Heading styles.
- *Master Document.* The Master Document mode is actually a method for collaborating on documents within a workgroup.

  ▶ **See** "Using Master Documents," **p. 1100**

To change the way the document appears, choose <u>V</u>iew followed by the desired display mode.

You also can use multiple windows to view a document. This is helpful when you need to view, for example, the first and last pages of a long document at the same time. By default, each document opens with only one window. To open another window for the document, choose <u>W</u>indow, <u>N</u>ew Window. Word opens another window containing the same document. To switch between windows, press Ctrl+F6 or select the desired window from the Window menu.

 TIP Keep in mind that you aren't working with two copies of the document, only with two *views* of the document. Changes to the document in one window are applied in the other as well. The document name will change in the title bar of each window to reflect the same name with a different window number, such as MYDOC.DOC:2.

If you simply want to split the current window into two panes, choose <u>W</u>indow, <u>S</u>plit. Word attaches a window splitter line to the pointer. Locate the pointer where you want the window split and click the left mouse button. Word splits the window into two panes as shown in Figure 4.3.

FIG. 4.3
You can split a window to view different parts of the document in one document window.

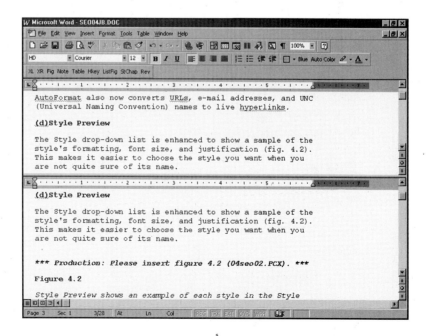

Part
II

Ch

4

> **T I P** To split the window with just the mouse, point to the split box just above the up arrow at the top of the
> vertical scroll bar. When the cursor changes to a double horizontal line, click and drag to split the
> window.

To move text from one area of the document to another, select the text in one pane and then copy or cut the text to the Clipboard. Click in the other pane, locate the insertion point where you want the text inserted, and then paste it from the Clipboard. You can also move text by selecting the text and dragging it from one pane to another. To close the split, either drag the edge of the pane all the way to the top or bottom of the document window or choose <u>W</u>indow, Remove <u>S</u>plit. Or, just double-click the border between the two panes.

Using AutoCorrect, AutoComplete with AutoText, and AutoFormat

Three of the most useful features in Word for automating text entry are AutoCorrect, AutoComplete, and AutoFormat. All three speed up document creation by automatically entering text for you, either from shortcuts that you type or correcting spelling errors. With a little customization, these features can save you an enormous amount of effort in document creation. First, consider what AutoCorrect can do for you.

Using AutoCorrect

AutoCorrect is designed to automatically replace typing and spelling errors as they occur. For example, if you always type "Widnows" instead of "Windows," as I often do, AutoCorrect will correct that for you. You just have to give AutoCorrect an example of the incorrect text and the appropriate correction. AutoCorrect includes hundreds of predefined AutoCorrect entries based on the most common spelling and typographical errors. AutoCorrect will monitor for and replace these common errors automatically by default. Just type, and AutoCorrect will fix errors as you go. To configure AutoCorrect, choose <u>T</u>ools, <u>A</u>utoCorrect to display the AutoCorrect property sheet shown in Figure 4.4.

The following check boxes on the AutoCorrect property page control how AutoCorrect functions:

- ▊ *Correct TWo INitial Capitals*. Enable this option to have AutoCorrect automatically replace double capitalized letters with an initial capitalization only. For example, TExas would be replaced with Texas.

- ▊ *Capitalize First Letter Of <u>S</u>entences*. Enable this option to have AutoCorrect automatically apply capitalization to the first character in the first word of a sentence. If you fail to capitalize the word, AutoCorrect will do it for you.

- ▊ *Capitalize <u>N</u>ames Of Days*. With this item enabled, AutoCorrect will automatically capitalize the days of the week for you.

- *Correct Accidental Usage Of cAPS LOCK Key.* Enabling this option causes AutoCorrect to detect when you are typing with the CAPS LOCK key down and automatically change the case of the text accordingly.

- *Replace Text As You Type.* Clear this check box to turn off AutoCorrect.

T I P Word doesn't try to correct words with just two characters, so state and other short abbreviations are not affected. You also can specify exceptions to AutoCorrect, preventing other unwanted changes.

FIG. 4.4
Use the AutoCorrect property sheet to control the types of errors AutoCorrect will correct.

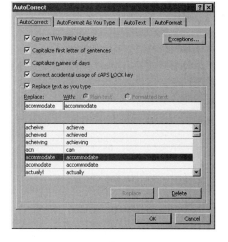

Part
II

Ch
4

Customizing AutoCorrect   To add your own custom AutoCorrect entry, simply type the incorrect text in the Replace text box on the AutoCorrect property sheet. Then, enter the correct text in the With text box and click the Add button. You also can add an entry by right-clicking an incorrect word in the document and choosing AutoCorrect. Word will suggest as many alternatives as it can, and choosing an alternative will add an entry to AutoCorrect with the selected correction.

T I P AutoCorrect recognizes and can replace phrases as well as individual words. To add a phrase, simply treat it the same way you would a single-word AutoCorrect entry. Type the incorrect phrase in the Replace text box, then type the correct phrase in the With text box and click Add. Note that the text to be replaced is limited to 31 characters.

To change an entry, type the name of the existing entry in the Replace box or scroll through the list of entries and select the one to change. Enter the change in the With text box.

Applying Exceptions to AutoCorrect   You can apply several exceptions to AutoCorrect to have it ignore things it would otherwise correct. To define exceptions, click the Exceptions button on the AutoCorrect property page. This displays the AutoCorrect Exceptions property sheet shown in Figure 4.5.

FIG. 4.5

Specify exceptions to AutoCorrect through the AutoCorrect Exceptions property sheet.

The First Letter page shown in Figure 4.5 lets you specify abbreviations after which Auto-Correct will not capitalize the first letter of the following word. If you added the text, "qty.," for example, AutoCorrect would not capitalize "of" in the sentence, "I ordered a qty. of 12 but received 2." AutoCorrect would normally attempt to capitalize "of" because it follows a period, and AutoCorrect would assume you were starting a new sentence.

You should clear the Automatically Add Words To List check box if you don't want exceptions that you allow in a document to be automatically added to the AutoCorrect exceptions list. If you make one exception in one document only, for example, leaving this option checked would cause that exception to be added to the AutoCorrect exception list. All further documents in which you typed the same text would also have the exception applied.

The INitial CAps property page (see Figure 4.6) lets you apply exceptions to the way AutoCorrect handles words with two initial capped letters. To add an entry, simply type the exception in the Don't Correct check box and click the Add button. Clear the Automatically Add Words To List check box to prevent exceptions that you make manually from being added to the list.

FIG. 4.6

Use the INitial CAps property page to apply exceptions to the way AutoCorrect handles words with double initial caps.

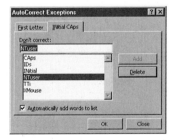

Copying AutoCorrect Entries Between Computers   Your AutoCorrect entries are stored in the *User*.acl file, where *user* is your Windows login name. This file is located in the Windows directory. If your user login name is **joeb**, for example, your AutoCorrect entries are stored in \Windows\Joeb.acl.

You might on occasion need to copy AutoCorrect entries from one computer to another to retain your settings. You might be reinstalling Office, moving your programs to another computer, or sharing your AutoCorrect entries with others.

To copy your AutoCorrect entries to another installation of Office, perform these steps (assume that **joe** is the user name on the source computer and **jane** is the user name on the destination computer and that Office 97 is already installed on both computers):

1. Close Word on both computers.

2. Copy the Joe.acl file from your Windows folder to the Windows folder on the destination computer.

3. Rename the acl file according to the user name you'll be using when you log on to the destination computer to use Office. For example, rename it from Joe.acl to Jane.acl. If you are simply moving your software from one computer to another and will continue to use your same login name, do not rename the file after copying it.

4. Choose Start, Run, and enter **REGEDIT** in the Run dialog box to start the Registry Editor.

5. In the Registry Editor, open the key HKEY_CURRENT_USER\Software\Microsoft\ Office\8.0\Common\AutoCorrect. Double-click the Path value and edit it to point to the acl file you renamed in step 2, such as C:\Windows\jane.acl.

6. Close the Registry Editor and start Word to verify that the AutoCorrect entries transferred properly.

TIP To share AutoCorrect entries among multiple users, place the acl file on a network server and edit each user's registry to point to the network copy of the acl file. The acl file could then have a generic name, such as Everyone.acl, and each registry would point to the same file name.

Using AutoComplete with AutoText

AutoComplete is new in Office 97 and works primarily as an extension of AutoText. When you begin to type a word that is included in the AutoText entries, a suggested completion for the text pops up near the text you're typing. Type **Sept**, for example, and AutoComplete suggests September as the completion. Instead of continuing to type, just press Enter. AutoComplete types the text for you. AutoComplete will automatically complete the following items:

- Current date
- Days of the week
- Month names
- AutoText entries

The first three types of entries are hard-coded into Word. You can define AutoText entries through the AutoText page of the AutoCorrect property sheet (shown earlier in Figure 4.4). Refer to the following section for complete information on creating AutoText entries.

T I P The Word Help file indicates that AutoComplete will automatically complete your name, and the natural assumption is that it takes your name from the User Information page on the Options property sheet. Either the Help file is incorrect or this feature doesn't work in Word 97. The only way to insert your name is to create an AutoText entry for it, just as you would any other AutoComplete entry.

To turn off AutoComplete, choose Tools, AutoCorrect and click the AutoText tab. Then, clear the Show AutoComplete Tip for AutoText and Dates check box.

Using AutoText

AutoText provides an excellent means for automatically inserting text into a document and saving considerable document creation time. You simply define the text you use often, and Word stores it for you. You can then use AutoComplete to automatically insert the text or choose to insert the text manually using the Insert menu or the AutoText toolbar.

 T I P To turn on or off the AutoText toolbar, right-click any toolbar and click AutoText.

Defining AutoText Entries To define AutoText entries, choose Insert, AutoText, AutoText to open the AutoText page of the AutoCorrect property sheet (see Figure 4.7). Or, if the AutoText toolbar is being displayed, click the AutoText button in the toolbar. In the Enter AutoText Entries Here text box, type the text you want to add to the list and click Add.

FIG. 4.7
You can define AutoText entries in the AutoText page, but you can't name them separately as you can using other methods for AutoText creation.

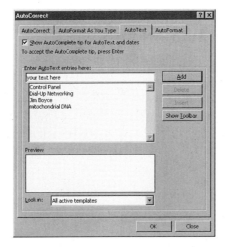

 T I P To display the AutoText toolbar, right-click any visible toolbar or the menu bar and put a check by AutoText.

If you want to include formatting in your AutoText entries, first type and format the entry in a document. Then, select the text to be included in the entry and press Alt+3. Or, select the text and click the AutoText button or choose Insert, AutoText, and New. Either action opens the Create AutoText Entry dialog box in which you name the entry (see Figure 4.8). The name you apply does not have to match the AutoText content in any way.

FIG. 4.8
Select text and press Alt+F3 if you want to apply a name to the AutoText entry that is different from the default name.

Inserting AutoText Entries   Inserting AutoText entries is easy. If AutoComplete is enabled, the text will appear near the insertion point as you begin to type it. Just press Enter when the AutoComplete tip appears to insert the text without typing all of it. To insert AutoText entries without AutoComplete, choose Insert, AutoText, AutoText. Select from the list the text you want to insert and choose Insert. If the AutoText toolbar is open, just select the text to be inserted from the drop-down list on the toolbar.

If you want to insert text automatically but don't want to use AutoComplete or go through the steps necessary to insert text from the AutoText list, use AutoCorrect instead. Create AutoCorrect entries with shortcut names that when typed will insert other text. For example, create an AutoCorrect entry named **dun** that inserts the text **Dial-Up Networking**. Enter **dun** in the Replace text box and **Dial-Up Networking** in the With text box of the AutoCorrect property page when you create the entry. Then, just type **dun** the next time you want **Dial-Up Networking** inserted in the text. AutoCorrect will replace the text as soon as you press the spacebar after typing **dun**.

Copying AutoText Entries Between Computers   AutoText entries are stored in Normal.dot, the default Word document template. You must copy Normal.dot from one computer to another to move the AutoText entries between them. The Normal.dot file is located in the Office\Templates folder.

Using AutoFormat

AutoFormat, which has been enhanced in Office 97 with a few new features, enables you to automatically format a document either as you type or after the document is created.

Formatting as You Type   To set AutoFormat options that apply as you type, choose Tools, AutoCorrect and then click the AutoFormat As You Type tab to display the AutoFormat As You Type page (see Figure 4.9).

Part
II

Ch
4

FIG. 4.9

Word treats automatic formatting as you type and global automatic formatting separately.

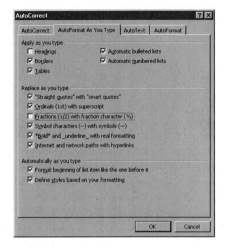

If an option is turned on (has a check by it) in the Replace As You Type dialog box, Word will automatically make the replacement indicated beside the option. The Replace As You Type options on the AutoFormat As You Type page are generally self-explanatory. The Internet And Network Paths With Hyperlinks option controls how Word formats Internet objects such as URLs, e-mail addresses, and paths to network devices. If enabled, this option causes Word to turn these objects into hyperlinks that, when clicked, open the associated object.

Typing **http://www.microsoft.com**, for example, converts the text to a hyperlink and underlines the text to indicate that link. If you click the link, Word launches your Web browser and takes you to the Web site. Clicking an e-mail hyperlink opens your e-mail application and begins composing a new message with the hyperlinked address in the To field. Clicking a network path such as **\\server\applications** opens the selected resource on the network.

The following list summarizes the Apply As You Type options:

- *Headings.* This option causes Word to automatically apply heading styles Heading1 through Heading9 to document heads.

- *Borders.* With this option enabled, Word automatically draws lines between paragraphs. Typing three or more dashes (–––) inserts a thin line. Typing three or more underscore characters (___) inserts a bold line. Typing three or more equal signs (===) inserts a double line. Typing these characters within a paragraph does not result in lines being drawn.

- *Tables.* Enabling this option causes Word to automatically create a table when you type a series of plus signs and dashes: +----+----+--------+. Word places column breaks at each plus sign, thus defining the width of the columns in the table. You can then click in the table to begin adding data in it.

- *Automatic Bulleted Lists.* With this option, Word automatically creates a bulleted item when you start the paragraph with an asterisk, dash, or lowercase **o** followed by a space or tab. When you press Enter at the end of the paragraph, Word automatically applies the bullet to the paragraph and starts another bulleted paragraph. To end bulleting, press Backspace without typing the new paragraph.

- *Automatic Numbered Lists.* Enabling this option causes Word to automatically create numbered or lettered lists. If you type at the beginning of a paragraph a letter or number followed by a period and a space or tab (**1.**) and then press Enter, Word automatically numbers or letters the following paragraph in sequence.

The following options are in the Automatically As You Type group:

- *Format Beginning Of List Item Like The One Before It.* With this option enabled, Word automatically formats the remainder of a bulleted or numbered item as the first part. If the first word of a bulleted or numbered item is bold and underlined, the first word of the following bullet or numbered item will be made bold as well.

- *Define Styles Based On Your Formatting.* As you type and apply formatting to paragraphs, Word can automatically turn those combinations of character and paragraph formatting into styles. You can then use those styles to quickly format other paragraphs.

For more information on using styles, refer to Chapter 5, "Using Outlines, Templates, and Styles."

Formatting a Document with AutoFormat In addition to formatting as you type, Word also can apply the AutoFormat options to a document as a whole in one operation. This is helpful if you have created or imported a document that does not contain the level of formatting you want. To apply global automatic formatting to the current document, choose Format, AutoFormat to open the AutoFormat dialog box (see Figure 4.10).

FIG. 4.10
You can specify the type of document on which you are working to refine the way AutoFormat treats the document.

To set options for the global AutoFormat process, click the Options button to display the AutoFormat property page (see Figure 4.11). Many of the same options you have in the AutoFormat As You Type property page appear in this page.

The following list explains the options included on the AutoFormat page that are not included on the AutoFormat As You Type page (discussed in the previous section):

- *Styles.* Enabling this option causes Word to retain the styles you have already applied in a document.

FIG. 4.11

You can apply formatting through AutoFormat on a global basis as well as when you type text.

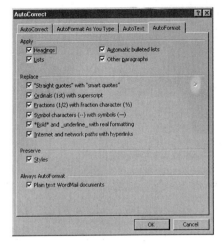

 TIP You can control whether or not styles update on an individual basis. To do so, choose Format, Style. Select the style to change and click Modify. Clear the Automatically Update check box.

■ *Plain Text WordMail Documents.* If enabled, this option causes e-mail messages in the WordMail editor to be formatted when you open the message. It does not affect documents in Word.

Using AutoSummarize

AutoSummarize, a feature new in Office 97, automatically creates a summary of the current document. AutoSummarize performs a statistical and linguistic analysis of the document to determine the most important sentences and then creates a summary based on that analysis. This is a very helpful feature for creating executive summaries of documents or in simply providing you with a working summary of a document's contents.

You configure AutoSummarize to base the summary on a percentage of the document's word count, specific number of sentences, or less than a specific number of words. Changing the percentage changes the summary and can help you fine-tune the summary. Also, you can choose from four different formats for the summary.

 TIP If you're using the Microsoft IntelliMouse, you can hold down the Shift key and move the roller to change the summary percentage.

To use AutoSummarize, choose Tools, AutoSummarize. Word performs the summary analysis and displays the AutoSummarize property sheet shown in Figure 4.12.

FIG. 4.12
Word first performs the
summary analysis, and
then lets you customize
the summary.

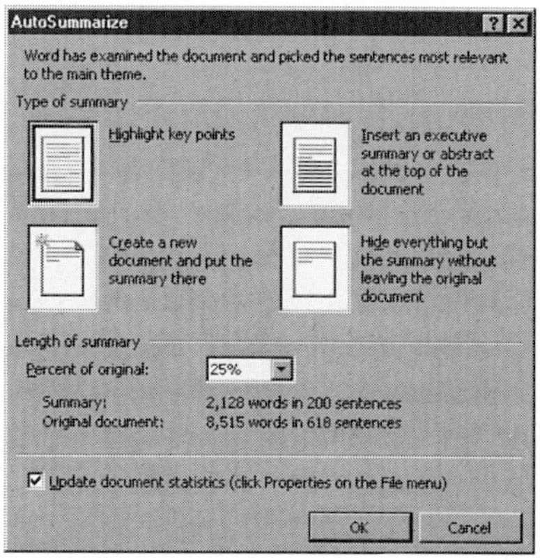

Use the controls in the AutoSummarize property sheet to configure the summary. Choose Tools, AutoSummarize to display the AutoSummarize property sheet. Choose one of the options described in the following list and then choose OK to display or create the summary. These are the options Word provides for the summary:

- *Highlight Key Points*. With this option, Word highlights the key elements of the document in yellow and displays the remainder of the document in gray. Use the small AutoSummarize dialog box that pops up to increase or decrease the word count percentage on which the summary is based.

- *Create A New Document And Put The Summary There*. This option creates a new document containing the text of the summary. This is similar to the previous option, except that the summary text is placed in a new document rather than highlighted in the current document. Use this option to create a summary that you can edit separately from the source document.

- *Insert An Executive Summary Or Abstract At The Top Of The Document*. This option creates the summary and inserts the summary as separate text at the top of the document.

- *Hide Everything But The Summary Without Leaving The Original Document*. This option summarizes the document and hides all but the summary text. It does not create separate summary text but simply turns off everything but the summary.

Two of the options create separate summary text: Create A New Document And Put The Summary There, and Insert An Executive Summary Or Abstract At The Top Of The Document. If you simply want to view a summary of the document, choose one of the other two options.

Creating Simple Macros

Macros offer a method of automating both simple and complex tasks. A *macro* is a set of instructions that a program runs to automatically perform tasks. So, a macro in an Office 97 application such as Word is essentially a program. You can create the macro by manually

Part
II

Ch

4

coding it the way a programmer develops an application or use the easy method and *record* the macro.

To record a macro, you first turn on recording and then perform the steps you want to automate. For example, assume you want to insert two short paragraphs with specific text and formatting. You use these two short paragraphs frequently in other documents. So, you record a macro that inserts the paragraphs for you. You name your new macro and turn on macro recording, and then type and format the text for the two paragraphs. You then turn off recording. Next, you place the insertion point where you want the material inserted and run the macro. Word executes the same steps you did when you recorded the macro and essentially types and formats the information for you. Instead of spending five minutes typing and formatting the material each time you want to use it, Word does it for you in a matter of seconds.

N O T E   Recording a macro actually results in a Visual Basic for Applications (VBA) program. VBA offers considerable power for creating custom applications within the Office 97 suite. Creating complex programs is very possible with VBA but goes beyond the scope of *Special Edition Using Office 97*. This chapter provides only a brief introduction to recording simple macros. For a more detailed discussion of Word macros, refer to Chapter 11, "Using VBA in Word."

For a more detailed discussion of VBA, refer to the VBA-specific chapters at the end of each application part in this book. Part X, "Introduction to Developing Office Applications," delves a little more deeply into VBA programming. For a complete treatment of the subject, consult *Special Edition, Using Visual Basic for Applications 5.0* from Que. ■

Recording a Macro

Recording a macro is simple. You turn on recording, perform the actions you want recorded, and then turn off recording. To begin recording a macro, choose Tools, Macro, Record New Macro. Or, click the Record Macro button on the Visual Basic toolbar. The first steps in the recording process are to give the macro a name, specify where it is to be stored, and add an optional description for it (see Figure 4.13). Use the following steps to create the macro:

FIG. 4.13
You can specify the template in which the macro is stored or store it in the Normal.dot template, making it available to all documents.

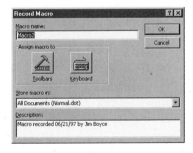

1. Name your macro. Choose a name that indicates the function of the macro, such as **Insert2Paragraphs**. Note that you can't use spaces in macro names but can use any combination of letters and numbers up to 80 characters.

2. Decide where to store the macro. If you want the macro available to all documents, store it in Normal.dot. Otherwise, you can store the macro in the current document. Select your choice from the Store Macro In drop-down list.

3. Add a comment to the macro that describes its function. This description appears in the Macros dialog box to help you identify specific macros (see Figure 4.14).

FIG. 4.14

The Macros dialog box lists all currently available macros and includes an optional description for each.

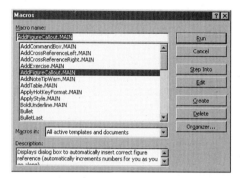

4. When you've specified the name, location, and description, you can begin recording the macro by clicking OK. You'll learn how to assign a macro to a toolbar or shortcut key later in this section.

Part
II

Ch
4

After you click OK, a small dialog box appears containing two buttons, Stop Recording and Pause Recording. The pointer changes to include a cassette to indicate that Word is recording your actions. Perform the steps you want recorded and then click the Stop Recording button. If you need to pause recording to perform a task you don't want recorded, click the Pause Recording button. Click the button again to resume recording. When you are finished, click the Stop Recording button.

Running a Macro

If you have assigned a macro to a toolbar or keyboard shortcut, just click the toolbar button or press the key combination assigned to the macro. The macro will immediately execute.

You also can run a macro by selecting it from the Macros dialog box (refer to Figure 4.14). Choose Tools, Macro, Macros to open the Macros dialog box. Select from the list the macro you want to run and click Run. To select a macro from a specific open document or from Normal.dot, choose the document or Normal.dot from the Macros In drop-down list. This enables you to weed out those macros you don't want to see in the list.

Editing a Macro

If you make a mistake while recording a macro, or simply decide later you would like to change part of it, you don't have to record it again. Instead, edit the macro. To do so, choose Tools, Macro, Macros or press Alt+F8 to open the Macros dialog box. Select the macro to edit and click <u>E</u>dit. Word opens the Visual Basic window with the macro opened for editing. Make the changes to the macro and then choose <u>F</u>ile, <u>C</u>lose And Return To Microsoft Word, or press Alt+Q. If you are editing a macro contained in a document, the macro changes will be saved the next time you save the document. If the macro is in a template, the macro will be saved when you close the template or close Word (in the case of Normal.dot).

N O T E   It isn't the purpose of this chapter to explain macros or Visual Basic for Applications in detail. Instead, the intent is to provide a brief overview of how to record macros. For a complete understanding of macro creation and editing, you need to understand VBA. Refer to Chapter 11, " Using VBA in Word," for an in-depth treatment of macros.

Using the Document Map

Word 97 includes a new feature called the Document Map, which helps you quickly navigate a document. The Document Map, which consists of a new pane at the left edge of the Word workspace, gives you an outline view of the document's headings while retaining the main document window in whichever view mode you prefer. For example, you can display the full document in Normal view but have the document's outline, based on its headings, displayed in the Document Map pane (see Figure 4.15).

FIG. 4.15

The Document Map effectively combines an outline view with any other view.

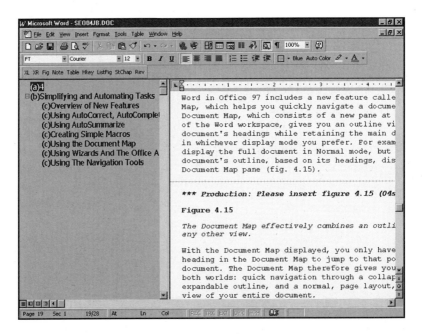

With the Document Map displayed, you only have to click a heading in the Document Map to jump to that point in the document. The Document Map therefore gives you the best of both worlds: quick navigation through a collapsible/expandable outline and a normal, page layout, or online view of your entire document.

To use the Document Map, choose View, Document Map. Or, click the Document Map button on the Standard toolbar. Word splits the display to show a new pane at the left side of the workspace (refer to Figure 4.15). The Document Map pane contains an outline view of the document based on its headings. To navigate through the document, just click a head in the map. Word jumps to that point in the document.

 You can control the map view just as you can an outline view. Clicking the plus sign beside a head expands that head and clicking a minus sign collapses the head. You also can right-click in the map pane for a context menu that lets you select the level of detail to display in the map pane (see Figure 4.16).

FIG. 4.16
Use the context menu in the map pane to control the level of detail in the map view.

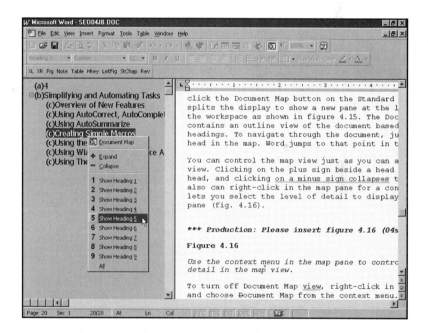

To turn off Document Map view, right-click in the map pane and choose Document Map from the context menu. Or, choose View, Document Map or click the Document Map button on the Standard toolbar.

Using Wizards and the Office Assistant

Chapter 2, "Using Common Office 97 Features," explained the use of the Office Assistant. Word includes several *wizards* that automate and simplify tasks, and these wizards work in conjunction with the Office Assistant to make it easier for beginners to accomplish the task. A wizard prompts you for information and uses that information to automatically create a document or document element. For example, the Letter Wizard automates the task of creating various types of letters. You don't need to know much, if anything, about the correct structure of a letter. The Letter Wizard handles that for you.

You have the option of including specific wizards when you install Word. These wizards include the following:

- *Envelope*. The Envelope Wizard automates the process of creating and printing envelopes.
- *Letter*. The Letter Wizard offers several styles of letters from which to choose and automates letter creation.
- *Fax*. The Fax Wizard helps you create and send faxes using a variety of options and cover pages.
- *Mailing Label*. This wizard automates the creation of mailing labels. You can create individual labels or use mail merge to create labels from a mailing list.
- *Memo*. This wizard helps you create a memo using various options and styles.
- *Pleading*. The Pleading Wizard helps you create legal pleading documents for submission to a court of law.
- *Newsletter*. This wizard automates the process of laying out a newsletter, offering three different styles and several other options.
- *Résumé*. The Resume Wizard will help you put together a professional-looking, attractive résumé.
- *Web Page*. This wizard automates the process of creating a Web page for publishing on the World Wide Web.
- *Avery*. The Avery Wizard automates the task of using and printing labels from Avery Dennison Corporation.
- *Agenda*. The Agenda Wizard helps you create agendas for meetings using various agenda styles and other options.
- *Calendar*. Use this wizard to create and print monthly calendars.

N O T E   The Avery, Agenda, and Calendar Wizards are included in the Value Pack, which is included on the Office 97 CD version only. Open the folder \Valupack\Template\Word on the CD and copy the desired template and wizard files to the Office\Templates folder. You also can download these wizards and others from the Microsoft Web site at **http://www.microsoft.com**.

The wizards installed with Microsoft Word appear in the New dialog box (see Figure 4.17). To run a wizard, choose File, New and click a tab on the New dialog box to choose the type of document you want to create. Search in the list of document types for a wizard icon and double-click the icon. To run the Newsletter Wizard, for example, click the Publications tab and then double-click the Newsletter Wizard icon.

FIG. 4.17
Wizards are repre-
sented by a different
icon from template files
in the New dialog box.

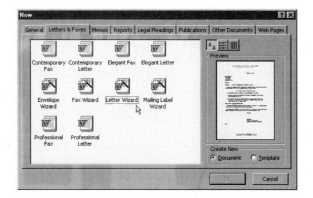

Creating Documents Using Wizards

To create a document using a wizard, choose File, New. In the New dialog box, select the type of document to be created by clicking the appropriate tab. Notice that near the right side of the dialog box are two option buttons, Document and Template. To create a document, just double-click the wizard icon as soon as it appears, or verify that the Document option button is selected and click OK.

N O T E Some wizards appear in Word's menus. You can start the Letter Wizard, for example, by choosing Tools, Letter Wizard. ■

What happens next depends on the wizard. Figure 4.18 shows the Letter Wizard. As with other wizards, the Office Assistant pops up to help you use the wizard to complete the task. It explains the options in the wizard and gives you hints on how to proceed.

Other wizards have been completely redesigned in Office 97 to give you a better overview of the task and enable you to skip steps in the process. Figure 4.19 shows the Résumé Wizard. The left edge of the wizard's dialog box contains a flowchart you can use to skip to a specific step in the task. The flowchart also serves as a road map to the task at hand. To skip to a specific step, just click that step in the flowchart. To proceed through the wizard sequentially, click the Next button. As you can see in Figure 4.20, most of the steps include examples to show you the effect of choosing a specific option.

The whole purpose of a wizard is to simplify a process, so there isn't any need to explain how to use each of the wizards provided with Office 97. Through the combination of automation and hints provided by the wizard and by the Office Assistant, you should have no trouble using each of the wizards.

Part
II

Ch
4

FIG. 4.18
The Office Assistant works in conjunction with many wizards to help you through the task.

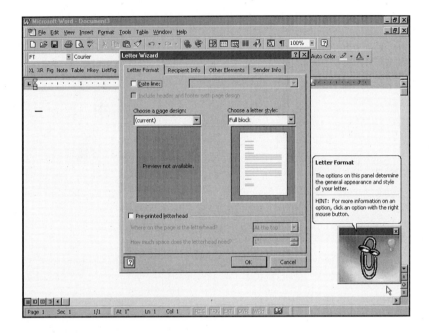

FIG. 4.19
The Resume Wizard, like many Office 97 wizards, has been enhanced to let you skip steps in the process.

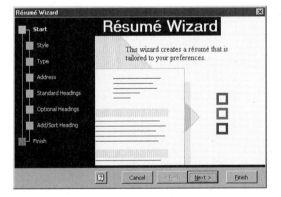

Creating Templates Using Wizards

In addition to creating a document from a wizard, you also can create a template. The primary difference is that the former creates a document file and the latter creates a template file. You would create a template from a wizard if you wanted to base more than one document on the outcome of the wizard. For example, you might run the Newsletter Wizard once to create a newsletter template you use each month to create that month's newsletter. The following month you would create a new document based on the template rather than running the wizard.

FIG. 4.20

Most steps in a wizard include illustrations to help you see the effect of choosing a specific option.

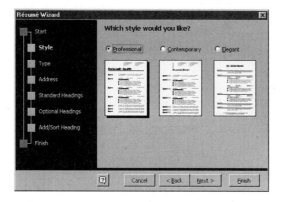

To create a template instead of a document file from a wizard, follow these steps:

1. Choose File, New.
2. Click the tab for the desired document type and then click the desired wizard icon once.
3. Click the Template option button and choose OK.
4. When you are finished using the wizard and the document appears, save the template file in the Office\Templates folder to make it easily accessible the next time you need it (it will appear in the New dialog box along with the others in the Templates folder).

   ▶ **See** "Creating and Using Templates," **p. 91**

Using the Navigation Tools

Word provides several toolbars that help you quickly access and use specific Word features. Just click the toolbar button and the associated command is executed. In addition, several new and enhanced features are provided for helping you navigate through a document. This section focuses on those features.

▶ **See** "Working with Toolbars," **p. 26**

Navigating in Word means much more than just scrolling through a document with the PageUp and PageDown keys or the scrollbars. Word includes several features that help you browse through a document using specific criteria to determine how you move through the document. This section focuses on those features, beginning with a brief explanation of Find, Replace, and GoTo.

Using Find, Replace, and GoTo

The Find feature helps you locate text in the document. To use Find, choose Edit, Find or press Ctrl+F. Word displays the Find and Replace dialog box shown in Figure 4.21.

Part

II

Ch

4

FIG. 4.21

Use Find and Replace to locate specific text in the document.

To simply find some text, type the text in the Fi*n*d What text box and click *F*ind Next. To find the next occurrence of the text, click *F*ind Next again. To apply further search criteria, click the *M*ore button to expand the dialog box as shown in Figure 4.22.

FIG. 4.22

Find and Replace offers additional criteria for locating and replacing text.

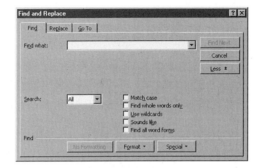

The options in the Find and Replace pages include the following:

- *Match Case*. Enabling this option causes Word to match the case of the text you type with the text in the document. **WORds** would match **WORds**, for example, but **WORDS** would not match **words**.

- *Find Whole Words Only*. Enable this option if you want the search text treated as a whole word. With this option enabled, a search for **fast** would match **fast** but not the word **faster**.

- *Use Wildcards*. Use this option to specify wildcard characters in your Find What text. For example, use **l*er** to search for **longer**, **later**, and other words that begin with *l* and end in *er*. Note that the Find Whole Words Only option becomes disabled, so a search for **l*er** would find strings in the document that began with *l* and ended with *er*, such as, "**L**ate at night is bett**er**." See the Sp*e*cial option in this list for more information.

- *Sounds Like*. Use this option to search for text that sounds like but is spelled differently from the search text. A search for **best** with this option, for example, would find **best**, **based**, and **beside**.

- *Find All Word Forms*. Use this option to replace all forms of a word. For example, use it to replace **fast, faster,** and **fastest** with **quick, quicker,** and **quickest**. You specify only fast in the Find What box, but Word actually locates the other forms of the word.

- *No Formatting*. Use this option to ignore the font, style, and other formatting characteristics of the text being located.

- *Format.* Use this drop-down list to select combinations of font, paragraph, style, and other criteria upon which to base your search.

- *Special.* Use this drop-down list to search for special document elements such as paragraph marks, tabs, fields, and so on.

The Replace page works much like the Find page except that you specify replacement text as well as the search text. You can selectively replace instances of the text or choose Replace All to replace all instances of the text. You can use all the same criteria for replace as you can for Find.

Go To is similar to Find except that it is designed to take you to a specific point in the document based on criteria other than (and in a addition to) content. To use Go To, choose Edit, Go To or press Ctrl+G. In the Go To page (see Figure 4.23), select from the Go To What list the criteria for your search. The text box on the page changes according to which criteria you select. Selecting Page from the Go To What list, for example, changes the text box as an input for the page number to go to.

FIG. 4.23
Use Go To when you
need to jump to a
specific point in the
document based on
a variety of search
criteria.

Part
II
Ch
4

The following list explains the search criteria available from the Go To page:

- *Page.* Use this option to move by pages. Enter a specific page number or +*n* or -*n*, where *n* is a number, to move a certain number of pages forward or backward.

- *Section.* Documents can be divided into different sections using *section breaks*. Use this option to move to a specific section or to move a certain number of sections forward or backward.

- *Line.* Use this option to move to a specific line in the document or to move a certain number of lines forward or backward.

- *Bookmark.* You can insert named bookmarks in a document by choosing Insert, Bookmark. Use this option to jump to a specific bookmark. Bookmarks can be used to identify sections of a document by name and are often used to automatically insert text in a document.

- *Comment.* Use this option in conjunction with revision marks to jump to revisions inserted by a specific person.

- *Footnote.* Use this option to jump to a specific footnote number or a certain number of footnotes forward or backward.

- *Endnote.* Endnotes are similar to footnotes except they typically appear at the end of a document. Use this option to jump to a specific endnote or a certain number of endnotes forward or backward.

- *Field*. Use this option to jump to a field. Select the field type from the Enter Field Name drop-down list.

- *Table*. Use this option to jump to a specific table number or certain number of tables forward or backward in the document.

- *Graphic*. Choose this option to jump to an image by specific number or forward or backward relative to the current location.

- *Equation*. Use this option to jump to an equation in the document by specific number or relative to the current position.

- *Object*. Use this option to jump to specific types of OLE objects such as bit maps, media clips, embedded sounds, and so on.

- *Heading*. Choose this option to jump to a specific heading number or move a certain number of headings relative to the current location.

Using the Navigation Toolbar

New in Word 97 is a navigation tool on the vertical scrollbar. The navigation tool consists of controls that work in concert with the Find and Go To features described in the previous section. You use these controls to browse through the document using many of the same search criteria described in the previous section (page, section, footnote, and so on.), with the exception of the Line and Bookmark selections. Two additional items, Go To and Find, are included in the browse objects.

At the bottom of the vertical scrollbar are three buttons (see Figure 4.24), described in the following list:

FIG. 4.24

The navigation tools reside at the bottom of the vertical scroll bar.

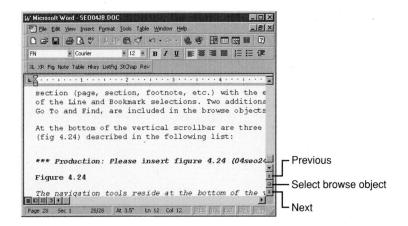

- *Previous*. Click this button to move back in the document to the previous occurrence of the selected browse object. If you're using the Find object, for example, use this button to find the previous occurrence of the word, phrase, style, and so on.

- *Select Browse Object.* Click this button to select the type of browse object to use for navigation. Word opens a dialog box at the cursor from which you select the type of browse object.

- *Next.* Click this button to move forward in the document to the next occurrence of the browse object.

A good example of a use for the browse tools is when you are performing a search for some specific text using the Find page of the Find and Replace dialog box. Instead of opening the dialog box each time you want to perform an additional search, you simply click the Next or Previous browse buttons to search forward or backward for the next occurrence of the text. ●

Part

II

Ch

4

CHAPTER 5

Using Outlines, Templates, and Styles

by Jim Boyce

Microsoft Word 97 provides several features that help you organize and create documents quickly and easily, both at the planning stage and when actually creating the document. This chapter examines these features. ■

Creating and using outlines

Word helps you plan and organize documents through its built-in outlining capability. Word 97 adds a few new features that make outlining even more powerful.

Creating and using templates

Templates enable you to automate much of a document's formatting and can considerably speed up the document creation process.

Using styles

Styles enable you to apply specific paragraph and font properties to text automatically by simply applying a style to the selection. ·

Overview of New Features

Word 97 includes a few new features to improve the use of styles. This section provides a brief overview of those new features. Later in this chapter you'll read about these features in detail.

Style Previews

Styles are named groups of settings that you can apply to paragraphs to quickly format text. A new feature in Word 97 is the presence of *style previews*. The Formatting toolbar includes a drop-down list from which you can choose a style to apply to the current paragraph. Previously, the drop-down list showed only the names of the styles. Word 97 now provides a preview of the style within the drop-down list. This preview can help you identify the style you want.

Automatic Style Definition

Word 97 makes style creation much easier by automating the process. Word automatically creates styles as you apply paragraph and character formatting. You can then use the style elsewhere in the document. Type a one-line, centered paragraph at the top of a document, for example, and Word assumes you are entering a title. Word will automatically apply a title style to the paragraph. Automatic style definition is controlled by the setting Define Styles Based On Your Formatting on the AutoFormat As You Type property page.

Automatic Style Updating

Each style has a selection of properties associated with it, including typeface, font size, character scale, indention, and much more. Word 97 adds a new property called *automatic update* to each style. This automatic update property enables Word to automatically update all instances where the style is used in a document when you change only one instance of the style. For example, assume you've created a heading style with 14-point font size and bold. You've marked the style for automatic updating. You create a document that uses the style in 50 locations. You then highlight all the text in the style and apply italic to it. The text in each of the other 49 locations also has italic applied to it. Thus, the style is updated throughout the document automatically.

▶ **See** "Using Word Templates," **p. 94**

Creating and Using Outlines

Writing a letter is usually a simple task. Writing longer documents such as short stories, long reports, or books is a much greater challenge. Having written and contributed to more than 30 books, I can assure you that a good outline is mandatory if you hope to accomplish the task with any sort of success.

Word offers an excellent set of features for creating and using outlines to organize your documents. Outlining the document not only helps you build the structure and flow of the document but also helps you navigate through it and modify the document much more quickly. This section explains how to make the best use of the outline features in Word 97.

N O T E   *Styles* are discussed briefly in this section of the chapter and discussed in more detail later in the section "Creating and Using Styles." If you're not familiar with styles, for now you just need to understand that a style is a set of named formatting characteristics that you can apply to a paragraph to control its appearance. You might create a style called ArialTitle, for example, with center justification, Arial typeface, and 16-point bold font. Whenever you want to use that paragraph and text formatting, you just apply the ArialTitle style and Word applies the formatting automatically. By naming styles, you make it easy to quickly apply the same style to many paragraphs within a document. ■

Understanding Outlines in Word

An outline is really little more than a hierarchical ranking of the headings in a document. This chapter, for example, is written using several different levels of headings to help organize the material and denote the relative importance of the topics. Figure 5.1 shows an example of a chapter outline from this book.

FIG. 5.1
An outline helps you organize large amounts of information into logical chunks.

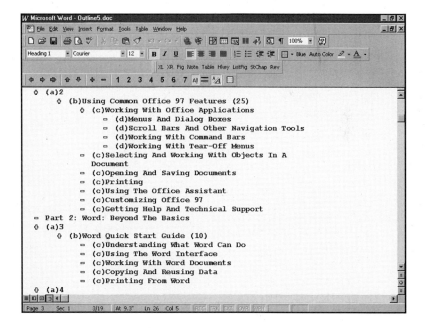

Part
II

Ch
5

Outlines in Word rely on Word's predefined heading styles. These heading styles, named Heading 1, Heading 2, and so on, each have a relative level of importance in the outline. The Heading 1 style represents the highest level in the outline. Heading 6 represents the lowest level. These different heading levels organize the structure of the document and provide a means for quickly navigating the document. Outline View, discussed in the next section, is one of the mechanisms that helps you navigate through the outline.

Using Outline View

Outline View displays the document headings in a collapsible or expandable, hierarchical tree. Figure 5.1 showed a document in Outline View. To select Outline View, choose View, Outline. To switch back to Normal View, choose View, Normal (or choose a different view mode from the View menu).

Because of the different formatting characteristics associated with each heading, headings automatically indent to show their relative importance to one another. Outline View therefore gives you a hierarchical view of the document. Headings are not the only document element that appear in Outline View, however. Outline View doesn't change the structure or content of the document; it changes only your view of the document.

You can control the level of detail you view in Outline View, thereby controlling how much of the document and/or outline structure you see. When you choose Outline View, Word opens the Outlining toolbar previously shown in Figure 5.1.

1. Click the 1 in the toolbar to view only level 1 (uppermost) headings.
2. Click the 2 to view levels 1 and 2, and so on.
3. To view all of the document, including those paragraphs that have styles other than the heading styles associated with them, click All.

If you want to view only the first line of each paragraph, whether heading or otherwise, click the Show First Line Only button on the toolbar. This is helpful when you want to view the first line of the normal paragraphs within each heading but not the entire paragraph content.

When you create an outline, you'll find that each heading has its own character formatting. If you prefer not to see the character formatting, click the Show Formatting button on the Outline toolbar.

 TIP   You can modify the heading styles to suit your own formatting preferences, changing typeface, font size, and other characteristics. To change a style's formatting, choose Format, Style. Select the style from the list in the Style dialog box and click Modify. For more information on using styles, see the section "Creating and Using Styles," later in this chapter.

Creating an Outline

The mechanics of creating an outline are simple—just apply to each paragraph the appropriate heading style based on the paragraph's level in the outline hierarchy. The heading will assume its correct level in the outline hierarchy. If necessary, you can change each paragraph's level in the outline. The slow method is to click in the paragraph and then choose the desired heading or other style from the style list in the Formatting toolbar. Here's the quick method: place the insertion point in the paragraph and press Alt+Shift+Right Arrow to decrease the heading's importance (increase its indention) or press Alt+Shift+LeftArrow to increase its importance (decrease its indention).

CAUTION

Promoting and demoting existing text in an outline automatically applies the heading styles, replacing any previous style associated with the paragraph.

Because you can apply the heading styles to each paragraph at any time, you can type the entire outline and then apply the desired heading levels to it. Or, you can apply the heading levels as you go along. When you're ready to start entering normal text within a heading, just insert a paragraph after the heading and format it using the Normal style or other nonheading style as appropriate.

Using Outline Paragraph Formatting

In addition to the Heading styles, Word also includes nine outline levels that you can apply to paragraphs. These outline levels are separate from the paragraph's style, which enables Word to do a better job of integrating body text into the hierarchical structure of a document. The outline levels also give you greater flexibility in formatting and viewing the document. Normal body text does not indent within the outline structure unless you specifically apply an indent within the paragraph's formatting. The outline levels essentially perform that indention for you while maintaining the nonheading style of the paragraph and its associated character and paragraph formatting.

To apply an outline level to a paragraph, right-click the paragraph and choose Paragraph from the context menu. Or, click in the paragraph and choose Format, Paragraph to open the Paragraph property sheet shown in Figure 5.2.

FIG. 5.2
Use the Paragraph property sheet to specify the outline level and other properties of the paragraph, including its formatting.

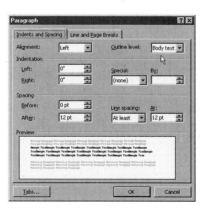

From the Outline Level drop-down list, select the outline level to apply to the paragraph. To apply no outline level to the paragraph, choose Body Text from the drop-down list.

TIP The outline levels provide an excellent mechanism for imposing a hierarchical outline structure to a document without affecting the appearance of the headings. The heading styles assume their associated formats in the heading. The outline levels apply the hierarchical structure without affecting the appearance of the text. Outline levels, therefore, provide an "invisible" method of outlining.

The outline levels offer a means for creating your own outline heading styles without affecting or requiring that you modify the existing heading styles defined by Word. You can create your own heading styles that use the outline paragraph levels to provide outline structure while retaining the special formatting you apply through the headings' styles. You might create an entire document using outline level assignments for all paragraphs and not use the body text property for any of the document. It is irrelevant whether or not the body text is actually formatted as body text. You can apply a sufficiently low outline level (level 9, for example) to retain the text's position in the document as the lowest level in the structure but not affect appearance or printing.

Navigating with the Outline

Outlines are important for organizing the logical structure of a document, but they also play an important role in helping you navigate through a document. As explained previously in this section, the outline hierarchy is expandable or collapsible to enable you to show only the level you want to see. If you have a very long document (and thus a very long outline), you can, for example, collapse the outline to show only Heading 1 level headings. This might enable all the first-level headings to appear on the display at one time. In effect, you're seeing the entire document with everything except the first-level headings hidden.

If you need to edit text within a specific heading, just click the heading to move the insertion point, then either choose Normal view or expand the outline view to show the entire document and begin working in the selected section. When you need to move to a section elsewhere in the document, collapse the outline by clicking a lower-numbered heading level button on the Outlining toolbar, select the heading in which you want to work, and then expand the document again to begin adding or editing text.

The Document Map, explained in Chapter 4, "Simplifying and Automating Tasks," offers another method for viewing the structure of an outline and navigating within the document. The Document Map uses the heading levels in the document to display the Document Map view. In effect, this gives you an outline view in the Document Map pane while you retain a normal view in the document pane. This gives you the best of both worlds: an outline view for navigation and a normal view for editing. Just click in the Document Map where you want to work, and Word jumps to that point in the document.

Printing an Outline

As handy as it is to be able to view a document in Outline View, it still is sometimes helpful to have a hard copy of an outline. The hard copy is much more portable than your computer, for example.

There is nothing mysterious or difficult about printing an outline, even when the document contains plenty of other text in addition to the headings. To print an outline, just select Outline view and expand or collapse the outline to show the amount of detail you want in the printed copy. Then, choose <u>F</u>ile, <u>P</u>rint and print the document as you would any other. Word will print the outline as it appears on your display, complete with formatting and indention, rather than the entire content of the document.

N O T E If you have configured Word to show only the first line of a paragraph in Outline view, Word prints the entire paragraph even if only one line is showing in the Outline view. ▪

TROUBLESHOOTING

When I print from Outline view, the entire document prints. How do I print only the outline? Before you print, make sure you select the desired level that includes only the information you want to appear on the printed page, such as Heading3 or Heading4. Also make sure not to print the document from a Print Preview window. Print Preview does not properly format the document using its outline structure.

Creating and Using Templates

In Word, a *template* is essentially a document containing styles, macros, AutoText entries, custom toolbars, shortcut keys, and boilerplate text you use as a basis for creating other documents. It serves as a template for the creation of other documents, which is where it gets its name. Documents have a dot file extension (compared to a document file's doc extension).

You can attach one template to a document at a time, and settings and resources stored in the template are available to the document to which the template is attached. If you have multiple documents open at one time, each with its own template attached, the resources in each template are available only to the document to which it is attached.

Word includes a defaultglobal template called Normal.dot that stores resources that are available to all documents. Normal.dot, which is stored in the Templates folder, is global by design and becomes available automatically when you start Word. Because it is global, all documents have access to the resources in Normal.dot. As you begin customizing settings, you should place in Normal.dot only those resources that you want available to all documents. Create custom templates for the specific types of documents that you create.

T I P You can restore the Normal.dot template to its default state (as it was when Word was installed) by closing Word, renaming or deleting the existing Normal.dot file, then restarting Word. Word will create a default Normal.dot file in the Templates folder.

You also can create your own templates that contain resources you want made available to all documents. These are called *global templates*. These templates are not any different from Normal.dot or other attached templates except in the way they are loaded. Rather than being attached to a specific document, you load them manually when you need them or configure Word to load them automatically (explained later in the section "Using Global Templates").

Part
II

Ch

5

Understanding How Word Locates Templates

Office 97 creates a specific folder structure to contain templates for the Office applications. Figure 5.3 shows the default folder structure for templates in Office 97. By default, general templates are stored in the Templates folder under the main Office folder. Other templates are stored in the subfolders within the Templates folder.

FIG. 5.3

Office stores all templates in a common folder structure under the primary Office folder.

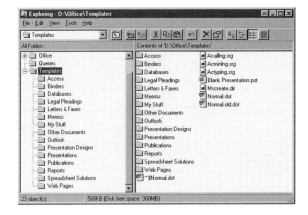

When you choose File, New, Word displays the New property sheet shown in Figure 5.4. The templates that appear in the New property sheet depend on the settings you have configured in Word for file locations (explained later in this chapter) as well as the templates stored in the specified folders.

The templates stored in the Templates folder appear in the General page. Templates in the subfolders under the Templates folder appear on their own tabbed pages in the New property sheet. If you add other folders under the Templates folder, those folders will appear as additional pages in the New property sheet if the folders contain template files. Thus, you can customize the organization of your templates simply by changing the folder structure in which the templates are stored.

FIG. 5.4

The New property sheet lists templates and wizards you can use as a basis to create other documents.

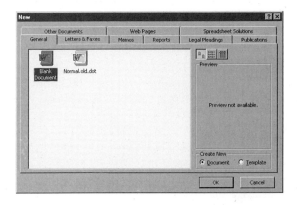

To specify the location in which Word looks for document templates, choose Tools, Options to display the Options property sheet and click the File Locations tab to display the File Locations page (see Figure 5.5). The User Templates setting points to the primary folder in which Word will look for templates when you choose File, New or begin the process of attaching a template to a document. The Workgroup Templates setting specifies the location of templates that are shared among a workgroup.

FIG. 5.5
Use the File Locations page to specify the location of templates, your documents, and other files.

 You can place a custom Normal.dot file in the workgroup template folder on a server, making the resources available in the template available automatically to all users in the workgroup. Each user then would not have his or her own Normal.dot file.

About Wizards

In Office, *wizards* automate tasks, often eliminating the need for you to understand how to perform a task. The wizard prompts you for the necessary information to complete the task and then performs the task for you. Word includes several wizards for creating envelopes, letters, resumes, and other documents.

▶ **See** "Using Wizards and the Office Assistant," **p. 75**

You might think that a wizard contains a lot of programming code. It does, but perhaps not in the form you think. A wizard is just a template file with a wiz file extension and all the macros, styles, and other resources necessary to automate the task for which the wizard is designed. Therefore, you can create your own wizards to automate tasks. Naturally, doing so requires an understanding of Visual Basic for Applications (VBA), the programming language used by Office 97. The point to understand, however, is that wizards are not something only a Microsoft programmer can create. Given a knowledge of VBA, you too can create complex wizards. The other point to understand is that there is no real difference between document files, templates, or wizards. The only difference is in how they are used.

▶ **See** "Creating Your Own Applications with VBA," **p. 1143**

▶ **See** "Using VBScript," **p. 1165**

N O T E   Although documents, templates, and wizards are essentially the same, Word does treat
them differently. You can't attach a template to another template or to a wizard, for
example. ▨

Using Word Templates

As explained earlier, Normal.dot is global by design and all its resources are available for every document. To use the resources in another template, you must either attach the template to the document or load the template globally. Attaching a template to a document makes its resources available only to that document. Loading a template globally makes its resources available to all open documents during the current Word session.

To attach a template to a document, complete the following steps:

1. Make the document active and choose <u>T</u>ools, Templates and Add-<u>I</u>ns. Word displays the Templates and Add-Ins dialog box shown in Figure 5.6.
2. Click the <u>A</u>ttach button to open the Attach Template dialog box (a standard File Open dialog box).
3. Locate and select the template and choose <u>O</u>pen. Word returns you to the Templates and Add-Ins dialog box and places the template path in the Document <u>T</u>emplate text box.

FIG. 5.6

Use the Templates and Add-Ins dialog box to attach a template to a document or load templates globally.

When you attach a template to a document, Word stores that association with the document. The next time you open the document, the template will still be attached and its resources available to the document.

The Automatically Update Document Styles check box on the Templates and Add-Ins dialog box determines whether or not Word automatically updates the styles in the active document when you load the document. If changes have been made to styles in the template, for example, and this check box is enabled, the styles in the document will be updated automatically each time you load the document. This helps ensure that the styles in the document are always up to date and is particularly helpful when you're working as part of a workgroup.

An administrator or supervisor can modify a single shared template, and all the documents across the workgroup to which the template is attached can be updated automatically just by loading the document and saving it again.

You also can base a document on a template when you start the new document. The New dialog box (choose File, New) contains two option buttons, Document and Template, that define the type of document to create. If you choose Document, Word starts the new document based on the selected template. Choosing the Template option starts a new template based on the selected template.

Using Global Templates

A global template is one that is available to all documents during the current Word session. You might create macros that you want to use in all documents and store those in a global template. Note that a template is global only because of the way you load it—any template can be loaded globally.

To make a template global, complete the following steps:

1. Choose Tools, Templates and Add-Ins. Any templates currently loaded globally appear in the Global Templates and Add-Ins list.

2. To load a template globally, choose Add. Use the resulting Add Template dialog box (a standard File Open dialog box) to locate and select the template.

3. Choose OK to place the template name in the global list.

4. Repeat the process for any other templates you want to load globally. Then in the Templates and Add-Ins dialog box, click OK.

 TIP Templates consume memory and other system resources. If you are finished using a template, consider removing it from the list of global templates to free its resources for the system and other applications.

Templates that you load using this method are available throughout the current Word session. When you close Word, those global templates are closed as well and are not reloaded automatically in the next Word session. They do, however, remain in the list. All you have to do to load them is open the Templates and Add-Ins dialog box and place a check mark beside the ones you want to load.

If you want one or more templates to be loaded globally and automatically as soon as you start Word, place those templates in the Startup folder. The Startup folder is located in *MSOffice\Office\Startup*, where *MSOffice* is your primary Office 97 folder. You don't have to do anything else to have the templates load automatically—placing them in the Startup folder takes care of it.

Creating Your Own Templates

Templates are a powerful mechanism for automating document creation. So, it's likely that you'll want to create your own templates that are tailored to the type of work you do and the way you work. The following sections examine the key issues involved in creating your own templates.

Part
II
Ch
5

To start a new template, complete the following steps:

1. Choose File, New to open the New property sheet.
2. Select the existing template on which you want to base the new template.
3. Choose the Template option button and choose OK. Word opens a new document window for the template.
4. Perform whatever customization you want, such as creating toolbars, styles, macros, shortcut key definitions, and boilerplate text. Then, save the template. Word will automatically apply a dot file extension to the file.

Using Boilerplate Text   Boilerplate text is text that typically remains the same from document to document. If you compose contracts, for example, much of the language in the contract remains the same. That's boilerplate text.

Any text you put in a template carries through to the documents that are based on that template. You might create a form letter, for example, and save it as a template. When you want to write a letter based on that form letter, you just start a new document based on the form letter template. The new document will have the text included in it automatically.

When you need to define boilerplate text, just open the template you'll be using for the documents. Type and format the text, and then save the template.

Storing Resources in a Specific Template   Generally, the easiest way to place resources such as custom toolbars in a specific template is to open the template, and then create the resource. In the case of custom toolbars, for example, you can store the toolbar either in Normal.dot or in the current document by selecting the desired template from the New Toolbar dialog box (see Figure 5.7). Choose Tools, Customize, Toolbars to open this property page.

FIG. 5.7

When creating a toolbar, you must specify whether the toolbar will be stored in Normal.dot or the current document (or template).

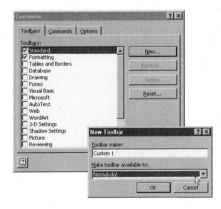

The following list explains how to specify the storage location other than in Normal.dot for specific types of resources:

- *AutoText*. Open the template in which you want to store the AutoText entry. Choose Insert, AutoText, AutoText to open the AutoText page of the AutoCorrect property sheet. From the Look In drop-down list, choose the template in which you want the entries stored. Click the Enter AutoText Entries Here text box and choose Add.

- *Macros*. Open the template in which you want the macro stored. Choose Tools, Macro, Record New Macro to open the Record Macro dialog box. From the Store Macro In drop-down list, choose the current template. Proceed with the macro recording process.

- *Styles*. Open the document or template in which you want the style to be stored. If you want the style stored in the current document, clear the Add to Template check box in the New Style dialog box. Place a check mark in this box if you want the style stored in the template that is attached to the current document.

- *Toolbars*. Open the template in which you want the toolbar stored. Right-click any toolbar and choose Customize or choose Tools, Customize to open the Customize property sheet. On the Toolbars page, click the New button. In the New Toolbar dialog box, select the current template.

- *Boilerplate Text*. Open the template in which you want the text created and simply type and format the text. Save the template. Any documents you create based on the template will include all the text in the template, complete with formatting.

- *Shortcut Keys*. Open the template in which you want the shortcut key definitions stored. Choose Tools, Customize to open the Customize property sheet. Select the Commands tab to display the Commands page. Choose the Keyboard button. Select the current template from the Save Changes In drop-down list.

The previous list is not intended as a complete explanation of how to create these types of resources. These topics are explored elsewhere in this book.

▶ **See** "Working with Toolbars," **p. 26**

▶ **See** "AutoText," **p. 59**

▶ **See** "Creating and Using Styles," **p. 98**

▶ **See** "Create Macros with the Macro Recorder," **p. 220**

Using the Organizer

You don't have to create resources in the template where they will reside. Instead, you can use the Organizer to copy resources from one document or template to another. The section "Copying, Deleting, and Renaming Styles," later in this chapter, explains how to use the Organizer to move styles between template files. You also can use the Organizer to copy AutoText entries, toolbars, and macros from one template to another.

To open the Organizer, choose Tools, Templates and Add-Ins, and then click the Organizer button. When the Organizer appears, click the tab for the type of resource you want to copy. Figure 5.8 shows the Toolbars page as an example.

Part

II

Ch

5

FIG. 5.8

Use the Organizer to copy resources between template files.

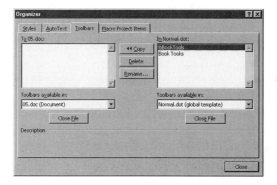

The process for copying resources is the same regardless of the type of resource. Open the two templates in the Organizer, select the source resource, and choose Copy to copy it to the other template.

Creating and Using Styles

A *style* is a named set of formatting characteristics. Styles provide a means of quickly and easily applying paragraph and character formatting to text. You define the style by giving it a name and various paragraph and/or character formatting properties. Then, instead of manually applying individual formatting characteristics through the Paragraph and Font property sheets, you simply apply the style to the paragraph or text.

The paragraph or selected text automatically takes on the formatting characteristics assigned to the style. Therefore, the primary purpose of styles is to simplify and standardize formatting. Using styles in your documents can speed up document creation considerably by automating most, if not all, of your paragraph and character formatting.

Word includes several paragraph styles and a few character styles by default, but you can create any number of styles to suit your needs. In fact, you can use styles to create templates that help you quickly create specific types of documents. If you happen to be a screenwriter, for example, you could create a set of styles that set up the paragraph formats for direction, dialog, action, and so on. When you want to write a specific body of text, such as dialog, you simply apply that style to the paragraph and begin typing. Word takes care of the formatting for you.

Understanding Word Styles

Word recognizes two types of styles: paragraph and character. A paragraph style applies to an entire paragraph and encompasses all of the formatting characteristics possible that control the paragraph's appearance. The following list includes some of the common paragraph formatting characteristics:

- Line spacing
- Indention

- Tab stops
- Borders
- Font properties

Every paragraph has a style associated with it. The default paragraph style is called Normal. Character styles apply only to selections of text, rather than to entire paragraphs (although you can select all of the text in a paragraph and apply a character style to that text).

Character styles apply to individual character formatting properties such as those in the following list:

- Typeface
- Font size
- Bold
- Underline

All of the properties you can apply with the Font property sheet (by choosing Format, Font) can be applied to a character style. Unlike paragraph styles, there is no default character style. This means that characters do not have to have a character style applied to them.

Text that has no character style applied to it assumes the character formatting inherent in the paragraph style for the paragraph in which it resides. Text that has a character style applied to it assumes the character formatting inherent in the character style as well as the character formatting inherent in its paragraph style. For example, assume you apply a paragraph style that specifies the text in the paragraph be 14-point Arial bold. Then you apply to some of the text in the paragraph a character style that specifies italic. The resulting text will be 14-point Arial bold italic.

The character style takes precedence over the font characteristics specified by the paragraph style. For example, assume you have a paragraph style that specifies Arial typeface and a character style named TNR that specifies Times New Roman typeface. Any text in the paragraph with no character style will be Arial. Any text with the TNR character style will use Times New Roman.

You can create character styles that inherit the font characteristics of the paragraph style in which they are applied but which also have their own font characteristics. You might create a style that inherits the typeface of the paragraph style, for example, but which applies bold, underline, and italic to the text. If you apply the character style in two paragraphs that each use a different typeface in the paragraph style, the text in each paragraph will inherit the typeface of its paragraph style, but all of the text to which the character style is applied, regardless of which paragraph it is in, will be bold, underlined, and italic.

Applying a Style

You can apply a style to a paragraph before or after you actually type the text in the paragraph. The paragraph and any text in it take on the characteristics of the style as soon as you apply the style. The easiest way to apply a style is to place the insertion point in the paragraph (click

Part

II

Ch

5

anywhere in the paragraph) and select the style from the Styles drop-down list in the Formatting toolbar (see Figure 5.9). You'll notice that the list provides a preview of each style within the list, including the typeface and font characteristics. Note that paragraph styles have a small paragraph mark at the right edge of the entry in the list. The four small lines indicate the alignment of the paragraph style (left, centered, right, aligned). The number indicates the primary point size defined for text by the style.

If you prefer to use the keyboard to apply styles, press Ctrl+Shift+S to highlight the current style in the Style drop-down list, and then type the name of the style to apply and press Enter. Or, press Ctrl+Shift+S and then press the up or down arrow key to scroll through the list.

FIG. 5.9

The Styles drop-down list provides a preview of each style's major properties.

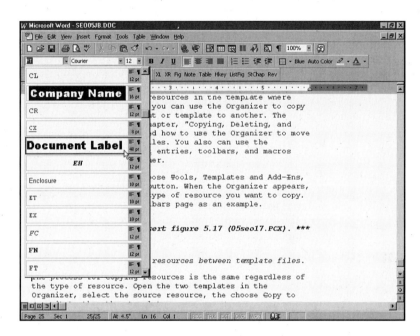

 TIP   Touch typists will find it easiest to use Ctrl+Shift+S to apply styles because you don't have to remove your hand from the keyboard. To quickly apply the Normal style to the current paragraph, press Ctrl+Shift+N. To activate the Font drop-down list to choose a typeface, press Ctrl+Shift+F.

You also can use the menu to apply styles:

1. Place the insertion point in the paragraph and then choose Format, Style to open the Style dialog box (see Figure 5.10). On the left side of the dialog box, Word displays the currently defined styles.

2. Choose from the List drop-down list the types of styles to show in the list. The Styles In Use option displays all built-in styles that you have applied or modified and any styles you have defined in the active document. The User-Defined Styles option displays only those styles you have defined in the active document. The All Styles option displays all styles available to the active document.

To view the properties of an existing style, select the style from the list. The Paragraph Preview box shows a sample of the paragraph formatting for the selected style. The Character Preview box shows a sample of the character formatting for the style. The Description area provides a description of the style's properties. Select the desired style from the <u>S</u>tyles list and click <u>A</u>pply.

T I P You can assign a shortcut key to each style to help you quickly apply styles. Just place the insertion point in the paragraph and press the key combination assigned to the style. To assign a shortcut key to a style, choose F<u>o</u>rmat, <u>S</u>tyle and then select the style to which you want to apply the shortcut key. Click <u>M</u>odify and then Shortcut <u>K</u>ey. Word opens a Customize Keyboard dialog box in which you can assign a key combination to the style.

FIG. 5.10

The Style dialog box lets you view, create, and modify paragraph and character styles.

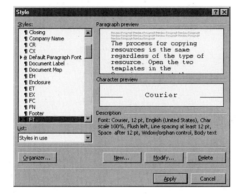

Creating a Style

As mentioned previously, Word includes several styles and you can modify these styles or create as many of your own as you need. Creating a style is a relatively simple process. You simply specify the name for the style and then specify the formatting characteristics of the style.

T I P If you want to base the new style's paragraph characteristics on an existing style, first click in the existing paragraph before opening the Styles dialog box. If you want the text characteristics for the style applied to a specific selection of text in the existing paragraph, highlight the text before opening the Styles dialog box.

To create a style, complete the following steps:

1. Choose F<u>o</u>rmat, <u>S</u>tyle. Word displays the Style dialog box previously shown in Figure 5.10.

2. Then click the <u>N</u>ew button to display the New Style dialog box (see Figure 5.11). If applicable, select a style on which you want to base the new style.

FIG. 5.11

Use the New Style
dialog box to create
your own styles.

3. In the Name text box, type the name for your new style. Style names retain their case in the list, so typing MyStyle, for example, will store the style by that name rather than all uppercase or all lowercase. The style names are not case sensitive, however. Using the previous example, you could press Ctrl+Shift+S to activate the Style drop-down list and then type **mystyle** or **MYSTYLE** to choose the style named MyStyle.

4. From the Style Type drop-down list, choose either Paragraph or Character depending on the type of style you want to create. The Based On list shows the style on which the new style will be based, which defaults to the style of the paragraph that was selected when you entered the Style dialog box.

5. From the Style For Following Paragraph drop-down list, select the style that you want applied to the paragraph immediately following the one to which the new style is applied. If you create a Figure Number style, for example, you might create a Figure Caption style for the paragraph that immediately follows. So, when you define the Figure Number style, you would select Figure Caption as the style for the following paragraph. When you press Enter at the end of the Figure Number paragraph, Word automatically applies the Figure Caption style to the next paragraph. If you don't specify a different following paragraph style, Word defaults to the same style.

6. Define the format for the paragraph and/or text. Click the Format button to open a menu from which you can select various paragraph and text style options for the paragraph. Most of the settings are self-explanatory. The following sections briefly describe those few that are not as obvious.

N O T E The following sections explain the formatting options that are less intuitively obvious. For additional explanation of other options not discussed here, use Help or the Office Assistant. ▪

Character Spacing   The Character Spacing page on the Font property sheet (see Figure 5.12) lets you control the spacing, scale, and other font characteristics that define the size and spacing of the text. Choose the Format button and then Font from the New Style dialog box to access this sheet. The following list explains these options:

FIG. 5.12

Use the Character Spacing page to define the scale, spacing, and kerning for the style's text.

- ■ *Scale*. This control lets you specify the scale of the text relative to a normal of 100%. Scale enables you to make the text larger or smaller, including spacing, than the default size of the typeface and font.

- ■ *Spacing*. This option specifies the spacing between characters and can be set to normal, condensed, or expanded. The associated By control lets you specify the percentage the text is condensed or expanded. The default unit is points, but you can use other measurements by appending their units to the number (such as 3cm for centimeters).

- ■ *Position*. Use this option to specify the position of the text relative to the baseline of the text, and the associated By control to the specify the amount above or below the baseline. The default unit is points, but you can use any unit of measure supported by Word.

- ■ *Kerning For Fonts*. *Kerning* adjusts the spacing between certain pairs of characters to provide a relative even spacing between characters. The amount of spacing depends on the design of the typeface. Use the associated Points And Above control to specify the size at which Word begins kerning the text.

Paragraph Choose Paragraph from the Format menu in the New Style dialog box to specify the indention and other characteristics of the paragraph. The following list explains some of the properties and controls on the Indents and Spacing page (see Figure 5.13):

- ■ *Outline Level*. Using this control, specify the outline level for the paragraph. The outline level enables you to assign a hierarchical level to the paragraph to build outlines. Refer to the section "Using Outlines," previously in this chapter, for more information regarding outline levels and how they are different from Word's heading styles.

T I P Word uses the default measurement units specified in the General page of the Options property sheet for spacing. You can choose between inches, centimeters, picas, or points. Type a number followed by **pt** to specify points. Use **cm** for centimeters and **pi** for picas.

Part
II

Ch
5

FIG. 5.13

Specify the general characteristics of the paragraph with the Indents and Spacing page.

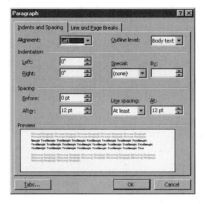

> ■ *Spacing.* Use these controls to specify the spacing between the current paragraph and the previous and next paragraphs. Also specify the spacing between lines in the paragraph with the Line Spacing control.

Use the Line and Page Breaks page (see Figure 5.14) to specify other general properties for the paragraph. The following list explains the options in the Line and Page Breaks page:

> ■ *Widow/Orphan Control.* The last line of a paragraph at the top of a page is called a *widow*. The first line of a paragraph at the bottom of a page by itself is called an *orphan*. Enable this check box to prevent Word from leaving widows and orphans with this paragraph style. Word adjusts the page breaks to move one or more lines preceding the widow to the same page as the widow or moves the orphan to the following page.

> ■ *Keep Lines Together.* Enabling this check box prevents Word from making page breaks within a paragraph. Instead, Word moves the whole paragraph to the following page. This can result in excessive white space on the page.

FIG. 5.14

Specify how Word handles page breaks and other paragraph characteristics with the Line and Page Breaks page.

> ■ *Keep With Next.* Enabling this option prevents Word from making a page break between the current paragraph and the following paragraph.

- *Page Break Before.* Enable this option to force Word to insert a page break prior to the paragraph (always start the paragraph on a new line).

- *Suppress Line Numbers.* Enable this option to prevent Word from displaying line numbers beside the lines in the paragraph. This setting has no effect if you aren't using line numbers.

- *Don't Hyphenate.* Enable this option to prevent Word from automatically hyphenating words in the paragraph.

Adding the Style to the Current Template The Add to Template check box on the New Style dialog box determines where Word stores the new paragraph style. If you enable this check box, Word stores the style in the template attached to the active document, which makes the style available to other documents that use the same template. If you clear this check box, Word stores the style only in the active document.

Modifying and Updating a Style

To modify a style, complete the following steps:

1. Choose Format, Style to open the Style dialog box.

2. Select the style to modify and click the Modify button. Word opens the Modify Style dialog box, which is virtually identical to the New Style dialog box.

3. Set the properties you want for the style and choose OK.

The Automatically Update check box on the New Style and Modify Style dialog boxes determines how Word handles the style globally throughout the document when you modify the style in one location. If this check box is enabled and you modify the formatting of a paragraph in the document, Word automatically applies those changes to the style and therefore to all occurrences of the style in the document.

Using the Style Area

The style of the active paragraph appears in the Style drop-down list of the Formatting toolbar, giving you a quick indication of the paragraph's current style. If you prefer, you can open the Style Area to display the style names of all paragraphs visible on the display. Figure 5.15 shows the Style Area open at the left of the document workspace.

To turn on the Style Area, you simply need to allocate some space to it. To do so, choose Tools, Options. On the View page of the Options property sheet, use the Style Area Width spin control to set the width of the Style Area. To turn off the Style Area, set its width to zero.

Using the Style Gallery

The Styleæ Gallery (see Figure 5.16) gives you a means of viewing the styles defined in all of the templates in the Templates folder and its subfolders. To open the Style Gallery, choose Format, Style Gallery.

Part

II

Ch

5

FIG. 5.15

The Style Area displays the style name of each paragraph; the width of the Style Area is user-definable.

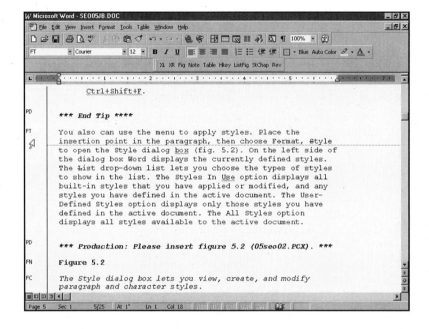

FIG. 5.16

Use the Style Gallery to preview and apply styles from other templates to the current document.

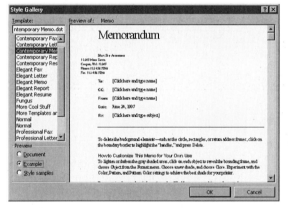

From the Template list, choose the template whose styles you want to preview. From the Preview group, choose one of the following option buttons:

- *Document*. Choose this option to view the active document with the styles applied from the selected template.

- *Example*. Choose this option button to view a sample document that uses styles from the selected template.

- *Style Samples*. Choose this option to view examples of specific styles in the selected template.

To copy the styles from a template to the active document, just double-click the template in the Template list. Word copies the styles to the active document and closes the Style Gallery. Or, select the template and choose OK. Choose Cancel to close the Style Gallery without applying any styles to the active document.

Copying, Deleting, and Renaming Styles

The Style Organizer provides a means by which you can copy, delete, and rename styles. The Style Organizer is actually a subset of the Organizer, which helps you copy objects between templates. You can use the Styles page of the Organizer to copy individual styles between documents and templates (unlike the Style Gallery, which copies all styles from the selected template to the active document). Figure 5.17 shows the Styles page of the Organizer.

FIG. 5.17

Use the Organizer to copy styles and other objects between documents and templates.

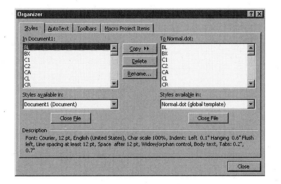

The Style Organizer displays the styles in two files at one time and enables you to copy individual styles between the two files. By default, the Style Organizer displays the active document and the default template, Normal.dot. To copy a style, select the style to be copied and click the Copy button. To delete a style, select the style and click Delete. Word will prompt you to verify the deletion. To rename a style, select the style and click Rename. To work with different files, click Close File to close the current file. Then click Open File to open a different file in the Organizer.

 TIP The Organizer also lets you copy AutoText, toolbar changes, and macros between documents and templates. For more information on using AutoText, refer to Chapter 4, "Simplifying and Automating Tasks." For more information regarding templates, see the section " Creating and Using Templates," earlier in this chapter. For more information regarding macros, refer to Chapter 11, "Using VBA in Word."

Part

II

Ch

5

Advanced Formatting and Graphics

by Jim Boyce

Knowledge of how to apply special character formatting, insert graphics, use watermarks and page backgrounds, use columns, and perform other types of page magic can make the difference between a good document and an outstanding one. This chapter helps you combine Word's powerful formatting and graphics features with your writing skill to create powerful, dynamic documents. ■

Work with sections

Word allows you to cordon off your documents into smaller areas so that you can apply different formatting to one section without affecting the other sections.

Use headers and footers

Many types of documents use headers and footers, and Word makes creating those elements an easy task.

Use watermarks, page borders, and textures

These elements not only spruce up printed documents, but also make a dramatic difference in the appearance of documents that you create for online viewing.

Use highlights, color, and graphics

Word makes applying highlighting and color to selected text easy, allowing you to set that text apart from the rest of your document. Working with graphics is somewhat more difficult, but a little background knowledge helps you use graphics effectively.

Use multiple columns in a document

Newsletters, brochures, and many other types of documents use multicolumn layout. Word offers several features to help you create multicolumn documents.

Overview of New Features

Word 97 includes several new features and enhancements of existing features to improve document formatting, placement of graphics, and the general appearance of your documents. This section offers a brief overview of the new features and enhancements. All these topics are covered in more detail later in this chapter.

Background Picture Rendering

Word now works more like a Web browser, loading text before loading graphics. This behavior enables the document user to begin browsing through a document before it is fully loaded and also emphasizes Microsoft's shift to Internet-enabled applications and documents.

Compressed Graphics

Word reduces memory and disk-space usage by automatically compressing graphics embedded in documents. Word stores JPEG images in their native format and converts all raster image formats to a new compressed format known as Portable Network Graphic (PNG).

Online Content

The Microsoft Web site includes additional content, such as clip art and templates, that you can download and use in your documents.

Text Wrapping and Formatting

Word 97 improves character formatting by supporting 90-degree text rotation in table cells, frames, and text boxes. Word 97 also enhances text wrapping around objects by adding new wrapping styles. These new options make wrapping text around irregular-shape objects easier.

Linked Text Boxes

Linked boxes enable text to flow from one page to another with other text or objects separating the boxes. A newsletter, for example, may contain a story that starts on page 1 and continues on page 4. Linked text boxes allow the text to be continuous but to appear on the two different pages. Changes flow between the two boxes automatically.

OfficeArt

OfficeArt, a new feature in Office 97, brings to all the Office applications the drawing tools that formerly were available only in PowerPoint.

Page Borders

Word 97 enables you to add a border to each page of a document to enhance the document's appearance. In addition to new border line styles, Word includes more than 150 art styles for border art that previously were included with Microsoft Publisher.

Text Borders, Shading, and Font Effects

Word offers several new features and improvements for controlling the appearance of text. Word allows you to apply borders and shading to entire paragraphs or to any selected text within a paragraph. Word also adds several new formatting options for text to create animated special effects. You can format text with blinking, flashing, sparkling, and other special effects. You apply these animated effects as you do any other character effects: by checking the Font dialog box for them (select the text and choose Format, Font).

Using and Formatting Sections

Sections are among the primary mechanisms in Word that enable to change formatting from one part of the document to another. Sections enable you to give each section its own page formatting. You can start a new section to use different page margins or columns, for example. For more information on inserting column breaks, see "Using Columns" later in this chapter.

Using Section Breaks

You create a new section by inserting a *section break* between the sections. Word supports three types of section breaks:

- *Next Page.* This type of section break causes the new section to start at the beginning of the next page and is useful for elements such as new chapters, lists, and other items that you want to start on the next page.
- *Continuous.* This section break starts on the same page. You can use this type of section break to begin using a different number of columns from the preceding section.
- *Odd Page or Even Page.* These types of section breaks start the next section on the next even- or odd-numbered page.

Section breaks appear in a document as a double line with the words Section Break in the middle of the lines, followed by a notation of the type of break. You can edit a section break like other characters in a document. You delete a section mark by putting the insertion point at the beginning of the section and pressing Delete or by placing the insertion point at the end of the section break and pressing Shift+LeftArrow to highlight the section mark, then Backspace to delete it.

Section breaks contain the settings for the text that precede them. When you delete a section break, the text before the section break becomes part of the following section and takes on that section's characteristics such as margins and page number settings.

N O T E Section breaks appear in Normal view but don't appear in Page Layout or in the printed document.

Inserting Section Breaks

To insert a section break, choose Insert, Break to display the Break dialog box (see Figure 6.1). Choose the type of section break that you want, then choose OK to insert the section break.

FIG. 6.1

Use the Break dialog box to insert section and column breaks.

After you insert a section break, place the insertion point in the section in which you want to change the formatting. Then choose File, Page Setup to display the Page Setup property sheet. In the Margins page, specify the margins for the section; then use the Apply To drop-down list to specify how to apply the margins. Choose This Section to apply the settings to the current section. Choose From This Point Forward to apply the margins to the current section and all sections following it. Choose Whole Document to apply the settings to the entire document.

You also can change the margins of a section with the mouse when viewing the document in Page Layout mode. The gray area in the vertical and horizontal ruler shows the current margin setting. Just click the edge of the margin and drag the mouse to change the margin. Drag the margin to the left to decrease the margin or to the right to increase the margin. As you drag the margin, a dashed vertical margin line appears on the document to serve as a guide for positioning the margin.

 In all viewing modes, you can set the left and right indents of individual paragraphs by using the horizontal ruler.

Inserting Page Breaks

Word automatically wraps text to the following page based on page margins, paragraph indents, and other criteria. You can insert a manual page break any time you want to force Word to start a new page. To insert a page break, press Ctrl+Enter. Page breaks appear as a single line in the document, with the words Page Break in the middle of the line. The breaks appear in Normal view but do not appear in Page Layout view or in the printed document. Delete page breaks the same way that you delete section breaks (described in the preceding section). You also can insert a page break from the Break dialog box (choose Insert, Break). Page Break is the default option on the Break dialog box.

Using Headers, Footers, and Page Numbers

Headers and footers appear at the top and bottom, respectively, of a document. Headers are often used for repeating the title or a document from page to page and for entering page numbers at the top of the document. Footers are often used for the same purpose, but at the bottom of a document. You have to enter the text for a header or footer only once; Word automatically repeats it from page to page. Headers and footers also are useful for placing backgrounds and watermarks on a page (explained later in this chapter in the section, "Using Watermarks, Page Borders, and Textures").

▶ **See** "Using Watermarks, Page Borders, and Textures," **p. 118**

Viewing Headers and Footers

The headers and footers in a document do not appear in Normal view but do appear in Page View as dimmed text. Dimming the text helps you recognize it as header/footer text and sets it apart from the document's body text.

To view a document in Header/Footer view, choose View, Header and Footer. Word switches to Page Layout mode, dims the document's body text, and brings the header area to the foreground for editing. The program also displays the Header and Footer toolbar (see Figure 6.2).

FIG. 6.2
You create and edit headers and footers by using a special view mode. You also can create other document elements in this mode.

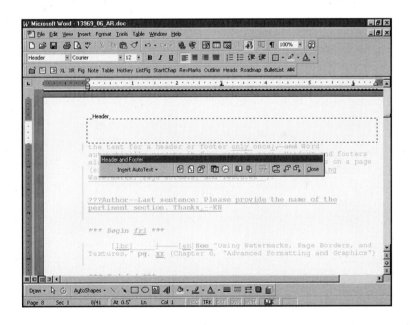

To switch to the footer, choose the Switch Between Header and Footer toolbar button or simply page down to the footer. To return to the preceding document view mode, choose Close from the Header and Footer toolbar. The other features of the Header and Footer toolbar are explained in the following sections.

Part

II

Ch

6

Using Page Numbers

You can insert page numbers into a document manually, but you wouldn't be putting Word's power to good use. Why not have Word place, format, and increment the page numbers for you?

Inserting Page Numbers   To number a document, choose Insert, Page Numbers to display the Page Numbers dialog box (see Figure 6.3). Your numbers always appear in either the header or footer.

FIG. 6.3

Use the Page Numbers dialog box to specify the location and format of page numbers.

By making choices from the Position drop-down list, specify whether you want the page numbers to appear at the top (header) or bottom (footer) of the document. Make choices from the Alignment drop-down list to specify the alignment on the page for the page numbers. The Left, Center, and Right options are relative to the page margins. The Inside and Outside options locate the page numbers relative to the document's bound edge. The Inside option places the text near the binding, and Outside places the page numbers toward the outside of the document (away from the bound edge).

Choose the Format button to open the Page Number Format dialog box (see Figure 6.4). Use this dialog box to specify the number format for the page numbers, as well as other properties.

FIG. 6.4

In the Page Number Format dialog box, you specify the style of page number to use. You also specify the starting number for the section.

From the Number Format drop-down list, you can choose one of five options to use numbers, letters, or Roman numerals for the page numbers. If you want to include the chapter number in the page number, such as 3-1 (chapter 3, page 1), enable the Include Chapter Number check box. This option relies on the built-in heading styles in Word to indicate the start of a new chapter (or other logical document-division element). From the Chapter Starts with Style drop-down list, choose the heading style that indicates the start of the document element that you want to use as the basis for numbering the pages. Then choose from the Use Separator drop-down list the character that you want Word to use as the separator between the chapter number and page number.

Next, choose how you want Word to determine the value of the first page number. If you want the page numbering to continue from the preceding section, choose Continue From Previous Section. If you want to specify your own starting letter or number, choose the Start At option button; then specify the starting number or letter by using the spin control to choose a starting number or letter.

> **T I P**   When you want to begin page numbering with a different number, letter, or format, start a new section by inserting a section break. Then use the Start At option to specify a starting page number for the new section.

Removing Page Numbers   Word inserts a page number into each page when you tell it to number the document. The page numbers adjust automatically to the document as you add and remove text, so you don't have to worry about renumbering pages as you insert or delete material. You may want to remove all the page numbers to insert a different format, however, or simply not have page numbers in the document.

To remove page numbers, choose View, Header and Footer. If the page numbers are in the document's footer, choose the Switch Between Header and Footer toolbar button or scroll down to the footer. Select the frame around the page number and press Del. Word deletes all the page numbers in the document.

If you want to remove the page numbers from only one area of the document, break the document into sections, placing section breaks above and below the area in which you want to remove the page numbers. Then use the method described in the preceding paragraph to remove the page numbers from the section.

Creating Headers and Footers

Headers and footers are useful for entering text and document elements other than page numbers. You may want to include a document title, your name, letterhead, graphics, or other elements at the top and bottom of a page, for example.

Creating headers and footers is easy in concept: just switch to Header and Footer view and then add the elements to the document. When you choose View, Header and Footer, Word switches to Header and Footer view and then opens the Header and Footer toolbar. The header editing box, a nonprinting dashed box around the header area, appears automatically. To enter text in the header, just click the header box and start typing. Do the same to enter text in the footer.

Part
II

Ch
6

> **T I P**   You can use the up and down arrow keys on the keyboard to switch between the header and footer.

Using the Header and Footer Toolbar

The Header and Footer toolbar (see Figure 6.5) appears automatically when you enter Header/Footer view. The Header and Footer toolbar provides several controls for adding and formatting page numbers, the time, date, and other information.

FIG. 6.5

Use the Header and Footer toolbar to insert dynamic text, such as page numbers, into a header or footer.

The following list describes the controls in the Header and Footer toolbar:

- *Insert AutoText*. Click this button to select AutoText entries for insertion into the header or footer.

- *Insert Page Number*. This button inserts a page-number field into the header or footer. Use this control when you want to place a page number in a location within the header or footer other than where Word automatically inserts the page number (such as within some other text).

- *Insert Number of Pages*. Use this button to insert a field containing the total number of pages in the document. You can use this control in conjunction with a page-number field to add the text *Page 2 of 24*, for example. The number 24 is the number-of-pages field and increments automatically as more pages are added to the document.

- *Format Page Number*. Click this button to open the Page Number Format dialog box, discussed in the section "Inserting Page Numbers" earlier in this chapter.

- *Insert Date*. This control inserts a field containing the current date.

- *Insert Time*. This control inserts a field containing the current time.

- *Page Setup*. Click this button to open the Page Setup property sheet, where you can set margins and other page properties.

- *Show/Hide Document Text*. Click this button to display the document's body text on and off. Normally, the body text appears dimmed. If the page is complex, turning off the body text can speed display.

- *Same As Previous*. Use this control to automatically create a header or footer that is the same as in the preceding section of the document.

- *Switch Between Header and Footer*. Use this button to switch between the header and footer.

- *Show Previous/Show Next*. Use these controls to switch to the preceding or following header or footer, respectively.

Using Graphics in Headers and Footers

You can insert graphics as well as text into a header or footer. You can insert a graphic into a header to create a letterhead, for example (see Figure 6.6).

FIG. 6.6
Use graphics in a header to create a letterhead.

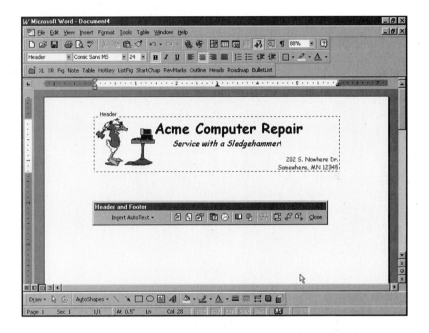

To insert the graphic, simply locate the insertion point in the header or footer at the point where you want the image to be inserted; then choose Insert, Picture. From the Picture cascade menu, choose the type of image that you want to insert; then follow Word's prompts to complete the process. Inserting graphics is covered in detail later in this chapter, in the section "Integrating Graphics."

The header/footer box enlarges as necessary to accommodate the image. You then can resize and relocate the image as necessary to fine-tune the layout.

 You're not limited to inserting just text and graphics within the header or footer. Although Word automatically makes the header and footer active when you enter Header and Footer view, you can add graphics and text to the body area of the document just as easily. The elements that you insert in this way show up within the body of the document and repeat from page to page (just like headers and footers), but are dimmed. You can edit these elements by opening Header and Footer view or by double-clicking the element. The following section offers more information on inserting text and graphics into the header or footer layer of a document.

Part
II

Ch
6

Using Watermarks, Page Borders, and Textures

Word offers several features for adding elements other than text to your documents, including background and repeating graphic elements. These elements can have a dramatic effect on the appearance of your documents. This section examines three such effects, beginning with watermarks.

Word defines a *watermark* as being any text or graphic that appears on top of or behind the text in a printed document. The term's origin stems from the use of special processes during paper manufacturing to add translucent designs that appear only when the paper is held up to the light. These designs are called watermarks. You can add the word *Confidential* to a document as a watermark, for example (see Figure 6.7, or you can add the word *Sold* across a real estate proposal. Whatever your use of watermarks, adding them is a simple process.

FIG. 6.7

Watermarks are just text and/or graphics inserted into the Header and Footer layer of a document.

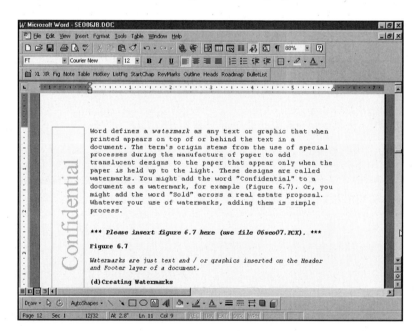

Creating Watermarks

You create a watermark by inserting the watermark elements (text and/or graphics) into the Header and Footer layer of a document. When you close Header and Footer view, the watermark elements move to the background along with the header and footer elements. Generally, you want to format the watermark so that the body text does not wrap around it (as though it were truly printed on the paper before the text was added), but you can apply text wrapping around the watermark as though it were part of the main-document body. In essence, watermark elements behave just like elements in the main body of the document, but simply exist on a separate layer of the document. Like headers and footers, watermarks carry through from one page to another automatically.

T I P To place a watermark on only one page of a document, create a new section to contain the page in which you want the watermark to appear.

To insert a watermark, first choose View, Header and Footer to open Header and Footer view; then begin inserting the elements that you want to use as the watermark. If you are inserting graphics, you can simply choose Insert, Picture and follow the same process that you use to insert graphics into the body of a document. To insert regular text as a watermark, however, you must insert the text into a text box. To insert a text box, open the Drawing toolbar by choosing View, Toolbars, Drawing. Click the Text Box button; then click and drag in the document to create the text box. Click the text box and begin typing the text.

N O T E Text boxes and frames are nearly identical in function in Word 97. Text boxes offer all the advantages of frames, plus many additional features that frames do not offer. In general, you use frames only when you need to include comments (through comment marks), footnotes or endnotes, and a very few types of fields that are not supported by text boxes. Perform a search in Help on the keyword frames for more information about the difference between text boxes and frames. ■

You can rotate the text in a text box to be vertical. To do so, select the text box and choose Format, Text Direction to open the Text Direction dialog box. Select the orientation that you want for the text; then choose OK. To move the text box, just click and drag its border.

To create text that is rotated at angles other than vertical, use WordArt. Choose Insert, Picture, WordArt to open the WordArt Gallery dialog box. Text that you create with WordArt can be rotated at any angle. After you create the WordArt object, click the Free Rotate button in the WordArt toolbar to rotate the text.

▶ **See** "Using WordArt," **p. 1048**

Controlling Watermark Transparency

Although the watermark elements appear dimmed in Word, they do not print dimmed; instead, they print at the same color depth and shading as they appear when you insert them. Typically, you want the watermark elements to be very light in shade so that they don't interfere with the visibility or readability of the main body of the document, so you often have to adjust the text and graphics to be much lighter.

To lighten text, change the text's color. Select the text and choose Format, Font. In the Font property sheet, choose from the Color drop-down list an appropriate color for the text. To adjust WordArt images, click the Format WordArt button in the WordArt toolbar. In the Colors and Lines page of the Format WordArt property sheet (see Figure 6.8), use the Fill and Line controls to choose an appropriate color or shade.

Adjusting graphics for use as watermarks typically means reducing the brightness and contrast of the image. Word makes it easy to apply the right brightness and contrast by providing a special color setting for the image. After you insert the image, right-click the image and then choose Format Picture from the shortcut menu to open the Format Picture property sheet. In the Picture page (see Figure 6.9), choose Watermark from the Color drop-down list. If you prefer, use the Brightness and Contrast controls to fine-tune the image's properties. When you're satisfied with the settings, choose OK to view the changes in the document.

FIG. 6.8

Use the Format WordArt property sheet to control the color and apparent transparency of WordArt objects.

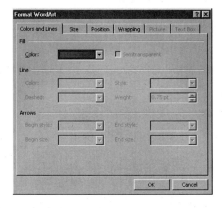

FIG. 6.9

Increase the image's brightness to make it more transparent.

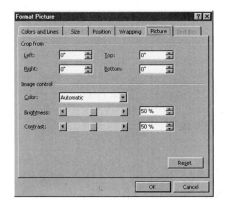

Using Page Borders

Word 97 enables you to apply a border to the pages of a document and includes several borders among which to choose. You can apply the border to one or more sides of the page and control other options, such as the border width and distance from the edge of the page and the document text.

To add a page border, choose Format, Borders and Shading. Click the Page Border tab to display the Page Border property page (see Figure 6.10).

Choose a border graphic from the Art drop-down list. Use the Width control to change the width in points of the border and graphic. Click the four buttons in the Preview area to turn on and off individual sides of the border (clicking one of these four buttons automatically selects the Custom option). When you're satisfied with the border, choose OK to apply the border to the page.

FIG. 6.10
Use the Page Border property page to specify a graphic border for a page and to control the border's properties.

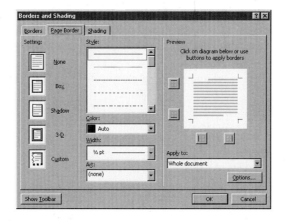

Using Page Backgrounds

Word includes several textures and other special effects that you can apply as the background for a document. These backgrounds appear in Online Layout view but do not appear in Normal or Page Layout view. Backgrounds are intended primarily for Web pages that you create with Word, but you can use borders with any documents that you view in Page Layout view.

To apply a background to a document, choose Format, Background. Choose a color from the resulting cascading menu or choose More Colors to select a custom color for the background. To apply a graphic or texture as the background instead of a color, choose Fill Effects from the menu to display the Fill Effects property sheet, shown in Figure 6.11.

FIG. 6.11
The Gradient page of the Fill Effects property sheet helps you apply a gradient fill to the page's background.

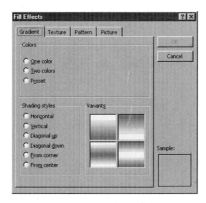

Part
II

Ch
6

Use the Gradient page to apply a gradient fill as the background. You can choose one color, two colors, or preset color combinations. From the Shading Styles group, choose a gradient fill pattern.

The Texture page (see Figure 6.12) allows you to choose an image to use as a background texture. Word includes 24 sample textures among which to choose, but you can use any graphic file in a wide variety of formats supported by Word. You can download a JPEG or GIF image from the Internet, for example, or create your own to use as the background texture. Word automatically tiles the image to fill the document's background.

FIG. 6.12

Use the Texture page to specify a graphics file as the background for the document.

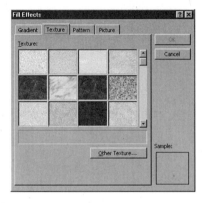

 T I P   The Office 97 CD-ROM includes several photos, clip art, and other images that you can use as textures. The images are located in the \Clipart folder on the CD-ROM.

The Pattern page (see Figure 6.13) allows you to choose a two-color pattern to apply as the document's background.

FIG. 6.13

Use the Pattern property page to apply a two-color pattern as the background.

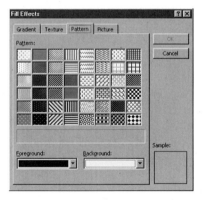

The Picture property page (see Figure 6.14) allows you to choose image files to use as the background of the document. You can choose the same types of images with this option that you can in the Texture page. The difference is that the Texture option tiles the image to fill the document. The Picture option centers and scales the image to fit the document.

To turn off the background, choose Format, Background, No Fill.

FIG. 6.14
Use the Picture
property page to
choose a background
image for the
document.

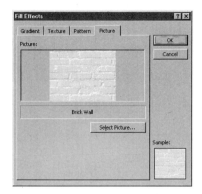

Using Highlighting and Color

Sometimes, background fills and other special effects are just too much. In some situations, all
you really need is a little highlighting or color. Word enables you to specify not only the typeface and other font characteristics of text, but also the color. In addition, you can highlight text
much as you can with a highlighter pen.

Using Colored Text

In Word, Color is a property of text, just like the typeface, font size, bold, italic, and so on. To
apply color to text, select the text and choose Format, Font. In the Font page of the Font property sheet, choose the color for the text from the Color drop-down list; then choose OK to
apply the text. Choosing Auto sets the text to black except when the background shading is 80
percent or more, in which case the text color is white.

 You can use the Font Color button in the Formatting toolbar to set font color. Select the text and then
click the Font Color button. To choose a different color, click the small down arrow beside the Font
Color button.

Highlighting Text

In addition to applying color to text, you can apply a color to the text's background. Applying a
color in this way is called *highlighting* and is similar to highlighting text on paper with a color
highlighter. To highlight text, click the Highlight button in the Formatting toolbar; then drag
the mouse over the text to be highlighted. (You can select the text first, if you want.) To change
the highlight color, click the small down arrow next to the Highlight button in the Formatting
toolbar. To turn off highlighting, click the Highlight button again.

Part

II

Ch

6

N O T E   All that highlighting really does is apply a background color to the text. You can use highlighting in combination with font color to achieve special effects. You can use blue text with a yellow highlight, for example, to make the text really stand out. ▪

To remove highlighting from text, simply highlight it again. Word changes the background color back to its default color.

Integrating Graphics

Graphics are important parts of many types of documents. Brochures and newsletters, for example, are incomplete without graphics. Word 97 has improved its graphics support, making the process of integrating graphics into your documents easier than ever.

Office 97 supports a wide range of graphics formats, including GIF, PCX, JPG, EPS, BMP, and many, many more. Office provides support for these graphics formats through graphics converters. To view the graphics filters that are currently installed, run Office 97 Setup and choose Add/Remove Programs. Select the Converters and Filters item; then click Change Option. The installed filters have a check beside them. Place a check beside any other filters that you want to add.

In most cases, inserting graphics is just a matter of placing the insertion point where you want the image to be inserted and then choosing Insert, Picture, followed by the type of image to insert. To insert clip art, for example, choose Insert, Picture, Clip Art to display the Microsoft Clip Gallery sheet, shown in Figure 6.15. From this property sheet, you can insert any of the clip-art images, photos, sounds, and video clips that are included with Word. If you installed any of Word's graphics files when you installed Office 97, the files will be located in the Clipart folder within the main Office folder. Additional multimedia clips are available if the Office 97 CD-ROM is in the CD-ROM drive when you open this sheet.

FIG. 6.15

Use the Microsoft Clip Gallery to insert multimedia clips into a document.

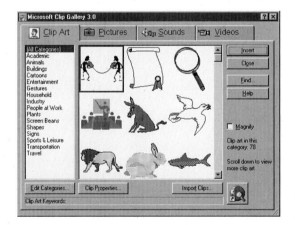

The Microsoft Clip Gallery is a utility that helps you organize multimedia clips, as well as preview and insert them. In Clip Gallery, click the tab for the type of clip that you want to insert; select the clip to insert; and then choose Insert.

> **N O T E** Clip Gallery doesn't actually contain clips—it simply provides a means for previewing and selecting clips. The clips reside on your hard disk or Office 97 CD-ROM. You can import additional clips into Clip Gallery. Doing so only adds the preview image to Clip Gallery; it does not actually add the clip to your hard disk (if the clip is not already on the disk). You can add to Clip Gallery clips that reside on a CD-ROM or a network server, for example. ▪

▶ **See** "Using Office 97 Clip Gallery," **p. 1053**

You also can insert graphics from files without using the Clip Manager. To do so, choose Insert, Picture, From File. Word displays the Insert Picture dialog box, shown in Figure 6.16. Locate and select the graphics file to be inserted, set any desired options in the dialog box, and then choose Insert.

FIG. 6.16
Use the Insert Picture dialog box to select and set properties for graphics files to be inserted into the document.

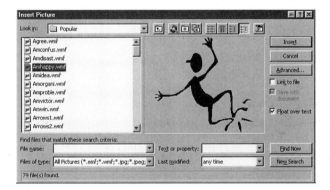

The following list describes a few key controls in the Insert Picture dialog box:

- ▪ *Link to File*. Enable this check box to link the image in the document rather than embed it. The image appears in the document but does not actually reside in the document. Instead, Word loads the image from its source file each time you load the document. Changes in the source image, therefore, automatically appear in the document the next time you open the document. To update links without reloading the document, choose Edit, Links.

- ▪ *Save with Document*. This check box is enabled by default and dimmed if the Link to File check box is cleared. When enabled, this option causes Word to save the image within the document file. Saving images in the document file makes the document file much bigger, but also makes it fully portable. Other users can view the graphics if they are embedded and saved in the document file.

- ▪ *Float Over Text*. Enabling this check box causes the image to be placed in the drawing layer of the document, where it can be manipulated with various buttons in the Drawing toolbar. You can move the image in front of or behind text, for example. Clearing this check box causes the image to be placed inline (within the paragraph) and treated like text. Even if you place the image in the drawing layer, you can still wrap text around the image in a variety of ways. Generally, placing the graphic in the drawing layer offers the best flexibility in editing the image.

N O T E   The Link to File and Save with Document options relate to the difference between embedding and linking objects in a document. Object Linking and Embedding (and updating links) goes beyond the scope of this book, because it is a general Windows 95 topic rather than a topic that is specific to Office. For a detailed discussion of linking and embedding, refer to "*Building Compound Documents with OLE*," Chapter 15, *Special Edition Using Windows 95.* ▪

N O T E   You can embed or link graphics in a document through the Clipboard. Place the graphics in the Clipboard; then choose Edit, Paste to embed or Edit, Paste Special, Paste Link to link the graphics in the document. ▪

Controlling Text Wrap and Other Properties

After you insert a graphic into a document, you'll probably want to change the way that text wraps around the image or to control other properties of the image. This section explains the ways in which you can modify an image's properties after you insert it into a document.

Moving and Sizing Graphics   To move an image in the document, just click the image and drag it to its new location. You'll notice that when you place the mouse pointer on the image, the pointer changes to a four-way arrow to indicate that you can move the image. If you're moving the image a long distance in the document (from one page to another, for example), cut the image to the Clipboard and then paste it in the new location.

T I P   Hold down the Ctrl key while dragging to copy an object. Hold down the Shift key while dragging to constrain the object's movement to horizontal and vertical movements.

Sizing images is equally easy. When you click the image, you see eight selection handles on the image, indicated by small squares on the border around the image. Click a handle and drag to resize the image. The four handles in the corner enable you to change the size of the image proportionally, and the handles on the four sides enable you to resize using only one side (stretching the image).

T I P   Click the Reset Picture button in the Picture toolbar to restore an image's original settings.

Changing Text Wrapping   The way that text flows around an image is called *text wrapping*. Word offers several options for controlling text wrapping, each of which is shown in example in the Wrapping page of the Format Picture property sheet. To display this sheet, click the image to select it and then choose Format, Picture. Alternatively, right-click the image and then choose Format Picture from the context menu. Click the Wrapping tab to display the Wrapping page. Figure 6.17 shows the Wrapping page of the Format Picture property sheet. The effects of the different wrapping options are evident in the examples.

FIG. 6.17

Control the way that text flows around an image with the Wrapping property page.

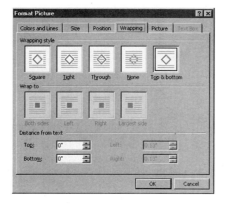

In addition to selecting the wrap method, you can modify the image's wrap points—points in the image that determine how close to the image text wraps. Click the Text Wrapping button in the Picture toolbar; then choose Edit Wrap Points to display the image's wrap points. The wrap points are shown as small, solid black squares connected by dashed lines, as shown in Figure 6.18.

FIG. 6.18

Wrap points enable you to control how close to an object text wraps.

Part

II

Ch

6

Click and drag existing wrap points to move them. Hold down the Ctrl key and click a wrap point to remove it. Click and drag anywhere in a dashed wrap line to create a new wrap point.

Adjusting Image Properties   Word offers a few additional options for formatting images. The Image Control button in the Picture toolbar allows you to format the image as grayscale, as black and white, or as a watermark. The More Contrast and Less Contrast buttons, when clicked, adjust the contrast of the image. The More Brightness and Less Brightness buttons adjust the brightness of the image. The Set Transparent Color button allows you to click a color in the image to make it transparent (not available with all image types). The Line Style button changes the border line around the image.

You also can control an image's properties through the Format Picture property sheet. Many of the controls in the Format Picture property sheet correspond to controls in the Picture toolbar; others enable you to fine-tune the position, size, and other properties of the image. The controls in the Format Picture property sheet generally are self-explanatory.

Cropping an Image   Cutting the edges off an image or trimming it to a different size is commonly known as *cropping*. You can crop images in Word through the Picture toolbar. After selecting the image, click the Crop button in the toolbar; then click and drag any of the resize points on the image's border. As you move the resize point, the image is cropped accordingly. Click the Crop button again to turn off cropping.

N O T E   The image is not really cropped, because the cropped portion remains; it is simply hidden behind the crop lines. Think of cropping in Word as being the process of adjusting the boundary of an invisible window around the image so that you view only a portion of the image. Note that cropping an image in Word does not reduce its file size. Crop the image in a drawing program such as Photo Editor if you want to reduce the file size. ▪

Using Captions

Word uses text boxes to create captions. To insert a caption with an image, first click the image to select it; then choose Insert, Caption to display the Caption dialog box (see Figure 6.19).

FIG. 6.19
The Caption dialog box enables you to insert a caption for an image quickly and easily.

From the Label drop-down list, choose the type of caption that you want to insert. Click the New Label button to create a new type of label. In the Caption text box, modify the text for the caption as desired. Use the Position drop-down list to choose between placing the caption above or below the image. Click the N̲umbering button to change the type of numbering method used for the caption. When you're satisfied with the caption, choose OK to insert it into the document.

Word automatically keeps track of and numbers captions for you. If you're inserting figures into a document, for example, Word automatically labels them Figure 1, Figure 2, Figure 3, and so on.

As mentioned earlier in this section, Word inserts captions into text boxes. The text box is not directly attached to the image, however, although Word places the caption directly above or below the image as you specify. When you move the image, the caption does not automatically move with it. Therefore, you may want to group the text box and the image so that they do move together. To group these elements, click the image and hold the Shift key while clicking the caption text box. Right-click the image and then choose G̲rouping, G̲roup from the context menu. After the image and the text box are grouped, they move as one. You still can edit the caption text just by clicking it, however.

Using Columns

Many types of documents use columns for formatting at least some of the text in the document. Newsletters and brochures are two common types of documents that use columns. Word offers good flexibility for the use of columns in a document. This section explains how to create and format columns.

Setting Up Columns

You can set up columns either before or after you type the text for the columns; the options available to you are the same either way. You can apply columns to an entire document or to a selection of text. To apply columns to a selection of text, you place that text in a separate section and then apply the column formatting to that section. When you select text and then apply column formatting to that selection, Word automatically creates a new section to contain the selected text. Whenever you need to use different column formats or to switch between using column and noncolumn format, just start a new section.

To apply columns to the entire document, place the insertion point at any location in the document and then choose F̲ormat, C̲olumns to display the Columns dialog box (see Figure 6.20). To apply columns to an existing selection of text, select the text before choosing F̲ormat, C̲olumns.

To begin using columns after a selection of text, place the insertion point after that text and start a new section by inserting a section break (choose I̲nsert, B̲reak). Then, with the insertion point in the new section, choose F̲ormat, C̲olumns.

In the Columns dialog box, choose the number of columns from one of the preset options or use the N̲umber of Columns control to specify the desired number of columns. Use the Width and Spacing controls to control the width of each column and the space between columns.

Enable the Equal Column Width check box to have Word automatically size the columns equally. Clear this check box to specify different settings for each column.

FIG. 6.20

Use the Columns dialog box to set column options and the extent to which the columns apply.

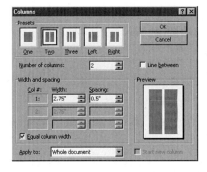

Use the Apply To drop-down list to specify the extent of the document to which the columns apply. The options include:

- *Whole Document.* This option applies the column formatting to the entire document.
- *This Point Forward.* This option starts a new section and applies the column formatting to the new section.
- *This Section.* This option applies the column formatting to the section in which the insertion point is located.

Starting a New Column

Occasionally, you want to force Word to begin a new column, moving the insertion point to the top of the next column. When you choose the This Point Forward option in the Columns dialog box, the Start New Column check box becomes available. Enabling this check box causes Word to begin a new column, which moves the text following the insertion point to the top of the next column. Word begins a new column by inserting a new column break.

You also can use two easier methods to insert column breaks. Choose Insert, Break, Column Break, and OK to insert a column break, or simply press Ctrl+Shift+Enter to insert the column break.

Using Lines Between Columns

In some situations, you want to include lines between columns. You could draw the lines manually, but why not have Word do the job for you? When you place a check in the Line Between check box in the Columns dialog box, Word automatically places vertical lines between columns. To place horizontal lines between paragraphs within a column, simply apply a border to the bottom of the preceding paragraph or to the top of the following paragraph (choose Format, Borders and Shading). If you're switching from columns to noncolumn format and want a horizontal line to appear between the columns and the following text, apply a top border to the paragraph immediately following the columns. Figure 6.21 shows an example.

FIG. 6.21

Apply a border to the first paragraph in the next section after columns to create a horizontal line separating the columns from the following text.

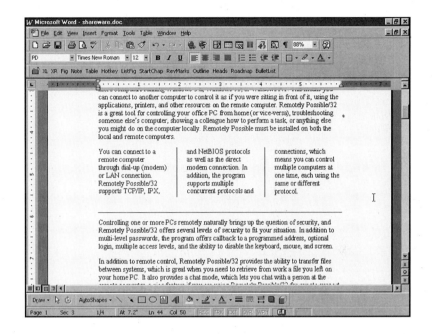

 When you apply a single border (one edge only) to a paragraph by clicking one of the four edge buttons on the preview area of the Borders and Shading property sheet, Word does not apply different border styles, width, or color to the border line. To apply different border properties to a single-edge border, first select the properties (color and so on) and then click the desired border button to apply the border. If you already have a border defined, select None. Then set the desired properties and click the desired edge button to turn on the border with the new properties.

Using Bullets and Numbering

Bulleted and numbered lists are common in many types of documents. Bulleted lists allow you to emphasize paragraphs by placing a graphical indicator called a *bullet* at the beginning of the paragraph. Figure 6.22 shows a bulleted list.

Numbered lists often are used to indicate sequential steps or processes. Figure 6.23 shows an example of a numbered list.

Both bulleted and numbered lists are commonly used throughout this book to organize steps and to draw attention to important points.

Word 97 simplifies the use of bullets and numbered lists by automating their formatting. If you apply bullet formatting to a paragraph, Word automatically applies the same bullet format to the following paragraph. When you finish adding bulleted paragraphs, you simply turn off bulleting and continue typing the next paragraph.

Part
II

Ch
6

FIG. 6.22

Bullets help emphasize a paragraph and often are used for such elements as checklists within a document.

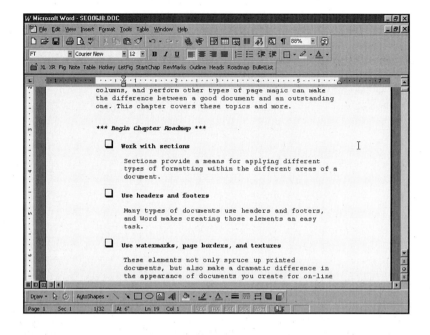

FIG. 6.23

Use numbered lists to describe sequential steps or processes.

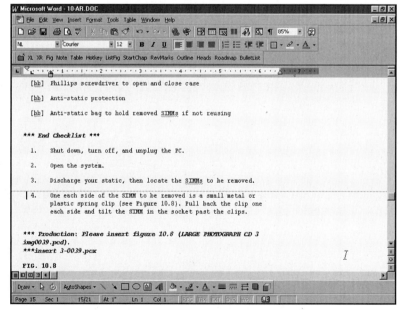

 TIP   Through AutoFormat, Word automatically converts a paragraph to bulleted format if the paragraph begins with an asterisk and a tab or space. So an easy way to start creating bulleted paragraphs is to start a new paragraph and then type an asterisk, followed by a tab or space. Type the paragraph and press Enter, and Word automatically applies bullet formatting to the paragraph.

Word also simplifies the use of numbered lists. You type a number at the beginning of the paragraph, followed by a tab or space, and then type the rest of the paragraph. When you press Enter, Word converts the paragraph to a numbered list, automatically entering the next sequential number at the beginning of the following paragraph. Note that you must enable these features on the AutoFormat Options dialog box to enable Word to perform them automatically.

You have quite a bit of control of the appearance of bulleted or numbered lists. This section of the chapter explains how to create and modify these types of document elements.

Creating a Bulleted List

As mentioned earlier in this chapter, all you have to do to start a bulleted list is type an asterisk, followed by a tab or space, and then type some additional text. Word converts the paragraph to a bulleted one when you press Enter. Alternatively, you can click the Bullets button in the Formatting toolbar to begin a bulleted list. You can format a bulleted paragraph before or after you type the text. Click the Increase Indent or Decrease Indent button in the Formatting toolbar to change the indent of the paragraph. Alternatively, right-click the paragraph and then choose either Increase Indent or Decrease Indent from the context menu.

You can use any character as the bullet character. To choose a different bullet or to modify other characteristics of the paragraph, select the paragraph and choose Format, Bullets and Numbering. Alternatively, right-click the paragraph and choose Bullets and Numbering from the context menu. Word displays the Bullets and Numbering property sheet, shown in Figure 6.24.

FIG. 6.24

You can use any character as the bullet, but Word provides several predefined choices.

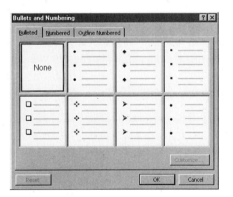

To use a predefined bullet character, select it and choose OK. To choose a custom bullet character or to set spacing and other properties, select a predefined type and then choose Customize to display the Customize Bulleted List dialog box, shown in Figure 6.25.

Choose the Bullet button to select a different bullet character. Word opens the Symbol dialog box, shown in Figure 6.26. Select the desired symbol and choose OK.

Choose the Font button to open the standard Font dialog box. Select the typeface from which you want to choose a bullet character; then choose other options, such as font size and bold or italic. Choose OK when you're satisfied with the selection.

FIG. 6.25

You can change the bullet character, the font from which the bullet comes, and the spacing properties in the Customize Bulleted List dialog box.

FIG. 6.26

Choose a new bullet type from the Symbol dialog box.

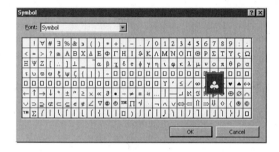

 T I P To turn off bulleting quickly, click in the paragraph for which you want to turn off the bullet and then click the Bullets button in the Formatting toolbar.

Creating a Numbered List

Creating a numbered list is as easy as creating a bulleted list. If you begin a paragraph with a number, followed by a period and tab or space, and then type other text, Word automatically starts a numbered list when you press Enter. Type each item in the list and then press Enter after the last item. Press Backspace to remove the last number.

You also can create a numbered list through the Bullets and Numbering property sheet. Choose Format, Bullets and Numbering, or right-click the paragraph and choose Bullets and Numbering from the context menu. When the Bullets and Numbering property sheet appears, click the Numbered tab to display the Numbered property page, shown in Figure 6.27.

To choose a different starting number or to set other numbering properties, click the Customize button in the Numbered page. As you can see in Figure 6.28, you can select the number format, font, number style, starting number, and other properties for the list. Changing one item in the list changes the other items in the list automatically.

The following list explains the two options for numbering lists:

- *Restart Numbering.* Choose this option if you want the list to begin at 1, A, or i.
- *Continue Previous List.* Choose this option to have the list begin with the next number after the preceding bulleted item. Word takes the last number or letter from the

preceding list, even if that list is separated from the current one by other text, and increments the counter to derive the new number or letter for the current list.

FIG. 6.27
Choosing a numbering style for the list from the Bullets and Numbering property sheet.

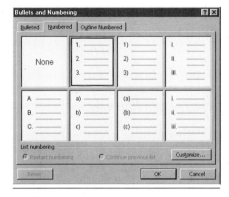

FIG. 6.28
Use the Customize Numbered List dialog box to control numbered-list properties.

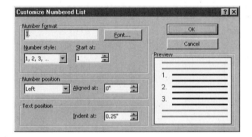

One of the most important advantages of using Word's automatic list numbering is that it truly is automatic. If you insert some items within the list, the numbers of following items adjust accordingly.

To turn off numbering, set the numbered list type to None.

Creating Outline Numbered Lists

An outline numbered list is similar to an outline created with Word's outlining features, except that it doesn't rely on Word's Heading styles or outline paragraph levels. The outline numbered list feature simply provides a quick way to create an outline-format numbered list.

To create an outline numbered list, choose Format, Bullets and Numbering, and click the Outline Numbered tab to display the property page shown in Figure 6.29.

You can choose from one of the predefined styles or customize a style to suit your preferences. To customize a style, select the one that you want to customize and choose the Customize button. Word displays the Customize Outline Numbered List dialog box. Click the More button to expand the dialog box to display all items, as shown in Figure 6.30.

FIG. 6.29

Use the Outline
Numbered page to set
the properties for an
outline numbered list.

FIG. 6.30

Modify outline
numbered list styles in
the Customize Outline
Numbered List dialog
box.

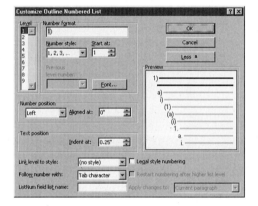

Choose a level from the Level list; then use the remaining controls to change that level's properties. Most of the settings in the dialog box are self-explanatory. The following list summarizes a few settings that are not self-explanatory:

- *Link Level to Style*. Choose from this drop-down list the style (if any) that you want to
  associate with the selected level in the outline list. Word automatically numbers with the
  appropriate level the paragraphs that you format with the selected style.

- *Follow Number With*. Choose from this drop-down list the character to follow the
  number. You can choose a tab, a space, or no character.

- *Legal Style Numbering*. Choose this item to convert numbers in the list to Arabic values
  (such as changing IV to 4).

- *Restart Numbering After Higher List Level*. Enabling this option causes Word to automatically start back at 1, a, or I when the selected list level follows a higher list level.

- *ListNum Field List Name*. This option allows you to use the ListNum field to insert
  multiple outline numbers on a single level. For more information about fields, refer to
  Chapter 7, "Fields, Forms, and Dynamic Content."

▶ **See** "Using Field Codes to Create Dynamic Content," **p. 140**

When you're satisfied with the settings, choose OK, then OK a second time to apply the formatting. You'll find that for the most part, Word's true outlining features that rely on the Heading styles offer the most flexibility in terms of navigating and viewing the document. You can use Outline View to expand and collapse the outline to quickly view large parts of the outline and move around in it. Nevertheless, the outline numbered lists offer an excellent means of creating legal documents and other documents that rely on structured outline numbering. ●

Part

II

Ch

6

Fields, Forms, and Dynamic Content

by Jim Boyce

Most of the documents that you've created up to this point probably have been static. Word, however, enables you to create documents that contain dynamic information that changes automatically, such as page numbers, dates, and indexes. You also can use Word to create forms that can be filled in on-screen, just as a paper form might be. This chapter examines these topics. ◼

Using field codes

Field codes are special types of objects that you can use to insert dynamic information into a document, such as page numbering and document statistics. Word supports numerous field codes and optional switches for each field.

Protecting the document

When using field codes and creating forms, you often want to protect the document so that others who view the document don't accidentally change the contents of the document.

Creating forms

Word includes several features that help you create printed forms and forms for use on-screen.

Using Field Codes to Create Dynamic Content

Much of the data you place in a document is static—text and graphics that do not change. However, you'll probably want to include dynamic data in your documents that changes as the document or other parameters change. For example, you might want the total editing time for the document to appear in the header or footer, along with the document author's name. Or you might want to build complex elements such as forms that automatically fill in areas of the form from information such as the date, time, or other information.

Field codes are the mechanism in Word that enable you to add that dynamic content. Field codes are particularly useful in creating document templates and forms. The field codes can automate much of the process of filling in the form or adding content to a document derived from a template. Most of Word's templates use field codes for much of their content. The following sections explain field codes and teach you to use them in your documents.

> **N O T E** Field codes are a powerful feature for automating document content creation. A complete treatment of all of Word's 70+ fields an their options would require multiple chapters and goes beyond the scope of *Special Edition Using Microsoft Office 97*. This section of the chapter provides a solid introduction to field codes and points you in the right direction to learn more. For a detailed look at field codes, check out *Special Edition Using Microsoft Word 97*, Best Seller Edition, also from Que. ▨

Understanding Field Codes

In Word, *field codes* are special objects you can insert into a document that act as placeholders for dynamic data—data that can change automatically. Word uses field codes to insert page numbers, for example. As new pages are added, the result of the page-number field code changes accordingly. Date and time field codes are other examples of Word field codes. These two field codes insert the current date and time into the document. If you load the document the next day and then update the field codes, you see the current date in the document again.

Word also uses field codes automatically for other features. When you create an index or table of contents in the document, for example, Word uses field codes to build those document elements.

Word supports more than 70 field codes that cover a wide range of data types. Word organizes these field codes into the following groups:

- *Date and Time.* Field codes in this group include the date when the document was created, the current date and time, the date printed, the date when the document was last saved, and total document-editing time.
- *Document Automation.* This group contains field codes for comparing values, performing conditional branching, inserting document variables, moving the insertion point, running macros, and downloading commands to a printer.

- *Document Information.* This group includes several field codes that insert information about the document. This information includes such items as author, comments, file name and size, and number of pages.

- *Equations and Formulas.* Field codes in this group enable you to insert formulas, equations, and symbols, as well as to offset the subsequent text after the field to the left, right, up, or down.

- *Index and Tables.* Use these field codes to insert tables of contents, indexes, and tables of authorities into the document. Generally, you use Word's automated features to insert these document elements instead of inserting the field codes yourself.

- *Links and References.* These field codes enable you to insert AutoText entries, hyperlinks, pictures, and other document objects.

- *Mail Merge.* Field codes in this group enable you to create mail-merge documents, which combine data documents with template documents to create individualized form letters (and other documents).

- *Numbering.* These field codes insert various numbering-related items into the document: bar codes, list elements, page numbers, number of times that the document has been saved, current section number, number of pages in the section, and more.

- *User Information.* These field codes insert various information from the User Information page of the Options property sheet (choose Tools, Options, User Information).

When you first insert a field code, Word calculates the result of the field code depending on the code that is inserted. When you insert a date field, for example, Word checks the current system date, and that information appears within the document. Load the document tomorrow, and the field still shows the previous day's date. To make the field current, you must update it. Use one of the following methods to update fields:

- To update a single field, click the field and then press the F9 function key.

- To update multiple field codes, select the extent of the document that contains the field codes to be updated and then press F9.

- To update all field codes in the document, choose Edit, Select All and then press F9.

Viewing Field Codes

It's important to understand that when you insert a field code, you're not inserting the data that actually appears in the document. Instead, you're inserting a code that results in the data's being displayed. The field and the resulting displayed information are different. If you are familiar with Microsoft Excel (the spreadsheet program in Office 97), you can draw an analogy between Excel spreadsheet cells and field codes. When you enter a formula in an Excel spreadsheet cell and press Enter, you see the results of the cell, not the formula that derived the results. Field codes are the same—you see the results of the field code, not the underlying code itself.

Part

II

Ch

7

As you work with documents that contain field codes, however, you occasionally need to view the field codes rather than their results. You may want to edit the field code's option so that it displays a different result or so that the result is formatted differently, for example. You must *turn on* field codes to view them.

You can turn on field codes globally throughout the document or turn on only selected field codes. To turn on all field codes, press Alt+F9. Figure 7.1 shows a simple document containing field codes. The first two field codes are turned off, and the next two field codes are turned on.

FIG. 7.1

The first two field codes in this document are turned off, and the second two are turned on.

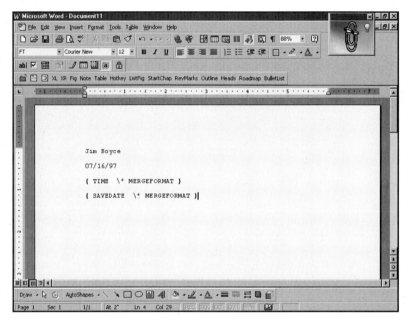

The Shift+F9 and Alt+F9 shortcuts toggle the field codes on and off. To turn off display of all field codes and view the results again, just press Alt+F9. Select individual field codes and press Shift+F9 to turn field codes off again.

Later in this chapter in the section "Formatting Field Codes," you learn about formatting field codes and using options, and understanding how to view the field codes can be important in those two tasks. Before getting into those topics, however, you need to learn how to add field codes to the document.

Inserting Field Codes

You insert field codes into a document in much the same way that you insert other document elements. To insert a field code, choose Insert, Field to display the Field dialog box (see Figure 7.2).

FIG. 7.2

Insert field codes and set their options by using the Field dialog box.

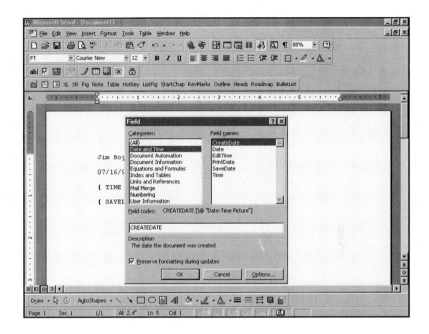

The Field dialog box groups the field codes by function in the <u>C</u>ategories list. Select a category from the list to view the field codes in that category. The field codes appear in the Field <u>N</u>ames list. Click (All) in the <u>C</u>ategories list to view all the field codes, sorted alphabetically. This option is helpful when you know the field name but not the category in which it resides.

Selecting a field places the field name in the <u>F</u>ield Codes text box of the Field dialog box. Word shows the syntax of the field in the area just above the text box, with optional parameters shown in square brackets. You then can click the <u>F</u>ield Codes text box and add optional switches or other parameters to the field code. These parameters and switches determine how the field's contents appear in the document and differ from one field code to the next. You can insert a formula from a Word bookmark, for example. In the <u>F</u>ield Codes text box, you add the bookmark name for the formula that you want to insert.

N O T E The <u>P</u>reserve Formatting During Updates check box determines how Word handles the formatting of the field-code results when the field is updated. This option is discussed in detail in "Formatting Field Codes" later in this chapter. ■

Using field codes effectively requires that you understand the optional parameters and switches for the field code. The syntax example in the dialog box eliminates the need to memorize each field—a good thing, because each of the more than 70 field codes is different. After you select a field code from the list, click the <u>o</u>ptions button to display the Field Options dialog box (see Figure 7.3). This dialog box lists the optional switches that you can add to the field code and describes their functions. Just select the switch that you want to add and click <u>A</u>dd to Field.

Part

II

Ch

7

FIG. 7.3

Use the Field Options dialog box to view and add optional switches for each field.

An in-depth discussion of each of the field codes and their optional settings would require several chapters. See *Special Edition Using Microsoft Word 97* Best Seller Edition for more information on using Word's field codes. For now, just remember these key points:

- Field codes enable you to insert dynamic data into a document.
- You can toggle field codes on or off to view either the result of the field code or the field code itself.
- Each field code can use optional switches that control its content (result) and appearance.
- Word shows a syntax example for each field code when you select the field code in the Field dialog box.
- Word uses field codes to build such elements as tables of contents, tables of authorities, and indexes.
- You must update field codes to make them show the most current information.

 If you need to include a backslash character (\) in a field code's optional information, replace single \ characters with \\. Here is an example of the INCLUDETEXT field, which includes the contents of another file—or portion thereof—in the current document:

```
{INCLUDETEXT "C:\\My Documents\\April\\Report"}
```

Exploring a Hands-On Example

In this example, you create a simple template for creating interoffice memos. Follow these steps to create the template and insert the field codes:

1. Open Word, and start a new template based on the Blank Document. To do so, choose File, New, and click the General tab on the New property sheet. Select the Blank Document icon, select the Template option button, and choose OK.

2. Choose a typeface, set the font size to 24, and type the text **Interoffice Memo**.

3. Start a new line and set the font size to 12.

4. Type **From:**, followed by a space.

5. Choose Insert, Field to display the Field dialog box and choose User Information from the Categories list.

6. Choose UserName in the Field Names list; then choose OK.

7. Start a new line and type **To:**, followed by a space.

8. Choose Insert, Field to display the Field dialog box, and choose Document Automation from the Categories list.

9. Choose MacroButton from the Field Names list.

10. In the Field Codes text box to the right of the field name, type **NoMacro "Enter recipient's name"** and choose OK.

11. Start a new line and type **Date:**, followed by a space.

12. Choose Insert, Field to display the Field dialog box, and choose Date and Time from the Categories list.

13. Choose Date from the Field Names list; then click the Options button to display the Field Options dialog box (see Figure 7.4).

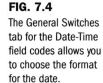

FIG. 7.4

The General Switches tab for the Date-Time field codes allows you to choose the format for the date.

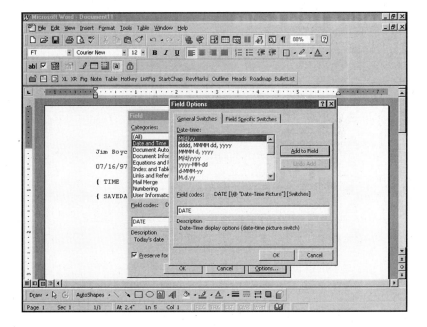

14. From the Date-Time list, choose MMMM d, yyyy.

15. Click Add to Field.

16. Choose OK twice to close both dialog boxes and insert the field into the document.

17. Start a new line and type **Time:**, followed by a space.

18. Choose Insert, Field to display the Field dialog box, and choose the Date and Time category; then choose the Time field.

Part

II

Ch

7

19. Choose <u>O</u>ptions, scroll through the list, and then choose h:mm am/pm from the <u>D</u>ate-Time Formats list.

20. Choose <u>A</u>dd to Field.

21. Choose OK twice to close both dialog boxes and insert the field.

22. Save the file in the Templates folder; then close the file.

Now you have a simple memo form. To test the form, choose <u>F</u>ile, <u>N</u>ew, and choose the template that you just created. Make sure that the <u>D</u>ocument option button is selected; then choose OK. Word starts a new document based on your template and automatically fills in your user name, as well as the current date and time. All you need to do is type the recipient's name in the Enter Recipient's Name box. Word replaces the field with the text that you type.

The MacroButton box is intended for running macros in the document, but you can use it to insert placeholder field codes by specifying **NoMacro** as the name of the macro to associate with the field. Using MacroButton with the NoMacro name is essentially like inserting an empty labeled field.

Formatting Field Codes

Just as you do with regular text, you can format field codes so that the results take on a specific typeface, font size, and other character formatting. When you update the field, the formatting can be retained or lost, depending on how you set up the field. You can format the results of field codes in either of two ways. The first way is to apply formatting directly to the results of the field code. After you insert the field code, you select its contents (results) and format its font characteristics as you would any other text. The second method of formatting field-code results involves including formatting switches when you define the field code. The following sections explore these two methods.

Formatting Field-Code Results Directly   As mentioned earlier, you can simply highlight the results of a field code and apply character formatting just as you would for any other text. Whether the formatting is retained the next time the field is updated depends on how you created the field. In the Field dialog box, you see a check box labeled <u>P</u>reserve Formatting During Updates. If this box contains a check, Word automatically appends the *MERGEFORMAT switch to the field. This option causes any formatting applied to the field results to be retained when the field is updated. Clearing this check box causes the formatting to be lost the next time that the field is updated.

Word adds the *MERGEFORMAT switch to some field codes automatically. Insert an AutoText field, for example, and Word includes the *MERGEFORMAT switch to the field, even though this switch doesn't appear in the Field dialog box when you define the field. *MERGEFORMAT is discussed in more detail in the following section.

Using Formatting Switches   You also can format the results of field codes by applying formatting switches to the field code. The following list describes general switches that you can apply to a field to control the appearance of its results:

- ■ * (Format). Use this switch to specify number formats, capitalization, and character formatting (bold, italic, and so on). Follow this switch with the formatting code, such as *Caps. This example capitalizes the first letter of each word.

- ■ \# (Numeric Picture). Use this switch to specify the characteristics (such as decimal places and currency symbols) of numeric results. Using \# $###.00, for example, formats the results as currency with two decimal places.

- ■ \@ (Date-Time Picture). Use this switch to format date and time results. Using \@MMMM, d, yyyy, for example, formats a date with the full month, the date without a leading zero, and a four-digit year, such as February 6, 1997.

- ■ \! (Lock Result). This switch prevents field codes contained in text inserted by the BOOKMARK, INCLUDETEXT, and REF field codes from being updated unless the field is first updated in its source document. Without this switch, Word updates the embedded field.

N O T E The general switches described in the preceding list cannot be applied to all field codes. For a complete list of field codes to which these switches do not apply, consult the Reference Information\Field Types and Switches section of the Word Help file. ■

Each of the general switches described in the preceding list must include additional parameters, which vary from one switch to another. The Caps parameter used in the sample Format (*)is an example of an additional parameter. For a complete list of these parameters and additional information about each switch, consult the Reference Information\Field Types and Switches section of the Word Help file.

Performing Calculations with Field Codes

In addition to pulling information from various sources—document statistics, other files, date, time, and so on—you may want to perform calculations in your documents. One method of performing calculations involves using the Formula field code. The syntax for the Formula field code is as follows:

```
{= formula [Bookmark] [\# Numeric Picture]}
```

N O T E The square brackets in the preceding syntax example indicate that the information within the brackets is optional. The brackets themselves should not be included in the formula. ■

The formula expression can contain a combination of numbers, bookmarks that reference numbers, other field codes that result in numbers, and numeric operators and functions. The expression also can reference values in tables and values returned by functions. The following example adds a static value to a value contained in the bookmark named "Sales", divides the number by 12, and formats the result as currency with two decimal places:

```
{= (Sales+24,389.75) / 12 \# "$#,##0.00"}
```

Part

II

Ch

7

The `Formula` field code enables you to perform calculations on the contents of the cells in tables. As in Excel, cells are referenced by column and row. Columns are labeled with letters and rows are labeled with numbers, as in the following example:

```
A1  B1  C1  D1
A2  B2  C2  D2

A3  B3  C3  D3
A4  B4  C4  D4
```

▶ **See** "Inserting Tables," **p. 167**

In Word, you reference a cell by combining the column and row with a colon. A:1, for example, references the first cell in the top-left corner of the table. When used in a formula, the cell reference is enclosed in parentheses. The following `Formula` field code sums a range of cells:

```
{=SUM(A1:A4)}
```

In this example, the field code must be located within the table, because no other information is included to identify the table itself— just the range within it. Use bookmarks to reference tables elsewhere in the document. The following example sums a range of cells in two different tables and then subtracts them:

```
{=(SUM(Sales B2:B7))-(SUM(Expense C1:C29))}
```

You also can reference an entire row or column. To reference a column, use its column letter twice, separated by a colon. The reference A:A, for example, identifies the entire column A. The reference 4:4 identifies all of row 4. You can use multiple cell references as well. The following example averages rows 2 and 4:

```
{=AVERAGE(2:2,4:4)}
```

 To identify a range, specify the first and last cells of the range, as in A1:F6.

In summary, you can use the `Formula` field code to perform many types of calculations. You can build a table containing sales information, for example, and summarize the table or reference the table data elsewhere in the document through calculations on the table's contents. You may need to use formulas to calculate page numbers, sections, or other items. In short, anything in Word that deals with numeric values is a good candidate for the `Formula` field code.

For a complete description of the `Formula` field-code options and the use of table cells, consult the Reference Information/Field Types and Switches/Field Codes: =(Formula) field item in the Word Help file.

 When you include fields in a document, you sometimes want to protect those fields from being changed or to protect an entire document from being modified. For more information on protecting fields and documents, refer to "Protecting the Document" later in this chapter.

Creating and Using Forms

Word provides several features for creating printed forms and forms to be used and filled in on-screen. You may create an invoice (see Figure 7.5) or sales form, for example, and then print it to fill in the blanks. Alternatively, you may fill in the blanks on-screen first and then print the form. In either case, Word makes creating the forms an easy task, and you end up with professional-looking forms. This section of the chapter explores features in Word for creating these forms.

FIG. 7.5

Using forms can help you create attractive forms, including this company invoice.

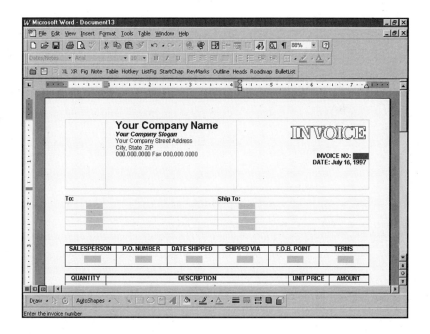

> **N O T E** This chapter focuses on creating printed forms and forms for use on-screen in Word. You also can create forms for use on the Internet with Word. For a detailed description of Internet-based forms, consult Chapter 47, "Internet Forms and Databases." ■

Exploring the Forms Controls

You could manually draw all the boxes and blanks in a form, and sometimes, you may need to do so, but Word provides a set of features just for creating forms. These features can considerably simplify the process of creating online forms. The first set of form controls that Word offers is located in the Forms toolbar (see Figure 7.6). Choose View, Toolbars, Forms to view the Forms toolbar.

Part
II

Ch
7

FIG. 7.6

Use the Forms toolbar to create on-screen or printed forms.

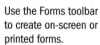

The following list describes the buttons in the Forms toolbar:

 ■ *Text Form Field.* Use this button to insert a text field in which the user enters text (on-screen) or fills in the blank in the printed document.

 ■ *Check Box Form Field.* This button inserts a box into the document. When used on-screen, these boxes act much like Windows check boxes. Clicking one check box places an X in the box; and clicking it again removes the X.

 ■ *Drop-Down Form Field.* Use this button to create a drop-down list from which on-screen users can make choices. This form field is not applicable to printed forms, although when printed, this form displays the first choice in the list of choices associated with the field.

 ■ *Form Field Options.* Use this button to set the properties of individual form fields in the document.

 ■ *Draw Table.* Use this button to open the Tables and Borders toolbar, with which you can draw custom tables and set their properties. The Tables and Borders toolbar is discussed later in this chapter.

 ■ *Insert Table.* Use this button to insert a table that has preset properties and equal-size table fields. When you select an existing table column, this button changes to the Insert Column button, with which you can add a column to the existing table. When you click a table cell, this button changes to the Insert Rows button, with which you can insert rows in a table column.

 ■ *Insert Frame.* Use this button to insert a frame into the document. Frames are handy for containing graphics and text, but you also can use text boxes to contain text, and text boxes offer additional features that are not provided by frames.

 ■ *Form Field Shading.* Use this button to turn on and off shading of form fields. Shading applies to printed forms as well as on-screen forms.

 ■ *Protect Form.* Use this button to protect the properties of the form fields from being changed. Turning on protection does not prevent data from being entered in the form fields, but simply protects the underlying form fields themselves from being modified.

Word also includes several ActiveX-based Controls that you can insert into documents. These ActiveX Controls are designed to work in conjunction with Visual Basic for Applications (VBA) to provide sophisticated programming and automation capabilities. You insert these controls by using the Control Toolbox toolbar (see Figure 7.7).

 T I P

Word includes several ActiveX Controls other than those shown in the Control Toolbox toolbar. These controls are provided by third-party vendors, and you typically must pay a license fee to enable and use them. For more information about ActiveX Controls, see Chapter 11, "Using VBA in Word."

FIG. 7.7

Insert ActiveX controls into a document by using the Control Toolbox toolbar.

Although these ActiveX Controls are most useful in conjunction with VBA to provide document automation, you also can use them as simple form controls without any underlying VBA code. If you want a set of check boxes in a document, for example, you can insert either the Check Box Form Field from the Forms toolbar or insert the Check Box ActiveX Control from the Control Toolbox toolbar.

Creating a Form

The first steps in creating a form are sketching out what you want the form to look like and listing the information that you want it to contain. If the form will include graphics, letterhead, or other document elements, make sure that you have those elements ready, or be prepared to create them as part of the form.

Whether you are creating a printed form or a form for use on-screen, you should consider creating the form as a template. Then you can base new form documents on this template, helping ensure that your original form remains unchanged until you are ready to revise it.

▶ **See** "Creating and Using Templates," **p. 91**

After you begin the new template, begin adding the static information (such as form title, letter-head, and graphics) and other elements of the form that will not change—that is, elements in the form that the form user will not modify.

When you're ready to start adding fields to the form, choose View, Toolbars, Forms to display the Forms toolbar. If you prefer to use ActiveX Controls, choose View, Toolbars, Control Toolbox. The following section explains how to use the various objects in the Forms toolbar. For more information about using the Control Toolbox, see Chapter 11, "Using VBA in Word."

Using Text Boxes and Check Boxes

Text fields and check boxes often make up the majority of the objects in a form. Use text fields when you want to create a fill-in-the-blank field in the form. Use check boxes just as you do in Windows to indicate choice of an option. If you're building an employee insurance sign-up sheet, for example, you use text fields for the employee's name, address, and other information, and use check boxes to have the employee choose a payment method or deductible option.

To insert a text form field, place the insertion point where you want the field to be inserted and click the Form Field Options button in the Forms toolbar. A shaded text box appears in the document. To set the text form field's properties, double-click the field, or single-click the field and then click the Form Field Properties button in the toolbar. In either case, you see the Text Form Field Options dialog box, shown in Figure 7.8.

FIG. 7.8

Use the Text Form Field Options dialog box to set the properties, such as length, of the text field.

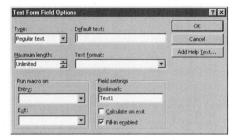

Use the Type drop-down list to choose the type of text that you want to associate with the field—regular text, numbers, a date, the current time, the current date, or a calculation. All but the current-date and current-time options enable you to specify the default value for the field. The default value appears in the form, and the user can change it. You also can use the default value to provide instructions, such as Enter your name here.

 Text fields default in width to about 3/8 inches. The field expands in size as the user types information. For printed forms, however, you probably want the text field to print at a fixed size. To expand the size of the text form field to suit the amount of space that you want in the form, use as many spaces as necessary as the default text to force the field to the desired size.

The following list describes the controls in the Text Form Field Options dialog box:

- *Type*. Choose from this drop-down list the type of text entry that you want in the field.
- *Default Text*. Type the default value for the text in this box. The default value appears in the form and is overwritten when your user enters his or her own information in the field.
- *Maximum Length*. Specify the maximum length of the field or choose Unlimited to allow the field to expand as much as needed.
- *Text Format*. Use this drop-down list to choose the format in which you want the text to appear. This drop-down list changes according to your choice in the Type drop-down list. Choose Number from the Type drop-down list, for example, and this control changes to Number Format, allowing you to choose among various numeric formatting options.
- *Entry*. Use this drop-down list to choose a macro to run when the user clicks the field.
- *Exit*. Use this drop-down list to choose a macro to run when the user exits the field by pressing the Tab key or by clicking outside the field.
- *Bookmark*. Assign a bookmark name to the field with this control.

- *Calculate on Exit.* Place a check in this box to have Word recalculate the results in the field when the user exits the field.

- *Fill-In Enabled.* Place a check in this box if you want the user to be able to fill in the blank on-screen. To prevent the field from being filled in, clear this check box.

- *Add Help Text.* Click this button to assign help messages to the field that appears in the Word status bar when the user presses F1 with the field selected. You also can define the message for a small message box that appears when the user presses F1 when the field is selected.

 TIP To provide vertical separation between text form fields, set the paragraph properties for each line to provide additional space before or after the paragraph, or change the line spacing.

To insert a check box into the form, place the insertion point where you want the check box to appear and click the Check Box Form Field button in the Forms toolbar. Then space or tab to the right and type a name for the check box.

 TIP Set the font size of a text form field or check box form field to control the size of the element in the form.

Using Tables in a Form

Tables sometimes are useful in forms for displaying information as well as prompting for information. How and whether you use tables in your forms depends on your needs and the contents of the forms.

To insert a table with uniform column and row arrangement, click the Insert Table button in the Forms toolbar. The control expands to allow you to choose from a 1×1 to a 4×5 table. Click the table of the size that you want. The resulting table is much like any other table that you would insert into a Word document and can be formatted as such. You can use the commands in the Table menu to modify the table.

▶ **See** "Formatting and Modifying Tables," **p. 175**

To insert rows into the table, click the table where you want the rows to be inserted and then click the Insert Rows button in the Forms toolbar. To insert a column, you must first select the column where you want a new one to be inserted and then click the Insert Row button in the Forms toolbar. Notice that this button replaces the Insert Table button, as does the Insert Rows button, when you select a column or row, respectively.

If you want more control of the table's initial structure or appearance, click the Draw Table button in the Forms toolbar; then click and drag to define the overall rectangular area of the table. When you release the mouse button, the Tables and Borders toolbox appears. Use the controls in the Tables and Borders toolbox to fine-tune the appearance of your table.

▶ **See** "Inserting Tables," **p. 167**

Part
II

Ch
7

After you create the structure of the table, you probably want to fill in at least some of the cells in the table. Some of the information, such as labels, is static. You may want the user to be able to fill in some of the table, however. If so, you need to add the appropriate type of text form field to each cell. Just click the cell and then click the Text Form Field button in the Forms toolbar.

 TIP   If you turn on document protection, you won't be able to modify the contents of a table. Turn off protection while you are designing the form; then turn it back on before you save it.

Using Drop-Down Form Fields

Windows (and, therefore, Windows applications) uses drop-down lists to enable you to choose among multiple options. The Forms toolbar includes a Drop-Down Form Field button that you can use to insert drop-down lists into your forms. These drop-down lists are applicable only to on-screen forms, of course.

To insert a drop-down list into a form, place the insertion point where you want the drop-down list to be inserted and then click the Drop-Down Form Field button. Word inserts a default-size drop-down list that initially looks much like a text form field, except for its greater width. Double-click the drop-down form field to open the Drop-Down Form Field Options dialog box, shown in Figure 7.9.

FIG. 7.9

Add choices to the drop-down list through the Drop-Down Form Field Options dialog box.

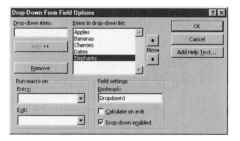

Type the first option for the list in the Drop-Down Items text box; then choose Add. Repeat this procedure to add all other options to the list. Select an item and then click the up or down arrows beside the Items In Drop-Down List area to change the order of the items in the list. Select an item and click Remove to remove it from the list.

As you can with text form fields, you can assign a macro to run when the user clicks the drop-down list or exits the list. Set these options with the Run Macro On group of controls. You also can assign a bookmark to the drop-down form field, set it to calculate on exit (applicable to formulas), and enable or disable the drop-down list. Click the Add Help Text button to add optional Help text for the status bar or F1 key, if desired. When you are satisfied with the drop-down list properties, choose OK.

Notice that the drop-down list won't actually function as a drop-down list until you turn on document protection; then it behaves just like a Windows drop-down list. Click the drop-down list and choose one of the options from the list.

Using the Form

When you finish creating the form template, save it in a folder accessible by those people who need to use it (either on-screen or to print it). As discussed in the following section, you need to make sure that you turn on protection for the document to prevent accidental changes to the form. With protection turned on, the person using the form on-screen can only fill in the blanks, check boxes, and other objects that you include in the form. With protection turned off, the user can modify any portion of the form, including deleting parts of the form.

 You can use sections in a form to segregate different sets of form fields. Then you can assign passwords to specific sections to prevent anything in those sections from being changed. The following section explains this topic.

Protecting the Document

As mentioned earlier, you need to protect forms to enable them to function properly and to prevent them from being accidentally changed by other people when they use the form. You also can protect a document in other ways. This chapter examines the methods available in Word for protecting documents. This chapter discusses how to protect a document's fields and form fields, as well as how to use passwords to protect a document. For information on using protection with revision marks and comments, see Chapter 55, "Document Collaboration."

Protecting Individual Fields

You cannot protect fields in a document per se, but you can temporarily lock them to prevent them from being updated. Nothing, however, prevents you or someone else from selecting the field and then deleting it or from overwriting its contents by clicking inside the field and typing. Locking the fields does, however, prevent the locked fields from being updated when the rest of the fields in the document are updated. To lock an individual field, click the field and press Ctrl+F11. Click a field and press Shift+Ctrl+F11 to unlock a field.

 You can protect a range of fields by using a workaround. Place the fields to be protected in their own section and then protect the section, as explained in "Protecting Sections" later in this chapter.

Protecting Forms and Form Fields

Essentially, the only time you want to turn protection off for a form is when you are designing the form. You want the form protected at all other times when the form is being used. Protecting the form prevents users from accessing or changing anything other than the contents of the form fields. In other words, all the user can do is fill in the form; the user cannot modify its structure or other content.

The easiest way to turn on form protection is to click the Protect Form button in the Forms toolbar. Alternatively, you can choose Tools, Protect Document to open the Protect Document dialog box (see Figure 7.10) and then choose the Forms button to turn on form protection. Save the document with protection turned on.

FIG. 7.10

Use the Protect Document dialog box to set document protection options.

Protecting Sections

If the document contains multiple sections, you can selectively protect each section, which means that you can lock entire sections to prevent them from being changed (other than form fields in the section). If you want a user to be able to modify only part of the contents of a document, divide the document into sections and protect the desired sections.

To define protection by section, choose Tools, Protect Document to open the Protect Document dialog box. Click the Sections button to open the Section Protection dialog box (see Figure 7.11). Place a check beside each section to be protected; then choose OK. Then choose OK in the Protect Document dialog box to turn on protection.

FIG. 7.11

You can protect certain areas of a document by using sections and the Section Protection dialog box.

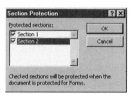

Using Passwords

You can use passwords in several ways to protect the contents of a document. These ways include the following:

- Protect a document from being opened without a password
- Protect a document from being modified without a password
- Protect a form with a password

You can protect a document with two passwords when you save the document (the first two options in the preceding list). The first password is required for opening the file. The second password is for modifying the file. If you apply both passwords, the user has to specify a password to open the file and then specify another password to modify it. Alternatively, you can use either password alone, depending on your needs.

To apply passwords to a document, open the document and choose File, Save As to open the Save As dialog box; then choose Options to display the Save property sheet, shown in Figure 7.12.

FIG. 7.12

Use the Save property sheet to specify options that control how the document is saved.

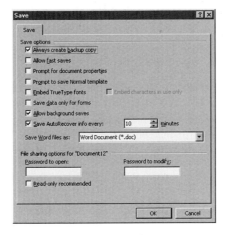

In the Password to Open text box, type the password that you want to apply to the document to protect it from being opened. Only those people who have the password can open the document. The password can be up to 15 characters long and can contain any combination of letters, numbers, spaces, and symbols. Passwords are case-sensitive.

In the Password to Modify text box, type the password that you want to use to protect the document from being modified. If the user doesn't have this password, he or she cannot modify the document but can view it. Choose OK and then choose Save to save the document with the new password.

CAUTION

Don't forget the passwords that you assign to a document. If you do, you won't be able to open or modify the document.

You use a different method to protect a form from changes. With the form open, choose Tools, Protect Document to open the Protect Document dialog box (refer to Figure 7.10). Type a password in the Password text box and choose OK. Word prompts you to confirm the password by typing it again. Do so and choose OK.

With the form protected by a password, the person using the form can still enter data in the form fields. The user has to know the password to turn off protection and modify other parts of the form, however.

Part

II

Ch

7

Creating Indexes and Tables of Contents

Word automates many tasks that would be extremely time-consuming to perform manually. These tasks include creating indexes, tables of contents (TOC), tables of figures (TOF), and tables of authorities (TOA). The following list describes these document elements:

- *Index.* An index summarizes the content of a document, listing words, phrases, and the pages on which those words and phrases appear.
- *Table of contents.* A table of contents summarizes the topics or headings in a document, and includes the page number on which each topic or heading begins.
- *Table of figures.* A table of figures summarizes the figures in a document, typically listing the figure caption and page number on which the figure is located. You also can use this feature to create a table of tables or a table of equations.
- *Table of authorities.* A table of authorities lists references to cases, statutes, rules, and so on in a legal document, and specifies the page number on which the reference appears.

The following sections explain how to create indexes, tables of contents, and tables of figures. Tables of authorities are not covered, because they apply to a smaller user segment. If you require help in creating a table of authorities, press F1 and perform a search for **table of authorities**. For additional help creating and using indexes, tables of contents, and tables of figures, refer to *Special Edition Using Microsoft Word 97*, Best Seller Edition from Que.

Creating an Index

You can insert an index at any point in a document, but indexes typically are included at the end of the document. Word inserts the index within its own section to separate it from the rest of the document, regardless of where you locate the index within the document.

The most important aspect of creating an index is marking the index entries, which means selecting the words or phrases within the document to be included in the index. Word offers two methods for marking index entries. You can mark the entries one word or phrase at a time directly in the document, or use a *concordance file* that contains information Word uses to mark the words and phrases automatically.

To create an index by marking individual entries, begin at the top of the document and locate the first word or phrase to be included in the index. Highlight the entry, then press Shift+Alt+X or choose Insert, Index and Tables; click the Index tab; and choose Mark Entry. The Mark Index Entry dialog box appears, as shown in Figure 7.13.

The selected word or phrase appears in the Main Entry text box automatically. Use the following controls in the Mark Index Entry dialog box to define the entry:

- *Subentry.* Use this text box to specify the text for an index subentry. The subentry text is added to the index below the Main Entry keyword or phrase, along with other subentries.
- *Cross-Reference.* Choose this option button if you want to insert a text reference, such as See *something else* instead of a page number.

- *Current Page.* Choose this option (the default) to have a page number inserted into the index for the selected entry.

- *Page Range and Bookmark.* Use the Page Range option button to have Word insert a range of pages rather than a single page number for the entry. The range must already be defined in the document by means of a bookmark. Choose the name of the bookmark from the Bookmark drop-down list.

- *Page Number Format.* Use these two check boxes to turn on or off boldface and italic for the page-number text for the entry.

- *Mark.* Choose this button to mark the current selection with the specified index settings.

- *Mark All.* Choose this button to mark all occurrences of the selected text in the document.

FIG. 7.13

Use the Mark Index Entry dialog box to mark words or phrases for inclusion in the index.

N O T E Word inserts an Index Entry (XE) field code as hidden text directly to the right of the selected word or phrase. You can view these field codes by turning on field codes.

If you work with documents that contain many of the same index keywords or phrases, you can use a concordance file to significantly speed the index-marking process. A concordance file consists of two columns, one entry per line. The left column lists the text that you want to index, and the right column lists the index entries to create for the text specified in the left column. After you create the concordance file, you can use it for multiple documents as required. There is no specific command or wizard to help you create a concordance file in Word. Instead, you simply create a Word document containing a two-column table, then fill the table with the index entries.

To mark a document by using a concordance file, first open the document to be indexed. Locate the insertion point where you want the index to be inserted; then choose Insert, Index and Tables, and click the Index tab to display the Index page of the Index and Tables property sheet (see Figure 7.14).

In the Index page, choose AutoMark. Word displays a standard Open dialog box. Locate and select the concordance file; then choose Open. Word searches the document for occurrences of the entries listed in the concordance file and marks them according to the right-column entries in the concordance file. Word marks only the first occurrence of the entry in each paragraph.

Part

II

Ch

7

FIG. 7.14

Use the Index page to specify a variety of settings that control the appearance of the index.

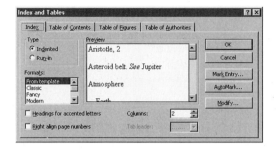

After the document has been marked by either of the methods described earlier in this section, you're ready to insert the index. Choose Insert, Index and Tables. Select the style of index that you want to use, using the Preview as a guide. When you're satisfied with the appearance of the index, choose OK to insert the index into the document.

As you continue to work on a document that has been indexed, the page numbers specified in the index entries are likely to become incorrect to some degree as text shifts within the document. An index is simply a table of field codes, so updating the index simply means updating the field codes. To update the index, place the insertion point anywhere in the index and press F9. Alternatively, right-click the index and then choose Update Field from the shortcut menu.

Using Word to Create a Table of Contents

Creating a table of contents requires that you perform a series of actions. These actions are summarized in the following list:

- Apply paragraph styles to the document to identify logical levels within the document. Or, you can add Table Entry (TC) field codes as hidden text in the document to identify index items.
- Specify the style of table you want to use.
- Specify settings that control the appearance of the TOC.
- Insert the TOC.

To create a table of contents you first apply paragraph styles to your document. Although you can create your own styles, probably the easiest method for you at first is to rely on the styles that are included with your default template.

T I P You can build a TOC by adding Table Entry (TC) field codes as hidden text at the end of each TOC entry throughout the document. Using styles is by far the easiest method, however, and is the one explained in this chapter. Notice that you also can build a TOC by using a combination of styles and TC field codes.

If the document is long enough to include a TOC, you are likely to have used outlining with the document. Assume that you've created a document and applied the predefined Heading 1, Heading 2, and Heading 3 styles to the appropriate headings in the document. The paragraphs with the Heading 1 style appear leftmost in the TOC, with the Heading 2 and Heading 3 headings being indented to the second and third stops in the TOC, respectively.

N O T E If you haven't used the Heading styles in the document, assign a style to each of the heads in the document that you want to be included in the TOC. Use a different style for each level of the document. All chapter titles, for example, have the same style; section heads all use their own style; and so on. ▨

To insert the TOC in Word, locate the insertion point where you want the TOC to be inserted; then choose Insert, Index and Tables, and click the Table of Contents tab (refer to Figure 7.14). From the Formats list, choose the style of TOC that you want. Word applies paragraph and font formatting to the TOC table according to your choice. If you want Word to use the default paragraph style in your document for the TOC, choose the From Template option.

Next, use the four controls at the bottom of the Index and Tables dialog box to specify options for the TOC. Enable the Show Page Numbers check box if you want the page number to be listed for each heading. Enable the Right Align Page Numbers check box to have the page numbers aligned at the right edge of the TOC. Use the Show Levels spin control to choose how many levels to include in the TOC. Finally, if the TOC style that you chose supports tab leaders, choose the desired tab leader from the Tab Leader drop-down list. The tab leader is the character, if any, that separates the page numbers from the heading.

Next, click the Options button to display the Table of Contents Options dialog box (see Figure 7.15). Make sure that the Styles check box is enabled; then scroll through the available styles list to locate the Heading 1 style. You find that Word has already assigned the appropriate TOC level to the style. If you're basing your TOC on other styles, locate the styles and assign to them the appropriate level by clicking the TOC Level text box next to the style and then typing the level number (1, 2, 3, and so on). When you've set all the necessary style levels, choose OK. Then choose OK in the Index and Tables dialog box to insert the TOC into the document.

FIG. 7.15

Set up the styles to be used for the TOC by using the Table of Contents Options dialog box.

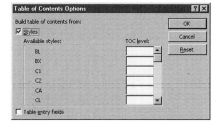

Most likely, your document won't remain static after you insert the TOC; page numbers may change, new headings come and old headings go, or you may just change a few words here or there. So understanding how to update the TOC is important. To do so, right-click the TOC table and then choose Update Field from the context menu to open the Update Table of Contents dialog box (see Figure 7.16). You can choose to update just the page numbers or update the entire TOC. Choose the desired option in the dialog box; then click OK.

FIG. 7.16

Specify whether you want to update a single field or the entire TOC.

Creating a Table of Figures

If your document contains several figures, you may want to include a table of figures (TOF) that lists the figures. You include a TOF in much the same way that you insert a TOC. As for a TOC, an easy way to mark the figure entries is to use a style. If you inserted captions for each figure, however, you can use the caption as the tag by which the TOF is defined. You can use Table Entry (XC) field codes as hidden text with each figure reference, but using the styles or caption method is much easier.

If you plan to use captions as the basis for the TOF, first insert a caption for each equation, figure, or table. If you are using styles as the basis for defining the TOF, apply the desired style to each figure caption.

To insert the TOF, locate the insertion point where you want the TOF to be located. Then choose Insert, Index and Tables, and click the Table of Figures tab to display the Table of Figures property page (see Figure 7.17).

FIG. 7.17

Insert tables of figures by using the Tables of Figures property page.

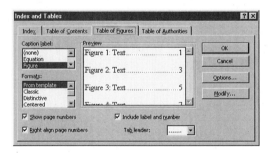

The following list describes the controls in the Tables and Figures page:

- *Caption Label*. Use this list to specify the type of caption element to use to define the TOF.

- *Formats*. Choose the overall style of the table from this list.

- *Show Page Numbers*. Place a check in this check box if you want each table entry to list the page number of the associated figure.

- *Right Align Page Numbers*. Place a check in this check box to force the page numbers to the right margin of the document. When this option is enabled, the Ta<u>b</u> Leader control becomes available.

- *Include Label and <u>N</u>umber*. Use this control to turn on or off the inclusion of the selected caption label in the entry.

- *Ta<u>b</u> Leader*. Use this drop-down list to choose the type of separator to place between the entry and its page number. This item is enabled only when <u>R</u>ight Align Page Numbers is checked.

If you are using styles or field codes to define the TOF, choose the <u>O</u>ptions button to open the Table of Figures Options dialog box. Click the <u>S</u>tyle check box; then choose the style associated with the figure caption or other document element that you want to be included in the TOF entry. Alternatively, click the Table <u>E</u>ntry Fields check box and choose the appropriate table identifier. Choose OK when you finish setting options.

When you are satisfied with your TOF settings, choose OK. Word inserts the TOF as a table of field codes. ●

CHAPTER 8

Using Tables

by Jim Boyce

Tables are important elements used in many types of documents. Word 97 provides several features that enable you to quickly create, fill in, format, and modify tables. This chapter explores tables in depth. ■

Creating tables

You can create equally-proportioned tables quickly in Word by specifying the number of rows and columns to create. Or, you can draw to quickly create tables with different column and row proportions.

Formatting and modifying tables

You can format tables manually or let Word autoformat the tables using several predefined table styles.

Sorting table data

Word makes it easy to sort the data in a table based on several different criteria.

Using formulas in tables

You can use tables in Word much like you use a spreadsheet in Excel by adding formulas to the cells. A cell can reference other cells in the table and you perform summation and other common spreadsheet functions.

Overview of New Features

Word 97 includes only a few new features relating to tables, but those few features offer considerable power. The following sections provide a brief overview of these new features.

Drawing a Table

In previous versions of Word, as in Word 97, you can quickly create a table by specifying the number of columns and rows for the table. Word creates the table with the same number of cells in each row. That is, the cells in each column are equally distributed (see Figure 8.1).

FIG. 8.1

A typical table created by Word's predefined table styles results in equally-spaced rows and columns.

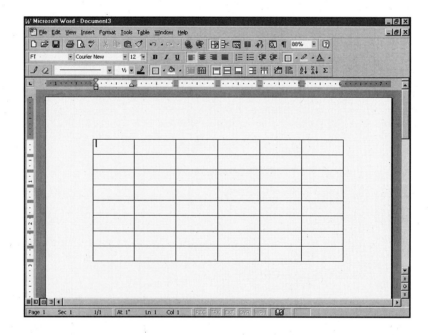

You can modify this type of table quite easily to change row and column spacing and consolidate cells, but Word 97 offers a new feature that lets you draw the table. You define the rectangular area for the overall table size, then begin drawing the row and column lines at any point desired in the table (see Figure. 8.2). This new feature makes it easy to create custom table layouts.

Tables and Borders Made Easier

Another change in the way Word handles tables is the integration of table and border commands in one toolbar called the Tables and Borders toolbar. Adding these border commands to the toolbar makes it easier to change table border styles and sizes.

FIG. 8.2
Quickly create custom table layouts using Word 97's new feature for drawing a table right in the document.

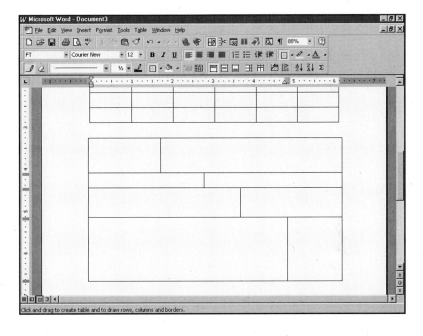

Merging Cells Vertically

Previous versions of Word allowed you to merge cells horizontally in a table. Word 97 also offers the ability to merge cells vertically in a table. You can merge cells using commands in the Table menu or by simply erasing the line that separates the two cells with the new Eraser tool in the Tables and Borders toolbox. See the section "Splitting and Merging Cells" later in this chapter for more information.

Vertical Text Alignment and Orientation

You can easily align the text in a table cell at the top, center, or bottom of the cell. Word 97 also lets you rotate the text vertically in the cell. You can adjust the alignment of the vertical text just as you can the horizontal text. See the section "Changing Text Orientation and Alignment" later in this chapter for more information.

Resizing and Alignment

Word 97 now lets you change the height or width of rows and columns by simply dragging the row and column borders. You also can easily align rows and columns to distribute them evenly within the table.

Inserting Tables

Tables in Word consist of rows and columns of cells in which you can enter text, formulas, and graphics. You can use tables to create a grid of images or even arrange side-by-side paragraphs. You can perform calculations not only within cells, but perform summation and other functions from one cell to another, making Word tables act much like a spreadsheet.

This section of the chapter explains how to create tables and enter data into them. Later sections explain how to format and manipulate table contents.

Creating Evenly-Distributed Tables

If you want a table with evenly-distributed cells—one in which the cells are horizontally and vertically aligned throughout the table, Word can create the table for you automatically. You only have to specify the number of columns and rows to include in the table. Word does the rest.

To create an evenly-distributed table, follow these steps:

1. Place the insertion point where you want the table inserted.
2. Choose Table, Insert Table to open the Insert Table dialog box (see Figure 8.3). Or, click the Insert Table button on the Standard toolbar.

FIG. 8.3

Quickly create evenly-distributed tables using the Insert Table dialog box.

3. Use the Number of Columns and Number of Rows controls to specify the number of columns and rows in the table.
4. If you want the columns equally spaced, choose Auto from the Column Width control. Or, type or select the column width from this same control.
5. Choose OK to insert the table in the document.

After the table appears in the document you can click in individual cells to begin entering data in the cells. For more information, refer to the section "Adding Data to the Table" later in this chapter.

Using the Table Drawing Tool

While the Insert Table dialog box offers a very quick way to create simple, evenly-distributed tables, you might need to create a more complex table. For example, you might need to structure the table cells to place a varying number of cells in each column. Word 97 includes a new feature that lets you draw a table one cell at a time.

Use the following steps to draw a complex, custom table in a Word document:

1. Choose Table, Draw Table. Word switches to Page Layout view and displays the Tables and Borders toolbar. The pointer changes to a pencil pointer.
2. Click and drag in the document to define the overall size of the table (see Figure 8.4).

FIG. 8.4
Draw the outline of the table first.

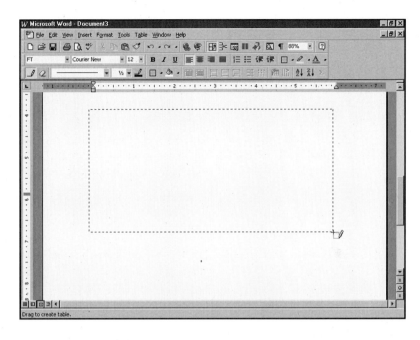

3. Use the pencil pointer to draw initial column and row lines (see Figure 8.5).

FIG. 8.5
Add cells to your custom table layout by simply drawing the cell borders with the pencil tool.

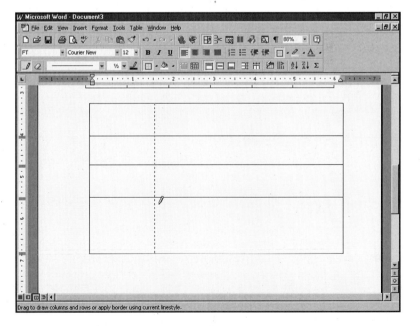

4. To remove lines, click the Eraser button on the Tables and Borders toolbox, then drag the resulting eraser pointer over the line to be erased.

5. Click outside the table to exit the Table Editor mode.

At this point you have a simple, custom table. You'll learn how to format the table and change its appearance later in the section "Formatting and Modifying Tables." Before learning how to insert data in a table, you must first learn how to select cells.

Selecting Cells in a Table

Word offers several methods for selecting cells individually and as a group. Use the following methods to select cells:

- *Select a cell.* Place the arrow cursor just inside the left edge of the cell and click.

- *Select a row.* Click to the left of the row.

- *Select a column.* Click the column's top gridline or border. The pointer will change to a vertical arrow when it is in the correct position to select a column.

- *Select multiple cells, rows, or columns.* Click the first cell and drag to the last cell of the desired selection. Or, click in the first cell, hold down the Shift key, and click in the last cell of your selection.

- *Select text in the next cell.* Press the Tab key or simply select the text using the pointer. You can use the arrow keys to move between cells.

- *Select text in the previous cell.* Press Shift+Tab or select the text using the pointer.

- *Select the entire table.* Click the table and press Alt+5 (use the 5 character on the numeric keyboard with NumLock turned off).

N O T E   You can select a row or column by placing the cursor in a cell, then choosing Table, Select Row or Select Column. Select the entire table by choosing Table, Select Table.

Adding Data to the Table

Adding data to a table is easy. In most cases, you simply click in the cell in which you want the data, then start typing. Word automatically wraps the text within the cell as you type. Word also automatically increases the row height if necessary to accommodate all of the text within the cell.

TIP   Word automatically changes the row height across the table when the amount of text in a particular cell requires more vertical space. You can't prevent the other cells in the row from also changing, but you can erase the row lines and draw them back in at the previous spacing.

You can format the text in a table cell in the same way you format text outside a table. Either set your formatting options before you begin typing, or select the text afterwards and apply formatting (bold, italic, and so on) to the text.

Part

II

Ch

8

You can insert graphics in a table cell almost as easily as text. Essentially, you click in the cell and insert the graphic. However, you can't use Insert, Picture to insert the image. Instead, use the following method to insert an image in a table cell:

1. Click in the cell.
2. Choose Insert, Object to open the Object dialog box (see Figure 8.6).

FIG. 8.6

Insert graphics or other OLE objects in a table using the Object dialog box.

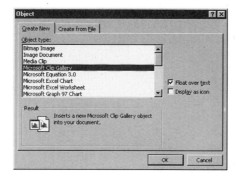

3. Scroll through the object list to find the type of object you want to insert (such as Microsoft Clip Gallery).
4. Clear the Float Over Text check box.
5. Choose OK.
6. Depending on the type of object selected, you might see an application, an Open dialog box to select a file, or in the case of Microsoft Clip Gallery, the Clip Gallery itself.
7. Select the image or file to insert, then choose OK or Insert depending on what is offered in the application or dialog box.

Depending on the size of the table cell and the image, the image may not fit inside the cell. If not, a right and/or bottom portion of the image might extend behind the next cell to the right or below the current cell. You can click the image and drag its resize handles to make it fit in the cell. Or, simply adjust the cell size as necessary. Click the cell's border and drag it to the desired size to resize the cell. To resize the height of a cell, you must resize the entire row. First select the row by moving the pointer to the left margin of the row until the pointer changes to point to the right, then click to select the row. After selecting the row, choose Table, Cell Height and Width. In the Cell Height and Width dialog box, specify the desired cell height and choose OK.

Importing Data from a Database

You don't need to create a table first to insert data from a database into the table. Instead, you can let Word create the table for you automatically. That way you don't have to worry about getting the number of columns or rows set beforehand.

To insert a database as a table, use the following steps:

1. Choose View, Toolbars, Database to open the Database toolbar.

2. Place the insertion point in the document where you want the table to be inserted.

3. Click the Insert Database button on the Database toolbar to display the Database dialog box (see Figure 8.7).

FIG. 8.7

Use the Database dialog box to begin the process of selecting the data to be inserted.

4. Choose the Get Data button.

5. Use the resulting Open Data Source file dialog box to locate and select the database you want to open. Choose MS Access Databases from the Files of Type drop-down list to view available Access databases. After you select the database, choose Open.

    Microsoft Access starts and displays a Microsoft Access dialog box similar to the one shown in Figure 8.8.

FIG. 8.8

Choose the table(s) from which to bring the data.

6. Select the desired table from the list and click OK.

7. Word returns to the Database dialog box. Choose the Query Options button to display the Query Options dialog box.

8. Click the Select Fields tab to display the Select Fields property page (see Figure 8.9).

9. Select the fields you want included from the database into the table, then choose OK.

10. Choose Insert Data. Word prompts you to select which records to insert (see Figure 8.10).

11. Choose All if you want all the records in the table, or specify the beginning and ending record numbers.

FIG. 8.9

Use the Select Fields page to choose the data to include from the database into the table.

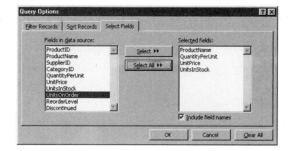

FIG. 8.10

You can insert a range of records or all records in the database.

12. If you want to be able to update the table records later, place a check in the Insert Data As Field check box. With this option selected, Word will insert the data in the table using field codes that can be updated later if the source data changes.

13. Choose OK to insert the table.

In step 13, you had the option of inserting the data using field codes. If you want to be able to update the data in the table from the database later if or when the database changes, insert the records using field codes. When you need to update the table, simply update the fields in the document. Word will retrieve the data from Access.

Finding Specific Records   If you have a long, complex table, it can be time-consuming to search through the table manually to find a specific record, particularly if the table is not sorted by the field in which you are searching. Word provides a search feature to help you quickly search through the table. Open the Database toolbar, then click the Find Record button. Word opens a dialog box in which you specify the search text and field in which you want to search (see Figure 8.11). Fill in the dialog box according to your search needs and choose Find First. The dialog box stays visible after the first record matching the search criteria is found. Choose Find Next to search for the next occurrence of the data.

FIG. 8.11

Specify the search text and the field in which to search to locate specific records.

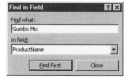

 Using a Data Form   Although you can add new entries simply by adding new rows and typing the data in the cells, it often is easier to use a data entry form, particularly if the table contains several columns. To add, modify, and delete records from a table using a data form, first click in the table. Then on the Database toolbar click the Data Form button. Word displays a Data Form dialog box similar to the one shown in Figure 8.12.

FIG. 8.12

A data form makes it easier to add records to a large table.

You can use the data form to browse the records in the table or modify the table. Click the Add New button to clear the form to add a new record. Fill in the data form and choose OK if this is the only record you want to add. Otherwise, choose Add New again and repeat the process for additional records. Note that the records won't appear in the table until you click OK in the Data Form dialog box. Use the Delete and Restore buttons, respectively, to delete records and restore a record's original values. Use Find to locate records. Use View Source to open the source table.

Converting Existing Text to a Table

If you have a document containing tabular data created without using tables, you can easily convert that text to a table. Word does all the hard work for you. To convert text to a table, first select all of the text to be converted. Then choose Table, Convert Text to Table. Word displays the Convert Text to Table dialog box shown in Figure 8.13.

FIG. 8.13

Specify the character that Word should use to locate the separator between table fields.

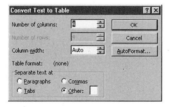

Word will determine the number of columns and rows required automatically, but you can change the number of columns if needed, as well as the column width. The key factor you must specify is the character Word will use when determining how to separate the text into different table columns. You can choose from Paragraph, Tab, Comma, or specify a different character using the Other option button. If the text uses tabs to separate columns of text, for example, choose the Tab option button. Then choose OK to convert the text to a table.

T I P Errors that occur while converting text to tables usually are caused by extra separator characters within the text. Be sure to use unique separator characters when creating or editing text that will be converted to a table or database format.

Formatting and Modifying Tables

Creating a table usually involves more than just defining the number of rows and columns and filling in the data. You'll probably want to use Word's formatting options to add borders, shading, and other formatting characteristics to the table. You also might want to make content changes to the table. This section focuses on Word features that enable you to format and modify tables.

AutoFormatting Tables

You can apply table formatting manually to achieve a custom look for a table, but Word offers a feature that can automatically format the table, saving you a lot of time and work. You can use the AutoFormat feature when you insert the table or afterwards. To use AutoFormat during table creation, set the row and column options in the Insert Table dialog box (choose Table, Insert Table), then click the AutoFormat button to display the Table AutoFormat dialog box (see Figure 8.14).

FIG. 8.14
Use the Table
AutoFormat dialog box
to set formatting
options for the table.

Word provides several predefined formatting schemes in the Formats list. Choose a scheme to view it in the Preview box. Use the check boxes in the dialog box to turn on and off various formatting aspects (the options are self explanatory). Choose OK to return to the Insert Table dialog box, then choose OK to insert the table with the specified formatting options.

To use automatic formatting to format an existing table, right-click the table and choose Table AutoFormat, or choose Table, AutoFormat from Word's menu. Word will open the Table AutoFormat dialog box with which you can specify formatting options.

Working with Borders

Word automatically places a single-line, thin border around a table and draws similar lines to separate the table cells from one another. You can apply a different border to the table and selectively turn off border lines around each cell (or change their line characteristics).

To change border properties, choose View, Toolbars, Tables and Borders to turn on the Tables and Borders toolbar. If you want to change the border around a cell or group of cells, click in the cell or select the group. Choose the line style and weight you want from the Line Style and Line Weight controls on the toolbar. Then click the small arrow beside the Border button on the toolbar, and choose the border style for the selection. To apply a border to the whole table, select the whole table by choosing Table, Select Table, then choose the border style using the Outside Border button.

You also can draw individual border lines. To do so, first select the line style and weight for the line, then click the Draw Table button. Draw the border lines by clicking and dragging over the existing border and cell lines. Click the Eraser button and drag over lines to erase them.

Numbering Cells in a Table

Word makes it easy to number the cells in a table. To number the first cell in each row, select the first column in the table and then click the Numbering button on the Formatting toolbar. Or, select the column and choose Format, Bullets and Numbering, then select the type of numbering method and choose OK. If you want to number the cells in a row instead of a column, choose the row to be numbered.

If you want to number a selection of table cells rather than a whole column, select the range of cells. Then click the Numbering button on the Formatting toolbar.

Changing Text Orientation and Alignment

Word places text in the table horizontally by default. This is the orientation you'll probably use most often. In some cases, however, you might want to align the text vertically in one or more cells. You might also want to change the alignment of text in the cell to the left, center or right (vertical text), or top, middle, or bottom (horizontal text).

To align text, click in the cell or select the range of cells to change. On the Tables and Borders toolbar, click the Align Top, Center Vertically, or Align Bottom toolbar buttons. Note that when you click in a cell containing vertical text, these buttons change to Align Left, Center Horizontally, and Center Right to reflect the alignment choices for vertical text.

To change the orientation of text, click in the cell or select a range of cells and click the Change Text Direction button on the Tables and Borders toolbar. This button acts a toggle, changing the text from horizontal to vertical left and vertical right.

Splitting and Merging Cells

Sometimes you might want to merge cells together or split a cell into multiple cells. To merge cells into a single cell, first select the cells to be merged. Then on the Tables and Borders toolbar, click the Merge Cells button. Or choose Table, Merge Cells. Word will automatically merge the cells.

 To split cells, first click in a cell to select it or select a range of cells. Then on the Tables and Borders toolbar, click the Split Cells button. Or choose Table, Split Cells from the menu. Word displays the Split Cells dialog box shown in Figure 8.15.

FIG. 8.15
Use the Split Cells dialog box to split one or more cells into additional cells.

Use the Number of Rows and Number of Columns controls to specify the number of rows and columns to create. Place a check in the Merge Cells Before Split check box if you want Word to merge together a selected range of cells before splitting them into the specified number of cells. Choose OK when you're ready to split the cells.

Controlling Tables Across Multiple Pages

Word offers a few handy options for controlling the way long tables flow onto multiple pages. The following sections describe those options.

Repeat Column Headings Across Pages   If you use column headings in a lengthy table, you probably want them to appear in the first row on each page of the table. All you have to do is specify the row to use as the table headings and Word takes care of the rest. Any changes you make to the headings are applied on each page.

To apply the headings, first select the row you want to use as the column headings. Then choose Table, Headings. Word automatically applies the headings to each page of the table.

Controlling Breaks Across Pages   Word determines where a table will break to the next page. You can, however, force the table to break at a specific location. Just click in any cell of the row you want placed on the next page, then press Ctrl+Enter. Word will move the row and its following rows to the next page. To prevent a row from breaking to the next page, choose Table, Cell Height and Width to open the Cell Height and Width dialog box (see Figure 8.16). Clear the Allow Row to Break Across Pages check box, then choose OK.

> **CAUTION**
> Inserting a table break causes headers on subsequent pages to be lost. You can insert a separate header table in Header/Footer view to compensate for the lost headers.

FIG. 8.16

Use the Cell Height and Width dialog box to prevent rows from breaking across pages and to set column and row width and height.

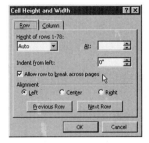

Sorting

The ability to sort a table is particularly useful when you have imported data into a large table. If the original data was not sorted, or you want to use a different sort method, Word will take care of the task for you.

You can sort using a single set of criteria or multiple criteria. You only have to select one column to perform the sort on the whole table. For example, if the table contains a list of first and last names for a group of people, you only have to select the last name column to sort the table. Word will keep the correct first names associated with the last names, because it sorts the rows, not the individual cells in the rows.

The options available to you when you sort a table depend on how much of the table you select. If you want the most options for sorting the table, just click in a cell to select the table. If you want to sort using a specific column only, select the column. Then, choose Table, Sort to open the Sort dialog box (see Figure 8.17).

FIG. 8.17

Use the Sort dialog box to specify options when sorting a table.

If you did not select a column prior to opening the Sort dialog box, the Sort By drop-down list will include all of the columns in the table, allowing you to select any column as the sort key. If you selected a column prior to opening the Sort dialog box, that column will be the only one listed in the drop-down list. Select the column on which you want the sort operation to be based, choose Ascending or Descending according to your desired outcome, then choose OK.

You also can sort the table based on multiple criteria. Assume, for example, that your table contains an address list with first and last names in separate columns with other address information in other columns. Also assume that you want to sort the table by last name, but also want the first names to be in order within each last name group. Bob Johnson, for example, should come before Karen Johnson.

To sort using multiple criteria, click in the table and then choose Table, Sort. In the Sort dialog box, select from the Sort By drop-down list the column you want to use as the primary criteria. Choose from the Then By list the criteria for the secondary sort operation. For example, you might select Last Name as the primary criteria and First Name as the secondary criteria. Choose OK to sort the table.

You can set two options when sorting a table. Choose Options on the Sort dialog box to view the Sort Options dialog box (see Figure 8.18). To make the sort case sensitive, choose the Case Sensitive option button. You can specify the language Word will use for the sort operation by selecting the language from the Sorting Language drop-down list.

T I P The Separate Fields At section of the Sort Options dialog box are applicable only to sorting data in delimited text.

FIG. 8.18
Choose a language and specify whether the sort is case sensitive using the Sort Options dialog box.

Using Formulas

In addition to placing text and graphics in a table, you also can use formulas to perform calculations. The calculations are not limited to the cell in which the formula is contained, but instead can reference other cells in the table or data marked in the document with a bookmark. Word uses field codes to create the formulas. This section of the chapter explains how to use formulas, beginning with an overview of cell referencing.

▶ **See** "Using Field Codes to Create Dynamic Content," **p. 140**

Understanding Cell References

In Word, you reference a cell by combining the column and row with a colon, with A:1, for example, referencing the first cell in the upper-left corner of the table. When used in a formula, the cell reference is enclosed in parentheses. The following Formula field code sums a range of cells (note that you do not type the brackets {}, but instead Word inserts these for you automatically):

`{=SUM(A1:A4)}`

N O T E Field codes are turned off by default. You can turn on field codes by choosing Tools, Options, and checking the Field Codes option on the View property page.

In this example, the field code must be located within the table because no other information is included to identify the table itself, but just the range within it. Use bookmarks to reference tables elsewhere in the document. The following example sums a range of cells in two different tables, then subtracts them:

```
{=(SUM(Sales B2:B7))-(SUM(Expense C1:C29))}
```

You also can reference an entire row or column. To reference a column, use its column letter twice separated by a colon. The reference A:A, for example, identifies the entire column A. The reference 4:4 would identify all of row 4. You can use multiple cell references, as well. The following example averages rows 2 and 4:

```
{=AVERAGE(2:2,4:4)}
```

Defining Formulas

You can insert a formula in a table cell by simply inserting a field code in the cell, but Word offers a slightly easier method. Click in the cell in which you want the formula placed, then choose Table, Formula to display the Formula dialog box (see Figure 8.19).

FIG. 8.19

Use the Formula dialog box to insert a formula in a table cell.

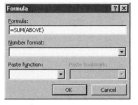

Type the desired formula in the Formula text box. If you aren't sure which functions you can use in your formulas, click the Paste Function drop-down list to view a list of available functions.

From the Number Format drop-down list choose the format you want to apply to the results of the calculation. If you have bookmarks defined in the document you can use them in calculations as well. The Paste Bookmark drop-down list contains all of the bookmarks defined in the document. When you're ready to apply the formula to the cell, choose OK.

N O T E   For more information about defining formulas, refer to the section, "Performing Calculations with Field Codes," in Chapter 7, "Fields, Forms, and Dynamic Content." ■

Creating a Chart from a Table

You can easily create a chart in Word using a table as the basis for the chart. To create the chart, first select the cells in the table that you want included in the chart. If the entire table contains chart information, click in the chart and then choose Table, Select Table to select the entire table. If you want the chart to have axis labels, make sure the table has column and row labels and include those in the selection.

After you have selected the chart or range of cells, choose Insert, Object. In the Object property sheet (see Figure 8.20) select Microsoft Graph 97 Chart from the Create New list. Make sure you place a check in the Float Over Text check box, and then choose OK. Word uses the data in the table as the basis for the chart, placing the chart in the document.

 TIP For better control over the placement of the chart in the document after you insert the chart, make sure the Float Over Text check box is selected. If this check box is cleared, Word inserts the chart in the document directly after the table and you'll have less flexibility in moving the chart on the page.

If the table includes column headings, those column headings appear as the X-axis labels for the chart. Row column headings, if any, are used as the chart legend. Figure 8.20 shows a simple chart created from a table in Word.

FIG. 8.20

Word can quickly create 3-D charts from the data in a table.

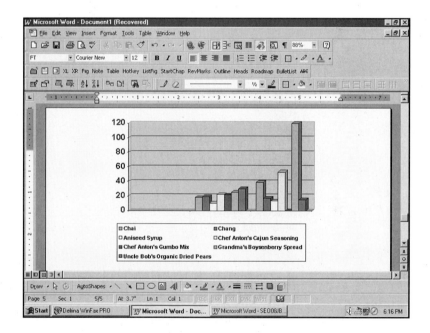

You can drag the chart on the page to relocate it as necessary. You also can change the content of the chart without changing the table data from which it was created. Double-click the chart to edit it. The Standard toolbar and menus change in Word as Microsoft Chart 97 becomes active. To change values in the chart, choose View, Datasheet. Word displays a data sheet similar to the one shown in Figure 8.21. As you can see, the datasheet is a simple spreadsheet. Use it to change the labels and other values on which the chart is based.

To change the chart type, choose Chart, Chart Type to display the Chart Type property sheet shown in Figure 8.22. Choose a chart type and click OK.

To control other chart options, choose Chart, Chart Options to display the Chart Options property sheet shown in Figure 8.23. The options on each of the tabbed property pages are generally self-explanatory. If you need more help with setting chart options, refer to Chapter 16, "Advanced Formatting and Charting."

FIG. 8.21

You can edit the contents of the chart using a data sheet that functions much like Excel.

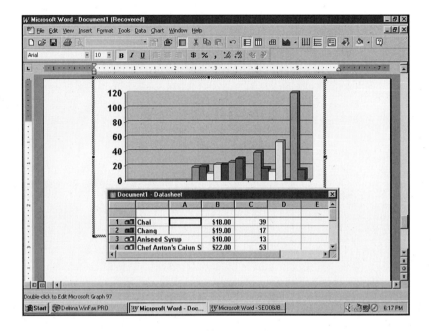

FIG. 8.22

You can choose from many different types of charts to change the chart's appearance.

FIG. 8.23

You can control a wide variety of options to fine-tune the appearance and content of the chart.

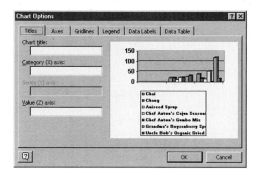

CHAPTER 9

Merging Documents

by Jim Boyce

Automation is one of the key functions of any computer program, and one task that Word automates is *document merging*. Document merging enables you to combine two documents to create a third. You can merge a list of addresses with a form letter, for example, to create a custom letter for a mass mailing. You can perform the same operation to create custom labels. Or you may simply need to insert one document into another.

This chapter examines the various ways that you can merge Word documents and other data sources. ■

Merging Word documents to create labels and form letters

You can merge a list or other data from one Word document into another.

Merging from the Outlook Address Book

Do you need a set of mailing labels or a form letter? You can address those documents by merging from your Outlook address book.

Merging data from an Access database

Merging from an Access database gives you considerable power to create many types of documents quickly and easily without duplicating your data.

Overview of New Features

Word 97 offers a few new features to make merging documents even easier. This section of the chapter provides a brief overview of these new features and enhancements.

Envelope and Label Wizards

Previous versions of Word enabled you to create envelopes and labels through commands in the Tools menu. Word 97 provides a new Label Wizard to step you through the process of creating labels. Word also provides an Envelope Wizard to help you set up and print envelopes. You get to these wizards just as you do to any new document—by choosing File, New.

Creating Custom Labels

You can create custom labels and save them by name for use later as the basis for other labels. The custom labels appear in the same list as Word's predefined labels (see Figure 9.1). In addition, Word 6.0 did not offer the capability to change the page size for a page of labels. Word 97 adds this capability, giving you even better control of size and placement of labels.

FIG. 9.1
Word 97 enables you to create and save custom label definitions, and you can use existing label definitions as the basis for your custom labels.

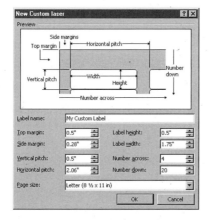

Merging Outlook and Word

Because integration is a theme throughout Office 97, you should expect to see integration between Outlook—the messaging and Personal Information Manager (PIM) included with Office 97—and Word. Word enables you to use the Outlook Contacts and Personal Address Book to import addresses and other information for addressing letters and creating mail-merge documents.

Merging Documents

In its simplest form, *merging* means bringing information from another application and incorporating that information into a Word document.

One form of document merging is bringing one document, or a portion thereof, into another document. You can achieve this in a few ways, depending on the type of document from which you are merging data and on whether you want to import the entire document. The following section briefly explains how to copy only part of a Word document to another.

Copying Between Word Documents

You can copy a portion of one Word document to another through the Clipboard. To do so, follow these steps:

Part

II

Ch

9

1. Open the source document and the destination document.
2. In the destination document, locate the insertion point where you want the other data to be inserted.
3. Press Ctrl+F6 to switch to the source document.
4. Select the information that you want to place in the other document.
5. Choose Edit, Copy (or press Ctrl+C) to copy the data to the Clipboard.
6. Press Ctrl+F6 to switch to the destination document.
7. Choose Edit, Paste (or press Ctrl+V) to copy the data into the document from the Clipboard.

Instead of copying the data into the destination document, you can link the data. Rather than placing the data in the destination document, linking places a reference to the data in the document instead. As the source document changes, the link in the destination document also changes, showing you the most up-to-date copy of the data. Use these steps to link data:

1. Open the source document and the destination document.
2. In the destination document, locate the insertion point where you want the other data to be inserted.
3. Press Ctrl+F6 to switch to the source document.
4. Select the information that you want to place in the other document.
5. Choose Edit, Copy (or press Ctrl+C) to copy the data to the Clipboard.
6. Press Ctrl+F6 to switch to the destination document.
7. Choose Edit, Paste Special to view the Paste Special dialog box (see Figure 9.2).
8. Choose the Paste Link option button.
9. Choose Formatted Text (RTF) from the As list; then choose OK.

Word inserts the data as the result of a field code. To update the data in the destination document after the source document changes, just update the field code. To do so, click the field code and press F9. Select the entire document and press F9 to update all fields in the document.

▶ **See** "Using Field Codes to Create Dynamic Content," **p. 140**

FIG. 9.2

Use the Paste Special dialog box to link data into Word.

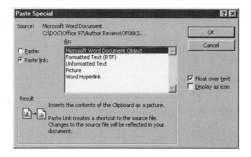

N O T E You can insert the text into the destination document as unformatted text by choosing the Unformatted Text option from the As list. To retain character and table formatting, make sure to choose the Formatted Text (RTF) option. You also can use the Microsoft Word Document Object to insert the data and retain its formatting. Using this option causes Word to insert the data in a format that enables you to double-click the data to edit it. This option is helpful for inserting or linking large bodies of text into the document. ▉

Through Word 97's new support for hyperlinks, you also can insert links to a portion of a document. Choose the Word HyperLink option in the Paste Special dialog box to insert a link to the data. Or choose Edit, Paste as Hyperlink.

Inserting One Word Document into Another

Sometimes, you want to insert or link an entire document into another. The process is simple. Follow these steps:

1. Open the destination document and place the insertion point where you want the other document to be inserted.

2. Choose Insert, File to display the Insert File dialog box (a standard Word Open dialog box).

3. Locate and select the file that you want to insert.

4. If you want to link the file instead of inserting it, place a check in the Link to File check box.

5. Choose OK to insert or link the selected document into the current document.

   ▶ **See** "Overview of Binders," **p. 986**

   ▶ **See** "Using Master Documents," **p. 1100**

Using Mail Merge

The term *mail merge* typically is used to describe the process of merging some form of address database with a form letter to create a group of individualized letters. You may want to send out a promotional offer, for example, but personalize each letter with the recipient's name, address, and other personal information. Mail merge allows you to do just that.

Although mail merge is designed to help you create these personalized form letters, you can use mail merge to merge any kind of data with any other kind of document to individualize the documents. This chapter explains how to use the mail-merge features in Word to merge data from Word, Access, and Outlook into a Word document.

Mail merge in Word consists of a few common steps, regardless of what type of data source you use. When the process is complete, you have a single document containing all the personalized documents and can print all the documents in a single operation. Alternatively, you can print individual documents in the set by printing only those pages or sections of the document that are relevant.

The following list explains the steps involved in performing a mail-merge operation:

- *Create the main document.* The first step is creating the main document that is used as the basis for your personalized documents. In the case of a form letter, for example, you first create the form letter.

- *Create the data source.* The next step is creating the external data source from which the names, addresses, or other information will come. You may already have this step completed if you are bringing information from Outlook or an Access database (if you've already created the address book or database, for example).

- *Define merge fields in the main document.* Next, you define merge fields in the main document. These fields tell Word where to insert specific data items from the data source. In a form letter, for example, you define merge fields for the first name, last name, address, and other information that appears in the address and salutation of the letter.

- *Merge the data with the main document.* When the main document and data source are ready, you can merge the two. The result is a single document containing all the personalized documents, with page breaks separating one document from another.

- *Print the document.* Because all the personalized documents are placed in a single document file, you can print all the documents in one operation just as you would any other type of document. Alternatively, you can select individual pages or sections for printing.

Types of Documents You Can Create

The main document in a mail-merge operation is the one that contains the boilerplate text and graphics, which are the same in all the resulting documents. In the case of a form letter, for example, the form letter itself is the main document. You then personalize the main document by using information from the data source, which may be another Word document, an Excel document, an Access database, or your Outlook contact list.

Word helps you create four types of main documents for a mail merge:

- *Form letter.* When you opt to create a form letter, Word merges the main document and the data source to create a single document that contains all the personalized letters, each letter in its own section. You then can modify each section separately, if you want, and print an individual letter simply by printing only its section. Print the entire document to print all the letters.

- *Envelopes.* Word automates the process of creating envelopes, enabling you to specify the envelope type, print options, and other variables. The resulting merged document contains all the envelopes, each in its own section.

- *Labels.* Word allows you to specify the type of label (size, number per page, and so on) and then creates a main document consisting of a page of labels. Each label cell contains the fields necessary to insert the address information that you specify. The resulting merged document contains multiple pages of labels, all in one section.

- *Catalog.* A catalog is much like a form letter, with one major exception: The resulting merged document contains all the data in one section, rather than individual sections. In other words, you create a single document from the data source, rather than one document per record. You can use this option to create membership lists, for example.

Using Different Data Sources

Word enables you to use several sources for mail-merge data. The following sections provide an overview of using Word, Access, and Outlook as data sources.

Using Word as a Data Source   To use a Word document as the source for the data that gets merged into another document, set up the Word source document by using columns, with each column representing a specific field (last name, first name, address, and so on). Each row represents a record. In the case of addresses, for example, each row represents all the information for one person's address. Figure 9.3 shows an example of a Word table used to store addresses.

You can set up the Word source document by using tabs to separate the fields, but you also can use a table. Because Word offers several features for editing and sorting tables, you should consider using a table whenever you want to create a mail-merge source document in Word.

Using Access as a Data Source   You can use Microsoft Query, dBASE, FoxPro, and Access databases as sources of mail-merge data. Because Access is included with Office 97, *Special Edition Using Microsoft Office 97* focuses on using Access.

Before you can use Access as a data source, you have to create a database that contains the information you want to import. You may have a product database that you want to use to generate a promotional flier, for example. Each record in the database may have a field called Sale, which specifies whether the item is on sale at the current time, and another field called SalePrice, which specifies the sale price. You could perform a mail merge and import information from only the records that were currently on sale to generate your sales flier.

When you import data from Access, you open the Access data table from which you want the data to come and then specify which record fields to merge into the document.

Using Outlook or Exchange as a Data Source   You can use Outlook as a data source to import contact information, such as names, addresses, and phone numbers. To use Outlook as the data source, you first must enter the contact information in Outlook. If you are using Outlook to maintain your contact addresses, the work of creating the addresses is already done.

FIG. 9.3

Use tables to simplify the process of creating mail-merge source documents in Word.

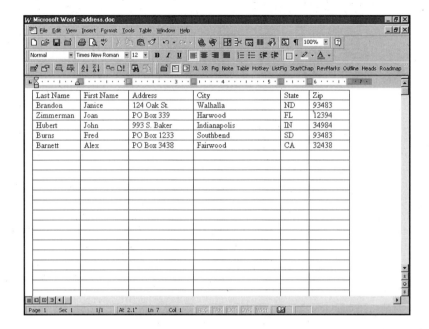

Last Name	First Name	Address	City	State	Zip
Brandon	Janice	124 Oak St.	Walhalla	ND	93483
Zimmerman	Joan	PO Box 339	Harwood	FL	12394
Hubert	John	993 S. Baker	Indianapolis	IN	34984
Burns	Fred	PO Box 1233	Southbend	SD	93483
Barnett	Alex	PO Box 3438	Fairwood	CA	32438

If you are using Exchange (Windows Messaging) as your e-mail program, you can import source data from your Personal Address Book. The process is virtually the same as for importing data from Outlook, so this chapter focuses on using Outlook.

Creating a Form Letter

You probably are familiar with form letters. Sweepstakes letters are a good example of form letters. These letters are mailed out to millions of people and contain the same information except for the address, salutation, and occasionally a few other details in the letter.

Creating a form letter by using Word is a relatively simple process. The first step is writing the body of the letter, containing all the text and graphics that you want to be included in every letter. Then you insert merge fields into the letter. These merge fields include the name and address for the address section of the letter, the addressee's name in the salutation, and sometimes other information that changes from one letter to another. When you merge the documents, Word fills in each merge field, using data from the data source to create personalized letters.

Follow these steps to create and mail-merge a form letter in Word:

1. Begin a new document, and type the body of the letter and all other text and graphics that you want to be included in each letter (see Figure 9.4).

FIG. 9.4

The main document includes all the text that you want to be printed in each letter.

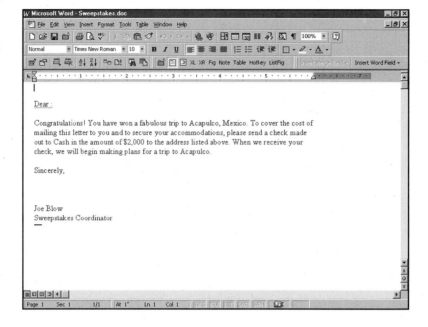

2. Create the data source, if it does not already exist. This means creating a Word or Excel document, Access database, Outlook contact list, or other data-source document supported by Word.

3. With the main document open, choose Tools, Mail Merge to open the Mail Merge Helper dialog box (see Figure 9.5).

FIG. 9.5

The Mail Merge Helper dialog box steps you through the process of creating a mail-merge document.

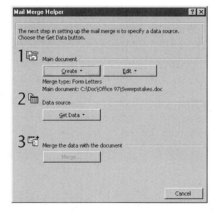

4. Choose Create, Form Letters. A simple dialog box with two options appears.

5. In this example, you already have opened the main document, so choose Active Window. If you want to start a new document to be the main document, choose New Main Document and type the letter's body text.

6. Choose Get Data; then choose from the drop-down list the source for the data that you will be importing into Word (see Figure 9.6).

You can create a new data source, open an existing source, specify header options, or use an address book. This example uses Outlook, so choose Use Address Book.

FIG. 9.6
Specify whether you want to create a data-source document or work with an existing data source.

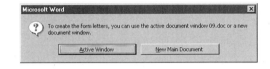

Word displays the Use Address Book dialog box (see Figure 9.7).

FIG. 9.7
Choose the address book that you want to use as the source for the merged data.

7. Choose the address book you want to use; then choose OK.

8. If you don't already have merge fields inserted into the main document, Word detects that fact and prompts you with a dialog box, asking you to edit the document to add the fields. The only option in the dialog box is Edit Main Document, so make that choice. Word switches to the main document and opens the Mail Merge toolbar.

9. Place the insertion point in the document where you want to insert the first field. (Place the insertion point where you want the address field to be located, for example.)

10. From the Merge Field drop-down menu, choose the field that you want to insert.

To create the address, for example, choose First_Name, press the spacebar, and open the drop-down list again to choose Last_Name. Press Enter and then choose Postal_Address from the Merge Field list.

11. Repeat step 10, inserting all the desired fields into the document. Figure 9.8 shows an address block defined with merge fields.

12. Choose Tools, Mail Merge to open the Mail Merge Helper dialog box.

13. Choose Merge. Word displays the Merge dialog box, shown in Figure 9.9.

14. Specify the desired options (explained in the following bulleted list).

15. Choose Merge to merge the source data with the main document and create the new merged documents.

The following list explains the options in the Merge dialog box:

FIG. 9.8

This form letter contains an address block that will be filled in when the document is merged.

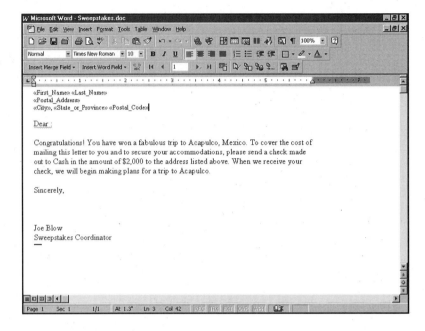

FIG. 9.9

Use the Merge dialog box to specify options before performing the mail-merge operation.

■ *Merge To.* Use this drop-down list to choose New Document, Printer, or Electronic Mail, depending on what you want to do with the resulting merged document. Choose New Document if you want to save the merged document for editing. If you don't want to save the document, choose Printer to print it or Electronic Mail to send it to other people through your e-mail program.

■ *Records to Be Merged.* Use the controls in this group to specify which records (all or a range) to include in the merge.

■ *When Merging Records.* The two options in this group determine whether Word ignores empty data fields. If you have some addresses with two lines and others with just one, for example, the records with only one address line include a blank second address-line field. You probably want Word to ignore the blank fields in most cases, which prevents those fields from being merged.

■ *Check Errors.* Choose this button to configure the way that Word handles any errors that occur during the merge operation.

■ *Query Options.* Choose this button to specify how Word filters the incoming data.

To specify how Word handles errors during the merge operation, click the Check Errors button to display the Checking and Reporting Errors dialog box (see Figure 9.10).

FIG. 9.10
You can specify how
Word handles any
errors that occur during
the merge operation.

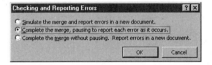

The following list explains the options in the Checking and Reporting Errors dialog box:

- *Simulate the Merge and Report Errors in a New Document.* Choose this option to test for errors before actually merging the documents. Word creates a new document containing a list of errors generated during the merge operation.

- *Complete the Merge, Pausing to Report Each Error As It Occurs.* Choose this option (the default) to have Word complete the merge operation and report any errors as they occur.

- *Complete the Merge Without Pausing. Report Errors in a New Document.* Choose this option to have Word perform the merge without pausing to report errors. Word creates a new document to contain the list of errors.

You can refine the way Word processes the incoming data by specifying query options. To do so, choose the Query Options button in the Merge dialog box to display the Query Options property sheet (see Figure 9.11).

FIG. 9.11
You can use the Query
Options property sheet
to set query filters and
other options that
control the way that
Word merges the
documents.

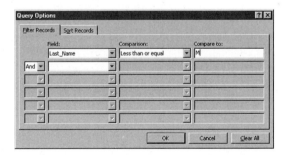

The Filters page, shown in Figure 9.11, enables you to filter out certain records based on criteria that you specify. You may want to merge only the records with last names ranging from A through M, for example. Choose Last_Name from the Field drop-down list, choose Less Than or Equal from the Comparison drop-down list, and then type **M** in the Compare To text box. You can specify multiple criteria by setting additional filters.

 For more help with filters, press F1 to open the Office Assistant search dialog box and perform a search using **filters** as the keyword.

The Sort Records page of the Query Options property sheet (see Figure 9.12) allows you to sort the data as it is coming in to be merged. You may want to merge the document so that the letters are sorted by postal code for quicker mail processing, for example. From the Sort By drop-down list, choose the field on which to base the sort operation. Then specify either Ascending or Descending. You can specify multiple sort criteria by using the Then By and Then By drop-down lists.

FIG. 9.12

Use the Sort Records page to sort the records before merging the document.

When you're satisfied with the filter and sort options, choose OK. Choose Merge in the Merge dialog box to merge the documents and create your personalized form letters.

Although this example uses Outlook as the source, the process of importing data from other sources (such as Access) is essentially the same. After you select the source document (and, in the case of Access, the desired data table), Word checks the selected source for all the available fields. These fields then become available from the Insert Merge Field drop-down list in the Mail Merge toolbar.

Creating Mailing Labels

The process of creating mailing labels is slightly different from that of merging a form letter. One primary difference is that you must specify the size and type of label to use. The other difference is that instead of multiple documents separated by sections, Word creates multiple pages of labels, one record per label.

To create mailing labels, first make sure that you have created the address information on which the labels will be based. Then follow these steps:

1. Choose Tools, Mail Merge in Word to display the Mail Merge Helper dialog box.
2. Choose Create, Mailing Labels on the Mail Merge Helper dialog box. Word prompts you to choose between the current document or creating a new main document.
3. Choose Active Window to create the labels in the active window, or choose New Main Document to start a new document for the labels.
4. Choose Get Data, and choose the desired source for the address data from the drop-down list.

   After you choose the data source, Word prompts you to set up the main document.
5. Click Setup to open the Label Options dialog box (see Figure 9.13).
6. Click the Details button to view the details for the label (see Figure 9.14).

FIG. 9.13

Choose predefined labels or define your own by using the Label Options dialog box.

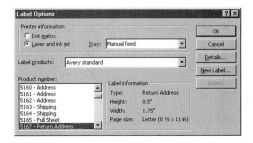

FIG. 9.14

You can view and change individual settings for the label to fine-tune it to your needs.

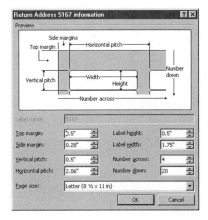

7. If you want to create a new label, choose the New Label button. The resulting dialog box is essentially the same as the one shown in Figure 9.14.

8. After you specify the label parameters, choose OK in the Label Options dialog box. Word opens the Create Labels dialog box, shown in Figure 9.15.

FIG. 9.15

Use the Create Labels dialog box to insert fields into the label.

9. Choose the Insert Merge Field button to open a menu of available fields.

10. Select the field that you want to insert into the label.

11. Repeat Steps 9 and 10 to insert all the desired fields; then choose OK.

12. If you want to include a delivery bar code in the label, click the Insert Postal Bar Code button to display the Insert Postal Bar Code dialog box, shown in Figure 9.16.

FIG. 9.16

You can insert delivery bar codes into your mail-merge labels and envelopes.

13. From the Merge Field with ZIP Code drop-down list, choose the field in the source data that contains the ZIP or postal code from which the delivery bar code should be generated.

14. From the Merge Field with Street Address drop-down list, choose the field in the source data that contains the street address; alternatively, leave this option blank.

15. Choose OK. Word creates a page of labels containing the necessary merge fields (see Figure 9.17).

FIG. 9.17

Word creates a page of labels that contain the specified merge fields.

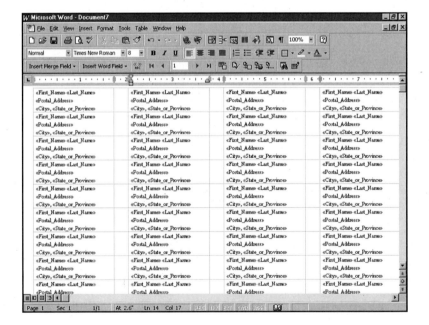

16. Set any desired filter options (explained in the preceding section).

17. Choose Merge to open the Merge dialog box.

18. Set any other desired options.

19. Choose Merge to merge the data.

TROUBLESHOOTING

The lines of each label are too far apart. How do I set the spacing between lines? Word uses the paragraph settings from the paragraph in which the insertion point is located when you start the process of creating the labels. So between steps 4 and 5 of the preceding example, set the paragraph-formatting options accordingly. You also can set the formatting after you create the labels, but setting it beforehand is easier, because you have only one paragraph to set.

Creating Envelopes

You create envelopes in much the same way that you create a mailing list. The only real difference is that you specify the type of envelope to use, rather than the type of label. To create mail-merge envelopes, choose Tools, Mail Merge to display the Mail Merge Helper dialog box. Choose Create, Envelopes. Use the process for creating mail labels described in the preceding section, except that in step 6, you specify the envelope settings rather than label settings. The remainder of the process is essentially the same.

Creating a Catalog

Unlike a form letter that, when merged, results in multiple documents, each document in its own section, a catalog results in a single document within one section. In a form letter, the data records are merged one to a document; in a catalog, all data records are merged into the same document. The catalog mail-merge option is useful for creating mailing lists, membership lists, product lists, and any other type of list in which you want to import data from another source into a single document.

The primary thing to remember when you are creating a catalog is that any boilerplate text that you type in the document is duplicated within the document for each record. You probably want to perform the merge first to insert the list and then edit the document to add any other text or graphics to it.

Using Other Field Codes

You may have noticed that the Mail Merge toolbar includes a menu labeled *Insert Word Field*. You can use this menu to insert various other Word field codes to customize the outcome of the merge process. For additional information regarding the use of field codes, refer to Chapter 7, "Field, Forms, and Dynamic Content."

▶ **See** "Using Field Codes to Create Dynamic Content," **p. 140**

CHAPTER 10

Customizing Word

by Jim Boyce

Office users have always enjoyed the capability to customize the applications in the Office suite to suit their preferences. Office 97 offers even more ways to customize the interface. Chapter 2, "Using Common Office 97 Features," explains how to customize the toolbars, menu, and keyboard in your Office 97 applications, including Word. This chapter examines customization issues that are specific to Word. ■

Copying custom settings between templates

Custom settings—such as toolbars, menus, and keyboard shortcuts—are associated with specific templates and documents. You can copy custom settings between these templates and documents to make them available when you work with these documents.

Setting Word options

Word offers numerous features that control the way that Word looks and functions.

Using Word startup switches

You can append command-line switches to the command that you use to start Word, such as in a desktop shortcut, to control the way that Word starts and to perform actions automatically.

Setting View Options

Word enables you to set a variety of options that determine the types of document elements that Word displays, which nonprinting characters to show, and which Word interface elements to show. To set these options, choose Tools, Options and then click the View tab to display the View page of the Options property sheet, shown in Figure 10.1. Note that the options that appear in the View property page vary slightly according to the type of document view you are using (Normal, Page Layout, and so on). All of the available commands for all modes are described later in this section.

FIG. 10.1

Use the View page to control the document elements and interface components that Word displays.

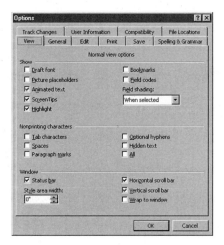

The controls in the Show group specify whether Word displays certain document elements. These controls enable you to turn on and off the display of these elements. The following list describes all the controls that can appear in the Show group:

- *Draft Font*. This check box causes Word to display most formatted text as underlined or bold, with graphics shown as empty boxes. Use this option to speed up display updating with heavily formatted documents.

- *Drawings*. This check box determines whether Word displays objects that you draw in a document by using the Drawing toolbar. You can clear this check box to hide drawing objects and improve the speed at which you scroll through documents that contain many drawings. Place a check in this box to have Word display the drawing objects.

- *Object Anchors*. *Object anchors* lock objects, such as pictures, to a paragraph. Anchors are represented in the document by small anchor icons. To view these anchors, place a check in this check box. Clear this check box to hide the anchors. You also can view anchors by clicking the Show/Hide button in the Standard toolbar.

- *Text Boundaries*. When this option is selected (checked), Word displays dotted lines to indicate page margins, text-column boundaries, and objects. You can think of these lines as being layout lines that help you view the boundaries of these objects. Clear this check box to turn off text boundary lines.

- *Picture Placeholders*. Documents that contain several pictures can display slowly on some computers. Place a check in this box to display a box in place of the image. The box acts as a placeholder for the image.

- *Animated Text*. When this box is checked, Word displays animated text, according to its animation formatting. Blinking text, for example, blinks on- screen. Clear this check box if you want to see how animated text appears when printed.

- *Screen Tips*. This setting applies to documents that have been edited with revision marks. If this option is turned on and you allow the mouse pointer to hover over a comment reference mark or text that has been modified by revision marks, Word will display a pop-up box containing the reviewer's comments.

- *Highlight*. You can highlight text in a document, changing the background color of the text. Changing this color is similar to highlighting text on a printed page by using a highlighter pen. Place a check in this box to view highlighting, and clear the box to turn off display of highlighting. Turning off display of highlighting does not remove the highlighting from the text.

- *Bookmarks*. Place a check in this box to have Word display bookmarks in the document. Bookmarks are displayed inside brackets [ ]. These bookmark indicators appear in the document but do not print, even when this option is turned on.

- *Field Codes.* Enable this check box to turn on the display of field codes, and clear the check box to hide field codes. You can achieve the same result by pressing Alt+F9.

- *Field Shading*. This drop-down list determines how Word shades field-code results. The default, When Selected, causes Word to shade a field on-screen only when you place the insertion point inside the field. Choose Always if you want the field-code results to be shaded even when they are not selected. Choose Never if you don't want the field-code results to be shaded.

Word uses several nonprinting characters to represent characters in the document that do not print. An example is the paragraph mark that you insert at the end of a paragraph when you press Enter. Sometimes, you need to view these nonprinting characters to help you format a document or determine why a document is not formatting the way that you expect it to.

The following list describes the check boxes in the Nonprinting Characters group of the View property page:

- *Tab Characters*. Tabs normally display as white space in the document. Place a check in this box if you want to view the tab character, which appears as a right arrow.

- *Spaces*. Spaces normally appear in a document as white space. Place a check in this box to view spaces as dots.

- *Paragraph Marks*. Placing a check in this box causes Word to display a special character to indicate the new line character (which you insert by pressing Shift+Enter) and paragraph marks (which you insert by pressing Enter).

- *Optional Hyphens*. Word can automatically hyphenate a document to break words at the end of lines, which is particularly useful in paragraphs that use justified alignment. You also can insert optional hyphens by pressing Ctrl+hyphen (-). These hyphens, which are hidden text, break the word only if it falls at the end of a line. Place a check in this box if you want Word to display the optional hyphen characters instead of hiding them.

■ *Hidden Text.* You can format text in a document as hidden text. Hidden text normally does not appear in a document (thus, its name). Place a check in this box to view hidden text as dotted-underline text.

■ *All.* Place a check in this box to turn on the display of all hidden and nonprinting characters. You also can click the Show/Hide button in the Standard toolbar to display all hidden and nonprinting characters.

The Window control group provides several controls that you can use to define the way the elements that appear as part of the Word document interface. These options vary slightly depending on the view mode you are using. The following list describes all options that can appear in the Window group:

■ *Status Bar.* Place a check in this box to turn on the Word status bar that provides page, section, line, column, and other information at the bottom of the Word document area.

■ *Style Area Width.* Use this control to specify the width of a scrap area at the left edge of the display to show the name of the style assigned to each paragraph.

■ *Vertical Ruler.* Place a check in this box to turn on a vertical ruler for the document area.

■ *Horizontal Scroll Bar.* Place a check in this box to turn on a horizontal scroll bar for the document area.

■ *Vertical Scroll Bar.* Place a check in this box to turn on a vertical scroll bar for the document area.

■ *Wrap to Window.* Place a check in this box to have the text wrap to the width of the window in Online Layout mode.

■ *Enlarge Fonts Less Than.* Use this control to have Word automatically enlarge in the document any text with a font size smaller than the specified size. This control appears only in Online Layout mode.

Setting General Options

Word offers several settings that allow you to control a variety of general options that determine how Word functions. To view and change these settings, choose Tools, Options and click the General property page of the Options property sheet (see Figure 10.2).

The following list describes the settings in the General Options property page:

■ *Background Repagination.* With this option checked, Word automatically repaginates the document as you work. Generally, background repagination does not affect performance, except on slow computers with large documents. This setting does not affect repagination in Page Layout view, and this control is dimmed when in Page Layout view.

■ *Help for WordPerfect Users.* When this option is checked, Word displays instructions or demonstrates an example of performing a task in Word when you press a WordPerfect for DOS key combination.

FIG. 10.2

The General property page contains several controls that specify a variety of general settings to control the way that Word functions.

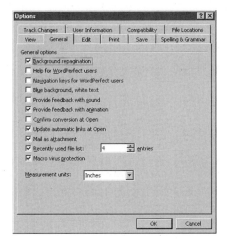

■ *Navigation Keys for WordPerfect Users.* Placing a check in this check box causes Word to change the behavior of the PgUp, PgDn, Home, End, and Esc keys to match the behavior of these keys in WordPerfect.

■ *Blue Background, White Text.* Choose this option if you want Word to display the document using white text on a blue background rather than black text on a white background. The white-on-blue option resembles the standard WordPerfect for DOS screen colors.

■ *Provide Feedback with Sound.* Word can emphasize certain events, such as the completion of a task, by playing a sound. If your computer contains a sound card, placing a check in this box turns on those sound notifications. You can set individual sounds through the Sounds object in the Control Panel.

■ *Provide Feedback with Animation.* With this option checked, Word animates the mouse pointer and other Word interface elements to indicate when tasks are being performed (such as printing and saving a document). Clear this check box to turn off animation.

■ *Confirm Conversion at Open.* Word can automatically detect document types and convert them to Word format when you attempt to open a file that is not a Word document. Enable this check box if you want Word to choose a converter automatically. Clear this check box if you want Word to prompt you to choose a converter.

■ *Update Automatic Links at Open.* With this check box selected, Word automatically attempts to update all links in a document when you open the document. Clear this check box if you don't want Word to update the links automatically. You then can direct Word to update the links whenever you desire.

■ *Mail As Attachment.* When this option is checked and you choose File, Send To, Mail Recipient, Word attaches the current document to the resulting e-mail message as an attachment. Clear this check box if you want Word to insert the current document into the message as text instead.

■ *Recently Used File List/Entries.* Place a check in the Recently Used File List to have Word list the most recently used (MRU) document files in the File menu. Use the Entries spin control to specify the number of MRU documents to appear in the menu (1 to 9).

■ *Macro Virus Protection.* Word documents can contain macros, customized toolbars, menus, and shortcuts. Macros can be designed to run automatically when the document opens, which means that macros can act as viruses, performing unwanted actions on your computer and files. Place a check in this check box if you want Word to warn you when you open a document that contains macros or other custom elements. You then have the option of opening the document without loading the macros loaded.

■ *Measurement Units.* Use this control to specify the default unit of measure. Choose inches, centimeters, points, or picas.

Setting Editing Options

You can set several options that control the way that Word handles text selection, text insertion, graphics editing, and other common document-editing tasks. To set these options, choose Tools, Options and then click the Edit tab to display the Edit property page, shown in Figure 10.3.

FIG. 10.3
Use the Edit page to specify how Word handles common document-editing tasks.

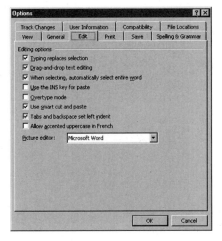

The following list explains the options in the Edit property page:

■ *Typing Replaces Selection.* If you select text and begin typing, the new text that you type replaces the selected text. If you want the new text to be inserted in front of the selected text, clear this check box.

■ *Drag-and-Drop Text Editing.* With this option selected, you can select text and move it around in the document by using the mouse. If you have a problem in accidentally moving text when you select it, clear this check box to turn off this feature.

- *When Selecting, Automatically Select Entire Word.* With this option checked, Word automatically selects the entire word when you select (with the mouse) a portion of the word, the following space, and part of the next word. Turning on this feature makes selecting text a little easier, particularly when the text is located at the left edge of the document.

- *Use the INS Key for Paste.* This option is off by default; turning it on causes Word to paste from the Clipboard when you press the Ins key.

- *Overtype Mode.* When overtype mode is turned on, new text that you type replaces the text to the right of the insertion point. You can turn this feature on and off by double-clicking the OVR button in the status bar.

- *Use Smart Cut and Paste.* With this item selected, Word removes extra spaces when you delete text and adds spaces when you insert text from the Clipboard. Clear this check box to prevent Word from adding or removing spaces during a cut or paste operation.

- *Tabs and Backspace Set Left Indent.* When this option is turned on, you can place the insertion point at the beginning of an indented paragraph and press Tab to increase the indent or press Backspace to decrease the indent. With this option turned off, these keys act as Tab and Backspace.

- *Allow Accented Uppercase in French.* This option applies to text that you format as French (set the language property of the text to French). With the option selected, the Word spell checker prompts you to suggest accent marks for uppercase letters. Clear this check box if you don't want Word to suggest accent marks.

- *Picture Editor.* Use this drop-down list to choose Microsoft Photo Editor or Microsoft Word as the application to use when you double-click an image to edit it.

Setting Print Options

The Print page of the Options property sheet (see Figure 10.4) allows you to specify settings that control the way that Word prints documents. To display this page, choose Tools, Options and click the Print tab.

The Print options are separated into four groups. The Printing Options group allows you to specify several options that control the way that Word prints. These options are explained in the following list:

- *Draft Output.* Some printers support a special draft mode that doesn't print some document-formatting characteristics, to provide faster printing. Choose this option if you want to print in draft mode.

- *Update Fields.* Choose this option if you want Word to update field codes in the document automatically before printing the document.

- *Update Links.* Choose this option if you want Word to automatically update all links in the document before printing the document.

Part
II

Ch
10

FIG. 10.4

Set printing options with the Print property page.

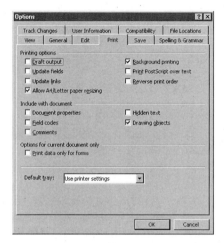

- *Allow A4/Letter Paper Resizing.* Place a check in this box if you want Word to automatically reformat documents formatted for A4 to letter, and vice versa, when the document is printed. This option affects only the formatting in the printed page, not the formatting in the document.

- *Background Printing.* With this option (the default) selected, Word prints documents in the background, enabling you to continue working on the document while it prints. Background printing uses additional memory and can slow the print process. For fastest printing when you don't need to continue working on the document, clear this check box.

- *Print PostScript over Text.* This setting applies only to Word for Macintosh documents. Choose this setting to print Word for Macintosh files that contain watermarks or other PostScript code.

- *Reverse Print Order.* Choose this option if you want Word to print the document beginning with the last page and working to the first page.

The settings in the Include with Document group of the Print property page allow you to control which document elements print and which do not. Generally, you want to print text and graphics and to omit hidden text and other support elements. Being able to print these normally hidden objects is necessary sometimes. The following list explains the elements that you can turn on or off for printing through the Include with Document group:

- *Document Properties.* Choose this check box to include the author's name, document-editing time, file size, file name, title, and other information from the Summary page of the document's properties (choose File, Properties to view document properties). Word prints the information on a separate sheet at the end of the print job.

- *Field Codes.* Choose this option if you want Word to print field codes instead of field-code results.

- *Comments.* Choose this option to print comments that have been inserted into the document through revision marks. Word prints the comments beginning with a new page at the end of the document.

- *Hidden Text.* Choose this option if you want hidden text in the document to be printed. Hidden text appears on the screen with a dotted underline, but this underline is omitted from the printed text.

- *Drawing Objects.* Choose this option to have Word print drawing objects (objects that you insert by using the drawing tools in the Drawing toolbar). Word prints an empty box as a placeholder for each drawing object.

The Print Data Only for Forms option in the Print page allows you to control the way that Word prints forms that you created using form fields. With this option selected, Word prints the data entered in the form fields but does not print the rest of the form. This option is handy for extracting the form data from the form.

 Turn on this option and print to a text file to extract data from a form to a text file.

The Default Tray drop-down list allows you to specify which printer tray to use by default.

Setting File Open and Save Options

The Save property page (see Figure 10.5) contains settings that allow you to specify the way that Word handles saving a document. You also can specify how Word is to handle automatic features related to saving documents, such as automatically saving a document after a certain period.

FIG. 10.5

Use the Save page to define how Word handles document-saving tasks.

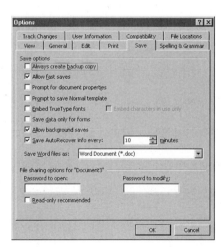

Part

II

Ch

10

The following list describes the controls in the Save property page:

- *Always Create Backup Copy.* Place a check in this box to have Word make a backup copy of the current document file before saving the changes from the current editing session. Word names the backup file *Doc.bak*, in which *Doc* is the name of the current file. If you open Barney.doc, for example, and then make changes and save the file, Word renames Barney.doc as Barney.bak and saves the changes in Barney.doc. You can restore the preceding file by opening Barney.bak and saving it as a document file (or simply renaming the .Bak file as a .Doc file).

- *Allow Fast Saves.* With this check box selected, Word saves only changes in the document file, rather than resaving the entire file. Turning on this option can reduce save time when you are working on a large document. You should turn off this feature and perform a full save when you finish working on the document, however. Unless you are working with a large document, leave this option turned off to ensure that Word saves the entire file each time you save.

- *Prompt for Document Properties.* Enable this check box if you want Word to prompt you to fill in the document properties (author, title, and so on) each time you save the document.

- *Prompt to Save Normal Template.* With this option selected, Word asks you when you exit Word whether you want it to save in Normal.dot the default font, menu, toolbar, and other settings modified in the current session. If you clear this check box, Word saves these changes to Normal.dot without prompting you.

- *Embed TrueType Fonts.* Choose this option if you want Word to store in the document file any TrueType fonts used in the document. This option enables other people to view the document with those fonts, even if they don't have the fonts on their systems. Embedding TrueType fonts in a document increases the size of the document file.

- *Save Data Only for Forms.* With this option checked, Word saves only the data from an on-screen form, placing the data in a tab-delimited text file.

- *Allow Background Saves.* Choose this option to allow Word to save a document in the background while you continue to work on the document. Generally, this option has a noticeable effect only when you work with large documents.

- *Save AutoRecover Info Every xx.* Place a check in this box to allow Word to automatically save the document to a special backup file. If the system or Word hangs, you can restart Word and have it automatically recover the document at the point of the last AutoRecover save.

- *Save Word Files As.* Use this drop-down list to specify the file format Word that uses as the default file type for saving new documents.

- *Password to Open.* Use this box to specify a password that a person must specify to open the file.

- *Password to Modify.* Use this box to specify a password that a person must specify to modify the file.

■ *Read-Only Recommended.* Place a check in this box to have Word suggest to anyone who opens the file that it be opened in read-only mode. If the person answers affirmatively, Word opens the document in read-only mode, preventing changes in the document.

Setting Spelling and Grammar Options

Word includes the capability to check the spelling and grammar in a document. The settings in the Spelling & Grammar property page (see Figure 10.6) determine how Word performs these spelling and grammar checks.

FIG. 10.6

You can configure Word's capability to check the spelling and grammar in a document.

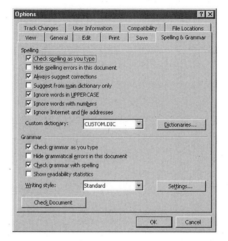

The following list describes the settings in the Spelling & Grammar property page that control Word's spell-checking features:

■ *Check Spelling as You Type.* Enable this check box if you want Word to check your spelling as you type, underlining questionable words in red.

■ *Hide Spelling Errors in this Document.* Choose this option to have Word ignore spelling errors in the current document.

■ *Always Suggest Corrections.* If selected, this option causes Word to automatically display a list of suggested alternatives to misspelled words when Word performs a spell check. This setting does not apply to Word's Check Spelling As You Type option.

■ *Suggest from Main Dictionary Only.* Choose this option to have Word suggest spelling alternatives only from the main dictionary. Clear this check box to have Word suggest spelling alternatives from all dictionaries.

■ *Ignore Words in UPPERCASE.* Choose this option to have Word ignore words in uppercase when it performs a spelling check.

■ *Ignore Words with Numbers.* Choose this option to have Word ignore words that contain numbers when it performs a spelling check.

■ *Ignore Internet and File Addresses*. This option, when selected, causes Word to ignore Internet URLs, e-mail addresses, and file path names when it performs a spelling check.

■ *Custom Dictionary*. Use this drop-down list to choose the current custom dictionary. When you direct Word to add a word to the dictionary during a spell check, Word adds it to the dictionary selected by this option.

■ *Dictionaries*. Click this button to add, remove, or modify custom dictionaries. Use custom dictionaries to contain words that are not included in Word's default dictionary.

The settings in the Grammar group specify the way that Word handles grammar checking. The following list describes the settings in this group:

■ *Check Grammar as You Type*. This option, when selected, causes Word to check for grammatical errors as you type. Grammatical errors are underlined with a wavy green line.

■ *Hide Grammatical Errors in this Document*. Choose this option to have Word ignore grammatical errors in the current document.

■ *Check Grammar with Spelling*. Place a check in this box to have Word check grammar whenever you perform a spell check on the document.

■ *Show Readability Statistics*. Readability statistics indicate the reading-difficulty level of a document. Choose this option if you want Word to display readability statistics after it completes a grammar check.

■ *Writing Style*. Use this drop-down list to indicate the writing style of the current document. Changing the style changes the way that Word checks the grammar of the document and reports readability level.

■ *Settings*. Click this button to display the Grammar Settings dialog box (see Figure 10.7). The controls in the Grammar Settings dialog box enable you to specify the types of things that Word looks for during a grammar check.

FIG. 10.7
Use the Grammar Settings options to specify which items Word checks during a grammar check.

Setting Options for Tracking Revisions

Word enables you to track revisions in a document, and also maintains information about which changes were made and by whom. Revisions are useful when more than one person works on a document or when you must submit a document for review to someone else. Changes made by each person reviewing the document appear as underlined text in a specific color. You can specify the colors used by Word to indicate revisions, as well as font characteristics and other revision settings, through the Track Changes property page of the Options property sheet (see Figure 10.8).

FIG. 10.8

Use the Track Changes page to specify how Word is to handle revision marks.

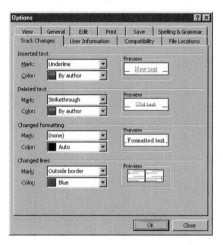

Part
II

Ch
10

The following list explains the settings in the Track Changes property page:

- *Inserted Text.* Use the two controls in this group to specify the color and font formatting that Word uses to indicate new text inserted into the document when revision marks are turned on. If you choose By Author, Word assigns a unique color to the first eight people who review the document.

- *Deleted Text.* Use these two settings to specify how Word should mark text for deletion during document review.

- *Changed Formatting.* By default, Word does not mark formatting changes during document review. Use these two controls to specify a desired formatting mark and color to apply to text when a user changes the formatting.

- *Changed Lines.* Word automatically marks paragraphs with a line at the left margin to indicate those that contain changes. This option makes it easier to locate changes, particularly those that are relatively insignificant and could be hard to find (a change in one character, for example). The Color setting specifies the color of the line. Use the Mark drop-down list to specify a different location for the change mark. Notice that this setting does not affect Normal view, in which Word always places the revision indicator at the left border.

Setting User Information Options

The User Information page of the Options property sheet (see Figure 10.9) enables you to enter your name, initials, and mailing address.

FIG. 10.9

Word uses your personal information in such tasks as revision marking.

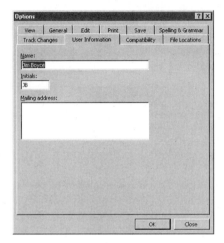

These settings are used throughout Word for various purposes, as indicated in the following list:

- ▪ *Name.* Word uses this name as the author in the document's properties (choose File, Properties to view document properties), in letters and envelopes, and when you insert revisions or comments into a document.

- ▪ *Initials.* Word uses these initials for letter and memo elements, as well as for comment marks.

- ▪ *Mailing Address.* Word uses this information as the default mailing address when you create an envelope or letter.

Setting Compatibility Options

Word has evolved considerably since its introduction in the late 1970s. The program's file formats have evolved as well to incorporate new features and support other hardware platforms, such as the Macintosh. Word 97 provides full backward compatibility with previous versions of Word. You can save a file by using a specific Word document format, but you can specify the parameters for each of the document file types to fine-tune compatibility between users.

The settings in the Compatibility property page (see Figure 10.10) enable you to specify settings for each of Word's native document file formats. To specify settings, choose a file format from the Recommended Options For drop-down list; then enable and disable check boxes in the Options group as desired.

FIG. 10.10

Use the Compatibility property page to fine-tune compatibility settings for other Word file formats.

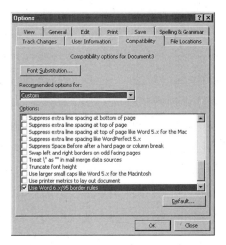

Part

II

Ch

10

If your system does not contain fonts that are specified in the current document, you can click the Font Substitution button to select which fonts on your system are used to represent the unavailable fonts.

Setting File Location Options

By default, Word looks in its own folders for its support files— templates, clip art, and so on. The program looks in the My Documents folder (which it creates during installation) for documents. If you are using a different folder to contain your document files, templates, or other files, or want to specify a different startup folder for automatically loaded templates, do so through the File Locations property page of the Options property sheet (see Figure 10.11).

FIG. 10.11

Specify your own locations for document files, templates, and other Word files by using the File Locations page.

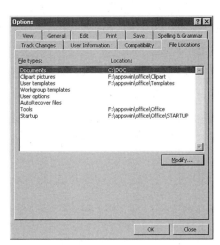

To change a folder setting, just double-click the item in the list or select the item and choose Modify. Word opens a standard browse dialog box that you can use to locate the desired folder.

 The Startup folder specifies the folder in which Word looks for templates and add-ins to load automatically as soon as Word starts. To make templates and the macros and other custom elements contained in the templates available to all documents, place the templates in the Startup folder. Notice that this folder is the Startup folder specified in the File Locations page in Word, not the Startup folder for Windows 95/Windows NT.

Using Word Startup Switches

Word support several command-line switches that control the way that Word starts. You can use some of these switches to make Word perform actions automatically at startup. Word supports the following command-line switches:

- ■ /a. The /a switch directs Word to not load add-ins and global templates, including Normal.dot, at startup. Use this switch when you want to start a clean copy of Word or when you suspect that something in an add-in or the global templates is causing a problem in Word. If Word functions properly after you start it with the /a switch, a problem exists with one of the add-ins or global templates. Close Word, rename Normal.dot to Normal.old.dot, and restart Word normally. If Word starts and functions normally, your Normal.dot file contained an error.

- ■ /l addinpath. Use this switch to load a specific add-in when you start Word. Replace *addinpath* with the path to the add-in file.

- ■ /m macroname. Use this switch to run a specific macro when Word starts. Use the /m switch by itself without a macro name to prevent Word from running any macros at startup. Using /m by itself is a good method for preventing a macro virus from executing when you load a document that you suspect contains one.

- ■ /n. The /n switch directs Word to start without opening a new document. Use this switch if you want Word to start with no document window.

- ■ /t document. Use the /t switch to direct Word to load a document as a template. Specify the document name in place of *document* after the /t switch.

You can use several methods to start Word with command-line switches. The first method is to start Word from a command prompt and include the switches in the command line that you use to start Word. To do so, open a command prompt window by choosing Start, Programs, MS-DOS prompt. When the DOS window opens, use the DOS CD command to change to the drive and folder containing the Winword executable file (Winword.exe). Typically, Winword.exe is located in *Officehome*\Office\, in which *Officehome* is the primary folder in which you installed Word. So if you installed Office to C:\Program Files\Office97, Winword.exe is located in C:\Program Files\Office97\Office. The following example starts Word without opening a new document window:

```
Winword.exe /n
```

The second way to start Word with a switch is to create a shortcut to Word and specify the switch in the command line of the shortcut. Follow these steps to create such a shortcut:

1. Right-click the desktop or the folder of your choice and then choose New, Shortcut to start the Create Shortcut Wizard.

2. In the Command Line text box, type (in quotes) the path to WINWORD.EXE, followed by a space, and include the desired switch at the end of the command line (example: "C:\Program Files\Office97\Office\Winword.exe" /n). See Figure 10.12 for an example.

FIG. 10.12
Use the Create Shortcut Wizard to create a shortcut that starts Word with a specific switch.

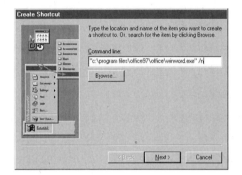

Part

II

Ch

10

3. Click the Next button to view the next page of the Wizard.

4. Type a name for your shortcut.

   This name appears below the shortcut's icon.

5. Click Finish.

You can create as many shortcuts to Word as you want, each with its own command line and optional switches. If you prefer to have only one shortcut, simply edit the shortcut to change the command line as needed. To edit a shortcut, right-click the shortcut's icon and then choose Properties from the shortcut menu. Click the Shortcut tab to display the Shortcut property. Modify the command line in the Target text box; then choose OK. ●

CHAPTER 11

Using VBA in Word

by Keith MacKay

Knowing how to create great-looking documents is only the beginning of efficient use of Word. Macros—recorded groups of actions that can be repeated as necessary—allow routine tasks to be reduced to a mouse click. Word 97 automatically records all macros in Microsoft's standard macro programming language, Visual Basic for Applications (VBA). This chapter introduces VBA and explains how to create, modify, run, and manage macros in Word through the use of the Macro Recorder and the Visual Basic Editor (VBE). The chapter also teaches you how to connect your macros to toolbars or have them run automatically whenever you open a document. ■

Create macros with the macro recorder

The macro recorder records a series of Word actions exactly so that they can be played back later.

Play recorded macros

When a macro has been recorded, Word 97 allows you to play it back as often as desired.

Modify recorded macros

Knowing how to modify a recorded macro opens a whole new world of possibilities.

Run macros from a toolbar button or menu option

For true customization of Word, you can create your own toolbar buttons and menu options, and connect them to your own macros.

Manage your macros by using the macro organizer

Some macros are so useful that you want them to be available in every document you create. Other macros are specific to the document that they are created in. The macro organizer allows you to determine the availability of your macros for every document.

Overview of New Features

Word 97 is the first release of Word to incorporate VBA, Microsoft's standard version of the Visual Basic programming language, for use within applications. VBA is also included in Excel, Access, and PowerPoint, allowing you to create routines in one application and then move them to other applications with little or no changes.

Older releases of Word (Word 95 and earlier) allowed macro programming by using a scripting language called WordBasic. Routines written in WordBasic are automatically converted to Visual Basic code when opened in Word 97. WordBasic's functionality is still available from the Word 97 VBA WordBasic object.

> **CAUTION**
>
> Word 97 automatically converts only WordBasic macros that have been saved in Word 6.0 or Word 95 format. If you have Word 2.0 documents with WordBasic routines, you first must open and save them in Word 6.0 or Word 95 format.

Create Macros with the Macro Recorder

The macro recorder allows the user to record a series of Word actions for later playback. For routine tasks, this easy-to-use tool proves to be a huge time-saver. If you are in the business of generating proposals, for example, judicious use of the macro recorder and a generic proposal template can save you hours each week. The rest of the chapter describes how a typical proposal process might be streamlined through the use of VBA macros in Word. Village Software, Inc. graciously allowed the use of a slightly modified version of the Details section from its *Proposal and Marketing FastPlan* for these examples.

N O T E You can find all sample files referenced in this chapter in this book's CD-ROM. ▉

For the example in this chapter, open the proposal details template (Details0.dot), which includes the generic proposal text. Notice that in the proposal, every place in which the client's company name should appear has been replaced by the generic text [Client] (see Figure 11.1).

You could choose Edit, Replace to replace each instance of [Client] with the actual client's company name—in this case, Acme Software, Inc. (see Figure 11.2).

Because you know that you need to customize every proposal that you create, and because you always replace the [Client] text, a better way to automate the customization task is available. Close Details0.dot and load a fresh copy of it (so that the [Client] references are intact). Now you're ready to record a macro.

By recording a macro, you can repeat the replacement procedure whenever you want. Recording a macro is a simple four-step process. Follow these steps:

FIG. 11.1
The text [Client] is used in every location where the client's company name should appear.

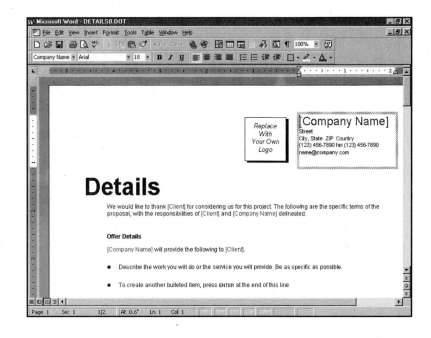

FIG. 11.2
This figure shows the Find and Replace dialog box.

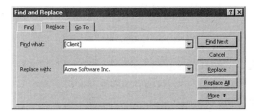

1. Start recording by choosing Tools, Macro, Record New Macro (see Figure 11.3).

2. Assign a name to the macro and click OK (see Figure 11.4.)

   In this case, use RenameClient as the name of the macro.

3. Perform your Word actions.

   For this example, choose Edit, Replace and fill in the Replace dialog box as shown in Figure 11.5.

4. Stop recording by clicking the Stop Recording button in the Stop Recording toolbar or by choosing Tools, Macro, Stop Recording (see Figure 11.6).

 TIP Word 97 also includes a Pause Recording button in the Stop Recording toolbar. If you're not sure what to do next while recording, click the Pause Recording button, try the action, and then undo it by choosing Edit, Undo. When you discover the correct action to take, click the Resume Recorder button (same button, new name) and continue recording. For complex macros, using the Pause/Resume Recorder technique is much easier than having to start over.

FIG. 11.3
Use the fly-out menu to begin recording a macro.

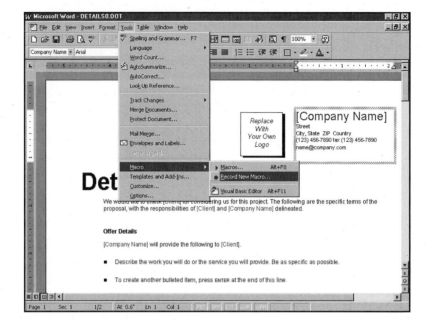

FIG. 11.4
Use this dialog box to name your macro.

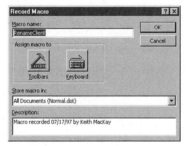

Using the Macros Dialog Box Macros

Choose Tools, Macro to display the Macros dialog box. You can also display the Macros dialog box by pressing Alt+F8. From this dialog box, you can run, test, edit, create, delete, manage, and even label your macros. The following list describes each option that is available in the Macros dialog box:

■ *Run*. In the left window, highlight the name of the macro that you want to run and then click the Run button to execute it. Notice that Run is the default operation, so you can also run a macro by double-clicking the macro name or by highlighting the name and then pressing Enter or the spacebar.

■ *Step Into*. The Step Into button allows you to run your VBA macro code one line at a time, to make sure that it is behaving as you expect at each step. When your macro doesn't behave quite right, this option allows you to determine where it's broken.

FIG. 11.5
Perform the steps that you want the macro to include.

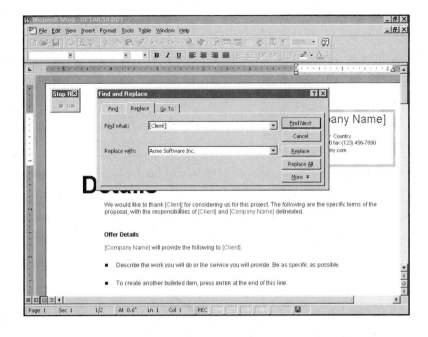

FIG. 11.6
Use this fly-out menu to stop recording.

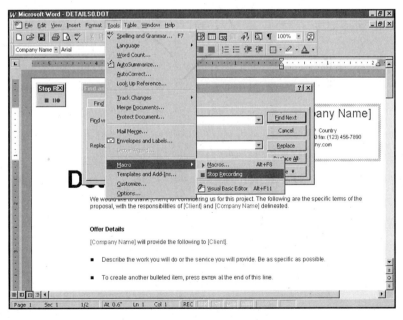

■ *Edit*. The Edit button allows you to view and modify your VBA macro code in Word's Visual Basic Editor (VBE). You can toggle back and forth between the VBE and your document window at any time by pressing Alt+F11. While you are in the document window, you can also choose Tools, Macro, Visual Basic Editor to display the VBE. The section "Modify Macros in the Visual Basic Editor" later in this chapter discusses the VBE in more detail.

N O T E   VBE opens in a separate window from Word, and allows direct editing and testing of Visual Basic for Applications macros. Excel and PowerPoint also have a VBE, and Access provides similar functionality from the Modules tab of the database. Outlook has a much more limited facility, called the Script Editor, that is used to edit VB Script (a light version of VBA).

■ *Create.* Clicking the Create button gives you the option of creating a new macro to replace the highlighted macro (see Figure 11.7).

FIG. 11.7

Click Yes to clear existing code for highlighted macro, click No to return to the Macros dialog box, or click Cancel to return to document.

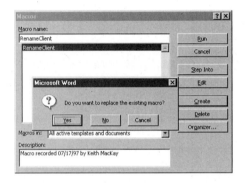

If you click the Yes button, the VBE appears, with the insertion point located in the macro that you highlighted. Any existing code in the macro is deleted.

■ *Delete.* Use the Delete button to delete a macro. You are asked to confirm that you really want to delete the macro.

■ *Organizer.* Clicking the Organizer button displays the Organizer dialog box, with the Macro Project Items tab brought to the front. You can easily move macros back and forth between templates and documents with this tool. "Manage Your Macros by Using the Macro Organizer" later in this chapter discusses the Organization dialog box further.

Notice that you can change the description for any of your macros at any time in the Macros dialog box. Making the description as specific as possible makes your life much easier a few months downstream when you don't remember exactly what the RenameClient macro actually does. To add or update a description, follow these steps:

1. Open the Macros dialog box by choosing Tools, Macro, Macros or pressing Alt+F8.

2. Highlight the macro that has the description to be added or changed.

3. Type the new description in the Description text box at the bottom of the dialog box.

   This description is added as a comment line at the beginning of your macro. The description is also used to help identify macros in the Customize dialog box and in the Organizer.

Modify Macros in the Visual Basic Editor

Knowing how to record macros can provide you tremendous power in your use of Word. You often find, however, that a recorded macro is not quite enough to solve the task at hand. In those cases, you need to dive a little deeper into using VBA in the VBE.

The Visual Basic Editor Windows

Open Details1.dot and choose Tools, Macro, Visual Basic Editor (or press Alt+Fll) to enter the VBE. The VBE has several windows that you can display or hide by making choices from the View menu. Figure 11.8 shows the Project Explorer, Properties, and Code windows.

FIG. 11.8

The VBE, displaying the Project Explorer, Code, and Properties windows (clockwise from top).

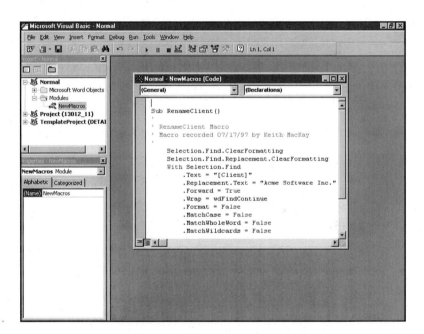

The Project Explorer allows you to view the components and code of every open document in Word. Click the plus sign (+) buttons to expand a document and the hyphen (-) buttons to collapse a document.

The Properties window allows you to customize particular preferences for this document. Typically, you need not make any changes in items in the Properties window.

The Code window displays the macros in the module highlighted in the Project Explorer. Double-click the title bar of the code window to have it fill the right portion of the editor window. Figure 11.9 shows the RenameClient macro in the editor window.

Changing Macro Code

In this section, you make some changes in the macro. First, you need to generalize the macro to work with any client, not just with Acme Software, Inc. One way to generalize the macro is to ask the user what company this proposal is being prepared for and then substitute that name in the macro.

FIG. 11.9

The VBE Code window displays Visual Basic Macro code (in this case, the RenameClient macro is shown).

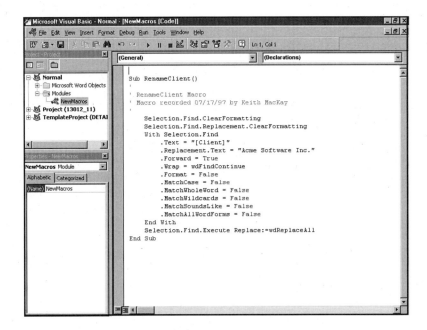

To implement the company request, you need two things: an input mechanism and a variable (a temporary storage bin for the company name). The new code is shown in Listing 11.1 along with the necessary changes. Just click the Code window and add or change the three lines as shown in the listing. The file Details2.dot contains this code with the changes already made.

N O T E   You can find all sample files referenced in this chapter in this book's CD-ROM.

Listing 11.1   A:LIST11_1.TXT (RenameClient macro using InputBox and variable)

```
Sub RenameClient()
'
' RenameClient Macro
' Macro recorded 07/17/97 by Keith MacKay
'
Dim cname As String          '**** add this row

cname = InputBox("Enter client's name", "Enter Name") '**** add this row

Selection.Find.ClearFormatting
Selection.Find.Replacement.ClearFormatting
With Selection.Find
  .Text = "[Client]"
```

```
    .Replacement.Text = cname        '**** change this row
    .Forward = True
    .Wrap = wdFindContinue
    .Format = False
    .MatchCase = False
    .MatchWholeWord = False
    .MatchWildcards = False
    .MatchSoundsLike = False
    .MatchAllWordForms = False
  End With
  Selection.Find.Execute Replace:=wdReplaceAll
End Sub
```

How the *RenameClient* Macro Works

This section steps through the code and describes what each section of the code does.

Every recorded macro is automatically given some header information. The macro is a Sub and is given the name that you chose at the beginning of the recording process. Any description given to the macro is added as a comment. By default, the description indicates the date and who recorded the macro. For instance, here are the first few rows of the RenameClient macro, as generated by the macro recorder.

```
Sub RenameClient()
'
'  RenameClient Macro
'  Macro recorded 07/17/97 by Keith MacKay
```

Now you tell the macro that you are going to use a variable that contains a String (any group of characters). Whenever you use a variable, declaring it this way is wise. For more information, see Dim in Microsoft Visual Basic Help. Here is RenameClient's variable definition section.

```
Dim cname As String        '**** add this row
```

Next, you add the command to display the input box. Notice that InputBox is a function, which means that it returns a value of some kind when it is run. In this case, InputBox returns whatever the user typed in it. The two arguments given to InputBox (the two items in parentheses) determine what the InputBox prints in the dialog box itself and in the title bar of the dialog box.

Setting cname equal to the InputBox function is important. This "set variable equal to function" technique is the way to tell VBA to run the InputBox function and put whatever it returns in the cname variable. Here is the code from RenameClient which displays the InputBox and assigns the InputBox return value to the variable cname.

```
cname = InputBox("Enter client's name", "Enter Name") '**** add this row
```

Now you come to the Find portion of the code, to which you make one minor (but significant) change: You assign Replacement.Text to become the variable cname, rather than a specific string of characters. The usage of the variable rather than fixed text gives the macro the flexibility to use whatever text is in cname every time the macro runs. The rest of the code is

Part

II

Ch

11

automatically generated by the macro recorder and provides explicit settings for every possible option of Word's replace feature. To make the code easier to read, you can delete those optional arguments, which are set to their default settings. (Typically, many optional arguments can be eliminated, because each Word action has many possible parameters, and you actually change few of them in most Word operations.) See Microsoft Visual Basic Help for Find to determine which settings meet these criteria. Here is the rest of the code as generated automatically by the macro recorder.

```
Selection.Find.ClearFormatting
  Selection.Find.Replacement.ClearFormatting
  With Selection.Find
    .Text = "[Client]"
    .Replacement.Text = cname          '**** change this row
    .Forward = True
    .Wrap = wdFindContinue
    .Format = False
    .MatchCase = False
    .MatchWholeWord = False
    .MatchWildcards = False
    .MatchSoundsLike = False
    .MatchAllWordForms = False
  End With
  Selection.Find.Execute Replace:=wdReplaceAll
End Sub
```

The End Sub statement is automatically provided for you by the macro recorder. Every Sub must have an End Sub statement to indicate when it is done.

T I P The Help provided for VBA generally is very good in Microsoft Office applications. To access Help at any time from within the VBE, choose Help, Microsoft Visual Basic Help or press F1. If you press F1 while the insertion point is on a word in the Code window, help for that particular word appears (if it exists). Use of the help system is an excellent way to learn Visual Basic fundamentals from recorded macros.

Test Your Changes

After making the changes in the macro, return to Microsoft Word by choosing View, Microsoft Word (or by pressing Alt+F11). To run your new macro:

1. Choose Tools, Macro, Macros (or press Alt+F8).

2. Highlight RenameClient.

3. Click Run.

Your input box appears, as shown in Figure 11.10.

FIG. 11.10

This figure shows the RenameClient input box.

Type a name and click OK, and the names are replaced. Run the macro a second time, and enter a different company name. Notice that no replacements occur. Why didn't the macro drop in the new name? The Find method is searching explicitly for [Client]. Because [Client] was replaced by a new company name, the Find method can't find any more instances of [Client]. In this example, being unable to replace a prior replacement isn't a problem, but in some cases, you may want to replace a placeholder multiple times.

N O T E You can solve the multiple-replacement problem by using Microsoft Word's bookmarks. Bookmarks allow you to tag text that you want to manipulate. VBA allows you to replace the text in a bookmark without obliterating the bookmark itself. This book leaves that example as an exercise for you. ▪

Now you are ready to test the Cancel button from the input box, just to make sure that every possible scenario works. First, choose Edit, Undo VBA, Find.Execute. Executing this Undo step restores the client names to be [Client]. Run the macro again and click the Cancel button. Now all the instances of Client have been replaced by nothing!

The InputBox function returns whatever the user typed if OK is clicked, but it returns a zero-length string ("", or nothing) when Cancel is clicked. (See the InputBox help page for more details on the behavior of the InputBox function.) Choose Edit, Undo VBA, Find.Execute again to restore your [Client] text; then return to the VBE.

N O T E Undo works in this case, but Undo typically undoes only the last Word action performed. Even though Word has a multiple Undo, as your macros get more complex, saving your document *before* testing becomes more important, because Undo undoes only part of your macro, not the entire thing. ▪

To solve this blank-replacement problem, add an If statement to the code after the InputBox line, as follows:

```
cname = InputBox("Enter client's name", "Enter Name")

 If cname = "" Then Exit Sub        '**** add this row
```

N O T E The file Details3.dot (included on the accompanying CD-ROM) contains this code modification, as well as the custom toolbar discussed later in this chapter in the "Run Macros from a Toolbar Button" section. ▪

This code checks to see whether Cancel was clicked. If so, it exits the subroutine, leaving the user back where he or she started. This sort of data-validation technique makes the difference between a robust application and one that breaks.

To make sure that this approach is the right one, return to Word and test the macro. If that the macro works appropriately, save the template.

Part

II

Ch

11

> **CAUTION**
>
> Saving the template after each macro change *before* you test it is wise. As your macros get more complex, you can crash Word, close Word, close the document, make changes that you can't undo, or otherwise lose the work that you just did.

Run Macros from a Toolbar Button

Custom toolbars can prove to be great time-savers. Being able to add your own macros to toolbar buttons gives you even greater flexibility and power. To add the `RenameClient` macro to a new toolbar, perform the following steps:

1. Choose Tools, Customize to display the Customize dialog box, shown in Figure 11.11.

FIG. 11.11

The Customize dialog box is used to customize toolbars and menus.

2. Click the New button to display the New Toolbar dialog box (see Figure 11.12).

FIG. 11.12

The New Toolbar dialog box is used to determine a toolbar's name and scope.

3. Type a name for your toolbar into the New Toolbar dialog box.
4. Choose DETAILS3.DOT from the Make Toolbar Available To drop-down list.

   Now you have a tiny gray toolbar with no buttons on it.
5. Click the Commands tab of the Customize dialog box, and in the Categories area, scroll down to Macros. You see a list of all currently available macros in the document.
6. Drag `TemplateProject.NewMacros.RenameClient` to your new toolbar. When you release of the mouse button, you should see the name of the macro fill the toolbar.

TIP Notice that you can't see the entire macro name in the Comman<u>d</u>s box and that you cannot resize the Customize box. The inability to resize the Customize box is another compelling argument for using good descriptions. (The description of each macro is displayed in the bottom of the dialog box when you select the macro.)

7. Right-click your new toolbar item to access its properties (see Figure 11.13).

FIG. 11.13
Right-click a toolbar in order to change the name and appearance of each toolbar item from the toolbar's properties menu.

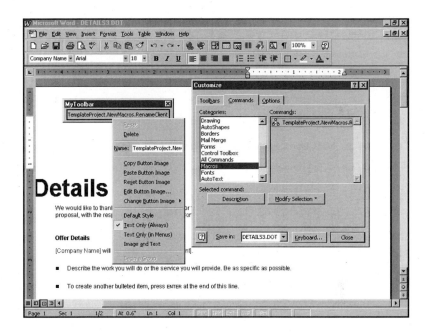

Part
II

Ch
11

8. From the right-button menu for your toolbar, you can optionally type a shorter or more descriptive name in the Name text box.

Notice that the name you assigned is used as a ToolTip for the button (it's displayed in yellow if you hover over the button's icon for a second or so). You can also manipulate button images and the format of your toolbar button from your toolbar's right-button menu.

9. Make any changes that you want and then click Close in the Customize dialog box.

Click your new toolbar button to make sure it works (click Cancel when the input box appears). The file Details3.dot on the accompanying CD-ROM contains the final `RenameClient` macro code and a toolbar called MyToolbar, which is connected to it. You can create toolbars of any number of buttons. If you are building toolbars for use by other people as well as yourself, it is better to keep the toolbars small and to group similar buttons, to keep them easy to use and understand.

Run Macros When a Document Opens

At this point, you can run your macro at the click of a mouse, but you are going to use this macro every time you open this template. You can get even more efficient and run the macro automatically whenever the template opens just by giving the macro an appropriate name. You can even run a macro whenever Word opens or whenever you exit a document or Word. This section discusses the five auto macros that Word recognizes, as shown in Table 11.1.

Table 11.1 Word's Five Auto- (Event) Macros

Macro	Runs If You...
AutoOpen	Open existing document.
AutoClose	Close document.
AutoExec	Start Word, load Normal template, or open global template from startup folder.
AutoNew	Create new document.
AutoExit	Quit Word or unload global template.

If you want to have the RenameClient macro run every time you open the proposal template, you can do so in two ways:

- Rename the macro RenameClient as AutoOpen in the VBE code window, and save the template.
- In the VBE, rename the NewMacros module AutoOpen, and change the RenameClient macro to Main.

The first option generally is the one used, although using the second technique can enhance the readability of a complex Word application that has many modules. Notice that in either case, you must save and close the template and then reopen it to test whether the macro is working (it runs only when the document is open, after all). The file Details4.dot on the accompanying CD-ROM demonstrates this technique.

N O T E All auto macros can live in any template or document, with the exception of AutoExec, which runs automatically only if it is stored in either the Normal template or another global template stored in the folder that Word references as its startup folder.

To prevent auto macros from running, hold down the Shift key while performing the operation that normally triggers the macro. If you have a document that contains an AutoOpen macro, for example, hold down the Shift key while you open the document until the document is completely loaded and the mouse pointer changes from an hourglass to an arrow. Within VBA, you can prevent auto macros from running by using the following instruction:

```
WordBasic.DisableAutomacros
```

Manage Your Macros by Using the Macro Organizer

The macro organizer provides an easy way to determine which macro modules are available to which documents. Limiting the scope (availability) of macro modules is an effective way to enhance productivity and prevent confusion. Although you can store all your macro modules in your Normal template, as their number grows, they are more difficult to find and manage. Also, specific macros that you want to have within a particular document do not merit cluttering your Normal template.

Start the Organizer

Choose Tools, Macro, Macros or press Alt+F8. Then choose the Organizer button. Choosing the Organizer button displays the Organizer dialog box, which is automatically open to the Macro Project Items tab (see Figure 11.14).

FIG. 11.14
The Organizer dialog box provides a facility for determining the availability of each macro module for each of your templates and documents.

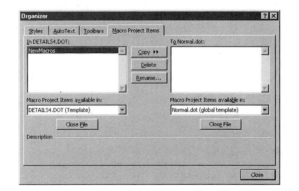

Part
II
Ch
11

Notice that three other tabs are available for managing styles, AutoText entries, and toolbars. Each of these tabs is used in the same way and for the same purpose: to determine the availability of your custom elements to each of your documents and templates.

Moving Macro Modules Between Documents

Macros that exist within a template are also available to any document based on that template. Macros that exist within the Normal template are available to each new document which is created based on the Normal template. For instance, any template created using File, New in which Blank Document is chosen from the General Tab will contain the macros from the Normal template.

When you enter the Organizer dialog box, the current document (and a list of any macro modules that it contains) is displayed on the left side, and the Normal template (and a list of its available macro modules) is shown on the right.

To move a macro module, click the name of the module to be moved and then click the Copy button to copy it to the other document. If the document to which you want to move the module is not displayed, click the Close File button that is displayed below the file that does *not* contain the desired module. When that document is closed, click the resulting Open File button, and browse to the file that you want to add the module to. When the correct origin and destination templates or documents are displayed, select the module name in the origin file and click the Copy button to add it to the destination file.

Deleting Macro Modules from Documents

Select a macro name in either document and click the Delete button to delete the macro. Notice that the macro module is removed only from the document in which it was highlighted. You can choose multiple modules for deletion at the same time by holding down Ctrl or Shift while you select the module names.

Renaming Macro Modules

To rename a macro module, select the existing name and then click the Rename button. Clicking the Rename button will prompt you with a dialog box in which to type the new name.

In practice, it usually is best to maintain consistent module names across documents, rather than name the same module with different names in several documents. Using consistent module names just makes it easier to keep track of which documents actually have which specific macros included.

Part III: Excel: Beyond the Basics

CHAPTER 12

Excel Quick Start Guide

by Patrice-Anne Rutledge

This Quick Start Guide introduces you to the basic concepts of using Microsoft Excel 97, including creating, opening, saving, and printing worksheets and workbooks. If you're already familiar with Excel, this material can serve as a brief review. ▬

Excel navigation

You can navigate your worksheets with the mouse, with the keyboard, or by scrolling.

Worksheet creation

Creating, saving, and reopening worksheets is simple and automatic in Excel as is entering text, numbers, and formulas.

Worksheet printing

You can set print parameters, preview your worksheets, and specify exact print areas.

Understanding What Excel 97 Can Do

Excel 97 is the spreadsheet application part of Microsoft Office 97. Excel's major strength is its ability to track, analyze, and perform calculations on data. With Excel you can create budgets, expense statements, forecasts, and other financial and analytical documents.

When you start Excel 97, a workbook opens that displays a blank worksheet. Figure 12.1 illustrates a sample blank worksheet.

FIG. 12.1

Excel worksheets include cells, rows, and columns.

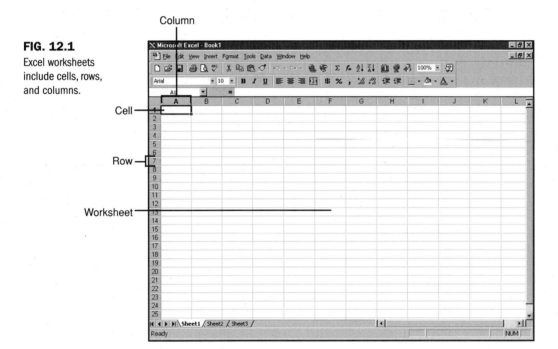

In Excel, you store and save data in a *workbook*. A new workbook contains three *worksheets*, labeled Sheet1, Sheet2, and Sheet3 in *sheet tabs* at the bottom of the worksheet. You can rename these sheet tabs to something more meaningful by highlighting them and typing in the new label. You can also add additional worksheets by choosing Insert, Sheet.

A worksheet consists of a series of *columns* and *rows*. Excel worksheets have 256 columns labeled across the top of the worksheet with a letter of the alphabet, such as A, B, C, and so on. After the letter Z, Excel continues with the following naming convention: AA, AB, AC, and so on. Each row has a numeric label along the left side of the worksheet. A worksheet has 65,536 rows.

In Excel, you store data in a *cell*, the intersection of a column and row. Each cell is identified by the combination of the column and row labels. For example, the cell in the upper-left corner of the worksheet is A1. This is referred to as the *cell reference*. You can always tell which cell or cells are active because the column labels are bolded. See Figure 12.1 column A and row 1.

Cell references are important in Excel because you use them to create formulas based on your worksheet data.

▶ **See** "Working with Formulas," **p. 276**

Working with the Excel 97 Interface

You can easily navigate around your worksheets using either the mouse or basic keyboard commands. Because Excel can contain up to 65,536 rows, you may often want to move quickly through worksheet data or to a specific cell. To do this, Excel offers worksheet scrolling and a Go To command that takes you to a designated cell.

Navigating with the Mouse

Navigating with the mouse is simple—just position the mouse pointer over the cell you want to activate and click the left mouse button.

Navigating with the Keyboard

You can use a variety of keys and key combinations to navigate in an Excel worksheet. Table 12.1 illustrates these keys and where they move.

Table 12.1   Keyboard Navigation

Key	Moves
Right arrow, Tab	One cell to the right
Down arrow, Enter	One cell down
Left arrow, Shift+Tab	One cell to the left
Up arrow, Shift+Enter	One cell up
Ctrl+right arrow	To the next nonblank cell to the right
Ctrl+left arrow	To the next nonblank cell to the left
Ctrl+down arrow	To the next nonblank cell down
Ctrl+up arrow	To the next nonblank cell up
Home	To column A of the active row
Ctrl+Home	To cell A1
Ctrl+End	To the last cell used
Page Up	Up one screen
Page Down	Down one screen
Alt+Page Up	One screen to the left

Part
III

Ch
12

continues

Table 12.1   Continued

Key	Moves
Alt+Page Down	One screen to the right
Ctrl+Page Up	To the next worksheet
Ctrl+Page Down	To the previous worksheet

Navigating with the Scroll Bar

To navigate row by row with the scroll bar, click the up or down scroll arrow. You can also navigate by dragging the scroll box up and down the scroll bar. When you do this, the row or column heading displays so you know your exact location in the worksheet.

 Scrolling moves the screen display, but doesn't change the active cell.

Navigating with the Go To Command

To quickly move to a specific cell, you can use the Go To command. Choose Edit, Go To or press F5 to open the Go To dialog box, shown in Figure 12.2.

FIG. 12.2

Move quickly to a specified cell with the Go To dialog box.

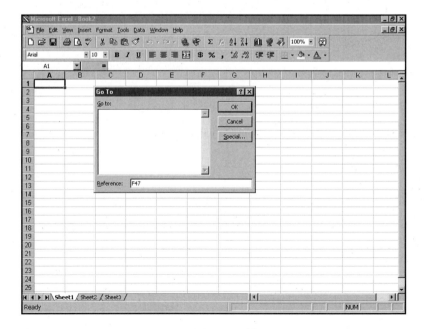

Enter the name of the cell to which you want to move in the Reference edit box and then click OK. To move to cell F47 for example, type F47 and click OK. The mouse pointer moves to F47, making it the active cell.

Working with Excel Documents

Once you've familiarized yourself with the basic parts of an Excel worksheet and how to navigate it, you'll want to create your own worksheets and enter text, numbers, and formulas in them. By planning the names of your worksheets and the folders you'll place them in before you save, you can make it easy to find and open them again in the future.

Creating Workbooks

 When you open Excel, a blank worksheet automatically displays. You can also create a new worksheet based on an existing template. A *template* is a workbook or worksheet you can use as the basis for another workbook or worksheet. To do so, choose File, New to open the New dialog box, shown in Figure 12.3.

FIG. 12.3
Choose a worksheet template in the New dialog box.

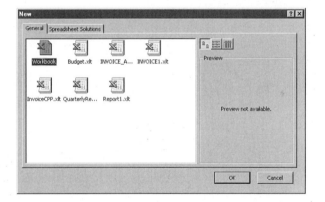

Choose the worksheet template you want to use as the basis for your new document and click OK.

▶ **See** "Using Templates," **p. 309**

NOTE Excel includes several built-in templates for expense statements, purchase orders, and invoices. You can also create your own templates. ■

Entering Workbook Data

Once you've created a workbook, activate a worksheet cell in which you want to enter data by positioning the mouse pointer over it and clicking the left mouse button. Cell A1 is activated by default when you create a new worksheet.

T I P   You can also enter data directly in the formula bar.

As you type in new data, this data appears in both the active cell and in the area above the worksheet called the *formula bar*. The insertion point, a blinking bar, displays in this active cell to show you where your next entry will appear. Figure 12.4 illustrates these areas of the worksheet.

FIG. 12.4
You can view and enter data in the formula bar.

Formula bar ———

Insertion point ———

Cancel button ———

Enter button ———

Edit Formula button ———

Three small buttons appear to the right of where your text displays in the formula bar.

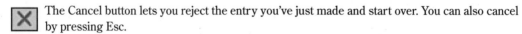
The Cancel button lets you reject the entry you've just made and start over. You can also cancel by pressing Esc.

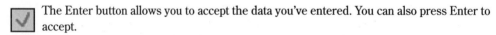
The Enter button allows you to accept the data you've entered. You can also press Enter to accept.

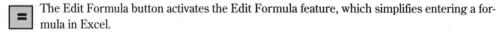
The Edit Formula button activates the Edit Formula feature, which simplifies entering a formula in Excel.

Entering Text   Entering text in an Excel worksheet is a straightforward task. Text entries can consist of a series of alphanumeric characters such as letters, numbers, and symbols. The combination of numbers and characters in, for example, an address lets Excel know you've made a text entry. An entry such as 100 Main Street, therefore, would be treated as text.

In general, when you enter text in a cell Excel recognizes that it's text data rather than numeric data and formats it properly. But in some cases numbers can actually be text fields. For instance, a ZIP Code consists of a series of numbers, but is really text data since you would never use it in calculations. To let Excel know that a series of numbers is a text entry, precede it with an apostrophe. As an example, you would enter the ZIP Code 94566 as '94566. The apostrophe displays in the Formula Bar, but not in the actual worksheet cell.

 TIP You can enter up to 32,000 characters in a single cell.

Entering Numbers A numeric entry in Excel consists only of numbers; you can't include regular text. You can enter the following kinds of numeric values:

▶ **See** "Formatting Numbers, Dates, and Times," **p. 328**

- Integers, such as 341
- Decimal fractions, such as 15.612
- Integer fractions, such as 1 1/4
- Values in scientific notation, such as 1.23E+08

 TIP If the cell displays ##### after entering a long number, double-click the right edge of the column to widen it.

Entering Dates and Times When you enter a date or time, Excel recognizes this and displays the date or time using the current default format. For example, if your default date format is 9/1/97, entering 9-1-97, 9/1/1997, or 9/01/97 would all convert to 9/1/97.

▶ **See** "Formatting Numbers, Dates, and Times," **p. 328**

When you enter a date or time, Excel converts the date entry to a serial number or the time to a decimal fraction so that you can perform calculations based on it. You don't see this format in your worksheet, though. It displays as a regular date or time.

 TIP Press Ctrl+; (semicolon) to enter the current date and Ctrl+: (colon) to enter the current time.

Entering Formulas The ability to calculate values using formulas is one of Excel's most important features. To enter a formula, first enter the equal sign (=) and then enter the specific formula. The formula displays in both the cell in which you're typing and in the formula bar. Press Enter to accept the formula. The active cell now displays the result, but the formula bar still displays the formula, illustrated in Figure 12.5.

For example, entering the formula **=A1+A2+A3** in cell A4 will sum the values of cells A1 through A3. If you change any of the values in these three cells, the summed value in cell A4 changes accordingly.

Part
III

Ch
12

FIG. 12.5

The formula bar displays
the formula on which the
active cell is based.

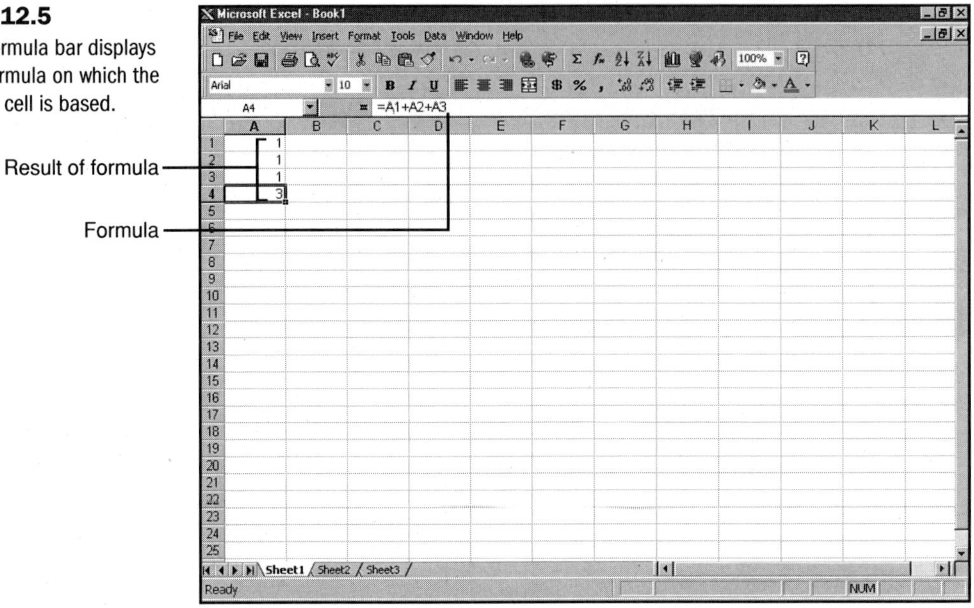

Result of formula

Formula

Saving Workbooks

When you create a new workbook, Excel assigns it the temporary name Book1 and continues to increment (Book2, Book3, and so on) as you open new workbooks. To permanently retain the contents of a workbook, you need to save it.

Saving is a simple process in Excel, so be sure to save your workbooks regularly. If you're going to be entering large amounts of data or creating complicated formulas, you should save every five to ten minutes. That way, if you should have a system failure or accidentally close your document, you'll only have several minutes' worth of work to repeat.

You'll also want to think carefully about the name you choose for your new workbook as well as the folder in which you want to save it. A descriptive name such as **1997 Compensation Analysis** is easier to find later than **97Cmp**. Also consider carefully the naming of your folders. When you first start creating workbooks decide whether you want to organize them in folders based on subject, year, and so on.

 T I P To save changes to a file you've previously saved, click the Save button on the Standard toolbar. Excel saves the changes automatically without opening the Save As dialog box.

To save a newly created workbook, follow these steps:

1. Choose File, Save to open the Save As dialog box, shown in Figure 12.6.
2. Choose the folder to Save In and enter the File Name.

FIG. 12.6

Choose the name and location of the file you want to save in the Save As dialog box.

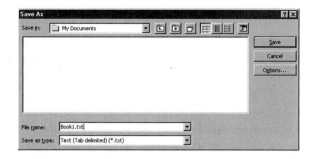

3. Microsoft Excel Workbook (*.xls) is the default file type, but you can also save your workbook as another file type, such as a template, previous version of Excel, text file, or Lotus 1-2-3 file.

 TIP If you want to save an Excel workbook to another format after an initial save or as a different file name, don't use the Save button, which automatically saves the changes to an existing workbook. Instead, choose File, Save As.

4. Click the Save button to save the workbook and return to the active worksheet.

Opening Workbooks

Once you've created and saved a workbook, you'll want to open it again. If you carefully thought out the organizational structure when saving your workbooks, it will be easier to locate them later. See "Saving Workbooks," earlier in this chapter, for tips that make finding workbooks you've saved an easy process.

To open a previously saved workbook, follow these steps:

1. Choose File, Open to access the Open dialog box, shown in Figure 12.7.

Part
III

Ch
12

FIG. 12.7

You can open and search for specific files in the Open dialog box.

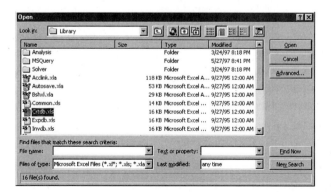

T I P   To limit a long list of files based on the type of file you want to open, select that type from the Files of Type drop-down list.

2. Choose the folder you want to Look In.

3. Select the file from the scroll list and click Open.

In some cases, finding the file you want to open might not be that simple. For example, you may not remember the file name or in which folder you placed it. Or, you may have thousands of files, which makes locating the appropriate one more difficult.

To narrow down the search in a particular folder, you can enter a portion of the file's name in the File Name field and then click Find Now. Excel displays all files that contain those characters. For example, entering **18** would find files named Chapter 18.xls, 18Aug.xls, and Release 18 Notes.xls. To start another search, click the New Search button.

Printing from Excel

To print a worksheet you've created, follow these steps:

1. Select the worksheet you want to print and choose File, Print to open the Print dialog box. Figure 12.8 illustrates this dialog box.

FIG. 12.8

Quickly print your Excel worksheets from the Print dialog box.

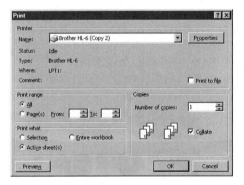

2. Choose the Name of your printer. The default printer displays automatically.

3. In the Print Range group box, determine whether you want to print All pages or only certain Page(s). If you want to print a certain range of pages, enter that range in the From and To scroll boxes. For example, to print only pages 5 through 10, you would enter **5** in the From scroll box and **10** in the To scroll box.

T I P   To preview your worksheet first, select the Preview button. See "Previewing Worksheets" later in this chapter for more details on Print Preview.

4. In the Print What group box, specify whether to print the specific Selection (group of cells you've selected), the Active Sheet(s), or the Entire Workbook.

5. Next, indicate the Number of Copies you want to print and whether or not you want to Collate them.

6. Click OK to print.

Printing a worksheet may not always be this simple, however. At times you'll want to print only certain areas, preview your worksheet first, or set other print parameters.

Previewing Worksheets

 Before printing, you may want to preview on-screen what your document will look like. To do so, select the worksheet you want to preview and choose File, Print Preview. Figure 12.9 illustrates a worksheet preview.

FIG. 12.9
You can preview and change your Excel worksheets.

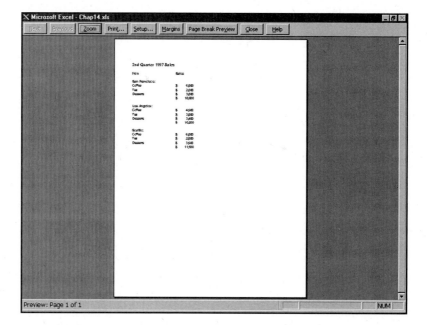

Print preview includes many options for viewing and customizing your printed worksheet, including the following buttons:

- *Next*. In multiple-page worksheets, moves you to the next page.
- *Previous*. In multiple-page worksheets, moves you to the previous page.
- *Zoom*. Enlarges the page for easier viewing; clicking Zoom again returns you to the regular page size.
- *Print*. Opens the Print dialog box.

- *Setup*. Opens the Page Setup dialog box, where you can specify page, margin, header/footer, and sheet parameters.

- *Margins*. Displays light gray lines where margins exist; you can adjust the margins by clicking the handle of the margin you want to change and dragging the handle to the new location.

- *Page Break Preview*. Displays page breaks; you can adjust these by clicking and dragging the breaks with your mouse.

- *Close*. Closes Print Preview and returns to the worksheet.

- *Help*. Opens Microsoft Excel help for the Print Preview feature.

Setting Print Parameters

To set print parameters such as page size, layout, margins, header/footer, and sheet details, choose File, Page Setup to open the Page Setup dialog box, shown in Figure 12.10.

FIG. 12.10

Set page orientation and scaling on the Page tab.

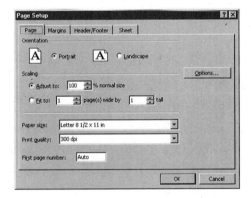

In the first tab, Page, you can set orientation, scaling, and size parameters. Orientation is particularly important for printing since changing the orientation of a worksheet from Portrait to Landscape can often help the entire sheet fit on one page.

On the Margins tab (see Figure 12.11), you can specify margins for the Top, Bottom, Left, Right, Header, and Footer of your document. You can also center the worksheet on the page either Horizontally or Vertically.

Choose from a number of predefined Headers and Footers on the Header/Footer tab, shown in Figure 12.12.

You can also create a Custom Header or Custom Footer if you prefer.

Finally, you'll set worksheet parameters on the Sheet tab. Figure 12.13 illustrates this tab.

On this tab, you'll probably want to remove the check from the Gridlines check box. Selecting Gridlines will print horizontal and vertical gridlines on your worksheets, something that you will probably want to avoid when creating professional-looking printed output from Excel.

FIG. 12.11
You can customize your margins for printing.

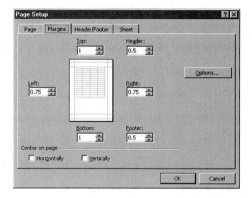

FIG. 12.12
Choose a predesigned header and footer or create your own.

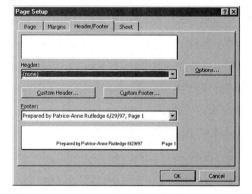

FIG. 12.13
Decide whether or not to display Gridlines on the Sheet tab.

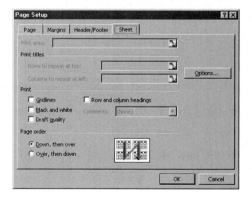

Part
III

Ch
12

Setting Print Areas

If you want to print only a certain section of a worksheet, you can set a print area. Print areas designate specific cells to print. All cells outside of the print area do not print. To set a print area, select the area you want to print and choose File, Print Area, Set Print Area. If you then preview your worksheet, you'll see that only the designated print area is set to print.

To clear this print area, choose File, Print Area, Clear Print Area. ●

CHAPTER 13

Workbooks, Worksheets, and Ranges

by Patrice-Anne Rutledge

Once you've created a basic Microsoft Excel 97 worksheet, you'll probably want to modify it. In Excel you can easily select cells and ranges and then edit, copy, move, insert, and delete them. You can also create many different views of your data: you can reduce or enlarge it, freeze and split panes for easier viewing, and even create a custom view. Finally, Excel enables you to name cells and ranges of data, a feature that you'll find very useful as you move forward and start creating formulas. ■

Multiple workbooks and worksheets

Excel provides many options for viewing worksheets and workbooks including row and column header, simultaneous, multiple workbook, and custom views.

Worksheet and range selection

In Excel 97, you can select worksheets, columns, rows, and single or multiple ranges of data.

Range names

Range names enable you to refer to ranges of cells by name for easier identification.

Range fills

You can use the AutoFill and Format Painter features to automate the filling of ranges with data and formatting.

Range modification

You can easily edit, delete, copy, move, and insert worksheets, ranges, and data.

Reference operators

Excel provides several specific reference operators that let you combine ranges of cells in calculations and formulas.

Working with Multiple Workbooks and Worksheets

In Excel, you can easily modify your workbooks and worksheets with special features that simplify the tasks of editing, copying, moving, inserting, and deleting.

Editing Worksheets

Excel provides two ways to edit cell contents you've previously entered. You can select the cell and edit the contents in the formula bar, or you can double-click the cell and edit the contents directly in the cell. Excel refers to this second option as *in-cell editing*. To be sure that in-cell editing is active, choose Tools, Options and verify that the Edit Directly in Cell check box is checked on the Edit tab.

Clearing Cell Contents   To clear cell contents, select the cell or range of cells and choose Edit, Clear to display a shortcut menu. From this menu you can choose from the following options, each clearing your cell contents in a different way:

- *All*. Clears everything including contents, formatting, and cell notes.
- *Formats*. Clears only cell formatting, not the contents.
- *Contents*. Clears the contents but leaves cell formatting.
- *Comments*. Clears comments only.

 TIP   As a shortcut, select the data you want to clear, right-click the mouse, and choose Clear Contents from the shortcut menu. This performs the same function as choosing Edit, Clear, Contents.

Checking Worksheet Spelling   An important part of editing any worksheet is to verify that the spelling is correct. Excel's spelling feature checks worksheets, macros, and charts for errors. To check the spelling in more than one worksheet, select the tab of each sheet you want to check by pressing and holding down the Ctrl key and clicking the tabs of the sheets you want to include.

 TIP   To spell-check only a specific worksheet range, select it before clicking the Spelling button.

 TIP   If Excel finds no spelling errors, it displays a dialog box telling you that the spell-check is complete for the entire sheet.

To start checking spelling, follow these steps:

1. Click the Spelling button on the Standard toolbar or choose Tools, Spelling.
2. When Excel encounters an error, the Spelling dialog box displays, shown in Figure 13.1.

FIG. 13.1
Excel provides many
different spell-check
options.

3. The misspelled word is highlighted in the Not in Dictionary field and potential suggested spellings, if any, display in the Change To box.

 TIP To add the selected word to the custom dictionary, click the Add Button.

4. Choose one of the suggestions or enter the correct spelling in the edit box and click the Change button to change this instance of the word or Change All to change all instances of the misspelled word.

Excel also offers several other options with the following buttons:

- *Ignore*. Ignores the suggested change and continues checking the spelling.
- *Ignore All*. Ignores all occurrences of the suggested change and continues checking the spelling.
- *Add*. Adds the word to the custom dictionary as it is currently spelled.
- *Suggest*. Offers additional suggestions related to the current selection in the Suggestions list.
- *AutoCorrect*. Add the misspelled word and its correction to the AutoCorrect list.

5. When Excel completes checking spelling, it displays a message box telling you so. Click OK to return to the worksheet.

Viewing Workbooks and Worksheets

Excel 97 offers many different ways you can view a worksheet once you've created it. With large worksheets, you can create frozen column and row headings that display as you scroll through your data. You can also split the worksheet to view different parts at the same time. Excel also provides the ability to hide specific rows, columns, and worksheets to make working with your data easier. Finally, you can also view multiple workbooks and worksheets at the same time.

Viewing Row and Column Labels

With long worksheets you'll often lose sight of your column labels as you scroll down your list of data. Scrolling to the right can make the row labels disappear. To avoid this problem, you can "freeze" the label row and column.

▶ **See** "Printing from Excel," **p. 246**

Part
III

Ch
13

To freeze only the horizontal pane (row labels), choose the row immediately underneath the one you want to freeze. For example, to freeze only the first row, you would select row 2. Choose Window, Freeze Panes. Now when you scroll down, this first row is frozen. Figure 13.2 shows an example of a frozen row (see row labels).

FIG. 13.2

Freezing panes makes it easier to identify column and row headers.

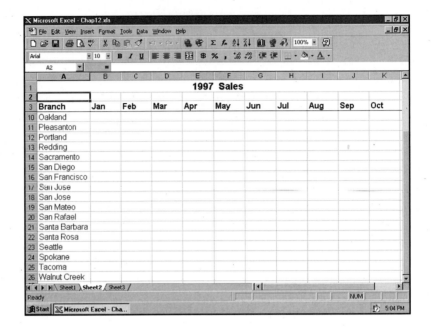

To freeze only the vertical pane (column labels), choose the column immediately to the right of the column you want to freeze. Choose Window, Freeze Panes to freeze it.

To freeze both the horizontal and vertical panes, select the cell immediately beneath and to the right of where you want to freeze the pane. For example, to freeze row 1 and column A, you would select cell B2. Choose Window, Freeze Panes to freeze.

 T I P To unfreeze all panes, choose Window, Unfreeze Panes.

N O T E Frozen panes don't display when you print a worksheet. For example, if you freeze the first row in what will print as a multiple page document, the frozen row won't print as a column heading after the first page. To print column headings, choose File, Page Setup to open the Page Setup dialog box. In the Print Titles group box on the Sheet tab, enter the Rows to Repeat at Top and Columns to Repeat at Left. ■

Viewing Two Parts of a Worksheet Simultaneously

You can view two parts of the same worksheet simultaneously. For example, you may want to view the top 5 rows and bottom 5 rows of a 50-row worksheet at the same time. To do this, you'll use the split boxes you find at the top of the vertical scroll bar or at the right of the horizontal scroll bar. Figure 13.3 illustrates an example of using split boxes (see row labels).

 T I P To remove these splits, drag the split bar back to the top or right of the worksheet window.

FIG. 13.3

Use split boxes to split your worksheet display.

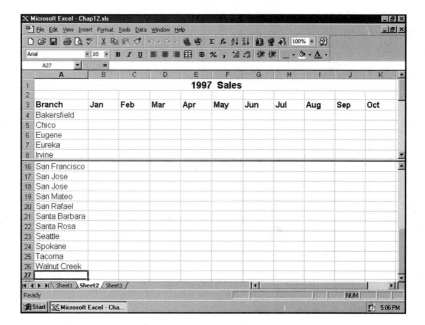

Point to the split box and drag the mouse to the location where you want to place the split. To display the top and bottom 5 rows in your worksheet, you would drag the vertical split box to just below row 5. Then you could scroll in the lower pane to the last five worksheet rows.

Enlarging or Reducing Worksheet View

To enlarge or reduce the view of your current worksheet, select an appropriate zoom percentage from the Zoom drop-down list. To enlarge the view of the selected cells only, choose Selection from the drop-down list.

 T I P In addition to the predetermined zoom percentages in the Zoom drop-down list on the Standard toolbar, you can also manually enter your own zoom percentage in this box. Excel supports zooms from 10 percent to 400 percent.

Part
III

Ch
13

Hiding Worksheets, Columns, and Rows

In Excel, you can hide worksheets, columns, and rows from view. This is useful if you temporarily want to work only with specific data and prefer to only view that data.

To hide a worksheet from view, select the Worksheet tab and choose F̲ormat, S̲heet, H̲ide. Excel removes the worksheet from view, but doesn't delete it. To view the worksheet again, choose F̲ormat, S̲heet, U̲nhide to open the Unhide dialog box, shown in Figure 13.4.

FIG. 13.4

Choose the worksheet
to unhide in the Unhide
dialog box.

Select the sheet you want to unhide in the U̲nhide Sheet list and click OK.

To hide rows, select the row or rows you want to hide and choose F̲ormat, R̲ow, H̲ide. To restore these rows, select the rows that surround the hidden rows and choose F̲ormat, R̲ow, U̲nhide. The hidden rows display again. Figure 13.5 shows a worksheet with rows 4, 7, and 10 hidden.

FIG. 13.5

Rows 4, 7, and 10 are
hidden.

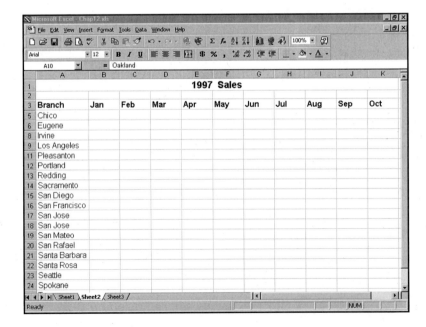

To hide columns, choose the column or columns to hide and select F̲ormat, C̲olumn, H̲ide. Similarly, to restore select the columns that surround the hidden columns and choose F̲ormat, C̲olumn, U̲nhide.

Creating a Custom View

If you've made numerous customizations to worksheets that you want to save in your workbook before exiting—such as hidden rows and columns, print settings, and filters—you can create a custom view. To do so, follow these steps:

1. Choose View, Custom Views to open the Custom Views dialog box, shown in Figure 13.6.

FIG. 13.6
You can create custom views in Excel.

2. Click the Add button to open the Add View dialog box, which Figure 13.7 illustrates.

FIG. 13.7
Specify what you want to include in your custom view.

3. Enter the Name of the view and then decide whether you want to include either or both of the Include in View options:

   - *Print Settings*. Saves the currently selected print settings with the view.
   - *Hidden Rows, Columns, and Filter Settings*. Saves the formatting of currently hidden rows and columns as well as any filters you've applied.

4. Click Close to return to your current worksheet.

To display a custom view, choose View, Custom Views. In the Custom Views dialog box select the view you want to display and click the Show button.

To delete a view, select a view in this same dialog box and click the Delete button. A message box confirms that you want to delete. Click Yes.

Viewing Multiple Worksheets and Workbooks

At times you may want to work with multiple worksheets or workbooks simultaneously.

> **CAUTION**
> Be careful about viewing too many workbooks or worksheets at once. Too much clutter can make your screen unreadable.

Part
III

Ch
13

To view multiple workbooks, follow these steps:

1. Open all the workbooks you want to view.

2. Choose Window, Arrange to open the Arrange Windows dialog box, illustrated in Figure 13.8.

FIG. 13.8
Excel offers four view styles—tiled, horizontal, vertical, and cascade.

3. Decide how you want to arrange your window. Excel offers four views:

- *Tiled*. Divides the window into tiled squares. For example, four open workbooks would display in two rows with two columns.

- *Horizontal*. Displays workbooks in horizontal rows.

- *Vertical*. Displays workbooks in vertical columns.

- *Cascade*. Layers the workbooks in overlapping rows.

4. Click OK to apply the view. Figure 13.9 illustrates a tiled view for three different workbooks.

FIG. 13.9
Viewing multiple workbooks and worksheets is easy.

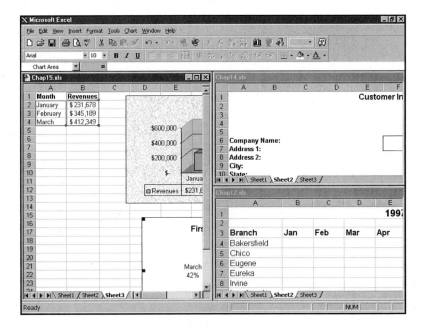

To display only one worksheet again, click the Maximize button of the worksheet you want to view.

To view multiple worksheets in the same workbook, follow these steps:

1. Open the workbook that contains the worksheet you want to view.

2. Choose Window, New Window. In the window that opens, click the tab of each worksheet you want to view.

3. Choose Window, Arrange to open the Arrange Windows dialog box.

4. Choose from the four options for arranging your worksheets: Tiled, Horizontal, Vertical, or Cascade.

5. Check the Windows of Active Workbook check box to be sure that you view only the currently selected workbook.

6. Click OK to apply the view.

The selected worksheets are arranged according to the option you chose. To change the arrangement you selected, simply apply a new arrangement. To view only one worksheet, maximize the worksheet you want to view.

Selecting and Using Ranges

In Excel 97 you can select entire worksheets or portions of worksheets including columns, rows, and ranges. To select an entire worksheet, click the rectangle that is diagonally to the left of cell A1.

 TIP Excel highlights the column and row headings of selected cells in bold text to help you easily identify selected cells and ranges.

You can also select specific rows and columns. To do so, click the row or column header. Row and column headers are the gray cells that border the active worksheet and use letters of the alphabet to represent columns and numbers to represent rows. To select nonadjacent rows and columns, press and hold down the Ctrl key as you make your selections.

Selecting Ranges

In Excel, you'll often want to group cells into ranges of data. You can select ranges with either the mouse or keyboard. To select a range of data with the mouse, select the upper-left cell in your range and drag the mouse to the lower-right cell in the range.

To select a range with the keyboard, go to the cell in the upper-left corner of the range. Press and hold down the Shift key and use the arrow keys to select the range.

Selecting Multiple Ranges

You can select more than one range of cells at a time using either the mouse or the keyboard. To use the mouse to select a multiple range of cells, click the first cell you want to include and drag the mouse over the entire range of cells. Press the Ctrl key and, while holding it down, select the other ranges in the same way. Figure 13.10 shows a worksheet with multiple ranges selected.

FIG. 13.10

You can select multiple ranges of data in Excel.

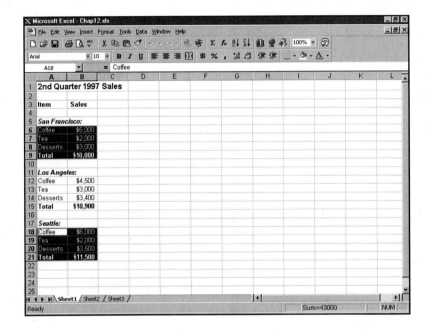

To select multiple ranges with the keyboard, follow these steps:

1. Press and hold down the Shift key and use the arrow keys to select your first range.

2. Press Shift+F8. The ADD indicator appears at the right of the status bar, letting you know that you can add additional ranges.

3. Go to the upper-left cell of the next range you want to select.

4. Press Shift and the arrow keys to select this next range. ADD disappears from the status bar, the long horizontal bar at the bottom of the screen directly above the taskbar.

5. To add additional ranges, continue to repeat steps 2 through 4.

Naming Ranges

CAUTION

Be sure that your range name starts with either a letter or underline and doesn't include any spaces. The remaining characters can be letters, numbers, periods, or underlines. Excel won't accept a range name that doesn't follow these standards.

You'll often want to name individual cells or ranges of cells for easier identification. Range names make it easier to understand how a worksheet is organized. They also are useful for referring to specific cells in a formula and for moving quickly to a specific worksheet location.

To create a range name, follow these steps:

1. Select the individual cell or range you want to name.
2. Click in the Name box on the left side of the formula bar.
3. Enter the name you want to give to the range.
4. Press Enter to save the range name.

 TIP You can also create a range name by choosing Insert, Name, Define to open the Define Name dialog box. Enter the range name in the Names in Workbook box, click the Add button and then select OK to exit.

Figure 13.11 illustrates an example naming an individual cell as Jun97_Sales.

FIG. 13.11

It's easy to name a cell or range using the name box in the formula bar.

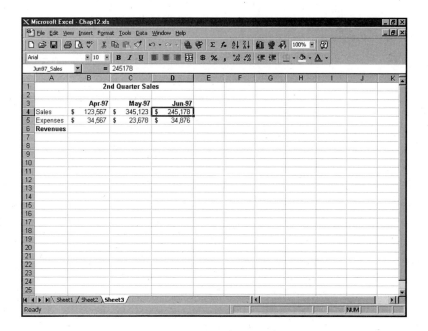

Part

III

Ch

13

Using Range Names in Formulas

Once you've created a range name, you can refer to it as you would a cell reference in a formula. For example, if you've named your sales and expense totals for June 1997 as Jun97_Sales and Jun97_Expenses, you could enter the following formula in the formula bar to determine total revenues for June 1997: =Jun97_Sales-Jun97_Expenses. Figure 13.12 illustrates this formula (see formula bar).

▶ **See** "Working with Formulas," **p. 276**

FIG. 13.12

Naming a cell or range makes creating formulas easier.

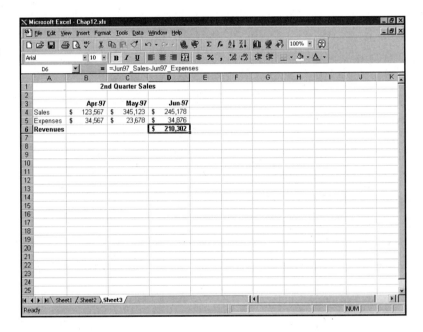

If you've created long or detailed range names, you can also enter them into formulas by using the Paste Name dialog box. To do so, follow these steps:

1. Select the cell in which you want to place your result, then enter = in the formula bar.

2. Choose Insert, Name, Paste to open the Paste Name dialog box, shown in Figure 13.13.

FIG. 13.13

Use the Paste Name dialog box to insert a range name into a formula.

3. Choose the range name you want to insert from the Paste <u>N</u>ame drop-down list.

4. Click OK to return to the formula bar.

5. Continue entering the formula, returning to the Paste Name dialog box whenever you need to select a range name.

Deleting Range Names

To delete a range name, follow these steps:

1. Choose <u>I</u>nsert, <u>N</u>ame, <u>D</u>efine to open the Define Name dialog box, shown in Figure 13.14.

FIG. 13.14
You can delete unwanted range names.

2. Select the range name to delete from the Names in <u>W</u>orkbook drop-down list.

3. Click the <u>D</u>elete button.

Filling a Range

You can, of course, manually fill a range with data or apply specific formats to it, but Excel offers two features to automate these common tasks.

Filling a Range with AutoFill

Excel's AutoFill feature lets you easily copy cell data to adjacent cells. In general, Excel copies the data exactly as it is in the original cells, but for series such as dates and numbers, Excel extends the data. For example, you could enter Jan and Feb in cells and use AutoFill to extend the remaining months. If you wanted to enter the numbers 1 through 100 in a column, you could enter the first two numbers and let AutoFill take care of the rest.

Part
III

Ch
13

 You can also combine text and numbers with AutoFill. For example, you could use AutoFill to extend Quarter 1 to Quarter 2, Quarter 3, and so on.

To use AutoFill, follow these steps:

1. Select the cells you want to copy or extend.
2. Position the mouse pointer on the handle in the lower-right of the selected area. A large plus sign appears.
3. Drag the handle to the last cell you want to fill or extend and release the mouse.

CAUTION

Be sure to drag the AutoFill handle in the lower-right corner rather than the edge of the cell, which moves data. When the AutoFill handle is active, you'll see a plus sign (+) next to it.

 T I P Holding down the Ctrl key reverses the fill effect from standard to series and vice versa. For example, in general, extending cells containing the numbers 1, 2, and 3 would extend the number series to include 4, 5, 6, and so on. Pressing Ctrl enables you to simply repeat the content of the existing cells again.

Figure 13.15 illustrates the use of AutoFill.

FIG. 13.15
With the AutoFill feature, you can automatically extend a series of data.

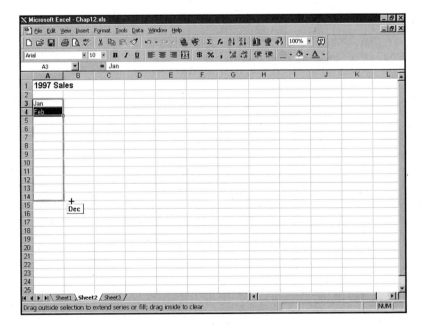

Filling Range Formats with the Format Painter

Format Painter is an Excel feature that lets you copy the formatting of a particular range of cells, but not the data itself. This is particularly useful if you've done extensive cell formatting and don't want to repeat the same steps again. To use Format Painter, follow these steps:

TIP To copy formatting to more than one additional location, double-click the Format Painter button. It remains active and continues to apply formats until you click it again.

1. Select the cells from which you want to copy the format.

2. Click the Format Painter button on the Standard toolbar. The area you've selected is surrounded by a flashing marquee.

3. Select the cells to which you want to apply the formatting and release the mouse button.

Figure 13.16 illustrates the process of using the Format Painter. The new cells take on the styles of the cells in the marquee. For example, bolding, italics, text style, and size are all copied with the Format Painter.

FIG. 13.16

Apply formatting options using the Format Painter.

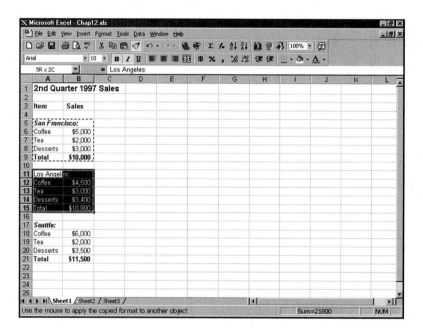

Moving, Copying, Inserting, and Deleting Ranges

Excel provides several options for manipulating ranges of data including techniques for moving, copying, inserting, and deleting.

Copying Worksheets and Worksheet Ranges

Excel makes it easy to copy worksheets and worksheet ranges. To copy an entire worksheet, follow these steps:

1. Select the sheet tab of the worksheet you want to copy.

2. Right-click the mouse and choose <u>M</u>ove or Copy from the shortcut menu. The Move or Copy dialog box appears, shown in Figure 13.17.

FIG. 13.17

Select the Create a Copy check box to copy the worksheet.

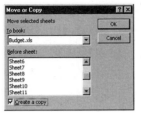

3. Select the workbook to which you want to copy the worksheet from the To Book drop-down list. Or, select (new book) to place the worksheet in a new workbook.

 TIP You can copy a worksheet only to an open workbook. Only open workbooks display in the To Book drop-down list.

4. Indicate where to place the worksheet from the Before Sheet scroll list. You can place this worksheet before any of the listed worksheets, or you can choose to move it to the end.

5. Be sure to select the Create a Copy check box. If you don't, you'll move your workbook rather than copy it.

6. Click OK to copy the sheet. Excel places a (2) after the original worksheet name. For example, if you copied a worksheet named Budget, Excel would name the copy Budget (2).

In addition to copying worksheets, you may also want to copy worksheet data. The four ways to copy data and formatting in Excel are included in the following list:

- Use the drag-and-drop method
- Copy and paste
- Use the AutoFill Method
- Use the Format Painter

Copying with Drag-and-Drop To copy using the drag-and-drop method, follow these steps:

1. Select the range of cells you want to copy.

2. Place the mouse pointer on the edge of the selected data. When the pointer changes from a large white plus sign to an arrow, press the Ctrl key. A small plus sign appears next to the mouse pointer.

3. Drag the selected cells to the new location and release the mouse.

 TIP If drag-and-drop won't work, choose Tools, Options and verify that the Allow Cell Drag and Drop check box on the Edit tab is checked.

Figure 13.18 illustrates the process of copying using drag-and-drop.

FIG. 13.18

You can see an outline of your data as you drag and drop it.

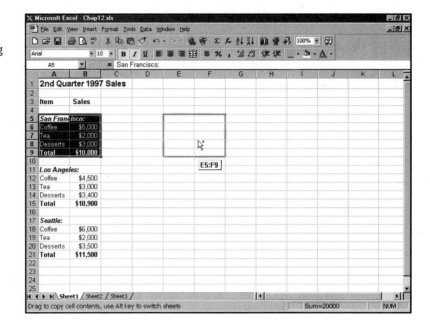

Copying with Copy and Paste   To use the copy and paste method to copy worksheet data, follow these steps:

1. Select the range of cells you want to copy.

2. Choose Edit, Copy. A flashing marquee surrounds the data you want to copy.

3. Select the cell in which you want to place the data you're copying. If you're copying a range of cells, select the upper-left cell in the new location range.

> **N O T E**   Excel provides a way for you to copy only certain characters within a cell rather than the entire contents. To do so, double-click the cell, choose the characters you want to copy either in the cell or in the formula bar, and then use the copy and paste method. ■

 You can also press Ctrl+C to copy and Ctrl+V to paste. If you make a mistake when copying data, choose Edit, Undo Paste or press Ctrl+Z. You can undo up to the last 16 actions. You can also right-click the mouse and choose Copy from the shortcut menu.

You can also right-click the mouse and choose Paste from the shortcut menu.

> **N O T E**   The marquee surrounding the data to copy remains until you press Enter or Esc. This allows you to continue copying the same data to multiple locations. ■

4. Choose Edit, Paste to paste the data in the new location.

Figure 13.19 demonstrates using copy and paste.

FIG. 13.19

Copying and pasting
data is simple in Excel.

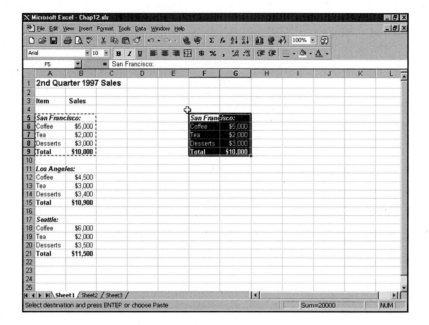

Moving Worksheets and Worksheet Ranges

Moving worksheets and range data in Excel is similar to copying. To move a worksheet, follow
these steps:

1. Select the sheet tab of the worksheet you want to move.

2. Right-click the mouse and choose <u>M</u>ove or Copy from the shortcut menu. Figure 13.20
   illustrates the Move or Copy dialog box which appears.

 You can move a worksheet only to an open workbook. Only open workbooks display in the <u>T</u>o Book
drop-down list.

FIG. 13.20

You can move a
worksheet within the
same worksheet or to a
new workbook using the
Move or Copy dialog box.

CAUTION
Don't select the Create a Copy check box. If you do, you'll copy your worksheet, not move it.

3. Select the workbook to which you want to move the selected worksheet from the To Book drop-down list. Or, select (new book) from the To Book drop-down list to place the worksheet in a new workbook. The existing workbook is the default.

4. Indicate where to place the worksheet from the Before Sheet scroll list. You can place this worksheet before any of the listed worksheets, or you can choose to move it to the end by selecting the (move to end) option in the Before Sheet scroll list.

5. Click OK to move the sheet. The sheet tab order changes based on your move.

In Excel you can move worksheet data in two ways. You can move it using the drag-and-drop method, or you can cut and paste.

Moving with Drag-and-Drop   To move worksheet data using the drag-and-drop method, follow these steps:

1. Select the data you want to move.

2. Place the mouse pointer on the edge of the selected data; an arrow appears.

3. Drag the selected cells to the new location and release the mouse.

Figure 13.21 illustrates how to use drag-and-drop to move data.

Moving with Cut and Paste   To use the cut and paste method to move worksheet data, follow these steps:

1. Select the cells you want to move.

 You can also right-click the mouse and choose Cut from the shortcut menu.

2. Choose Edit, Cut. A flashing marquee surrounds the data you want to move.

3. Select the cell to which you want to move the data. If you're copying a range of cells, select the upper-left cell in the new location range.

4. Choose Edit, Paste to paste the data in the new location. The data no longer remains in its original location; it's removed.

 You can also press Ctrl+K to cut and Ctrl+V to paste.

 If you make a mistake when moving data, choose Edit, Undo Paste.

FIG. 13.21

An arrow appears when you're ready to drag-and-drop.

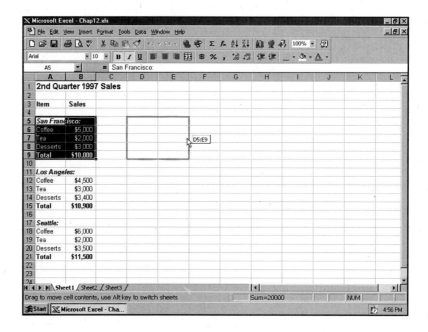

Inserting Worksheets, Columns, and Rows

To insert a new worksheet into a workbook, select Insert, Worksheet. Excel inserts a new sheet before the currently selected worksheet and automatically names it. For example, if you already have three worksheets in a workbook, Excel would name the new sheet Sheet 4 regardless of its position in the workbook.

> **CAUTION**
>
> If you don't select a sheet tab before right-clicking the mouse, the shortcut menu that displays will apply to inserting rows and columns rather than the worksheet itself.

You can also add a new worksheet by selecting a sheet tab, right-clicking the mouse, and choosing Insert from the shortcut menu. The Insert dialog box appears, shown in Figure 13.22.

Select the Worksheet icon on the General tab and click OK. Depending on the installation options you chose and the templates you've created, your Insert dialog box may vary from the one illustrated in Figure 13.22.

You can also insert new columns, rows, and cells in Excel. This ability is useful when you've already created a worksheet and decide to add additional data.

FIG. 13.22

You can insert a new worksheet using the Insert dialog box.

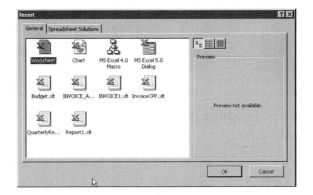

Inserting Columns   To insert a new column, select the column that occupies the location where you want to add the column. Choose Insert, Columns to insert the new column, which appears to the left of the currently selected column. You can also select the column header, right-click the mouse, and choose Insert from the shortcut menu.

 TIP To insert more than one column at a time, select the number of columns you want to insert before choosing Insert from the menu. For example, if you want to insert three columns before Column C, you would select Columns C, D, and E and then choose Insert, Columns.

Inserting Rows   To insert a new row, select the row above which you want to add the row. Choose Insert, Rows to insert the new row. You can also select the row header, right-click the mouse, and choose Insert from the shortcut menu.

 TIP To insert more than one row, select the number of rows you want to add before proceeding with insertion.

Inserting Cells   To insert new cells in a worksheet, select the cell or cell range where you want to insert and choose Insert, Cells. The Insert dialog box appears, illustrated in Figure 13.23.

 TIP You can also insert a new cell by selecting where you want to insert, right-clicking the mouse, and choosing Insert from the shortcut menu to open the Insert dialog box.

FIG. 13.23

Excel provides several options for inserting data.

Part
III

Ch
13

This dialog box gives you the following options for inserting new cells:

- *Shift Cells Right*. Inserts new cells to the left of the selection.
- *Shift Cells Down*. Inserts news cells above the selection.
- *Entire Row*. Inserts a new row.
- *Entire Column*. Inserts a new column.

Deleting Worksheets, Columns, and Rows

At times you'll want to delete the worksheets and data in your Excel workbooks. You may have made a mistake, the data is no longer needed or valid, or you simply want to reorganize how you've presented your data.

> **CAUTION**
>
> Choosing Edit, Delete only deletes rows, columns, and data, not the entire sheet.

Deleting Worksheets　To delete a worksheet from a workbook, select the worksheet tab and choose Edit, Delete Sheet. Figure 13.24 displays the warning box that appears.

Click OK to continue with the deletion or Cancel to cancel it.

FIG. 13.24
A warning box appears when you delete a worksheet.

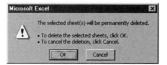

Deleting Columns　To delete a column, select the column header of the column or columns you want to delete and choose Edit, Delete. The remaining columns move to the left. You can also select the column header, right-click the mouse, and choose Delete from the shortcut menu.

Deleting Rows　To delete rows, choose the row header of the row or rows you want to delete and choose Edit, Delete. The remaining rows move up. You can also select the row header, right-click the mouse, and choose Delete from the shortcut menu.

Deleting Ranges　To delete specific cells from a worksheet, select the cells and choose Edit, Delete. This opens the Delete dialog box, illustrated in Figure 13.25.

FIG. 13.25
There are several deletion options for deleting worksheet cells.

T I P You can also delete cells by selecting them, right-clicking the mouse, and choosing Delete from the shortcut menu to open the Delete dialog box.

This dialog box gives you the following deletion options:

- *Shift Cells Left*. Moves existing cells to the left of the deleted cells.
- *Shift Cells Up*. Moves existing cells up.
- *Entire Row*. Deletes the selected row or rows.
- *Entire Column*. Deletes the selected column or columns.

Using Reference Operators

In Excel, you'll want to be able to combine ranges of cells for use in calculations and formulas. *Reference operators* let you determine how to group cells or ranges in these calculations.

Table 13.1 lists the reference operators you can use.

Table 13.1   Reference Operators

Operator	Description
: (colon)	Defines a range, encompassing all cells between and including the two referenced cells
, (comma)	Defines a union, combining multiple references into one
single space	Defines an intersection, which calculates one result for cells included in both references

For example, SUM(B12:B15) would sum the range of cells between B12 and B15—B12, B13, B14, and B15. SUM(B12:B15,C5) would sum all the cells between and including B12 and B15 as well as cell C5.

Intersections are a bit more complicated. SUM(A1:A5 A4:A9) would find the cells included in both references (A4 and A5) and sum only those two cells. ●

Part

III

Ch

13

CHAPTER 14

Formulas and Functions

by Joe Habraken

Formulas and functions are used to perform calculations in your Excel 97 worksheets. Formulas are the calculations that you build yourself using cell addresses and mathematical operators such as + (addition). Functions are the built-in formulas that Excel provides for use in basic (such as the Sum function) to very sophisticated calculations (like the IF function). Excel provides the ability to copy and move formulas and functions and use range names in your calculations. Excel even provides you with array formulas and functions that can calculate a range of results based on several different cell addresses. ■

New features

Excel 97 offers many new formula and function features that both simplify and enhance the calculations you do in your worksheets.

Creating your own formulas

Building formulas in Excel can be easy; you can use the point method for entering cells addresses, while features like copy and move allow you to re-use your formulas in the same worksheet or copy them to another workbook.

Using range names, links, and arrays

You can simplify complex calculations by using range names to refer to cell groupings in your formulas and functions.

Auditing your worksheet

Once you've created your formulas and used Excel functions for your worksheet calculations, you can identify the cells involved in the formulas and functions and troubleshoot your calculations using the Excel Audit toolbar.

Using Excel functions

You can use functions to calculate sums and averages and even use functions, like the IF statement, that give you results based on conditions that you set.

Overview of New Features

Excel 97 provides a number of new features that make working with formulas and functions a very straightforward process. These enhancements include:

- *Formula Palette.* This new tool provides you with help in editing formulas that contain an Excel function. Select the cell that holds the formula and then click on the Edit Formula button on the Excel Formula Bar The Formula Palette will appear detailing the type of function you are using and the cell ranges involved. Use the Palette to edit the cell ranges or get additional help from the Office Assistant.

- *Paste function.* With the help of the Office Assistant, you can enter a text description of the type of function you want to use to return a calculation and Excel will suggest the formula that you should use in Excel's Paste function dialog box. Open the Paste function dialog box and then click the Office Assistant button for help.

- *Range Finder.* When you edit a formula or function in Excel, the cells and ranges associated with the formula or function will be highlighted.

- *Natural-language formulas.* You can use your column and row headings to designate cells in a formula. For instance, a cell could be designated by East Total, where East would be the Row heading and Total would be the column title for the total value that was entered for the East region.

Two other improvements found in Excel 97 aren't directly related to formulas and functions but may also help you design fool-proof calculations in your worksheets. Data validation allows you to specify what type of data goes in a particular cell, such as text, whole numbers, or dates. Placing restrictions on cell data entry can assure that your formulas will return correct values. The Auditing Toolbar also provides a Circle Invalid Data button that will find any invalid data entered in your spreadsheet cells.

Taking advantage of these improvements requires a basic understanding of how formulas and functions do their jobs in an Excel worksheet. Formulas in particular can be tricky because you must design them yourself.

Working with Formulas

A *formula* is an expression or equation that you design to perform calculations in your Excel worksheets. You can use your formulas to add, subtract, multiply, and divide the numerical values that you place in the worksheet cells. You can also design formulas that will complete more complex calculations. In many cases, however, you will find that Excel provides a built-in function that will handle more difficult calculations like mortgage payments, or conditional statements, or complex statistics like a linear trend.

A good rule to follow is to create your own formulas only when Excel does not provide a function that will do the same job. You can usually limit your formula writing to include simple math like subtraction, multiplication, and division.

The real beauty of Excel formulas is the fact that you can design them so that they do their calculations on the contents of cells. You do this by specifying the cell address in the formula. That way you can change the values in the cells that are involved in the formula without needing to edit the formula.

Some people use this technique for "what if" analysis. For instance, you can set up an Excel spreadsheet using the PMT function that can show you the monthly payment for a car at different car prices and loan interest rates. In effect, you are saying what if the car is 20,000 and the interest rate is 8 percent? Can I afford the calculated monthly payment? Each time you type a different interest rate into the interest rate cell or a different car price in the price cell, you are analyzing the potential monthly payment; each set of values returns a different payment amount. You are using "what if."

The formulas that you enter into your worksheets will consist of cell references and the appropriate operators. When you enter a formula into a spreadsheet it must always start with an equal sign (=). This tells Excel that the information in the cell is an equation and will return a value. The most commonly used operators are shown here:

Operator	Performs	Examples
+	Addition	=A1+B1
−	Subtraction	=A1–B1
*	Multiplication	=A1*C12
/	Division	=A1/B3
*	Exponentiation	=A*12

You can also combine operations in one formula using parentheses such as (A1+B1)/C1. These compound formulas can be a little trickier than a straightforward addition or subtraction formula (see "Understanding and Controlling Operator Precedence" for more information on operator use).

You can enter your formulas into your worksheet two different ways: You can enter the formula including the cell references via the keyboard; or you can use the mouse to point to the cells that will be involved in the formula.

For instance, you may have a worksheet that contains two columns of numerical data (see Figure 14.1). One column holds the total sales (in dollars) achieved for the year by each of your regional salespersons. The second column contains the commission percentage that you pay each person (the commission is different for each employee because commission is based on the number of years of employment with the company). With Excel, it is easy to calculate the actual dollar amount of the commissions that you will have to pay out to each person.

The formula will be:

total sales×commission percentage = commission amount

Part

III

Ch

14

FIG. 14.1

This spreadsheet requires a simple multiplication formula to return the dollar amount of the commission that will be paid to each of the sales staff.

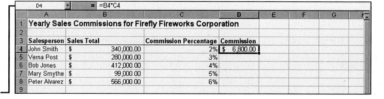

To type the multiplication formula into the worksheet:

1. Click the cell in which you want to place the formula (D4).

2. Type the formula—in this case, **=B4*C4**.

3. Press Enter to enter the formula in the cell. The actual value that the formula calculates will appear in the cell. The formula itself will appear on the Formula Bar as shown in Figure 14.2.

> **TIP** The numeric keypad on your keyboard provides you with the easiest access to the math operators that you will use in your formulas (*, +, /, and so on). Make sure that your Num Lock is on before you try to use the keypad.

FIG. 14.2

The formula multiplies the total sales by the commission percentage and calculates the commission amount.

Formula Bar —

You can also create your formula using the point-and-click method to identify the cells that you want to include in the expression. We'll use the spreadsheet shown in Figure 14.2 for this example:

1. Click the cell in which you want to place the formula (D5).

2. Type = (equal sign).

3. Click the first cell you want to appear in the expression (B5), then type * (multiplication sign).

4. Click the second cell you want to appear in the expression (C5). Then click the Enter icon on the Formula Bar. The formula will be placed in the cell and display the result of the calculation.

> **TIP** Using the point method to select the cells that will appear in a specific formula can help cut down on incorrect cell references and typographical errors in your formulas.

You can also use the methods described previously to create addition, subtraction, and division formulas. All you have to do is make sure that you reference the correct cells and use the appropriate operator.

You will find that you need to create your own formulas for many simple situations such as subtraction, multiplication and division. For more complex equations you will want to use one of Excel's built-in functions. Refer to the section "Understanding and Using functions" later in this chapter.

Understanding and Controlling Operator Precedence

Designing your own formulas requires that you understand the natural order of math calculations or operator precedence. Order of precedence is a set of rules for carrying out calculations, meaning that certain operations must be carried out before others. Excel follows the order of precedence rules and they are especially important for formulas that contain more than one operator.

For instance, in the formula A2+B2*C2, the multiplication sign takes precedence over the addition sign. This means that B2 will be multiplied by C2 and then A2 will be added to their product. The order of precedence operations is the following:

Order	Operator	Symbol in Excel
1	Exponent	*
2	Multiplication	*
	Division	/
3	Addition	+
	Subtraction	−

So, in the formula A2*B2 + C23, the first operation calculated will be C2 raised to the third power, the second will be A2*B2, and the third will be the product of the multiplication cells A2 and B2 added to the exponentiation of C2.

When a formula contains more than one operator of the same type or precedence value, Excel computes the result from left to right. In the formula A2*A3/A4 the multiplication and division operators have the same precedence value. So Excel will multiply A2 by A3 and then divide the result by A4.

You can control operator precedence in your formulas using parentheses. Operations enclosed in parentheses take precedence over operations that are not. In the formula (A1+A2)*B2, the parenthetical calculation takes precedence over the multiplication operator. So, A1 and A2 will be added and their sum will then be multiplied by B2.

Part
III

Ch

14

 TIP A good way to test your understanding of the order of precedence is to create several formulas on paper that use numerical values rather than cell references. For instance, 5*5+2 will return the result 27, while the formula 5*(5+2) returns the result 35.

Keeping the rules of operator precedence in mind when working in Excel will help you design formulas that do not return unexpected or unusual results. Remember that you can use the parentheses to change the natural order of calculations in any formula that you create.

Understanding and Using Functions

Functions are the ready-made formulas that are built into Microsoft Excel. Excel functions exist for almost every type of calculation; there are financial functions, statistical functions, logical functions—even database functions.

Functions can do everything from add a range of numbers, to count the number of entries in the range, to provide you with a conditional statement that can return an either/or result depending on the particular value in each cell of the range.

A function consists of two parts: the name of the function and the range of cells that you want the function to act upon. For instance, the function =AVERAGE(B4:B8) will give the average of the cells in the range B4 to B8.

 TIP   Functions are built to calculate simple and complex equations. It is a good idea to use functions whenever you can; you can count on a function returning the correct answer, while formulas that you design yourself can potentially be incorrect.

Table 14.1 gives you a list of a number of the Excel function categories, example functions from the category, and the purpose of the function.

Table 14.1   Excel Function Categories

Category	Function	Purpose
Financial	PMT	Calculates loan payments.
	PV	Calculates current value of an investment.
Date and Time	NOW	Returns the current date.
	WEEKDAY	Identifies a text day entry by a number 1–7.
Math and Trig	COS	Calculates the cosine of an angle.
	EVEN	Rounds a number to the nearest integer.
Statistical	AVERAGE	Calculates the average for a range of cells.
	COUNT	Counts the number of cells with entries in a particular range.

Category	Function	Purpose
Database	DMIN	Returns the smallest number in a column of cells.
	DMAX	Returns the largest number in a column of cells.
Logical	IF	Returns a true or false answer to a conditional statement.

Obviously, the category or categories of functions that you use most often will depend on the type of worksheets you develop. If you are involved in a tree population study in the Amazon rainforest, you would probably use a number of the statistical functions. If most of your spreadsheets are used to track loans and investments, you will use the financial functions.

Commonly Used Functions

You will find that while Excel offers a great number of functions for your use, you will probably end up using only a small number of those available. The most commonly used Excel function is the SUM function; this function adds a specified range of cells:

=SUM(cell range)

Other commonly used functions are described in Table 14.2:

Table 14.2 Commonly Used Excel Functions

Function	Example	Description
AVERAGE	=AVERAGE(cell range)	Calculates the statistical mean or average for the range of numbers.
COUNT	=COUNT(cell range)	Counts all the cells in a specified range.
MAX	=MAX(cell range)	Returns the maximum (largest) value in the specified range of cells.
MIN	=MIN(cell range)	Returns the minimum (smallest) value in the specified range of cells.
PMT	=PMT(interest rate cell, # of payments cell, loan value cell)	Calculates the periodic payment of a loan with a fixed term and a fixed interest rate.
IF	=IF(logical test, true value, false value)	Evaluates a conditional statement to either true or false. Being equal to or less than a certain number (<=50) may be the conditional statement and the actual value returned to the cell will depend on the True/False values you specify.

continues

Part

III

Ch

14

Table 14.2 Continued

Function	Example	Description
COUNTIF	COUNTIF*(range,criteria)*	Counts the cells in a range that meet the function criteria. For instance, you could establish the criteria. The function will then return a count of only the cells in the designated range that have a value of less than 5000.
HLOOKUP	HLOOKUP*(lookup_value, table_array,row_index_num, range_lookup)*	Enables you to look up information in a data table based on a row of values in the worksheet. A lookup value could be the total sales for a particular region. This value is then cross-referenced in the designated lookup table (the table array and row index number). The value found in the lookup table is returned to the cell holding the HLOOKUP function.
VLOOKUP	VLOOKUP*(lookup_value, table_array,row_index_num, range_lookup)*	Enables you to look up information in a data table based on a column of values in the worksheet. VLOOKUP functions the same as HLOOKUP and will return a value from a lookup table based on a lookup value (a particular cell in the spreadsheet).
COUNTA	=COUNTA*(cell range)*	Counts all the cells in a range that hold data, including numerical and text entries. COUNTA differs from COUNT in that COUNT only counts the cells in a range holding numerical information.
HYPERLINK	HYPERLINK*(link_location)*	Specifies the location and file name of an object linked to a particular cell in an Excel worksheet. The hyperlink can consist of a Microsoft Word document, another Excel spreadsheet, or any OLE-compliant object.
ROUND	=COUNTA*(cell range)*	Counts all the cells in a range that hold data, including numerical and text entries. COUNTA differs from COUNT in that COUNT only counts the cells in a range holding numerical information.

Function	Example	Description
NOW	=NOW	Returns the numeric value of the current date. Each day is assigned a number with January 1, 1900, serving as the start point. This numeric system of returning the date allows you to use dates in formulas. To format the NOW numerical value, use the Date format.
RANK	=RANK(number,ref,order)	Assigns a ranking number to the value in a particular cell based on the other values in the range of cells (ref) specified. The order can be set at descending by placing a zero in the order position of the function. To set the order to ascending, use the number 1.
ROUND	=ROUND(number,num_digits)	Rounds a value to a particular number of digits. For instance, ROUND would take the value 2.16 and round it to 2.2 if the number of digits (num digits) specified in the function is set to 1, meaning you want to round the number to the first decimal place.

When you enter functions into an Excel worksheet, you can type the function into a cell, specifying the function name and the range of cells you want the function to act upon, or you can use function entry tools like AutoSum and Paste function. Both of these features are available as buttons on Excel's standard toolbar.

 TIP If you want a truly exhaustive list of Excel functions, refer to Que's *Special Edition Using Microsoft Excel 97, Best Seller Edition.*

Using AutoSum

 SUM is definitely the most used Excel function. Cognizant of this fact, Microsoft has placed a button on the Excel Standard toolbar called AutoSum.

AutoSum is particularly useful in that it will try to anticipate the range of cells that you want to add. Use the AutoSum in a cell at the bottom of a column of cells you want to add, and AutoSum automatically selects the cells above it for inclusion in the SUM range. AutoSum will also select the range of cells to add when you use it to place the SUM formula to the right of a row of cells.

Part
III

Ch
14

To total a range of numbers using AutoSum:

1. Click the cell where you want to place the SUM function.

2. Click the AutoSum button. The SUM function will be entered in the cell, and a possible range of cells to be totaled will be designated by a marquee box as shown in Figure 14.3.

FIG. 14.3

The AutoSum button provides you with a quick way to add a range of numbers in your worksheet.

AutoSum button

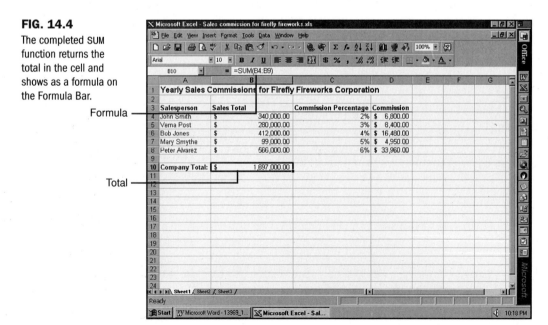

3. If the cell range selected by AutoSum is the correct range, press Enter to complete the formula. If the cell range is incorrect, use the mouse to select the correct range of cells, then press Enter to place the function in the current cell. A completed SUM function is shown in Figure 14.4.

FIG. 14.4

The completed SUM function returns the total in the cell and shows as a formula on the Formula Bar.

Formula

Total

4. If you want to edit the range in the function, select the cell holding the function. Use the mouse to select the new cell range then click the Enter icon on the Formula Bar, or press Enter.

The result of the formula or function appears in the cell and the formula or function appears on the Formula Bar. You can edit any formula or function by double-clicking in the cell and editing the equation in the cell, or by clicking in the Formula Bar and editing the equation there.

Entering Functions Using Paste Function

Excel gives you access to a very large number of functions. The easiest way to insert these functions into your worksheets is via the Paste function button on the Standard toolbar. Once the function itself is inserted into a particular cell, it is up to you to provide the cell addresses that the function will act upon.

To insert a function into your worksheet:

1. Click the cell you want to place the function in, and then click Paste function. The Paste function dialog box appears as shown in Figure 14.5.

FIG. 14.5

The Paste function dialog box allows you to view and select functions by category.

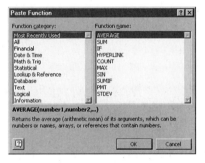

2. The Paste function dialog box is divided into two panes. Click the Category pane to view the functions in each category, which appear in the Name pane.

 TIP Excel keeps track of your most recently used functions. Click Most Recently Used in the Category Pane and then select the function you want to use from the Name pane.

3. When you've found the function that you want to use, select it in the Name pane. A short description of the function appears at the bottom of the Paste dialog box.

4. To paste the selected function into the worksheet, click OK. The function will be pasted into the cell and the Formula Palette appears.

The Formula Palette shows the range of cells that the function selected for use (not all functions will designate a possible range) and provides you with information on the function. The function result based on the current range of cells is also listed in the Formula Palette (see Figure 14.6).

Part
III

Ch
14

FIG. 14.6

The Formula Palette appears when you paste a function into your spreadsheet. It's designed to help you build foolproof formulas.

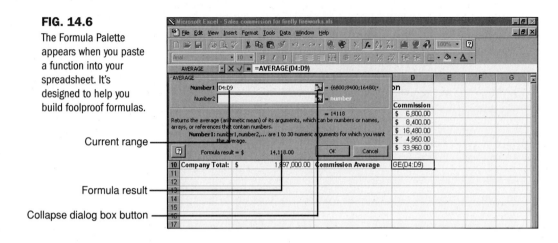

Current range

Formula result

Collapse dialog box button

 T I P The Formula Palette also provides a function button at the top of the dialog box that you can use to change the currently selected function.

---

5. To change the current range, click the Collapse dialog box button next to the range box. The Formula Palette will collapse, allowing you to see your worksheet. Select the appropriate range of cells for the function, then press Enter or click the Enter button on the Formula Bar.

6. The Formula Palette re-appears showing the newly selected range and the new result of the function based on the range. If the range is correct, click the OK button. The function is inserted into the cell and the result is returned.

Getting Help with a Function

To get help with a function, follow these steps:

1. If you need more help with a particular function when you are in the Paste function dialog box, click the Office Assistant button in the Paste function dialog box. The Office Assistant appears, as shown in Figure 14.7.

2. In the Office Assistant's balloon click Help with this Feature. For help specific to the currently selected function, click Help with Selected Function in the balloon.

3. The Excel Help system opens a page with specific help on the selected function. When you're finished with the Help page, close it and return to the Excel window, where you can paste the selected function into your worksheet.

N O T E You can also insert functions via the Insert menu. Choose Insert, Function. ▪

FIG. 14.7

Use the Office Assistant to get more information about the Paste function feature or for specific functions.

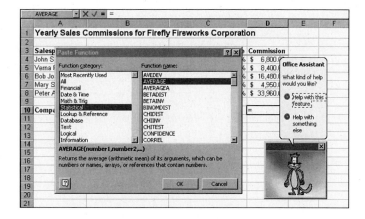

Copying and Moving Formulas and Functions

You can copy and move formulas and functions in your Excel worksheets using several different tools such as the Edit menu, various toolbar buttons, and the Excel Fill handle. Because many of your worksheets are designed to give you comparative data on sales figures, stock performances, or population growth over time, being able to copy formulas and functions can save you time typing or inserting the same formula or function over and over again.

For instance, the worksheet shown in Figure 14.8 details the sales performance of a particular company's sales force. The worksheet also computes the commission that each sales representative will receive for the year. While the sales total and commission rate (a percentage) are different for each salesperson, the formula that you use to compute their commission will be the same.

FIG. 14.8

The formula used to compute the commission for each of the sales people will be the same.

	A	B	C	D
1	Yearly Sales Commissions for Firefly Fireworks Corporation			
2				
3	Salesperson	Sales Total	Commission Percentage	Commission
4	John Smith	$ 340,000.00	2%	$ 6,800.00
5	Verna Post	$ 280,000.00	3%	
6	Bob Jones	$ 412,000.00	4%	
7	Mary Smythe	$ 99,000.00	5%	
8	Peter Alvarez	$ 566,000.00	6%	
9				
10	Company Total:	$ 1,697,000.00		
11				
12				
13				

The only difference in the formula is that John Smith's commission is computed by =B4*B4, and Verna Post's is computed by =B5*B5. The formula is exactly the same—only the cell references differ.

Part
III

Ch
14

Excel allows you to copy the formula from D4 (John's commission) to D5 (Verna's commission) and still get the correct answer because of the way Excel sees the formula. Excel sees the formula as, "Multiply the two cells that are to the left of this formula." So when you copy the formula to other cells where you want to compute the same type of answer, Excel adjusts the cell references in the formula to take into account the formula's new location.

The ability of Excel to change the cell addresses in a formula when you copy it is called *relative cell referencing*. Excel adjusts the cell references depending on where you copy the formula.

The easiest way to copy a formula that will adjust to its new location because of relative cell referencing is to use the Fill handle:

1. Click the cell that holds the formula or function you want to copy. In the lower right-hand corner of the cell box, a small black handle will appear. This is the Fill handle.

2. Drag the Fill handle to select the cells to which you want to copy the formula as shown in Figure 14.9.

3. When you release the mouse button, the formula or function will be pasted into the selected cells and the cells will be highlighted. Click in any cell to deselect the cells.

FIG. 14.9

Drag the Fill handle to select the cells to which you want to copy the formula.

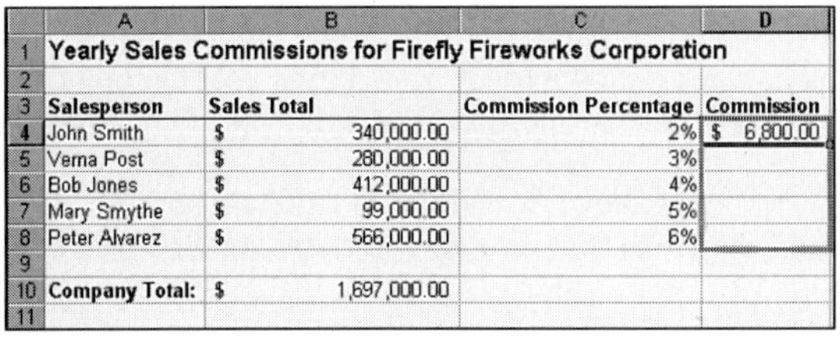

	A	B	C	D
1	Yearly Sales Commissions for Firefly Fireworks Corporation			
2				
3	Salesperson	Sales Total	Commission Percentage	Commission
4	John Smith	$ 340,000.00	2%	$ 6,800.00
5	Verna Post	$ 280,000.00	3%	
6	Bob Jones	$ 412,000.00	4%	
7	Mary Smythe	$ 99,000.00	5%	
8	Peter Alvarez	$ 566,000.00	6%	
9				
10	Company Total:	$ 1,697,000.00		
11				

You will notice that when you click the cells to which you pasted the formula, Excel has adjusted the cell references so that the formula returns the correct answer. The Fill handle works very well for copying formulas across columns or down rows that hold similar data.

In some worksheets, you will design formulas or use functions where you do not want all of the cells referenced in the formula to adjust to their new location. In fact, if the cell reference does change, your formula or function will no longer return the correct answer. To keep a cell address from changing as you copy the formula to a new location, you must make the cell address an *absolute reference*. This tells Excel not to use relative referencing on that particular cell address in the formula.

A good example of absolute referencing would be a worksheet where you are calculating your sales force's yearly commission and all the commissions are figured using just one percentage rate (cell B12) as shown in Figure 14.10. The formula used to compute the total commission would be =B4*$B$12. The absolute referenced cell is designated by typing a $ in front of the column designation and a $ in front of the row designation.

N O T E   When you place a cell address in a formula or function, you can make it an absolute reference by pressing the F4 function key. Excel will place the $ sign before the column and row designations. ▮

Once you've correctly entered the formula using the absolute reference, you can use the Fill handle to copy the formula to other cells as detailed earlier in this section.

CAUTION

A value contained in a single cell that is referenced in a formula or function that you copy to multiple locations on the spreadsheet must be designated as an absolute reference. Otherwise, the copied formula will adjust to its new location and incorrectly reference a cell other than the cell you specified in the original formula or function.

 T I P   Financial functions such as PMT will require you to use absolute referencing if you want to calculate payments for a particular loan amount at different interest rates. Because the loan amount does not change, the cell holding this information must be an absolute reference.

FIG. 14.10

To copy some formulas and functions, you must make sure that you've designated which cell addresses in the formula should be absolute references.

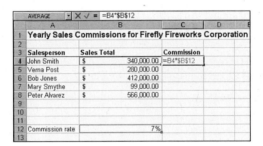

Copying and Pasting a Formula

You can also use the copy and paste commands to copy a formula or function to another location or locations. To copy a formula from one cell to another:

1. Click the cell that holds the formula or function you want to copy. Click the Copy button on the Standard toolbar.

2. A selection marquee will appear around the cell as shown in Figure 14.11. Click in the cell that you want to copy the formula to and click the Paste button.

3. To copy the formula to several cells, select the cells and then click Paste. When you are finished pasting, press the Esc key to remove the selection marquee from the copied cell.

 T I P   Use Ctrl+C to copy a cell's contents and Ctrl+V to paste the contents into another cell(s).

Part

III

Ch

14

FIG. 14.11

A selection marquee will appear around cells that you copy.

Yearly Sales Commissions for Firefly Fireworks Corporation			
Salesperson	Sales Total	Commission	
John Smith	$ 340,000.00	$ 23,800.00	
Verna Post	$ 280,000.00		
Bob Jones	$ 412,000.00		
Mary Smythe	$ 99,000.00		
Peter Alvarez	$ 586,000.00		

————Selected cell

Moving a Formula or Function

You can also move a formula or function from one cell to another in Excel. This is particularly useful if you've inadvertently placed a formula in the wrong cell. Moving a formula or function does not change the cell references in the formula; they remain the same as when you input them during the creation of the formula. You will remember that the Fill handle and the copy command change the cell references in the formula to relate to their new location.

Moving a formula or function in Excel is mouse work. To move a formula or function:

1. Click the cell that holds the formula or function you want to move.

2. Place the mouse pointer on any of the selected cell's border. The mouse pointer will become an arrow.

CAUTION

Do not inadvertently drag the Fill handle of the formula cell you want to move. This will copy the formula to the new location instead of moving it.

3. Drag the formula cell to the new location and then release the mouse. The formula or function has been moved.

 To move a formula or function from one worksheet to another in a workbook, hold down the Alt key when dragging the formula. You access the other worksheets by dragging the formula onto the appropriate worksheet tab.

 To move a formula or function via the keyboard, press Ctrl+X to cut the cell contents and Ctrl+V to paste it into another cell.

Using Range Names

Range names can be used to specify a range of cells in an Excel formula or function. You've already worked with range names in Chapter 13. Naming a range of cells is just a matter of selecting the cell range and then choosing Insert, Name to create the range's name.

Using range names in your formulas not only saves you time as you design your formulas, but it will also help make sure that you designated the correct range in your formula or function.

TIP You will find that you will use Range names more often in Excel functions, which usually act on a number of cells to return an answer.

To use a range name in a function:

1. Click the cell that will hold the function. Click the Paste button. Select the function in the Paste dialog box and then click OK.

2. The Formula Palette will appear, and the range in its range box will be selected. To designate a range name as the range in the function, choose Insert, Name, Paste. The Paste Name dialog box appears as shown in Figure 14.12.

3. Select the range name you want to use in the function and then click OK in the Paste Name dialog box. The range name appears in the Formula Palette.

4. To complete the function, click OK in the Formula Palette. The completed function will return the appropriate answer in the designated cell.

To use a range name in a formula:

1. Click the cell that will hold the formula. Begin your formula with =.

2. When you are ready to designate a cell range for the formula to act upon, choose Insert, Name, Paste. The Paste Name dialog box appears.

3. Select the range name you want to use in the formula and then click OK. The range name will be placed in the formula; add the appropriate operators or other cell addresses or range names and then press Enter to complete the formula.

FIG. 14.12
The Paste Name dialog box lists all the range names that you have defined for the current workbook.

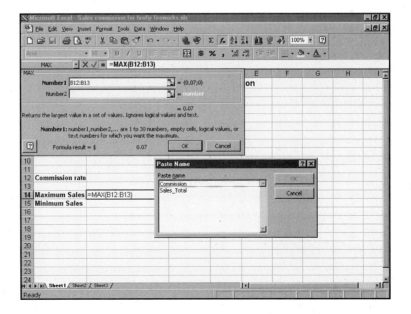

Using Arrays

An *array formula* is a single formula that can produce multiple results. An array formula does this by operating on a group of cells containing arguments or values and returning the answers to the equation to another group of cells.

For instance, you may want to create one formula to compute the payment that you would make on a new car at different interest rates. One array formula (using Excel's PMT function) could be created to show the payments at different interest rates; the array formula would do this by referencing an *array constant*, which is the group of cells that hold the different interest rates that the PMT function would use in its calculations.

Cells that share an array formula are called an *array range*. In Figure 14.13, the array range is the cells where the various payments on the car based on the different interest rates appear.

Array formulas can be very useful in that you only have to design one formula or set up one function to get multiple results. This can cut down the need to troubleshoot multiple formulas later.

To create an array formula using an Excel function:

1. Select the array range (the cells that will hold the array formula) as shown in Figure 14.14.

2. Use the Paste Insert button to open the Paste function dialog box. Select the function you want to use and then click OK.

FIG. 14.13

The array range is the cells where the various car payments appear.

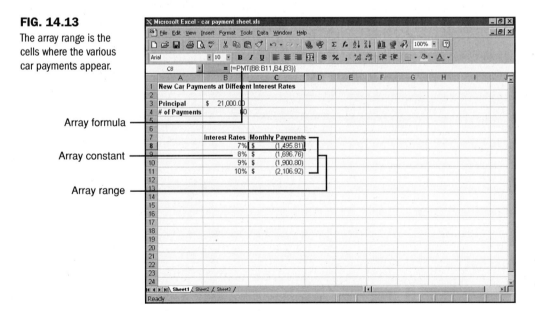

FIG. 14.14

Select the cells (the array range) in which you want to place the array formula.

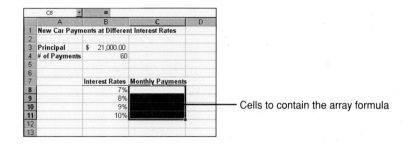

Cells to contain the array formula

3. The Formula Palette will open displaying the various ranges that must be entered to complete the formula. To specify the array constant, select the range of cells that hold the constant values as shown in Figure 14.15.

4. Enter any other cell addresses or ranges required by the Excel function in the Formula Palette and then click OK to close the Formula Palette. The array formula will only appear in the first cell of the array range.

5. To complete the array formula, click in the Formula Bar next to the right of the formula. Press Ctrl+Shift+Enter. The array formula appears in all the cells of the array range as shown in Figure 14.16. Click in any worksheet cell to deselect the array range.

You will notice that an array formula has braces around it. This signifies the fact that it is a formula that is shared by an array range of cells.

FIG. 14.15

The array constant is the range of cells that hold the constant values you will use in the array formula.

Constant values

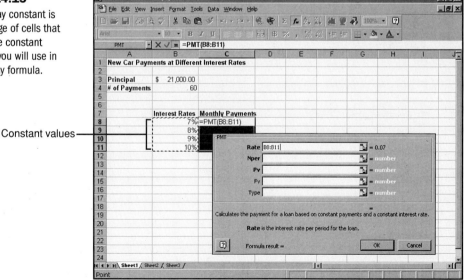

FIG. 14.16

The array formula appears in each of the cells in the array range.

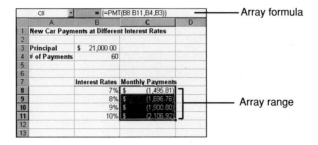

You can also use array formulas when you must create a formula from scratch, such as a simple formula for multiplication or division.

1. Select the cells in the array range.

2. Type = to begin the formula. Enter operators and cell addresses as you would for any other formula.

3. When you need to enter the array constant range, select the range with the mouse.

4. When you've complete the array formula, press Ctrl+Shift+Enter. The array formula appears in the cells of the array range. Click anywhere in the worksheet to deselect the array range.

You can create array formulas from any formulas that you normally design, or from any of Excel's functions. You can even create compound array formulas where the constant range of the array formula consists of the return from another formula or Excel function.

Using Links

Excel provides you with the ability to link to data that resides outside of the current worksheet. This data can be on another worksheet in the current workbook or in an entirely different workbook (for more about workbooks and worksheets, see Chapter 13). Links can also be made to external data on company intranets or even the Internet.

You can use links to pull data into a worksheet so you don't have to re-enter the information. Using links in your worksheets can be particularly useful when you are building formulas and functions that summarize information contained on other worksheets or in other workbooks.

For instance, a company may have used a different worksheet each quarter to track their profits and losses. This means that four spreadsheets would be created for each year, one every three months.

Using links, you can pull data from the four quarterly reports and use them in formulas and functions on an end-of-year summary worksheet. You can use linked data as values in cells or place the link directly into a formula.

To create a link to external data:

1. Select the cell where you will place the linked data.

2. Type = to begin the link. If the data is on another worksheet in the same workbook, click the tab for that sheet or open the other workbook. Click the cell to which you want to link.

3. Press Enter. You will be returned to the worksheet and cell that holds the new link. The cell will show the data from the link as shown in Figure 14.17.

FIG. 14.17

Linked data will appear in the cell as data, while appearing as a link formula in the Formula Bar.

Linked formula ──

Linked data ──

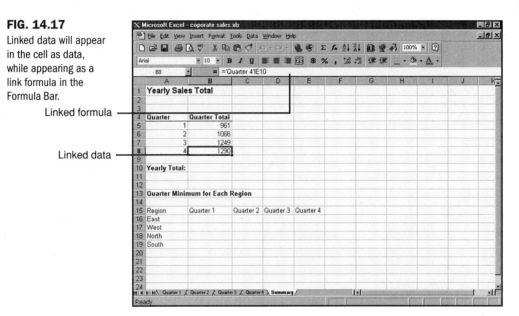

The great thing about linked data is that if you change the data in the cell to which you have linked, the link will update itself the next time you open the workbook containing the link.

The real power of links is unleashed when you use them in your formulas and functions. Data from several different worksheets or workbooks can conceivably be included in the same formula or function.

Placing a link in a formula is very similar to placing a link in a cell.

1. Begin the formula with =. To insert a link, go to the worksheet that holds the data, select the cell(s), and then return to the worksheet that holds the formula you are building.

2. Place the appropriate operator or operators in the formula. If you need to add another link, go to the worksheet holding the information that you want to link to the formula and select the appropriate cell or cells.

Part
III

Ch
14

T I P Use the worksheet tabs to move from worksheet to worksheet within a workbook. If you need to switch to another open workbook, open the Window menu and select the appropriate workbook file.

3. When you complete the formula, press Enter. The result of the formula appears in the formula cell. If you want to view the links in the formula, you can view them in the Formula Bar.

Links can also be used in Excel functions. To place a link in a function:

1. Use the Paste Insert button to open the Paste function dialog box. Select the function you want to use and then click OK.

2. The Formula Palette opens, displaying the various ranges that must be entered to complete the formula. To use a link for one of the function ranges, go to the worksheet that holds the cell or cell range for the link.

3. The Formula Palette will accompany you to the worksheet. Select the cell or cells for the link as shown in Figure 14.18. The cell range appears in the Formula Palette. If you need to enter more cell addresses or ranges to complete the function, return to the worksheet where you are building the function and continue.

4. If the linked cell or range completes the function, click OK in the Formula Palette. The completed function appears in your worksheet and returns the appropriate answer. The actual function with the link appears in the Formula Bar (see Figure 14.19).

T I P Another easy way to link to data on other worksheets is by using the range names that you created for cells and ranges on the particular worksheet.

FIG. 14.18

The Formula Palette will be available in the worksheet you want to use for the function link; select the cell(s) for the link.

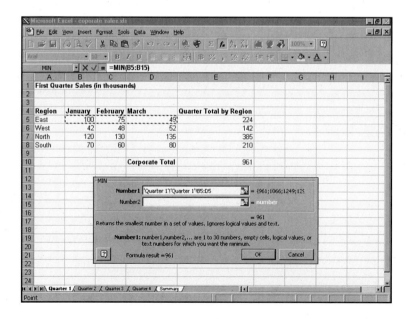

FIG. 14.19
The completed function will contain the link to the external data.

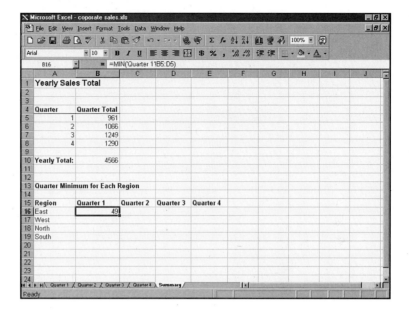

Auditing Formulas and Functions

Excel also provides you with a set of tools to check the soundness of the formulas and functions that you build in your worksheets. These auditing tools allow you to trace the cells that are referenced in a particular formula or function, or trace all the formulas or functions that reference a particular cell. An auditing tool also exists that can be used to trace formulas that return an error code.

The Auditing tools are reached either by the Tools menu and the Auditing command or by the Auditing toolbar:

Auditing Tool	Purpose
Trace Precedents	Points out all the cells that are referenced in the selected formula or function.
Trace Dependents	Points out all the formulas or functions that reference the value in the currently selected cell.
Trace Error	Points out the cells involved in a formula or function that return an error message.
Remove All Arrows	Clears the arrows and lines drawn by the tracing tools.

Cells referenced in a particular formula or function are called *precedents*. Tracing precedents enables you to see exactly which cells and ranges are involved in a particular formula.

Part

III

Ch

14

To trace the precedents for a formula or a function in a worksheet:

1. Select the formula or function. Choose Tools, Auditing, Trace Precedents.

2. Arrows will be drawn from the formula or function to the cells and cell ranges that are referenced in the equation, as shown in Figure 14.20.

FIG. 14.20

The Auditing feature can locate the precedents for a particular formula or function.

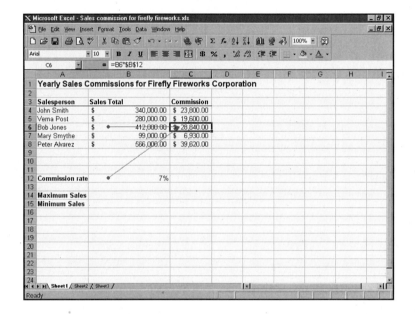

There may be occasions when you want to see all the formulas and/or functions that use a value in a particular cell. These formula and function cells are called *dependents*; they are dependent on the value in the cell.

To trace dependents for a particular formula or function:

1. Select a cell containing a particular value. Choose Tools, Auditing, Trace Dependents.

2. Arrows will be drawn from the cell to all the cells that contain formula or functions that reference the particular cell as shown in Figure 14.21.

You can also trace the cells involved in a formula or function that returns an error message. An *error message* means that the formula could not return an appropriate answer using the cells or cell ranges referenced in the formula.

An example would be the #DIV/0! error message. This error message appears when you inadvertently create a formula in which you divide a value by a cell that currently has no value (0).

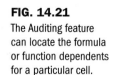

FIG. 14.21

The Auditing feature can locate the formula or function dependents for a particular cell.

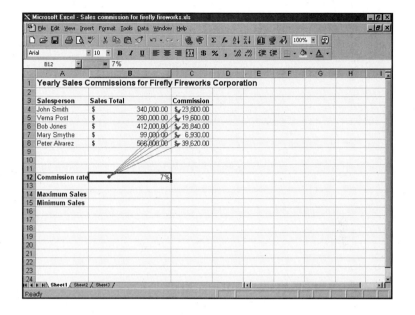

To trace an error message:

1. Select a formula cell containing an error message. Choose Tools, Auditing, Trace Error.

2. Arrows are drawn from the cell containing the error-yielding formula to all the cells involved in the formula.

3. Once you have used the Auditor to trace precedents, dependents, or errors, you can easily remove the arrows from the worksheet. Choose Tools, Auditing, Remove All Arrows.

Excel also provides tools that you can use in conjunction with the auditing tools. Whenever you double-click a formula to edit it, the Range Finder feature highlights all the cells and cell ranges involved in the particular formula. This is not unlike tracing precedents via the Auditor.

Another feature that can help you troubleshoot your formulas and functions is Excel's ability to display the *formulas* in your worksheet rather than the *results*. To display the formulas in your worksheet:

1. Choose Tools, Options, and then click the View tab. To display formulas in cells, select the Formulas check box.

2. Click OK to return to the worksheet. Cells containing formulas will display the actual formulas and functions.

3. When you want to return the worksheet to Normal and view the results of formulas and functions, return to the View tab and clear the Formulas check box.

Part

III

Ch

14

CHAPTER 15

Using Outlines, Templates, and Forms

by Patrice-Anne Rutledge

In Microsoft Excel 97, you can use outlines, templates, and forms to make data easier to view, use, and enter. Excel includes many advanced features including automatic outlining, built-in templates, and a Form toolbar for adding form controls to worksheets. In addition, you can use the Template Wizard with Data Tracking to enter data in an Excel form and store it for reporting and analyzing in another database. Finally, Excel also provides security for your data with protection for worksheets and workbooks, including a new macro virus protection feature. ∎

Outlines

In Excel 97, you can create both automatic and manual outlines of worksheet data.

Data protection

You can protect worksheets, workbooks, and shared workbooks. You can also activate macro virus protection to help detect potential macro viruses.

Templates

Create your own templates, use Excel's detailed built-in templates as a model, or link templates to other databases for simplified data entry and data analysis.

Forms

Use forms as an additional data entry tool. You can use the Forms toolbar to enhance and add controls to forms.

Using Outlines

Excel 97 enables you to create outlines that group data automatically based on summary formulas or manually based on your exact specifications. Creating an outline is a good idea if you have a long list that contains numerous subtotals. By creating an outline, you can more easily view summary information or specific sections of data.

> **N O T E** Another way to summarize a long list of data is to create a PivotTable. A PivotTable is an interactive report that summarizes and analyzes data. To create a PivotTable from your list, select it and choose <u>D</u>ata, <u>P</u>ivotTable Report. ▨

▷ **See** "Creating PivotTables," **p. 368**

You can also create an outline automatically by using Excel's subtotal feature. This feature creates subtotals and an outline at the same time. To use it, select the data you want to subtotal and choose <u>D</u>ata, Su<u>b</u>totals to open the Subtotal dialog box. Note that you must sort your data before subtotaling.

▷ **See** "Creating List Subtotals," **p. 362**

 Once you've created an outline, Excel makes it easy to display the outlined data as a chart. To do this, select the data you want to chart and click the Chart Wizard button on the Standard toolbar to open the Chart Wizard dialog box.

▷ **See** "Creating Charts with the Chart Wizard," **p. 337**

Creating an Automatic Outline

Excel 97 creates an automatic outline if your list data includes cells with summarized information. For example, if cells A1 through A3 include numeric data and cell A4 includes a formula such as =SUM(A1:A3), Excel will automatically outline the data. Figure 15.1 displays an Excel list in a format that will accept automatic outlining.

> **CAUTION**
>
> If the data you want to outline isn't in the proper format, you'll receive an error message. Either reformat the Excel list to include summarized cells or manually create an outline.

To have Excel create an automatic outline, follow these steps:

1. Position the cell pointer in the list you want to outline.
2. Choose <u>D</u>ata, <u>G</u>roup and Outline, <u>A</u>uto Outline.
3. Excel automatically applies an outline based on the summarized cells you created. Figure 15.2 displays an outline of the list data illustrated in Figure 15.1.

  Use the Hide Detail Level and Show Detail Level buttons to hide and display the detail in an outline.

FIG. 15.1
This Excel list is in a
format that will accept
automatic outlining.

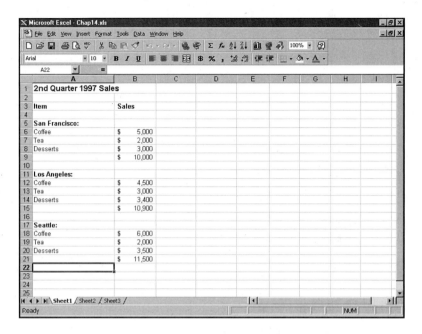

FIG. 15.2
Click the Hide Detail
Level button to hide
summary detail.

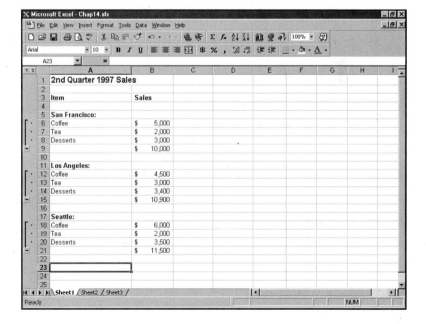

Creating a Manual Outline

If you can't create an automatic outline because of the way your list is designed, or you want control over how you create the outline, you can outline your data manually. You might also want to use manual outlining to outline the content of a book or report, for example, that doesn't include summarized numeric data.

To manually create an outline, follow these steps:

1. Select the rows you want to group in an outline. Do not include the row that contains the summary formula.

2. Choose Data, Group and Outline, Group to group the selected items.

3. The Group dialog box appears, as shown in Figure 15.3.

4. Choose to group either by Rows or Columns and then click OK to return to the worksheet.

FIG. 15.3

In the Group dialog box you can group by either rows or columns.

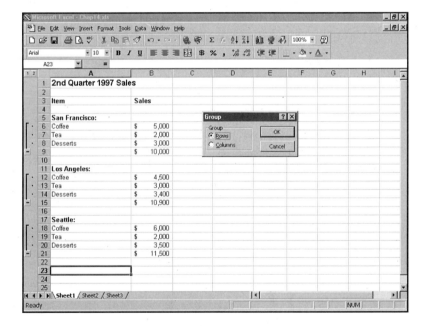

   T I P   If you've made a mistake or no longer need to view grouped data, you can remove a grouping. To do so, select the data you grouped and choose Data, Group and Outline, Ungroup.

Modifying an Outline

If you want to display your data in outline format but don't want to show the outline buttons, you can hide them. Choose Tools, Options and select the View tab. Figure 15.4 displays this tab.

FIG. 15.4
On the Options View tab, you can choose to hide outline buttons.

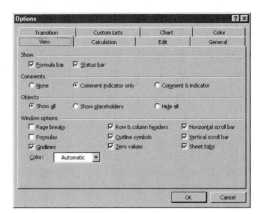

Clear the check from the Outline Symbols check box and click OK. Your summarized outline format remains, but the outline button symbols no longer display.

Removing an Outline

To remove an outline, choose Data, Group and Outline, Clear Outline. Excel removes the outline and outline buttons.

Protecting Documents and Data

Excel 97 includes several tools for protecting your data from other users' changes as well as from macro viruses. Before working with templates and forms, it's a good idea to understand how Excel's security features work.

▶ **See** "Using Resource Sharing and Security," **p. 1076**

Protecting Worksheets

You can protect individual worksheets in Excel 97. To do so, follow these steps:

1. Select the worksheet you want to protect and choose Tools, Protection, Protect Sheet to open the Protect Sheet dialog box, shown in Figure 15.5.

FIG. 15.5
You can protect worksheet content, objects, and scenarios.

2. Choose to protect any or all of the following worksheet elements:

N O T E   You can unlock specific cells in a worksheet you're going to protect to allow users access only to those specific cells. For example, in a form you could allow access only to data entry cells. To do this, select the cells you want to unlock, right-click the mouse, and choose Format Cells from the submenu to open the Format Cells dialog box. In the Protection tab, clear the Locked check box.

- *Contents.* Protects locked cell contents, formulas and cells you've hidden, and chart elements.
- *Objects.* Protects graphic objects, maps, charts, and comments.
- *Scenarios.* Protects scenarios, used for generating different answers for what-if analysis.
  - ▶ **See** "Evaluating What-If Scenarios," **p. 414**

CAUTION

Remember that passwords are case sensitive. If you enter a password for a protected worksheet and it doesn't work, try entering the password again with the exact case for each character. If you forget your password, there is no way to recover it, so be very careful about storing passwords for essential documents in a safe place.

3. You can enter an optional Password if you want to require users to enter a password to have access to the worksheet.

4. Click OK to return to the worksheet. If you chose to require a password, the Confirm Password dialog box, shown in Figure 15.6, asks you to Reenter password to proceed.

T I P   To hide the contents of certain cells before protecting a worksheet, select those cells, right-click the mouse, and choose Format Cells. On the Protection tab of the Format Cells dialog box, click the Hidden check box.

5. Enter the password again and click OK.

FIG. 15.6

Reenter your password to confirm it.

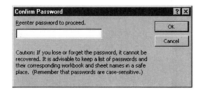

CAUTION

You'll receive an error message if you try to run a macro that changes cell contents on a protected worksheet.

To unprotect a worksheet, choose Tools, Protection, Unprotect Sheet. If you required a password for this worksheet, the Unprotect Sheet dialog box displays, shown in Figure 15.7.

FIG. 15.7

You have to enter a password to unprotect a sheet you've password protected.

Enter the Password and click OK to unprotect.

Protecting Workbooks

In addition to protecting individual worksheets, you can also protect entire workbooks. Protecting a workbook is different from protecting a worksheet. Excel lets you protect either the workbook structure, the workbook windows, or both.

Protecting the structure of a workbook prevents users from adding, deleting, or changing worksheets; creating macros; displaying PivotTable source data; creating a summary report with the Scenario Manager; or using Analysis ToolPak tools. Protecting the workbook windows prevents users from resizing, moving, or closing windows.

To protect a workbook, follow these steps:

1. Select the workbook you want to protect and choose Tools, Protection, Protect Workbook to open the Protect Workbook dialog box, shown in Figure 15.8.

FIG. 15.8

Excel lets you protect the structure and windows in a workbook.

2. Choose to protect either or both of the following workbook elements:

- *Structure*. Protects worksheets. Users can't add, delete, hide, move, copy, or rename worksheets.
- *Windows*. Protects windows. Users can't move, resize, or close windows.

3. You can enter an optional Password if you want to require users to enter a password to have access to the workbook.

4. Click OK to finish. If you chose to require a password, the Confirm Password dialog box asks you to Reenter password to proceed.

5. Enter the password again and click OK.

To unprotect a workbook, choose Tools, Protection, Unprotect Workbook. If you required a password for this workbook, the Unprotect Workbook dialog box displays. Enter the Password and click OK to unprotect.

TIP You can also protect shared workbooks. To use this feature, select Tools, Protection, Protect and Share Workbook to open the Protect Shared Workbook dialog box.

▶ **See** "Collaborating in Excel," **p. 1110**

Protecting from Macro Viruses

A *macro* is a series of commands that allow you to automatically perform specific tasks in Excel. A macro virus is a type of computer virus that's stored in a workbook or template macro and can cause damage to your data when you open the workbook or template. By disabling unknown macros, you can avoid infection.

▶ **See** "Using the Excel Macro Recorder," **p. 444**

To activate the macro virus protection feature, choose Tools, Options and select the General tab on the Options dialog box. Figure 15.9 illustrates this tab.

FIG. 15.9
The General tab includes an option for macro virus protection.

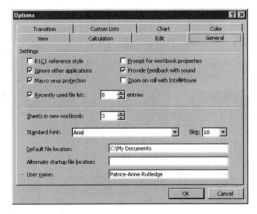

Select the Macro Virus Protection check box to enable detection. When you open a workbook, Excel displays a warning dialog box if it contains any macros. Figure 15.10 displays this warning.

FIG. 15.10
Excel displays a warning if you open a worksheet that contains macros.

You can choose from the following options:

- *Disable Macros*. Opens workbooks and deactivates all macros. No macros in this workbook will run.
- *Enable Macros*. Opens workbooks and activates all macros.
- *Do Not Open*. Closes both warning and workbook.

If you don't want Excel to tell you when macros are present in a workbook, clear the check from the Macro Virus Protection check box.

TROUBLESHOOTING

My worksheet macros won't work. If you activated macro virus protection and chose the Disable Macros option in the warning dialog box that displays when you open a worksheet, your worksheet macros won't function. If you're sure that these macros are virus-free, you can reopen the worksheet, choosing the Enable Macros option.

Using Templates

In Excel, a *template* is a saved workbook that you can use as the basis for other similar workbooks. At the most basic level you can create an Excel worksheet or workbook, save it as a template, and then reuse it as the basis for other like documents.

You can also use Excel's built-in templates to create sophisticated worksheets for invoices, purchase orders, and expense statements. In addition, Excel lets you create form templates to use for data entry that you link to a database—in either Excel or another application, such as Access—for analysis and reporting.

Creating a Template

Creating a template is a good idea for worksheet and workbook types that you routinely use. For example, let's say that every quarter you create a detailed sales report. You've applied a lot of special formatting that you don't want to redo every time. You can save a formatted workbook as a template and then reuse it.

T I P You can also reuse a worksheet by simply saving it with another name and replacing the contents.

Excel templates store the following settings: cell and worksheet formatting, cell styles, page formats, print areas, headers, row and column labels, data, formulas, graphic objects, macros, hyperlinks, custom toolbars, ActiveX controls, worksheet and workbook protection, calculation options, and window display options.

To create a template based on an existing worksheet or workbook, follow these steps:

1. Open the worksheet or workbook you want to save as a template.
2. Choose File, Save As to open the Save As dialog box, shown in Figure 15.11.

FIG. 15.11

Save your worksheet as a template in the Save As dialog box.

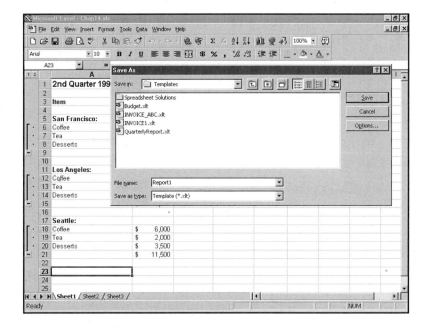

3. Be sure the Save In drop-down list points to the Templates folder.

 T I P *.xlt is the file extension for Excel templates.

4. Enter the File Name and choose Template(*.xlt) as the Save as Type.
5. Click the Save button to return to the worksheet.

To use the template, choose File, New to open the New dialog box, illustrated in Figure 15.12.

Select the new template and click OK to open a new document based on this template.

FIG. 15.12
You can open the template you've saved in the New dialog box.

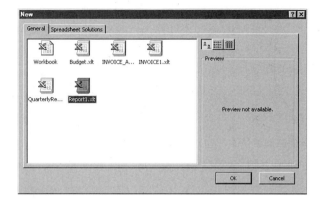

Using Excel's Built-In Templates

Excel 97 includes several built-in templates that you can use to create common business forms such as invoices, purchase orders, and expense statements. To use one of the templates as a basis for your own worksheet, follow these steps:

1. Choose File, New to open the New dialog box. Figure 15.13 illustrates the second tab, Spreadsheet Solutions.

FIG. 15.13
Excel includes three built-in templates for invoices, expense reports, and purchase orders.

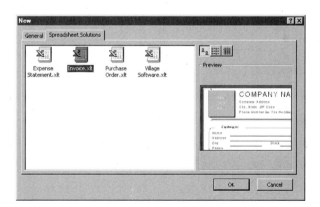

2. In this example, you'll choose the Invoice template, Invoice.xlt, to create an invoice form. Click OK to open the template.

 TIP See "Protecting Documents and Data" earlier in this chapter for more information on macro virus protection.

3. A warning box appears, telling you that the template you're about to open contains macros. Figure 15.14 displays this dialog box.

FIG. 15.14
Excel warns you that the template contains macros.

4. Click the <u>E</u>nable Macros button to continue.

5. A ready-made invoice form displays, as shown in Figure 15.15.

FIG. 15.15
You can modify this invoice form to suit your needs.

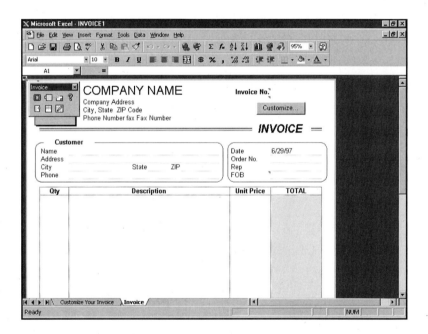

6. To customize the invoice, click the Customize Your Invoice worksheet tab. Figure 15.16 displays this tab.

7. Enter your company's name, address, and other information in this worksheet.

8. When you've completed your customizations, you can lock in your changes and save the template with another name. To do this, click the Lock/Save Sheet button to open the Lock/Save Sheet dialog box, illustrated in Figure 15.17.

FIG. 15.16

Enter your company's own information on the Customize Your Invoice worksheet tab.

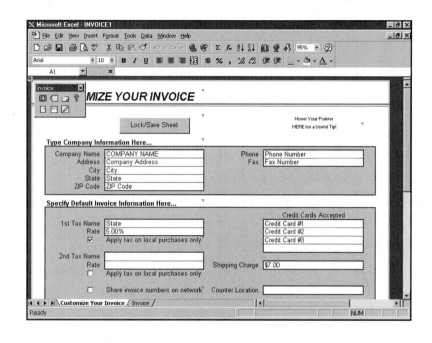

FIG. 15.17

You can lock and save changes you've made to the template.

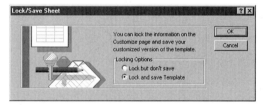

9. You can choose to Lock But Don't Save or to Lock and Save Template. In this case, select Lock and Save Template and click OK.

10. The Save Template dialog box appears, shown in Figure 15.18. Enter the new File Name of your template and click OK.

FIG. 15.18

Save your new template for later use.

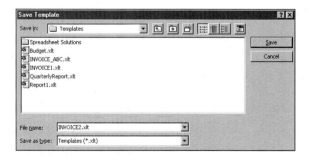

TIP To make additional customizations, click the Customize button in the upper-right corner of the invoice.

11. Excel saves the template and returns to the Invoice worksheet tab.

To use the new template you've saved, choose File, New and open it from the New dialog box.

Using the Template Wizard

Excel 97 includes a feature called the Template Wizard with Data Tracking, which enables you to link specific worksheet cells to database fields. The invoice template you just used to create your own invoice has already been linked to an Excel database named Invdb.xls. Figure 15.19 illustrates this worksheet.

FIG. 15.19

You'll use the Invoice database to store your data.

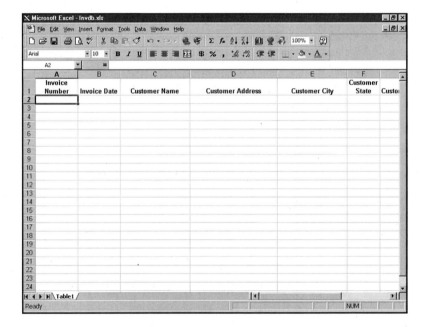

Invdb.xls includes the following fields which have been linked directly to cells in the Invoice template:

- Invoice Number
- Invoice Date
- Customer Name
- Customer Address
- Customer City

- Customer State
- Customer ZIP
- Customer Phone
- Total Invoice
- Rep

▶ **See** "Access Quick Start Guide," **p. 583**

▶ **See** "Using Access Data in Excel," **p. 1023**

N O T E You can also store your data in applications other than Excel. For example, you could enter the data in your Excel form and store it in Access or FoxPro. ▪

The Invoice form provides an easy way to enter this information and also provides a well designed document to send to customers. For data tracking and analysis, the database is a more suitable format. Using the Template Wizard with Data Tracking, you can enter the information once and use it in both ways.

To get a clearer understanding of how this works, look at how the Template Wizard was set up to work with the Invoice form and database.

To do so, follow these steps:

1. Choose Data, Template Wizard to open the Template Wizard, shown in Figure 15.20.

FIG. 15.20

The Template Wizard offers step-by-step guidance.

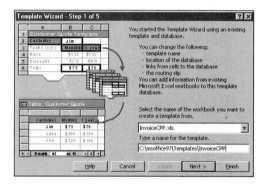

2. In step 1 of the Wizard, you select the name of the workbook that is the basis for the template and then assign a name to the template. Click Next to continue.

3. Figure 15.21 illustrates step 2. In this step, you enter the name and location of the database in which to store your data. In this case, you've elected to store your data in the invdb.xls database.

4. Next, continue to step 3, illustrated in Figure 15.22. In this step, you determine which cells to store in which database fields.

5. First, choose the worksheet from which to select cells in the Sheet drop-down list.

T I P Before you link worksheet cells to database fields, it's a good idea to create a paper map of how you want to link this data, particularly if your template is complex.

FIG. 15.21

Enter information about the database in which you'll store data.

FIG. 15.22

Step 3 lets you link cells to field names.

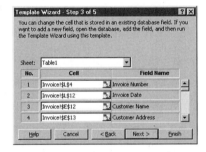

 TIP Use the Cell Reference button to return to the worksheet to select the cells to link.

6. For each cell that you select, enter a corresponding database field name. In this example, you'll see that ten worksheet cells have been linked to database field names. Remember that when you initially set up linked fields, you enter field names in the Field Names edit boxes; here they appear dimmed.

 TIP In order to add information from other workbooks, you must have organized your data in exactly the same way as in the existing template. Otherwise, the data won't match up properly.

7. Step 4, shown in Figure 15.23, asks if you want to include information from existing Microsoft workbooks to your database. If you answer No, Skip It, step 5 displays when you click the Next button.

FIG. 15.23

You can include data from an existing worksheet in your database.

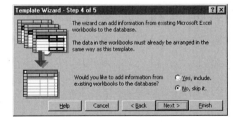

8. If you answer Yes, Include, a revised step 4 displays when you click the Next button. Figure 15.24 illustrates this revised step 4.

FIG. 15.24

You can select, delete, and preview other worksheets.

9. Click the Select button to open the Select Files to Convert dialog box, shown in Figure 15.25.

FIG. 15.25

Choose the file you want to convert.

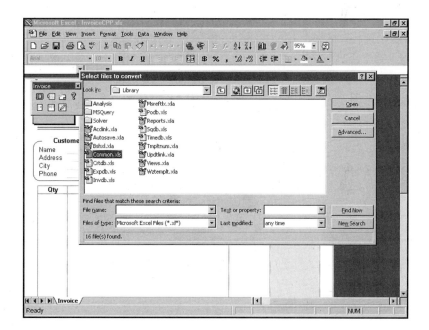

TIP You can also Delete and Preview the workbook you've selected.

10. Choose the file you want to add to the database and click Open to return to the Template Wizard.

   ▶ **See** "Using Message Providers," **p. 743**

11. Figure 15.26 displays step 5 of the Template Wizard. In this step, you can choose Add Routing Slip to send a message to others via electronic mail each time you create a new workbook based on this template.

FIG. 15.26

You can send notices via e-mail when you create a new workbook based on this template.

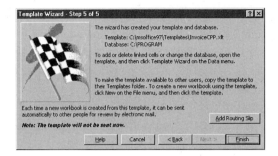

12. Click Finish to return to the worksheet. The Invoice form is set up to enter data in the Invoice database.

As you enter data in the Invoice form, you can click the Capture Data in a Database button on the Invoice toolbar to save data in the database. Figure 15.27 illustrates the Create and Interact with Database dialog box.

FIG. 15.27

You'll update your database with new information you enter on your form.

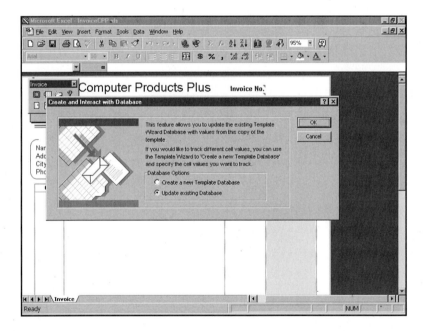

Select the Update Existing Database option button and click OK. The Template File-Save to Database dialog box appears, shown in Figure 15.28.

Indicate that you want to Create a New Record and click OK. Excel copies the data you entered on the Invoice form to the Invoice database.

FIG. 15.28
Create a new record in the database you've specified.

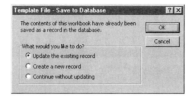

TROUBLESHOOTING

The New dialog box doesn't display a template I created. You must place templates in the Templates subfolder in the folder in which you installed Office 97. Alternatively, you can place templates in the Alternate Startup File Location you specified in the Options dialog box General tab.

I can't find the Expense Statement, Purchase Order, or Invoice templates in the New dialog box. You need to reinstall Office 97, adding the Expense Report Template, Invoice Template, and Purchase Order Template in the Excel, Spreadsheet Templates window.

The Template Wizard doesn't work. Reinstall Office 97, adding the Template Wizard with Data Tracking option in the Excel, Add-ins window.

Creating Forms in Excel

In Excel 97 you can create forms to automate and standardize many data entry tasks. You can create online forms that are meant to collect and analyze data in Excel, forms designed to be printed, and forms to collect information from a Web site. You can also create your own forms for other users to use as a template.

▶ **See** "Exporting Excel Data to the Web," **p. 922**

▶ **See** "Creating a Form," **p. 937**

 To create an Excel form to use on the Web, choose Tools, Wizard, Web Form to open the Web Form Wizard.

 Use the built-in Excel form templates as examples when creating your own forms. You'll find these templates by choosing File, New and selecting the Spreadsheet Solutions tab.

To create a simple form template that tracks customer information, follow these steps:

1. Click the New button on the Standard toolbar to create a new worksheet.
2. Enter your form title, such as Customer Information.
3. Next, create a list of fields you want users to enter. Figure 15.29 displays your form so far.

FIG. 15.29

Creating forms is simple in Excel.

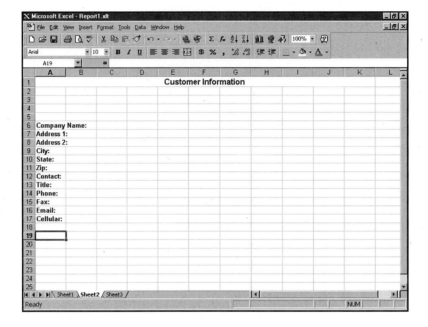

4. To make it easier for users to tab through the fields they need to enter in your form, you can unlock only those cells in which users are to make entries, and protect the rest of the worksheet. See "Protecting Documents and Data," earlier in this chapter to learn more about using Excel's protection features. In this step, select the cells you want to unlock.

5. Choose Format, Cells to open the Format Cells dialog box. Figure 15.30 displays the Protection tab.

FIG. 15.30

Unlock cells on the Protection tab.

6. Clear the check mark by the Locked check box and click OK to return to the worksheet.

7. Choose Tools, Protection, Protect Sheet to open the Protect Sheet dialog box, shown in Figure 15.31.

FIG. 15.31

You can protect
worksheet data in
Excel.

8. Specify whether you want to protect for Contents, Objects, and/or Scenarios. For more information on which protection options to choose, see "Protecting Worksheets" earlier in this chapter.

9. Enter an optional Password, if you want to password protect your worksheet, and click OK.

10. If you selected to use a password, the Confirm Password dialog box opens. Reenter the password and click OK to return to the worksheet.

 To remove worksheet protection, choose Tools, Protection, Unprotect Sheet.

CAUTION

Remember that if you password-protect a worksheet, you'll have to enter this password whenever you open it in the future.

Users now tab only from one data entry field to another, rather than to the next cell.

11. To hide the gridlines on your form, choose Tools, Options to open the Options dialog box. On the View tab, clear the check mark by the Gridlines check box. Figure 15.32 displays this dialog box. Your cells remain, but you now have a blank background.

FIG. 15.32

Removing gridlines
creates a blank form
background.

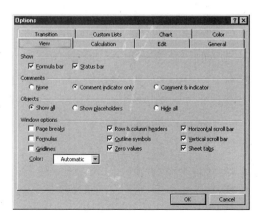

12. To save your file as a template, choose <u>F</u>ile, Save <u>A</u>s to open the Save As dialog box.

13. Enter your template name in the File <u>N</u>ame box and choose Template (*.xlt) in the Save As <u>T</u>ype box.

When you want to use this template, choose <u>F</u>ile, <u>N</u>ew and select this template in the New dialog box.

Using the Form Toolbar

You can add controls to your forms to automate or simplify tasks. Check boxes, drop-down lists, and option buttons are all examples of controls. In Excel 97 you can use the Form toolbar to add controls to forms. These controls are similar to the controls that you use in Access to create a form.

Another way to create a drop-down list of possible options in Excel is by using the data validation feature.

N O T E   Data validation has other uses beyond simply creating a list of possible data choices. Using this feature you can also validate and limit numeric entries as well as date and time formatting. Open the Data Validation dialog box by choosing <u>D</u>ata, Va<u>l</u>idation. ▪

▶ **See** "Using Data Validation," **p. 350**

▶ **See** "Designing a Form," **p. 649**

▶ **See** "Adding Controls to a Form," **p. 652**

Table 15.1 displays the buttons you'll find on the Form toolbar.

Table 15.1   Buttons on the Form Toolbar

Button	Description	Button	Description
Aα	Label		Combination List-Edit
ab|	Edit Box		Combination Drop-Down Edit
	Group Box		Scroll Bar
	Button		Spinner
✓	Check Box		Control Properties

Button	Description	Button	Description
	Option Button		Edit Code
	List Box		Toggle Grid
	Combo Box		Run Dialog

These buttons enable you to place controls on your forms that you'll use to perform tasks or run macros. Look at Excel's built-in form templates for examples of how to use controls on a form. For instance, choose File, New and open the Purchase Order template from the New dialog box. Figure 15.33 displays this template.

This form includes many form controls including buttons, option buttons, and group boxes.

FIG. 15.33

You can add buttons, group boxes, and option buttons to a form.

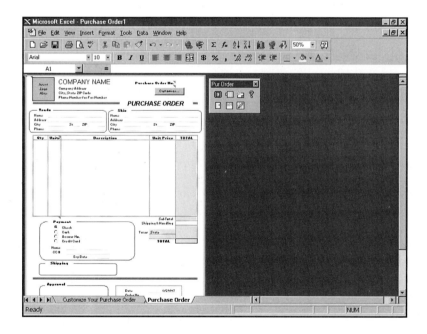

Adding a Control to a Form

To add a basic control to a form, follow these steps:

1. Choose View, Toolbars, Forms to open the Forms toolbar if it isn't already open.

2. Select the button of the control you want to add. For example, to add a list box to your form, select the List Box button and then drag the mouse across the worksheet area in which you want to place it. Figure 15.34 illustrates the empty list box.

FIG. 15.34

Users can choose from several predefined options in a list box.

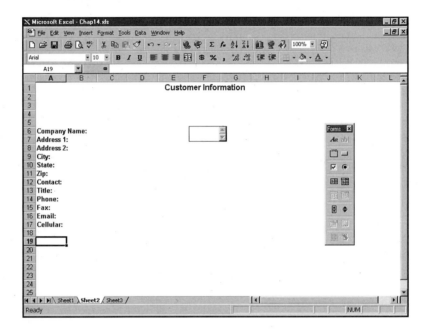

3. Select the list box, right-click, and choose Format Control from the submenu. Figure 15.35 displays the Control tab on the Format Control dialog box.

FIG. 15.35

The Format Control dialog box lets you set parameters for your form control.

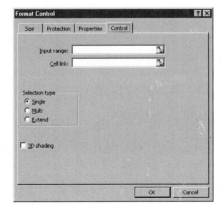

N O T E You must create a list of possible values in an Excel worksheet before you format the control. If this data is on the same form or worksheet, you can hide it from view later by selecting it, opening the Format Cells dialog box, and choosing Hidden on the Protection tab.

4. In the Input Range, enter the cell range that contains the values you want to include in the drop-down list. You can click the Cell Reference button to return to the worksheet to select this data.

5. If you want to return a value representing the selected drop-down list item, enter the cell in which to place this value in the Cell Link field.

6. Next, determine your selection type—Single, Multi, or Extend—depending on whether you want to be able to select one or more than one item in the list.

7. Finally, you can apply 3D Shading to this list box if you want.

8. Click OK to return to the worksheet.

Users can now choose from the designated values in the list box when they use your form. You can continue adding form controls until you've completed the form.

CHAPTER 16

Advanced Formatting and Charting

by Patrice-Anne Rutledge

Excel 97's sophisticated formatting and charting options enable you to easily create dynamic, aesthetically pleasing reports and presentations with your worksheet data. Formatting options include numerous text and number styles, as well as the capability to rotate text and apply conditional formats to your worksheets. And the Chart Wizard walks you step by step through the creation of a basic chart that you can later modify and customize. ■

New features

Excel 97 offers many new formatting and charting features that enable you to create high-quality worksheets.

Data formatting

Excel provides options for both basic text and numeric formatting, as well as advanced options such as rotations, merged data, and conditional formats.

Chart Wizard

Use the Chart Wizard as a guide through the process of creating complex charts.

Chart customization

After you create a basic chart, you can change it or enhance it with a multitude of formatting options, including background textures, WordArt, and 3-D.

Overview of New Features

Excel 97 includes numerous new formatting and charting features that both simplify procedures and enhance the appearance of charts and worksheets. These features include:

- *Conditional formatting.* Excel 97 includes a new feature that allows you to apply specific formatting to the contents of cells under certain conditions.

- *Rotated text.* You can rotate text within cells by using this new feature.

- *Merge cells.* By merging the contents of one or more cells, you can create one cell.

- *Chart Wizard enhancements.* Excel 97 consolidates all charting options into one wizard, including the capability to select subtypes and preview the chart in step 1.

- *Chart menu.* This new menu consolidates many common chart-formatting options, including the capability to modify the chart type, location, and source data.

- *Chart toolbar enhancements.* The toolbar includes new features that automate chart modifications.

- *New chart types.* New types include bubble, pie of pie, and bar of pie, as well as three 3-D shapes: pyramid, cone, and cylinder.

- *Chart Tips.* When the mouse pointer hovers over a particular element, a Chart Tip tells you the name of the chart element, as well as its value.

- *Single-click selection.* Rather than having to double-click a chart to activate it and then click the selection that you want to modify, you can now simply select a chart element with a single click.

- *Time-scale chart axes.* Excel 97 includes special formatting options for charts based on a time scale such as month, day, or year.

- *Chart data tables.* You can combine a graphical representation of data as well as the data itself in a single chart.

- *Additional graphical enhancements.* Now you're able to add pictures, textures, and gradient fills to your Excel 97 charts.

Formatting Numbers, Dates, and Times

To apply numeric formatting options, select the cell or range of cells that you want to format and then click the appropriate button(s) described in Table 16.1.

Table 16.1   Numeric Formatting Buttons

Button	Description
$	Currency Style
%	Percent Style

Button	Description
	Comma Style
	Increase Decimal
	Decrease Decimal

To display revenue data as a currency amount with no decimal places, for example, first select the Currency Style button and then click the Decrease Decimal button twice.

TIP   You can also open the Format Cells dialog box by right-clicking the data you want to format and choosing Format Cells from the shortcut menu.

For more complex numeric formatting, choose Format, Cells to open the Format Cells dialog box (see Figure 16.1).

FIG. 16.1
When you choose the type of format to apply, the options on the right side of the screen change. If you choose the Currency Category, for example, you can determine the number of decimal places, the current Symbol, and the Negative Numbers format.

Excel also recognizes common date and time formats, and converts them to the current default format when you enter data. If your default date format is 9/1/97, for example, the entries 9-1-97, 9/1/1997, or 9/01/97 would all be converted to 9/1/97. From the Format Cells dialog box, select either Date or Time in the Category list, then choose from among the default Types listed.

Creating a Custom Numeric Format

If you need a numeric format that Excel 97 doesn't include, you can create it yourself by using a custom format. To do so, choose the Custom Category in the Number tab of the Format Cells dialog box. Enter the custom format codes in the Type text box, using the samples in the drop-down list as a starting point.

If you want to create a custom date or time format, for example, you can use date and time format codes to design a format that is specific to your needs. Table 16.2 lists these codes.

Table 16.2   Date and Time Format Codes

Code	Description
m	Month as a number with no leading zero
mm	Month as a number with leading zero
mmm	Month as a three-letter abbreviation
mmmm	Month as a full name
d	Day of week with no leading zero
dd	Day of week with leading zero
ddd	Day of week as a three-letter abbreviation
dddd	Day of week as a full name
yy	Year as a two-digit number
yyyy	Year as a four-digit number
h	Hour with no leading zero
hh	Hour with leading zero
m	Minute with no leading zero
mm	Minute with leading zero
AM/PM	AM or PM indicator

Using these format codes, you can enter **d-mmm-yy h:mm** to represent 30-Aug-97 0:00, for example.

Formatting Alignment

 TIP   To center your text across columns, select the cells that you want to center and then click the Merge and Center button on the Formatting toolbar.

   From the Formatting toolbar, you can right-align, left-align, or center your text. For other kinds of alignment formatting, select the cells to format and then choose Format, Cells to open the Format Cells dialog box. Figure 16.2 displays the Alignment tab of this dialog box.

FIG. 16.2
You can change the alignment of data in the Alignment tab of the Format Cells dialog box.

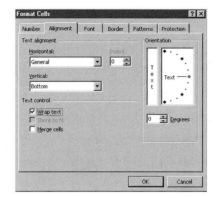

 To activate the Indent scroll box, choose Left (Indent). You can then specify an exact amount of indentation.

From the drop-down lists, you can choose the <u>H</u>orizontal and <u>V</u>ertical text alignment that you prefer.

The Alignment tab offers several options for controlling text:

- *Wrap Text*. Wraps the text within a single cell, adjusting row height accordingly.
- *Shrin<u>k</u> to Fit*. Shrinks the text to fit the size of the existing cell.
- *<u>M</u>erge Cells*. Creates one cell by merging the contents of one or more cells.
- *Rotate Text*. Rotates text from 90 to -90 degrees.

Figure 16.3 illustrates each of these options.

N O T E In the Orientation group box of the Alignment tab, you can choose either vertical or horizontal orientation. If you choose vertical orientation, you also must choose a specific vertical alignment (Top, Center, Bottom, or Justify) from the <u>V</u>ertical drop-down list.

Customizing Fonts

The Formatting toolbar contains several options for customizing the fonts in your worksheet. Table 16.3 illustrates these options.

Table 16.3   Font Formatting Buttons

Button	Description	Enables You To:
Arial	Font	Choose a new font from the drop-down list.

continues

Table 16.3   Continued

Button	Description	Enables You To:
10 ▼	Font Size	Choose a new font size—from 8 to 72—from the drop-down list.
B	Bold	Bold the selected text.
I	Italic	Italicize the selected text.
U	Underline	Underline the selected text.
A ▼	Font Color	Choose a font color from the palette that displays.

If you require more flexibility than the Formatting toolbar offers, you can select the text that you want to format and choose Format, Cells to open the Format Cells dialog box. The Font tab, displayed in Figure 16.4, provides additional options for underlining and other effects, such as strikethrough, superscript, and subscript.

FIG. 16.3

In Excel 97, you can wrap text, shrink text to fit, merge cells, or rotate text in a worksheet.

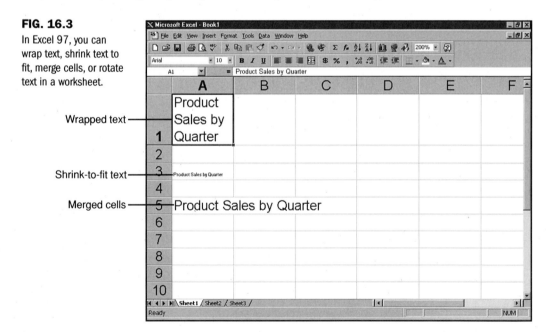

FIG. 16.4

The Font tab includes several advanced formatting options including effects such as strikethrough, superscript, and subscript.

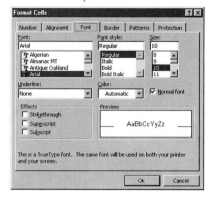

Applying a Border and Pattern

Borders serve as visual separators between worksheet areas and can also enhance the appearance of printed reports.

TIP A shortcut for applying borders is selecting the cell or range that you want to format and then clicking the arrow next to the Borders button to display the Borders palette.

To apply a border, select the Border tab of the Format Cells dialog box, illustrated in Figure 16.5. You can open this dialog box by choosing Format, Cells.

FIG. 16.5

In the Format Cells dialog box, select a border to add to a cell.

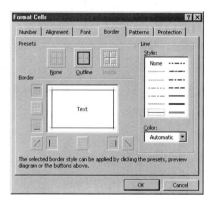

The simplest way to apply a border is to use one of the preset borders:

- *None*. No border—choose to remove an existing border.
- *Outline*. Border around the outside edge of the selected cells.
- *Inside*. Border on the inside grid of the selected cells.

The preview area displays what the border will look like.

You can also design your own border with the border buttons that appear in the bottom half of the dialog box. These buttons give you the option to create top, bottom, left, right, or diagonal borders.

You can enhance your worksheet even more with patterns and colors. The Patterns tab of the Format Cells dialog box allows you to choose among a variety of colors and patterns (see Figure 16.6).

FIG. 16.6

Apply patterns and colors to a cell with the Format Cells dialog box.

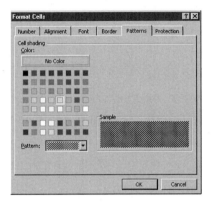

Choose a Color from the selection of available colors. Click the arrow next to the Pattern box to display the Pattern palette. The Sample box displays the effects of your selected color and pattern.

Using Automatic Formatting

Using Excel's AutoFormat feature enables you to choose among predesigned templates that include preformatted numbers, cell alignments, column widths, row heights, fonts, borders, and other options.

To use AutoFormat, follow these steps:

1. Select the range that you want to format.
2. Choose Format, AutoFormat. The AutoFormat dialog box appears, as shown in Figure 16.7.

FIG. 16.7

The AutoFormat dialog box displays preformatted templates.

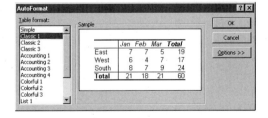

3. Select one of the format types in the Table Format list box. You can view the selected format in the Sample box.

4. Choose OK to apply the format.

Using Conditional Formatting

Excel 97 includes a new feature called *conditional formatting*, which allows you to apply specific formatting to the contents of cells under certain conditions. Excel automatically applies the format that you specify (such as a certain color) to the cell if a condition is true. You can use conditional formatting to highlight values that you want to track or the result of a formula. You can display a cell in red if it contains a negative number, for example.

To use conditional formatting, follow these steps:

1. Choose Format, Conditional Formatting to open the Conditional Formatting dialog box, shown in Figure 16.8.

FIG. 16.8

Using Excel 97's conditional formatting feature, you can specify the conditions under which to apply a particular format.

2. From the Condition 1 drop-down list, choose either Cell Value Is or Formula Is, depending on whether you want to track a cell value or formula.

3. If you choose to track a cell value, select a condition from the second drop-down list.

4. Enter the conditional data in the adjacent text box, or click the Cell Reference button to return to the worksheet to select the appropriate cell.

   You must enter data in two text boxes if you choose a condition that evaluates between two values. In this example, you want to apply formatting if the cell content is greater than 0.

5. Click the Format button to open the Format Cells dialog box.

6. Select the desired formatting options and click OK to return to the preceding dialog box. In this case, you want to set the color to red.

7. To include additional conditions, click the Add button, which adds Condition 2 below Condition 1 in the dialog box.

8. When you finish, click OK to return to your worksheet.

When you enter data that matches one of your conditions, Excel formats that data as you specify. A negative amount in the cell that you just formatted displays in red, for example; a positive amount displays in the default color.

To delete a condition, follow these steps:

1. Choose the <u>D</u>elete button in the Conditional Formatting dialog box, which opens the Delete Conditional Format dialog box, shown in Figure 16.9.

FIG. 16.9
Deleting conditional
formatting is simple in
Excel 97.

2. Select the condition that you want to delete and click OK to return to the Conditional Formatting dialog box.

3. When you finish, click OK to return to your worksheet.

Turning Data into Charts

When you finish entering and analyzing data in a worksheet, you may want to represent this data visually in a chart. Excel 97 offers a variety of chart types that you can easily create with its Chart Wizard. Table 16.4 lists these chart types.

Table 16.4   Chart Wizard Chart Types

Chart Type	Description
Column	Compares a set of values across categories in vertical columns.
Cylinder	Creates a column chart with a cylindrical shape.
Cone	Creates a column chart with a cone shape.
Pyramid	Creates a column chart with a pyramid shape.
Bar	Compares a set of values across categories in horizontal bars.
Line	Displays a line with a marker at each data value.
Pie	Displays the amount contributing to a total as a numeric value or percentage.
Doughnut	Functions as a pie chart, but can contain multiple series of data.
(XY) Scatter	Compares pairs of values with scatter marks.
Bubble	Similar to a scatter chart, but compares three sets of values.
Area	Displays a contribution trend for each value.
Radar	Creates markers at each data point.
Surface	Creates a 3-D surface showing value trends.
Stock	Displays three sets of values as stock high, low, and close.

T I P Cylinder, cone, and pyramid charts are new variations of a column chart and provide an enhanced way to depict column data.

Choosing the right chart type is an essential first step in creating a meaningful chart, because all other chart formats and options depend on this selection. Suppose that you want to graphically represent your company's revenue over the past three months. A column, bar, or line chart is a good choice for this kind of data. Figure 16.10 illustrates the same information displayed in these three kinds of charts.

FIG. 16.10

In Excel charts, the x axis is the category axis and the y axis is the value axis. In the column chart, the category axis is horizontal and the value axis is vertical. In the bar chart, the opposite is true.

Data that charts are created from

Bar chart

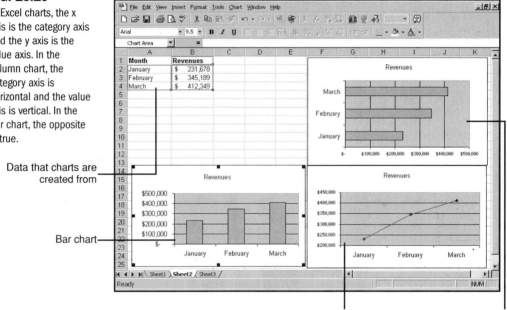

Line chart   Column chart

A pie chart is a good way to represent separate values that make up a whole. Figure 16.11 illustrates a sample pie chart.

Creating Charts with the Chart Wizard

 Using Excel's automated Chart Wizard, you can quickly and easily create sophisticated charts from your existing worksheet data. To create a chart by using the Chart Wizard, follow these steps:

 T I P You can include nonadjacent data ranges in your chart by holding down the Ctrl key as you select additional ranges.

FIG. 16.11

A pie chart can represent percentages of a whole.

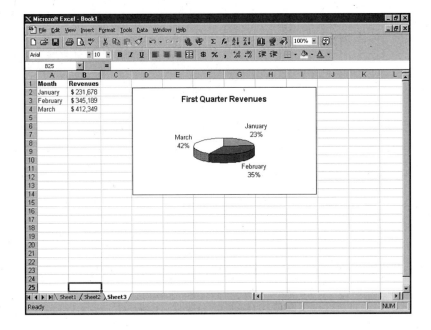

1. Select the data to be included in the chart (including column and row labels).

2. Click the Chart Wizard button in the Standard toolbar to open the wizard. Figure 16.12 displays step 1 of the wizard.

FIG. 16.12

You can choose from among 14 chart types in step 1 of the Chart Wizard.

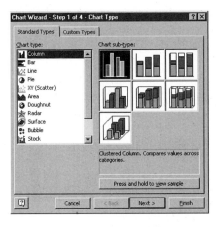

TIP   For additional chart-type choices, look at the Custom Types tab in step 1 of the Chart Wizard.

The Standard Types tab includes a list of 14 chart types, each with a number of chart subtypes that appear on the left side of the dialog box.

TIP After you identify a potential chart type and subtype, click the Press and Hold to <u>V</u>iew Sample button, which displays a larger sample of this chart type on the left side of the dialog box.

3. Click Next to continue to the second Chart Wizard step, in which you select source data. Figure 16.13 illustrates this dialog box.

4. Determine whether to display your data in Rows or Columns.

   The preview box illustrates how each option would appear in a chart.

Part

III

Ch

16

FIG. 16.13

The range of cells that you initially selected appears in the <u>D</u>ata Range box. You can change this range, if you prefer.

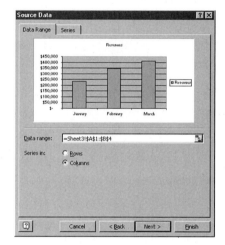

N O T E In Excel, a *data series* is the set of data that a chart element (such as a column, bar, or pie slice) graphically represents. You can have multiple data series. The Series tab of the Source Data dialog box provides more options for determining the data series in your chart. ▣

5. Click Next to continue to the third step of the wizard; each tab offers a different charting option for determining titles, axes, gridlines, legends, data labels, and data labels.

6. In the <u>T</u>itles tab, specify a Chart Title, which centers across the top of a chart. Figure 16.14 displays this tab.

FIG. 16.14

You can also specify the <u>C</u>ategory (X) Axis label and a <u>V</u>alue (Y) Axis label. If available, you can also specify Second-Category (x) and Second Value (y) axes.

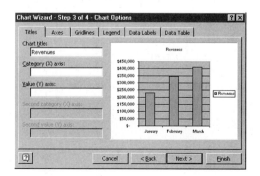

The other tabs in step 3 allow for the following:

- *Axes.* In this tab, you determine whether to display the Category (x) axis, the Value (Y) axis, or both axes.

  If you decide to display a category (x) axis, you then need to choose among the following formatting options: automatic, category, or time-scale.

- *Gridlines.* In this tab, you can choose to display or hide the gridlines in your chart (which can make your chart easier to read). You can add major or minor gridlines to either the category (x) axis or the value (y) axis. The default for most charts is to include major gridlines for the value (y) axis.

- *Legend.* In this tab, you can specify whether to show a legend in your chart. (A *legend* associates descriptive text with the colors or patterns of data in your chart.) You can place your legend at the bottom, corner, top, right, or left of your chart.

- *Data Labels.* Often, you want to display a descriptive label next to its graphical representation in a chart. You can do this in the Data Labels tab, shown in Figure 16.15.

FIG. 16.15

Using the Data Labels tab, you can choose to display actual monetary amounts in a chart, rather than just display them visually.

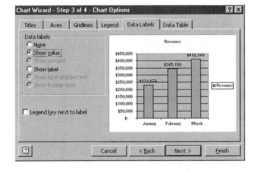

- *Data Table.* Finally, you have the option of displaying a data table below your chart. A *data table* includes the actual data that you're representing graphically, in a format similar to the original data range in your worksheet. Figure 16.16 shows the Data Table tab.

FIG. 16.16

A data table displays detailed data in your chart.

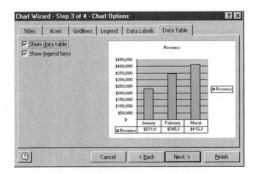

7. Click Next to continue to step 4 of the Chart Wizard, where you determine the location of your chart—either as a New Sheet or as an Object in an Existing Sheet (see Figure 16.17).

FIG. 16.17
You can place your chart in the same worksheet or a different one.

8. Finally, at the end of step 4, click the Finish button to complete your chart.

 T I P To deactivate Chart Tips, choose Tools, Options and then deselect the Show Names and Show Values check boxes in the Chart tab of the Options dialog box.

 To identify each section of your new chart, hover the mouse pointer over the particular section to allow the Chart Tips feature to tell you the name of the chart element, as well as its value.

Modifying Charts

After you create a basic chart, you'll probably want to modify it in some way. The easiest way to modify a chart is to use the buttons in the Chart toolbar, which appears after you create your chart. Table 16.4 describes the buttons in this toolbar.

N O T E Not every toolbar button is available at all times. Angle Text Upward and Angle Text Downward, for example, are active only when you are choosing a text field. ▪

Table 16.4   Chart Toolbar

Button	Name	Description
Chart Area ▼	Chart Objects	Lists available chart objects.
	Format	Opens Format dialog box, which contains available formatting options.
	Chart Type	Displays the Chart Type palette, in which you can change the chart type.
	Legend	Activates and deactivates the chart legend.
	Data Table	Activates and deactivates the chart data table.

continues

Table 16.4 Continued

Button	Name	
	By Row	Displays the data by row.
	By Column	Displays the data by column.
	Angle Text Downward	Rotates selected text down.
	Angle Text Upward	Rotates selected text up.

TIP Right-clicking a chart produces a shortcut menu that lists many of these same options.

97 The Chart menu also includes many options for modifying a chart after you create it. From this menu, you can modify the chart type, source data, location, and other options.

Modifying the Chart Type

To modify the chart type, click the arrow to the right of the Chart Type button in the Chart toolbar. A chart palette (see Figure 16.18) displays the available types of charts. Select the new chart type, and the chart updates automatically.

FIG. 16.18

Choose a new chart type from the palette.

Moving a Chart

To move an existing chart, click inside it to activate it and then drag it to a new location in the worksheet.

TIP To copy the chart rather than cut it, choose Edit, Copy or press Ctrl+C.

To move a chart to another worksheet in your workbook, select it and then choose Edit, Cut. Move to the new worksheet and choose Edit, Paste to paste the chart to the new location.

Resizing a Chart

To resize an existing chart, follow these steps:

1. Select the chart by clicking it.
2. Position the mouse pointer over a chart handle until the mouse pointer becomes a double arrow.

 TIP To maintain proportions while resizing, hold down the Shift key.

3. Drag the chart handle to increase or decrease the chart to the desired size.

Formatting Charts

To perform basic formatting of your chart, choose the chart area that you want to format from the Chart Objects drop-down list in the Chart toolbar. Then click the Format button to open the Format dialog box. The complete names of the Format button and the Format dialog box change, depending on the chart object that is currently selected. If you selected the Chart Title object, for example, the button and dialog box are named Format Chart Title. The tabs of the Format dialog box also vary, depending on the selected chart object.

Suppose that you want to format the font of the chart title—a common formatting task. To do so, select Chart Title as your chart object and then click the Format Chart Title button to open the Format Chart Title dialog box, shown in Figure 16.19.

FIG. 16.19
You can format the pattern, font, and alignment of your chart title.

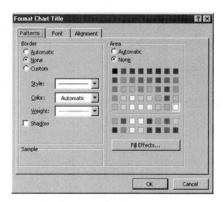

This dialog box has three tabs: Pattern, Font, and Alignment. In the Font tab, you can make any necessary font changes.

Enhancing Charts

After you create a chart and make basic modifications in it, you may want to make further enhancements to improve its aesthetic appearance. Here are some suggestions:

- Change the gradient, texture, or pattern of your chart's background by selecting it and then clicking the Fill Color button in the Formatting toolbar. From the Fill Color palette, select <u>F</u>ill Effects to open the Fill Effects dialog box, shown in Figure 16.20.

FIG. 16.20

In the Fill Effect dialog box, you can change a gradient, texture, or pattern.

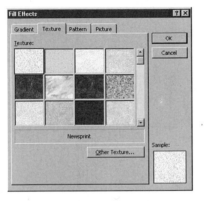

You can choose among a variety of fill options in the Gradient, Texture, Pattern, and Picture tabs. Figure 16.21 shows a sample chart that uses the Newsprint texture.

FIG. 16.21

Applying a textured background to a chart can enhance its appearance.

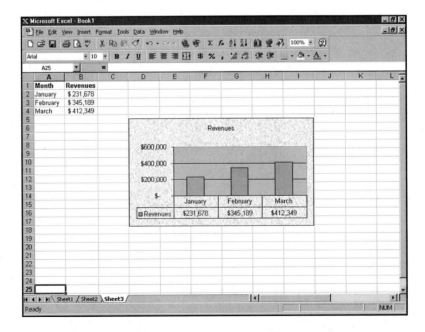

> ▶ **See** "Using WordArt," **p. 1048**

- Incorporate WordArt into your charts by choosing Insert, Picture, WordArt to open the WordArt Gallery, where you can choose among many WordArt styles.

- Rotate a text element by selecting it and then clicking the Angle Text Downward or Angle Text Upward button in the Chart toolbar.

Part **III**

Ch **16**

CAUTION

Be sure to make enough room for this rotated text; otherwise, it can overlap other chart elements.

If you selected a 3-D chart subtype, Excel 97 provides additional formatting options. To work with these additional options, choose Chart, 3-D View to display the 3-D View dialog box (see Figure 16.22).

FIG. 16.22
You can adjust a chart's elevation, rotation, or perspective in the 3-D View dialog box.

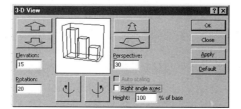

T I P   To remove all customizations that you made in the 3-D options, click the Default button.

You can change the Elevation—the level at which you view the chart—either manually by entering a value in the text box, or by clicking the elevation control to increase or decrease the value incrementally.

In addition, you can adjust the Rotation of the 3-D chart—its angle—in the same way. Either enter a manual rotation level in the text box or adjust by using the rotation controls.

N O T E   The perspective option doesn't appear if you selected the Right Angle Axes check box in the 3-D View dialog box. ■

The Perspective feature allows you to set depth. Again, enter the level manually or use the controls. Check the Right Angle Axes box to remove perspective from the chart.

Enter Height as a percentage of the base. If you select Auto Scaling, Height defaults to 100 percent.

Saving Customized Chart Formats

After you make extensive customizations in a chart, you may want to reuse the format. To create a custom chart format, follow these steps:

1. Select the chart that you want to use as a custom format.

2. Choose <u>C</u>hart, Chart <u>T</u>ype to open the Chart Type dialog box, shown in Figure 16.23.

FIG. 16.23

Add a user-defined chart type in the Chart Type dialog box.

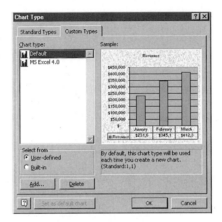

3. Select User-Defined in the Custom Types tab. A list of user-defined chart types appears, and the Add button is activated.

 T I P Click the Delete button to delete a user-defined chart.

4. Click the <u>A</u>dd button to open the Add Custom Chart Type dialog box, shown in Figure 16.24.

FIG. 16.24

You can enter a name and description of your custom chart.

5. Enter a Name and Description for this custom chart type.

6. Click OK.

The user-defined custom chart is now available for selection the next time you create a new chart. ●

CHAPTER 17

Using Lists and Databases

by Patrice-Anne Rutledge

Excel 97 offers numerous features for creating lists and databases. Using data forms, you can simplify basic data entry tasks. For more complex entries, data validation helps you to ensure entry accuracy. Excel also includes the ability to apply sophisticated sorting, filtering, and subtotaling to any list. ■

New features

Excel 97 includes several new features that enhance list and database creation, including data validation.

List and database overview

Once you create a list in Excel, you can sort and filter it like a database.

List data entry

Using Excel's data form, you can simplify data entry tasks. The new data validation feature makes it easier to avoid data entry errors and improve accuracy.

List modification

You can display, find, edit, and delete records using the data form.

List sort and filter

Excel includes both basic and advanced sorting and filtering features.

List subtotals

You can subtotal your list data after you've sorted and then expand or collapse the detail in which you want to view the summaries.

Overview of New Features

Excel 97 includes a few new features that further automate list and database entry:

- *Data validation.* To ease entry and help avoid entry errors, data validation lets you specify entry parameters by field.

- *Custom data entry messages.* In Excel 97 you can customize input and error messages when using data validation.

Understanding Lists and Databases

In Excel 97, a *list* is a series of rows in a worksheet containing similar data. A worksheet with client names and addresses, a series of stock performance data, or a project to-do list are all examples of lists. In each case the columns contain similar information based on each column label. Figure 17.1 shows two list examples.

FIG. 17.1

In Excel 97, a list contains a series of rows with like data.

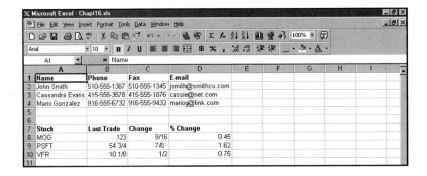

Excel automatically considers any data in a list format to be a database and enables you to find, sort, or total this data—common database functions. When using a list as a database, each *column* is a database field that determines the type of information required for data entry. Excel considers the column label to be a field name and each *row* to be a database record.

Designing and Creating a List

You can create a basic list in any Excel worksheet. To create a list, enter the column labels in the first row. For example, let's say that you want to create a project to-do list for a design firm. You want to include the following columns:

- Project
- Due Date
- Customer
- Designer
- Estimated Revenue
- Estimated Hours

> **TIP** You can use formatting features such as bolding, italics, or cell borders to differentiate parts of your list.

> **CAUTION**
>
> Be sure that your worksheet doesn't include other data in the area beneath your new list. If the list grows, it may collide with the data you've entered below it.

You'll enter the data for each individual project in a separate row. Because Excel considers all consecutive rows to be part of the same list, avoid blank rows between sections or between the column labels and the list data. Figure 17.2 illustrates the first few rows of this project list.

FIG. 17.2

Organize list data in columns.

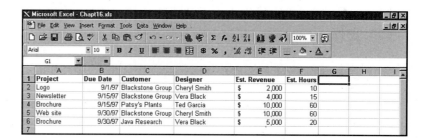

Entering List Data

Once you've created an Excel list, you can continue entering data in the worksheet, or you can create a data form to simplify your data entry tasks. A *data form* displays field names in a database format and allows you to enter information in text boxes. In a data form, you can add, modify, find, and delete records.

▶ **See** "Using Templates," **p. 309**

N O T E If more than one user is going to enter data in your Excel database, the Template Wizard with Data Tracking can make this easier. To open this wizard, choose Data, Template Wizard and follow the prompts that appear for each step.

Entering Data with the Data Form

A data form uses the column labels from your list as text box labels and enables you to quickly add new data records.

To enter data using the data form, follow these steps:

1. Position the cell pointer in any cell in your list.

CAUTION

Before choosing Data, Form, you must first select any cell within the list you want to modify, otherwise Excel displays an error message stating that no list was found.

2. Choose Data, Form. Figure 17.3 displays the Data Form dialog box.

FIG. 17.3
A data form can simplify data entry tasks.

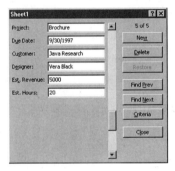

3. Click the New button to add a new row or record to the list. Excel displays a new blank record.

N O T E   If you make a mistake and want to erase your current entry, click the Restore button on the data form to remove the entry from the form. You must click Restore before pressing Enter to avoid saving the record. ▪

 T I P   Press Tab to move forward to the next text box. Press Shift+Tab to move to the previous text box.

4. Enter your data in each text box.
5. Press Enter to save the record and display another blank record once you've completed entering data.
6. Click the Close button to return to the worksheet.

Using Data Validation

CAUTION

Any data validation you set doesn't apply to entries you make using the data form.

CAUTION

You can't set data validation options if you're currently entering data or if you've applied protection to your worksheet; the Validation option on the Data menu appears dimmed. Complete your data entry and unprotect your worksheet by choosing Tools, Protection, Unprotect Sheet and then try to access the Validation menu again.

Using Excel 97's data validation feature, you can specify the exact information you can enter in your list, reducing the chance for data entry errors. For example, you can limit entries to a select list of choices, ensure that a user enters a valid date in a date column, and prevent numeric entries outside set parameters you've specified.

 T I P

To remove data validation criteria, select the column from which you want to remove validation and choose Data, Validation to open the Data Validation dialog box. Then click the Clear All button in the Data Validation this dialog box. To remove data validation from the entire worksheet, select the worksheet and then click Clear All.

To set data validation criteria, select the column whose data entry you want to validate and choose Data, Validation to open the Data Validation dialog box. To validate the data only in part of a column, select the specific cells you want to validate rather than the entire column. Figure 17.4 displays this dialog box.

FIG. 17.4

Set parameters for data entry in the Data Validation dialog box.

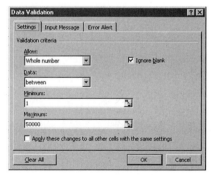

You can choose to Allow the following criteria:

- Any value
- Whole number
- Decimal
- List
- Date
- Time
- Text length
- Custom

Part III
Ch
17

Note that the default selection in <u>A</u>llow depends on the data in the column that you're validating.

Validating Numeric, Date, and Time Entries   If you choose Whole Number, Decimal, a numeric, Date, or Time as the <u>A</u>llow criteria, you have the following <u>D</u>ata operator options:

- Between
- Not between
- Equal to
- Not equal to
- Greater than
- Less than
- Greater than or equal to
- Less than or equal to

You'll enter <u>M</u>inimum and Ma<u>x</u>imum values for numeric values, or start and end parameters for date and time. Click the Cell Reference button, located to the right of the <u>M</u>inimum and Ma<u>x</u>imum fields, to return to the worksheet to select these values.

For example, in the project list you might want to specify that a user must enter a date between the current date and **1/1/99** for the project due date. You could also specify that the estimated project cost must be at least $1 and no more than $100,000 to help avoid data entry errors. If you enter an invalid value, Excel displays an error message, shown in Figure 17.5.

FIG. 17.5

An error message appears telling you that you've entered invalid data.

Validating List Data   To create a drop-down list of values from which a user must choose, first select the entire column that you want to validate. Next, choose List as Your <u>A</u>llow option in the Data Validation dialog box, and then enter your <u>S</u>ource list. By clicking the Cell Reference button, you can return to your worksheet and select your list of valid values. For example, if the only project types you'll want to enter are those that currently exist in your list, you can select those options. Then when you enter your next value in the Project column, a drop-down list displays the values from which you can choose, shown in Figure 17.6.

CAUTION

Only choose a validation list when you don't want to enter any data other than the list values. Otherwise, it's better not to use data validation and let Excel's AutoComplete feature finish your entries after you type in the first few characters of a value you've previously entered.

Specifying Input and Error Messages   To specify an input message to display when a user makes an entry in a column you've validated, go to the Input Message tab in the Data Validation dialog box. Figure 17.7 illustrates this tab.

FIG. 17.6

Choose from the list of valid values.

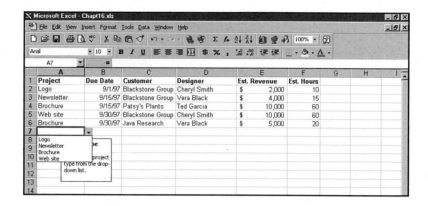

CAUTION

Be sure you select an entire column to validate rather than just one cell in the column or Excel may not display an error message when users enter invalid data. If you select only a specific cell, Excel applies data validation only to that cell.

FIG. 17.7

You can specify the exact input message you want the user to see.

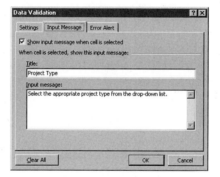

Select the <u>S</u>how Input Message When Cell Is Selected check box. Enter your desired <u>T</u>itle and Input Message. Click OK to return to the worksheet. Figure 17.8 illustrates how this message displays when you enter a value.

To display a custom error message when a user enters invalid data, choose the Error Alert tab. Figure 17.9 illustrates this tab.

Select the <u>S</u>how Error Alert After Invalid Data Is Entered check box. Select an error alert <u>S</u>tyle: Stop, Warning, or Information. Then enter your <u>T</u>itle and <u>E</u>rror Message. Click OK to return to the worksheet. Figure 17.10 shows a sample custom error message.

FIG. 17.8

When users enter data, they'll see the input message you've created for that field.

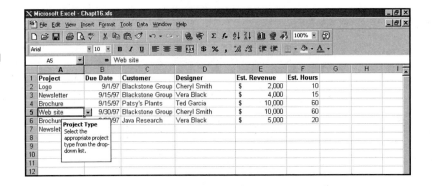

FIG. 17.9

Specify a custom error message on the Error Alert tab.

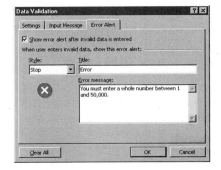

FIG. 17.10

When a user enters an invalid value, Excel displays the custom error alert you've created.

TROUBLESHOOTING

After I choose Data, Form, Excel displays an error message stating that no list was found. Before choosing Data, Form, you must first select any cell within the list you want to modify.

I set data validation parameters, but didn't receive an error message when I entered invalid data. Be sure you selected an entire column to validate rather than just one cell in the column. If you only select a specific cell, Excel only applies data validation to that cell.

The Validation option on the Data menu appears dimmed. You can't set data validation options if you're currently entering data or if you've applied protection to your worksheet. Complete your data entry and unprotect your worksheet by choosing Tools, Protection, Unprotect Sheet and then try to access the Validation menu again.

Modifying Records

Once you've entered data in your list, either directly on the worksheet or using the data form, you'll probably want to modify the list data in some way. You can use the data form to display, delete, edit, and search for specific records. You can also choose Data, Subtotals to use the **subtotal** feature to create subtotals based on your list data.

Displaying and Finding Records

In Excel 97, you can use the data form to locate and display records in your list. Position the cell pointer in a cell in your list and choose Data, Form. Table 17.1 lists the navigational commands for locating data in a data form.

 You also can use the scroll bar to view each record in your list.

Table 17.1 Data Form Navigational Commands

Command	Result
Find Next button	Displays next record
Find Prev button	Displays previous record
Page Up	Displays first record
Page Down	Displays blank record

 You can use multiple criteria when searching for records. Just enter the criteria values in the appropriate text boxes.

When searching for data, you can specify a single criterion or multiple criteria. Entering multiple criteria creates an AND condition. You can't use the data form to search using an OR condition. In addition to searching for exact matches, you can use a number of comparison operators in your search criteria. Table 17.2 illustrates the available search comparison operators.

 You can also use the ? wildcard to search for any single character or the * wildcard to search for any group of characters. For example, news* would locate newsletter, newsletters, newspaper, and so on.

 To search for blank column fields, enter the = in the text box of the field you want to search. Don't include any other characters in the box, only the = with no additional criteria.

Table 17.2 Comparison Operators

Button	Description
=	Equals
>	Greater than
<	Less than
>=	Greater than or equal to
<=	Less than or equal to
<>	Not equal to

For example, to locate projects with an estimated revenue greater than $5,000, you would enter **>5000** in the Est. Revenue text box. To find all records for Newsletter projects, enter **Newsletter** as your Project criterion.

To locate records in a data form, follow these steps:

1. Select a cell in the list.
2. Choose Data, Form.
3. Click the Criteria button.
4. Enter the search criteria in the text box of the field you want to search, illustrated in Figure 17.11.

FIG. 17.11

In this example, the search criterion is an Estimated Revenue amount greater than 5000.

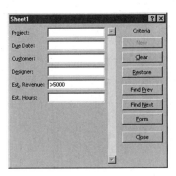

5. Click the Find Next button to locate the next match. Excel emits a beep if no matches exist.
6. Select the Close button to return to the worksheet.

Editing Records

Once you've located the record you want to edit, make any desired changes and either Close the data form or move to a new record to save the changes. You can also edit the data in a list directly in the worksheet as you would any other data.

Deleting Records

In the data form, you can also delete records from your list. You can only delete one record at a time using the data form, not multiple records.

To delete a record from the data form, follow these steps:

1. Position the cell pointer in any cell in your list.
2. Choose <u>D</u>ata, F<u>o</u>rm to open the data form.
3. Click the Find <u>N</u>ext button to locate the record you want to delete.
4. Click the <u>D</u>elete button to delete the record.

    Excel displays a warning box, illustrated in Figure 17.12, to verify that you really want to delete the record.

FIG. 17.12

A message box appears reminding you that the record will be permanently deleted.

5. Click OK to delete the record; click Cancel to cancel the deletion.
6. Select the C<u>l</u>ose button to return to your worksheet.

Sorting and Filtering Lists

Excel enables you to both sort and filter your list data based on a number of criteria. You can sort by up to three fields and apply sophisticated filtering options to locate very specific list information.

Sorting List Data

 In Excel 97, you'll sort based on the column fields you created in your list. The fastest way to quickly sort a list is to select the column by which you want to sort and then click the Sort Ascending or the Sort Descending button on the toolbar.

 T I P To sort only selected records in a list, highlight the records you want to sort and then apply sorting.

CAUTION

If you don't select the entire list (for example, you select only a few cells in a column), Excel displays a Sort Warning dialog box asking if you want to only sort the selection you've made or if you want to expand the selection to include the entire list. It's important to avoid sorting only certain columns in a list while excluding others. Excel doesn't sort columns that aren't selected and the result can be mismatched data across rows.

Part
III

Ch
17

To sort a list by more than one field, follow these steps:

1. Position the cell pointer in the list you want to sort.

2. Choose <u>D</u>ata, <u>S</u>ort. Figure 17.13 displays the Sort dialog box.

FIG. 17.13

You can sort based on up to three different fields.

 TIP To undo a sort you applied by mistake, choose <u>E</u>dit, <u>U</u>ndo Sort to redisplay the original order. You must choose this command immediately after performing the sort and before performing another action.

3. At the bottom of the Sort dialog box, indicate whether your list has a Header <u>R</u>ow or No Header Ro<u>w</u> in the My List Has section. If you have a header row, you don't want Excel to think this row is part of your data and sort it.

4. In the Sort By drop-down list choose the name of the column field by which you want to sort. You can sort in either <u>A</u>scending or <u>D</u>escending order.

5. To sort records using additional fields, select additional sort fields in the two following Then By drop-down lists. You can sort by up to three fields.

6. Click OK to apply the sort. Figure 17.14 illustrates the result of sorting by project.

FIG. 17.14

The worksheet data is now ordered based on specifications to sort by Designer.

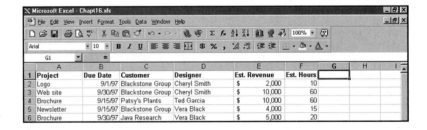

Setting Sort Orientation Normally, you'll want to sort your list data from top to bottom. Occasionally, however, you may want to sort data from left to right. To do so, select the <u>O</u>ptions button on the Sort dialog box to open the Sort Options dialog box, shown in Figure 17.15.

In the Orientation group box, select Sort <u>L</u>eft to Right to change the sort orientation.

FIG. 17.15
Set sort orientation in
the Sort Options dialog
box.

Sorting Days and Months To customize the format of days of the week or months, choose Tools, Options and select the Custom Lists tab. If none of the existing lists are formatted the way you prefer, choose New List under Custom Lists, enter the new list items in the List Entries box and click the Add button to add your new list.

When you sort a text field, Excel sorts in alphabetical order. If your field is a day of the week or a month, this produces undesirable results. To sort dates appropriately, click the Options button on the Sort dialog box to access the Sort Options dialog box. From the First Key Sort Order drop-down list, illustrated in Figure 17.16, select the date order in which you want to sort.

FIG. 17.16
You can sort days of
the week and months
in chronological order.

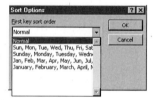

Filtering List Data

When you want to view only a portion of the data in a list, you can apply filters to hide the selected data that is outside of the selected filter parameters. Excel 97 doesn't delete this data; it just prevents you from viewing it until you remove the filter.

In Excel, you can use the AutoFilter feature to apply a basic filter or create a custom filter to match specific criteria.

Using AutoFilter To filter a list using AutoFilter, follow these steps:

 Once you've applied filters, to remove AutoFilter filters, choose Data, Filter, AutoFilter again.

1. Select a cell in the list you want to filter.
2. Choose Data, Filter, AutoFilter. You'll see drop-down lists next to each column heading, shown in Figure 17.17.

FIG. 17.17

Excel displays drop-down arrows next to each column heading.

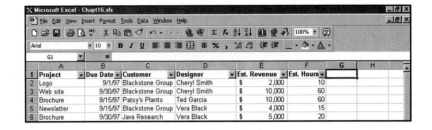

3. Click the drop-down list in the column that you want to filter. For every column, you can choose to filter on a unique item in the column; display all items, the top ten items in the list, blank items, or nonblank items; or create a custom filter. Figure 17.18 displays this drop-down list.

FIG. 17.18

You can choose the item to display from the drop-down list.

4. Select the item you want to display. If you select Top Ten, the Top 10 AutoFilter dialog box displays, as shown in Figure 17.19.

FIG. 17.19

You can filter based on the top or bottom items.

Choose whether to display the Top or Bottom Items or Percents and then indicate the quantity to display. Click OK to return to the worksheet.

5. Repeat the previous two steps for each additional column you want to filter.

TIP To remove a filter from a specific column, select All from the drop-down list of that column.

Excel displays the records that match your filter criteria and hides all other records.

Creating a Custom AutoFilter   If you want to apply specific criteria to your filter, you can create a custom AutoFilter. To do so, follow these steps:

1. Select a cell in the list you want to filter.

2. Choose Data, Filter, AutoFilter.

3. Select the drop-down arrow in the column you want to filter and choose Custom from the list. Figure 17.20 displays the Custom AutoFilter dialog box which opens.

FIG. 17.20

The Custom AutoFilter dialog box lets you create a custom filter.

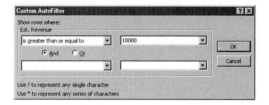

4. The first drop-down list includes all available comparison operators from which you can choose. Select the appropriate operator.

5. In the second drop-down list, select the data you want to compare.

 T I P You can also enter specific criteria in this text box using wildcard characters rather than selecting an item from the list. The ? wildcard searches for any single character; the * wildcard searches for any group of characters.

6. To include a second set of criteria, choose <u>A</u>nd to indicate that the records must meet both sets of criteria. Choose <u>O</u>r to indicate that the records need only match either set of criteria. Select the second set of criteria as described in steps 4 and 5.

7. Choose OK to return to the worksheet. Excel applies the filter and displays the records that match the criteria you entered. Figure 17.21 illustrates the filtered list.

FIG. 17.21

Excel displays the filtered list of Revenue greater than or equal to 10,000.

N O T E For even more sophisticated filtering capabilities, you can use Excel's Advanced Filter feature which lets you filter based on calculated criteria and apply detailed AND and OR criteria. Choose <u>D</u>ata, <u>F</u>ilter, <u>A</u>dvanced Filter to access this feature. ▪

Subtotaling List Data

When you sort data in a list, Excel enables you to summarize the data with subtotals. When you summarize a list, Excel calculates subtotals based on subsets of the data and also calculates a grand total.

Creating List Subtotals

To create list subtotals, follow these steps:

1. Sort your list data in the order in which you want to create subtotals. For example, if you want to create subtotals based on the amount of revenue generated by each designer, first sort your list by designer. The earlier section in this chapter, "Sorting List Data," covers the basics of sorting.

2. Select a cell in the list you want to subtotal.

3. Choose Data, Subtotals. The Subtotal dialog box opens as illustrated in Figure 17.22.

FIG. 17.22

Use the Subtotal dialog box to create data subtotals.

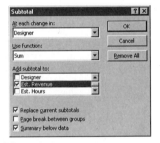

4. Specify the field by which to subtotal from the At Each Change In drop-down list.

5. From the Use Function drop-down list, select Sum to create subtotals. You can also select average, count, and other summary functions.

6. In the Add Subtotal To box, choose the data to subtotal. For example, if you want to subtotal all estimated revenues, select the Est. Revenue check box.

7. Select any of the following options if you want to apply them: Replace Current Subtotals, Page Breaks Between Groups, or Summary Below Data.

8. Click OK to create the subtotals and return to your worksheet, illustrated in Figure 17.23.

FIG. 17.23

The worksheet now displays subtotal lines for each Designer's Estimated Revenue.

Level 1, 2, 3 buttons

Hide Detail Level button

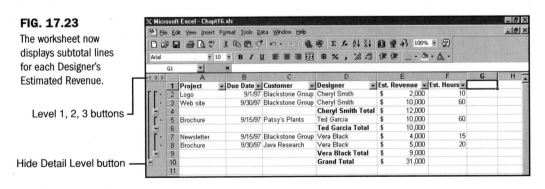

Subtotaling List Data **363**

Controlling Data Display in a Subtotaled List

Excel displays subtotaled data in Outline view. Using this view, you have control over the amount of data you want to display. For example, you can display only the data subtotals and grand totals or all the detail data as well.

▶ **See** "Using Outlines," **p. 302**

 To display only the subtotal, select the Hide Detail Level button for that subtotal. Excel hides the detail and displays only the summary data, illustrated in Figure 17.24.

FIG. 17.24
The Hide Detail Level button lets you hide subtotal detail.

Show Detail Level button

Hide Detail Level button

 To restore the data detail, select the Show Detail Level button. Excel displays the full detail again.

Removing Subtotals from a List

To remove list subtotals, select a cell in the subtotaled list and choose Data, Subtotals to open the Subtotal dialog box again. Click the Remove All button to restore the original list.

TROUBLESHOOTING

After sorting the database, Excel sorts the column titles along with the data in the list. To prevent the column titles from sorting with the rest of the list, choose Header Row in the My List Has section of the Sort dialog box.

Excel created a subtotal for each entry in my list rather than by group. You must sort on the field on which you want to subtotal first. To do so, choose Data, Sort.

III

Ch
17

CHAPTER 18

Using Pivot Tables

by Patrice-Anne Rutledge

Microsoft Excel 97's Pivot Table feature enables you to easily create interactive reports that summarize and analyze data found in Excel lists as well as external databases. With Pivot Tables you can drag and drop table elements to quickly view data in different ways. Once you create a Pivot Table, you can use Excel's advanced features to enhance, modify, and customize it even further. ■

New features

Excel 97 offers many new Pivot Table features that both simplify and enhance Pivot Tables, including the ability to preserve formatting and select only specific data.

PivotTable basics

With Pivot Tables, you'll combine four main elements—rows, columns, pages, and data—to analyze information in a multitude of ways.

PivotTable Wizard

Use the PivotTable Wizard to guide you step-by-step through the process of creating a Pivot Table.

PivotTable formatting

Once you've created a basic Pivot Table, you can format its labels, text, and numbers.

PivotTable customization

You can refresh the data in your Pivot Table to update it without changing its structure, or drag and drop fields to analyze data in entirely different ways.

Overview of New Features

Excel 97 provides a number of new features that make Pivot Tables a more powerful data analysis tool. These features include the following enhancements:

- *Persistent formatting*. This option lets you apply formatting such as bolding or color enhancements that the Pivot Table maintains when you refresh data.
- *Page field layout options*. You can now place multiple page fields in either columns or rows in a Pivot Table.
- *PivotTable selection*. Using the Pivot Table selection feature, you can select only specific PivotTable data for formatting or analysis.
- *Dates displayed in order*. Excel 97 displays dates in the appropriate order rather than alphabetically.
- *Enhanced PivotTable options*. Step 4 of the PivotTable Wizard includes an Options button that opens a detailed PivotTable Options dialog box for advanced users.
- *AutoShow and AutoSort capabilities*. Excel 97 includes options for sorting Pivot Table data as well as filtering the top and bottom data-field entries.
- *Calculated fields and items*. You can create formulas using Pivot Table data and store them as calculated fields and items.
- *External data access improvements*. Excel 97 offers server-based page fields to enhance memory and performance when accessing large amounts of external data.

Understanding Pivot Tables

A Pivot Table is an interactive report that summarizes and analyzes data in an Excel worksheet or an external database. Using Pivot Tables, you can quickly and easily analyze data in a variety of ways without creating a new report each time. A Pivot Table cross-tabulates data in columns and rows with the option to filter and sort the display data as well as to expand on its detail.

The layout of a Pivot Table includes four main areas:

- *Row*. Displays the field items in a row.
- *Column*. Displays the field items in a column.
- *Data*. Summarizes a field by row, column, and page.
- *Page*. Allows you to filter Pivot Table data.

You can create a Pivot Table from four different types of sources:

- An existing Excel database or list
- An external data source, such as an Access database
- Multiple consolidation ranges
- Another Pivot Table

Before creating a Pivot Table, particularly if you're new to the idea of Pivot Tables, it helps to create a diagram of what you want your Pivot Table to look like and what you want it to summarize. This makes it easier to determine what fields to place in the row, column, page, or data areas.

Figure 18.1 illustrates an Excel list and its accompanying Pivot Table. The list includes four columns—the name of a salesperson, the product that salesperson sold, the month the salesperson sold the product, and the product sales amount. In the Pivot Table you've summarized and totaled this data.

FIG. 18.1

A Pivot Table can summarize and analyze the data in an Excel list.

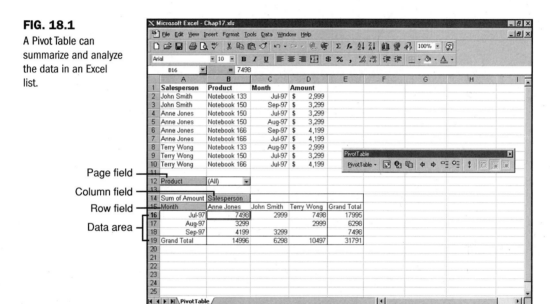

In this example, you've placed the Month field as a Pivot Table row, the Salesperson field as a column, the Amount as your summarized data, and the Product as the page field on which you can filter. With the page field you're able to adjust the contents of the Pivot Table based on product. You can display the data for all products combined or for a single product. To display a single product, click the arrow next to the page field and select that product.

You could also switch the row and column fields by switching Month and Salesperson. The amount in the cell that intersects between these two fields will remain the same. If you want to filter based on Salesperson or Month, you could move either of these to the page field and move the existing page field, Product to a row or column. Pivot Tables are extremely flexible and allow you to view data in many ways.

Part III

Ch

18

Creating Pivot Tables

Excel's PivotTable Wizard simplifies Pivot Table design. The PivotTable Wizard guides you through the four steps of creating a Pivot Table. Depending on your choice of data source in Step 1, the second step differs as it assists you in selecting this data source. The following example shows you how to create the Pivot Table illustrated in Figure 18.1, which uses an existing Excel list as its data source.

To create a Pivot Table from an Excel list or database, follow these steps:

1. Select the data you want to analyze in the PivotTable.

2. Choose <u>D</u>ata, <u>P</u>ivotTable Report to open Step 1 of the PivotTable Wizard, shown in Figure 18.2.

FIG. 18.2

In Step 1 of the PivotTable Wizard, you can specify what kind of source data to use.

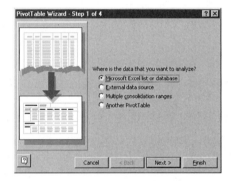

3. Indicate that you want to analyze data in a <u>M</u>icrosoft Excel list or database.

4. Click Next to continue to Step 2, shown in Figure 18.3.

FIG. 18.3

In the PivotTable Wizard's Step 2, you'll select the data range to include in the Pivot Table.

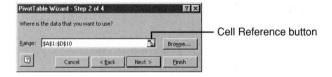

Cell Reference button

T I P Excel automatically selects the data range for you if you position the cell pointer in your list before activating the PivotTable Wizard.

5. The cell references of the data you previously selected appear in the <u>R</u>ange edit box. You can change this data by selecting the Cell Reference button, to the right of the <u>R</u>ange edit box, to return to your worksheet.

CAUTION

If you didn't select your column headings when you created your Pivot Table, they won't display in Step 3. You won't see field names, just row data. Go back to Step 2 and include these headings in your data range. Otherwise, Excel recognizes the first row of data as your field button names.

6. Continue to Step 3 of the wizard, illustrated in Figure 18.4, by clicking the Next button.

FIG. 18.4

You can define your Pivot Table layout in Step 3.

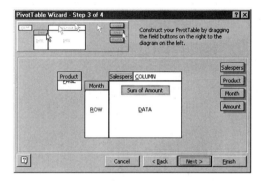

 TIP Double-click a field button to customize it. The PivotTable Field dialog box opens in which you can specify subtotal, formatting, sort, display, and page field options.

7. Drag the field buttons on the right of the dialog box to the appropriate location on the diagram. In this example, you want to place the Month field as a Row, the Salesperson field as a Column, the Product field as the Page, and the Amount field as your summarized Data.

8. Click the Next button to go to Step 4, shown in Figure 18.5.

FIG. 18.5

You can place your Pivot Table in a new or existing worksheet.

9. Determine whether you want to place your Pivot Table in a New worksheet or an Existing worksheet. If you choose to place it in an existing worksheet, you can specify its exact location by clicking the Cell Reference button to return to the worksheet.

10. To set advanced PivotTable options, click the Options button to open the PivotTable Options dialog box. For details on these options, see the section "Setting Advanced PivotTable Options" later in this chapter.

11. Click the Finish button to complete and create your Pivot Table.

Creating a Pivot Table from Another Pivot Table

To create a new Pivot Table from an existing Pivot Table, choose the Another PivotTable option in Step 1 of the PivotTable Wizard. Step 2 then differs from the previous example. Figure 18.6 illustrates Step 2 based on this selection.

FIG. 18.6

You can create a new PivotTable from the data in an existing PivotTable.

In Step 2, indicate Which PivotTable contains the data you want to use. Click Next to continue to Steps 3 and 4.

Creating a Pivot Table from Multiple Consolidation Ranges

You can create a single Pivot Table from multiple ranges or worksheets. To do so, follow these steps as you complete Step 1 of the PivotTable Wizard.

1. Select the Multiple Consolidation ranges option in Step 1 of the PivotTable Wizard. Step 2a then displays, as illustrated in Figure 18.7.

FIG. 18.7

Excel 97 will create a single page field for you or you can create your own.

2. When creating a Pivot Table from multiple ranges you can include from zero to four page fields. In Step 2a, you can choose one of the following options:

   - Create a Single Page Field for Me.
   - I Will Create the Page Fields

3. Depending on your selection here, Step 2b varies. If you chose to have Excel create a single page field, Step 2b displays as illustrated in Figure 18.8.

FIG. 18.8

Select the ranges to include in Step 2b.

TIP To delete a range you've chosen, select it and click the Delete button.

To choose each range to consolidate, enter it in the Range edit box and click the Add button to move it to the All Ranges box. You can use the Cell Reference button to return to a worksheet for selection.

If you chose to create your own page fields, Step 2b displays as illustrated in Figure 18.9.

FIG. 18.9

You can set up to four page fields when you consolidate multiple ranges.

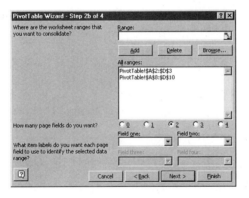

Part III

Ch 18

Step 2b expands to include options for selecting page fields. First, determine the number of page fields you want—from zero to four.

4. The Field One, Field Two, Field Three, and Field Four drop-down lists display based on the corresponding number of page fields you selected. For example, if you chose to display only two page fields (2), Excel 97 would activate only Field One and Field Two. If you chose to display four page fields, Excel would activate all four drop-down lists. Enter or select the item label you want to associate with each data range in the Field drop-down lists.

5. Click Next to continue to Steps 3 and 4, which are identical to the instructions in the "Creating Pivot Tables" section earlier in this chapter.

Creating a Pivot Table from an External Data Source

In many cases you'll use an application such as Microsoft Access to track and store large amounts of data. You can then use the quantitative power of Excel to analyze this data in a Pivot Table. For example, if you have an order-entry database in Access, you can use a Pivot Table to analyze sales by customer, employee, data, or geographic area.

To create a Pivot Table from an external data source, such as an Access database, follow these steps as you complete Step 1 of the PivotTable Wizard.

> **CAUTION**
>
> Be sure that you've installed Microsoft Query with Excel 97 before trying to create a Pivot Table from an external data source or you'll receive an error message. To install this feature, return to Microsoft Office 97 Setup and choose the Data Access, Microsoft Query Option.

1. Select the External Data Source option in Step 1 of the PivotTable Wizard. Figure 18.10 illustrates Step 2 of the wizard based on this data-source selection.

FIG. 18.10

Excel 97 lets you create a Pivot Table from an external data source.

2. Click the Get Data button to open the Choose Data Source dialog box, shown in Figure 18.11.

FIG. 18.11

Specify your external data source in the Choose Data Source dialog box.

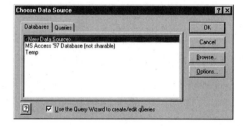

 T I P You can also select queries you've already created as your data source. You'll find these in the Queries tab of the Choose Data Source dialog box.

3. In this example, you'll choose MS Access '97 Database on the Databases tab and click OK to continue.

4. The Select Database dialog box opens, as illustrated in Figure 18.12.

FIG. 18.12

Identify the Access database to use in the Select Database dialog box.

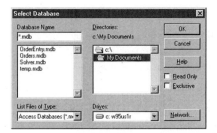

5. Select the Database <u>N</u>ame and click OK.

▶ **See** "Performing a Query," **p. 432**

▶ **See** "Using Other Data Sources," **p. 437**

> **N O T E** Microsoft Query, with its Query Wizard, is an optional feature for Excel 97. Using the Query Wizard enables you to select specific information from external data sources to use in Excel. ▨

6. The Query Wizard opens. Use the wizard to select the Access database data you want to include in your Pivot Table.

7. Once you finish your query and click the Finish button in the PivotTable Wizard, you'll return to Step 2.

8. Continue with Steps 3 and 4 of the wizard. Excel 97 connects to your data source and completes your Pivot Table.

Excel 97 includes several new options for improving memory performance when accessing large external databases. To set these options, select the Pivot Table, click the Pivot Table Field button on the Pivot Table toolbar to open the PivotTable Field dialog box, and click the Ad<u>v</u>anced button.

The PivotTable Field Advanced Options dialog box includes the following Page Field options:

▨ <u>R</u>etrieve external data for all page field items (faster performance). Speeds up data retrieval by accessing all items at once.

▨ <u>Q</u>uery external data source as you select each page field item (requires less memory). Retrieves the data for each page field item as it's displayed. Excel requires less memory to do this.

▨ Di<u>s</u>able pivoting of this field (recommended). If you move a page field to a different part of the Pivot Table and you've chosen to query the external data source as you select each page field, the data for all items is instead retrieved at once. This requires more memory and slows down performance. Checking this option helps you avoid this problem.

Setting Advanced Pivot Table Options

To specify additional Pivot Table options, click the Options button on Step 4 of the PivotTable Wizard. Or, right-click a finished Pivot Table and choose Options from the shortcut menu. Figure 18.13 illustrates the PivotTable Options dialog box.

FIG. 18.13

You'll set advanced options in the PivotTable Options dialog box.

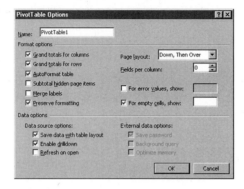

The PivotTable Options dialog box includes a variety of formatting options you can set:

- *Grand Totals for Columns*. Calculates and displays column item grand totals.
- *Grand Totals for Rows*. Calculates and displays row item grand totals.
- *AutoFormat Table*. Applies the default AutoFormat formatting to the Pivot Table.
- *Subtotal Hidden Page Items*. Includes page field items you hid in the PivotTable Field dialog box in Pivot Table subtotals.
- *Merge Labels*. Merges cells in all Pivot Table outer row and column labels.
- *Preserve Formatting*. If you select this option, you'll preserve any formatting you made if you refresh your data. If you don't select this option, your Pivot Table reverts back to its original unformatted version.
- *Page Layout*. You can display page fields in a single column (Down, Then Over) or across columns (Over, Then Down).
- *Fields Per Column*. Determines the number of page fields you want to include in a Pivot Table row or column.
- *For Error Values, Show*. You can indicate the value to display for errors, such as #.
- *For Empty Cells, Show*. You can indicate the value to display for empty cells, such as 0.

The PivotTable Options dialog box also includes several data source options:

- *Save Data with Table Layout*. Saves a copy of the external data on which you based the Pivot Table. You'll want to select this option if you plan to customize your Pivot Table later, otherwise you'll have to refresh your data to perform any additional customizations or analysis.

■ *Enable Drilldown*. Drilldown enables you to display the source data a particular cell summarizes when you double-click it.

■ *Refresh On Open*. Refreshes data automatically when you open the Pivot Table.

If you've accessed an external data source, you can also set the following options in this dialog box:

■ *Save password*. Saves the password used to access an external data source as part of the query. You then won't need to enter the password again when you refresh your Pivot Table.

■ *Background query*. Runs the query in the background so that you can continue working in Excel. Useful for complex queries that take a long time.

■ *Optimize memory*. Optimizes Pivot Table memory performance. Useful when creating a Pivot Table from an external database and the system tells you it doesn't have enough memory.

Formatting Pivot Tables

Once you've created your Pivot Table, you'll probably want to customize its format.

To preserve the formatting you apply to Pivot Tables once you refresh them, select the Preserve Formatting option in the Pivot Table Options dialog box. Also be sure to enable selection, by right-clicking the mouse on the PivotTable and choosing Select, Enable Selection from the menu.

If the PivotTable toolbar doesn't display, choose View, Toolbars and select PivotTable from the submenu.

The PivotTable toolbar provides several ways to easily format and modify your Pivot Table. Table 18.1 lists the PivotTable toolbar buttons and their use.

Table 18.1   PivotTable Toolbar Buttons

Button	Name	Description
PivotTable ▾	PivotTable	Displays a submenu with the most common PivotTable options.
🖼	PivotTable Wizard	Opens the PivotTable Wizard.
🖼	PivotTable Field	Opens the PivotTable Field dialog box for the field selected.

continues

Table 18.1   Continued

Button	Name	Description
	Show Pages	Opens the Show Pages dialog box in which you can choose to Show all pages of any of the page fields you specified in Step 3 of the PivotTable Wizard.
	Ungroup	Ungroups PivotTable items you grouped.
	Group	Groups selected PivotTable items.
	Hide Detail	Hides PivotTable details.
	Show Detail	Displays PivotTable details.
	Refresh Data	Refreshes PivotTable based on current source data.
	Select Label	Using the selection feature, selects specific field labels.
	Select Data	Using the selection feature, selects specific data.
	Select Label and Data	Using the selection feature, selects both labels and data.

In Excel 97 you'll use the PivotTable toolbar buttons as well as other features to format the overall appearance of a Pivot Table, its text, and numeric data.

Changing the Appearance of a Pivot Table

To easily change the overall appearance of your Pivot Table, place the cell pointer in the Pivot Table and then choose Format, AutoFormat from the Excel menu. This opens the AutoFormat dialog box, as shown in Figure 18.14.

Choose a new format from the Table Format list and then click OK to return to the worksheet.

 TIP If you don't want autoformatting to apply to all areas of your Pivot Table, click the Options button on the AutoFormat dialog box to expand it. You can then specify exactly which formats to apply.

FIG. 18.14
Use the AutoFormat feature to apply a variety of predesigned styles to your Pivot Table.

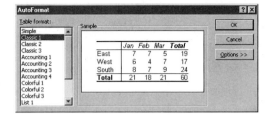

Formatting Numeric Data

 To format the numbers in the Pivot Table data area, select a cell in the data area and click the PivotTable Field button on the PivotTable toolbar. Figure 18.15 displays the PivotTable Field dialog box.

▶ **See** "Formatting Numbers, Dates, and Times," **p. 328**

FIG. 18.15
The PivotTable Field dialog box offers a multitude of options for formatting numeric data.

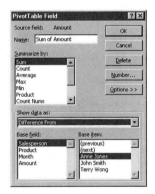

 T I P You can also right-click and select Field from the submenu to open the PivotTable Field dialog box.

In this dialog box you can Summarize in the following ways:

- *Sum*. Sums the values (default setting)
- *Count*. Counts the number of instances the item occurs
- *Average*. Averages the values
- *Max*. Displays the maximum value
- *Min*. Displays the minimum value
- *Product*. Displays the product of the values
- *Count Nums*. Counts the number of rows that include numeric data

- *StdDev*. Estimates the standard deviation
- *StdDevp*. Displays the standard deviation
- *Var*. Estimates the variance
- *Varp*. Displays the variance

As an example, let's say that instead of showing the total amount of sales for each salesperson in the Pivot Table, you now want to display the number of products each salesperson sold. By changing the summarization option to Count, your Pivot Table automatically reflects this. Figure 18.16 illustrates this change.

FIG. 18.16

You can apply several different numeric summary options, including Count.

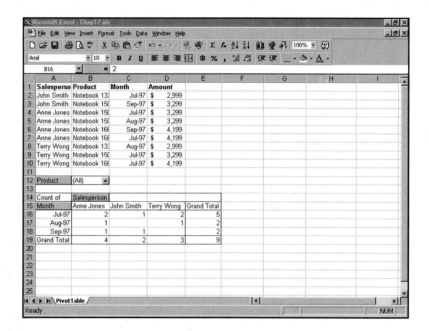

Click the Options button to expand the dialog box, providing more choices. You can choose to show your data in the following ways:

- *Normal*. Displays default format
- *Difference from*. Displays data as the difference from a selected base field and item
- *% of*. Displays data as a percentage of the value for a selected base field and item
- *% Difference From*. Displays data as a percentage difference from a selected base field and item
- *Running Total in*. Displays successive items as a running total based on the selected base field
- *% of Row*. Displays data as a percentage of the row total

- *% of column.* Displays data as a percentage of the column total
- *% of total.* Displays data as a percentage of the grand total of all PivotTable data
- *Index.* Displays data using the following formula:((value in cell) × (grand total of grand totals)) / ((grand row total) × (grand column total))

If you choose Difference from, % of, or % Difference from, you'll activate the Base Field and Base Item fields. Depending on which base field you select, the Base Item drop-down list includes the option of comparing the base field to a specific field item, the previous item, or the next item.

TIP Click the Number button to open the Format Cells Number tab, in which you can set other numeric formatting options.

N O T E In addition to formatting numeric data in a Pivot Table, you can also create calculated fields and items in a Pivot Table by defining formulas using existing Pivot Table data. For example, you could create a new field called Quota Percentage, which compares a salesperson's sales totals for a period of time as a percentage of the required sales quota. To create calculated fields and items, select PivotTable, Formulas, Calculated Field or Calculated Item from the PivotTable toolbar. ■

Formatting Pivot Table Fields

You can also easily format Pivot Table text fields, including options on how to display and sort field data.

 To format a PivotTable field, select a designated field such as Salesperson, and click the PivotTable Field button on the PivotTable toolbar. Figure 18.17 displays the PivotTable Field dialog box.

FIG. 18.17

You can also format text fields in the PivotTable Field dialog box.

N O T E In addition, you can set subtotal options in the PivotTable Field dialog box. For more information on setting summarization options, see the "Formatting Numeric Data" section earlier in this chapter. ■

In this dialog box you can change the orientation for the selected field Name by Row, Column, or Page.

If you want to hide specific items and not display them in the Pivot Table, select those items in the Hide Items list.

Select Show Items with No Data if you want to display empty data cells.

Setting AutoSort Options   Click the Advanced button to open the PivotTable Field Advanced Options dialog box, shown in Figure 18.18.

FIG. 18.18
You can set AutoSort and AutoShow options in Pivot Tables.

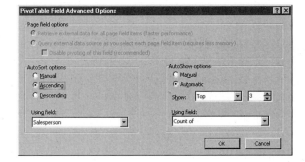

N O T E   Excel 97 displays dates in chronological order, rather than alphabetical order. ■

In this dialog box you can set automatic sorting and display options. You can sort on the selected field in Manual (default), Ascending, or Descending order. If you choose to sort in ascending or descending order, Excel activates the Using Field drop-down list, from which you can choose the field to sort.

Setting AutoShow Options   Use the AutoShow feature to display only a certain number of entries for the selected field. To use this feature, select the Automatic option button and then specify whether you want to Show the Top or Bottom entries. Next, indicate the number of entries you want to display. Select the field on which to base this display in the Using Field drop-down list. For example, if you had twenty salespeople, you could display only the top three by total sales in a Pivot Table and then quickly change this to show only the bottom three.

Formatting Selected Pivot Table Data

Excel 97 includes a new feature that lets you format items or fields based on data, labels, or both data and labels.

TIP You can also use the selection feature to select data for formulas.

To enable PivotTable selection, first select the Pivot Table you want to format. Then choose PivotTable, Select from the PivotTable toolbar. From the Select submenu, choose the Enable Selection option. Selecting the data you want to format activates the following toolbar buttons: Select Label, Select Data, and Select Label and Data.

For example, if you want to bold all the Month item labels, you would select the Month field button. This highlights all the Month item labels. To include the data as well, click the Select Label and Data button on the PivotTable toolbar. To select only the data, click the Select Data button. Once you've made your selection, click the Bold button on the Formatting toolbar. Figure 18.19 illustrates the effect of bolding all the Month labels using this technique.

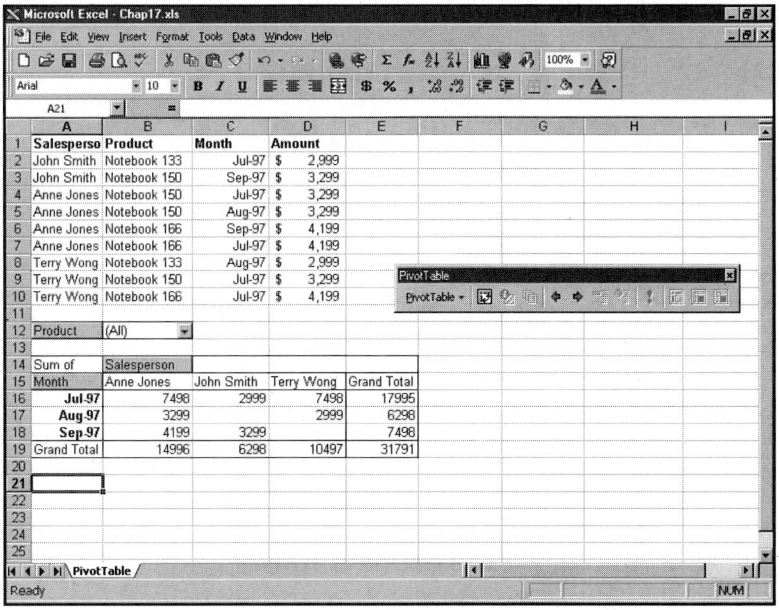

FIG. 18.19 Data selection enables you to format only specific PivotTable data such as all the month labels in this figure.

To highlight all data for "Jul 97" in red, select that row and apply the appropriate color format with the Font Color button.

You can also apply any other formatting option to specific data using the selection feature. Set selection options from the shortcut menu that displays when you choose PivotTable, Select from the PivotTable toolbar.

Modifying Pivot Tables

Once you've created a Pivot Table, you can easily modify both its source data and its layout. If you change the data source, an Excel list for example, you can select the Pivot Table and click the Refresh Data button on the PivotTable toolbar. Excel immediately updates the Pivot Table with the new information.

Rearranging a Pivot Table

Drag the Field buttons to a new column or row location to rearrange the Pivot Table. For example, let's say you want to rearrange the Pivot Table in Figure 18.19 to move the page field Product to the row level. To do so, select the Product field button and drag it next to the Month row field button. The Pivot Table automatically rearranges, as illustrated in Figure 18.20.

FIG. 18.20

You can quickly modify Pivot Table columns and rows by dragging field buttons to a new location.

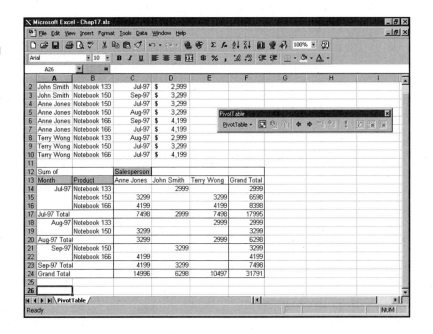

To do more complex rearrangements, you can select the Pivot Table and click the PivotTable Wizard button on the toolbar to reopen the PivotTable Wizard. From the PivotTable Wizard you can make more extensive modifications.

Adding or Removing Fields

To add or remove a Pivot Table field, select the Pivot Table and click the PivotTable Wizard button on the PivotTable toolbar. Step 3 of the wizard displays. You can drag new fields to the Pivot Table layout diagram or drag existing fields off the layout and back to the field button list on the right side of the dialog box.

TROUBLESHOOTING

I lost my formatting when I refreshed data. To preserve the formatting you apply to Pivot Tables once you refresh them, select the Preserve Formatting option in the PivotTable Options dialog box. Also be sure to enable selection by right-clicking the mouse and choosing Select, Enable Selection from the menu.

I made a mistake in formatting or modifying my PivotTable, and my data is gone. In many cases you can undo your modification by choosing Edit, Undo. If this command isn't available, return to the PivotTable Wizard to recreate your Pivot Table based on your original specifications.

CHAPTER 19

Analyzing Spreadsheet Data

by George Lynch

After you've entered your data in Excel, there may come a time when you want to analyze that data from different perspectives. Excel 97 contains several tools to enable you to perform different types of analyses, from the simple to the complex. For example, you might want to see how different rates will affect the monthly payments on a loan. Or you might want to know how what costs you can reduce in order to achieve a specific goal. This chapter explains Excel's analysis tools in detail.

You might find that some tools are rather complex, but if you follow the examples closely, you should gain an understanding of how Excel analyzes data and gives you the results you need. ■

New analysis and quality-of-life features in Excel 97

Become acquainted with the powerful new features that will let you use Excel in a way you might not have thought possible.

Use Data Tables to analyze different financial variables

Data tables enable you to vary certain terms in a formula to compare results.

Goal Seek and Solver features

If you need to arrive at a specific answer, Goal Seek recalculates your formulas to achieve that answer by changing a condition you specify.

Understand circular references

If you've ever had a circular reference error in your spreadsheet, or you tried to calculate a circular reference unsuccessfully, this section is for you.

Use Excel's Scenario Manager to evaluate different possibilities

You can create a "model," where you define certain terms (such as a loan rate or a loan amount, for example), then use formulas to calculate those terms. Excel's Scenario Manager lets you vary the terms to compare results. You can save each scenario you create to compare all the scenarios against each other.

Overview of New Features

Excel 97 has a number of interesting new features, which enhance the model-building power of Excel.

Excel and the Web

Web Query enables you to retrieve data from the Internet into a spreadsheet. Several sample queries are included with Excel 97 to demonstrate the power of this new feature. Using these sample Web Queries you can perform the following tasks:

- Retrieve stock price information directly into a spreadsheet cell from a stock information service on the Internet.

- Retrieve timely information directly into your spreadsheet to update a portfolio model with current pricing information.

- Create your own Web Queries, which can function on a local-area network to update your spreadsheets from databases within your company.

Excel is also "Web Aware" in other ways. It contains the following tools:

- A Web toolbar

- Web based help extensions (links to Microsoft's Web site at points relevant to Excel users)

- A Hyperlink button to enable you to insert references to files on the World Wide Web

- A local Web server (intranet) or a file on a local or network file service

You can also use the enhanced Save As feature to publish your worksheet as an HTML page for viewing with a browser like Microsoft Internet Explorer. You can even use Excel itself to browse the Internet.

Multiple Level Undo

Excel now provides a multiple level undo so you can step back through changes you have made. You can undo up to the last 16 actions you have taken. Remember, though, that some actions cannot be undone (for example, deleting a sheet from the workbook).

Dialog Boxes

Some dialog boxes have been enhanced to include a collapse feature. This enables you to minimize the dialog box to make it easier to find a range on the spreadsheet. (To see an example, choose File, Page Setup. In the Page Setup dialog box, select the Sheet tab. Note the buttons at the end of the Print Area and the Print Title boxes. If you clicke of those buttons, the Page Setup dialog box collapses.)

Formula Enhancements

Excel 97 contains several new and exciting improvements for working with formulas. What follows is a description of some of the most interesting new features:

■ The new Formula AutoCorrect automatically fixes 15 of the most common formula entry errors. You have the option of accepting or rejecting any change that Excel proposes.

■ Excel now automatically uses column and row headings (that are part of the table) as substitutes for cell references in Natural Language formulas. This can reduce common errors and simplify entry and readability of formulas.

■ When you edit a formula cell by pressing F2 (or double-clicking the formula cell), Excel displays color-coded frames and text in the formula to aid in identifying the cells, which are used as inputs. This new feature is called the Range Finder.

N O T E The Range Finder feature is available only if you enable the Edit Directly in Cell option. To do this, select Tools, Options, then click the Edit tab and enable the Edit Directly in Cell option.

Some experienced Excel users have preferred to disable this option in previous versions. The reason is that when this option is disabled and you double-click a formula cell, Excel will select all the precedent cells (cells that contribute to the formula). Some users find that to be a better auditing tool.

Disabling the Edit Directly in Cell option still holds one advantage over the new Range Finder—Range Finder only indicates precedent cells on the same worksheet as the formula cell, whereas using the double-click method selects precedent cells from other worksheets.

As you can see, each option has its own advantages. ■

■ An enhanced Formula Palette incorporates features of the Function wizard and the formula bar into a single more intuitive tool. The Formula Palette appears automatically when you activate the formula bar.

■ Excel 97 has enhanced tools for tracking and eliminating unnecessary circular references. A warning appears when a formula is entered which causes a cell to refer directly or indirectly to itself and the Circular Reference toolbar opens automatically. The Circular Reference toolbar contains a Navigate Circular Reference list box, and a Trace Dependents and Trace Precedents tool to help locate cells which are part of a circular reference.

Part
III
Ch
19

A Few Definitions

Before we begin looking at Excel's analysis tools, it might be helpful if we review a few definitions that we will be using in this chapter (see Table 19.1).

Table 19.1   Definitions

This Term	Means
Function	A built-in calculation that comes with Excel 97. Functions take *Arguments*, which are specific values that you need to enter in a specific order for the function to work properly. (Excel's Function Wizard guides you through entering arguments for functions.)
Argument	Most functions in Excel require numbers or values in order to return an accurate answer. These are called arguments. Arguments must be entered in a specific order for the function to work correctly. Some functions have both required arguments (which you must enter) and optional arguments (which you can enter to modify the way the particular function works).
Formula	A calculation that you create to resolve a problem. You can create complex formulas that contain several functions.
Absolute/ Relative References	Excel uses relative references when you first create a formula. A relative reference tells Excel the location of the referenced cell (for example, the referenced cell is two columns to the left and one row up) instead of using a cell address. Thus, when you copy a formula that uses relative references, the formula will change the referenced cells according to where you paste the copied formula. An absolute reference, on the other hand, refers to a specific cell address, regardless of where you copy the formula. Absolute addresses show dollar signs (for example, $A$1, $C$225). You can mix absolute and relative references (for example, $A1, A$1, A1, $A$1).
Syntax	This term relates to the order of a function's arguments.

Building and Using Data Tables

Data tables allow you to calculate many values within a function by varying one or two of the function's arguments. Excel expects data tables to be organized in a specific layout. You need to understand how Excel expects data tables to be constructed in order to create meaningful data tables of your own.

Purpose of Data Tables

Data tables provide a method for creating a set of similar or related formulas arranged in a rectangular array. They are generally used as part of a larger model. There are two types of data tables: one variable and two variable.

A one variable data table enables you to change the values for a single argument within a function and calculate answers for all the values. For example, you could calculate the monthly payments on a loan for a number of different interest rates in a one variable data table.

To do this, you would need to know the total amount of the loan, the interest rate and the number of payments to be made. Then you can use the PMT function (this function calculates payments based on amount, rate, and number of payments) to calculate the monthly payment. You could then set up a one variable data table, listing different interest rates and calculate the monthly payments on each interest rate.

A two variable data table enables you to change the values for two arguments within a function. The table lists the different arguments and the results of each. For example, you could calculate the monthly payments on a loan for both different interest rates and different periods of time for repaying the loan.

Data Dialog Box

When you create a data table, whether one or two variable, you need to use the Data dialog box (see Figure 19.1).

FIG. 19.1

This figure shows the Data Table dialog box.

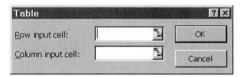

You need to first construct your data table before opening the Data dialog box. Once you have your data table, select the appropriate table range and select Data, Table. In a one variable table, you need to enter either the column or row input cell, while in a two variable table, you need to enter both the column and row input cells.

Excel uses the cells you enter to calculate the variables you list in your data table. You need to be sure you enter the correct cells to insure correct calculations. This may seem a little confusing now, but the following examples should make it clear.

Data Table Layout

When you create a data table, whether one variable or two variable, you need to pay attention to the layout of the table itself. Your data table will not return accurate calculations unless it is laid out exactly the way Excel expects.

A one variable data table can be constructed down a column or across a row. The next three examples illustrate a one variable data table using a column to list the variables (see Figures 19.2, 19.3, and 19.4).

Part
III

Ch
19

FIG. 19.2

This example lists interest rates from 6.00 percent to 8.25 percent in a one variable data table. The rates are in a single column (D). Note that cell E4 contains a function (the NPV function, which is explained in The One Variable Data Table, below).

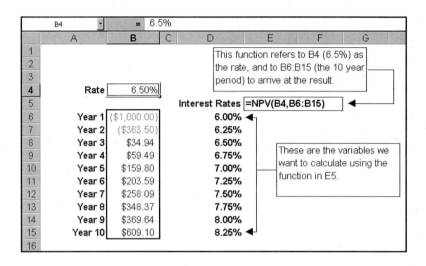

FIG. 19.3

This example shows how to select the entire data table. Note particularly that you need to select all the cells that compose the data table, including the cell that contains the function and the blank cell to its left, and the blank cells under the function and to the right of the rates.

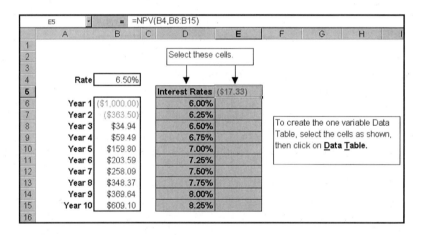

FIG. 19.4

This example shows the Table dialog box.

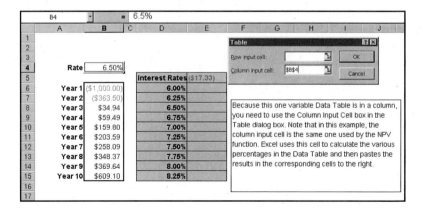

You first select the table (see Figure 19.3), then select Data, Table. Note that you would use the Column Input Cell box because this table was constructed down a column. You can also create a one variable data table that uses a row rather than a column to list the variable data (see Figure 19.5). In this case, you type the cell reference for the input cell in the Row Input Cell text box in the Data dialog box. This is illustrated more completely in the following section about two variable data tables.

FIG. 19.5

This example shows a one variable data table constructed along a row rather than down a column. Note that the formula here is in cell D4, one cell below and to the left of the first cell of the interest rates.

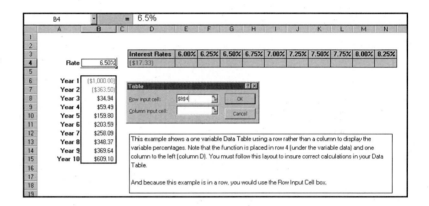

Two variable data tables use both rows and columns to list the two variables. You need to be sure you enter the correct cells in the Data dialog box in order to ensure correct calculations.

The One Variable Data Table

The one variable data table is a useful and efficient method of entering and managing a group of related formulas. This type of data table enables you to vary one of the arguments of a function so you can compare the results quickly. So, for example, you could see how different interest rates could affect your repayments on a loan.

We will use the NPV function as an example. This is the Net Present Value function which calculates the net present value of an investment (a number by which different cash flows from investments can be compared). It takes two arguments, the "discount" or interest rate, and the list of payments, positive (income) and negative (payments), which represent the stream of cash flows from the investment.

The syntax of the NPV function is: NPV(rate,value1,value2,...). The value arguments represent the list of payments. You can enter up to 29 values.

Setting Up the Table Begin by preparing a spreadsheet as shown in Figure 19.6, with the cash flows from five alternative investments listed in columns C5:C14 through G5:G14.

Preparing the Table The cash flows all begin with a value of –$1000, indicating that all investments require an initial outlay of $1000. All five cash flows are initially negative in the first couple of periods before becoming positive.

Part
III

Ch
19

FIG. 19.6

This is an example of the projected cash flows for five different investments. You can calculate the Net Present Value (NPV) for each of these cash flows, assuming the projected interest rate is the same for each investment, in order to compare the investments.

	B17		=	6.48%		
	A	B	C	D	E	F	G
2		Cash Flow Forecasts					
4			Project A	Project B	Project C	Project D	Project E
5		Year 1	($1,000.00)	($1,000.00)	($1,000.00)	($1,000.00)	($1,000.00)
6		Year 2	($363.50)	($177.72)	($409.19)	($326.36)	($127.20)
7		Year 3	$34.94	($68.30)	($82.85)	($216.49)	($5.95)
8		Year 4	$59.49	$173.20	$62.45	$177.22	$37.69
9		Year 5	$159.80	$177.36	$195.12	$289.32	$109.13
10		Year 6	$203.59	$108.82	$200.31	$292.61	$110.56
11		Year 7	$258.09	$264.61	$278.13	$312.50	$261.16
12		Year 8	$348.37	$289.40	$294.70	$361.15	$404.58
13		Year 9	$369.64	$391.14	$573.01	$461.68	$454.34
14		Year 10	$609.10	$431.46	$704.06	$501.99	$457.94
16		Expected Interest Rate					
17		6.48%					
18			NPV Project A	NPV Project B	NPV Project C	NPV Project D	NPV Project E
19		Interest Rates					
20		6.00%					
21		6.25%					
22		6.50%					
23		6.75%					
24		7.00%					
25		7.25%					
26		7.50%					
27		7.75%					
28		8.00%					
29		8.25%					

This is typical of investment projects that initially require money to be spent and then eventually begin to generate money as they grow. The NPV function provides a way of comparing these streams of income and expense over time and determining which is the most profitable.

The way the NPV function reduces a stream of payments to a single number is by combining the present value of each payment (or expense). The present value of an expense or payment is determined by the interest rate. Future payments and expenses are reduced or "discounted" based on interest or "discount" rate.

Using this example (see Figure 19.6), in cell B17 enter the Expected Interest Rate, which is 6.48 percent. This is the value you will use to calculate the NPV for the five Projects. In the range B20:B29 enter a range of alternative interest rates, from 6.00 through 8.25 percent. You will use this column of alternative rates to calculate a table of NPV values for each of the five Projects.

Setting Up the Data Table   You could create a block of formulas manually by entering a formula in each cell in the range C20:G29 (see Figure 19.7). In C20 you would enter the formula =**NPV(B20, C5:C14)** and then in D20 you would enter =**NPV(B20, D5:D14)** and so on (see Figure 19.8).

This would be tedious, time consuming, and could lead to many errors, which might be difficult to track down. It would also be inefficient in terms of the time required to recalculate your spreadsheet, because Excel has to calculate each formula individually. The one variable data table is a better way to accomplish this task.

Entering the Table Formula   To create the one variable data table to calculate the NPV values for your projects based on the range of alternative discount rates you have specified, begin by entering the reference formulas in cells C19 through G19.

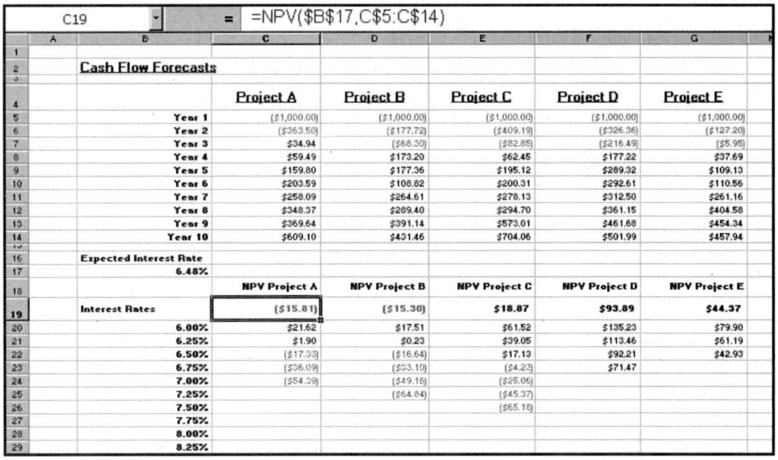

FIG. 19.7

This example shows how you could begin creating individual formulas to calculate the NPV for each project and for each projected interest rate.

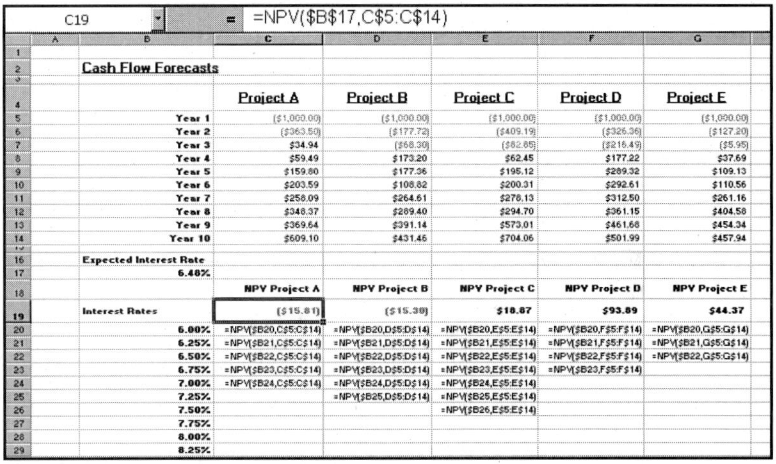

	C19		=	=NPV($B$17,C$5:C$14)			
	A	B	C	D	E	F	G
1							
2	**Cash Flow Forecasts**						
3							
4			Project A	Project B	Project C	Project D	Project E
5		Year 1	($1,000.00)	($1,000.00)	($1,000.00)	($1,000.00)	($1,000.00)
6		Year 2	($363.50)	($177.72)	($409.19)	($326.36)	($127.20)
7		Year 3	$34.94	($68.30)	($82.85)	($216.49)	($5.95)
8		Year 4	$59.49	$173.20	$62.45	$177.22	$37.69
9		Year 5	$159.80	$177.36	$195.12	$289.32	$109.13
10		Year 6	$203.59	$108.82	$200.31	$292.61	$110.56
11		Year 7	$258.09	$264.61	$278.13	$312.50	$261.16
12		Year 8	$348.37	$289.40	$294.70	$361.15	$404.58
13		Year 9	$369.64	$391.14	$573.01	$461.68	$454.34
14		Year 10	$609.10	$431.46	$704.06	$501.99	$457.94
15							
16		**Expected Interest Rate**					
17		6.48%					
18			**NPV Project A**	**NPV Project B**	**NPV Project C**	**NPV Project D**	**NPV Project E**
19		Interest Rates	($15.81)	($15.30)	$18.87	$93.89	$44.37
20		6.00%	$21.62	$17.51	$61.52	$135.23	$79.90
21		6.25%	$1.90	$0.23	$39.05	$113.46	$61.19
22		6.50%	($17.33)	($16.64)	$17.13	$92.21	$42.93
23		6.75%	($36.09)	($33.19)	($4.23)	$71.47	
24		7.00%	($54.39)	($49.16)	($26.06)		
25		7.25%		($64.84)	($45.37)		
26		7.50%			($65.18)		
27		7.75%					
28		8.00%					
29		8.25%					

FIG. 19.8

This example shows the same approach as does Figure 19.7, except here you can see the formula in each cell rather than the result.

	C19		=	=NPV($B$17,C$5:C$14)			
	A	B	C	D	E	F	G
1							
2	**Cash Flow Forecasts**						
3							
4			Project A	Project B	Project C	Project D	Project E
5		Year 1	($1,000.00)	($1,000.00)	($1,000.00)	($1,000.00)	($1,000.00)
6		Year 2	($363.50)	($177.72)	($409.19)	($326.36)	($127.20)
7		Year 3	$34.94	($68.30)	($82.85)	($216.49)	($5.95)
8		Year 4	$59.49	$173.20	$62.45	$177.22	$37.69
9		Year 5	$159.80	$177.36	$195.12	$289.32	$109.13
10		Year 6	$203.59	$108.82	$200.31	$292.61	$110.56
11		Year 7	$258.09	$264.61	$278.13	$312.50	$261.16
12		Year 8	$348.37	$289.40	$294.70	$361.15	$404.58
13		Year 9	$369.64	$391.14	$573.01	$461.68	$454.34
14		Year 10	$609.10	$431.46	$704.06	$501.99	$457.94
15							
16		**Expected Interest Rate**					
17		6.48%					
18			**NPV Project A**	**NPV Project B**	**NPV Project C**	**NPV Project D**	**NPV Project E**
19		Interest Rates	($15.81)	($15.30)	$18.87	$93.89	$44.37
20		6.00%	=NPV($B20,C$5:C$14)	=NPV($B20,D$5:D$14)	=NPV($B20,E$5:E$14)	=NPV($B20,F$5:F$14)	=NPV($B20,G$5:G$14)
21		6.25%	=NPV($B21,C$5:C$14)	=NPV($B21,D$5:D$14)	=NPV($B21,E$5:E$14)	=NPV($B21,F$5:F$14)	=NPV($B21,G$5:G$14)
22		6.50%	=NPV($B22,C$5:C$14)	=NPV($B22,D$5:D$14)	=NPV($B22,E$5:E$14)	=NPV($B22,F$5:F$14)	=NPV($B22,G$5:G$14)
23		6.75%	=NPV($B23,C$5:C$14)	=NPV($B23,D$5:D$14)	=NPV($B23,E$5:E$14)	=NPV($B23,F$5:F$14)	
24		7.00%	=NPV($B24,C$5:C$14)	=NPV($B24,D$5:D$14)	=NPV($B24,E$5:E$14)		
25		7.25%		=NPV($B25,D$5:D$14)	=NPV($B25,E$5:E$14)		
26		7.50%			=NPV($B26,E$5:E$14)		
27		7.75%					
28		8.00%					
29		8.25%					

In cell C19, enter **=NPV($B$17, C5:C14)**. Then Click the button in the lower-right corner of cell C19 (your pointer should change to a crosshair) and drag it to G19 to fill the formula across the range C19:G19.

N O T E $B$17 is an absolute reference to cell B17, required for the Formula Drag in the next step to work correctly. You can make a relative reference absolute by selecting the reference in the formula bar and pressing F4. If you repeatedly press F4, you will see that it is a four-way toggle (A1, $A$1, A$1, $A1).

Also, if you don't see the small button on the lower-right corner of a selected cell, select Tools, Options, and then select the Edit tab and put a check mark next to Cell Drag and Drop. This option enables you to use the Fill handle, so you can simply grab the handle and use it to fill in formulas and other items across or down a range of cells.

Alternatively you could enter **=NPV(B17, D5:D14)** in D19, **=NPV(B17,E5:E14)** in E19, and so on to G19. This approach eliminates the need to create an absolute reference, but it is a little less elegant in that you need to enter the NPV function five times instead of once.

Next, select the range B19:G29, and select Data, Table to open the data table dialog box (see Figure 19.9).

FIG. 19.9

This is an example of the Data Table dialog box.

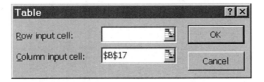

Click in the Column Input Cell edit box, and then either type **B17** or click the spreadsheet cell B17. Click the OK button and the table will fill in as shown in Figure 19.10.

FIG. 19.10

Completed one variable data table.

	Project A	Project B	Project C	Project D	Project E
Cash Flow Forecasts					
Year 1	($1,000.00)	($1,000.00)	($1,000.00)	($1,000.00)	($1,000.00)
Year 2	($363.50)	($177.72)	($409.19)	($326.36)	($127.20)
Year 3	$34.94	($68.30)	($82.85)	($216.49)	($5.95)
Year 4	$59.49	$173.20	$62.45	$177.22	$37.69
Year 5	$159.80	$177.36	$195.12	$289.32	$109.13
Year 6	$203.59	$108.82	$200.31	$292.61	$110.56
Year 7	$258.09	$264.61	$278.13	$312.50	$261.16
Year 8	$348.37	$289.40	$294.70	$361.15	$404.58
Year 9	$369.64	$391.14	$573.01	$461.68	$454.34
Year 10	$609.10	$431.46	$704.06	$501.99	$457.94

Expected Interest Rate 6.48%

Interest Rates	NPV Project A	NPV Project B	NPV Project C	NPV Project D	NPV Project E
	($15.81)	($15.30)	$18.87	$93.89	$44.37
6.00%	$21.62	$17.51	$61.52	$135.23	$79.90
6.25%	$1.90	$0.23	$39.05	$113.46	$61.19
6.50%	($17.33)	($16.64)	$17.13	$92.21	$42.93
6.75%	($36.09)	($33.10)	($4.23)	$71.47	$25.11
7.00%	($54.39)	($49.16)	($25.06)	$51.22	$7.73
7.25%	($72.24)	($64.84)	($45.37)	$31.45	($9.24)
7.50%	($89.65)	($80.14)	($65.18)	$12.15	($25.78)
7.75%	($106.63)	($95.08)	($84.49)	($6.69)	($41.93)
8.00%	($123.19)	($109.66)	($103.31)	($25.09)	($57.69)
8.25%	($139.35)	($123.89)	($121.67)	($43.05)	($73.07)

The value of a data table is its use within a larger model. In our example we have entered constant values in each cell indicating payment or expense expected for each project in each year. In a real model these values would be calculated based on a number of different conditions.

The Two Variable Data Table

A two variable data table enables you to vary two arguments of a function. You could, for example, create a two variable data table that shows you what your monthly payments would be for different interest rates over different amounts of time.

For this example you will use the DB function. The DB function in Excel calculates the cost of depreciation on an asset for a given period based on an initial value and a final or "salvage" value, using the Fixed-Declining Balance method of calculating the depreciation. See Table 19.2 for an explanation of the arguments for the DB function.

Table 19.2 DB Function Arguments

This Argument	Means
Cost	The initial value of the asset.
Salvage	The final value of the asset (for example, the amount for which it could be sold after it had been used for the period specified by the Life argument).
Life	Represents the useful lifetime of the asset.
Period	Used to specify for which year in the asset's useful lifetime the depreciation cost is being calculated.
Month	(optional) Indicates that the depreciation cost is to be calculated for a specific month of the year.

Setting Up the Input In cell B2, enter the initial value of the asset, **$1000**. In cell B3, enter the final salvage value of the asset, **$100**. In cell B4, enter the expected life of the asset in years, **10**. In cell B5, enter the number **1** to indicate the year in the life of the asset for which you want to calculate the depreciation cost. In cell E4, enter the formula **=DB(B2,B3,B4,B5)** and press Enter. The result displayed in cell E4 should be **$206.00** (see Figure 19.11).

The depreciation formula can only return the depreciation cost for a single year (or month) in the life of an asset. In a financial model, which spans several historical and forecast years, the cost of depreciation for assets would be needed for each year and for each asset.

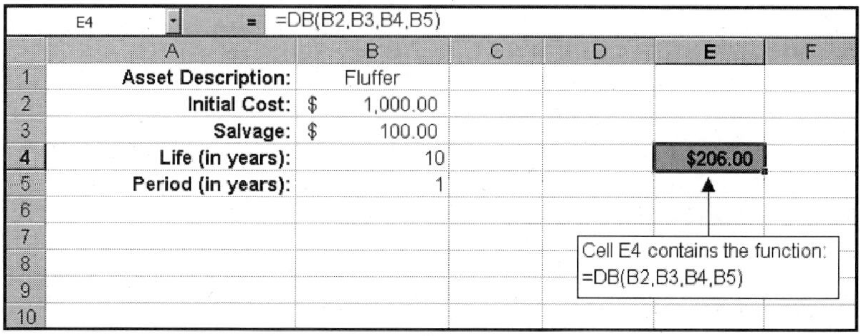

Part III

Ch 19

FIG. 19.11
This is an example of the DB function. Note that the inputs are entered in their own cells (B2:B5), and that the DB function refers to those cells. That way, if you decide to change one of the input figures, the function will recalculate automatically.

	E4	▪	= =DB(B2,B3,B4,B5)				
	A		B	C	D	E	F
1	Asset Description:		Fluffer				
2	Initial Cost:	$	1,000.00				
3	Salvage:	$	100.00				
4	Life (in years):		10			$206.00	
5	Period (in years):		1				
6							
7							
8						Cell E4 contains the function:	
9						=DB(B2,B3,B4,B5)	
10							

You could enter the formula separately for each period as described previously, or you could use a single input table to calculate the depreciation for the entire life of the asset. You might have many assets with many initial costs, purchased at different times (therefore at different periods in their useful life). You could set up separate tables for each or you could use a two variable data table for efficiency (see Figure 19.12).

FIG. 19.12

This is one example of a two variable data table. Here the period is varied from one to ten years in Column E, while the initial cost is varied from $1,000 to $3,000 in row 4. Now we can create a table that will calculate all the values based on these varied inputs.

	E4			=	=DB(B2,B3,B4,B5)					
	A	B	C	D	E	F	G	H	I	J
1	Asset Description:	Fluffer								
2	Initial Cost: $	1,000.00								
3	Salvage: $	100.00			Reference Formula	Cost				
4	Life (in years):	10			$206.00	1000	1500	2000	2500	3000
5	Period (in years):	1			Period	1				
6						2				
7						3				
8						4				
9						5				
10						6				
11						7				
12						8				
13						9				
14						10				
15										

In cells E5 through E14, enter the numbers **1** through **10** for the number of years in the life of the asset. These values will be used as the Period variable in the DB formula for the table.

In cells F4 through J4, enter the values **1000, 1500, 2000, 2500,** and **3000.** These values will be used as the Cost variable in the DB formula for the table.

With the mouse, select the area for the table E4:J14, which is bordered on the top by the Cost values and on the left by the Period values. The DB formula is in the upper-left corner of the table area, which is how Excel chooses the formula to use for the two-way table. You need to construct your two variable data table in this manner for it to return accurate calculations.

Select Data, Table to open the data table dialog box. The data table dialog box contains two input text boxes: the Row Input Cell box and the Column Input Cell box. For a two-input table, both of these boxes will be filled in. Click in the Row Input Cell box and then click cell B2. Then click in the Column Input Cell box on the dialog box and click cell B5 (see Figure 19.13); then click the OK button.

FIG. 19.13

This example shows the data table area selected and the Data dialog box with the appropriate cell entries. Note that the Row Input Cell is B2. This is because you varied the initial cost along a row.

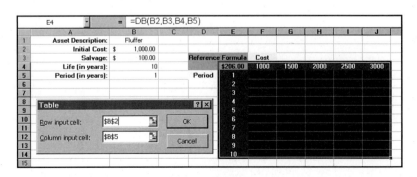

The table will fill in with values (see Figure 19.14). Each cell in the table indicates the depreciation cost for an asset, with the initial cost indicated by the value at the top of the column; the period in the asset's life cycle is indicated by the number at the left side of the table.

FIG. 19.14

This is an example of the completed two variable data table.

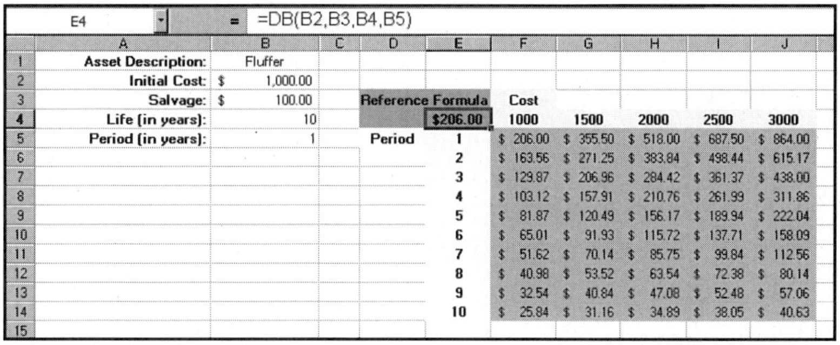

	E4		=	=DB(B2,B3,B4,B5)					
	A	B	C	D	E	F	G	H	I	J
1	Asset Description:	Fluffer								
2	Initial Cost: $	1,000.00								
3	Salvage: $	100.00		Reference Formula	Cost					
4	Life (in years):	10		$206.00	1000	1500	2000	2500	3000
5	Period (in years):	1		Period	1	$ 206.00	$ 355.50	$ 518.00	$ 687.50	$ 864.00
6					2	$ 163.56	$ 271.25	$ 383.84	$ 498.44	$ 615.17
7					3	$ 129.87	$ 206.96	$ 284.42	$ 361.37	$ 438.00
8					4	$ 103.12	$ 157.91	$ 210.76	$ 261.99	$ 311.86
9					5	$ 81.87	$ 120.49	$ 156.17	$ 189.94	$ 222.04
10					6	$ 65.01	$ 91.93	$ 115.72	$ 137.71	$ 158.09
11					7	$ 51.62	$ 70.14	$ 85.75	$ 99.84	$ 112.56
12					8	$ 40.98	$ 53.52	$ 63.54	$ 72.38	$ 80.14
13					9	$ 32.54	$ 40.84	$ 47.08	$ 52.48	$ 57.06
14					10	$ 25.84	$ 31.16	$ 34.89	$ 38.05	$ 40.63
15										

You can check the calculation by entering the DB function in cell D17, for example: **=DB(2000, 100, 10, 7)**. Compare the value in cell D17 to the value in cell H11. They should both read $85.75. Now change the formula in cell D17 to read **=DB(J5, 100, 10, E9)**. The value should match the value in cell J9, $222.04.

This check formula does the same substitution that the data table does. You could duplicate the calculation done by the two-way table by setting up an area with formulas referring to the top row of each column for the Cost parameter and the left column of each row for the Period parameter.

This would require entering the formula in each cell in the table, which would be tedious and could lead to errors that would be difficult to find. The resulting set of formulas would slow down calculation of your spreadsheet because Excel calculates data tables more efficiently than a group of formulas entered separately in adjacent cells.

Deeper Inside Two Variable Data Tables   The data table dialog box labels are somewhat cryptic and are the causes of most of the confusion people have with data tables. The data table is based on a formula in the Reference Formula cell, which is the top-left corner cell of the data table area you select. The formula in this cell must use at least two arguments, and the two arguments that you want to substitute must be entered into the formula as cell references.

The top row of the table to the right of the Reference Formula cell must have values, which will be substituted in the formula for one of the arguments. You can choose to set up the table with either of the arguments on the top row and the other in the left column. In the previous example (see Figure 19.14), you could have used "Period" across the top row and "Cost" down the left column, or you could have substituted for another argument, say Salvage instead of Cost. The order of the arguments in the function in the Reference Formula cell is not related to the way you set up your table. What is important is that you select the appropriate cells when setting the Row Input and Column Input in the data table dialog box.

The first argument in the function is substituted in each cell with the value in the top row of the column, and the fourth argument is substituted in each cell with the value in the left column of the table. When you set up the data table you arranged the Cost values on the top row of the table and the Periods down the left column (see Figure 19.14).

Because Cost is in the top row of the table area, you selected the cell that the table reference formula (the DB function in cell E4) uses for its Cost argument (cell B2) as the Row Input Cell. The Period values are in the left column of the table area, so you selected the cell that the table reference formula uses for the Period argument (cell B5) as the Column Input Cell. (See Figure 19.13 to see the Table dialog box.)

The values substituted for the Period argument are listed in the left column of the table. In the data table dialog box, select the cell used by the Reference Formula cell for the Period parameter (cell B5) as the Column Input Cell.

The values substituted for the Cost parameter are listed in the top row of the table. Therefore, in the data table dialog box, you select the cell used by the Reference Formula cell for the Cost parameter (cell B2) as the Row Input Cell.

Remember that the Row Input Cell means the cell used by the Reference Formula for that argument (the top row of the table), and Column Input Cell means the cell used by the Reference Formula for that argument (the left column of the table).

Using Goal Seek

Goal Seek is a quick and easy approach to arriving at a desired result by changing the value of another cell. The purpose of Goal Seek is to find a desired value for a cell that contains a formula.

Using Goal Seek in a Worksheet

Although the Goal Seek feature can be used with a chart (see the following section), it is most commonly used in a worksheet. One way to see how Goal Seek can be used in a worksheet is to use a financial function such as the Rate function.

The Rate function calculates the interest rate per period of an annuity. The Rate function can take up to five parameters: Nper, Pmt, PV, FV, Type, and Guess, as shown in Table 19.3.

Table 19.3 Rate Function Arguments

This Argument	Means
Nper	The number of periods in the life of the annuity (required).
Pmt	The value of the payments from the annuity each period (required).
FV	The future value (required).
Type	Indicates whether payments are made at the end of the period (if Type=0 or is omitted) or at the end (if Type=1) (optional).
Guess	Used to help the function determine the correct value (optional).

Using the example shown in Figure 19.15, you would enter the number of periods—in this case, 72—into cell B2. In cell B3, enter the amount of the periodic payments from the annuity, –136 (negative to indicate payment). In cell B4, enter the present value of the annuity, **4,000**. In cell B6, enter the rate formula **=RATE(B2,B3,B4)**. The value displayed should be approximately 4.32 percent.

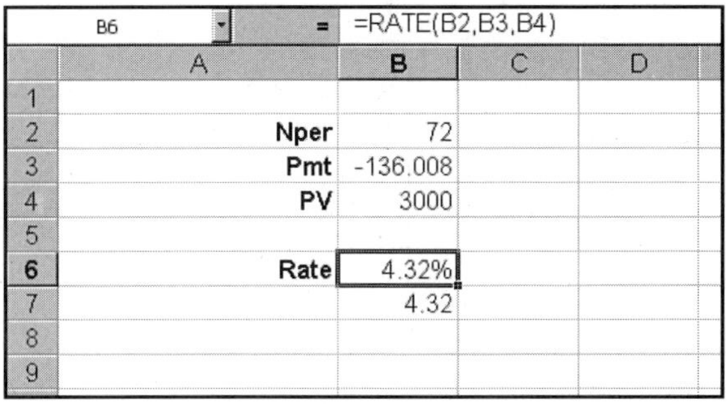

FIG. 19.15
Rate function example.

Suppose that you want to find the payments, which would cause the rate of the annuity to equal 6.50 percent. You could begin trying different values manually, changing cell B3 until cell B6 shows the desired value. It would probably take quite some time to reach the correct value. Instead you could use Goal Seek to find this payment level very quickly.

To use Goal Seek, select Tools, Goal Seek from the menu bar. The Goal Seek dialog box opens and prompts you to enter the information required to find the payment (see Figure 19.16). Click in the Set Cell text box and click the worksheet in cell B6. Then click in the To Value text box and type **6.5%**. Then click in the By Changing Cell text box and click cell B3. Click OK and Excel will quickly display the dialog box indicating that a solution was found. You can click OK and the change will be saved to cell B3, or if the value is not correct you can click Cancel and revert to the previous value.

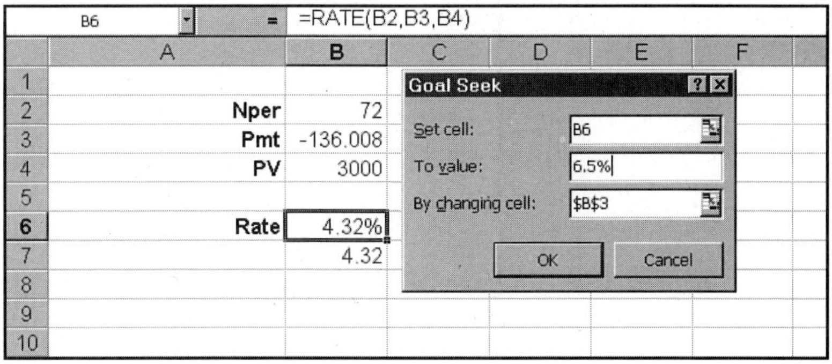

FIG. 19.16
This is one example of the Goal Seek dialog box and how to use it.

If you have problems finding a solution with Goal Seek, you can create a custom formula that contains a different but related value. In this example, the value of the rate you are trying to find is a fairly small number. You could put a formula in cell B7: **=100*B6**. Then you could use the Goal Seek dialog box to set B7 to value 6.5 by changing cell B3.

Using Goal Seek in a Chart

Another way of using the Goal Seek tool is to invoke it automatically when working with a chart. Given a chart like the one in Figure 19.17, you can select a data point and drag it to a desired level (see Figure 19.18).

FIG. 19.17

This shows a sample chart embedded on a worksheet. Note the data to the left of the chart. These data are not numbers that were typed in. Rather, they are the results of formulas.

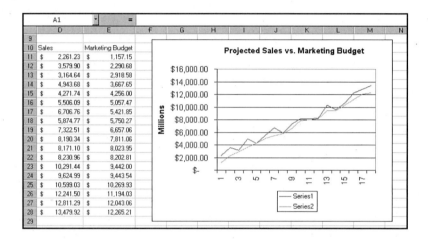

FIG. 19.18

This example shows the effect of selecting a specific data point on one of the lines and dragging that data point to a different value.

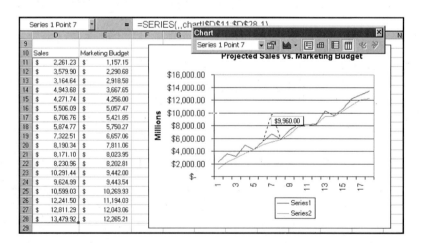

This causes the Goal Seek dialog box to open and prompt you for the cell to change to cause the change (see Figure 19.19), which you indicated by moving the data point on the graph.

N O T E You should note that charts which are created from numbers that are typed into cells will not use the Goal Seek feature when you drag a data point on the chart. In this case, Excel will just change the underlying number.

The Goal Seek feature can be used only on charts where the underlying numbers on the worksheet are the results of formulas. When you change a data point on a chart like this, Excel displays the Goal Seek dialog box so you can indicate where you want the change in the underlying data to occur. ■

FIG. 19.19

This example shows the Goal Seek dialog box, which Excel displays automatically as a result of changing the data point.

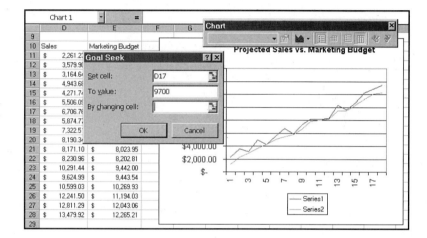

There may be no way to achieve the result you have requested, in which case Goal Seek will indicate that a solution may not have been found. If the value displayed is "good enough" you can accept the change, otherwise you can revert to the original value by canceling the dialog box.

Using Solver

The Solver utility is similar to the Goal Seek tool, except that the features and flexibility it offers are much greater. The types of problems Solver can be used to solve are very diverse. You could use Solver in the same way as the Goal Seek tool, to set a single cell to a particular value, or to a maximum or minimum value. However, Solver can modify many more cells in attempting to find the desired solution. Solver can be required to find a solution that meets criteria you specify. For instance, a particular input cell may be required to be greater than 0, or the solution could require an integer value.

For example, the Solver tool can be used to model complex problems in engineering, economics, or finance. It can also be used to find solutions for optimal distributions of goods among warehouses or to schedule employees to minimize expenses while making sure that all work shifts have minimum required staff.

Loading Solver

You need to be sure that the Solver is available to you when you want it. To do this, select the Tools menu and look for the Solver command. If it is not there, you will first need to use the Add-Ins command.

To load the Solver add-in, select Tools, Add-Ins. Scroll through the list of add-ins to Solver Add-In and click the check box. If the Solver add-in doesn't appear in the list you will have to browse for it. If it was not installed during your Office 97 installation process, you may have to install it separately.

After the Solver add-in is loaded Solver appears on the Tools menu. Select Tools, Solver to open the Solver tool.

Setting Up a Sample Problem

To demonstrate the Solver tool you can use this simple example. Given a fixed budget of $1,000, you want to find an optimal mix of commodities that could be purchased at given costs. To set up the problem, enter the values as shown in Figure 19.20.

FIG. 19.20

This example shows a list of commodities, their individual costs, and the overall budget.

			E9		=	=SUM(E3:E6)	
	A	B	C	D	E	F
1						
2			Unit Cost	Units	Total Cost	
3		Car	220	0	0	
4		Telephone	35	0	0	
5		Food	29	0	0	
6		Clothes	104	0	0	
7						
8						
9		Budget	1000		0	
10						
11						
12		Constraints				
13		None				
14						

Using Figure 19.20 as an example, you would enter =D3*C3 into cell E3. In cell E4 enter = D4*C4 and so on through cell E6. The range D3:D6 represents the number of units purchased of each commodity, and the range E3:E6 represents the total amount spent on each commodity. In cell E9 enter the formula =SUM(E3:E6), to represent the total amount spent on all commodities.

You can enter different values in the range D3:D6 to indicate different mixtures of the commodities purchased. The problem is to figure out how to spend the entire budget but no more.

The Solver dialog box (see Figure 19.21) prompts for several parameters, which you can set. The most important is the Target Cell, which is the cell that contains the formula for which you want to find a particular value.

FIG. 19.21

The Solver dialog box.

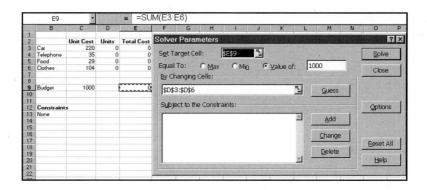

NOTE The Target Cell must be a single cell on the current sheet. ▨

You can click in the Set Target cell text box and then click the cell that contains the formula. In this case, that is E9. The next choice is whether Solver is to find a particular value or find a minimum or maximum for the model. For this example, in the Equal To options, click the Value Of button and enter **1,000** in the box (see Figure 19.21).

NOTE All Precedents of the Target cell must be on the same sheet as the Target cell. ▨

Next, you need to specify the cells that are to be changed in order to set cell E9 to a value of 1000. Click in the By Changing Cells text box and type **D3:D6,** or select the range D3:D6 on the spreadsheet.

CAUTION

Solver will overwrite a cell formula with a constant value if the cell is one of the "Changing Cells" you specify. You can lose your formulas if you are not careful.

Having entered the minimum information necessary you can now click the Solve button (in the upper right part of the dialog box). Solver now displays the solution shown in Figure 19.22.

Solver displays a dialog box indicating that a solution has been found and offers several choices. You can choose to keep the values Solver found (they are displayed in the cells D3:D6). Or you can choose to restore the original values in the cells. You can create a *scenario* with the values Solver has found by clicking the Save Scenario button, after which you will be prompted for a scenario name. (See the section "Scenarios" later in this chapter).

Solver also offers a list of three reports, which it can generate and add to the current workbook. The three reports are called Answer, Sensitivity, and Limits. You can select any combination of these from the list and click OK to generate the reports. Each report you select inserts a new worksheet in the workbook with an appropriate sheet name.

FIG. 19.22

A Solver solution.

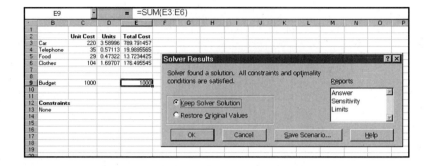

The Solver Reports give detailed technical information about the solution that was found including the final value, the input values, and the constraints applied on the solution. In the first case, you did not apply any constraints, and as a result, the values found may not represent realistic choices. You can refine the Solver solution by adding constraints.

Adding Constraints

The process of using the Solver tool is often iterative. That is, the best solution to the original problem may not be found in a single attempt. Observing the results of our first attempt to find an optimal mix of commodities, notice that the values suggested are not integral values. It may be that you can't have fractional values for the commodities purchased, so add constraints to the Solver dialog box.

The values you originally entered are remembered by Solver, so you only need to modify the settings you have already created. Select Tools, Solver to open the Solver dialog box, and in the Subject to the Constraints section, click the Add button (see Figure 19.23).

The Add Constraint dialog box opens and prompts you to enter the Cell reference and the condition which must hold. In this case, select the range D3:D6 in which the Units for each commodity are entered. In the middle list box change the operator from "<=" to "**int.**" This will also change the constraint box to "integer" (see Figure 19.24). Click the OK button to save the constraint and return to the Solver dialog box. The Subject to Constraints list should now include the item $D$3:$D$6 = integer (see Figure 19.25).

If you choose the Solve button now, the Solver will determine a combination of goods that can be purchased at the stated prices so that the total equals $1000 and all of the units are whole numbers (see Figure 19.26).

FIG. 19.23

This is an example of the Add Constraint dialog box.

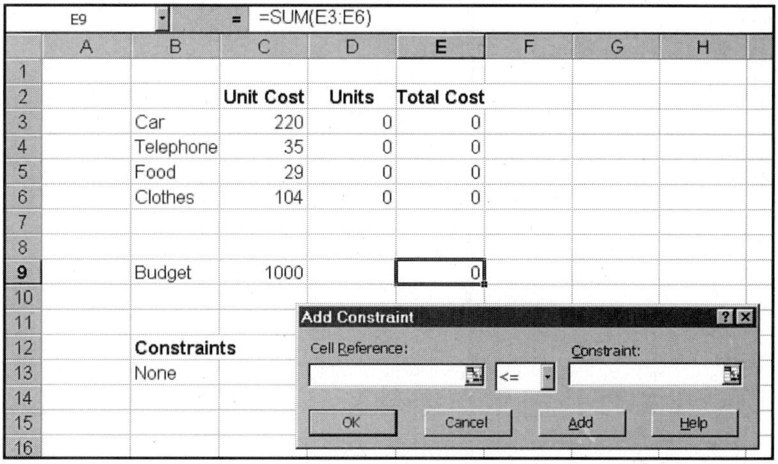

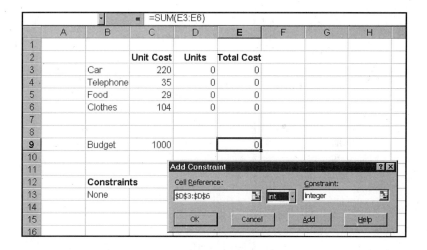

FIG. 19.24

This is an example of the Add Constraint dialog box after a constraint has been added.

FIG. 19.25

This example shows the Solver dialog box with added constraints. Each time you need to add a constraint, you need to use the Add Constraints dialog box.

FIG. 19.26

This shows Solver's resolution of the problem after having added the constraints.

		E9		=	=SUM(E3:E6)	
	A	B	C	D	E	F
1						
2			Unit Cost	Units	Total Cost	
3		Car	220	-12	-2640	
4		Telephone	35	0	0	
5		Food	29	0	0	
6		Clothes	104	35	3640	
7						
8						
9		Budget	1000		1000	
10						
11						

The results are not perfect, however, because the value Solver chose for Car is a negative number. This would violate the sense of the problem, so we need to add further conditions to the Solver Constraints. To do so, follow these steps:

1. Select <u>T</u>ools, Sol<u>v</u>er to open the Solver dialog box again and click the Add button to open the Add Constraints dialog box.

2. In the Cell Reference text box, select cells D3:D6.

3. Change the <= sign to >=.

4. In the Constraint text box type **0** and click OK.

A list of constraints is displayed (see Figure 19.27). The list indicates that the solution Solver can reach is now limited to non-negative, integer units. If you click the Solve button, Solver recalculates and finds a new combination subject to the conditions you have specified (see Figure 19.28).

FIG. 19.27

This is an example of the Solver dialog box showing the new constraints.

You can continue to refine the model, adding, changing, or deleting constraints as appropriate. For the final step you will add a set of minimum values for each of the units, to insure that the solution not only satisfies the budget constraint of $1,000 but also satisfies requirements of the uses of the commodities in the model.

To perform the final step in this example, look at Figure 19.29 and note the values entered in cells B17:C21. Enter these values in your worksheet. You are preparing to tell Solver to use these values when calculating the problem.

FIG. 19.28

This example shows the new results that Solver came up with based on the new constraints you added.

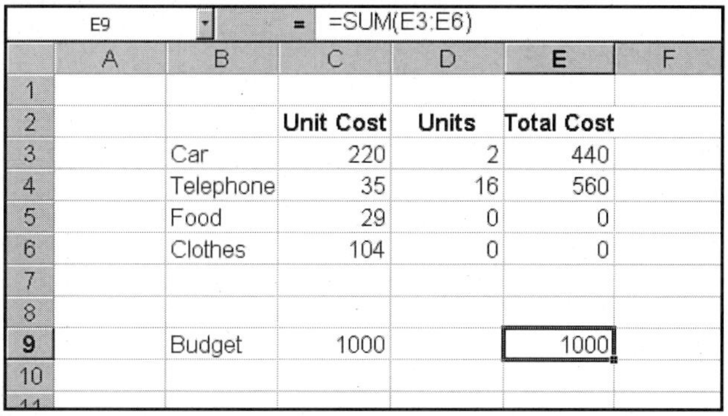

	A	B	C	D	E	F
					=SUM(E3:E6)	
1						
2			Unit Cost	Units	Total Cost	
3		Car	220	2	440	
4		Telephone	35	16	560	
5		Food	29	0	0	
6		Clothes	104	0	0	
7						
8						
9		Budget	1000		1000	
10						

FIG. 19.29

This example shows several new constraints in cells B17:C21. You can enter these in your worksheet and then add them to Solver from the worksheet.

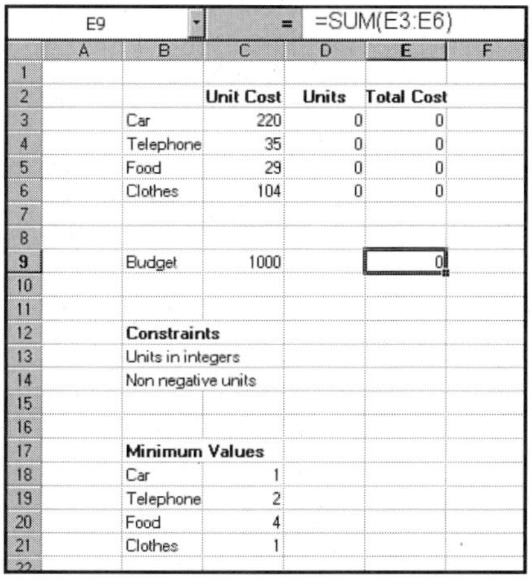

	A	B	C	D	E	F
					=SUM(E3:E6)	
1						
2			Unit Cost	Units	Total Cost	
3		Car	220	0	0	
4		Telephone	35	0	0	
5		Food	29	0	0	
6		Clothes	104	0	0	
7						
8						
9		Budget	1000		0	
10						
11						
12		Constraints				
13		Units in integers				
14		Non negative units				
15						
16						
17		Minimum Values				
18		Car	1			
19		Telephone	2			
20		Food	4			
21		Clothes	1			

To add the minimums as constraints to the Solver, follow these steps:

1. Select Tools, Solver to open the Solver dialog box again and click the Add button to open the Add Constraints dialog box.

2. In the Cell Reference box, click in cell D3.

3. Change the operator box to >=.

4. Click in the Constraints box and click cell C18.

5. Click Add to save the constraint condition and add another.

6. Repeat the process for cells D4:D6. Be sure to select the correct constraint cell for each commodity.

7. Click OK on the last constraint (D6 >= C21) instead of Add.

The Subject to the Constraints list displays the conditions you have set. You can scroll through the list to verify that all constraints are present and correct. If you click the Solve button, Solver will search for a new solution using the new constraints (see Figure 19.30).

Part
III

Ch
19

FIG. 19.30

This example shows that Solver reached a new solution based on the latest set of constraints.

	A	B	C	D	E	F
					=SUM(E3:E6)	
			Unit Cost	Units	Total Cost	
1						
2			Unit Cost	Units	Total Cost	
3		Car	220	1	220	
4		Telephone	35	16	560	
5		Food	29	4	116	
6		Clothes	104	1	104	
7						
8						
9		Budget	1000		1000	
10						
11						
12		Constraints				
13		Units in integers				
14		Non negative units				
15						
16						
17		Minimum Values				
18		Car	1			
19		Telephone	2			
20		Food	4			
21		Clothes	1			

You can continue to add or modify conditions as necessary. You can also add formulas to the model, which may simplify the way you specify certain types of constraints.

As you work with Solver you will find that a combination of constraints set in Solver and formulas on the worksheet that calculate comparisons, differences, and sums of other inputs allow the greatest flexibility in modeling a problem and satisfying complex sets of conditions. As the model gets more complex, calculation may slow down, and it will be even slower if you do not model some constraints as formulas to keep the list of Solver constraints to a minimum.

Setting Solver Options

Solver enables you to control the way that it works through the Solver Options dialog box. To open this dialog box, select Tools, Solver and when the Solver dialog box is displayed, click the Options button (see Figure 19.31).

FIG. 19.31

This example shows the Solver Options dialog box.

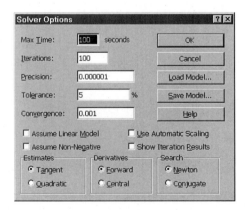

Once you open the Solver Options dialog box, you can modify the settings to affect the way Solver works. See Table 19.4 for an explanation of the Solver options.

Table 19.4 Solver Options

This Option	Means
Max Time	You can specify that Solver should not continue to search for a solution to the problem forever by entering the number of seconds allowed for calculation in the Max Time text box. If Solver has not found a solution within the specified time it will halt and display a message that it could not find a feasible solution. You can keep or discard the value reached within the allowed time.
Iterations	In the Iterations text box you can specify that Solver should stop searching for a solution after recalculating the changing cells in the worksheet any number of times (100 is the default). If a solution has not been found, Solver notifies you with a Show Trial Solution dialog box that offers the options of Saving a Scenario with the Current Values, Continuing to Search for the Solution, or Canceling the Search. If you continue, solver will ignore the Iterations value as it continues to search for the solution.
Precision	The Precision value is used to control how Solver evaluates the conditions you have set. It is used to determine whether the value in a constraint cell satisfies the condition of the constraint, being equal to, less than, or greater than a value. The value must be between 0 and 1. Larger values speed up searches at the risk of increasing errors in the constraints.
Tolerance	The Tolerance Value is used only in problems involving integer solutions. It is the percentage by which the target cell can vary from the true optimal value (possibly a non-integer) and still be considered acceptable. The default is 5 percent.
Convergence	Convergence is used by Solver to determine when a solution has been reached in a nonlinear model. When the ratio of the previously calculated value of the target cell to the currently calculated value is less than the convergence value for 5 iterations, Solver stops searching, whether it has found a solution or not. The value must be between 0 and 1 (default 0.001) and smaller values will require longer search times.
Linear Model	If the problem you are modeling is linear you can speed calculation by setting the Assume Linear Model option. The simple model, used in this chapter, is a linear model, and could safely use this option. If you set this option on a nonlinear model Solver will not calculate correctly and probably will not reach the correct solution.

Part

III

Ch

19

continues

Table 19.4   Continued

This Option	Means
Assume Non-Negative	The Assume Non-Negative option forces Solver to treat all changing cells as if they have a constraint to be greater than or equal to 0. You can reduce the number of constraints by selecting the Assume Non-Negative option. This should only be set when all or most of the adjustable cells in the model are non-negative because Solver will ignore possible negative values for those variables that are allowed to be less than 0.
Use Automatic Scaling	The Use Automatic Scaling option is useful when you have a model in which the target cell and the changing cells contain values that differ greatly in size. Using this option allows Solver to adjust for these large variations automatically. Choose this option if Solver is not able to find a solution for a problem with these conditions.
Show Iteration	Show Iteration Result causes Solver to pause after each iteration and display the currently calculated value. This can be useful in troubleshooting a problem for which Solver doesn't reach a solution, or in seeing the way Solver reaches a particular solution. This option slows calculation dramatically because you will be prompted to continue at each step. Calculation will not continue until you have clicked the Continue button. You can also stop calculation at any iteration and save a scenario.
Estimates/Derivative/ Search	The Estimates, Derivative, and Search method options are advanced features that control the way Solver attempts to find a solution. The explanation of these methods is beyond the scope of this chapter. You can try different methods if Solver is having difficulty finding a solution, or if you want to try to speed up the search. The defaults are Tangent Estimates, Forward Derivatives, and Newton Search.

From the Solver Options dialog box you can also choose to Save and Load the constraints and conditions you have specified. You only need to save the model if you will be evaluating multiple sets of constraints.

To save the current set of constraints, for example, click the Save Model button. You need to choose a range of cells large enough to contain all the formulas in the Solver constraints, so click cell I2 and click OK. Solver starts in the specified cell and fills formulas down as needed. If you select more than one cell you must select a range large enough to hold all the formulas. If you select a range that is too small, Solver prompts you with the number of cells necessary to save the current set of constraints.

CAUTION

Solver will overwrite any cells in the range you specify or from the cell you specify to the end of the range necessary to store the constraint formulas.

You can choose to load the set of constraints by clicking the Load Model button and selecting the entire range of saved formulas (I2:I13) and clicking OK (see Figure 19.32).

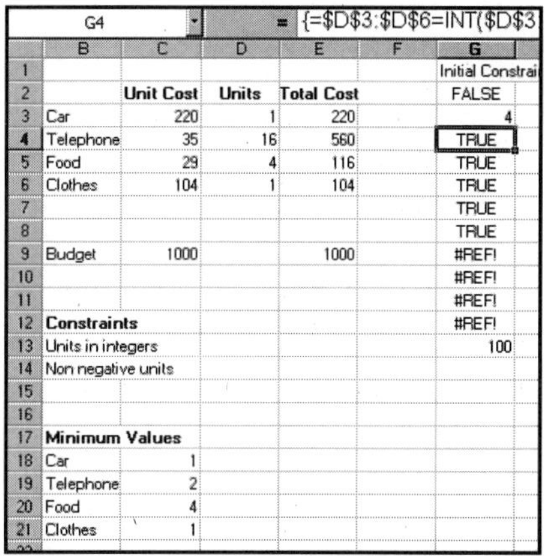

FIG. 19.32

This is an example of a worksheet displaying a list of constraints.

	B	C	D	E	F	G
				G4		={=$D$3:$D$6=INT($D$3
1						Initial Constrai
2		Unit Cost	Units	Total Cost		FALSE
3	Car	220	1	220		4
4	Telephone	35	16	560		TRUE
5	Food	29	4	116		TRUE
6	Clothes	104	1	104		TRUE
7						TRUE
8						TRUE
9	Budget	1000		1000		#REF!
10						#REF!
11						#REF!
12	Constraints					#REF!
13	Units in integers					100
14	Non negative units					
15						
16						
17	Minimum Values					
18	Car	1				
19	Telephone	2				
20	Food	4				
21	Clothes	1				

N O T E The Save Model feature enables you to store many different sets of constraints for the same problem. If you use the Save Model feature often, you will find that naming the range of cells that contains a set of constraints as well as labeling them in a cell will make them much simpler to manage and maintain. To label the set of constraints in this example, go to cell I1 and type Initial Constraints. Then select the range I1:I13 and choose Insert / Name / Create and choose Create Names in Top Row (the default) and click OK. Now you can load the set of constraints by entering the name **Initial_Constraints** in the Load Model dialog box instead of selecting the range.

Circular References and Iteration

A circular reference is created when a formula in a cell refers directly or indirectly to the cell in which it is contained. The simplest example of a circular reference is a cell that refers to itself. If the cell B2 contains the formula: =B2, this is known as a circular reference. An example of several cells that form a circular reference is shown in Figure 19.33.

Excel will warn you when you enter a circular formula and provides a toolbar for tracking down circularity in a worksheet. Circular references can be a big problem when they occur unintentionally because Excel can't fully complete calculating all the formulas in the worksheet.

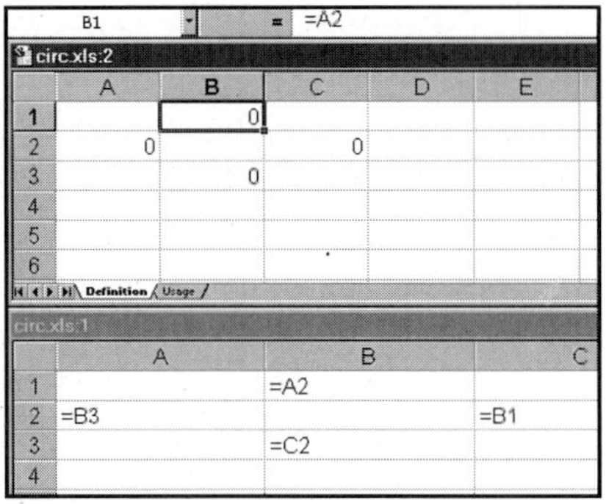

FIG. 19.33

Two views of a worksheet containing circular references. (One view shows formulas, the other view shows results.)

Circular references are not always a problem, however, and some problems require circular references in order to model them correctly. A system of simultaneous equations, such as those that commonly occur in engineering models, or a complex iterated function in economics are examples of problems that require circular references. These types of problems also require special calculation methods to solve them.

A simple example of a system of simultaneous equations is shown in order to illustrate the problem. This example uses a pair of equations to solve the following:

$$X = 9 + Y / 7$$
$$Y = 1 + 2 * X$$

You can put these formulas directly into Excel as shown in Figure 19.34:

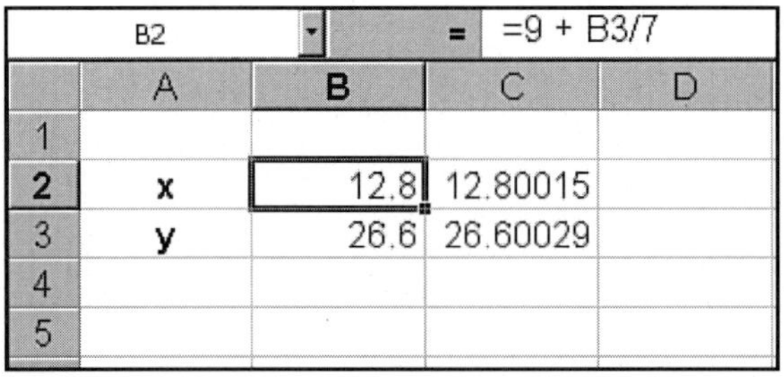

FIG. 19.34

This is an example of a pair of sample equations.

In cell B2 enter **=9 + B3/7** and in cell B3 enter **=1 + 2* B2**. If you do not have the Iteration option checked (in the under the Calculation tab), Excel will warn you of the circular dependency you have just entered. This is useful for avoiding accidental circularity, but you have the choice of dismissing the dialog box and continuing working with the circular formulas without being reminded again.

In order to calculate values for these cells Excel must calculate repeatedly until it gets close to the correct value. To allow this you must turn on Iteration by selecting Tools, Options and clicking the Calculation tab (see Figure 19.35). The values in the Maximum Iterations text box and Maximum Change text box can be left at the default values of 100 and .001 for this example (see Figure 19.35). With these settings Excel will quickly display the values for X and Y.

In B2 the value 12.8 will be displayed, while in cell B3, the value 26.6 will be displayed. To see what is going on, change the Maximum Iterations value from 100 to 1. This causes Excel to stop calculating after a single attempt to calculate the cells. Select cell B2 and re-enter the formula =9+B3/7 and press Enter. The value displayed will not equal 12.8 and cell B3 will not equal 26.6. Repeatedly pressing F9 will show the values used in the intermediate calculation or "iteration" of the calculation procedure.

At each stage of the calculation process, Excel uses the value of the referenced cells in a formula as if they were constant values. Excel calculates the value of B2 and treats B3 as if it were a constant value. Then Excel calculates the value of B3, treating B2 as if it were a constant.

After B3 has been calculated, B2 would normally be recalculated (because a cell it is dependent on has changed value), but you set iterations to 1, effectively telling Excel to stop at this point. Pressing F9 tells Excel to recalculate the worksheet again, and the values in B2 and B3 will change again. When Iteration is on, Excel will recalculate repeatedly until either it has recalculated the worksheet the number of times specified in the Maximum Iterations box (default 100), or until all the values being calculated change by an amount less than the amount specified in the Maximum Change box. (The default is 0.001.)

FIG. 19.35

This shows the Tools Options dialog box with the Calculate tab selected. Note the default values for Maximum Iteration and Maximum Change.

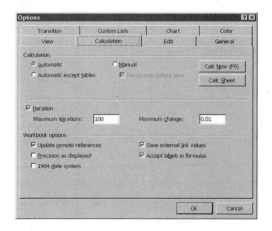

Not all equations like this will reach a final value. If you change the formula in B2 to =2+B3^2, and the formula in B3 to =SQRT(2+B2), the values will never reach a stable value for the two equations. In this case the values will continue to grow without bound, but in other cases the problem may not be as obvious. The values in a set of cells with circular references could bounce up and down erratically without ever settling down to the "true" value. This is another reason to be careful with circular references and be sure you understand the process you are attempting to model.

Evaluating What-If Scenarios

One of the most common uses of spreadsheets is for what-if analysis. You can create a model of a problem in Excel by preparing a spreadsheet with formulas that calculate results based on *input* cells. When you change the values of the input cells to reflect different conditions for the model and recalculate, you are performing a what-if analysis. You can use this analysis to see the values that the model produces under different conditions, or scenarios.

The Scenario Manager is a tool for manipulating worksheets for what-if analysis. Typically, there are multiple cells that change with each set of conditions. Using Scenario Manager you can do the following:

■ select up to 32 cells per scenario to define as changing cells

■ specify values for each of those cells

■ save the entire set of cells and values with a descriptive name

■ reload the values from a saved scenario to set the values of the changing cells to a known value

To illustrate the use of the Scenario Manager you can use the sample worksheet shown in Figure 19.36.

FIG. 19.36

This worksheet shows a simple model that might require what-if analysis.

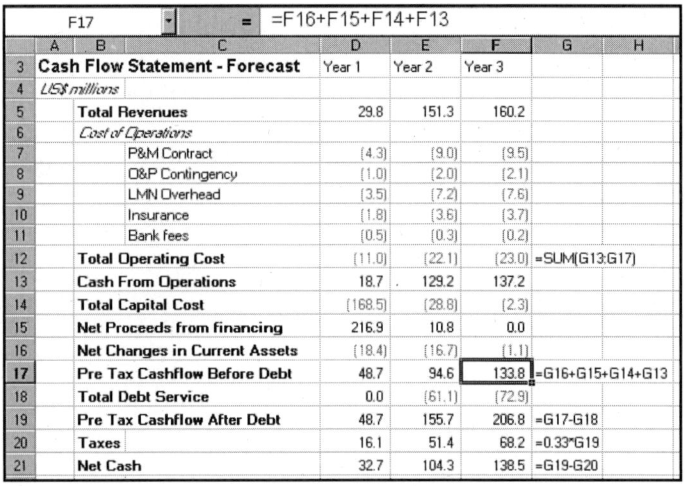

F17		=	=F16+F15+F14+F13					
A	B	C	D	E	F	G	H
3	**Cash Flow Statement - Forecast**		Year 1	Year 2	Year 3		
4	*US$ millions*						
5	**Total Revenues**		29.8	151.3	160.2		
6	*Cost of Operations*						
7		P&M Contract	(4.3)	(9.0)	(9.5)		
8		O&P Contingency	(1.0)	(2.0)	(2.1)		
9		LMN Overhead	(3.5)	(7.2)	(7.6)		
10		Insurance	(1.8)	(3.6)	(3.7)		
11		Bank fees	(0.5)	(0.3)	(0.2)		
12	**Total Operating Cost**		(11.0)	(22.1)	(23.0)	=SUM(G13:G17)	
13	**Cash From Operations**		18.7	129.2	137.2		
14	**Total Capital Cost**		(168.5)	(28.8)	(2.3)		
15	**Net Proceeds from financing**		216.9	10.8	0.0		
16	**Net Changes in Current Assets**		(18.4)	(16.7)	(1.1)		
17	**Pre Tax Cashflow Before Debt**		48.7	94.6	133.8	=G16+G15+G14+G13	
18	**Total Debt Service**		0.0	(61.1)	(72.9)		
19	**Pre Tax Cashflow After Debt**		48.7	155.7	206.8	=G17-G18	
20	**Taxes**		16.1	51.4	68.2	=0.33*G19	
21	**Net Cash**		32.7	104.3	138.5	=G19-G20	

The sample worksheet shows a simplified and abbreviated Cash Flow statement. Column G displays sample formulas for the rows that are not constant values.

The range D7:F11 represents the detailed information of the Operating Costs for this fictional company. Because this is a forecast of future events, the Operating Costs aren't known in advance. For this reason, a great deal of effort can go into creating complicated models to predict these and other forecast values. Even so, predictions can be high or low, and scenarios can be useful for investigating the effect on the company under different conditions.

For this example, you can use a simplified version of this analysis. To begin, you need to create a scenario from the values, which we have initially entered in the spreadsheet. To do this, select the range D7:F11 and choose Tools, Scenarios to open the Scenario dialog box (see Figure 19.37).

FIG. 19.37

This example shows the Scenario dialog box.

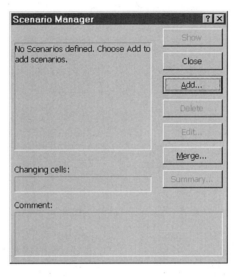

Click the Add button in the Scenario Manager dialog box to open the Add Scenario dialog box (see Figure 19.38).

FIG. 19.38

This example shows the Add Scenario dialog box.

Part

III

Ch

19

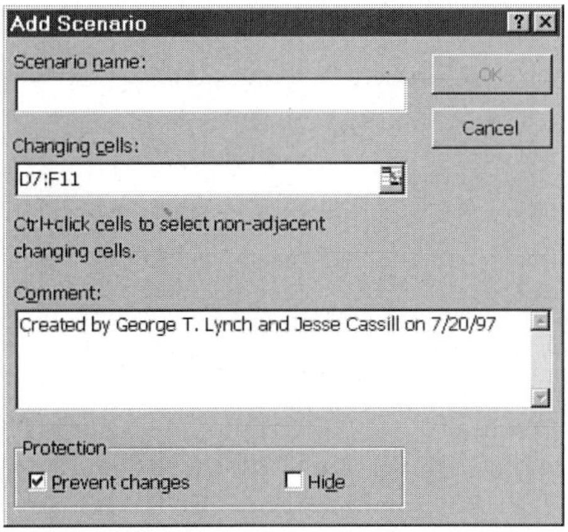

Adding a Base Case Scenario

The Add Scenario dialog box prompts you for a name for the Scenario. In the Scenario Name text box, type **Base Case**. The range of Changing Cells is D7:F11; it was previously selected. You could add other cells as necessary, but in this case there is no need.

In the Comment text box enter a descriptive comment that will be useful in distinguishing this scenario from others you might create. Enter: **This scenario contains the values for Cost of Operations which represents the most likely case given status quo** and click the OK box to save the scenario.

The Scenario Manager then prompts you with a list of the Changing Cells and the values to be saved for this scenario. You can keep the values listed by just clicking the OK button. The Base Case scenario is now saved and appears in the Scenario Manager list. Close the Scenario Manager dialog box and return to the spreadsheet (see Figure 19.39).

FIG. 19.39

This sample worksheet shows a base case Scenario. Note the values in cells D7:F11.

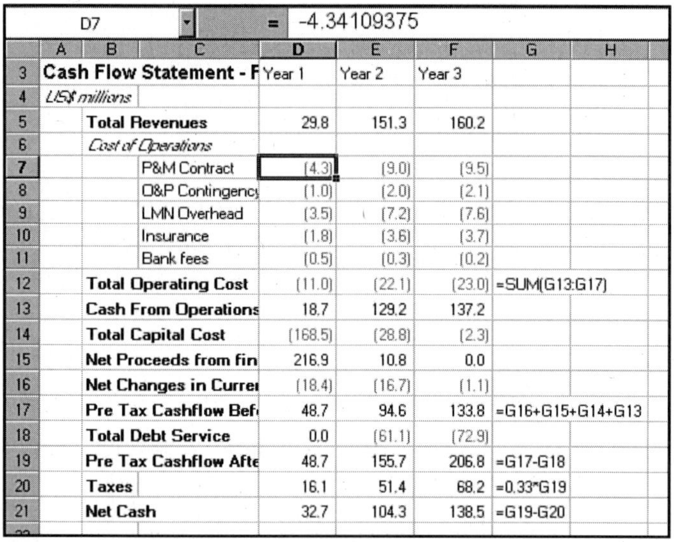

	A	B	C	D	E	F	G	H
	D7		▾	=	-4.34109375			
3	**Cash Flow Statement - F**			Year 1	Year 2	Year 3		
4	*US$ millions*							
5		Total Revenues		29.8	151.3	160.2		
6		*Cost of Operations*						
7			P&M Contract	(4.3)	(9.0)	(9.5)		
8			O&P Contingency	(1.0)	(2.0)	(2.1)		
9			LMN Overhead	(3.5)	(7.2)	(7.6)		
10			Insurance	(1.8)	(3.6)	(3.7)		
11			Bank fees	(0.5)	(0.3)	(0.2)		
12		Total Operating Cost		(11.0)	(22.1)	(23.0)	=SUM(G13:G17)	
13		Cash From Operations		18.7	129.2	137.2		
14		Total Capital Cost		(168.5)	(28.8)	(2.3)		
15		Net Proceeds from fin		216.9	10.8	0.0		
16		Net Changes in Currei		(18.4)	(16.7)	(1.1)		
17		Pre Tax Cashflow Befi		48.7	94.6	133.8	=G16+G15+G14+G13	
18		Total Debt Service		0.0	(61.1)	(72.9)		
19		Pre Tax Cashflow Afte		48.7	155.7	206.8	=G17-G18	
20		Taxes		16.1	51.4	68.2	=0.33*G19	
21		Net Cash		32.7	104.3	138.5	=G19-G20	

With only a single Scenario defined you can do what-if analysis by editing the values in any or all of the changing cells in the range D7:F11. You can then reset all of the values to the Base Case by selecting Tools, Scenarios, and then selecting the Base Case Scenario in the scenario list, and clicking the Show button. All the values you stored will be pasted back into the range and your spreadsheet will be back to the initial state you saved.

Adding a Worst Case Scenario

The real value of the Scenario Manager, however, is in storing many scenarios. Now you will create a Worst Case Scenario.

Begin by changing the values in the range D7:F11.

1. In cell C1 enter the value **1.3**.

2. Right-click C1 and select Copy from the shortcut menu.

3. Select the range D7:F11. Right-click the selected range and select Paste Special from the short-cut menu.

4. Choose the Multiply option from the Paste Special dialog box and click OK. This increases the values in the range by 30 percent.

Because these are costs, this represents a situation of higher expense, which represents a Worst Case Scenario. Now we need to add this scenario to the Scenario Manager.

Select the range D7:F11 and select Tools, Scenarios from the menu to open the Scenario Manager dialog box. Click the Add button in the Scenario Manager to open the Add Scenario dialog box and enter **Worst Case** for the Scenario name. Enter a comment, such as **This scenario includes a 30% increase in Operating Costs.** Click OK to save the scenario and return to the Scenario Manager dialog box. The Worst Case scenario should appear below the Base Case in the scenario list. Click Close to close the Scenario Manager dialog box. Your sample worksheet should now show the values that represent a worst case scenario (see Figure 19.40).

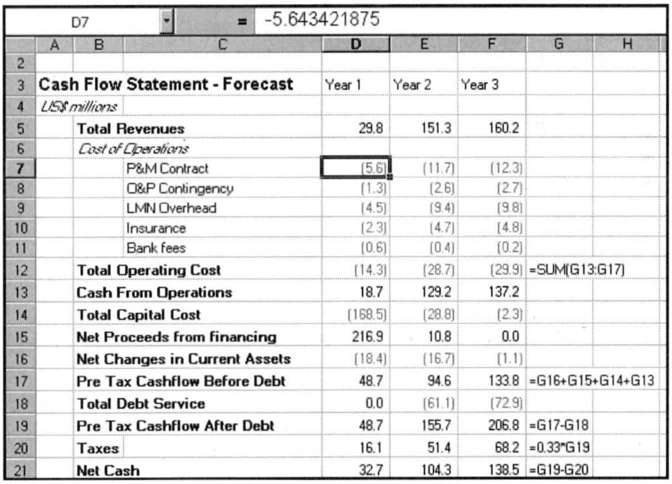

FIG. 19.40

This sample worksheet shows a worst case Scenario. Note the values in cells D7:F11.

	D7		=	-5.643421875				
	A	B	C	D	E	F	G	H
2								
3	**Cash Flow Statement - Forecast**			Year 1	Year 2	Year 3		
4	*US$ millions*							
5		Total Revenues		29.8	151.3	160.2		
6		*Cost of Operations*						
7			P&M Contract	(5.6)	(11.7)	(12.3)		
8			O&P Contingency	(1.3)	(2.6)	(2.7)		
9			LMN Overhead	(4.5)	(9.4)	(9.8)		
10			Insurance	(2.3)	(4.7)	(4.8)		
11			Bank fees	(0.6)	(0.4)	(0.2)		
12		**Total Operating Cost**		(14.3)	(28.7)	(29.9)	=SUM(G13:G17)	
13		**Cash From Operations**		18.7	129.2	137.2		
14		**Total Capital Cost**		(168.5)	(28.8)	(2.3)		
15		**Net Proceeds from financing**		216.9	10.8	0.0		
16		**Net Changes in Current Assets**		(18.4)	(16.7)	(1.1)		
17		**Pre Tax Cashflow Before Debt**		48.7	94.6	133.8	=G16+G15+G14+G13	
18		**Total Debt Service**		0.0	(61.1)	(72.9)		
19		**Pre Tax Cashflow After Debt**		48.7	155.7	206.8	=G17-G18	
20		**Taxes**		16.1	51.4	68.2	=0.33*G19	
21		**Net Cash**		32.7	104.3	138.5	=G19-G20	

Adding a Best Case Scenario

Now that you have a base case scenario and a worst case scenario, you can add a best case scenario. In this example, that would mean a scenario where the operating costs are lower.

Follow these steps to add a Best Case Scenario:

1. Select Tools, Scenario to open the Scenario Manager dialog box.

2. Click the Base Case scenario and click the Show button to reset the Operating Cost items in the range D7:F11 to the original values. Then click Close to close the dialog box.

3. In cell C1 enter the value **0.8**.

4. Right-click C1 and select Copy from the shortcut menu.

5. Select the range D7:F11. Right-click the selected range and select Paste Special from the shortcut menu.

6. Choose the Multiply option from the Paste Special dialog box and click OK. This will decrease the values in the range by 20 percent.

Because the costs are lower, these values will represent a best case scenario.

Now create another scenario following the steps just described. Name this scenario the **Best Case** and enter a description, such as **This scenario represents a 20% decrease in Operating Costs**. When you close the Scenario Manager dialog box, your worksheet should show the values that represent the best case scenario (see Figure 19.41).

FIG. 19.41

This sample worksheet shows a best case scenario.

	E10		=	-2.88360427970355				
	A	B	C	D	E	F	G	H
3	**Cash Flow Statement - Forecast**			Year 1	Year 2	Year 3		
4	US$ millions							
5		**Total Revenues**		29.8	151.3	160.2		
6		Cost of Operations						
7			P&M Contract	(3.5)	(7.2)	(7.6)		
8			O&P Contingency	(0.8)	(1.6)	(1.7)		
9			LMN Overhead	(2.8)	(5.8)	(6.1)		
10			Insurance	(1.4)	(2.9)	(3.0)		
11			Bank fees	(0.4)	(0.2)	(0.1)		
12		**Total Operating Cost**		(8.8)	(17.7)	(18.4)	=SUM(G13:G17)	
13		**Cash From Operations**		18.7	129.2	137.2		
14		**Total Capital Cost**		(168.5)	(28.8)	(2.3)		
15		**Net Proceeds from financing**		216.9	10.8	0.0		
16		**Net Changes in Current Assets**		(18.4)	(16.7)	(1.1)		
17		**Pre Tax Cashflow Before Debt**		48.7	94.6	133.8	=G16+G15+G14+G13	
18		**Total Debt Service**		0.0	(61.1)	(72.9)		
19		**Pre Tax Cashflow After Debt**		48.7	155.7	206.8	=G17-G18	
20		**Taxes**		16.1	51.4	68.2	=0.33*G19	
21		**Net Cash**		32.7	104.3	138.5	=G19-G20	

You now have created three scenarios for Operating Costs in this simple model. You can quickly replace an entire group of cells with values that represent different assumptions about the future.

In a real model you might want to create multiple scenarios for Revenues, and a separate set for Expenses. You could then show a best case Revenue scenario with a worst case Expense scenario, for example. You can mix and match scenarios to explore different possibilities.

> **CAUTION**
>
> Remember that a scenario stores information for each cell you specify, so if two scenarios store different values for the same cell the last scenario you show will set the value for that cell. This could lead to results that are inconsistent with the assumptions you are trying to model.

Merging Scenarios

If you have created scenarios in the past that will exactly fit a current model, you can merge them into the current worksheet. You will find, however, that if the models aren't identical that merging an existing set of may not give you the results you want.

To merge scenarios, you need to have at least two workbooks open: one that contains the existing scenarios and one in which you want to create scenarios.

If it isn't open already, open the workbook that contains the existing scenarios. Make the current workbook (the one in which you want to create scenarios) active. (You can do this by clicking the Window menu and selecting the appropriate workbook from the list at the bottom of the pull-down menu.) Then, with the current workbook active, select Tools, Scenarios and click the Merge button. This opens the Merge Scenarios dialog box (see Figure 19.42).

Select the worksheet that contains the scenarios you want to merge and click the OK button.

FIG. 19.42

This example shows the Merge Scenarios dialog box.

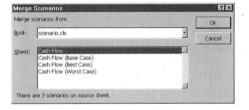

The scenarios will be merged into the current workbook.

Scenario Summaries

After you've created your scenarios, you can create summaries of the different scenarios on additional worksheets. To do this, select Tools, Scenarios to open the Scenario Manager dialog box. Click the Summary button to open the Scenario Summary dialog box (see Figure 19.43). The Scenario Summary offers two options:

- Scenario Summary
- Scenario Pivot Table

Use Scenario Summary to create a new worksheet that displays the changing cells and their results. It is best to select this option when your scenarios have only one set of changing cells.

FIG. 19.43

This example shows the Scenario Summary dialog box. Note that you can create either a Scenario Summary or a Scenario Pivot Table from here.

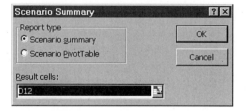

If your scenarios have more than one set of changing cells and more than one user creates scenarios, you can create a Scenario Pivot Table instead. This will give you the ability to obtain an instant what-if analysis of the existing scenarios. The Scenario Manager creates a new worksheet with a pivot table containing the scenarios on the active sheet.

Scenarios Notes

Scenarios are stored in the worksheet and can contain cells only in one worksheet. You can create scenarios on each sheet in a workbook, but you must activate the worksheet in order to change the scenario for that worksheet. Scenarios are limited to 32 changing cells.

Printing Scenarios

There are a couple of methods you can use to print scenarios. Perhaps the simplest is to create a Scenario Summary sheet (see the previous section on Scenario Summaries), define the print area, and print the summary.

One other method you can use is the Report Manager. You can store as many scenarios as you create and print them using the Report Manager.

To do this, select View, Report Manager to open the Report Manager dialog box. Click the Add button to open the Add Report dialog box. Here is where you add your scenarios to the Report Manager.

1. Type a name for the report in the Report Name text box.

2. In the Section to Add portion of the dialog box, click the down arrow to the right of the Sheet list box. This will display a list of the sheet names in the workbook. Select the sheet that contains the scenarios you want to add to the report.

3. Click the down arrow to the right of the Scenario list box. This will display a list of the scenarios you have defined on that worksheet. Select one of the scenarios by clicking once on it.

4. Click the Add button to add that scenario to the Sections in this Report text box at the bottom.

5. Repeat steps 3 and 4 until you have added all the scenarios you want to this report.

6. Click OK to close the Add Report dialog box and return to the Report Manager. Note that now all the options are available.

7. Repeat steps 1 through 6 to create new reports.

8. To print a report, select it in the Report Manager and click the Print button.

N O T E When you use the Report Manager to print scenarios, you cannot use print preview to see what will print. You should use print preview before you add the scenario to the Report Manager to see how it will print. Make any necessary modifications before adding the scenario to the Report Manager. ▪

CHAPTER 20

Using Microsoft Query

by Joe Habraken

Microsoft Query provides you with the ability to import database information and other external data into Microsoft Excel. You can then analyze the data using Excel features such as Pivot Tables, functions, and charts. Using Microsoft Query, Excel can even retrieve data from the World Wide Web, such as stock reports. ■

What is Microsoft Query

Microsoft Query is an optional tool that you can use to retrieve database information into Microsoft Excel for analysis.

Installing and configuring Microsoft Query

Microsoft Query is installed as an optional feature when you install Microsoft Office on your computer. Because Query works directly with Excel, configuring Query is easy.

Retrieving information from data sources

The external data that you retrieve using Microsoft Query can come from a variety of sources, such as Microsoft Access, Borland's dBASE or any other database for which you have the ODBC driver.

Setting up queries using Microsoft Query

Because Microsoft Query is integrated seamlessly with Microsoft Excel, you can set up a new external data query via the Excel data menu and the Get External Data command.

Overview of Microsoft Query and ODBC

Microsoft Query is a powerful yet easy-to-use data import tool that allows you to retrieve external information into Microsoft Excel. *External* simply means that the data is not in an Excel Workbook. The information can be in a database such as Microsoft Access or Borland dBASE, or it can reside in a custom made client server application that uses Microsoft's SQL Server software. Microsoft Query also now allows you to pull information from the World Wide Web, such as stock reports, into Excel.

A *query* is a question. Microsoft Query allows you to ask questions about data in external databases and then retrieve the data that fits the parameters you specify in the query. Microsoft Query uses an ODBC (Open Database Connectivity) driver to read the data that is in the external database. The information in the external database is called the *data source*.

To retrieve information from a particular data source, you must have the appropriate ODBC driver. The driver helps Query identify the type of source data you want to search, such as an Access database, and the actual location of the files. A number of ODBC drivers ship with the Microsoft Office software. Other drivers are available from Microsoft.

N O T E   You may find that some external data sources require you to enter a password and user identification before you can access the database with Microsoft Query. Get all the information that you need for a particular database from your system administrator or the actual administrator of the external database. ▪

Microsoft Query can do much more than just retrieve the information from the data source into an Excel Workbook. Because you can design a query that asks the data to be treated in a certain way, you can manipulate the type of data that is retrieved and format the data for your particular use. The list below shows some of the possibilities that Microsoft Query offers.

- You can design a query that will limit the data that is imported into Excel. For instance you can import data only on stocks that show positive growth over a certain period of time.

- You can perform calculations on the data as you import it. You may want to calculate a monthly total or an average sales figure and pull it in with the external data.

- You can sort the data that you retrieve in your query. The information can be sorted alphabetically, by date, or by some other criteria that you set in the query.

- You can change the look of the data that you import. You can use fonts and other layout features to display the data in a way that means the most to you.

Microsoft Query gives you access to a large number of external data sources and allows you to manipulate the data via your queries. But before you can take advantage of the queries that this powerful Excel add-on has to offer, you must install and configure it.

Installing and Configuring Query

Microsoft Query is one of the optional software tools found in Microsoft Office. It is not installed on your computer if you chose typical or minimum during your initial installation of Office. You can install Query along with all the other Office components by doing a Custom installation. If you've already installed Office, don't worry; you can also add Query to your Office installation relatively easily.

Installing Microsoft Query with the Office Installation

To include Microsoft Query when you install Office for the first time, you must do a Custom installation.

1. Insert the Office CD in your CD-ROM drive. The Office CD will automatically load and provide you with three choices: you can install Office, read information for users upgrading to Office from an earlier version, or you can explore the extras that have been included as part of the CD's "ValuPack."

2. Click the Install Microsoft Office. The Office Setup dialog box will appear as shown in Figure 20.1. Click the Custom button to do a Custom installation.

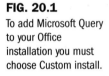

FIG. 20.1

To add Microsoft Query to your Office installation you must choose Custom install.

3. The Office Custom dialog box will appear. It contains an options list for all the components of Microsoft Office as shown in Figure 20.2.

Components that are not selected for installation won't have a check mark in their respective check box. Some components of Office will be selected for installation by a checkmark, but the check box will be gray. This means that not all of the add-ons and tools associated with that particular component of Office will be installed.

Part

III

Ch

20

FIG. 20.2

A list of all the Office components appears in the Setup dialog box. Click a feature that you want to add to the Custom installation.

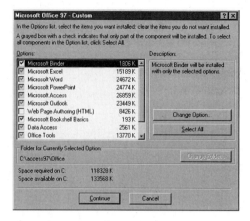

To add Microsoft Query to the installation list:

1. Click the Data Access component to select it. Then click the Change Option button. The components that make up the Data Access portion of Office will appear in a list. Two of the listed components—Database Drivers and Microsoft Query—are needed if you want to run Microsoft Query as part of Office.

 You can install all the optional components of Office by clicking the Select All button. This type of installation takes up the most disk space, but it also ensures that absolutely all the components of Office will be installed.

2. Select the check boxes for Database Drivers and Microsoft Query, then click OK. You will be returned to the Office Custom installation box.

3. To complete your installation of Office, which will now include Microsoft Query and the ODBC drivers that ship with Office, click the Continue button and follow the instructions provided.

Adding Microsoft Query to Your Office Installation

If you've previously installed Microsoft Office and did not do a Custom installation, you can add Microsoft Query and the ODBC drivers to your PC fairly easily. Place the Office CD in your CD-ROM drive and you're ready to begin (if the Office CD automatically loads, select the Add/Remove Programs button and proceed to step 2):

1. Click the Menu button on the top Office toolbar (the button will be on the far left if your Office toolbar is displayed horizontally on the Desktop). Select Add/Remove Office Programs as shown in Figure 20.3.

 If you don't use the Office toolbar you can also start the Office setup program via the Run command on the Start menu. In the Setup box type **D:setup**, where D: is the drive letter of your CD-ROM drive. If the D: drive is not your CD ROM drive, type in the appropriate letter designation.

FIG. 20.3

To change your Office installation, use the menu on the Office toolbar.

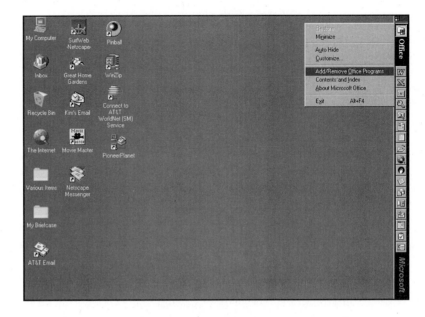

2. The Office Installation Maintenance dialog box will appear as shown in Figure 20.4. This dialog box allows you to add and remove components from your Office installation.

3. To add Microsoft Query and the ODBC drivers to your Office installation, click the Add/ Remove button.

FIG. 20.4

You can add and remove Office components from your installation via the Maintenance Dialog Box.

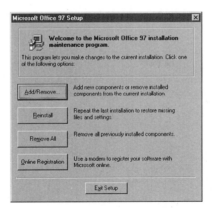

Part

III

Ch

4. The Component list for Office will appear. Click the Data Access component to select it. Then click the Change Option button.

5. Select Microsoft Query and Database Drivers as shown in Figure 20.5. Once you've selected these components click OK. To continue with the installation and the addition of Query and the ODBC drivers to your Office installation, click Continue.

FIG. 21.5

You need to add Microsoft Query and the Database Drivers to your Office installation if you want to use Microsoft Query with Excel.

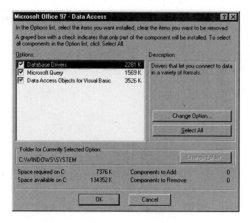

Configuring Microsoft Query

Configuring Microsoft Query to import data from various database sources is more a matter of having the correct ODBC drivers than changing any settings in Query itself. The Office CD provides you with five ODBC drivers for use with Query. These drivers will be installed when you select Database Drivers during the Office installation process:

- Microsoft Access driver
- Microsoft Excel
- dBASE and Microsoft FoxPro driver
- Microsoft SQL Server driver
- Text and HTML driver

> **CAUTION**
>
> In some cases you may need a custom ODBC driver if you are using a special database as your Query data source. Request the appropriate driver from the developer of the database. Also make it very clear that you are requesting the 32-bit version of the current driver.

You can check which ODBC drivers are installed on your computer using the Windows Control Panel.

1. Click Start and then point to Settings. Click Control Panel to open the Control Panel window as shown in Figure 20.6.

2. Double-click the 32-bit ODBC icon (if other ODBC icons appear in the Control Panel, they are for earlier versions of Microsoft Access or Query). The ODBC Data Source Administrator opens. Click the ODBC Driver tab. The Administrator provides you with a list of all the ODBC drivers that are currently installed on your PC, as shown in Figure 20.7.

3. When you have finished viewing the ODBC drivers, click the Cancel button to close the ODBC Data Source Administrator.

The ODBC Data Source Administrator can also be used to configure data source types related to each of the drivers that are installed on your computer. To configure one of the default data sources, select the data source on the User DSN tab and then click Configure.

The dialog box that appears enables you to specify a database name to be associated with the selected data source type. Configuring data sources can also be done within Microsoft Query. This second method of defining your data sources is actually the most straightforward and is described in the next section.

FIG. 20.6

You can check your ODBC drivers and identify data sources for Microsoft Query via the 32-Bit ODBC icon in the Windows Control Panel.

FIG. 20.7

The ODBC Data Source Administrator provides you with a list of the ODBC drivers currently installed on your computer.

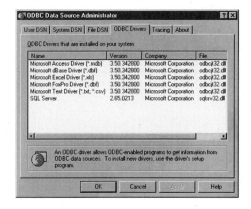

Part

III

Ch

20

Defining Data Sources

Your Data Sources will be databases that exist locally on your computer or on a network to which you connect. Data Sources can also consist of online information found on the World

Wide Web. To query a Data Source you must first define that Data Source. This means that you must let Query know the name and location of the Data Source and the ODBC driver that it will use. Fortunately, Microsoft Query makes it easy to define your Data Sources from inside Microsoft Excel.

To define a new data source:

1. Make sure that Excel is running and that you have a blank worksheet open.

2. Choose Data, Get External Data. On the submenu that appears click Create New Query.

3. Microsoft Query will open the Choose Data Source dialog box as shown in Figure 20.8. Use this box to select existing Data Sources or to define new ones.

FIG. 20.8

The Choose Data Source dialog box allows you to define a new Data Source or use an existing one for your query.

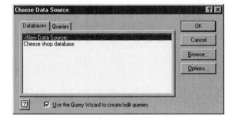

 T I P   The procedure to build a new query that uses an already existing Data Source is the same as that shown above for defining a new Data Source.

4. To define a new Data Source, double-click <New Data Source> in the Choose Date Source dialog box. The Create New Data Source dialog box appears.

5. Type the name you want to give this Data Source in the What Name do you Want to Give this Data Source? box. As soon as you designate the name for the Data Source, you will be required to identify the ODBC driver for the Data Source.

6. Click the drop-down arrow in box 2 (the driver type selection box) as shown in Figure 20.9. A list of the available ODBC drivers appears.

FIG. 20.9

You must select an ODBC driver for your new Data Source.

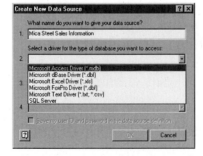

7. Once you've designated the ODBC driver, you can connect to the database that will serve as the new Data Source. Click the Connect button in the Create New Data Source dialog box.

8. A ODBC dialog box will open that is specific for the ODBC driver that you chose for your new Data Source. For instance, if you had chosen the Microsoft Access ODBC driver, the ODBC Microsoft Access dialog box appears as shown in Figure 20.10.

9. In the Access ODBC dialog box you can Select, Create, Compact, or Repair an Access database. Click Select to open a database.

FIG. 20.10

The ODBC dialog box is specific to the ODBC driver that you chose and allows you to identify the database that will serve as the Data Source.

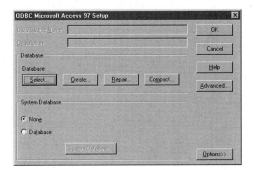

N O T E The choices in the ODBC dialog box depends on the type of database to which you will connect. The Access ODBC dialog box allows you to execute several different database commands related to Access databases such as Create, Compact, or Repair. If you choose the FoxPro or dBASE ODBC drivers your only choice is to select the database that will serve as the Data Source. ▓

10. In the Access ODBC dialog box you can Select, Create, Compact, or Repair an Access database. Click Select to open a database that will serve as the Data Source.

11. A Select Database dialog box appears. Use it to browse your computer or the network to which you are attached. Select the database for the new Data Source as shown in Figure 20.11. Click OK to complete the selection.

FIG. 20.11

The Select Database dialog box allows you to identify the database that will serve as the new Data Source. The database can be on your computer or a network.

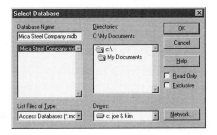

Part
III

Ch
20

12. Click OK again to close the ODBC dialog box (the name and location of your database will now appear in the box). You will be returned to the Create New Data Source dialog box.

13. If you want, you can specify a particular table in the database to serve as the data source in box 4 (this is optional). Choose OK.

The new Data Source appears in the Choose Data Source dialog box. You are now ready to perform a query based on the data your new Data Source contains.

 You can delete Data Sources that you no longer use or need. Use the Windows Explorer to open C:\Program Files\Common Files\ODBC\Data Sources. Select and delete the Data Sources that you want to remove.

Performing a Query

When you perform a query using Microsoft Query, you will be asking a Data Source questions about the data that it holds. These questions or queries can be very straightforward such as asking the external Data Source to show you all the data that it holds in a particular table by placing the information into an Excel spreadsheet. Your queries can also filter the data, meaning that you will import a subset of the data available. This subset will be based on criteria that you set such as invoice data that was input during a specific time frame, or sales figures that exceed a certain amount. Your queries can also provide you with subtotals based on numerical information. You can also sort the imported data based on a certain field of information.

To perform a new query, make sure that you open a new Excel Workbook or that the current worksheet is blank. To perform a query using Microsoft Query:

1. Click the Data menu, then point at Get External Data. On the submenu that appears click Create New Query.

2. Microsoft Query opens the Choose Data Source dialog box. Choose an existing Data Source or define a new data source as detailed above in "Defining Data Sources."

3. After selecting the Data Source, you are ready to begin the query. Make sure that the Use the Query Wizard check box is selected in the Choose Data Source dialog box, then click the OK button.

4. The Query Wizard dialog box appears. Select the table you want to include in the Query and click the Add button. This will add all the columns (also known as fields) to the Columns in your Query box as shown in Figure 20.12.

5. If you want to include only certain fields from a table or tables in the Data Source, click the plus symbol (+) next to the table name.

6. The plus symbol will turn into a minus symbol (-) and the fields in the table will be listed. Select the fields you want to include and click the Add button to add them to the Columns in Your Query box.

FIG. 20.12

The Query Wizard dialog box allows you to select the table and the columns in the table that you will import into Excel via Microsoft Query.

Table list

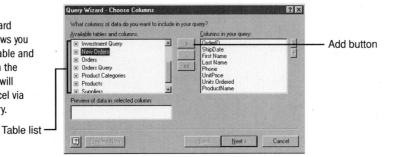

Add button

7. Once you have selected the columns that you want to import from the tables in the Data Source, click the Next button. The Query Wizard's Filter Data dialog box appears. This box allows you to filter data by a column or columns of the data found in the Data Source. For instance, if you only want to import sales data that is associated with units of your product that have sold over a certain quantity, you would select the column related to quantity sold in the Column to filter box.

8. Once you select the data column or columns from the Data Source table that you will use for your data filter, you must specify how the Query Wizard will actually filter the data. In the Only Include Rows Where drop-down box, select an operator to filter the data. The filter operator can be equals, does not equal, is greater than, is less than, and a number of other conditional statements.

9. After selecting the operator statement in the Only Include Rows Where drop-down box, you must specify the criteria that the operator uses in the drop-down box on the right.

10. Click the right-most drop-down arrow and a list of the data in the column of the table appears. Select the data that you will use with the filter operator. For instance, if you chose greater than, select the data amount in the drop-down box that the filter will use to select the greater than data by. Figure 20.13 shows a completed Query filter.

FIG. 20.13

The Query Wizard Filter Data box asks you to choose a column of data, an operator, and an actual data value for filtering the Data Source information that you will import into Excel.

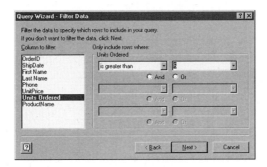

Microsoft Query provides a number of operator statements for filtering your data. Consult the following table for help with these query filter operators.

Operator Statement	Use When:
Equals	Records are to be filtered by a direct match of data in a particular field.
Does not equal	Records are filtered by designating data you do not want the query to filter by in a particular field.
Greater than	Use when you want to filter by numerical data and want to select records by data that exceeds a particular value.
Is greater than or equal to	Filters by numerical data; selects records that equal or exceed a specified value in a specific field.
Less than	Use when you want to filter records that have data in a field that is less than a particular value.
Is less than or equal to	Filters records by selecting those that old data in a particular field that is less than or equal to a specified value.
Begins with	Filters records by matching the beginning of a specified text or numerical string.
Does not begin with	Filters records that hold data in a particular field that do not begin with a specified text or numerical string.
Ends with	Filters records by a field containing data that ends with a specified text or numeric string.
Does not end with	Filters records by a field containing data that does not end with the specified text or numeric string.
Contains	Use to filter records when a field contains a specified text or numeric string.
Does not contain	Filter records using a specified text or numeric string that is not contained in the data found in the field.
Like	Filter records by specifying a numeric or text string that is like the data you want to match in a particular field (Smyth for Smith).
Not like	Filter records that do not contain data in a particular field that is like the specified text or numeric string.
Is Null	Select records that do not have data in the specified field.
Is not Null	Select records that do have data in the specified field.

11. Once you've completed designing your data filter, click the Next button to continue. The Query Wizard Sort Order dialog box appears. Use the drop-down box to select a column in the Data Source that you want to sort the data by. You can sort the information in Ascending or Descending order by clicking the appropriate option button. A Sort Order for a Data Source column is shown in Figure 20.14.

FIG. 20.14

You can sort the information that you import via Microsoft Wizard in the Query Wizard Sort Order box.

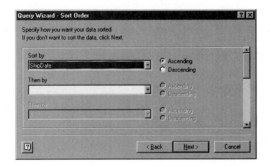

 You can sort the import data in the Data Source table by up to three sort parameters.

12. Once you've selected your sort order for the Data Source, click the Next button to continue. The final screen in the Query creation process appears.

The Query Wizard provides you with three different possibilities as you prepare to complete your query. You can:

- Save the query, allowing you to use the query at a later date.
- View the data using Microsoft Query and edit the query if necessary.
- Import the data into Excel for further analysis.

If you need to analyze the data in your Data Source on an ongoing basis, you may want to save the Query. This will allow you to recall the query using Microsoft Query and negates the need for redesigning the query. To save the query select the Save Query button and name the query to save it.

If you choose to view the data in Microsoft Query and edit the query, choose the View the data using Microsoft Query option button and then click Finish. Query provides you with a table view of the query results and provides you with a number of tools to further manipulate the data. You can adjust your filter parameters and change the column that you sorted the information by. A query in Microsoft Query is show in Figure 20.15. Once you have manipulated the query you can save it for later use. You can then retrieve the query when you invoke Microsoft Query from the Excel Data menu.

You can also import the data from the revised query into Excel. To do so, choose File, Return Data to Microsoft Excel.

Part III
Ch
20

FIG. 20.15

Microsoft Query allows you to manipulate the query further before saving it. You can then retrieve the revised query to import data into an Excel spread-sheet.

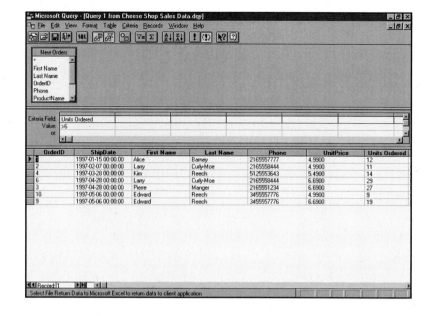

In most cases, because you are using Query to import data into Excel for analysis, you will want to select the Import the Data into Excel option button and then click Finish. This places the data into a blank Excel spreadsheet.

Integrating the Query Results into Excel

You can import the query data into Excel two ways. One way is to select the Import the Data into Excel option button and then click Finish on the last screen of the Query Wizard's query creation process. This will cause the data to be returned to Excel in the form of a spreadsheet. You can also return query data to Excel from Microsoft Query itself as discussed above via the Query File menu.

1. When you choose to retrieve Query data into Excel from the Query Wizard screen or from Microsoft Query the Returning External Data to Microsoft Excel dialog box appears as shown in Figure 20.16.

2. You can place the data into the current Worksheet at a designated cell, or click the option button to place the data into a new worksheet. You can also place the data directly into an Excel Pivot Table report, which provides you with a great deal of flexibility if you want to analyze the imported data. After you designate your preference, click OK.

    ▶ **See** "Using Pivot Tables," **p. 365**

3. The data will be placed into Excel as a spreadsheet (or Excel PivotTable if you selected the PivotTable report option).

FIG. 20.16
The Returning Data to
Excel dialog box allows
you to designate where
the data where will be
pasted into the current
spreadsheet or select a
new worksheet. You can
even have the data
placed in an Excel
PivotTable.

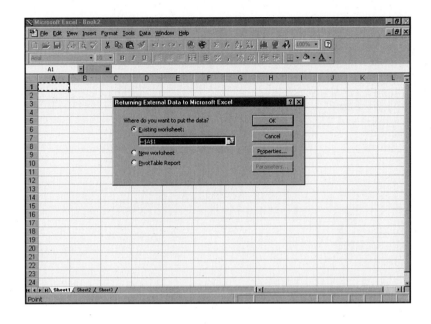

 TIP If you chose to retrieve the data into Excel as a PivotTable, the PivotTable Wizard will appear to help you place the data in the appropriate rows and columns.

Once the data is in an Excel spreadsheet, you can treat it as you would any other information that you place in Excel. You can add formulas to the sheet, set up what if scenarios, and chart the data. Figure 20.17 shows data imported via Microsoft Query that has been charted and totaled after it was imported into Excel.

Using Other Data Sources

Microsoft Query also allows you to import data into Excel from data sources other than databases. You can now use information on the World Wide Web as a Query Data Source and retrieve it into Excel.

To run a Web query you must be able to connect to the Internet via an Internet Service Provider or an Online Service such as America Online or the Microsoft Network. Excel then connects to the Web when you request a Web query.

Excel comes with four Web queries—three of the queries can be used to download data related to investments and stock market information. The fourth query is actually designed to help you download additional queries from the Web. The following table gives you information on each of the available queries.

Data Source	Data Retrieved
PC Quote Stock Quotes	Detailed Information on Specific Stocks
Dow Jones Stocks	Data for Dow Jones Industrial Stocks
More Web Queries	Retrieve Additional Web Queries
Multiple Stock Quotes	Retrieve information on Multiple Stocks from PC Quote, Inc.

FIG. 20.17

When you retrieve external database data into Excel, you can use Excel's tools—such as the Chart Wizard and various formulas—to analyze the information.

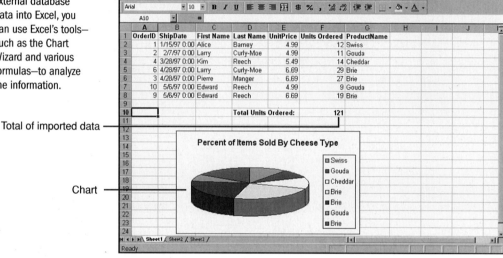

Total of imported data

Chart

Running a Web Query

Running a Web Query to retrieve data into an Excel spreadsheet is every bit as straightforward as running a database query. Once again the process is started via the Excel Data menu.

1. Make sure that Excel is running and that you have a blank worksheet open. Connect to your Internet Service Provider or Online Service via your modem dial up connection or network.

2. In Excel choose Data, Get External Data. On the submenu that appears, click Run Web Query. The Run Query dialog box opens.

3. To run a particular query, select it as shown in Figure 20.18, and then click Get Data.

4. To run a particular query, select it and then click Get Data as shown in Figure 20.18. The Returning External Data to Excel dialog box will open. Select the worksheet and location that you want to place the imported data, and then click OK.

5. A title line will appear in the Excel spreadsheet, meaning that the stock data is being retrieved from the Web. Once the data has been imported it will appear in your spreadsheet as shown in Figure 20.19.

Once you download the information you can print it, graph it or analyze it using other tools in Excel. The data that is retrieved from the Web stock Data Sources in this manner is no more than 20 minutes old when you download during business hours. This means that the Web query is providing you with real time stock information that you can work with in Excel.

FIG. 20.18
Select the Web query you want to run and then select Get Data.

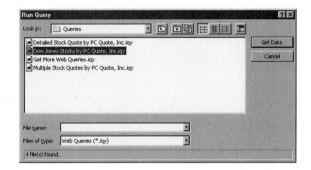

FIG. 20.19
The Dow Jones Stock Web query provides you up-to-date information on stocks that makeup the Dow Jones Industrial Average.

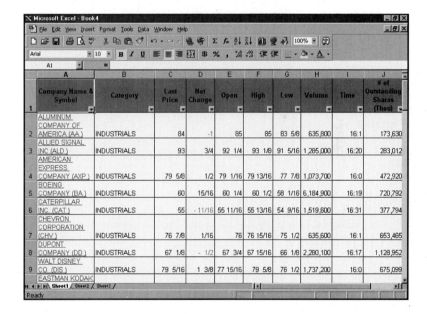

Part
III

Ch
20

Downloading Additional Web Queries

You can also download additional Web queries for Microsoft Excel. These Web queries consist of data on additional stock reports, foreign currency exchanges, and consumer loan interest rates.

To download additional Web Queries, make sure that you are connected to the Internet via your Internet Service Provider or Online Service. The commands for downloading the additional Web Queries are found on the Excel Data menu.

1. Click the <u>D</u>ata menu, then point at Get External <u>D</u>ata. On the submenu that appears click Run <u>W</u>eb Query. The Run Query dialog box will open.

2. Select Get More Web Queries in the Run Query dialog box. Then click Get Data. The Returning External Data to Excel dialog box opens; click OK to continue.

3. The additional Web queries will be downloaded from the Web in the form of an Excel spreadsheet. This spreadsheet contains detailed information on Excel Web queries and provides links that you can use to download additional Web Queries as shown in Figure 20.20.

TIP You can print or save the Web Query spreadsheet that you downloaded. Then you can download the Web Queries at your leisure or peruse the list to decide which Web Queries you would like to download and install on your PC.

4. When you click a link for one of the listed Web Queries, your default Web browser will open (in most cases this will be Microsoft Internet Explorer) and move to the Web site referenced in the link. A Save dialog box will appear that you can use to save the new Web Query. Designate a location for the Web Query download and click Save.

FIG. 20.20

When you choose to get more Web Queries, a spreadsheet containing links to a number of new Web Queries is retrieved into Excel. Click a link to download a specific query.

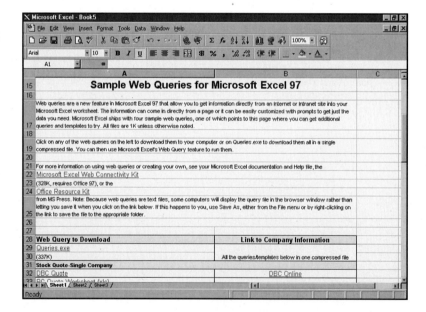

CAUTION

When you download individual Web Queries using the links in the Web Query worksheet, make sure you place the queries in your default query directory. This is usually the C:\Program Files\Microsoft Office\Queries folder. This will make it much easier to find the queries when you want to run them in Excel.

The new Web Query will be downloaded to your computer. The next time you run a Web Query in Excel the recently downloaded query will be listed with the other Web Queries in the Run Query dialog box.

 You can download all the additional Web Queries found in the Web Query hyperlink worksheet by downloading the Queries.exe file. It is the first link listed on the Web Query worksheet. This file contains all the Web Queries listed on the sheet. To install queries after downloading Queries.exe, double-click this executable file using the Windows Explorer and install the queries to your default query folder.

CHAPTER 21

Using VBA in Excel

by John Green

Macro procedures increase your productivity through automation. If you carry out the same series of steps in your worksheet repeatedly or on a regular basis, you can have a macro do that for you automatically. The process might be as simple as formatting some cells or as complex as consolidating your company reports.

After you have created your macros, you can execute them in many ways. You can run a macro by clicking a button on a worksheet or toolbar, choosing a menu item, or even by actions such as clicking a cell. ■

Increase your productivity

You can automate you regular Excel operations by writing macros to carry out the same tasks at the press of a button.

The Macro Recorder

The Macro Recorder is the easiest way to create a macro.

Beyond the Macro Recorder

You need to know VBA programming concepts and the Excel Object Model to make your macros flexible and powerful.

User-defined functions

You can use VBA to write your own functions that you can use in spreadsheet calculations to simplify complex formulas.

Putting it all together

Through the code examples and the explanations in the text, you will see how the power of VBA can be harnessed to reach your goals.

Using the Excel Macro Recorder

The easiest way to create a macro is to use the macro recorder. This is like turning on a tape recorder that will register everything you do until you turn it off. The recorded operation can then be played back by using Tools, Macro, Macros or by a keyboard shortcut consisting of the Ctrl key plus a single letter key that you choose.

Recording the Macro

Say you want to create a macro to format the cells that are currently selected in a worksheet. Figure 21.1 shows how the spreadsheet might look before you apply the formats.

FIG. 21.1

You can start the Excel macro recorder by clicking the Record Macro button on the VBA toolbar.

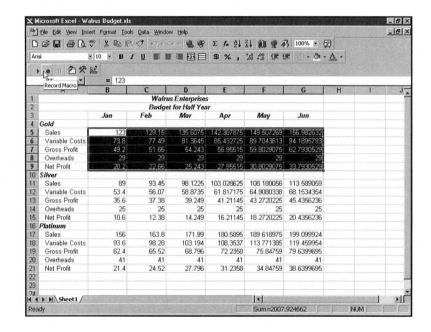

 TIP Before you start to record a macro, it is a good idea to prepare a mental plan of what you want to achieve. Think about the sequence of commands you will use to achieve your goal. Determine which steps you want to perform as normal manual operations and at what point you want to turn the recorder on and at what point you want to turn it off.

In this case, you would not record selecting the cells because you want to apply the formats to any cells that have been selected before the macro is executed. Therefore, you start the recorder after selecting the cells.

To record a macro, follow these steps:

1. Choose Tools, Macro, Record New Macro or click the Record button on the Visual Basic Toolbar, which you can see in Figure 21.1. You will see a dialog box, similar to the one shown in Figure 21.2.

2. Type in the macro name you want to use so that it replaces the name Macro1. Do not put a space or any special characters in the name. In this example, you could use FormatCells.

3. Edit the Shortcut Key to a letter of your choice. It can be a lower- or uppercase character. In this example, you could use a lowercase f.

4. Choose where you want to store the macro. Macros stored in the hidden file Personal.xls are automatically saved and loaded for future Excel sessions. This is appropriate for often-used utility macros but not for application-specific macros where it is preferable to store the macro in the application workbook or a completely separate workbook. In this example, you could choose to store the macro in This Workbook.

5. Click OK to start the recording process. The word Recording appears on the status bar at the bottom of the screen. This feature gives you a visual reference for whether the recorder is switched on.

6. Carry out the steps you have planned to record. In this example, you could use Format Cells and, under the Number tab, choose a Currency format, under the Font tab, choose Color as dark blue and then click OK to apply the formats.

7. Stop the recorder using Tools, Macro, Stop Recording or by pressing the Stop Recording button. You will find that, while you are recording, the Macro Record button on the VBA toolbar changes to the Stop Recording button. You might also have seen another Stop Recording button appear on its own special Stop Recording toolbar.

T I P   When you assign Ctrl key shortcuts to macros, you can use a lowercase letter, but that could replace one of the standard keyboard shortcuts. (Ctrl+C is the shortcut for Edit, Copy for example.) If you choose an uppercase character, you need to hold down both the Ctrl key and the Shift key when you run it, but it will not conflict with the standard shortcuts.

CAUTION

It is important to remember to turn off the Macro Recorder. If you do not turn off the recorder it will continue to record everything you do, including your attempt to run the macro later. A macro that tries to run itself can create an infinite loop. If you do accidentally create such a macro and run it, or if you want to stop any macro for any reason, press the Esc key to interrupt the macro and press End to terminate it.

Part

III

Ch

21

FIG. 21.2

The Record Macro dialog box appears when you start recording.

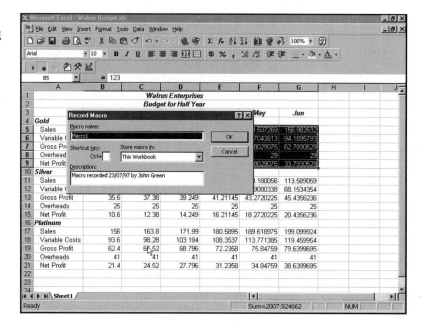

Running the Macro

After you have recorded a macro, you can execute it as often as required. In this example, you could select some more cells to be formatted, such as B11:G15. To run the macro using its short cut key, press Ctrl+F.

Alternatively, if you have not assigned a short cut, or if you have forgotten the short cut, you can run the macro from the Macro dialog box. To run the macro from the Macro dialog box, follow these steps:

1. Choose Tools, Macro, Macros or press the Run Macro button on the left side of the VBA toolbar. This opens the Macro dialog box that you can see in Figure 21.3.

2. Click the name of the macro to highlight it.

3. Press the Run button.

 If you want to change the short cut key for your macro, you use the same Macro dialog box as you use to run your macro. Use Tools, Macro, Macros and select the macro and click Options. The macro Options dialog box opens, and you can change the short cut key.

Modifying Code Using the Visual Basic Editor

The Macro Recorder is certainly the quickest and easiest way to create new macros. However, the result is not very flexible and the resulting code is usually not as efficient as it could be. It is often desirable to modify the code.

FIG. 21.3

The Macro dialog box can be used to run your macros.

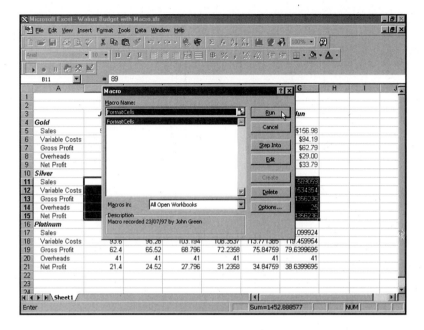

You can examine and edit your macro code in the VBE (Visual Basic Editor) window. To open the VBE window, use the following steps:

1. Choose Tools, Macro, Macros or press the Run Macro button on the left side of the VBA toolbar to open the Macro dialog box.

2. Click the name of the macro to highlight it.

3. Click Edit. This activates the VBE window and positions your cursor at the selected macro code.

Figure 21.4 shows the FormatCells macro from the previous example. Note that the macro starts with the Sub keyword followed by the name of the macro and a pair of parentheses. Also note that some lines are preceded by an apostrophe to indicate that they are comment lines which are not operational. They are there for documentation purposes only.

The comments are followed by VBA macro language statements that perform actions. Although you will probably not fully understand these statements at first, you can see that they use terms which are similar to Excel menu choices.

The first action performed by the macro is to set the number format of the selected cells. The rest of the macro code is contained in a With/End With construction, which sets the font characteristics of the selected cells.

Note that the code sets every possible option in the Font dialog box, not just the color option that was used in the example. This might be what you want, but is more likely to be unnecessary. This code will override any existing font settings.

Part
III

Ch
21

FIG. 21.4

You can examine and edit your macros in the VBE window.

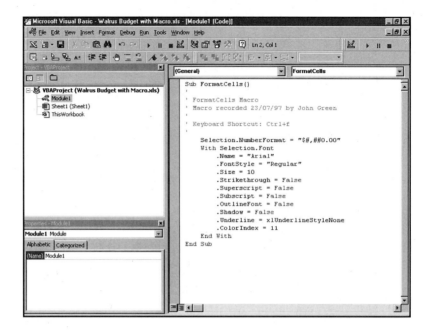

For example, if you wanted to use this macro to change only the color of cells that had been deliberately formatted as Times New Roman. This code would set the font to Arial. The problem is easily fixed. You can edit out the rows that are not required by selecting and deleting them. The final macro might look like Listing 21.1.

Listing 21.1   Format Macro

```
Sub FormatCells()
'
' Keyboard Shortcut: Ctrl+f
'
    Selection.NumberFormat = "$#,##0.00"
    With Selection.Font
        .ColorIndex = 11
    End With
End Sub
```

Absolute and Relative Recording

There are two modes you can use when recording macros in Excel. They are Absolute and Relative Recording. The mode only makes a difference if you are recording the selection or activation of cells. If you choose Absolute Recording, Excel always selects the same range of cells as the ones you selected when recording. If you use Relative Recording, Excel selects relative to the previous selection.

For example, if you select the A4 cell, turn on the recorder, and use Absolute Recording and select the cell under A4, the resulting code is

```
Range("A5").Select
```

which always selects the A5 cell regardless of which cell was previously active.

If you record the same action using Relative Recording, the resulting code is

```
ActiveCell.Offset(1,0).Range("A1").Select
```

which selects the cell underneath whichever cell was previously active. It is probably not obvious to you at this stage how this code works. You will see the details explained as you read through the following sections.

You can switch between Absolute and Relative Recording at any time while you are recording by clicking the Relative Reference button on the Stop Recording toolbar that you can see in Figure 21.5. When the button is selected, you get Relative Recording. When it is not selected, you get Absolute Recording.

FIG. 21.5

You can switch between Absolute and Relative Recording using the Relative Reference button on the Stop Recording toolbar.

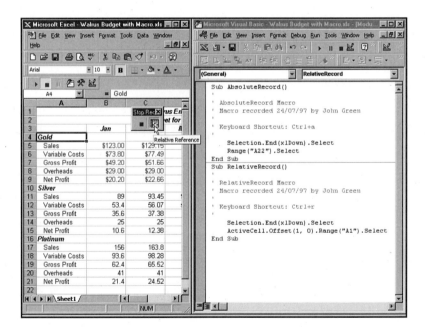

TROUBLESHOOTING

What should I do if the Stop Recording toolbar does not appear? The Stop Recording toolbar should appear when you start recording and disappear when you stop recording. If you don't see the Stop Recording toolbar when you start recording, or if it is permanently on the screen, use the following method to return it to normal operation.

Part
III

Ch
21

continues

continued

If the Stop Recording toolbar is permanently on-screen, choose View, Toolbars, Customize and click the Stop Recording check box to deactivate it. Whether the last step was necessary of not, now record a dummy macro by starting the macro recorder. As soon as the recorder is running, use View, Toolbars and click the Stop Recording toolbar name to activate it. Now stop recording. Go to the VBE window and delete the macro.

Figure 21.5 shows the macros recorded when trying to find the first empty cell in the A column below A4. Before starting the recorder, the A4 cell was selected. The recorder was switched on and the last item in the A column was then found using Ctrl+down arrow. Following that, down arrow was used to select the empty cell below the last cell. The `AbsoluteRecord` macro was recorded entirely in Absolute mode. The `RelativeRecord` macro was recorded entirely in Relative mode.

The code in the AbsoluteRecord macro will always result in selecting A22.

The code in the `RelativeRecord` macro is much more useful. As long as the active cell contains data and has at least one cell with data under it, running the `RelativeRecord` macro will find the first empty cell underneath the active cell. It will work in any column, even if rows are added or deleted.

Storing Macros in Personal.xls

Macros that you use often and with different spreadsheets are best kept in the Personal.xls workbook. We have seen that one of the options when recording a macro is to record directly into this workbook. If Personal.xls does not exist and you elect to record a macro into it, Excel automatically creates the workbook for you. Personal.xls will be automatically opened when you open Excel, so any macros stored there are always available.

At the end of your session, when you exit from Excel, you are prompted to store the changes to Personal.xls. By default, Excel stores this workbook in a directory called Xlstart. On a standard C drive installation of Office 97, the path to this directory is

```
C:\Program Files\Microsoft Office\Office\Xlstart
```

If you use a network version of Excel, you might need to create an alternative startup directory using Tools, Options and clicking the General tab. In the edit box labeled Alternate Startup File Location, you can enter the path to any directory where you have read/write access. If you then save a workbook in this directory, giving it the name of Personal.xls, it behaves as the standard Personal.xls workbook. If you also hide the workbook using Window Hide, and save this change when exiting Excel, it remains hidden.

CAUTION

Don't nominate a directory you use for storing your normal workbooks as your alternative startup directory, unless you want all those workbooks to open automatically when you start Excel. Any workbooks, apart from templates, stored in Xlstart or your alternative startup directory are opened at the same time you open Excel.

If you want to edit or delete macros in Personal.xls, just unhide it using <u>W</u>indow, <u>U</u>nhide. It behaves like any normal workbook. You should hide it again before the end of your Excel session if you want it to be normally hidden.

Assigning Macros to Toolbar Buttons

You have seen how you can run a macro using the <u>T</u>ools menu or using a Ctrl key short cut. Another very convenient way to run a macro is to attach it to a button on a toolbar.

If you want to attach a macro to a toolbar button, it is best to place it in Personal.xls. You can have the macro in another workbook if you want, but Excel has to load the workbook when the button is clicked. This can take time and can be visually disruptive. If the macro is in Personal.xls, it will be ready for use all the time and access will be transparent.

Say you record a macro in Personal.xls that is identical to the RelativeRecord macro in Figure 23.5, naming it **FindEmptyCell**. You could attach it to a button on a toolbar and run it in any worksheet to find the next empty cell down any column. You could create a new toolbar for the purpose, or add it to an existing toolbar.

To create a new toolbar and add a custom button to it, use the following steps:

1. Choose <u>V</u>iew, <u>T</u>oolbars, <u>C</u>ustomize to open the Customize dialog box.
2. Click the Tool<u>b</u>ars tab and click <u>N</u>ew.
3. Enter a name for the new toolbar, such as **Utilities**, and click OK.
4. Click the <u>C</u>ommands tab in the Customize dialog box and, under Categories, scroll down and select Macros as shown in Figure 21.6.
5. Drag the Custom Button icon from the Comman<u>d</u>s box and drop it on your new toolbar.
6. While the Customize dialog box is still open, either right-click the new toolbar button or click <u>M</u>odify Selection to display the pop-up menu shown in Figure 21.6.
7. Click Assign <u>M</u>acro and select the desired macro in the Assign Macro dialog box and click OK.
8. You can also use <u>N</u>ame to change the name of the button in the pop-up menu. This determines the ToolTip message that is displayed when you rest the mouse pointer on the button. You can also select <u>E</u>dit Button Image to touch up the icon or Change <u>B</u>utton Image to select a new image from a set.
9. Click Close to dismiss the Customize dialog box.

The changes you have made to the toolbars will be permanent. You can now run the attached macro in any worksheet in any future session in Excel.

FIG. 21.6

While the Customize dialog box is open, you can create new toolbars and add custom buttons to run your macros.

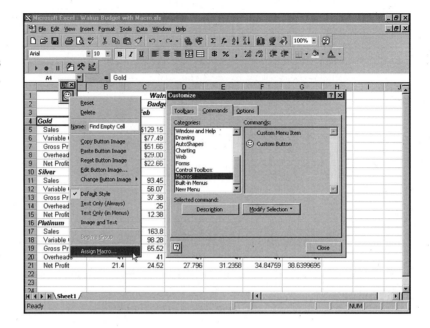

User-Defined Functions

When you use the Macro Recorder, VBA creates a block of macro code that starts with the Sub keyword followed by the name of the macro and a pair of parentheses. The block of code is terminated by the End Sub key words. This block of code is referred to in VBA as a *Sub procedure*.

So far you have dealt only with VBA Sub procedures. Sub procedures carry out actions such as formatting spreadsheet cells or saving workbooks. VBA also supports one other type of procedure called a Function procedure. *Function procedures* start with the Function keyword and end with the End Function keywords.

The difference between a Sub procedure and a Function procedure is that Function procedures calculate a result or a return value. When you run a Function procedure, it produces a numeric value or some text that you can use in a worksheet calculation. You can use Function procedures in your worksheet formulas in the same way that you can use the SUM function or the IF function to calculate a result in a worksheet formula.

There are already hundreds of functions built into Excel. You will be familiar with the SUM function and possibly many others such as IF and VLOOKUP. Using VBA, you can write your own worksheet functions that you can use in your cell calculations.

By writing your own functions, you can make many complex calculations much easier for yourself and others in your organization. For example, the calculation of personal or company taxes can be quite complex in some countries and involve a number of subsidiary calculations and table lookups. All of this could be built into a single function with enough input arguments to define all the possible alternative situations. All you have to do then is use the function in a cell, defining each input argument, and it will return the appropriate result.

For example, say you wanted to convert degrees Centigrade to degrees Fahrenheit. You could write your own function to do that. Figure 21.7 shows the VBE window containing two user-defined functions. The top function starts with

```
Function CToF()
```

that defines a function procedure called CToF (short for Centigrade to Fahrenheit). The spreadsheet that uses the CToF function to perform the conversion calculation is shown on the left of Figure 21.7. You can see the formula used in the B3 cell by looking at the formula bar above the worksheet:

```
=CToF(A3)
```

The A3 cell, containing 100, is used as the input argument of the CToF function. The calculated result, 212, is returned to the B3 cell.

FIG. 21.7

You can write your own VBA functions that you can use in your spreadsheet calculations.

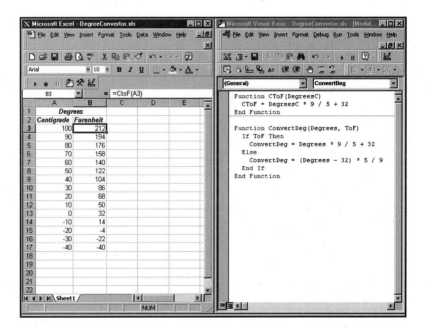

There is no way that you can record a user-defined function. It must be written from scratch. To create a function, use these steps:

1. Activate the workbook that will contain the function and press Alt+F11 to activate the Visual Basic Editor window.

2. If the workbook does not already contain a module, use Insert, Module to create a new VBA module.

3. Type in the function.

The function starts with the keyword Function, followed by the name of the function. Start the name with a letter and do not use spaces or special characters in the name. In parentheses, following the function name, you create names for all the required input parameters. The parameter names follow the same rules as the function name but, apart from that, can be any names you like.

In the body of the function, you can perform all the necessary calculations to get the required result. To return the result to the worksheet, you set the name of the function equal to the result.

The second function in Figure 21.7, ConvertDeg, is a little more complex than CToF. It allows conversion in either direction. If the second parameter, ToF is set equal to True, it converts the Degrees input argument to Fahrenheit. If ToF is False, it converts Degrees to Centigrade. To convert 75 degrees Fahrenheit to Centigrade, you could enter the following formula into a worksheet cell:

```
=ConvertDeg(75,False)
```

The Excel Object Model

VBA programming is virtually the same in all Office 97 applications as far as programming structures and principles are concerned. The differences between the products lie in their object models. When you record macros, you don't need to be familiar with the Excel object model. But, if you want to modify recorded macros or create macros that can't be recorded, knowledge of the Excel object model is essential.

VBA is an object-oriented programming language. It deals with objects. *Objects* are the components you find in an application. In Excel, some examples of objects are WorkBooks, WorkSheets, Ranges, Charts, CommandBars and CommandButtons. Some objects belong to *collections*. For example, there is a collection called the WorkBooks collection. It contains all the currently open WorkBook objects in memory.

Objects are arranged in a hierarchy. At the top level, you find the Application object which is Excel. Under Application you find the WorkBooks collection. Under the WorkBooks collection there is the individual WorkBook object. Under the WorkBook object there is the Range object. This hierarchy describes the relationships between all the objects in the application and is referred to as the *application object model*.

You can find the Excel object model represented in a diagram in the help screens. To see it, follow these steps:

1. Starting from either the Excel window or the VBE window, choose Help, Contents and Index.
2. Click the Contents tab and from near the bottom of the list of topics, double-click Microsoft Excel Visual Basic Reference to open the subtopics beneath it.
3. Double-click either Visual Basic Reference or Shortcut to Visual Basic Reference. This opens a new help dialog box for VBA.

4. Double-click Microsoft Excel Visual Basic Reference to open the subtopics beneath it.

5. Double-click Microsoft Excel Objects. You should now see the diagram shown in Figure 23.8.

6. Click the red arrow to the right of Worksheets (Worksheet) to see the details on the worksheet object, which is shown in Figure 21.9.

FIG. 21.8

The Excel object model as it appears in the Office 97 help screens.

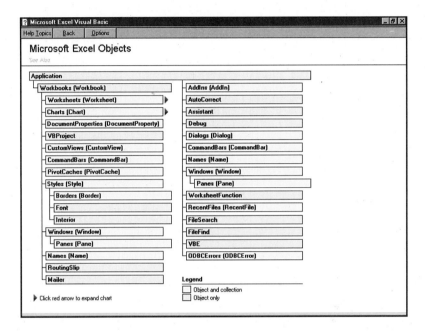

The object model is important because it gives you the names of the objects you need to reference in your VBA code. It also gives you the position of each object in the object hierarchy. You often need to qualify an object by specifying the objects above it, and you need to know the correct order.

If you want to manipulate an object in VBA code, you need to know what properties and methods it has. *Properties* are the measurable characteristics of the object and methods are the actions that the object can perform or have performed on it. For example, a Workbook object has a Name property which defines its file name, and an ActiveSheet property which defines which sheet in the workbook is currently active. A Workbook object has an Open method to load it into memory and a Close method to remove it from memory.

Many objects can respond to system events. Events include most of the actions that you can perform on objects. For example, when you click a CommandButton object, the Click event takes place. You can write a macro which runs when this event occurs.

FIG. 21.9

Details of the Excel worksheet object.

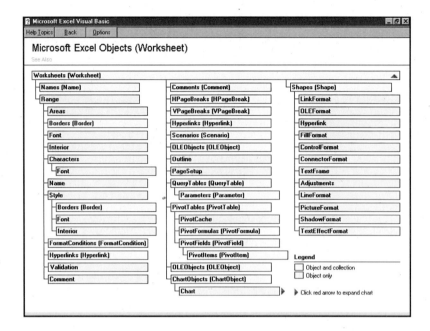

After you have found the object you want in the help screen diagram, you can click its name to move to a detail screen that describes the object. This screen also lets you see a list of the properties and methods for the object and you can jump to detailed descriptions and examples. Where applicable, you can also get a list of the events for the object.

Object Browser

The Object Browser provides another valuable source of information on application objects. You can display the Object Browser in the VBE window by using View, Object Browser or by pressing F2. You can see the Object Browser in Figure 21.10.

You can select which object library to browse in the drop-down menu in the top left section of the Browser. When you click an object in the Classes list, you see its methods, properties and events displayed to the right. You can get help on the currently selected item by clicking the ? icon in the top-right section of the Browser.

Immediate Window

The Immediate window, shown in Figure 21.10, enables you to experiment with VBA code. It is a valuable learning tool that you will use to look at the most important Excel objects. You can display the Immediate window using View, Immediate Window or by pressing Ctrl+G. If you arrange the Excel window and the VBE window side by side, as shown in Figure 21.10, you can observe the effects of your experiments.

FIG. 21.10

The Object Browser and the Immediate window. You can use the Immediate window to experiment with VBA code.

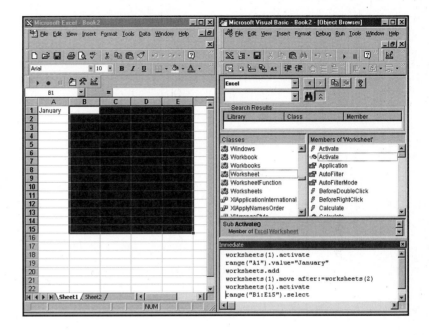

If you want to execute a method such as Activate on an object such as the first worksheet, you type the following in the Immediate window and press Enter:

```
Worksheets(1).Activate
```

VBA is not case-sensitive and can be entered in any combination. If you want to execute the same line of code again, click anywhere in the line and press Enter again. You do not have to be at the end of the line.

If you want to set the value of a property, such as the Name property of the first worksheet to myData, you type the following and press Enter:

```
Worksheets(1).Name = "myData"
```

If you want to display a property such as Count of an object such as the Worksheets collection, you type either of the following:

```
Print Worksheets.Count
```

or

```
? Worksheets.Count
```

When you press Enter, the value will be printed on the next line in the Immediate window.

As you are typing, you will often be prompted with lists of properties and methods or parameter values. If you want to choose from a list, select the item you want and press Tab. If you prefer, ignore the prompts and keep typing normally.

Part
III

Ch
21

The *Workbooks* Collection

The Workbooks collection consists of the workbooks that are currently open in the Excel window. As with most collections, you can determine the number of open workbooks with the Count property. You can add a new empty workbook to the collection with the Add method or open an existing workbook with the Open method. You can use the Close method to close all the workbooks in the collection.

 You can get help about any VBA object or keyword while you are in the VBE window. As soon as you have typed any object name or keyword, press F1 to bring up the help screen. Alternatively, you can click anywhere in an existing word and press F1.

If you want to experiment, make sure you can see both the Excel and VBE windows. In the Immediate window, type

> **Workbooks.Close**

Remember to press Enter to execute the command. This closes all the open workbooks. You might be prompted to save changes. Now type

> **Workbooks.Add**

This creates a new empty workbook such as Book2. Place your cursor back on the same line and press Enter again. Do this once more so that you have created three workbooks. To make the workbooks all visible, type

> **Windows.Arrange xlArrangeStyleCascade**

Here you are using the Arrange method of the Windows collection. XlArrangeStyleCascade is an intrinsic constant used to define the first parameter of the Arrange method.

> **CAUTION**
>
> When you type the XlArrangeStyleCascade constant, do not use the number one (1) as the second letter. It is a lowercase letter l.

To determine the number of open workbooks, type

> **?Workbooks.Count**

The number will be printed on the next line.

The *Workbook* Object

The Workbooks collection contains Workbook objects. To specify a particular workbook, you use the item property of the collection.

```
?Workbooks.Item(1).Name
```

This returns the name of the first workbook. However, the item property is the default member for the `Workbooks` collection and can be left out.

```
?Workbooks(1).Name
```

This is a shortcut way to specify the `Item` property. As with most collections, you can use either the index number of the item or the text ID of the item. To activate Book3, you could type

Workbooks("Book3").Activate

To save the second workbook using a new name, type

Workbooks(2).SaveAs "Data.xls"

You can use the `ActiveWorkbook` property of the `Application` object as a shortcut to refer to the currently active workbook.

```
?ActiveWorkbook.FullName
```

The `FullName` property gives the complete path and name for the workbook file.

Close the saved workbook so that you can open it again using the `Open` method of the `Workbooks` collection.

Type the following to close the workbook:

Workbooks("Data.xls").Close

Type the following to open the workbook:

Workbooks.Open "Data.xls"

CAUTION

It is tempting to think you are dealing with a collection when you are dealing with an object in a collection. A construction such as `Workbooks("Data.xls")` generates a reference to a `Workbook` object. To find the properties and methods of this object, you must look at the `Workbook` object in the Object Browser or help screens, not the `Workbooks` collection object.

The *Worksheets* Collection

Each workbook has a `Worksheets` collection. If the workbook is not the active workbook, you need to qualify the `Worksheets` collection with a reference to the specific workbook. To count the worksheets in the second workbook, type

?Workbooks(2).Worksheets.Count

If you want to refer to the active workbook, you can leave out the workbook reference. To add a new worksheet to the active workbook and put it after the first sheet, type

Worksheets.Add After:= Worksheets(1)

Part
III

Ch
21

Here you are defining a parameter by name. Previously, you have defined parameters by position. Click the word Add that you typed in the last example and press F1. This will bring up the help screen for the Add method. Click Worksheets to get specific help for Worksheets.Add. Notice that the After parameter is the second parameter. To specify it by position, you need to type

Worksheets.Add ,Worksheets(1)

The comma is required to make it clear that the first parameter is missing. On the other hand, if you specify the parameter by name, you do not need to worry about its position in the parameter list. It is also an advantage when writing code in your modules to include the parameter name. This makes the code easier to understand.

The *Worksheet* Object

As with the Workbook object, you can refer to a Worksheet object as a member of the Worksheets collection by index number or name. The index number follows the order of worksheets in the workbook with the name appearing as it does on the worksheet tab.

```
?Worksheets(2).Name
```

returns the tab name of the second worksheet in the workbook.

```
?Worksheets("Sheet2").Index
```

returns the position of Sheet2 in the Sheets collection.

> **CAUTION**
>
> Be careful using the index property of the worksheet object as it returns the position of the worksheet in the sheets collection. The Sheets collection includes worksheets, charts that are on their own sheets, and other older style sheets from previous versions of Excel such as dialogsheets. If you have two worksheets and a chart, arranged in the order Sheet1, Chart1, Sheet2, then Worksheets(2).Name returns Sheet2. However, Worksheets("Sheet2").Index returns 3. Even Worksheets(2).Index returns, 3, which is even more confusing.

You can refer to the currently active sheet by the ActiveSheet property of the Application object.

```
?ActiveSheet.Name = "Sales Data"
```

This defines the sheet tab of the active sheet as Sales Data.

The *Range* Object

The Range object is the one that you will probably refer to most in your VBA code. The two main ways to generate a reference to a range object are by using the Range property and the Cells property.

The *Range* Property   The Range property of the Application, Worksheet, or Range object enables you to generate a range object reference using text.

```
Range("B2:D10").Select
Range("C3").Activate
```

The first statement selects the B2:D10 range in the active worksheet with the B2 cell as the active cell. The second statement leaves the selection unchanged but activates the C3 cell within the selection.

N O T E   There is no such thing as a cell object in the Excel object model. A single cell is a range object, just as a block of cells is a range object. There is, however, a cells property, which can be used to generate a reference to a Range object. ▩

The Range property can take two arguments to generate a reference to a block of cells.

```
Range("B1","D10").Select
```

The previous line selects the range B1:D10 in the active worksheet.

The Range property is convenient if you want to refer to a single specific range by cell reference or name.

```
Range("B2:C5").Name = "myData"
Range("myData").Value = 100
```

creates the name myData and enters the value 100 into each cell in the range.

You can refer to part of a range using the following construction:

```
Range("myData").Range("A2").Select
```

If myData starts in B2, the previous code selects the B3 cell, acting as if myData is a mini worksheet with its own A1 cell in its upper-left corner.

 TIP   [A1] is equivalent to Range("A1") and [myData] is equivalent to Range("myData"). This syntax can be used to shorten your code. Many macro writers prefer to use the longer form because the syntax is consistent with other object reference syntax.

Part
III

Ch
21

The *Cells* Property   If you want to loop through a series of cells in a Do/Loop or For/Next programming structure, it is convenient to use the `Cells` property to generate range object references. This is because it is most convenient, when writing code, to refer to rows and columns by number. You can refer to a cell using `Cells(RowNumber,ColumnNumber)`.

```
Cells(2,3).Value = "January"
```

enters the label **January** into the C2 cell in the active worksheet.

If you want to refer to a cell within another range, you can do so with the following:

```
Range("myData").Cells(2,2).Font.ColorIndex = 3
```

Assuming that `myData` starts in B2, this sets the font color of the C3 cell to red.

You can use the `Cells` property with the `Range` property to refer to a block of cells.

```
Range(Cells(2,2),Cells(4,5)).Clear
```

clears the data and formats from the range B2:E4.

Other Useful Properties and Methods   You can refer to the active cell using the `ActiveCell` property of the `Application` object.

```
ActiveCell.Formula = "=A1*10"
```

The `Selection` property of the `Application` object refers to the currently selected cells.

```
Selection.Interior.Color = RGB(0,255,0)
```

This sets the background color of the selected cells to green. The `RGB` function returns colors by specifying the values of red, green, and blue in the range of 0 to 255.

The `Offset` property of a range generates a reference to a range object with the same number of rows and columns as the original range object, but offset by a specified number of rows and columns. It is often used to select the next cell to the active cell.

```
ActiveCell.Offset(1,0).Activate
```

activates the cell that is one row down and zero columns to the right of the active cell.

The `End` property can be used to emulate the effect of holding down Ctrl while pressing one of the cursor movement keys, or pressing End followed by a cursor movement key. In a worksheet, this activates the last cell in a row or column of data in the direction indicated.

If you have a column of data in A1:A10 and A11 is empty, you can use

```
Range("A1").End(xlDown).Activate
```

to activate the A10 cell. You can use `xlUp`, `xlToRight`, and `xlToLeft` to go in other directions. You can use the following to refer to a block of cells.

```
Range("A1",Range("A1").End(xlDown)).Font.Bold = True
```

bolds the cells in A1:A10, assuming A11 is empty.

If you need to know how many rows and columns have been used in a worksheet, you can use the `UsedRange` property of the worksheet. The `UsedRange` includes all columns and rows containing data or other cell information such as formatting and all columns and rows between.

> **CAUTION**
>
> You can't assume that the used range starts in A1. There could be rows at the top of the worksheet that have no data, or columns on the left, although this is unusual.

```
ActiveSheet.PageSetup.PrintArea = ActiveSheet.UsedRange.Address
```

can be used to set the print area to the cells containing data.

Knowing the used range, you can determine the first and last rows and columns that have been used in the worksheet. However, it is more convenient to find the last row and column using the `SpecialCells` method with the `xlCellTypeLastCell` constant.

```
LastRow = Cells.SpecialCells(xlCellTypeLastCell).Row
?LastRow
```

This code creates a variable, `LastRow`, containing the row number of the last row in the used range and then displays the value.

TIP Because Excel considers cells with formatting as part of the used range, the last cell returned by the `SpecialCells` method might not be what you want. If you want to find, and apply a name to the last cell of the range that contains data, you can use the code in Listing 21.2.

Listing 21.2   Finding the Last Data Cell

```
Sub NameRealLastCell()
    Dim RealLastRow As Long
    Dim RealLastColumn As Long
    RealLastRow = _
      Cells.Find("*", [A1], , , xlByRows, xlPrevious).Row
    RealLastColumn = _
      Cells.Find("*", [A1], , , xlByColumns, xlPrevious).Column
    Cells(RealLastRow, RealLastColumn).Name = "RealLastCell"
End Sub
```

Another very useful property is the `CurrentRegion` property of the range object. This returns a reference to a table of data. A table is defined as an area of worksheet containing data that is separated from surrounding data by at least one empty row and column. The table itself can have empty cells, so long as there is not an entirely empty row or column. Figure 21.11 shows the effect of selecting the `CurrentRegion` property of the A12 cell.

Part
III

Ch
21

FIG. 21.11

You can use the `CurrentRegion` property of the range object to refer to a table of data in a worksheet.

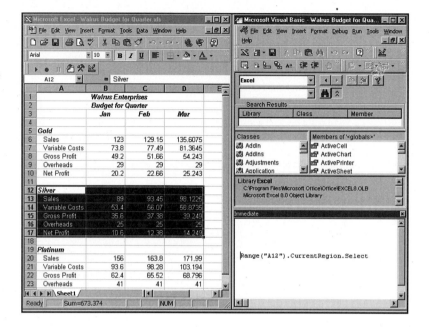

Creating Sub Procedures

You will now see how you can incorporate some of the object references you have investigated into some useful code. You will also make use of some VBA looping structures to repeatedly execute similar code and also see how to go about writing efficient code.

One undesirable outcome from using the macro recorder is that you get the most inefficient code possible. The problem is that the recorder can only record what you can do manually and that involves selecting objects so that you can make changes to those objects. In VBA code, it is seldom necessary to select anything in order to change it, but the recorder slavishly does what you do. If you want to write the most efficient code, you should try to avoid selecting anything.

A Macro that Selects

Figure 21.12 shows the top of a list of product data. If you want to make it easy to spot the premier product, Iridium, you need a macro to scan the list and give the Iridium cells a bold font.

FIG. 21.12

This list of products goes down to row 500; in this example, the macro finds every occurrence of Iridium and makes it bold.

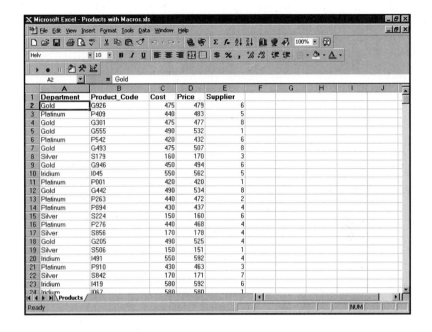

Before you write your macros, you need to open the VBE window and insert a code module. Figure 21.13 shows how the module will eventually appear. To insert a new module, follow these steps:

1. Starting in the Excel window, press Alt+F11 to activate the VBE window.

2. If you don't have the Project Explorer window visible, use View, Project Explorer (or Ctrl+R). The Project Explorer gives you an overview of the VBA components you are working with, so it is a good idea to have it open.

3. You might also like to open the Properties Window, if it is not already open, using View, Properties Window (or F4). The Properties Window is useful when you design user forms or want to change the properties of worksheets, workbooks, and embedded controls in sheets.

4. Use Insert, Module to create a new code module.

 TIP If you need to delete a module, right-click it in the Project Explorer and choose Remove Module. You will be given the opportunity to export its contents to a separate file. You can also use drag and drop in the Project Explorer to copy a module to another project.

Part

III

Ch

21

FIG. 21.13

Macro Sub procedures to loop through the A column and bold the Iridium entries.

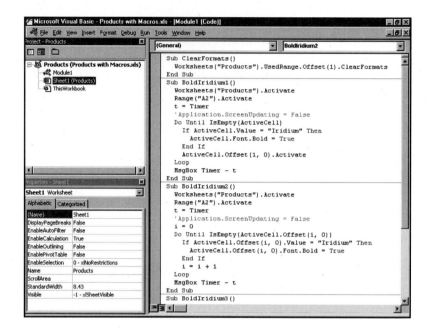

You can now type Listing 21.3 into the module.

Listing 21.3   Bolding the Iridium Cells

```
Sub BoldIridium1()
  Worksheets("Products").Activate
  Range("A2").Activate
  t = Timer
  Do Until IsEmpty(ActiveCell)
    If ActiveCell.Value = "Iridium" Then
      ActiveCell.Font.Bold = True
    End If
    ActiveCell.Offset(1, 0).Activate
  Loop
  MsgBox Timer - t
End Sub
```

The first two lines in the procedure activate the Products worksheet and the A2 cell. You want to time the running of the macro, so the third line captures the start time. At the end, the MsgBox statement displays the elapsed time in seconds.

The body of the macro is a Do/Loop structure, which repeats the code between Do and Loop until the condition on the Do is satisfied. That is, it tests to see if the active cell is empty on each pass through the loop and exits the loop when this is true. Note that just before the Loop statement, you activate the cell underneath the currently active cell. The block If sets the font to bold if the cell contains Iridium as text.

To run the macro, activate the Excel window and use Tools, Macros, Macro. Select the macro name and press Run. As the macro runs, you will notice that the screen flickers as the cells are selected and the screen scrolls. The runtime will depend on your processor. Using a mid-range Pentium processor, it might take about five seconds to process the 500 rows.

If you want to remove the formatting from the cells, you can use the following macro:

```
Sub ClearFormats()
  Worksheets("Products").UsedRange.Offset(1).ClearFormats
End Sub
```

The offset of one row is used to ensure that the first row headings remain bold.

A Macro that Does Not Select

Now, write a new version of the macro that does not select cells using Listing 21.4.

Listing 21.4 Avoiding Selecting Cells

```
Sub BoldIridium2()
  Worksheets("Products").Activate
  Range("A2").Activate
  t = Timer
 i = 0
  Do Until IsEmpty(ActiveCell.Offset(i, 0))
    If ActiveCell.Offset(i, 0).Value = "Iridium" Then
      ActiveCell.Offset(i, 0).Font.Bold = True
    End If
    i = i + 1
  Loop
  MsgBox Timer - t
End Sub
```

This macro activates the A2 cell like the first one. From then on, it uses the Offset property to examine cells below the active cell and change them. A counter variable, i, is established to hold the row offset values and it is increased by one each time round the loop.

When you run the macro, there will be no screen flicker or scrolling. It should run in about 0.5 seconds on a mid-range Pentium, about ten times faster than the previous macro.

Screen Updating

There is another way to cut down on screen flicker and speed up the macro. This is by adding the following statement

```
Application.ScreenUpdating  = False
```

near the beginning of the macro, perhaps after the Range("A2").Activate. This freezes the screen until the macro finishes. This does increase the speed of the first macro dramatically. It should bring the time down to about 0.8 seconds on a mid-range Pentium.

This takes a little gloss off the second macro example, but the second macro is still significantly faster than the first. Interestingly enough, even though the second macro does not update the screen, it can be sped up using the same technique. However, the increase is minor, with the modified macro running in about .48 seconds

For Each/Next Loop

There is another technique that you can use to process every member of a collection. This is a For Each/Next loop. The macro could be written again as Listing 21.5.

Listing 21.5   Using a For Each/Next Loop

```
Sub BoldIridium3()
  Worksheets("Products").Activate
  Range("A2").Activate
  t = Timer
  For Each rngCell In Range("A2", Range("A2").End(xlDown))
    If rngCell.Value = "Iridium" Then
      rngCell.Font.Bold = True
    End If
  Next rngCell
MsgBox Timer - t
End Sub
```

rngCell is just an arbitrary object variable name that is automatically assigned to each cell in the range, one by one, as the macro loops between the For and the Next statements. It takes about .25 seconds on a Pentium, so is significantly faster than the previous macros.

This type of loop is very useful in VBA. You can process all the Workbook objects in the Workbooks collection or all the Worksheet objects in the Worksheets collection of a workbook, for example.

Basic Output and Input

If you want to display a message or get input from a user, there are two available functions that are easy to use. They are MsgBox and InputBox. If you want to get more sophisticated, you can design your own user forms with the full complement of controls including list boxes, option buttons, and check boxes.

The *MsgBox* Function

You have already used MsgBox to display the execution times for your macros. By default, it shows a dialog box with the time and an OK button. In this format, MsgBox is useful for displaying warnings or information. The dialog box is modal, which means processing ceases while it is showing, and the user can't do anything until the OK button is pressed.

MsgBox has a number of options that can increase its effectiveness. As well as a message, or prompt, you can specify an icon and a number of different button combinations including OK, Cancel, Yes, No, Abort, Retry, and Ignore. If you examine the help screen for MsgBox, you will see that these options are specified by assigning numeric values to the second parameter, or you can use intrinsic constants, such as vbQuestion and vbYesNo.

There is also a third parameter, which defines a title to go at the top of the dialog box. The fourth and fifth parameters are used to specify help screens and are only useful if you know how to use the Windows help compiler.

Figure 21.14 shows two macros that use MsgBox. The dialog box shown was generated by running Message2. Rather than clutter up the MsgBox code with the parameter details, Message2 assigns the required text and values to variables.

FIG. 21.14

The Message2 macro uses the MsgBox function to generate this simple dialog box asking about personal details.

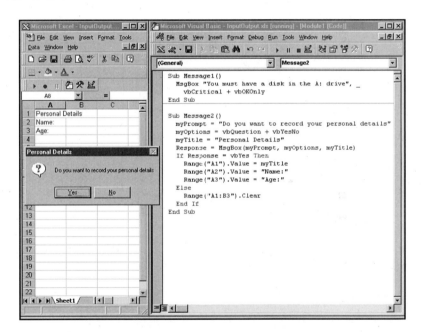

Message2 shows how you capture the return value from MsgBox. Once again, if you examine the help screen for MsgBox, you will see that there are intrinsic constants, such as vbYes and vbNo, provided to enable you to find out which button the user pressed. Here, the return value is assigned to a variable, Response, and there is a test to see if it is equal to vbYes. If so, some headings are placed in the active sheet to prepare for the next step, which will be addressed later. If the user has not pressed Yes, the active sheet is cleared.

Part

III

Ch

21

> **N O T E**   The Message1 macro does not have parentheses around the arguments for MsgBox,
> whereas Message2 does use parentheses around the MsgBox arguments. This illustrates
> an important rule that you must be aware of in VBA. If you assign the return value of a function or
> method to a variable, or use it as input to another function or method, the arguments must be in
> parentheses. If you do not make use of the return value, its arguments must not be in parentheses.

The *InputBox* Function

MsgBox enables you to distinguish between button presses, but it does not let you ask for input data in the form of text or numbers. Listing 21.6 shows how to use the InputBox function prompt the user for input data.

Listing 21.6   Format Macro

```
Sub Message3()
  myPrompt = "Do you want to record your personal details"
  myOptions = vbQuestion + vbYesNo
  myTitle = "Personal Details"
  Response = MsgBox(myPrompt, myOptions, myTitle)
  If Response = vbYes Then
    Range("A1").Value = myTitle
    Range("A2").Value = "Name:"
    Range("A3").Value = "Age:"
    UserName = InputBox("Please enter your name", myTitle)
    If UserName = "" Then Exit Sub
    Range("B2").Value = UserName
    UserAge = InputBox("Please enter your age", myTitle)
    If UserAge = "" Then Exit Sub
    Range("B3").Value = UserAge
  Else
    Range("A1:B3").Clear
  End If
End Sub
```

The dialog box generated by InputBox has a text box in it. Here the user can type input data. The dialog box has an OK button and a Cancel button. If the user clicks OK, InputBox returns the text in the text box. If the user clicks Cancel, InputBox returns a zero-length string. In the previous code, the If test was used to see if a zero-length string has been returned. If so, the Sub procedure is terminated. Otherwise, the data is inserted into the active sheet.

CAUTION

When entering the Message3 macro code, make sure you enter the zero-length string as two double quotes with nothing in-between. Don't put a blank space between the quotes.

Event Procedures

Excel 97 has extended the power of VBA macros by exposing a number of workbook and worksheet events. These events include opening workbooks, activating and deactivating workbooks and worksheets, double-clicking cells, selecting cells, and many more.

This means that you can write code for any of these events. The code runs when the event occurs. Figure 21.15 shows the code written for the SelectionChange event of Sheet1. To write an event procedure like this, use the following steps:

1. Use Alt+F11 to activate the VBE window.

2. In the Project Explorer, double-click the workbook or sheet object in which you want to write your code. For this example, double-click Sheet1. This opens the code module for that object.

3. Click the Object drop-down at the top of the code module and choose Workbook or Worksheet. In this case choose Worksheet.

4. If necessary, use the Procedure drop-down list at the top of the code module to choose the event you want to respond to. In this case the SelectionChange event should have been automatically selected when you chose Worksheet from the Object drop-down. The first and last lines of the Worksheet_SelectionChange Sub procedure will be automatically generated.

FIG. 21.15

By writing an event procedure for a worksheet, you can generate an error message when users attempt to access sensitive areas of the worksheet.

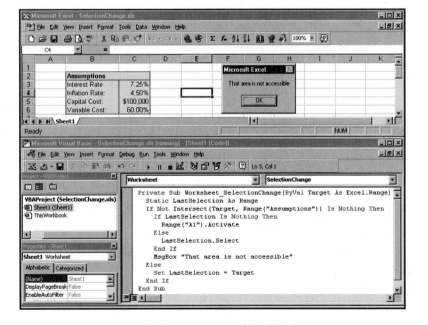

Part

III

Ch

21

The event procedure in Figure 21.15 detects when a user clicks into the Assumptions area of Sheet1, which has been given the name Assumptions. When this happens, the selection is returned to the previous selection and an error message is displayed by MsgBox.

This event procedure runs every time the user selects a new cell or range of cells. Target is an input parameter automatically supplied by the system and contains a reference to the range object just selected. LastSelection is an object variable used to store the last area selected. It is declared as Static so that its value will not be lost each time the Sub ends.

The Intersect method is used to generate a Range object containing all the cells that are common to the Target and the Assumptions range. The If test is true if there is something in common (when the overlap is not nothing). If the test is true, there is then a test to see if LastSelection contains anything. If the file has just been opened and the user clicks immediately on Assumptions, LastSelection contains nothing. In this case A1 is selected. Otherwise, LastSelection is selected. The message is then displayed. If the cells selected are not in the Assumptions range, the selected range is recorded in the LastSelection object variable.

The ability to detect and respond to a wide range of system events greatly enhances your ability to customize the user interface. You can prevent users from accidentally or deliberately corrupting data. More importantly, you can help users and increase their productivity. ●

Part IV: PowerPoint: Beyond the Basics

CHAPTER 22

PowerPoint Quick Start Guide

by Read Gilgen

These days communication is the name of the game. Whether you're trying to sell a product, teach an academic subject, or convince your boss to fund your project, you need to be able to convey your ideas clearly and convincingly. Unfortunately, today's audiences don't usually have the time or patience to pore through pages of printed material. But they just might sit through an overview presentation, especially if it can capture and hold their attention.

Fortunately you have Microsoft PowerPoint at your disposal. In no time at all you can create presentations that not only communicate ideas but also captivate audiences and motivate them to action. ■

What PowerPoint is and what it can do

Learn how to enhance your presentations with slides, printouts, or even on the Web.

Navigating in PowerPoint

The look of PowerPoint is different, yet similar to other Microsoft Office 97 products. Learn where to find the features you need.

Starting a PowerPoint presentation

Choose from several presentation options as you start up PowerPoint.

Saving and printing a PowerPoint presentation

Knowing the basics can save you time and frustration.

Understanding What PowerPoint Can Do

PowerPoint is a tool that extends your own ability to communicate. The better you know how to use PowerPoint, the more likely you are to be successful in making effective presentations.

Communicating Ideas More Effectively

A PowerPoint presentation is similar to a Word outline in that it reduces your subject to the bare essentials. As a result, you must focus more on the structure of the presentation including:

- What is the main purpose of the presentation?
- Who is my audience?
- What do I want them to know?
- What do I want them to do?

Once you understand what you are trying to communicate, you then proceed to present information in a concise, easy-to-understand way. For example, rather than listing all 15 reasons your client should buy your product, you might focus instead on the top three or four reasons.

Finally, once you have determined the content of your presentation, you then begin to format the presentation in such a way that audiences will want to listen. PowerPoint enables you to add the following:

- Color-coordinated backgrounds that can match the tone and purpose of your presentation
- Consistent font styles so that the audience gets the message without being distracted by the presentation of the text
- Animated slide elements that wake up the audience, or that highlight important points
- Multimedia objects such as graphics, sound, or video to increase audience attention and understanding

Your PowerPoint presentation is more likely to be successful if you focus first on the content and organization of your presentation and then add a design and other formatting.

What Skills Do You Bring to PowerPoint?

PowerPoint is just a tool that extends your ability to communicate. If you were applying for a job as a PowerPoint presentation designer, you might see the following job description:

PowerPoint Designer Wanted. Must know subject thoroughly. Must understand intended audiences. Must have experience communicating subject to intended audience. A sense of graphic design helpful but not required.

You can do this! You are the expert and PowerPoint is there to help. After you create your first presentation, you'll be amazed at how easy it is to add a professional look to what you present.

What Kinds of Presentations Can I Create?

PowerPoint enables you to create anything from one-page presentations, such as posters, to multipage slide shows. However, PowerPoint is not a genuine graphics design program; other programs do a better job of designing and editing graphic objects. PowerPoint's real strength lies in being able to put together various textual and graphical elements to create superior slide shows.

Single-page presentations include posters, flyers, signs, or advertising layouts.

Slide show applications are much more extensive, including the following:

- Presentations designed for face to face contact, such as board meetings, classroom training, or sales contacts
- Unattended presentations, such as an information kiosk or a Web-based presentation

How Do I Make the Presentation?

All presentations can be printed or presented electronically. For example, you probably will want to print, duplicate, and distribute flyers, posters, and signs.

However, you have several options for distributing or showing your PowerPoint presentation:

- If you have a computer and a data projector or data display panel, you can run your PowerPoint presentation from the computer. This gives you a great deal of flexibility to make last minute changes to your presentation and also to adjust the rate of presentation to match your audience. Increasingly, businesses and educational institutions do have this type of display equipment and make it available if you need it for your presentation to them.
- Using the Pack-and-Go feature, you can prepare a slide show that you can take with you on the road, or that you can send to anyone. You, or someone else, can even play the show on a computer that doesn't have PowerPoint installed.
- You can print your PowerPoint slides onto overhead transparencies or convert them to 35mm slides for traditional overhead or slide presentations.
- You can print PowerPoint slides in handout format, complete with slides and speaker notes, or in outline format.
- You can publish your slide show to the World Wide Web. PowerPoint enables you to export your slides, including graphics, to an HTML format that you can use on any Web server, thus making your slide show available to the whole world.

Working with the PowerPoint Interface

The PowerPoint interface is much like any other Windows program, so if you are familiar with other Windows programs, you should have no problem using PowerPoint.

Starting PowerPoint for the First Time

If you performed a typical installation of the Office 97 suite, you will find two buttons on your Start Menu: New Office Document and Open Office Document. If you click New Office Document, you see the dialog box shown in Figure 22.1. Three of the ten tabs pertain to PowerPoint documents:

FIG. 22.1

To create a new PowerPoint document, choose New Office Document from the Windows 95 Start menu, and choose the type of presentation you want to create.

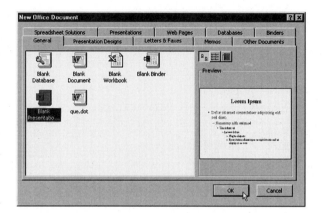

- *General.* Double-click the Blank Presentation icon to start a new, blank presentation.
- *Presentations Designs.* Click a design to preview it, then double-click a design to start a new presentation using that design. You create the content.
- *Presentations.* Click a presentation template to preview it, then double-click a template to create a new presentation based on typical predefined slides. PowerPoint suggests the content and presentation structure.

Looking Over the PowerPoint Screen

Assuming you choose a Blank Presentation, PowerPoint starts and asks you what type of layout you want. For now, just click OK. You then see the screen shown in Figure 22.2. The PowerPoint screen includes typical Windows elements such as a menu, several toolbars, an editing screen where you create and modify your slides, and a status bar that shows information about your slideshow.

Understanding PowerPoint's Default Toolbars and Buttons   A default PowerPoint screen includes the following toolbars:

- *Standard toolbar.* This contains buttons common to all Office 97 programs, such as Open, Save, Print, and so on. The right side of this toolbar offers buttons commonly used in PowerPoint, for example, New Slide. Point at a button to see a ToolTip describing that button.

FIG. 22.2

The PowerPoint screen offers many tools for working on your presentation.

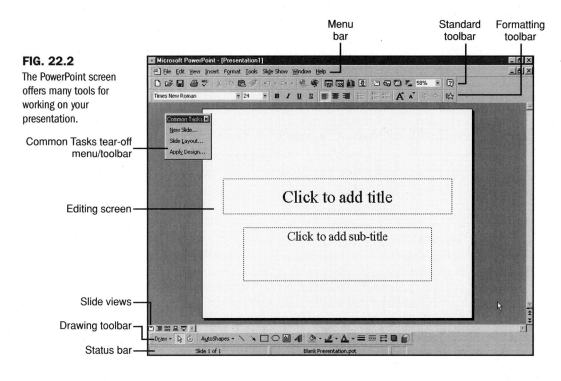

- Menu bar
- Standard toolbar
- Formatting toolbar
- Common Tasks tear-off menu/toolbar
- Editing screen
- Slide views
- Drawing toolbar
- Status bar

- *Formatting toolbar.* Font and alignment buttons are the most common buttons on this toolbar. These buttons are also common to all Office 97 programs.
- *Drawing toolbar.* This contains aids to adding graphic elements to your slides and is located at the bottom of the editing area.
- *Common tasks.* By default, this toolbar displays as a floating palette. As with all toolbars, you can drag the title bar of this toolbar to any side of the screen and display it as a toolbar.

One important bar that isn't a typical toolbar is the row of Views buttons displayed to the left of the horizontal scroll bar at the bottom of the screen. Clicking one of these buttons displays your slides in outline, slide, slide sorter, or notes views. The last button plays the current slide as a slide show.

Adding/Removing Toolbars Typical of all Office 97 applications, you can add or remove PowerPoint toolbars by right-clicking the toolbar and selecting or deselecting toolbars from the list.

You also can drag a toolbar from its location to any other side of the screen or into the editing area to display it as a floating tool palette.

Where to Go for Information

PowerPoint's online help is invaluable as you begin working with the program, and even after you become a seasoned PowerPoint user.

The core of PowerPoint's help is the Office Assistant, which, depending on how you have it set up, offers suggestions or asks you questions to better help you. For more information on the Office Assistant, see Chapter 2, "Using Common Office 97 Features."

PowerPoint also offers indexed help, as well as a link to the Microsoft Web site where you can receive updates and other helpful information.

Hidden in an unlikely spot is the very useful PowerPoint Central. Choose Tools, PowerPoint Central, and PowerPoint runs a slide show that offers ideas, tips, and access to additional resources that help you create the best slide shows possible. For example, PowerPoint Central includes "The Four P's for Better Presenting," a tutorial from the Dale Carnegie Training Institute. If it has been some time since you accessed PowerPoint Central, PowerPoint offers to connect you to the Microsoft Web site to update PowerPoint Central with new information and additional resources.

N O T E Don't forget to refer to other chapters in this book. For example, Chapter 2, "Using Common Office 97 Features," includes vital information needed to work in all of the applications included in the Office 97 suite. ■

Working with PowerPoint Documents

If you normally create only word processing documents, working with PowerPoint documents may take some getting used to. Before launching into your first project, take some time to become familiar with the various elements of a PowerPoint presentation.

Understanding Slide Layers

Each PowerPoint slide consists of three basic layers:

- The *design* layer is also the *master slide* level that provides the *background* graphics, color scheme, text fonts, and location of slide elements for your slides. The design layer is the same for all slides in a presentation, thus providing a consistent look.

- The *layout* layer is based on the type of slide you are creating, such as title, bullet, chart, table, or blank slides. The layout determines where various slide elements are located. Layout elements can be modified or ignored on any individual slide.

- The *slide* layer is where you add your own *content*. Each slide's content is unique, so text or graphics added to the slide appear only on that slide.

Although you can modify the design, or master layer, at first you should just use the formats provided by PowerPoint and focus on the content, or slide layer. As you become more experienced, you can begin making modifications to the background layers or even create your own.

N O T E One option for starting a presentation is to use the AutoContent Wizard. However, if you understand how a PowerPoint presentation is built, you will be able to take better advantage of the AutoContent Wizard. See Chapter 25, "Creating a Slide Show and Making the Presentation" for more information on the AutoContent Wizard. ▓

Choosing an Initial Layout

When you first start PowerPoint, you can choose a blank presentation, start with a design, or use one of PowerPoint's templates. If you start with a blank presentation, PowerPoint asks you first what layout you want to use (see Figure 22.3).

FIG. 22.3

Choose a layout for your slide from the Slide Layout dialog box.

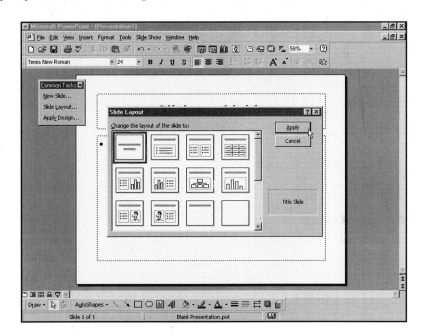

Generally, your first slide will be a title slide. If you are creating something other than a slideshow, such as a poster or flyer, you may want to choose some other layout, such as blank slide.

N O T E You can choose from 12 layouts, including title, bulleted list, or blank (the most commonly used), and several combinations of charts, text, and clip art. ▓

 You can change the layout by choosing Format, Slide Layout, or click Slide Layout on the Common Tasks tool palette. Choose a different layout style by clicking it to select it and then clicking the Apply button.

Choosing an Initial Design

If you start with a blank slide, regardless of the layer you choose, you still need to choose some sort of background or design layer.

 To choose a background layer, choose F<u>o</u>rmat, Apply Design, or click Apply Design on the Common Tasks tool palette. PowerPoint displays the Apply Design dialog box shown in Figure 22.4. Click a design file on the list at the left, and PowerPoint previews it for you on the right. When you find just the design you want, click the Apply button. If the design you choose isn't quite what you had hoped for, repeat this process until you find what you need.

FIG. 22.4

Choose a master background design from the Apply Design dialog box.

N O T E   Although you can change the design layer of a slide at any time, doing so may affect the position of text or graphics you have already created. If you don't like the result, you can change the design layer back to your original selection. You can also reposition graphics, or reposition or edit text to match better the new design layer. ▪

Adding and Editing Text

Once you have chosen your design and layout layers (see Figure 22.5), you can begin adding your own text and other objects to your slides.

To edit a title slide, for example, click the title box. The title box prompt disappears and a blinking insertion point appears. At this point you can use most of your typical word processing editing procedures, such as typing, deleting, selecting, changing font or other attributes, and so on. Remember also that you can use E<u>d</u>it, <u>U</u>ndo if you don't like the results.

FIG. 22.5
Use Slide view to modify elements of your slide after applying a design and layout.

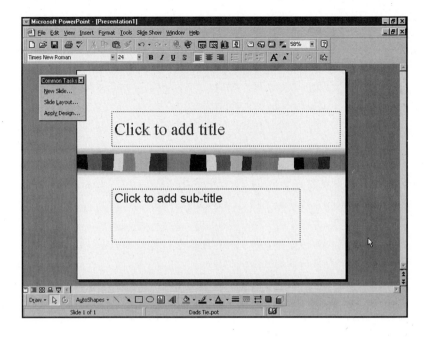

Click the mouse anywhere on the slide to deselect the text box you have just created. To return to a box to edit its content, simply click that box. To add text to another text box, for example, the subtitle, simply click the box and enter text.

Using PowerPoint Views

The basic element of a slideshow is the slide itself. However, to give you a better sense of what your slideshow looks like, PowerPoint offers several different *views* of your presentation. Each view is accessed by choosing View, and then by choosing the type of view you want. You also can click a view button on the View bar (to the left of the horizontal scroll bar).

The following list shows the five views and their purposes:

- *Slide.* The basic editing view is the Slide view (refer to Figure 22.5). Here you edit slide objects such as text or graphics. Note the two buttons at the bottom of the vertical scroll bar. Click these to go to the previous or next slide.

- *Outline.* The structure of your slide presentation is similar to an outline (see Figure 22.6). The slide's title is a main outline heading, and bulleted text items are outline subheadings. You can use this view to create the entire slide show, switching to Slide view later to modify specific slide objects.

N O T E Even in this view, PowerPoint displays a Preview box so you can see the general look of the slide you are creating in Outline view. ■

FIG. 22.6

The Outline view enables you to focus on the structure and content of your slide show.

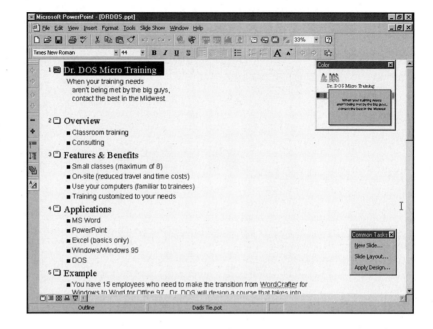

■ *Slide Sorter.* The slide sorter displays miniature versions of your slides, enabling you to see the general organization of your slideshow (see Figure 22.7). In this view you can quickly change the order of your slides, or modify slide transitions—the way PowerPoint changes from one slide to the next. (See Chapter 26, "Using VBA in PowerPoint," for more information on slide transitions.)

■ *Notes Page.* You prepare speaker notes to help you remember what to say during your presentation. If you do create speaker notes, you can view them along with the slide in the Notes Page view (see Figure 22.8). To go to a different slide, click the Previous Slide or Next Slide buttons. (For more information on speaker notes, see Chapter 27, "Access Quick Start Guide.")

■ *Slide Show.* When you play your slide show, the slides fill the entire screen. The Slide Show view enables you to see what the slides will look like when played. To exit Slide Show view, press the Escape key.

Copying and Reusing Data

PowerPoint uses all of the same Windows procedures you use in Word and other Windows programs, to select and manipulate text or graphics images, or to cut, copy and paste material. Learning to take advantage of the Windows environment can help make creating PowerPoint presentations easier and faster.

FIG. 22.7
The Slide Sorter view gives you an overall view of your slide show.

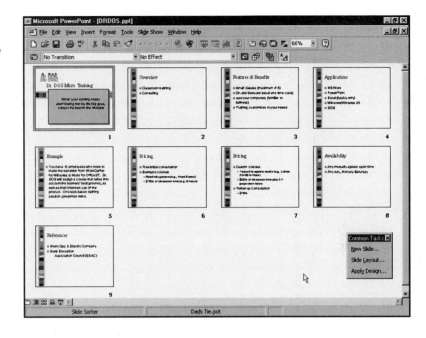

FIG. 22.8
View speaker notes along with the slide in Notes Page view.

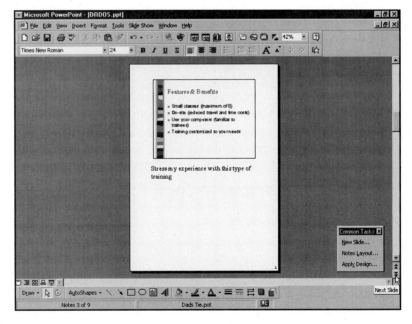

Selecting and Manipulating Screen Objects

Text and graphics are contained inside boxes, and these boxes with their content become slide *objects*. Each object can be moved or resized.

For example, the box that surrounds the text in a title slide can be sized or moved to make your text fit where you want it. Use the mouse to drag the sizing handles to reshape the text box. To move the entire box without changing its shape, position the mouse pointer on any edge of the box until it changes to a four-headed arrow, then drag the box to a new location.

Cutting, Copying, Deleting Objects

Slide objects can be cut or copied, and pasted onto any other slide. To select an object, click the edge of the object box. Then choose Edit, Copy (or Cut), or use any other Windows method for copying (or cutting). Windows places a copy of the object in the Windows clipboard.

To delete an object, first select it then press Delete. If you delete a text box, PowerPoint deletes only the contents of the box, replacing the text with a prompt for new text, for example, "Click to add title" (refer to Figure 22.5). If you really don't want text in the box, you can ignore the prompts since they do not display when you play the slide show, nor do they print.

Using Paste versus Paste Special

When you choose Edit, Paste, PowerPoint retrieves a copy of the object from the Windows clipboard and places it on the screen. You then can drag the object (drag the edge of the object) to the desired location.

Some objects, especially graphic images, have special characteristics that you may want to maintain. For example, if you use a chart that was produced in Excel, you may want to maintain the ability to update the chart should the underlying data be changed. In such cases you copy the chart as you normally do while in Excel. However, to paste it in PowerPoint, you choose Edit, Paste Special. In the Paste Special dialog box (see Figure 22.9), you choose Paste link to paste a copy of the chart while maintaining its link with the spreadsheet from which it came.

Printing from PowerPoint

Whether you need a backup copy for your own records or you want to provide handouts for your audience, chances are that at some point you'll need to print your slide show.

Previewing Documents

There is no separate print preview. Instead, the slide show itself is the preview. However, you can see what your slide will look like when printed in black and white.

 Choose View, Black and White, or click the Black and White (B&W) View button on the toolbar. This view removes the background layer and converts color elements to shades of gray. For reference, PowerPoint also displays a color version in a separate small window (see Figure 22.10).

FIG. 22.9

Use the Paste Special option to maintain links between graphic objects and the programs that created them.

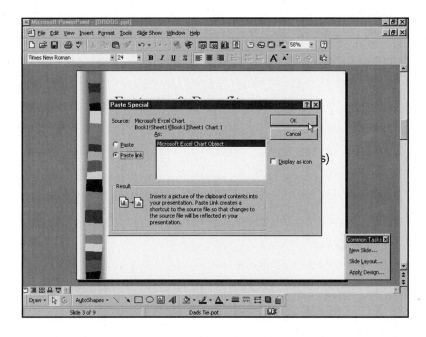

FIG. 22.10

Preview how your slide will print by using the Black and White view.

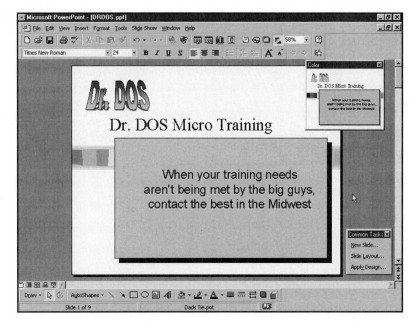

Default Printing

To print your slides, choose File, Print, or press Ctrl+P. The Print dialog box appears (see Figure 22.11). By default, PowerPoint prints one copy of each of your slides in black and white. Choose OK to print using these default settings.

FIG. 22.11

Choose Print dialog box options to print your slide show.

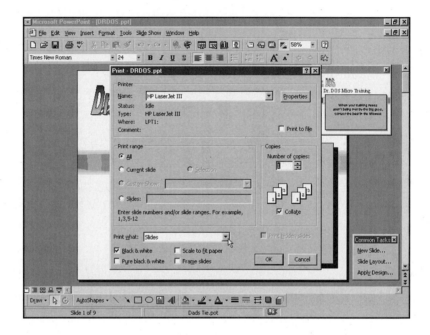

Choosing Printing Options

In the Print dialog box you can specify the printer you are printing to, the number of copies you need, and which slides you want to print.

Using the Print what drop-down menu, you can also choose to print full slides, handouts (with 2, 3, or 6 slides per page), notes pages (one slide per page along with speaker notes), or the outline view of the slide show.

If you have a color printer and want to print your slides in color, uncheck the Black & White box. Doing this prints the background layer of your slides.

Finally, you can adjust the slide to print Pure Black & White (no gray shades), Scale to Fit Paper, or you can add a thin frame line to Frame slides.

N O T E If you uncheck the Black & White box when using a black and white printer, the background prints in shades of gray. However, if your printer doesn't have enough memory, PowerPoint may not be able to print the entire slide. The background may also obscure text or other images when printed this way. ■

CHAPTER 23

Building PowerPoint Presentations

by Read Gilgen

You've probably sat through presentations that put you to sleep almost as soon as the lights were dimmed. But you've also seen presentations that grab your attention from beginning to end.

Compelling presentations don't just happen by accident. Usually they're the result of lots of planning. They also reflect careful thought about what must be said and what elements go along with the content to make the presentation more effective. PowerPoint can help you come up with just the right combination to combat drowsiness during your presentations. ■

Organize your presentation with Outline view

You can organize your thoughts better when you can see the structure of your presentation in outline form.

AutoContent Wizard gets you started quickly

The wizard asks you questions about your presentation, such as the title and the audience, and prepares a slideshow based on your answers.

Save time with templates

Templates provide a consistent look to your presentation. They also save you time, since you don't have to recreate the layout for each slide.

Add text and graphic objects

A well-chosen picture or graphic illustration can go a long way toward communicating your ideas more effectively. Dress up your presentation with clip art images, graphic shapes, or artistic word shapes.

Using Outlines to Plan and Organize a Presentation

No amount of pizzazz can compensate for a poorly organized presentation. Your job is to make it easier for audiences to grasp concepts, understand processes, or to see how pieces of information fit together.

An outline is an excellent tool to help you organize your thoughts and to give structure to your PowerPoint presentation. If you can clearly see your presentation's structure, it's quite likely your audience will too.

Starting PowerPoint in Outline View

As you learned in Chapter 22, you can start PowerPoint in several different ways. If you don't want to be distracted by fancy layouts or designs, your best option is to begin with a blank presentation screen in Outline view. Follow these steps:

1. From the Windows 95 Start menu, click New Office Document to display the New Office Document dialog box.

2. Choose the General tab and double-click the Blank Presentation file. PowerPoint starts, and the New Slide dialog box appears.

N O T E   Alternatively, you can start PowerPoint from the Start menu by choosing Programs and then Microsoft PowerPoint. From the opening dialog box, choose Blank presentation and click OK. ▧

3. Since you're just getting started, click OK to accept the Title Slide layout.

4. Finally, switch to the Outline view by choosing View, Outline or click the Outline View button on the View menu. PowerPoint displays the Outline View screen (see Figure 23.1)

 T I P   In Outline view, the Common Tasks tool palette can be in the way. Drag the tool palette (click and drag its title bar) to the lower-right of the screen to uncover the outline editing screen. If the Common Tasks tool palette is not visible, choose View, Toolbars, Common Tasks.

Creating Outline Text

An outline helps you organize your presentation into major sections or headings, along with subsections or subheadings. Once you see the overall structure of your slide show, you can then fill in the details and work on polishing the slides themselves.

Let's suppose you're creating a brief presentation to show clients what your company is all about. Since your first slide is a title slide, you'll probably want to use your company name as the title, and some sort of motto as the subtitle.

To enter outline text, follow these steps:

FIG. 23.1

The outline view helps you organize your presentation without being distracted by layouts and designs.

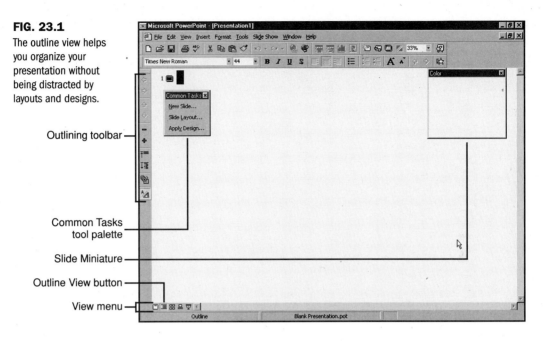

Outlining toolbar

Common Tasks tool palette

Slide Miniature

Outline View button

View menu

Part

IV

Ch

23

1. Begin by typing the title, for example "The Company Store." Note that what you type also appears in the Slide Miniature box. When you have typed the title, press the Enter key. PowerPoint adds a new slide.

2. Press the Tab key to *demote* slide 2 so it becomes the subtitle for slide 1. Type the subtitle, for example, "We Sell Only the Best."

3. Now when you press Enter, PowerPoint remains at the subtitle level. Press Shift+Tab to *promote* the subtitle to become the title for a new slide (see Figure 23.2).

Setting Outline Levels

Although promoting and demoting sounds rather complicated, it's really not. In a typical outline you have major headings, along with various levels of subheadings. All of this helps you to clearly see the organization of your material.

Suppose your second slide is a bulleted list showing what your company is all about. Begin by typing the major heading for slide 2, for example, **The Company Store ...**. Then press Enter.

To add bulleted subheadings (there is no subtitle on a bulleted slide), you can press the Tab key or you can click the Demote button on the Outlining toolbar to establish that the next lines you type are at the second outline level. As you type each item, simply press Enter to add a new item at the same subheading level. (See Figure 23.3 for sample text.)

N O T E Only titles, subtitles, and bulleted text items appear in the Outline view. You must switch to the Slide, Slide Sorter, or Slide Show views to see other objects such as charts, graphics, or text objects. ▪

FIG. 23.2

Promote and Demote outline levels to create slides with subtitles or bulleted lists.

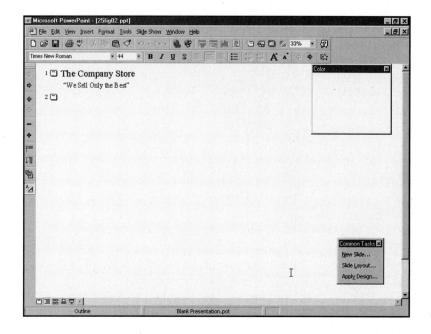

FIG. 23.3

The complete outline for a presentation includes only essential text.

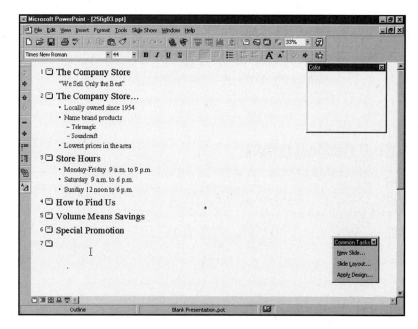

PowerPoint's promote and demote options are shown in the following list:

 ■ *Demote*. Press Tab or click the Demote button on the Outlining toolbar. This moves the insertion point to the right and creates a subheading to the current outline level.

■ *Promote*. Press Shift+Tab or click the Promote button. This moves the insertion point to the left and returns to next higher subheading, or to the slide title.

■ *Move Up*. Click the Move Up button to switch the order of the current outline item with the one that precedes it. The item maintains its subheading status.

■ *Move Down*. Click the Move Down button to switch the order of the current outline item with the one that follows it.

Finally, to get a better overview of your outline, you can use the following options:

■ *Collapse*. Click the Collapse button to hide all of the subheadings of the current slide.

■ *Expand*. Click the Expand button to display all of the subheadings of the current slide.

■ *Collapse All*. Click the Collapse All button to hide all subheadings of all slides in the presentation. Slides that have subheadings appear underlined in gray.

■ *Expand All*. Click the Expand All button to display all of the subheadings of all of the slides in the presentation.

To add a new slide, promote a blank line until a slide and number appear. Alternatively, you can click New Slide on the Common Tasks tool palette and choose the slide layout you want for the next slide.

Editing Outline Text

Editing text in the outline view is simple. Click the text area you want to edit and use typical word processing editing procedures including backspace, delete, or cut and paste.

To change a subheading level, click anywhere on the subheading text and use promote or demote.

If you want to change the order of a slide, click the slide icon in the Outline view and drag it to its new location. The pointer changes to a four-headed arrow and a thin horizontal line indicates the new position of the slide (see Figure 23.4).

> **CAUTION**
>
> Creating a presentation requires a lot of thought and effort. Be sure to save your presentation early and then save it often as you build your presentation. Reward your creativity by not losing your work!

Importing Outline Text from Word

The Outline view helps you visualize and organize your presentation. However, you may already have material organized in a Word document that uses headings and subheadings. If so, you can import that material directly into the PowerPoint Outline view by following these steps.

FIG. 23.4

Change the slide order in a presentation by dragging the slide to a new location in Outline view.

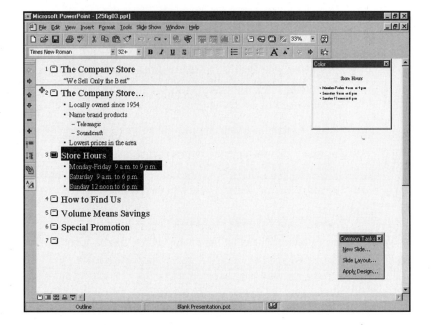

1. In Microsoft Word, make sure the Word document uses outline headings and that you have saved the outline.

2. In Word, choose File, Send to, Microsoft PowerPoint. Word starts PowerPoint and transfers the data to PowerPoint.

3. Check the outline in PowerPoint. If the Word headings have been prepared properly, all first-level headings become slide titles, second-level items become subtitles or bullet items, and so on.

4. In PowerPoint, edit the text as necessary, promoting or demoting items as needed.

CAUTION

Don't forget to save your PowerPoint presentation or modifications to the imported outline will be lost.

Applying a Slide Layout

When you complete your presentation outline, you're ready to add the appropriate layouts and design to fit the material you're presenting.

The first slide you create in Outline view is, by default, a title slide. Subsequent slides, by default, are bulleted list slides.

In the sample slideshow (refer to Figure 23.3), the last four slides are neither standard title nor bulleted list slides. For example, the "How to Find Us" slide will include a title, no subtitle, and a graphic map and text to give directions. Thus, each slide must have its own layout. To change the layouts for the last four slides, follow these steps:

1. Click the slide 4 icon. PowerPoint highlights the slide title.

2. Click Slide Layout on the Common Tasks tool palette. Alternatively, you can choose Format, Slide Layout from the menu bar. PowerPoint displays the Slide Layout dialog box and highlights the Bulleted List layout since that is the default slide layout (see Figure 23.5).

FIG. 23.5
Change the layout of a slide in the Slide Layout dialog box.

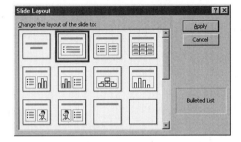

3. Click the slide layout you want to change to, for example, Title Only (the third slide layout on the bottom row).

4. Click Apply to change the layout of the currently selected slide. Although it may appear that nothing has happened, when you view your slide you will note the layout change.

5. Repeat steps 1–4 to change slide 5 to the Chart layout.

6. Repeat steps 1–4 to change slide 6 to the Title Only layout.

7. Repeat steps 1–4 to change slide 7 to the Blank layout.

 TIP Use the scroll bar to see all 24 layouts. These include everything from blank slides to combinations of titles, subtitles, bullets, data and organization charts, clip art images, and media clips.

Applying a Slide Design

Now that you've prepared the content and selected appropriate layouts for each slide, you're ready to choose a slide design. PowerPoint offers several predefined slide designs that coordinate text, layout, graphic objects, and colors to provide a consistent look throughout your entire presentation.

To choose a design, follow these steps:

1. Click Apply Design on the Common Tasks tool palette. Alternatively, you can choose Format, Apply Design from the menu bar. PowerPoint displays the Apply Design dialog box (see Figure 23.6).

2. Browse the list of design files and click one to see what it looks like in the Preview Box at the right side of the dialog box.

FIG. 23.6
Choose a master design for your presentation from the Apply Design dialog box.

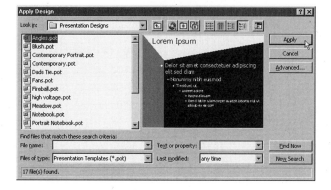

3. When you find a design you like, choose A̲pply. PowerPoint applies the design to each and every slide in your presentation.

N O T E PowerPoint normally opens the Presentation Designs folder on your hard drive. More designs can be found in the Presentations folder. Click the Up One Level button, then choose the Presentations folder.

Viewing the Presentation from the Outline View

After you apply a design to your slides, PowerPoint displays the currently selected slide from the outline in the Color View miniature view (see Figure 23.7). To view a different slide, simply click that slide in the outline.

FIG. 23.7
The Color View window enables you to see the currently selected outline slide in miniature.

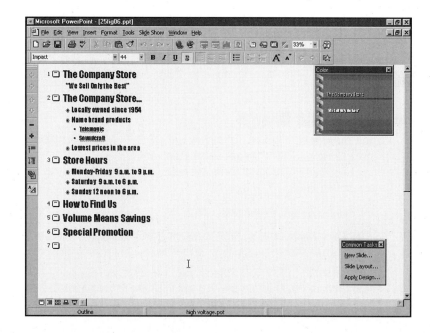

However, what looks good in miniature may not look so good in a full-sized view. To change the view of your presentation, choose View from the menu and then choose one of five views: Slide, Outline, Slide Sorter, Notes Page, and Slideshow. (See "Using PowerPoint Views" in Chapter 22 for a complete description of these different views.)

Using the AutoContent Wizard

If you're not feeling particularly well organized or creative, PowerPoint's AutoContent Wizard can help guide you through the required steps to a successful presentation. It asks you what kind of presentation you are making, suggests what you need to include, and then provides you with a predefined design and style template.

Starting the AutoContent Wizard

Earlier you learned how to start PowerPoint by choosing New Office Document from the Start menu. You also can start PowerPoint by clicking the Start button, choosing Programs, and then choosing Microsoft PowerPoint. When you use this method, PowerPoint starts and presents you with the PowerPoint dialog box containing the choices shown in Figure 23.8. Choose the AutoContent Wizard to assist you in putting together your slideshow and click OK. PowerPoint displays the AutoContent Wizard dialog box shown in Figure 25.9.

FIG. 23.8
When you start PowerPoint, you can choose how you want to create your new presentation.

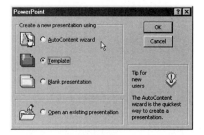

FIG. 23.9
The AutoContent Wizard helps you get started with your presentation.

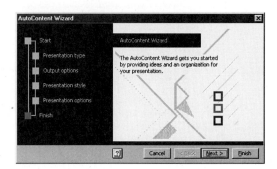

Providing Initial Information

The AutoContent Wizard first asks you basic questions about your presentation. Each time you click Next, you provide additional bits of information such as the following:

- *Presentation type.* PowerPoint offers several presentation categories and topics. For example, you might choose a presentation that helps you recommend a corporate strategy. You could even choose one of the Carnegie Coaches to learn or teach others specific human relations skills, such as how to introduce a meeting or thank a speaker. (See Table 23.1 for a list of PowerPoint's predefined presentation types.)

- *Output options.* Do you plan to make this presentation yourself, in a meeting, using handouts? Or do you plan to place the presentation by itself on the Internet, or in a kiosk-style setting?

- *Presentation style.* If you are making the presentation yourself, will you use a computer to make an on-screen presentation, or will you rely on black and white or color overheads or 35mm slides? Will you print handouts?

- *Presentation options.* If you choose to make the presentation yourself, PowerPoint asks you to provide information for the title slide. If the presentation is to be an Internet or kiosk presentation, you can specify copyright information, your e-mail address, or when the presentation was last updated.

Table 23.1   PowerPoint's Predefined Presentations

Category	Presentation Type
General	Recommending a Strategy Generic
Corporate	Company Meeting Financial Overview
Projects	Status Project Overview
Operations/HR	Information Kiosk Organization Overview
Sales/Marketing	Marketing Plan Product/Services Overview
Personal	Announcement/Flyer Personal Home Page
Carnegie Coach	Facilitating a Meeting Introducing a Speaker

Category	Presentation Type
	Managing HR's Changing Role
	Motivating a Team
	Presentation Guidelines
	Presenting a Technical Report
	Selling Your Ideas
	Thanking a Speaker

N O T E You do not need to click Next, nor do you have to complete each of the questions in order. Simply click directly on the box to the left of any of the questions and click Finish when you are ready to view the slideshow. ■

After you complete the information for these initial questions, choose Finish. PowerPoint generates a slideshow for you and takes you directly to the Outline view (see Figure 23.10).

FIG. 23.10
The AutoContent Wizard creates a complete slideshow that you edit to fit your needs.

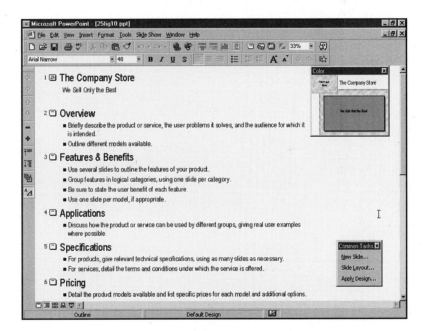

Editing Suggested Content

Suppose, for example, you choose to create a Sales Marketing Plan (refer to Figure 23.10). PowerPoint can suggest the organization and format, but you must now provide the information you will present.

Begin by clicking each slide and changing the data to fit your corporation. The miniature slide preview box shows you what each slide looks like, but for now, focus on the content of each slide.

 Finally, switch to the Slide view by choosing View, Slide, or click the Slide view button on the View menu. Beginning with the title slide, change slide elements as necessary (see Figure 23.11). For example, you can move text boxes or other objects to make them fit more neatly on the screen.

FIG. 23.11
Switch to the Slide view to make sure all slide elements look the way you want them to.

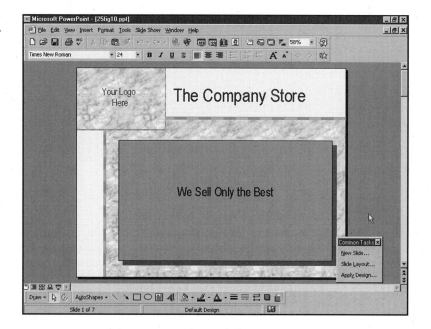

N O T E Some presentations contain more complex slide objects, such as clip art images or embedded Word tables or Excel charts. See "Creating Static Presentations" later in this chapter for information on changing these objects. ▨

Applying Layout and Design

Although PowerPoint suggests the layout and design for each type of presentation, you can change these to match your sense of what will appeal to your audience.

For example, if you intend to add a clip art image to one of your bulleted slides, you would follow these steps:

1. Switch to the slide you want to change, for example to slide 5, which contains a bulleted list.

2. Choose Format, Slide Layout from the menu, or choose Slide Layout from the Common Tasks tool palette. PowerPoint displays the dialog box shown in Figure 23.12.

FIG. 23.12

The Slide Layout dialog box enables you to choose a different layout for each slide.

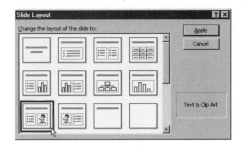

3. Select the layout you want, such as Clip Art and Text or Text and Clip Art.

4. Choose Apply. PowerPoint changes the slide layout as shown in Figure 23.13.

FIG. 23.13

Layouts can include text, bullets, and even clip art images.

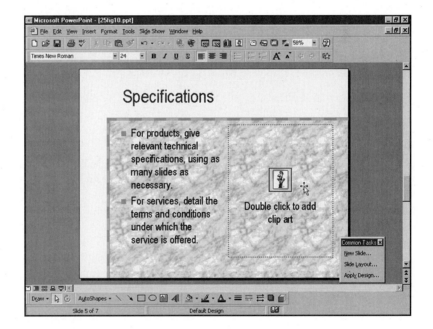

5. As prompted, double-click the Clip Art box. PowerPoint presents a gallery of clip art images (see Figure 23.14).

N O T E   If you did not install the entire clip art gallery on your computer, and if the Office 97 CD-Rom is not in your CD drive, PowerPoint notifies you that you can obtain additional clip art from the CD-Rom. Otherwise, PowerPoint simply shows all the available clip art. ▦

6. Select a clip art category and image and choose Insert.

7. Position the clip art image where you want it on the slide.

FIG. 23.14

Microsoft's Clip Gallery offers you hundreds of clip art images for your presentations.

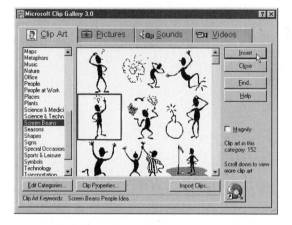

For more information on adding graphic and other objects to your slides, see "Creating Static Presentations" later in this chapter. You also can change the overall background and design of your slideshow by following these steps:

1. Choose Format, Apply Design from the menu, or choose Apply Design from the Common Tasks tool palette. PowerPoint displays the Apply Design dialog box shown in Figure 23.15.

FIG. 23.15

Choose just the design you want in the Apply Design dialog box.

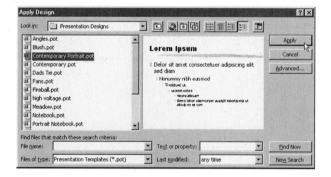

2. Click a design. In the design list at the left of the dialog box, PowerPoint displays that design, with sample text, in the preview box.

3. Choose the design you want and then choose Apply. PowerPoint changes the design of all the slides in your presentation.

Having changed the design, you should also review your slides to make sure the title and other slide objects are positioned appropriately. For example, in Figure 23.16 changing the design resulted in a larger font, which caused the title to wrap in the text box. If necessary, resize or reposition slide objects until the slide appears the way you want it.

FIG. 23.16
Changing a slide design may also force you to make additional changes to your slides.

Using Templates

Templates are nothing more than predefined layouts and designs for your presentation to which you add your own material. You've already been using templates in this chapter, although we haven't referred to them as such. For example, the AutoContent Wizard uses templates, and you added both layout and design templates to the slideshow you created from the Outline view.

Selecting a Template

If you start PowerPoint from the Start Menu, you can choose to begin with a blank presentation, use the AutoContent Wizard, or use a template (refer to Figure 23.8). If you are already in PowerPoint, simply choose File, New and the New Presentation dialog box appears (see Figure 23.17).

If you start PowerPoint from the New Office Document option on the Start Menu, you have the same PowerPoint options, plus other options related to Word and Excel.

Finally, if PowerPoint is already running, you can choose File, New and the New Presentation dialog box appears (refer to Figure 23.17).

PowerPoint's templates fall into three general categories:

- ■ *Blank presentations.* When you use this template, nothing is provided. You have to create the content and add layouts and designs of your choosing.

FIG. 23.17

Choose a template from the New Presentation dialog box to begin your presentation with a predefined layout or design.

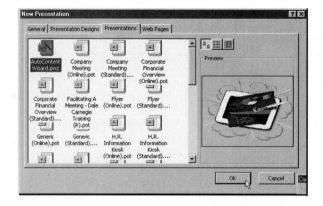

■ *Presentation Designs.* These templates provide color schemes, font designs, and background graphics. While these provide a consistent look to your presentation, you must determine the entire content and what layouts to use.

■ *Presentations.* These are complete templates that include the design as well as suggested layouts, along with suggested content. These are the same templates used by the AutoContent Wizard.

■ *Web Pages.* These templates can be used when developing a World Wide Web page.

Providing Template Information

If you use any of the Presentations templates, you must add basic template information yourself. You also have to know which template is designed for which application. For example, the Marketing Plan (Online) is designed to be used on the Web and already includes buttons and links that connect from one slide to another.

Generally, if you plan to use a Presentation template, you're better off using the AutoContent Wizard to help you choose the right template and fill in basic template information.

On the other hand, if all you want is a design template, select a design from the list of templates and choose OK. Before you can begin, PowerPoint requires you to select the layout for the first slide. Select a layout, for example, the Title layout, and choose OK. PowerPoint displays the first slide with blank text objects (see Figure 23.18).

Changing Template Objects

Changing template objects is really quite simple. For example, to add title text to your title slide, just click the Click To Add Title box, and PowerPoint displays a text editing box (see Figure 23.19). Type the text you want. You may need to adjust the size or position of the template object (for example, the text box). However, usually you should try to make your additions match the suggested size and location of the original template objects.

FIG. 23.18
A template contains blank objects that you fill in.

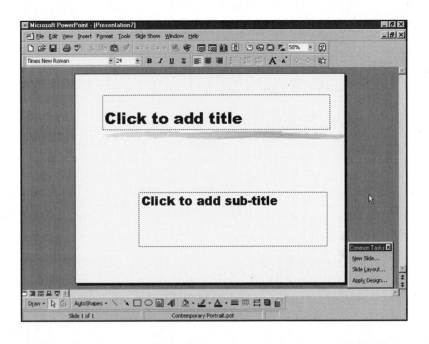

FIG. 23.19
Click a blank object and then type the text you want to insert.

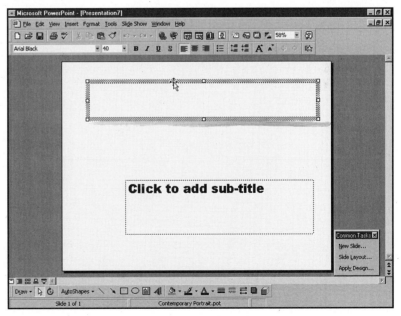

Creating Static Presentations

Whether you create a flyer based on the Flyer template, create a sign from a Blank template, or simply want to enhance or modify any slide, you need to know how to add elements or *objects*, such as text boxes, graphic images, tables, or charts.

Adding Text Objects

Text boxes are perhaps the most common of all slide objects. Although most templates have ample text objects, you can add more. For this exercise (and all others in this section), after having started PowerPoint, choose File, New, choose the General tab, then choose the Blank Presentation template, and select the Blank layout.

To add a text object, follow these steps:

1. Choose Insert, Text Box.
2. Position the mouse pointer where you want to begin your text box and click. PowerPoint displays a text editing box.
3. Type the text you want, for example, **Sale Today!** (see Figure 23.20).

FIG. 23.20

A text box is just one of many objects you can add to a PowerPoint slide.

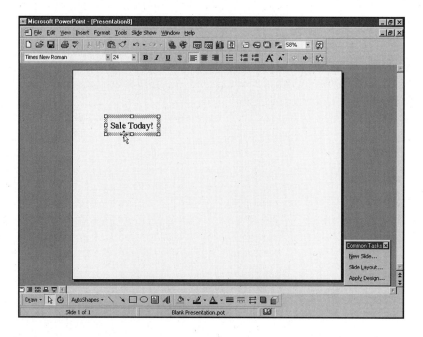

To edit the content of text boxes, simply click the text box. You can then edit the text, or select text within the box and choose Format, Font to change the font or the size, style, or color of the font.

To change the size of a text box, click and drag any of the sizing handles (the eight hollow boxes around the edge of the text box). Text size does not change, but where it wraps within the box does change depending on the size of the box.

To move a text box, you must position the mouse pointer on one of the box edges so that the mouse pointer changes to a four-headed arrow (refer to Figure 23.20). Then click and drag the box to its new location.

 TIP If you accidentally resize the box instead of moving it, just choose Edit, Undo and try again, being careful not to drag a sizing handle.

You can further modify text boxes in many creatively different ways. For example, suppose you want your text to appear in a shaded box, at a 45 degree angle, and in a larger and different font (see Figure 23.21). You would follow these steps:

FIG. 23.21

You can modify text boxes in many creative and useful ways.

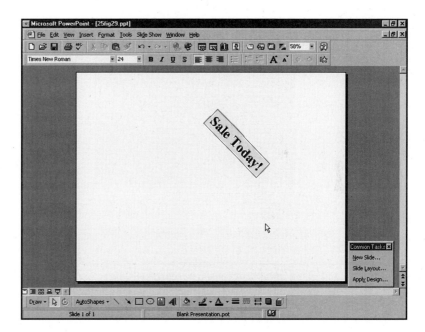

1. Click the text box and choose Format, Text Box. Alternatively, you can right-click the text box and choose Format Text Box from the menu. PowerPoint displays the Format Text Box dialog box (see Figure 23.22).
2. Click the Colors and Lines tab if it isn't already selected. Then choose Color or click the drop-down menu for the Fill Color (see Figure 23.23). Here you can simply choose a fill color you like, for example, yellow.

FIG. 23.22

The Format Text box dialog box lets you change fill colors, line styles, and more.

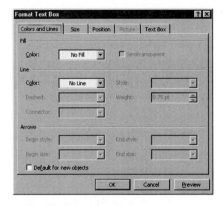

FIG. 23.23

Fill styles include colors, patterns, and special effects.

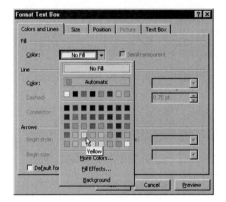

3. Objects are stacked on top of each other, with the most recently created objects on top. If you want objects from the back to appear through the fill color you have chosen for your text box, choose Semit̲ransparent.

 You can add special gradient color effects, or add textures, patterns or pictures as fill backgrounds to your text box, by choosing F̲ill Effects from the drop-down menu. Don't be afraid to explore PowerPoint's many formatting options.

4. Choose the Line Co̲lor, S̲tyle, W̲eight (thickness), and D̲ashed (whether the line is solid, dashed, or dotted). For example, change the line color to Automatic, which gives you a single, solid black line around the text box.

5. Click the Size tab to display the information shown in Figure 23.24. Change Rota̲tion to 45 degrees.

6. Click the Text Box tab and change the box's internal margins, if necessary (see Figure 23.25). For example, since you are using a filled background, you may want more space between the text and the edges of the box.

FIG. 23.24

You can rotate text boxes as needed.

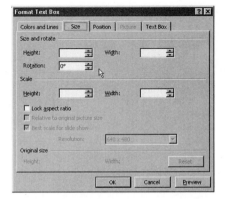

FIG. 23.25

Change the box's internal margins for more space between the box edge and the text.

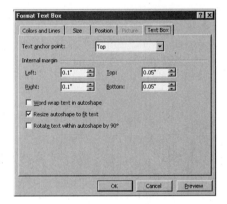

7. If you want to make your changes apply to all new text boxes, on the Colors and Lines tab choose Default for new objects.

8. Choose OK to apply the changes to your text box.

Adding Clip Art Objects

Well-chosen graphic images can enhance your presentation in ways that words alone cannot. PowerPoint comes with several standard clip art images, as well as many more on the Office 97 CD-ROM. In addition, you can insert graphic files from other sources, such as scanned images or PowerPoint's own AutoShapes and Draw features. You can even connect to the Web for more clip art images.

 To add a clip art image, choose Insert, Picture, Clip Art, or click the Insert Clip Art button on the toolbar. PowerPoint displays the Microsoft Clip Gallery (see Figure 23.26). Click the category you want, find and select the image you want, and choose Insert (see Figure 23.27).

FIG. 23.26

Insert clip art images from the Microsoft Clip Gallery.

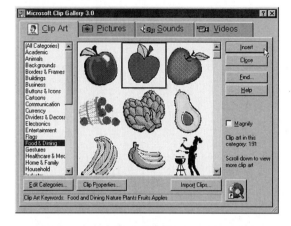

FIG. 23.27

Clip art images appear in boxes that you can size and move.

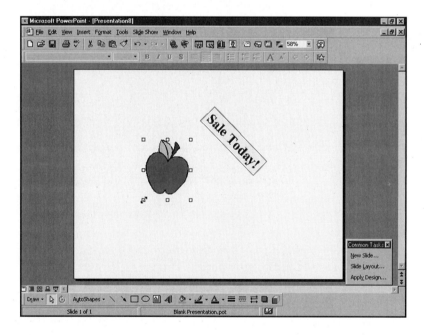

You manipulate clip art images the same way you size and move text boxes, although there are some differences. For example, dragging the sizing handles to change the size of the image box also changes the size of the image inside the box. For example, if you drag a side handle, you stretch the image horizontally. Dragging a corner handle changes the size proportionally. Also, you can click anywhere on the image and drag it to a new location.

To change the format of a clip art image, choose Format, Picture. PowerPoint displays the Format Picture dialog box (see Figure 23.28). The fill and line options are the same as for text boxes (see "Adding Text Boxes" earlier in this section).

FIG. 23.28

Modify an image using the Format Picture dialog box.

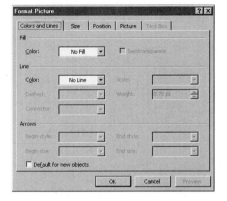

Click the Picture tab to display options used exclusively with clip art images (see Figure 23.29). Here you can adjust the following:

FIG. 23.29

Crop an image's edges or change its colors.

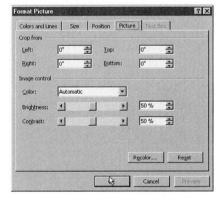

■ *Crop From*. Move the box edges in from the left, right, top, or bottom to hide part of the image.

 If you want more space between the edge of the image and the box, set the cropping to a negative number. For example, a cropping measurement of –0.1 inch places an extra .1 inch between the edge of the box and the image.

■ *Color*. When set to Automatic, the image displays in its original colors. You can also choose Grayscale (shades of gray), Black and White (no gray), or Watermark (lightly shaded, with greater brightness and less contrast).

■ *Brightness*. If the image is too dark or too light, you can adjust its brightness.

■ *Contrast*. If you increase or decrease the brightness, you may also need to adjust the contrast so the image doesn't look washed out.

Part

IV

Ch

23

■ *Recolor.* This option enables you to exchange one color in an image for another. For example, you could change the red car to a yellow one by substituting yellow for red.

■ *Preview.* As you make changes, you can preview those changes before actually applying them to the image. You may have to drag the Format Picture dialog box out of the way to see the preview.

■ *Reset.* Choose this option if you don't like how you've changed the settings and you want to start over again.

Adding Draw Objects

You can add graphic shapes to your presentations by using Office 97's Draw features. Many of these features can be accessed from the Insert, Picture menu. However, it is much quicker and easier to use the Drawing toolbar, which normally is displayed toward the bottom of the PowerPoint editing screen. If it's not displayed, choose View, Toolbars, and choose the Drawing toolbar. 23

Table 23.1 describes each of the Drawing toolbar buttons and their functions. In addition to creating graphic objects, you also can modify them using the Drawing toolbar.

Table 23.1 The Drawing Toolbar Options

Tool	Tool Name	Description
Draw ▾	Draw	This pop-up menu gives you options to group or ungroup objects, to change their order in the stack of objects, to rotate or flip an object, and so on.
▱	Select Objects	Before you can make changes to an object, you must select it. When an object displays sizing handles it has been selected.
↻	Free Rotate	Use this option to drag a corner sizing handle and rotate the object.
AutoShapes ▾	AutoShapes	This tool allows you to add many predefined shapes, including basic shapes, flow chart symbols, block arrows, stars and banners, and callouts.
╲	Lines	This is for straight lines only. For multisegment or curved lines, use the AutoShape menu.
↖	Arrows	This is a single-line, straight arrow, with the arrowhead appearing at the end of the line as you draw it.
▭	Rectangles	This shape can be square or rectangle, filled with a solid color.
○	Ovals	This shape can be a circle or oval, filled with a solid color.

Tool	Tool Name	Description
	Text Box	This tool creates a box into which you type text.
	WordArt	With this tool you can add shapes and color schemes to words or phrases.
	Fill Color	This button fills the fills the selected object with the color displayed on the button. Click the drop-down menu to the right of the button to choose a different color.
	Line Color	This button changes the line around the object to the selected color. Click the drop-down menu to the right of the button to choose a different color.
	Text Color	This tool changes the color of the text in the selected text box to the color displayed on the button. Click the drop-down menu to the right of the button to choose a different color.
	Line Style	Use this tool to select the thickness and style of line surrounding an object.
	Dash Style	Use this tool to choose whether a line is solid, dotted, or dashed.
	Arrow Style	This button allows you to add arrow heads or tails to lines.
	Shadow	Add a background shadow to the object with this tool.
	3-D	Use this tool to add a three-dimensional look to the object.

Part
IV
Ch
23

T I P The Drawing toolbar is available in all Office 97 programs. What you learn here can be used also in Word documents, for example.

To insert a graphic shape, choose the shape type and click and drag on your screen to get the location and the size image you want.

You can modify the shape of any of these graphics by right-clicking the object and choosing the Format option from the menu. For example, right-click a WordArt image and choose Format WordArt from the menu. The options you see are similar to those you learned when working with clip art and text boxes (see "Adding Text Objects" and "Adding Clip Art Objects" earlier in this chapter).

In addition, from the Drawing toolbar you can modify specific image features directly, without going first to a formatting dialog box. For example, you first select an object by clicking it, then you can change the line style or color, the fill color, and so on.

Let's try something practical using these tools. Suppose you want to create a "No Smoking" sign. (see Figure 23.30). Follow these steps:

FIG. 23.30

Create signs like this one using PowerPoint's drawing tools.

1. Create the International "No" symbol by choosing AutoShapes from the Drawing toolbar Choose Basic Shapes and then select the "No" symbol.

2. Move the mouse pointer to the editing screen and click and drag the mouse pointer to create the size symbol you want.

T I P To drag an autoshape proportionally, hold down the shift key while dragging.

3. With the shape selected, click the Fill Color menu (the arrow just to the right of the Fill Color button) and choose a different color, for example, red.

4. Finally, click the Shadow settings button and from the dialog box choose a shadow you like, for example, lower left.

5. Choose the Text Box button and click the editing screen to insert a text box.

6. From the Formatting toolbar, choose Center and change the Font Size, for example, to 60 points.

7. Type **No**, press Enter twice and then type **Smoking**.

8. Click the Free Rotate button on the Drawing toolbar and drag the corner rotate handle on the text box until it aligns as shown in Figure 23.31.

9. Click the Shadow settings button on the Drawing toolbar and choose the same shadow you did for the graphic image, for example, lower left.

You've barely scratched the surface when it comes to creating and manipulating graphic images. Explore and play with other images and settings until you're able to get exactly the images you want in your PowerPoint presentations.

Importing Data from Word

You're probably already used to moving text from one Office 97 program to another. For example, in Word you simply select the text you want to copy and choose Edit, Copy. Then move to PowerPoint, position the insertion point in a text box, and choose Edit, Paste.

Copying Word objects such as tables, however, isn't quite that simple. The reason is that the size of objects in a PowerPoint slide are considerably larger than those same objects in a Word document.

The key, then, is to create the object in Word at roughly the same size that you expect it to appear in PowerPoint. For example, if you create a table, make the font size about 36 points. Also, add lines (thicker than usual) and any other formatting features such as fills *before* copying the table to PowerPoint.

After creating and copying the table, you have two options for pasting the table in PowerPoint:

- ▧ Paste, by choosing Edit, Paste.
- ▧ Paste Special, by choosing Edit, Paste Special. You then can choose Paste Link and paste a Microsoft Word Document Object. This method has the advantage of linking the original table with the PowerPoint copy so that changes in the Word table automatically appear in the PowerPoint table.

 If your table contains relatively little data, you should consider creating the table directly in PowerPoint. Choose Insert, Picture, Microsoft Word Table and then follow the same procedures you use when creating a Microsoft Word table (see Chapter 8, "Using Tables," for more information on how to create and format tables).

Importing Data from Excel

You also can insert worksheets or charts created in Excel into your PowerPoint presentations. Once again, the key to successfully moving data or charts from Excel to PowerPoint is to first create the data carefully and completely in Excel.

To move data from Excel to PowerPoint, first select the cells you wish to copy from Excel and choose Edit, Copy. Switch to PowerPoint and choose Edit, Paste, or choose Edit, Paste Special if you want to create an active link between the Excel worksheet and the PowerPoint copy.

The same procedure works for charts created in Excel.

Generally the size of worksheets and charts you can see on an Excel screen is similar to the same objects in a PowerPoint presentation. Thus you don't need to take unusual steps to create larger data cells or charts before copying them to PowerPoint.

Finally, you can import an entire Excel worksheet to a PowerPoint screen (see Figure 23.31). Make sure you save your Excel worksheet, then in PowerPoint choose Insert, Object, Create From File. Supply the file name of the worksheet and choose OK. PowerPoint imports the data, along with any special formatting and charts or graphics you added.

FIG. 23.31

You can link Excel worksheets to your PowerPoint presentations.

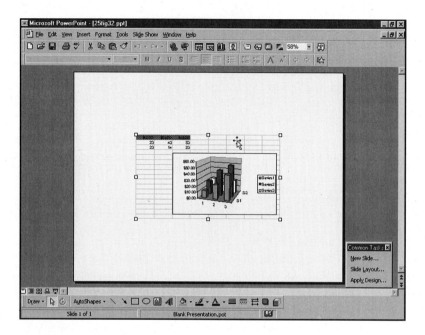

CAUTION

When you insert an Excel file into PowerPoint, the entire active area of the worksheet is inserted. Thus, you want to be sure that the worksheet contains relatively few columns and rows, or the data will appear very small.

CHAPTER 24

Advanced Techniques and Graphics

by Read Gilgen

Good slide shows begin with good content and organization. But great slide shows also use elements that make your audiences sit up and take notice.

In place of static slides, you can add transitions to them to make the change from one slide to another more interesting. You can add actions and animation to objects on the screen, and you can even add sound or video clips for true multimedia presentations. ■

Add transitions to your slides

Changing from one slide to the next need not be as boring as a traditional slide show. Use fades, wipes, or dissolves to add interest.

Animate slide objects

Learn how to drive home a point by making objects move on the screen.

Integrate sound and video in your slide show

Learn how much more effective a presentation can be when you insert sound or video clips at the appropriate places. Let your audience use all of its senses to experience your presentation.

Using Slide Transitions

In an old-fashioned slide show, moving from one slide to another created a brief flash and a noise from the slide projector. Computer slide shows, on the other hand, are quick and noiseless. PowerPoint enables you to use special transition effects so that your audience clearly sees that you are changing from one slide to the next.

Choosing a Slide Transition

Suppose you are continuing work on "The Company Store" slide show that you began in Chapter 23, "Building PowerPoint Presentations." In PowerPoint, open that slide show, or any other you want to work on. In Outline view, your slide show appears as shown in Figure 24.1.

FIG. 24.1

The overall structure and major headings of your presentation are best seen in the Outline view.

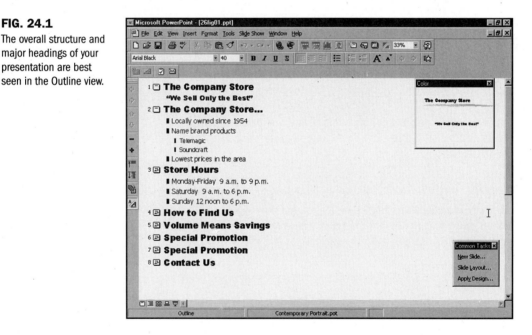

You can choose a slide transition while in any view, but for this exercise, switch to Slide Sorter view by choosing View, Slide Sorter, or click the Slide Sorter View button on the View menu. PowerPoint displays the slide show as seen in Figure 24.2.

To add a slide transition to the currently selected slide, complete the following steps:

1. Choose Slide Show, Slide Transition. PowerPoint displays the Slide Transition dialog box shown in Figure 24.3.
2. Choose the transition you want by clicking the Effect drop-down menu.
3. Choose other effects, such as transition speed, method for advancing the slide, and sound.
4. Choose Apply to add the transition to your slide.

FIG. 24.2
You can see the overall layout of your slide show in the Slide Sorter view.

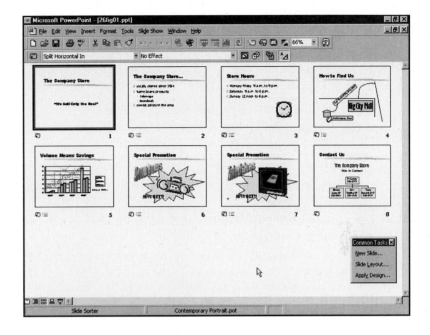

FIG. 24.3
The Slide Transition dialog box helps you determine how your presentation moves from one slide to the next.

 T I P You can preview the effect of your transition by choosing Effect or by clicking the preview box at the upper-left corner of the dialog box. PowerPoint displays the transition from a dog to a key, or vice versa.

You can choose from the following transition effects:

- *No Transition.* The slide show simply moves from one slide to the next, like an old-fashioned slide projector.

- *Blinds (Horizontal, Vertical).* This effect looks like venetian blinds, closing on one slide and opening to another.

- *Box (In, Out).* Here a box shape grows from the center outward, or from the edges toward the center.

- *Checkerboard (Across, Down).* This transition causes the new slide to appear in small, checkerboard-like squares that grow in the direction selected.

- *Cover (Down, Right, Left, Up, Left-Down, Left-Up, Right-Down, Right-Up).* This transition looks like a window shade, with the new slide on it, being drawn in the selected direction.

- *Cut.* This transition is the same as No Transition.

- *Cut Through Black.* This effect cuts to black, then cuts from black to the next slide. However, the transition is so quick that it appears the same as Cut, or No Transition.

- *Dissolve.* Here the slide slowly dissolves, gradually revealing the next slide.

- *Fade Through Black.* This effect causes the slide to fade to black, then the second slide gradually appears.

- *Random Bars (Horizontal, Vertical).* In this transition, the second slide begins to appear in randomly placed bars of varying widths. At first the bars look like a bar code.

- *Split (Horizontal In, Horizontal Out, Vertical In, Vertical Out).* With the split in effect, the first slide seems to shrink from the outside edge to the center. With the split out effect, the second slide grows from the center to the edge.

- *Strips (Left-Down, Left-Up, Right-Down, Right-Up).* This transition is like a typical wipe, but diagonal. The second slide replaces the first slide with a jagged line of strips, from one corner to another.

- *Uncover (Down, Right, Left, Up, Left-Down, Left-Up, Right-Down, Right-Up).* This effect is the opposite of the Cover transition. Here it's as if the window shade, with a slide on it, is being opened to reveal a slide behind it.

- *Wipe (Down, Left, Right, Up).* A wipe looks like the first slide is being erased to reveal the second slide.

- *Random Transition.* PowerPoint selects the transition, randomly. If you want to control the effect of your transitions, this is not a good choice.

Additionally, you can choose these options:

- *Speed.* You can choose a Fast, Medium, or Slow transition.

- *Advance.* The default is to require you to click the mouse or press a key to advance a slide. However, you can let PowerPoint advance your slides Automatically after a specified number of seconds.

- *Application.* You can apply the slide transition to the current slide only, or you can Apply to All slides in your presentation. If you choose to apply the transition to all slides, you still can change the transition for any single slide in your presentation by selecting the slide, choosing a transition, and choosing Apply.

> **CAUTION**
>
> Transitions are fun and easy to use, but too many different transitions can distract the viewer. Pick one transition and stick with it, except when you feel that a particular slide would benefit from something different.

- *Sound.* You can specify a WAV file to play as background music for your slide. You can even have it *loop* (repeat) until you play another sound. For more information on adding sounds to your presentation, see "Adding Sound," later in this chapter.

N O T E PowerPoint slide background sounds start over at each slide transition and stop playing altogether when another sound is introduced.

Checking Transitions in Slide Sort View

You can easily view how your transitions look while in Slide Sorter view. Beneath each slide, PowerPoint displays tiny icons that represent special effects that you add to your slides. Click the icon that looks like a screen with an arrow (refer to Figure 24.2). PowerPoint shows the transition each time you click, briefly displaying the preceding slide and making the transition to the current slide.

Using Preset Animations

PowerPoint enables you to add movement to otherwise static slides, thus adding appeal to your presentation. Although animations can get complex, PowerPoint offers several preset animations that are quick and easy to use, and that make you look like a professional.

Creating Animation Objects

The content of each slide consists of several *objects* that appear on top of a design. These objects include text objects (titles, subtitles, bullets, or text boxes), graphic images, and even multimedia objects (sound or video). For more information on creating slide objects, see Chapter 23, "Building PowerPoint Presentations."

Adding a Preset Animation

N O T E You can edit objects only in the Slide View. Therefore, before adding animations, switch to Slide view.

Suppose you want to make the title of your second slide look *and* sound like it is being typed, one character at a time.

To add a preset animation to an object, while in Slide view follow these steps:

1. Click the object you want to animate.

2. Choose Slide Show, Preset Animation. PowerPoint displays a menu with the choices shown in Figure 24.4.

FIG. 24.4
PowerPoint offers easy-to-use animation effects right from the menu.

3. Choose the animation you want—for example, Typewriter.

Although PowerPoint does not appear to do anything, it has quietly added the animation and sound effect you requested. PowerPoint also has determined that the animation will occur only after you click the mouse (or press a key) while playing the slide.

To view the animation, choose View, Slide Show; or simply click the Slide Show button on the View menu. The slide appears but does not display the title. Click the slide or press any key and PowerPoint displays the title one character at a time, while making a typewriter sound.

N O T E   All references in this chapter to playing multimedia clips (sound or video) assume you have the necessary hardware and software installed on your computer. If you don't, you see the animation motion, but do not hear the sound effect. ▓

Using Animated Bullets

One of the most common uses for animation is with bulleted text objects. Adding animation to a bullet causes each bulleted item to appear on the screen one at a time.

Suppose, for example, you want the bullets on your second slide to appear as if painted from left to right. Complete the following steps:

1. Click the bullet text you want to animate.

2. Choose Slide Show, Preset Animation. Refer to Figure 24.4 for the 14 possible choices.

3. Choose the animation you want, for example, Wipe Right.

PowerPoint adds the Wipe Right animation effect you requested. This particular effect does not have sound associated with it. PowerPoint also has determined that each first-level bulleted item will appear along with its subgroups only after you click the mouse (or press a key) while playing the slide.

Adding Customized Animation Effects

Using preset animation may be adequate for most presentations, but you can also customize your animation for clever and very interesting effects.

N O T E Adding animation effects is a creative, artistic endeavor. Don't be afraid to explore and try out various animation until you get just the effect you want. ▪

Suppose you want to animate the three objects you find on your third slide (see Figure 24.5). In Slide view, with none of the objects selected, choose Sli̲de Show, Custo̲m Animation. PowerPoint displays the dialog box shown in Figure 24.6.

FIG. 24.5
You can customize animation for slide objects such as title, bullet list, and graphic image.

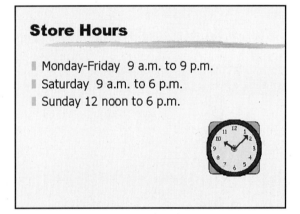

FIG. 24.6
Custom animation enables you to animate any or all of the objects on a slide.

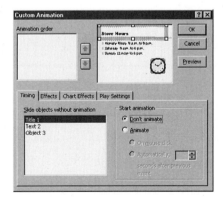

Setting an Object's Animation Timing

There are three objects in the sample slide: the Title, the Bullet List, and a graphic image. None of these objects is currently animated. Click Title 1 in the S̲lide Objects Without Anima- tion box to select it. PowerPoint highlights the title in the preview box at the top-right of the

Custom Animation dialog box with what looks like an edit box. This also brings up the Start animation buttons.

To animate the title, first click Animate. PowerPoint places the Title Object in the Animation Order box and shows the Animate options. By default, during a slide show, you must click the mouse on a slide or press any key to start the animation. If you choose Automatically, you can specify that the animation take place automatically after any number of seconds.

Adding Special Effects

Adding animation to an object does nothing more than cause it to appear on the screen, either after a mouse click or automatically after a specified number of seconds. You can make the animation much more interesting by adding special effects to change the way the object enters the screen.

Click the Effects tab and PowerPoint changes the dialog box, as shown in Figure 24.7.

FIG. 24.7

The Effects tab provides many special effects that you can add to slide objects.

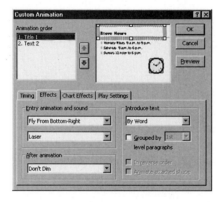

Suppose you want the title to fly in from the bottom-right, one word at a time, making a laser sound as it does. Complete the following steps:

1. Click the Entry animation and sound drop-down menu and choose from over 50 effects the animation effect you want, for example, Fly From Bottom-Right. PowerPoint starts the other dialog controls.

2. Click the sound drop-down menu and choose Laser from the list.

3. Click the Introduce text drop-down menu and choose By Word.

4. Click the Preview button to view and hear the animation effect.

Other options shown in this tab of the dialog box are usually for bulleted text objects. To change the animation for the bulleted list in the sample slide, first click the Timing tab (refer to Figure 24.6). Then click the Text 2 object to add it to the Animation Order list. Click Animate and click the Effects tab (refer to Figure 24.7).

Some of the options you have for animating the bulleted text items are included in the following list:

- *Entry Animation and Sound.* Choose the animation (for example, Fly From Bottom-Right), but unless you want to distract your audience, you may want to leave the sound setting at [No Sound].

- *Introduce Text.* For example, if you choose All at Once, whole lines of bulleted text will appear instead of one word at a time.

- *Grouped By.* Unless you specify otherwise, first-level bullets appear accompanied by their subheadings. If you want subheadings to appear by themselves, click the level at which they should do so, for example, 2nd. If you want the entire bulleted list to appear at once, clear the Grouped by box.

- *In Reverse Order.* You can have the bulleted items appear last item first, as in a Top 10 Countdown list.

- *After Animation.* You can specify that each bullet, after entering the screen, changes color, hides, or hides after the next mouse click. If you are lecturing while displaying the slide, this option enables you to make the current bullet distinguishable from the bullets you have already presented.

> **N O T E** To animate just a single object on a slide, click the object to select it before choosing Custom Animation. This takes you directly to the Effects tab of the Custom Animation dialog box. Selecting an effect for the object automatically adds the object to the Animation Order box and turns on animation in the Timing tab of the dialog box.

Setting Order of Appearance

Although you have three objects on your slide, you added animation to only two of them. The third, the graphic image, simply appears along with the slide.

The two animated objects appear on the screen in the same order you added animation to them. If you want to change the order in which they appear, simply click the item you want to change in the Animation Order box (refer to Figure 24.6) and then click the up or the down arrow.

Figure 24.8 shows a slide that, when played, appears to display an animated map that leads, street by street, to the Company Store. To create that effect, each street in the map, beginning at the right, is added one at a time, using the Wipe Left animation effect.

Chart Effects

You can add data charts to the slide's animation order, but the animation effects you use are different than those used for text and graphics. Consider, for example, the slide shown in Figure 24.9.

FIG. 24.8

Using animation effects, you can make a map appear to lead to your store.

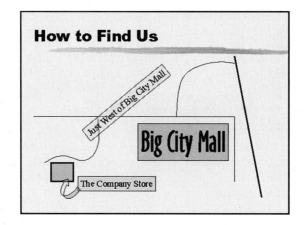

FIG. 24.9

Even charts like this one can benefit from animation effects.

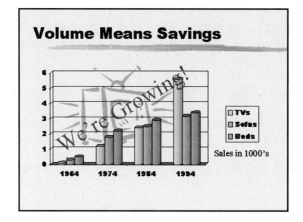

To add animation to the data chart, first click the chart to select it and then choose Slide Show, Custom Animation, or right-click the data chart and choose Custom Animation from the menu. PowerPoint displays the Custom Animation dialog box with the Chart Effects tab selected (see Figure 24.10).

Begin by selecting the Entry animation and sound effect, if any, you want for your data chart. For example, if you want to make the bars in the chart appear to be growing, choose the Wipe Up effect.

Having added animation to your chart, you can now specify how the various elements of the chart are introduced by choosing one of the options listed below:

- *All at Once*. All of the bars of the chart appear at the same time, using the animation effect you selected.

- *By Series*. In the sample chart, all of the bars representing TVs would appear at the same time, followed by the sofa bars, and then the bed bars.

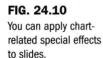

FIG. 24.10
You can apply chart-related special effects to slides.

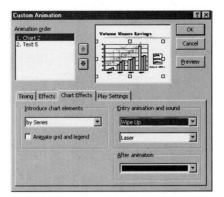

- *By Category.* In the sample chart, all of the bars for 1964 would appear, followed by the 1974 bars, and so on.

- *By Element in Series.* In the sample chart, the TV bar for 1964 would appear first, then the TV bar for 1974, and so on. After all the TV bars appear, then the Sofa bar for 1964 appears, and so on.

- *By Element in Category.* In the sample chart, each bar for 1964 appears in sequence, followed by each bar for 1974 and so on.

You also can choose to Animate the grid and legend. Otherwise those elements appear immediately before the appearance of the data chart bars.

Finally, you can choose how the chart will appear when the next animated object appears. For example, suppose you want to add text that says "We're growing!" You can make the data chart dim (change to a single color) as the text appears on the screen (see Figure 24.11). Choose After Animation and then choose the color the chart will change to, for example, black. You also can choose to hide the chart after it is animated or to hide it at the next mouse click.

Play Settings

The options found in the Play settings tab of the Custom Animation dialog box apply to multimedia clips such as sound or video (see "Adding Multimedia," later in this chapter). Some of these options are explained in the following list (see Figure 24.12):

- *Play Using Animation Order.* If this box is not checked, the media object is not played.

- *Pause Slide Show.* If you do choose to animate the media object, you can pause the slide show while it plays.

- *Continue Slide Show.* If the media clip is particularly long, and you allow the slide show to continue, you may need to stop the media clip before it is finished playing.

- *After Current Slide.* The media clip stops playing as soon as you move to the next slide.

- *After Slides.* This option specifies the number of slides that must play before the media clip stops playing.

FIG. 24.11

The Dim feature enables you to change the color or hide an object after it is displayed.

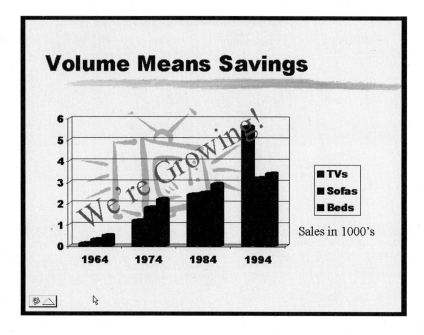

FIG. 24.12

Multimedia clips have extra animation options that determine how they play in a presentation.

You also can choose the <u>M</u>ore options button, and PowerPoint displays the Play Options dialog box shown in Figure 24.13. Here you can choose from the following options:

- *Loop Until Stopped*. The media plays over and over until it is stopped by another media action.

- *Rewind Movie When Done Playing*. The video clip can stop and continue to display the last frame, or it can rewind and display the first frame as a static image.

If the media being played is an audio CD, you can specify the track or tracks to play and the precise starting and ending time for the audio selection.

FIG. 24.13

Control how a media clip is played during a presentation.

Creating Actions

Besides making objects dance on your screen or make noise, you also can make them do practical things, such as jumping to another slide, navigating to a Web site, or starting another program.

Selecting an Action Object

Actions can be attached to nearly any object, including graphic images, text boxes, or entire bulleted lists or organization charts.

However, you cannot attach an action to just a portion of an object. For example, in the organization chart shown in Figure 24.14, you can attach an action to the entire organization chart but not to individual names in that chart.

FIG. 24.14

You can create action links to any area of your slide, including each person in an organization chart.

The way around this limitation is to create "dummy" objects that can't be seen when playing the slide show but that will allow action to occur when you click them. In the sample slide, complete these steps to create a clickable object:

1. Choose the Rectangle tool from the Drawing toolbar.

2. Drag from one corner of an organization chart box name to the opposite corner and release the mouse button. PowerPoint creates a filled rectangle that covers the organization chart box (see Figure 24.15).

FIG. 24.15

"Dummy" objects, even when hidden, can serve as action links.

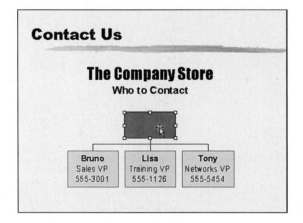

3. Choose Format, AutoShape, or right-click the rectangle and choose Format AutoShape from the menu.
4. Click the Colors and Lines tab.
5. Choose Fill Color and select No Fill.
6. Choose Line Color and select No Line.
7. Choose OK to add the invisible rectangle to the slide.
8. Repeat steps 1-7 for each action area of the object.

PowerPoint hides the rectangle and its border line but does display the sizing handles for the rectangle. If you click anywhere else, PowerPoint deselects the rectangle. To select the rectangle again, you must click the mouse pointer right on the edge of the box.

 You can also select an invisible object by choosing the Select Objects tool from the Drawing tool bar, and dragging an area that includes the object. When you release the mouse button, PowerPoint displays the object's sizing handles.

Adding a Link to a Web Site

With the box selected, you now can attach an action to it. For example, to link the Company Store's owner to his Web page on the company's Web site, follow these steps:

1. Choose Slide Show, Action Settings, or right-click the rectangle and choose Action Settings from the menu. PowerPoint displays the Action Settings dialog box (see Figure 24.16).

FIG. 24.16

Action links can take you to slides, to the Web, and more.

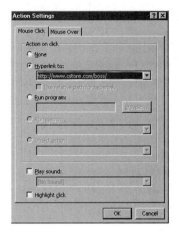

2. Choose Hyperlink To.

3. In the Hyperlink To: edit box, type the full URL of the Web site, for example http:// www.cstore.com/boss/.

4. If you want, you can choose Play Sound and specify a WAV file to play when this object's action is chosen.

You also can tell PowerPoint to highlight the object when you click it. However, since the sample rectangle is invisible, this setting will have no effect.

Using Other Actions

Several of the actions PowerPoint offers are included in the following list:

■ *Hyperlink.* This enables you to jump to the previous, next, first, last, or any slide. You also can jump to a URL (Web site), to another PowerPoint slide show, to a file, or to a Custom Show (a subset of the current show).

■ *Use Relative Path for Hyperlink.* This option is grayed out if the link requires a full path name (for example, http://..., and so on) or if the selected object image is saved with the slide show. For details, see "relative links in hyperlink addresses" in PowerPoint's Help, Contents and Index.

■ *Run Program.* Clicking an action object can launch another program, such as Notepad, the Calculator, a game, a statistics program, and so on.

■ *Run Macro.* Plays a macro you create for use in the slide show. If you have not created a macro, this option is grayed out.

■ *Object Action.* If you select an embedded, editable object, such as the organization chart, you can edit the object while playing the slide show. For example, you could replace a clip art image, edit a data chart, or play a media clip.

■ *Play Sound.* You can play a WAV sound file, in addition to any other action you have chosen.

▪ *Highlight Click*. Choose this option if you want to highlight an action object after you click it.

Using Mouse Over to Start an Action

By default, PowerPoint requires you to click the object during a slide show to make the action take place, for example, to go to a Web site. But you also can make an action take place by merely passing the mouse pointer over it. For example, to add a sound effect to the VP for Training box, complete these steps:

1. Select the rectangle that covers the organization chart box. This is the action object.

2. Choose Slide Show, Action Settings, or right-click the rectangle and choose Action Settings from the menu. PowerPoint displays the Action Settings dialog box.

3. Click the Mouse Over tab. PowerPoint displays the same information as shown in Figure 24.16.

4. Choose Play Sound.

5. From the Play Sound drop-down menu, choose the sound effect you want to play, for example, Camera.

6. Click OK.

CAUTION

Passing a mouse over an object is the easiest way to start an action. Unfortunately, it can be too easy. Reserve the Mouse Over feature for actions that are quick, such as a sound effect. Use the Mouse Click option for actions that should be chosen deliberately, such as jumping to a Web site or to another slide.

Adding Multimedia

PowerPoint keeps up with today's powerful computers by enabling you to include sound and video clips in your presentation. The combination of graphics, text, sound, and video constitutes a multimedia presentation.

Deciding to Use Multimedia

Before integrating media clips into your presentation, you should consider whether you really need them. Do the clips add to the understanding of the presentation's content? Do they add necessary pizzazz that holds your audience's attention? Or are they merely window dressing that could just as easily be left out?

Make sure the need justifies the effort it takes to add multimedia effects.

Finding Media Clips

The simplest of multimedia effects are text and the clip art image. As you learned in Chapter 23, Office 97 comes with an extensive clip art gallery.

However, when you do use the gallery, you'll notice that there are other media types as well. The collection that is installed on your computer is quite limited, but if you leave the CD-ROM in your CD drive, you have access to thousands of clips. These include the following types of images and sounds:

- *Clip Art*. The gallery contains 3,184 clip art images, grouped from academic to weather categories.

- *Pictures*. PowerPoint includes 144 photo-quality pictures.

- *Sounds*. Twenty-nine sounds are available for your use.

- *Videos*. You can choose from 21 sample videos, most of which last only 3–4 seconds.

In addition, there are many other media clips you can find on the Internet, in other programs, or from commercial sources. You can even create your own media clips (see "Adding Sound" later in this chapter.)

CAUTION

While copying images and media clips from the Web is technically easy to do, you will usually be in violation of copyright laws if you take images from a public site without permission. Although many people do not know it, you cannot reuse photographs, clip art, or media clips that you find in public sources without the permission of the creator.

Be sure to e-mail the administrator of the site where you find clip art and ask his or her permission prior to using images you find.

Choosing the PowerPoint Player (Clip) or the Media Player

You can insert PowerPoint media clips in two ways. One method uses the Windows 95 Media Player, while the other uses the PowerPoint Player.

The PowerPoint Player is internal to the PowerPoint program and generally does a better job of playing clips. However, it is limited to starting, pausing, or resuming a sound or video. You can insert media clips most easily from the Office 97 CD-ROM using the PowerPoint Player by choosing Insert, Movies and Sounds and selecting the appropriate media type.

The Windows 95 Media Player can handle the same kinds of clips but is an external program that doesn't always work as well as the PowerPoint player. However, it does enable you to start, stop, pause, fast forward, and rewind your clip. To insert media clips using the Media Player, choose Insert, Object and then choose the media file you want to play.

Generally, you should use the PowerPoint player. However, if you can't insert a media clip any other way, use the Media Player. The following sections assume you are using the PowerPoint Player.

CAUTION

Be aware that a bug in PowerPoint sometimes causes PowerPoint to stop working if both sound and video players are being used to play objects on the same PowerPoint slide. Be sure to test your slides thoroughly and, if necessary, use only one player or the other on any given slide.

Adding Sound

You have already learned how to associate sounds with animated objects as well as action objects. However, you also can insert sounds by themselves as objects.

Suppose, for example, you want to insert a sound clip into a PowerPoint presentation from the Clip Gallery. Complete these steps:

1. Choose Insert, Movies and Sounds, Sound from Gallery. PowerPoint displays the dialog box shown in Figure 24.17.

FIG. 24.17

The Microsoft Clip Gallery 3.0 provides clip art, photographs, sound clips, and video clips.

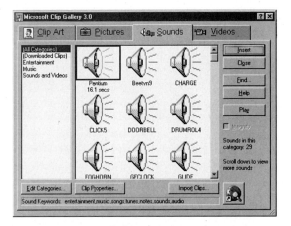

CAUTION

If you choose a sound (or other media clip) from the Office 97 CD, PowerPoint will look for that sound on the CD when you play your slide show. To ensure that all of your media clips are available when you make your presentation, you should copy them to the same folder on your computer where you save your PowerPoint presentation.

2. Select the sound clip you want.
3. Choose Play to preview the sound.
4. Choose Insert to place the sound in your presentation. PowerPoint displays a small audio speaker icon.

5. Drag the icon to the location on the slide where you want it and size it as desired (see Figure 24.18).

FIG. 24.18

Clicking a speaker icon plays a sound.

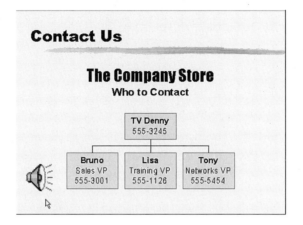

To play the sound clip while running your slide show, simply click the speaker icon.

You also can change a few of the special effects for the sound icon. For example, you can add animation effects or change the play action to Mouse Over, and so on.

Recording and Editing Sound Clips

If you have a microphone attached to your computer's sound board, you also can record your own clips to add to your presentation.

Suppose, for example, you want to include the Company Store's sales manager telling people to "Save 50% on boomboxes and TVs!" Complete these steps:

1. Prepare your "script" and make sure your microphone is properly connected.

2. Choose Insert, Movies and Sound, Record Sound. PowerPoint displays the Record Sound dialog box shown in Figure 24.19.

FIG. 24.19

Record your own sounds in PowerPoint.

3. Type a description for the sound you are about to record, for example, "Special Deal."

4. Click the Record button (the button with the red dot).

5. Speak into the microphone.

6. Click the Stop button (the button with the square black box).

7. Click the Play button (the one with the triangle) to hear the recording.

N O T E   If you don't like the recording and want to do it over again, you must Cancel and start over. Otherwise, what you record a second time is added to the first recording. ▪

8. Click OK to insert the sound, along with the sound icon, in your presentation.

T I P   You can also record sounds using the Sound Recorder that comes with Windows 95. The Sound Recorder has the advantage of being able to edit your recording and to save it as a separate WAV file. If you have the Sound Recorder installed, you'll find it on the Start Menu, Programs, Accessories, Multimedia. If you don't find it there, you must install it from your Windows 95 CD-ROM.

The sound clip is saved with your presentation, and therefore it can be used anywhere that you need a sound in your current slide show only. For example, if you want to hear the sound when you click a photograph of the sales manager, complete these steps:

1. Select the photo object and choose Slide Show, Action Settings, or right-click the photo object and choose Actions Settings. PowerPoint displays the Actions Settings dialog box (refer to Figure 24.16).

2. Check the Play Sound check box.

3. Click the Play Sound drop-down menu and from the list choose the sound you just recorded.

4. Click OK.

Now when you play the slide show, clicking the photo object plays the sound you recorded.

Suppose you have a 2-minute recording of music, but you want only about a 10-second introduction to your slide show. PowerPoint itself does not have the capability to edit an audio clip, but the Sound Recorder that comes with Windows 95 does.

You can open the sound clip in the Sound Recorder, edit it as desired, and then save the resulting clip with a new name.

N O T E   If you see a green and black waveform box in the Sound Recorder, you can edit the sound. However, some of the WAV files that come with the Office 97 Clip Gallery must be converted to an editable file format before you can edit them. To do this in the Sound Recorder, open the WAV file and choose File, Properties. Then choose Convert now and click OK twice. ▪

Using Audio CDs

In addition to sound clips, you can add audio tracks, or just parts of audio tracks from audio CDs. Unlike sound clip files, you cannot associate CD tracks to animated objects or to slide transitions. Instead, you must insert a CD track as an object and then tell PowerPoint how to play it.

To insert a CD track into your presentation, complete these steps:

1. Make sure the CD you want to use has been placed in the CD-ROM drive.

CAUTION

If you play a CD track during your slide show, make sure nothing else is demanding use of the CD-ROM drive. For example, if the Windows 95 CD Player is running, even if it is stopped or paused, PowerPoint cannot access the CD at the same time.

2. Choose Insert, Movies and Sounds, Play CD Audio Track. PowerPoint displays the Play Options dialog box (see Figure 24.20), which indicates how many tracks the CD contains and the CD's total playing time.

FIG. 24.20

Play audio CD tracks, or just portions of a track.

3. Specify the track number you want to start with and the one you want to end with. If you want to play just one track, the number should be the same in both the Start Track and the End Track boxes.

4. If you want to play just a portion of a track, indicate the Start At and the End At times.

 PowerPoint does not offer any way to preview the CD track to determine exactly where you want to begin or end a track. However, you can use the CD player that comes with Windows 95 to play the CD and to note the beginning and ending times you want. Be sure to close the CD player before returning to PowerPoint.

5. If you want the track to play continuously until you stop it, check the Loop Until Stopped box.

6. Click OK to insert the CD audio track as an icon in your presentation.

To enable the CD track to be played, you must use Custom Animation to include the track and to specify how it is to be played. See "Adding Customized Animation Effects," earlier in this chapter, to learn how to include and play a media clip.

Adding Video

The "multi" part of multimedia is particularly evident when you use video clips in your presentation. A video segment can add significant impact if it is used appropriately.

> **CAUTION**
>
> Most video clips are recorded to play back in a small window on the screen. A short segment, for example, three to four seconds, even when played in a small window, can require a huge amount of disk space. Before committing resources to a video clip, make sure you really need it.

Unless you have the facilities for converting video into a digital format, you must use clips already prepared by others. In addition to the 21 video clips that come with Office 97, you can find others on the Web. Remember, however, that copyright restrictions often apply to multimedia material you find on the Internet.

Suppose you want to add impact to the slide that shows your TVs on sale (see Figure 24.21). You can use the Cost Cutting video clip that comes with Office 97.

FIG. 24.21

Carefully chosen video clips, such as this cost-cutting video, can add impact to your presentation.

To add a video clip, complete these steps:

1. Choose Insert, Movies and Sounds, Movie from Gallery. PowerPoint displays the videos in the Clip Gallery (see Figure 24.22).

2. Select the video clip you want to use and, if you want, choose Play to preview it.

3. Choose Insert to place a copy of the video clip in your presentation.

4. Select the video object and move it or resize it as needed.

5. Choose Edit, Movie Object, or right-click the object and choose Edit Movie Object from the menu. PowerPoint displays the Play Options dialog box (see Figure 24.23).

6. If you want the video to continue repeating itself until you stop it, choose Loop Until Stopped.

7. If you want the movie to display the first frame after it plays, choose Rewind Movie When Done Playing. However, if you want the movie to display the ending frame, for example the dollar bills cut in half, leave this box unchecked.

8. Click OK to return to PowerPoint.

FIG. 24.22
The Clip Gallery
provides 21 video clips.

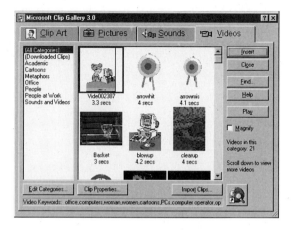

FIG. 24.23
Control how you want to
play a video clip.

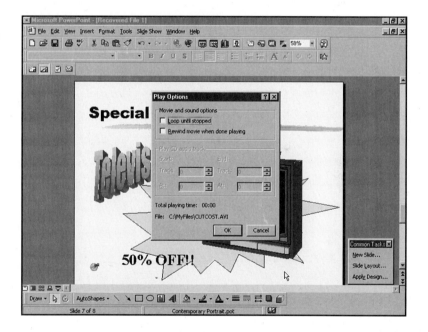

You can preview the video clip by double-clicking it on the screen. However, to enable the video clip to be played during a presentation, you must use Custom Animation to include the clip and to specify how it is to be played. See "Adding Customized Animation Effects," earlier in this chapter, for how to include and play a media clip.

Part
IV
Ch
24

CAUTION

If you choose a video clip from the Office 97 CD, PowerPoint will look for the video clip on the CD when you play your slide show. To ensure that all of your media clips are available when you make your presentation, you should copy them to the same folder on your computer where you save your PowerPoint presentation.

CHAPTER 25

Creating a Slide Show and Making the Presentation

by Read Gilgen

The moment of truth has arrived. After hours of careful planning and preparation, you face an eager audience. Will your slide show do what you hope it will do? Will your audience go away informed, convinced, or motivated? Or will they leave wishing they'd stayed at the office to catch up on their e-mail?

To be sure, the slide show itself is the most important part of your presentation. But as you discover in this chapter, how you make the presentation is almost as important. You learn that you can create and use speaker notes, time your slide show, add narrations, and prepare handouts so that you enter the meeting with confidence, knowing that you're ready to make a good impression. ■

Use speaker notes

Speaker notes help you remember what you intend to say. Speaker notes can be printed and used as one type of handout.

Practice the timing and control of your slide show

You can practice presenting your slide show, then time how long each slide takes. When you make the presentation, you can monitor whether you're going too fast or too slow.

Create narrated and other custom shows

If you make your presentation to different audiences, you can select which slides to present to fit each audience. In addition, you can add a recorded narration and let the slide show run by itself.

Prepare handouts, create 35mm slides, or publish your slide show to the Web

You can print handouts from your slide show for your audience. If you don't have access to a computer display, you can convert your slide show into 35mm slides. You can even reach a worldwide audience by publishing your show to the World Wide Web.

Creating the Slide Show

In preceding chapters you learned how to create slides, add transitions, and organize your slides into a complete presentation. PowerPoint offers yet more tools to help you complete the preparations for your slide show.

Creating and Using Comments

As you create your slides, you may find that you're missing a bit of needed information, or you're not quite sure whether to include a particular item.

If you were creating such a presentation on paper, quite likely you'd use a sticky note to remind yourself to resolve the problem before finalizing the project. To avoid interrupting your train of thought, or putting a damper on your creative process, you can use the PowerPoint Comments feature to make notes for yourself.

Suppose, for example, that you're preparing a presentation for your employer about the Company Store, and you can't remember the Sunday hours. To create a comment on the store hours slide, you follow these steps:

1. Go to the slide where you want to create a comment—for example, the store hours slide.

2. Choose Insert, Comment; alternatively, if the Reviewing taskbar is displayed, click the Insert Comment button. PowerPoint displays a yellow-shaded text box and the name of the person adding the comments (see Figure 25.1).

FIG. 25.1

Use the Comment feature to add notes to yourself or others during the review of your presentation.

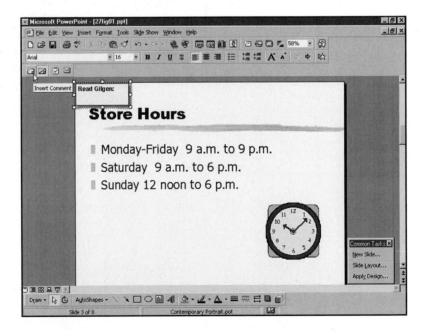

3. Type your comments in the comment box.

4. Position and size the comment box the same way you do any text box.

5. Click outside of the comment box to deselect it.

 By default, PowerPoint displays any comments that have been added to a slide. If you want to hide the comments, choose <u>V</u>iew, <u>C</u>omments and the comment boxes disappear.

> **CAUTION**
>
> If you don't hide your comments, they appear during your presentation and print out on your handouts.

Creating Speaker Notes

If you're making your presentation in person, you may need help remembering what to say during each slide. That's where Speaker Notes come in handy.

To add Speaker Notes to your presentation, follow these steps:

1. Go to the first slide.

 2. Choose <u>V</u>iew, <u>N</u>otes Page; or click the Notes Page View button on the View menu. PowerPoint displays your slides as shown in Figure 25.2.

FIG. 25.2

View your speaker notes in the Notes Page view.

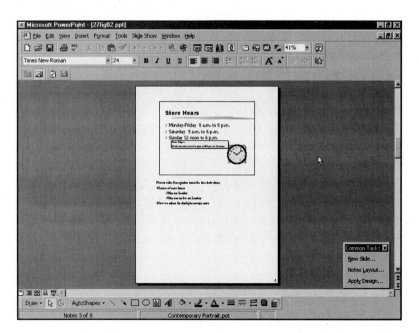

3. Choose <u>V</u>iew, <u>Z</u>oom; or click the Zoom button and choose a larger zoom size—for example, 100%. PowerPoint now displays the Notes text box in a size you can read.

4. Type your notes in whatever manner they work best for you. For example, if you work best from detailed outlines, click the Bullets button on the Formatting toolbar.

TIP Although it's tempting to prepare everything you plan to say ahead of time, presentations that the viewer must read word for word tend to be very boring. If you can, learn to make a presentation from an outline to maintain a measure of spontaneity.

Generally you print your speaker notes rather than view them during your presentation. If you choose F<u>o</u>rmat, Notes <u>L</u>ayout you can choose to display just the slide, just the notes, or both (see Figure 25.3). The other options under the F<u>o</u>rmat menu (Notes <u>C</u>olor Scheme and Notes Background have no effect either during the slide presentation or on your printed speaker notes. See "Using Conferencing" later in this chapter for situations where you might display speaker notes or use color schemes for your notes during a presentation.

FIG. 25.3

You can view your speaker notes and slides together as you review your presentation.

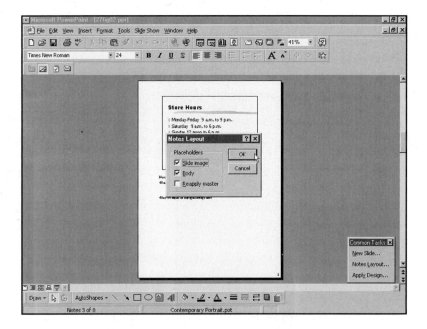

Setting Up the Show

Before presenting the slide show for the first time, you need to set up how you want the show to run. Choose Sli<u>d</u>e Show, <u>S</u>et Up Show to display the dialog box shown in Figure 25.4. You can choose three basic approaches to your slide presentation:

■ *Presented by a Speaker (Full-Screen)*. If you plan to show the presentation using a computer and a data projector, this option enables you to use the full screen to do so.

FIG. 25.4
Use the Set Up Show dialog box to specify how you will show your presentation.

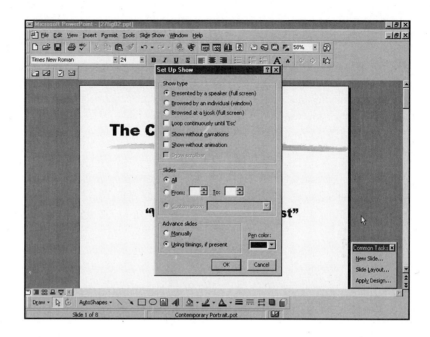

- *Browsed by an Individual (Window)*. Choose this option if you want viewers to control the slide show. During the presentation the viewer sees a browser-like interface (see Figure 25.5).

FIG. 25.5
You can show your presentation using a browser-like interface.

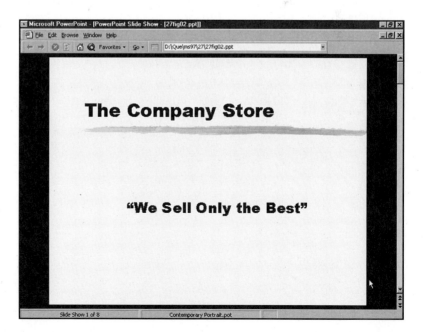

- *Browsed at a Kiosk (Full-Screen)*. Choose this option if you intend to leave the show running on its own and if you don't want viewers to control the show with a mouse or the keyboard.

Each of the previous is affected by other settings you make in this dialog box and elsewhere. For example, an unattended (kiosk) presentation requires automatic timings for each slide since the viewer cannot advance the slide manually.

Other options in the Set Up Show dialog box include:

- *Loop Continuously Until ESC*. Checking this option means the show will repeat itself until someone presses the Esc key. A kiosk-type presentation assumes the slide show will loop.
- *Show Without Narrations*. Use this option if you're at a trade show and you don't want to bother the people in the booth next to you.
- *Show Without Animation*. If you get an audience that reacts adversely to busy multimedia screens, choose this option to display only the completed slides.
- *Choose Which Slides to Display by Choosing All, or Specifying the Starting and Ending, From and To Slide Numbers*. You also can choose a Custom show if any are defined (see "Creating Custom Shows" later in this chapter).
- *Advance the Slides Manually (Requiring a Keystroke or Mouse Click), or by Using Timings, If Present*. Advancing a slide manually suppresses, but does not delete, any automatic timing you may have set for a slide transition. It does not affect object animation within a slide.
- *Choose the Pen Color You Will Use When Highlighting Your Slide During a Presentation.*

Playing the Slide Show

To play your slide show, choose Slide Show, View Show. This starts the presentation with the first slide, using the settings you chose in the preceding section.

N O T E   Choosing View, Slide Show, or clicking the Slide Show button on the View menu displays the presentation, beginning with the current slide, not at the beginning of the slide show. ■

To advance to the next slide you can:

- Click the left mouse button
- Press the Page Down key
- Press the N (Next) key
- Press the right cursor or down cursor keys
- Press the spacebar

When you press any of these keys, PowerPoint makes the next transition, whether it is to advance to a new slide, or to activate an animation sequence.

To back up to the previous slide, you can:

- Press the Page Up key
- Press the P (Previous) key
- Press the left cursor or up cursor keys
- Press the Backspace key

There are so many slide control options, you may find it difficult to remember them all. To get a quick list of options, press F1 (Help) at any time during the slide show. PowerPoint displays the dialog box shown in Figure 25.6.

FIG. 25.6

Press F1 to get a list of slide control options while showing your presentation.

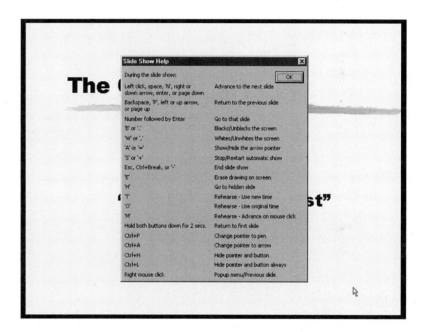

You can also access many of the slide control options by clicking the right mouse button. PowerPoint displays the shortcut menu shown in Figure 25.7. From this menu you click the left mouse button to choose any of the options shown.

TIP Clicking the small button at the lower left of the screen also displays the slide controls shortcut menu.

The first group of menu options (Next, Previous, and Go) change slides. Choose <u>G</u>o to jump directly to any slide in the presentation.

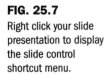

FIG. 25.7
Right click your slide presentation to display the slide control shortcut menu.

Using the Screen Pen

By default, PowerPoint displays a pointer. You can use the pointer to direct the audience to notice specific parts of your slide. However, the pointer is easy to lose track of, especially when used with a data display.

Instead of relying on the pointer, use the Pen option, which enables you to draw on the slide show screen much as you would with a marking pen.

To use the screen pen, follow these steps:

1. Right-click the screen to display the slide controls menu (refer to Figure 25.7).
2. Choose Pen. PowerPoint displays a pointer shaped like a pencil.
3. Click and drag on the screen to draw a freehand line.
4. Right click and choose Arrow from the menu to turn off the pen.

Using the pen to highlight areas of your screen takes some getting used to. However, with a little practice you can learn to make a point by drawing on the screen.

By default, PowerPoint uses a color that complements the screen design you have chosen. If you want to change the color of the pen, right click the screen and choose Pointer Options, Pen Color.

Using a Black Screen

During your presentation you may want to conduct a discussion without the distraction of a slide behind you. If you know when these discussions will occur, you can add blank slides at the appropriate places in your slide show.

However, if you encounter an unplanned need for a blank slide, you can right click the screen and choose Screen, Black Screen. To display the current slide again, choose Screen, Unblack Screen.

 Instead of using the mouse, you can simply press the B key to black the screen, and press B again to display the slide.

Using Speaker Notes

Earlier you learned how to create speaker notes. During a slide show you can refer to these notes, or even add to them. To view the speaker notes, simply access the shortcut menu (right click the screen) and choose Speaker Notes to open the Speaker Notes dialog box.

All formatting, such as bulleted lists, is lost in this view. Likewise, if you add text, you are limited to adding plain text without formatting.

Using the Meeting Minder

The Meeting Minder is a handy tool for taking minutes and recording assignments made during a presentation. You can even prepare assignments ahead of time.

Suppose you are making a presentation to your sales staff, and you want to note that everyone agreed to increase sales by 100 percent. Further, Karen agreed to publish a daily bar chart showing progress toward this goal. To write Meeting Minutes and to create Action Items, follow these steps:

1. Right-click the screen and choose Meeting Minder from the Menu. PowerPoint displays the dialog box.
2. On the Meeting Minutes tab, enter any notes you want to record, for example, "Everyone agreed to increase sales by 100 percent."
3. Click the Action Items tab to see the Action Items page.
4. Type a Description of the action item, for example, **Prepare bar chart to track sales increases**. Your description can be much longer than the space you see on the screen.
5. Type the name of the person to whom the task is assigned in the Assigned To box.
6. Modify the due date, if appropriate.
7. Choose Add to add this particular action item to the list of items created for this presentation.

As you add action items, PowerPoint builds a final slide that appears at the end of the show summarizing action items noted during the presentation.

Also, after you complete the presentation, you can then Export the minutes and the action items to Word (see "Using Other Output Methods" later in this chapter).

Part
IV

Ch
25

Timing Your Presentation

Every speaker lives in fear that his or her presentation will be too long or too short. Good timing is essential if you don't want a lot of "dead time" by ending too early, or if you don't want to rush and skip over important material because you're taking too long. PowerPoint can help.

Rehearsing Timings

You can rehearse your presentation using the Rehearsal feature. Choose Slide Show, Rehearse Timings and PowerPoint starts your slide show and displays the Rehearsal dialog box.

The overall length of your presentation is displayed at the upper left, while the length of the current slide is shown at the right. You can use the following options:

- *Pause*. Click the pause button to suspend the timing. Click it again to resume the timing.
- *Repeat*. If you want to time the current slide over again, click repeat to reset the timing for the current slide to zero.
- *Advance*. When you're ready to advance to the next slide, click the Advance button and PowerPoint records the time and moves on.

N O T E   The Advance button moves to the next animated object, and not necessarily to the next slide. The timing you see indicates the elapsed time since the last animated object or slide. ■

As you rehearse each slide, repeating as necessary, you gradually gain confidence in your delivery and the amount of time it takes you to present the material. When you complete the slide show, PowerPoint tells you the total elapsed time and asks if you want to save the timings. If you do, the timings are added to each slide as timed transitions.

PowerPoint also asks if you want to review the timings in the Slide Sorter View. If you do, you see the actual elapsed time recorded beneath each slide.

Finally, when you play the show, the slides and animated objects change automatically based on your rehearsed timings.

Using the Slide Meter

If you have set automatic or rehearsed timings for your slides, you can use the PowerPoint Slide Meter to gauge how closely you're staying with the targeted time. To turn on the Slide Meter, while playing the slide show, right-click the slide and choose Slide Meter from the menu. PowerPoint displays the Slide Meter.

More likely than not you'll use the Slide Meter only for rehearsal, since you don't really want to distract your audience with an on-screen meter. Besides being a distraction, the Slide Meter could curb spontaneous discussion. For example, if you rehearsed and set the transition time for a slide at 25 seconds, but someone asks a question, you could quickly get far behind.

If you use the Slide Meter during the slide show, and also want to allow for audience participation, you can pause the show, and the meter, by right-clicking the slide and choosing Screen, Pause from the menu. To resume the slide show, and also set the meter in motion again, right-click the slide and choose Screen, Resume.

Using a Recorded Narration

Another method for timing your show, but also for enabling the show to run by itself, is to record a narration. Then when you play the slide show, slides advance in synch with your narration.

Recording the Narration

To record a narration, your computer must have a microphone connected to its sound board. Then, follow these steps:

1. Prepare and rehearse your narrative script before attempting to record it.
2. Choose Slide Show, Record Narration. PowerPoint displays the Record Narration dialog box.
3. Adjust the recording Settings if needed. By default PowerPoint records at a medium ("radio") quality. The dialog box shows you how many minutes you can record based on the space on your hard disk and the quality of the recording.
4. Choose Link narrations in if you want to keep the recorded material in a separate .Wav file. If you don't check this box, the narration is embedded in your presentation, thus making the presentation file considerably larger.

N O T E If you link your narrations to a file, the resulting .Wav file is placed in the same folder as your slide show. Remember that if you move the slide show file elsewhere, you must also move the .Wav file that accompanies it.

5. Choose OK and PowerPoint begins to play the slide show beginning with the first slide.
6. Record your narration, advancing through the slide show as you normally do.
7. At the conclusion of the slide show, tell PowerPoint whether to save the narration timings with the slide show.
8. Also indicate whether to view the slides and their timings in the Slide Sorter view.

Playing the Recorded Narration

Playing a slide show along with its recorded narration is easy. Simply choose Slide Show, View Show. PowerPoint presents the slides along with the narration, and also advances the slides at the same pace you did when you recorded the narration.

If you want the slide show to play over and over again, choose Slide Show, Set Up Show and select the Loop Continuously Until 'ESC' box.

Part

IV

Ch

25

N O T E The narration is a .Wav sound file. Because PowerPoint can play only one .Wav file at a time, other .Wav files you may have included in your presentation (such as sound effects) will not play if you use recorded narration. ▄

CAUTION

Removing a narration from your slide show can be a rather tedious process unless you use Undo right away. To remove narration from your slides later you must remove the media object (a speaker icon) from each slide that contains a narration.

Creating Custom Shows

If you repeat your presentation often, you may find that sometimes you have to modify it to better suit your audience. In some cases you need to remove slides, but for other situations you must put them back in.

PowerPoint enables you to create one single slide show, and to hide, expand, or summarize slides as needed. You also can create custom slide show lists so that you don't have to set up individualized presentations each time you need them.

Hiding Slides

When you hide a slide, you simply prevent it from being shown during the slide show. However, the slide remains part of the total presentation file. To hide a slide, follow these steps:

1. Switch to Slide Sorter view. Although you can perform these steps in any view, the Slide Sorter View helps you see the overall presentation, thus enabling you to choose the proper slides to hide.

2. Click the slide you want to hide.

3. Choose Slide Show, Hide Slide; or click the Hide Slide button on the Slide Sorter toolbar. In Slide Sorter view, beneath the selected slide, PowerPoint displays a page icon with a line through it.

To unhide a slide, repeat the preceding steps.

Expanding Bullet Slides

For some of your audiences, you may want to expand on the information presented in a bullet slide. Or, you might want to create a table of contents slide, and use its bulleted items as titles for the next several slides.

To expand a bulleted list, simply go to the slide you want to expand and choose Tools, Expand Slide. PowerPoint leaves the original bulleted slide intact, but inserts a new slide for each bulleted item from the original.

You then can hide the original, or you can add objects to the expanded slides. If you don't want the expanded slides to display, you can hide them as well.

N O T E You can't unexpand a slide but it's relatively easy in Slide Sorter view to delete the expanded slides. Hold down the Shift key and click each of the slides you want to delete. Then release the Shift key and press Delete. ▪

Creating an Agenda Slide

If you want to create a summary slide—one that lists several slide titles in one bulleted list—follow these steps:

1. Switch to Slide Sorter view. (This procedure does not work in other views.)
2. Select the titles of the slides you want to include in the summary slide.

3. On the Slide Sorter toolbar, click the Summary Slide button.

PowerPoint creates a Summary Slide, with a bulleted list of the selected slide titles, and inserts the slide immediately preceding the first of the slides you selected. You then can edit or enhance the summary slide, or you can drag the slide to any position you want.

Inserting Slides from Other Shows

Another way to customize your slide show is to insert slides from another show. Suppose, for example, you want to create an agenda for a meeting and you want to discuss slides from last month's Board of Directors meeting.

After starting a new show and selecting the design you want, follow these steps to insert slides from another show.

1. Choose Insert, Slides from Files. PowerPoint displays the Slide Finder dialog box (see Figure 25.8).

FIG. 25.8
You can insert slides directly from previously created slide shows.

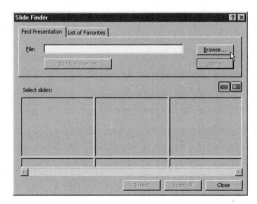

2. Type the File Name of the slide show that contains slides you want to use, or Browse to find the file.

3. Choose Display to view a thumbnail sketch of all of the slides in the show.

4. Select the slides you want to include and choose Insert. If you want to use all of the slides, choose Insert All.

5. If you want to include slides from other shows, repeat steps 1–4. Otherwise, choose Close to return to your slide show.

If you are creating an agenda—and the inserted slides contain titles that serve as agenda items—you can create a summary slide as described in the preceding section.

Saving and Using Custom Shows

Another method for creating a custom show is to make a custom slide list based on the current slide show and save the list for when you need it. Suppose, for example, you want to create a presentation for the company's board of directors, changing the order of some slides and leaving others out altogether.

To create and save a custom show, follow these steps:

1. Choose Slide Show, Custom Shows. PowerPoint displays the Custom Shows dialog box.

2. Choose New. PowerPoint displays the Define Custom Show dialog box (see Figure 25.9).

FIG. 25.9

Create custom slide lists using the Custom Show feature.

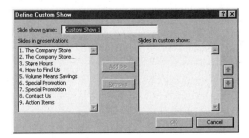

3. Type the name of your custom show in the Slide show name box—for example, **Board of Directors**.

4. Click the first slide you want to use to select it.

5. Choose Add to copy the slide from the left column to the right column.

6. Repeat steps 4 and 5 until your slide list is complete.

7. To remove a slide from the Slides in Custom Show column, select the slide and choose Remove.

8. To change the order of a slide, click the slide to select it and click the up or down arrows to move the slide up or down in the list.

9. Choose OK to save the custom show list. In the Custom Shows dialog box (see Figure 25.10) PowerPoint adds the custom show to any others you have created.

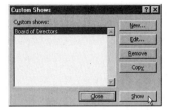

FIG. 25.10
Save your tailor-made presentations to use at any time.

10. Choose <u>C</u>lose to close the Custom Show dialog box.

To play a custom show, simply choose Sli<u>d</u>e Show, <u>C</u>ustom Shows, then select the show you want to play and choose <u>S</u>how.

Using Branching

When you present a slide show, typically you move sequentially from one slide to the next. PowerPoint also enables you to branch, which means to jump from one slide to another, out of sequence.

Designing a Branched Slide Show

Using a branched presentation requires careful planning. The easy part is setting up links to jump from one slide to another. But if you're not careful, you can create a maze from your slide show so that you get sidetracked or even lost altogether.

The key to a well organized, branched, presentation is to create a home slide which becomes the reference point for the entire slide show. You branch out from the home slide, and then always provide for yourself a way to get back to the home slide.

An example would be an agenda slide where you might not want or need to discuss each agenda item in sequence. You would create a link from the agenda slide to the first slide for a given agenda item. At the last of the slides for an agenda item, you create a link to return to the agenda slide.

Before you begin creating branched links, stop and sketch out an actual diagram of what you want to do. Then creating the branched presentation will be relatively simple and you won't leave out important links.

 T I P If you print an outline view of your presentation, you can use the printout to draw and redraw your planned links, until you're sure the branching roadmap is complete. See "Printing a Slide Show" later in this chapter for information on printing various views of your presentation.

Adding Action Settings to Slide Objects

You can link any object on your slide to any other slide in your presentation. Whatever object you link, however, should clearly suggest where that link leads. On an agenda slide, for

Part
IV

Ch
25

example, you might link bulleted items to slides that illustrate or explain the agenda item in greater detail.

Suppose, for example, you want to link the bulleted items shown in Figure 25.11. Follow these steps:

FIG. 25.11

Bulleted lists make great presentation agendas.

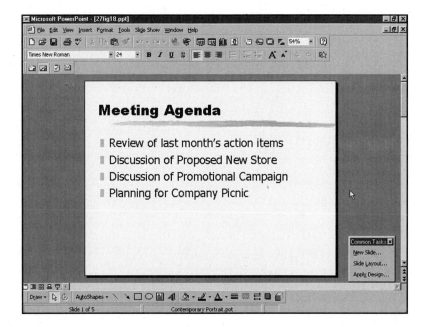

1. Go to the agenda slide and switch to Slide view.
2. Click the bulleted slide list.
3. Select the bulleted item you want to link.
4. Choose Slide Show, Action Settings. PowerPoint displays the Action Settings dialog box.
5. Choose Hyperlink To, and click the Hyperlink To drop-down list (see Figure 25.12).
6. Select Slide and PowerPoint displays the Hyperlink to Slide dialog box (see Figure 25.13).
7. Select the target slide you want to link to, and choose OK.
8. Choose OK again to return to your slide. PowerPoint adds the action link, and also highlights the bulleted item (see Figure 25.14).

When you play the slide show, you simply click the highlighted bulleted item to jump to the target slide.

 TIP If you don't like the look of the highlighted item, you can create an invisible "dummy" object over the bulleted item, and link that object to the target slide. See "Selecting an Action Object" in Chapter 24 for information on creating invisible action objects.

FIG. 25.12
You can branch to many different locations inside or outside of your presentation.

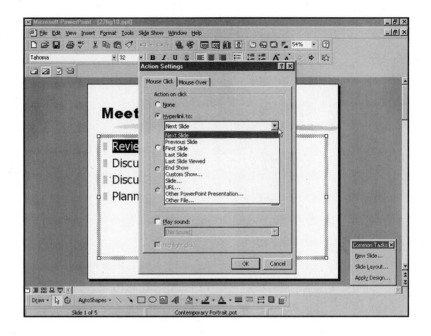

FIG. 25.13
A hyperlink enables you to quickly jump from one slide to another.

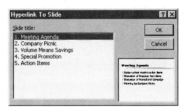

Adding Action Buttons

Getting to the target slide is easy because the home slide contains a reference to it. However, the target slide might not contain anything that remotely suggests returning to the home slide.

A common method for providing linking clues is the action button, often an arrow or some other visual indicator that tells you where you'll go if you click it. For example, suppose you want to add an action button that links the Action Items list to the home slide. Follow these steps:

1. Go to the slide where you want to create the link, for example, the Action Items list.

2. Choose Slide Show, Action Buttons, and from the menu list shown in Figure 25.15, choose the button you want to insert, for example the Home button. PowerPoint displays a cross-hairs mouse pointer in the slide editing area.

3. Drag the mouse pointer to create a button. PowerPoint then displays the Action Settings dialog box (see Figure 25.16).

FIG. 25.14
Linked bulleted items appear underlined, like links in a Web browser.

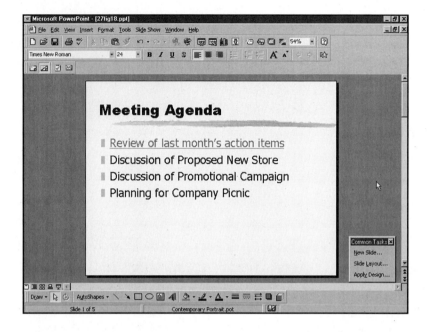

FIG. 25.15
PowerPoint's ready-made action buttons make it easy to create action links.

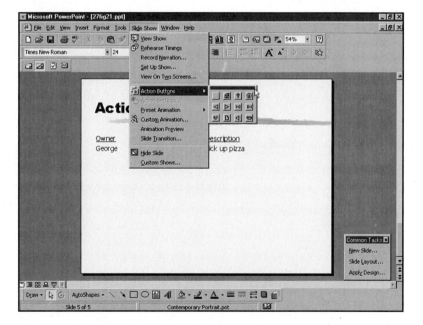

4. Click the Hyperlink To drop-down list, and choose the slide you want to jump to.

5. Choose OK to return to your slide. PowerPoint displays a button similar to the one shown in Figure 25.17.

FIG. 25.16

The Action Settings dialog box enables you to associate an action with an action button or with any action object.

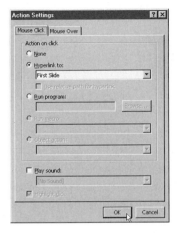

FIG. 25.17

You can size or move a button, and even increase or decrease its three-dimensional look.

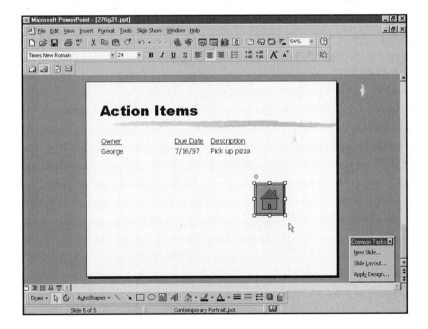

6. Drag the sizing handles to size the button.

7. Drag the button to the location you want it to appear.

8. Drag the yellow diamond near the button to increase or decrease the three-dimensional effect of the button.

Now when you play the slide show, you click the Home button to return to the home slide.

Many of the action buttons (refer to Figure 25.15) are more useful for stand-alone slide shows that will be run by the viewer, such as at a trade convention or in a kiosk setting. Action buttons include:

Icon	Description
	Custom
	Home
	Help
	Information
	Back or Previous
	Forward or Next
	Beginning
	End
	Return
	Document
	Sound
	Movie

You can customize each button by choosing Format, AutoShape, then changing color, line style, and so on.

Using Conferencing

PowerPoint for Office 97 has added conferencing capabilities that enable you to control a presentation on your computer, while displaying it on other computers. While running the slide show, you can use your Meeting Minder or Speaker Notes without displaying those items on the other computers.

Viewing on Two Screens

If you want to connect your computer to just one other computer—for example, from your notebook computer to a computer with a larger monitor—you can connect the two with a null-modem (serial) cable and run the View on Two Screens feature.

After connecting the computers (see your local computer support person for details on connecting two computers using a serial cable), choose Slide Show, View on Two Screens. PowerPoint displays the dialog box shown in Figure 25.18.

FIG. 25.18

You can view your presentation simultaneously on the screens of two interconnected computers.

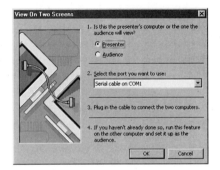

Follow the directions in the dialog box for each of the two connected computers. Then, on the Presenter's computer, run the slide show.

Conferencing with Others over the Network

If you want to connect several computers, you can use the Presentation Conference feature. For example, you want an entire training classroom to see on their screens the slide show you are presenting. Or perhaps you want to conduct a conference among several colleagues from around the country.

The key requirement for conferencing is that each computer must be connected by local area network, or by the Internet.

To set up a Presentation Conference, follow these steps if you are an audience member:

1. Choose Tools, Presentation Conference. PowerPoint displays the Presentation Conference Wizard (see Figure 25.19). Choose Next to advance to each of the following steps.

2. Indicate that you are the Audience.

3. You are prompted for the connection type. If you are connected to a local server (Windows NT, NetWare, Windows for Workgroups), you should specify Local Area Network. If you are connecting through the Internet, even if you're also connected to a Local Area Network, choose Dial-in to Internet.

FIG. 25.19

The Presentation Conference Wizard helps you set up a conference of online audience members.

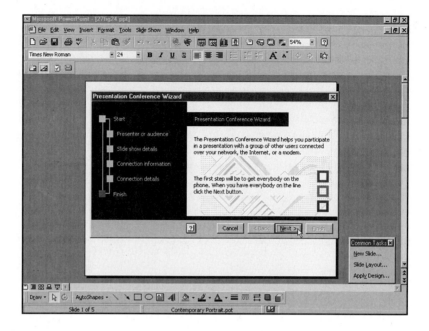

4. Note the name of your computer, which the presenter must know in order to include you in the conference. If you are connecting over the Internet, this name takes the form of an IP number, a network address that consists of four sets of numbers separated by periods. If the connection is via a Local Area Network, the name will be something more recognizable, such as George or Mary.

5. Choose Finish to set yourself up as a member of the conference. Then wait for the presenter to begin the slide show.

If you are the presenter, you follow slightly different steps:

1. Choose Tools, Presentation Conference. PowerPoint displays the Presentation Conference Wizard (refer to Figure 25.19). Choose Next to advance to each the following steps.

2. Indicate that you are the Presenter.

3. PowerPoint indicates what slide show setup is currently set. To change the setup, choose Cancel and go to Slide Show, Set Up Show and change the slide show settings. Otherwise continue to the next step.

4. If you are connecting through a modem to an Internet service provider, you must now connect with that service. When you are connected, or if you already are connected to the Internet through a local network, choose Next.

5. Type each participant's Computer name or Internet address (IP number), choosing Add for each person you add.

N O T E The wizard may not report correctly to audience members what their network address is. If conferencing does not work for an audience member, ask her to run Winipcfg.exe which reports her correct IP number and other information about her network connection. ▧

6. When the conference list is complete, ensure that all conference participants have clicked <u>F</u>inish. Then choose <u>F</u>inish yourself to establish the connections and begin the slide show.

Once the show is running, you control how the presentation advances. You also can use the Meeting Minder or your speaker notes without the audience seeing them. See Figure 25.20 to see the presenter's view of the conference.

FIG. 25.20

As the presenter in an on-line conference, you have complete access to speaker notes, the Meeting Minder, and so on.

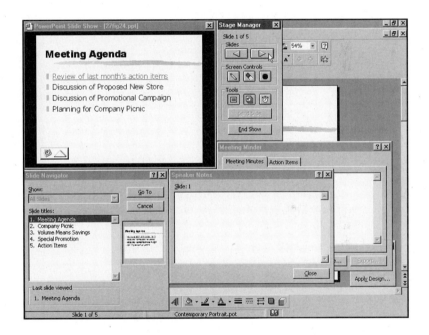

Using the Pack and Go Wizard

Not always do you have the luxury of making your presentation using your own computer. If you want to transport your presentation to be used on another computer, you should ask these questions:

- Does the other computer use Windows 95, Windows NT, or an older version of Windows?
- Does the other computer have Office 97 and PowerPoint installed on it?
- What resolution does the other computer's display use?

If the answers to all of the above match your computer's setup exactly, you are very lucky. You can simply copy your show to a floppy disk and run it on the other computer.

If the answers don't match, in many cases you still can take your show with you and play it on the other computer by using the Pack and Go feature.

To prepare your presentation to play on the other computer, follow these steps:

1. Choose File, Pack and Go. PowerPoint displays the Pack and Go Wizard. Each time you choose Next, you advance to the next item on the wizard's list.

2. In the Pick Files to Pack, indicate whether you want to include the active (open) presentation, or specify another file to pack. You can pack more than one file.

3. Choose the destination. Typically you save the packaged file to a floppy disk, but you can also specify a local hard drive, a network drive, or some other location.

4. Under links, choose Include Linked Files if you want to make sure sounds and other clips get packed with the show.

5. If you want to ensure that fonts display properly, whether they're installed on the other computer of not, choose Embed TrueType fonts.

6. If the remote computer does have PowerPoint installed, you need not install the viewer. Usually it's best to include the viewer, just in case, by choosing Viewer for Windows 95 or NT.

N O T E   If you intend to play the show on a computer running Windows 3.1, you will need to make a separate viewer disk and follow other special instructions. Click the Help button on the Pack and Go Wizard for details. ▨

7. Choose Finish to pack the show.

If you choose to include the viewer and prepare the show for Windows 95 or NT, PowerPoint creates a file with a name that ends in .Ppz. In addition, PowerPoint also places the setup file Pngsetup.exe on the destination disk.

To play the show on another computer, copy the two files to the other computer's hard disk, then from the Start menu, choose Run and run the PNGSETUP program, which unpacks, then plays, your PowerPoint presentation as it would on your own computer, complete with transitions, sounds, and so on. If you included more than one slide show, upon completion of the first, the second begins, followed by the third, and so on.

Printing a Slide Show

You've just dazzled your audience with an entertaining and motivating presentation. Now you want them to walk away with something that keeps the presentation fresh in their minds.

PowerPoint enables you to print your presentation in a variety of formats.

Printing Handouts

To print a presentation, simply choose File, Print; or press Ctrl+P. PowerPoint displays the Print dialog box (see Figure 25.21). In addition to typical print options, such as destination printer or number of copies, you have the following options:

FIG. 25.21

PowerPoint helps you print your presentation in many different formats.

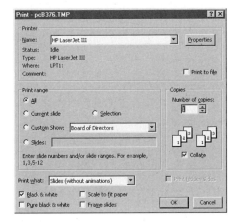

- ▪ *All*. Print all of the slides in the presentation.
- ▪ *Current Slide*. Print just the currently displayed slide.
- ▪ *Selection*. If you are in Slide Sorter view and have one or more slides selected, this option prints just the selected slides.
- ▪ *Custom Show*. If you have defined custom shows, you can choose to print only the slides for a given show.
- ▪ *Slides*. Specify by slide number the slides you want to print.

You also can specify just what you want to print from your slides. For example, from the Print What drop-down list you can choose:

- ▪ *Slides (without animations)*. This is the default printout choice.
- ▪ *Slides (with animations)*. Print a slide's hidden action objects.
- ▪ *Handouts*. You can print summary pages, with 2, 3, or 6 six slides per page.
- ▪ *Notes Pages*. Print speaker notes for yourself, or even as handouts for your audience.
- ▪ *Outline View*. Print the outline as a summary for yourself or for your audience.

Finally, you can fine tune the output as well:

- ▪ *Black & White*. Optimizes the output of color slides to a black and white printer, or prints in black and white shades on a color printer.
- ▪ *Pure Black & White*. Prints only black and white, with no gray shading.
- ▪ *Scale To Fit Paper*. Adjusts the size of the image to fit your paper, but does not change the shape of the actual presentation slides.
- ▪ *Frame Slides*. If you are in Slide view, this option prints a frame border around the slide.

Part
IV
Ch
25

Printing Overhead Transparencies

You can also print your slides to overhead transparencies in case you don't have a working display computer where you will be making your presentation. You can print them in black and white or in color, depending on the printer and the overhead film you have available.

For example, you can purchase special overhead film that you can use in your laser printer. Choose the best black and white option, and print directly on the overhead film. You can also print overheads using ink jet printers. However, ink jet printers require a special, more expensive film that allows the ink to dry without smearing.

> **CAUTION**
>
> Don't try to use your laser printer to print on regular transparency film. The heat from the laser printer's fuser roller will melt the film, and can cause serious damage to your laser printer.

In any case, it's not a bad idea to have a set of overhead transparencies as an emergency backup to your computer presentation.

Using Other Output Methods

In addition to printing in PowerPoint, you also can print some of your presentation in Word, publish your slide show to the Web, or send your slides to a slide service to be converted to 35mm slides.

Exporting to Word

To create specially formatted notes or handouts, you can send your presentation to Microsoft Word. Choose File, Send to, Microsoft Word and PowerPoint displays the Write-Up dialog box (see Figure 25.22). Printout options include:

FIG. 25.22

You can create special speaker or audience notes by sending your slide presentation to Microsoft Word.

■ Print notes along with the slides, either to the right or below.

■ Print blank lines for audience note taking, either to the right or below the slides.

■ Print only the presentation's outline.

You also can export minutes and action items created with the Meeting Minder. Simply choose Tools, Meeting Minder, and in the Meeting Minder dialog box choose Export. Output options include:

■ Post action items to Microsoft Outlook

■ Send meeting minutes and action items to Microsoft Word

If you choose to send the information to Word, you get the document shown in Figure 25.23.

FIG. 25.23
Export Meeting Minder information to Microsoft Word for a summary of minutes and action items.

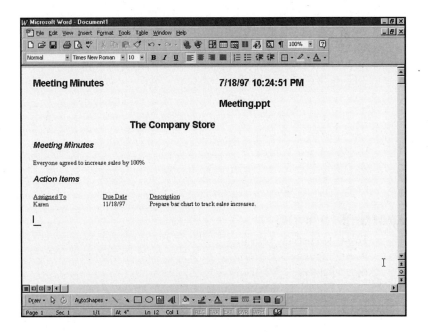

N O T E Your audience also can take with them the entire presentation, including graphics, media clips, and interactive links. In addition, you can save some natural resources by not providing them with paper printouts.

You accomplish this amazing feat by publishing your presentation to the World Wide Web. You then provide your audience with a Web address (URL), and they use their favorite browser to play your slide show on their own computer.

For details on publishing a presentation to the Web, see Chapter 46, "Creating and Publishing Web Documents." ■

Exporting a Presentation to a Slide Service Bureau

If you're taking your slide show someplace where they don't even have computers (there are such places still), you can convert your presentation into 35mm slides or crystal clear color overheads.

Some slide service bureaus can take your PowerPoint file and do the rest of the work for you. Often you can send your file by e-mail and within a matter of days (or hours) you receive a package of slides in the mail.

PowerPoint also includes a special wizard that can help you prepare and submit your presentation to Genegraphics, a service bureau that can produce slides, overheads, and full-color handouts. To use this service, you must first install the Genegraphics wizard by performing a custom install of Office 97, and choosing Genegraphics from the PowerPoint options.

To use the Genegraphics wizard, simply choose File, Send to, Genegraphics. You then can choose the exact type of output you need and how quickly you need to have it. You can even contact Genegraphics 24 hours a day, seven days a week. For current information on Genegraphics, visit their Web site at **http://www.genegraphics.com**. ●

CHAPTER 26

Using VBA in PowerPoint

by Ford Cavallari

As you've already learned, PowerPoint contains a number of powerful automated features, such as Slide Masters. But there will be times when the built-in automation may not be quite right to solve your specific problems. Fortunately, Microsoft includes Visual Basic for Applications (VBA) in PowerPoint 97 for such situations. This chapter will leverage some of the VBA concepts introduced in the Word and Excel chapters and show you how they can now be used to automate your PowerPoint work. ■

Create PowerPoint macros with the built-in macro recorder

Use macro recorder to capture a series of PowerPoint actions into a simple VBA program.

Play the recorded macro

After recording, learn to play back the VBA macro through a simple menu selection.

Learn the essential objects in PowerPoint

Dissect the recorded macro and learn the basics of the PowerPoint object structure—the key to VBA programming.

Create a new VBA program using the built-in editor

To illustrate the versatility and power of VBA and the built-in Visual Basic Editor (VBE), you'll write a quick program from scratch.

Connect macros to toolbar buttons

After you've written the new VBA utility for PowerPoint, you'll attach it to a toolbar button to complete the task.

Overview of New Features

Officially, PowerPoint 97 is the first PowerPoint version to include VBA. Unlike Word and Excel, which have included a macro or scripting language since the earliest releases, PowerPoint had no scripting support until Windows 95. But as of Office 97, Microsoft has equipped all Office applications with the same powerful VBA language. From a practical perspective, this means that you now can record, write, and play macros in PowerPoint. But it also means that macros created for other Office applications can be ported with relative ease to PowerPoint.

N O T E Actually, PowerPoint 95 contains a full but officially unsupported version of VBA. If you never found it (it was well hidden by Microsoft), don't feel too badly. PowerPoint 97's VBA is *very* different from PowerPoint 95's unofficial version, and there are no supported conversion tools or compatibility modes between the two versions. ▨

Creating a Macro with the Macro Recorder

Just as with Word and Excel, you can easily record actions inside PowerPoint with the macro recorder. These recorded macros can be useful in themselves, but they are best used to "jump-start" the creation of more powerful VBA programs. If your work with PowerPoint involves repetitive text editing, searching/replacing, placement of graphics/objects, or any other recurrent activities, you'll find that VBA will save you time and make your work less tedious.

To illustrate how VBA macros can improve your work with PowerPoint, you'll work through an example similar to what you did with Word in Chapter 11, "Using VBA in Word." Again, you'll use a section of the Village Software Proposal and Marketing FastPlan. With this PowerPoint template, you'll add VBA code to streamline and automate your activities—creating a simple, straightforward, and time-saving presentation-generation system.

N O T E The files referred to in this chapter are all included on the book's CD-ROM. ▨

To start, open your standard presentation file, Presentation0.ppt. This PowerPoint template includes four slides, including the title slide. On each slide there are several text boxes holding the actual presentation text. One text box on each page will ultimately hold the name of the specific client; for now, it has only the placeholder text, [Client] (see Figure 26.1).

In Chapter 11, "Using VBA in Word," you use the macro recorder to register the VBA commands associated with selecting Edit, Replace, and then filling in the Replace dialog box. In PowerPoint, you need to use a somewhat different approach. Each page in the PowerPoint presentation has a text box with the placeholder [Client]—it's always in the lower-right corner. You need to select that text box and change the text, page by page, to the real company name—Acme Software Inc. We'll give this a try on page 1.

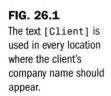

FIG. 26.1
The text [Client] is used in every location where the client's company name should appear.

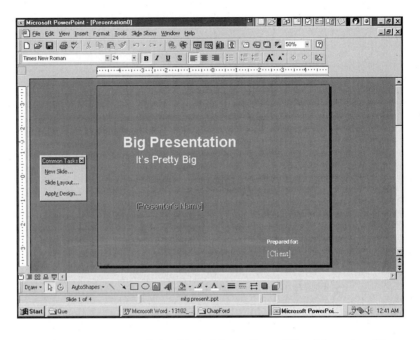

1. Start Recording by choosing PowerPoint Tools, Macro, Record New Macro (see Figure 26.2).

FIG. 26.2
Begin recording your first macro in PowerPoint.

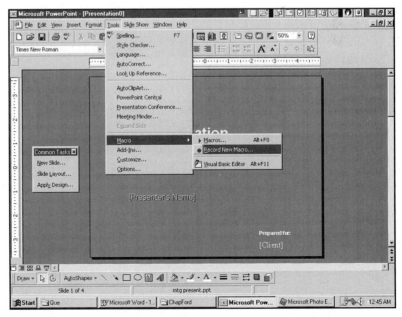

2. Assign a Name—in this case, **RenameClient1**—to the macro and click OK (see Figure 26.3).

Part

IV

Ch

26

FIG. 26.3

Assign a name to the macro, as shown here.

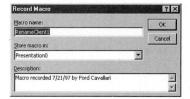

3. Select the bottom-right text box and change the text to **Acme Software Inc.** (see Figure 26.4).

FIG. 26.4

Select the bottom-right text box and change the text to **Acme Software Inc.**.

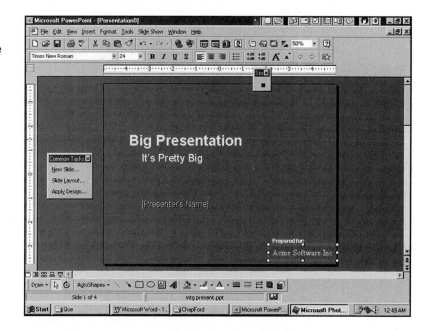

4. Click the Stop Recording button on the Stop Recording toolbar (see Figure 26.5).

N O T E You might have wondered why we didn't record for PowerPoint exactly what we recorded for Word—namely the Edit, Replace sequence. Unfortunately, as the newest Office 97 application to adopt VBA, PowerPoint is not quite as VBA-complete as are Excel and Word. There are several command sequences that just do not record—and Edit, Replace is one of them. ■

FIG. 26.5
When you have finished recording your macro, click the Stop Recording button on the Stop Recording toolbar.

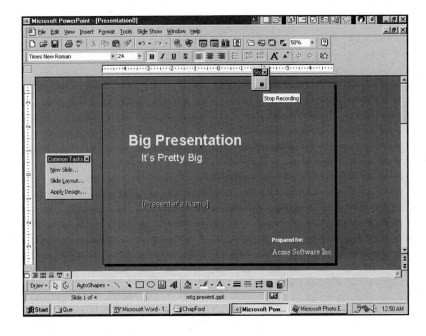

Using PowerPoint's Macro Dialog Box

Now that you've recorded your "jump-start" macro, check the macro by playing it. Select Tools, Macro, Macros to display the Macro dialog box. PowerPoint's Macro dialog box should look familiar because it's almost identical to the Macro dialog boxes of Word and Excel (see Figure 26.6).

Part

IV

Ch

26

FIG. 26.6
PowerPoint's Macro dialog box is almost identical to those of Word and Excel.

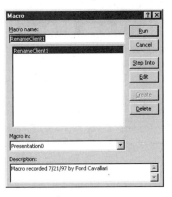

N O T E   Note that PowerPoint does not include an Organizer command or the associated functions. Again, PowerPoint is playing VBA catch-up to a large extent with Word and Excel. ▪

To run the macro you just recorded, follow these steps:

1. Open the file Presentation1.ppt from the CD-ROM. This file contains the macro, RenameClient, that you just recorded.

2. Press Alt+F8 (or choose Tools, Macro, Macros) and select Run to activate the recorded macro.

   [Client] is replaced by Acme Software Inc., as shown in Figure 26.7.

FIG. 26.7
The recorded
RenameClient1 macro
changes specific text on
page 1 only.

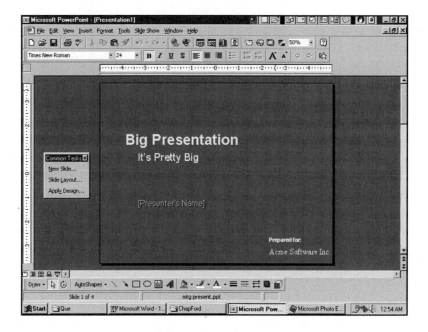

Modifying Macros to Make Them More Useful

Recording macros is only the first step in creating truly useful automation for Office 97. The next step is learning from and then modifying your recorded macros. First, you'll take a look at what you recorded and learn some of PowerPoint's macro fundamentals from the RenameClient1 macro.

Use the Visual Basic Editor to View Your Macro

With Presentation1.ppt still loaded, choose Tools, Macro, Visual Basic Editor (or press Alt+F11) to activate the VBE. On the right side will be the Project Explorer window. Click the + buttons if necessary to expand the document and navigate to the Module1 line. Clicking this line opens a Code Window displaying the VBA code associated with the RenameClient1 macro (see Figure 26.8).

FIG. 26.8

The RenameClient1 macro as shown in the VBE code window.

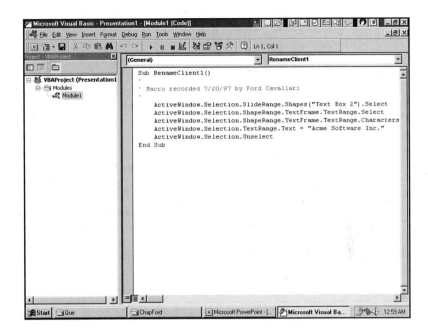

Take a close look at the macro to learn about how PowerPoint programming works. Listing 26.1 shows the RenameClient1 macro. This simple macro steps through a sequence of selections—the slide, the text box, and the text in the text box—and then puts its text (Acme Software Inc.) into that text box.

Listing 26.1   Module1.txt—Original Recorded RenameClient1 Macro

```
Attribute VB_Name = "Module1"
Sub RenameClient1()
Attribute RenameClient1.VB_Description = "Macro recorded 7/20/97 by Ford
Cavallari"
'
' Macro recorded 7/20/97 by Ford Cavallari
'
    ActiveWindow.Selection.SlideRange.Shapes("Text Box 2").Select
    ActiveWindow.Selection.ShapeRange.TextFrame.TextRange.Select
    ActiveWindow.Selection.ShapeRange.TextFrame.TextRange.Characters(Start:=1,
Length:=15).Select
    ActiveWindow.Selection.TextRange.Text = "Acme Software Inc."
    ActiveWindow.Selection.Unselect
End Sub
```

Part
IV

Ch
26

> **TIP** To make sense of this macro, it's useful to take a quick, simplified look at the PowerPoint object model. The object model for an application is the representation of how to access each type of object in the application. PowerPoint's object hierarchy consists of presentations, slides, and shapes, respectively. As a result, you can modify the attributes of an individual presentation, an individual slide, or an individual shape using VBA.
>
> A fully qualified object reference for a shape on the first slide of Presentation1.ppt would be `Presentations(1).Slides(1).Shapes(1)`. *Fully qualified* means that the reference includes the entire tree that must be "walked" to find the given object, without using any shortcuts. The macro recorder is able to create shortcuts through working from current *selections*, such as `Selection.SlideRange`, which accesses the currently selected slide, and `Selection.ShapeRange` for the currently selected shape. For more information on object models, see Chapter 57, "Creating Your Own Applications with VBA."

Here's what the macro does, line-by-line:

1. The first line of this macro records the name of the module. The second line opens the Sub, and the following two lines are comments. The actual macro code begins on the fifth line, which selects the Shape (in this case a Text Box) containing the placeholder string `[Client]` (selected manually when recording the macro).

2. The sixth line goes inside the Text Box and accesses the text (TextRange, in PowerPoint terms) associated with it.

3. The seventh line selects the characters within the TextRange (as well as reselecting the `TextRange` selected by the previous line—efficiency is not an attribute of the macro recorder).

4. The eighth line actually changes the text.

5. The ninth line deselects the Text Box.

Upgrading the Macro

The recorded macro takes a straightforward approach to accessing the target object (the Text Box with `[Client]` in it, selected manually) and changing its value explicitly and directly. Using the same basic concept as the recorded macro, the rewritten macro in Presentation2.ppt loops through each slide in the presentation and makes the text change on each sheet (see Listing 26.2).

Listing 26.2 Module2.txt—Rewritten RenameClient2 Macro

```
Attribute VB_Name = "Module1"
Sub RenameClient2()
For Each sld In Application.ActivePresentation.Slides
    For Each shp In sld.Shapes
        shp.TextFrame.TextRange.Replace FindWhat:="[Client]", _
```

```
            Replacewhat:="Acme Software Inc."
        Next shp
    Next sld
End Sub
```

Using For Each loops, the rewritten macro loops through each slide within the active presentation, and then within each of those slides it loops through the different shapes. Within each of these shapes, the macro looks for the target text, [Client], and replaces it with Acme Software Inc.. The macro follows this procedure, line by line:

1. The third line (after the module and macro definition lines) starts a For Each loop that goes through the slides.

2. The fourth line starts a second For Each loop that goes through the shapes in the slide. Note that this loop goes through all shapes—Text Boxes, Rectangles, and other objects.

3. Line five is the final control line apart from the loop-closing Next statements. This line checks the shape for the target text and replaces it with the new text. Note that this single line does what several lines did in the recorded macro, and that it uses the Replace method, which cannot be recorded.

 TIP The For Each construct, one of the most powerful and useful features of VBA, is designed to step through collections of objects. Because most Office applications contain many such collections (cells inside sheets inside workbooks in Excel, shapes inside slides inside presentations in PowerPoint) For Each is a simple and efficient way of cycling through these collections.

Finishing the Macro

As with the Word example, you should generalize the PowerPoint example to work with any client, not just Acme Software, Inc. As with Word, you can ask the user what company the proposal is being written for. To do this, you need an input mechanism and a place to put the input. The new code, shown in Listing 26.3, incorporates those two additions.

Listing 26.3   Module3.txt—Improved RenameClient2 Macro with Input Box

```
Attribute VB_Name = "Module1"
Sub RenameClient2()
Dim cname As String
cname = InputBox("Enter client's name", "Enter Name")
For Each sld In Application.ActivePresentation.Slides
    For Each shp In sld.Shapes
        shp.TextFrame.TextRange.Replace FindWhat:="[Client]", _
            Replacewhat:=cname
    Next shp
Next sld
End Sub
```

The client's name is stored in the variable cname, which is in turn used as the replacement value.

```
cname = InputBox("Enter client's name", "Enter Name")
shp.TextFrame.TextRange.Replace FindWhat:="[Client]", Replacewhat:=cname
```

Try the new macro by either making these changes manually or by loading Presentation3.ppt. Run the macro by hitting Alt+F8 or by choosing Tools, Macro, Macros and highlighting RenameClient2. Click Run. The input box will appear as shown in Figure 26.9.

FIG. 26.9

The RenameClient input box appears when the modified macro is run.

Type a name and click OK, and that name will replace all instances of [Client] on each slide. Try this yourself. Now, what do you think will happen if you try to run this macro a second time? Or if you hit the Cancel button on the Input dialog box? We'll leave finding these answers as an exercise for you.

Finally, this macro works well on the PowerPoint presentation as is. But what happens if you add additional objects or pictures to any slide? If you add an object such as a line, the macro will no longer work.

One disadvantage of the For Each construct is that it goes through *all* members of the collection, in this case Shapes. It happens that all the shapes that you were using were either Text Boxes or Rectangles with text frames—so each had a text frame. But many objects such as lines have no text frames. If such a shape is added to *any* slide, the Replace within the For Each loop fails.

There is a simple fix, however. Adding a check for a text frame as shown in the following If statement is all that's needed to restore the macro to perfect health.

```
If shp.HasTextFrame Then shp.TextFrame.TextRange.Replace FindWhat:="[Client]",
Replacewhat:=cname
```

The final macro with the new Replace line reads as follows:

```
Attribute VB_Name = "Module1"
Sub RenameClient2()
Dim cname As String
cname = InputBox("Enter client's name", "Enter Name")
For Each sld In Application.ActivePresentation.Slides
    For Each shp In sld.Shapes
        If shp.HasTextFrame Then shp.TextFrame.TextRange.Replace
FindWhat:="[Client]", _
            Replacewhat:=cname
    Next shp
Next sld
End Sub
```

Activating the Macro from a Toolbar

Now that the macro is working well, all you need to do is increase its accessibility (not that pressing Alt+F8 and run is so inaccessible.) You can add your macro to a custom toolbar just as you did with Word. The procedure is exactly the same. To add RenameClient2 to a PowerPoint custom toolbar, do the following:

1. Choose Tools, Customize. This will bring up the Customize dialog box (see Figure 26.10).

FIG. 26.10

The Customize dialog box, used to customize the PowerPoint toolbars

2. Click the New button to create a new custom toolbar. Type in a name (such as MyToolbar) for your new toolbar.

3. Note that you now have a buttonless mini-toolbar. To add a button to the toolbar, click the Commands tab on the still-open Customize dialog. Select Macros from the category list on the left. That will reveal a macro button (RenameClient2) that you'll be able to add to your toolbar.

4. Drag the RenameClient2 macro button to the toolbar with your mouse. When you let go of the mouse button, the macro button will drop onto your toolbar.

5. If you would like an image on the button, left-click the button after it's on the toolbar and select menu item Change Button Image. Just drag the cursor over the image of your choice and it will be added to the button.

6. Click Close on the Customize dialog box. Your toolbar is now ready.

Part
IV

Ch
26

Part V: Access: Beyond the Basics

CHAPTER 27

Access Quick Start Guide

by Scott Fuller and Kevin Pagan

Access 97 is the relational database component of Office 97. This chapter, which starts the Access section of this book, explores some basic database concepts and the uses of Access. If you are new to databases or to Access, you may want to spend some time studying the database concepts presented in this chapter. ■

Learning the parts of a database

First, we explore the parts of database, and discuss the basic database terminology.

Types of databases

This section explores the different types of databases and briefly discusses their functionalities.

Exploring Access 97

After covering the "basics" in the previous two sections, the section takes a look at Access 97.

Opening an Access database

Here, we discuss the procedure of opening database files in Access 97.

Creating an Access database

In this section, we cover the process of creating an Access database from scratch.

Saving an Access database

This section discusses the way databases are saved in Access 97.

Basic steps in creating an Access database

This sections covers some basic database design issues.

Learning the Parts of a Database

In order to fully understand the uses of Access, you should understand some basic database concepts. These concepts apply to all databases, not just to Access. All databases, large or small, are built around these concepts.

A *database* is an organized collection of data. It is considered an organized collection because the data is stored in categories that are accessible in a logical (or practical) manner. Every entry of data is referred to as a *record*.

Table 27.1 illustrates a simple database.

Table 27.1 A Simple Phone Number Database		
Last Name	**First Name**	**Phone**
Denver	Bob	234-2344
Hale	Alan	956-2222
Louise	Tina	678-1937
Backus	Jim	578-4884

Each column (Last Name, First Name, and Phone) is a *field* in the database. The data in this database is divided into these three categories or fields. Each row of data in the database (exclusive of the column headings) is a *record*. One record is equal to one complete name entry (last name, first name, and phone number) in the database.

Another important part of a database is the *index*. An index is a unique value in a field. Not all databases have an index. An index performs two functions: it prevents records from being duplicated, and it accelerates the process of "looking up" (or searching) records.

Access is often referred to simply as a "database," but is more accurately a *DBMS (database management system)*. A DBMS is a computer database software application that helps to store, retrieve, sort, filter, print, and present the information contained in a database. In a DBMS, data is stored in tables similar to Table 27.1. However, a DBMS offers much more to the user. For example, data is often presented on the computer screen in *forms*. Forms are screen templates used to present data in an easy-to-understand fashion for data input or other user interaction.

A DBMS uses templates for the printer as well. In Access, for example, these printing templates are referred to as *reports*.

Types of Databases

There are two basic types of databases:

- *Flat file databases* are sequential access databases. They store all information in one large table, often duplicating data. Flat file databases are sequential, meaning they do not access the data via an index. Instead, flat file databases scan the data from beginning to end.

- *Relational databases* are much more popular. Relational databases enable data to be stored in multiple tables and linked together via data indexes. Because data can be divided into several tables, relational databases are faster and easier to maintain than flat file databases.

As mentioned earlier, Access is a relational database. It enables the user to divide data into multiple tables.

Tables 27.2 and 27.3 show two tables that are linked together via the EmployeeID field.

Table 27.2 An Employee Table

EmployeeId	Name	Address	City	State	Zip	Phone
E001	Anna Adams	123 Main St	Dallas	TX	75243	555-123-1234
E002	Billy Barnes	456 Hick Ave	Tulsa	OK	34533	555-484-4848
E003	Chad Church	5858 48th	NYC	NY	22342	555-234-1110
E004	Edgor Egg	234 Hatch St	Bird	WY	01283	555-948-9494

Table 27.3 A Business Trip Database

Trip Location	Purpose	EmployeeID	Cost
London	Sales	E002	$1599
Paris	Sales	E004	$2357
Rome	Sales	E003	$2108
The Haag	Sales	E003	$1529

Part
V

Ch
27

The benefit of linking these two tables is that the data from the Employee table is not dupli-cated in the Business Trip table. The EmployeeID field in the Business Trip database links all the information in the Employee table to it. The DBMS manages this link and the cross-references of the records. Thus, if a manager wants to access information about an employee's business trips, the manager simply references the employee by Employee ID, thus preventing having to store duplicate data in both tables.

Exploring Access 97

Access 97 is a relational database system that was designed to take full advantage of the Win-dows 95 operating system. It has the following enhancements from its predecessor, Access 95:

> Improved performance
>
> VBA (Visual Basic for Applications) enhancements
>
> More database templates
>
> New macro commands
>
> Internet/intranet connectivity

In this section, we review the components of an Access database, basic operations of Access, and how to create, open, and save an Access database. Because Access is a DBMS composed of many parts, Table 27.4 describes the components or (objects) found in an Access database.

Table 27.4   The Components of an Access Database

Object	Description
Table	The object in which the data is stored. Looks much like a spreadsheet.
Form	Display template used to make data more readable and understandable on the screen.
Report	Printing template used to design printouts of the data stored in a table.
Query	Extracts data from the table based on user definable criteria.
Macro	Automates database objects based on commands or events.
Module	VBA procedures written to automate more complex operations that cannot be handled with macros.

These database objects work together to create an Access database. However, not all Access databases use all objects. For example, macros and modules are used only when some sort of automation is needed in the database.

Opening an Access Database

When Access is started, a dialog box appears similar to that in Figure 27.1.

FIG. 27.1
The initial dialog box gives you three choices.

From the bottom part of this dialog box, you can select an Access file to open. If you select the More Files option, Access launches an Explorer window that enables you to browse for additional files.

If you closed this dialog box without making a choice, or if you need to open another file, there are two other methods of opening files. You can select Open Database from the File menu or click the Open Database button on the toolbar.

Creating an Access Database

As shown in Figure 27.1, Access enables you to create a new database from the startup dialog box. The top portion of the dialog box gives you the choice of a Blank Database or launching the Database Wizard.

If you choose Blank Database, you will be prompted for a name for the database and Access will create the database structure. Figure 27.2 illustrates the blank database.

FIG. 27.2
A blank or empty database has a file name, but does not contain any database objects.

Part
V

Ch
27

From this point you can create any tables, forms, reports, queries, macros, and modules that you need in your database. These are the *objects* of the database.

If you choose <u>D</u>atabase Wizard, Access launches a dialog box that lists all the Database Wizards available on your system. Figure 27.3 shows this dialog box with a list of wizards.

FIG. 27.3

The default list of wizards included with Access 97 is quite extensive.

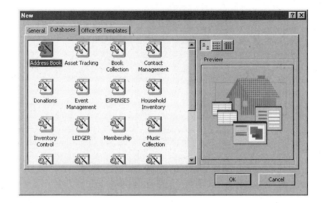

From this list, you choose the Database Wizard that best fits the design of the database you want to create, and Access will launch the wizard. Before the wizard starts, however, Access asks you to name the new database. The Database Wizard then guides you through a series of questions that will help Access customize the creation of the database to your needs.

The dialog screen, illustrated in Figure 27.4, shows the Database Wizard enabling you to select the fields that you want to use in your database.

FIG. 27.4

You also have the choice of adding sample data to the database.

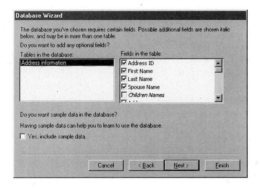

After the fields have all been specified, you select the style of the database, which is the next step of the wizard (see Figure 27.5).

FIG. 27.5
By selecting a style, you create a unified "look" throughout the database.

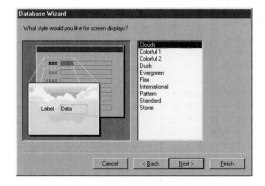

You can also change the font used in the database. The next step in the wizard is to select the font that you want used throughout the database (see Figure 27.6).

FIG. 27.6
The Compact font enables you to find more information on the screen with forms.

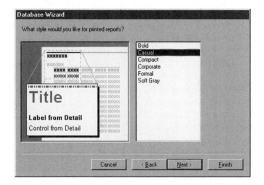

The final step in the Database Wizard is to select the name that is going to be used, as shown in Figure 27.7. This is the name that will appear on the Title bar and the Properties sheets. The file name for this database is still what you originally named it.

This completes the steps of the Database Wizard. After selecting Finish, the wizard creates the tables, forms, reports, and any other database objects that you need. The steps in the Database Wizard will vary some depending on the nature of the database that the wizard is creating.

If you close the initial dialog box, you can initiate the Database Wizard by choosing File, New Database or by clicking the New Database button on the toolbar.

Part
V

Ch
27

Saving an Access Database

Unlike a lot of other applications (such as Word), with Access you do not have to consciously save your database. Saving is done automatically after you name a database. Access writes the data out to disk whenever records are entered or when you make changes to a database objects. This is why Access requests a name for the database upon initial creation.

FIG. 27.7
From this dialog box you can also select a picture to be used throughout the forms and reports in the database.

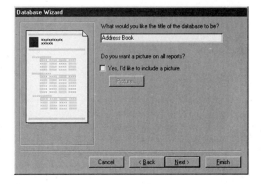

T I P As you will see in later chapters of this book, you must save the objects within your database after they are created or edited—for example, forms, reports, queries, tables, macros, and modules.

As you enter new information into your database after the tables and forms have been created and saved, the data is saved to disk after each new record is entered.

Basic Steps in Creating an Access Database

If you choose to create your new database without using the Database Wizard, there are some basic design guidelines that can help you in the creation process. The order that you create the database objects in the database is important.

Here is the suggested creation order:

Tables	Tables contain fields that hold the data of the database and are referred to by all other objects. Tables act as the foundation of the database. Any table linking should be done at this step.
Queries	Queries further connect information between tables and filter the data that will be seen on-screen or in a report.
Forms	Forms are the screen or user interface of your database. Generally speaking, you design the screen of your database before going on to reports. New to Office 97 is a special kind of form called a *switchboard*. A switchboard acts as a main menu for your database, giving the user a push-button selection for all the forms and reports.
Reports	After you have designed the user interface, which usually acts as the data input portion of the database, you design the reports, which are the output portion.
Macros & Modules	Macros and Modules add automation to controls and to the database objects. You will have already created some macros or modules during the form creation when placing controls such as command buttons on the forms. At this point, you would create any macros or VBA modules that are needed anywhere else in your database.

CHAPTER 28

Creating and Formatting Data Tables

by Scott Fuller and Kevin Pagan

Now that you have a general understanding of database concepts, you can use Access to create tables within a database and input data into those tables. Tables are the primary building blocks of your database. All the other objects in your database—forms, reports, and so on—use the data stored in your tables.

In this chapter, you see how to create basic tables, perform simple modifications on your tables, and set basic properties for the tables. In addition, you see how to input your data into the tables that you have created. ■

Creating tables

Learn how to use MS Access' tools to create tables for your database.

Modifying tables

Learn how to modify the tables that you create to suit your needs.

Working with data

Explore different ways to get your data into your database.

Creating a New Table

To create new tables, you should first open the database for which you want the tables to be created. Next, select the Table tab and click the Ne̲w button. Access displays the New Table dialog box, as shown in Figure 28.1.

FIG. 28.1

You create new database tables by using one of the methods in this dialog box.

Following is a brief description of each method by which you can create a new database table:

Datasheet view. In this method, you create a new table by entering data directly in a blank database, similar to entering data in a spreadsheet. When you finish entering the data and save the sheet, Access automatically reviews the data and then creates the appropriate field types and formats for you. If you have never created a table or if you have data ready to go, you may find this method to be helpful.

Design view. In this view, you create a table from scratch, selecting the field names, field types, and formats that you want. This method gives you the most direct control of your table creation and allows for maximum flexibility in creating tables.

 TIP   Even if you plan to use the more automated table creation methods described later in this section, you should be somewhat familiar with design view so that you can more effectively use the automated methods.

Table Wizard. This wizard provides automated table creation based on a predefined list of common tables. You provide the wizard information about the table that you want, and the wizard helps you create the table.

Import Table. If the data that you need in Access is already stored in another application or in another Access database, *and* if you plan to permanently store the information in the new table, importing the data may be best. With this method, Access copies the data in the other location and automatically creates a table for the data based on the old location's characteristics.

Link Table. This method is similar to the Import Table option. Linking, however, leaves the data in its current location (such as another application) and creates a table in your current Access database. From the new table, you can access, edit, and view the data.

N O T E   In previous versions of Access, Link Table was called *attaching* a table.

Creating a Table in Datasheet View

Creating a table in datasheet view is similar to entering data in an Excel spreadsheet. When you select Datasheet View in the New Table dialog box (refer to Figure 28.1), Access creates a "blank" datasheet, such as the one shown in Figure 28.2.

FIG. 28.2

A blank datasheet view table is similar to a spreadsheet. You can enter data directly in this screen.

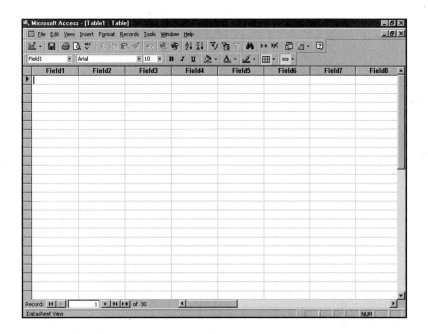

Using the blank screen, you can enter your data directly in the datasheet. When you finish, you simply save the datasheet, and Access automatically creates the table for you, assigning appropriate field types, formats, and so on.

In Figure 28.3, data has been input directly into the blank datasheet.

Access also looks for a primary-key field when it creates the table from your datasheet. *A primary-key field* is a field that is unique to each record and that helps Access index and otherwise organize the data in your table. If it cannot locate a primary key, Access tries to add a field to your table and create its own primary key, as shown in Figures 28.4 and 28.5.

When Access creates its own primary key, it simply adds an automatically numbered ID field, as shown in Figure 28.5.

 TIP When your table is created and saved, you may find that you need to edit the table, which can do in Table Design view.

Part

V

Ch

28

FIG. 28.3

Data is entered directly in the datasheet.

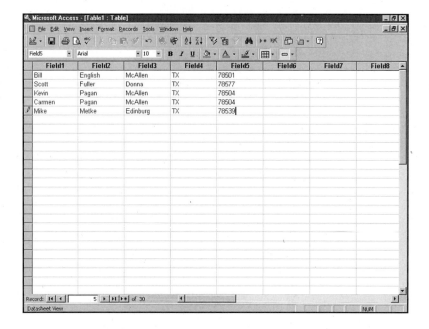

FIG. 28.4

Access creates its own primary key if your datasheet does not contain an appropriate field.

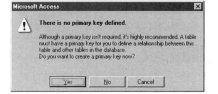

Follow these basic steps to create a table by using datasheet view:

1. Open the database window.

2. Click the New button in the Table tab. The New Table dialog box appears.

3. Double-click the Datasheet View option and a blank datasheet appears.

4. Enter your data in the blank fields of the datasheet.

 T I P   Don't forget to save the table after inputting a few rows (records) of data.

5. After you enter and save the table, create the primary key, if necessary, and save the table again.

6. After Access creates your table, check the fields and data to make sure that Access did not inappropriately alter your data during the table-creation process.

7. Make any changes that you want by using Design view to modify field types.

8. Save the table after you enter all your data.

FIG. 28.5

Access creates its own ID field to use as a primary key.

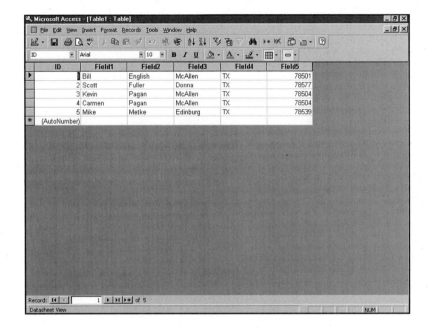

Creating a Table by Using the Table Wizard

If you want to take a more step-by-step approach to table creation but still want a significant amount of Access automation, try using the Table Wizard option.

When you click the Table Wizard button on the toolbar (or select Table Wizard and click OK), Access presents the main Table Wizard dialog box, shown in Figure 28.6.

FIG. 28.6

The main Table Wizard dialog box gives you sample tables and fields to help you create your own tables.

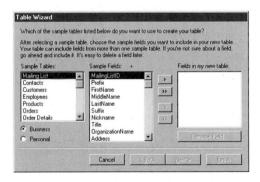

In this dialog box, you can select sample *Business* and *Personal* tables and their related fields. To change from *Business* to *Personal*, simply select the option button beside the appropriate table type.

Part
V

Ch
28

You can choose to take one of the sample tables and all of its related fields as is—that is, use the table in its predefined format—or you can choose various fields from various sample tables in a mix-and-match manner.

Clicking the Add All Fields button with the Mailing List sample table selected, for example, moves all the predefined fields to your new table.

On the other hand, you can select a few fields in the Mailing List table, click the Personal option button, and then use the Video Collection sample table to select other appropriate records.

In Figure 28.7, for example, all the data fields from the sample *Business Table Category* have been selected, followed by additional fields from the *Suppliers Table*.

FIG. 28.7

You can use various fields from various tables (Business or Personal) for your new table.

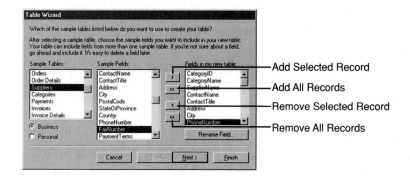

After you select the fields that you want to use, click Next.

T I P   Instead of clicking Next, you can click Finish at this point (and throughout the remainder of the process) and create your table based on the information that you have provided so far. The first time you create a table by using the wizard, you may want to go through the entire process. As you create more tables in this manner, however, you may decide that information up to some point is all that you really need for your situation and cut the process short by choosing Finish somewhere along the way.

As shown in Figure 28.8, the wizard next asks for a table name, which you can enter based on the naming criteria (up to 64 characters, letters, numbers, and spaces). Alternatively, you can use the name that Access has chosen for you.

As described in the preceding section, Access creates a primary key for you, if you so choose. Otherwise, if you want to set the primary key yourself, the wizard guides you through the appropriate series of steps.

After you click Next, Access asks whether your new table is related to other tables in the database. (Note that if this is the first table that is created in the database, Access does not ask if your new table is related to other tables in the database.) Related tables have records that match based on a primary key from one table and another key (called a *foreign key*) in the other table. The category number in the new table, for example, may be the primary key in that table and may also appear in the Product table, where it would be the foreign key. (The Product ID number may be the primary key in that table.)

FIG. 28.8

Name the table (or use the Access-generated name) and tell Access whether you want a primary key to be generated for you.

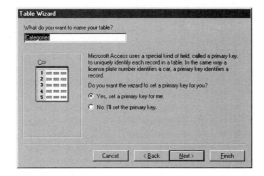

If Access finds relationships with other tables, it lists them for you to choose or allows you to define additional relationships, as shown in Figure 28.9.

FIG. 28.9

The wizard allows you to create relationships among tables in your database.

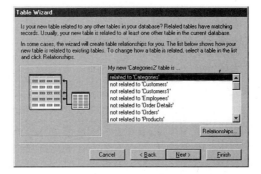

When you finish modifying the relationships, click Next; the final wizard box appears. If you still need to modify the table, you can choose that option by clicking the appropriate button. Alternatively, you can enter data directly in the table or you can ask the wizard to create a data-input form in which you can enter data (see Figure 28.10).

FIG. 28.10

The Table Wizard creates your table and allows you to enter data or creates a form for you.

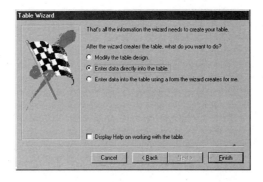

Part
V

Ch
28

Creating a Table by Importing

If your data is located in another location (such as another application), and you want to move the data to your Access 97 database and maintain the data there, you can import the data. The supported file types for importing are:

- Access (MDB)
- Text (TXT, CSV, TAB, and ASC)
- Lotus 1-2-3 (WK*)
- Excel (XLS)
- HTML files
- Paradox (DB)
- dBASE III, IV, 5 (DBF)
- FoxPro (DBF)
- FoxPro 3 (DBC)
- ODBC databases

If your file is not in the supported list, see whether you can export the file in its resident application into one of the supported application formats.

Follow these steps to import a table by using the Import Table option:

1. Open the database window.
2. Select the Tables tab.
3. Click New. The New Table dialog box appears.
4. Choose the Import Table option and then click New. The Import Table dialog box (shown in Figure 28.11) appears.

FIG. 28.11

The Import dialog box allows you to select the file format, location, and specific file that you want to import.

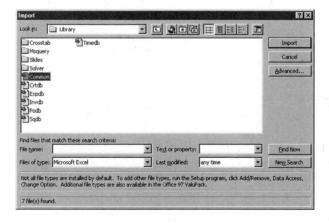

5. From the File of Type drop-down list, choose the file type (format) that you want to import, specify the location, and select the file that you want to import.

6. Choose Import.

   The table appears in the Table tab of your database. If problems occur, Access displays error dialog boxes and helps you try to fix the problems.

TIP As you can with tables created by other methods, you can use the Design view to modify your imported table.

Creating a Table by Linking

Linking is similar to importing. With linking, however, you leave the original data in its original location and simply use an Access table to view and edit the data.

> **CAUTION**
>
> The supported file types for linking are similar to those for importing, but although you can import a FoxPro 3 (DBC) or Lotus 1-2-3 (WK*) file to Access 97, you cannot link these files to Access 97 tables.

Follow these steps to link data from another source into your table:

1. Open the database in which you want the linked table to appear.

2. Select the Tables tab.

3. Click New and the New Table dialog box appears.

4. Select Link Table and click OK.

   A dialog box like the one shown in Figure 28.12 appears.

FIG. 28.12
The Link dialog box allows you to specify the type of file that you want to link to.

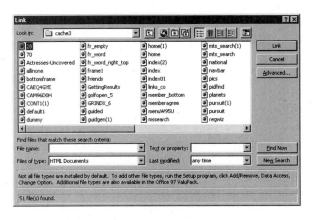

5. From the File of Type drop-down list, choose the file format that you want to use (HTML, for example), as shown in Figure 28.12.

6. Specify the file location and file name.

7. Choose Link. The new table appears in the Table tab of your database. (If problems occur, Access tells you and tries to help you fix them.)

Creating and Modifying Tables in Design View

Regardless of the method that you use to create a table, you can modify the table by using Design view. (Be aware that Design view is where you change your table. Design View is not to be confused with Datasheet view, which is where you input data.)

TIP

You can also create new tables from scratch in Design view simply by creating a blank table. To create a blank table, click the Tables tab and then click New. Next, choose Design View. Access creates a blank table in Design view, ready for you to modify.

Working in Design View

To enter Design view for an existing table, open the database and select the desired table. Next, click the Design button on the right side of the window. You can also open the table in Datasheet view and choose View, Table Design.

Figure 28.13 shows a table created in Design view.

FIG. 28.13

This table is displayed in Design view.

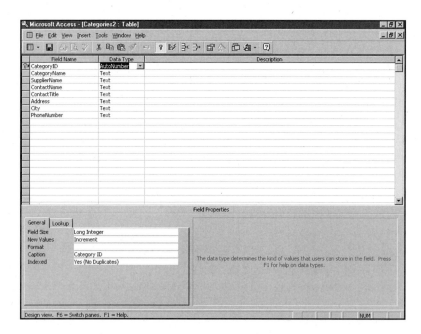

Design view contains three major areas: the toolbar, the Field Grid pane, and the Field Properties pane.

Using the Design View Toolbar

The main area of Design view is the Field Grid pane. You modify this pane by using the Design View toolbar. The main toolbar buttons are shown in Table 28.1.

Table 28.1   The Design View Toolbar

Button Name	Description
Datasheet View	Displays the table in Datasheet view
Save	Saves the table
Cut	Removes the selected object or text to the Clipboard
Copy	Copies the selected object or text from the Design window to the Clipboard
Paste	Places a copy of the Clipboard contents in the currently selected location
Primary Key	Enables users to select a column as the primary key; toggles the primary key on and off
Indexes	Displays the index sheet for the currently selected object
Insert Row	Inserts a row above the currently selected row
Delete Row	Deletes the selected row or rows
Properties	Opens or closes the property sheet for the currently selected object
Build	Helps create an item or property, such as a field or input-mask property
Database Window	Displays the Database window
New Object	Displays a drop-down list of new objects that you can create, such as tables, forms, reports, queries, and macros
Office Assistant	Calls up the Windows Office Assistant

Using the Field Grid Pane

The Field Grid pane is the main part of the Design view window. In this pane, you can define field names, data types, and descriptions. The pane (refer to Figure 28.13 earlier in this chapter) consists of the row-selector column (on the far left), the Field Name column, the Data Type column, and the Description column.

Part
V

Ch
28

Field Names   You can change (or create) your field names by using this column. Again, the names can have up to 64 characters, numbers, and spaces. Your field names must be unique within the table.

Data Types   The type of data that you can store in a given field is determined by the Data Type setting for that field. You cannot enter incompatible data in a field. You cannot put text in a numeric field, for example. The data types used in Access are as follows:

- *Text:* alphanumeric characters
- *Memo:* alphanumeric characters (up to 65,535 characters)
- *Number:* any numeric type
- *Date/Time:* dates and times (up to 8 bytes)
- *Currency:* rounded numbers for dollars and cents
- *AutoNumber:* unique sequential (increments of 1) or random numbers used by Access to automatically number each record that you enter
- *Yes/No:* logical values, such as True/False and On/Off
- *OLE Objects:* OLE objects, graphics, or other binary data
- *Hyperlinks:* text and numbers that define a path to a document, Web page, or other specific location in a document
- *Lookup Wizard:* wizard that walks you through the process of creating a field that displays a drop-down list of acceptable values from another table

 TIP   The default data type is Text, and Access automatically assigns that type to a newly created field. To change the type, click the down arrow in the record that you want to change in the Data Type column and choose the data type you need from the list that appears, as shown in Figure 28.14.

Field Descriptions   Use the Field Description column to provide information about the field.

Field Properties   The fields that you create, like other objects, have properties. You can set these properties to define the way that data is stored in a field and the way the data is displayed. The fields that you set by using Design view are applied to other database objects that use the table, such as forms, reports, and queries.

You modify field properties in the Field Properties pane by using the General and Lookup tabs. Figure 28.15 shows sample field properties for a field that contains the PhoneNumber data in the sample table.

Following are brief descriptions of the field properties in the General tab depending on which data type is selected:

- *Field Size:* sets the maximum number of characters in a text field and limits numeric fields to a range of values
- *New Values:* determines how new values for AutoNumber fields are handled (incrementally or randomly, for example)

- *Format*: sets the display format for dates, numbers, and so on
- *Decimal Places*: sets the number of decimal places in Number and Currency fields
- *Input Mask*: used for Text and Date fields only; sets the formatting specific for the field
- *Caption*: provides a label that is used in forms and reports, as well as a header for datasheets that contain the field
- *Default Value:* sets a default value to be entered automatically in new fields
- *Validation Rule*: Restricts data entry to values that meet the validation criteria (a maximum number, a valid date no later than today, and so on)
- *Required*: If set to active, the user must enter data in the selected field
- *Allow Zero Length*: Allows Text and Memo fields to have null strings
- *Indexed*: creates an index based on this field

FIG. 28.14
This list provides the data types used in Access.

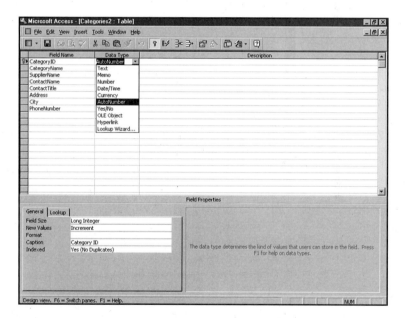

The Lookup tab contains additional property settings. These property settings depend on what data type you have in the field and the value of the first Lookup field property: Display control.

Following are the properties in the Lookup tab:

- *Display Control.* Sets the type of control to use to display the field in a form. The types of controls include Text Box (default), List box, and Combo Box.
- *Row Source Type.* Determines whether the values in the List Box or Combo Box come from a table or query, from a list you type in, or list of fields from a table or query.
- *Bound Column.* This property specifies the column number that appears in the Row Source.

Part
V
Ch
28

- *Column Count.* The number of columns for the Combo or List Box is set using this option.
- *Column Heads.* Displays the names of the fields from the Row Source.
- *Column Width.* Specifies the width of the drop-down list or list-box column.

To set field properties in Design view, simply select the field for which you want to set properties; the Field Property pane displays the General tab for the properties for that field.

Next, click the specific property that you want to set; enter the property value (or choose it from the drop-down list); and continue with other properties.

FIG. 28.15

The Field Properties pane at the bottom of the window allows you to define the way that data is stored and displayed in your table.

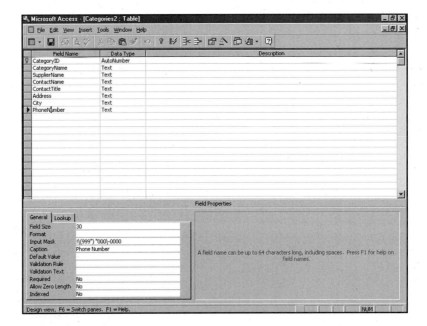

Working with Other Settings

In addition to the settings described in the preceding section, you can change other settings and make other modifications in your table from Design view. Following is a brief overview of those settings (for more detailed information, see Que's *Special Edition Using Access 97*):

- *Primary key.* Although doing so is not required, creating a primary key in every table is a good idea. The Primary Key helps Access work with your data efficiently and also makes creating relationships and links to other tables much easier. To set the primary key, click the Primary Key toolbar button or choose Edit, Primary Key.
- *Index properties.* Like keys, indexes help Access find values and organize data. Access automatically indexes your primary-key fields. You can create indexes for other fields by

selecting the field that you want to index in the Field Grid pane, selecting the Indexed property in the Field Properties pane, and then choosing the type of index from the drop-down list.

 TIP As you can see, Access allows you to make a variety of changes in tables by using the Design view. Be careful, however, when you make certain changes in existing tables. Deleting a field, renaming a field, or changing certain field properties (such as data type) can affect other objects, such as related tables, forms, reports, and queries.

Importing and Linking Data

Now that you have learned how to set up the framework of your database by using Access' tables. you can explore various ways to create and manipulate the actual data in your database.

The data for your database can come from a variety of sources. You usually find, however, that your data is one of two general types: data from an existing source in a computer system (such as an old database) or data that comes from a noncomputer source (such as printed information). Existing data in computer form is much easier to work with, mainly because it does not require all that typing. With Access, however, you find the flexibility to work with various data sources.

This section explores various data sources and explains how to get that data into your Access database.

Many times, you discover that the data you need for your Access database already exists in some other database. Your organization may have an older Paradox database, for example, or an Excel spreadsheet may contain data that you want to use in your database. Access supports a variety of data formats and allows you to import or link that data to your database.

At the outset, you need to decide whether you want to import or link the data. The following paragraphs explain the difference.

When you *import* data, you actually retrieve the data from the source location and create a new copy of the data within your Access database. You can then manipulate, update, and otherwise change the data without affecting the data at the source. Thus, importing data can be useful (and perhaps necessary) if you do not have the authority to change the source data, or if you simply want to keep the source data intact. The main thing to remember about importing is that after the data is imported, changes that you make in your new copy do not change the data in the original source data.

Linking data allows you to use the source data directly in your database. With linking, you do not create a new copy of the data, but simply use the original data. If you have update rights in the original data, you can also change the original data source directly from your Access database.

Part
V

Ch

28

TIP Deciding whether to link or import data is an important first consideration. Generally, if the data that you need in the source is not likely to change, or if you just want a snapshot of the data, importing probably is the better bet. (Likewise, you may have only one-time access to the data, such as data in a purchased mailing list, in which case importing is the way to go.)

On the other hand, if the data source is continually being updated in the original program or location, and if having up-to-date versions is important for your database applications, linking may be better.

If either choice seems to be equally acceptable, keep in mind that Access works much faster on its own tables than it does on linked data—so when in doubt, import.

Access 97 allows you to import or link data from a variety of sources, including the following:

- Other Access databases—versions 1.x, 2.0, 7.0 (95), and 8.0 (97)
- Microsoft Excel
- dBASE III, III+, IV, and 5
- FoxPro
- Paradox
- ODBC databases (with an appropriately configured ODBC driver)
- HTML tables and lists
- Lotus 1-2-3 files

N O T E   Not all the import and link drivers are automatically installed when you install Access 97. Most notably, the drivers for Paradox and Lotus 1-2-3 are not included in the setup, but they are available through the Office 97 ValuPack. If you need data from these sources, be sure to load the drivers from the ValuPack on the CD-ROM provided with the Access program or obtain these drivers from Microsoft's Web sites. (To access the information on the Web, choose Help, Microsoft on the Web, Free Stuff in Access 97.) ▨

How to Import or Link Data

Now that you've located compatible data and decided that you want to link or import that data, here are the steps you need. The exact steps vary somewhat, depending on the location and type of the data that you are importing or linking, but this section gives you the general steps. (Notice that the steps are almost identical whether you are linking or importing, except for step 2.)

To import or link data, follow these steps.

1. Open the database in which you want to use the imported or linked data, and make sure that the database window is visible.

   Figure 28.16 shows the database window of the Access sample Northwind database.

2. If you are going to import data, choose File, Get External Data, Import.

You can also right-click anywhere in the database window and then choose Import from the shortcut menu, or you can click the New button in the database table window and then choose the Import Table option from the list that appears.

FIG. 28.16

Before importing or linking data, be sure that the database you want to use is open and that the database window is visible.

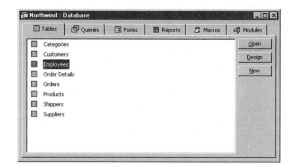

You see the familiar Open dialog box, like the one shown in Figure 28.17. Using this dialog box, you can choose the type of data that you want to import by using the Files of Type drop-down box, then locate the specific file containing the data you want to import. Here, we have selected Microsoft Access and several files appear.

FIG. 28.17

This is an Import dialog box for selecting the file you want to import.

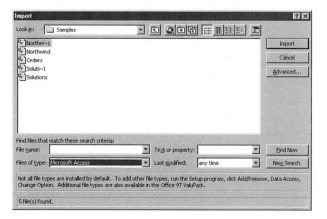

If you are going to link data, the process is similar. Choose File, Get External Data, Link Tables. (As you can in the import process, you can also right-click the title area of the database window and then choose Link Tables from the shortcut menu, or click the New button in the Tables window and double-click the Link Table option in the New dialog box.) Select the location of the data file, the type of data, and the specific file in the Link dialog box, shown in Figure 28.18.

3. After you locate the file that you want to use for linking or importing, select the file and then click the Link (or Import) button in the dialog box (or simply double-click the filename).

Part

V

Ch

28

4. Respond to any further dialog boxes that appear, such as the one which appears in Figure 28.19 when you double-click the Northwind file in the Link dialog box.

In the box shown in Figure 28.19, choose the table of data that you want to link (or import, if you are importing data) and then click OK.

FIG. 28.18

The Link dialog box is similar to the Import dialog box.

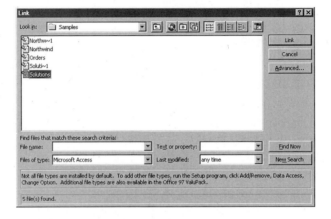

FIG. 28.19

In this box, select the specific data that you want to link to from the selected file.

Access creates the linked data entry in the database table window. (Because you used a table with the same name, Access added the number 1 to the name to create a new linked table called Categories1, as shown in Figure 28.20.)

FIG. 28.20

You can see the new linked table in the updated Database table window.

Linked table—

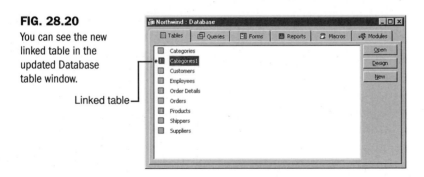

Notice that Access uses a different icon to represent linked tables. As shown in Figure 28.20, those icons have a small arrow to their left, indicating the link.

 TIP The examples used here create duplicate copies of the same data within the Northwind sample database—a procedure that you may actually use from time to time. As you can with most other filenames in Windows 95, you can right-click the table name and choose Rename from the shortcut menu to use a different name for the newly created, duplicate data file, if you don't care for the 1 extension added by Access. You can use this technique to rename any object in Access 97.

How to Use Linked or Imported Data

After you import data from another source, you can use that data just as though it had been created in Access.

Your use of linked data, on the other hand, can be restricted depending on a variety of factors, including the type of data, the location, and your rights to the data. Although you cannot add, delete, or change the fields of a linked data table, you can change some properties of the table using Design view.

Managing Linked or Imported Data

From time to time, the source file containing linked data may be moved to a new location. Because Access stores the information about the link to your data along with the table in your database, if the source is moved, the program can't find the data. You can fix this problem by using Access' Linked Table Manager. Choose Tools, Add-Ins, and choose Linked Table Manager. If you installed this option at Setup, a list of linked tables appears, and you can use the check boxes to select the tables that you want to update. Then click OK. The Table Manager displays a dialog box that allows you to select the new location of the linked table.

Notice that the Linked Table Manager cannot help you if the linked data is deleted or if the table has been renamed. In those cases, you generally have to delete the link and start over with a new link.

Adding and Editing Original Data

In the previous sections, you learned how to import data from existing data sources. In this section, you learn how to add and edit data directly in a table.

You can add, edit, and delete individual data records from Access tables by using either of two views: Datasheet view or Form view. In Datasheet view, the program displays several records at the same time in table format. When you click the Open button in the Tables window with the Customers table highlighted, you see the Northwind Customers table in Datasheet view (as shown in Figure 28.21).

Using Form view, Access displays the records one at a time in a format that you design for those records. To see an example of Form view, click the Forms tab in the Northwind database window, select the Customers form, and click Open (see Figure 28.22).

Part
V
Ch
28

Customer ID	Company Name	Contact Name	Contact Title	
ALFKI	Alfreds Futterkiste	Maria Anders	Sales Representative	Obere Str. 57
ANATR	Ana Trujillo Emparedados y helados	Ana Trujillo	Owner	Avda. de la Cons
ANTON	Antonio Moreno Taquería	Antonio Moreno	Owner	Mataderos 2312
AROUT	Around the Horn	Thomas Hardy	Sales Representative	120 Hanover Sq.
BERGS	Berglunds snabbköp	Christina Berglund	Order Administrator	Berguvsvägen 8
BLAUS	Blauer See Delikatessen	Hanna Moos	Sales Representative	Forsterstr. 57
BLONP	Blondel père et fils	Frédérique Citeaux	Marketing Manager	24, place Kléber
BOLID	Bólido Comidas preparadas	Martín Sommer	Owner	C/ Araquil, 67
BONAP	Bon app'	Laurence Lebihan	Owner	12, rue des Bouc
BOTTM	Bottom-Dollar Markets	Elizabeth Lincoln	Accounting Manager	23 Tsawassen Bl
BSBEV	B's Beverages	Victoria Ashworth	Sales Representative	Fauntleroy Circus
CACTU	Cactus Comidas para llevar	Patricio Simpson	Sales Agent	Cerrito 333
CENTC	Centro comercial Moctezuma	Francisco Chang	Marketing Manager	Sierras de Grana
CHOPS	Chop-suey Chinese	Yang Wang	Owner	Hauptstr. 29
COMMI	Comércio Mineiro	Pedro Afonso	Sales Associate	Av. dos Lusíadas
CONSH	Consolidated Holdings	Elizabeth Brown	Sales Representative	Berkeley Garden
DRACD	Drachenblut Delikatessen	Sven Ottlieb	Order Administrator	Walserweg 21
DUMON	Du monde entier	Janine Labrune	Owner	67, rue des Cinqu
EASTC	Eastern Connection	Ann Devon	Sales Agent	35 King George
ERNSH	Ernst Handel	Roland Mendel	Sales Manager	Kirchgasse 6
FAMIA	Familia Arquibaldo	Aria Cruz	Marketing Assistant	Rua Orós, 92
FISSA	FISSA Fabrica Inter. Salchichas S.A.	Diego Roel	Accounting Manager	C/ Moralzarzal, 8
FOLIG	Folies gourmandes	Martine Rancé	Assistant Sales Agent	184, chaussée de
FOLKO	Folk och fä HB	Maria Larsson	Owner	Åkergatan 24
FRANK	Frankenversand	Peter Franken	Marketing Manager	Berliner Platz 43
FRANR	France restauration	Carine Schmitt	Marketing Manager	54, rue Royale

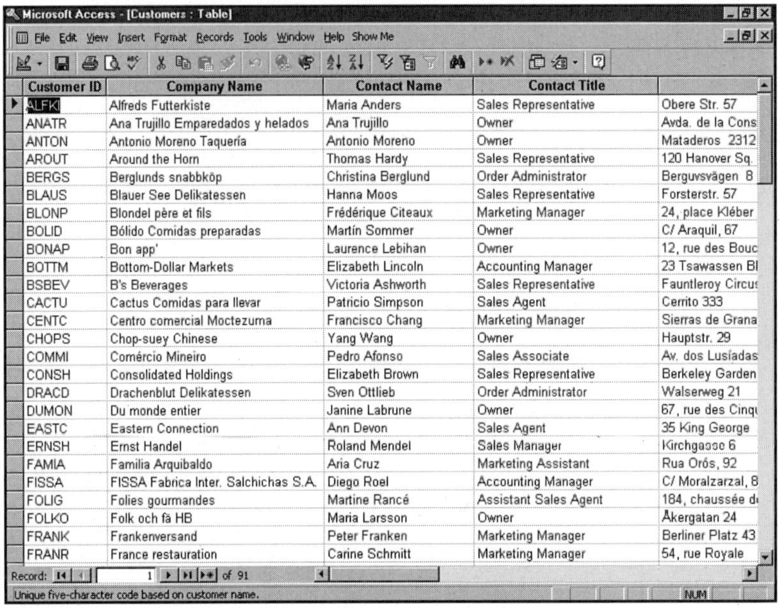

FIG. 28.21
Datasheet view shows several records in a table at the same time.

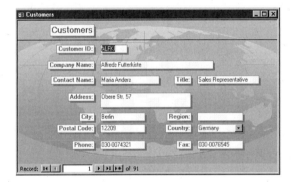

FIG. 28.22
Form view shows one record at a time and sometimes is easier for users to work with, because it is similar to using paper forms.

Creating Forms

If you want to view data in Form view, you need to create forms for the data tables that you want to view in that format. Creating custom forms can be quite an art form; the intricacy of form design is beyond the scope of this chapter. For more information about form design, **see** Chapter 30, "Designing and Using Forms."

Fortunately, Access has a nice feature that allows you to quickly create basic forms if you prefer Form view but don't want to do a great deal of work. To use this feature, select the table (or query) for which you want a form and then click the drop-down arrow button next to the New Object button (the next-to-last button from the right end of the Database toolbar).

From the list that appears, choose AutoForm. Access creates a simple form for you.

Switching Between Views

If you have created a form for certain data tables, you can view that data in either Form or Datasheet view at any time.

To open the data in Datasheet view, click the Tables tab and then double-click the table that you want to view, or select the table and then click Open. You can also right-click the table and then choose Open from the shortcut menu. This opens the view shown Figure 28.21.

To open the same data in Form view, click the Forms tab and then double-click the form that you want to open. Just as you can in Datasheet view, you can also select the form that you want to use and then click the Open button, or right-click the form and then choose Open from the shortcut menu. This opens the form view as shown in Figure 28.22.

When you are in Form view, you can quickly switch to Datasheet view by clicking the View toolbar button, which is the first button at the left end of the main Access toolbar. When you click this button in Form view, you can choose among Datasheet view, Form view, and Design view.

N O T E Form view is *not* available from the View drop-down button if you originally opened the table in Datasheet view. Design view is always available, however. Design View is not used to manipulate data; it is simply used for working on the form itself. ▨

Customizing the Datasheet View

If you need to see several records at the same time but aren't crazy about the plain-vanilla Datasheet view, you can customize Datasheet view. To do so, open the table in that view and then use the Formatting (Datasheet) toolbar to customize the format.

Normally, when you are in Datasheet view, the Formatting (Datasheet) toolbar is visible; if it's not, simply right-click the main toolbar (while you're in Datasheet View) and click the Formatting toolbar, or use the View drop-down menu's Toolbar option to do the same thing.

By using this toolbar, you can change the appearance of the datasheet in several ways, including the following:

- ▨ Change the font and/or font size for all text in the datasheet by using the Font and/or Font Size drop-down lists.
- ▨ Underline, italicize, and/or boldface all text by clicking the appropriate toolbar button.
- ▨ Change the background color of the sheet by clicking the drop-down arrow next to the Fill/Back Color button and choosing your favorite color. You change the foreground (text) and gridline colors in the same way by using the appropriate drop-down arrow.
- ▨ You can customize the gridlines or hide them by using the drop-down arrows next to the Gridlines and the Special Effects buttons. (You should experiment with various combinations to get the look that you want, because not all grid effects are available with the various hide/show combinations.)

Part
V

Ch
28

Moving Around the Data

Now that you have seen the two views used to view data, you want to move around within your database. Navigating from record to record in a form or a datasheet is simple. By using the navigation buttons at the bottom of the Form or Datasheet window or by choosing Edit, Go To, you can go to the First, Last, Next, or Previous records. You can also select New Record to move to a blank form in Form view or to a new record line in Datasheet view. The navigation buttons and the Edit, Go To options are both shown in Figure 28.23.

FIG. 28.23

The navigation buttons at the bottom of the screen duplicate the functions of the Edit, Go To command.

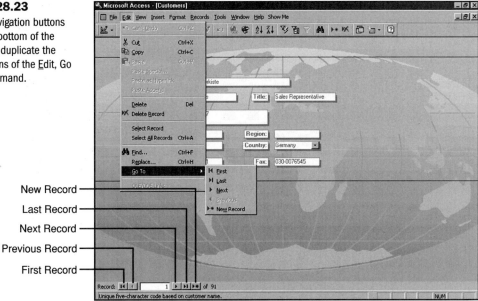

New Record
Last Record
Next Record
Previous Record
First Record

In Datasheet view, you can also use the scroll bars (if visible) to scroll the data records. Use the vertical scroll bar on the right side of the screen to scroll up and down records. You can scroll through the various columns in Datasheet view by using the horizontal scroll bar at the bottom of the window.

 TIP   If your Datasheet view contains more columns than you can view at a time, critical columns may scroll off the left side of the screen. To correct this problem, you can freeze one or more columns so that they always stay on-screen.

To freeze columns, simply select the column(s) that you want to freeze and choose Format, Freeze Columns, or right-click anywhere in the column and then choose Freeze from the shortcut menu. When these columns are frozen, the other columns scroll off the left, but those frozen columns are always visible. You can unfreeze the columns by choosing Format, Unfreeze All Columns.

Adding Data

After you learn how to manipulate the data views and move around the data in your tables, adding data is a straightforward process. Simply move to a blank record in either Datasheet or Form view and type the contents of each field for which you want to add data.

In Form view, for example, click the New Record navigation button and type the information that you want to put in the first field, as shown in Figure 28.24.

FIG. 28.24

This figure shows a new record in the Northwind database with only the first field complete.

New record —

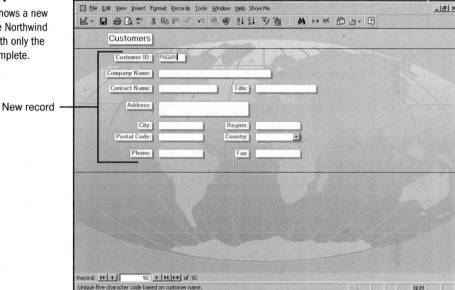

Press Tab or Enter to move to the next field or, if you want to skip around, click the next field that you want to fill in. Access saves your new record when you move to another record. If you made any mistakes (such as leaving a critical field blank), Access does not allow you to leave the new record until you correct the error or confirm that you want to leave.

Figure 28.25 shows the same partially completed record in Datasheet view.

N O T E In Access, you do not need to insert a record between any other records. Access sorts the records any time you ask it to; therefore, you just place new records in the table by using the New Record feature described and sort it out later. ▪

Editing Data in a Table

With a few minor things to keep in mind, editing data in an Access table is simple. Select the data that you want to change by locating the record and clicking the appropriate field, and use your text-editing skills to change the information.

FIG. 28.25

Datasheet view contains a partial new record. Notice the small pencil icon, which reminds you that this record has not yet been saved.

Pencil icon —

Keep one matter in mind, though: When you are in a particular field, you may be in edit mode or navigation mode. If you used the keyboard to reach a particular field, that field's entire contents are selected instantly. If you begin to type at that moment, you delete the selected contents and insert new data. On the other hand, if you jumped to a field by clicking the mouse, you are in edit mode, and the insertion point blinks. Typing now simply inserts new data without deleting the existing contents. To switch back and forth between the edit and navigation modes, press the F2 key.

 TIP Most of your Windows-style word processing editing features work while you are editing records in Access. A few extras can come in handy, however. You can use the ditto marks (Ctrl+") to copy the data from the same field of the preceding record. These features can be big time-savers if several records contain similar data. Also, the Ctrl+semicolon (;) combination inserts the current date. If a field has a default value, pressing Ctrl+Alt+space bar inserts that value.

For more editing keys and other data-entry information, view the Data Entry subtopics in the Help index.

You can also change the order of columns in Datasheet view. To accomplish this task, use the mouse to drag and drop the column in the desired location. (Frozen columns cannot be dragged.)

Rearranging the columns (as opposed to freezing) may be desirable for several reasons. For example, the nature of the presentation of the data may require a different column order, or performing multiple-column sorts (described in "Sorting Data" later in this chapter) may necessitate changing the order of the columns to achieve the desired sort.

Deleting Data

From time to time, you need to delete data from your database. To do so, simply select the record that you want to delete and then choose Edit, Delete Record, or move to that record and press Ctrl+hyphen (-). Access deletes the current record after confirming that you want to do so.

Likewise, you can select several records for deletion (in Datasheet view) by clicking the first record and then selecting the records that you want to delete, then choose Edit, Delete Record, or move to that record and press Ctrl+hyphen (–). Access deletes the current record after confirming that you want to do so.

Sorting Data

When you have all your data imported, linked, or entered in your database, the real power of Access begins to kick in. You can now sort and filter your data. In addition, you can create queries, reports, and other forms of output for your data; these are discussed in subsequent chapters.

Sorting data, as the name implies, means putting the data records in your table in some type of order (such as ascending or descending order, based on the number in one of the table's fields).

Simple Alpha Sorts

The most common of all sorts is the *alphabetical* (or *alpha*) *sort*. Alpha sorts can be either ascending (A to Z) or descending (Z to A).

In Figure 28.26, you see the first of several records in the Northwind Customer table as they probably appear on your system (if you loaded the sample database). You can easily see that the records are sorted alphabetically by the Customer ID field. Notice that the column-freezing technique discussed earlier in this chapter is used to freeze the Customer ID field and scrolled over so that the Country field is right beside it.

FIG. 28.26
These records have been sorted in an ascending alphabetic sort by Customer ID.

Customer ID	Country	Phone	Fax
ALFKI	Germany	030-0074321	030-0076545
ANATR	Mexico	(5) 555-4729	(5) 555-3745
ANTON	Mexico	(5) 555-3932	
AROUT	UK	(171) 555-7788	(171) 555-6750
BERGS	Sweden	0921-12 34 65	0921-12 34 67
BLAUS	Germany	0621-08460	0621-08924
BLONP	France	88.60.15.31	88.60.15.32
BOLID	Spain	(91) 555 22 82	(91) 555 91 99
BONAP	France	91.24.45.40	91.24.45.41
BOTTM	Canada	(604) 555-4729	(604) 555-3745
BSBEV	UK	(171) 555-1212	
CACTU	Argentina	(1) 135-5555	(1) 135-4892
CENTC	Mexico	(5) 555-3392	(5) 555-7293
CHOPS	Switzerland	0452-076545	
COMMI	Brazil	(11) 555-7647	
CONSH	UK	(171) 555-2282	(171) 555-9199
DRACD	Germany	0241-039123	0241-059428
DUMON	France	40.67.88.88	40.67.89.89
EASTC	UK	(171) 555-0297	(171) 555-3373
ERNSH	Austria	7675-3425	7675-3426
FAMIA	Brazil	(11) 555-9857	
FISSA	Spain	(91) 555 94 44	(91) 555 55 93
FOLIG	France	20.16.10.16	20.16.10.17
FOLKO	Sweden	0695-34 67 21	
FRANK	Germany	089-0877310	089-0877451

Record: I◄ ◄ | 1 | ► ►I ►* of 91

Unique five-character code based on customer name.

Part

V

Ch

28

What if you want to view the list sorted so that all the customers in a particular country appear adjacent to one another? This type of sort is a simple ascending (or descending) alphabetic sort. Follow these steps:

1. Open the Customer table in the Database window in Datasheet view.

2. Click Country so that this column is selected.

3. Click the Sort Ascending or Sort Descending toolbar button, or choose Records, Sort, Sort Ascending (or Sort Descending).

    You can also right-click the column and make the same choices from the shortcut menu.

Figure 28.27 contains the result.

FIG. 28.27

This figure shows the same list sorted in ascending alphabetical order, this time by the Country field.

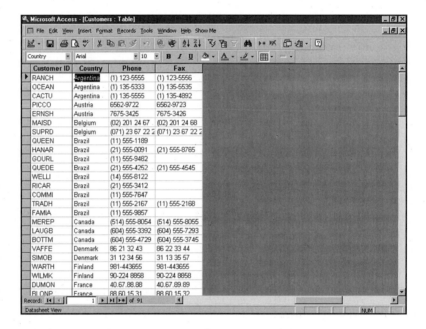

Multiple Sorts

You can also perform sorts on more than one field at a time—a procedure sometimes called a sort within a sort. You need to keep in mind several limiting factors:

- Access sorts only on *adjacent* fields (or columns).

- The sort is performed on the leftmost column of fields first, and then on the next to the right, and so on.

- Because of the first two factors in this list, you may have to change the order of one or more of the columns in your datasheet to accomplish the desired sort.

In the next sort, you want to arrange the Northwind customers alphabetically, first by country (thus grouping all customers in a country) and then alphabetically by Customer ID within each country.

To accomplish this task, follow these steps:

1. Unfreeze the Customer ID column, if you still have it frozen.

2. Drag and drop the Customer ID so that it is *to the right of and adjacent to* the Country column.

3. Click the Country column; then Shift+click the Customer ID column so that both columns are selected.

4. Click the Sort Ascending toolbar button.

Notice the difference between the result of these steps (see Figure 28.28) and the result of the preceding steps.

FIG. 28.28

In this Figure, the data is sorted first by Country, then by Customer ID by moving the columns so they are in that order and then sorting on both columns at the same time.

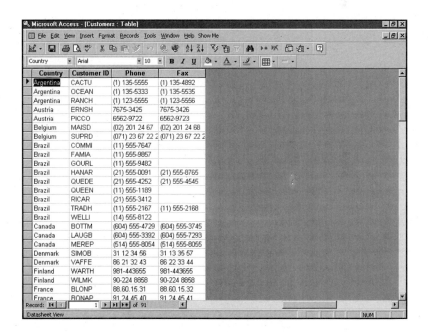

This type of sort within a sort is particularly useful for a large list of names in which several people have the same last name (similar to a telephone book).

 You can also perform sorts in Form view in much the same manner. The examples in this section use Datasheet view, however, so that the results are more immediately apparent.

Part

V

Ch

28

To remove the effect of the sort, choose Records, Remove Filter/Sort. Removing the sorts returns the records to their original order—that is, unsorted. You can also right-click anywhere in the sheet and then choose Remove Filter/Sort from the shortcut menu.

Data Filtering

Filtering is the process by which you locate and isolate one or more records that you want to view, and hide the rest of the data. In the preceding examples, you may want to view only customers in a particular country and (temporarily) hide all the rest. A filter is the way to accomplish this goal.

Simple Filters   To apply a filter to the Northwind Customer data so that only customers from Germany are displayed, go to the Customer table and click Open. Move to the Country column and click a record with the data record Germany filled in. Next, click the Filter by Selection toolbar button or choose Record, Filter, By Selection.

The result is a list of only those customers who are located in Germany, as shown in Figure 28.29.

FIG. 28.29

This figure shows the Northwind database of customers filtered by Germany in the Country field.

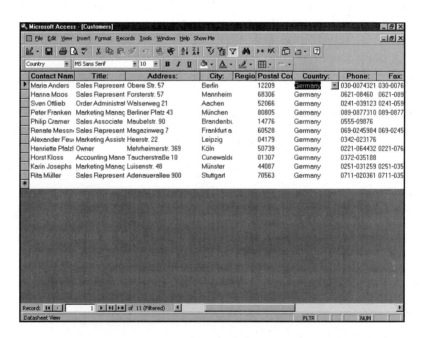

Likewise, you can filter by *excluding* the selection— by excluding all the customers in Germany, for example, to produce a list of only those customers in countries other than the selected criterion. Don't forget to choose Remove Filter/Sort before moving on.

TIP You can apply a filter within a filter (in other words, further filter your data) by first applying a filter (as you did earlier) and then applying another filter (a selection or exclusion) to the newly filtered list. You can continue this process as many times as needed (or until you run out of data that meets the filter criteria).

More Complex Filtering   Your filter criteria need not be an entire field record; you can filter by a portion of a record, or by using Access' new Filter by Input feature. You can also select filter criteria using *wild cards* and *masks*. You can use the wild card symbol *, for example, to search for all records starting with the letter *P* by entering **P***, or you can search for all the names in a list that begin with the letters A–F by using the symbol **<G** as the criteria.

User Input Filters   Figure 28.30 shows the Customer table in the Customer ID field after right-clicking and filling in `less than C` by using <c in the Filter For box.

FIG. 28.30

By right-clicking the Customer table, you can use the Filter For (input) feature.

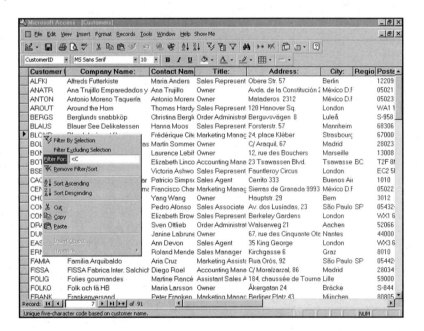

Figure 28.31 shows the result of this process.

Form Filters   If you prefer, you can create form filters by choosing Records, Filter, Filter by Form. A blank filter form appears, along with a revised toolbar and new tabs near the bottom of the form. To begin creating the filter form, first click one of the fields; then, from the drop-down list of records, choose the criteria that the record must contain to pass the filter. You can choose more than one criterion in the initial form; the criteria are considered to be *And criteria*. In other words, a record must match the criteria in *all* the fields to pass the filter.

Part
V

Ch
28

FIG. 28.31

This figure shows the result of the Filter For search using <C.

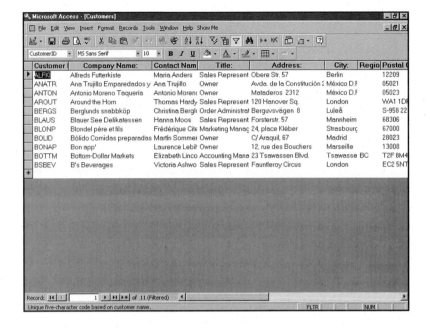

Figure 28.32 is created using the Country field with "Germany" as the criterion, *and* City field using "Berlin" as the criterion. Thus, in order to pass this stage of the filter, the record must contain *both* Germany and Berlin.

FIG. 28.32

This Figure is created using the Filter by Form feature.

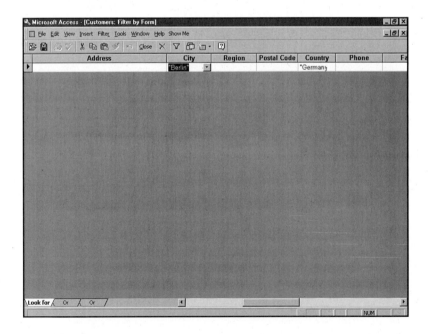

Notice that the Form window has tabs near the bottom. Now you want, *in addition* to all the customers in Berlin, Germany, all the customers in Austria, this time without regard to city. You accomplish this task by clicking the first Or tab, clicking the Country field, and then choosing Austria from the list of records, as shown in Figure 28.33.

FIG. 28.33
Here the Or tab is used to include customers from Austria in our filter form.

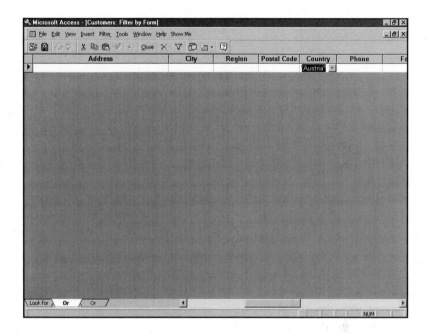

Finally, click the Apply Filter toolbar button to obtain the results shown in Figure 28.34.

You may recall that previous examples showed a total 11 customers in Germany, and in this example the data is filtered down to one German customer in Berlin, *plus* the two Austrian customers.

 TIP If you design a particularly complex filter form and plan to use it frequently, you should choose File, Save As Query feature and save the filter as a query.

Advanced Filters and Sorts Using the Advanced Filter/Sorts feature of Access, you can perform many of the features described in the preceding sections at the same time, in a single window.

To launch this feature, make sure that your table is open; then choose Records, Filter, Advanced Filter/Sort. A window similar to the one shown in Figure 28.35 appears.

FIG. 28.34

This figure shows all the customers in either Berlin, Germany, or any city in Austria.

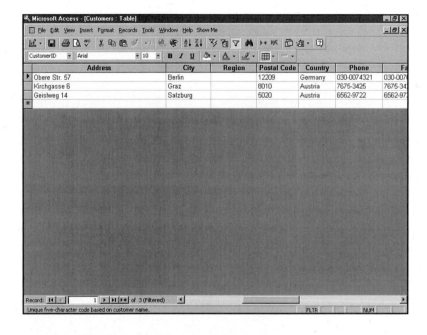

FIG. 28.35

In the Advanced Filter/ Sort window, you can perform several filter and sort functions at the same time.

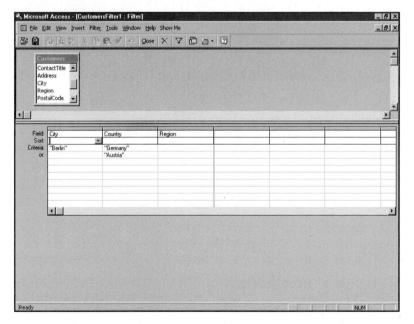

This Advanced Filter/Sort window contains the leftover criteria from the latest filter. In this window, you can add to the grid any field(s) for which you want to specify sort order or filter criteria.

To specify a sort order for the Customer ID field, for example, double-click the Customer ID field in the box in the top-left corner; that field is added to a new column in the grid. Next, click the row labeled Sort and choose Ascending. Now the filter looks like Figure 28.36.

FIG. 28.36

You can add additional sort or filter criteria, such as an ascending Customer ID sort.

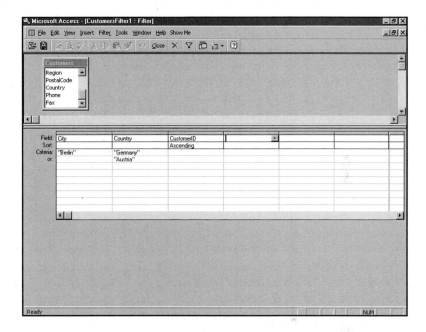

Finally, you can save the filter as a query by choosing File, Save As and then apply the filter by choosing Filter, Apply Filter/Sort or clicking the Apply Filter toolbar button.

By using a combination of logical operators (less than, greater than, between, and so on), exact criteria matches, and sorts, you can create complex filters. For more information about this process, see Que's *Special Edition Using Microsoft Access 97.* ●

Part

V

Ch

28

CHAPTER 29

Query Techniques for Finding and Sorting Data

by Scott Fuller and Kevin Pagan

After creating your database and entering data, you can retrieve that data in a variety of useful ways. In this chapter, we will look at *queries,* which are simply ways of retrieving your data by asking structured questions. ■

Overview of new features

In this section, we examine what is new in Access 97 as compared to the previous version.

Exploring queries

Here we look at the different types of queries and we examine dynasets and how they are used.

Creating and using queries

This section looks at the query creation process and the use of query wizards.

Editing a query

Here we explore the query window, QBE (Query by Example) grid, the query toolbar, totaling fields, and sorting.

Modifying records through queries

This section discusses the use of Action queries, and the concept of Cascading Deletes.

Creating crosstab queries

Here we look at the creation process of Crosstab queries.

Overview of New Features

Users of Access 97 will find a variety of improvements to Access 95, including:

New properties

RecordSetType	Enables you to set the result of a query to a snapshot or another type of recordset.
FailOnError	Controls the way to handle errors with ODBC data sources.
MaxRecords	Limits the number of records that will return from a ODBC database.

Menu commands

Many menu commands in the query menus have been made easier to understand. For example, the Make Table menu command is now the Make-Table Query command. The various rewording of the menus and menu commands help new users to better understand the menu commands.

Exploring Queries

Queries enable you to extract data from your database. Performing a query is much like asking a question of the tables in the database. How many boxes of product did we ship to California last month? What are the names of our customers who spent more than $10,000 with us over the past year? Being able to ask questions like these are what make databases useful. This is what queries do.

Queries have functionality beyond just asking questions. They also merge data, filter data, alter tables, and create tables. Because queries can bring information together from multiple tables, forms and reports are often based on queries. When forms and reports are created from queries, the underlying query executes to provide the form or report with the latest information from the tables.

Types of Queries

Here is a list of the various queries in Access and a brief summary of each:

Select Query	The most common type of query. Select queries enable you to gather data from fields in tables, calculate fields, and summarize data from tables. Select queries are similar to filters (which is discussed in a later section in this chapter) except that they can query more than one table, create new fields from calculations, and summarize data.

Make Table Query	Creates a new table from the queries dynaset. A make table query is a good way of archiving data from a table before deleting records. For example, if you have a sales table that contains sales information for the past ten years, which is really slowing down your invoicing. You might consider moving the older data to another table with a make table query. This query is considered an action query.

T I P An action query is any Access query that moves, copies, creates, or deletes data.

Update query	An update query makes global changes to the data in the underlying table or tables. They are commonly used to make sweeping changes to data across the entire database. For example if the price of an item needs to be changed throughout the entire database, an update query finds all occurrences of the desired item and updates the price. This is also considered an action query.
Append query	This query adds records from one or more tables to another table. This type of query enables you to take groups of records from a table and add them to the end of another table. This is a copy function, not a move function. An append query is considered an action query.
Delete query	As the name suggests, a delete query deletes selected records from one or more tables. When used in combination with the append query, these two queries jointly function as a move query. Records can be copied from one table to another with the append query, and the delete query can delete the same records from the original table. This is the last type of action query in Access 97.
Crosstab query	This query groups data together from one or more tables into a spreadsheet-like table with summary information. This type of query is commonly used to compare values, spot data trends, and group data for graphs.
Pass-Through query	A pass-through query sends SQL commands directly to a SQL database server.
Data-Definition query	This type of query uses SQL commands to create or edit database objects.
Union query	With the use of SQL commands, this query combines fields from two or more tables into a single field.

Dynasets

When a query is run, Access collects the data that query gathers in a dynaset. A *dynaset* acts and looks like a table. Dynasets are similar to recordsets, but with one major difference. *Recordsets* are collections of records that you can treat as an object. If you change the records in a recordset, the change is only effective in the recordset. Recordsets are not updateable objects. On the other hand, dynasets are a dynamic collection of data. If the records in a dynaset are altered, the records in the underlying table are also altered, so changes that take place when a query is run affect the associated tables and the entire database.

Creating and Using Queries

In Access 97, there are two ways to create queries: design view and the query wizards. Figure 29.1 shows the dialog box that is displayed after selecting Ṉew under the Queries tab in a database.

FIG. 29.1
This dialog box shows the available query wizards, as well as the option for design view.

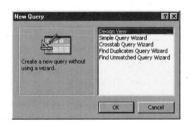

We will explore the use of query wizards first.

Exploring Query Wizards

Query wizards can help guide you through the creation of several useful queries. Each of the available wizards is listed and briefly summarized below:

Simple Query Wizard	A simple query wizard creates a select type query on one or more tables. This wizard can also guide you through the selection of data, calculation of sums and averages from the data, and counts of the data from the tables. This query is the most commonly used query wizard because it is multifunctional.
Crosstab Query Wizard	This is a special purpose query wizard which builds a crosstab query. Because crosstab queries can be difficult to understand initially, this query wizard is very useful when creating crosstab queries for the first time.

Find Duplicates Query Wizard	As the name suggests, this query wizard locates all the duplicate records in a table. This query can be used to help eliminate redundant records.
Find Unmatched Query Wizard	This query wizard is used to create a query that finds records in one table that are not found in another. This would be useful to compare two customer tables to find out which table contains customers who are not found in the other table.

Query wizards help to create the basic query that you need, but sometimes you may find it necessary to finish up using Design view. Design view is discussed in the next section.

Creating Queries using Design View

To create a query in design view, choose Design View in the New Query dialog box. Access prompts you for the tables that you are going to use in a query with the Show Table dialog box, as shown in Figure 29.2.

FIG. 29.2

From this list, you add tables to your query.

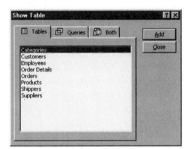

Select the tables that you want to add to your query by either double-clicking the table or by highlighting the table name and choosing the Add button. Notice in Figure 29.2 that you can also select Queries or Both (tables and queries) to build your query. Because queries produce a table-like object called a dynaset, you can use these them to build other queries. When a query executes, it first executes the underlying queries to get the updated dynaset.

After you have selected the desired tables or queries, Access adds them to the query and displays the Query Design View window as shown in Figure 29.3.

At this point let's briefly examine the Query Design View window. Figure 29.4 shows the Query Design View window with two tables.

The bottom portion of the Query Design View window is known as the *QBE* or *Query by Example* grid. The QBE portion of the windows enables you to define your query by providing examples of the data for which the query is going to search. For example if you wanted to find all the customers from Iowa, you would use the example "Iowa" or "IA."

FIG. 29.3

Notice that Access automatically identifies and displays any relationships found between the tables.

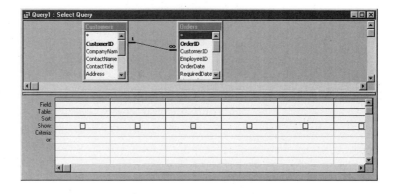

FIG. 29.4

The top portion of this window has the two tables that we added in the previous step.

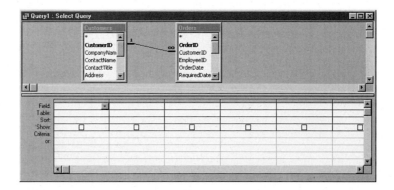

To add fields from one of the tables in our example to the QBE grid, you select the field (or fields) and drag it to the grid. Figure 29.5 shows the QBE grid after dragging the necessary fields to the grid.

FIG. 29.5

Only the fields dragged to the QBE are in the dynaset generated by this query.

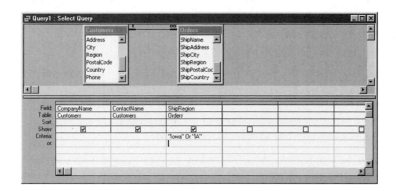

The ShipRegion field has the following criteria set:

"Iowa" or "IA"

In these examples, we are using string values, shown here enclosed in quotes. (Quotes would not be necessary if we were querying for numerical values.) The example also includes a logical operator, OR. There are additional operators commonly used in queries, (AND & NOT). The OR operator enables us to search for either occurrences of the state that we are searching for; that is, the state name or its two-letter abbreviation.

Also notice in Figure 29.5 that the Show check boxes are all selected. If you do not want the ShipRegion field to show in the resulting dynaset, you unselect the Show checkbox for that field.

To view the dynaset the query builds, select the datasheet View from the View drop-down list on the toolbar. Figure 29.6 shows the datasheet for this query. Notice we could easily show the ShipRegion field in the datasheet.

FIG. 29.6

Queries display the resulting dynasets in datasheets.

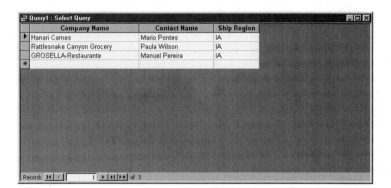

In this datasheet, data from the Orders table is used to select certain data from the Customers table. The relationship between the two tables and the QBE functionality of Access' queries made this query simple to create.

Editing a Query

Once queries are created, either by Design view or by a wizard, you may find it necessary to go back and edit them. To edit a query from the Queries tab in the database, highlight the query and select the Design button.

Back in Design view, you can add tables to the query, change QBE examples, or add and delete fields. The Query Toolbar available in Design view makes editing a query easier.

The Query Toolbar

These buttons on the Query Toolbar provide shortcuts to the query tools that Access offers.

Table 29.1   Query Toolbar Buttons Available in Design View

Button	Button Name	Description
	View	Enables the various views of the query. Choose among Design, Datasheet, and SQL views.
	Save	Saves the query design. Any changes that you make to the query are not saved until you choose Save.
	Print	Prints the resulting datasheet.
	Print Preview	Shows how the resulting query datasheet will look when printed.
	Spelling	Invokes the spelling checker.
	Cut	Moves the selected object to the Windows clipboard.
	Copy	Copies the selected object to the Windows clipboard.
	Paste	Places what is currently on the Windows Clipboard to the cursor location.
	Undo	Reverses the last action.
	Query Type	Enables you to change the type of query. The choices are Select, Crosstab, Make Table, Update, Append, and Delete.
	Run	Executes the query.
	Show Table	Displays the Show Table dialog box, so additional tables or queries can be added to the existing query.
	Totals	Toggles the view of the Totals row in the QBE grid.
	Top Values	Enables you to filter values. The choices are 5, 25, 100, 5%, 25%, and All.

Button	Button Name	Description
	Properties	Displays the Properties windows of the selected object.
	Build	Starts the Expression Builder.
	Database Window	Displays the Database window.
	New Object	Enables you to create new database objects. The choices in this drop-down list are AutoForm, AutoReport, Table, Query, Form, Report, Macro, Module, and Class Module.
	Office Assistant	Invokes the Office Assistant for Access 97.

As with all Office 97 products the Toolbar can be customized. To customize the Query Design View Toolbar, select View, Toolbars, Customize.

Prompting the User for Input

At times when you create or edit queries, you might find it necessary to prompt the user for the QBE criteria example. In our previous query example if we wanted to make our query capable of selecting any ShipRegion, we would enter the following into the ShipRegion criteria field.

The brackets surrounding the user prompt causes Access to invoke the User Dialog Box. Figure 29.7 shows the resulting dialog box at run time.

FIG. 29.7
The user enters the example at run time.

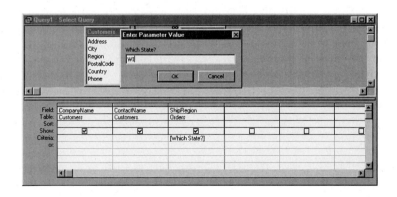

There is no limit to the number of user prompts that can be used in a single query. Prompting the user for information is an excellent way to make your queries more flexible.

Totaling Data

Queries can also perform group calculations based on individual fields. Totaling invoice values, counting customers, and averaging shipment costs can also be very useful. All these calculations are performed in the Total row of the QBE grid. By default, the QBE grid does not contain the Total row. To enable the Total row, select the Totals button on the Toolbar or choose View, Totals. Figure 29.8 shows the QBE grid with the Total row enabled.

FIG. 29.8

By default, the Total row has the value Group by.

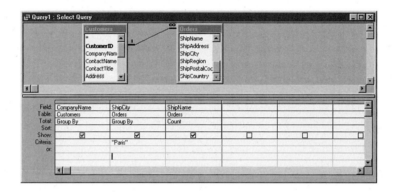

To count the number of orders from the Paris customers, select the drop-down list in the ShipName field and set it to *count*. In the ShipCity criteria field, enter **Paris**.

Figure 29.9 shows the resulting datasheet of this query.

FIG. 29.9

The CountofShipName field tells us that this one customer from Paris has placed four orders.

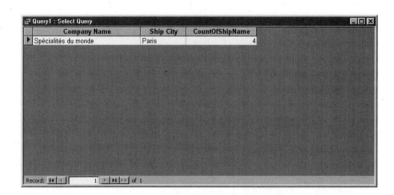

The Total row enables you to perform several operations on your data. Each of these operations is selectable from the drop-down list. The Total drop-down list contains the following values:

Sum	Totals the field values. Works with numerical fields.
Avg	Averages the field.
Min	Finds the minimum value for this field.

Max	Finds the maximum value for this field.
Count	Counts the number of occurrences of this field.
StDev	Computes the Standard Deviation.
Var	Computes the variance.
First	Finds the first occurrence of data in this field.
Last	Finds the last occurrence of data in this field.
Expression	Creates a calculated field.
Where	Uses the SQL Where command.

Sorting Data

Access places the records on the datasheet in the order that they were found. These records can be sorted by using the Sort row on the QBE grid. To sort a name field, for example, in ascending order, select the drop-down list in the sort row for the CompanyName field and choose Ascending. Figure 29.10 shows the resulting QBE grid.

FIG. 29.10

The CompanyName field will now be displayed in alphabetical order.

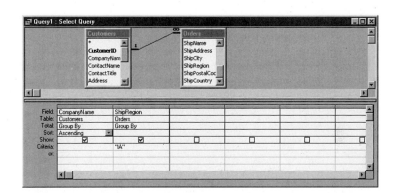

You can select multiple fields for sorting. Access will, by default, first sort the resulting data from the left-most field to the right-most field. For example, Figure 29.11 shows an additional field added to the query.

FIG. 29.11

The ContactName field has been added to the query.

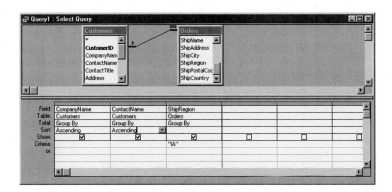

In this query, Access first sorts the resulting data by CompanyName and then by ContactName. The overall sort order is left to right on the QBE grid.

T I P You can change the order of the fields in the queries by selecting a whole column and dragging it to the new location.

Modifying Records through Queries

Action Queries are a group of queries that perform special functions. As described earlier in this chapter in the Query type section, Access 97t uses the following action queries:

Make Table

Update

Append

Delete

Creating an Action Query

To create an action query follow these steps:

1. Create a Select query that selects the records that you wish to manipulate.

2. Change the query to an Action query by selecting desired Action query from the Query Type drop-down list on the toolbar.

3. If a Make Table or Append query type is chosen, Access prompts you for a table name See Figure 29.12.

FIG. 29.12

Enter the name of the table in this dialog box. Notice you can specify another database as well.

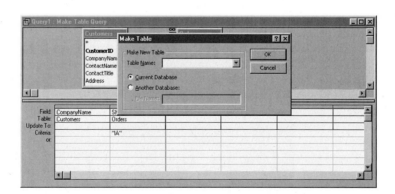

4. Select the Run button from the toolbar to run the action query.

T I P Action queries move and delete data, so they should be well-planned and carefully used to prevent unwanted data loss or data corruption.

Understanding Cascading Deletes

With Referential integrity and Cascade Delete Records selected in the database relationship window, Access can potentially delete data from tables that are not even in your action query. Referential integrity is a set of database rules that helps Access manage related data between two linked tables. Figure 29.13 shows a table relationship with Referential integrity selected.

FIG. 29.13

Referential integrity manages the relationship between these two tables.

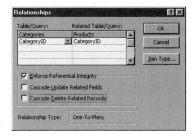

Notice in Figure 29.13 that there is a selection for Cascade Delete Related Records. If this choice is enabled, records deleted via query from the Categories table will automatically have related records deleted in the Products table. This type of relationship is powerful; be careful when performing action queries on tables that are part of a Referential Integrity relationship, or you may delete more records than you intended.

Creating Crosstab Queries

Crosstab queries enable you to cross-tabulate data in a row by column layout. Crosstab queries add another row to the QBE grid. Figure 29.14 shows a query with the Crosstab row enabled in the QBE grid.

FIG. 29.14

The Crosstab row shows, each field's value in the roll it plays in the crosstab.

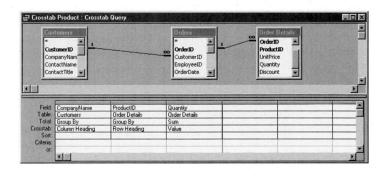

When creating a Crosstab query, you have to tell Access which fields are to be used as row headings, column headings, and summary values. To create a Crosstab query, follow these steps:

1. Select New from the Queries tab in the database window.
2. Select the tables that you wish to use for your crosstab.

3. Drag and drop the fields that you are going to use for the query in the QBE grid.

4. Set any field criteria or sorting that you need.

5. Click the Query Type button on the toolbar and then select Crosstab.

6. Select the field that will be the Column Heading and set the Crosstab setting to Column Heading via the field's drop-down list.

7. Select the field that will be the Row Heading, and set the Crosstab row to Row Heading via the field's drop-down list.

8. Set the Crosstab setting to Value via the field's drop-down list. This field's Total setting must be set to sum or average. Figure 29.15 shows the completed Design view of this Crosstab query.

N O T E   In this example we didn't use the query wizard because the wizard does not allow the use of multiple tables. The wizard requires that a multiple table query be created beforehand to consolidate the data for a crosstab query. ▪

FIG. 29.15

This Crosstab query answers the question: Who brought how much of what product?

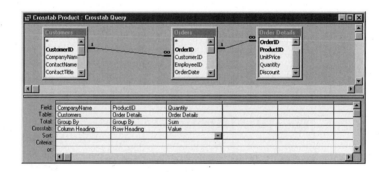

9. Select the Run button from the toolbar to view the results. Figure 29.16 shows the resulting datasheet.

FIG. 29.16

Crosstab queries are a very useful tool to analyze your database.

Product	Alfreds Futterkiste	Ana Trujillo	Antonio Moreno	Around the Horn
Chai				
Chang			20	15
Aniseed Syrup	6			
Chef Anton's Cajun Seasoning				
Chef Anton's Gumbo Mix				
Grandma's Boysenberry Spread	16			
Uncle Bob's Organic Dried Pears				
Northwoods Cranberry Sauce				
Mishi Kobe Niku				
Ikura				
Queso Cabrales		2	74	
Queso Manchego La Pastora				
Konbu		10		20

Record: 1 of 77

A variation of the Crosstab query is to add two or more row headings. Figure 29.17 shows the Design View of a Crosstab query.

FIG. 29.17

This query answers the question: To which cities and states are the products being shipped?

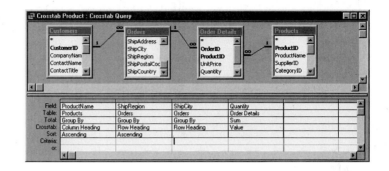

Figure 29.18 shows the resulting datasheet.

FIG. 29.18

Notice that the rows are sorted by state then by city.

Ship Region	Ship City	Alice Mutton	Aniseed Syrup	Boston Crab Meat	Camembert Pierrot
AK	Anchorage	20			
BC	Tsawassen	56	20	50	75
BC	Vancouver				
CA	San Francisco				
Co. Cork	Cork			40	6
DF	Caracas				
Essex	Colchester				15
IA	Albuquerque				
IA	Caracas				
IA	Rio de Janeiro				
ID	Boise	204		82	115
Lancashire	Hedge End				21
Lara	Barquisimeto				43
MT	Butte			10	
NM	Albuquerque	73	4		23
Nueva Esparta	I. de Margarita		70	50	24
OR	Elgin	2			
OR	Eugene				15
OR	Portland				

Record: 1 of 73

CHAPTER 30

Designing and Using Forms

by Scott Fuller and Kevin Pagan

Forms are the user interface part of an Access database. They are what the user works with when entering and editing the database records. It is important that forms be well designed, or even the best designed tables and queries will go under-utilized. Forms are used to collect information from the user, and display information to them. This chapter will help you understand form creation and form design. ◼

Overview of new features

Explore the new features that Access 97 offers for form design and use.

Using AutoForm to create Forms

Explores the use of AutoForm and the three basic AutoForm types: Columnar, Tabular, and Datasheet.

Using the form wizard

Here we examine the full use of the form wizards that are available in Access 97.

Designing a form

We explore the Form Design View window and the toolbar.

Adding controls to a form

We look at the procedures for adding controls to a form and how to work with control properties.

Working with multiple forms

This section looks at the challenges of working with multiple forms.

Overview of New Features

Access 97 has the following form design enhancements over Access 95:

Tab control   You can now create and use Tabs in form design. Tabs enable you to divide an ordinary form into sections that are navigated via tabs along the edge of the form.

Chart Wizard   You can now create 20 different types of charts on your forms to help display information to the user in a more useful manner.

Using AutoForm to Create Forms

AutoForm is a tool available in Access that quickly generates forms. There are three basic AutoForm designs:

Columnar   Places all the fields from the query or table on the form in a top to bottom single column manner.

Tabular   Places the fields from the query or table on the form in a tablet-like manner.

Datasheet   All the fields from the query or table are placed on the form and the form is displayed in a datasheet view.

The following sections explore the creation of these three AutoForm designs. In each section, the Autoforms are based on the same table to help demonstrate the differences in the three AutoForm designs.

Columnar AutoForm

To create a Columnar AutoForm, follow these steps:

1. From the Forms tab of the Database window select New.

2. In the New Form dialog box select AutoForm: Columnar and the table or query from which it will be based. Figure 30.1 shows this completed dialog box.

FIG. 30.1
Choose the table or query from the drop-down list.

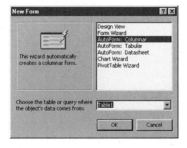

Access generates the Columnar AutoForm. Figure 30.2 shows how this completed design looks.

FIG. 30.2
AutoForm will select the background style based on the style used in other forms and reports in this databas

Columnar forms like this one generated by the AutoForm tool are useful for a quick data entry interface. The order of the fields on the form corresponds to the order of the fields in the table or query. The first field in the table or query is the first field on the form.

Tabular AutoForm

To create a Tabular AutoForm follow these steps:

1. From the Forms tab of the Database window select New.
2. In the New Form dialog box select AutoForm: Tabular and select the table or query from which it will be based.

Access generates the Tabular AutoForm. Figure 30.3 shows how this completed design looks based on the same table used in the previous figure.

FIG. 30.3
The Tabular AutoForm uses the same background and style that is used in other forms and reports in the same database.

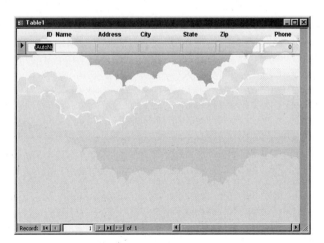

Tabular forms enable you to see more than one record at a time. This can be helpful if you are designing a quick lookup form. The user will be able to see more than one record at a time on the form and will be able to quickly scan through the list.

Datasheet AutoForm

To create a Datasheet AutoForm, follow these steps:

1. From the Forms tab of the Database window select New.

2. In the New Form dialog box select AutoForm: Datasheet and the table or query from which it will be based.

Access generates the Datasheet AutoForm. Figure 30.4 shows how this completed design looks based on the same table used in the previous two examples.

FIG. 30.4
The Datasheet AutoForm
is a no-nonsense kind
of form.

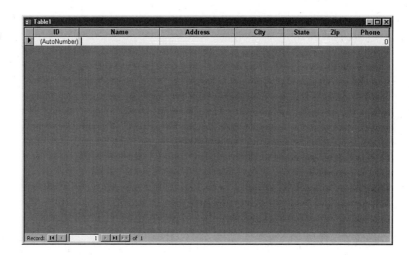

Datasheet forms, as with Tabular forms, enable you to see more than one record at a time. The main difference is the datasheet is just that—a database. There are no fancy bitmaps or layouts, just the data in a datasheet. This can be a good option for users with slower workstations.

Using the Form Wizard

Form Wizards can help you quickly create a form. The difference between AutoForms and the Form Wizard is that with the Form Wizard you can make more decisions during the creation process thereby giving you more flexibility of design. With the Form Wizard, field selection, style selection, form layout, and even the ability to work with multiple tables or queries is given to you.

To start the Form Wizard follow these steps:

1. From the Forms tab of the Database window select New.

2. In the New Form dialog box select Form Wizard and the table or query from which the new form will be based.

3. Select the fields that you want placed on the form.

4. Choose the basic layout of the form. You have the following choices:

- *Columnar.* Fields are placed on the form in a column-like manner.
- *Tabular.* Fields are in spreadsheet-like manner.
- *Datasheet.* Fields are displayed in a datasheet.
- *Justified.* Fields are evenly spread out on the form.

5. Choose the style for your form.

 TIP It is a good idea to keep the same style throughout one database. Otherwise, forms and reports can look misplaced among others.

6. Title your form and select Finish. The Form Wizard creates the form per your instructions.

The Form Wizard creates forms quickly and with more flexibility than AutoForm. However, further customization may still be necessary. The section "Designing a Form" later in the chapter covers editing forms.

Exploring Charts and the Chart Wizard

Access enables you to analyze your database records via line charts, pie charts, bar charts, and several other chart types. These charts can help you more effectively relate the data to the users of you database. The chart wizard helps you to assemble your chart on the form. Before we examine the chart wizard, we look at some basic chart terminology and definitions.

Parts of a Chart

The most important elements of a chart are described in Table 30.1

Table 30.1   Chart Terminology

Term	Definition
Axis	Axes are the lines in a graph along which values are plotted. The *x-axis* is the horizontal line and the *y-axis* is the vertical line. 3-D graphs use a third axis called the *z-axis*.
Series	A series is a set of data plotted on a chart. A line chart with three lines drawn representing three different sets of data is said to have three series.
Titles	Titles are the labels on the various axes and on the entire chart as well.
Tick Marks	Tick marks are the markings on the axis that represent different values on that axis. For example, an axis that represents dollar may have tick marks for every $1,000 along that axis.
Gridlines	Gridlines are optional lines that extend out from the tick marks. Gridlines can make a chart more readable.

continues

Table 30.1   Continued

Term	Definition
Labels	Labels appear at each tick mark to identify the values of the tick marks.
Scale	The scale defines the range of values on an axis and the increments of the tick marks.
Slice	A slice is part of a pie chart that represents a particular series or group of data in that chart.
Legend	A chart legend shows which plot color or symbol is related to which data series.
Floor	The floor is the bottom part of a 3-D chart from which the data series will grow.
Wall	The wall is the back of a 3-D chart. The gridlines extending from the y-axis are found on the wall.

The Chart Wizard

To start the Chart Wizard follow these steps:

1. From the Forms tab of the Database window select New.

2. In the New Form dialog box select Chart Wizard and the table or query from which the chart will be based.

3. Select the fields that you want plotted on the chart.

4. The Chart Wizard prompts you for the information it needs to build a chart. Figure 30.5 illustrates the choices of the chart types available in Access.

FIG. 30.5
The Chart Wizard prompts you for the chart type.

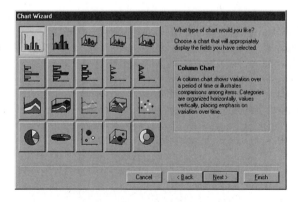

5. After selecting the chart type, the Chart Wizard asks you to verify which field is plotted along which axis and any other charting decisions.

6. Name and save the chart.

Figures 30.6 to 30.9 show some basic chart types plotting the same data.

FIG. 30.6
Standard Bar Chart.

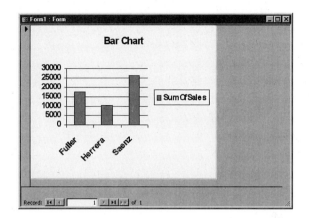

FIG. 30.7
A 2-D Pie Chart.

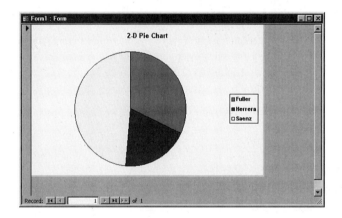

Figures 30.6 and 30.7 are standard two-dimensional charts. 2-D charts can only plot two series of data. The next two figures (Figures 30.8 and 30.9) are three-dimensional charts. 3-D charts can plot three data series. For purposes of comparing the different chart type, all the examples here have only two data series—Salesmen and Sales.

FIG. 30.8
A 3-D Bar Chart.

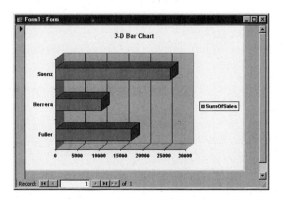

FIG. 30.9
A 3-D Pie Chart.

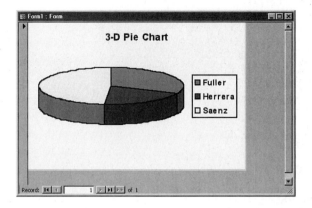

Using Excel's PivotTable Wizard with Access

PivotTables are powerful tools for analyzing large amounts of information. PivotTables are similar to CrossTab queries, but they enable you to dynamically change the columns and rows headings. This makes it possible to sort through large amounts of data on the fly, dynamically switching the columns and rows around to help you see the data better.

To start the PivotTable Wizard follow these steps:

1. From the Forms tab of the Database window select New.
2. In the New Form dialog box select PivotTable Wizard and the table or query from which the PivotTable will be based.
3. Select the fields that are going to be used in the PivotTable.
4. Excel 97 is launched. Figure 30.10 shows dialog box after Excel takes over.

FIG. 30.10
The creation of the PivotTable is a drag and drop process.

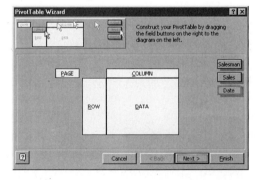

5. Drag the fields to the desired locations on the PivotTable. Figure 30.11 shows the fields Salesman, Sales, and Date dropped into the various locations in the PivotTable Wizard.
6. After selecting next, the PivotTable is ready to be created. Figure 30.12 shows the completed PivotTable.

FIG. 30.11
This example will show
us who sold how much
when.

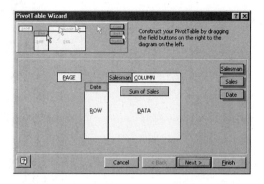

FIG. 30.12
After the completion of
the PivotTable Wizard
control is given back to
Access and the
PivotTable remains an
OLE object in Access.

Sum of Sales	Salesman			
Date	Fuller	Herrera	Saenz	Grand Total
1/1/97		2342	6874	9216
1/2/97	1231			1231
2/5/97	4233			4233
2/10/97			4422	4422
3/12/97			1294	1294
3/15/97			8353	8353
3/25/97	1893			1893
3/27/97		5858		5858
4/3/97	8783			8783
4/9/97			1231	1231
4/25/97		2362		2362
5/15/97	1239			1239
5/30/97			4242	4242
Grand Total	17379	10562	26416	54357

Edit PivotTable

To edit the PivotTable, select the Edit PivotTable button on the bottom of the PivotTable window. Since the PivotTable is actually an Excel OLE object, Excel launches and enables you to change the column and rows in the PivotTable.

 TIP OLE enables Office programs to share data. For example if a datasheet is embedded in a Word document, the embedded datasheet in the Word document is automatically updated whenever it is changed in the database. OLE manages this process of sharing and updating information.

See Chapter 18, "Using Pivot Tables," for more information on PivotTables.

Designing a Form

If you are more experienced in form design or if you are creating a complex form and the Form Wizard offers no time saving advantages, you can create a form by going directly to design view. Once in design view you can add controls to forms and apply formatting from a free hand environment. To enter Form Design View for a new form follow these steps:

1. From the Forms tab of the Database window select New.
2. In the New Form dialog box select Design View and the table or query from which the form will be based.

You can also edit an existing form in design view.

To enter Form Design View for an existing form follow these steps:

1. From the Forms tab of the Database window select the form that you wish to edit.
2. Select <u>D</u>esign.

Form Design Terminology

Before we look at the process of form design, let's examine some form-related terminology.

Field List	Lists the table or query fields that are available to place on the form.
Controls	Controls are form objects that are placed on the form. Examples include: fields, text boxes, command buttons, labels, and so on.
Toolbox	The Toolbox is a collection of buttons for adding controls to your form.
Grid	The grid is the background of the form in design view. It represents the size of the form. Controls are placed on the grid in design view.
Property Sheet	The Property Sheet contains all the properties for a form object or the form itself. A property sheet is divided into the following sections—Format, Data, Event, Other, and All.

Exploring Form Design View

Some basic form creating and editing functions can be explored by examining Figure 30.13.

FIG. 30.13
This in the Form Design View windows with a blank unnamed form loaded.

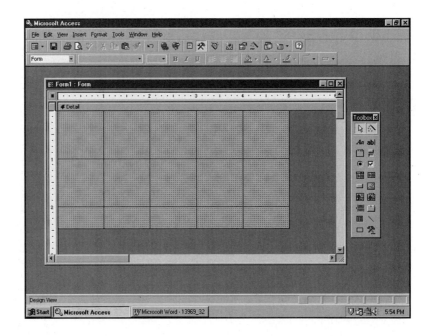

The grid located in the middle of Form Design View window is the size of the form when the form is run. To change the size of the form, select the edge of the grid and drag it to the desired size. Notice that the rulers along the top and the left-hand side help in determining the finished size of the form.

To change the properties of the form itself, right-click the Form Select box that is at the intersection of the two rulers. From this list, choose Properties. Figure 30.14 shows the property sheet for a form.

FIG. 30.14

This property sheet contains all the settings for the form itself.

To change a property on the properties sheet follow these steps:

1. Open the property sheet if it is not already opened.

2. Select the tab for the type of property that needs to be changed. The following is a list and a brief description of the tabs on a form's property sheet.

   Format. This tab has the appearance related properties of the overall form. Some of the Format properties are changed automatically when you resize the form with the mouse.

   Data. This tab contains the data source, default values, and the value ranges.

   Event. Enables you to control what happens when certain event occur. For example, the On Click event determine what will happen when the user clicks on the form.

   Other. This tab is the catch-all category. Certain features such as AutoCorrect can be toggled on or off.

   All. The All tab places all the above categories into one big list of properties.

3. Select the text box next to the property that you wish to change and enter the value. Some properties will give you the ability to launch a Macro or Expression builder. This builder is discussed in Chapter 35, "Using VBA in Access."

4. Close the property sheet and the changes are saved.

The grid that the controls are placed on, by default, snaps the controls in place. This helps in keeping control lined up on the form. Sometimes this control snapping can actually be counterproductive. The controls keep snapping into the wrong place, or you find it difficult to resize a control.

To disable control snapping, toggle the Snap to Grid setting in the Format menu. You can also temporarily deactivate Snap to Grid by holding the Ctrl key while moving or resizing controls on the grid.

Adding Controls to a Form

Controls are the fields, buttons, check boxes, and labels that are placed on the form. Placing these controls onto the form (or grid) is a drag and drop process. The controls are selected from the toolbox and are dropped onto the grid. When a control is selected from the toolbox, the cursor turns into a crosshairs pointer that enables you to set the two opposing corners of the control on the grid. Once the control is on the grid, the mouse returns to a normal selector type pointer. Figure 30.15 shows the Toolbox that is available in Form Design View.

FIG. 30.15

The top two buttons of the toolbox perform special functions and are not controls themselves.

The arrow-like pointer the top left button toggles on or off depending on the focus the window. Toggling the top left button on forces the mouse pointer to select objects.

The magic wand looking button on the top right toggles Control Wizards on or off. Some controls, such as Command Buttons, have wizards associated with them. This toggle button turns these wizards on or off.

Table 30.2 describes each of the default controls found in the toolbox.

Table 30.2	Controls in the Toolbox
Name	**Description of Function**
Label	Enables you to place text on the form.
Textbox	Gives a place to enter or view data.
Option Group	Frames a set of check boxes, option buttons, or toggle buttons.
Toggle Button	Acts as an on/off button.
Option Button	Also called a Radio button, this control can be either cleared or selected by the user.
Check box	Similar to the above, this control can either be checked or unchecked.
Combo Box	Gives the user a list to choose from or the user can enter the text.

Name	Description of Function
List Box	Gives the user a list of choices, only allowing one of the choices to be selected.
Command Button	Runs a macro or a VBA procedure that calls another form, report, or some other automation function.
Image	Displays a picture file on the form.
Unbound Object Frame	Displays a picture, graph, or OLE object that in not stored in the underlying table or query.
Bound Object Frame	The same as above, but the object is stored in the underlying table or query.
Page Break	Creates a page break on the form.
Tab Control	This control has tabbed pages.
Subform	Inserts a form into the current form.
Line	Enables you to draw lines on the form.
Rectangle	Draws a rectangle.
More Controls	Displays a menu of other special purpose controls.

Part

V

Ch

30

As previously mentioned, some of the controls have wizards associated with them. The Command Button is widely used to call other forms. The following steps show how to add a Command Button onto a form and how to use the associated wizard.

1. Select the Command Button control from the Toolbox.
2. Place the control on the form, setting two opposing corners. The Command Button Wizard launches (see Figure 30.16).

FIG. 30.16

The first screen of the Command Button Wizard has two lists. One is a category list and the other is a list of actions under the selected category.

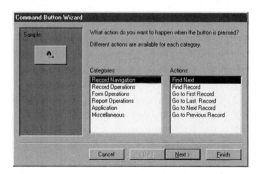

3. From the list on the left, choose the category of the action that you wish to have the Command Button perform.
4. Select the desired Action from the list on the right, and select Next.

5. Enter the desired text label or select a picture for the Command button.

6. Enter a name for the Command Button, and select Finish.

At this point, the Command Button control can be moved or resized to fit the desired location on the form.

Working with Control Properties

Each control has a property sheet. A control's property sheet is very similar to the form's property sheet. Figure 30.17 shows the property sheet for a Command Button control.

FIG. 30.17

The property sheet for a control is divided into the same sections as the form's property sheet.

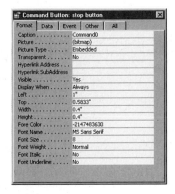

The property sheet is a little different for every control, but the overall layout of the sheet is the same. This makes it easier for new user's to change the property settings. To illustrate this point, Figure 30.18 shows the property sheet for a Line control.

FIG. 30.18

The Data and Event sections exist in this property sheet, but they are blank because a Line control can not hold any data or have an event associate with them.

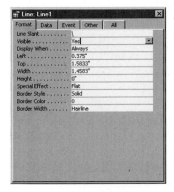

As you can see from the previous figure, the layout of the property sheet for a Line control is the same as the layout for the Command Button. The difference between the two is the Command Button has many more properties associated with it.

To change a property on a property sheet for a control, follow these steps:

1. Open the property sheet by right clicking the control and select Properties.

2. Select the tab for the type of property that needs to be changed.

3. Select the text box next to the property that you wish to change and enter the value. Some properties will give you the ability to launch a Macro or Expression builder. This builder is discussed in Chapter 35, "Using VBA in Access."

4. Close the property sheet and the changes you made are saved.

Working with SubForms

A subform is a form that is within another form. Subforms enable you to create forms within other forms that help to show more information on a single screen. The form that contains the subform is referred to as the *main form*. Figure 30.19 show an orders form that contains a subform.

FIG. 30.19

The details section of the order is actually a subform.

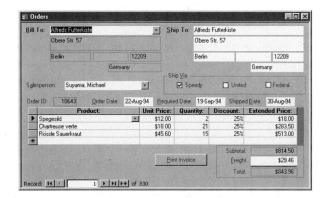

Figure 30.20 show the same orders form in design view.

FIG. 30.20

The subform area is where the subform is placed.

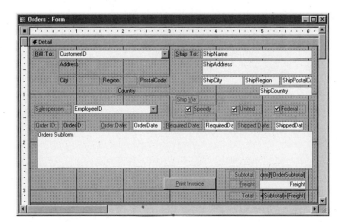

The subform is maintained on its own and is listed in the Forms tab of the Database window. The relationship between the tables underlying both the main form and subform keeps the data on the two forms in sync with each other. Here are some considerations when working with subforms:

1. The underlying tables or queries generally will have a one-to-many relationship. The table or query underlying the subform is on the 'many' side of this relationship and the table or query that is underlying the main form is on the 'one' side.

2. The subform has to be created first and saved before it can be placed into the main form.

3. You can have more than one subform in a form.

4. Subforms can be nested. That is to say a subform can have a subform.

5. You can have only two subforms that contain subforms themselves in a main form.

To create a subform in a form follow these steps:

1. Open the main form in design view by selecting it in the Forms tab of the Database window and select the Design button.

2. Select Tile Vertically from the Window menu. This places the Database window and the Form Design View window side by side. Figure 30.21 illustrates this side by side view.

FIG. 30.21

From this layout, dragging and dropping is much easier.

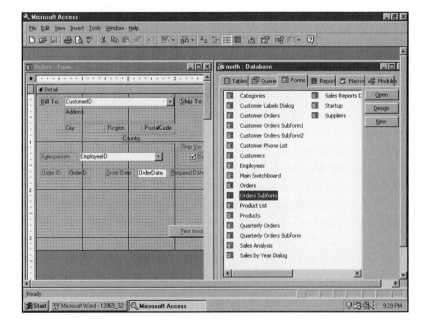

3. From the Forms tab in the Database window drag and drop the desired form that will become the subform to the desired location on the main form.

4. Save and close the main form.

Generating Reports

by Scott Fuller

In previous chapters, you learned how to create your own Access database, import or input data, and query the data. In this chapter, you explore various ways to output your data in reports.

Access reports are especially useful for providing organized data in a user-friendly format. This chapter describes a variety of ways to lay out and create reports. ■

Create reports

Get an overview of Access reports and how they are created.

Create AutoReports

Learn the quick and easy way to create simple but effective reports.

Use Report Wizard and create mailing labels

Explore Access sophisticated wizards that help you create reports and mailing labels that are tailored to your needs.

Customize reports

Briefly look at some of the complex, sophisticated design tools that are available to help you create custom reports.

Publish your reports

When your report is complete, you want other people to see it. Explore how to publish your report in HTML for use on the Internet or via e-mail, and learn other ways to get your report out to those who need it.

Understanding Access Reports

Before you create *any* type of report, you should carefully consider several matters, such as the following:

- Who will use the report?
- What will they use it for?
- What data (both fields and records) must be included, and which must be excluded?
- What types of tables, forms, and queries do I have in my database?
- Do I really need a report (output), or do I need a form (for input)?
- What types of reports are the users already using to obtain this information, and will my new report improve on those reports (or at least not be any worse)?
- Have I talked to the people who will use the report to find out what *they* want?

When you have carefully planned your report by considering all the important factors, you are ready to start work on your report.

Creating Reports with AutoReport

If you need a quick and easy report to produce a plain listing of certain data, or maybe just to start deciding what kind of report you may eventually want to use, consider using Access' AutoReport feature.

AutoReport is really a wizard with no (or few) user options. By using AutoReport, you can create Columnar (or vertical) reports and Tabular reports. Figures 31.1 and 31.2 show examples of each type of report, using the Northwind sample database.

The columnar format of AutoReport allows you to pick a table from which this special wizard places each field on a separate line with the field label printed to the left.

Figure 31.2 provides the same information as Figure 31.1, but uses the AutoReport Tabular feature. If you have just a few fields and want to put as much as you can on a single page quickly, you may find this layout to be useful.

Creating an AutoReport Columnar Report

Using AutoReport is fairly simple. To create a columnar report by using AutoReport, first open the database for which you want the report and then follow these steps:

1. Choose Insert, Reports to access the Reports dialog box, shown in Figure 31.3.

   You can also click the New Object toolbar button.

2. Choose AutoReport: Columnar.

FIG. 31.1

A columnar (or vertical) report created with the AutoReport feature.

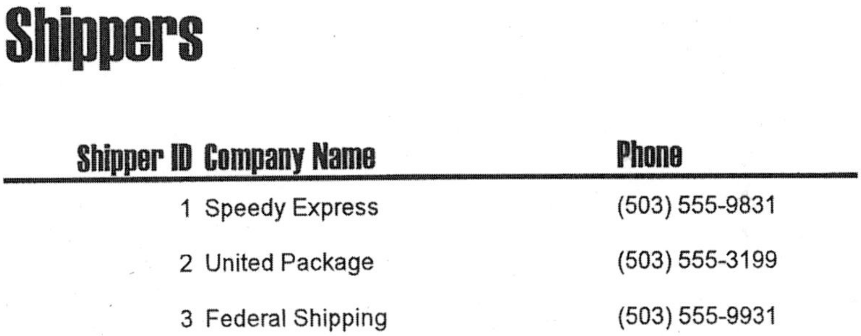

Shippers

Shipper ID	1
Company Name	Speedy Express
Phone	(503) 555-9831
Shipper ID	2
Company Name	United Package
Phone	(503) 555-3199
Shipper ID	3
Company Name	Federal Shipping
Phone	(503) 555-9931

FIG. 31.2

An AutoReport-created Tabular report.

Shippers

Shipper ID	Company Name	Phone
1	Speedy Express	(503) 555-9831
2	United Package	(503) 555-3199
3	Federal Shipping	(503) 555-9931

3. From the drop-down list at the bottom of the dialog box, choose the table from which you want to create the report.

4. Click OK.

   The AutoReport Columnar Wizard creates a simple report for you, as shown in Figure 31.4.

From here, you can use the Design View toolbar button and many other report-editing features to customize your report, as described in more detail later in this chapter. You can also use the File menu to save the report with file name.

Part

V

Ch

31

FIG. 31.3

In the Reports dialog box, you can choose the AutoReport Columnar option.

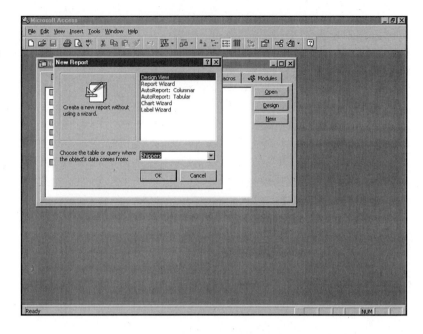

FIG. 31.4

This report is a preview of the report created with AutoReport: Columnar.

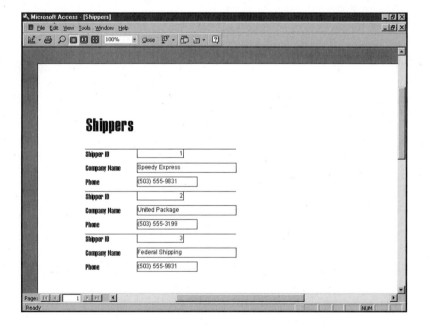

Creating an AutoReport Tabular Report

The steps for creating an AutoReport Tabular report are similar to those for creating a Columnar Report. (Again, be sure that you have a database open before beginning.)

1. Choose Insert, Reports or click the New Object toolbar button to access the Reports dialog box.

2. Choose AutoReport: Tabular, as shown in Figure 31.5.

FIG. 31.5
This time, the AutoReport: Tabular option is selected.

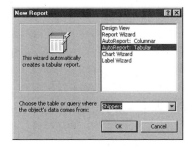

3. From the drop-down list at the bottom of the dialog box, choose the table from which you want to create the report.

4. Click OK.

The AutoReport: Tabular Wizard creates the report for you, as shown in Figure 31.6.

FIG. 31.6
You can customize the report, edit the layout, and so on, using the tools shown in this figure.

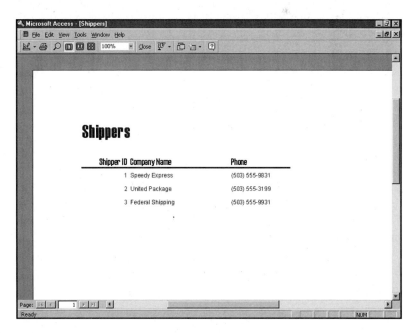

As you can see, using the AutoReport features is an easy way to start creating reports or to create final versions of simple reports. If you want a bit more control of the design of your report, move to the following section, which discusses the Access Reports Wizard.

Using Access Reports Wizard

As with many Office 97 applications, using the wizards in Access 97 can be a quick and easy way to create a useful report. In this section, you look at several types of reports that the Access wizards help you create.

If you have used wizards in any other Office 97 applications, the Reports Wizard will look familiar. The exact procedures that you use depend on what you want your report to look like, the data you want that it to contain, and so on. Following are the general steps for creating a report by using the Reports Wizard:

1. To use an existing table, open your database and click the Tables tab.

2. Select the table that you want to use.

3. If you want your report to include a filter or sort that is associated with the table, open the table in Datasheet view and make sure that the filter or sort is in place. If so, the report automatically includes the sort or filter. Figure 31.7 shows the Northwind database Tables tab with the Suppliers table selected.

FIG. 31.7

The Tables tab of the Northwind sample database is used to create a sample report in the Reports Wizard.

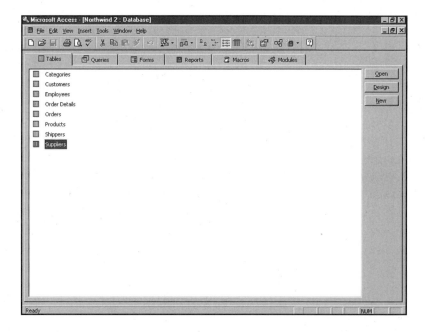

4. If you want to use an existing query to create your report, click the Queries tab and select the query that you want to use.

You can also open the query in Datasheet view.

For this example, use the Suppliers table for the report.

5. Choose Insert, Report or click the New Object toolbar button, shown in Figure 31.8. The New Report dialog box appears.

FIG. 31.8

Use the New Object toolbar button to access the New Report panel. (Notice that the New Object button changes as items are chosen from that drop-down list.)

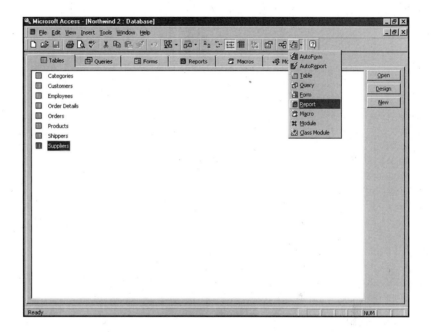

Part

V

Ch

31

6. Select Report Wizard. Notice that the table that you selected is displayed in the drop-down list, as shown in Figure 31.9.

FIG. 31.9

This time, you use the Report Wizard dialog box shown here to create a report.

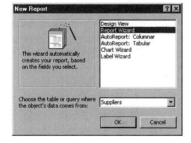

(Notice that in this wizard (unlike the AutoReport feature), you can change your mind about the table or query that you want to use by changing the selection in the Tables/Queries drop-down list.) Figure 31.10 shows what the Report Wizard dialog box looks like before any selections or other changes have been made.

FIG. 31.10

The Report Wizard dialog box gives you choices about the table or query that you want to use and which fields you want to use in your report.

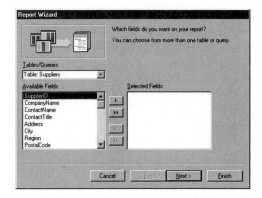

7. Select the fields that you want to include in your report.

   To add one field at a time, click the > button; to add all the available fields, click the >> button.

   To remove selected fields one at a time from click the < button; to remove all the selected fields at the same time, click the << button. In Figure 31.11, a few fields have been added, one at a time, for our report.

FIG. 31.11

Use the Report Wizard dialog box to choose the fields that you need for your report.

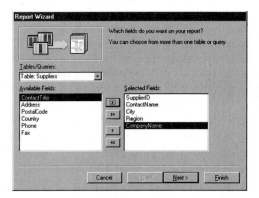

8. After you select your fields, click Next to move to the next series of wizard options.

   The first possible option to appear (if it is needed) is the Grouping Levels dialog box. Using this dialog box, you can group your report by additional levels. You may want to group your company's supplier by region, so that users of the report can tell at a glance which supplier are located in the various regions. Figure 31.12 shows the results.

9. To choose the grouping field, either double-click the field or select the field and then click the > button.

   If you choose more than one grouping field, you can move the grouping levels up and down by clicking the Priority buttons.

After you choose a grouping field, the Grouping Options button becomes active, and you can click it to select the interval that you want to use for your grouping, as shown in Figure 31.12.

FIG. 31.12

Use the Grouping feature to select the Region field to group our suppliers.

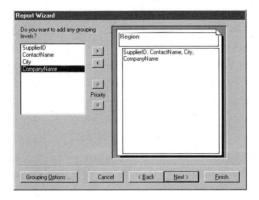

Part

V

Ch

31

10. When you have the groupings to your liking, click Next to move to the Sort Order and Summary Information screen.

In this case, the report is sorted in alphabetical order by the suppliers' company names, as shown in Figure 31.13.

FIG. 31.13

Use the sort order dialog box to sort your report by up to four fields.

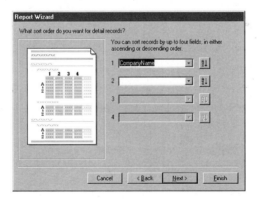

Notice that the sort order dialog box does not have the Summary Options button, because no numeric fields exist in the report. If your report has numeric fields, the box looks like the one shown in Figure 31.14.

If you click this button, a typical Summary Options dialog box appears (see Figure 31.15).

FIG. 31.14

This dialog box has the Summary Options button available because numeric fields were selected for the report.

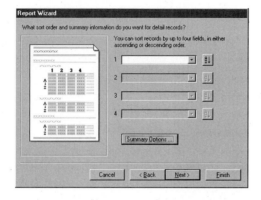

FIG. 31.15

Access this dialog box by clicking the Summary Options button, when it is available. You have summary options for each numeric field in your report.

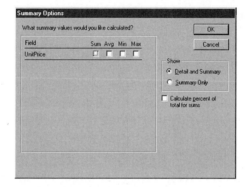

11. When you have your sorts and summaries selected, click Next to access the Report Wizard Layout dialog box.

The appearance of the dialog box depends on whether you selected groupings. If so, the dialog box looks like the one shown in Figure 31.16.

FIG. 31.16

Use this dialog box to choose layouts for a grouped report.

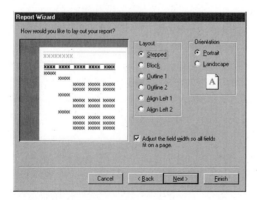

If you do not have groupings, the dialog box looks more like Figure 31.17.

FIG. 31.17
Use this dialog box to choose layouts for a nongrouped report.

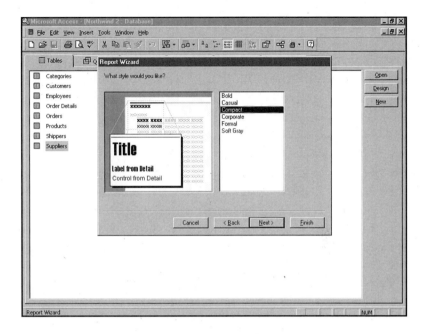

12. In either event, select the style that you want and click Next.

13. Experiment with the available styles, as shown in Figure 31.18.

FIG. 31.18
This dialog box displays the available report styles. The preview window is useful for deciding which one you like best.

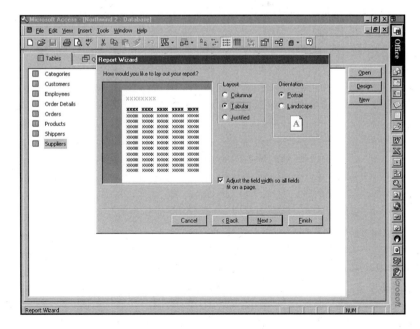

14. Choose the style that you want to use and then click Next.

15. Notice the suggested title and make any changes that you want.

     Keep in mind that this title is used for the report title, the report name in the database file, and the report caption.

16. Click Finish.

     The wizard creates your report (see Figure 31.19).

FIG. 31.19

When all the settings are correct, click Finish in this dialog box to complete your report.

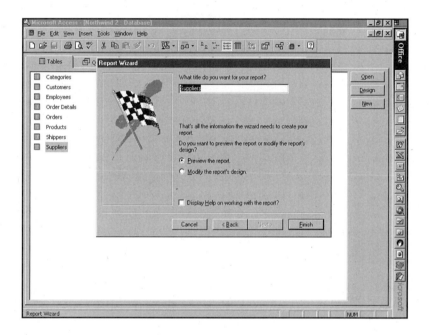

When Access completes the report, the report appears in Print Preview, as shown in Figure 31.20.

From this view, you can do several things with your report, including the following:

- *View the report in a variety of formats.* You can use Design or Layout Preview view to make changes in your report. In addition, you can view one or several pages of the report on- screen at the same time by clicking the Multiple Pages, One Page, or Two Pages toolbar button.

- *Print the report.* You probably want to print your new creation so that you can provide hard copies to certain users. Use the normal Windows printing functions (choose File, Print or click the Print toolbar button) to print your report.

     You see a printed version of the sample report in Figure 31.21. Your report may look different from Figure 31.21, depending on which options you chose.

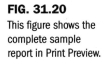

FIG. 31.20
This figure shows the complete sample report in Print Preview.

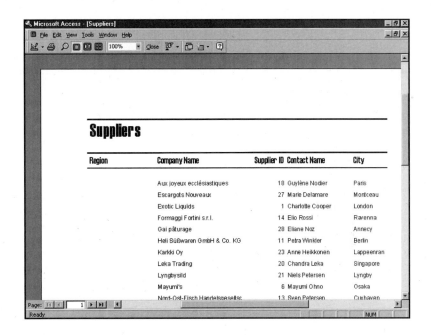

Part
V

Ch
31

- *Send the report to another Office application.* By clicking the OfficeLinks toolbar button, you can send the report to Word or Excel for use in those applications.

- *Publish the report in HTML format.* See "Integrating Documents and Databases" in Chapter 51 for more information on this topic.

- *Send the report via your e-mail system.* To send your report via your e-mail system, choose File, Send. Choose the format that your e-mail system uses, and follow the instructions for sending your report.

Customizing Reports

In the preceding sections of this chapter, you saw how Access' features can help you create nice-looking reports, especially those reports that are typical for most organizations.

At times, however, you may need to modify the standard reports created by the wizards or to create a report from scratch. In that case, Access provides a variety of powerful tools to help you create your reports.

N O T E Creating custom reports is almost identical to creating custom forms. Therefore, if you are already familiar with that process, creating reports is much easier. ■

Although the intricacies of creating complex custom forms are beyond the scope of this book, basic familiarity with some of the design tools may prove to be useful. For more information about form design, refer to Que's *Special Edition Using Microsoft Access 97.*

FIG. 31.21

The printed version of the two-page sample report of the Northwind Suppliers, grouped by region.

Suppliers

Region	Company Name	Supplier ID	Contact Name	City
	Aux joyeux ecclésiastiques	18	Guylène Nodier	Paris
	Escargots Nouveaux	27	Marie Delamare	Montceau
	Exotic Liquids	1	Charlotte Cooper	London
	Formaggi Fortini s.r.l.	14	Elio Rossi	Ravenna
	Gai pâturage	28	Eliane Noz	Annecy
	Heli Süßwaren GmbH & Co. KG	11	Petra Winkler	Berlin
	Karkki Oy	23	Anne Heikkonen	Lappeenran
	Leka Trading	20	Chandra Leka	Singapore
	Lyngbysild	21	Niels Petersen	Lyngby
	Mayumi's	6	Mayumi Ohno	Osaka
	Nord-Ost-Fisch Handelsgesells	13	Sven Petersen	Cuxhaven
	Norske Meierier	15	Beate Vileid	Sandvika
	Pasta Buttini s.r.l.	26	Giovanni Giudici	Salerno
	PB Knäckebröd AB	9	Lars Peterson	Göteborg
	Plusspar Lebensmittelgroßmärk	12	Martin Bein	Frankfurt
	Refrescos Americanas LTDA	10	Carlos Diaz	São Paulo
	Specialty Biscuits, Ltd.	8	Peter Wilson	Manchester
	Svensk Sjöföda AB	17	Michael Björn	Stockholm
	Tokyo Traders	4	Yoshi Nagase	Tokyo
	Zaanse Snoepfabriek	22	Dirk Luchte	Zaandam
Asturias				
	Cooperativa de Quesos 'Las Ca	5	Antonio del Valle Saave	Oviedo
LA				
	New Orleans Cajun Delights	2	Shelley Burke	New Orlean
MA				
	New England Seafood Cannery	19	Robb Merchant	Boston
MI				
	Grandma Kelly's Homestead	3	Regina Murphy	Ann Arbor
NSW				
	G'day, Mate	24	Wendy Mackenzie	Sydney

Region	Company Name	Supplier ID	Contact Name	City
OR				
	Bigfoot Breweries	16	Cheryl Saylor	Bend
Québec				
	Forêts d'érables	29	Chantal Goulet	Ste-Hyacint
	Ma Maison	25	Jean-Guy Lauzon	Montréal
Victoria				
	Pavlova, Ltd.	7	Ian Devling	Melbourne

Figure 31.22 shows some of the available tools for the Suppliers sample report, this time opened in Design view.

FIG. 31.22

This figure shows a report in Design view.

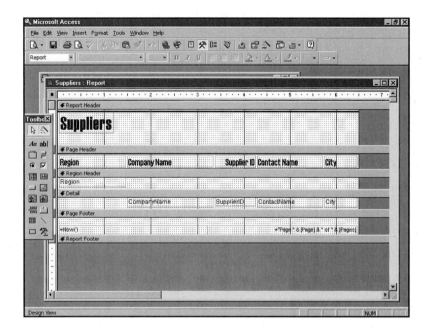

As you can in most layout applications, you can perform a variety of sophisticated functions on the layout of your report. You can drag the field headings to new locations; change the font, font size, color, and other attributes of the labels; and generally redesign the report layout to suit your needs and taste.

You can also use the AutoFormat feature to apply predefined styles to your report. To use AutoFormat, choose Format, AutoFormat; then choose a style to apply to your report.

 TIP You can also customize the AutoFormats from here, so that when you use the Reports Wizard, the styles available to you are those that you customized.

If you want to apply individual styles to only certain areas of your report, you can select only the controls to which you want to apply styles. You select the controls you want to work with by using Select Objects in the toolbox. Click the Select Objects tool in the toolbox; then click any object in the report. You can select multiple objects by dragging the tool over several controls, or by dragging the tool along the left or top borders to sweep a group of controls. Then you can apply the styles to only the selected controls.

In Figure 31.22, shown earlier in this chapter, you can select the Region header and apply a style only to that control.

All the functions that are available in the wizards are also available in Design view. Figure 31.23 shows the Grouping and Sorting functions as they appear in Design view. To access these features, choose View, Sorting and Grouping.

Notice that this figure contains the leftover sorts and groups from previous examples.

FIG. 31.23

This is in the Sorting and Grouping dialog box Design view.

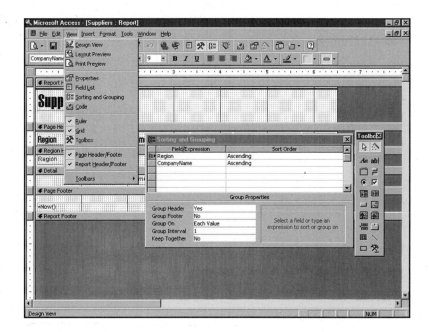

The possibilities of using Design view to create custom reports are almost endless. Try it yourself to get the hang of it.

> **T I P** If you are new to customizing reports, you should start with a report created with a wizard or AutoFormat, just to ensure that the basic building blocks of your report are present.

Creating Mailing Labels

A specialized type of report you can create using the Access Report Wizard is the mailing label report. This type of report allows you to print standard Avery-type mailing labels and further allows you to customize the layout of your labels and perform other functions, such as sorting your label list.

> **T I P** If you use labels other than Avery, you may be able to save some time in designing your label reports by contacting the supplier or manufacturer of your labels. Often, even nonstandard-size labels have an Avery equivalent, and you can use this setting to avoid designing your label reports from scratch.

Creating mailing labels is similar to using the Report Wizard, but with several fewer steps. Again, be sure that the appropriate database is open; then start from the database window with a table or query selected. (You can also start in the Reports window of your database and choose New.)

Click the New Object toolbar button and choose Report from the list that appears. Click the Label Wizard in the New Report dialog box (see Figure 31.24).

FIG. 31.24
Select the Label Wizard in the New Report dialog box.

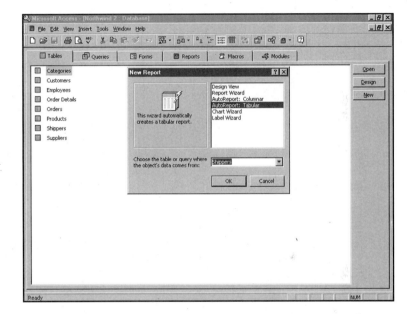

Choose the appropriate label format from the lists (see Figure 31.25), or click the Customize button if your organization uses some other type of labels.

After you select your label type, click Next to select the font and font size that you want, along with color and other options.

When you complete that process, click Next to access the layout portion of the Label Wizard dialog box. Using this dialog box, you can select the fields that you want to use in your labels. In Figure 31.24 earlier in this chapter, you see a typical label layout. Notice that the Prototype label is sized to fit the labels that you chose; therefore, if you can't fit all the fields that you want to use on your label, the label cannot hold all the data.

TIP If your label does not seem to be large enough to hold all the fields that you want to use, try reducing the font size. You can also eliminate some unnecessary fields to make the others fit.

The Prototype label is similar to what you see is what you get format; therefore, be sure that your fields appear exactly as you want your labels to appear, as shown in Figure 31.26.

FIG. 31.25

Select your label size or create your own custom-size label layout.

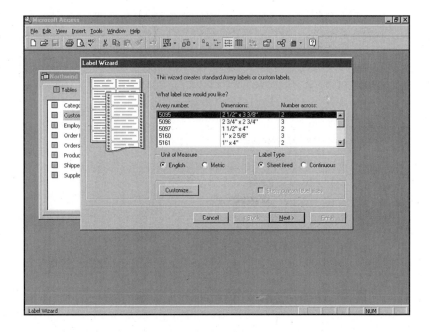

FIG. 31.26

Select the fields you need and move them around to get the label look that you want.

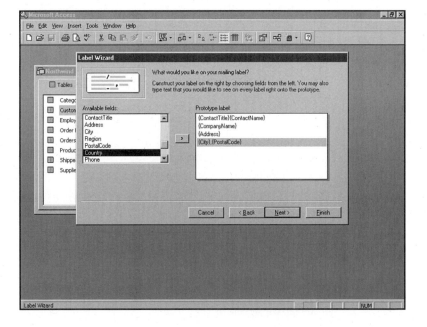

Notice that you can move around the Prototype by pressing the arrow keys. Also, you can type directly in the Prototype if you need to insert characters, such as a comma between the City and PostalCode fields.

Click Next to move to the sort portion of the Label Wizard dialog box. If you want your label report to be sorted, choose the field and sort order, as shown in Figure 31.27.

FIG. 31.27

You can sort your labels in this dialog box.

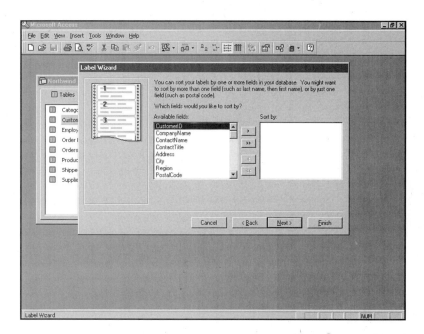

Click Next again and select a title for your label report or accept the default value. Click Finish. Access creates your label report (see Figure 31.28).

FIG. 31.28

This figure shows the complete label report. You are ready to print the report on mailing labels.

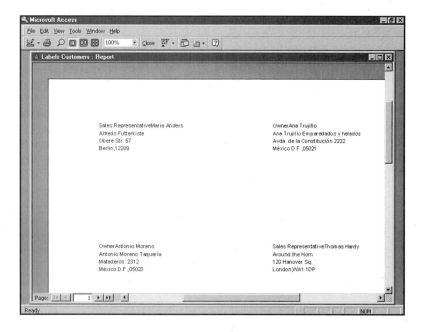

T I P Don't forget to send the report to the correct printer and load the appropriate labels before printing, especially if you have a long list of records to print.

CHAPTER 32

Using Multiple Tables

by Scott Fuller and Kevin Pagan

Access provides three table relationships for you to use. We'll explore these in detail and also focus on the use of relational models. ∎

Relational Models

Learn how to use Relational Database Models.

Table relationships

Explore the three table relationships available in Access.

Building Multiple Table Relational Models

In general, Access tables in a database should contain only fields about one topic. This concept is referred to as being Imperial. For example, a Customer table should contain the fields that are associated with customers (*Name, Address, Customer type,* and so on), and a Salesperson table should contain fields such as *Salesperson name, Employee Number, Department,* and so on. While both sets of fields could function in one table, it would be sloppy and difficult to maintain.

The best way to create a database is to separate data (fields) into tables where they are associated only with other fields that relate to a particular topic. The term *Relational Database* refers to a database with multiple tables wherein each relates to a particular subject or topic.

This chapter explores the three basic models of relational databases.

One-to-Many Model

A one-to-many relationship is the most common type of relationship. In a one-to-many relationship, a record in Table A can have many matching records in Table B, but a record in Table B has only one matching record in Table A.

Figure 32.1 shows a one-to-many relationship in the MS Access relationship editor.

FIG. 32.1
This is a one-to-many relationship and it is the most common relational database model.

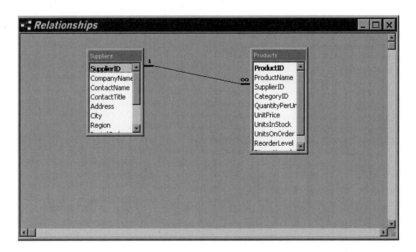

In this example, each one of the Suppliers (One) can have multiple Products (Many). This would follow the real-life relationship between a supplier and the inventory. One supplier may provide several products in the inventory.

In Microsoft Access, a one-to-many relationship is created if only one of the related fields is a primary key or has a unique index. The link in this example is created with the *SupplierID* field, which is a field in both tables, and is the primary key in the Suppliers table.

Many-to-Many Model

A many-to-many relationship is really two one-to-many relationships with a third table. In a many-to-many relationship, a record in Table A can have many matching records in Table B. A record in Table B can have many matching records in Table A. This type of relationship is only possible by defining a *junction* table whose primary key consists of two fields: the key fields from both Tables A and B.

Figure 32.2 shows an example of this type of relationship.

FIG. 32.2
In this example, the Order Details table is the junction table.

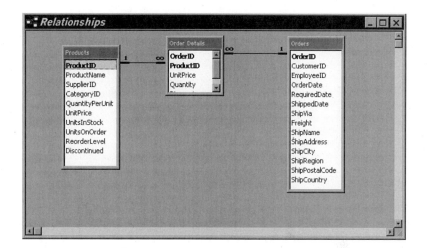

In this example, the Orders table and the Products table have a many-to-many relationship that's defined by creating two one-to-many relationships to the Order Details table. Each record in the Orders table can have many matching records in the Order Details table. This is because each order (one record in the Orders table) will have multiple products sold (each represented by a record in the Order Detail table).

In turn, each record in the Products table can have many matching records in the Order Details table. This is because each product item (one record in the Products Table) will be sold more than once (assuming there is more than one in the inventory), so each product item will have many matching records in the Order Details table.

One-to-One Model

A one-to-one relationship is created if both of the related fields are primary keys or have unique indexes.

A one-to-one model dictates that each record in Table A can have only one matching record in Table B, and each record in Table B can have only one matching record in Table A. Figure 32.3 is an illustration of this type of relationship.

Part
V

Ch
32

FIG. 32.3

The information on the clients is divided into two tables.

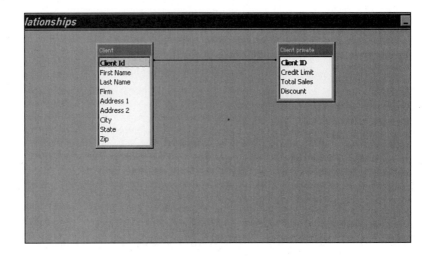

This type of relationship is not very common, because most information related in this way would be in one table. However, one might use this one-to-one relationship model to divide a table for security reasons as in our example. The client fields that are sensitive, such as credit limit, discount, and so on, are stored in a separate table. This enables you to password protect the Client Private table and keep unauthorized users out. The client fields that are not sensitive are stored in another table. This table (Clients) can be accessed by anyone for purposes of mailing labels and the like.

Another reason to use this type of relationship model would be to divide a very large table into two tables. Sometimes when tables contain many fields, dividing the overloaded table into separate tables enhances database performance.

Table Relationships

In Microsoft Access, table relationships are created and modified in the Relationships window. In this section, we will examine each of the previously mentioned relationship types. Because one-to-many relationships are the most popular, we will create this type as the first example in this section.

To create any relationship, you must first open the Relationship window by selecting Relationships from the Tools menu. Figure 32.4 shows the Relationship windows upon opening.

In this example, we will add both the databases shown in the Open Database window in Figure 32.4. Because our employees in the Employee table work in various departments that are represented in the Department table, we will link the two tables. At this point, we drag the field Department Name from the Department table and drop it on the Department field in the Employees table. Figure 32.5 shows the resulting window.

FIG. 32.4

If there are no previous relationships in your database, an Open Database window pops up when you first enter the Relationships window.

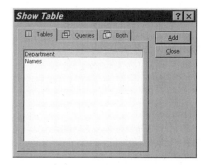

FIG. 32.5

The Relationship Editor pops up after you drag and drop the field.

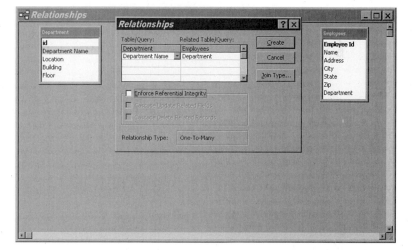

Part
V

Ch

32

Now check off the Enforce Referential Integrity box and click Create. A one-to-many relationship has now been created. Figure 32.6 shows the relationship between these two tables.

FIG. 32.6

Notice that the line between the tables shows the type of relationship that has been created.

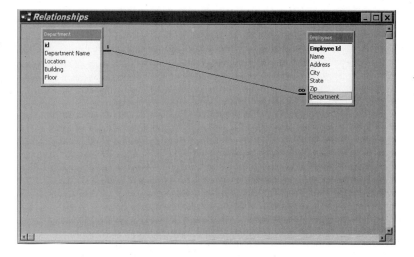

In this example, we checked the Enforce Referential Integrity box. *Referential Integrity* is a system of rules that is particular to Access. This system of rules is used to ensure that relationships between records in related tables are valid, and that you don't accidentally delete or change related data in the database.

Creating a many-to-many relationship requires the use of a junction table. The classic example of this is the Order and Product tables with an Order Details table acting as the junction table.

Figure 32.7 shows the Relationship window with the three tables unlinked.

FIG. 32.7
At this point you link the Orders and the Products tables to the Order Details table.

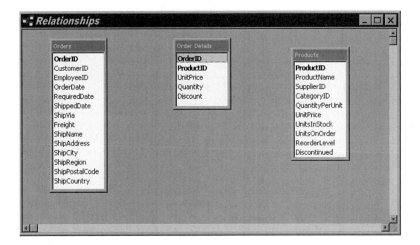

The first step to create this many-to-many link is to link the OrderID field. Drag the OrderID field from the Orders table to the OrderID field in the Order Details table.

Figure 32.8 shows the setting that you would use in this link.

FIG. 32.8
Here are the appropriate settings for a relationship of this type.

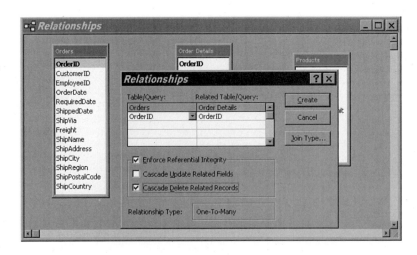

The next step is to create the link between the Products table and the junction table (Order Details). The Product ID field is the linking field. Drag the ProductID field from the Products table to the ProductID field in the Order Details. Figure 32.9 shows the settings for this relationship.

FIG. 32.9
This link also uses
Referential Integrity.

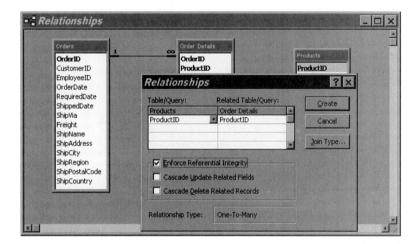

A many-to-many relationship now exists between the Orders and Products tables. Remember that in the junction table both the fields that are linked to the other tables must be both indexed. Figures 32.10 and 32.11 show the field settings for the OrderID and the ProductID fields in the Order Details table respectively.

FIG. 32.10
These are the settings
for the OrderID field.

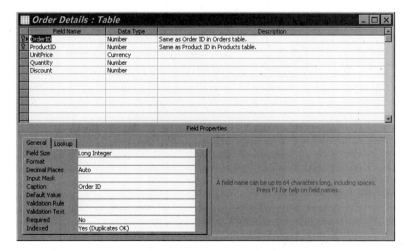

FIG. 32.11

These are the settings for the ProductID field.

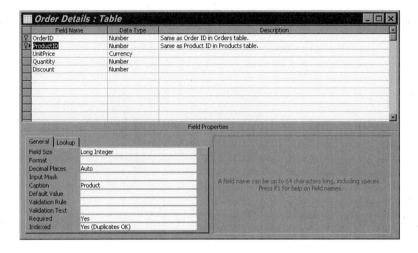

Notice in the previous two figures that both the fields are designated as Primary keys. This is done automatically when Access realizes that the table is a junction table.

The final type of relationship that we are going to explore in this section is the one-to-one relationship. To create a one-to-one relationship between two tables, we will drag the Client ID field from the Client table onto the Client ID field in the Client Private table. Figure 34.12 shows the settings for this relationship.

FIG. 32.12

Select the Enforce Referential Integrity box.

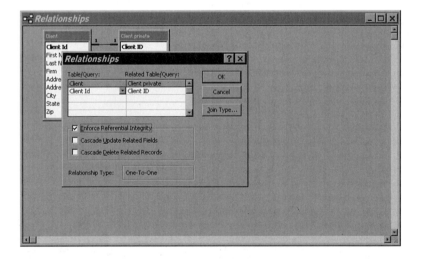

This one-to-one relationship enables you to separate the information on the clients into two categories: public and private. The private table can be password protected to prevent unauthorized access.

Multiple Table Queries

Another way tables can be linked is by using a query. By adding more than one table to a query, you can create a powerful link between the tables. In this section, we explore some queries where multiple tables are used.

In Figure 32.13, you will notice an example of a query that consists of two tables.

FIG. 32.13
When two or more tables are used in a query, Access will display the relationship between the tables.

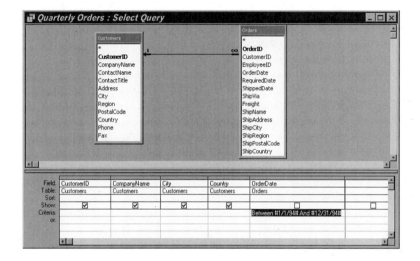

When two or more tables are used in a query, data from any table can be selected or filtered based on selection criteria from any of the other tables. In the previous example, the OrderDate field from the orders table has the following selection criterion:

    Between #1/1/94# And #12/31/94#

This selection criterion will filter the data that both tables will produce in the query to the orders that fall between the dates specified. This is how using multiple tables in a query enables you to create powerful database queries.

In the next example, we will look at a larger multiple table query. Figure 32.14 shows a query with six tables used to bring data from the various tables together to create an invoice.

This query brings the necessary fields from all six tables together to enable you to create a form or a report. The relationships that exist between the tables create the selection criteria.

For example, the CustomerID field links the Orders and the Customers tables together so that for each record in the query the correct customer and order are together.

Part
V

Ch
32

FIG. 32.14
Some multiple table queries are used just to bring related data together from various tables with no selection criteria.

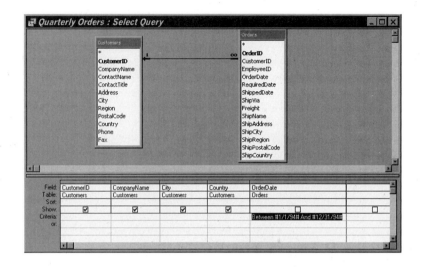

Multiple Table Forms

If your design doesn't call for a query to bring fields from multiple tables together for the purpose of building a form, you can add fields from multiple table to your form. When you create a form, Access will ask you for a form or a query from which to build the form. Figure 32.15 shows this dialog box.

FIG. 32.15
This dialog box will not allow you to initially base your form from multiple tables.

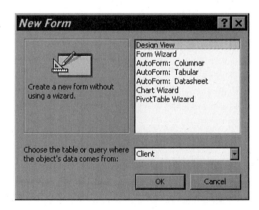

As a matter of practice, you should select the table or query that has the majority of the fields that you are planning to use. After the form is created, you can add fields from other tables via the Expression builder. Figure 32.16 shows the basic form with a text box field being created.

FIG. 3.16
Adding a text box and assigning the control source to a field in another table is a way of linking information to this form.

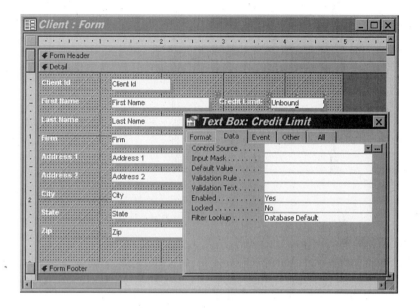

In the Control Source property field, you click the "..." button, and the Expression Builder comes up and enables you to select fields from any table in the database. Figure 32.17 shows the Expression Builder listing the fields from another table in this example database.

FIG. 32.17
The Expression Builder assigns the field to the text box's Control Source field.

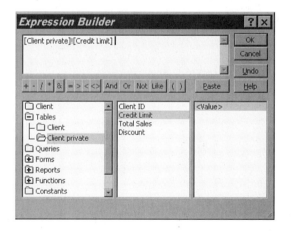

Because the tables in this example are linked with a one-to-one relationship, the link with Referential Integrity will keep the Credit Limit field in sync with the other fields in our form.

Multiple Table Reports

The method of using multiple tables in reports is the same as in forms.

Figure 32.18 show the dialog box that you use to choose the table or query to base your report on.

FIG. 32.18

As with forms, you can only select one table from this dialog box.

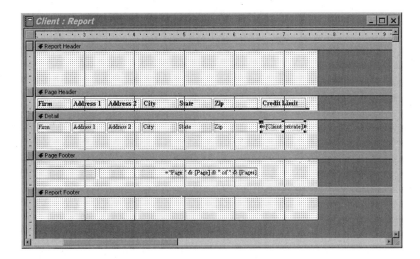

After you have based your report on a table and you have created its basic layout, you create a field on your report and assign its control source to the desired table and field via the Expression Builder.

As in forms, the link between the tables keeps the data in sync. This is assuming that the link uses Referential Integrity. ●

CHAPTER 33

Using Access Add-Ins

by Scott Fuller and Kevin Pagan

Access is a flexible database application. One of the reasons it is so flexible is that Access can "add" small applets and wizards to its default library. These "after market" applets and wizards are referred to as *add-ins*.

Access is shipped from Microsoft with some add-ins of its own. These are specialized tools to help you manage your databases. This chapter explores add-ins and the use and the administration of the add-ins included with Access 97.

To find after market add-ins, search the Internet with the term Access Add-in. This search will produce quite a list of Web sites that will point you to a wide array of Add-ins produced by various independent software developers. ■

Using the Add-in Manager

Explores the use and the purpose of the Add-in Manager in Access 97.

Using the Database Splitter

Explores the need to split a database, and the procedure for splitting a database in Access to improve performance and/or add functionality.

Using the Linked Table Manager

This section examines the use of the Linked Table Manager.

Using the Switchboard Manager

In this section, we examine Switchboards and the Switchboard Manager, including creating and editing Switchboards.

Using the Database Documenter

This section explores the tool that automatically documents the database and gives you an edge in development.

Installing Adds-Ins with the Add-In Manager

Add-ins are actually library files. That is, they are programming libraries that are stored in files with the extension of *.mda*. (Access databases are stored in files that have an extension of *.mdb*.) Access has a tool that helps manage these library files called the *Add-in Manager*.

Figure 33.1 shows the Add-in Manager with one add-in installed.

FIG. 33.1

This particular add-in enables information sharing between Access and Outlook. This particular add-in does not come with Access, but can be downloaded from Microsoft's Web site.

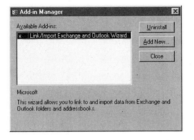

The check mark next to the Add-in indicates it is installed. Add-ins can be on the list of available Add-ins, but can be uninstalled for the current database.

To add a new Add-in to the list of available Add-ins follow these steps:

1. Choose Tools, Add-Ins.
2. From the Add-Ins menu, choose Add-In Manager.
3. Select the Add New button.
4. The Windows Explorer is launched and you can browse for the Add-in that you want to install. Once you find the desired Add-in select it and then select Open.

   The new Add-in is added to the list and is installed ready to use.

Uninstalling an Add-In

Occasionally, you may find it necessary to uninstall an Add-in. This might be necessary because you don't need a particular Add-in's functions for the current database or perhaps you are designing a database for someone that does not have that Add-in available to them. Uninstalling an Add-in does not remove the library file from the hard disk. The Add-in is simply removed from the list of available Add-ins.

To uninstall an Add-in follow these steps:

1. Choose Tools, Add-Ins.
2. Select Add-In Manager from the Add-Ins menu.
3. Select the Add-in you wish to uninstall button.

4. Select Uninstall.

5. The check mark next to the Add-in is removed indicating it is currently uninstalled.

In the previous version of Access, the Add-In Manager was used to customize wizards. This function has been handed over to the wizards themselves in Access 97.

Using the Database Splitter

The Database Splitter is a default Add-in tool to help you divide large databases. For example, you might want to split a database for use on a network. The Database Splitter is a wizard that divides a database into two files—one that contains the tables and one that contains everything else (the queries, forms, reports, macros, and modules). With the tables all in one file, the database performance is boosted.

The advantage of splitting the database is that users can manipulate forms and queries without slowing down the database responsiveness to the other network users.

To run the Database Splitter wizard follow these steps:

1. Choose Tools, Add-Ins.

2. Select Database Splitter from the Add-Ins menu.

3. The Database Splitter wizard will prompt you to make sure that you have backed up your database before proceeding. If you are ready to split the database, select Split Database.

4. Enter the new file name for the back-end of the database and select Split.

N O T E The term *back-end* refers to the portion of the database that houses the data. It is the part the user never sees, at least not directly.

The term front-end refers to the part(s) of the database the user does see, such as forms, reports, queries, etc.

5. The wizard informs you on successful completion.

Figure 33.2 shows a *front-end* database after a back-end file has been created.

FIG. 33.2

This figure shows a front-end database after a back-end file has been created.

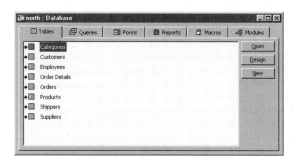

Notice the arrows in front of the tables in the Tables tab of the Database window in Figure 33.2. These arrows indicate that this database is now a front-end database to a back-end database that actually contains the tables.

Using the Linked Table Manager

Access stores all the information about table links in the database. If you move the file that contains a linked table to another folder, Access will not be able to find it, and the link will be broken.

The Linked Table Manager can find tables that have been moved and automatically recreate the link.

To start and use the Linked Table Manager, follow these steps:

1. Choose Tools, Add-Ins.
2. Select Linked Table Manager from the Add-Ins submenu. At his point Access launches the wizard and the following dialog box appears, as shown in Figure 33.3.

FIG. 33.3

This dialog box contains all the linked tables in the current database.

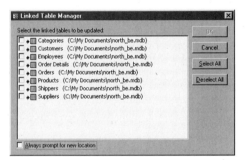

3. Select the tables where you want updated links by clicking the check box in front of the table.
4. As a matter of good procedure, select Always Prompt for New Location to force the Linked Table Manager to request the file locations.
5. Select OK.
6. The wizard will prompt you for a location of the new files with a dialog box. Enter the location of the file that contains the linked table. This step repeats for every table selected in step 3. The Linked Table Manager informs you of its successful completion.

Using the Switchboard Manager

The Switchboard Manager helps you to administer the switchboards in your database. *Switchboards* are the menu-like forms that launch the other forms and reports in the database.

To start the Switchboard Manager follow these steps:

1. Choose Tools, Add-Ins.

2. Select Switchboard Manager from the Add-Ins submenu. Access launches the Switchboard Manager wizard and the following dialog box appears, as shown in Figure 33.4.

FIG. 33.4

This dialog box lists all the switchboards that are found in the current database.

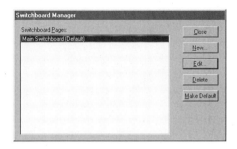

Alternatively, some switchboards will have a Change Switchboard Items button that you can select that launches the Switchboard Manager.

Here is a brief description of the command buttons on the Switchboard Manager:

Close	Closes the Switchboard Manager wizard.
New	Creates a new blank switchboard.
Edit	Enables you to edit an existing switchboard.
Delete	Removes a switchboard from the list.
Make Default	Makes the currently selected switchboard the Default switchboard. The default switchboard is the one that runs automatically when the database first opens.

After selecting a switchboard to edit and the Edit button, the Edit Switchboard Page dialog box appears (see Figure 33.5).

FIG. 33.5

This dialog box enables you to add, edit, delete, and change the order of the items on the switchboard.

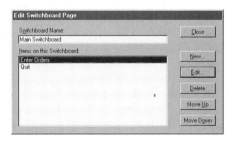

From this dialog box select the switchboard item that you want to edit and select the Edit button. (This process is also the same when you select the New button.) The Switchboard Manager launches another dialog box (see Figure 33.6) with three fields.

Part
V

Ch
33

FIG. 33.6

This dialog box enables you to change the appearance and functionality of the individual switchboard items.

The first field is a text box field called Text. In this field you enter or edit the text or the label that will appear next to the button on the switchboard.

The second field is a drop list field called Command. In this drop list you select the command function that you want this switchboard item to carry out. For example, open a form in edit mode.

The third field, which is also a drop list, is called Form. In this field, you select the form that the command in the previous field will work on.

After all the changes have been made, select OK, and you are returned to the Edit Switchboard Page dialog box.

The buttons Move Up and Move Down move the select switchboard items up or down on the list. The order that they appear on the list is the same as they appear on the switchboard.

Using the Database Documenter

Access has another useful tool called the Database Documenter. Databases have many settings that are located in the various properties sheets of the database, forms, report, queries, and modules. The Database Documenter creates a printout of these database properties and settings, table relationships, field properties, and so on, making it much easier to administer the database and serving as a good hard copy back-up of your database properties.

Documenting the database, while always recommended, can be extra helpful in the following circumstances:

- Handing over a database to another developer to finish the database design.
- If you are taking over the development of a database, and you need to see its current design and properties.
- If you are having problems with the development of the database, it can be very helpful to see the entire list of settings of a database all "spread out" before you.
- After converting a database from an older version of Access, it may be handy to check the properties of the various objects.

To start and use the Database Documenter follow these steps:

1. Choose Tools, Analyze.
2. From the Analyze submenu select Documenter. Figure 33.7 shows the Database Documenter dialog box.

FIG. 33.7

The Database Documenter dialog box is divided into tab sections for the various components of the database.

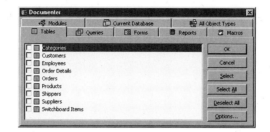

3. Select the tab for the type of database object that you wanted to have documented.

4. Select the individual objects that you want documented by checking off the associated check box.

5. When all the desired objects have been selected, select the Print button to print the documentation.

Part

V

Ch

33

CHAPTER 34

Customizing, Tuning, and Repairing Access Databases

by Kevin Marlowe

After you have a database in place, you may want to consider taking a look at your design and making some modifications to improve the reliability and performance of your system. This process can start at any point in the development process; in fact, modifying the database often helps ensure good design and trouble-free use. Access provides several tools that can help you get the most out of your database and out of the Access environment. ■

Use the Performance Analyzer

The Performance Analyzer inspects the design of each object in your database and makes recommendations as to how it can be improved.

See how to decrease disk space requirements

As you create and delete database objects, the space that Access has allocated for them becomes free, but Access saves room until you tell it to stop.

Use the Repair tool to resolve corruption

In rare cases, objects in your database may become corrupted and cause errors in the operation of your system. The Repair tool fixes some of the more likely problems.

Set Overall options for the database

Instead of writing special code to open a form on startup, prevent users from changing forms, and so on, Access includes a dialog box that sets options for the entire database at the outset.

Consider other performance-related issues

There are several things you can do to improve the performance of your application without the help of automated tools.

Using the Performance Analyzer

The Performance Analyzer tool, new in Access 97, inspects the objects in your database that you specify and recommends changes to improve the operation of your database. Its changes may not necessarily improve the appearance or maintainability of your database, however. For example, one of the Performance Analyzer's favorite suggestions is that you convert SQL statements in code modules to saved queries. While this may improve performance marginally, it certainly increases the clutter in the Database window when you're trying to find a particular query to edit. You have to take the Analyzer's recommendations at face value and apply the power of your developer's intuition to its suggestions to decide whether the recommendations are worth taking.

To run the Performance Analyzer on an existing database:

1. Open the database. From the Database window, click the Tools menu, then select Analyze, and then Performance.

2. You can select any specific object in the database by choosing a tab (Form, Table, Query, Report, Macro, Module) and clicking the check box next to the names of the objects you want analyzed. There are two special tabs:

   - The All tab lists all of the objects in the database in one pane (making it easy to select all of the objects at once)

   - The Current Database tab lists the Relationships and VBA Project objects, which are maintained separately from the user objects but can still be analyzed

   You also can use the Select, Select All, and Deselect All buttons at the right side of the Performance Analyzer window if you prefer. Choose OK to continue after you've selected the objects to be analyzed.

3. The Performance Analyzer runs and you'll see the Analysis Results window On the right side of the window, in addition to buttons for selecting specific problems, is an Optimize button marked; if you select a problem that Access can fix all by itself (like converting a SQL command to a stored query), clicking Optimize will make it happen.

The Analysis Results window (see Figure 34.1) includes a top pane (the Analysis Results pane) that contains a list of identified problems and a bottom pane (Analysis Notes) that gives details on each problem as you select it.

Each problem is marked by one of four icons representing the severity or status of the problem:

Recommendations are solutions for major problems that will adversely impact the operation of the database if not corrected. Access can automatically implement Recommendations.

Suggestions point out less severe problems that should be fixed for optimum performance, but they may have significant side effects to consider. Access can automatically implement Suggestions.

Ideas are general comments about database design that may improve performance, but are not simple to implement. Access cannot automatically implement Ideas.

Fixed items are corrected by clicking the Optimize button after selecting them. If you run the Performance Analyzer again, they won't appear.

While the recommendations of the Performance Analyzer may seem esoteric or to have minimal impact when taken individually, you may see quantifiable results from implementing a group of recommendations. Certainly, there's rarely any reason why you shouldn't take action on a Suggestion as identified by the Analyzer, and you should almost always follow recommendations given as Recommendations.

FIG. 34.1

The results of an analysis of the Northwind database. Naturally, there are no Recommendations or Suggestions to fix.

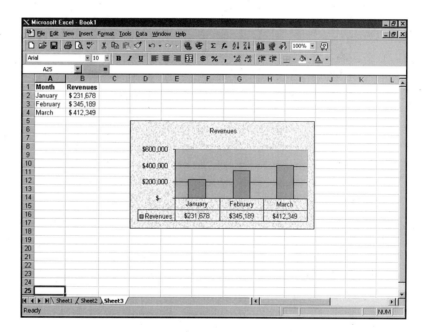

Compacting and Repairing

Databases, like any disk-based program, can sometimes get damaged by the forces of nature and the vagaries of PC architecture. Lost clusters, power surges, network confusion, and small gremlins that live in Windows 95 and NT that feed on programmer anxiety are all to blame; fortunately, Access provides a method for fixing databases that are corrupted by one or more of these things.

The Database Repair tool provided by Access isn't a panacea, however. Its biggest limitation is that it only repairs damaged tables and queries; if a corrupt element in a form or report is making your database act flaky, Repair can't help. For those times when a database application just doesn't seem to be working right, though, Repair may be able to help.

Part
V

Ch
34

A less serious, though related problem, is the issue of database bloat. Whenever you create objects in your database, Access allocates space for them in memory. When your database is saved to disk (as happens frequently in Access), space also is allocated on the disk. When you delete an object, Access reports to Windows that it's done with the memory that object was using, and Windows reclaims available memory from Access. However, the size of your database on disk won't necessarily decrease without some user intervention, because Windows keeps putting the (now smaller) database file back in the same place on the disk, and that place may be too big for the database after a few deletions. When you compact your database, you ask Access to make a copy of it in a new place on the disk, using only the space it really needs instead of the maximum space it's needed in the past.

A new feature in Access 97 enables you to compact and repair databases that you haven't yet opened. The procedures for repairing or compacting a closed database are almost identical to the procedures for fixing an open one.

To compact or repair a database that's already open in Access:

1. Click the Tools menu, then select Database Utilities, then either Compact Database or Repair Database.

2. Access closes the open database and performs the action you selected, replacing the current database in memory and on disk with the fixed one. If you select Repair, you'll see a confirmation message telling you that the database was successfully repaired, even if no errors were found.

To compact or repair a database that's not open:

1. Close any database you have open.

2. Click the Tools menu, then select Database Utilities, then either Compact Database or Repair Database.

3. Access opens a file selection dialog box, allowing you to select a database file and then click OK. If you select Compact, Access opens a second file selection dialog box and recommends db1.mdb as the destination for the compacted database; generally, you'll ignore the recommendation and click the same database file you chose before. Select Save and then Yes when asked for confirmation to replace the file.

4. Access performs the action you selected, replacing the database you selected with the fixed one. If you chose Repair, you'll see a confirmation message telling you that the database was successfully repaired, even if no errors were found.

If you're sure your database is corrupted and you can't fix it using these tools, make a copy of your database and try to figure out which database object is causing the problem, working from the copy. If you have problems consistently while working with a particular object, try to delete that object and re-create it from scratch. If you're using any custom controls (including the problematic Tab control), try deleting those. If all else fails, create a new database and import the objects from the problem database one by one (click the File menu, then Get External Data, then Import from the menu; choose the database to import from and select each object to import). After importing each object, test the new database and make sure it's working correctly until you find the offending object.

Setting Database Options

While the Options dialog box doesn't strictly impact the performance of your database (as measured by its speed or size), it has a great effect on the behavior of the database as you develop your application. It's relevant as a performance issue because setting these options appropriately can significantly ease your development effort, making development faster and more efficient, and the operation of your application more streamlined. Because the amount of time it takes to develop an application may affect the bottom line as much as the actual running of the delivered product, why not optimize the development process?

To view and change Access' options, click the Tools menu, then select Options. The Options dialog box appears with ten tabs pertaining to different parts of the database. Many are self-explanatory (and pressing F1 while the cursor is in a particular pane gives application-specific help), but some highlights of each tab's options are discussed here:

- *View.* The visibility of certain database objects can be changed with options on this sheet. For example, if you frequently create macro groups, you may want the Macro Names column of the Macro Builder visible by default.

- *General.* The default location where databases are stored is saved in a text box on this sheet; if you don't normally save your databases in C:\My Documents, you can change this option to make it easier to load database files into Access. Other options available on this sheet include the default page margins for reports and a toggle to turn sound effects on or off.

- *Hyperlinks/HTML.* The appearance of hyperlinks in tables and forms is set here, as well as the options for database objects saved as HTML. These options are also set as part of the Save as HTML process.

- *Edit/Find.* Several options for searches and filters are set here, but the most useful options to change on this sheet are the Confirm Record Changes, Document Deletions, and Action Queries options. All are on by default, but you can turn one or all of them off here if the confirmation dialog boxes annoy you.

 TIP It's not a good idea to change these options if you're developing a database you intend to distribute, because the options may not be set the same in the users' copies of Access. These confirmations also can be modified in VBA code, which you know will get distributed with your application by using the SetWarnings action.

- *Keyboard.* When users enter a text box on a form, the arrow and Enter keys have certain default behaviors. This sheet enables changing those defaults, which may be confusing to some and beneficial to others.

- *Datasheet.* The default Access datasheet looks like an Excel spreadsheet—black Arial text on a white background, with gridlines separating rows across 1-inch columns. If you prefer gaudy colors and/or fonts and textured cells (a la Quattro Pro?), you can set those options on this sheet.

■ *Tables/Queries.* When you create a table, Access assumes that each field you create is of type Text, length 50. If you change a field to the data type Number, Access assumes it's a Long Integer. If you're creating a table and you know from the start that all (or most) of the fields will be numeric, you can change the default field type on this sheet and save a lot of clicking during table design.

■ *Forms/Reports.* If you're creating a form or report, create a control, and edit the control's properties, sometimes a small ellipsis button appears in the Property sheet. This means that a Builder is available for this property. Usually, you're prompted to run the Macro Builder, the Query Builder, or the Code Builder when you click that button. Most of the time, you want to create an Event Procedure, so you almost always choose the Code Builder. Selecting Always Use Event Procedures on this sheet bypasses that selection process and always starts the Code Builder during form or report design. Other options on this sheet include the behavior of marquees drawn around multiple objects and the default templates for forms and reports.

■ *Module.* The appearance of the code development environment (colors, fonts, and so on) is defined on this sheet. You also can turn off the hints and syntax checking that Access performs by default while you enter code (see Figure 34.2). A useful option, turned on by default, is Require Variable Declaration. This option forces programmers to declare variables instead of letting Access guess as to their data types, preventing potential problems during program execution.

FIG. 34.2

The Options dialog box, opened to the Module sheet. You can customize most aspects of the Access environment with the options available under the tabs in this dialog box.

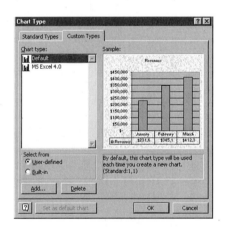

■ *Advanced.* These options concern the way Access handles requests from external applications (using ODBC and DDE) and users connected via a network. You'll rarely be concerned with any of these.

It's important to realize that changes made in the Options dialog box affect only the local installation of Access. If you're developing applications for distribution, or setting up a system for training, you'll probably want to stick with the defaults to prevent the problems that will arise when your database (or customers) use different machines.

Other Performance Considerations

The Performance Analyzer and Repair and Compact tools work well, but they only affect the performance of a specific database. In Access there are several things you can do to improve the performance of your applications. Many of these recommendations are common sense to experienced developers, but all of them can have a real impact on the performance of your application:

■ *Don't skimp on system memory.* Surprisingly, a dearth of available memory will slow your system down more severely than an underpowered CPU will. Access 97 runs quite capably on an older 486 CPU with 32M of memory, but it's a dog on a Pentium Pro with 12M. At this writing, memory is cheap (about $5 per megabyte), and adding memory increases development speed and decreases programmer frustration considerably. Also try to limit the number of applications you run while you're running Access. Access is a resource hog, both for system memory and disk activity. You don't want to try to download an enormous file from the Internet while you're timing an Access application.

■ *Cut down on the glitz.* Background images and bitmaps look nice on forms and reports, but they take time to load and they eat memory like candy. If you use a 1M bitmap as a form background, you increase the size of your database by slightly more than 1M both on disk and in memory. On a 16M machine, a couple of bitmaps can bring the system to a crawl.

■ *Use MDE files.* If your application is essentially finished and you're running it more than changing it, consider saving it as an MDE file. MDE files are the same as normal database files, but Access removes all editing capabilities from them. This "lightening" of the application usually improves performance noticeably, but at a cost—you can't edit an MDE file. Save the original MDB file for modifications and development, and give users the MDE version instead.

■ *Pretend you're a server.* If you're running Windows 95, your machine is probably not configured for maximal use of its CPU and RAM resources. You can make a simple change to help this:

1. Open Control Panel and select the System applet.
2. Click the Performance tab and click the File System button at the bottom of the window.
3. If the typical role of this machine is set to Desktop Computer, change it to Network Server.
4. Click OK twice and close Control Panel.

You can check Access help for many more ideas that may help improve database performance. From the menu, click Help, then select Contents and Index, then type **Performance** in the search box. ●

Part
V

Ch
34

CHAPTER 35

Using VBA in Access

by Keith MacKay

Macros are a mechanism for automating Access. You can connect them to buttons and use them to perform most Access operations. If you wish to work with VBA in Access, Macros can help smooth the transition. By recording a Macro and converting it to VBA, you can often gain some insight into how VBA routines are put together, and which routines to use for particular tasks. ■

Using Access macros

Create, play, and edit Access Macros to automate your work.

Macros versus VBA

There's a time and a place for each—here's how to know which is most efficient for your needs.

Creating VBA code in Access

Create, play, and edit VBA code in Access to take best advantage of Microsoft's standard application programming language—Visual Basic for Applications.

Using VBA in Access reports

Some of the trickiest and most important aspects of any Access system are the reporting modules. A real-world example demonstrates many of the techniques you need to know to automate the process.

> **N O T E**   To help mitigate confusion between Access Macros and VBA macros, we will use capitaliza-
> tion (capital M for Access Macros) and we will avoid using the term *macros* to refer to VBA
> Subs and Functions in this chapter.

Getting into the Macro Design Window

Creating Macros is fairly straightforward. From the database window, click the Macros tab
(see Figure 35.1).

FIG. 35.1

This is the Macros tab in
the Database window.

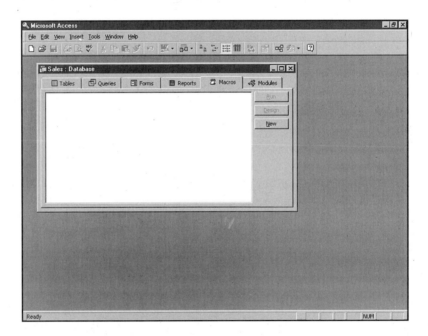

Click the New button on the Macros tab and the Macro design window appears (see Figure
35.2).

Macro Design Window Components

Now you need to use the tools provided in the Macro design window to build your Macro up
from its individual components. You will often find this step goes easier if you tile the Macro
design window and the Database window, as shown in Figure 35.3. To do so, choose Window,
Tile Horizontally, and then resize the two windows as desired by dragging their borders.

The Macro design window enables you to build macros from several different pieces: actions,
arguments, conditions, names, and comments.

■ Actions are the instructions as to what you wish Access to do (for example, print a report
or open a form).

■ Arguments are the settings specific for this action—sometimes referred to as the *parameters* of the command. When opening a form, for example, one of the arguments will be which specific form to open, and another will be what mode to open the form in (Form, Design, and so on).

FIG. 35.2

The Macro design window is ready for macro creation.

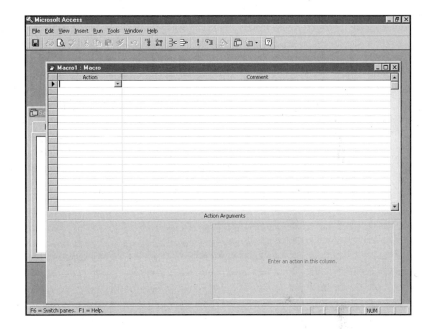

FIG. 35.3

Tiling the Macro design window and Database window simplifies the Macro design process. After tiling them, you can drag the borders of each to make more room for the Macros dialog box.

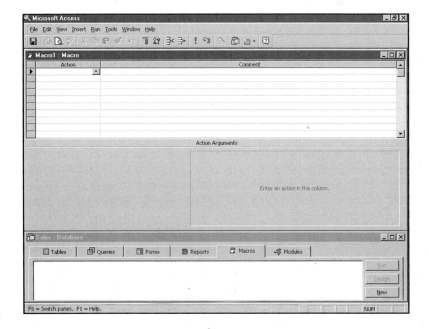

- Conditions are used to determine when a particular Macro (or piece of a macro) executes.

- Names are "tags" for your Macros so that you have a way to call them from each other (to chain them).

- Comments enable you to document your macros so that you remember their purpose when you revisit them later.

We will describe each of these in more detail as we build a macro to evaluate sales performance on entry into our Sales database (file Sales.mdb on the CD-ROM included with this book).

Building Your Macro

All Macros are based on an action. To see the list of all available actions, open the drop down list that appears in the Macro Actions column (see Figure 35.4). You can scroll through this list to select the action you would like to perform.

FIG. 35.4

Select an action from the Macro Action drop-down list.

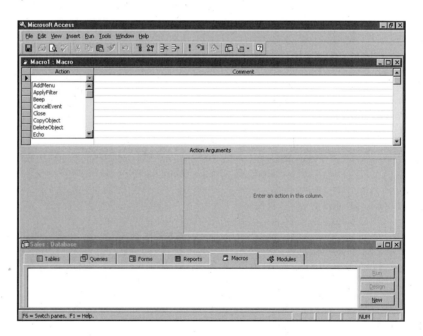

If you know the name of the action that you want to use, you can simply begin typing in the name you want (Access fills in the rest for you). One last alternative for many "open" actions is to drag the object you wish to open from the Database window into the Macro design window. For instance, in Figure 35.5, the Sales form from the Forms tab of the Database window was dragged into the Macro design window.

FIG. 35.5
Access 97 has automatically filled in much of the Macro after the Sales form was dragged from the Database window to the Macro design window.

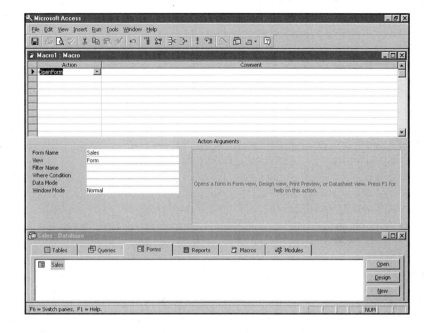

Now let's add a condition to show only our top performers. Click in the cell beside Where Condition and click the ellipsis (…) button to display the Expression Builder dialog box (see Figure 35.6).

In the Expression Builder, type in the phrase:

    [Sales]>50000

and click OK.

 When you need comprehensive information on a Macro action, select the action and click F1 to enter Microsoft Access Help.

Now that you have written your Macro, save it by clicking the Save toolbar button or choose File, Save. This will bring up a dialog in which you can enter a name for the Macro (see Figure 35.7). Call your new macro **SalesOver50K**.

After we discuss how to run your new Macro, we will describe how to create Macros that are conditional.

Playing Macros

You can run your Macro in several ways. While still in the Macro design window, you can click the Run button on the toolbar or choose Run, Run. From the Database window, go to the Macros tab and either double-click the desired Macro name or highlight it and click the Run

Part
V

Ch
35

button. In any case, when you run your new macro you will get a filtered form, as shown in Figure 35.8.

FIG. 35.6

The Expression Builder dialog box, with our expression filled in.

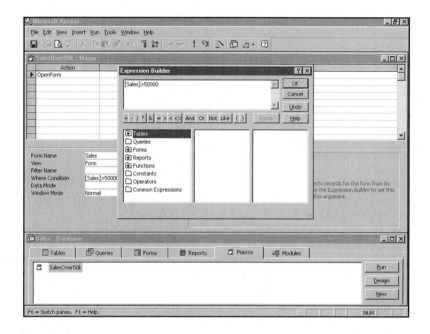

FIG. 35.7

Enter a descriptive name for your Macro. This name will appear in the Macros tab.

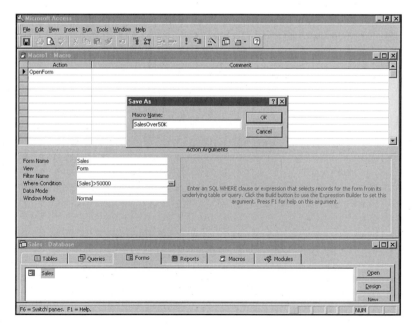

FIG. 35.8
The Sales form has been opened and a filter has been applied to show those salespeople with sales more than $50,000.

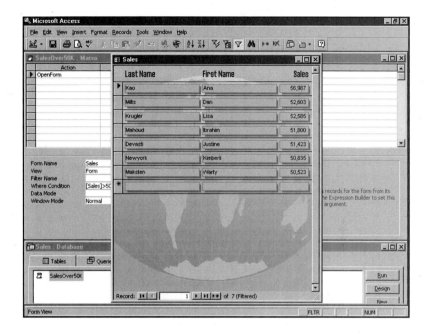

Adding Conditional Macro Code

Conditional Macro code enables you to determine whether a macro will execute, based on criteria that you establish. Now create a new macro that analyzes sales figures as they're entered, and displays a message box depending on the value. If you want to work along with this exercise, load Access database Sales2.mdb from the CD-ROM accompanying this book.

First, write the conditional macro, and then attach it to a button on the entry form. To display conditional information in the Macro design window, select View, Conditions, or click the Conditions button on the toolbar. You will note that the Condition column appears in the window.

In Figure 35.9, we have added the conditional Macro `AnalyzeSales` to analyze sales. Type the macro shown as follows into the Sales2 database (or open the SalesEntry form in the Sales3.mdb database for the final product, containing the Macro and a button to launch it). Note that the message and title for each MsgBox need to be entered in the Message and Title edit boxes that appear in the Action Arguments panel of the window when a MsgBox has been selected in the Action column. The macro should have the following elements entered in the following columns:

Macro Name	Condition	Action
AnalyzeSales	[Sales]>50000	MsgBox
	...	StopMacro
	[Sales]>40000	MsgBox
	...	StopMacro

Part

V

Ch

35

[Sales]<=40000	MsgBox
...	StopMacro

The Message for the first MsgBox should be `Excellent Sales Job!` and the Title should be `Goal Exceeded`. The Message for the second MsgBox should be `Good Sales Job!` and the Title should be `Goal Met`. The Message for the third MsgBox should be `Sales goal not met this month.` and the Title should be `Goal Unmet`.

> **CAUTION**
>
> It is important to note the ellipses on the StopMacro rows. An ellipsis in the conditional column indicates that that row should only be run if the prior row's condition was met. If you leave out the ellipses, the macro will always stop on the second row.

FIG. 35.9

Conditional Macro to analyze sales and provide an appropriate message.

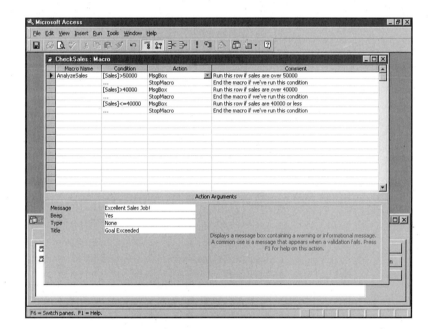

Note that we have also made the Names column visible by choosing View, Macro Names. It is important to note that these names differ from the name under which you save a Macro. The saved name refers to the entire Macro, while the Macro Names column in the Macro design window enables you to name the various different sections of a given Macro (this is analogous to named subroutines in other programming languages).

Attaching a Macro to a Button

Now create a button to launch the Macro. Save the Macro, close the Macro design window, and open the SalesEntry form in Design View (see Figure 35.10).

FIG. 35.10

This figure shows the SalesEntry form in Design mode. We've just expanded the background of the form a bit to make room for our new button.

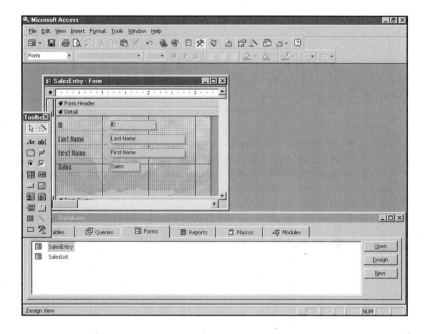

Make sure that the control wizards button in the Toolbox is selected. Click the Command Button icon in the Toolbox, and click the form to indicate where you would like to drop the button. The Command Button Wizard appears, and asks you all the questions necessary to construct your button. The first step is to determine what action is taken when the button is clicked. Select Miscellaneous and Run Macro (see Figure 35.11). Click Next.

FIG. 35.11

Step 1 of the Command Button Wizard.

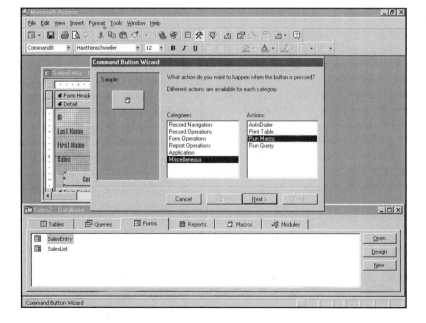

Part
V

Ch
35

The wizard will ask you which Macro to run. Select CheckSales.AnalyzeSales, as shown in Figure 35.12. Note that selecting CheckSales would perform the same task at the moment. However, if you add further Macro names to the CheckSales Macro sheet, it can begin to get confusing. It is best to be as specific as possible. Click Next.

FIG. 35.12

Select the desired Macro (Command Button Wizard, Step 2).

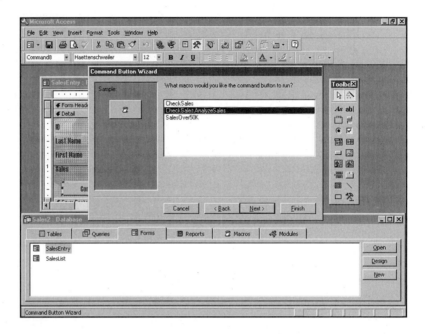

Now select whether you want to have text or a picture on the button. Many users typically use text because it tends to give a clearer description of the button's purpose (see Figure 35.13). If you want to use a picture, you can select from the two default pictures (MS Access Macro or Run Macro), from a variety of other pre-defined pictures (check Show All Pictures), or from graphics files on your file system (click the Browse... button). After you have made your selection between putting text and putting a picture on the button face, click Next.

Now name the button. This step is particularly important if you are planning to manipulate the button under VBA (see Figure 35.14). Many developers use standardized naming conventions for each object available to them for manipulation because it makes their code easier to read. For instance, button names are often prefaced with btn (so a button that generates a sales report might be named btnSalesReport). Click Next.

After naming the button, click Finish to drop the completed button onto your form. Save the form and return to Form View mode. Cycle through the salespeople using the form, and click the button. For those with sales greater than $50,000, you'll get one message (see Figure 35.15), for those between $40,000 and $50,000 you'll get another (see Figure 35.16), and for those less than $40,000 you'll get another.

FIG. 35.13
Select whether to put text or a picture on the button (Command Button Wizard, Step 3).

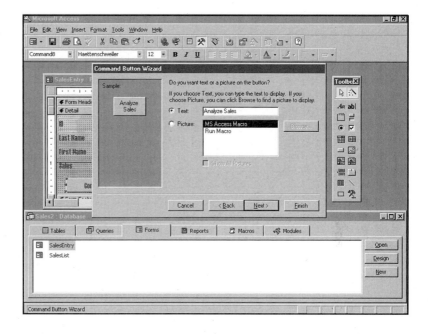

FIG. 35.14
Step 4 of the Command Button Wizard enables you to name the button.

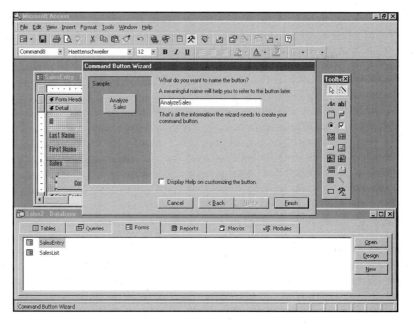

Debugging Macros

If you are accustomed to programming in a visual development environment, Access provides little in the way of Macro debugging tools. It does provide a single step capability from within the Macro design window (switch from the Forms tab to the Macro tab, and from the Run menu select Single Step or click the Single Step icon on the toolbar).

FIG. 35.15

A message from our conditional macro for a salesperson with more than $50,000 in sales.

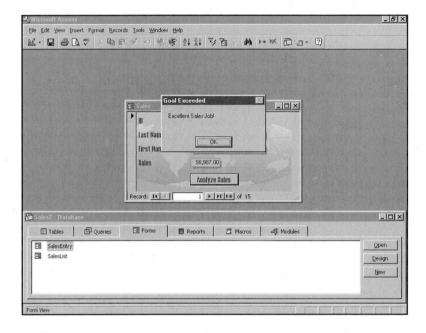

FIG. 35.16

This message shows our conditional macro for a salesperson with between $40,000 and $50,000 in sales.

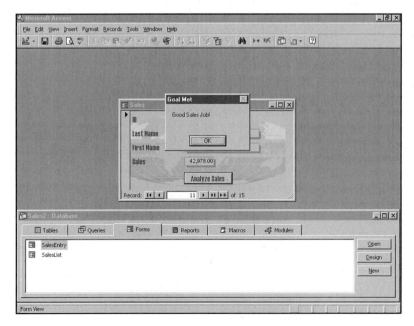

Single-stepping enables you to observe each line of macro code and its effect before executing the next line of macro code. This makes it much easier to determine where a macro is misbehaving. Just single step through the macro and make sure that the expected behavior occurs at each step. After turning Single Step on, note that it stays on within the current Access session until you turn it off again. You can even close your database and open another database—single step will remain on.

Should I Use Macros or VBA?

Macros are great solutions if you do not wish to learn VBA, and if your automation needs consist of performing repetitive tasks that don't require variable storage or information from external programs. If you find that you run up against some walls in your macro system, it's time to move to VBA. VBA gives you much more complete control of Access, and enables a lot more power in general.

Macro Limitations

Table 35.1 indicates a variety of reasons that you might want (or need) to switch to VBA to handle a particular programming task.

Table 35.1   Access Macro Limitations and VBA Solutions

Access Macro Limitation	VBA Solution
No variables	VBA enables variables and parameter-passing
Limited to built-in constructs	User-defined functions, Windows API calls
Can't "walk" a table	Can process a table one record at a time
No transaction processing	Can perform transaction processing
No error-trapping	VBA has error-trapping
Very limited debugging	Module tab has rich debugging environment
No external communication	Automation, DDE commands
Can't create database at runtime	Can create database at runtime
No replication	Replication control under code

That being said, if you want to redefine some keystrokes in your application (for instance, to launch a particular routine when you hit Alt+B), you can only do so using Access Macros. To display a dialog box when the user presses Ctrl+B, do the following:

1. Make the Macro Names column visible (either check View, Macro Names or press the Macro Names toolbar button).

Part

V

Ch

35

2. In the Macro Names column, type **^B**. You must name the macro with the keystroke combination that you want to capture. See AutoKeys in the Access Help index for details on available keystroke combinations and their representation.

3. Select MsgBox from the Action drop-down menu.

4. In the Action Arguments Message text box, enter **Ctrl+B keystroke detected**. In Title, enter **Keystroke Detected**.

In general, it's best to do as much of your coding in VBA as possible. Writing code first as an Access Macro and then converting to VBA is not a terrible approach to get code written in a hurry, though the resulting code will not always be as efficient as code that you write from scratch.

Converting Macros to VBA

Access 97 provides a simple facility for converting Access Macros to VBA. This can prove tremendously useful both for making your existing Access Macros more robust (for instance, you can add error-trapping), and for learning which VBA construct to use to obtain results that you formerly obtained with an Access Macro. To convert a Macro to VBA, follow the following steps:

1. Open the Macro in the Macro design window.

2. From the File menu, select Save As/Export.

3. In the Save As dialog box, select the Save as Visual Basic Module option button and click OK (see Figure 35.17).

FIG. 35.17
This is the Save As dialog box, as used to convert an Access Macro to a Visual Basic Module.

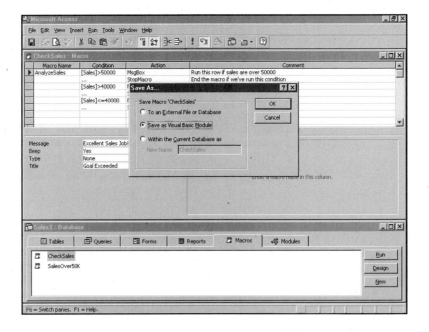

4. In the Convert macro dialog box, click Convert (see Figure 35.18).

FIG. 35.18
The Convert macro dialog box. Select whether you wish default error handling and your comments to be included.

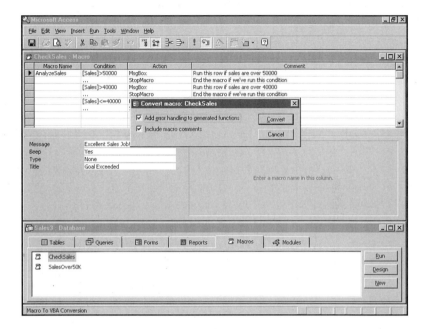

5. When the Macro conversion is complete, click OK and close the Macro design window. Go to the Modules tab.

6. Double-click the Converted Macro-CheckSales module, or highlight it and click the Design button. This will display the converted code for you (see Figure 35.19).

Code as converted in this fashion is not necessarily structured in the best possible way to the task at hand. As an example, you can take a look at the difference in this code as rewritten by hand in Sales4.mdb. Note that in Sales4 we've attached the module code directly to the SalesEntry form's AnalyzeSales button Click event. To see the code, enter the form in Design View, right-click the button, select Properties, select the Event tab, scroll down to Click, click [Event Procedure] and click the ellipsis (...) button. As this is a small routine, the code savings are small. Nevertheless, in a complex system with many routines, the savings can be significant. Also, readability can often be greatly enhanced by using the appropriate coding constructs.

Access VBA Example: Bonus Reporting

Here's a sample application that demonstrates how powerful VBA can be when processing reports. The reporting environment in Access has changed very little since Access 2.0, but the "hooks" into reporting from VBA enable tremendous control.

To walk along with this example, start from the Sales4.mdb database on the CD-ROM accompanying this book.

Part
V

Ch
35

FIG. 35.19

Voila! The Access Macro is converted into VBA.

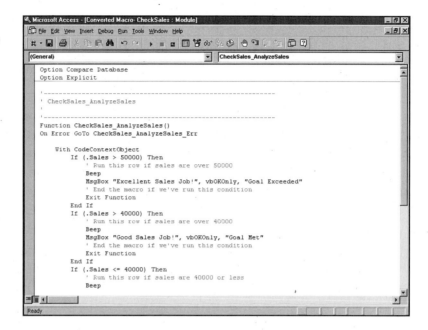

To begin, use the Report Wizard (from the Reports tab, click <u>N</u>ew) to create a tabular AutoReport from the Sales table. A report like that shown in Figure 35.20 will be generated for you.

FIG. 35.20

This is a tabular AutoReport from the Sales table.

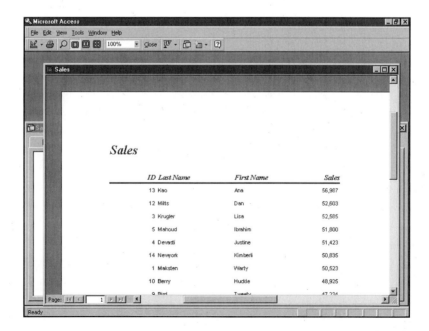

Enter Design view, and add a text box to the right end of the report detail section, as shown (see Figure 35.21). Delete the label control that is attached to the added text box. Rename the report **Sales This Month**, stretch the report header underline far enough to cover your new text box, and add the **Goal Met?** heading.

FIG. 35.21

The sales report in Design View mode, with the new additions.

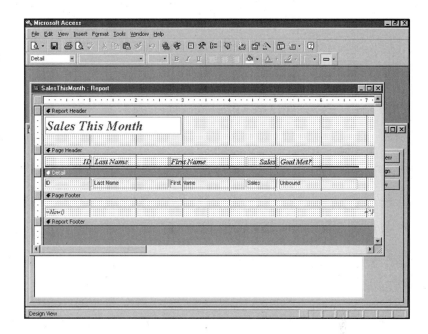

Now, right click your new text box and click <u>P</u>roperties. Go to the All tab, and name the text box **GoalMetMsg**. Close the Properties control.

For this next step, it's important to understand the concept of an *event*. Whenever Access performs an action of any kind, an event is triggered. The whole trick to designing Access code is deciding which event should kick off your code. Add the code, and then we'll discuss what's happening.

Right-Click (click the right mouse button) in the Details header on the report (the gray bar labeled Details) and click Build <u>E</u>vent. Choose Code Builder from the Choose Builder dialog box and click OK. This brings up a new Class Module window (see Figure 35.22).

Note that the module dialog box that appears has two drop-down boxes. The left drop-down box reads Detail, and the right drop-down box reads Format. Below, the shell of a Sub has been dropped into place for you. The name of each routine indicates what object it is tied to as well as which event will trigger the routine. In our case, this routine will run for each Detail row when the Format event runs. In Access, as each row is built to be printed, the Detail_Format event runs. When the row is actually printed, the Detail_Print event runs.

FIG. 35.22

A Class Module window, ready to insert code that operates in response to a report's Detail Format event.

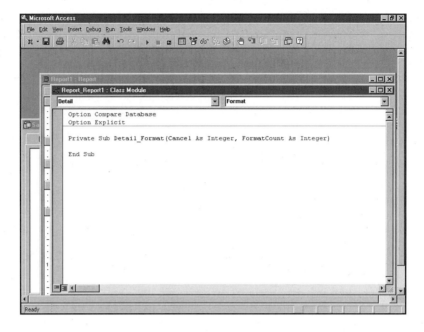

 TIP If you are using events to calculate running page totals, be sure to tie your code to the `Print` event. If the code is tied to the `Format` event, a row might get formatted but not get printed until the following page, resulting in incorrect page totals. The `Retreat` event is fired if a row has been formatted but is not printed.

Complete the `Detail_Format` routine, as shown in the Listing 35.1.

Listing 35.1   Sales5.mdb—Code for the *Detail_Format* Event of the *SalesThisMonth* Report

```
Private Sub Detail_Format(Cancel As Integer, FormatCount As Integer)
    Select Case Me!Sales
    Case Is > 50000
        Me!GoalMetMsg = "Exceeded!"
    Case Is > 40000
        Me!GoalMetMsg = "Met."
    Case Else
        Me!GoalMetMsg = "Not Met"
    End Select
End Sub
```

N O T E   What's `Me` in the routine? For Access, `Me` is shorthand for "whatever object called this routine". As a result, `Me` represents the current Detail row to be printed, and as each row changes, `Me` is reassigned to the new row. ■

Close the Class Module, Save the report, and switch to Report View mode. With just that small bit of code that we've added, you can get feedback on-the-fly as the report is created. This same technique can even be used to change the font style or color of text that is printed. ●

VI

Part VI: Outlook: Beyond the Basics

CHAPTER 36

Outlook Quick Start Guide

by George Lynch

Outlook is a new application that makes its debut with Office 97. Microsoft describes Outlook as a desktop information management program, which it most certainly is. If you've been considering getting a PIM (Personal Information Management) system, you probably don't need to look any further. Microsoft Outlook is a remarkably robust application.

You can use Outlook for a variety of tasks, including sending and receiving e-mail, and keeping and maintaining schedules, tasks and contact lists. Outlook also allows you to keep a journal to track events on a timeline. You can even post the electronic equivalent of those ubiquitous yellow "post-its"® on your desktop with Outlook. ∎

What exactly is Outlook?

See what all the fuss is about. Become familiar with the different Outlook components.

The Outlook interface

Note the different ways you can view and lay out your data in Outlook.

User profiles

Learn how to create and modify a profile in Outlook.

Outlook properties

Understand what Outlook properties are and how to modify them.

Outlook and e-mail

Use Outlook as your e-mail editor.

Understanding What Outlook Can Do

Outlook is a powerful tool for organizing the various types of information that you work with throughout the typical workday. Outlook can be used to:

- Manage your calendar, contact lists, and task lists
- Record events such as telephone calls in a journal as they occur throughout the day
- Send and receive electronic mail
- Schedule meetings
- Record freeform notes

The previous tasks require managing all kinds of different data and storing and displaying them in a variety of ways. The type of information which Outlook manages (for example schedules, task lists and contacts) can vary greatly from person to person.

Even the way you use a single tool such as the Contact List might vary, depending on whether you are using a personal phone list or a business contact list. With a personal list you may decide not to record the company name and work telephone number of someone, while those items would be crucial to a business contact list.

One of the great strengths of Outlook is its flexibility. You can adapt Outlook to work the way you want it to, and have it match the needs of your work environment and your preferences.

Using the Outlook Interface

Because Outlook combines several tools in one, it is important to understand how to select tools and how the menus, toolbars and keyboard functions change when different tools are selected. Like most programs, Outlook has a menu at the top of its window and a toolbar below it. In addition to these standard features, Outlook also has another toolbar located on the left side of the window, called the Outlook bar. Figure 36.1 shows the Outlook bar.

FIG. 36.1

The Outlook Bar allows you to quickly switch between tools.

Outlook bar —

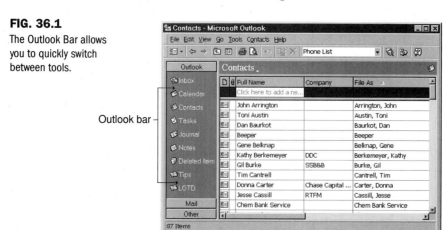

The Outlook bar is used for selecting the Inbox, Calendar, Contact List, and other tools that are combined into Outlook. To the right of the Outlook bar is the Information viewer. When the Inbox is selected in the Outlook bar, the Information viewer shows the list of electronic messages in the Inbox. When the Calendar tool is selected in the Outlook bar, the Information viewer displays the calendar. You can switch between tools by clicking the icons in the Outlook bar.

N O T E You can also switch tools by clicking the <u>G</u>o menu and selecting the Outlook component you want. ▨

When you change between components in the Outlook bar, the menus and toolbar at the top of the window change to match what you have selected. Also, note that the leftmost button on the toolbar also changes, depending on which component you select. If you select Calendar, for example, the button changes to New Appointment; if you select Contacts, the button changes to New Contacts. In other words, the leftmost toolbar button always creates a new item for whatever component you currently have selected.

N O T E The Ctrl+N keyboard combination always creates a new item for the tool that you are currently using. ▨

Views

Each Outlook component has a default "View" associated with it, but you can easily change this view to suit the way you work. A view is the particular display of data for the selected Outlook component. With the Inbox, for instance, you can use the default Messages view which gives you a list of message headers only or you can choose other views, such as "Messages with AutoPreview," which shows message headers and the first few lines of unread messages.

You can switch between views simply by selecting the Views drop-down list on the Toolbar or by choosing <u>V</u>iew,<u>C</u>urrent <u>V</u>iew from the menu and clicking another view (see Figure 36.2). The views available in the list vary depending on the component you have selected.

Different Views of Outlook Components

The Calendar views vary between the traditional grid and day planner views, and various types of tables which filter different groups of schedule items together in lists that can be sorted. You can choose to view Active Appointments, Events, Annual Events, Recurring Appointments or list items By Category.

In the list views, the lists can be sorted in ascending or descending order on any of the fields displayed in the column heading simply by clicking the field heading (clickce to sort in ascending order, click again to sort in descending order).

FIG. 36.2

Change views to find information more easily.

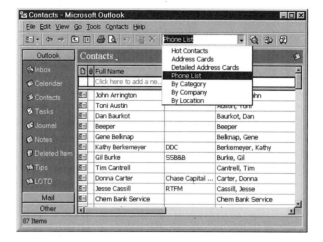

Contacts can be viewed as brief Address Cards, showing only partial information and as Detailed Address Cards showing more information. You can also view a Phone List which displays the name and various telephone numbers in a list format that can be sorted, or views for Category, Company and Location.

The Task List offers a number of different views:

- Simple List
- Detailed List
- Active Tasks
- Tasks for Next Seven Days
- Overdue Tasks
- Tasks by Category
- Only those tasks you have assigned to people (Assignments)
- Completed tasks
- A Task Timeline displaying a listing of tasks arranged on a horizontal timeline showing Start and Due date

In the Journal the Default view is a timeline showing Journal entries By Type. This view groups Phone calls, conversations, e-mail, meeting requests and other types of Journal entries together. In addition, you can select between different views such as grouping By Contact, By Category, Entry List (which is a chronological list of Journal entries), entries made in the Last Seven Days, or Phone Calls.

Notes are displayed as Icons by default, but you can choose to view them in a list showing Subject, Time Created, and Category. You can also view only those from the last seven days, or those organized by Category or Color.

Creating Your Own Views

In each of the Outlook components you can create your own views in addition to using the built-in views. The simplest way to do this is to start with an existing view and modify it.

In the Calendar you could select the Active Appointments view, which is sorted by Start Time in ascending order and change it to sort by subject. To save the current view, choose View, Define View. In the Define Views for Calendar dialog box, select the <Current view settings> and click the Copy button.

This opens a Copy View dialog box which prompts for a view name and offers choices of whether the view can be used on other folders or only the current folder, and whether it is visible to other users (in a network environment with shared folders). After you name and save the view, it is added to the list of views available for that folder. When defining a view you can specify the following:

- Fields displayed
- How items are grouped
- The sort order used
- The view filter (the criteria which displayed items must match)
- The format of the fonts of columns or rows

Introducing the Outlook Tools

You don't have to use all of Outlook's tools to accomplish your work, but they are all available to help you work better and faster. Choose the tools that make your job easier and help you accomplish more. The following sections introduce you to Outlook's tools. Read them and decide which Outlook tools are for you.

Electronic Mail

With electronic mail you can send and receive messages and files over the Internet or a local network. Incoming messages are delivered to your "Inbox," which is shown in Figure 36.3. They are listed in a table which indicates who the message is from, the subject of the message, when it was received, if there are any files attached and if the message has been read.

You can open a message by double-clicking it. This displays the entire message in its own window, which is shown in Figure 36.4. From the message window you have many options. You can simply close the message window, or you can choose to respond to the message, forward it to someone else, print the message, and extract a file if one is attached to the message.

FIG. 36.3

The Inbox displays the messages that you have received.

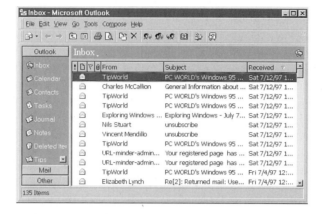

FIG. 36.4

Outlook comes with its own message editor.

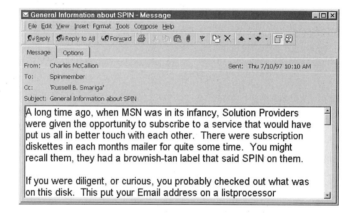

Composing and Sending E-Mail

To create an e-mail message, select the Inbox from the Outlook bar and click the New Message button on the toolbar. This opens a new message window. The cursor will be in the "To:" field and you can type an e-mail address directly in this box or you can click the "To:" button to open your address book to select an existing e-mail address.

If you haven't yet created an address for the person to whom you are sending a message you can click the New button to create a new entry. This is useful if you will be sending e-mail to the same person in the future. You can provide a "Display Name" which can be the person's name, for instance, or, for those people who have multiple e-mail addresses, you can add a descriptive bit of text, such as "at work" or "on the Internet" to the person's name, making it easier to distinguish between multiple entries for the same person.

If the person's name is in your Contact list you can click the name and click the "To:" button to add that person to the list of addressees. If you are sending the message to more than one person, add each addressee in the same way.

TIP You can also add people to the list of recipients of a "cc" or "carbon copy" or "bcc", a "blind carbon copy". (Recipients on the "bcc" list will receive a copy of the message including the list of recipients except for those on the "bcc" list).

You can fill in a subject and then compose the text of your message. When you are done composing the message you can click the Send button on the toolbar. If you are not on a network the message will be placed in the "Outbox" folder until a connection can be made. Once Outlook connects to the e-mail service (either on the Internet or on your local network) the message will actually be sent from your computer.

Outlook allows you to set various options on a message which affect the way the message is displayed when it is delivered. (These options will be effective only on a network using an e-mail system like Microsoft Exchange and when the addressee is also using Outlook.)

The Options tab for the message is below the menu and toolbar, shown in Figure 36.5. Here, you can set the "Importance" to "High", "Normal", or "Low", which will display an icon in the list of mail in the recipient's Inbox. You can also set the "Sensitivity" to "Normal", "Personal", "Private" or "Confidential". You can set flags on messages, by clicking the flag icon in the toolbar.

Choices of flags include:

- "Follow Up"
- "No Response Necessary"
- "Reply"
- "Review"

In addition, you can select a date by which the reply is expected, which will set a reminder for you so you can track whether the requested response has been made.

FIG. 36.5

Message options.

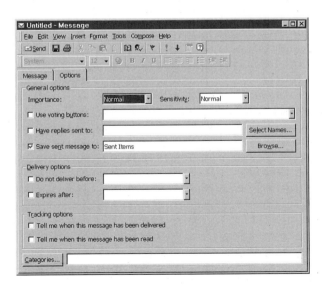

Reading E-Mail

If you are on a computer connected directly to a network your e-mail will be delivered to your Inbox automatically. If you are using Outlook on a computer with a modem your e-mail will be sent and delivered when you check for it. You can specify whether you want Outlook to check for new mail automatically by dialing the modem periodically and connecting to your e-mail service, or you can manually send and receive mail by choosing Tools, Check for New Mail (or press the F5 function key). When the modem connects to the e-mail service provider, your outgoing mail will be sent and any new messages for you will be placed in your Inbox folder.

To read an e-mail message, click the Inbox on the Outlook bar, then double click the message in the message list. This opens a separate window with the entire message, which you can scroll. Once you've read the message you can close the window. It is easy to distinguish unread messages from those you have already read because unread messages appear in the Message list in bold, while those that have been read are not bold.

Outlook allows you to respond to a message while you are reading it. By clicking the "Reply" button on the toolbar at the top of the message window you can create a new e-mail message. Outlook automatically fills in the "To:" field with the address of the person who sent you the original message, and enters the subject of the original message in the "Subject:" field.

> **N O T E**   To send a message that you have received to someone else, click the "Forward" button. A new message is prepared that contains the message that you were viewing. You can then edit the message and enter recipients as you normally would, but without having to retype an entire message.

Your cursor will be in the body of the message, ready for you to begin typing, and the original text will be included at the bottom of your message. If you receive a message which was sent to a list of recipients, you can respond to the same list by using the "Reply to All" button, which does the same thing as the "Reply" button, except the "To:" field includes the entire list of the original message. You can also manually add to the "To:" field, or to the "CC:" or "BCC" field if you want to include other addressees.

> **N O T E**   Sort the Inbox by clicking the Field headers at the top of the Inbox view. The field headers act like buttons and sort the contents of the Inbox when clicked. Clicking a field header once will sort the Inbox in descending order on that field, and clicking the same field header again will sort the list in the opposite order.

Another way of browsing your e-mail is to open a message, such as the oldest unread message, and using the Previous Item button on the Toolbar (or Ctrl + <) to "catch up" by reading your e-mail in the order in which it arrived. Note that the behavior of the Previous Item (or Ctrl + <) and Next Item (or Ctrl + >) toolbar buttons are consistent with the sort order currently selected in the Inbox. In other words, if the Received field of your Inbox is sorted in descending order (most recent messages at top), Ctrl + < moves to the next most recent message. So, if something unexpected happens when using the Next and Previous Item buttons remember to check the sort order of your Inbox.

Filing Your E-Mail

You can file your e-mail in different folders to keep it organized. If you have a message open you can choose to file it in another folder by selecting File, Move to Folder (Ctrl + Shift + V). This displays a list of available folders, as shown in Figure 36.6. Select a folder to move the message to and click the OK button, or you can create a new folder by clicking the "New..." button.

FIG. 36.6

The Move Item dialog box lets you place messages into folders other than the Inbox.

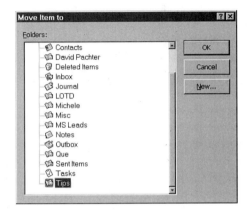

If you choose to create a new folder, the Create New Folder dialog box appears. This dialog box, shown in Figure 36.7, prompts you for a name and location for the new folder. It is usually a good idea to make the folder a subfolder of the Inbox, so that your e-mail is arranged in a logical, hierarchical structure. If you move messages to subfolders after reading them your Inbox will contain only unread messages.

FIG. 36.7

Create new folders to organize your messages.

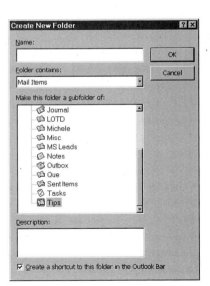

Attachments

In addition to simple messages, files of any type can be attached to a message and sent or received. When you receive a message with an attachment it will indicate the attachment with a small paper clip icon next to the "From" field. When you read the message you will see icons at the bottom indicating the type of file that was sent.

You can save an attachment to the disk by choosing File, Save Attachments from the menu, or you can launch the associated application by double-clicking the icon itself. You can attach a file to a message you are sending by clicking the paper clip icon from the toolbar when you are composing the message, and selecting the file to attach. Note that sending a message with an attachment over a modem can take a long time depending on the speed of your modem and the size of the file.

The Calendar

Use the Calendar, shown in Figure 36.8, to organize information about appointments, events, and meetings. Appointments have Location, Start and End dates and times. When you enter an Appointment, any information on the Subject line is also displayed in the Calendar.

FIG. 36.8

The Outlook Calendar organizes your appointments in a format you are probably already familiar with.

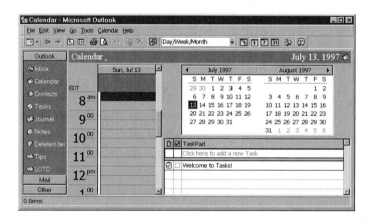

NOTE   If your computer is connected to a network using Microsoft Exchange Server, Outlook can display the free/busy time of the people you want to invite to the meeting, as well as send meeting requests directly to the invited participants. ■

You can view the Calendar in a traditional Day/Week/Month format or by lists of appointments, events or categories of events, appointments and meetings. In the Day/Week/Month view you can choose to see one day, a full week or a full month at a time.

Contact List

Outlook's Contact List can be used to record names, telephone numbers, and addresses, as well as e-mail addresses, fax numbers, pager numbers, World Wide Web home page URL, and a huge variety of other types of contact information. You can also define your own fields of information if the built-in fields aren't adequate for you.

The Address Cards view is the default view for the Contact list. It resembles a personal telephone book, as shown in Figure 36.9. This view includes an alphabetic tab column on the right side to navigate quickly through a large list.

FIG. 36.9

The Contact list has several views, with the Address Cards view being the default.

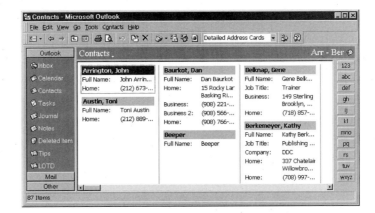

N O T E The contact list can easily be used as the data source in a mail merge with Microsoft Word 97.

Task List

Outlook's Task List, shown in Figure 36.10, allows you to record, sort, prioritize, and track tasks that you need to accomplish. You can also assign tasks to others and track their progress. The task list can show you which tasks are overdue, which are complete, and which are partially complete. The task list can be viewed by itself or in the default Calendar view, integrated with the view of the current day.

The default view of the Task list is a simple list of tasks, including a check box to mark the job complete, the task subject, and the due date. You can change the view to include more detailed information.

FIG. 36.10

The Task List keeps track of items that need to completed.

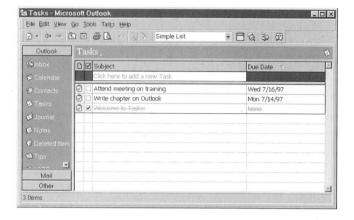

Journal

Outlook's Journal (see Figure 36.11) allows you to record events as they occur, such as telephone calls. You can also set the journal to automatically record events, such as the use of other Office 97 programs and the documents opened, or e-mail sent to or received from individuals in your address book.

FIG. 36.11

Events can be recorded in the Journal to record your actions and track your time.

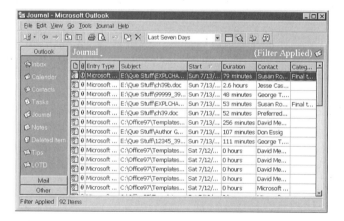

Journal entries can include text and even have files of any type embedded in them. As with the other Outlook components, you can select from a number of different views.

Notes

MS Outlook also has a tool for recording random scraps of information in a freeform manner similar to the yellow paper sticky notes that proliferate on computer monitors in many offices. As shown in Figure 36.12, Outlook Notes are not quite like their paper counterpart. However, like their paper equivalent, these notes can be useful for recording bits of information, but their organization is up to you.

FIG. 36.12
Notes record information that is not easily categorized.

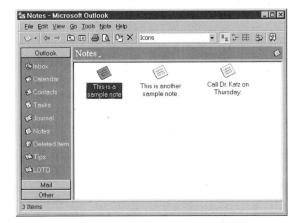

Outlook gives you various ways of organizing the notes that you want to save (by color, by category or by date). You also can search through the notes for a particular word, and you can drag a note to your desktop so you can see it when you start your computer.

File Management

Outlook allows you to browse your file system just as you would with Windows Explorer or My Computer. You can move files from your hard drive to a floppy disk, for instance, or connect to other machines across your network. You can also customize the Outlook bar to include special folders, drives, and icons for other programs that can be launched directly from Outlook with a single click. You can choose to use Outlook as your primary navigational and file management tool instead of Explorer.

Creating and Modifying a User Profile

If more than one person uses the same computer, you can keep separate Outlook configurations for each user by creating separate user profiles. User profiles store the configuration settings for Outlook, so by creating a profile for each user, the computer can be shared without users changing each other's settings. A default profile is created when Outlook is installed, but you can add other profiles at any time.

It is most commonly the case that only one profile is used for Outlook. The default setting in Outlook is to use the default profile setting from the Mail Control Panel program.

Within Outlook you have two other alternatives:

- You can choose to use a different profile as the default.
- You can be prompted for which profile to select each time you start Outlook.

Overriding the default with another default is useful if you have another e-mail program which uses the default settings but is not compatible with the settings needed for Outlook. Prompting the user on startup would be useful if more than one person uses the same system. By asking the user to choose a profile, personal settings can be kept separate from other users.

Creating a New User Profile

The first step is to select the services which the new profile will provide. Specifically, this means the type of e-mail connections that will be supported. One of the main functions of Outlook is to act as an interface to e-mail systems. Outlook can connect to different types of e-mail services, and the information about those connections is stored in the User Profile.

To create a new User Profile, click the Start button, then select Settings, Control Panel and double-click the Mail (or Mail and Fax) Icon. Next, click the Show Profiles button. Choose Add and the Setup Wizard will begin to guide you through the process of creating a new profile.

On a standalone computer, at home or in a small office you will most likely install the Internet Mail service. (If you don't install an e-mail service you won't be able to send and receive e-mail, or to communicate directly with other computers.) You can install the Personal Folders service and you will be able to use the other features of Outlook as a stand-alone system.

▶ **See** "Configuring and Using Microsoft Mail," **p. 744**

▶ **See** "Using Mail from Online Services," **p. 754**

On a computer connected directly to a network, you may be able to use the Microsoft Exchange service (if your network has a Microsoft Exchange Server available). With this service you can use the advanced features of Outlook and Exchange to share certain information, such as Free/Busy time or schedule details, with other designated users on your system.

Once you have selected the services which comprise the Profile, you will be prompted for a Profile Name. You should provide a name which will allow you to distinguish the profiles based on functionality, or based on user name if you are using profiles to keep individuals services separate.

N O T E Check with your network administrator for any configuration information that you are unsure of. ▪

Modifying a User Profile

You can add, remove or reconfigure services for a User Profile by selecting the profile you want to modify and clicking the Properties button. You may then modify settings for any of the existing services or add new ones. For example, you may need to modify your profile if your mail server is changed.

Setting General Outlook Properties

Customizing and configuring Outlook to match the way you work is the key to getting the most out of Outlook. Each of the tools can be configured separately, as we saw in the views. In addition, you can set general options for each component and for Outlook as a whole through the Options dialog box. Choose Tools, Options to open the Options dialog box, which is shown in Figure 36.13. This is a complex dialog box with 11 tabs. It allows you to configure, among other things:

- The way Outlook handles User Profiles

- The services it checks for e-mail

- How it notifies you when new messages arrive

- Default settings for messages you send

- The days and times which Outlook should display as part of the work week

- The events which are automatically recorded in the Journal

FIG. 36.13

Customize Outlook using the Options dialog box.

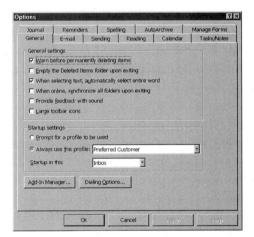

You can set the notification method which Outlook uses to tell you when new e-mail arrives by choosing Tools, Options from the menu and clicking the E-mail tab. You can choose to Display a notification message (a dialog box), briefly change the mouse cursor, or play a sound, or any combination of these methods.

From the Sending tab you can specify the default font and size of text used when you compose a new e-mail message. You can change the default settings for "Importance" and "Sensitivity" which you assign to the messages you send. You can also choose whether you want to receive notification when messages are delivered and when they are opened. These options only work on a local network and can generate many extra messages in your Inbox. You can set these on individual messages for which this information might be useful.

You can select a sound to play when Outlook reminds you of an appointment or overdue task by choosing the Reminders tab and browsing for an appropriate sound file. Reminders of Tasks which are due can be set on the Tasks/Notes tab. This is also where you would set the default size and font of the notes you create.

Use the right mouse button as a shortcut in configuring and customizing Outlook. Right-clicking almost any object or icon will display a menu. If that object can be configured, there will be a Properties item on the menu. ●

CHAPTER 37

Using Message Providers

by Nancy Warner

Outlook organizes your contacts and the electronic correspondence that you have with them. It keeps a record of all messages that you send and receive.

There are a number of different information services that can be used to send and receive e-mail messages. They range from the Microsoft Mail service that is included with Outlook to the mail systems provided by online services, such as America Online or your local Internet service provider (ISP). All of these types of information services can be accommodated by Outlook. ■

Create Microsoft Mail post offices

Create and administer Microsoft Mail post offices, including create mailboxes.

Send and receive messages with Microsoft Mail

Messages can be sent to other Microsoft Mail users in your workgroup. Microsoft Mail provides many options to customize your use of the service.

Use Internet e-mail

Use Outlook with the Internet to send and receive messages to people around the world.

Get e-mail from online services

Use Outlook with your e-mail account from an online service, such as CompuServe or Microsoft Network.

Use Remote Mail

Remote mail lets you preview messages waiting for you by initially downloading only the message header.

Configuring and Using Microsoft Mail

When using Microsoft Mail, messages are sent to workgroup members using a post office, which is located on one of the computers in the workgroup. A member of the workgroup is the administrator of the post office. The administrator creates mailboxes that store messages. Each member of the workgroup must have at least one mailbox to send or receive messages.

Depending on your situation, your workgroup may already have a post office. If so, go to the "Working with Microsoft Mail Service" section later in this chapter. If you do not have a post office, see "Working with Workgroup Post Offices" section in this chapter for information on creating a post office and administering its mailboxes.

A workgroup post office is the file that handles messages sent to users through Microsoft Mail. The post office has at least one mailbox for each user, just like you might have a P.O. Box at a post office. Messages that are sent to a user are placed in his or her mailbox until he or she retrieves them.

N O T E The post office must be in a folder that is accessible by all members of the workgroup. ■

Creating Post Offices

Before creating a post office, create or choose a folder for the post office. Eventually that folder must be shared so that other members of the workgroup can access it. To create the post office, follow these steps:

1. If Outlook is running, choose Exit and Log Off from the File menu.

2. Choose Control Panel from the Settings menu on the Start menu.

3. Double-click the Microsoft Mail Post office icon to open the Microsoft Workgroup Post office Admin Wizard's first dialog box, shown in Figure 37.1.

FIG. 37.1

The first step in the Microsoft Workgroup Post Office Admin Wizard.

4. Click the Create a new Workgroup Post office option button and click the Next button. Figure 37.2 shows the next dialog box in the wizard.

FIG. 37.2
A folder's path must be
provided for the post
office's location.

CAUTION

Click the Cancel button if a post office location appears in the dialog box shown in Figure 37.2. A value only shows up here if a post office already exists.

---

5. Type in the path of the folder to contain the post office or click the Browse button to use the Browse for Post office dialog box to select a folder.

   ▶ **See** "Sharing Peer Resources," **p. 1077**

6. Click the Next button to go to the next dialog box of the wizard, shown in Figure 37.3. This dialog box shows the post office's location.

FIG. 37.3
The dialog box displays
the name generated
for the post office folder.

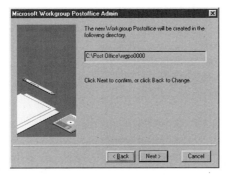

7. Click the Next button to accept the location of the post office and open the Enter Your Administrator Account Details dialog box, shown in Figure 37.4.

8. Enter your name and other information in the Enter Your Administrator Account Details dialog box, including a name for the administrator's mailbox and a new password.

 TIP   Don't use a name that relates the administrator's mailbox to you. Use a name such as admin so that you can have your own mailbox. That way it's easy to keep your personal mail separate from administrative mail.

FIG. 37.4

Mailboxes store information about their user.

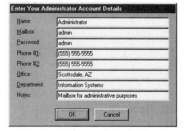

CAUTION

If you forget the administrator's mailbox name or password, you can no longer administer the post office and have to create a new post office. Remember that you can only have one post office.

9. Click the OK button to complete the process of creating a workgroup post office.

Adding Post Office Mailboxes

After the post office is created, the next step is to create mailboxes for members of the workgroup. To create mailboxes, follow these steps:

1. Choose Control Panel from the Settings menu on the Start menu.

2. Double-click the Microsoft Mail Post office icon to open the Microsoft Workgroup Post office Admin Wizard's first dialog box, shown in Figure 37.1.

3. Click the Administer an Existing Workgroup Post office option button and click the Next button.

4. Click the Next button in the dialog box that appears if the location of the post office is correct. Figure 37.5 shows the dialog box that appears next.

FIG. 37.5

You must know the administrator's mailbox name and password to administer a post office.

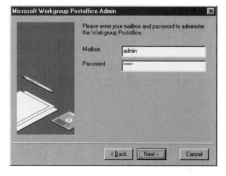

5. Enter the mailbox name and password for the administrator's account and click the Next button to open the Post Office Manager, shown in Figure 37.6.

FIG. 37.6

Mailboxes are controlled in the Post Office Manager.

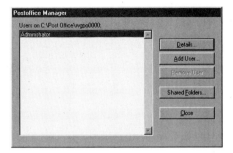

6. Click the Add User button to display the Add User dialog box shown in Figure 37.7.

FIG. 37.7

The Add User dialog box should look familiar.

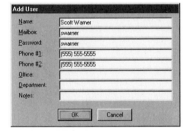

7. Enter the information for a user and click the OK button to create their mailbox.

 Use a combination of a user's name or other information to name their mailbox. Initially, assign all users the same password or use a system similar to the one suggested previously. Then, tell users to change their passwords as soon as they can. That way, only they know their password.

8. Repeat steps 6 and 7 as many times as necessary and click the Close button when finished.

Modifying and Deleting Post Office Mailboxes

After creating post office mailboxes, you may need to modify or delete some of the mailboxes for various reasons. For example, a phone number might change or someone might leave your workgroup. To modify or delete mailboxes, follow these steps:

1. Follow steps 1 through 5 in the "Adding Post Office Mailboxes" section to open the Post office Manager. Figure 37.8 shows the Post Office Manager with several mailboxes listed.

2. Select the mailbox that you want to modify or delete.

3. Click the Details button to view the information for the selected mailbox. The dialog box shown in Figure 37.7 appears.

Part

VI

Ch

37

FIG. 37.8

All mailboxes are listed in the Post Office Manager.

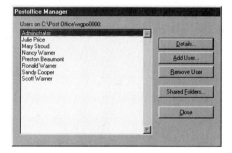

NOTE To delete the selected mailbox, click the Remove User button and click the Yes button in the confirmation dialog box that appears. ▇

  4. Make your changes to the information for the mailbox and click the OK button to accept them.

  5. Click the Close button to close the Post Office Manager.

 TIP You cannot view the password for a mailbox in the Details dialog box because it appears as a group of asterisks. However, if a user forgets their password, you can give them a new one by deleting the asterisks and entering a new password.

Working with Microsoft Mail Service

Creating a post office gives everyone a place to send and receive messages. To use the post office, each user must add the Microsoft Mail service to their Outlook profile—if it is not installed already. After the Microsoft Mail service is added to a user's profile, it can be configured for that user's needs.

▶ **See** "Creating and Modifying a User Profile," **p. 739**

▶ **See** "Setting General Outlook Properties," **p. 741**

Adding Microsoft Mail Service

Users can send messages to other users and receive messages from other users after adding the Microsoft Mail service to their profiles. To add the Microsoft Mail service to a profile, follow these steps:

  1. Start Outlook.

  2. Choose Services from the Tools menu to open the Services dialog box, shown in Figure 37.9.

  3. Click the Add button to open the Add Service to Profile dialog box, shown in Figure 37.10.

FIG. 37.9
Services are added in the Services dialog box.

FIG. 37.10
Many different services can be added to a profile.

4. Select Microsoft Mail in the Add Service to Profile dialog box and click the OK button. The service is added to the profile and the Microsoft Mail dialog box is opened. The "Configuring Microsoft Mail Service" section discusses how to use the Microsoft Mail dialog box.

Configuring Microsoft Mail Service

Microsoft Mail has many configuration options. These options control the behavior of Outlook when working with Microsoft Mail messages. The following sections review the different options that are used when connecting to a post office on a local machine. To open the Microsoft Mail dialog box, choose Services from the Tools menu and double-click the Microsoft Mail service. Click OK to save any changes that you make and close the dialog box.

> **CAUTION**
> Clicking the Apply button saves all of the changes that have been made in the Microsoft Mail dialog box to that point. Clicking the Cancel button does not reverse the changes.

Configuring Microsoft Mail Connection

Click the Microsoft Mail dialog box's Connection tab to set the location of the post office and how to connect to it. Figure 37.11 shows the Connection page.

Enter the location of the post office in the edit box. You can either type it in or click the Browse button to specify it. Select the Automatically Sense LAN or Remote option to cause Outlook to determine the method to connect to the post office and automatically search for it. If Outlook can't connect to a post office, it prompts you for the location.

FIG. 37.11

The post office can be local or on a remote network.

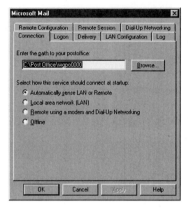

> **N O T E**   Outlook normally locates the workgroup post office for you automatically. If Outlook doesn't find a post office and you know that one exists, contact your workgroup administrator. ▓

Configuring Microsoft Mail Logon

Click the Microsoft Mail dialog box's Logon tab to automatically logon to your mailbox. Figure 37.12 shows the Logon page of the Microsoft Mail dialog box. Enter your mailbox name and password.

FIG. 37.12

Outlook can be configured to logon on the post office automatically.

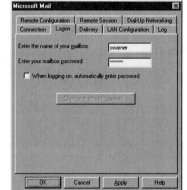

   You can have your password changed automatically the next time you connect to the post office by clicking the change password check box and clicking the Change Mailbox Password button.

Configuring Microsoft Mail Delivery

The Microsoft Mail dialog box's Delivery page, shown in Figure 37.13, enables or disables the delivery of messages. In addition, this page can cause Outlook to automatically retrieve messages and notify other users when they are sent mail.

N O T E   Your network must have the NetBIOS protocol in use to have recipients alerted when they receive a message. NetBIOS is Microsoft's network protocol, but it is not required to use Windows. ▪

FIG. 37.13

Microsoft Mail can be configured to allow only incoming or outgoing messages.

Enable or disable the delivery of messages using the check boxes at the top of the page. You can limit the types of addresses that can be delivered to by clicking the Address Types button and deselecting undesired address types by clicking their check box. Change the interval for mail retrieval to cause your mailbox to be checked more often or less frequently.

Configuring Microsoft Mail Log

The mail log records unusual or important events that occur while using Microsoft Mail. You must specify a location for the log or one is automatically placed in the Windows directory. To disable logging, click the check box at the top of the Log page.

T I P   Keeping a log makes it easier to troubleshoot problems that you might encounter while using Microsoft Mail.

Changing User Passwords

Most of the time you are assigned a temporary password when you are first assigned a mailbox. You should change your temporary password immediately after establishing your Microsoft Mail service. To change you Microsoft Mail password, follow these steps:

1. Choose Change Mailbox Password from the Microsoft Mail Tools submenu of the Tools menu to display the Change Mailbox Password dialog box.

2. Type the current password in the Old Password edit box.

3. Type the new password in the New Password and Verify New Password edit boxes.

4. Click the OK button to change the password.

Using Microsoft Mail to Send and Receive Messages

After you install the Microsoft Mail service and configure it for your needs, you can create and send messages to other users in your workgroup. In addition to any automatic delivery you might have configured, you send and receive messages the same way that you would for other mail services.

▶ **See** "Using Microsoft Mail to Send and Receive Messages," **p. 752**

Internet Mail can be used to exchange messages with people around the world or with people down the hall. It doesn't matter if they are connected to your network or even if they use the same type of computer. Standards for Internet Mail allow computers and networks of different types to communicate with each other.

In order to facilitate the communication possible using Internet Mail, you must install and configure the Internet Mail service in your profile. To do this, you need some information about the mail server that is used on your network or by your ISP. At a minimum, you need to know your e-mail address, your mail server's name or IP address, your account name, and your password. To add the Internet mail service to your profile, follow these steps:

1. Start Outlook.

2. Choose Services from the Tools menu to open the Services dialog box, shown in Figure 37.9.

3. Click the Add button to open the Add Service to Profile dialog box and add the Internet mail service. The Add Service to Profile dialog box is shown in Figure 37.10.

4. Select Internet Mail in the Add Service to Profile dialog box and click the OK button. Figure 37.14 shows the Internet Mail dialog box that is displayed.

5. Enter your name and e-mail address at the top of the dialog box, and enter your mail server's name or IP address, your account name (usually the first part of your e-mail address), and your password. The two buttons are used to set advanced options, but the default values are those usually chosen.

 T I P   Your name and e-mail address is included in messages for the recipient. They are not used to connect to your mail server.

6. Click the Connection tab to determine how to connect to your Internet mailbox. Figure 37.15 shows the Internet Mail dialog box's Connection page.

7. Click the option button for the method you want to use to connect to your mail server. If you have an ISP, choose to use a modem and select the connection for your ISP from the drop-down list box.

FIG. 37.14

Internet mail can be configured for different accounts and servers.

FIG. 37.15

Mail servers can be on a local network or on remote computers.

 TIP Click the Schedule button to arrange to have Outlook automatically and periodically check for messages.

8. Click the OK button to save your changes.

To modify the settings for the Internet mail service, you would double-click the service in the Services dialog box and use the Internet Mail dialog box. The service is deleted by selecting it in the Services dialog box and clicking the Remove button.

After Internet mail is properly configured, you can send and receive messages using your Internet mail account. Use the Check for New Mail On feature to specifically use the Internet mail service.

▶ **See** "Using Microsoft Mail to Send and Receive Messages," **p. 752**

Using Mail from Online Services

Online services such as CompuServe and The Microsoft Network are very popular. Many users might get their e-mail services through one of these providers. While these providers supply software to access e-mail accounts, you might want to use Outlook to handle your e-mail for these services.

If MSN is your service provider, the installation of MSN software sets up a service for using its e-mail services in your profile. After installing MSN, you don't need to do anything except open outlook to use it with your MSN e-mail account.

N O T E   MSN mail service has options, just like other mail services. Double-click the service in the Services dialog box to modify its settings. ■

CompuServe mail can be accessed using software provided by CompuServe. The software is a modified Microsoft Exchange client that allows Outlook to communicate with CompuServe's mail system. To obtain the software, use the **GO** word **CIS:MAP-36**. The file is named CSMAIL.EXE. Download the file and run it. Follow the instructions to install and configure the service.

Other online services may also provide software that allows Outlook to use their mail services. Contact your provider to find out if they have any such software. After any service is successfully added to a profile, messages can be sent and received using that service.

Using Remote Mail

Outlook's Remote Mail feature allows you to limit the amount of time that you spend connected to a mail server. This can be useful when you have to use Dial-Up Networking to connect to your mail server. You can save time and money using Remote Mail.

The Remote Mail feature initially downloads only the headers for messages. Message headers contain the subject, sender, time received, importance, and size of a message. They also indicate if there are any attachments with the message. You can use the information from the message header to decide which messages to download and which messages can wait. For example, an unimportant message with a large attachment might be able to wait until you can connect to the mail server locally or during an off-peak calling period.

N O T E   Some services may need some configuration changes before they can be used with Remote Mail. ■

To use Remote Mail to send and receive messages, follow these steps:

1. Start Outlook.
2. Choose Connect from the Remote Mail submenu of the Tools menu to start the Remote Connection Wizard, shown in Figure 37.16.

FIG. 37.16

You can select which information services to connect to.

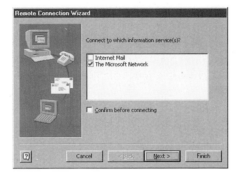

Part

VI

Ch

37

3. Select which information services to connect to.

 TIP Click the Confirm Before Connecting check box to verify the connection information for services before they are dialed.

4. Click the Next button to continue to the dialog box shown in Figure 37.17.

FIG. 37.17

The number of messages sent or services that messages are received from can be controlled.

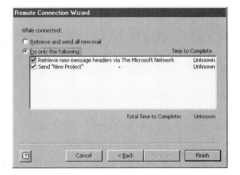

5. Select the actions that you want performed while connected to the information services that you selected in the first dialog box.

6. Click the Finish button to connect and exchange messages using the instructions that you provided in the two message boxes of the Remote Connection Wizard.

 TIP To limit the amount of time spent online, configure remote mail and the information services being used to disconnect after sending and receiving messages.

After you connect to your information services and retrieve the headers for the messages that you have waiting, you must decide which messages should be downloaded and which should be left on the server. Marked messages are downloaded from the mail server to your computer the next time that you connect using remote mail. Figure 37.18 shows the Remote toolbar that can be used to connect, disconnect, and mark and delete messages. The Remote toolbar matches the Remote Tools submenu of the Tools menu exactly. In fact, the Remote Tools submenu is a tear-off menu.

FIG. 37.18

The Remote toolbar provides quick access to the remote mail tools.

N O T E   If you mark a message to retrieve a copy, a copy of the message is downloaded to your computer and the message is left on the mail server.

Outlook allows a number of different services to be used for sending and receiving messages. It also provides several different ways for these services to communicate. All of these services are controlled and configured using the Services dialog box. ●

CHAPTER 38

Managing Microsoft Fax with Outlook

by Joe Habraken

Microsoft Outlook provides an easy-to-use interface for managing the Windows 95 Microsoft Fax feature. When you start using Outlook as your e-mail and fax manager, in fact, you will never miss Microsoft Exchange. You can send, receive, and manage your faxes right in the Microsoft Outlook window, and access all your sent and received messages quickly by using the Outlook Bar. Outlook even provides you all the tools you need to configure Microsoft Fax for your use. ■

New features

Microsoft Outlook replaces Microsoft Exchange as your Windows 95 fax and electronic-mail manager.

Configuring Microsoft Fax

You can use Microsoft Outlook to set all the Microsoft Fax parameters. You decide the type of cover page for your faxes, how your fax is sent, and how faxes are received.

Sending and receiving faxes

The Compose menu makes creating and sending a new fax easy. The Outlook Bar gives you easy access to your Inbox and Sent box, so you can track all your sent and received faxes.

Selecting your modem or network fax server

Outlook gives you complete control of the modem that you use to send and receive your faxes. If you're on a network, Outlook can help you configure Microsoft fax to send and receive faxes over the network fax server.

Using fax-on-demand systems

You can use Microsoft Outlook to receive faxes from fax-on-demand systems that provide fax libraries on a certain subject, such as troubleshooting a particular type of computer system.

Accessing Microsoft Fax

To access Microsoft Fax from Outlook, you must install Microsoft Fax and Microsoft Exchange from your Windows 95 CD-ROM, if they were not installed with the 95 operating system. To install Microsoft Fax and the Exchange components that it needs to operate:

1. Access the Windows Control Panel by clicking the Start button and then choosing Settings, Control Panel.

2. In the Control Panel, double click the Add/Remove Programs icon; then select the Windows Setup tab.

3. Select the check boxes for Microsoft Fax and Exchange in the dialog box. Make sure that your Windows 95 CD-ROM is in the CD-ROM drive; then click OK. Follow the on-screen prompts to complete the installation.

Configuring Microsoft Fax

To use Microsoft Fax when you are in Outlook, you must configure its features so that your computer can send or receive faxes over a modem or a network that uses a network fax server. Configuring Microsoft Fax for the first time from Microsoft Outlook is a two-step process; you must include Microsoft Fax as an Outlook service, and then you must configure Microsoft Fax to send and receive faxes over your modem or network.

When you first configure Microsoft Fax as a service, you will need to specify whether you are sending and receiving your faxes by modem or over a network. The installation below assumes that you are using a modem. If you need to add a network fax server to your installation, see "Configuring Microsoft Fax for Use on a Network Server" later in this chapter.

Adding the Microsoft Fax Service and Configuring Your Modem

Adding the Microsoft Fax service to Outlook is a straightforward process if you installed Microsoft Fax during your Windows 95 installation. New services such as Microsoft Fax are added via the Outlook Tools menu.

During the configuration of Microsoft Fax, it is quite easy to set up the modem that you will use to send and receive your faxes. However, you must first give Outlook the ability to control the Microsoft Fax Service.

1. Double-click the Outlook icon on the desktop to open Microsoft Outlook.

2. In the Outlook window, choose Tools, Services. The Outlook Services dialog box opens (see Figure 38.1). This dialog box allows you to control the services set for the Outlook user profile that is currently in use.

3. Click the Add button to add a new service. The Add Service to Profile dialog box appears. All the available services, such as Microsoft Fax, are listed in this dialog box.

FIG. 38.1

The Outlook Services dialog box allows you to add, remove, and control the properties of the services included in your Outlook user profile.

 TIP When you add, remove, or edit the services in Outlook, you are changing the services available to the current user profile.

Part

VI

Ch

38

4. To add Microsoft Fax to the Outlook services, select Microsoft Fax and click OK, as shown in Figure 38.2.

FIG. 38.2

Select the service that you want to add to Outlook and then click the OK button.

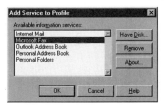

A Microsoft Fax message box appears, telling you that you must provide certain information (such as your fax number and modem type) before you can send and receive faxes in Outlook.

5. Click Yes to continue.

 TIP If you don't want to configure the fax parameters now or don't have all the configuration information handy, you can choose to set up the fax information later. To do so, click the No button.

The Microsoft Fax Properties dialog box appears as shown in Figure 38.3. This dialog box is where you supply the information that Outlook needs to send and receive faxes via Microsoft Fax. (You will configure the Microsoft Fax Properties in the section "Setting the Fax Preferences.")

FIG. 38.3

The Microsoft Fax Properties dialog box is where you set the parameters that are needed to send and receive faxes.

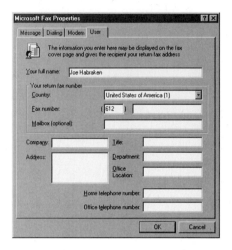

Configuring Microsoft Fax for Use on a Network Server

If you are using a PC that is connected to a network, you probably will be sending and receiving your faxes over a network fax server. Outlook and Microsoft Fax have no problem sending and receiving faxes over the network, but you must add a network fax server to the modem list to which Outlook and Microsoft Fax connect.

To add and configure a network fax server, follow these steps:

1. Choose Tools, Microsoft Fax Tools, Options to open the Microsoft Fax Properties dialog box.

2. Select the Modem tab.

3. Click the Add button. The Add a Fax Modem dialog box appears. This dialog box allows you to add a new modem or a network fax server.

4. Select Network Fax Server, as shown in Figure 38.4.

FIG. 38.4

Select Network Fax Server in the Add a Fax Modem dialog box.

5. Click OK. The Shared Network Directory dialog box appears. You must specify the directory that the server uses as a holding place for sent and received faxes. You probably need to get this information from your network administrator.

6. Enter the shared directory information, as shown in Figure 38.5.

FIG. 38.5

Specify the shared fax directory on the network.

7. Click OK. You return to the Microsoft Fax Properties dialog box, and your network fax server appears in the list of available modems.

8. Select the network fax server and then click the Set As Active Modem button.

9. Click OK to close the Microsoft Fax Properties dialog box.

The network fax server is now used to send and receive the faxes that you send with Microsoft Outlook and Microsoft Fax.

TIP If you closed the Microsoft Fax Properties dialog box after you added the Microsoft Fax service to Outlook, you can reopen it by choosing Tools, Microsoft Fax Tools, Options.

Part

VI

Ch

38

Setting the Fax Preferences

When Microsoft Fax has been included as one of your personal information services, you can configure the Outlook fax-related preferences. The Microsoft Fax Properties dialog box includes four tabs:

- *User*. The User tab is where you provide information about yourself. This information includes your name, your return fax number, and information about the company you work for. Much of the information is optional; you must provide your name and a return fax number in this tab, however.

- *Modem*. The Modem tab provides a list of the modems (and network Fax Servers) that are currently installed on your PC. Select the modem that you want to use to send and receive your faxes.

- *Dialing*. The Dialing tab allows you to set the number of retries that the modem makes when dialing a fax number. This tab also gives you access to other dialing properties, such as dialing to access an outside line or using a calling card when dialing.

- *Message*. The Message tab is where you select the time to send the fax, the type of cover page to use, and the page format to use for the message.

To configure the settings in the Microsoft Fax Properties dialog box, follow these steps:

1. Select the User tab and enter your name in the Full Name text box.

2. Choose your country's name from the Country drop-down list.

3. Enter a return fax number. All the other information in the User tab is optional.

T I P   If you work on a network and your network uses mailboxes to receive new faxes, you must include your
network mailbox name in the User tab. Your network administrator provides this information to you.

4. When you complete this tab, click the Modem tab. The Modem tab lists the modems that
   are currently available to you for sending and receiving faxes.

5. Select the appropriate modem and click the Set As Active Fax Modem button, as shown
   in Figure 38.6.

FIG. 38.6

The Modem tab is where
you select and configure
the modem that you use
to send and receive your
faxes.

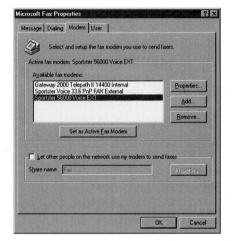

6. If you want to change any of the parameters associated with the modem, click the
   Properties button. This allows you to change the number of rings before the modem
   answers the phone, as well as the modem volume. Click the OK button to return to the
   Modem tab.

7. If you are on a network, you can choose to share your modem with other people on the
   network by clicking the check box titled Let Other People on the Network Use My
   Modem to Send Faxes.

8. After you select your modem and modem preferences, click the Dialing tab.

9. In the Dialing tab, set the number of retries and the time between retries that you want
   your modem to use.

10. If you must dial a number to get an outside line, click the Dialing Properties button.

    The Dialing Properties dialog box appears. Set the location that you are dialing from,
    your area code, and the number that you must dial to get an outside line.

11. You can select a check box to use a calling card or disable call waiting, as shown in
    Figure 38.7.

FIG. 38.7
The Dialing Properties dialog box is where you set the parameters for how Outlook dials your modem.

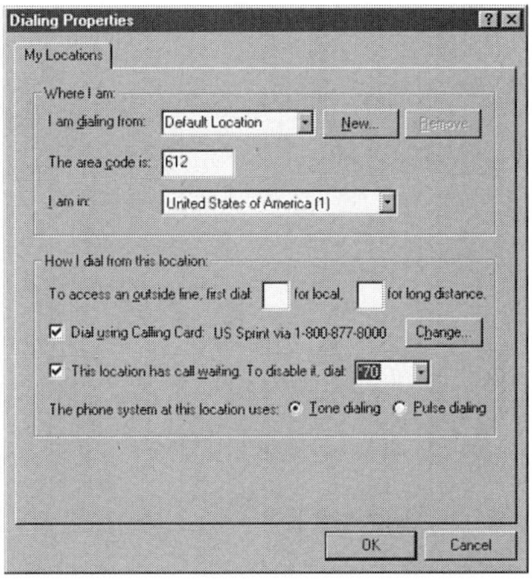

12. After you set your dialing properties, click OK to return to the Microsoft Fax Properties dialog box.

13. Click the Message tab.

14. Select the Time to send options for your faxes by clicking the appropriate radio button.

    To send all new faxes immediately, for example, click As Soon As Possible.

15. If you want to send faxes to other users of Microsoft Fax so that they can edit the faxes, choose Editable, If Possible from the Message Format box.

16. If you want to automatically send a fax cover page with all your faxes, click the Send Cover Page check box and then choose the type of cover page from the Cover Page list box, as shown in Figure 38.8.

FIG. 38.8
The Message tab allows you to set when faxes will be sent and whether all faxes include a fax cover page.

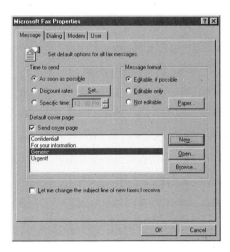

You can create your own fax cover pages. In the Message tab, click the New button. The Fax Cover Page Editor appears; you can use it to design and save your own fax cover sheets. For more detailed information on creating your own cover pages, see "Creating and Editing Cover Pages."

17. When you finish setting properties, click OK to close the dialog box.

18. To close the Services dialog box (which is still open), click OK.

Microsoft Fax has been added as an Outlook service and has been configured to send and receive faxes via your modem or network.

 If you configure and use Microsoft Exchange to send and receive faxes, the same settings are available in Outlook. You can use Microsoft Fax immediately via Outlook if none of the fax-service parameters (such as your modem type and dialing preferences) has changed.

Sending Faxes

After you configure Microsoft Fax, you are ready to send faxes by using Microsoft Outlook. New faxes are launched via the Outlook Compose menu.

Outlook makes it very easy to send a new Fax by supplying you with a New Fax Wizard. To create a new Fax via the New Fax Wizard:

1. To create a new fax, choose Compose, New Fax. The Compose New Fax Wizard appears.

2. Choose your dialing location (which usually is the default setting, unless you are using a portable computer) from the drop-down list in the wizard window.

 If you are not using a portable , you can remove the opening window from the Compose New Fax Wizard so that it won't appear in the future. Click the check box titled I'm Not Using a Portable Computer, So Don't Show This to Me Again on the initial window of the New Fax Wizard.

3. Click Next to continue. The next screen is where you enter the information that pertains to the person (or people) to whom you want to send the fax to.

4. Type the person's name in the To text box.

5. From the Country drop-down list, choose the country to which you are sending the fax.

6. Type the Fax number in the Fax # text box (see Figure 38.9).

 You can also enter the person (or people) to whom you are sending the fax by using your Outlook Address Book or Contacts list. Click the Address Book button and then double-click to choose the name or names to add to the list. Make sure that you included the person's fax number in his or her Address Book entry before using this method of selecting names.

FIG. 38.9

Enter the person's name and fax number and then click Add to List to place that person in the Recipient box for your fax.

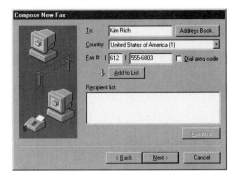

7. When you complete the entries, click Add to List. The person's name is added to the recipient box.

8. Repeat the procedure for any other people to whom you want to send the fax.

9. When you complete the recipient list, click Next. The next screen allows you to select a cover-page style for your fax.

10. Click the appropriate radio button to select your fax cover-page style. If you don't want a fax cover page, click the No radio button.

11. If you want to change the settings for when the fax will be sent, click the Options button.

    You can edit the Message parameters for this fax (such as the time sent and the message format) that you set when you first configured Microsoft Fax.

12. After you change the fax settings, click OK to return to the Compose New Fax Wizard.

13. Click Next to continue.

14. In the next screen, type the subject of your fax in the Subject text box.

15. If you want to include a note in the cover sheet, type it in the Note text box, as shown in Figure 38.10.

FIG. 38.10

Type the subject of your fax and any note you want to include in the cover page.

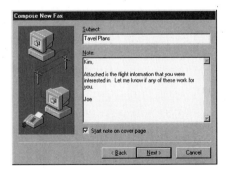

16. When you complete your note, click the Next button to continue.

The next screen is where you designate the body of your fax message. You can attach a document, spreadsheet, or any other file type to a fax in Outlook such as an HTML file. The added file serves as the pages of the fax and is included with your fax cover page.

> **CAUTION**
>
> When you attach large files to your faxes, you increase the transmission time required to send the fax. Large faxes also run a greater risk of transmission errors and lost data.

17. Click Add File to browse your hard disk, and select the file, as shown in Figure 38.11.

FIG. 38.11

The Compose New Fax Wizard allows you to attach the body of your fax to the cover page by using a previously created file stored on your hard disk.

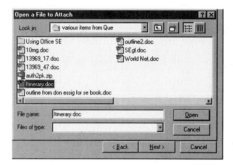

18. Click Open to add the file to the fax and return to the Compose New Fax Wizard.
19. Click Next to continue. You've completed the fax composition and are ready to send the fax.
20. Click Finish. The Microsoft Fax Status dialog box appears.

The fax is formatted to be sent. If you attached files to the fax, the file's application opens (a Word document opens in Word, for example), and the item is readied to be sent with the fax cover page.

When the fax is formatted, the phone number that you specified is dialed. When the connection is made, your fax is sent, as shown in Figure 38.12. When the fax is sent, the Microsoft Fax Status dialog box disappears.

FIG. 38.12

The Microsoft Fax Status box keeps you apprised of how the sending of your new fax is going.

> **CAUTION**
>
> If Microsoft Fax does not access the modem correctly and your fax is aborted, you may need to troubleshoot the configuration that you set up to send and receive faxes. Choose Help, Microsoft Fax Help Topics, Contents tab, and double-click the Troubleshooting icon. The help system walks you through your fax and modem setup to help you fix any problems.

Receiving and Processing Faxes

The faxes that you receive eventually are available in the Outlook Inbox. How Microsoft Fax answers the call for an incoming fax depends on whether you are using a modem with its own line and whether you share one line between your phone and modem.

Receiving Faxes Automatically

If your modem is attached to its own phone line, you can set it to automatically incoming fax calls.

To set the modem to automatically answer the incoming call, you must set the Modem properties as detailed below.

1. Choose Tools, Microsoft Fax Tools, Options to open the Microsoft Fax Properties dialog box.

2. Select the Modem tab.

3. To set the fax properties of the modem, click Properties. The Fax Modem Properties dialog box appears.

4. To set the answer mode to automatic, click the Answer After radio button and then set the number of rings for which you want to wait before the modem answers the incoming fax call, as shown in Figure 38.13.

FIG. 38.13

The Fax Modem Properties dialog box allows you to set up your modem to automatically answer the phone when you have an incoming fax.

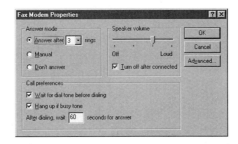

5. You can set the modem speaker volume by dragging the speaker volume switch.

6. After setting your answer options and speaker volume, click OK. You return to the Microsoft Fax Options dialog box'and the Modem tab.

7. Click OK to close the Microsoft Fax Properties dialog box.

Now your fax modem automatically answers any calls that come in on your fax line. If you share one phone line between your fax and telephone, you will want to answer the incoming calls manually by using the Microsoft Fax Status dialog box, as detailed in the following section.

Receiving Faxes Manually

To receive a fax manually, you need to know that the incoming call on your phone line is a fax rather than a voice call. You should verify with the sender of the fax when he or she plans to sending the fax to you, so that you can use Microsoft Fax to answer the fax call manually.

When you open Microsoft Outlook, a fax machine icon is placed at the right end of the Windows taskbar. This icon allows you to answer your fax calls.

To answer an incoming Fax call:

1. Click the fax machine icon on the taskbar. The Microsoft Fax Status dialog box opens, as shown in Figure 38.14.

FIG. 38.14
The Microsoft Fax Status dialog box allows you to answer incoming fax calls manually.

2. When your telephone rings, click the Answer Now button. Microsoft Fax directs your modem to answer the incoming call. The Idle status message in the Microsoft Fax Status dialog boxes changes to Answering Call.

   When the connection is established, the dialog box displays the status of each page of the fax as it is received, as shown in Figure 38.15.

FIG. 38.15
The status of the incoming fax is detailed in the Microsoft Fax Status dialog box.

When the fax transmission is complete, the Answering Call designator returns to Idle.

3. Click the Close button to close the dialog box.

After you receive a fax, either by having your modem answer the call automatically or by answering the call manually, you need to download the received fax to Microsoft Outlook. When the fax is in the Outlook Inbox, you can read it, print it, or move it to another Inbox folder.

To download the new fax to the Outlook Inbox, follow these steps:

1. Choose Tools, Check for New Mail. New faxes and e-mail are downloaded into your Inbox.

2. To add new faxes only to your Inbox, choose Tools, Check for New Mail On. The Check for New Mail On dialog box appears.

3. Since you only wish to download new faxes to your Inbox, click the Microsoft Fax check box as shown in Figure 38.16.

FIG. 38.16
Use the Check for New Mail On dialog box to download items from selected services.

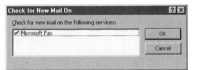

Whichever method you use to download the new fax, it appears in your Outlook Inbox. When the fax is in your Inbox, you can process it; processing a fax can include reading, printing, deleting, or even moving the fax to a new Outlook folder.

Reading a Fax

You open a new fax in the Outlook Inbox the same way that you read the other items that appear in your Inbox, such as your new e-mail messages.

To open and read a new Fax in Outlook:

1. In the Outlook Inbox, double-click the fax message that you want to read. A Fax Viewer window opens, displaying the fax, as shown in Figure 38.17.

FIG. 38.17
When you double-click the fax in the Inbox, the Fax Viewer opens, displaying the fax.

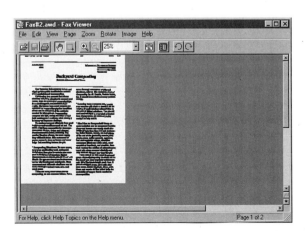

2. To zoom in on the fax to get a better view, click the Zoom In button (the magnifying glass with the plus symbol) on the Viewer toolbar.

3. Click the Zoom In button until you can easily read the text in the Fax (see Figure 38.18). To Zoom Out, choose the Zoom Out button on the viewer toolbar. Click the Zoom Out mouse pointer on the Fax to zoom away from the document.

FIG. 38.18

Use the Zoom In (or Zoom Out) button to change the view of your fax.

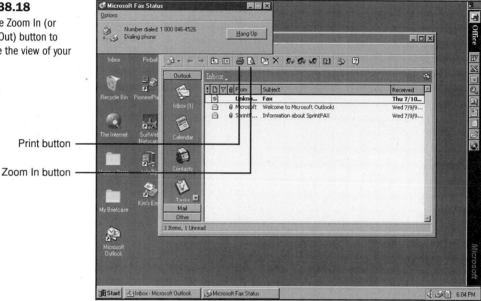

Print button

Zoom In button

 TIP You may want to click the Fax Viewer's Maximize button when you zoom in on the fax to read it. This will supply you with the maximum amount of window space in which to view your Fax.

4. If you want a hard copy of your fax, click the Print button.

The file version of the fax is formatted as a facsimile of the original document by the Viewer and your printer.

5. When you finish viewing or printing your fax, close the Fax Viewer by clicking its Close button. You return to the Outlook Inbox.

Using Request a Fax

Microsoft Outlook and Microsoft Fax offer you the capability to electronically request faxes from various fax-on-demand and fax-back services. These services usually are libraries of technical support or sales documents that you can receive via your fax machine.

TIP In some cases, you must navigate a series of menus to receive a particular document from a fax-on-demand service. Navigating the fax back menus requires the use of your touch-tone phone, and you cannot directly request the fax via Outlook. You can use the Microsoft Fax system and Outlook, however, to receive the fax when the fax-on-demand system sends it to you.

To access a fax-on-demand system, you must know the phone number that you use to connect to the system when requesting a fax. In many cases, these systems' numbers are toll-free and are available to you because you purchased a particular product or service.

It is not uncommon for you to find that a fax-on-demand service contains only one document or one set of documents, such as information on a particular product. Other fax-on-demand services (also referred to as *fax-back systems*) house huge libraries of documents; the Internal Revenue Service's system, for example, provides a fax-back system for tax forms. You may need to contact the provider of the fax-back service to obtain a catalog of the documents that are available on the service.

To connect to a fax-on-demand service by using Outlook, follow these steps:

1. Choose Tools, Microsoft Fax Tools, Request a Fax.

   The Request a Fax dialog box appears. In this dialog box, you must specify whether you want to receive any document that is available on the fax-on-demand service or whether you want to receive a certain document by using a document code or name.

2. Click the appropriate radio button and type the name or code for the document, if necessary (see Figure 38.19).

FIG. 38.19
You can specify whether you want the fax-on-demand service to send you whatever is available, or you can specify one document in the service's library.

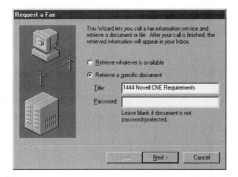

3. Click Next to go to the next screen—the Company name and phone number screen. This screen is where you provide the company name and the phone number that you want Microsoft Fax to dial to request your fax.

4. Type the company name and the phone number for the fax-on-demand system, as shown in Figure 38.20, and then click the Add button.

Part
VI

Ch
38

FIG. 38.20

Type the company name and the phone number you will use to request the fax document using the Request a Fax feature.

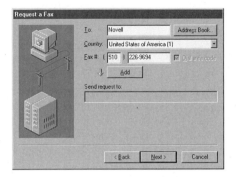

5. The contact information appears in the Send Request to: box. Click the Next button to continue.

   In the next screen, you are asked when you want to send the request: as soon as possible, or during another period.

6. Select the radio button for the time when the fax-on-demand request should be sent.

7. Click the Next button. The screen tells you that the request is ready to send.

8. Click the Finish button to initiate the fax retrieval. The Microsoft Fax Status dialog box opens. and the number of the fax-on-demand system is dialed.

   Upon connection, your request is transmitted via your fax; then the Microsoft Fax Status dialog box closes the connection and returns to Idle.

   Depending on how busy the service that you contacted is, you phone may ring in a matter of moments. The call is from the fax service and means that your request was honored and that the system is sending the requested fax.

9. Click the Answer Now button. Your requested fax is download via your modem. Your new Fax will appear in your Outlook inbox.

When you receive your requested fax, you can view it or print it just as you would any other fax. Be aware, however, that some fax-back documents are large, so you may have to be patient while your modem receives a lengthy fax.

Creating and Editing Cover Pages

You can send optional cover pages with the faxes that you send by using Microsoft Outlook and Microsoft Fax. You can edit the existing cover pages or create new ones for your faxes.

To modify an existing cover page or create a new cover page, follow these steps:

1. Choose Tools, Microsoft Fax Tools, Options to open the Microsoft Fax Properties dialog box.

2. Select the Message tab.

3. To edit an existing cover page such as the Generic cover page, select the particular cover page and click Open, as shown in Figure 38.21.

If you want to create a new cover page, click New.

FIG. 38.21

You can modify the current cover pages or create new ones.

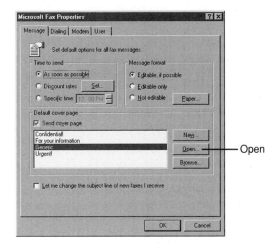

Both of these choices open the Fax Cover Page Editor, as shown in Figure 38.20.

The Editor is a text and graphic layout tool that you can use to modify or create fax cover pages. Each object that you create, whether it is text or a graphic, can be selected and moved in the cover page. Objects can also be selected and grouped and then moved in the cover page as a single entity.

To create new text and graphic items for the fax cover page, follow these steps:

1. Click the Text button in the toolbar (ToolTips are provided for the buttons on the toolbars, so use your mouse to identify the various buttons).

2. Click and drag using the text tool to create a text box (dragging down and then to the right is the easiest way to create the rectangle).

3. An insertion point appears in the new text box. Type the text you want in the box.

4. After you type the text, change the font type and size by selecting the text box (click its border). Sizing boxes will appear on the text box, letting you know that it has been selected. To change the font type and size, click the Format menu, then click Font. Use the Font dialog box to specify the font size and format.

5. To add a graphic to the fax cover page, select any of the graphics tools (circle, rectangle, and so on) provided on the toolbar. To select the circle, click the circle button.

6. Click and drag the mouse pointer on your cover page screen to create a circle on the fax cover page, as shown in Figure 38.22.

7. To modify the circle's (or other graphic object's) line and shading, right-click the circle and choose Line Fill and Color from the shortcut menu.

   The Line, Fill and Color dialog box appears. This dialog box allows you to modify the appearance of the object.

FIG. 38.22

The Fax Cover Page Editor provides you all the tools to modify and create fax cover pages; the circle tool allows you to draw a circle on your cover page.

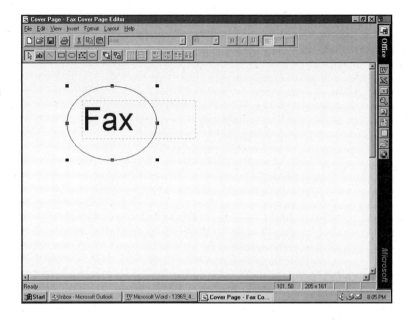

8. Choose a new line thickness and fill color from the drop-down lists. Then click the close button to close the dialog box.

9. To place text on a graphic, type the text in a text box and then drag it onto the graphic.

10. Select the graphic and click the Send to Back button in the toolbar (the seventh button from the right). This allows the text to sit on top of the graphic.

   To specify where Microsoft Fax places information about the receiver (name, fax number, address, and so on) or the sender (you), you must insert codes for these items from the Insert menu.

11. Choose Insert, Recipient. A text box appears with the Recipient code in it. You can drag the box to the place on the cover page where you want the recipient name to appear.

12. Click Name to place in the fax cover sheet a code that accepts the receiver's name when you create a new fax, as shown in Figure 38.23.

13. Use the Insert menu to insert the other receiver and sender codes that you want to have in your cover page. Each receiver and sender code such as Address or Fax Number will appear in a separate text box when you insert them.

14. When you complete your new or modified cover page, click the Save button and then exit the Fax Cover Page Editor by clicking its Close button.

   You return to the Microsoft Fax Properties dialog box. If you created a new cover page, it is listed in the Cover Page list box.

15. Click OK to close the dialog box and return to the Outlook window.

FIG. 38.23

The Insert menu provides the codes that place the sender and receiver information in the fax cover page when you compose a new fax in Outlook.

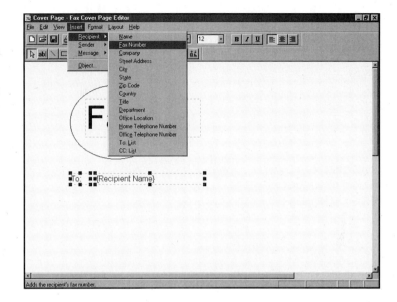

CHAPTER 39

Advanced Messaging

by George Lynch

E-mail has become a major fact of life for most of us in today's business world. Most of us have more than one e-mail address (as well as an office number, one or more home numbers, a cell phone number, a beeper number and so on). Trying to keep messages organized has in itself become a significant task.

Fortunately, Microsoft Outlook contains a number of messaging features you can use to organize and automate your e-mail messages. This chapter covers Outlook's messaging features. ■

Customizing Outlook's interface

Learn how to customize the Outlook interface, including how to design your own interface.

Powerful sorting and storing features

Outlook enables you to sort your messages according to whatever method appeals to you and gives you the ability to group your messages by common themes

Message filtering and processing

You can filter your messages by conditions that you set up, such as displaying only messages from one sender.

Powerful tracking features

Organize your mail, appointments, and contacts by using Categories.

Automate your correspondence

Outlook enables you to automate message processing, signatures, receipts, and auto-responses.

Customizing the Interface

Outlook provides the tools that enable you to customize its appearance to fit a variety of different personal preferences and work styles.

Viewing the Folder List

You can customize the way you navigate through the tools in Outlook by having the Folder list displayed in a split window instead of a drop-down list.

To do this, select View, Folder List to keep the hierarchical tree list of folders visible. The View, Folder menu item is a toggle. If the Folder List is visible and you select it from the View menu, you will hide the list, as shown in Figure 39.1. The next time you select View, Folder, the Folder list will be displayed, as shown in Figure 39.2.

FIG. 39.1

Outlook without the Folder list.

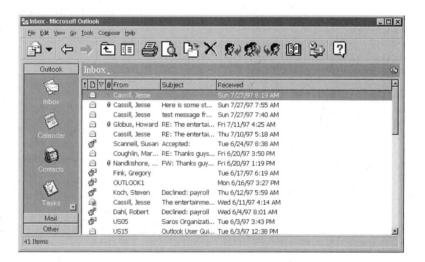

The Folder list is useful for navigating with the keyboard instead of the mouse. This can be useful on a laptop or for those who prefer to keep their hands on the keyboard for speed.

When the Folder list is displayed, you can tab between the Folder list and the messages in the Inbox, for instance, and use the cursor arrow keys to change to the Calendar or any other Outlook component.

FIG. 39.2
Outlook shows the
Folder list.

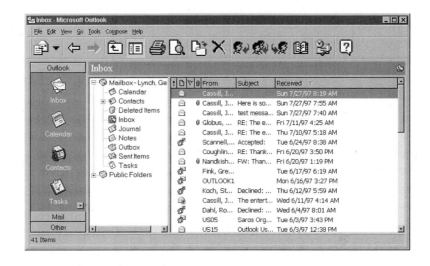

Hiding the Outlook Bar

You can even hide the Outlook bar completely. To hide the Outlook bar, select View, Outlook
Bar. This toggles off the view of the Outlook bar, as shown in Figure 39.3. To bring it back,
select the same menu item to toggle the view back on. Hiding the Outlook bar can be useful if
you are working on a laptop with limited screen real estate.

Part
VI

Ch

39

FIG. 39.3
Outlook with Outlook
bar hidden.

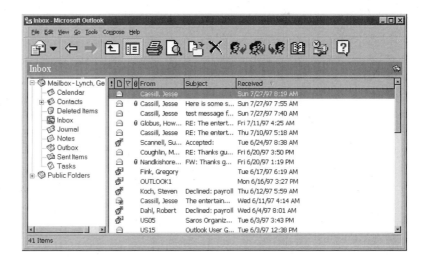

You can hide the status bar to squeeze out a couple of extra pixels by selecting the View, Status
Bar. This toggles the status bar.

Creating Your Own E-Mail Folders

You can use subfolders as one method of organizing your e-mail. For example, you might wish to create a folder for a project on which you are working. You could store all messages you receive regarding the project in the folder, or you could create folders for the most common types of e-mail you receive, or for the people who frequently send you e-mail which you wish to receive, such as your boss or your spouse.

To create a subfolder, select the Inbox on the Outlook bar and click File, Folder, Create Subfolder. Figure 39.4 shows the New Folder dialog box that appears. Type a name for the folder and choose a location within the hierarchy. Select the default Mail Items from the list marked Folder Contains to create a folder into which you can file your e-mail.

FIG. 39.4

Use the Create New Folder dialog box to name and choose a location for new folders.

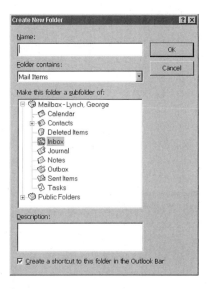

After you have created all the folders you need, you can move messages into them to keep your Inbox and all your e-mail messages organized.

Views

A view is a group of settings that control the display of data in Outlook. The simplest and quickest way to customize Outlook is by changing your view from the default to one of the several other built-in views. You can select one of the built-in views by selecting View, Current View from the menu and choosing from the menu of available views.

Changing views varies the way the data in the Inbox is displayed, the amount of text, and the ordering of the messages. The built-in views of the Inbox and their descriptions are listed in Table 39.1.

Table 39.1 Built-In View of the Inbox

View	Description
Messages	Displays a list of messages in a table with a single line for each item. Fields include:Importance, Icon (indicating message type), Flag status (indicating action on the message is required), Attachment, From, Subject, and Received.
Messages with AutoPreview	Displays three lines of the message so that you can decide whether you want to open the message or ignore it.
By Message Flag	Groups messages based on the message flag status field. Flags can be set by the sender to a variety of settings, including Call, Do not Forward, Follow-up, and so on.
Last Seven Days	Displays only those messages received in the last week. This view automatically cleans up your Inbox and is most useful for catching up on e-mail after a vacation.
Flagged for Next Seven Days	Typically, e-mail messages older than a week are not in need of as much attention as those sent more recently. The "Flagged for the next seven days" view gives a quick list of upcoming deadlines as assigned in your e-mail.
By Conversation Topic	Groups messages by subject line with replies sent and follow-ups. This is also sometimes called message threading. Groups of messages are arranged by subject. See Figure 39.5 for an example of an Inbox sorted by Conversation topic.
By Sender	Groups messages on the "From:" field.
Unread Messages	Hides all messages you have already opened, allowing you to see only those you haven't yet read.
Sent To	The Sent To includes the "To:" field as a column so you can see messages also sent to others as well as yourself.
Message Timeline	Shows icons with partial subject lines as captions arranged from left to right on a calendar timeline. Older messages are to the left and you can scroll through a list of the entire history of your Inbox. The messages are arranged vertically to indicate order of arrival within the day received. See Figure 39.6 for an Inbox sorted into Timeline view.

Part VI

Ch 39

N O T E The recipient of a flagged message can mark it as completed. The By Message Flag groups flagged, completed and unflagged (normal) messages and displays additional fields: the Message Flag text and the Due By date field. ■

FIG. 39.5
Outlook Inbox, By Conversation Topic view.

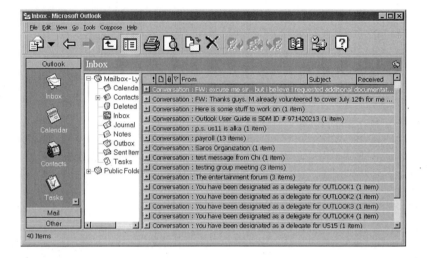

FIG. 39.6
Inbox by Timeline View.

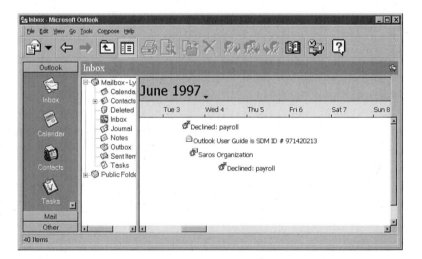

Designing Your Own Custom View

It's easy to create your own views of the Inbox. There are five standard types, or structures, of views:

1. Table formats data into columns and rows.

2. Timeline displays data chronologically.

3. Card displays fields as they might appear on an index card.

4. Day/Week/Month displays items in a calendar view.

5. Icon displays icons that represent items.

You can create a view of your Inbox based on any of these, and although some may be more useful than others, it may be interesting and useful to see your Inbox in Calendar or Card format.

Defining a View

Select <u>V</u>iew, <u>D</u>efine Views from the menu to open the Define Views for "Inbox" dialog box (see Figure 39.7). Click the New button to create a new view (see Figure 39.8).

FIG. 39.7

Define Views for "Inbox" dialog box.

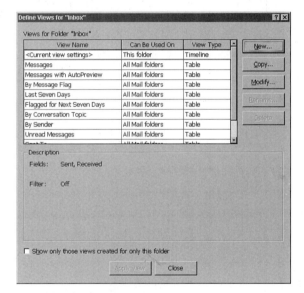

FIG, 39.8

Use the New View dialog box to create definitions for new views.

In the Create New View dialog box, enter a name for the view, for example E-mail Calendar. Select the Day/Week/Month type of view and click OK. This opens the View Summary dialog box. Click OK on the View Summary dialog box to accept the settings (see Figure 39.9).

FIG. 39.9
Review available views in the View Summary dialog box.

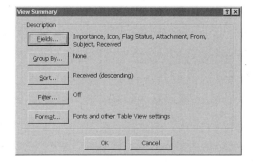

You can now review your Inbox as you would a calendar (see Figure 39.10). You might find this type of view to be useful, depending on the way you work.

FIG. 39.10
Use the Day/Week/Month view to organize the messages in your Inbox.

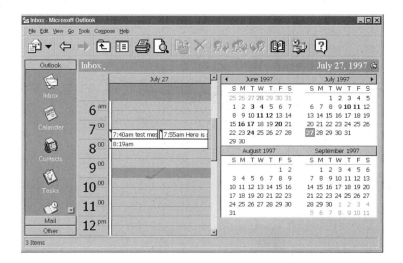

If this view is useful, but not quite exactly the way you want to display your messages, you can modify the view, by selecting View, Define Views from the menu. Select the view you wish to modify (in this case E-mail Calendar) and click the Modify button. Click the Format button to modify the fonts and icons used in the view.

You can experiment with this and other custom views to find those which meet your needs. You can also copy and modify built-in views to create custom views.

Sorting Messages

Perhaps the best way organizing your e-mail is to file it immediately. Most of us are not so organized, or we receive so much e-mail that it quickly piles up. Fortunately, Outlook provides many tools for organizing your Inbox and other e-mail folders.

Sorting Within a Folder

The default Messages view uses the Windows List control to display the list of e-mail messages in the Inbox. This control enables you to sort the messages in a variety of ways. Each column heading acts as a button which, when clicked, sorts the messages into order based on the data in that column. Clicking the Column Heading button once sorts the list in the default order for that column; this may be ascending or descending based on the data. Clicking the Column Heading button again reverses the sort order, and each time you click the Column Heading button it again reverses the order.

Virtually all of the columns can be used to sort a list of items in a view in any of the Outlook tools. This is an amazingly powerful, useful, and intuitive tool for quickly organizing your messages. Figure 39.11 shows an inbox that has been sorted by sender.

FIG. 39.11

The faint triangle to the right of the word From in the column heading Shows that the messages are sorted by Sender.

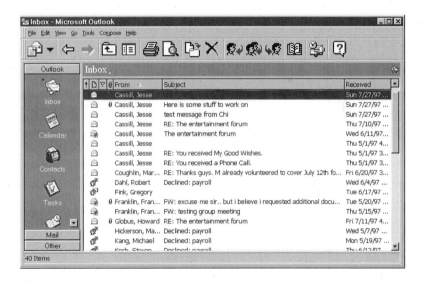

The Messages view contains columns indicating the following:

- who sent the message ("From:")
- the subject of the message
- the time and date you received the message
- the urgency level the sender assigned (the "!" icon column heading)

- a Flag column
- an Attachment column indicating messages that have files attached
- an Icon column indicating the type and status of the message

The normal sort order for this list view is in descending order, by time and date received. Incoming messages are added to the top of the list in the Inbox and older messages are pushed down. This is perfectly useful for reading messages as they arrive because new messages will be grouped together and can be quickly browsed or read in order of arrival. It can also be good for finding a message sent on a particular day.

This is not the only way of viewing new mail, however. Your personal preference may be to see new messages added to the bottom of the list. To achieve this, simply click the Received: Column Heading button.

When you click a column header, a triangle appears next to the column header text (if there is room to display it) indicating that sorting is applied to this field, and the order of the sort. A triangle with the point down indicates Descending sort order, that is Reverse Alphabetic (Z's first, A's last) for text fields and Most Recent to Oldest for date-type fields such as Received. An up-pointing triangle indicates Ascending sort order which reverses the order of the sorting. For iconic columns, such as Flagged or Attachments the sort order simply groups similar messages together, that is all messages with attachments will appear at the top of the list when sorted by Attachment in Descending order (right-click the paper clip icon; select Descending Order from pop-up menu). This can be used on other fields to find, for example, all the messages in the Inbox flagged as completed.

FIG. 39.12
Inbox Mail Symbols (Part 1).

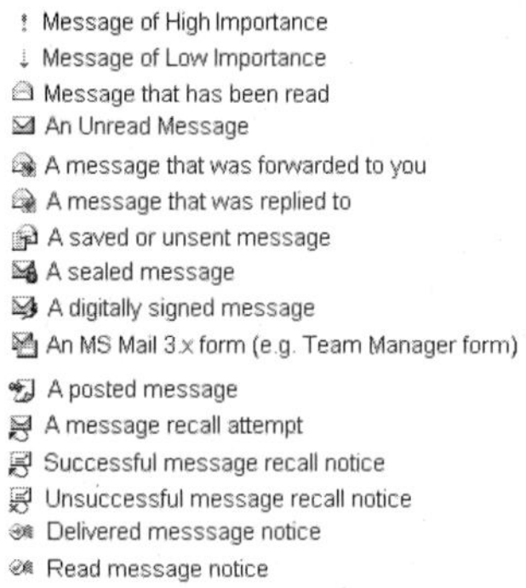

! Message of High Importance
↓ Message of Low Importance
⊖ Message that has been read
☑ An Unread Message
A message that was forwarded to you
A message that was replied to
A saved or unsent message
A sealed message
A digitally signed message
An MS Mail 3.x form (e.g. Team Manager form)
A posted message
A message recall attempt
Successful message recall notice
Unsuccessful message recall notice
Delivered messsage notice
Read message notice

FIG. 39.13
Inbox Mail Symbols (Part 2).

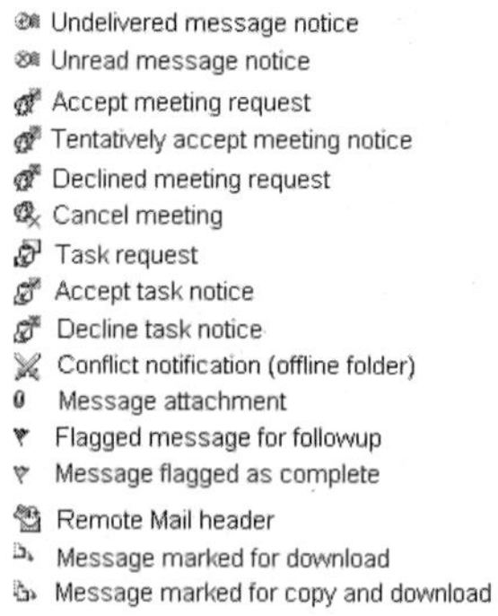

Undelivered message notice
Unread message notice
Accept meeting request
Tentatively accept meeting notice
Declined meeting request
Cancel meeting
Task request
Accept task notice
Decline task notice
Conflict notification (offline folder)
0 Message attachment
▼ Flagged message for followup
▽ Message flagged as complete
Remote Mail header
Message marked for download
Message marked for copy and download

NOTE You can also use all of the sorting techniques described in this chapter on other mail folders, such as the Sent folder, or any other custom folders you have created. ▪

Sorting Using the Sort Dialog Box

You can sort by up to four fields, each with its own ascending or descending order by using the Sort dialog box. Choose View, Sort to open the dialog box (see Figure 39.14).

FIG. 39.14

The Sort dialog box is used to sort Outlook data.

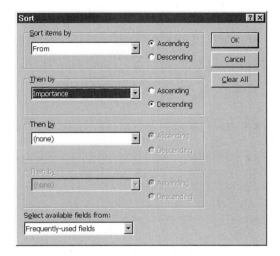

The items in the Sort Items By list box and Then By list boxes are controlled by the Select Available Fields From list box at the bottom of the dialog box. By default, the available items are shown in each of these list boxes from the Frequently-Used Fields list. You can select an item in the Sort Items By list box, choose Ascending or Descending, and sort the list or add additional sorting criteria. As you select a field to sort by at each level, the next level in the list is activated. If you wish to sort by fields that don't appear in the list, select a different set of fields in the Select Available Fields From list box.

You can remove the sorting criteria by selecting the Clear All button, which sets all the Sorting list boxes back to (none).

Finding Messages

When you accumulate a large quantity of e-mail, finding a particular message can be a real chore. Outlook's searching capabilities can make the process easier with its flexible and powerful Find tool. (In fact, it may take a little time and practice to become fully familiar with all the searching tools Outlook provides. Fortunately, they are mostly intuitive and even fun to use). To find a particular message, select the Find tool from the toolbar (or Ctrl+Shift+F or Tools, Find Items). Figure 39.15 shows the Find dialog box.

You can enter text to search for in the Subject field, or expand the search to also include text in other related fields. The From and Sent To buttons enable you to pick from your address list for IDs to match. You can also search by one of several time fields, including Received, Sent, Due, and Expiration Date. The time criteria ranges from Today to Last Month. Other search criteria include Messages With Attachments, Unread Messages, and messages marked important.

With advanced searching you can select from any field for a wide range of criteria (see Figure 39.16). You can combine multiple criteria to narrow your search to precisely the messages you wish to find.

Part
VI

Ch
39

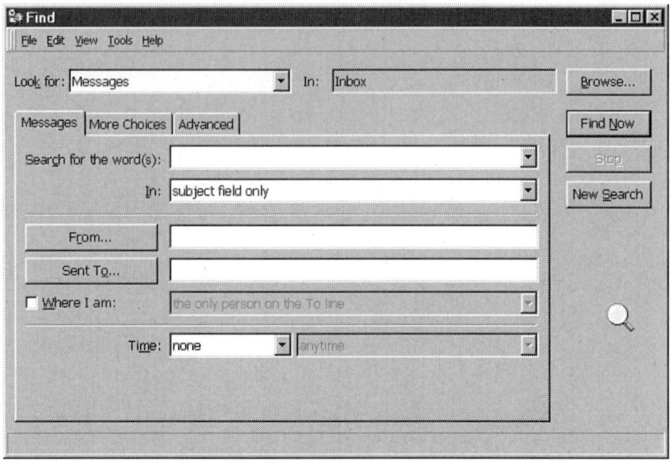

FIG. 39.15

Use Find dialog box to locate data quickly.

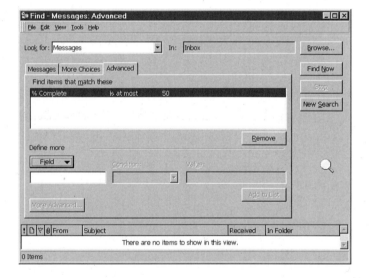

FIG. 39.16

The Advanced tab of the Find dialog box has options for narrowing searches.

To build an advanced search, click the Advanced tab; click the Field button and select a field from the list. Next, select a criteria in the Condition field based on the data type you have selected, and finally enter a value if applicable.

For example, to find messages which were due yesterday, select the Due By field from the Date/Time list. In the Condition list, scroll until the word Yesterday appears. Then click the Add to List button. The new search criteria will be copied to the box at the top of the dialog box. Then click the Find Now button.

You can also add additional criteria. One example is Incomplete Status. To do this, select the All Task Fields list and choose %Complete from the top of that list. In the Condition list choose Is at Most and in the Value field enter 50. Click the Add button to save. This will add the condition to the query. Click Find Now to see a list of messages that meet the criteria you specified.

Grouping Messages

You can group messages by right-clicking a Column Heading button and choosing Group By This Field from the pop-up menu. This displays the Group By box at the top of the list of messages, with the selected field above the other fields (see Figure 39.17).

N O T E The Group By area at the top of the message list is not displayed by default in Outlook at first, so don't bother looking for it until you right-click a column heading and select Group By This Field from the pop-up menu. Alternatively, you can click View, Group By box to toggle the Group By area on and off. ■

FIG. 39.17

View Group By box menu item.

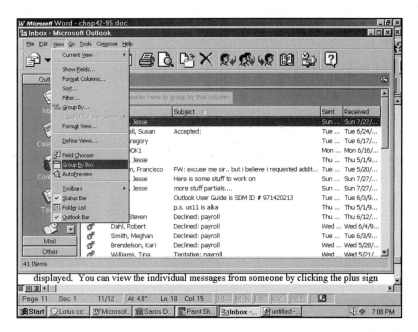

If you are in the Messages view and right-click the From: column heading and choose Group By, the list of messages collapses and displays a single line for each person who sent you messages (see Figure 39.18). In other words, you are grouping your messages by the sender. To the left of each message line an Expand button appears and the name of the sender is displayed. You can view the individual messages from someone by clicking the plus sign to expand the list for that grouping.

FIG. 39.18

Outlook Inbox messages can be grouped by Sender.

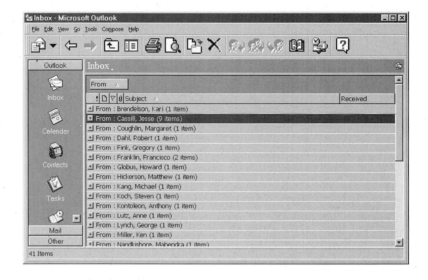

Using the Group By Dialog Box

If you want to group your messages by a category that isn't currently displayed in the Inbox, select View, Group By from the menu to open the Group By dialog box (see Figure 39.19).

FIG. 39.19

Use the Group By dialog box to group data.

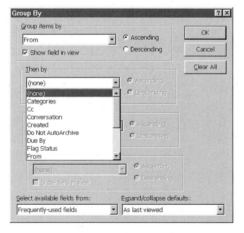

In the Group By dialog box, you can nest groupings up to four fields, with each grouping sorted independently, either ascending or descending within the group. Grouping creates an indented list with the Group By box at the top of the list and a sort order indicator for each grouping field (see Figure 39.20).

FIG. 39.20

Here is an example of 3-level Grouping of Messages (note that the Sent group is in descending order, while the From and Subject groups are in ascending order.)

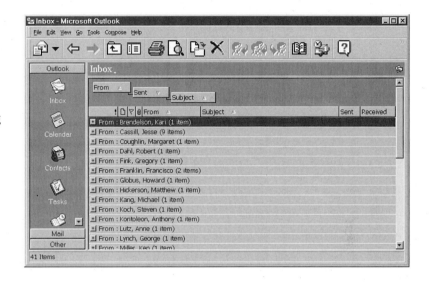

Adding Column Headings

When you group your messages, you may find that the column headings Outlook uses don't provide enough information for you. In this case, you can add more column headings, which in turn will provide more information about each message. For example, you might not have a column heading named Sent. This column will display the date and time the message was sent to you. In this case you can simply add the new column heading by using the Field Chooser window.

Open the Field Chooser window by right-clicking any existing column heading and then selecting Field Chooser from the pop-up menu. Alternatively, you can click the View menu and select Field Chooser from there. In either case, the Field Chooser window appears (see Figure 39.21).

To add a field to the existing columns, simply click and drag the field you want out of the Field Chooser dialog box to the column headings. The new field will immediately appear. Be careful, however, to drop the field where you want it.

Deleting Column Headings

To delete a column heading for grouped messages, simply click and drag the heading you want to remove until you see an "X" appear over the heading. When you release the mouse button, the column heading will disappear. Remember, however, to click and drag *down*. If you drag up, you will add the column heading to the grouping area. If you drag left or right, you will reposition the column heading instead of deleting it.

FIG. 39.21

Customize columns using the Field Chooser.

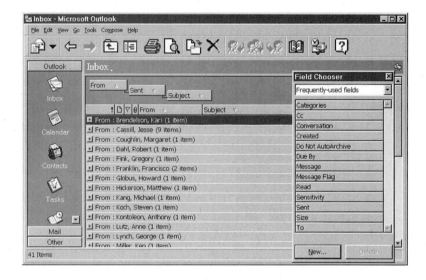

Filtering Messages

Filtering messages is similar to querying a database. You specify criteria based on fields, and Outlook displays only the messages that satisfy the criteria. To create a filter, select View, Filter from the menu (see Figure 39.22).

FIG. 39.22

Messages are filtered using the Filter dialog box.

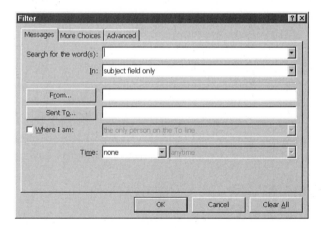

For example, you can specify a text string to search for in the subject field, such as "Financial" to display messages that contain that text in their subjects. Other sample filters you can create might include the following:

■ An expanded filter to include messages with the specified text in the body of the message by changing the selection in the **In** list

■ A filter displaying the messages from a particular sender by entering the sender's name in the From box

■ A filter to display only recent messages by selecting Received in the Time list box and Today in the next list box

You can filter any combination of Categories by selecting the More Choices tab (see Figure 39.23) and entering categories, or selecting categories from the list displayed when the Categories button is clicked (see Figure 39.24). If you are diligent in assigning categories to messages, you can create filters that will be more useful and flexible than a hierarchical folder structure. Other basic filtering features include *importance, attachments* and *size.*

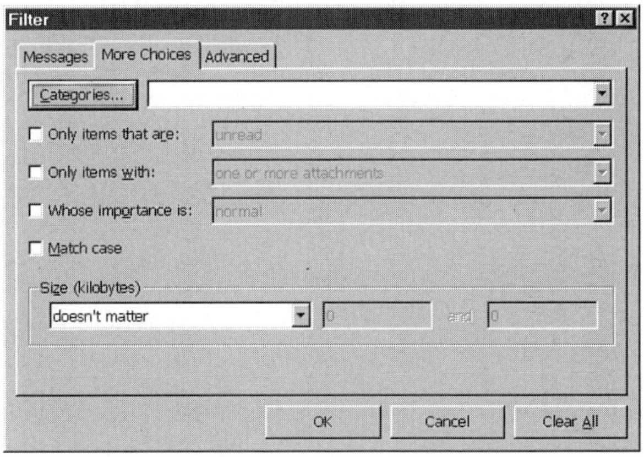

FIG. 39.23
The Filter dialog box has many choices.

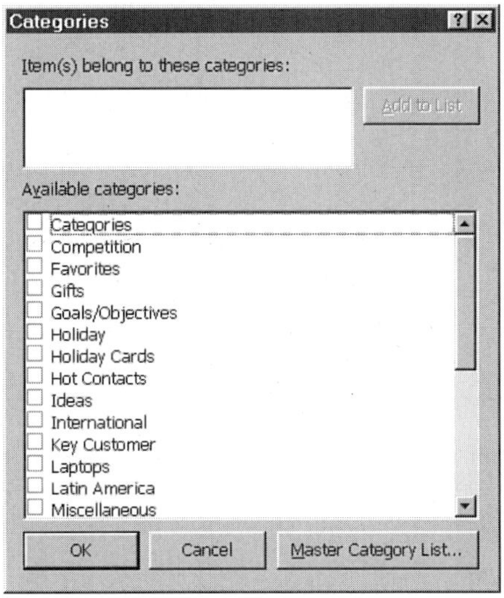

FIG. 39.24
The Categories dialog box can be used to help filter messages.

The Advanced tab enables you to create complex criteria based on any field defined in Outlook (see Figure 39.25). The list of possible choices under Conditions depends on the type of data in the selected filter field, whether it is a date, text or status field. To enter criteria here, click the Field button and select a field. Next, select one of the listed conditions in the Condition list. Finally, enter a value in the Value text box. For example, you might select Subject as the field to filter, Contains as the condition, and then you might type text that would be in the Subject field of some messages.

FIG. 39.25

The Filter dialog box has Advanced options.

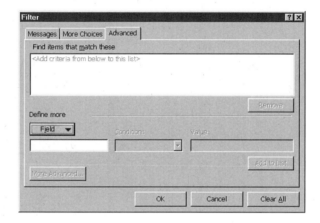

Using Categories

You can put messages in categories that you can later use to find and group messages. You can use categories on messages you send as well as marking messages you receive with the categories you choose. In effect, categories in Outlook provide you with a more powerful method of organizing your messages, tasks and other items.

Adding Items to a Category

You have to select whatever you want to add to a category. For example, if you want to add several messages to a category, first select the messages. As with many Windows 95 items, you can select contiguous messages by clicking the first one, pressing the Shift key, then clicking the last one in the list. That selects all the messages between the first one you selected and the last one you clicked. You can select noncontiguous messages by selecting the first one, then pressing the Ctrl key and clicking each other message you want to add to the selection.

When you've selected the messages, click the Edit menu and select Categories to open the Categories dialog box. Alternatively, you can right-click any of the selected messages and select Categories from the pop-up menu (see Figure 39.26).

> **CAUTION**
> Be sure you right-click a selected message. If you right-click elsewhere, you will lose your selection, and you won't get the appropriate menu.

FIG. 39.26
Items are placed into categories using the Categories dialog box.

Select the category you want and click OK. The selected messages will now be in that category.

Removing Items from a Category

To remove an item from a category, first select the messages, and then open the Categories dialog box. If all the messages you selected were assigned to a category, that category will show a check mark. Simply clear the check mark to remove the message from that category.

N O T E If you select several messages you might find that when you open the Categories dialog box that one or more categories have shading in the check box instead of a check mark or being completely clear. This is because some of the messages you selected, but not all, have been assigned to that category. You can click each shaded check box to add or clear the check mark so that the entire selection will be assigned to or removed from that category. ▪

Creating Categories

If Outlook's built-in categories are not sufficient for your needs, you can create your own. Click the Edit menu and then select Categories to open the Categories dialog box. Then type the new category name in the text box above the list of currently available categories. Finally, click the OK button to add the new category to the Master Category list.

Deleting Categories

You can delete any category, including the built-in ones that come with Outlook. In order to delete a category, you need to open the Master Category list. Begin by clicking the Edit menu and then selecting Categories to open the Categories dialog box. Next, click the Master Category List button at the bottom of the dialog box. When the Master Category List window opens, you can select any category and click the delete button on the right (see Figure 39.27). This removes the category from the Master Category list, but leaves it in the Available Categories list.

FIG. 39.27

All categories are in the Master Category list.

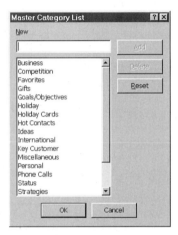

When you delete categories, however, you need to remember that any messages that were assigned to those categories will still be assigned. You will have to take an extra step to remove the category assignment from those messages. To do this, select the appropriate messages, open the Categories dialog box and remove the check mark from the appropriate category.

Note that there is a Reset button in the Master Category List dialog box. You can use this to restore categories that you deleted, but only if they were originally part of Outlook's built-in categories. If you delete a category that you added previously, the Reset button will not restore that category for you.

Finding Messages by Category

One of the major benefits of assigning messages to categories is that you can find them when you want them. If you are diligent about assigning categories, you should find that you have little trouble finding important messages, regardless of who sent them, the subject, or the dates.

Begin by clicking the Tools menu and selecting Find Items (see Figure 39.28). In the Find dialog box, click Any Type of Outlook Item (the first item in the list) in the Look For box. In the Folders box, select the check boxes next to the folders you want to search, and clear the check boxes next to the folders you don't want to search.

FIG. 39.28

Use the Find dialog box to quickly locate messages.

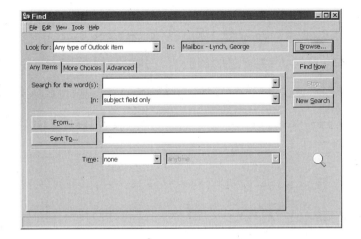

If the folder you want to search does not appear in the In box, or you want to search more than one folder, click Browse to select from a list (see Figure 39.29).

FIG. 39.29

You can browse for other folders.

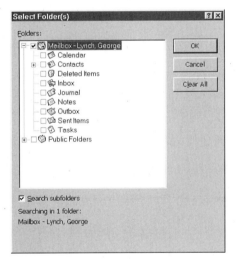

Part
VI

Ch
39

Click OK, and then click the More Choices tab. Click Categories, and then select the check box next to the category you want.

N O T E If the category you want isn't available in the Available categories box, click Master Category list, type a name for the category, click Add, and then click OK. ■

Finally, click OK, and then click Find Now.

Filtering Messages by Category

As with finding messages by category, you can filter your messages by category so that only those you have in a particular category will be displayed by Outlook.

Begin by selecting the folder you want to filter. Click the View menu, select Filter. Then, click the More Choices tab (see Figure 39.30) and choose how you want to filter the data.

FIG. 39.30

The Filter dialog box shows the More Choices tab.

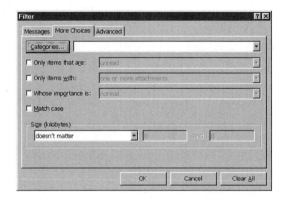

Click the Categories button to open the Categories dialog box. Then click the check box next to the category you want to use as a filter. Then click OK.

Archiving

Archiving is the process of moving data from the Inbox and other folders into other storage (for example, older data might be saved on a CD or tape backup). You may have messages that are no longer current but you want to keep them for your records. Archiving is the process of moving those important, but older, messages off-line and out of your way without losing them forever. Archiving can be done either manually or automatically.

Manually Archiving

To manually archive a folder, click the File menu and select Archive. This opens the Archive dialog box (see Figure 39.31).

Select Archive This Folder. (The first option, Archive All Folders According to the AutoArchive Settings, is only for use when you have set up an AutoArchive system.) Type a name and a location for the archived items in the Archive File box, or click Browse to scroll through a list of folders. Enter a date in the Archive Items Older Than box, or click the down arrow to see a calendar to select the date. Messages older than the date you enter will be archived.

FIG. 39.31
Archive dialog box.

AutoArchiving

AutoArchiving means that you set the conditions for Outlook to automatically move messages and other items to another folder (or permanently delete them, if that's what you wish). There are two elements to setting up AutoArchiving:

- Setting AutoArchive options in the Options dialog box (this is where AutoArchiving is turned on or off)
- Setting AutoArchive options for each folder you want AutoArchived

Begin by clicking the Tools menu and select Options. In the Options dialog box, click the AutoArchive tab (see Figure 39.32). Here you enable and disable AutoArchive and set the basic AutoArchive options (how often, whether or not you are prompted, where the files are stored, and so on). The options you set in this dialog box will apply to all AutoArchived items in Outlook.

After you've set the basic options, you need to apply AutoArchiving to the specific Outlook folders you want automatically archived. AutoArchiving does not apply to individual messages or subfolders, but only to the folders listed in the Outlook bar.

Begin by right-clicking the folder you want to AutoArchive (such as Inbox or Calendar). Be sure you right-click the item that is listed in the Outlook bar (see Figure 39.33). Then click Properties on the shortcut menu. This opens the Properties dialog box. Click the AutoArchive tab (see Figure 39.34).

Part
VI

Ch
39

FIG. 39.32

The Options dialog box with the AutoArchive tab selected.

FIG. 39.33

Right-clicking the Inbox in the Outlook bar opens its shortcut menu.

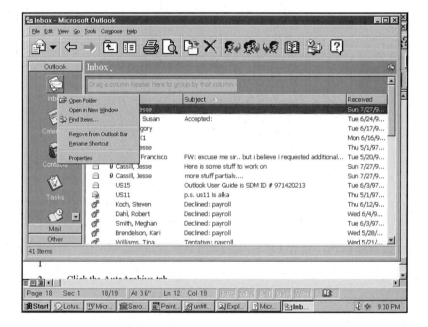

Set the AutoArchive properties as you desire. Note that you can opt to permanently delete the items rather than save them to another folder. When you have selected the options you want, click OK.

FIG. 39.34

The AutoArchive tab lets you automatically archive older information.

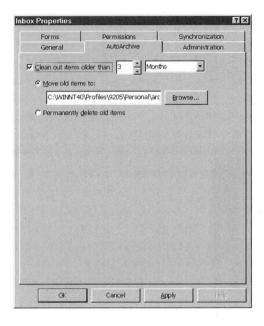

Retrieving Archived Items

To bring messages back into your Inbox or other active folders, click the File menu, select Import and Export (see Figure 39.35) to start the Import and Export Wizard. The Wizard will step through the process of importing a file and will enable you to control the way in which the items are restored.

FIG. 39.35

The Import and Export Wizard walks you through the steps.

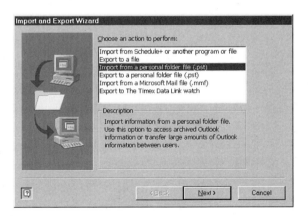

Select Import from a Personal Folder File from the list of actions to perform. Click the Next button. Select the file to import (see Figure 39.36). This should be the file to which AutoArchive is saved or the file to which you chose to archive. You can browse for the file at this point, or you can cancel the Import and Export Wizard to check the name of the AutoArchive file from the AutoArchive tab on the Options dialog box. You can set the actions to handle creation of duplicates, but because the AutoArchive process removes messages from your active folders when it archives you don't have to worry about duplicate items.

FIG. 39.36

Select the folders to import.

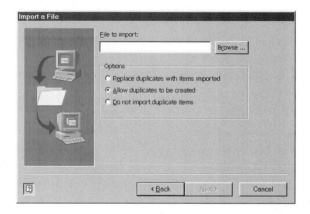

After you have selected a file to import, Outlook reads the structure of the file and prompts you to select folders within the file from which you can import items. You can select the folder into which the items will be placed, and you can create a filter to limit the import to only those items that meet the criteria you specify. Click Finish to perform the retrieval.

If you don't wish to bring messages back into your active folders you can choose to load the archive as a separate file. Outlook can treat the file as an information service, displaying the archive as a separate tree within the Folder list. This keeps the messages separate from your active folders and gives you full access to the archive.

To add the archive as an information service, begin by selecting the Tools menu. Select the Services item. Click the Add button on the Services tab of the Services dialog box (see Figure 39.37). From the list of items in the list labeled Available Information Services choose Personal Folders.

FIG. 39.37

Add the Personal Folders service.

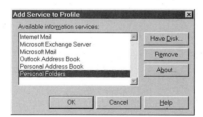

If Personal Folders does not appear in this list it means that the service was not installed. In order to proceed you will have to load the service by clicking the Have Disk button and entering the path to your Office 97 installation disk.

After adding the Personal Folders service, browse to and select the archive file and click OK. In the name field enter Archive. Click the OK button and the Archive service will be displayed in the list of services available in your profile. Click OK to complete the process.

You can view the Archive service by selecting the View menu, and selecting the Folder List item (see Figure 39.38). Archive appears in the Folder list along with the other services in your profile. You can click the Expand button next to the Archive title to display available subfolders in the Archive service.

FIG. 39.38

View folders with the Archive service loaded.

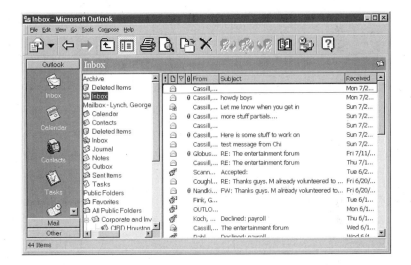

You can navigate to the Inbox in the Archive and select individual message items. These can be copied or moved into other folders, including your active Inbox.

To add the Archive service to your Outlook bar, click the Archive title in the Folder list and drag it to the Outlook bar. The cursor displays an insertion bar between the icons in the Outlook bar indicating that the Archive icon can be placed between the selected icons. Release the mouse button to drop the Archive icon on the Outlook bar. The Folder icon is displayed with the title Archive. You can now navigate to the Archive folder by clicking the icon in the Outlook bar. Select the View menu, and select the Folder List item to close the Folder list.

To remove the Archive service from the Folder list you must remove it from the list of available services for the profile. Select the Tools menu, and select Services. Click Archive in the list of services and click the Remove button. Click OK and the item will be removed from the Folder list.

Part

VI

Ch

39

Using Rules for Automated Processing of Messages

Often the best way to deal with large quantities of e-mail is to have an assistant deal with it for you. Outlook provides *assistants* to manage rules for automatically handling messages. There is an Inbox Assistant, which can automatically process messages as they arrive, and an Out of Office Assistant, which can deal with your mail when you will not be able to access it for some time. The Out of Office Assistant is designed to be activated when you are preparing to leave the office, as for a vacation or business trip. The Inbox Assistant is always active, if you have defined any rules for it to use on your incoming mail.

Rules in Outlook are instructions for handling events. An event is typically the delivery of a message to the Inbox. When a message arrives in the Inbox, the rules for the Inbox Assistant provide the instructions on how it should be handled. The rules are applied in order from top to bottom as they appear in the list of rules the assistants maintain. The assistants use the conditions you define to determine whether a rule applies to a particular message. If it does, then the action you define for the rule is performed on the message. Typical actions include moving the message to a special folder or sending a "Thank you for your message" message back to the sender.

To create a rule for the Inbox Assistant, select the Tools menu, and select Inbox Assistant. Click the Add Rule button to specify the conditions and actions of the rule (see Figure 39.39).

FIG 39.39

Set conditions and actions in the Edit Rule dialog box.

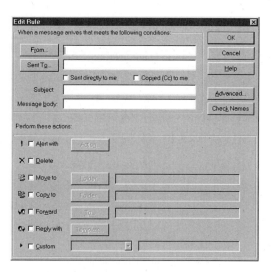

You can specify a name in the From edit box by clicking the From button and selecting from names in your Address list, or you can leave the box blank to indicate that the rule applies to messages from any sender. You can specify a text string to search for in the subject of a message or in the message body. In the Advanced dialog box you can choose the check box labeled Only Items That Do Not Match These Conditions.

The bottom half of the Edit Rule dialog box is for defining actions to perform on the message if the conditions specified are met. Click the Reply With check box and then click the Template button to compose a standard message to be sent as a reply to any and all messages you receive. In the body of the Reply Template, type Thanks for sending me e-mail!. Click the Save icon and close the template. Click OK to save the rule. Outlook will prompt you with the information that the reply will be sent to all incoming messages and ask for confirmation. This warning is helpful because a rule to reply to all messages can cause situations where e-mail is sent automatically back and forth between mailboxes that both have automatic responses defined.

Rather than clicking OK to save the rule you have created, click the Edit Rule button to change the rule to another more useful function. Click the From button and select a name from your Address Book. Click the Move To check box and click the Folder button. Select the Inbox and select the New Folder button. Enter the name you have selected from your Address Book and click the OK button. Select the new folder in the list and click OK. The name of the new folder appears in the Move to Folder box.

Click OK to save the rule and OK again to close the Inbox Assistant. The rule you created is active and it will be executed when you receive a message from the person you specified. Messages from that sender will automatically be moved to a separate folder. To test this rule you have to wait until some mail arrives from that person.

You can create multiple rules to the Inbox Assistant. Rules are processed from the top of the list down, so messages that might fit multiple conditions in different rules will be processed by the assistant based on the order of the rules. If this causes unwanted results you can experiment with different orderings for the rules in your Inbox Assistant. To change the Rule list, use the Move Up and Move Down buttons on the right side of the Rules list. To disable a rule, remove the check mark on the left side of the rule definition in the Rule list.

To delete a rule, select the rule in the Inbox Assistant Rule list and click the Delete Rule button.

The Out of Office Assistant is similar to the Inbox Assistant, except that it is customized to deal with your absence from the office (see Figure 39.40). You can activate the Out of Office Assistant easily by clicking the I Am Currently Out of The Office button. You can enter text that will be sent only once to each sender (to avoid ping-ponging messages from autoresponding mailboxes). This text is usually some helpful information about the fact that you are not reading your mail and how long you will be gone.

Creating rules for the Out of Office Assistant is the same as the process described for the Inbox Assistant. By using the Out of Office Assistant to deal with the load of mail you normally receive you can avoid some of the unpleasantness that can accompany returning to work after a nice long vacation. If all your mail is neatly filed and messages went out to notify people that you were not available, the process of catching up with your mail will be that much simpler.

FIG. 39.40
Use the Out of Office
Assistant when traveling
or on vacation.

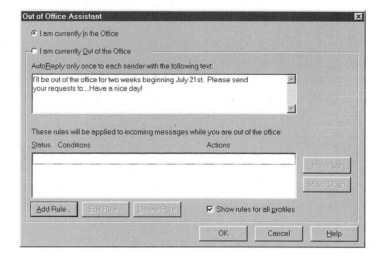

Using Recipient Groups

If you frequently send messages to a group of people you can create a Personal Distribution list that will simplify addressing and help you avoid forgetting to send the message to all of the people who should receive a particular message (see Figure 39.41). To create a Distribution list, select the Tools menu, and choose the Address Book. On the Address Book menu choose the File menu, and select New. Select the Personal Distribution list from the list of types of entries.

FIG. 39.41
Personal Distribution
lists make it easier to
send messages to large
groups.

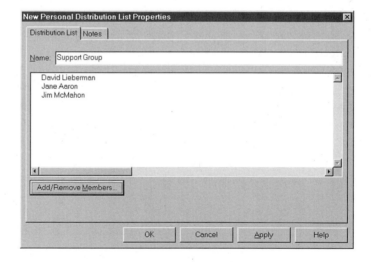

This will open a dialog prompting you for a name for the distribution list. Enter a name that applies to the list you want to create. Click the Add/Remove Members button to display a list of addresses from your default address list. Select the names of the people you wish to include in the list you are creating. When you have added all the names you want in the list click OK.

The list will be stored in your personal Address Book or your Outlook Address Book. You can compose a message as usual and select the list from your address book to create a message that will be sent to an entire group. This saves time and reduces the chance that you will forget to send an important message to one member of the group.

Using Signatures

Signatures are text that is automatically inserted at the end of messages you compose. They can contain any text you want, but remember they are attached to each message you send. The readers of your e-mail messages will see the Signature on each message they receive from you. A signature of this type can be a great way to personalize your messages and to express yourself or to convey some important information, but you should be cautious of abusing the possibility. A long signature text can quickly become stale.

To create a signature and attach it to all sent messages select the Tools menu, and select AutoSignature (see Figure 39.42). Click the box marked Add This Signature to The End of New Messages. Click in the Edit box and type the text of your choice. You can optionally elect to leave the signature text off when replying or forwarding a message. Although you can format the text by selecting the font, font color, paragraph alignment, and so on, be aware that this formatting may not remain as you intended it when sending to mail services outside your network.

FIG. 39.42

The AutoSignature dialog box lets work with your signature.

Some examples of signatures that you could use are the business card style, which consists of contact information, or a quote from a favorite author, or one that expresses your view of life.

You can insert your AutoSignature into a message by selecting the Insert menu from the Compose Message screen. Selecting AutoSignature inserts the text at the current cursor location.

Part VI Ch 39

Using Receipts

A receipt in Outlook is a message that is sent automatically to the sender of a message, by the Exchange server notifying when the recipient has received or opened a message. The sender must specify before sending the message that a Receipt is requested.

To request a receipt on a message, create a new message and select the Options tab on the Message form (see Figure 39.43). Under the Tracking options you can check either Tell Me When This Message Has Been Delivered or Tell Me When This Message Has Been Read, or both.

FIG. 39.43

Customize the action of messages with the Message Options dialog box.

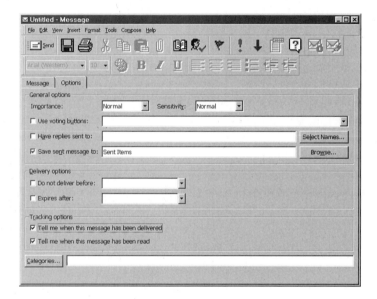

This can be useful when you are waiting for a response or you need confirmation that the recipient actually opened the e-mail message.

Receipts are delivered to the Inbox just like regular e-mail, except the icon identifying the type of message is different. For a delivered message, instead of an envelope icon there is a small, metered mail stamp with a green arrow in the center. For a message that has been read, the Return Receipt icon is a mail stamp with a green check mark in the center.

You can turn on message tracking by default from the Options dialog box on the Sending tab. If you select Automatic Notification of Every Receipt you will probably want to create a rule to file the receipts in a folder automatically, to keep your Inbox from being overfilled with receipts.

To review the results of the tracking request open the message you sent from the Sent Items folder and click the Tracking tab.

Working with Public Folders

Public folders are shared storage space on a Microsoft Exchange server, which is typically visible to all or many of the users of the server. Public folders can be set up to allow any user to post messages, files, contact lists, calendars, and so on for all to see or update. Message forums or bulletin boards are examples of public folders. A message forum is a mail folder to which users can send messages that are readable by anyone with access to the folder. Forums typically exist to serve as a place to discuss a single topic or a group of related topics. Forums can be set up to allow anyone to post messages without anyone reviewing or approving the message before it is readable by all forum users, or they can be moderated, in which case no message is visible until the moderator approves it.

Creating a public folder requires that you have sufficient permissions granted by your Microsoft Exchange Administrator for creating new folders in an existing public folder. To determine whether you have been granted permission to create a subfolder within a particular public folder, begin by selecting the View menu, and select the Folder List button. Right-click the folder you want to check and click the Properties menu. Select the Permissions tab. Under the Permissions section, the check box for Create subfolders must be checked in order for you to do so (see Figure 39.44).

FIG. 39.44

Be sure to check Exchange public folder permissions.

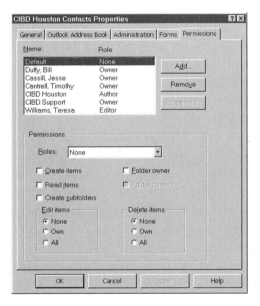

To create a public folder select a folder on which you have been granted Create Subfolder permissions. Select the File menu and click New. Click Folder from the menu. In the Name text box enter a name for the folder you are creating (see Figure 39.45).

Part
VI

Ch
39

FIG. 39.45

Name the subfolder that you are creating.

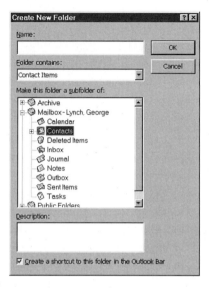

Select Mail Items in the Folder Contains box to create a folder for a forum. This limits the type of items that can be placed in the folder to messages. Users with permission can post messages to the forum that can be read by all the forum users.

Voting

You can collect others' opinions on a question in a simplified manner by using the Voting buttons. Rather than reading lengthy responses to a question that you want to pose to a group you can offer the group a limited number of choices that they can pick from. Yes or No, Approve or Reject are simple examples of choices that you might want to offer, or you might want to allow responses of 1 to 5 that indicate a level of approval to some proposition.

To send a message with Voting Buttons, begin by composing the message. Click the Inbox and click the New Message Icon in the toolbar. Click the Options tab and select the Use Voting Buttons and select from the list or enter your own. If you enter your own text be careful. The text in the Voting Buttons box indicates which buttons will appear with what text. The text is divided into the caption for each button at the semi-colons, so if you enter: "Excellent;Good;Neutral;Bad;Very Bad" in the Voting Buttons box a toolbar with five buttons will appear on the message when the recipient opens it. By clicking the appropriate button a response can be sent with the button caption in the subject line of the message.

You can set delivery options to schedule the sending of the message and move responses to another file automatically or to redirect responses to a different ID. You can set the message to expire at a certain time so that if it is not yet delivered when the expiration time comes, delivery will be canceled. These delivery options can be very useful in combination with Voting to run a kind of election or referendum without having responses trickle in over time. ●

CHAPTER 40

Scheduling with the Calendar

by Liz Tasker

Microsoft Outlook enables you to keep a complete schedule of appointments, meetings, and events. You create, view, and maintain your schedule by managing these items within Outlook's calendar folder. Appointment items are activities that you block time for in your calendar that do not involve inviting other people or resources. A meeting is a special type of appointment item to which you can invite people and resources. An event is a special type of appointment item that lasts 24 hours or longer.

If you were previously a Microsoft Schedule+ 95 user, you can continue to use Schedule+ as your default calendar.

If you are connected to a Microsoft Exchange Server, you can share your schedule with other users who are connected to an Exchange server.

This chapter explains how to configure and use the Microsoft Outlook Calendar. ■

Use a variety of views to look at your calendar, schedule, and tasks

Using a variety of scheduling views, you can keep track of what you need to do and when you need to do it.

Configuring your calendar

Outlook provides a collection of options and properties for customizing your calendar.

Setting up appointments, meetings, and events

Use appointments to schedule time for business or social activities, such as having your computer fixed or getting a massage. Use events to schedule activities that last 24 hours or longer, such as a conference or a family reunion. Use the Meeting Planner to invite people to meetings and to reserve a location and equipment.

Setting calendar options

Outlook provides calendar options that help you stay on top of your schedule.

Overview of Calendar

Outlook's Calendar acts as an online, automated appointment book that helps you schedule and manage your time. The Calendar folder contains three types of appointment items: appointments, meetings, and events. Although they are similar, each type of item has its own special attributes.

By default, Outlook presents these items in a graphical Day\Week\Month view that provides three calendar formats, the Date Navigator, and the Taskpad. The Day\Week\Month view is powerful, fun, and easy to use, and is where you are likely to spend most of your time. Figure 40.1 shows the Day format of the Day\Week\Month view.

FIG. 40.1

The Day\Week\Month
View in Day Format.

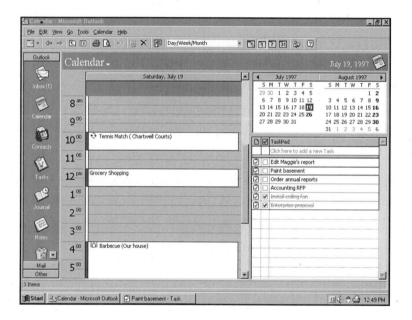

The Day\Week\Month view consists of these three main areas:

- *Calendar.* You can display this area in three formats: day, week, and month. The month format hides the Date Navigator and Taskpad areas of the view.

- *Date Navigator.* This is the small calendar next to the appointment area in Calendar. It provides a quick and easy way to navigate to different dates.

- *Taskpad.* This area displays a daily To-Do list of tasks, which you can add to and monitor.

Viewing the Calendar

Like all Outlook folders, the Calendar folder has a set of predefined views. In addition to the Day\Week\Month view, Outlook also provides several other predefined, table-type views, which you may also want to use from time to time.

To select a different view for the calendar, follow these steps:

1. Click the Calendar icon in the Outlook Bar.
2. Select View, Current View, the view you want. Table 44.1 lists the predefined views for the Outlook Calendar.

Table 40.1 lists the predefined views for the calendar.

Table 40.1 Views for the Contact List

View	Description
Day\Week\Month	The default view, which provides three screen areas: the calendar, Date Navigator, and Taskpad.
Active Appointments	Displays chronologically sorted list of appointments.
Events	Spreadsheet style table with one line per contact, sorted alphabetically.
By Category	Expandable table of contacts, grouped by category.
By Location	Expandable table of contacts, grouped by country.

The Day\Week\Month gives you a choice of three different calendar layouts. The Day layout, as shown previously in Figure 44.1, lets you zoom in on the scheduled activities for a particular day. The Week layout lets you view the activities for an entire week.

The Month layout lets you view the activities for an entire month. If you want to view all of your upcoming appointments, you can use the Active Appointments view. You can use the Events view to display all upcoming events on your calendar. You can use the Annual Events view to display those events that occur yearly on your calendar.

The Recurring Appointments view lets you display all recurring appointments, meetings, and events.

You can use the By Category view to display all recurring appointments, meetings, and events organized by category.

Configuring the Calendar Folder

The Calendar folder provides two areas of configuration, which you can customize:

- ■ Calendar options
- ■ Calendar properties

When you install Outlook, the system provides default settings for both your calendar options and properties so that you can use Outlook without ever changing your configuration. However, you should be familiar with the calendar options and properties to take advantage of configuration settings that could be helpful to you.

Part
VI

Ch
40

Calendar options enable you to define how your personal calendar looks and behaves. Calendar options are relevant and can help you in any work environment, whether you are using Outlook with Microsoft Exchange in a network environment, using Outlook as an e-mail manager, or using Outlook strictly as a personal information manager.

While calendar properties are most important if you are using Outlook to share appointments and schedules on an Exchange server or through e-mail, the properties you use to configure the Calendar folders will depend on your operating environment and how you interact with e-mail and network file servers.

If you use Outlook primarily as a remote user to access e-mail, you will want to set different options and properties than if you are usually connected to a Microsoft Exchange Server.

Setting Calendar Options

You will probably want to customize your calendar options as soon as you start using your calendar. Calendar options enable you to define the days and hours of your workweek, define holidays and time zones, and set group scheduling options. The Options dialog box, shown in Figure 40.2, is where you set Calendar options.

FIG. 40.2

The Options dialog box.

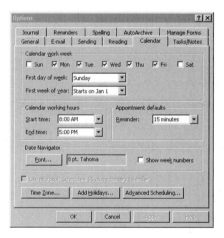

To set calendar options, follow these steps:

1. Select Tools, Options
2. Click the Calendar tab.
3. Select and fill in Calendar Work Week and Working Hours options.
4. If desired, set options to change the appearance of the Date Navigator.
5. If you want to use Microsoft Schedule+ as your primary calendar, make sure that the check box is selected. If you want to use the Outlook calendar, deselect the check box.
6. If you want to see an additional time zone in your calendar, click the Time Zone button. For more information, see the "Setting Time Zones" section in this chapter.

7. If you want to add national holidays for another country to your calendar, select the Add Holidays button, select the countries whose holidays you want to add, then click OK.

8. If you want to set options for processing meeting requests or change the default settings for publishing your free and busy time, click the Advanced Scheduling button. For more information, see the "Setting Advanced Scheduling Options" section in this chapter.

9. When you are finished setting calendar options, click OK.

N O T E As you can see from the other tabs on the Options dialog box, calendar options are only a subset of the Outlook options that you can set. Remember that none of your new settings on any of the Options tabs will take effect until you click OK on the Options dialog box. When you click OK, all new settings take effect. ▓

Setting Time Zone Options   Outlook enables you to select from a complete list of international time zones for viewing the hours on your calendar. When you install Outlook, you select a primary time zone, which you can change at any time. In addition to the primary time zone, you can display a second time zone within the Daily format of the Day\Week\Month view in your Calendar. For example, if you live in the eastern United States but frequently travel to the central U.S. for business meetings, you can set up eastern time as your primary time zone and central time as your additional time zone, as shown in Figure 40.3.

FIG. 40.3

The Time Zone dialog box.

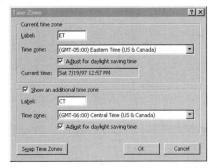

N O T E The additional time zone only displays in the Daily format of the Day\Week\Month calendar view. ▓

You access the Time Zone dialog box by selecting Tools, Options on the menu bar, then clicking the Time Zone button. Table 40.2 describes the areas of the Time Zone dialog box and how to use them.

Table 40.2   Areas of the Time Zone Dialog Box

Area	Description
Current time zone	A set of options that enable you to select a current time zone from the international list of time zones. You can assign a time zone label, which appears as the Time Zone heading in the daily calendar format, and select whether to adjust for daylight savings in time zones where it is used.
Show an additional time zone	A set of options that enable you to select a second time zone to display. You can remove the display of the second time zone at any time by simply deselecting the check box.
Swap time zones	A button that swaps your selections for the current and additional time zone. For example, you might use this option when you are on a trip in the geographical area of additional time zone.

TIP Outlook updates changes to your time zone setting as soon as you click OK in the Time Zone dialog box, even if you subsequently click Cancel to reject the changes you make on the tabs in the Options dialog box.

Setting Advanced Scheduling Options   Advanced scheduling options fall into two categories: meeting processing options and settings for free/busy time. You set these options in the Advanced Scheduling dialog box as shown in Figure 40.4.

FIG. 40.4

The Advanced
Scheduling dialog box.

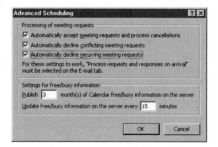

You access the Advanced Scheduling dialog box by selecting Tools, Options on the menu bar, then clicking the Advanced Scheduling button.

TIP For meeting processing options to work, you must select the Process Requests and Responses on Arrival Option on the E-mail tab of the Options dialog box.

Outlook enables you to publish your availability for meetings to other Outlook users. Within the Advanced Scheduling Options dialog box, you can specify the number of months of free time and busy time you want to make available to other users. You can also specify the frequency that you want to update your published free/busy time on the file server.

Setting Calendar Properties

The Calendar Properties dialog box is where you define configuration properties for the Calendar folder. Calendar properties include general options, automatic archiving options, folder access options, and forms associated with the Calendar folder. Typically, you set Calendar properties when you install your system and change them infrequently. Figure 40.5 shows the Calendar Properties dialog box.

FIG. 40.5

The Calendar Properties dialog box.

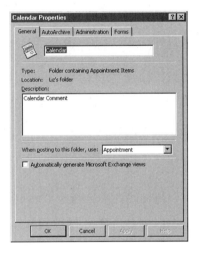

To access the Calendar Properties dialog box, follow these steps:

1. On the Outlook bar, click the Calendar icon. The Calendar folder opens.

2. Select File, Folder, Properties.

TIP Another way to access the Calendar Properties dialog box is to right-click the Calendar icon in the Outlook bar.

The Calendar Properties dialog box provides these four option tabs for configuring your Calendar folder: General, AutoArchive, Administration, and Forms.

The three fields on the General tab are described in Table 40.3.

Table 40.3 Calendar Properties: General

Property	Description
Description	Optional comment about the folder.
When Posting to This Folder, Use:	The form and item type used to create and store items in the current folder. The default value is Calendar.
Automatically Generate	
Microsoft Exchange Views	An option for public folders that allows views created in Outlook to be available in Microsoft Exchange.

The AutoArchive tab sets options for how Outlook handles old calendar items (that is, appointments, events, and meetings) during the automatic archiving process. The fields on this tab are described in Table 40.4.

Table 40.4 Calendar Properties: AutoArchive

Property	Description
Clean out Items Older Than	Enables automatic archiving of items in the Calendar folder based on the age you enter.
Move old documents to	Specifies that aged items should be archived and allows you to select the location and name of the archive file.
Permanently Delete Old Documents	Removes old items from the system; select this option if you do not want to archive items in your Calendar folder.

TIP To activate automatic archiving, select Options from the Tools menu, and then go to the AutoArchive tab and fill in the information.

Most of the fields on the Administrative tab involve options for configuring access and processes for public folders, as described in Table 40.5.

Table 40.5 Calendar Properties: Administrative

Property	Description
Initial View on Folder	The default view for the selected Calendar folder.
Drag/Drop Posting Is A	Determines which user appears as the owner of appointment copied to public folders. The Forward

Property	Description
	option specifies that the appointment is posted by the user who copied it. The Move/Copy option specifies that the appointment appears exactly as it was in its original location. The user who copied the appointment to the public folder is not indicated.
Add Folder Address To	Adds the folder address to your Personal Address Book so that you can send mail directly to the folder.
This Folder Is Available To	Allows access to all users who have the appropriate permission or Owners only.
Folder Assistant	Edits the processing rules for posting items in Exchange public folders. This button is not available if you are working offline.
Folder path	Shows the folder location.

The Forms tab contains options for managing the forms associated with the folder. Unless you need to use customized forms to view your appointment items, you won't need to change any properties on this tab. Table 40.6 describes the properties.

Table 40.6   Calendar Properties: Forms

Property	Description
Forms Associated with This Folder	Lists the forms copied or installed in the folder. These forms are located in the Folder Forms Library.
Manage	Copies a form from a different forms library to the Folder Forms Library, or installs a new form in the Folder Forms Library.
Allow These Forms in This Folder	Specifies which forms can be stored in the Calendar folder.

Part
VI

Ch
40

Creating and Modifying Appointments

The Appointment window provides a form-based interface for you to enter and edit appointment items. This window is one of the predefined forms supplied with Microsoft Outlook. The Appointment window consists of a multipaneled form and set of menu options for entering and editing Appointment information, as shown in Figure 40.6.

FIG. 40.6
The Appointment
window.

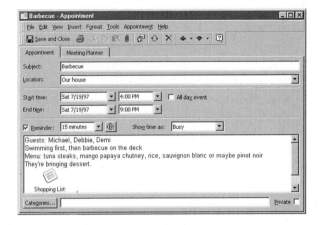

The Appointment window provides these two tabs of options for creating appointments:
Appointment and Meeting Planner.

Entering New Appointments

To enter a new appointment, follow these steps:

1. Select File, New, Appointment or press Ctl+Shift+A. An untitled Appointment window
   appears.

Alternatively, if you have the Calendar folder open, you can use one of these methods to display an
untitled Appointment window:

- Click the New Appointment icon in the toolbar.

- Select Calendar, New Appointment (or if you already have the Appointment window open, select
  Appointment, New Appointment).

- Press Ctrl+N.

- Double-click in a blank area of the Calendar.

2. Type a subject for the Appointment in the Subject field.

3. Type a location, or select a location from the list. All locations that exist in your calendar
   will appear in the location list.

4. Select or type a start and end date.

5. Enter any additional information that you want on Appointment tab as follows:

   - Reminder—Turn on Reminder check box, specify how long prior to the appoint-
     ment you want to be reminded, and click the bell icon to select the WAV file to use
     as the reminder sound.

   - Show Time As—Select how the time will appear on your published
     calendar—busy, free, tentative, or Out of Office.

- Comments—In the large white text box, type any information you might want to remember for the appointment.
- Categories—Select or type one or multiple categories under which you want to file this appointment.
- Private—Specify that subject and location of this appointment should not appear on your public calendar.

6. Click the Save and Close button; select File, Save; or press Ctl+S.

 If you want to quickly enter many appointments, you can type them directly into the calendar in the time slots provided in the Day format of the Day\Week\Month view. While you might eventually want to open each appointment item to adjust the duration and specify a location, this direct typing approach is very efficient when you have many appointments and little time to enter them.

Editing an Appointment

To edit an appointment, follow these steps:

1. Click the Calendar icon on the Outlook bar. The Calendar folder opens, displaying the appointments for the day.
2. Use the Date Navigator to locate the day of the appointment.
3. Double-click the appointment you want to edit.
4. Make any changes to the appointment.
5. Click Save and Close.

 If you only want to edit the subject of an appointment, you can do so directly on the calendar without opening the appointment item. You must be viewing the calendar in the Day format. Then, you can find the appointment, insert your cursor on the text line next to the time slot, and type your changes directly on the line.

Scheduling Events

An event is a special type of appointment item that lasts at least one full day. When you schedule an event, you can still schedule appointments and meetings during the time of the event, unless you specify otherwise when you set up the event.

To enter a new event, follow these steps:

1. Click the Calendar icon on the Outlook bar.
2. Select Calendar, New Event. An untitled Event window appears.

N O T E   The Event window is identical to the Appointment window except that the All Day Event
check box is selected and there are no fields for entering start and end times. If you
deselect, the All Day Event check box, the title bar changes to Untitled—Appointment and the date
fields appear.

3. Type a subject for the Event in the Subject field.

4. If desired, type a location, or select a location from the list. All locations that exist in your calendar will appear in the location list.

5. Select or type a start and end date.

6. Enter any additional information that you want on the Appointment tab, including reminders, comments, and categories.

7. Click the Save and Close button; select File, Save; or press Ctl+S.

T I P   If you want to quickly enter one or multiple events, you can type them directly into the calendar in the
slots provided in the Week and Month formats of the Day\Week\Month view. This direct typing
approach is very efficient for entering events on your calendar, especially if the events do not require
additional detailed information.

Scheduling Meetings

In Outlook, a meeting is a special type of appointment item in which you select attendees, view their schedules, and then create the appointment. Outlook automatically sends invitations to the attendees by generating a mail message. Attendees can respond to a meeting invitation message by accepting or rejecting the meeting.

In addition to people, attendees can also include resources, such as rooms and equipment. Resources must be set up with an Outlook profile. For example, your system might have two resources established: Conference Room A, and Conference Room B. Each conference room would have its own schedule. The department's administrative assistant could have read/write permission to the conference room resources and could process all reservation requests.

To set up a meeting, follow these steps:

1. Click the Calendar icon on the Outlook bar.

2. Select Calendar, Plan a Meeting. The Plan a Meeting dialog box appears. This dialog box enables you to check the availability of the people and resources required for your meeting before you send out invitations.

3. Invite attendees. If you know the contact names or e-mail addresses of the people and resources you want to invite, you can type them directly into the All Attendees list. If you are not sure, click Invite Others and use the Select Attendees and Resources dialog box to look them up.

4. Select Autopick to determine a meeting time that is available for all required attendees.

5. Click Make Meeting. The Plan a Meeting dialog box closes to reveal an Untitled Meeting window that is partially filled. The To field contains all the attendees that you have selected, and the date and time are filled in as you have specified.

6. Type a subject for the meeting in the Subject field.

7. If you did not schedule a room, type a location, or select a location from the list.

8. Enter any additional information that you want on the Appointment tab, including reminders, comments, and categories.

 TIP If you want to send an agenda or a document for the attendees to read in preparation for the meeting, you can insert an item or a file into the comments box by selecting either the Insert, Item or Insert, File menu option.

9. If you decide to add attendees, change the meeting time, or want to check attendee status, select the Meeting Planner tab, and edit the meeting information as needed.

10. Click the Save and Close button; select File, Save; or press Ctl+S.

Creating Recurring Appointments, Meetings, and Events

Outlook provides the ability to create recurring appointments, meetings, and events. This feature can be handy for scheduling regular business activities, such as filling out expense reports, coordinating weekly staff meetings, or scheduling an annual conference for a team of people to attend. This feature can also help you schedule recurring personal activities, such as paying monthly bills or holding an annual picnic.

There are several ways to create recurring appointment items:

■ You can create a new recurring appointment, meeting, or event by using those options provided on the Calendar menu.

■ You can create a new nonrecurring appointment, meeting, or event and then optionally add recurrence information to it by selecting the Appointment, Recurrence menu option.

■ You can turn an already existing, nonrecurring appointment, meeting, or event into a recurring appointment at any time by opening the item and selecting the Appointment, Recurrence menu option.

Whatever method you choose to make an item recurring, all methods eventually lead you to the Appointment Recurrence dialog box, as shown in Figure 40.7.

The Appointment Recurrence dialog box enables you to specify the following information about an appointment, meeting, or event:

■ *Appointment time.* Including start time, end time, and duration. End time and duration are mutually dependent on each other. That is, if you change the end time it affects the duration, and if you change the duration it affects the end time. Outlook will not let you create recurring events less than 24 hours long.

Part
VI

Ch
40

- *Recurrence pattern.* The four main choices are daily, weekly, monthly, yearly. Within each of those choices, you can specify particular days or dates.

- *Range of recurrence.* Including the start date and a milestone for ending the recurrence, which can be based on number of occurrences, an end date, or never ending.

FIG. 40.7

The Appointment
Recurrence dialog box.

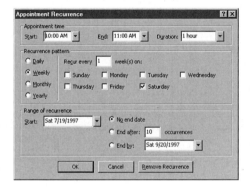

CHAPTER 41

Maintaining a Contact List

by Liz Tasker

Microsoft Outlook provides a Contacts folder in which you can keep a database of contact items. Each contact item contains the name of a person or organization, along with other pertinent information, such as addresses and phone numbers. The Contacts folder acts as an intelligent online directory of contacts and helps you automate communications with them. You can keep one list of contacts in Outlook's Contacts folder, or if you prefer to have multiple lists of contacts, you can set up additional Contacts folders. ■

Configuring the Contacts folder

You set properties for the Contacts folder to specify how it interacts with e-mail, provides public access on a Microsoft Exchange file server, and displays information.

Creating contacts

You can create an online directory of people, companies, and organizations, including e-mail addresses, mailing addresses, phone numbers, and just about any note or fact that you want to file away under a name.

Telephoning contacts

Outlook provides automatic-dialing and call-recording facilities.

Integrating contacts with e-mail

Contacts can be linked to your Outlook Address Book to help automate the sending of e-mail messages.

N O T E Although Outlook enables you to set up multiple contacts folders, you can only record automated journal entries for contacts that you have entered in Outlook's Contacts folder. Unless you have a special need to keep separate lists of contacts, you may want to keep all of your contacts in Outlook's predefined Contacts folder, both for simplicity's sake and to take advantage of automated journal entries. ■

This chapter explains how to configure and use the Contacts folder to set up and manage your contacts.

Working with the Contacts Folder

The Contacts folder allows you to set up, view, and work with a list of contacts within your Outlook application. For each contact, you can view e-mail, address, and telephone information, as shown in Figure 41.1.

FIG. 41.1

The Contacts folder.

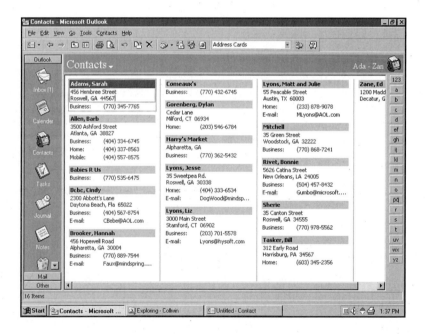

Additionally, you can keep job-related information, personal facts, and journals of the interactions that you have with contacts.

By default, Outlook provides one Contacts folder, which you cannot delete. But you can create additional contacts folders if you want to keep separate lists of contacts for different purposes. You may want to keep business-related contacts in the Contacts folder provided with Outlook, create a separate contacts folder for friends and relatives, and create yet another contacts folder for people who belong to a club or organization in which you are active. If possible, however, you should keep all contacts in the predefined Contacts folder supplied by Outlook, both for simplicity and to take advantage of all Outlooks automation features.

N O T E   Some of the automated features for contacts, such as automated journal entries, work only for the default Contacts folder supplied by Outlook. ■

When you install Outlook, the Contacts folder is available for your immediate use. You can create contacts by typing them directly in Microsoft Outlook or by importing contact information from another source, such as Microsoft Schedule+ or a file downloaded from a mail server. You can start adding or importing contacts immediately. Before you begin, however, you may want to take look at how your Contacts properties are configured.

Viewing the Contact List

Like all Outlook folders, the Contacts folder has a set of predefined views that provide a predefined presentation and organization of items or—more specifically, in this case—the contacts. The default view for the Contacts folders is Address Cards, as shown in Figure 41.1 earlier in this chapter.

To select a different view for the contact list, follow these steps:

1. Click the Contact icon in the Outlook bar to open the Contacts folder.
2. Choose View, Current View, *the view you want.*

Table 41.1 lists the predefined views for the Contact List.

Table 41.1   Views for the Contact List

View	Description
Address Cards	Small cards that list the following general information for each contact: name, mailing address, all e-mail addresses, and all phone numbers
Detailed Address Cards	Larger cards that list all general information for each contact
Phone List	Spreadsheet-style table with one line per contact, sorted alphabetically
By Category	Expandable table of contacts, grouped by category
By Location	Expandable table of contacts, grouped by country

Part
VI

Ch
41

The Address Cards view provides an easy-to-read screen format for your contacts, as shown in Figure 41.2.

FIG. 41.2

Address Cards view.

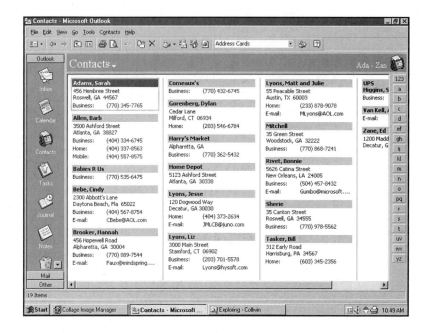

The Detailed Address Cards view, as shown in Figure 41.3, also provides an easy-to-read screen format, but displays more contact information than the Address Cards view.

FIG. 41.3

Detailed Address Cards view.

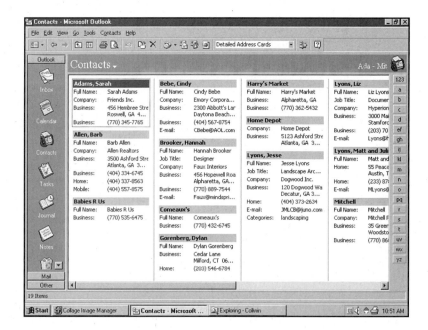

The Phone List view, as shown in Figure 41.4, with its alphabetically-sorted table of contacts, is useful for quickly looking up business phone numbers.

FIG. 41.4

Phone List view.

The By Category view, as shown in Figure 41.5 is useful for viewing all the contacts that fall under a particular category, such as business or personal.

FIG. 41.5

By Category view.

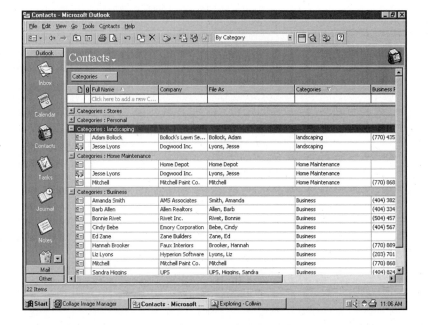

The By Company view, as shown in Figure 41.6 is useful for viewing all the contacts that work for a particular company.

FIG. 41.6

By Company view.

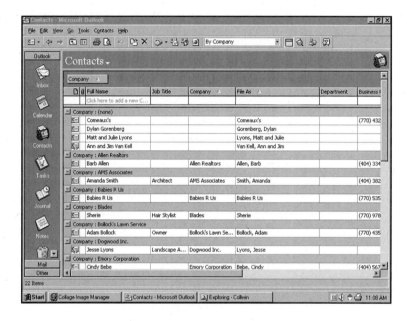

The By Location view, as shown in Figure 41.7, is useful for viewing all the contacts located in a specific country.

FIG. 41.7

By Location view.

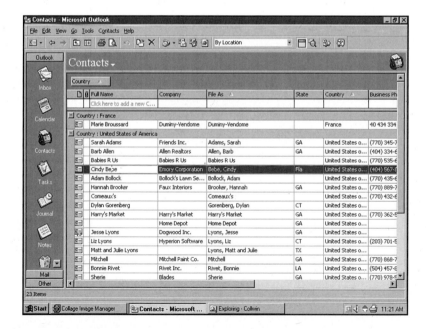

Configuring the Contacts Folder

The properties that you use to configure the Contacts folder depend on your operating environment and on whether you interact with e-mail and Microsoft Exchange file servers. If you use Outlook primarily as a remote user to access e-mail, you want to set different options than you do if you usually are connected to a Microsoft Exchange Server.

The Contacts Properties dialog box is where you define properties for the Contacts folder. Contact properties include general options, address-book options, folder-access options, and forms associated with the Contacts folder, as shown in Figure 41.8.

FIG. 41.8

The Contacts Properties dialog box.

Typically, you set contact properties when you install your system and change them infrequently.

To set properties for the Contacts folder, follow these steps:

1. Click the Contacts icon.

2. Choose File, Folder, Properties for Contacts.

   The Contacts Properties dialog box appears, displaying these four tabs of properties for configuring the Contacts folder: General, Outlook Address Book, Administration, and Forms.

TIP Another way to access the Contacts Properties dialog box is to right-click the Contacts icon, then click Properties

3. Edit the default values of the text boxes in each tab, as needed. See Tables 41.2– 41.4 for descriptions of these text boxes.

4. Click OK to save changes to the contact folder properties or Cancel to discard them.

The three text boxes in the General tab are described in Table 41.2.

Table 41.2   Contacts Properties: General

Property	Description
Description	Optional comment about the Contacts folder.
When Posting to This Folder, Use:	The form and item type used to create and store contact items in the current folder. The default value is Contact.
Automatically Generate Microsoft Exchange Views	An option for public folders that allows views created in Outlook to be available in Microsoft Exchange.

The Outlook Address Book tab helps define the integration between the Contacts folder and e-mail. The text boxes in this tab are described in Table 41.3.

Table 41.3   Contacts Properties: Outlook Address Book

Property	Description
Show This Folder As an E-Mail Address Book	Allows the contacts in the current folder to appear in the Address Book dialog box
Name of the Address Book	Contacts-folder identifier that appears in the Show Names From box of the Address Book

Most of the fields in the Administration tab involve options for configuring access and processes for public folders, as described in Table 41.4.

Table 41.4   Contacts Properties: Administration

Property	Description
Initial View on Folder	The default view for the Contacts folder.
Drag/Drop Posting Is a	Determines which user appears as the owner of contacts copied to public folders. The Forward option specifies that the contact is posted by the user who copied it. The Move/Copy option specifies that the contact appears exactly as it was in its original location. The user who copied it to the public folder is not indicated.
Add Folder Address To	Adds the folder address to your Personal Address Book so that you can send mail directly to the folder.
This Folder Is Available To	Allows access to all users who have the appropriate permission or only to owners of the folder.

Property	Description
Folder Assistant	Edits the processing rules for posting items in Ex change public folders. This button is not available if you are working offline.
Folder Path	Shows the folder location.

The Forms tab contains options for managing the forms associated with the folder, as described in Table 41.5.

Table 41.5   Contacts Properties: Forms

Property	Description
Forms Associated with This Folder	Lists the forms copied or installed in the folder. These forms are located in the Folder Forms Library.
Manage	Copies a form from a different forms library to the Folder Forms Library or installs a new form in the Folder Forms Library.
Allow These Forms in This Folder	Specifies which forms can be stored in the contacts folder.

Creating and Modifying Contacts

The Contacts window provides a form-based interface for you to enter and edit contact items. This window is one of the predefined forms supplied with Microsoft Outlook. The Contacts window consists of a multiple-panel form and a set of menu options for working with contacts, as shown in Figure 41.9.

FIG. 41.9
The Contacts window.

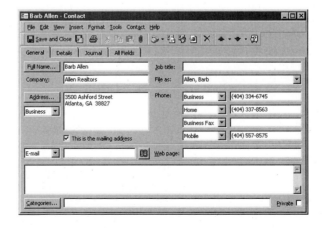

The Contacts window provides four tabs of options for configuring your Contacts folder: General, Details, Journal, and All Fields, as described in Table 41.6.

Table 41.6 Tabs of the Contacts Window

Tab	Description
General	Collects name, address, phone, and e-mail information about a contact.
Details	Collects other business-related information about a contact (such as department and manager) and personal information (such as the contact's birthday).
Journal	Displays journal entries for a contact. Additionally, the Journal tab provides several text boxes that assist you in setting up and maintaining journal entries for a contact.
All Fields	Displays attributes about the text boxes in the Contacts window and allows you to add new customized text boxes for a particular contact.

Entering New Contacts

To enter a new contact, follow these steps:

1. Choose File, New, Contact or press Ctl+Shift+C.

   An untitled Contacts window appears.

 TIP Alternatively, if you have the Contacts folder open, you can use one of these methods to display a untitled Contacts window:

- Click the New Contact icon in the toolbar.
- Choose Contacts, New Contact.
- Press Ctrl+N.
- Double-click a blank area of the Contacts folder workspace.

2. In the Full Name text box, type a name for the contact.

NOTE To see how Outlook parses the full name into multiple-name fields, click the Full Name button to view the Check Full Name dialog box.

3. If desired, type a job title and company for the contact.

4. Choose a File As option.

   This option determines the how the contact is listed in Address Cards and Detailed Address Cards views. The File As box gives you several choices for filing the contact, based on the information that you entered in the Full Name and Company boxes.

5. Enter any additional information that you want to keep for that contact in the General tab in the following fields:

- *Address.* You can enter up to three addresses, including business, home, and other. The information stored for an address is a combination of these fields: street address, city, state, ZIP code, and country. You can type all this information directly in the Address text box supplied in the Contact window, and Outlook will subdivide it into the fields automatically, or you can click the Address button to enter each address line in a separate text box.

- *Phone.* You can enter multiple phone numbers, including business, home, mobile, pager, and fax.

- *E-mail.* You can enter up to three e-mail addresses.

- *Web Page.* You can enter a URL for the contact and access it at any time by choosing Contacts, Explore Web Page.

- *Categories.* You can enter multiple categories for each contact. Categories are attributes that you can use to group contacts together. For example, you might group your contacts into the following categories: business, family, and friends. Outlook comes with a list of predefined categories, which you can modify to meet your needs.

- *Private.* You can specify that the contact is not viewable by other users who have access to this folder.

6. Click the Detail tab and enter any additional information that you want to keep for that contact in the following text boxes: Department, Office, Profession, Assistant's Name, Manager's Name, Birthday, Anniversary, Nickname, and Spouse's Name.

7. Click the Journal tab and enter any additional information that you want to keep for that contact in the following fields:

- *Automatically Record.* automatically records actions for this contact, based on your journal recording selections in the Options dialog box. Only contacts in the predefined Contacts folder provided with Outlook can be recorded automatically.

- *Show.* allows you to filter the type of journal entries that appear in the large text box on the Journal panel.

- *AutoPreview.* displays the first three lines of the notes for each journal entry.

N O T E   When a contact is saved, you can also use this tab to manually enter and delete journal entries for the contact. ▨

8. To enter and view values for any additional fields, including user-defined fields, that you want to keep for that contact, click the All Fields tab, choose a Select From option to display a list of fields, scroll through the list to the field you want to enter, and type the value in the Value column. If you want to create a new field, see the Maintaining User-Defined fields procedure in this chapter.

9. Click the Save and Close button.

Part

VI

Ch

41

When entering multiple contacts, you can reduce data entry time, eliminate mouse clicks, and combine steps by using these options for saving contacts:

- *File, Save and New.* This option saves and closes the current contact and then opens a new untitled Contact window, ready for you to add another contact.
- *File, Save and New Company.* This option goes one step further by copying the company name, address, and phone number from the current contact to the new contact.
- *Contacts, New Contact from Same Company.* This option is the same as the Save and New Company option.

Editing Contacts

Outlook provides two main methods for making changes in contacts: editing in a view of the Contacts folder or editing in the Contacts window. Editing in a view of the Contacts folder can be faster, but not all fields are available. Editing in the Contacts window provides access to all information about a contact, but you may not need to see everything, and viewing only one contact at a time slows your work.

The easiest way to edit contacts depends on the changes that you want to make. If you want to edit one particular field (such as the address) for one or multiple contacts, editing directly in a view of the Contacts folder probably is easier. If the field that you want to edit does not appear in any view that you have, however, or if you want to review and modify many details about a particular contact, you need to use the Contacts window.

Editing in the Contacts Window   The Contacts window provides a multiple-panel form that allows you to view and edit all contact information.

To edit a contact in the Contacts window, follow these steps:

1. Click the Contacts icon in the Outlook bar.

    The Contacts folder opens, displaying the list of contacts, as shown in Figure 41.10

2. Double-click the contact that you want to edit.

Editing Directly in a View of the Contacts Folder   Outlook provides six predefined views of the Contacts folder, with each view displaying a subset of contact information in a prescribed format. Some views present contacts as individual cards, and others present contacts as rows in a table. Each of the predefined views allows you to edit all or most of the visible fields. In Address Cards view, for example, you can edit all visible fields except the name under which the contact is filed. In By Category, By Company, and By Location views, you can edit all the visible fields, but you must use drag-and-drop editing to change the value of the fields by which the contacts are grouped.

 If you want to add a field to a view, choose View, Define Views. In the Define Views dialog box, click the Fields button. Then, in the Show Fields dialog box, click the New Field button.

FIG. 41.10

The Contacts folder.

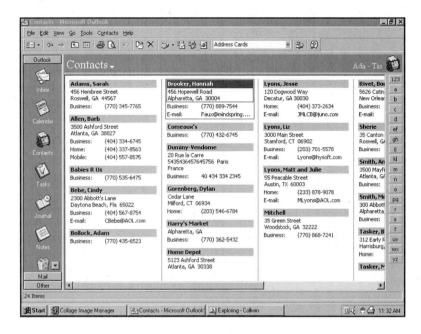

Editing Field Text   Editing a contact directly in a view of the Contacts folder is like editing any other text box in a Microsoft Windows applications; the same user-interface rules apply. To insert text, simply click to position the insertion point and start typing. To delete text, use the Backspace key or highlight the text and press the Del key. You can also choose Cut, Copy, and Paste from the Edit menu to edit entries.

Editing by Drag and Drop   In views in which contacts are formatted in grouped tables, you can drag and drop contacts to edit the groups to which they belong. Moving a contact in this way modifies the value or values of the field by which the contact is grouped.

You can use this dragging and dropping technique in the By Company, By Category, and By Location predefined views or in any grouped table view that you create. This drag-and-drop feature is quick and useful for organizing your contacts. You may have multiple contacts at the same company, for example, but you entered the company name in three variations. When you access the By Company view, these variations are listed as three separate companies. You can use drag-and-drop editing to regroup all the contacts under your favorite variation of the company name. When you move a contact to a different company name, Outlook edits the value of the contact's Company field.

This drag-and-drop capability works slightly differently in By Categories view. Because a contact can be associated with multiple categories, the drag-and-drop function does not move a contact from one category to another, but adds a new category to the contact's Categories field. The contact then appears in multiple groupings in By Category view.

Part
VI

Ch
41

Maintaining User-defined Fields

You can add your own customized fields to the Contacts folder. For example, you might want to keep track of your clients favorite drinks and restaurants so you know how to entertain them. Any customized fields that you add are available for every contact in the folder.

To maintain user-defined fields for Contacts, follow these steps:

1. Click the Contacts icon in the Outlook bar to open the Contacts folder.

2. Either create a new contact or edit an existing contact, as described in the previous procedures in this chapter.

3. Before closing the Contact window, click the All Fields tab, as show in Figure 41.11.

FIG. 41.11

The All Fields tab.

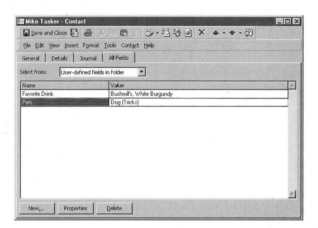

4. Modify user-defined fields as needed:

- To add a new user-defined field, click New. The New Field dialog box appears, as shown in Figure 41.12. Enter the name, type, and format for the field, and then click OK.

FIG. 41.12

The New Field
dialog box.

- To modify an existing user-field, click the field in the table, and then click Properties. The Field Properties dialog box appears, as shown in Figure 41.13. Edit the type or format for the field, and then click OK.

- To delete a user-defined field, click the field in the table, and then click Delete.

FIG. 41.13

The Field Properties
dialog box.

5. Click New to add your own customized fields to the Contacts folder. Any customized text boxes that you add are available for every contact in the folder.

Importing and Exporting Contacts

If you already have a list of contacts stored in another file on your computer, you can use the Import and Export Wizard to load them into Outlook. The Import and Export Wizard makes it easy to import contacts and even easier to export them.

Importing Contacts   You can import names, addresses, and other contact information from another Outlook application or any of these sources: Microsoft Schedule+, Access, Excel, FoxPro, Lotus Organizer, dBASE, and comma-delimited and tab-delimited DOS- or Windows-based files.

To import a contact list or a file from another Office program, follow these steps:

1. Choose File, Import and Export. The Import and Export Wizard appears, as shown in Figure 14.14.

FIG. 41.14

The Import and Export
Wizard.

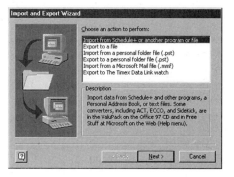

2. Select the import option for type of file format that you are importing.

3. Follow the instructions in the Import and Export Wizard.

 T I P   If you import from a file used in Microsoft Word or PowerPoint, the file should be formatted with tab-separated values or comma-separated values.

Part
VI

Ch
41

Exporting Contacts   You can export contact information to an ASCII file for use in other external programs, to a personal folder file (.pst) to share with other Outlook applications, or to the Timex DataLink.

To export contacts, follow these steps:

1. Choose File, Import and Export. The Import and Export Wizard appears.
2. Choose a file format.
3. Click the Contacts folder and then specify any filtering options for contacts that you want to export.
4. Specify the destination file name and location.

Telephoning Contacts

Before Outlook can make phone calls for you, you must set up your computer and a modem for automatic phone dialing. Then Outlook can dial phone numbers, including numbers for your contacts in the Outlook contact list.

You can automatically create a journal entry to record the duration of your phone call and add notes from your conversation to the journal entry. You can also create a speed-dial list of phone numbers that you call frequently.

To use Outlook to make a new phone call, follow these steps:

1. Choose Tools, Dial, New Call.

    The New Call dialog box appears.

2. If you want to call someone in your Contact list, type a name in the Contact box and then press Tab.

    If the name is in the Outlook contact list and you have already entered phone numbers, the first phone number for the contact appears. If the name is not in the Outlook contact list or does not have a phone number already, type the phone number in the Number box.

3. If you want to call the contact at a different phone number, select another phone number from the Phone Number list or type the number in the Number text box.

 TIP   To add this number to your speed-dial list, click Dialing Options, type the person's name in the Name text box and the phone number in the Number text box, click Add, and then click OK.

4. To keep a record of the call in a Journal, click Create New Journal Entry.

    If you select this check box, after you start the call, a journal entry opens with the timer running. You can type notes in the text box of the journal entry while you talk.

5. Click Start Call.

6. Pick up the phone handset and then click Talk.

7. If you created a journal entry for the call, when you finish, click Pause Timer to stop the clock and then click Save and Close.

8. Click End Call and then hang up the phone.

Integrating Contacts with E-Mail

You can set up your Contacts folder to work with Outlook's Address Book so that you can avoid entering long e-mail addresses every time you want to send a contact a message. After you integrate the Contacts folder with the Outlook Address Book, the Address Book displays any of the contacts in the folder who have e-mail addresses.

To integrate the Contacts folder with the Address Book, follow these steps:

1. In the Outlook bar, click the Contacts folder that you want to add to the Address Book.

2. Choose File, Folder, Properties. The Contacts Properties dialog box appears.

3. Click the Outlook Address Book tab.

4. Select the check box titled Show This Folder As an E-Mail Address Book.

5. In the Name of Address Book text box, type the name for the Contacts folder. This name appears in the Show Names From text box in the Address Book dialog box.

CHAPTER 42

Managing Tasks and Your Time

by Liz Tasker

When you have a busy schedule, one good way to get organized is to jot down the things you need to do. If you are like many people, you probably have at least one "to-do list," or maybe several. You've probably also experienced the anxiety of misplacing your to-do list. In Outlook you can keep an electronic to-do or task list that offers the advantages that you can always find it and you can update it and print it as often as you like.

Outlook's task lists provide some additional benefits as well. You can use the task list to organize and categorize your tasks, specify due dates, and track progress. If you are using Outlook with e-mail or on an Exchange network, you can also assign tasks to other people.

This chapter explains how to configure and use the Microsoft Outlook Tasks folder. ■

Viewing tasks

Outlook provides a set of predefined views for the task list, which you can modify as needed.

Configuring the Tasks folder

You can set options and properties to customize your Tasks folder.

Creating and modifying tasks

You can create one-time and recurring tasks for yourself and others and then track the status of the tasks as progress is made.

Generating status reports

You can automatically or manually generate status reports, which are specially formatted mail messages that provide information about a specific task.

Overview of the Tasks Folder

Outlook's Tasks folder acts as an online to-do list that you can use to keep track of any task that needs to get done, whether it's a business task or a personal chore.

By default, Outlook presents the Tasks List in the Simple List view, as shown in Figure 42.1.

FIG. 42.1

The Simple List view.

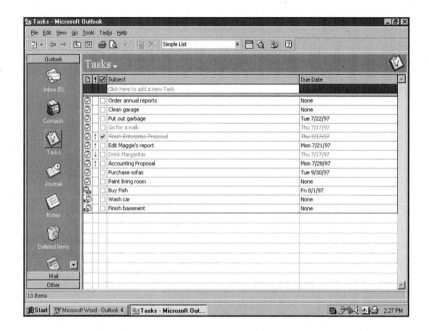

Like most of the predefined views for the Tasks folder, the Simple List view is a table that contains multiple rows for displaying tasks and multiple columns for displaying different information about the tasks. Notice the exclamation point icon in the heading for the second column. This column indicates the priority level for a task. An exclamation point next to a task indicates that it has a high priority and a down arrow indicates low priority. Those tasks without a symbol in the second column have a normal priority.

Viewing the Task List

Like all Outlook folders, the Tasks folder has a set of predefined views. In addition to the Simple List view, Outlook also provides several other predefined views, which you may also want to use from time to time.

To select a different view for the tasks list, follow these steps:

1. Click the Tasks icon in the Outlook bar.
2. Choose View, Current View, and then choose the view you want. Table 42.1 lists the predefined views for the Tasks list.

Table 42.1   Views for the Tasks List

View	Description
Simple List	The default view, which provides a list of all tasks with their due dates.
Detailed List	A list of all tasks, with more detailed information, including status, due dates, percent complete, and category.
Active Tasks	A detailed list of all tasks except those that are completed or deferred.
Next Seven Days	A detailed list of all tasks due within the next seven days.
Overdue Tasks	A detailed list of all overdue, uncompleted tasks.
By Category	A detailed list of all tasks grouped by category.
Assignment	A list of all tasks assigned to others.
By Person Responsible	A detailed list of all tasks, grouped by owner.
Completed Tasks	A detailed list of all completed tasks.
Task Timeline	A graphical time-line, showing all tasks.

The Simple List is useful for viewing a list of all tasks, along with their priorities and due date.

If you want more details in your task list, such as task status and percent complete, you can use the Detail List view.

The Active Task view is useful for viewing all outstanding tasks that have not been deferred.

You can use the Next Seven Days view to display the tasks that are due in the near future.

The Overdue Tasks view, allows you to get a list of overdue, uncompleted tasks, which is useful when you have a long, outdated task list that you need to update. Using this view, you can quickly view overdue tasks and determine whether to mark them complete, defer them, extend the due date, or take some other action.

The By Category view, is useful for viewing all the contacts that fall under a particular category, such as business or personal.

If you are using Outlook to share task assignments, you can use the Assignment view, to view all tasks assigned to other users.

The By Person Responsible view allows you to view all tasks grouped by their owners. This view is useful for assessing the workloads of multiple users and for separating your own tasks from other people's tasks.

The Completed Tasks view allows you to quickly see what work has been finished.

Part
VI

Ch
42

The Task Timeline view allows you to have a graphical picture of task durations and simultaneously-occurring tasks. This pictorial representation can be useful to assess peak workload occurrences.

Configuring the Tasks Folder

The Tasks folder provides two areas of configuration that you can customize: task options and task properties. When you install Outlook, the system provides default settings for both Task options and properties so you can use Outlook without changing your configuration. However, you should be familiar with the Task options and properties to take advantage of configuration settings that could be helpful to you.

Task options allow you to define how your task list looks and behaves. Task options are relevant and can help you in any work environment, whether you are using Outlook with Microsoft Exchange in a network environment, using Outlook as an e-mail manager, or using Outlook strictly as a personal information manager.

Task properties are most important if you are using Outlook to assign tasks and share task lists on an Exchange server or through e-mail. The properties you use to configure the Tasks folders will depend on your operating environment and how you interact with e-mail and network file servers. If you use Outlook primarily as a remote user to access e-mail, you will want to set different options and properties than if you are usually connected to a Microsoft Exchange server.

Setting Task Options

You will probably want to customize your Task options as soon as you start using your task list. Task options allow you to define defaults for reminders and assigned tasks and set display colors and working hours. The Task/Notes tab in the Options dialog box, shown in Figure 42.2, is where you set Task options.

FIG. 42.2

The Options dialog box.

To set Task options, follow these steps:

1. Choose Tools, Options.

2. Click the Task/Notes tab.

3. Type or select a daily Reminder time for Outlook to remind you of outstanding tasks. If you have task reminders enabled, Outlook automatically displays a note at this time to remind you of the tasks that are due to be completed on that day.

N O T E For Outlook to display any reminders, you must select the Display the Reminders check box on the Reminders tab of the Options dialog box. ▪

4. If you want a daily reminder to complete tasks that are due, select Set Reminders on Task with Due Dates.

5. If you want to track the progress of tasks you assign to others, select Keep Updated Copies of Assigned Tasks on My Task List.

6. If you want to receive a message when tasks assigned to others are complete, select Send Status Reports When Assigned Tasks Are Completed.

7. Select the colors you want to display for Overdue tasks and Completed tasks.

8. Enter your working hours, per day and per week. Outlook uses these hours to calculate days in the Total Work and Actual Work fields of a task.

N O T E The Tasks/Notes tab also allows you to set default display options for Outlook's electronic sticky notes. For more information on notes, see Chapter 43, "Using Journals and Notes." ▪

9. When you are finished setting Task options, click OK.

N O T E As you can see from the other tabs on the Options dialog box, Task options are only a subset of the Outlook options that you can set. Remember that none of your new settings on any of the Options tabs will take effect until you click OK on the Options dialog box. When you click OK, all new settings take effect. ▪

Setting Task Properties

The Task Properties dialog box is where you define configuration properties for the Tasks folder. The properties are grouped on four panels as listed:

- ▪ *General panel*, which allows you to edit the folder description and set general processing properties for the folder.

- ▪ *Automatic Archiving panel*, which allows you to specify properties for backing up and purging items in the folder.

- ▪ *Administration panel*, which allows you to define access and processing properties for public folders.

- ▪ *Forms panel*, which allows you to define the forms associated with the folder.

Typically, you set task properties when you install your system and change them infrequently. Figure 42.3 shows the Tasks Properties dialog box.

FIG. 42.3

The Tasks Properties dialog box.

To access the Tasks Properties dialog box, follow these steps:

1. On the Outlook Bar, click the Task icon. The Tasks folder opens.
2. Choose File, Folder, Properties for Tasks.

 TIP Another way to access the Tasks Properties dialog box is to right-click the Task icon in the Outlook bar.

The Tasks Properties dialog box provides four tabs of options for configuring your Tasks folder: General, Autoarchive, Administration, and Forms.

The three fields on the General tab are described in Table 42.2.

Table 42.2   Task Properties: General

Property	Description
Description	Optional comment about the folder.
When Posting to This Folder, Use:	The form and item type used to create and store items in the current folder (default value is Task).
Automatically Generate Microsoft Exchange Views	An option for public folders that allows views created in Outlook to be available in Microsoft Exchange.

The Autoarchive tab sets options for how Outlook handles old Task items (that is, appointments, events, and meetings) during the automatic archiving process. The fields on this tab are described in Table 42.3.

Table 42.3   Task Properties: AutoArchive

Property	Description
Clean Out Items Older Than	Enables automatic archiving of items in the Tasks folder, based on the age you enter.
Move Old Documents To	Specifies that aged items should be archived and allows you to select the location and name of the archive file.
Permanently Delete Old Documents	Removes old items from the system; select this option if you do not want to archive items in your Tasks folder.

 TIP

To activate automatic archiving, choose Tools, Options and then go to the AutoArchive tab and fill in the information.

Most of the properties on the Administrative tab are options for configuring access and processes for public folders, as described in Table 42.4.

Table 42.4   Task Properties: Administrative

Property	Description
Initial View on Folder	The default view for the selected Tasks folder.
Drag/Drop Posting Is A	Determines which user appears as the owner of tasks copied to public folders. The Forward option specifies that the task is posted by the user who copied it. The Move/Copy option specifies that the task appears exactly as it was in its original location. The user who copied the task to the public folder is not indicated.
Add Folder Address To	Adds the folder address to your Personal Address Book so you can send mail directly to the folder.
This Folder Is Available To	Allows access to all users who have the appropriate permission, or Owners Only.
Folder Assistant	Edits the processing rules for posting items in Exchange public folders. This button is not available if you are working offline.
Folder Path	Shows the folder location.

Part
VI

Ch
42

The Forms tab contains options for managing the forms associated with the folder. Unless you need to use customized forms to view your task items, you won't need to change any properties on this tab. Table 42.5 describes the properties.

Table 42.5   Task Properties: Forms

Property	Description
Forms Associated with This Folder	Lists the forms copied or installed in the folder; these forms are located in the Folder Forms Library.
Manage	Copies a form from a different forms library to the Folder Forms Library, or installs a new form in the Folder Forms Library.
Allow These Forms in This Folder	Specifies which forms can be stored in the Tasks folder.

Creating and Modifying Tasks

You can create and modify tasks in the Task window, which provides a form-based interface for entering and editing task items. The Task window, as shown in Figure 42.4, is one of the pre-defined forms supplied with Microsoft Outlook.

FIG. 42.4

The Task window.

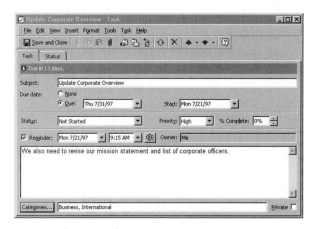

Within this window you can create new tasks and task requests and then edit and track them as their status changes. You can also specify options for task recurrence.

Entering New Tasks

You can create new tasks whenever you like. When you create a new task, Outlook automatically adds it to your task list.

To enter a new task, follow these steps:

1. Choose File, New, Task or press Ctrl+Shift+K. An untitled task window appears.

 TIP Alternatively, if you have the Tasks folder open, you can use one of these methods to display an untitled Task window:

- Click the New Task icon in the toolbar.
- Choose Task, New Task.
- Press Ctrl+N.
- Double-click in a blank area of the task list.

2. Type a subject for the Task in the Subject field.

3. If you want to specify a due date, click Due, enter a due date, and optionally enter a start date.

4. Enter any additional information that you want on the Task tab as follows:

- *Status*. Select from the following predefined choices to provide a general indication of how the task is progressing: Not Started, In Progress, Waiting On Someone Else, Deferred. This field can be useful when viewing the task list, both as a column to display and as a field to sort by.

- *Priority*. Select High, Medium, or Low. This field can also be useful when viewing the task list, both as a column to display and as a field to sort by.

- *% Complete*. Select or type a number that represents the percentage of the task you think is complete.

- *Reminder*. Select the Reminder check box, specify the date and time you want to be reminded, and click the speaker icon to select .WAV file to use as the reminder sound.

- *Comments*. In the large white text box, type any information you might want to remember for the task or insert another Outlook item, such as a note, to reference.

- *Categories*. Select or type one or multiple categories under which you want to file this task.

- *Private*. Specify that subject and location of this appointment should not appear to others who have access to this folder.

5. Select the Status tab and enter any additional information that you want as follows:

- *Date completed*. Enter the date if you have completed the task.

- *Total work*. Enter the number of hours you think it will take to complete the task.

- *Actual work*. Enter the number of hours that have been spent working on the task.

- *Mileage*. If applicable, enter the number of miles you traveled to perform the task.

- *Billing information*. If applicable, enter billing information, such as an account number or an hourly billing rate.

- *Contacts*. If applicable, enter the names of contacts associated with this task.
- *Companies*. If applicable, enter the names of companies associated with this task.

6. Click the Save and Close button, choose File, Save, or press Ctrl+S.

 TIP If you want to quickly enter many tasks, you can type them directly into the task list by clicking the first line of the task list, typing the task subject, and pressing enter. While you might eventually want to open each task item to edit the due date or assign it to someone else, this direct typing approach is very efficient for quickly creating a to-do list.

Editing or Updating a Task

To edit a task, follow these steps:

1. Click the Task icon on the Outlook bar. The Tasks folder opens, displaying the appointments for the day.

2. Double-click the task you want to edit.

3. Make any changes to the task, such as updating the status, percentage complete, or actual hours.

4. Click Save and Close.

 TIP You can also edit any information that appears in a view by typing directly on the task list. For example, in the Detailed List view, you could edit the % Complete field for each task just by clicking the % Complete cell in the row of each task you want to edit, and then typing the new percentage directly into the cell.

Task Assignments and Requests

If you use e-mail with Outlook, you have the ability to assign tasks and send task requests to other Outlook users. You also can receive task requests and status reports from them. The person who receives the task request can accept the task, decline the task, or assign the task to someone else.

When you send a task request, the person who receives the task request becomes the owner of the task. Although you can keep an updated copy of a task in your task list and receive status reports on it, you cannot make changes to a task once you've assigned it to someone else. Only the owner of the task can make changes to it.

If you own a task that was assigned to other people before you accepted it, every time you make a change your change is automatically made to the copies of the task in their task lists. And when you complete the task, Outlook sends automatic status reports to the other people who were assigned the task and requested status reports.

Assigning a Task   If you have a task in mind for someone else, you assign it to him or her by creating a new task request. You can also assign one of your existing tasks to someone else, which will also create a new task request. Either way, Outlook will send your task request to that person. The task request will appear in the recipient's Inbox and on his or her task list.

To enter a task request, follow these steps:

1. Choose File, New, Task Request or press Ctrl+Shift+U. An untitled Task window appears.

 Alternatively, if you have the Tasks folder open, you can use one of these methods to start a new task request:

- Choose Task, New Task Request.
- Double-click an existing task that you want to assign to someone else and then choose Task, Assign Task.
- Double-click in a blank area of the task list and then choose Task, Assign Task.

2. Type the name of the person you want to receive the task request or click the To button to look up the name in an address book.
3. If this is a new task, type the Subject.
4. Specify Due date, Start date, Status, Priority, and % Complete as desired.
5. If you want to track the task you are assigning, select Keep an Updated Copy of the Task on your My Task List.
6. If you want to receive a copy of the status report on task completion, select Send Me a Status Report When This Task Is Complete.
7. Select the Status tab and fill in or update any pertinent information.
8. Click Send. Outlook sends the task request to the person you specified. Based on the options you selected, the task will either disappear from your task list or be viewable in the Assignment view.

Responding to a Task Request   When you receive a task request, you can accept the task, decline the task, or assign the task to someone else. Based on your actions, the task workflow will continue as follows:

- If you accept the task, you become the new owner of the task and are the only person who can edit it.
- If you decline the task, it is returned to the person who sent you the task request.
- If you assign the task to someone else, you can keep an updated copy in your task list and receive status reports, but ownership is transferred to the person who receives the assignment.

To respond to a task request, follow these steps:

1. From your Inbox, double-click the message that contains the task request.

2. Accept, decline, or reassign the task by selecting the appropriate option.

3. If you want to add a comment, click Edit the Response Before Sending and type your comment in the text box.

4. Click Send. Your response will be delivered to the person who sent you the task request.

Recurring Tasks

Outlook provides the ability to create recurring tasks. This feature can be handy for reminding yourself and others to do things like prepare for a weekly meeting, take out the garbage, or get your haircut. Once you set up a recurring task, Outlook provides options for skipping an occurrence or removing recurrence altogether.

Creating Recurring Tasks   When you create a new task or a task request, you can specify that it is recurring, or you can turn a nonrecurring task into a recurring task at any time.

To make a task or task request recurring, follow these steps:

1. Click the Task icon on the Outlook Bar.

2. Choose Task, New Task to create a new task or task request or double-click an existing task to open it.

3. Choose Task, Recurrence. The Task Recurrence dialog box appears, as shown in Figure 42.5.

FIG. 42.5

The Task Recurrence dialog box.

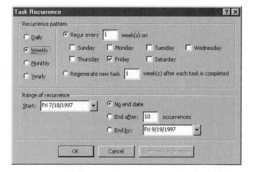

4. Click Daily, Weekly, Monthly, or Yearly. This selection determines your choices for specifying exactly when the task recurs. For example, if you select Monthly, you have three options for specifying recurrence:

   • Task recurs on a specific day within an interval of months. For example, you can set up a task to recur monthly, such as the 15th day of every month, or you can set up a task to recur quarterly, such as the 1st day of every 3rd month.

- Task recurs on a specific day of a specific week within an interval of months. For example, you can set up a task to recur monthly, such as the first Monday of every month, or you can set up a task to recur quarterly, such as the first Monday of every third month.
- Task recurs on a number of months after the current task is complete. For example, you can specify that the system regenerate a new task one month after the current task is complete.

5. Specify a Range of recurrence, including the Start date and a milestone for ending the recurrence. You can set up a recurring task with No End Date, or you can end task recurrence based on a specified number of occurrences or on a particular date.

6. Click OK when you are finished entering recurrence information.

7. Click Save and Close.

Skipping an Occurrence   Occasionally, you may want to skip a recurring task. For example, if you set up a task to remind you to send a status report to your boss every week, you can skip a week when your boss is on vacation. Or, maybe you are taking the summer off from a weekly activity that you do the rest of the year, such as attending a dance class.

When Outlook generates the next occurrence of a recurring task, you can skip the occurrence and remove it from your task list. To skip an occurrence, follow these steps:

1. Double-click the row containing the occurrence of the task you want to skip.

2. Choose Task, Skip Occurrence.

> **CAUTION**
>
> Do not delete the task if you just want to skip an occurrence. Deleting the task will delete all future occurrences.

Removing Recurrence   You can easily change a recurring task into a one-time task by following these steps:

1. Double-click the row containing the recurring task you want to change.

2. Choose Task, Recurrence.

3. Click Remove Recurrence.

4. Click Save and Close.

Sending Status Reports

You can send a status report on any task to any other e-mail user whenever you like. Additionally, when you complete a task assigned to you by another user, Outlook automatically sends the user a status report upon task completion.

Part
VI

Ch
42

To send a status report for a task, follow these steps:

1. From the task list, double-click the task you want.
2. Choose Task, Send Status Report.
3. Type recipient names or click the To and CC buttons to select them from an address list.

N O T E   If the task was assigned to you, names of people on the update list are already filled in. ▧

4. Click Send. Outlook generates and sends an e-mail message to the recipients.

CHAPTER 43

Using Journals and Notes

by Liz Tasker

Journal entries and notes are two other types of Outlook items that you can use to collect and manage information.

Journal entries enable you to keep a record of your communications with specific contacts and the activities you perform on Microsoft Office documents. One great feature of Outlook is its ability to create automatic journal entries. Thus, your Journal becomes an automated diary of your communications and activities.

Notes are items that you manually create to jot down ideas. Notes are simply text objects that are equivalent to online sticky notes. Like paper sticky notes, you can attach them to other Outlook objects and documents.

This chapter describes how to use Outlook journals and notes. ■

Viewing your journal

Your Journal is a special Outlook folder that enables you to view and track e-mail, your to-do lists, meetings, phone calls, and any Microsoft document.

Creating automatic journal entries

As you perform tasks in Microsoft Office, Outlook generates automatic entries in your journal based on the options you set.

Creating manual journal entries

You can create manual journal entries in your journal, in addition to the journals automatically generated by Outlook.

Working with notes

You can create notes about any subject, fact, or thought that you want to remember, then attach those notes to any other Outlook item, including mail messages, contacts, appointments, and journal entries.

Overview of Journals and Notes

Journals and notes are two additional items that Outlook provides to help you track information, activities, and ideas happening in your business and personal life. Outlook organizes all of your journal entries into a folder, which is called your Journal, and all notes into a Notes folder.

Journal enables you to keep a personal audit trail of your communications and other activities. Communications can include phone calls, e-mail messages, meeting and task requests, faxes, and even offline conversations. Other activities can include changes to any Microsoft Office document. Journal is useful in that it lets you chronologically organize and view Outlook items, Microsoft Office documents, and other miscellaneous communications in one place.

Notes enables you to quickly jot down any miscellaneous facts or ideas that you might have, which could include anything from a grocery list to an idea for improving your business. Like the other Outlook items, journal entries and notes are both kept in their own Outlook folders, which appear in the Outlook bar.

Viewing Your Journal

By default, Outlook presents Journal in the By Type view, which provides a time line of journal entries categorized by journal type, as shown in Figure 43.1.

FIG. 43.1

The By Type view is the default view.

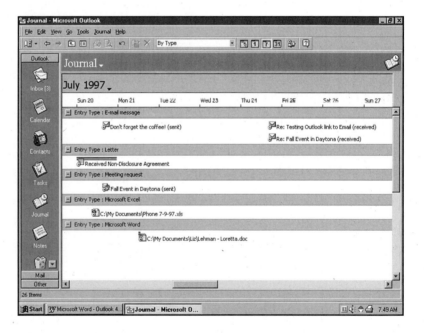

Like most of the predefined views for your Journal, the By Type view is a time line, which is very useful in giving you a complete chronological picture of the various activities in which you are involved. This can be a valuable tool in assessing if you are spending your time effectively and really doing the things you want and need to do.

In addition to the By Type view, Outlook also provides several other predefined views, which you may also want to use from time to time.

To select a different view for your Journal, follow these steps:

1. Click the Journal icon in the Outlook bar.
2. Select View, Current View, and the view you want.

Table 43.1 lists the predefined views for Journal.

Table 43.1 Views for Journal

View	Description
By Type	The default view, which provides a chronological time line of all journal entries grouped by entry type.
By Contact	A chronological time line of all journal entries grouped by contact.
By Category	A chronological time line of all journal entries grouped by category.
Entry List	A detailed list of all journal entries.
Last Seven Days	A detailed list of all journal entries for the last seven days.
Phone Calls	A detailed list of phone call entries, indicating subject, time, duration, and contact information.

Configuring Your Journal

You configure your Journal through journal options and journal properties. When you install Outlook, the system provides default settings for both so that you can use Outlook without ever changing your configuration. However, you should be familiar with the Journal options and properties to take advantage of configuration settings that could be helpful to you.

Journal options are very important if you are interested in generating automatic journal entries. You will probably want to customize your Journal entry options as soon as you start using your Journal.

Journal properties are also important, but you can probably stick with the defaults unless you want to change the automatic archiving options for your journal items. You can also set properties for sharing your Journal and using other forms, but these tasks are not something most users will likely want to do.

Setting Options to Generate Automatic Journals

Journal options enable you to define the activities that cause Outlook to generate automatic journal entries, as well as general behavior, and archiving rules for your Journal. Through the Journal options you select, Outlook can automatically generate journal entries to record correspondences with particular contacts and to record the creation and editing of Microsoft Office documents. The Journal tab in the Options dialog box, shown in Figure 43.2, is where you set Journal entry options.

FIG. 43.2

The Options dialog box is where you define rules for generating automatic journal entries.

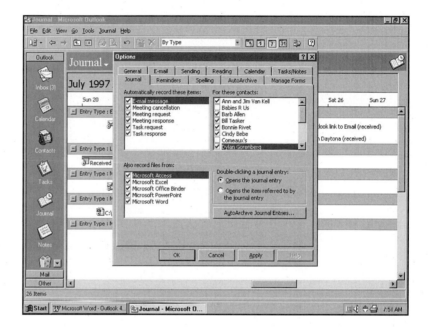

To set Journal entry options, follow these steps:

1. Select Tools, Options.

2. Click the Journal tab.

3. Click your selections in the list of items and the list of contacts. Your selections indicate the e-mail, meeting correspondence, and task correspondence items that you want to record for your contacts. You can select all contacts or a subset of contacts. For example, you could record all e-mail messages and correspondences regarding meetings and tasks for all contacts who are coworkers or clients.

N O T E Outlook will not automatically record a task or appointment that you create for yourself. You must create a manual journal entry to record these items. ▪

4. Click the Microsoft Office applications that you want Outlook to track. Outlook will create a journal entry anytime you use the application to create or edit a document. The journal entry will include a link to the document.

5. Click the option you want to specify for the behavior of double-clicking journal entries. You can either double-click to open the journal entry or open the item itself.

6. Click the AutoArchive Journal Entries button to display and specify properties for automatic archiving of journal entries.

 TIP The AutoArchive Journal Entries button is just another way to navigate to the Journal Properties dialog box and access the AutoArchive properties. Accessing and setting journal automatic archiving properties from within the Options dialog box works the same as directly accessing them from the Outlook desktop. When you select OK in Journal Properties dialog box, any new property settings take effect, even if you cancel the changes that you make in the Options dialog box.

7. When you are finished setting Journal options, click OK.

NOTE As you can see from the other tabs on the Options dialog box, Journal options are only a subset of the Outlook options that you can set. Remember that none of your new settings on any of the Options tabs take effect until you click OK on the Options dialog box. When you click OK, all new settings take effect.

Setting Journal Properties

The Journal Properties dialog box is where you define configuration properties for the Journal. Journal properties include general options, automatic archiving options, folder access options, and forms associated with the Journal. Typically, you set Journal properties when you install your system and change them infrequently. Figure 43.3 shows the Journal Properties dialog box.

To access the Journal Properties dialog box, follow these steps:

1. On the Outlook bar, click the Journal Entry icon. The Journal opens.

2. Select File, Folder, Properties.

 TIP Another way to access the Journal Properties dialog box is to right-click the Journal icon in the Outlook bar.

The Journal Properties dialog box provides these four tabs of options for configuring your Journal: General, AutoArchive, Administration, and Forms.

The three fields on the General tab are described in Table 43.2.

FIG. 43.3

The Journal Properties dialog box contains settings for automatic archiving, folder access, and other general properties.

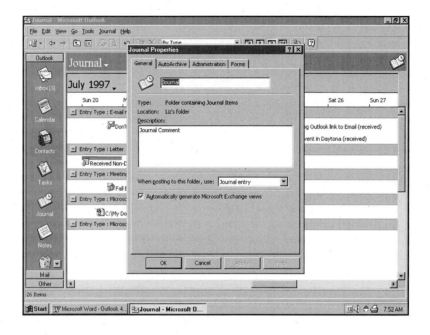

Table 43.2   Journal Properties: General

Property	Description
Description	Optional comment about the folder.
When Posting to This Folder, Use:	The form and item type used to create and store items in the current folder. The default value is Journal.
Automatically Generate Microsoft Exchange Views	An option for public folders that allows views created in Outlook to be available in Microsoft Exchange.

The AutoArchive tab sets options for how Outlook handles old Journal entry items during the automatic archiving process. The fields on this tab are described in Table 43.3.

Table 43.3 Journal Properties: AutoArchive

Property	Description
Clean out Items Older Than	Enables automatic archiving of items in your Journal based on the age you enter.
Move Old Documents To	Specifies that aged items should be archived and enables you to select the location and name of the archive file.
Permanently Delete Old Documents	Removes old items from the system; select this option if you do not want to archive items in your Journal.

TIP To activate automatic archiving, select Options from the Tools menu, then go to the AutoArchive tab and fill in the information.

Most of the fields on the Administrative tab involve options for configuring access and processes for public folders, as described in Table 43.4.

Table 43.4 Journal Properties: Administrative

Property	Description
Initial View on Folder	The default view for the Journal.
Drag/Drop Posting Is A	Determines which user appears as the owner of journal entries copied to public folders. The Forward option specifies that the journal entry is posted by the user who copied it. The Move/Copy option specifies that the journal entry appears exactly as it was in its original location. The user who copied the journal entry to the public folder is not indicated.
Add Folder Address To	Adds the folder address to your Personal Address Book so that you can send mail directly to the folder.
This Folder Is Available To	Allows access to all users who have the appropriate permission, or to owners only.
Folder Assistant	Edits the processing rules for posting items in Exchange public folders. This button is not available if you are working offline.
Folder Path	Shows the folder location.

The Forms tab contains options for managing the forms associated with the folder. Unless you need to use customized forms to view your journal items, you won't need to change any properties on this tab. Table 43.5 describes the properties.

Table 43.5 Journal Properties: Forms

Property	Description
Forms Associated with This Folder	Lists the forms copied or installed in the folder. These forms are located in the Folder Forms Library.
Manage	Copies a form from a different forms library to the Folder Forms Library, or installs a new form in the Folder Forms Library.
Allow These Forms in This Folder	Specifies which forms can be stored in your Journal.

Creating and Editing Journal Entries

The Journal Entry window provides a form-based interface for you to enter manual journal entries and edit journal entry items. This window is one of the predefined forms supplied with Microsoft Outlook. The Journal Entry window consists of a form and set of menu options for entering and editing Journal Entry information, as shown in Figure 43.4.

FIG. 43.4

The Journal Entry window enables you to enter manual journals.

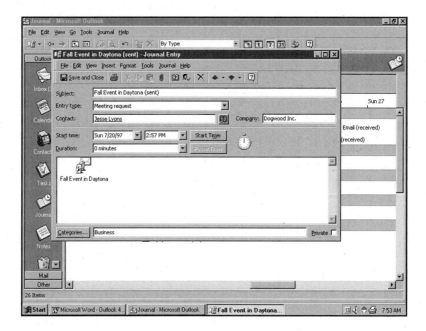

Within this window you can create new manual journal entries and edit any existing journal entries. These procedures are described in the next several sections.

Creating Manual Journal Entries

Although Outlook provides options to generate automatic journal entries for some Outlook items, you must manually record journal entries for other items, including your own tasks and appointments. Additionally, you might want to create manual journal entries to make note of documents that you receive, such as letters and faxes, and conversations you have in person or on the phone.

To enter a new journal entry, follow these steps:

1. Select File, New, Journal Entry or press Ctl+Shift+J. An untitled Journal Entry window appears.

Alternatively, if you have your Journal open, you can use one of these methods to display an untitled Journal Entry window:

- Click the New Journal icon in the toolbar.
- Select Journal, New Journal Entry.
- Press Ctrl+N.
- Double-click in a blank area of the Journal.

2. Type a subject for the Journal entry in the Subject field.

3. Select the appropriate entry type from the drop-down list.

4. Optionally, enter any other information for the journal entry as follows:

   - Type or select one or multiple contact names to associate with the journal entry.
   - Type a company name.
   - If the entry type is a phone call or meeting, record the exact length by clicking the Start Timer and Pause Timer buttons, or enter an approximate length by typing or selecting a value in the Duration field.
   - Type a text entry in the big white comment box, or attach a note, Outlook document, or other object using the Insert menu.
   - Select one or multiple Categories for the journal entry.
   - Select Private to keep others from viewing this journal entry in a public folder.

5. Select the Status tab and enter any additional information that you want as follows:

   - Date Completed   If you have completed the journal entry, enter the date.
   - Total Work   Enter the number of hours that you think it will take to complete the journal entry.
   - Actual Work   Enter the number of hours that have been spent working on the journal entry.
   - Mileage   If applicable, enter the number of miles you traveled to perform the journal entry.
   - Billing Information   If applicable, enter billing information, such as an account number or an hourly billing rate.
   - Contacts   If applicable, enter the names of contacts associated with this journal entry.
   - Companies   If applicable, enter the names of companies associated with this journal entry.

6. Click the Save and Close button; select File, Save; or press Ctl+S.

Editing a Journal Entry

You can edit a journal entry if you want to modify any of the information about the journal. For example, you might edit a journal entry for a meeting request to add a document describing the results of the meeting.

To edit a journal entry, follow these steps:

1. Click the Journal icon on the Outlook bar. The Journal opens, displaying a list of journal entries.
2. Double-click the journal entry you want to edit.
3. Make any changes to the journal entry, such as updating the date or duration, or adding a contact, category, or document.
4. Click Save and Close.

Tracking Phone Calls

Outlook's automatic phone dialing capabilities can create journal entries. If you want to automatically time a call and type notes in Outlook while you talk, you can set an option before you start the call to create a journal entry for the call. For example, you might want to use this option if you bill clients for your time spent on phone conversations.

To track a phone call, follow these steps:

1. Select Tools, Dial, New Call. The New Call dialog box appears.
2. To have Outlook look for a number in the contact list, type a name in the Contact text box.
3. If the name you type in the Contact text box is in the Outlook contact list and you already entered phone numbers for that contact, click the phone number you want in the Number text box.
4. If the name is not in the Outlook contact list or does not have a phone number already, type the phone number in the Number text box.
5. Select the Create New Journal Entry When Starting New Call check box.
6. If you select this check box, after you start the call, a journal entry opens with the timer running. You can type notes in the text box of the journal entry while you talk.
7. Click Start Call.
8. Pick up the phone handset, and then click Talk.
9. When you are finished, click Pause Timer to stop the clock.
10. Click Save and Close.

Working with Notes

Outlook provides a Notes folder where you can keep online notes about anything that you want to jot down. Notes can be useful to record a miscellaneous thought or idea that you can later insert into a mail message, task, appointment, or other Outlook item.

Viewing Notes

By default, Outlook presents the Notes folder in the Icons view, as shown in Figure 43.5.

FIG. 43.5

The Notes Folder in Icons view.

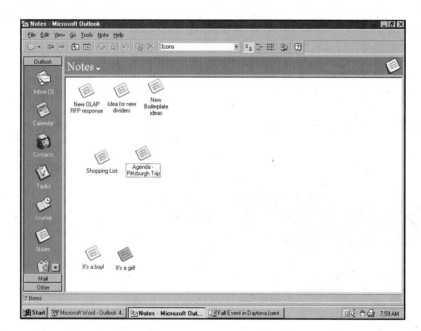

In addition to the Icons view, Outlook also provides several other predefined views, which you may also want to use from time to time.

To select a different view for the Notes folder, follow these steps:

1. Click the Notes icon in the Outlook bar.
2. Select View, Current View, and the view you want.

Table 43.6 lists the predefined views for the Notes folder.

Table 43.6 Views for Notes

View	Description
Icons	The default view, which provides an icon and title for each note. You can arrange the icons by dragging and dropping.
Notes List	A detailed list of all notes that displays the first three lines of each note.
Last Seven Days	A detailed list of all notes for the last seven days.
By Category	A detailed list of all notes grouped by category.
By Color	A detailed list of all notes grouped by color.

Configuring Notes

You configure the Notes folder through notes options and notes properties. When you install Outlook, the system provides default setting for both so that you can use Outlook without ever changing your configuration.

N O T E   Note properties are identical to the properties for journals and all other Outlook items. For a description of these properties, see the Setting Journal Properties section in this chapter. ▨

Notes options define the default appearance of Notes. The Tasks/Notes tab in the Options dialog box, shown in Figure 43.6, is where you set note options.

FIG. 43.6

The Options dialog box is where you define the default appearance of notes.

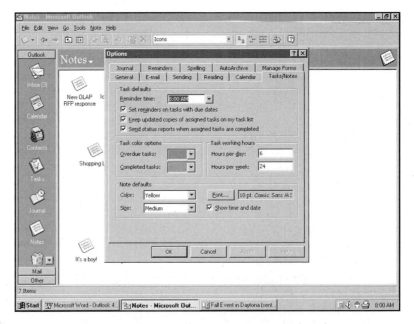

To set note options, follow these steps:

1. Select Tools, Options.
2. Click the Tasks/Notes tab.
3. Select a default color and size for your notes.
4. Click the Font button to change the default font type, size, and style for your notes.
5. Select or deselect the Show Date and Time option, as desired.
6. When you are finished setting Notes options, click OK.

N O T E   As you can see from the other tabs on the Options dialog box, Note options are only a subset of the Outlook options that you can set. Remember that none of your new settings on any of the Options tabs will take effect until you click OK on the Options dialog box. When you click OK, all new settings take effect.

Creating and Editing Notes

The Notes window provides a form-based interface for you to enter and edit notes. This window is one of the predefined forms supplied with Microsoft Outlook. The Notes window is simpler than the forms for other Outlook items. It consists of an area for typing text, a Note icon, and a Close icon, as shown in Figure 43.7.

FIG. 43.7

The Note window is like an online sticky note.

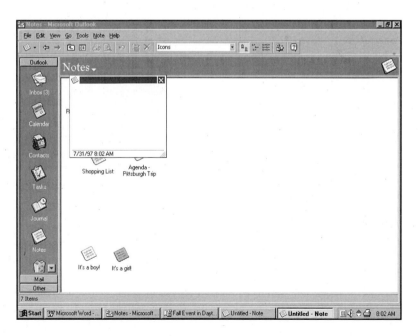

The Note window does not contain a menu bar, as other forms for other Outlook items do. Instead, the Note icon drops down to reveal a few menu items, as shown in Figure 43.8.

FIG. 43.8.

The drop-down menu in the Notes window.

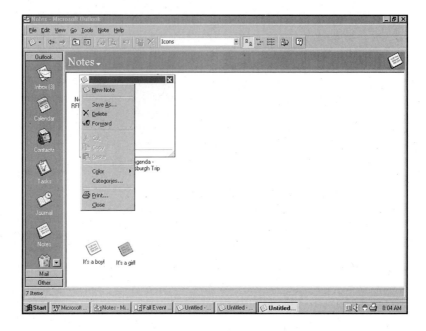

Creating Notes   To create a new note, follow these steps:

1. Select File, New, Note or press Ctl+Shift+N. An untitled Note window appears.

T I P   Alternatively, if you have the Notes folder open, you can use one of these methods to display an untitled Note window:

- Click the New Note icon in the toolbar.
- Select Note, New Note.
- Press Ctrl+N.
- Double-click in a blank area of the Notes folder.

2. Type the text for your note.

3. If you want to change the color of your note, select a category for it, or print it, click the Note icon, and select the appropriate menu option.

4. Click the Close icon.

Editing Notes   To edit a note, follow these steps:

1. Click the Note icon on the Outlook bar. The Note folder opens.

2. Double-click the note you want to edit.

3. Type your changes to the note text.

4. Click the Close icon.

CHAPTER 44

Working with Forms

by Liz Tasker

Outlook provides forms and templates to assist you in the creation and management of your Outlook items. Forms are windows in Outlook that you can use to enter and display item information for any of the six types of Outlook items (messages, contacts, appointments, tasks, journal entries, and notes). Templates are predefined reusable items that have some fields already filled in.

This chapter describes how to work with templates and forms. ■

Using existing forms and templates

Outlook provides a set of predefined forms and templates. Some of these are available when you install Outlook, while others are accessible on your Office 97 CD or from the World Wide Web.

Creating and using templates

Templates provide a quick way to create multiple Outlook items that contain some of the same field values, text, or attachments.

Creating new forms

If you need forms that contain additional fields or perform custom validations and calculations, you can create new customized forms based on Outlook's predefined application forms.

Overview of Templates and Forms

When you install Outlook, you get a set of predefined application templates and forms for working with Outlook items.

You can customize the existing templates by changing the values stored in the fields, or you can create new templates from Outlook items. You can create customized forms based on the predefined application forms, but you can't replace the original application forms with a modified copy. Within customized forms, you can add, remove, and rearrange controls, as well as write custom validations, calculations, and other user-defined events in Visual Basic script.

This chapter focuses on the special tools that Outlook provides for building forms and templates. For a more detailed discussion of Visual Basic script, see Chapter 57, "Creating Your Own Applications with VBA," and Chapter 58, "Using VBScript."

Guidelines for Templates and Forms

Whether you need to use a template or form depends on your specific scenario and requirements. Table 44.1 provides some guidelines about when to use templates, Outlook's predefined application forms, or customized forms.

When to Use Templates You should create a template when you want to keep a reusable master copy of an item that is already filled with certain field values, text, or inserted objects. For example, you might have a standard letter that you send new clients. In this letter, you always use the same body text and enclose the same attachment documents, including a welcome package and a contract.

When to Use Forms When you have a need to collect customized item information, you can either modify Outlook's predefined forms or create customized forms. You should use a predefined Outlook form when you just want to include additional fields with an item every once in a while. Although you can add pages and fields to the particular item you are creating, you will not be able to save your modifications to the predefined Outlook form. For example, you might have a few people in your contact list for which you want to add some miscellaneous information, such as gift ideas or the names of their pets.

You should create a new form when you want to create a reusable, master form in which you want to add, remove, and rearrange fields and add customized calculations and validation. For example, you might want to create a special calendar form for household employees to calculate a projected bimonthly bill based on the hours that they are scheduled to work.

Predefined Outlook Forms

Outlook comes with eight predefined forms in the Application Forms library. Table 44.1 lists these predefined forms.

Table 44.1 Outlook Application Forms

Form	Description
Message	The default form for the Inbox.
Appointment	The default form for the Calendar.
Contact	The default form for Contact folder.
Task	The default form for the Task folder.
Journal entry	The default form for the Journal.
Note	The default form for the Notes folder.
Post	The form that Outlook uses to post a note to another folder.
Standard Default	The form that Outlook uses when the correct form cannot be found.

The Message, Appointment, Contact, Task, Journal Entry, and Notes forms are described in detail in the previous Outlook chapters.

Changing the Default Form for a Folder

You can change the default form for a folder to any form that is based on the same item type as the folder. To change the default form for a folder, follow these steps:

1. Right-click the Outlook item in the Outlook bar and choose Properties.
2. Select the General tab.
3. Select the form you want in the When posting to this folder field.

Additional Predefined Forms

You can install several additional sets of sample forms that are available on the Office 97 CD. Even if you don't need these specific forms, you can see if you might want to use them as templates to create a different custom form. This is especially valuable if you find the forms have some specially coded behavior that you can take advantage of.

Table 44.2 lists the five sets of sample forms.

Table 44.2 Guidelines for Using Templates and Forms

Form Set	Description
Classified Ads	A response form used to purchase items in the classified ads, this form comes with a sample database.
Sales Management	A set of forms used to manage any generic sales process; the forms synchronize with Calendar, Tasks, Contacts, and Journal.

continues

Table 44.2   Continued

Form Set	Description
Training Management	A set of forms used to schedule and enroll students in courses; the forms synchronize with Calendar.
Vacation and Sick Leave	A set of forms used to report vacation and sick leave; the forms synchronize with the user's Calendar.
While You Were Out	A form that can be used to take a message for another Outlook user and send it to their Inbox.

When you install these sample forms, the installation program creates a file called **forms.pst** in the Microsoft Office\Office subdirectory on your hard drive. That file contains an Outlook message item for each of the five form sets. Each message gives you an overview of the sample forms within the set and tells you how to configure them on your system.

To view the forms.pst file, follow these steps:

1. Install the Outlook sample forms from the Office 97 CD.

2. Start Outlook, if it's not already running, and click the Inbox icon.

3. Select File, Open Special Folder, then click Personal Folder.

4. Double-click forms.pst. The Sample folder opens.

5. Display the subfolders by clicking the Sample Folder heading or selecting View, Folder List. The subfolders for the five sample forms should appear.

6. Double-click the message for the sample folder you want to explore, and follow the instructions in the message.

Working with Templates

Templates save you time in creating similar or identical items because they allow you to fill information in the fields and save it. This reduces what you need to type in each time you create another item. When you create an item using a template, the information is already filled in. Templates are stored with an .oft extension.

You can create your own templates from items and also use the templates provided with Outlook. For example, you might want to save several message templates with special headings in the top few lines of the text area.

Creating a Template

To create a template, follow these steps:

1. Open a new or existing form.

2. Enter or edit values in the form.

3. Select File, Save As.

4. In the Save As File Type field, select Outlook Template and make sure to save the form in the Templates folder, as shown in Figure 44.1.

FIG. 44.1
Use the Save As Dialog Box to save the file to the Templates folder.

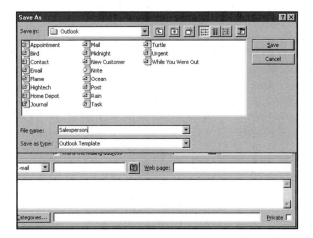

 If you save a template in the wrong place, you can easily delete it. To delete a template, access the folder in which you saved the template and press Delete.

Using a Template to Create an Item

The purpose for creating Outlook templates is so that you can use them to more quickly create Outlook items. To create an item based on a template, follow these steps:

1. Select File, New, Choose Template.

2. Double-click the template you want to use. An untitled item appears with already filled fields.

3. Enter the rest of the item information as needed, then click Save and Close.

Working with Customized Forms

All Outlook forms, including application forms and new forms you create, must be associated with one of the six Outlook item types. Furthermore, you cannot create a new form from scratch. When you create a new form in Outlook, you must base it on an existing form.

Depending on your needs, expertise, and interest level, creating customized forms can be as simple as adding a new text field to an Outlook application form and publishing the form under a new name. Or it can involve fairly extensive modifications, including new pages, fields, properties, and custom processing written in Visual Basic script.

The forms design capabilities provided within Outlook are similar to the forms design function-ality available in Visual Basic for Applications (VBA); however, Outlook VB Script is more limited and specific to managing Outlook items. If you are familiar with designing forms and writing script in VBA, Outlook forms design will seem very familiar, although somewhat quirky.

Outlook Design Mode

You must be in design mode to modify or create a form. When you are in design mode, you have access to a set of forms design commands and tools that are not visible at any other time.

To access design mode, from the menu bar of any blank Outlook form, select Tools, Design Outlook Form.

 TIP The Design Outlook Forms menu option is only available on the Tools menus in the Outlook forms windows. This menu option does not appear on the Tools menu of the Outlook folder windows.

After you select the Design Outlook Form menu option, the look of the form window changes. Figure 44.2 shows a blank Contact form in Design mode.

FIG. 44.2

The Contact Form is in Design Mode.

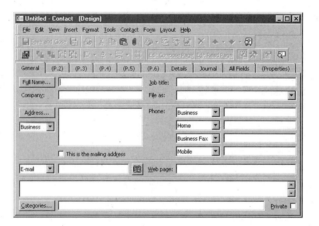

Any time you are in Design mode on a Outlook form, the title bar displays the word "(Design)." Additionally, the following user interface objects become available for customizing a form when it is in Design mode:

- A Form menu, which contains commands for setting page level options, accessing control properties, and displaying and hiding design tools.
- A Layout menu, which contains commands useful for formatting and grouping controls on a page.
- A design toolbar, which contains icons for many of the options on the Form menu.

- A new set of tabs, including five blank pages and three special design tabs: All Fields, Properties, and Actions. Parentheses around a tab label indicate the page is hidden.

- Field Chooser, a floating dialog box that allows you to drag predefined fields onto the form. These fields are controls that already have set properties—they are already assigned, or "bound," to a data type and field.

- Toolbox, a floating dialog box that allows you to drag controls onto a page. You set the properties for the controls and bind them to fields as needed.

- Script Editor, a tool that displays a window for writing visual basic script for the form and its controls. A separate help file is available on the Outlook Visual Basic Script Editor, but you need to install it. You can find it on the Office 97 CD in the ValuPack\MoreHelp folder, or on the World Wide Web by selecting Help, Microsoft on the web, Online Support in any Office97 application.

Creating New Outlook Forms

You can create new forms, but you cannot create them from scratch. New forms must be based on an existing form. Through this approach, every Outlook form is inherently associated with one of the six Outlook item types.

When you're designing a new form, you should start with a blank instance of the form upon which you are basing it. If you use an instance of the form that contains an existing item, all of the field values for that item will become default values for the new form you are designing.

To create a custom form, follow these steps:

1. Select File, New, Choose Form. The New Form dialog box appears, as shown in Figure 44.3.

FIG. 44.3

In, the New Form Dialog Box, you choose an existing form to use as a model for your new form.

2. Select the forms library that contains the form you want to use to create a new form, then double-click the form. An untitled blank form appears for the item you selected.

 T I P Another way to open a blank item for creating a form is to select the item icon on the Outlook bar, then select the form you want to base your new form on from the Item menu.

3. From the menu bar on the blank form, select Tools, Design Outlook Form.

4. Add and remove fields and controls as needed:

- To add a field, click the field in the Field Chooser box, then drag the field onto a page.
- To remove a field, press Ctrl, click the control and label associated with the field, and click Delete.

N O T E You cannot add, remove, or modify the fields on the General page and other preformatted pages of the form. (Although you can hide preformatted pages. See step 8.) Those pages that are editable appear with a gray dotted background. ▪

5. Add and remove controls as needed:

- To add a control, click the control in the Control Toolbox, then drag the control onto a page.
- To remove a control, select the control and press Delete, or right-click the control and then click Delete on the shortcut menu.

6. To set properties for a control, right-click the control and then click Properties on the shortcut menu, or click the control and select Form, Properties. For more information, see the Control Properties section in this chapter.

7. To set additional display properties, right-click the control, and then click Advanced Properties on the shortcut menu. Edit property values as needed.

8. Hide or show pages on the form by selecting Form, Display This Page. If you drag a field or control to a hidden page, the page automatically shows.

N O T E You cannot show the (Properties) or (Actions) pages. ▪

9. Select the (Properties) tab and set properties for the form. For more information, see the Form Properties section in this chapter.

10. To create custom actions for a form, select the (Actions) tab, then click New. For details on creating custom Actions, see the Creating Custom Actions section in this chapter.

11. If you need to code additional custom behavior for the form or a control on it, select Form, View Code to access the VB script editor. You can use the VB script editor to write visual basic instructions for the form or for a control on the form. For example, you might add a button to a form, and you want the button to display a group of text boxes when the user selects it. You could write VB script to cause the additional text boxes to display when the user presses the button. For more information on creating Outlook VB script, see Chapter 58, "Using VB Script," or select Help in the Script Editor window.

12. Save the form using one of the options described in Table 44.3.

13. To toggle out of design mode and test the form, select Tools, Design Outlook Forms. To toggle back to Design mode and make changes, select the menu option again.

Table 44.3 Saving a Form

To Save the Form...	Select...
As an item in the open folder	File, Save. Use this option when you do not plan to share the form, or you want to send it to others by e-mail.
As a file	File, Save As, then enter the destination path, file name, and file type in the Save As dialog box. Use this option when you want to work with the form in another program or use the form as a template.
As a new custom form	File, Publish Form As, then type the name of the form in the Form Name box. You can use the Publish in button to change the library where the form is stored. To save the form in the Organization Forms Library, click Organization in the Forms Library box. To save the form in the Folder Forms Library, click Folder Forms Library, and then click the folder where you want the form saved. Use this option when you want to save a form to a library for easy access by you and others.

Control Properties

Each control has properties that you can set and display in the Properties dialog box. Figure 44.4 shows the Properties dialog box for a text box control.

FIG. 44.4

The Properties Dialog box displays the properties for a control.

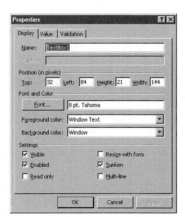

While each control has its own nuances, all have properties that are grouped under the same set of tabbed pages:

- The Value page allows you to bind the control to a field or to set initial and calculated values.
- The Display page allows you to set font and format properties.
- The Validation page allows you to set field validation settings and formulas, click, and then select the options you want.

Form Properties

The Properties page, as shown in Figure 44.5, allows you to set properties for a form when you are in Design mode. This page is not visible outside of Design mode.

FIG. 44.5

The Properties Page contains the properties of the form.

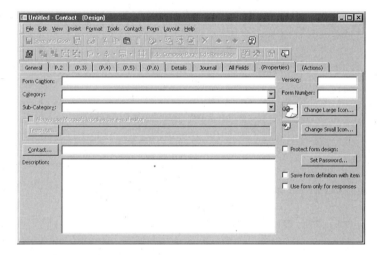

- To rename a form, in the Form Caption box, type the name that you want to appear in the title bar of the form.
- To protect your form with a password, select the Protect form design check box, and then type a password in the Password and the Confirm boxes. Click OK.
- To enable the form for e-mail, select the Save form definition with item check box.
- To have the form show only for replies to messages, select the Use form only for responses check box.

Form Actions

You can use actions to open other forms, even forms of a different type. For example, you can create a message form with an action that opens a contact form. You can also use actions to create new items, such as a message form with an action that creates a new contact. The new item is created in the open folder, not in the Contacts folder.

The Actions page is not visible outside of Design mode. Figure 44.6 shows the Actions page of a Contact form in Design mode.

FIG. 44.6

The Actions Page allows you to create automatic actions for a form.

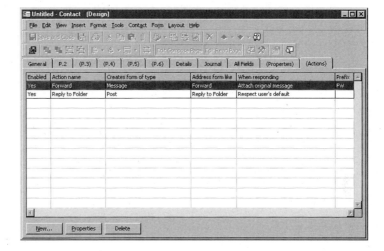

Creating an Office Form

This procedure requires that you be in an Outlook folder for items or a public folder, not a file folder.

1. On the File menu, point to New, and then click Office Document.
2. Double-click the icon for the type of file you want to start.
3. Select an option for posting the document:
   - To create a form that you can post to a public or private folder and that contains only a Document page, click Post the document in this folder.
   - To create a form that you can send and that contains Document, Message, and Options pages, click Send the document to someone.
4. Create the document text. If you are creating a Word document, you can use the Insert menu to paste in an existing document.
5. From the menu bar on the blank form, select Tools, Design Outlook Form.
6. Follow the rest of the steps for creating a form, as described in the Creating a Form section of this chapter.

Tracking and Managing Forms

Outlook has three types of forms libraries for storing Outlook forms:

- *Personal Forms Library.* Forms saved in this library are accessible to only you and are stored in your mailbox. These forms are available on the item menu from the Choose

Form command. Use this library when you have created a form for your own personal use, such as a form to track the hours of household employees, such as a housekeeper, baby-sitter, dog walker, or lawn care service.

- *Folder Forms Library.* Forms saved in this library can be accessible to everyone (in a public folder) or only to you (in a private folder). If the form is saved in a library on your hard disk, it is accessible to you only while in the folder. These forms are available on the item menu while you are in the folder. Use this library when saving forms to a specific folder, generally a public folder. For example, in a public folder used for a particular project, you could have a status report form and an instructions form.

- Organization Forms Library. Forms saved in this library are accessible to everyone in your organization and are stored on the Microsoft Exchange server. (You must have write permission to save to the server; for information, see your administrator.) These forms are available on the item menu from the Choose Form command. Use this library for forms that are needed by many people, such as an expense report form. Saving to this library provides a quick and easy way to distribute and update forms.

You can move sample forms into a forms library. Open the sample form, and then save it in a forms library by using the Publish Form As command on the File menu. ●

Part VII: Internet and Intranet Integration

CHAPTER 45

Integrating with the Internet

by Joe Kraynak

You are probably accustomed to using applications to access files locally, either on your own computer or on your company's network. You have used the familiar File, Open command to open files for editing, and have used the File, Save command to save completed files to your hard drive or to the network server.

With the recent popularity of the Internet (and the Web), you have had to use specialized applications, including Web browsers and FTP clients, to access files and Web pages stored on remote Internet servers. To work on a file, you have had to save it to your hard drive, open it in a specialized editor, and then upload the file to the remote server. This forced you to jump back and forth from your desktop applications to your Internet programs and learn many new commands and procedures.

Microsoft Office has introduced several new features in Office 97 to integrate your local PC and the Internet. The most significant feature, the Web toolbar, allows you to open Web pages (and other files stored on the Internet) in your Office applications, view them inside the application's window, and edit those files using the Office application. You can even use Internet Explorer to open your Office documents; Internet Explorer displays the document, along with the application's toolbar and menus, so you can edit the document right inside the Explorer window! ■

Use the Internet from Office

Learn how to open Web pages in Word, Excel, PowerPoint, and Access.

Access Office Documents with Internet Explorer

Learn how to open Office 97 documents in the Internet Explorer window, and use Internet Explorer 4.

Add Web page objects to your documents

You can copy and paste graphics, animations, and other objects from Web pages to your Office 97 documents.

Download and upload files with FTP

Find out how to open and save Office 97 documents on remote FTP servers.

Search for files with Find Fast

Find files on your computer or on your company intranet with Find Fast and Web Find Fast.

Accessing the Internet from Office Applications

Like most recent Microsoft products, the majority of the new features in Office 97 are directed toward taking advantage of the Internet, especially the World Wide Web. Every application in Office 97 allows you to save your documents as Web pages, insert links, and publish your pages electronically. In addition, the Office 97 Web toolbar provides easy access to files on your computer, your company's intranet, or the Web.

In order to use any of these advanced features, you must first install Internet Explorer. When you installed Microsoft Office 97, it placed an icon on your desktop called Setup for Microsoft Internet Explorer. Insert your Office 97 CD and double-click the icon to install Internet Explorer. Then, follow the on-screen instructions. The installation places an icon, called The Internet, on your Windows desktop, which you can double-click to set up your Internet connection and run Internet Explorer.

N O T E The following sections explain how to use Internet Explorer 3.x, included on the Office 97 CD. However, if you work primarily on the Internet or on your company's intranet, you should upgrade to Internet Explorer 4, as explained later in this chapter. Internet Explorer 4 includes additional desktop integration tools that provide near seamless integration between your desktop PC and the Internet. ▪

Using the Web Toolbar

All Office 97 applications (except Outlook) feature the Web toolbar, which offers controls for opening and navigating Web pages, as well as your Office documents. To display the toolbar, click the Web Toolbar button in the Standard toolbar, or right-click any toolbar and select Web. The Web toolbar appears just below the Formatting toolbar, as shown in Figure 45.1. If you have used Internet Explorer to browse the Web, the Web toolbar should look familiar.

Table 45.1 provides a list of the buttons on the Web toolbar, along with a brief description of each button.

Table 45.1 Web Toolbar Buttons

Button	Name	Description
⇦	Back	Opens the previously opened page or document.
⇨	Forward	If you click the Back button to view the previous page, Forward takes you to the next page.
⊗	Stop Current Jump	Aborts the page that is currently loading and displays any contents that have been downloaded.

Button	Name	Description
	Refresh Current Page	Reloads a page in the event that the page did not load properly or you aborted the page loading.
	Start Page	Opens the starting page, which you can set up in your browser.
	Search the Web	Opens a search page in your Web browser.
Favorites ▾	Favorites	Lets you add the currently opened page or document to the Favorites menu, and displays the names of pages and documents you added.
Go ▾	Go	Provides several options for navigating the Web, including Back, Forward, Start Page, and Search.
	Show Only Web Toolbar	Hides the other toolbars, giving your Office application more room for displaying Web pages.
(see Figure 45.1)	Address	Lets you quickly go to a Web page or open a document by entering its address, and provides a list of addresses for pages you have recently visited.

Part
VII

Ch
45

FIG. 45.1

The Microsoft Office Web toolbar allows you to navigate Web pages and Office documents in your application window.

Address ——

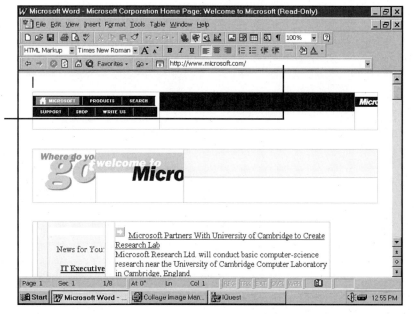

Entering Page Addresses

You can use the Web toolbar to open pages stored on the Web and to jump to documents (Office documents or Web pages you have previously opened). Take the following steps:

1. Drag over the address in the Address text box, and type the address of the Web page you want to open.

2. Press Enter. This automatically establishes the Internet connection (if required) and calls up Internet Explorer, which then loads the Web page.

3. To display the page in Word so you can edit it, click Internet Explorer's Edit button. Internet Explorer automatically runs Word and opens the file as a read-only file (see Figure 45.2). You can then click links (icons or highlighted text on Web pages) to navigate the Web. As you click links, the Web pages open in the Word window, not in Internet Explorer.

TROUBLESHOOTING

The Web page opens in a different text editor, instead of Word. If you have another Web page editor set up as the default editor, the Web page will open in that editor, not in Word. To use Word as the default Web page editor, run My Computer or Windows Explorer, select View, Options, and click the File Types tab. Scroll down the list of file types, select Internet Document (HTML), and click the Edit button. In the Actions list, click Edit, and click the Edit button. Next to the Application Used to Perform Action text box, click the Browse button, and select the Winword.exe file (it is in the \Program Files\Microsoft Office\Office folder). Keep clicking OK to back out of the dialog boxes and save your changes.

FIG. 45.2

When you click Internet Explorer's Edit button, the page appears in Word, where you can navigate the Web by clicking links, or edit the page.

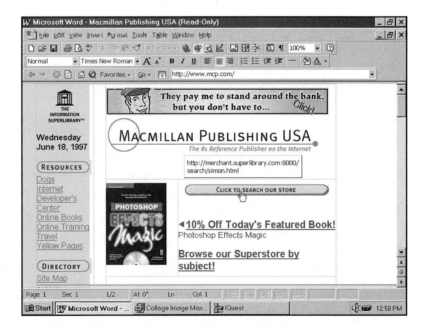

> **CAUTION**
>
> Web browsing with your Office applications may not seem all that smooth at first. Entering a Web address when an Office document is opened kicks you out to the browser, Internet Explorer, which opens the file. If you click Explorer's Edit button, the page opens in Word. When you click a link on the page, the next page opens in Word, not in Internet Explorer, and you can then browse the Web with Word as you would with your browser. Just keep in mind that when you use the Web toolbar when an Office document is opened, it initially calls up Internet Explorer.

Flipping Back and Forth

As you click links to move from one Web page to the next, the Back and Forward buttons on the Web toolbar become active. Click the Back button (the leftmost button on the Web toolbar) to display the previous page. When you back up, the Forward button becomes active. Click the Forward button to return to a page you backed up from.

As you open Office documents and Web pages, their addresses are added to the Address drop-down list. To return to a document you recently opened, open the Address drop-down list and select the address of the desired document or Web page. The selected document or page is opened in the application's window.

Stopping and Reloading Pages

To the right of the Back and Forward buttons are two buttons that give you control over the page that is currently loading: the Stop and Refresh buttons. Click the Stop button if a page is taking an extremely long time to download. This aborts the download and displays as much of the page as has been downloaded (typically most of the text and links).

If a page transfer is interrupted for any reason, click the Refresh button to reload the page. In most cases, Refresh succeeds in downloading any graphics and other objects that may have been lost in the initial download.

Searching the Internet

Internet Explorer is set up to use a page at Microsoft's Web site to search the Internet. In the Web toolbar, click the Search the Web button (just to the left of the Favorites list). This runs Internet Explorer, which opens the search page, as shown in Figure 45.3. Enter two or three unique words to compose your search instruction, select the desired Web search tool, and click the Search button. The search tool finds pages that match your search instruction and displays a list of links. You can click the links to browse with Internet Explorer or click the Edit button to display the list in Word, and then click links to browse.

N O T E Your Office application may try to open the Search page and will often botch the task, displaying a blank page. You will get better results by clicking the Search button in Internet Explorer. ▪

FIG. 45.3

When you click the Search button in the Web toolbar, Internet Explorer runs and displays Microsoft's Search page.

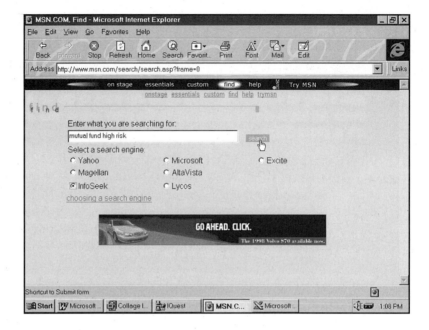

Adding Documents or Pages to the Favorites Menu

Internet Explorer offers a feature called Favorites that allows you to add the names and addresses of Web sites to a menu so you can quickly return to the sites later. The Web toolbar provides this same quick access to your Office documents.

To add an Office document to the Favorites menu, complete the following steps:

1. Open the Office document, and then select Favorites, Add to Favorites.

2. In the Add to Favorites window, type the title of the document as you want it to appear on the Favorites menu.

3. Click the Add button.

Whenever you want to open the document, open the Favorites menu in any Office application or in Internet Explorer and select the document. The document is then opened in the application you used to create it.

Browsing Office Documents with Internet Explorer 3

Internet Explorer 3 and your Office 97 applications have built-in support for ActiveX documents. This means that you can open Office documents right inside the Internet Explorer window. (ActiveX is a file/program sharing technology, designed to help integrate programs and files on the Internet. See Chapter 48, "Using ActiveX Controls.")

To open an Office document in Internet Explorer, complete the following steps:

1. Run Internet Explorer.

2. Choose File, menu Open, or press Ctrl+O. The Open dialog box appears.

3. Click the Browse button. A folder list appears, prompting you to select the file.

4. Open the Files of Type drop-down list and select All Files.

5. Change to the drive and folder in which the document is stored. The drive can be on your computer, a network, or your company's intranet.

6. Double-click the name of the document and then click the OK button. The document opens in the Internet Explorer window. The application's menus are added to Internet Explorer's menu bar.

7. To view the Office application's toolbars, click the Tools button, as shown in Figure 45.4. The application's toolbars appear just below Internet Explorer's toolbars.

8. Edit and save the file as you normally would in your Office application.

Part
VII

Ch
45

FIG. 45.4

With ActiveX document support, Internet Explorer allows you to open and edit documents created in Office applications.

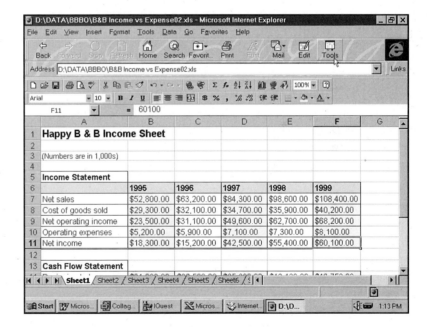

In addition to using the File, Open command, you can use links to open Office documents. If you connect to a page on the Internet or on your company's intranet that has links pointing to Office documents, simply click a link for the document you want to open. Internet Explorer opens the document, just as if you had used the File, Open command. You can then use Internet Explorer's toolbar to navigate your Office documents, just as if they were Web pages:

- Click Back to move back to the previous document or Web page.

- If you clicked the Back button, click Forward to move to the next document or Web page.

- Open the Address drop-down list and click the name of the document you want to open.

- If you know the name and location of a document you want to open, enter its path in the Address text box. For example, **d:\data\business\ledger97.xls**.

If you are using Internet Explorer to access your company's intranet or a Web page that contains links to Office documents, whenever you click a link to open a Word document or Excel worksheet, Internet Explorer opens the document. If you would rather have the document opened in the Office application, you can edit the file associations for these Office document types. The following steps provide instructions on how to edit the file associations for your Office documents:

1. In My Computer or Windows Explorer, choose <u>V</u>iew, <u>O</u>ptions.

2. Click the File Types tab.

3. Scroll down the list of file types and select the file type that has an association you want to edit: Microsoft Excel Worksheet or Microsoft Word Document. (PowerPoint slide shows and Access databases do not open automatically in the Internet Explorer window.)

4. Click the <u>E</u>dit button. The Edit File Type dialog box appears, as shown in Figure 45.5.

5. Click Open We<u>b</u> Documents in Place (at the bottom right of the dialog box) to remove the check from its box.

6. Click OK to return to the Options dialog box, and then click OK to save your settings.

FIG. 45.5

You can edit the file association for an Office document to prevent it from automatically opening in Internet Explorer.

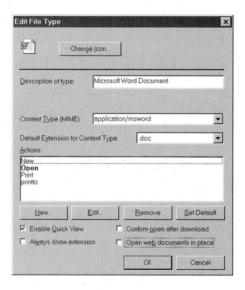

Enhanced Internet Integration with Internet Explorer 4

Although Internet Explorer 3 provides a few tools for integrating your Office applications with the Internet, Internet Explorer 4 provides tools that integrate your entire Windows desktop with the Internet. If your work requires you to frequently access the Web or your company's intranet, you should consider upgrading to Internet Explorer 4. This latest version of Internet Explorer offers the following desktop enhancements:

- *Single-click access to applications and documents*. Instead of double-clicking an icon to run an application or open a document, you click once, just as you click links on Web pages.

- *Internet integration for My Computer and Windows Explorer*. You can use My Computer or Windows Explorer to browse the Web, your computer's hard drive, or your company's intranet from a single window.

- *Additional taskbar features*. You can place document shortcut icons in the Windows taskbar, toggle applications on or off, and quickly return to the Windows desktop.

- *Site subscriptions*. Subscribe to Internet sites, and have content automatically delivered to your desktop.

The following sections show you how to download a copy of Internet Explorer 4, install it, and use its desktop integration features to make your computer look and act more like the Web.

Part

VII

Ch

45

Downloading and Installing Internet Explorer 4

Before you can take advantage of Internet Explorer 4's enhanced desktop integration features, you must download a copy from Microsoft. You can download the installation file using Internet Explorer 3.

Complete the following steps to download Internet Explorer 4 and install it on your system:

1. Run Internet Explorer and establish your Internet connection.

2. Click in the Address text box, type **www.microsoft.com/ie**, and press Enter. This connects you to the Internet Explorer home page.

3. Click the link for downloading Internet Explorer 4. You may have to click several links to access the download page.

4. Click the link for downloading the Active Setup file. This is a 4M file that will run the installation and download the remaining Internet Explorer 4 files. A form appears, prompting you to select a version.

5. Select the desired version of Internet Explorer 4 (be sure to select the version that includes desktop integration features) and click Next. A list of download sites appears.

6. Click the link for the ie4setup file at the download site nearest you. The File Download dialog box appears, prompting you to save the file or open it.

7. Click Save to Disk, and click OK. The Save As dialog box prompts you to select a folder for the file.

8. Select the folder in which you want the file stored, and click Save. Internet Explorer saves the file to your hard drive; this may take a few minutes.

9. Once you have the installation file, double-click its icon to run the installation. Follow the on-screen installation instructions.

The Internet Explorer 4 installation utility gives you three options for installing Internet Explorer:

■ Standard Installation (11M) includes Internet Explorer (Web browser), Outlook Express (for e-mail), and ActiveMovie (for playing video clips on the Web).

■ Minimum Installation (8.5M) includes only the Internet Explorer Web browser and the components it needs to play media files.

■ Enhanced Installation (15M) provides everything that the Standard installation offers but also includes FrontPage Express (for creating and editing Web pages) and Outlook Express (both e-mail and newsgroup components).

■ Full Installation (20M) includes everything: Internet Explorer, Outlook Express for e-mail and newsgroups, ActiveMovie, FrontPage Express (for creating and editing Web pages), NetMeeting (for virtual conferences), NetShow (for live video broadcasts), Microsoft Chat, Web Publishing Wizard, and Microsoft Wallet.

Because you downloaded Internet Explorer plus the desktop integration features, you can select any of the installation options listed here. You do not have to perform the full installation.

N O T E Internet Explorer with desktop integration features requires 8M more RAM than Internet Explorer without desktop integration features. If you decide that you no longer want to use the desktop integration features, you can uninstall them using Add/Remove Programs in the Windows Control Panel. ■

Using Internet Explorer's Desktop Integration Features

When you install Internet Explorer, it automatically makes changes to your Windows desktop, the Start menu, My Computer, and Windows Explorer to integrate your desktop with the Web. You will notice the following changes (see Figure 45.6):

■ Internet Explorer's Active Desktop is enabled, displaying a Web page as your Windows background. See "Working with the Active Desktop" later in this chapter for details.

■ The Channel Bar appears on your desktop. You can use the Channel Bar to "tune in" to popular Web sites by clicking buttons on the Channel Bar.

■ The Windows taskbar now includes icons for launching Internet Explorer, Channels (for tuning in to popular Web sites), Outlook Express for e-mail, and Desktop (for quickly returning to the Windows desktop from any application).

- The Start, Find menu contains options for searching the Internet.

- You can now single-click shortcuts to run applications or open files.

- My Computer and Windows Explorer are completely revamped and now include a toolbar that looks and acts like the toolbar in Internet Explorer. See "Browsing Files with My Computer" and "Browsing Files with Windows Explorer" later in this section.

FIG. 45.6

After installing Internet Explorer with desktop integration, your Windows desktop takes on a new look.

Single-click shortcuts to run applications and open documents

Start menu contains new options

Active Desktop displays the Channel Bar

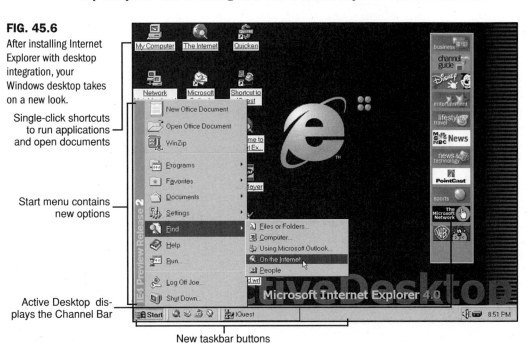

New taskbar buttons

Start Menu Changes   Internet Explorer has placed a couple of new commands on the Start menu. Open the Start menu and point to Find. The Find submenu now has a couple of additional options: Computer lets you search another computer on your network or intranet for files; People allows you to use Internet search tools to track down friends, family members, and business associates on the Web.

In addition to the new commands, you can now rearrange program icons on the Start menu simply by dragging them. Drag any program icon up or down on the menu or drag it over the name of the submenu on which you want it placed and release the mouse button.

 Taskbar Changes   The Windows 95 taskbar has a couple of new features as well. Just to the right of the Start button is a new toolbar (called Quick Launch) that initially contains four icons named Launch Internet Explorer Browser, Launch Mail (for e-mail and newsgroups), Show Desktop, and View Channels. Show Desktop allows you to quickly return to the Windows desktop when you are working in other applications.

You can take control of this new toolbar and your new taskbar in several ways:

■ Drag the slider on the right side of the toolbar to make it take up more or less space on the taskbar. See Figure 45.7.

FIG. 45.7

Your new Windows taskbar is much more powerful.

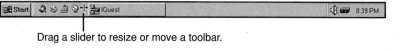

Drag a slider to resize or move a toolbar.

■ Drag the slider to the left or right of another toolbar's slider to move the toolbar.

■ Drag document icons or shortcut icons onto the Quick Launch toolbar to create buttons for the applications you run most often or for documents you frequently access.

■ You can add toolbars to the taskbar. Right-click a blank area of the toolbar, point to Toolbars, and select any of the following options:

● Address places the Address text box on the taskbar. You can enter the address of a Web page into this text box to open a page.

● Links inserts a bar that contains buttons pointing to helpful Web pages. You can add buttons for your own favorite pages.

● Desktop displays a toolbar containing buttons for all of the shortcuts on your Windows desktop.

● New Toolbar lets you transform a folder into a toolbar. For example, you can select New Toolbar and choose Control Panel to create a toolbar that contains icons for all the tools in the Windows Control Panel.

■ To remove a toolbar, right-click a blank area of the toolbar and select Close.

■ To view larger icons in the toolbar, right-click a blank area of the toolbar and choose View, Large.

■ To turn text descriptions of the toolbar buttons on or off, right-click a blank area of the toolbar and choose Show Text.

You might also notice that the taskbar now toggles running applications. For instance, if you click the button for a running application, Windows moves the application's window to the front so you can start working (which Windows has always done). However, when you click the button again, Windows minimizes the application window, so you can return to the previous application or to the Windows desktop.

Browsing Files with My Computer   Click the My Computer icon in the upper-left corner of the Windows desktop and keep an eye on the screen. You now see the new improved My Computer, a two-paned window with an attractive background. If the Standard Buttons toolbar, shown in Figure 45.8, is not displayed, choose View, Toolbar, and select Standard Buttons. Drag the bottom of the toolbar to display the Address text box in its own bar. The new toolbar looks more like a toolbar you might find in a Web browser; in fact, you can use this toolbar to navigate the Web.

FIG. 45.8

My Computer helps you navigate your File system as if it were a Web page.

Click back and forward to navigate your folders

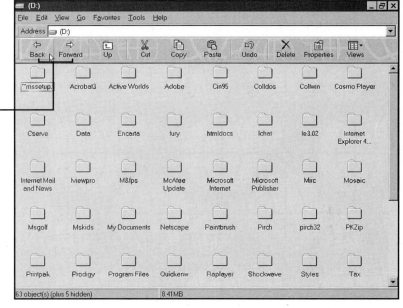

The left pane displays information about the currently highlighted icon. For instance, if you rest the mouse pointer on a drive icon, My Computer displays disk space details: Total Size and Free Space. To turn off the pane, Select View, As Web Page.

To access your files and folders with the new My Computer, use the following steps:

- Click a file to run an application or open a document.
- Click a folder to open it.
- Don't click a file to select it; clicking opens the file or runs it (if it is a program file). To select a file, rest the mouse pointer on the file (point to the file). My Computer highlights it.
- To select additional files, hold down the Ctrl key while pointing to other files you want to select.
- To select a group of neighboring files, point to the first file and then hold down the Shift key while pointing to the last file in the group.
- To deselect a file, point to it.
- You can still right-click a selected file to display a shortcut menu with commands for opening, cutting, copying, and pasting files.
- To rename a file, right-click it and select Rename.
- You can click the Back button to return to the folder you previously opened. If you backed up, you can click the Forward button to move ahead.
- The Up button moves you up one level in the folder tree.

Part
VII

Ch
45

- The File menu keeps track of which folders (and Web pages) you have opened, so you can quickly return to a folder by selecting it from the File menu.

- The View menu is nearly the same as the old My Computer View menu; it contains options for arranging icons in the window.

The Address text box performs the same task as it does in Internet Explorer. You can use the toolbar to navigate the Web, your company's intranet, and your hard drive.

 TIP If My Computer opens a new window every time you open a Web page or folder, your desktop will quickly become cluttered. Choose View, Folder Options. On the General tab, click Custom, Based on Settings You Choose, and click the Settings button. Under Browse Folders as Follows, select Open Each Folder in the Same Window. Click OK.

Browsing Files with Windows Explorer Windows Explorer has the same enhancements you find in My Computer. Windows Explorer provides one-click access to applications and files and offers the Internet Explorer toolbar, which you can use to browse the Web or your company's intranet. To run Windows Explorer, complete the following steps:

1. Click the Start button, and choose Programs.
2. Click Windows Explorer.
3. If the toolbar is not displayed, choose View, Toolbar, and select the desired toolbar option: Standard Buttons (the navigation buttons), Address Bar (for entering page addresses), Links (for creating buttons for your favorite pages), and/or Text Labels (to turn the button descriptions on or off).

You have probably worked with Windows Explorer before, and you are comfortable with its two-paned approach. The left pane displays a list of drives and folders, and the right pane displays the contents of the selected drive or folder.

However, you can now run Internet Explorer right inside the Windows Explorer window. From the left pane of Windows Explorer, labeled All Folders, click The Internet. This runs Internet Explorer in the right pane of the Windows Explorer window, as shown in Figure 45.9. You can now navigate the Web by clicking links or entering page addresses.

Returning My Computer and Windows Explorer to "Normal" If you dislike the changes to My Computer and Windows Explorer, you can return them to the way they were. First, make sure you are not viewing a Web page; click a drive or folder icon. In My Computer, choose View, Folder Options. Click the General tab and select either of the following options under Windows Desktop Update:

- To make the window look and act as it did before, click Classic Style.

- To enter custom settings, click Custom, Based on Settings You Choose, click the Settings button, and enter your preferences. For example, you can turn the Web backgrounds off and retain the single-click access to folders and files.

FIG. 45.9

Windows Explorer and Internet Explorer team up to provide single-click access to Web pages.

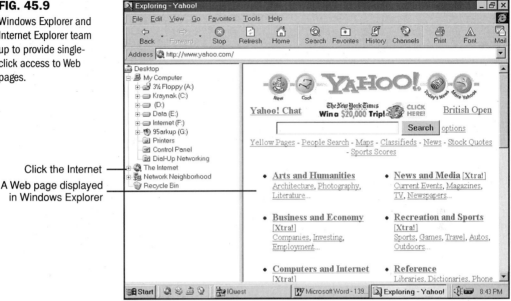

Click the Internet ——

A Web page displayed in Windows Explorer

Working with the Active Desktop

Internet Explorer's Active Desktop transforms your Windows desktop into a Web page on which you can place additional Web pages, ActiveX components, and other active content. This makes your desktop more like an information kiosk than a tool for simply accessing files and applications.

Before you can use the Active Desktop, first make sure it is on. If you see the Channel Bar in the upper-right quadrant of your desktop, Active Desktop is on. If this bar is not there, right-click a blank area of the Windows desktop and choose <u>A</u>ctive Desktop, View as <u>W</u>eb Page from the context menu.

Adding Desktop Components   To add desktop components, you must download them from the Web using Internet Explorer. Microsoft has set up a Desktop Component Gallery on the Web where you can go to download samples. The following steps show you how to access the gallery, download a desktop component, and place it on your Windows desktop:

1. Right-click a blank area of the Windows desktop, select <u>P</u>roperties, and click the Web tab. The Items on the Active Desktop list displays the names of any installed desktop components.

2. Click <u>N</u>ew. The New Active Desktop Item dialog box appears, asking if you want to go to the Active Desktop Gallery.

3. Click <u>Y</u>es. This runs Internet Explorer and connects you to the Internet, if you are not already connected. Internet Explorer loads the Active Desktop Gallery Web page.

4. Click the link for the desktop component you want. Another page appears, describing the component and displaying a link for downloading it.

5. Click the link to download it and place it on your desktop. Internet Explorer displays a couple of dialog boxes, asking for your confirmation and allowing you to specify how often you want your desktop component to update information. Enter your preferences.

Figure 45.10 shows the MSN Investor ticker as it appears on my Active Desktop. Once a desktop component is on the desktop, you can move it. Point to its title bar to display a gray bar, and then drag the bar to move the component. To resize the component, drag a corner of its window. As these desktop components become more popular, you will start to find desktop components sprinkled all over Web pages.

FIG. 45.10

Desktop Components make your desktop an active area where you can receive the latest news and information.

Point to the title bar to display a gray bar

Drag a corner to resize the component's window

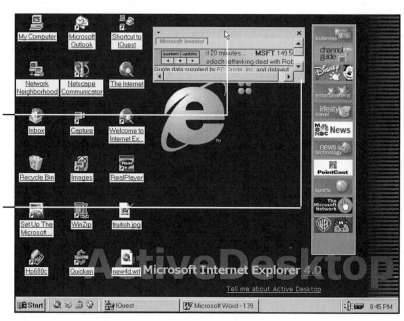

Removing Desktop Components   Turning off or deleting a desktop component is a little more difficult than adding one. Complete the following steps:

1. Right-click a blank area of the desktop and select Properties. The Display Properties dialog box appears.

2. Click the Web tab. This tab contains a list of desktop components, as shown in Figure 45.11, including the Internet Explorer Channel Bar.

3. To turn off a component, click its check box to remove the check mark.

4. To completely remove a component, select it and then click the Delete button.

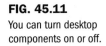

FIG. 45.11

You can turn desktop components on or off.

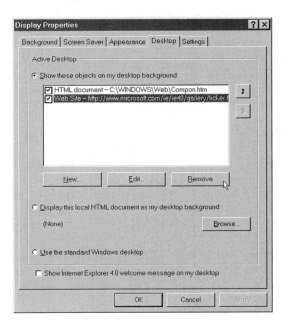

The Web tab contains some additional options for controlling the appearance of your desktop:

- View My Active Desktop as a Web Page turns on the Web Page wallpaper and all of the Active Desktop components. You can restore your desktop to its original condition by removing the check mark.

- Properties displays the settings for the currently selected desktop component (not available for all components).

- Reset All deletes all desktop components except the Channel Bar.

- Folder Options saves the current desktop settings, closes the Display Properties dialog box, and opens the Folder Options dialog box. This is the same dialog box that appears when you choose View, Folder Options in My Computer or Windows Explorer.

The black background that Internet Explorer displays on the desktop is actually a Web page set up as a background. To use a standard Windows background instead, click the Background tab in the Display Properties dialog box, and select the desired background. You can select (None) at the top of the list to turn off the Windows background and display a solid color.

Adding Internet Objects to Documents

As you browse the Internet, you find pages that contain links, graphics, video clips, audio re-cordings, and other objects that you may want to include in your own Office documents or Web pages. With Internet Explorer, you can quickly and easily copy these objects from Web pages or other Internet sources and insert them into your documents.

The following sections show you how to save entire Web pages, copy and paste hyperlinks, and drag and drop graphics, sounds, and video clips from Web pages into your Office 97 documents.

> **CAUTION**
>
> Before you copy material from an existing Web page, you should obtain permission from the Web page author. Original material, including graphics and video clips, may be copyrighted. When in doubt, check with the creator.

Saving Web Pages

As you open pages on the Web, you may want to save the page to your hard drive to use it as a template for creating your own Web page. You can then modify the page in Word or in one of your other applications and publish it to the Web (as explained in Chapter 46, "Creating and Publishing Web Documents").

To save a Web page, open the page in Internet Explorer and then choose File, Save As. Use the Save As dialog box to select the folder in which you want the file saved and click the Save button.

If you displayed the page in Word by opening the page and clicking the Edit button, you can use the File, Save As Word Document command to save the file as a Word document, instead of in the HTML format, which is used for Web pages.

When you save a file in Internet Explorer or Word, the program might drop the graphics or other files associated with the page. You may need to save the graphics files separately, as explained in the section "Inserting Graphics, Sounds, and Video" later in this chapter.

N O T E Internet Explorer 4 comes with its own Web page editor, called *FrontPad*. When you click the Edit button, Internet Explorer 4 displays the page in FrontPad (not Word), complete with graphics. You can then use FrontPad to edit the page and save it as an HTML file, or you can open the file in Word using the File Open command. ▪

Copying and Pasting Text

Occasionally, youmay not want to download or use an entire Web page. Perhaps the page contains some text you would like to quote or some information that supports one of your documents. Instead of saving the entire document, you can copy the portions you want to use.

To copy text in Internet Explorer, perform the same steps you would take to copy text in any of your other applications. Drag over the text and click the Copy button. You can then switch to your Office application and use the Paste command to insert the text.

Because Web page text may have some unique formatting, you will probably need to adjust the text after pasting it. For instance, it may include some line breaks that do not work properly in your Office document.

Copying and Pasting Hyperlinks

Most Web pages contain hyperlinks, highlighted text or graphics that you can click to open pages that the links point to. The easiest way to include hyperlinks in your Office documents or in Web pages you are creating is to drag the hyperlink and drop it into your Office document.

To use drag and drop, complete the following steps:

1. Display the destination document in your Office application.
2. Display the Web page that contains the hyperlink in Internet Explorer.
3. Drag over the hyperlink to select it. Point to the hyperlink, hold down the mouse button, and drag the link to your Office document. When you release the mouse pointer, your Office application inserts the link.
4. To change the link's name, drag over the link to select it and then type a name for the link. The underlying address still points to the designated Web page or Internet resource, but the link's name (which you see in the document) is the name you typed.
5. To edit a link, right-click it, point to Hyperlink, and select Edit Hyperlink. Use the Edit Hyperlink dialog box, shown in Figure 45.12, to change the address of the page or file that the link points to.

▶ **See** "Inserting and Editing Hyperlinks," **p. 913**

FIG. 45.12

You can change the address of the page or file that the selected link points to.

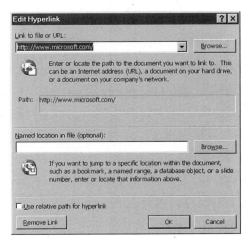

You can also copy and paste hyperlinks. In Internet Explorer, drag over the link, right-click the link, and choose Copy Shortcut. Change to your Office document, right-click where you want the link inserted, and choose Paste.

Part

VII

Ch

45

Inserting Graphics, Sounds, and Video

The Web is packed with images, audio recordings, video, and other media files. To add any of these media clips to your Office documents, you can copy them from Web pages in Internet Explorer and then paste them into your Office documents.

To copy and paste an image, run Internet Explorer and open the Web page that contains the image. Right-click the image and choose Copy. Change back to your Office application, right-click where you want the image inserted, and click Paste. If the Paste command is unavailable, you may need to save the graphic to your hard drive and then insert it using the Insert, Picture, From File command.

To use audio or video clips, or other media file types, you must first download the clip. In Internet Explorer, right-click the link that points to the media clip and choose Save Picture As or Save Target As. Use the Save As dialog box to save the file to a folder on your hard drive. You can then insert a link that points to the file, as explained in Chapter 46, "Creating and Publishing Web Pages" in the section "Inserting and Editing Hyperlinks."

 Instead of placing a large video clip in your document, you may want to create a link to it instead. By creating a link, you don't have to clutter your disk or Web server with a copy of the file. The file stays on its original server. When the user clicks the link for playing the clip, the clip downloads and plays from the remote Web server.

Opening and Saving Files with FTP

With the current focus on the Web, discussion of FTP (File Transfer Protocol) is often omitted. Fortunately, Microsoft didn't omit FTP from the long list of Internet features included in Office 97. You can now open Office documents and upload documents you've created to FTP servers assuming, of course, that you have been granted access to the server.

To access an FTP server, you must first enter the server's address and logon information. You can do this by choosing File, Open or File, Save As. In the resulting dialog box, open the Look In or Save In drop-down list and select Add/Modify FTP Locations (under Internet Locations/FTP). The Add/Modify FTP Locations dialog box appears, as shown in Figure 45.13.

Enter the address of the FTP server in the Name of FTP Site text box. Under Log on As, select Anonymous if the server allows anonymous access (no user name or password required) or click User, type your user name in the User text box, and enter a password in the Password text box. Click Add. You can repeat the steps to add other FTP servers to the list.

To open (download) a file from an FTP server, use the File, Open command in any of the Office applications. Open the Look In drop-down list and select the FTP server where the file is stored. You can then change to the desired directory and open the file as you normally would. Office handles the logon operation for you.

FIG. 45.13

If you have access to an FTP site, either anonymously or through a password, you can open documents or save files to the FTP server as easily as you do on your hard drive.

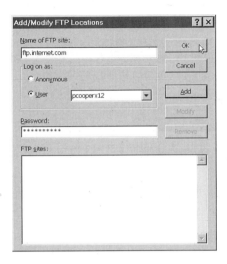

To save a file to an FTP server, you perform similar steps. Choose File, Save As to display the Save As dialog box. Open the Save In drop-down list and select the FTP server to which you want to save the file. You can then change to the desired directory and save the file as you normally would.

N O T E If you are accustomed to using an FTP program to use a personal directory on the server, the FTP program typically logs you on to your personal directory. However, the Office 97 FTP utility logs you on to the FTP server's root directory. You'll have to select folders and subfolders to open your personal directory. ▓

Using Find Fast and Web Find Fast

Office 97 includes a tool called Find Fast that indexes all your Office documents. When you search for a file from the File, Open dialog box, your Office application uses the Find Fast index to locate the specified file on your local PC or on the network drive.

Web Find Fast is a more advanced tool that works only on Windows NT servers or workstations configured as Web servers. Instead of prompting you for your search instructions via a dialog box, Web Find Fast displays a Web page form that you complete to enter your search instructions. Web Find Fast then searches the index on your intranet to find the specified file.

Searching for Documents with Find Fast

Find Fast does not require much intervention on your part. When you performed the Typical installation of Office 97, Find Fast was installed. Find Fast then automatically indexes your Office documents and other common files, such as HTML (Web pages).

Part
VII

Ch
45

To use Find Fast to search for a file, choose File, Open. At the bottom of the Open dialog box are options that allow you to search for files by name, file type, text or property (contents), or by the date the file was last modified. Use these lists and text boxes to enter your search instructions, as shown in Figure 45.14. Then, click the Find Now button.

You are then presented with a list of files that match your search instructions. Double-click the name of the file you want to open.

FIG. 45.14

The Search options at the bottom of the Open dialog box allow you to search the Find Fast index to find files.

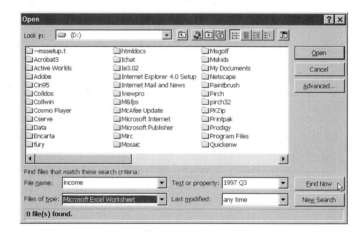

In Outlook, the procedure for finding files differs. Complete the following steps to search for document file in Outlook:

1. Open Outlook. Choose Tools and select Find Items, or press Ctrl+Shift+F. The Find dialog box appears.

2. Click the Advanced tab.

3. Open the Look For drop-down list and select Files.

4. Click the Browse button, select every drive and folder you want to search, and make sure Search Subfolders is selected. Click OK.

5. On the Files tab, enter the name of the file you are looking for in the Named text box, or click in the Search for the Word(s) text box and type a unique word or phrase that the document contains.

6. Click the Find Now button. Outlook searches the specified files and displays the names of all files that match your search instructions.

7. Double-click the name of a file to open it in its associated Office application.

Searching for Documents with Web Find Fast

If you work on an intranet, your intranet administrator may have set up Web Find Fast to help you and other users track down Office documents and HTML files on the intranet. Unlike Find Fast, which indexes Office documents and Web pages automatically, Web Find Fast requires the administrator to initiate the indexing operation for selected drives and folders. The administrator also must set up one of the Web Find Fast Web pages included with the Microsoft Office Service Pack.

To install Web Find Fast, double-click the Setup.exe in the Srvpack folder on your Office 97 CD.

To access and use Web Find Fast, you must open the Web Find Fast search page in Internet Explorer (or whichever browser you are using). If you are using a Windows NT workstation that is set up as a Web server, the file may be on your local drive. Otherwise, you can access it from the Windows NT Server. When you open the page, a form appears prompting you to enter your search instructions.

The Office 97 Service Pack comes with two forms: standard and advanced query. The Advanced Query form is shown in Figure 45.15. Enter your search instructions in the blanks, as your would in any Internet search form, and click the Search button.

Web Find Fast finds the documents that match your search instructions and displays a list of links for the documents. Click a link to open the document in its associated Office application.

Part
VII

Ch
45

FIG. 45.15

Web Find Fast displays a Web page form that you complete to enter your search instructions and execute the search.

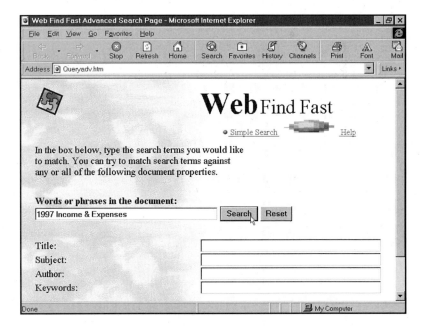

CHAPTER 46

Creating and Publishing Web Documents

by Joe Kraynak

The Internet is no longer reserved for large corporations, government agencies, and universities. The Web, with the help of some very innovative developers, has made the Internet accessible to anyone with a computer and even the most modest Internet connection. Now, small businesses and even individuals can establish their presence and express themselves on the Web by creating and publishing their own Web pages.

Up to the release of Office 97, however, the business of creating and publishing Web pages was still in the hands of the more sophisticated Web user. If you studied HTML and had a great deal of patience, you could compose a Web page in Notepad or WordPad by typing the required HTML codes yourself. For the less ambitious, developers created popular HTML editors, such as HotDog and FrontPage, that could handle some of the complex HTML coding for you and even lead you through the process of publishing your page on the Web. But these programs still intimidated some users.

With Office 97, there's no longer an excuse to avoid Web page publishing. Every Office 97 application allows you to transform existing documents into Web pages and easily

Using Word to create Web pages

You can convert existing Word documents into Web pages, and create Web pages from scratch using the Web Page Wizard.

Customize Web pages

Spruce up your Web pages with hyperlinks, tables, lists, graphics, sounds, and video clips.

Transform Excel worksheets into Web pages

Place your Excel worksheet data and charts on Web pages.

Publish Access reports on the Web

Use the Publish to the Web Wizard to convert your database into Web pages and place the pages on the Web.

Create an online slide show

Transform a PowerPoint presentation to an online slide show, allowing users to flip slides by clicking buttons or links.

Publish Web pages electronically

Use Microsoft's Web Publishing Wizard to place your Web page files on a Web server, making them available to other users.

place them on a Web server or your local intranet. In addition, Word comes with a Web Page wizard to help you create pages from scratch, along with several tools for inserting hyperlinks, graphics, video clips, and other objects to give your Web page a professional look.

N O T E Although the Office applications can convert existing documents into Web pages, the conversion often inserts improper HTML tags (the codes that control formatting for the Web page). Ideally, you should create your Web page from scratch rather than convert existing documents. However, you can use the conversion tools and then modify the codes using a text editor. ▨

Creating Web Pages with Word

Throughout its evolution, Word has become more of a desktop publishing program than a simple word processor. It has introduced advanced graphics and table features, text boxes with rotating text, WordArt, and page layout features that make it easy to create your own paper publications. With the current trend to publish electronically via the Web, Word has become a Webtop publishing tool as well.

When creating a Web page in Word, you will use many of the same tools you use to create paper publications. Like standard publications, Web pages require you to add headings, running text, lists, and graphics, and to format your text to make it more attractive. However, the Web provides another dimension, allowing you to insert video clips, hyperlinks, scrolling text, and other objects that can animate your document and make it more interactive.

Using the Web Page Wizard

If you have a document you want to use as your Web page, skip to the next section, "Transforming a Word Document into a Web Page," to learn how to convert the document to HTML. If you don't have a starting document, you can create a Web page from scratch using the Web Page wizard.

Like other Office wizards, the Web Page Wizard leads you step-by-step through an otherwise complicated procedure. The Web Page Wizard comes with several templates for creating different types of Web pages, including forms, a calendar, a table of contents, or a personal Web page. With the Web Page Wizard, you can create a simple, professional-looking Web page in a matter of minutes. You can then modify the page by deleting existing elements and adding your own text and graphics.

To run the Web Page Wizard, complete the following steps:

1. Choose File, New to open the New dialog box.
2. In the New dialog box, click the Web Pages tab and then double-click the Web Page Wizard icon. A sample Web page appears in the viewing area, and the wizard prompts you to select a page layout.

N O T E When you first use the Web Page Wizard or a template, Word may prompt you to download the latest version of the Web Page Authoring Tools. Click Yes to connect to Microsoft's Web site and download the update.

3. Click the desired layout to preview it. When you've selected an appealing layout, click Next.

   The Web Page Wizard prompts you to select a style to control the overall look of the page, including the background and typestyles.

4. Click the desired style to preview it in the document viewing area. Figure 46.1 shows the Personal Home Page layout with the Contemporary style applied to it.

5. After selecting the style you want, click Finish. Word displays the document.

You can now edit the document as you would normally edit a Word document. As you edit and format your document, Word inserts the corresponding HTML codes for you. See "Editing and Formatting Web Pages" later in this chapter for details on how to add to your page and change its look.

FIG. 46.1
The wizard asks two questions, and then creates a starting page for you.

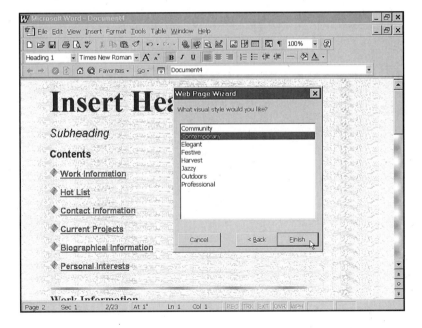

T I P You can also start with a blank Web page. Choose File, New, click the Web Pages tab, and double-click Blank Web Page.

Transforming a Word Document into a Web Page

If you have an existing Word document that has content you want to place on the Web, it makes little sense to start a page from scratch. You can convert the existing document into an HTML document suitable for the Web.

HTML stands for *HypertText Markup Language* and is a set of tags (codes) used to format the text, create lists, insert graphics and audio and video clips, insert hyperlinks that connect your page to other pages, and much more. For example, HTML includes a paired tag that makes text bold: **This is bold**. The first tag turns on bold, and the second turns it off. Although Word inserts the required codes for you when you format text or insert objects, you should have a general understanding of HTML tags, so you can edit the codes if you encounter formatting problems on your Web page.

To convert an existing document, first open the document in Word. Then, Choose <u>F</u>ile, Save as <u>H</u>TML. Use the Save As dialog box to select the drive and folder in which you want the file stored. You can also rename the file, if desired. When you save the file, Word automatically adds the HTML extension to the file's name; for example, if you name the file MyPage, Word saves it as MyPage.html. Click OK.

Once the file is saved, you can edit and format it as you do with any Word document. See the next section, "Editing and Formatting Web Pages."

Editing and Formatting Web Pages

Chances are that the Web page you created using the wizard, a template, or an existing document is not complete. You may want to add links, graphics, headings, and other items to your Web page to finish it. This section shows you how to add these items to your page and format your text.

The techniques covered in the following sections work for pages created in any Office application, so if you create a page using Excel or an online presentation using PowerPoint, as explained later in this chapter, you may want to refer to this section to learn the basics of inserting links and graphics and applying formats.

As you edit and format a Web page, your Office application automatically inserts the required HTML codes in place of the standard codes for formatting Office documents. For instance, when you press Enter to start a new paragraph, the application inserts the HTML code <P>. Your Office application keeps the codes in the background, so you don't have to work with them directly.

Organizing Your Page with Tables

Initially, you might think that tables are objects you insert as part of a Web page. Although you can use tables in this way, you can also use them to structure your Web page.

Due to the limitations of HTML formatting, overall page layout is difficult. HTML does not support tab settings or columns, so you cannot use the word processing tools you are accustomed to for controlling text and graphics on a page. HTML tables allow you to overcome some of these limitations. For instance, you can create a table, like the one shown in Figure 46.2, that controls the overall layout of your page.

As shown in the figure, links appear in the left column and the rest of the page is displayed in the right column. When a user clicks a link in the left column, the right column displays the related contents.

You can also use small tables to create your own button bars. For instance, you might add a table to the top of your page that contains links to other pages or documents. In each cell, you insert a link. You can also color the cells to make them look more like clickable buttons.

For details on creating and editing tables, see Chapter 8, "Using Tables." After creating tables, you can use the techniques described here to insert links, graphics, and text into the cells.

FIG. 46.2
Consider using the tables feature to control the overall layout of your Web page.

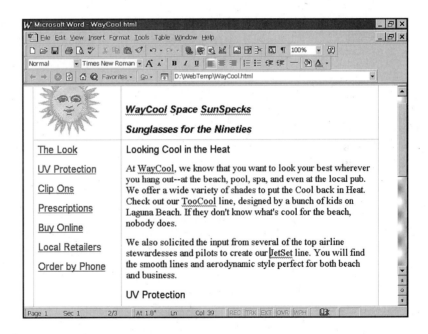

Inserting and Editing Hyperlinks

If you used the wizard or a template to create your Web page, your page already contains a few links to other sections of the Web page. However, you will probably want to insert additional links pointing to other pages on the Web or other documents at your Web site.

 The Standard toolbar in Word, Excel, Access, and PowerPoint has an Insert Hyperlink button that allows you to quickly insert links into your documents. The links might point to other Web pages, to other Office documents, or to any files on your hard drive or network. You can use links to stitch your documents together even if you're not on the Internet! Whenever you click a link to a file, Windows opens the file in the associated application.

The procedure for inserting a link varies depending on whether you are linking to a different section of the same document or to a different file (on your hard drive, the network, or the Internet). When creating a link to an external file, you simply mark the link text and then specify the address or path of the file you are linking to.

To create a link to an external file or Web page, complete the following steps:

1. Highlight the text or select the object that you want to use as the link. (You can use text or a graphic.)

2. Click the Insert Hyperlink button in the Standard toolbar (or choose Insert, Hyperlink, Ctrl+K). The Insert Hyperlink dialog box appears, as shown in Figure 46.3, prompting you to specify the address of the page you want the link to point to.

FIG. 46.3

Specify the address of the Web page or file that you want the link to point to.

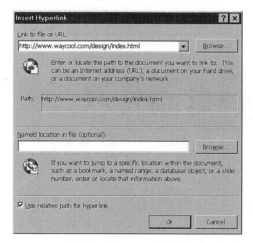

3. In the Link to File or URL text box, type the page's address. (If you are linking to a file on your hard drive or on the network, you can click the Browse button and select the file from a list.)

4. If you want to point to a specific location in the selected document or file (and you inserted a bookmark to mark it), click the Browse button next to Named Location in File. The Bookmark dialog box prompts you to select the bookmark to which you want the link to point.

5. Select the bookmark and click OK. If the document contains no bookmarks, the list is empty. (See the section, "Linking Within a Document," for details.)

6. Leave the Use Relative Path for Hyperlink option on if you plan on keeping all the connected files in the same folder. If you are creating a link to a file in a specific folder,

and you don't plan on moving that file, turn this option off. If you turn the option off, the entire path and name of the file are used as the link. (See the next section, "Relative and Absolute References," for details.) Click OK.

7. The selected text is transformed into a link and appears blue and underlined.

If you decide to remove the link from your page, select the link, click the Insert Hyperlink button, and click Remove Link.

N O T E   You can have your Office application automatically transform Web page and e-mail addresses into links. Choose Tools, AutoCorrect. Click the AutoFormat As You Type tab and make sure there is a check mark next to Internet and Network Paths with Hyperlinks. Click OK. With this option on, whenever you type a page address, network path, or e-mail address (and press the spacebar), the Office application converts the text into a link.

Relative and Absolute References   When specifying file locations for links, you must consider where the linked file will be stored on the Web server. If you store all your files in the same directory on the server, you can simply enter the file name of the link. When the user clicks the link, the file opens from the same directory which stores the Web page.

However, if the linked files are stored in different directories from the Web page, you must enter a directory path that specifies the file's location. You can enter paths as *absolute* or *relative references*.

An absolute reference gives the entire URL (address) of the file, including its Web server name, the complete path to the directory where the file is stored, and the name of the file; for instance, http://www.mcp.com/travel/frommers/alternate.html.

Relative references are used if the linked file is on the same Web server as your Web page. The relative reference provides only the path and file name; for example, /travel/frommers/alternate.html. Relative references help you manage complex Web sites consisting of files stored in multiple directories. By using relative references, you can move an entire directory tree on the server without having to edit file references.

Linking Within a Document   If you have a long document that uses several subheadings, you may want to include a table of contents at the beginning of the document that contains links to the various sections of the document. Creating an internal link is a two-step process; you must insert a bookmark to mark an area of the document that you want a link to point to and then insert the link that points to the bookmark.

First, mark each section you want to link to, using a bookmark. To do this, complete the following steps:

1. Highlight the destination text.
2. Choose Insert, Bookmark. The Bookmark dialog box appears.
3. Type a name for the bookmark and click the Add button. The name is added to the list of bookmarks in this document.

Part
VII

Ch
46

You can now follow the steps in the previous section to insert a hyperlink that points to the new bookmark. (In HTML terms, *bookmarks* are referred to as *anchor names*.)

> **N O T E** If you have a long document and you use bookmarks to help the user navigate, you should place a bookmark at the bottom of each section that returns the user to the top of the document or to the table of contents. ▪

Editing Links   You can edit a link to change the address of the document or to point the link to a different bookmark. Right-click the link, choose Hyperlink, Edit Hyperlink. This displays the Edit Hyperlink dialog box, which provides the same options you used to insert the link.

> **CAUTION**
>
> You must be a little careful when clicking links to edit them. If you click a link in your document, your Office application tries to open the linked file. To select a link, move the mouse pointer to the left or right of the link, so the mouse pointer does not appear as a hand. You can then highlight the link to select it.

Adding Headings, Paragraphs, and Lists

When you create a Web page, the styles list in the Formatting toolbar contains styles for quickly applying HTML formatting to your text. As with any formatting options, you can apply the HTML style before or after you type the text.

When applying styles and other formatting to your text, you should be aware that some of the formatting options available for Word documents do not work well in HTML documents. For instance, tabs are taboo, and fancy fonts that may look great in Word may not appear on the screens of the people who open your Web page. The following sections show you how to format using HTML-friendly options.

Formatting Headings   HTML supports six levels of headings. To add a heading to your page, open the Style drop-down list and select the heading level you want to apply. Then, type the heading. If you have already typed the text for a heading, select it and then select the heading level from the Style list.

Creating Normal Paragraphs   In most cases you will want to add a paragraph after a heading. To create a new paragraph, simply press Enter. To format the paragraph as normal text, open the Style list and select Normal. You can format selected text within the paragraph by using the Bold, Italic, and Underline buttons in the Formatting toolbar. You can also change the alignment of the paragraph (or a heading) by clicking the desired Align button.

Adding Numbered and Bulleted Lists   You can add numbered or bulleted lists to your Web page by using the Numbering or Bullets button in the Formatting toolbar. In addition to using the standard Office bullets, you can use more graphical bullets on Web pages. Choose Format,

Bullets and <u>N</u>umbering and click the Bulleted tab. You are presented with a list of graphical bullets you can use. When you save your Web page, your Office application automatically converts any graphical bullets to GIF (Graphic Interchange Format) images, making them compatible with most Web browsers. GIF is a popular format for storing images on the Web.

N O T E   The Formatting toolbar changes slightly when a Web page is opened. For instance, the Font Size drop-down list is replaced with two buttons: Increase Font Size and Decrease Font Size. Because each Web browser interprets the HTML codes differently to determine how to display a page, the Office application provides more general formats for text on Web pages. ▪

Inserting Horizontal Lines

When you work on a Web page, the Formatting toolbar includes a new button called Horizontal Line. This button allows you to insert graphic dividers between sections of your document. To insert a horizontal line, position the insertion point at the end of a paragraph and then click the Horizontal Line button.

To see a list of additional horizontal lines, choose <u>I</u>nsert, <u>H</u>orizontal Line. Select the desired graphical divider and click OK. (To quickly insert another horizontal line of the same type you just selected, click the Horizontal Line button in the Standard toolbar.)

Once the line is in place, you can drag it to move it, or drag one of its edges to make it longer or wider.

N O T E   When you use the <u>I</u>nsert, <u>H</u>orizontal Line command, the first line in the <u>S</u>tyle list inserts an HTML code that tells the visiting Web browser to display the line. All the other lines are graphic images stored as GIF files. Because graphic images are relatively large, using these graphic images as your horizontal dividers will slow down the page transfer slightly. If you're looking for speed, use the first line. If you must use one of the graphics, use the same one throughout your document. When a Web browser opens your document, it downloads only one copy of the graphic image and uses it to render the remaining horizontal lines in your document. ▪

Part VII

Ch 46

Inserting Pictures

When using graphics on a Web page, you must consider the file format of your images. Most Web browsers are capable of displaying graphics in the GIF and JPG (JPEG) file formats. If you use a graphic from Microsoft's Clip Art Gallery, Microsoft Office automatically converts the image to the GIF format when you save your document as a Web (HTML) page.

N O T E   GIF and JPG (Joint Photographic Experts Group) are the two most popular file formats used on the Web for storing images. ▪

When you access the Clip Art Gallery (using the Insert, Picture, Clip Art command), the Connect to Web for Additional Clips button appears in the lower-right corner of the window, as shown in Figure 46.4. You can use this button to download additional clip art from Microsoft's Web site. Complete the following steps:

1. Open the Clip Art Gallery, and click the Connect to the Web for Additional Clips button.

2. Read the license agreement and click Accept, if you agree to abide by the terms. A drop-down list appears, allowing you to select a clip art category.

3. Open the drop-down list and select the desired category; for instance, Academic or Business. Click the Go button. A Web page displays a collection of clip art images in the selected category.

4. Click the link for the image you want to download. A dialog box appears, asking if you want to save the file or open it.

5. Select the Open option, and click OK. (If you select the Save option, your Web browser saves the image file to disk, but does not add it to your Clip Art Gallery.)

Any clip art you download is automatically added to the Clip Art Gallery and placed in the appropriate category. A copy of the image also appears in the Downloaded Clips category.

FIG. 46.4

You can download additional clip art from Microsoft's Web site.

Click this button to access Microsoft's Clip Art Gallery on the Web

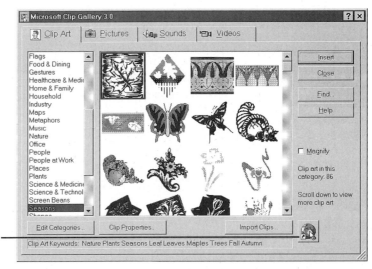

In addition to using Microsoft's clip art, you can drag-and-drop most graphics from a Web page into the Web page you are creating in your Office application. Display the Internet Explorer window and your Web page side by side, and then drag the graphic from the Explorer window into your Web page.

 When you are working on a Web page, the Insert, Picture menu offers another command called Browse Web Art Page. Click this option to connect to Microsoft's Web site and access additional graphics, including graphical bullets, images, backgrounds, and sounds.

> **CAUTION**
>
> When dragging and dropping any material from existing pages, keep in mind that you cannot use any original graphics, text, or other material without permission from its creator.

Adding Sound Clips and Background Audio

To give your page another dimension, you can add audio clips either as links or as background audio. Background audio automatically starts to play when a user opens your Web page.

To insert a Microsoft sound clip as a link, complete the following steps:

1. Position the insertion point where you want the link inserted.
2. Choose Insert, Picture and select Clip Art.
3. Click the Sounds tab. Select one of the sound icons in the list (you can click Play to preview the sound if you have a sound card and speakers).
4. Click the sound you want to insert and click the Insert button.

 TIP You can also copy and paste sounds clips from Web pages displayed in Internet Explorer. Right-click the link for the sound clip and select Save Target As. Save the file to your hard drive in the same folder as your Web page. Then create a link that points to the file.

To insert an audio file that plays in the background, complete the following steps:

1. Save your HTML document. If you don't save the document, your Office application will prompt you to save the document when you take the next step.
2. Choose Insert, Background Sound Properties. The Background Sound dialog box appears, as shown in Figure 46.5.

FIG. 46.5
You can add an audio clip from the Media folder to play in the background when your Web page is opened.

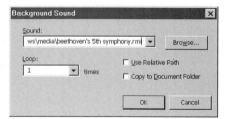

3. Click the Browse button and use the resulting dialog box to select a clip from the Office 97 Media folder, or from another folder on your drive.
4. In the Loop spin box, set the number of times you want the clip to play.
5. If you plan on including your Web page and all related files in a single directory on the Web server or in the same relative directories in which they are stored on your hard drive, make sure the Use Relative Path box is checked.

6. To have the selected sound file placed in the same folder as your Web page, make sure Copy to Document Folder is checked.

7. Click OK.

The only way to remove the background sound is to edit the HTML source (the codes behind the Web page). Choose View, HTML Source. Delete the code `<BGSOUND SRC="file name">`, and click the Exit HTML Source button in the toolbar.

 TIP If you have a sound card with a microphone attached, you can record a sound and place it on your page as a WAV file (which most browsers can play). Choose Insert, Object, select Wave Sound, and click OK. This runs Windows Sound Recorder, which you can use to record a voice message or music clip.

Adding a Background Color or Image

If you have wandered the Web much, you have seen pages with colored or textured backgrounds. Perhaps you have even seen pages that display a background image. You can add backgrounds to your Web pages in Office.

To add a background color, complete the following steps:

1. Choose Format, Background and select the desired color. For additional color options, you can click More Colors on the Background submenu.

2. To use a textured background, select Fill Effects from the Background submenu.

3. Select the desired texture or click Other Texture to select an image to use as the background.

The Office textures are actually small graphics that are tiled on the background to give the impression that the entire background is one big graphic. (This helps reduce the file size.) If you use the Other Textures command to use a special image on your hard drive, Office will tile the image, if needed, to fill in the background. If the image is large enough to fill the background, your Office application will not tile it.

Inserting Video Clips

If you have a video clip, you can insert it on your Web page as an inline video clip (which starts to play when the page is opened) or as a link. Keep in mind, however, that not all browsers support inline video. Also be aware that video clips are typically very large and will take a long time to download over a slow Internet connection.

 TIP If the video clip is already stored on a remote Web server, it's a good idea to create a link to it rather than placing a copy of the file on your own Web server. This saves you some storage space on your Web server. However, it may take longer to load the clip from the remote server, and if the creator of the clip decides to move or delete the clip, your link to the clip will no longer work.

If you have a video clip on your computer, or you know the URL of a video clip stored on a remote server, take the following steps to add it to your page:

1. Choose Insert, Video. The Video Clip dialog box appears, as shown in Figure 46.6.
2. In the Video text box, type the URL that points to the clip you want to play, or click the Browse button and select the video file from your hard drive. (Sample files are included on the Office 97 CD in the Clipart/Mmedia folder.)

FIG. 46.6
You can add a video clip to your Web page that starts playing when the page is opened.

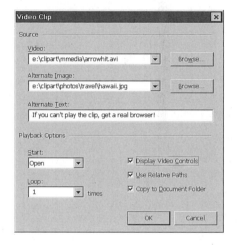

3. The Alternate Image text box allows you to specify an image to display in place of the video clip if the visitor's browser cannot display inline video.
4. The Alternate Text dialog box allows you to enter a text message to display if the visitor's browser cannot display the clip. For instance, you might type **Sorry, get a real browser**.
5. Click the Start drop-down list and select Open (to run the video when a visitor opens the page), Mouse Over (to start the video when the visitor points to it), or Both.
6. Click the Loop drop-down list and select the number of times you want the clip to play.
7. To have Start and Stop buttons displayed for the video when you are working on the page, click the Display Video Controls check box.
8. Make sure Use Relative Paths and Copy to Document Folder are checked. This ensures that when you publish your Web page the video clip is included with your Web page and is placed in the proper directory on the server.
9. Click OK.

Adding Scrolling Text

In Internet Explorer, Microsoft introduced an extension to the standard HTML code called the *marquee*. A marquee can display scrolling text on a Web page, assuming the browser supports it. If the browser does not support the marquee extension (Netscape Navigator does not support this extension), the text is displayed on the page, but does not scroll.

To add scrolling text to your page, complete the following steps:

1. Position the insertion point where you want the scrolling text inserted.

2. Choose Insert, Scrolling Text. The Scrolling Text dialog box opens (see Figure 46.7).

3. Highlight the entry inside the Type the Scrolling Text Here text box and type your text, as shown in Figure 46.7.

FIG. 46.7
You can include scrolling text on your Web page.

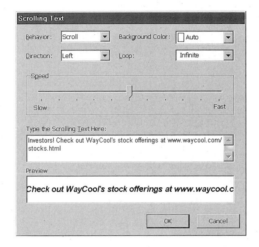

4. Use the controls at the top of the dialog box to change the speed, direction, movement, and background color for the scrolling marquee.

5. Click OK.

Exporting Excel Data to the Web

Not many worksheets find a home on the Web. They are usually too wide to fit inside a standard Web browser window, and they rarely contain enough graphics and links to hold the attention of a casual Web user. However, if you work at a company that has an intranet where fellow workers commonly share data, you might need to place your worksheets (or portions of them) on the Web.

Excel comes with an Internet Assistant that can help you transform an existing worksheet into a Web page or insert a portion of a worksheet into a Web page as a table.

In both cases, Excel's Internet Assistant codes the Excel data using special HTML table codes to arrange the data entries in columns. In the past, few Web browsers were capable of interpreting these table codes correctly. However, now that table codes have been in use for a while, most Web browsers, including Internet Explorer and Navigator, can display tables.

Part
VII

Ch

46

> **TIP** If you are working on an intranet where all users have Excel, you may not want to convert your Excel worksheet into a Web page. Instead, simply create a link to the Excel file. When someone clicks the link, your worksheet will automatically open in Excel.

Turning an Excel Worksheet into a Web Page

The easiest way to convert Excel data into an HTML Web page is to convert the entire file. Complete the following steps:

1. Open the worksheet that you want to convert into a Web page and highlight all the data you want to place on the page.

2. Choose File, Save As HTML.

3. The Internet Assistant Wizard Step 1 dialog box appears, showing the range of cells that the wizard is about to transform into a table (see Figure 46.8). You can click the Add button and highlight additional data to have the wizard convert it. Click the Next button.

FIG. 46.8
To transform Excel data into a Web page, you must first select the range of cells that contain the data you want to use.

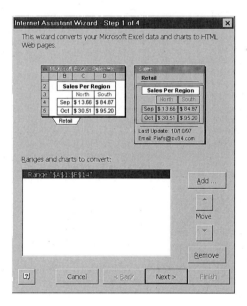

4. The Step 2 dialog box asks if you want to create a separate Web page or insert the data as a table in another Web page. Click Create an Independent, Ready-to-View HTML Document and click the Next button.

5. The Step 3 dialog box asks you to type a title, header, description, and footer information for the new page. In the Title text box, type a title for your page. Type any other entries as desired in the remaining text boxes and set any additional preferences. Click the Next button.

6. The Step 4 dialog box asks if you want to save the result as an HTML file or save it to your FrontPage Web. If you have a FrontPage Web, select Add the Result to My FrontPage Web. If you don't have FrontPage, select Save the Result as an HTML File.

7. Click the Browse button, use the Save dialog box to select the desired name and folder for the new file, and click Save.

8. Click the Finish button. The Internet Assistant Wizard creates a new HTML file including the title and any other information you chose to include on the page.

Inserting Excel Data or Charts in a Web Page

In most cases you will want to insert only a portion of a worksheet or a chart you created in Excel into your Web page. Although you can use Excel's Internet Assistant to convert the data for you, there is a much easier way.

First, open the worksheet that contains the chart or data you want to include on your Web page. Select the chart, or highlight the desired data, and choose Edit, Copy to copy the selected item.

Switch to Microsoft Word and open the Web page into which you want to place the copied data. Right-click where you want the chart or data inserted and click Paste. Word inserts the chart or data and automatically inserts the required HTML codes to format it.

Publishing from Access to the Web

Like Excel, Access comes with its own wizard, called the Publish to the Web Wizard. This wizard is truly amazing. With it, you can transform your entire Access database into a collection of Web pages, complete with a home page that provides links to all your reports, datasheets, and forms. You can even transfer the entire collection of Web pages to your Web server.

To use the Publish to the Web Wizard to convert your database into HTML-coded pages and publish those pages, complete the following steps:

1. Open your database in Access.

2. Choose File, Save as HTML. The opening Publish to the Web Wizard dialog box appears, indicating what it will do.

3. Click Next. The wizard prompts you to select the items (tables, queries, forms, and reports) that you want to include in your publication.

4. Click the check box next to each item you want to include (see Figure 46.9). Click Next. You are now prompted to select a template, to provide a consistent look for all your Web pages.

5. Click the Browse button, click the desired template, and click Select. (To use different templates for some pages, place a check mark next to I Want to Select Different Templates for Some of the Selected Objects.) Click Next. You are now asked how you want to output the database (see Figure 46.10).

FIG. 46.9
You can select all the
database objects you
want to present as Web
pages.

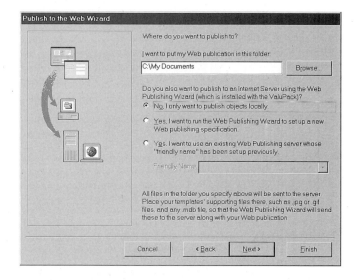

FIG. 46.10
The wizard prompts you
to select a format for
your pages.

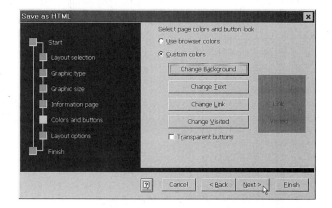

6. To create static Web pages, which can be placed on any Web server, click Static HTML.
    Static pages do not enable the database to perform queries and do not accept input from
    people viewing your pages.

    To publish dynamic datasheets, which allow users to input data, select Dynamic HTX/
    IDC (you must place the pages on a Microsoft Internet Information Server). See
    "Linking Forms to Your Database" in Chapter 47, "Internet Forms and Databases," for
    details about dynamic forms and databases. To publish the pages on a Microsoft Active
    Server, which allows users to input data using forms or datasheets, click Dynamic ASP.
    (To use different formats for some pages, place a check mark next to I Want to Select
    Different Format Types for Some of the Selected Objects.)

7. Click <u>N</u>ext. The next dialog box asks if you want to place the resulting Web pages in a folder on your hard drive or upload them to a Web Server (see Figure 46.11). Choose one of the following steps:

- Select N<u>o</u>, I Want to Publish Documents Locally, and then click the B<u>r</u>owse button and select the folder in which you want the Web pages stored. The remaining steps assume that you have selected this option; you can then publish the pages as explained later in this chapter.

- Select <u>Y</u>es, I Want to Run the Web Publishing Wizard to Set Up a New Web Publishing Specification. This tells the wizard that you want to upload to a Web server you haven't used before.

- Select <u>Y</u>es, I Want to Use an Existing Web Publishing Server Whose "Friendly Name" Has Been Set Up Previously, if you have already used the Web Publishing Wizard to publish Web pages. A later section in this chapter, "Publishing Your Page on the Web," provides details about publishing to a Web server using the Web Publishing Wizard.

8. Click <u>N</u>ext. The wizard asks if you want to create a Home page with links to your other Access Web pages. Click Yes, I Want to Create a Home Page, and then type a file name for the Home page in the designated text box.

9. Click <u>N</u>ext. You are now asked if you want to save your settings as a profile so you can use the same settings for other Web publications. If desired, click <u>Y</u>es and then type a name for the profile.

10. Click the <u>F</u>inish button.

FIG. 46.11

You can immediately upload the converted database files to a Web server, but you should save the pages locally and then test them in a Web browser before going public.

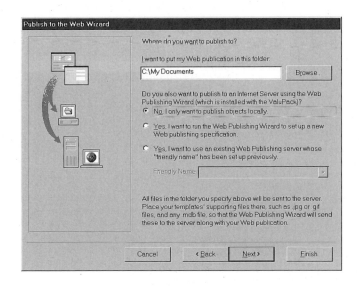

Putting PowerPoint Presentations on the Web

As you wander the Web, you might notice and appreciate the fact that many Web pages are relatively compact. Web developers know that users rarely scroll down lengthy pages to find the information they need. Users typically look at the opening screen, find a link that catches their eye, and click it to move to another page.

When you are creating your own Web pages and sites, you should try to keep your Web pages compact and provide links to help visitors flip back and forth to Web pages at your site.

PowerPoint's slide show approach is perfect for creating compact pages and providing a smooth flow from page to page at your Web site. With PowerPoint you transform a series of slides into a collection of text-light Web pages stitched together with links. When someone opens your Web slide show, the person can advance from one slide to the next with a simple click of the mouse.

Like Word, PowerPoint offers several ways to create Web documents, as explained in the following sections.

 For access to additional Web tools and information about using PowerPoint on the Web, run the PowerPoint Central presentation. Choose Tools, PowerPoint Central. This opens a Web presentation, complete with links to PowerPoint content at Microsoft's Web site.

Part
VII

Ch
46

Using AutoContent Wizard to Create a Web Slide Show

You have probably used PowerPoint's AutoContent Wizard to create presentations. You can now use it to create slide shows for the Web. To create a Web slide show using the AutoContent Wizard, complete the following steps:

1. When you start PowerPoint, the opening dialog box asks how you want to create your presentation. Click AutoContent Wizard and click OK. Or, choose File, New, click the Presentation tab, and double-click AutoContent Wizard.

2. Follow the wizard's series of dialog boxes to select the type of presentation you want to create. When asked how you plan to use the presentation, click Internet, Kiosk.

3. Continue answering the wizard's questions and supplying the requested information. After you respond to the last dialog box and click the Finish button, the wizard creates the presentation and displays it, just as any other presentation.

As with any document, you should save your presentation to prevent losing your work in progress. Complete the following steps to save your presentation:

1. Choose File, Save as HTML. The Save As HTML Wizard appears.

2. Click Next. The wizard prompts you to create a new layout or use an existing layout. If this is the first time you are using the wizard, you have no existing layouts.

3. Select New Layout, or select Load Existing Layout and choose the layout you want to use. Click Next. The next dialog box prompts you to select a standard page layout or frames.

N O T E Frames divide the user's browser window into two frames. The left frame displays a list of slides in the presentation, and the right frame displays the selected slide. This makes it easy for the user to navigate the presentation. However, not all Web browsers support frames, and some users just don't like frames. ■

4. Select the desired layout: Standard or Browser Frames, and click Next. You are now prompted to specify the desired graphic file format for your slides. See Figure 46.12.

FIG. 46.12

Select the desired format for the images used in your presentation.

5. Select GIF, JPEG, or PowerPoint Animation. GIF and JPEG store the images in a format that most browsers can display. PowerPoint Animation requires the user to download and install the PowerPoint Animation Player and use it to display the on-screen slide show. Click Next. The wizard prompts you to select a display resolution.

6. Click the desired display resolution, keeping in mind that higher resolutions display larger images. If you select a high resolution such as 1024×768, and the person who is viewing the presentation has his display set to 640×480, the slide won't fit on his screen. In addition, higher resolutions result in larger files, which take longer to download. Click Next. The wizard now prompts you to enter any additional information about yourself.

7. (Optional) Type your e-mail address in the E-Mail Address text box, and type the address of your home page in the Your Home Page text box. You can type additional information in the Other Information text area.

8. (Optional) Select <u>D</u>ownload Original Presentation to insert a button that allows the user to download the entire presentation (in its original format, before it was converted to HTML). Select <u>I</u>nternet Explorer Download Button to include a button that allows the user to download the latest version of Internet Explorer. Click <u>N</u>ext. The wizard prompts you to pick a color scheme for your presentation.

9. Click <u>U</u>se Browser Colors, to allow the visiting Web browser to determine the display colors to use for your slides (this makes your slide show download more quickly). Or, choose <u>C</u>ustom Colors, and use the color buttons to specify colors for the background, text, links, and visited links. Click <u>N</u>ext. The wizard prompts you to select a style for advance slide buttons.

10. Click the desired button style and click <u>N</u>ext. The wizard prompts you to specify the location of the buttons.

11. Select the desired button layout. You can display the buttons above or below the slides or to the left or right of the slides. Click <u>N</u>ext. You are now prompted to pick a folder in which you want the presentation folder placed.

12. Click the <u>B</u>rowse button, select the desired folder, and click the <u>S</u>elect button. A new folder will be created inside the selected folder, and each slide will be saved as a separate HTML document in that folder. Click <u>N</u>ext. The last dialog box appears.

13. Click the <u>F</u>inish button. The Save as HTML dialog box appears, asking if you want to save these settings to use again later.

14. Type a name for the settings, and click <u>S</u>ave. The wizard starts to convert the slides to HTML format, and displays the progress of the operation. When the operation is complete, a dialog box appears, informing you that you are done.

15. Click OK.

Your presentation consists of several files stored in a folder whose name is based on the presentation's file name. You can open the file called Index.html in Internet Explorer to see how it will look and act on the Web. Figure 46.13 shows a sample PowerPoint slide displayed in Internet Explorer.

Converting an Existing Slide Show into Web Pages

If you have already created the presentation you want to place on the Web, you can use the <u>F</u>ile, Save As <u>H</u>TML command to convert it into a series of Web pages. When you enter the command, the Save As HTML Wizard appears. Click the <u>N</u>ext button to proceed.

The Wizard displays a series of dialog boxes asking if you want to change the slide layout, use frames, specify a graphic format, select a display resolution, add your e-mail address, and control the look of your background, text, and control buttons (for advancing slides). Enter your preferences in each dialog box and click <u>N</u>ext. See Figure 46.14.

The last dialog box prompts you to specify a drive and folder for storing the Web pages that make up the slide show. It's a good idea to place the pages in a separate directory, apart from other files, to make it easier to publish the slide show later. After you select a directory, click the <u>F</u>inish button.

FIG. 46.13
A sample PowerPoint presentation displayed in Internet Explorer.

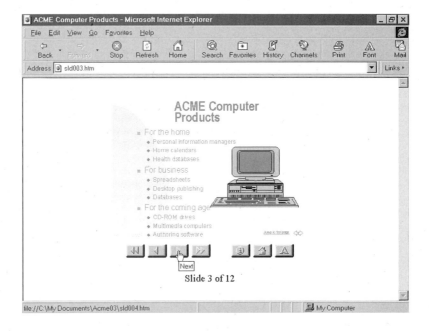

FIG. 46.14
You can change the look of the Web version of your presentation without affecting the original presentation.

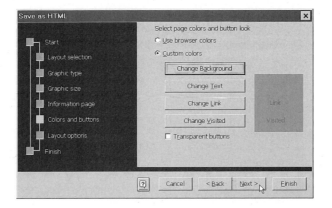

TIP   When you use the Save as HTML Wizard, it offers you the option of saving the presentation as a PowerPoint Animation. You may want to choose this option if you have a timed slide show that you want to run automatically in the user's browser window.

Making a New Presentation with an Online Template

You can also create a new Web presentation using one of PowerPoint's many online templates:

1. Choose File, New.

2. In the New dialog box, click the Presentations tab to view a list of templates. The templates that have (Online) in their names are designed for the Web.

3. Click one of the Online templates and click OK.

4. Make sure you choose File, Save as HTML when you save your new presentation.

Linking Slides

When you create an online slide show using the AutoContent Wizard, it adds buttons to each slide so a person can advance from one slide to the next. For less linear navigation, you might want to insert links on your slides that point to other slides.

To insert a link, complete the following steps:

1. Type the text or insert the object that you want to act as a link. (This is the text or graphic the user will click to activate the link.)

2. Right-click the text or object you want to use as a link, and select Action Settings. The Action Settings dialog box appears, as shown in Figure 46.15.

FIG. 46.15
Use the Action Settings dialog box to create hyperlinks that point to other slides in your presentation.

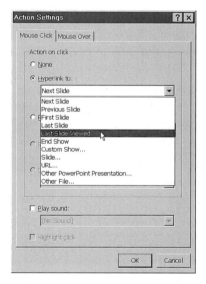

3. If the Mouse Click tab is not in front, click it.

4. Click the Hyperlink To option to turn it on.

5. Open the Hyperlink To drop-down list and select the slide to which you want this object or text to point. You can select the first or last slide or the next or previous slide, or click Slide and pick the specific slide you want this link to point to. (You can also choose to point a link to another file, a page on the Web, or another PowerPoint presentation.)

6. Click OK.

PowerPoint transforms the selected text or object into a hyperlink. (To learn more about links, see "Inserting and Editing Hyperlinks" earlier in this chapter.)

Publishing Your Page on the Web

You have created your own Web page, but it's not going to do you any good on *your* computer. You need to place it on a Web server where fellow Web surfers from all over the world can open it and experience your vision.

If you work for a company that has its own Web server, you can save your Web pages to the server. If you are not so fortunate, you can usually post a relatively small Web document on your Internet service provider's Web server. Most service providers and many of the major online services (America Online, CompuServe, and The Microsoft Network) allow members to post their personal pages in a special area on the server. Obtain the following information from your service provider:

- Does your service provider make Web space available to subscribers? If not, maybe you should change providers.

- How much disk space do you get and how much does it cost, if anything? Some providers give you a limited amount of disk space, which is usually plenty for one or two Web pages without video clips or large graphics.

- What is the URL of the server you must connect to in order to upload your files? This can be an FTP or Web server. Write down the address.

- What user name and password do you need to enter to gain access to the server? (This is usually the same name and password you use to establish your Internet connection.)

- In which directory must you place your files? Write it down.

- What name must you give your Web page? In many cases, the service lets you post a single Web page and you must call it **Index.html**.

- Are there any other specific instructions you must follow to post your Web page?

- After posting your page, what will its address (URL) be? You'll want to open it in your Web browser as soon as you post it.

You will have to *upload* your Web document and all associated graphics files to the service provider's computer. You can publish pages using Microsoft's Web Publishing Wizard, but first, you should check your page, as explained in the following section.

Test Your Page

Before you place your finished page on the Web, complete the following steps:

1. Run a spell check, and read the page again, just as if you were creating a paper document.

2. Open your page in Internet Explorer to make sure it looks okay.

3. Click the links to see if they work; you might have to edit them.

4. Make sure all the graphics are being inserted properly. Sometimes, the page might look fine in Word, but have problems in real life (on the Web).

Installing and Using the Web Publishing Wizard

Microsoft's Web Publishing Wizard is on the Office 97 CD, but it is not installed when you install Office. To install the wizard, insert the Office CD and use My Computer or Windows Explorer to change to the ValuPack\Webpost folder. Double-click the file named Webpost.exe and follow the installation instructions.

> **CAUTION**
>
> When publishing a Web page, you need to consider any associated files, such as graphics, that you used in that page. It's a good idea to place your Web page and its associated files in a single folder and then publish the entire folder. If you place only the Web page on the server, any links to graphics will not work.

Once you have installed the Web Publishing Wizard, you can run it and use it to place your page(s) on the Web. Complete the following steps:

1. Open the Start menu, choose Programs, Accessories, Internet Tools, and select Web Publishing Wizard. The Welcome dialog box appears.
2. Click Next. You are prompted to select the folder or file you want to place on the Web.
3. To place an entire folder full of files on the Web server, click Browse Folders and select the folder that contains your Web page and any associated files. (You can click Include Subfolders if the subfolders contain associated files, such as graphics.)

   To place a single file on the Web server, click the Browse Files button, and select the Web page file.
4. Click Next. The wizard prompts you to specify your Web server and provides a list of popular Web servers, such as CompuServe's Our World.
5. Open the drop-down list and select your Web server, or click New if your server is not on the list. If you clicked New, the wizard prompts you to type a name for your Web server.
6. Type a name for the server and then open the drop-down list and select one of the servers, or click <Other Internet Provider>. Click Next.
7. If you selected <Other Internet Provider>, you are now prompted to enter the Web server address, as shown in Figure 46.16. Obtain this address from your Web administrator or Internet Service Provider and type it in the URL or Internet Address text box. Click Next. The wizard prompts you to specify your Internet connection type.
8. If you are publishing your page on an intranet, select Use Local Area Network (Intranet). If you are using an Internet service provider, select Use Dial-Up Networking to Access the Internet and select your Dial-Up Networking connection. Click Next. The wizard indicates that it will now verify the information.
9. Click Next to start the verification process and publish your page.

Part
VII

Ch
46

FIG. 46.16

You must enter the URL of your Web server.

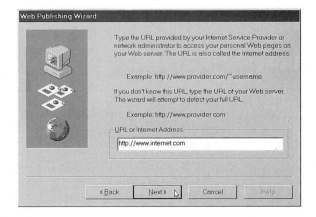

In this chapter, you learned some of the basics of creating Web pages in the various Office applications. If you create many Web pages or need to manage a complex collection of Web pages, you should learn more about HTML and the tools you can use to create and edit Web pages. You should also consider purchasing a dedicated Web page editor and Web management tool, such as Microsoft's FrontPage. ●

CHAPTER 47

Internet Forms and Databases

by Joe Kraynak

Microsoft Office 97 is no stranger to forms. Word, Excel, and Access all have features that allow you to create custom forms for entering data in your tables, worksheets, and databases.

What's new in Office 97 is that you can now convert your forms into Web pages and then place them on a Web server or intranet. A visitor to your site or a coworker can then pull up your Web form in his Web browser and use it to enter data, request specific information, search your Web site or intranet, or view related content via the Internet. ■

Understand Web forms

Take a look at a simple form and understand how online forms allow users to enter records into your database.

Create a form

Create forms in Word, Excel, and Access and customize forms by adding form controls.

Linking an online form to a database

Set up the required connection between the form you created and your Access database.

Use an online form

Link your Web page to a form, open the form in your Web browser, and use the form to enter data into your database.

Overview of Forms

You have no doubt encountered forms on the Web, even if you've done nothing more than connect to Yahoo or Lycos to perform a search. You type one or two entries to specify the topic of interest and then click a button to execute the search. The Web site then returns a list of links you can click to open specific pages. Perhaps you have used forms to register your software on the Web or to submit an entry for an online contest. You may have even used forms to place credit card orders or play archaic, interactive games.

Figure 47.1 shows a typical Web form. As you can see, the form is similar to a dialog box you might encounter in Windows or in one of your applications. It can contain text boxes, option buttons, check boxes, command buttons, and even drop-down lists. You make your selections, type entries in the required blanks, and then click a command button to send the information to the server.

FIG. 47.1

Forms provide a way for users to interact with a Web site by selecting options and entering data.

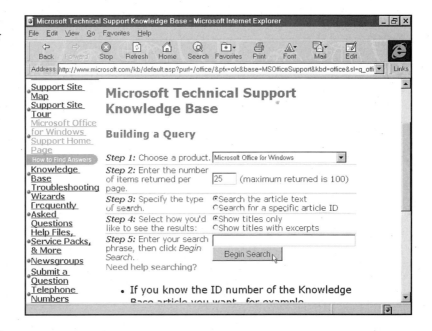

Mention of the server brings up another, more complex, aspect of forms. Eventually, you need to link the form to your database, either to allow users to enter data into the database or retrieve data from the database, or both.

To connect to a database, the form works along with a Web server—Microsoft's IIS (Internet Information Server)—and the database itself. When a user completes the form and submits it, the data travels to the IIS just as if the user clicked a link to request a page from the server. In the case of form data, however, the server passes the data along to the IDC (Internet Database Connector), which acts as a bridge between the Web server and the database. IDC then processes the data and either initiates a query or posts a new record.

This chapter provides the instructions you need to not only create the form but also establish the required links between the form, Web server (IIS), IDC, and your Access database.

NOTE If you simply wish to place data from your Access database on the Web, you can transform portions of your database into static Web pages, as explained in Chapter 46, "Creating and Publishing Web Documents." However, if you want users to be able to access up-to-date information in your ever-changing database, and enter information into it, you must establish a form/database link, as explained in this chapter. ■

Creating a Form

Before you even start thinking about linking a form to your database, you need to create the form you want to use. In the past, creating a form required some expertise with HTML codes. For example, the simple form shown in Figure 47.2 required the following complex codes:

```
<HTML>
<HEAD>
<META HTTP-EQUIV="Content-Type" CONTENT="text/html; charset=windows-1252">
<TITLE>pizzaordr</TITLE>
<META NAME="Template" CONTENT="C:\PROGRAM FILES\MICROSOFT
OFFICE\OFFICE\html.dot">
</HEAD>
<BODY LINK="#0000ff" VLINK="#800080">
<H1>Pizza Order Form</H1>
<FORM ACTION="URL">
<P>Choose Your Toppings: </P>
<P>
<INPUT TYPE="CHECKBOX" VALUE="pepperoni">
Pepperoni
<INPUT TYPE="CHECKBOX" VALUE="sausage">
Sausage
<INPUT TYPE="CHECKBOX" VALUE="anchovies">
Anchovies
<INPUT TYPE="CHECKBOX" VALUE="greenpeppers">
Green Peppers</P>
<P>
<INPUT TYPE="CHECKBOX" VALUE="onions">
Onions
```

```
<INPUT TYPE="CHECKBOX" VALUE="mushrooms">
Mushrooms
<INPUT TYPE="CHECKBOX" VALUE="blackolives"
Black Olives
<INPUT TYPE="CHECKBOX" VALUE="green olives">
Green Olives</P>
<P>Choose a crust (only one, please): </P>
<P>
<INPUT TYPE="RADIO" NAME="crust" VALUE="standard">
Standard<BR>
<INPUT TYPE="RADIO" NAME="crust" VALUE="deepdish">
Deep Dish<BR>
<INPUT TYPE="RADIO" NAME="crust" VALUE="thickcrust">
Thick Crust<BR>
<INPUT TYPE="RADIO" NAME="crust" VALUE="thincrispy">
Thin 'n Crispy</P>
<P>
<INPUT TYPE="submit"  VALUE="Order Pizza">
<INPUT TYPE="reset">
</P></FORM></BODY>
</HTML>
```

Fortunately, you can avoid these HTML form codes by creating your form in one of the Office 97 applications. Word, Access, PowerPoint, and Excel provide the tools you need to insert most of the common form controls, including text boxes, option buttons, check boxes, and Submit buttons. Which application should you use? The following list will help you decide:

- For collecting or distributing data on the Web, use Access. Access provides powerful tools that automate the process of creating forms, linking the forms to your Access database, and giving users the tools they need to query your database.

- If you are working on an intranet where everyone is using Excel, you can create Web forms and link them to an Excel data list or to an Access database. When a user clicks a link to open the Excel form, the form opens in Excel. Microsoft does not recommend using Excel forms for gathering data outside an intranet, where people may not use Excel.

- Word is useful for creating a Web form, but it does not provide tools for linking the form to a database. After creating the form, you need to go behind the scenes with the coded document and manually type additional codes.

FIG. 47.2
This form seems simple on the surface, but the HTML codes needed to create it are long and complex.

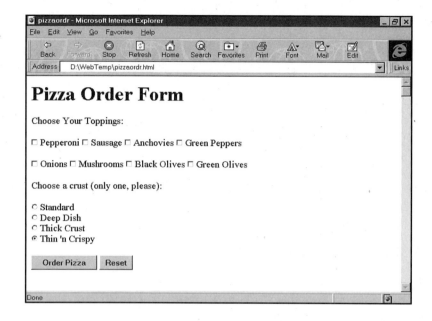

Adding Form Controls to Your Web Page in Word

When you open a Web page in Word, the Forms submenu appears on the Insert menu, and the Form Design Mode button appears on the Standard toolbar. You use these two tools to add form controls to your Web page.

To insert an item from the Forms menu, position the insertion point where you want the control inserted. Choose Insert, Forms, and select the desired control. Table 47.1 describes the controls listed on the Forms menu, and Figure 47.3 shows some of the uses for the various controls.

Part VII
Ch 47

 Word's Web Page Wizard, described in Chapter 46, "Creating and Publishing Web Documents," offers standard Web page forms named Registration, Survey, and Feedback. You can modify one of these predesigned forms instead of starting from scratch.

Table 47.1 Form Controls

Select This Control	To
Check Box	Insert a check box. Check boxes are useful for allowing users to select more than one item in a group of options.

continues

Table 47.1 Continued

Select this control	To
Option Button	Insert an option button, which is useful for allowing users to select only one option in a group. For example, if you are creating an online order form for T-shirts, you might use option buttons for sizes: Small, Medium, Large, and Extra Large.
Dropdown Box	Inserts a list that hides all options except the topmost option. To select an item, the user clicks the arrow on the right side of the box to display the list and then selects the desired option.
List Box	Inserts a list that displays all the available options. The user does not have to open the list to see the options.
Text Box	Provides a space for the user to type information. Text boxes are often used on registration forms, allowing the user to enter her name, phone number, and other information.
Text Area	Inserts a large text box, which allows the user to type a longer entry. Text areas are useful for collecting comments and feedback.
Submit	Adds a button that the user can click to submit any entries and selections made on the form.
Image Submit	Adds a graphic image in place of the Submit button. This allows you to use any suitable graphic as a button. If you select Image Submit, Word prompts you to select the image you want to use.
Reset	Inserts the Reset button, which the user can click to reset the form and start from scratch.
Hidden	Inserts a hidden control that can perform a task such as collecting information about the visitor's computer. The control is not displayed on the form when the user opens it.
Password	Displays a text box into which the user can type a password. When the user starts typing, asterisks appear in place of the typed characters, so someone cannot steal the password by looking over the user's shoulder.

Once you have inserted the control, a selection box appears, allowing you to move the control (by dragging it) or resize the control (by dragging one of its handles). To delete a control, simply click it and press the Delete key.

FIG. 47.3
The Form Controls in use.

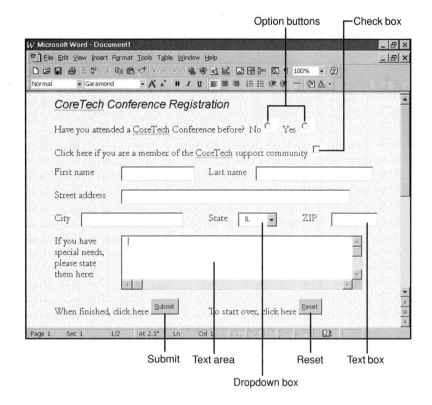

Option buttons
Check box

CoreTech Conference Registration

Have you attended a CoreTech Conference before? No ◯ Yes ◯

Click here if you are a member of the CoreTech support community ☐

First name [   ] Last name [   ]

Street address [   ]

City [   ] State [IL ▾] ZIP [   ]

If you have special needs, please state them here: [   ]

When finished, click here [Submit] To start over, click here [Reset]

Submit   Text area   Reset   Text box
Dropdown box

Toggling Form Design Mode   When you insert a control, Word automatically switches to Form Design Mode, displaying the controls as objects and displaying two horizontal lines that show where the form begins and ends. Word also displays the Control Toolbox and the Exit Design Mode button.

 You can turn off Form Design Mode by clicking Exit Design Mode or by clicking Form Design Mode in the Standard toolbar. This displays your form as it will appear on the Web page.

Using the Control Toolbox   In Form Design Mode, Word displays the Control Toolbox, which provides buttons for the same options you encountered on the Insert, Forms menu. This allows you to quickly insert controls without having to pull down menus. To add controls using the toolbox, complete one of the following steps:

- Click a control in the toolbox and then click where you want the control placed.
- Double-click a control in the toolbox.

Changing Properties of Form Controls   The Control Toolbox offers an additional option, the Properties button, which allows you to change the way the control behaves. Click Properties to display the Properties window for the selected control (or double-click the control in Design view). Figure 47.4 shows the properties for the check box control for the City field. Table 47.2

Part
VII

Ch
47

lists the properties for the controls. This window remains on-screen as you click other controls, so you can check and change properties for all the controls without having to open and close the window.

FIG. 47.4

You can change the properties of your form controls as you work.

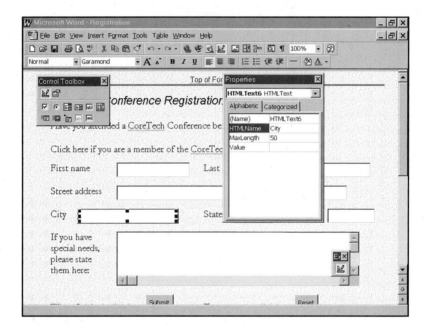

Table 47.2   Form Control Properties

Form Control	Properties
Check Box	**Checked** specifies the default check box setting: True for checked, False for unchecked. **HTMLName** is the name you give the control. **Value** is the entry that the control returns when checked. (If the box is not checked, no value is returned.)
Option Button	**Checked** specifies the default setting: True for selected, False for unselected. **HTMLName** is the name you give the control. Use the same name for all buttons in the group. **Value** is the entry that the option button returns when selected.
Dropdown Box	**DisplayValues** specifies the items in the list. Separate items with semicolons, no spaces: for example, **Option1;Option2;Option3 MultiSelect** specifies whether the user can select more than one item. False means only one item can be selected; True converts the drop-down list into a list box, which allows multiple selections. **Selected** specifies whether the first item in the list is selected by default. True means the item is selected; False means the item is

Form Control	Properties
	unselected. **Size** specifies the font size. **Value** is the entry that the list item returns when selected. Type the values in the same order as the DisplayValues and separate the values with semicolons, no spaces between value names.
List Box	**DisplayValues** specifies the items in the list. Separate items with semicolons, no spaces: for example, **Option1;Option2;Option3 MultiSelect** specifies whether the user can select more than one item. The default setting is True, allowing multiple selections. If you enter False, the following Selected options are unavailable. **Selected** specifies whether the first item in the list is selected by default. True means the item is selected; False means the item is unselected. **Size** specifies the size of the list box in relation to the number of items. The default setting is 3, making the box tall enough to display 3 entries at a time. If the list has more than 3 entries, a scroll bar appears. **Value** is the entry that the list item returns when selected. Type the values in the same order as the DisplayValues and separate the values with semicolons, no spaces between value names.
Text Box	**HTMLName** is the name you give the text box. **MaxLength** is the maximum length of the entry. The default setting is 0, allowing the user to type an entry of any length. **Value** allows you to display default text in the text box. (This is optional.)
Text Area	**HTMLName**is the name you give the text area. **Rows** specifies the height of the text area in rows. **Columns** specifies the width of the text area in columns. **Value** is any text that you want to appear in the text area when the user opens the form. **WordWrap** lets you specify whether text should wrap in the text area. Virtual and Physical turn on WordWrap for Web browsers that support it. Off turns WordWrap off for all browsers.
Submit	**HTMLName** is the hidden name you give the button. **Action** is the location of the database file that form is linked to. You can use the mailto: command (for instance, mailto:bfink@internet.com) to have the form entries e-mailed to you. **Caption** is the name of the button. You can use the default name, "Submit," or change the button's name. **Encoding** specifies the MIME type used to encode the submitted entries. **Method** specifies the HTML submission method: POST (to post entries) or GET to query a database.

Part
VII

Ch
47

continues

Table 47.2   Continued

Form Control	Properties
Image Submit	**HTMLName**, **Action**, **Encoding**, and **Method** are the same as for the Submit button. Image Submit performs the same function as the Submit button. **Source** is the name and location of the image used as the Submit button.
Reset	**HTMLName** is the hidden name you give the Reset button. **Caption** is the name of the button. You can use the default name, "Reset," or change the button's name.
Hidden	**HTMLName** is the name you give the hidden control. **Value** is the default text that's sent to the server when the user submits the form.
Password	**HTMLName** is the hidden name you give the Password text box. **MaxLength** is the maximum length of the entry. The default setting is 0, allowing the user to type an entry of any length. **Value** is set to display asterisks in place of the characters that the user types.

Linking Your Word Form to an Access Database

Although you can change the properties of controls, these properties do not link your form to your database. To use the form for users to enter data into your database or perform queries, you must enter additional codes manually.

Before entering these codes, work through the section "Linking Forms to Your Database," later in this chapter, to learn how to set up a dynamic relationship between your Access database and forms or queries. Access creates the files required to establish the link between the form and the database.

Once you have done that, you can add the required codes to the form you created in Word. These codes will reference the files created in Access to link the form to the database. The following sections explain the codes you must add to link your form or query to your Access database.

N O T E   The following section assumes that you are using Word along with Access and Microsoft's IIS to link your form to your database. If you are using a different type of server, for example, UNIX, you must enter different codes and use CGI scripts to establish the link. ■

Creating a Simple Query   To add codes manually, you must first display the source code for the form. Open the form in Word and then choose View, HTML Source. The following list provides an example of creating a simple query. The code shown here displays a form with two text boxes, which allow the user to type the first and last date for the range of records they want to view. The query then returns a list of employee sales by country for the dates specified.

```
<HTML>
<HEAD>
<TITLE>Employee Sales by Country</TITLE>
<BODY>
<FORM METHOD="GET" ACTION="Employee Sales by Country.ASP">
Beginning Date <INPUT TYPE="Text" NAME="Beginning Date"><P>
Ending Date <INPUT TYPE="Text" NAME="Ending Date"><P>
<INPUT TYPE="Submit" VALUE="Run Query">
</FORM>
</BODY>
</HTML>
```

Focus on the area between <FORM METHOD= and </FORM>. These codes create the query form. <FORM METHOD="GET" ACTION="Employee Sales by Country.ASP"> specifies that when the form is submitted, it will "get" data from the database using the file Employee Sales by Country.ASP. This file is created by Access when you export a table as an ASP (Active Server Page). You will learn how to export tables and other database objects as Active Server Pages later in this chapter.

The two date codes, <INPUT TYPE=>, create the text boxes into which the user types the beginning and ending dates. Word inserts these controls for you whenever you insert a form control on your page, as explained earlier.

The Final code, <INPUT TYPE="Submit" VALUE="Run Query">, creates the Submit button, named Run Query, that the user clicks to submit the query. After entering changes, be sure to save your page.

Integrating Your Form with an Access Database   To use a form to post data to your Access database requires more advanced techniques. In addition to your HTML form file, you must create two text files with the .idc and .htx extensions to create the link between your form and the database. You must save these files to a subdirectory of the /scripts directory on your Web server. Following is the code from a sample .idc file:

```
Datasource:NorthwindDSN
Template:Customers.htx
Password:
Username:Admin
SQLStatement:
+ INSERT INTO Customers
+ (CustomerID, CompanyName, ContactName, ContactTitle, Phone)+
VALUES('%CustomerID%', '%CompanyName%', '%ContactName%', '%ContactTitle%',
'%Phone%');
```

Part

VII

Ch

47

Let's dissect the code:

- *Datasource* specifies the ODBC data source (which links to the database). See "Creating a New Data Source," later in this chapter for instructions.
- *Template* is the .htx file you will create next.
- *Password* is required only if you need a password to access the database (here it is left blank).
- *Username* is your logon name, if required (Admin is the default entry).
- *SQLStatement* specifies the action that will be performed when the user submits the form. In this case, the SQLStatement specifies that the data must be inserted into the Customers table of the specified data source.
- The remaining entries indicate the fields in the destination database. In this example, the form will post entries to the CustomerID, CompanyName, ContactName, ContactTitle, and Phone fields in the database.

The .htx file, which acts as a template for returning a response to the user is pretty simple. Here's a sample of the .htx file used with the .idc file described above:

```
<HTML>
<HEAD><TITLE>Registration</TITLE></HEAD>
<BODY>
<H3>Customer Form</H3>
<H2>Information registered. Thanks!</H2>
</BODY>
</HTML>
```

When the user successfully submits the form, "Customer Form Information registered. Thanks!" appears on the user's screen. You can replace this text with any reply you want to return. You may also wish to include a link that returns the user to your home page. For example, <A HREF="http://www.internet.com/index.html">Click here to return home</A>.

You then need to take one last step: modifying your HTML form file. Open the file in Word and choose View, HTML Source. At the top of the form area, just above the first INPUT code, insert the following line:

```
<FORM METHOD="POST" ACTION="http://webservername/scripts/IDCdirectory/
filename.idc">
```

Replace *webservername* with the address of your Web server, *IDCdirectory* with the name of the directory in which you saved your .idc and .htx files, and *filename* with the name of the .idc file you created. Be sure to save your modified form. Here's a sample form with the line added (in bold):

```
<HTML>
<HEAD>
```

```
<TITLE>Customer Registration Form</TITLE>
<BODY>
<FORM METHOD="POST" ACTION="http://www.internet.com/scripts/
Customers/Customers.idc">
Customer ID: <INPUT TYPE="Text" NAME="CustomerID"><P>
Company Name: <INPUT TYPE="Text" NAME="CompanyName"><P>Name: <INPUT
TYPE="Text" NAME="ContactName"><P>
Title: <INPUT TYPE="Text" NAME="ContactTitle"><P>
Phone: <INPUT TYPE="Text" NAME="Phone">
<INPUT TYPE="Submit" VALUE="Submit">
</FORM>
</BODY>
</HTML>
```

Creating Web Forms in Excel

When you create a Web form in Excel, the form is created as an Excel file, not as a standard HTML file. When another person opens the form, Internet Explorer automatically opens the form in Excel. Because of this, Excel Web forms are not the best tools for gathering information on the Web. However, they are useful if you are working on an intranet where people who need to enter information into your worksheets or a corresponding Access database are all using Excel.

Excel comes with a Web Form Wizard that can lead you through the process of creating the form you need. Complete the following steps:

1. Use Excel's Forms toolbar to create your form, as explained in Chapter 15, "Using Outlines, Templates, and Forms." Make sure you use the Forms toolbar, not the Control Toolbox.

2. Choose Tools, Wizard and select Web Form. The Web Form Wizard-Step 1 of 6 dialog box appears.

3. Click Next. The next dialog box prompts you to select the cells and controls you want to use on your Web form. All form controls are automatically added to the list of controls that will appear on the form. To remove any controls, click the control and click Remove.

4. To add cells to the Web form, click Add a Cell, click the cell you want to use, and click OK. For example, if you want users to enter their first name in a cell, you would click the cell into which the user would type his or her first name. When you click OK, you are returned to the Wizard.

5. Double-click inside the Field Name of the Selected Control text box, type the name of the database field in which you want this entry posted, and click Change Name. See Figure 47.5.

FIG. 47.5

You must assign a name to each control to specify the field name in which the control value will be posted.

Database field name

Control name

Controls and cells are listed here

Type the database field name for the selected control and click Change Name button

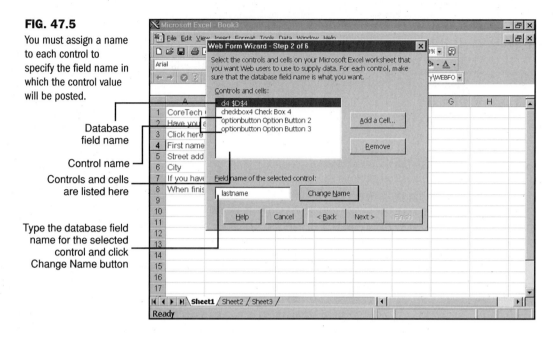

6. After adding all the desired controls and cells, and assigning them field names, click Next.

7. The Step 3 dialog box prompts you to specify the server you will use to manage the form. If you use Microsoft's IIS as the interface between the Web server and your database, select Microsoft Internet Information Server. If you use CGI (Common Gateway Interface), choose Common Gateway Interface. Click Next.

8. The Step 4 dialog box prompts you to specify the form's format and location. If you use FrontPage to manage your Web, select Add the Result to Your FrontPage Web. If you don't have FrontPage, use the default selection: Save the Result as a Microsoft Excel File.

9. In the File Path text box, type the path to the folder in which you want the form and related files stored. (When the Wizard creates the form, it creates four files: an .xls file (the form itself), an .mdb file (Access database), and an .idc and .htx file (for managing the link between the form and the database).

10. The Step 5 dialog box lets you type a message that will pop up on the user's screen after the user submits the form. Type the following entries:

Title appears in the title bar of the message window.

Header appears as the first line in the message window.

Text is the message itself.

URL Path is the address that points to the folder in which you want the data posted.

11. Click Next. The Step 6 dialog box appears, providing additional information about placing your form and associated files on the Web. Click Finish.

The Wizard creates the form and all the other files required to use the form to collect information. However, in order for your Excel form to work, you must perform the following additional steps:

- Move the .htx and .idc files that the Wizard created to a separate directory in the /scripts directory on your Web server.

- Create a new system data source for the .mdb file that the Wizard created. See "Creating a New Data Source," later in this chapter, for details.

- Place your new .xls file on your Web server and create a page that contains a link to this file. For example, if you created a form for collecting health insurance data from employees, you might place a link to the .xls file on the Human Resources Home Page.

- Open the .idc file in a text editor, such as Notepad, and look for "Datasource: Your datasource" at the top of the file. Replace "Your datasource" with the name of the system datasource you created.

NOTE Because of differences in how a Web or network administrator sets up a Web server, check with your administrator if you have any questions on where to place the files on the Web server. ■

Creating Web Forms in Access

In Chapter 30, "Designing and Using Forms," you used Access to create forms for entering data into your database. You can use the Publish to the Web Wizard to convert these forms into Web pages. However, the process requires a little preparation and planning to ensure that the form will run on your Web server.

Part VII Ch 47

To cover the preliminaries, read the following section, "Linking Forms to Your Database." This section leads you through the process of specifying a data source on the Web server, so you can enter the correct data source name when the Publish to the Web Wizard requests it.

At the end of the following section, you will learn how to create and publish Web forms from Access.

 TIP Access data entry forms are typically too wide or too long to fit inside a standard Web browser window. Before you convert forms into Web pages, open the form in Design view and move the fields closer together and nearer to the left margin.

Linking Forms to Your Database

To establish a dynamic relationship between a form and database, Office uses IDC (Internet Database Connector) or ASP (Active Server Page) to act as an interface between the Web server and your database. This allows you to manage your database as before and provide Web users with the access they need to view up-to-date information and post new records to your database.

The following sections explain what is involved in creating a dynamic relationship between your Web forms and your Access database.

Web Server Requirements

To use IDC or ASP files, you must have access to a Web server that can handle them. The steps in the following sections assume that you have one of the following operating systems and Web server environments:

- Windows NT Server version 3.51 or later running Microsoft Internet Information Server (IIS) version 1.0, 2.0, or 3.0. For information about the latest version of IIS, visit Microsoft's Web site at **http://www.microsoft.com/iis/**.

- Windows NT Workstation version 4.0 with Peer Web Services installed.

- Windows 95 and Personal Web Server installed. You can use Personal Web Server to test your pages locally (on your computer). To make your form available on the Web, you will then need to publish your form and associated files on a Windows NT Server running IIS. You can download a copy of Personal Web Server at **http://www.microsoft.com/ ie/iesk/pws.htm**.

If you are using the Personal Web Server, the installation creates a folder on drive C called WebShare. Placing folders or files in the WebShare folder places them on your Web. To find out the URL of your Web server, right-click the Personal Web Server icon in the taskbar tray and select Properties. The URL is displayed at the top of the General tab.

Integrating Access and IIS—the Internet Database Connector

As you saw in Chapter 46, "Creating and Publishing Web Documents," and earlier in this chapter, you can use the Publish to the Web Wizard in Access to save database objects and forms as dynamic Web pages. However, to create a link between these dynamic pages and the database itself requires two additional steps:

1. Create a new system ODBC data source on the Web server. The ODBC (Open Database Connectivity) provides a link between the server and the database.

2. Move files to the appropriate directories on the server. When you save files as dynamic IDC/HTX or ASP files, your Office application places all of the associated files in a single folder. You must move them to appropriate directories on your Web server to make them available.

The following sections lead you through the process of setting up your Web server and moving your files to the required directories.

Creating a New Data Source   To use the IDC/HTX or ASP files, you first need to create a new system ODBC data source on your Web server. Complete the following steps:

1. On the system running IIS, open the Windows Control Panel and double-click the 32-bit ODBC icon.

2. Click the System DSN tab to view a list of existing data sources, as shown in Figure 47.6.

FIG. 47.6

The ODBC Data Source Administrator dialog box displays the names of existing data sources.

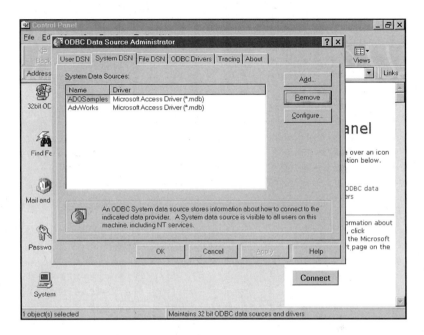

3. Click Add. The Create New Data Source dialog box appears, displaying a list of ODBC driver types.

4. Click Microsoft Access Driver (*.mdb), and click Finish. The ODBC Microsoft Access 97 Setup dialog box appears, prompting you to enter a name for the data source.

5. In the Data Source Name text box, type a name for the data source. You can type a description of the source in the Description text box.

6. Click Select and use the resulting dialog box to change to the folder that contains your Access database. Select the database file and click OK. This returns you to the ODBC Microsoft Access 97 Setup dialog box, as shown in Figure 47.7.

7. Click OK. You are returned to the Select Data Source window, and the name of the new system data source is added to the list.

8. Click OK.

Setting the Default ODBC Data Source in Access   Whenever you use the Publish to the Web Wizard, the Wizard prompts you to specify the data source you want to use. To have the Wizard enter the data source name you set up in the previous section as the default, complete the following steps:

1. Run Access and choose Tools, Options. The Options dialog box appears.

2. Click the Hyperlink/HTML tab.

Part
VII

Ch
47

3. In the Data Source Name text box, type the name you gave to your data source in the previous section (see Figure 47.8).

FIG. 47.7

You must set up a data source for using IDC/HTX files.

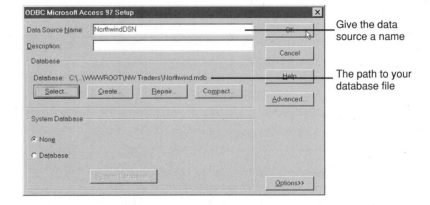

Give the data source a name

The path to your database file

FIG. 47.8

You can specify a default data source, so you don't have to enter it when using the Publish to the Web Wizard.

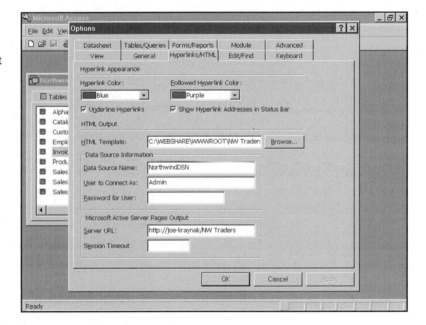

4. In the User to Connect As text box, type your username only if you need to enter a username to access the server. The default name, Admin, provides access if you don't need to log on.

5. If you typed a username in Step 4, click in the Password for User text box, and type your password.

6. Click OK.

Setting Up Directories on the Server   In order for your IDC/HTX and ASP files to work on the server, they must be placed in the appropriate directories. Although you can specify the destination directory using the Publish to the Web Wizard, the Wizard does not always place the files in the correct directories. For instance, when you publish dynamic content to the Web from Access, it places the IDC, HTX, and HTM files all in the specified directory. However, the IDC and HTX files must be in a separate subdirectory of the /scripts directory on the Web server.

Before you use the Publish to the Web Wizard to convert Access database objects into Web pages, you should create two directories on your Web server. If you are using IIS, create the directories below the InetPub directory on the server. If you are using the Personal Web Server, create the directories below the WebShare directory. The new directories should have the following paths:

- **\InetPub\wwwroot***subfolder* or **\WebShare\wwwroot***subfolder*, where *subfolder* is the name you give to your database folder on the Web server. When you publish from Access to the Web, the .htm, .idc, and .htx files will be placed in this directory.

- **\InetPub\scripts***subfolder* or **\WebShare\scripts***subfolder*. You must place .idc and .htx files in a subdirectory of the \scripts directory in order for them to run.

After creating these folders, use the administrator tools in IIS or Personal Web Server to make sure the folder for the IDC file provides read and execute access.

Creating a Template   When you export forms or queries as dynamic Web pages, Access prompts you to select a template to control the appearance of the form or query. You can use an existing template or create a new template. Save the template as a text-only file with the .html extension. The following is the HTML code for the sample form template used in the following sections:

```
<HTML><HEAD><TITLE><Form Template></TITLE></HEAD>
<BODY>
<BR><P ALIGN = CENTER>
<A HREF = "Default.htm">Return to Menu</A></P>
</BODY></HTML>
```

The code <A HREF "Default.htm">Return to Menu</A> displays a link at the bottom of the form page that the user can click to return to the home page, called Default.htm (assuming you choose to create a home page).

Publishing Dynamic Web Pages from Access

Now that you have set up your data source, specified the default data source, and set up directories on your Web server, you can use the Publish to the Web Wizard to convert your database or a portion of it into dynamic content on the Web. Complete the following steps:

1. Open your database in Access.

2. Choose File, Save as HTML. The opening Publish to the Web Wizard dialog box appears, indicating what it will do. (Leave I Want to Use a Web Publication Profile box unchecked.)

3. Click Next. The Wizard prompts you to select the items (tables, queries, and forms) that you want to include in your publication. (You can create static publications for reports, but you cannot create dynamic reports.)

4. Click the check box next to each table, query, or form you want to include. Click Next. You are now prompted to select a template, to provide a consistent look for all your Web pages.

5. (Optional) Click Browse, click the desired template, and click Select. (To use different templates for some pages, place a check mark next to I Want to Select Different Templates for Some of the Selected Objects. Access will prompt you to choose a template for each object.) Click Next. You are now asked how you want to output the database.

6. To publish dynamic datasheets, which allow users to access the most up-to-date information in your database, select Dynamic HTX/IDC. To publish the pages on a Microsoft Active Server, which allows users to input data using forms or datasheets, click Dynamic ASP. For details about Active Server Pages, see the next section, "Creating Active Server Pages."

7. Click Next. Assuming you specified a default data source (see "Setting the Default ODBC Data Source in Access," earlier in this chapter), its name appears in the Data Source Name text box. The User Name and Password entries are required only if you must enter a username and password for access to a secure Access database.

8. Click Next. The Next dialog box asks if you want to place the resulting Web pages in a folder on your hard drive or upload them to a Web server. Complete one of the following steps:

   Select No, I Want to Publish Documents Locally, and then click Browse and select the folder in which you want the Web pages stored. Select the subdirectory you created below the \wwwroot directory in the previous section. The following steps assume you selected this option. Select Yes, I Want to Run the Web Publishing Wizard to Set Up a New Web Publishing Specification. This tells the Wizard that you want to upload to a remote Web server you haven't used before. Select Yes, I Want to Use an Existing Web Publishing Server Whose "Friendly Name" Has Been Set Up Previously, if you have already used the Web Publishing Wizard to publish Web pages to a Web server in the list.

9. Click Next. The Wizard asks if you want to create a home page with links to your other Access Web pages. Click Yes, I Want to Create a Home Page, and then type a file name for the home page in the designated text box. (You can leave the name default.htm so the page will open automatically when a user accesses its directory, or you can create your own home page later.)

10. Click <u>N</u>ext. You are now asked if you want to save your settings as a profile, so you can use the same settings for other Web publications. If desired, click <u>Y</u>es and then type a name for the profile.

11. Click <u>F</u>inish.

 TIP Creating a profile helps you skip several steps if you run the Publish to the Web Wizard again. Instead of stepping through all the dialog boxes to specify your preferences, simply select the saved profile in the first dialog box to enter the same preferences for other publications.

The Publish to the Web Wizard creates the required files and stores them in the specified subdirectory on the Web server. To access your new dynamic database using a Web browser, you must perform two additional steps:

1. Move the IDC and HTX files from the subdirectory of \wwwroot*subfolder* to \scripts*subfolder*.

2. Use a text editor, such as NotePad, to open the file named Default.htm in \wwwroot\subfolder. Edit the line <A HREF="DataName.idc?"> to include the path to the .idc file. For instance, you might type <A HREF=/scripts/subfolder/DataName.idc?">. Save the file as a text-only file and be sure to retain the extension .htm.

Once you have performed these steps, you can run Internet Explorer and access your dynamic database. Use Internet Explorer to go to the address http://*servername*/*subfolder*/, where *servername* is the name of your Web server and *subfolder* is the name of the directory where default.htm is stored. Figure 47.9 shows an example of a default.htm file created by the Publish to the Web Wizard.

FIG. 47.9
Default.htm contains links to your other dynamic database files.

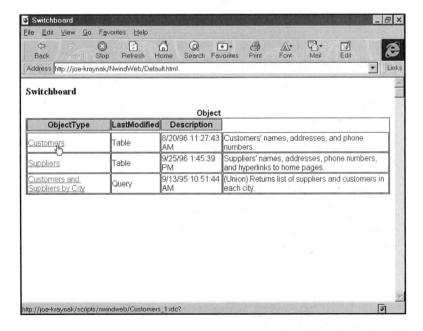

Creating Active Server Pages

Microsoft's Active Server Page is a component of IIS 3.0 and provides a much more efficient way of dealing with dynamic databases on the Web. When you output an object to the dynamic ASP files format, Microsoft Access creates an ActiveX Server Page (.asp) file. The .asp file contains HTML codes along with one or more queries and the information needed to connect to an ODBC data source.

The ASP file handles all the communication between the Web server and the database. When a user completes the ASP form in her Web browser and submits it, the ASP file opens the Microsoft Access database and runs the queries in the ASP file. It then merges the results and HTML codes in the ASP file into an HTML file and sends the resulting HTML file back to the Web browser.

Microsoft's Active Server Page is a component of IIS 3.0 and later, but it will also work with Personal Web Server and Peer Web Services. If you are using Personal Web Server or Peer Web Services, you can download the Active Server Page component from http://www.microsoft.com/iis/ and install it on your computer. (Download *only* the Active Server Page component.) You can then run and test your ASP forms locally before moving them to your Web server.

Making Directories for Your ASP Files   In "Setting Up Directories on the Server" you learned how to set up separate directories on your Web server for the .htm, .idc, and .htx files that the Publish to the Web Wizard creates. Before you create .asp files, you should create a separate subdirectory, \InetPub*subfolder* or \WebShare*subfolder*, for storing your .asp files.

After creating the required folder, use the Administrator tools in IIS or Personal Web Server to turn on Read and Execute access for the folder. Without Execute access, the .asp will be unable to process the request from the user, or may return the source code for the .html page to the user.

Exporting a Query as an Active Server Page   ASP provides a much more intuitive interface for users to perform queries on the Web. Exporting queries with ASP is also much easier than using IDC/HTX.

Before you convert a query into an ASP file, you should consider how you want the query to work. When you design your query, you enter criteria that might specify a range of values for one of the fields (for instance, a beginning and ending date). If you type specific criteria, Access creates a single ASP file that performs the query using the specified criteria. However, if you enter field names instead of specific values, as shown in Figure 47.10, Access creates two files: an ASP file and an HTML file. The HTML file is a form that allows users to type the range of values.

You can output queries as ASP files using either File, Save As/Export or File, Save As HTML. When outputting a single database object, the File, Save As/Export method is more efficient. The following steps show how to use the File, Save As/Export option:

1. Open your Access database file and select the query you want to convert into an Active Server Page.

2. Choose File, Save As/Export.

3. Select To an External File or Database and click OK. The Save Query dialog box appears.

4. Change to the folder you created for storing your ASP files.

5. Open the Save as Type drop-down list and select Microsoft ActiveX Server (*.asp). Click Export. The Microsoft Active Server Pages Output Options dialog box appears, as shown in Figure 47.11.

FIG. 47.10

To create an HTML query form that allows the user to perform the query on a specified range of values, use field names when you specify your criteria.

Here, field names are included in brackets

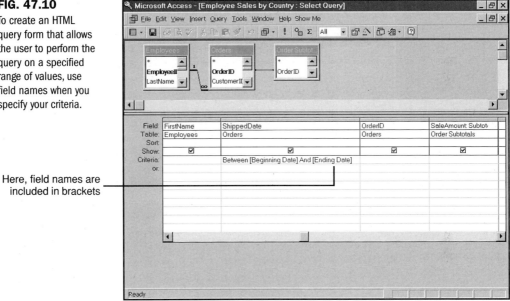

6. (Optional) If you have a Web page template you want to use to control the appearance of the page, type its location and name in the HTML Template text box, or use Browse to select it.

7. In the Data Source Name text box, type the name of the data source you want this query to use. See "Creating a New Data Source," earlier in this chapter, for details.

8. In the Server URL text box, type the server's address. For example, type **http:// servername/***subfolder* where *subfolder* is the name of the folder that will store your ASP files.

9. Click OK. Access converts the query into an ASP file and places it in the specified folder.

To see your new query in action, run Internet Explorer. Enter the address of your new ASP page or HTML page in the Address text box. Remember, if you used field names rather than specific values when specifying the criteria, Access creates an ASP and HTML file. Figure 47.12 shows a sample HTML query page displayed in Internet Explorer.

Part
VII

Ch
47

FIG. 47.11

Specify a data source and server URL to save as export.

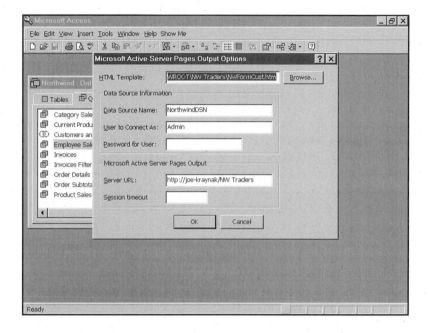

FIG. 47.12

An Active Server Page query displayed in Internet Explorer.

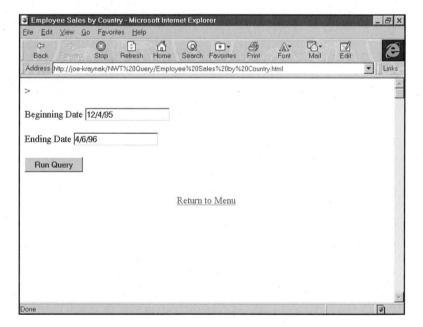

Converting an Access Form into an Active Server Page   As with queries, Access allows you to save existing forms as Active Server Pages. Access converts any text boxes and controls in the existing form into HTML controls on the ASP form and adds the standard form buttons for navigating records.

 TIP When you create your forms in Access, keep in mind that most Access forms are based on individual tables. If you want to use your form to enter data into more than one table, base the form on a query when creating it.

You can output queries as ASP files using either File, Save As/Export (as shown in the previous section) or File, Save As HTML. The following steps show how to use the File, Save As HTML option:

1. Open the Access database that contains the form you want to use.
2. Choose File, Save as HTML.
3. Click Next.
4. Click the check box next to each form you want to use as an Active Server Page. Click Next.
5. (Optional) Click Browse, select the desired template, and click Select. Click Next. You are now asked how you want to output the database.
6. Click Dynamic ASP.
7. Click Next. Assuming you specified a default data source (see "Setting the Default ODBC Data Source in Access" earlier in this chapter), its name appears in the Data Source Name text box. The User Name and Password entries are required only if you must enter a username and password for access to a secure Access database.
8. Click Next. The next dialog box asks if you want to place the resulting Web pages in a folder on your hard drive or upload them to a Web server. Perform one of the following steps: Select No, I Want to Publish Documents Locally, and then click Browse and select the folder in which you want the Web pages stored. Select Yes, I Want to Run the Web Publishing Wizard to Set Up a New Web Publishing Specification, and then follow the on-screen instructions. Select Yes, I Want to Use an Existing Web Publishing Server Whose "Friendly Name" Has Been Set Up Previously, and select the name of the server.
9. Click Next. The Wizard asks if you want to create a home page with links to your other Access Web pages. You can click Yes, to create a simple home page, but you will probably want to link to the form from a more attractive home page.
10. Click Next. You are now asked if you want to save your settings as a profile so you can use the same settings for other Web publications. If desired, click Yes and then type a name for the profile.
11. Click Finish.

To see your new form, run Internet Explorer and type the address of your new ASP page in the form **http://servername/***subfolder*/*formname***.html** where *subfolder* is the name of the folder that stores the ASP file and *formname* is the name of the ASP file you created. Figure 47.13 shows a sample ASP form page displayed in Internet Explorer.

Part
VII
Ch
47

FIG. 47.13

The HTML form that the Wizard creates is nearly identical to a form displayed in Access.

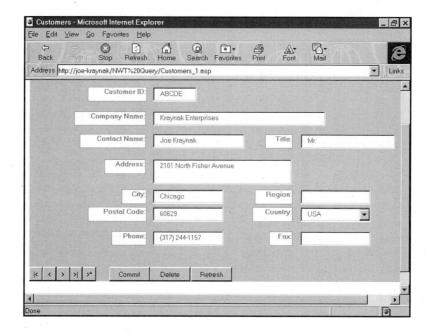

Removing the Record Navigation Buttons   Chances are when you place a form on the Web you do not want to give users access to existing records. You want the user to be able to use the form only to enter new records. You can remove the record navigation buttons from the bottom of the form by completing the following steps:

1. Open the *formname*_alx.asp file in a text editor, such as Notepad.

2. Scroll down the page, and look for the tag <OBJECT ID="nav_btn_MoveCancelUpdate." This tag and several tags that follow it create the buttons you want to remove.

3. Delete the following tags, being sure to delete from the first <Object> tag to the last </Object> tag for each button, but do not delete the <Object> tags for the New Record button: <OBJECT ID="nav_btn_MoveAddRecord" ... </Object>.
   <OBJECT ID="nav_btn_MoveCancelUpdate" ... </OBJECT>
   <OBJECT ID="nav_btn_MoveDeleteRecord" ... </OBJECT>
   <OBJECT ID="nav_btn_MoveCommitRecord" ... </OBJECT>
   <OBJECT ID="nav_btn_MoveLastRecord" ... </OBJECT>
   <OBJECT ID="nav_btn_MoveNextRecord" ... </OBJECT>
   <OBJECT ID="nav_btn_MovePrevRecord" ... </OBJECT>
   <OBJECT ID="nav_btn_MoveFirstRecord" ... </OBJECT>

4. You might also want to change the size and name of the Add Record button. The following shows changes (in bold) to the MoveAddRecord code to make the button wider and change its name from >* to Add Record:

```
<OBJECT ID="nav_btn_MoveAddRecord"
CLASSID="CLSID:D7053240-CE69-11CD-A777-00DD01143C57"
STYLE="TOP:434;LEFT:112;WIDTH:100;HEIGHT:28;ZINDEX:3;">
<PARAM NAME="BackStyle" VALUE="0">
<PARAM NAME="Caption" VALUE="Add Record">
<PARAM NAME="ParagraphAlign" VALUE="3">
<PARAM NAME="ForeColor" VALUE="0">
<PARAM NAME="Size" VALUE="728;728">
<PARAM NAME="SpecialEffect" VALUE="0">
<PARAM NAME="VariousPropertyBits" VALUE="2"></OBJECT>
```

5. Scroll to the top of the file and look for the following:

```
Sub UpdateRefreshBtn()
nav_btn_MoveCancelUpdate.Caption = "Cancel"
End Sub
```

6. Delete the middle line so that the new text appears as follows:

```
Sub UpdateRefreshBtn()
End Sub
```

7. Save your file and close it. Figure 47.14 shows the modified code.

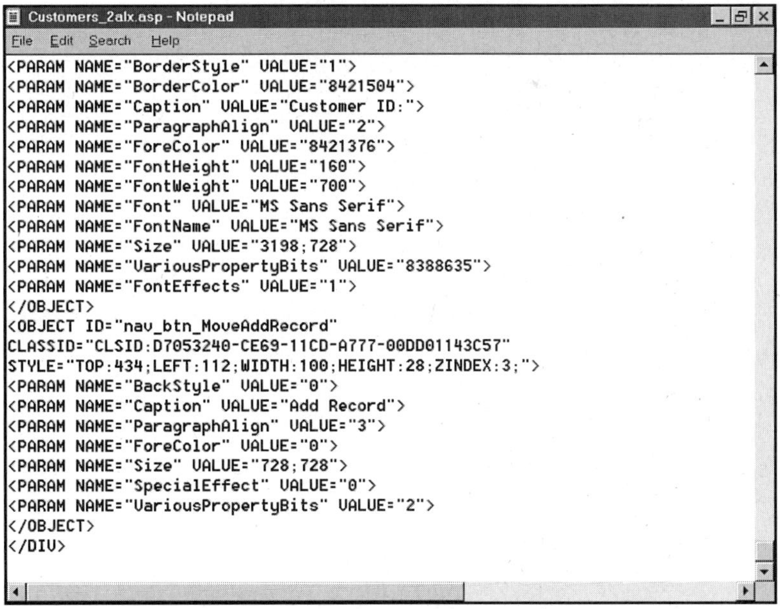

FIG. 47.14

You can modify the *formnamealx.asp* file to remove, rename, and resize buttons.

```
Customers_2alx.asp - Notepad
File   Edit   Search   Help
<PARAM NAME="BorderStyle" VALUE="1">
<PARAM NAME="BorderColor" VALUE="8421504">
<PARAM NAME="Caption" VALUE="Customer ID:">
<PARAM NAME="ParagraphAlign" VALUE="2">
<PARAM NAME="ForeColor" VALUE="8421376">
<PARAM NAME="FontHeight" VALUE="160">
<PARAM NAME="FontWeight" VALUE="700">
<PARAM NAME="Font" VALUE="MS Sans Serif">
<PARAM NAME="FontName" VALUE="MS Sans Serif">
<PARAM NAME="Size" VALUE="3198;728">
<PARAM NAME="VariousPropertyBits" VALUE="8388635">
<PARAM NAME="FontEffects" VALUE="1">
</OBJECT>
<OBJECT ID="nav_btn_MoveAddRecord"
CLASSID="CLSID:D7053240-CE69-11CD-A777-00DD01143C57"
STYLE="TOP:434;LEFT:112;WIDTH:100;HEIGHT:28;ZINDEX:3;">
<PARAM NAME="BackStyle" VALUE="0">
<PARAM NAME="Caption" VALUE="Add Record">
<PARAM NAME="ParagraphAlign" VALUE="3">
<PARAM NAME="ForeColor" VALUE="0">
<PARAM NAME="Size" VALUE="728;728">
<PARAM NAME="SpecialEffect" VALUE="0">
<PARAM NAME="VariousPropertyBits" VALUE="2">
</OBJECT>
</DIV>
```

Part
VII

Ch
47

Using a Form

Now that you have a form, you and other users can use the form to enter information into your database and query the database via the Web. The following sections explain how to link your home page (or another Web page) to your form, open the form in your Web browser, and use it for data entry and queries.

Linking Your Web Page to a Form

Once your form is on the Web server, you can insert a link on your Web page that points to the form. To do this, open your page in Word or one of your other Office applications. Type the text or insert the graphic you want to use as the link, select the text or graphic, and then click Insert Hyperlink to insert the link, as explained in Chapter 46, "Creating and Publishing Web Documents."

Assuming you place your Web page in the same directory as your form, you can simply enter the form's file name as a relative reference. When inserting a link to an ASP form, remember that the file's name ends in .asp, not .html. If you exported a query as an ASP file, then the filename's extension is either .asp or .html.

 TIP   If you chose to create a home page when publishing your form as an IDC/HTX or ASP file, open the home page in Internet Explorer and open your Web page in Word. Then copy and paste the link into your Web page.

Opening a Form in Your Web Browser

After you place your form (and the Web page that links to it) on the Web server, you should test the link to the form and the form itself. To open the form, run your Web browser and open the page that contains the link to the form. Click the link to open the form. If you did not create a link to the form, type the form's URL in the Address text box. Press Enter. Internet Explorer opens and displays the form. Figure 47.15 shows a sample HTML form opened in Internet Explorer.

Using a Form to Post Data

If you exported a form as an ASP page, you can use it to enter data into the linked database, just as you do in Access. When you open a form, it initially displays the first record in the database. To create a new record, click Create New Record, as shown in Figure 47.16. Type entries into the blanks to complete the form, and then click Commit or Submit to post your entries to the database.

You can also use the form to display existing records in the database, just as you do with an Access form. Click the buttons in the lower-left corner of the form to display the next or previous record or to jump to the first or last record in the database.

After posting your record, open your database to make sure that the record was posted to your database properly.

If you created a form in Word or Excel, simply fill out the form and click Submit to post your record to the database.

FIG. 47.15
Your form appears inside the Internet Explorer window.

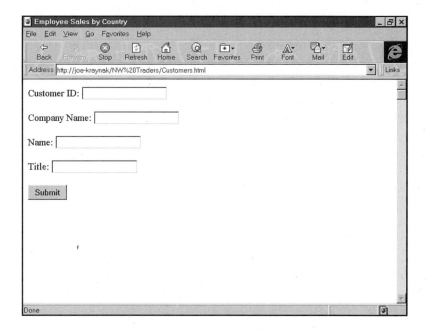

FIG. 47.16
Your Web form looks and acts as an Access form.

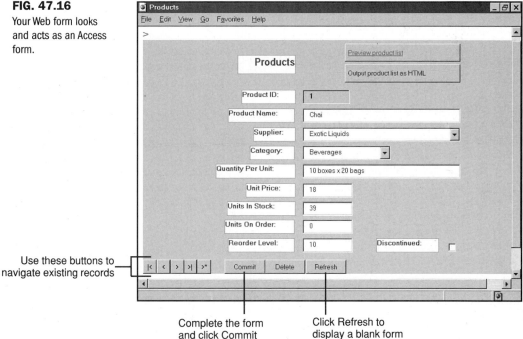

Part
VII

Ch
47

Use these buttons to navigate existing records

Complete the form and click Commit

Click Refresh to display a blank form

N O T E   You may notice that it takes some time for your browser to display records as you move
from one record to the next. Each time you add a record, display a new record, or move
from one record to another, the server must send your changes and requests to the database and
retrieve updated data. ■

Using a Form to Request Data

If you created a query, rather than a form, you can use it to query the database by specifying
the range of values for the desired field. When you open the query page, it displays familiar
text boxes prompting you to enter your query instructions. Type your entries and click Run
Query or Submit Query. The query returns the results in a table, as shown in Figure 47.17.

FIG. 47.17

After you submit your
query, the query results
are returned to you as a
table.

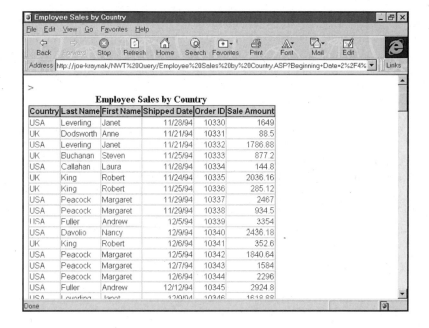

If you created a simple query in which you entered the range of values as the filter, you simply
open the ASP file you created. It immediately performs the query and returns the results in a
table. ●

CHAPTER 48

Using ActiveX Controls

by Joe Kraynak

If you've wandered the Web much with Internet Explorer, you surely have encountered a few ActiveX controls. Whenever you open a page that contains an ActiveX component that requires an ActiveX control you have not already downloaded and installed, a license agreement pops up on your screen, prompting for your permission to install it.

Once you have given Internet Explorer your okay, Internet Explorer automatically downloads the ActiveX control, installs it on your system, and uses it to play the ActiveX component that is on the page. This makes it easy to play active content on the Web without having to download and install separate helper applications and plug-ins.

However, ActiveX is much more than just an answer to Netscape plug-ins. It is also a tool that allows ActiveX-friendly applications to share documents. And it allows you to add active content to your Web pages. ■

Understand ActiveX

Understand ActiveX technology, including ActiveX controls and ActiveX documents.

Insert ActiveX controls in documents

Use ActiveX controls that are included with Office 97, use ActiveX controls in Access, and understand the limitations of ActiveX in Office 97.

Use the ActiveX Control Pad

Insert and manage ActiveX controls on your Web pages using the ActiveX Control Pad.

Write your own ActiveX scripts

Activate and integrate ActiveX controls with the Script Wizard.

Overview of ActiveX

ActiveX is a data-sharing, cross-platform, modular architecture designed to make it easy for Web developers (both novice and expert) to enhance their pages with programs, animation, video clips, virtual worlds, documents, games, and other dynamic objects that play right inside the Web browser window. The goal of ActiveX is to make the Web as rich and interactive as a CD playing on your local computer.

What makes ActiveX so attractive to the average Web page author is that it allows them to add powerful programming code to their Web pages without knowing much about programming. Novice Web page authors can use existing ActiveX components created by third-party developers, instead of having to write the programs themselves.

What makes ActiveX so attractive to programmers is that it allows them to use any of several popular programming languages—Visual Basic, C++, or even Java—to create ActiveX controls. And because these controls are cross-platform, the programmer need not modify the code for different platforms.

ActiveX consists of the following five technologies:

- *ActiveX Controls* are like plug-ins. They reside on your computer and enable your Web browser to play ActiveX components. For example, Internet Explorer comes with the ActiveMovie ActiveX control that plays most types of audio and video clips.

- *ActiveX Documents* are documents that you can open and edit in any application that supports ActiveX. For example, you can open a Word document or an Excel spreadsheet right in Internet Explorer.

- *ActiveX Scripting* is a programming language that allows you to write and insert small applications on your Web pages and coordinate other ActiveX components. JavaScript and VBScript are the two ActiveX scripting languages.

- *Java VirtualMachine* enables any browser that has built-in ActiveX support, such as Internet Explorer, to run Java applets.

- *ActiveX Server Framework* provides Web server support for functions such as database access and security. If you read Chapter 47, "Internet Forms and Databases," and exported Access database objects as Active Server Pages, you worked with the ActiveX Server Framework.

As you will see in this chapter, the beauty of ActiveX is in its modular approach, which allows you to assemble a complex, dynamic Web page simply by inserting one or more preprogrammed controls into your page.

Inserting ActiveX Controls in Office Documents

Microsoft Office 97 comes with several ActiveX controls, which you have probably used in previous chapters. For example, all the Web form controls discussed in Chapter 47, "Internet

Forms and Databases," are ActiveX controls. You insert the controls simply by selecting them from the Control Toolbox. You can then change their size and position and modify their properties to control their behavior.

You may have also used the Marquee control in Chapter 47 to insert a text box on your Web page that displayed scrolling text, as shown in Figure 48.1.

There are already over 2,000 ActiveX controls, created by Microsoft and third-party vendors, which you can use to add active content to your Web pages, and many of these controls are free. These controls let you do everything from animating text to including inline video clips. In the following sections, you will learn how to use the ActiveX controls that are built into Office 97 and how to obtain additional controls.

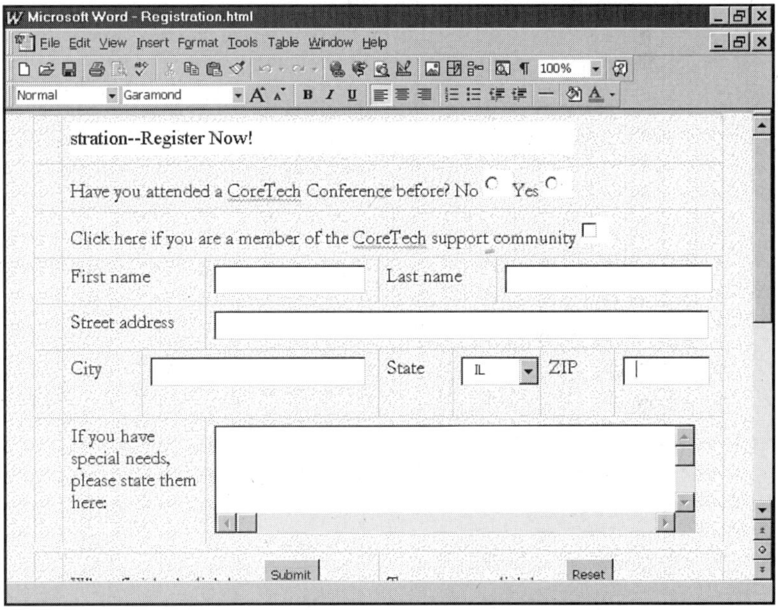

FIG. 48.1

Form controls and the scrolling marquee are ActiveX controls that are seamlessly integrated into your Office applications.

Inserting Office 97 ActiveX Controls

Office 97 supports both ActiveX controls and ActiveX documents. The various Office 97 applications have built-in ActiveX controls, some of which are shared between the applications and some of which are unique to particular applications. For example, the form controls appear in all the applications, via the Control Toolbox (or the Toolbox in Access). Additional controls, such as the scrolling text marquee in Word and the Action buttons in PowerPoint, are available only in certain Office applications.

The Control Toolbox offers controls only for inserting form elements, such as option buttons and text boxes, into your documents. To display the Control Toolbox, choose View, Toolbars and select Control Toolbox. The Control Toolbox appears, as shown in Figure 48.2. You can then insert a control by clicking the button for the desired control and then clicking the place in your document where you want it inserted.

FIG. 48.2

The Control Toolbox in Word, Excel, and PowerPoint provide ActiveX form controls.

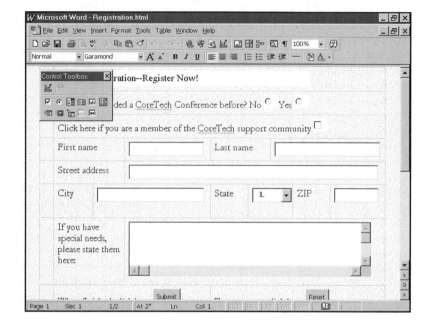

ActiveX Limitations in Office 97 Applications

 The More Controls button in the Control Toolbox displays a list of additional controls you may or may not be able to insert. This list includes any ActiveX controls you may have downloaded and installed in your Web wanderings. To insert a control, click the More Controls button and select the desired control from the list.

Unfortunately, most of the Office 97 applications (except Access) have strict limitations on the types of ActiveX controls you can use in your documents. You cannot insert many of the common ActiveX controls, including Label, Calendar, and ActiveMovie, into your Web documents (or Office documents). You can, however, add these controls to your Web pages using the ActiveX Control Pad, as explained later in this chapter.

N O T E Word, Excel, and PowerPoint implement ActiveX controls using the IDataObject interface rather than the IViewObject interface to draw the controls. ActiveX controls that require IViewObject support do not work in Word, Excel, or PowerPoint. However, Access does provide IViewObject support. Likewise, UserForms you create in PowerPoint, Word, or Excel provide IViewObject support. ▓

Using ActiveX Controls in Access

Of all the Office 97 applications, Access provides the broadest support for ActiveX controls. To insert a control into a form, first open the form in Design view. If the Toolbox is not displayed, choose View, Toolbox. The Toolbox is similar to the Control Toolbox used in the other Office 97 applications, but it includes several additional controls, including controls for inserting images, page breaks, and tabbed pages.

To view additional controls, click More Controls. This opens the submenu, shown in Figure 48.3, that lists all of the ActiveX controls installed and registered on your system. The list includes all the form controls built into Office 97, along with any additional controls you may have downloaded.

FIG. 48.3
When you click More Controls, a menu of all installed and registered ActiveX controls appears.

Registered ActiveX controls

The More Controls button

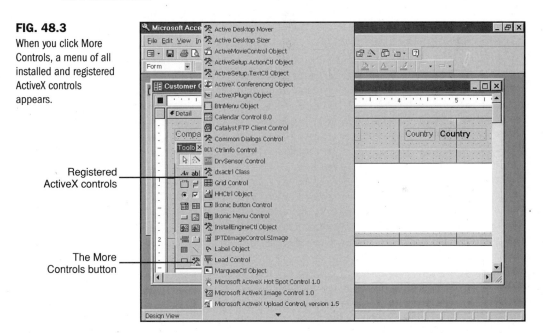

To insert a control, select it from the list and click the form where you want the control placed. Figure 48.4 shows the Calendar control, included with Access, placed on a form. See "Inserting the Calendar Control," later in this chapter, for detailed instructions on how to insert the control on a Web page and change its properties.

If you downloaded a control with its own installation utility, the installation program registers the control so that it appears on the More Controls menu. However, if you downloaded a control with the .dll or .ocx file extension, you must register the control first. To add a control to the Windows Registry, complete the following steps:

1. Choose Tools, ActiveX Controls. The ActiveX Controls dialog box appears, displaying a list of all the registered ActiveX controls.

2. Click <u>R</u>egister. The Add ActiveX Control dialog box appears, prompting you to select the ActiveX control you want to register.

3. Select the control you want to register. Most controls are placed in the \Windows\System or \Winnt\System32 folder.

4. Click Open. The control is now registered and should appear on the list of registered controls.

FIG. 48.4

The Calendar control is installed as part of Access.

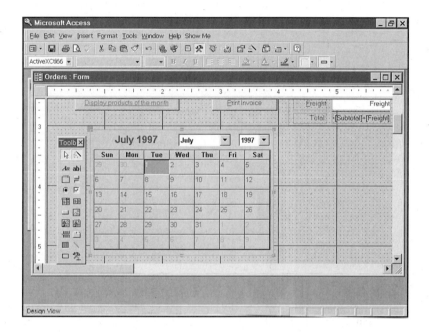

You can also register controls from the other Office applications. In the Control Toolbox, click More Controls, scroll down to the bottom of the list, and select Register Custom Control.

N O T E   To remove ActiveX controls from your system, you should first Unregister the control and then delete the control's .ocx or .dll file. To unregister a control, choose <u>T</u>ools, ActiveX <u>C</u>ontrols, click the control you want to unregister, and click <u>U</u>nregister. ■

Using the ActiveX Control Pad

The ActiveX Control Pad is essentially a text editor for Web pages that helps you insert ActiveX controls, change the look and layout of the controls, and write scripts to bring your controls to life.

Although the Control Pad is not included with Office 97, it's easy enough to obtain a copy off the Web. You can download ActiveX Control Pad from Microsoft at **http://**

www.microsoft.com/workshop/author/cpad/ or from PC World at **ftp://ftp.pcworld.com/pub/internet/applets_and_controls/setuppad.exe**. After downloading and installing ActiveX Control Pad, it appears on the Start, Programs, Microsoft ActiveX Control Pad menu.

When you start the Control Pad, you will notice that it's not a high-end, WYSIWYG, HTML editor. It displays the raw HTML code behind a Web page, as shown in Figure 48.5. This figure shows the page that the Control Pad displays on startup. You can open a page you've created, as explained in the next section.

FIG. 48.5

On the surface, ActiveX Control Pad appears as a simple text editor.

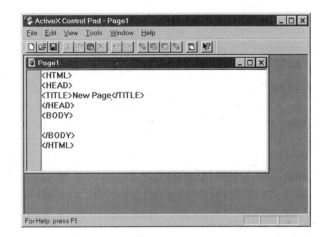

The real power of the ActiveX Control Pad is that it helps you with the complicated procedures of adding ActiveX controls and scripts (Visual Basic or JavaScript) to your HTML documents and with creating objects that you can reuse in other pages.

Opening an Existing HTML File

Because the ActiveX Control Pad is not the best tool for creating Web pages, you should first create your Web page using one of your Office 97 applications, as explained in Chapter 47, or a dedicated HTML editor, such as FrontPad.

After creating the page, you can then open it in the ActiveX Control Pad and use the Control Pad to add controls and scripts. To open your Web page, choose File, Open and use the resulting dialog box to select your Web page. The Control Pad displays the coded page in a separate document window, where you can start inserting controls.

Inserting Controls

Office 97 and the ActiveX Control Pad include a few sample controls, such as Label and Calendar, which you can insert into your document right away. You can also download additional controls created by Microsoft and other vendors. For an excellent list of controls, visit CNET's ACTIVEX.COM at **http://www.activex.com.**

Part
VII

Ch
48

Most ActiveX controls are packaged as .exe files. To install the control, you simply run the .exe file. This places the control (with the .ocx or .dll extension) on your hard drive and adds the control to the Windows Registry. If you download only the control (the .dll or .ocx file), you must register the control to make it available. See "Using ActiveX Controls in Access," earlier in this chapter, to learn how to register your controls.

To insert a control, complete the following steps:

1. Position the insertion point in your HTML file where you want the control inserted. Be careful not to insert the control inside existing codes. Insert it before a beginning or after an ending code.

2. Open the Edit menu and select Insert ActiveX Control. The Insert ActiveX Control dialog box appears, as shown in Figure 48.6, providing a list of available controls.

3. Select the desired control and click OK.

FIG. 48.6

When you choose to insert an ActiveX Control, you are presented with a list of installed controls.

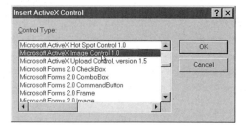

After you insert a control, the ActiveX Control Pad displays two windows (see Figure 48.7). In the window on the left (the Object Editor), you can drag the object's border to move it, or drag a handle to change its size and dimensions. In the window on the right (the Properties window), you can type entries to change the properties of the objects. These properties vary depending on the object you inserted. The following sections show you how to change the appearance and properties of some sample controls.

When you are done modifying the control, click Close (X) in the Object Editor and in the Properties window. The ActiveX Control Pad inserts the codes required to display the control. The beginning of the control is marked with the <OBJECT> tag, and the end is marked with the </OBJECT> tag. The <PARAM> tags specify the control properties.

In some cases, the control works without any additional input. However, other controls require that you assign *actions* to the control. For example, if you insert a command button, you must then assign an action to the button, specifying what the button should do when a user points to it or clicks it. See "Using the Script Wizard," later in this chapter, for instructions on how to assign actions to controls.

Inserting the Label Control   Your Office applications provide powerful tools for inserting and formatting headings, lists, and paragraphs into your Web pages. However, if you want to display text on an angle, sideways, or upside down, you need another tool—the Label control. To insert the control, complete the following steps:

1. Position the insertion point where you want the label added.

2. Choose <u>E</u>dit, <u>I</u>nsert ActiveX Control.

3. From the list of controls, select Label Object and click OK. The Object Editor and Properties windows appear for resizing the control and changing its properties.

4. In the Object Editor, drag the control's corner to make its frame larger. Inside the frame, you should see the word "Default."

5. In the Properties window, double-click Caption Default, type the text you want to use as your label, and press Enter.

6. Double-click Angle near the top of the properties list, type the number of degrees you want the text rotated, and press Enter (see Figure 48.8).

FIG. 48.7

After you choose a control, the ActiveX Control Pad displays two windows for changing the appearance and properties of the control.

Use this window to change the size and position of the control

This window lets you change the control's properties

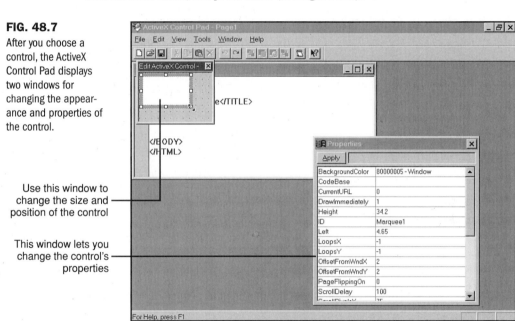

7. Continue selecting properties you want to change and typing the desired settings for those properties. You can change the text color, font, font size, and other properties. Some properties, such as alignment, allow you to scroll through a list of settings. Double-click the property to change its setting. For example, you can double-click FontBold to turn bold on (1-True) or off (0-False).

8. When you are done, click Close (X) to close both windows. The ActiveX Control Pad inserts the codes required to generate the object into your HTML document. In the left margin of the window, you should now see a cube icon, which marks the beginning of the Label control code(see Figure 49.9).

9. Choose <u>F</u>ile, <u>S</u>ave to save your changes. You can now open the page in your Web browser to see the Label control in action.

Part
VII

Ch
48

FIG. 48.8

You can change the size and properties of the Label control.

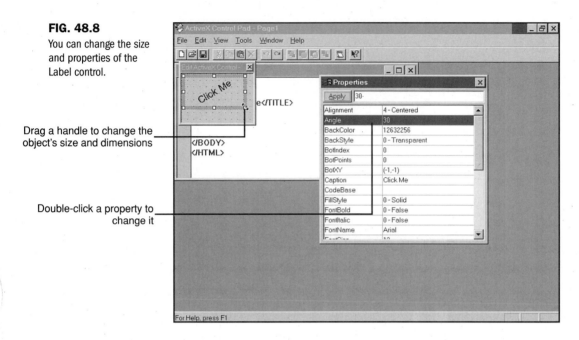

Drag a handle to change the object's size and dimensions

Double-click a property to change it

You can change the properties and size of the control at any time by clicking the cube icon in the left margin. This displays the Object Editor and Properties window you used to create the control. Later in this lesson, you will learn how to assign events to the Label object to make it perform actions when the user points or clicks the control.

FIG. 48.9

These codes generate the Label object on your Web page.

The cube icon marks the control you added

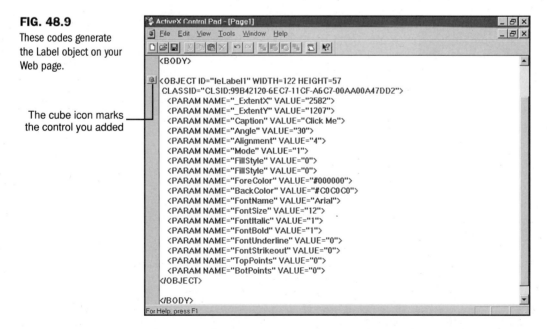

Setting the CodeBase Property   If someone pulls up your page and does not have the ActiveX control required to play an object on your page, a red X will appear in place of the object. However, if you specify the location of the control, the user's browser can automatically download the control. To specify the control's location, double-click CodeBase in the properties list and enter the URL for the control. For example, you might type the following for the Label control:

http://www.*servername*.com/*serverdirectory*/MSpert10.cab#Version=1,0,5,1">

If you store the control in the same folder as your Web page, you can enter a relative reference to the control simply by typing the control's filename (a file with the .ocx, .dll, or .cab extension).

For the following controls, you can enter the URL **http://activex.microsoft.com/controls/mspert10.cab** as the CodeBase:

Microsoft ActiveX Hot Spot Control 1.0

Microsoft ActiveX Image Control 1.0

Microsoft Forms 2.0 CheckBox

Microsoft Forms 2.0 ComboBox

Microsoft Forms 2.0 CommandButton

Microsoft Forms 2.0 Image

Microsoft Forms 2.0 Label

Microsoft Forms 2.0 ListBox

Microsoft Forms 2.0 OptionButton

Microsoft Forms 2.0 ScrollBar

Microsoft Forms 2.0 SpinButton

Microsoft Forms 2.0 TabStrip

Microsoft Forms 2.0 TextBox

Microsoft Forms 2.0 ToggleButton

Microsoft Forms 3.0 HTML Document

 TIP When downloading controls you want to use in your own Web pages, consider downloading and saving the control's installation file to your hard drive. You can then place the file in a directory on your Web server and use the CodeBase attribute to point to it. If you point to the file on the Web server from which you downloaded it, your pointer won't work if the file is moved.

Inserting the Calendar Control   The Calendar Control allows you to place a monthly calendar right on your Web page. If you are creating a registration form or another page in which a user might need to quickly look up dates, this control can be very useful. To insert the control and change its properties, complete the following steps:

1. Position the insertion point where you want the calendar inserted.

2. Choose Edit, Insert ActiveX Control.

3. From the list of controls, select Calendar Control and click OK. The Object Editor containing the Calendar Control and Properties windows appear (see Figure 48.10).

FIG. 48.10

The Calendar appears in the left window.

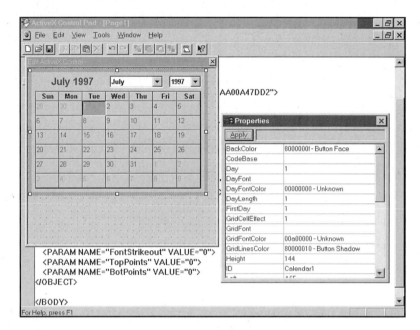

4. Drag a corner of the Object Editor window to enlarge it and then change the calendar's size or shape by dragging one of the calendar's corner handles.

5. In the Properties window, change of few of the calendar's properties. First, double-click DayLength and enter 0 (to display only the first letter of each day's name), 1 (to display common abbreviations, including Sun, Mon, Tue), or 2 (to display each day's full name). Be sure to press Enter or click Apply to apply your change to the calendar.

6. Double-click the FirstDay property and enter the day of the month you want selected when the user opens the calendar. Enter 0 to display no selected day. (You can change the starting year by changing the Year property setting.)

7. Enter any other changes to the property settings, as desired. For instance, you can double-click BackColor and select the desired background color from the list that appears when you double-click.

8. When you are done, click Close (X) to close both windows. The ActiveX Control Pad inserts the codes required to generate the object into your HTML document. In the left margin of the window, you should now see a cube icon, which marks the beginning of the Calendar control code.

9. Open the File menu and select Save to save your changes. You can now open the page in your Web browser to see the Calendar control in action (see Figure 48.11).

FIG. 48.11
You can use the drop-down lists on the Calendar to view different years and months.

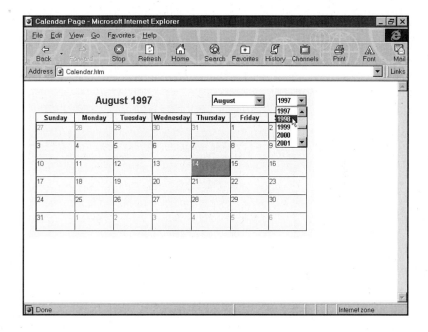

Navigational Controls   Although you can easily add links to point to other pages, you might want to provide alternative navigational tools for your visitors to use. For example, you can add command buttons that allow visitors to click buttons rather than link text. To insert the Command Button control, complete the following steps:

1. Position the insertion point where you want the button inserted.

2. Choose Edit, Insert ActiveX Control.

3. From the list of controls, select the Microsoft Forms 2.0 Command Button and click OK.

4. In the Object Editor, drag a corner of the control to enlarge it.

5. In the Properties window, double-click Caption and type the text that you want to appear on the button.

6. Enter any other changes to the property settings, as desired.

7. When you are done, click Close (X) to close both windows.

8. Choose File, Save to save your changes. You can now open the page in your Web browser to see the Command Button control. However, because you have not assigned any events or actions to the control, clicking the button does nothing. See "Using the Script Wizard," later in this chapter, to learn how to activate the control.

Part
VII

Ch
48

The ActiveX Control Pad features additional navigational controls, including pop-up menus, tabs, scroll bars, and hot spots (which you can use to mark areas of an image or a page as clickable).

Getting Help for Controls

The ActiveX Control Pad has its own help system, which provides basic instructions on how to use the controls, along with some helpful reference material about the controls included with ActiveX Control Pad.

To view reference material for a specific control, choose Help, Control Pad Help Topics. Click the Contents tab, double-click Developer's Reference, and double-click Controls. This displays a list of controls for which help is available. Double-click the control to display a page of reference information.

If you are using a control not included with the Control Pad, you won't find help for it in the Control Pad's help system. However, many controls come with their own Windows help file. Use the Windows Find feature to search for *.hlp files (usually stored in the \Windows\System folder).

Using the Script Wizard

As you saw in the previous sections, many controls you insert do nothing at first. In order to activate these controls, and integrate them with other controls, you must assign actions to the controls. You do this using the Script Wizard.

To display the Script Wizard, click the Script Wizard button in the toolbar, or choose Tools, Script Wizard. The Script Wizard window appears, as shown in Figure 48.12. The Script Wizard window consists of the following three panes:

- The *event* pane, on the left, displays a list of all the controls on your page. Click the plus sign next to a control to display a list of events that the control supports. An event is initiated by the user performing an action, such as clicking the control.

- The *actions* pane, on the right, also displays a list of controls, but displays the *properties* and *methods* assigned to the control. Methods are actions that the control supports; for example, the ActiveMovie control supports the Stop and Play actions. Click the plus sign next to a control to view a list of its methods and actions. Methods are displayed with a yellow exclamation point icon (!). Properties are marked with a blue document icon.

- The *scripts* pane, at the bottom, displays any actions you assign to the object via scripts. Two options below this pane allow you to change to List view to display brief descriptions of the actions, or Code view to display the script codes that perform the action.

To assign an action to a control, complete the following three steps:

1. In the events pane, you expand the events list for the desired control and select the event (for example, Click).

2. Specify that the action the control should initiate when the user performs the event (for example, Go to Page). In most cases, when you double-click an action you are prompted to enter a parameter.

3. Type the parameter (for example, if you selected Go to Page, you would type the destination page address) and click OK.

FIG. 48.12

The Script Wizard displays three panes.

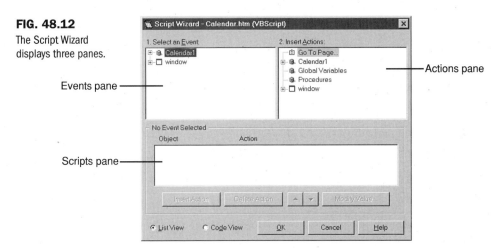

The following sections provide step-by-step instructions on how to use the Script Wizard to change the actions and properties of two sample controls. Although the procedures vary depending on the control, these examples provide you with the basic skills you need to script your controls.

Adding a Script for the Label Control As you saw earlier in this chapter, you can use the Label control to display text at an angle on your page. However, the Label control is much more powerful when you assign actions to it. Complete the following steps to use the Script Wizard to make it more interactive:

1. Insert the Label control, as explained earlier in this chapter (in the section named "Inserting the Label Control"), and close the Object Editor and Properties window.

2. Click the Script Wizard button. The Script Wizard appears.

3. Click the plus sign next to leLabel1 in the events pane to expand the list of events.

4. Let's turn the label into a link. Select DblClick in the events pane, and double-click Go To Page in the actions pane. The Go To Page dialog box appears, prompting you to type an entry.

5. Type the URL of a Web page (for example, http://www.yahoo.com), and click OK. The specified action is added to the scripts pane, as shown in Figure 48.13. (When the user double-clicks the label, the person's browser will open the specified page.)

Part
VII

Ch
48

FIG. 48.13

When you assign an action to an object, the action appears in the scripts pane.

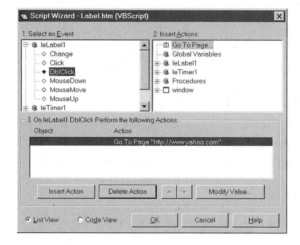

6. Let's add another action to the control. Click in the events pane.

7. Click the plus sign next to leLabel1 in the actions pane, and double-click ForeColor. A dialog box appears, prompting you to type a number to specify the color.

8. Click Color, select the desired color for the text, and click OK. (When the user clicks the label, its color will change to the specified color.)

9. Double-click Caption, type the desired label text (for example, type **"Double-click for Yahoo!"**), and press Enter. When the user clicks the label, it will display the new text.

10. Click OK, and then click Save to save your changes.

You can now open the page in Internet Explorer to view and test it. When you click the label, it should change color and display the text you entered for the second caption. When you double-click the label, Internet Explorer will open the specified page.

Creating a Menu Button   In the next example, we will create a menu button that displays a list of pages from which the user can choose. In this example, you get to work directly with VB scripting. To work through this example, you need the Microsoft IE30 Button Menu control. If you do not already have this control, you can download it from CNET **(http://www.activex.com)** or Microsoft **(http://www.microsoft.com)**.

Once you have downloaded and installed the control, you can insert it into your Web page and add the required script by taking the following steps:

1. In the ActiveX Control Pad, open your Web page, and position the insertion point where you want the control inserted.

2. Choose Edit, Insert ActiveX Control.

3. Scroll down the list of controls, and double-click Microsoft IE30 Button Menu Control.

4. In the Object Editor, drag a corner of the control to change its size.

5. In the Properties window, double-click Caption, type a name for the button, and press Enter. Double-click CodeBase, type **http://activex.microsoft.com/controls/ iexplorer/btnmenu.ocx**, and press Enter.

6. Close the Properties window and Object Editor, and click the Scripts button in the toolbar.

7. Click Code View at the bottom of the Script Wizard window. This displays the scripts pane in Code View, so you can type scripts directly into the pane.

8. In the events pane, click the plus sign next to Window, and click onLoad. (You will assign an action to the browser window which will load the menu items when it opens the page.)

9. Type the following codes in the scripts pane, as shown in Figure 48.14, replacing the text inside the quotes with the names of the menu items you want on your menu:

   pmenu1.AddItem "Go to Home Page"

   pmenu1.AddItem "Visit Yahoo!"

   pmenu1.AddItem "Check Out These Books"

FIG. 48.14

You can type script codes directly into the scripts pane in Code View.

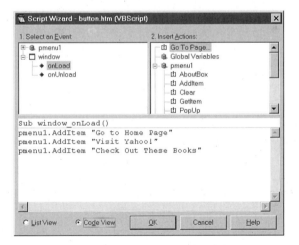

10. Click onUnload in the events pane, and type the following line: pmenu1.Clear()

    This tells the browser to clear items from the menu when the page is unloaded, preventing duplicate entries from appearing on the menu if the user backs up to the page.

11. In the events pane, click the plus sign next to pmenu1, and click Select. You will now assign page addresses to the items on the menu.

Part
VII

Ch
48

12. Type the following codes, replacing the URLs (between quotation marks) with the URLs of the pages you want your menu items to point to. The menu items are assigned case numbers, starting with case 1 for the first menu item:

Select Case item

case 1

Window.location.href = "http://www.microsoft.com"

case 2

Window.location.href = "http://www.yahoo.com"

case 3

Window.location.href = "http://www.mcp.com"

End Select

13. Click OK, and then click Save to save your changes.

Once you have saved your changes, open your page in Internet Explorer. The button appears on your page. When you rest the mouse pointer on the button, a down arrow appears, indicating that the button will open a menu. Click the button to display the menu you created, as shown in Figure 48.15. Select an item from the menu to open the page it points to.

FIG. 48.15

When you click the Button Menu control, it opens a menu that displays the items you added.

Creating and Inserting HTML Layouts

Although the ActiveX Control Pad is not a bona fide WYSIWYG HTML editor, it does provide one feature, called the HTML Layout Control, that can help you design and lay out portions of Web pages, such as forms and button bars. You can then save these layouts as .alx files and insert them into your Web pages. To create an HTML layout, complete the following steps:

1. Choose File, New HTML Layout. In the ActiveX Control Pad, two windows appear—the Layout window and the Toolbox.

2. To insert an object from the Toolbox, click the desired object, and then drag inside the Layout window, where you want the control inserted. When you release the mouse button, the control appears in the Layout window (see Figure 48.16).

3. Double-click the control to view its properties. The Properties window appears.

4. Change the object's properties, as desired. For example, if you inserted a command button, you may want to type a caption to name the button. Close the Properties window when you are done.

5. Repeat steps 2 to 4 to insert additional controls. Choose Edit, Insert ActiveX Control to insert controls that are unavailable in the Toolbox.

6. To assign actions to your controls, click the Script Wizard button in the toolbar, and use the Script Wizard, as explained earlier, to add scripts for making the controls interactive.

7. When you have completed the layout, choose File, Save. The Save As dialog box appears, prompting you to save the layout as an .alx file.

8. Select the folder in which you want to save the file, type a name for the file, and click Save.

FIG. 48.16

The HTML Layout Control allows you to position controls on your page.

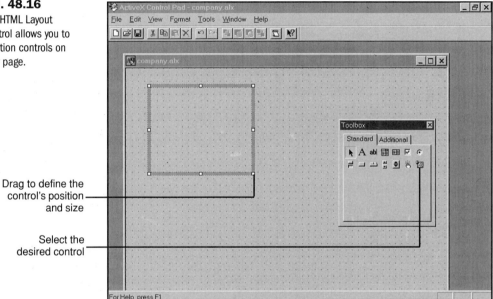

Drag to define the control's position and size

Select the desired control

Once you have created the HTML layout, you can easily insert it into an existing Web page. Complete the following steps:

1. Open the page in the ActiveX Control Pad, and position the insertion point where you want the layout placed.

2. Choose Edit, Insert HTML Layout.

3. Use the resulting dialog box to select the HTML Layout file you want to insert, and click Open. The ActiveX Control Pad inserts a code that refers to the .alx file, as shown in Figure 48.17. To the left of the code is an icon with an A, a circle, and a square on it. Click this icon to edit the .alx file at any time.

N O T E   Because ActiveX Control Pad inserts only a pointer to the .alx file, when placing pages on your Web server, make sure the reference to the .alx file points to the correct directory on the server. ▪

Part

VII

Ch

48

FIG. 48.17

When you insert an HTML layout, ActiveX Control Pad inserts a reference to the file, not the entire code.

This icon marks the HTML layout

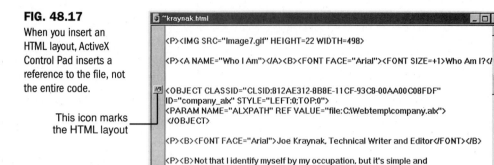

```
<P><IMG SRC="Image7.gif" HEIGHT=22 WIDTH=498>

<P><A NAME="Who I Am"></A><B><FONT FACE="Arial"><FONT SIZE=+1>Who Am I?</

<OBJECT CLASSID="CLSID:812AE312-8B8E-11CF-93C8-00AA00C08FDF"
ID="company_alx" STYLE="LEFT:0;TOP:0">
<PARAM NAME="ALXPATH" REF VALUE="file:C:\Webtemp\company.alx">
</OBJECT>

<P><B><FONT FACE="Arial">Joe Kraynak, Technical Writer and Editor</FONT></B>

<P><B>Not that I identify myself by my occupation, but it's simple and
quick, and relatively accurate.</B>

<P><B>Key responsibilities</B>

<P><B>Coaching soccer, writing funny computer books, fixing problems</B>
```

CHAPTER 49

Using Binders

by Joe Kraynak

As you work on reports, books, or other lengthy documents, you may find yourself using the advanced tools in the various Microsoft Office applications to create separate documents. For example, a report may require the advanced text editing and layout tools of Word, but it might also require Excel spreadsheets and graphs, and perhaps a few PowerPoint slides or Access tables.

You could create your overall document in Word and then cut and paste objects from the other Office applications. However, this can make the document too long and difficult to manage and strain your system resources, slowing your computer to a crawl.

Fortunately, Microsoft Office comes with an excellent document management tool called *Microsoft Binder* that lets you "clip" related documents together. For example, if you have a report that consists of a cover letter, one or more Excel worksheets, and a PowerPoint slide show, you can add all these files to a binder in order to work with them as a single document.

Once you've bound several documents together, Microsoft Binder allows you to rearrange the documents, number the pages, check spelling, add a header and footer, and perform other tasks to give your bound documents a consistent look and feel. You can even print all the documents with a single Print command. ■

Binder basics

Treat two or more Office documents as a single document.

Create and open binders

Make a binder, add documents to it, and edit your documents from the Binder window.

Binder printing basics and tips

Print documents in the Binder as a single document, printing a common header and footer on all of the pages.

Binder templates

Create binder templates that you can reuse for future projects.

Work with binders on the Internet

Save and open files on FTP servers, and add Web pages and other Internet files to your binder.

Overview of Binders

To understand Microsoft Binder, take a look at Microsoft Binder in action, as shown in Figure 49.1. Note that the Binder window is divided into two panes. Each document you add to the binder is shown as an icon in the left pane (you'll learn how to add documents later in this chapter). The icons appear in the order in which you joined the documents to the binder.

FIG. 49.1

Using Microsoft Binder, you can stitch together documents from different Office applications to create a single document.

Binder displays an icon for each document you add to the binder

The contents of the selected document appear here

Toolbars and menus change to provide tools for editing and formatting the selected documents

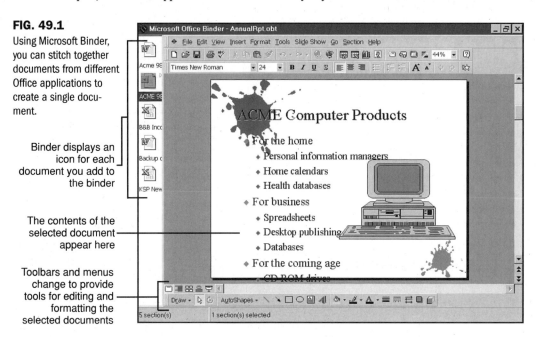

When you select a document's icon, the contents of the document appear in the right pane, where you can edit and format the document. The toolbar and menu bar change according to the application you used to create the document. For example, if you click an icon for a Word document, the menu bar and toolbar appear as they do in Word.

As you can see, the document editing pane is fairly small. However, Binder allows you to hide the left pane to give the document the entire window. You can also view any document in its own application window, outside Binder. After you edit the document, you can return to Binder to perform your organizational tasks.

Binder places each document in its own *section*, which contains page formatting settings for that section. The Section menu in Binder lists options and commands for controlling the selected section.

Creating a Binder

There's no trick to creating a binder. When you run Microsoft Binder (Start, Programs, Microsoft Binder), Binder automatically creates an empty binder for you. You can immediately start adding documents to the binder as explained in the following section.

If you are creating a report, you might wish to start with Microsoft Binder's Report template, which contains an outline for a sample report, including three sample Word documents (cover letter, executive summary, and analysis), a PowerPoint presentation (slide show), and an Excel workbook (data). To create a binder using this template, complete the following steps:

1. If Binder is not running, choose Start, Programs, Microsoft Binder. Binder opens a blank binder.
2. Choose File, New Binder or press Ctrl+N. The New Binder dialog box appears.
3. Click the Binders tab and select Report.obt. This is the Binder template.
4. Click OK. The new binder appears, as shown in Figure 49.2, displaying several icons for existing documents.
5. To view the contents of a document, click its icon in the left pane.

You can also create an empty binder at any time by selecting the General tab in step 3 and selecting Blank Binder, or by running Microsoft Binder again.

FIG. 49.2

You can use Microsoft Binder's Report template instead of starting from scratch.

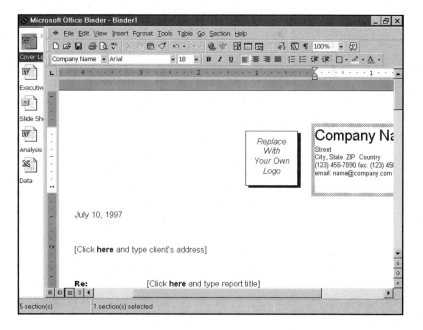

T I P If the Office 97 toolbar is displayed, click the New Office Document button, click the Binders tab, and double-click Report.obt.

Adding Existing Documents to a Binder

Once you have created a binder, you can start adding documents to it. You add documents to the binder either by copying existing documents to the binder or by creating new documents from Binder. (The procedure for creating new documents is covered in the following section.)

You can easily add existing documents by dragging and dropping their icons from a folder in My Computer or Windows Explorer into the left pane in Binder, as shown in Figure 49.3. Hold down the left mouse button as you drag. As soon as you release the mouse button, the document's icon appears on the left and its contents appear on the right.

FIG. 49.3
You can drag and drop icons from My Computer or Windows Explorer into the left pane in Binder.

Change to the folder that contains the document file you want to add to your binder

Drag the document icon into the left pane in Binder

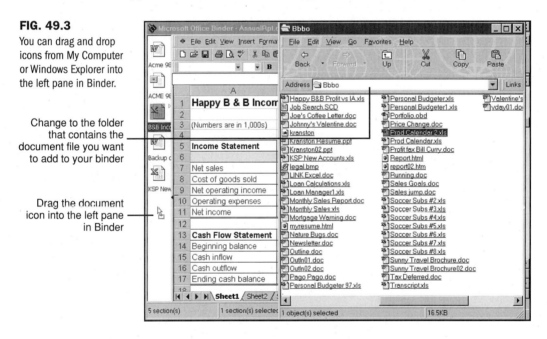

You can also add documents to your binder using a command on the Section menu. Complete the following steps:

1. In Binder's left pane, select the icon where you want the new document added. The new document will be inserted below the selected document.

2. Choose Section, Add from File. The Add from File dialog box appears, prompting you to select the document.

3. Change to the folder that contains the document you want to add and click the file.

4. Click Add. The left pane displays an icon for the added document.

TROUBLESHOOTING

I cannot add a file to my binder. If you have trouble adding documents of a certain type to your binder, Binder may not support that document type. Binder supports Word, Excel, and PowerPoint file types. Try saving the file as a Word, Excel, or PowerPoint file before adding it to the binder.

Creating New Documents from Binder

Because Binder is essentially a document management tool, you will typically create your documents in Excel, Word, or PowerPoint and then add them to a binder, as explained in the previous section. However, as you work on your bound document, you may need to add a document that you have not yet created.

Instead of leaving Binder and creating the document in another Office application, you can create the document from within Binder. To create a new document from Binder, complete the following steps:

1. Click the document icon where you want the new document added. The new document will be inserted below the selected document.

2. Choose Section, Add. The Add Section dialog box appears, prompting you to select the type of document you want to add. (This dialog box is similar to the New dialog box that appears when you select File, New in Excel, Word, or PowerPoint.)

3. Click the tab for the type of document you want to add: General, Letters & Faxes, Memos, Reports, Other Documents, or Web Pages. Each tab contains icons for two or more templates.

4. Click the desired template and then click OK. An icon for the selected document appears in the left pane.

If your binder already contains a document that is similar to the new document you want to add, you can duplicate the existing document and then modify it. To duplicate a document, first click the icon where you want the duplicate placed. Select Section, Duplicate. The Duplicate Section dialog box prompts you to select the document you want to clone. Click the desired document and click OK.

 Although the Section menu contains all the commands you need for adding documents to your binder, you may find it easier to use a context menu. Right-click a document icon in the left pane to display a context menu, which provides the following options: Add, Add from File, Delete, Duplicate, and Rename.

Part
VII

Ch
49

Saving and Opening Binders

You save a binder just as you save a file in most Office applications: select File, Save Binder or press Ctrl+S. This opens the Save Binder As dialog box. Provide a file name, location, and file type.

When you save a binder, any changes to the individual documents are saved only in the binder. When you add documents to a binder, those documents are copies of the originals. If you edit the document in binder and save your changes, the original document remains unchanged.

To save changes to the original document, complete the following steps:

1. Click the document's icon in the left pane.

2. Choose Section, Save as File. The Save As dialog box appears.

3. Select the folder in which you want the file saved, type a name for the file, and click Save.

Unbinding a Binder

To save all the documents in a binder as separate files, display the icon for the binder file in My Computer or Windows Explorer. Right-click the binder file and select Unbind, as shown in Figure 49.4. Windows extracts the sections of the binder and saves each section as a separate file in the same folder as the binder file. The original binder remains intact.

FIG. 49.4

When you unbind a binder, Binder saves each section of the binder as a separate document file in the same folder.

Right-click the binder file

Select Unbind

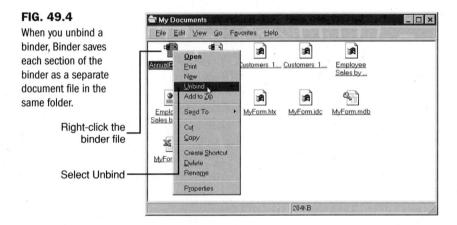

N O T E   In Windows NT Workstation 3.51, the Unbind option is not available. To save sections as separate documents, you must save each section individually using the Section, Save as File command. ▨

To open a binder, choose File, Open Binder. In the Open Binder dialog box, select the folder in which you saved the binder and click the name of the binder file (binder file names end in .obd). Click Open, and the binder is opened giving you access to all of its documents.

Working with Documents in a Binder

When you add documents to your binder, Binder creates a separate section for each document. When you click a document's icon in the left pane, its contents appear in the right pane. Binder displays the toolbars and menus for the application you used to create the file. You can edit and format the document in the Binder window, just as if it were displayed in its original Office application.

 To provide more room on the screen for working on a document, click the Show/Hide Left Pane button (just to the left of the File menu). The left pane disappears. To bring the pane back into view, click Show/Hide Left Pane again. Another way to turn off the left pane and the Show/Hide Left Pane button is to enter File, Binder Options. Click Show Left Pane and Left Pane Button to clear the check box and then click OK.

The following sections provide additional instructions on how to organize, delete, rename, and perform other binder management tasks.

Selecting Sections

If you are working with individual sections and the left pane is displayed, selecting sections is easy—you click the icon for the section you want to work with. However, if you have multiple sections and you need to rearrange them or work with selected sections as a group, you need to know how to select two or more sections:

- To move from one section to another, open the Section menu and select Next Section or Previous Section.
- To select adjacent sections, click the icon for the first section and Shift+click the icon for the last section in the group.
- To select nonadjacent sections, click the icon for one section and then Ctrl+click icons for additional sections.
- To select all sections, choose Section, Select All.

Organizing Sections in a Binder

The feature that makes Binder so powerful is its ability to quickly rearrange sections simply by dragging and dropping them in the left pane. If you chose to hide the left pane in the previous section, turn it back on when you need to move sections. You can then take the following steps to move, delete, or rename sections in your binder:

1. To move a section, drag its icon in the left pane up or down to where you want it placed. A black arrow appears on the right side of the pane to point out where the section will be moved. See Figure 49.5.
2. Release the mouse button. The section is moved to the specified location.

Part
VII

Ch
49

3. To rename a section, right-click its icon and select <u>R</u>ename. Type the desired name and press Enter.

4. To delete a section, right-click its icon and select <u>D</u>elete. Click Yes when asked to confirm.

FIG. 49.5

The left pane provides a convenient way to rearrange and manage sections in a binder.

Drag a section icon up or down to move it

This arrow shows where the section will be moved

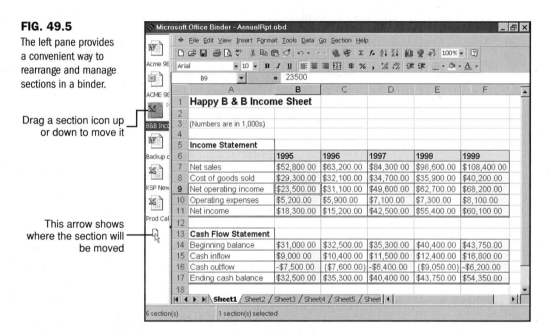

T I P   To quickly rearrange sections, open the <u>S</u>ection menu and select <u>R</u>earrange. This displays a dialog box listing the names of all the sections. Click the section you want to move and then click Move <u>U</u>p or Move <u>D</u>own to move it to the desired position. Click OK.

Hiding and Unhiding Sections

When reorganizing your binder, you may wish to hide some sections to bring other sections into view as you organize them. You can also hide sections to prevent them from printing, but you can do this more easily by setting print options for the binder, as you will learn later in this chapter.

To hide a section, click the icon for the section you want to hide, and choose <u>S</u>ection, <u>H</u>ide. To unhide a section, choose <u>S</u>ection, U<u>n</u>hide Section. This displays a dialog box that lists the names of all sections you have chosen to hide. Click the section you want to bring into view and then click OK.

Editing a Document Outside Binder

Although you can quickly hide the left pane to provide more screen space for editing a document, there may be times when you want to work on the document in a separate application window. For example, if you need to make significant changes to a Word document, you may wish to work in Word instead of in Binder. To view the document outside of the binder, complete the following steps:

1. Click the icon for the section you want to display in its own application window.

2. Select Section, View Outside. Binder opens the document in its Office application: Word, Excel, or PowerPoint.

3. Return to Binder. You cannot view the section in Binder and in the application window at the same time. When you select a section in Binder that is open in another application, Binder displays the message shown in Figure 49.6, indicating that the section is opened in another application.

4. Return to the application in which the section is opened. As you work with the section in the other application window, you can save your changes to the binder. Choose File, Update or press Ctrl+S. (To save the section as a separate document, you can choose File, Save Copy As.)

5. When you are done modifying the document, choose File, Close & Return to Bindername. This returns you to Binder, where you can now view the section.

FIG. 49.6

If a section is opened in another application, you cannot view its contents in Binder.

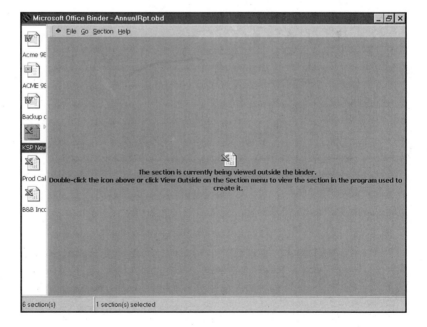

Checking for Typos and Misspellings

As you work with sections in a binder, you should keep in mind that this is a separate document and it requires the same keen editorial eye you use to check other documents before printing them or sending to other people.

 Fortunately, Binder includes the Office spelling checker. Unfortunately, you must spell-check each section in the document separately. Click the section and then click the Spelling and Grammar button, or choose Tools, Spelling and Grammar.

Printing Techniques for Binders

As you have seen in the previous section, Binder provides powerful tools for rearranging sections in lengthy documents. Even more powerful is Binder's ability to output the sections as a single document. You can add consistent headers and footers that print on every page of the document and number the pages consecutively throughout the document.

With Binder you can even hide sections to prevent them from being printed, allowing you to quickly customize your document for different audiences. For example, if you are creating a report, you may want to include an introduction for customers but omit the introduction for internal use.

The following sections explain how to prepare your binder for printing, preview it, and use some of Binder's more advanced printing options.

Adding Headers and Footers

Headers and footers help tie the pages of a document together and provide your audience with a tool for quickly finding the information they need. The Headers and Footers feature also allows you to include page numbers.

With Binder you can add headers and footers for all sections of your document. You can choose to print the same header and footer on all sections of the document, or you can print a different header or footer on selected sections.

N O T E   If you added an existing document with a header and/or footer to your binder, that header and footer are used for the section. You can override the header or footer by applying Binder's header or footer to the section, as explained in the following steps. ▪

To use the same header and/or footer for all sections of your document, complete the following steps:

1. Choose File, Binder Page Setup. The Binder Page Setup dialog box appears, displaying the Header/Footer tab in front.

2. Under Apply Binder Header/Footer To, select All Supported Sections. Or, select Only Sections Selected Below and select the sections for which you want to use the header or footer you are about to create.

3. To add a header, open the Header drop-down list and select the desired header format, as shown in Figure 49.7. If none of the listed formats appeals to you, skip to step 5.

FIG. 49.7

Binder offers several header and footer formats from which to choose.

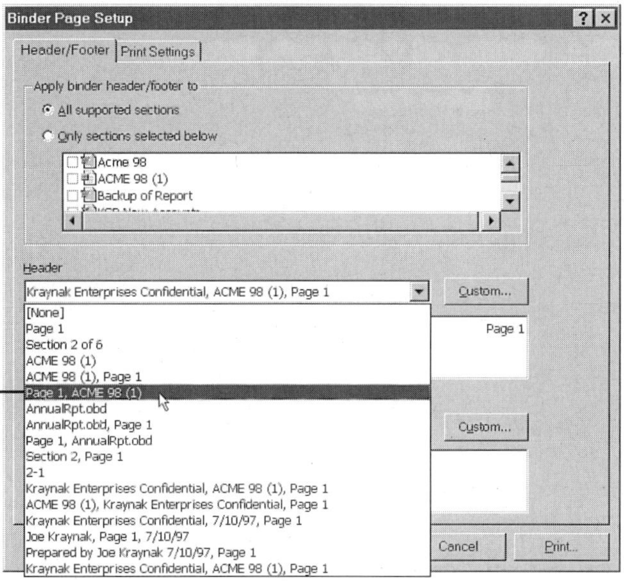

Select a format for your header or footer

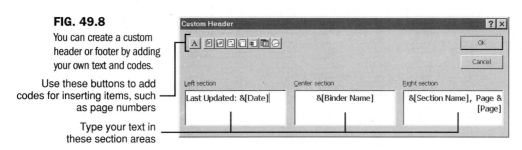

4. To add a footer, open the Footer drop-down list and select the desired format for your footer. If none of the formats appeals to you, move on to the next step.

5. To modify or create your own header or footer, click Header Custom or Footer Custom. This displays the Custom Header or Custom Footer dialog box, shown in Figure 49.8. As you can see, the header and footer consist of three sections: Left, Center, and Right.

FIG. 49.8

You can create a custom header or footer by adding your own text and codes.

Use these buttons to add codes for inserting items, such as page numbers

Type your text in these section areas

6. To delete text or codes from one of the section boxes, drag over it and press the Delete key.

7. To insert text, click in the section area where you want the text inserted and start typing. (You can press Ctrl+Enter to start a new line of text.)

Part
VII

Ch
49

8. To add a field code that performs a special task, such as inserting a page number or date, click where you want the code inserted and then click one of the buttons listed in Table 49.1.

Table 49.1   Header and Footer Code Buttons

Button	Button Name	Function
![Insert Page Number button]	Insert Page Number	Numbers the pages consecutively, and inserts the correct page number for each printed page.
![Insert Section Number button]	Insert Section Number	Numbers the sections consecutively and inserts the correct section number on each page.
![Insert Number of Sections button]	Insert Number of Sections	Inserts the total number of sections.
![Insert Section Name button]	Insert Section Name	Inserts the name of each section. It's a good idea to print the section name at the top of each page to help people locate sections easily.
![Insert Binder Name button]	Insert Binder Name	Inserts the name of your binder on each page.
![Insert Date button]	Insert Date	Inserts the current date on each page.
![Insert Time button]	Insert Time	Inserts the current time.

TIP   Consider combining field codes in the header and footer. For example, you might include the section name and page number as *Section Name*, Page, 1. Your entry would look something like this:

&[Section Name], Page &[Page]

9. To change the typestyle, size, or attributes for any text or codes, select the text or codes and click the Font button. Select the desired font, style, size, and attributes and then click OK.

10. When you are done entering your custom header or footer, click OK to return to the Binder Page Setup dialog box.

11. Click the Print Settings tab to enter settings that control page numbering.

12. Under Page Numbering, select Consecutive to number the pages as in a book, or select Restart Each Section to number the pages of each section separately. (The Start Numbering At option lets you specify the page number to start with.)

13. Click OK to save your header, footer, and page numbering settings.

CAUTION

You can create only one custom header or footer in a binder. If you want to use a different header or footer for a section, make sure that section is not selected in step 2. You can then create a custom header for that section.

Although you can add a code that inserts the section name into the header or footer, you may wish to create an entirely different header or footer for a section. To create a separate header or footer for one section, however, you must use the header/footer feature in that application (Word or Excel).

If you created a header or footer for all the sections in the binder, you must first turn off the header or footer for the section. Choose File, Binder Page Setup. Under Apply Binder Header/ Footer To, select Only Sections Selected Below and select all the sections except the section for which you want to create a unique header or footer. Click OK.

The procedure for creating a header or footer for a single section varies depending on whether the section is a Word or Excel document. First, select the section in Binder and then perform one of the following steps:

- If the section is a Word file, select View, Header and Footer. Use Word's header and footer tools to create the header or footer.

- If the section is an Excel workbook, choose Section, Page Setup. Click the Header/ Footer tab and create your header or footer as you would in Excel.

N O T E Binder's headers and footers do not work with documents created using previous versions of Word or Excel. They work only with current versions (your Office 97 documents). To print headers and footers for these documents, you must set up the headers or footers in Word or Excel. ■

Previewing a Binder Before Printing

Before you print your binder, you should display it in Print Preview to ensure that the pages are laid out as desired and that the headers and footers look right. To display the binder in Print Preview, choose File, Binder Print Preview.

Binder displays the first section of the document in Print Preview, as shown in Figure 49.9. A toolbar appears, displaying options for moving to the Previous Section or Next Section. Note that the Print Preview screen will vary depending on the selected section. Binder uses Excel's Print Preview screen to display Excel worksheets and Word's Print Preview screen for Word documents. (Print Preview is not available for PowerPoint sections. Open your slide show in PowerPoint to preview it.)

When you are done previewing the document, click Close in the Print Preview toolbar or click Exit Preview in the Binder Print Preview toolbar.

Part

VII

Ch

49

FIG. 49.9

When you select Binder Print Preview, Binder uses the Print Preview feature of the appropriate application.

Use these options to move to other sections

An Excel worksheet in Print Preview

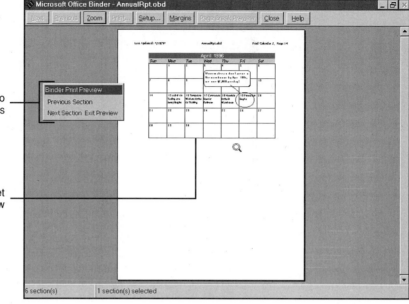

  To quickly preview a specific section, click the icon for the section and then choose Section, Print Preview.

Printing Your Binder

Once you are satisfied with the organization and appearance of your binder, you can print it. The procedure for printing binders is similar to printing in other Office applications. You choose the File, Print Binder command (or press Ctrl+P), enter your preferences, and click OK.

However, because a Binder document typically consists of two or more sections, Binder offers additional options for printing individual sections. For example, you may want to omit a section that contains background material that your audience does not need to see.

To print from Binder, complete the following steps:

1. If you hid any sections that you now wish to print, unhide them (Section, Unhide Section). Hidden sections are not included in the printout.

2. To prevent some sections from printing, select only the sections you want to print. (See "Selecting Sections," earlier in this chapter.)

3. Select File, Print Binder or press Ctrl+P. The Print Binder dialog box appears, as shown in Figure 49.10, prompting you to enter your preferences.

4. Under Print What, select All Visible Sections (to print all sections displayed in the left pane) or Section(s) Selected in Left Pane.

5. Under Numbering, select Cons_e_cutive to number the pages as in a book, or select Res_t_art Each Section to number the pages of each section separately. (The Sta_r_t Numbering At option lets you specify the page number to start with.)

6. Enter any additional printing preferences, such as the number of copies to print.

7. Click OK. Binder starts printing your document.

T I P

To print a single section, select it and then choose _S_ection, _P_rint.

TROUBLESHOOTING

Printer cannot print all document types in Binder. Some printers cannot print an entire binder full of different document types. If your printer cannot print the binder, select _F_ile, Binder Opt_i_ons. Click _P_rint Binder as a Single Job to turn off this option and then click OK.

FIG. 49.10
The Print Binder dialog box offers additional options for printing sections.

Choose to print all sections or only selected sections

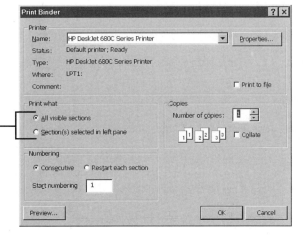

Creating and Using Binder Templates

If you frequently use Binder to create the same types of reports, you can save time by creating a binder template. The template stores the overall structure of your binder so that you can quickly plug in replacement documents. It also stores your header and footer settings and your default print settings so that you don't have to re-enter them.

Part
VII

Ch
49

To create a template from an existing binder, complete the following steps:

1. Choose _F_ile, _O_pen Binder and use the Open Binder dialog box to select the binder file you want to use as a template. Click _O_pen.

2. Modify the binder as desired by adding new or existing documents to it. (See "Creating a Binder," earlier in this chapter, for details.)

3. Choose File, Save Binder As to display the Save Binder As dialog box.

4. Open the Save As Type drop-down list and select Binder Templates (*.obt; *.obz).

5. Type a name for the template in the File Name text box.

6. If the Microsoft Office Templates\Binders folder is not selected, select it, as shown in Figure 49.11. The path to this folder is typically C:\Program Files\Microsoft Office\Templates\Binders. If you store the template in a different folder, it will not be listed on the Binders tab in the New Binder dialog box.

7. Click Save.

FIG. 49.11

To make it easy to access your new binder template, place it in the Templates\Binders folder.

The Binders folder is selected

To use your template to create a new binder, run Binder and select File, New Binder. In the New Binder dialog box, click the Binders tab, click the template you created, and then click OK.

  You can modify the template at any time by opening it in Binder, making your changes, and clicking Save or pressing Ctrl+S.

CHAPTER 50

Building Compound Documents

by Joe Kraynak

Each Microsoft Office 97 application offers specialized tools. Word excels in text editing and layout; Excel specializes in numbers, calculations, and charts; PowerPoint provides superior tools for creating presentations; and Access is best for database management.

As separate components, these applications are very powerful. However, if you want to tap the full power of the Office synergy, you need to use the applications together.

As you create reports, slideshows, brochures, and other documents, you will start to see a need to share data between documents. For example, you may need to insert a chart from Excel into a PowerPoint presentation or insert a portion of an Excel worksheet into a report. This chapter shows you various techniques for using the Office applications together in this way to create dynamic documents, share data on a network, and save time updating documents. ■

Understanding OLE

Share data dynamically between documents created in various Office applications.

Pasting data as embedded objects

Make text, graphics, and worksheets from one document an integral part of another document.

Linking documents

Create dynamic links between two or more Office documents for automatic updates.

Maintaining links

Use advanced techniques to keep linked data up-to-date.

Sharing data without OLE

Share data between applications that do not support OLE.

Overview of Compound Documents

Compound documents are documents that contain data from two or more applications that support OLE (*object linking and embedding*, pronounced oh-LAY). With OLE, applications and documents can share data dynamically. If you copy and paste data from an Excel worksheet into a Word document, for example, the pasted worksheet data is inserted as an OLE object in the Word document.

If you paste the object as a *link*, whenever you edit the worksheet in Excel the changes automatically appear in the Word document. If you paste the data as an *embedded object*, the link to the source document is broken but the object still retains a relationship with the application used to create it. You can edit the embedded object in its source application by double-clicking it.

When you copy and paste data as OLE objects, one document acts as the *destination (container)* and the other as the *source (server)*. The document that receives the pasted data is called the *destination document*. The contributing document is called the *source document*. By copying objects from a source document and pasting them into a destination document, you create a *compound document*.

Copying and Pasting Between Applications

Simple copy/paste or drag-and-drop operations typically use the Windows Clipboard to transfer the copied object to the destination document. This terminates the relationship between the source and its copy and between the copy and the application that was used to create it. In many cases this is just what you want to do; you can then edit the copy without changing the source.

In other cases you may wish to preserve the relationship between the source and the copy so that when you change the source its copy is automatically updated. For example, if you paste a portion of an Excel worksheet into a Word document, you may want the pasted worksheet data automatically updated whenever you edit the worksheet in Excel. This prevents you from having to enter your changes in two documents. It also saves storage space because you do not have to store the same data in two files.

Linking and Embedding

As you copy and paste data between Office documents, you need to be aware of the available options and question how you want the source and the copy related. You can share data in any of the following three ways:

■ *Link*. If you're using Office 97 applications or any other applications that support OLE, you can share data between documents by creating a link. With a link, the file into which you pasted the data does not actually contain the linked data; the linked data is stored in a separate (source) file. Whenever you edit the linked file (the source), any changes you make to it appear in all other documents that contain links to the source. For example, if you insert an Excel chart into a Word document as a link, whenever you change the chart in Excel, the modified chart appears in the Word document.

■ *Embed.* With OLE, you can also embed data from one file into another file. With embedding, the pasted data becomes a part of the file into which you paste it. If you edit the source, the changes do not show up in the copy. Likewise, if you edit the copy, the changes are not made to the source. In short, embedding breaks the link between the copy and the source. However, the pasted data retains a connection with the program that you used to create it. So if you double-click the embedded object, Windows automatically runs the associated application and you can edit the data.

■ *Paste.* You can paste data in any number of ways (including pasting the data as an embedded or linked object). However, not all applications support OLE. For those applications that do not support OLE, you can still share data between documents by copying and pasting the data, assuming the application supports the file format of the pasted data. However, the pasted data will have no connection with the source document or with the application that you used to create it.

■ *Hyperlink.* If you work on an intranet, you can create online documents with hyperlinks that point to other documents on your computer or on the intranet. To view a document with the most up-to-date information, the user clicks the hyperlink. Although hyperlinks do not display data from a source file in the destination file, they do make it easy to access related information and they are very easy to manage.

In-Place Editing

One of the major advantages of OLE in Office 97 is that you can edit objects in place. When you choose to edit an embedded or linked object in an Office document, the Office application does not kick you out to another application. Instead, the application used to create the source data takes over the current application window, displaying its own toolbars and menus (see Figure 50.1). You can then edit the object right inside the same window that displays the destination document.

Format Options for Links and Embedded Objects

When you choose to paste data as a link or as an embedded object (using Edit, Paste Special), the Paste Special dialog box (see Figure 50.2) displays several formats from which to choose. For example, if you paste Excel worksheet data into a Word document, you can choose to paste it as an Excel Worksheet Object, as Formatted Text (as a Rich Text File), or as a picture. Use the following list to help you decide which format to choose:

■ *Object.* In most cases you should choose the option with "Object" in its name (for example, Microsoft Excel Worksheet Object or Microsoft PowerPoint Slide Object). This inserts the object as a Windows Meta File (WMF), which displays a graphic representation of the source data. You can edit the object by double-clicking it.

■ *Formatted Text (RTF).* This option inserts the object as formatted text. For example, if you paste data from a spreadsheet into a Word document or a PowerPoint slide, the text is formatted using the Tables feature. With RTF, you can edit individual entries in the linked or embedded object. However, if you edit a linked object and then close and reopen the document that contains the link, any edited entries revert back to the entries used in the source document.

■ *Unformatted Text.* Select this option to insert text without formatting. This is not a very practical option, especially for pasting Excel worksheet data, because the data no longer appears in columns. However, if you are pasting data from a document that contains incompatible formatting codes, this may be your only option.

■ *Picture.* This option inserts the data as a high-quality graphic image that requires relatively little storage space and displays quickly in the destination document. If you choose to embed pasted data and share the destination document with other users, this option is best in terms of speed, storage, and quality.

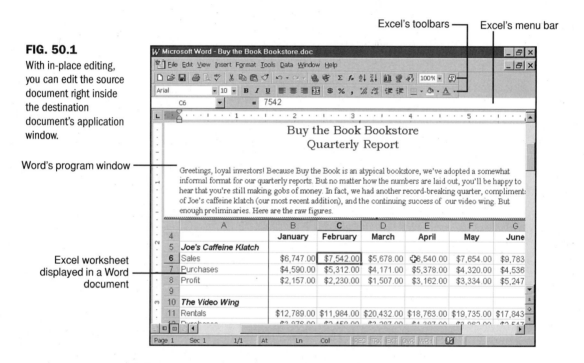

FIG. 50.1

With in-place editing, you can edit the source document right inside the destination document's application window.

Word's program window

Excel worksheet displayed in a Word document

Excel's toolbars

Excel's menu bar

Embedding Objects in a Document

When you want to share data between documents but keep the source file from being altered, you can copy and paste the data as an *embedded object*. The copy becomes the sole possession of the destination document. If you edit the source data, the copy does not reflect the changes.

Another consideration with embedded objects is file size. When you embed objects in a document, those objects contain the copied data. As you embed objects, the file size of the destination document grows. If you are concerned about file size, you may wish to paste the copied data as a link. See "Inserting Linked Objects in Documents," later in this chapter.

To insert data as an embedded object, choose one of the following:.

■ You can copy existing data from a document and paste it as an embedded object.

■ You can create a new embedded object, using the Insert, Object command. You use Insert, Object if the object you want to insert does not yet exist. The following sections provide instructions on how to copy and paste embedded objects and create new embedded objects.

Copying and Pasting Data as an Embedded Object

All of the Microsoft Office 97 applications support OLE, so you can paste data as embedded objects from a document you created in any of your Office applications into any document created in another Office application. In addition, you can share data with any other Windows application that supports OLE, such as WordPerfect, Lotus, Windows Paint, or CorelDraw! To insert data as an embedded object, complete the following steps:

1. Open the document that contains the data you want to copy and select the data. For example, you might drag over the cells you want to copy in an Excel worksheet or select PowerPoint slides in Slide Sorter view.

2. Choose Edit, Copy or click the Copy button.

3. Open the document in which you want to embed the copied data. Move the insertion point to the location where you want to paste the copied data.

4. Choose Edit, Paste Special. The Paste Special dialog box appears, as shown in Figure 50.2.

FIG. 50.2

The Paste Special dialog box lets you specify how you want the object inserted.

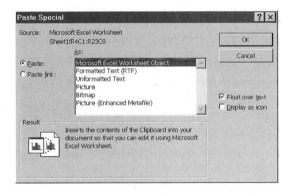

5. Make sure Paste (not Paste Link) is selected.

6. In the As list, select the desired format for the pasted object. See "Format Options for Links and Embedded Objects," earlier in this chapter, for details.

7. By default, Float Over Text is on (checked). This places the object on the drawing layer so that you can position it over existing text or other objects in the document. If you want to treat the object as text, choose the Float Over Text check box to turn it off (clear the check).

8. To display the inserted object as an icon that people can click to view the object, select Display As Icon.

9. Click OK. The object is inserted. The preferences you entered control the object's appearance and position.

TROUBLESHOOTING

Embedded object appears cropped. If the embedded object is too large to fit inside its frame, it may appear cropped. To make the object fit inside the margins, reformat the data in the source application to make it smaller, for example, reduce the font size. Or, paste the data as Formatted or Unformatted Text and then change the formatting in the destination document.

N O T E When you insert data from an Excel worksheet into a Word document, Word can display data from only one worksheet at a time. ■

Creating a New Embedded Object

The most convenient way to insert an embedded object is to copy data from an existing document. If you have not yet created the document, you can create and paste the embedded object on the fly, using another OLE compatible application, such as one of the Office applications.

In addition, Office comes with several *OLE applets*, such as MSGraph, that act as *mini-server applications*. You cannot execute these applets as stand-alone applications; they run only from within a destination document. To use them to create embedded objects, you must create the embedded object as a new object.

To create a new embedded object, complete the following steps:

1. Open the document in which you want to embed the object and position the insertion point where you want the object inserted.

2. Choose Insert, Object. (In some non-Office applications, you may have to select Edit, Insert Object.) The Object dialog box appears, displaying the Create New tab in front.

3. Select the type of object you want to insert and click OK. The application for the type of object you selected starts. If you look at the toolbar and menu commands, you can see that you are in a different application.

4. Create the object using the commands and features of that application.

5. When you complete the object, click anywhere inside the document. This closes the application you used to create the embedded object. You cannot open the embedded object as a separate file, but you can edit the object by double-clicking it.

Working with Embedded Objects

When you insert cut or copied data as an embedded object (by selecting the Object or Picture option from the As list), the data appears as part of the document. When you select an embedded object (usually by clicking it), selection handles appear around the object, as shown in Figure 50.3. You can then do any of the following to modify the object:

- To move the object, move the mouse pointer to a border (but not a selection handle) and drag the object to where you want it.

- To resize an object, move the tip of the mouse pointer over a selection handle and drag the handle to change the object's size or dimensions. Drag a corner handle to resize the object proportionally.

- To edit the object, double-click it. Windows runs the application associated with the object, allowing you to use the application's tools to modify the object.

- To delete an object, select the object and then press the Delete key.

- To convert an object from an icon to content or vice versa, select Edit, *ObjectName* Object, Convert. Select Display As Icon to turn it off or on, and click OK. If you turn Display As Icon off, the pasted object appears instead of the icon.

If you pasted Word text or Excel worksheet data as Formatted Text (RTF), no selection handles appear around the object when you click it. Also, you cannot double-click the object to edit it in its source application.

FIG. 50.3

You can select an embedded object to move or resize it.

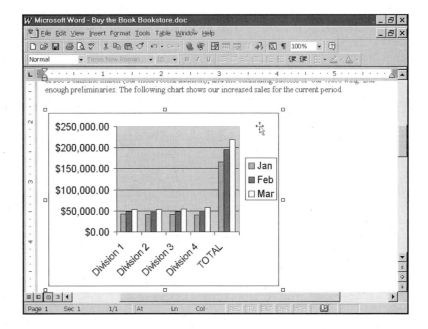

TIP

When you're working with the Office 97 applications, don't forget one of the data sharing features built right into Windows 95—*scraps*. If you select data in a document and then drag it to a blank area on the Windows desktop, Windows creates a shortcut for the data and marks it as a scrap. You can then drag this scrap into another document to insert it.

Inserting Linked Objects in a Document

Links are excellent if you need to share data on a network, or if you must use data from the same source document in several documents. You simply edit the source document and the updated data automatically appears in all of the documents in which you have inserted its data as links. However, links do have a couple of drawbacks:

- When you link data, you have two separate documents stored in two separate files: the destination and source documents. If you send someone the destination document, you must also send the source document. And, because the link specifies the location of the source document, that document must be stored on the same drive and in the same folder where your system stored the document.

- A link extracts data from a source document stored in a specific folder. If someone renames or moves the file, the link will no longer work. This can be a problem if someone else is in charge of maintaining the source document.

Despite these drawbacks, links are a very valuable tool, especially if you work on a network and need to share files with other departments or coworkers. The following sections provide instructions on inserting links, working with linked data, and using hyperlinks as an alternative to links.

Inserting Links

Before you can insert data from one document as a link in another document, you must make sure you have access to both documents. If you work on a network and you need to link to a document on the network, you must know the location of the file and have permission to open and modify it. You can then complete the following steps to create the link:

1. Open the document that contains the data you want to copy and select the data. For example, you may select one or two slides of a PowerPoint presentation or select a range of cells or a chart in Excel.

2. Select <u>E</u>dit, <u>C</u>opy or click the Copy button.

3. Open the document in which you want to paste the data. Move the insertion point to the location where you want the data pasted.

4. Select <u>E</u>dit, Paste <u>S</u>pecial. The Paste Special dialog box appears.

5. Select Paste <u>L</u>ink, as shown in Figure 50.4. If you do not select this option, the data will be pasted as an embedded object.

6. In the <u>A</u>s list, select the desired format for the pasted object. See "Format Options for Links and Embedded Objects," earlier in this chapter, for details.

7. By default, Float Over <u>T</u>ext is on. This places the object on the drawing layer so that you can position it over existing text or other objects in the document. If you want to treat the object as text, select Float Over <u>T</u>ext to turn it off.

8. To display the inserted object as an icon that people can click to view the object, select <u>D</u>isplay As Icon.

9. Click OK. The object is inserted. The preferences you entered control the object's appearance and position.

FIG. 50.4
The Paste Special
dialog box lets you
determine how the data
will be pasted.

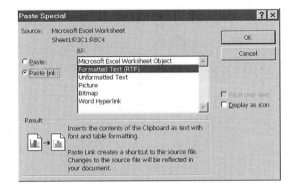

FIG. 50.4
The Paste Special
dialog box lets you
determine how the data
will be pasted.

Editing Links

If you inserted data as a linked object or picture, you can select it by clicking it and then move or resize it, just as if you were working with an embedded object. To edit the object in the source application, double-click the object.

However, if you inserted the link as Formatted Text, you cannot select the object or double-click the object to edit it. To format or edit the data, you must first open the link in the source application by performing the following steps:

1. Choose Edit, Links. A list of links in the current document appears, as shown in Figure 50.5.

FIG. 50.5
You can view a list of
links in the current
document.

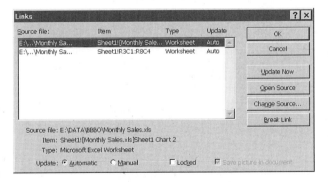

2. Click the link you want to edit or format and select Open Source. This displays the source document in the application used to create it.

3. Enter your changes to the source document.

4. Choose File, Exit (or File, Close if you want to continue working in Excel).

TROUBLESHOOTING

Cannot edit the link. If you receive an error message indicating that you cannot edit the link, check the following:

- If you are working on a network, make sure no one else has the source document open.

- Make sure the source document has not been moved or renamed. If it has, see "Relinking When Files Move," later in this chapter, to learn how to redirect the link.

- In order to edit the link, you must have a copy of the source application and your system must have sufficient memory to run both applications.

- Make sure no dialog boxes are open in the source application.

TIP You can quickly edit a linked object in any format by right-clicking the linked object, choosing Linked ... Object, and selecting Edit Link. If the linked object is an Excel table pasted as RTF, first make sure the insertion point is inside the table but that nothing in the table is highlighted.

Using Hyperlinks

If you are working on an intranet, you may wish to insert hyperlinks rather than pasting data as embedded or linked objects. The user can then click a hyperlink in your document to view updated data. This keeps the size of the destination document small. It also makes it easy to maintain the links; you simply need to make sure that the link always points to the correct location of the file.

N O T E Do not confuse *hyperlinks* with *links*. Hyperlinks are used in Web documents to link one document to another. They point to a specific file stored on another drive, Web server, or other Internet server. Links are used in Office documents to pull data from one document into another document.

There are two ways you can insert hyperlinks. The easiest way is to insert a hyperlink as if you were linking to a Web page. Complete the following steps:

1. Type the text or insert an image that you want the user to click to view the linked data and select the image or text.

2. Select Insert, Hyperlink (Ctrl+K) or click the Insert Hyperlink button on the Web toolbar. This opens the Insert Hyperlink dialog box, as shown in Figure 50.6.

3. In the Link To File Or URL text box, type the path to the file you want the link to point to or click Browse to select the file from a list.

4. In the Named Location In File text box, enter the bookmark name, range name, database object, or slide number you want the link to point to or click Browse to select the object from a list.

CAUTION

Do not type anything in the Named Location in File text box or use the Browse button next to it unless you have already inserted bookmarks in the document to which you are linking. Otherwise, you will receive an error message indicating that no bookmarks exist.

    5. Click OK. Your application displays the link as blue text or places a blue border around the image.

FIG. 50.6

You can create a hyperlink to a specific area in a document.

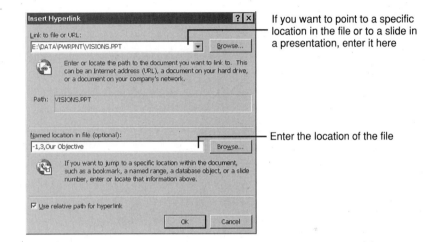

If you want to point to a specific location in the file or to a slide in a presentation, enter it here

Enter the location of the file

You can also insert copied data as a hyperlink by choosing Edit, Paste As Hyperlink. However, this inserts the entire object as a hyperlink. For example, if you paste a portion of an Excel worksheet as a hyperlink, all the cell entries in the pasted object appear blue and all point to the same Excel file.

Maintaining and Updating Links

Because links (not hyperlinks) allow you to share data dynamically, you must maintain them to ensure that they work properly and that your destination document always has the latest data from the source document. If you work on a network and someone moves the source document, you must edit the link's properties so it points to the document's new location.

In addition, links may be too automated for your purposes. When you open a document that contains links, the links automatically extract the latest data from the source document and insert it into the destination document. However, you might not always want the latest data. For example, if you are working on a quarterly report, you may want the link to insert last quarter's figures. To do this, you can lock the link to prevent the link from automatically updating itself.

Office provides several options for maintaining your links and for specifying how automated you want them to be. The following sections explain these options in detail.

Relinking When Files Move

If you work with Web documents, you know that a hyperlink works only as long as the file that the hyperlink points to does not move. The same is true with links. Links contain information about the location and name of the source document. If you or someone else moves the source document, you must redirect the link to point to the source document's new location. Complete the following steps to redirect the link:

1. Choose Edit, Links. The Links dialog box appears, displaying a list of links in the current document.

2. Click the link you want to redirect and click Change Source. The Change Source dialog box appears, allowing you to select the source document.

3. Change to the folder where the source document is stored, select the source document, and click OK. This returns you to the Links dialog box.

4. Click OK to save your changes.

Locking Links

To prevent links from automatically extracting updated data from the source document, you can lock the link. Locking the link is like turning it into a temporary embedded object. To lock one or more links in a document, complete the following steps:

1. Choose Edit, Links. The Links dialog box appears, as shown in Figure 50.7, displaying a list of links in the current document.

2. Click the link you want to lock. Ctrl+click to select additional links.

3. Select Locked to place a check in its check box.

4. Click OK to save your changes.

When you lock a link, the data from the source document remains fixed and you cannot manually update the link. Perform the same steps to unlock the link.

FIG. 50.7

You can lock links to prevent them from showing updated data from the source document.

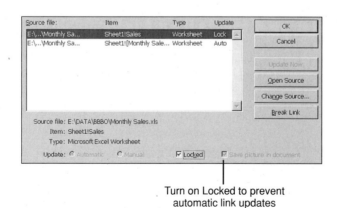

Turn on Locked to prevent
automatic link updates

Updating Links

By default, links are set to automatically update themselves. However, you can change the properties of the link so that the link updates itself only when you enter the update command. To set a link for manual updates, complete the following steps:

1. Choose Edit, Links. The Links dialog box appears, displaying a list of links in the current document.

2. Click the link you want to manually update. Ctrl+click to select additional links.

3. Next to the Update option, select Manual.

4. Click OK to save your changes.

When you set links for manual updates, you can pull updated data from the source document by performing one of the following steps:

- In the destination document, select Edit, Links. Select the links you want to update and click Update Now.

- You can update the links automatically when you print the container document. Select Tools, Options and click the Print tab. Under Printing Options, click Update Links. Click OK.

 TIP To quickly update a single link, select the link and press F9.

Unlinking Links

You can terminate the relationship between the link and the source document by breaking the link. This essentially transforms the link into an embedded object, preventing any changes to the source document from appearing in the container document.

To break a link, select Edit, Links. Select the link you want to break and click Break Link.

N O T E When you unlink a link, the link is broken. The only way to reestablish the link is to insert it again.

Using Data from Non-OLE Applications

Most new applications, such as CorelDraw! and WordPerfect, are OLE compatible, allowing you to paste data as a link or embedded object. However, some applications do not support the dynamic data-sharing capabilities of OLE. In such cases, you can still copy and paste data between documents by using the Windows Clipboard.

Copying and pasting via the Clipboard does not activate any dynamic data sharing capabilities. It simply pastes the copied data into your document. You can't double-click the copy to edit it in its source application, and the pasted data does not reflect changes made to the source document.

Complete the following steps to copy data from a non-OLE document into your Office document:

1. In the non-OLE application, open the document that contains the data you want to copy.
2. Select the data.
3. Use the application's Copy command to place the data on the Windows Clipboard.
4. Run your Office application and open the document into which you want to paste the Clipboard contents. Move the insertion point to where you want the data to be pasted.

5. Choose Edit, Paste or click the Paste button.

N O T E Although Office has several file format converters, you may run into problems if you try to paste data in a format that Office does not support. If you encounter problems with incompatible file formats, open the file in the program used to create it and save the file in a format that your Office application supports. ▪

Other Ways to Share Data in Office

Word, Access, PowerPoint, and Excel offer additional tools that allow you to share data and make the most of the specialized tools available in each application. For example, you can use an outline you created in Word to create a PowerPoint presentation or use Word's advanced page layout tools to format and print a report you created in Access. The following sections provide details on how to use the Office applications together.

Exporting a PowerPoint Presentation as a Word Outline

Not only does PowerPoint allow you to view and edit a presentation in Outline view but you can also export the presentation as a Word outline. You can then modify the outline in Word and add text and other objects to flesh out your document. To convert a PowerPoint presentation into a Word outline, complete the following steps:

1. Open the presentation in PowerPoint.
2. Choose File, Send To, Microsoft Word. The Write-Up dialog box appears, asking how you want the slides and text laid out on Word pages (see Figure 50.8).
3. Under Page Layout In Microsoft Word, select the desired slide and text layout. To export the presentation as an outline (without slides), select Outline Only.
4. If you chose to include slides in the Word document, you can select Paste Link to paste the slides as a links. (This option is unavailable if you selected Outline Only in step 3.)
5. Click OK. PowerPoint converts the presentation into a Word document and displays the document in Word, where you can start working on it.

FIG. 50.8
PowerPoint lets you
export a presentation as
a Word document.

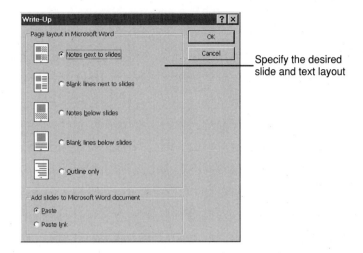

Specify the desired
slide and text layout

You can also transform an outline you typed in Word into a PowerPoint presentation. Open the outline you created in Word. Select File, Send To, Microsoft PowerPoint. Select the desired slide layout and click OK.

Analyzing Access Data in Excel

Although Access is the best tool to use for storing and extracting data, Excel provides superior tools for performing calculations and for analyzing data. If you have tried entering formulas in your Access report, you know how difficult it can be to enter the correct formula using the correct field codes. It's much easier to enter formulas in Excel using cell addresses or the point-and-click method.

In addition, Excel offers scenarios that allow you to play "What if?" with a set of values. You can change one or more values to see how the changes will affect the net result. And you can create several scenarios to see how they compare.

 To send a table, form, query, or report to Excel, first open it in Access. Then, select Tools, Office Links, Analyze It With MS Excel (or click the OfficeLinks button and select Analyze It with MS Excel). See "Using Access Data in Excel," in Chapter 51, "Integrating Documents and Databases," for details.

Publishing Access Reports with Word

Access provides excellent tools for storing and managing data, but its page layout features are inadequate and difficult to master. For more control over the look and layout of your reports, consider converting the report into a Word document.

 To convert an Access report to Word format, first open the report in Access. Click the Office Links button and select Publish It With MS Word. Access exports the report to Word, creating a new document (see Figure 50.9). You can now format the document using Word's advanced formatting tools, and you can add graphics and other objects to enhance the document.

FIG. 50.9

You can export an Access report to create a Word document.

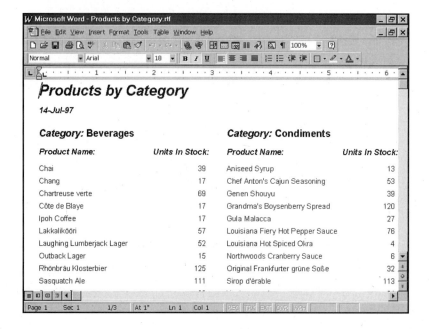

You can also use Access and Word together to merge your Word documents with an Access database. For example, you can merge a form letter created in Word with an address list stored in Access or automate the creation of mailing labels. See "Using Access Data in Word" in Chapter 51, "Integrating Documents and Databases," for details. ●

Integrating Documents and Databases

by Joe Kraynak

Access is a powerful application for storing, organizing, and retrieving data. It provides the tools you need to extract data from various sources, and then combine, sort, and filter that data to create both simple and complex reports.

However, Access lacks the tools available in the other Office applications for designing, presenting, and analyzing data. For instance, Access reports are excellent for presenting the data itself, but Word provides much better tools for adding text and graphics, and for arranging the data on pages. By combining Access' database tools with Word's superior publishing tools, you can create attractive reports that include summaries, graphics, and charts.

Access also comes up short in the data analysis department. Excel provides superior tools for analyzing data, including pivot tables and scenarios. Excel worksheets also make it much easier to perform complex calculations on data using formulas and functions.

In addition, Access has no presentation tools. If you need to present data in a slide show, you must use PowerPoint to create the presentation and lay out your slides. You can then extract data from your Access database to place it on your slides as supporting material.

Merge Word documents with Access databases

Leverage the power of your database by integrating it with Word's superior document management features.

Analyze your Access data with Excel

Access makes it easy to manage data, but when you need to analyze it, export your data to an Excel worksheet.

Export data from Access to Excel

Convert existing worksheet data into Access tables to take advantage of the powerful relational database tools in Access.

Use Access data in PowerPoint presentations

Effective presentations require good supporting data. Learn how to extract that data from Access and place it on your slides.

In this chapter, you learn how to use Access along with the other Office applications to exploit the full potential of your database. ▨

Using Access Data in Word

By itself, a database is of little use. It simply stores a collection of data and enables you to sort and extract that data in various ways. A database is useful only when you start to place the data in a meaningful context such as a report, or use it to create specific documents such as mailing labels and form letters.

Access provides several tools that enable you to use Word to place your data in a meaningful context and create documents. For instance, if you have created a report in Access, you can choose to publish the report with Word, where you can use advanced formatting and page-layout tools to modify the report. Access also enables you to merge your database with a Word document to create form letters, mailing labels, and other documents.

The following sections provide details on using Access along with Word to perform these tasks.

Publishing Access Reports with Word

An Access report is fairly basic. It contains a report title and data arranged in rows and columns. You can add graphics to the report and insert other objects, but the procedure is somewhat complicated.

To avoid the complexities of creating and printing complex reports from Access, you can export the report to Word. You can then use Word's advanced tools to add headings, additional text, graphics, charts, headers and footers, and other objects to make your report more complete and more attractive.

To publish an Access report with Word, complete the following steps:

1. Open your Access database and select the name of the table, query, form, or report you want to publish with Word. (To include only selected records in a table, highlight the desired records.)

2. Choose Tools, Office Links, Publish It with MS Word, or click the arrow to the right of the Office Links button, and select Publish It with MS Word. Access saves the file as ReportName.rtf in your default directory and displays the new document in Word (see Figure 51.1).

3. (Optional) In Word, choose File, Save As. From the Save As Type list, select Word Document (*.doc), and click the Save button.

You can now use Word to reformat the report and to add headings, running text, graphics, charts, and other objects to flesh it out. When you are finished, you can print the report just as you would print any document in Word.

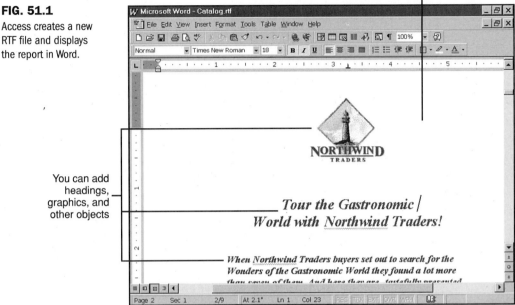

FIG. 51.1
Access creates a new
RTF file and displays
the report in Word.

Access report displayed in Word

You can add
headings,
graphics, and
other objects

NOTE When you choose to publish a report with Word, Access saves it in a separate file. Any
changes you make to the report in Word do not affect the original report in Access. In
addition, any changes you make to the report in Access or to the database on which the report is
based are not reflected in your new report. ▪

Pasting Records into a Word Document

The easiest way to use data from an Access database in Word is to copy the records from a
datasheet or query and paste them into your Word document. Pasted records are displayed in
a Word table with field names inserted in the top row. To copy records and paste them into a
Word document, complete the following steps:

1. Open the table or query that contains the records you want to copy and highlight the
   records.
2. Click the Copy button or press Ctrl+C.
3. Open the Word document into which you want the records pasted, and move the
   insertion point to the desired position.
4. Click the Paste button or press Ctrl+V. The records are pasted as a table into your Word
   document, as shown in Figure 51.2.
5. Format the table as desired.

FIG. 51.2

Pasted records appear in a table with field names as column headings.

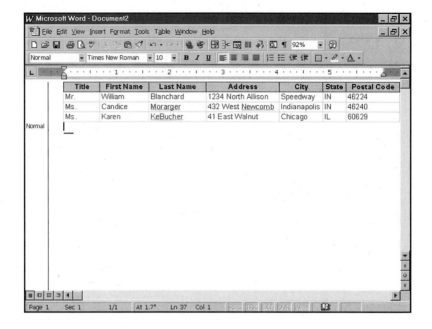

Title	First Name	Last Name	Address	City	State	Postal Code
Mr.	William	Blanchard	1234 North Allison	Speedway	IN	46224
Ms.	Candice	Morarger	432 West Newcomb	Indianapolis	IN	46240
Ms.	Karen	KeBucher	41 East Walnut	Chicago	IL	60629

N O T E The simple copy/paste operation inserts the records as RTF (Rich Text Format). There is no dynamic relationship between these records and your Access database. If you edit the database, changes will not appear in the table. To create a dynamic link between the pasted data and the Access database, use Edit, Paste Special. ■

Merging a Word Document with an Access Database

In Chapter 9, "Merging Documents," you learned how to use Word's Mail Merge feature to merge a form letter with data in a table, and how to create mailing labels. You can also call up Word's Mail Merge feature from Access to merge your Access data with a new or existing Word document.

Access features the Microsoft Word Mail Merge Wizard, which initiates the process. The wizard uses a table or query as the data source for the merge, and enables you to create a new main merge document in Word or use an existing Word document.

N O T E Running Mail Merge from Access uses DDE (Dynamic Data Exchange) to transfer data from Access to Word. You cannot use Word's Query feature to filter or sort Access database records. If you do, you break the DDE link. In order to create mailing labels, form letters, or other merged documents using a specific set of records (or to sort the merged documents), first create a query in Access, and then base your merge on the query rather than on a table. ■

To merge your database with a new Word document, complete the following steps:

1. Open your database and select the table or query to use as the data source.

 2. Choose Tools, Office Links, Merge It with MS Word, or click the arrow to the right of the Office Links button, and select Merge It with MS Word. The wizard appears, as shown in Figure 51.3.

FIG. 51.3
The Microsoft Word Mail Merge Wizard helps you merge your database with a Word document.

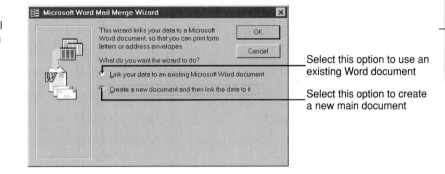

Select this option to use an existing Word document

Select this option to create a new main document

3. Select Create a New Document and Then Link the Data to It, and click OK. This launches Word, which opens a new, blank main document. A DDE (Dynamic Data Exchange) link is created between the Word document and the Access database.

4. Type any text you want to appear in the main document. For example, if you are creating a form letter, you might want to type your address at the top of the page.

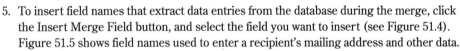 5. To insert field names that extract data entries from the database during the merge, click the Insert Merge Field button, and select the field you want to insert (see Figure 51.4). Figure 51.5 shows field names used to enter a recipient's mailing address and other data.

 6. Click the View Merged Data button in the Mail Merge toolbar to preview your form letter with actual data entries instead of merge fields.

 7. You can click the Next Record and Previous Record buttons to flip through the documents resulting from the merge.

 8. To merge the document and database and create a new document, click the Merge to New Document button—this enables you to preview the new merged documents before printing them. To merge directly to the printer, click the Merge to Printer button.

If you have already created the Word document you want to use for the mail merge, the Microsoft Word Mail Merge Wizard can merge your database with the existing document to avoid having to start from scratch. To merge a database with an existing Word document, complete the following steps:

1. Open your database and select the table or query to use as the data source.

 2. Choose Tools, Office Links, Merge It with MS Word, or click the arrow to the right of the Office Links button, and select Merge It with MS Word. The wizard appears, as you saw in Figure 51.3.

FIG. 51.4
You can insert merge fields to extract data entries from the database and insert them in your Word document.

A list of field names in the Access database

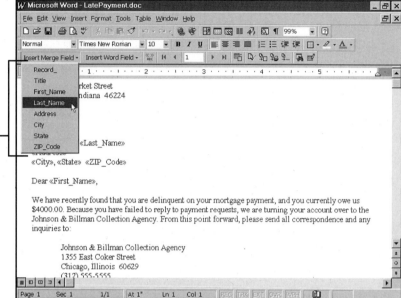

FIG. 51.5
Merge fields in a sample form letter extract field entries from the database.

Use punctuation and spaces as you normally would to format the address

Insert merge fields in place of specific information, such as the city, state, and ZIP Code

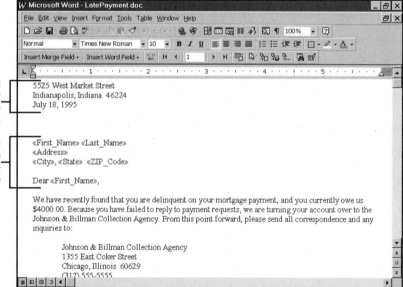

3. Link Your Data to an Existing Microsoft Word Document is selected by default. Click OK. The Select Microsoft Word Document dialog box appears.

4. Change to the drive and folder where the document is stored, select the document, and click Open. If you previously merged your document with a different data source, the Mail Merge Wizard dialog box appears, prompting you to confirm that you want to use a different data source (see Figure 51.6).

FIG. 51.6

If you merge a document that you have already merged with a different data source, Access prompts you to confirm changing the data source.

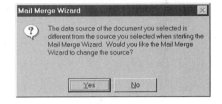

5. Click Yes. Word displays the selected document. The Insert Merge Fields drop-down list now contains a list of field names from the Access table or query.

6. Edit the document as desired. You can delete existing merge fields, or you can add fields by selecting them from the Insert Merge Fields drop-down list. You can also edit any text in the document.

7. Click the View Merged Data button in the Mail Merge toolbar to preview your form letter with actual data entries instead of merge fields.

8. You can click the Next Record and Previous Record buttons to flip through the documents resulting from the merge.

9. To merge the document and database and create a new document, click the Merge to New Document button. (This enables you to preview the new merged documents before printing them.) To merge directly to the printer, click the Merge to Printer button.

◆ TROUBLESHOOTING

When you change the data source, you will encounter problems if the field names in the new data source differ from those in the previous data source. When you click the View Merged Data button, Word displays the Invalid Merge Field dialog box indicating that a field merge code in your document does not match any field name in the data source. You can then Remove Field to delete the field in the document, or select a field that matches a valid field name in the data source.

Using Access Data in Excel

At a very basic level, Access and Excel are very similar. Both applications enable you to store data in a tabular format, typing entries in columns and rows. In Excel, you can treat worksheet data as a simple database and sort and filter your records using elementary database tools. In Access, you can use basic formulas to perform calculations on values in your tables or queries.

However, Excel does not provide the advanced tools for selecting and sorting data that you will find in Access. Excel's forms pale in comparison to the forms you can create with Access, and creating a report from an Excel worksheet is much more difficult than creating a report from Access.

Conversely, Excel provides superior tools for performing calculations and analyzing data. Excel's pivot tables and scenarios enable you to quickly rearrange data, and examine it from different perspectives using different values. (See Chapter 18, "Using Pivot Tables," for details.) In addition, Excel's formulas and functions enable you to perform complex calculations that are impossible to perform in an Access database.

The following sections show you how to use Access and Excel together to make greater use of both applications.

Pasting Access Records in an Excel Worksheet

One of the easiest ways to share data between Access and Excel is to use Copy and Paste. Because Access stores records in tables using the same row/column format used in Excel worksheets, the data transfers smoothly between the two applications.

To copy records and paste them into an Excel worksheet, complete the following steps:

1. Open the Access table or query that contains the records you want to copy, and highlight the records.

2. Click the Copy button or press Ctrl+C.

3. Open the Excel worksheet into which you want the records pasted, and select the cell in which you want the first column heading in the database inserted. When you paste records from Access, column headings are pasted in the top row, and records are pasted in the following rows.

4. Click the Paste button or press Ctrl+V. The records are pasted into your Excel worksheet, as shown in Figure 51.7.

5. Adjust the column widths as desired.

> **N O T E** Using the Edit, Paste command simply inserts a static copy of the records. To insert records that are automatically updated when you edit entries in the database, use the Edit, Paste Special command. ▨

Analyzing Access Data in Excel

If you store values in your Access database, you know that Access provides few tools for working with those values. You can use expressions to perform basic calculations on field entries to enter totals and subtotals, and you can use the Chart Wizard to graph values. To do anything more advanced, you need to use a dedicated spreadsheet application, such as Excel.

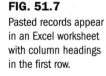

FIG. 51.7

Pasted records appear in an Excel worksheet with column headings in the first row.

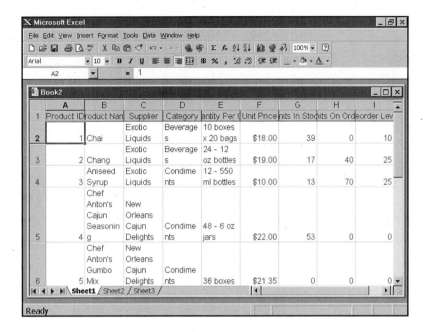

Fortunately, Access provides an Office Link that makes it easy to export tables, queries, forms, and reports as Excel worksheets. When you export the object to Excel, Access transforms the object into a separate Excel file (with the XLS extension). You can then edit the file without affecting the original object. You can also use Excel's formulas and functions to perform calculations, and use pivot tables, scenarios, and charts to analyze the data.

The easiest way to export a database object to Excel is to use the Office Link. Complete the following steps:

1. Open the database that contains the table, query, form, or report that you want to view in Excel.

2. Select the table, query, form or report.

3. Choose Tools, Office Links, Analyze It with MS Excel, or click the arrow to the right of the Office Links button, and select Analyze It with MS Excel. Access converts the object into an Excel worksheet, and displays it in Excel (see Figure 51.8).

N O T E When you choose to analyze Access data with Excel, Access saves the selected table, query, form, or report as an Excel file. By default, the file is stored in the My Computer folder. Access does not prompt you to specify a name or location for the file. ■

4. Use Excel to edit the worksheet or use any of Excel's advanced tools to perform calculations or analyze the data.

For details on how to use Excel's advanced data analysis tools, see Chapter 18, "Using Pivot Tables," and Chapter 19, "Analyzing Spreadsheet Data."

FIG. 51.8

When you choose to analyze Access data in Excel, Access converts the selected object into an Excel file.

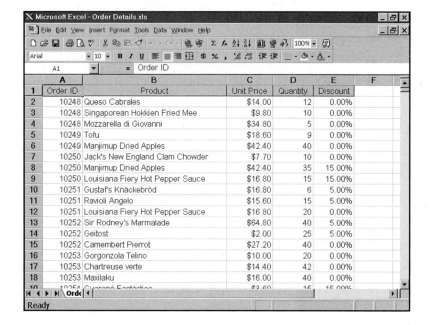

You can also export a table or query to an Excel file. Select the table or query you want to export to Excel. Choose File, Save As/Export. Make sure To an External File or Database is selected, and click OK. From the Save As Type list, select Microsoft Excel 97 (*.xls), and select an existing Excel file, or type a file name in the File Name text box. Click Export.

Importing Excel Data Into Access

Many businesses are just realizing the value of relational databases, such as Access. These businesses have relied on spreadsheets for storing and managing their data. The problem with spreadsheets is that they lack the tools for extracting and merging data from two or more spreadsheets. With a relational database, you can create a query that merges the data, sorts it, and filters it, making the data much more flexible.

Because of this, many businesses that have relied solely on spreadsheets for managing data are converting their large spreadsheets into relational databases. Fortunately, Access simplifies the process with its Import Spreadsheet Wizard. You can import a spreadsheet as a table in an existing database or in a new database.

CAUTION

If your worksheet contains formulas, you should freeze the values in the cells that contain formulas. Otherwise, Access imports the cells as blank data cells. First, use Excel's File, Save As command to save your Excel workbook under another name, and use this workbook for importing (this prevents changes from affecting the formulas in your original workbook). Highlight the cells that contain the formulas you want to freeze. Press Ctrl+C. Choose Edit, Paste Special, select Values, and click OK. The calculated values are pasted into the cells, rather than pasting the formulas into the cells. Save your new workbook.

To perform the conversion, complete the following steps:

1. Start Excel, and open the worksheet you want to import. (If you froze values as explained in the caution, open the worksheet that contains the frozen values.)

2. Above the first row of data, type a row of column headings (field names). These entries cannot include periods, exclamation points, or brackets.

3. (Optional) To include only selected records in the new Access table, highlight the column headings row and all the rows you want to include. Choose Insert, Name, Define, and name the range.

4. Save your Excel file and exit Excel.

5. Start Access and open the database into which you want to import the Excel data.

6. Choose File, Get External Data, Import. The Import dialog box appears prompting you to select the file you want to import.

7. Select the Excel file you want to import, and click Import. The first Import Spreadsheet Wizard dialog box appears, as shown in Figure 51.9.

FIG. 51.9
The Import Spreadsheet Wizard leads you through the import process.

You can import entire worksheets or named ranges

The Import Spreadsheet Wizard displays sample data from the worksheet here

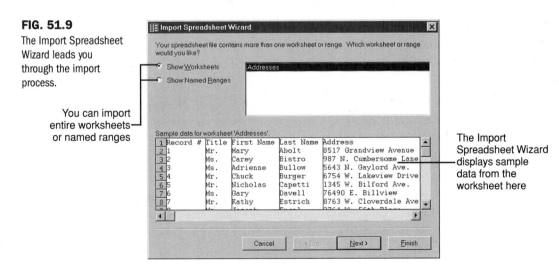

8. To import an entire worksheet, select Show Worksheets. If you named a range of rows to include in step 3, select Show Named Ranges. The names of the worksheets or ranges appear in the list to the right of these options.

9. Select the worksheet or named range you want to import. The Import Spreadsheet Wizard displays sample data from the worksheet or range at the bottom of the dialog box.

10. Click Next. The Import Spreadsheet Wizard prompts you to confirm that the first row of the worksheet contains column headings.

11. Make sure First Row Contains Column Headings is checked, and click Next. The Import Spreadsheet Wizard asks if you want to add the data to an existing table or use it to create a new table.

12. To create a new table, select In a New Table. To add the data to an existing table, select In an Existing Table, and select the table from the drop-down list (read the following caution). Click Next. If you chose to create a new table, you are prompted to specify properties of each field (see Figure 51.10). If you are adding data to an existing table, skip to Step 21.

FIG. 51.10

You can exclude columns from the table, change the names of column headings, choose an indexing option for each column, and set a column's data type.

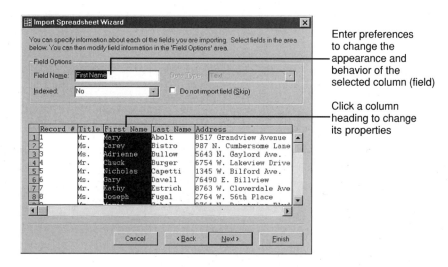

Enter preferences to change the appearance and behavior of the selected column (field)

Click a column heading to change its properties

CAUTION

Importing data into an existing table is tricky. The column headings you entered in Step 2 must match the field name entries in the destination table. If the column headings and field names do not match, you receive error messages and need to rename your column headings or delete them.

13. To exclude a column from the table, click the column heading, and select Do Not Import Field (Skip) to place a check in the box. (You can repeat this step to exclude additional columns.)

14. To change a field name (column heading) click the column heading, and type a new name in the Field Name text box. (If you typed the correct field names in Step 2, this step is unnecessary.)

15. To index a field, click its column heading, and choose the desired index type from the Indexed drop-down list: No, Yes (Duplicates OK), or Yes (No Duplicates). You can repeat this step to index additional fields.

16. If the entries in a column do not have a data type assigned to them, you can select a data type from the Data Type drop-down list. Click the column heading, and select the desired data type.

17. Repeat Steps 13-16 for each column in the worksheet. Click Next. The Import Spreadsheet Wizard prompts you to specify a primary key for the table (see Figure 51.11).

FIG. 51.11
The wizard prompts you to select a field to act as the primary key.

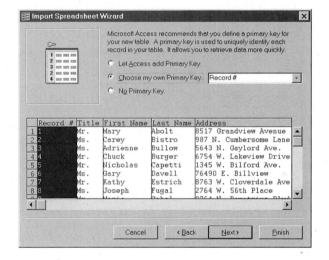

18. Select one of the following options: Let Access Add Primary Key, to have Access number your rows (records); Choose My Own Primary Key, and then select the field you want to use as the primary key, if an existing column in the worksheet can function as the primary key; No Primary Key, if this table does not need to be related to other tables in the database.

19. Click Next. The final Import Spreadsheet Wizard dialog box appears, prompting you to name the new table. By default, the wizard uses the worksheet name or the name of the named range, but you can change it (see Figure 51.12).

20. To rename the table, type the name you want to use. To split the table after importing it, select the check box labeled I Would Like a Wizard to Analyze My Table After Importing the Data.

21. Click Finish. Access imports the data and then displays a dialog box indicating that the process has been successfully completed. Click OK.

FIG. 51.12

You can enter a different name for the Access table.

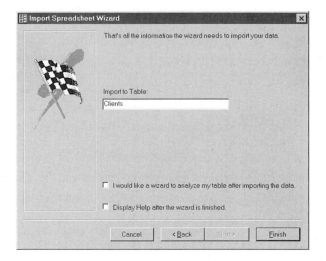

Using Access Data in PowerPoint

PowerPoint slides are not well suited to receive data from Access, especially if the data is stored in a large table or query. If you paste records from an Access table or query onto a PowerPoint slide, the data is inserted as formatted or unformatted text, and is difficult to format. However, if you use Access to store the data that you want to include in a presentation, you need to be able to extract that data and paste it on your slides.

To overcome the limitations of using Access data in your presentations, use one of the following workarounds:

■ Copy and paste small data selections. If you try to paste all the entries in a lengthy record, columns will be nearly impossible to control.

■ After pasting data from Access, select all the text (choose Edit, Select All or press Ctrl+A) and choose a much smaller font size for the selected text. The goal is to make the text small enough to enable the columns to align properly.

■ Copy records from your Access table or query and paste them in a Word document or Excel worksheet, as explained previously in this chapter. In Word, this creates a table. Copy the table or worksheet data, and paste it on your slide. This creates an embedded object, as shown in Figure 51.13. Double-click the object to format it in Excel or Word. In most cases, you need to reduce the font size to make the columns align properly.

If you are creating an online presentation, you can create a hyperlink to the table or query you want to include in your presentation.

▶ **See** "Inserting and Editing Hyperlinks," **p. 913**

FIG. 51.13
You can transfer Access data via Excel or Word to a PowerPoint slide as a table.

Access data pasted as a table in PowerPoint

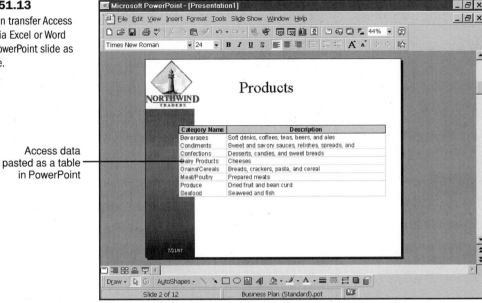

Unfortunately, you cannot create a hyperlink to a specific table or query in the database. The hyperlink points to the Access database file. When the user clicks the link during the presentation, Access runs and opens the database file. This brings up another issue: The user must have Access installed in order to view the database, and the database file must be stored in a folder that is accessible to the user.

> **CAUTION**
> When you create a hyperlink to a database file, you face some security issues. You might not want the person viewing the database to edit records or otherwise modify the database. See Chapter 54, "Sharing and Securing Resources," in the section named "Applying Database Security in Access," for instructions on how to secure your database.

Part VIII: Using Office 97 Tools

CHAPTER 52

Using Drawing Features

by John Purdum

Office 97 has been an incredible upgrade since it's previous version. It has become a lot more than just a word processor or an accountant's tool. Office 97 has allowed for the use of graphic editors, 3-D drawing tools, photo editors, painting programs, and so on in order to make your presentations more powerful. The following sections will give you a detailed overview of the new graphics capabilities of Office 97. ■

Using Microsoft Map

Learn how to create statistical maps to represent data within a document or presentation.

Using Photo Editor

Learn how to edit and manipulate photos.

Using Office Art

Office 97's introduction of Office Art will allow you to create graphics for presentations or the Web.

Using Word Art

Learn how to Create fantastic text effects with Word Art.

Using Other Drawing Tools

Look to this section to find out how to perform various tasks that will enhance your presentations.

Using Microsoft Map

Using Office 97's Microsoft Map feature is a helpful tool used to display data in a particular geographical area. By Using Microsoft Map, you can present your data in an efficient and organized manner. Suppose you are giving a presentation that involves a numerical statistic within a certain state, country, or province. You want the data to be displayed in a way that the interpreter can easily understand. You probably don't want to inaccurately display the data using pie charts or bar graphs. By using the actual geographic location in accordance with the data, you are able to provide a clearer representation.

Preparing the Data to Map

An important guideline you must follow in order to produce a Data Map involves the way the data is arranged in your worksheet. States, countries, and regions must be in the same column on the worksheet you are creating. The geographical maps available in the Data Map feature are Australia, Canada, Europe, Mexico, North America, Southern Africa, UK and ROI Countries, United States, and World Countries. The United States map can include Hawaii and Alaska, but only if specified.

 TIP   In order for your Data Map to be correctly created by Excel, you must always use the correct names or abbreviations. To see a list of spellings and abbreviations for different map features, there is a sample workbook Mapstats.xls in the Data folder within the folder where Microsoft Map was installed. This will save you from having to correct any misspellings in your worksheet.

N O T E   If the data you are presenting contains numeric postal codes, you must format the postal codes as text and not numbers. This prevents the removal of zeros from the postal codes included in your data.

Follow the next three steps in order to successfully map your data.

1. Arrange the data such as countries, states, regions, provinces, and so on, in columns on the worksheet you are using.

 TIP   If the data you enter follows a certain pattern, such as static numerical increments, the Autofill feature will save time filling the data.

2. In a separate column enter the numeric data that coincides with the countries, states, or regions. You can see an example of this step in Figure 52.1.

N O T E   Additional data can be entered in several columns relating to the geographical area your data is representing. For example, if the data you are presenting includes more than two variables, that is fine. Microsoft Map will accept several variables to be displayed within your map.

3. If you would like to have your data's titles included on the Data Map, you can enter them as column headings. This will allow the titles to show up on the map's legend.

FIG. 52.1

Be sure to separate your data in a columnar fashion

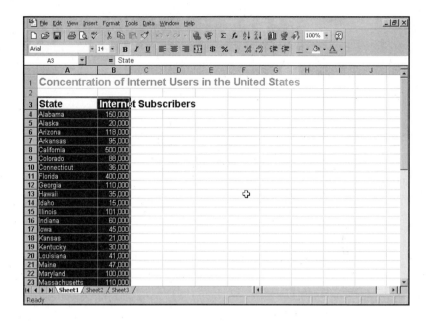

Displaying the Data

Once you have created all of the necessary columns of data on your worksheet, it's time to plot the data on to the map. The following steps will provide you with the necessary information.

1. Drag your selection area to include all of the data you would like included in the Data Map. You must include all numeric values and geographic selections.

2. Click the map icon included on the toolbar or choose Insert, Map to display the map layout crosshair.

3. Use the crosshair pointer to determine the size of the map you would like to display your data. Figure 52.2 illustrates this task.

   The Unable to Create Map dialog box appears if Excel was unable to recognize the data you have provided. For instance, suppose your data had two column headings named "Colorado" and "Michigan." The Unable to Create Map dialog box will appear because your data will be represented on a map of the United States, but the computer does not know if you wish to have Hawaii and Alaska included within the map. There are nine different geographic maps you are able to choose from. Choose the map that coincides with your particular data. The previously mentioned dialog box will also show if the Microsoft Map feature was not properly installed.

   If the data provided matches with more than one map style, the Multiple Maps Available dialog box will appear on your screen. Simply click the map choice that will best display the data to fit your needs.

Part

VIII

Ch

52

FIG. 52.2
Use the crosshair
pointer to determine
the size.

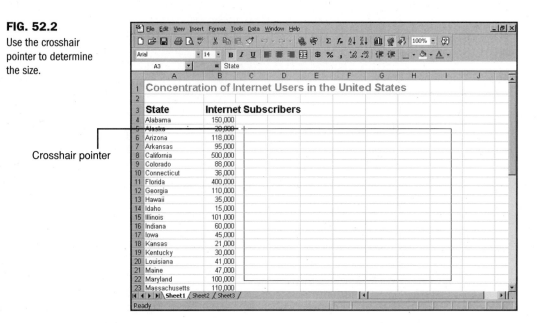

Crosshair pointer

4. Once you have completed steps one through four, the Data Map should show up on-screen, along with the Microsoft Map Control Dialog box and the Microsoft Map toolbar. This can be seen in Figure 52.3.

FIG. 52.3
The Microsoft Map
toolbar will help you to
customize your data.

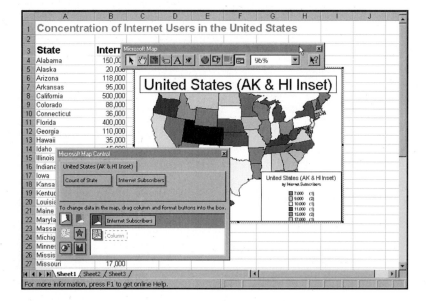

5. The Microsoft Map Control box allows you to decide how you would like to display the data on the Data Map. To change how the data appears on the Data Map, simply drag the icons into the white box at the bottom of the dialog box. To drag the items, just click the icon, and the mouse pointer will turn into a hand pulling a small handle. Drag the selected icon to the white box, and your data will be displayed as you selected.

The format section in the white box describes how your data will appear. The six buttons to the left are your choices. They include: value shading, category shading, dot density, graduated symbol, pie chart, and column chart. These six buttons can only be used to define the format you would like to use. See the following Table 52.1 for descriptions and functions of each button. The column section within the white box is used to define which column of data on your worksheet will be defined with which format type, as described earlier. The headings that you supplied for the data on your worksheet will show up on draggable boxes in the upper section of the Microsoft Map Control box. To see a visual description of this process, please refer to Figure 52.4.

Part VIII

Ch 52

FIG. 52.4

Dragging the icons will change the way your data is displayed

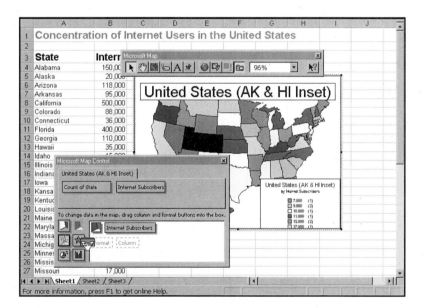

Table 52.1   Data Choices

Button	Name	Description
	Value Shading	This icon allows you to shade your data's numeric values within the Data Map
	Category Shading	This icon colorizes the category your data represents. (Country, State, Region, and so on)

continues

Table 52.1   Continued

Button	Name	Description
	Dot Density	Displays numeric value per category such as Internet users per state. Users being the numeric value and the state being the category.
	Graduated Symbol	A round symbol that changes with increase or decrease in numeric value.
	Pie Chart	The pie chart will increase or decrease in size relative to differences between numeric values.
	Column Chart	The bar graph shows differences, per category, between numeric values.

T I P If you would like to change the color of certain attributes within your map you can do this by double clicking inside the white box of the Microsoft Map Control box. The Format Properties box will appear and allow you to define properties for the legend within your Data Map or the format properties.

6. Once you have completed the format and column properties of your data map just close the Microsoft Map Control box by clicking its Close button, the (X).

N O T E When adding a Data Map to a Word Document or PowerPoint Presentation you must have first saved your data in Access or Excel. After you choose Insert, Object, Microsoft Map, it will ask you to select an external data source. You must retrieve the data files you created in Access or Excel. Once that is completed, you can return to the normal map creation processes. ■

Customizing Your Map

Once you have completed the steps in creating your Data Map, you may want to change its appearance. To reopen the Data Map main toolbar, double click the Data Map. The toolbar will allow you to customize your Map by using the tools shown in Table 52.2:

Table 52.2   Data Map Tools

Button	Name	Description
	Select Objects	You are able to drag and select certain parts of the map for repositioning or selecting.
	Grabber	The Grabber allows you to reposition the map within it's specified frame. Just position the grabber over the map, click, then move to selected area.
	Center Map	The Center Map feature allows you to center the map in accordance to the position of the pointer.

Data Map Tools	Name	Description
	Map labels	The Map Labels feature allows you to name, with text, the state, province, country, and so on. by just dragging the pointer over the selected area. When the text of the selected area you have chosen pops up, just click again and it will remain on the map.
A	Add Text	The Add Text feature allows you to position the pointer anywhere on the map and type in text.
	Custom Pin	This feature allows you to place pins anywhere on Map the map. Position the pointer over the desired area and click the mouse.
	Display Entire	The Display Entire feature allows you to return the magnification value to full or 100%.

Part

VIII

Ch

52

TIP When working with a map you have access to Microsoft Map Help Topics. This is found under the Help menu. It should answer any questions you may need addressed.

Insert a Scanned Picture

If you have a scanner, a collection of Kodak PhotoCD images, or if you work with images on Web pages, then you are able to use this excellent image-editing program-Microsoft Photo Editor. This application can be used through Word, Excel, or PowerPoint.

In order to use the Photo Editor, first you need to select an image or photo that you would like to include in your presentation. After inserting the selected image or photo into your document, you will then be able to change its size, texture, color, or shape accordingly.

1. Select the area within the PowerPoint presentation, Excel Worksheet, or Word Document where you would like the scanned photo to be placed.

2. Choose Insert, Picture, then Scanner. At that point, the Microsoft Photo Editor application will be brought up on the screen.

3. Scan your picture. Different instructions will be given with different scanners, so make sure you follow your scanner's proper procedures.

4. Once the image has appeared in Microsoft Photo Editor, you are able to make changes to the image. Photo Editor allows you to crop the picture, add special effects, adjust color, contrast, or brightness. If you need additional help, just go under the Help command and click Photo Editor Help.

5. Once you have edited the picture to your liking, click Exit and Return To on the Photo Editor File menu. Figure 52.5 shows an example of a photo placed in a Word Document.

FIG. 52.5

Photos can really spice up a document.

N O T E If you did not install Microsoft Photo Editor during your initial installation, just rerun the setup program and reinstall the additional software.

Inserting an Existing Image

Suppose you are developing a Web site that displays your favorite hobby, sport, movie star, and so on. To make the Web site much more interesting you would probably want to include photos and other types of graphics. Microsoft Photo Editor is a great tool to prepare images for the Web. The following steps will aid you in the creation of photos to Web graphics.

1. Click the Start menu, go to Microsoft Photo Editor and click. The main Photo Editor screen will appear.

2. Next, you either have to scan your photo or open an existing photo file. To scan a photo simply go to File on the main menu bar, then Scan Image. At this time you will either have to use your hand-held scanner or your flatbed scanner to collect the photo.

3. Once you have scanned your image you are ready to manipulate the image to your liking. You have several different choices by using toolbars or menus.

 T I P It's important that you save your Web files as either a JPEG or GIF. These two file types are the most common file types on the Web. They are accepted by every browser available on the market. JPEGs are used for photographs because of their high compression capabilities. JPEGs also save photos in 16.7 million colors as opposed to GIFs 256 colors. This makes for a much more realistic photo. As for the GIFs, they are used more for saving graphics that you create using a paint program such as Paint Shop Pro 4.12.

Using Microsoft Photo Editor Features

To enhance the quality of your photo, Photo Editor has an array of tools available. Along with image-enhancing capabilities, Photo Editor also comes with many tools that will manipulate your photos. You can change the texture, add a transparent background, emboss, and much more. Take time to explore the possibilities.

To help you understand the capabilities of Photo Editor you need to familiarize yourself with the icons you probably have never worked with before. The icons and their functions are listed in the Table 52.3.

Table 52.3   Photo Editor Buttons

Button	Name	Description
	Scan	This icon allows you to automatically scan a photo.
	Select	This allows you to select certain ranges on the photo. Once a selection has been made, you are able to manipulate the selected area by using the desired tools.
	Zoom	Allows you to zoom in or out from the photo. Figure 52.6 shows a selection that has been zoomed in on.
	Smudge	This allows you to manipulate the photo by dampening the sharpness of the photo.
	Sharpen	This feature allows you to heighten the quality of the photo.
	Image Balance	This allows you to increase or decrease the brightness.
	Set Transparent Color	This allows you to set a color for the back ground. This is especially useful if you plan to insert your photo on the Web. You can match the photo's background to your Web Page's background.
	Rotate	Allows you to rotate your image in any direction.

Part **VIII**

Ch **52**

 TIP   Under the Image and Effects menus of Photo Editor you will find many additional photo manipulating tools. Some include Negative, Despeckle, Posterize, Edge, Chalk and Charcoal, Emboss, texturizer, crop, resize, and so on. These tools are very useful for inserting photos in presentations and are especially useful for creating images for the Web.

If you are making photo files for the Web, make sure you save them as JPEG file types. It allows for a more realistic photo, and it is accepted by all browsers.

FIG. 52.6
The selection tool allows you to choose a section and perform any function.

Using Office Art

With the increased user capabilities of PowerPoint 97, there has been a new addition of Office Art drawing and graphics features. These capabilities allow you to create charts and add text to graphics. Plus, you can use 3-D and drop shadow effects, along with transparent fills, textures, and other picture modifying elements.

The Updated and Enhanced Features of Office Art

Office Art is the new set of drawing tools that are shared by all of the Office 97 programs. These tools allow you to create enhanced presentations, drawings, and creative shapes for logos, headlines, and letters.

In the following list you will find a list of some of the Office Art features along with a description of their capabilities.

Perspective Shadows   There is now a large selection of shadows with perspective that you can adjust the depth and angle of in order to make your pictures more realistic.

Connectors   You can enhance the effectiveness of your flowcharts and diagrams by adding straight, angled, and curved connectors between the shapes. The shapes are able to be moved while still keeping the connectors intact.

Bezier Curves   The new curve drawing tool allows you to create exact curves on documents.

AutoShapes   This new tool has added features that help make drawing diagrams, creating flowcharts, adding navigation buttons, and annotating documents much easier. The new AutoShape categories are block arrows, flowchart symbols, stars and banners, action buttons, connectors, and callouts.

Object Alignment   You are now able to space objects horizontally and vertically.

Precise Line-Width Control   You can select preset options or even customize line widths.

Image Editing   You are now able to adjust the brightness or contrast of a picture which makes for easier viewing.

3-D Effects   You are now able to transform two dimensional shapes into realistic 3-D objects. You are now able to even adjust the lightsource.

Transparent Backgrounds   If you want to insert an image or bitmap into a presentation or web page without having the image stand out, you can change the background color.

Office 97 Drawing Features

As we mentioned earlier in the section about Office Art, Office 97 has maximized the drawing capabilities in order for presentations and documents to have a more interesting effect. This drawing tool can also be used to create images for your Web pages. The new drawing features can be used with Excel, Word, and Powerpoint. Each application has the drawing toolbar available.

To get the Drawing toolbar (see Figure 52.7) to appear click the Drawing icon on the main toolbar in Powerpoint, Excel, or Word.

The Drawing toolbar and it's buttons perform many functions as shown in Table 52.4.

Table 52.4   The Drawing Toolbar

Button	Name	Description
Draw ▾	Draw	Allows you to choose predetermined shapes, called Autoshapes(described previously). Also allows you to manipulate the position of the image you are creating.
▵	Selections	Allows you to select an image or a part of an image to perform certain editing tasks such as a drop shadow or color change.
↻	Free Rotate	Allows you to rotate an image.
AutoShapes ▾	Autoshapes	Choose from a list of several different shapes in order to create an image.
\	Line	Allows you to insert a line.
↖	Arrow	Allows you to insert an arrow.
▢	Rectangle	Allows you to insert a rectangle.
○	Oval	Allows you to insert an oval.
▤	Text Box	Allows you to enter a text box on or surrounding an image.
◢	Insert WordArt	Allowsyou to pull up the WordArt dialog box and enter word art onto an image.
◇	Fill Color	Allows you to fill a shape or text. You can also choose a selection and use this function to fill the selection with the desired color.

continues

Table 52.4   Continued

Button	Name	Description
	Line Color	Allows you to choose a color before entering a line into your image.
	Font Color	Allows you to change color of text.
	Line Style	Allows you to choose from 1 different styles of lines. Most of them only differ by thickness.
	Dash Style	You can choose from 8 different types of dash lines.
	Arrow Style	You can choose from 13 different arrow types.
	Shadow Settings	This function allows you to create a drop shadow from an image. There are 20 different styles to choose from.
	3-D	The 3-D button allows you to turn any 2-D object into a 3-D object. There are 20 different styles to choose from.

TIP The selection button enables you to choose a certain section of an image and perform any of the above editing tasks in that section alone.

Creating an Image

To create an image using the Office 97 Drawing feature, complete the following steps.

1. Click the Drawing icon from the main toolbar in order to display the Drawing toolbar.
2. Select which shape or text you would like to create. This can be done by using the Autoshapes feature or the WordArt application. Each reside within the Drawing toolbar. Figure 52.7 illustrates this procedure.

FIG. 52.7
Using the Authoshape feature can save time.

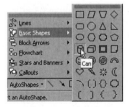

3. Choose what characteristics you would like to add to your image. Examples would be 3-D, drop shadow effect, or adding lines to your image. There are numerous characteristics you may add to an image. Figure 52.8 illustrates the creation of a 3-D image.

Using the Office 97 Advanced Drawing Features

To create a Drop Shadow drawing feature, follow these directions:

1. Choose a shape by selecting the AutoShapes button or Draw button from the Drawing Toolbar.

2. Edit the shape to your specifications by adding lines, text, color, and so on. All of these manipulation features are available on the Drawing Toolbar.

3. Click the Shadow button from the toolbar. A menu of several different styles of drop shadows should appear off of the toolbar.

4. Select the type of shadow you would like. This is done by selecting the shadow button< as described earlier, from the Drawing Toolbar.

5. Edit the image to your specifications. This is done by using the many editing features available on the Drawing Toolbar.

FIG. 52.8

3-D images can be easily created and edited with the Office 97 Drawing feature.

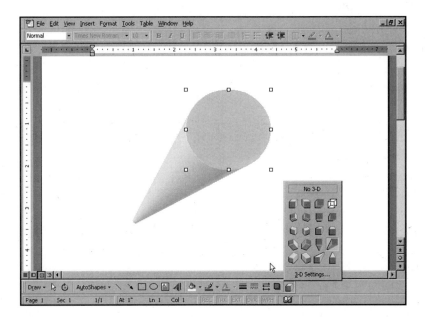

N O T E When creating a 3-D object using the Shadow feature, it will only work with a few of that available shadow selections. This happens because of the properties of the shape you have chosen sometimes don't coincide with the production of a shadow. ▪

Microsoft Office 97 has enabled the user to create realistic 3-D objects with minimal effort. Through the use of advanced toolbars, and manipulation tools, you can make even a boring presentation interesting.

Complete the following procedures to produce a 3-D image.

1. Click the AutoShapes button or the Draw button on the Drawing Toolbar.
2. Choose the shape you would like to create.
3. Click the 3-D button on the Drawing toolbar and choose the type of 3-D position you would like.

To change the light source of the 3-D object you have chosen, click the 3-D Settings button from the 3-D toolbar button menu. Then click the lighting button from the 3-D Settings toolbar. The 3-D settings toolbar will also allow you to adjust the length, direction, surface, color, and tilt of your object. Figure 52.9 show the 3-D Settings toolbar.

FIG. 52.9
The 3-D Settings toolbar has many editing functions.

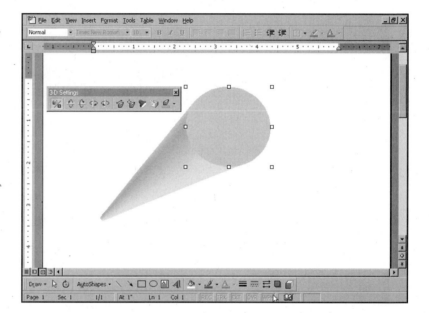

Using WordArt

Microsoft Office comes with an application called WordArt. WordArt can create different text effects that can be added into presentations, documents, worksheets, and so on. You can even create different text effects and add them to your Web pages. This application can easily take the place of any sort of text editor. With WordArt, the user is allowed to add text effects such as 3-D, different shapes and styles, shading, and more.

FIG. 52.10
You can add a 3-D image to a presentation in PowerPoint.

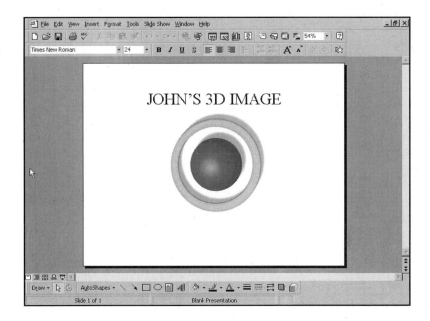

To use WordArt to complete some of these different effects just complete the following instructions.

1. Within the application you choose, locate the destination you would like your text to appear.

2. Choose Insert, Picture, WordArt or just click the WordArt icon on the Drawing toolbar. The WordArt Gallery dialog box should appear within your application. The dialog box should have 36 different text effects styles available. Figure 52.11 shows you the different text effects.

FIG 52.11
The WordArt application has a wide range of text effects to choose from.

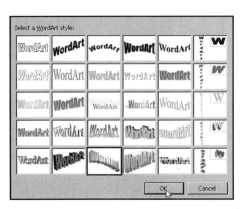

3. From the list of text styles choose the one you would like to use and click OK, or double click the text style. Once you have done this, the Edit WordArt Text dialog box will appear. Type in the text you would like to alter. Figure 52.12 shows you how this will look.

FIG. 52.12

Use the Edit WordArt Text dialog box to type your message or word.

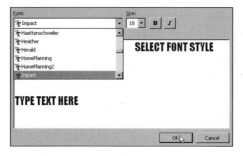

FIG. 52.13

The WordArt toolbar.

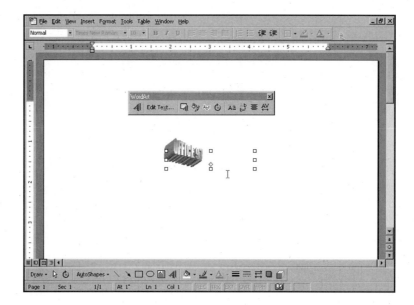

Customizing WordArt

After you have followed the procedures to get your WordArt on your document, presentation, or worksheet, you are able to customize it by using the WordArt toolbar. To activate the toolbar, double click the WordArt you are working with. Figure 52.13 illustrates the WordArt toolbar and it's buttons.

The WordArt toolbar and its buttons are shown in Table 52.5.

Table 52.5 The WordArt Toolbar

Button	Name	Description
	WordArt	Displays the WordArt Gallery.

Button	Name	Description
	Edit Text	Allows you to edit the text you chose for your WordArt.
	WordArt Gallery	Displays the WordArt Gallery.
	Format WordArt	Allows you to change the characteristics of the WordArt you have chosen. The Format WordArt dialog box includes the following tabs: Colors and Lines, Size, Position, Wrapping, Picture, and Text Boxes.
	WordArt Shape	This allows you to manipulate the shape flow of the text.
	Free Rotate	This function allows you to rotate the text you have chosen.
	Same Letter Heights	This allows you to align the height of the text equally throughout the entire word.
	WordArt Vertical Text	This allows you to align the text vertically one letter on top of another.
	Word Art Alignment	This allows you to right, center, or left align the chosen WordArt text.
	WordArt Character Spacing	This allows you to manipulate the spacing between the text characters.

Part

VIII

Ch

52

The size of the WordArt you are working with can be changed by enlarging the edit box surrounding the image. This is done by positioning the mouse pointer over the edit box until it becomes a double arrow. Move the pointer until the desired size is achieved.

TIP Using the WordArt application can be very beneficial when making text images for Web pages. Files can be saved as .GIFs and .JPEGs, the two most common image file types on the Web.

Using Other Drawing Tools

Along with the previous drawing and editing tools mentioned, Office 97 comes with an array of drawing tools. These tools let you create freehand images for PowerPoint presentations, Word Documents, and Excel Worksheets.

Using Microsoft Drawing 1.01

Another drawing feature that Office 97 is equipped with is the Microsoft Drawing feature. Compared to the Office 97 Drawing feature Microsoft Drawing 1.01 can't perform the amount of functions, but can still provide images, usually simple ones, within the documents you are creating.

In order to get the Microsoft Drawing 1.01 application to appear, just choose Insert, Object, then Microsoft Drawing 1.01. The application will appear as it does in Figure 52.14.

FIG 52.14
Microsoft Drawing 1.01 allows you to create simple drawings to insert into your documents.

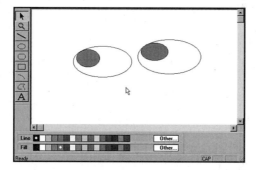

Microsoft Drawing 1.01 toolbar and it's functions are very simple. The toolbar buttons available on Microsoft Drawing 1.01 perform the same tasks as the similar icons in the Office 97 Drawing feature. Figure 52.15 shows what the Microsoft Drawing 1.01 toolbar looks like.

FIG 52.15
The functions this application performs are quite simple, but can still provide helpful visual aids.

 You are able to edit images in the Microsoft Drawing 1.01 application by choosing File, Import, then choosing which image you would like to edit. Figure 52.16 shows an imported picture within Microsoft Drawing 1.01.

FIG 52.16
An imported image from a separate file can be edited.

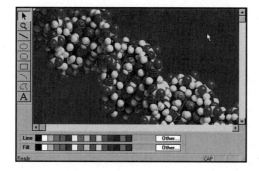

Using Office 97 Clip Gallery

Along with being able to create very intricate images using several drawing features, Office 97 also comes equipped with Art already created. You can choose from Clip Art, Pictures, Sounds, and Videos. Each of these choices has hundreds of examples to choose from.

Opening Microsoft Clip Gallery

Follow these steps to open the Microsoft Clip Gallery.

1. In your document select the area you would like the object displayed.

2. Choose Insert, Object, Microsoft Clip Gallery. The Microsoft Clip Gallery dialog box will appear.

3. There are four different tabs to choose from. You can choose from Clip Art, Pictures, Sounds, or Videos. Click the tab of the appropriate object and on the right side of the window a list of object categories will appear. This helps you to easily find the picture you are looking for. Figure 52.17 shows the Microsoft Clip Gallery application within a Word Document.

4. Once you have chosen the object you want just click Insert and you will return to the document you are currently working in.

5. When you return to the document you will notice the Picture toolbar appears by the image. Figure 52.18 displays the toolbar within the document.

FIG 52.17
Microsoft Clip Gallery has literally thousands of objects to choose from.

Editing Art from Microsoft Clip Gallery

Once the art has been placed in your document, spreadsheet, and so on, you may want to change some of the characteristics of the image. This can be done by using the Picture toolbar.

The Picture toolbar is shown in Table 52.6.

FIG. 52.18

The Picture toolbar allows you to edit the picture within your document.

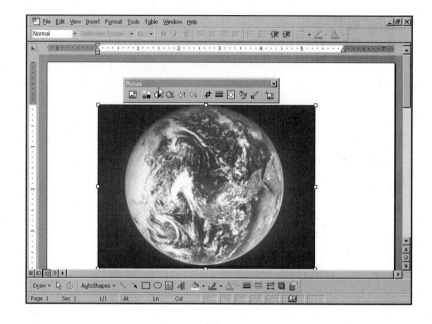

Table 52.6 The Picture Toolbar

Button	Name	Description
	Insert Picture	This allows you to insert another picture on top of the picture already placed in a document.
	Image Control	This lets you change the shading and lighting characteristics of a picture.
	More/Less Contrast	Increase or decrease the contrast of the picture.
	More/Less Brightness	Increase or decrease the brightness of the picture.
	Crop	You can crop certain parts of an image.
	Line Style	Choose from several different types of line styles.
	Word Wrapping	You can choose from several different text formats to place onto an image.
	Format Picture	Allows you to change the color, size, and so on, of the picture.
	Set Transparent Color	You can select a transparent background so the image blends in with your document's background.

Button	Name	Description
	Reset Picture	Allows you to revert to the normal style of the picture. It will erase all editing you had done.

Quickly Inserting a Bar Chart

When creating a document or presentation you may have several bits of data that you have to describe. Describing data such as population per time zone within the United States is hard to describe by just writing the information out. Sometimes using graphs or bar charts will aid in relaying data.

Using Microsoft Graph 97 Chart

Microsoft Graph 97 Chart is a tool that can quickly add a bar graph to an application.

To create a bar chart follow these steps:

1. Select where you would like to place your bar chart.
2. Choose Insert, Object, Microsoft Graph 97 Chart. At this time a small group of Excel cells and a bar chart will appear as they do in Figure 52.20. Default values are already present within the cells and the chart.
3. Tailor the default values to fit you data's content.

TIP In order for the data to change, you must click off of the cell you are editing and on to another cell. This will change the data represented in the bar graph.

4. Once you are done tailoring the bar chart just close the application by clicking the close box (X).

Using Microsoft Note-It

Office 97 has added a plethora of interactive applications for the user. One such application is Microsoft Note-It. This application allows the presenter of the presentation or document to place a picture within the document with the desired text within the picture. Once the user double clicks the picture the pre-formatted text appears within the document or presentation.

FIG. 52.19

Inserting pictures can easily increase the effectiveness of your document or presentation.

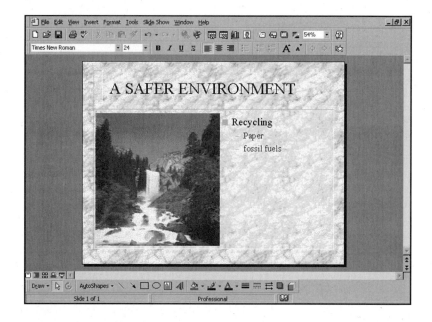

FIG.52.20

Data can be displayed more clearly using a bar chart.

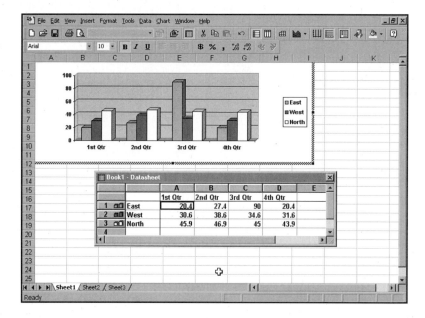

Adding the Clickable Caption

The ability to add pre-formatted text adds interactivity to a document or presentation. You can use the caption feature to add text to a certain image, document, or presentation. Use the next steps to add this feature.

1. Select the position where you would like the caption picture to appear.

2. Choose Insert, Object, Microsoft Note-It. The Microsoft Note-It application will appear within your document, presentation, or spreadsheet. Figure 52.21 illustrates the Microsoft Note-It Application box.

FIG 52.21

Adding interaction with Microsoft Note-It can make any document or presentation more interesting.

3. In the Choose A Picture box, select the picture you would like to use.

4. In the Type Your Caption Here box, type the text you would like to accompany the picture.

5. In the Type Your Note Here box, type the text you would like to appear once the user double clicks the caption picture.

6. Choose whether or not you would like Big or Small text.

These tools and applications in Microsoft Office 97 have been provided in order to make creative 3-D images, text, presentations, spreadsheets and documents. Take advantage of the many uses that these tools provide. ●

CHAPTER 53

Charts and Equations

by John Purdum

Microsoft Office 97 has added and updated many features that allow you to compile and present data and statistical information in a convenient way, for both the user and the audience. Presenting data through the use of charts or equations, whether they are bar charts, pie graphs, or line graphs, allows for a clearer representation. The point of any presentation is to get an idea across in a way that will leave an impact and convince the audience that your data is factual and practical. Or you might want to present statistical data to yourself to aid you in a decision. The next few sections illustrate how to create statistical information in this way. ■

Microsoft Chart

Use Microsoft chart to effectively display information to viewers. Complex and simple graphing tools will aid you in this process.

Microsoft Equation Editor

Use the Microsoft Equation Editor to display complex equations by using a variety of critical mathematical symbols and templates.

Microsoft Organization Chart 2.0

Use Microsoft Equation Editor to display hierarchies of many types—anywhere from a family tree to the flow chart of a Fortune 500 company.

Using Microsoft Chart

Office 97 comes equipped with an array of charting and graphing tools, but Microsoft Chart is the most complete and comprehensive charting application. Microsoft Chart allows the user to present data in a quick, professional manner that allows the viewer to comprehend the data easily. Microsoft Chart can be used in Excel, Word, and PowerPoint.

Suppose you want to compare the amount of money you spend on your electric bill per month. You are not only able to create a chart that will illustrate the monthly payments, but you could manipulate the chart in a way to compare that data with another variable such as season. This would then allow you to compare the obvious fluctuation of your electric bill because of factors such as temperature.

Creating a Chart

Follow these steps to create a chart:

1. Find the location in your presentation where you would like to place your chart.

2. Choose Insert, Object, Microsoft Excel Chart. This opens a default chart as illustrated in Figure 53.1.

FIG. 53.1

Notice the default statistical labels Food, Gas, and Motel.

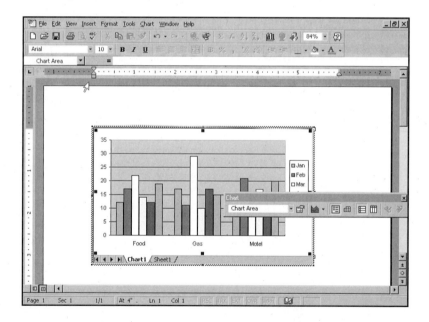

A toolbar should appear along with the default chart style, as shown in Figure 53.2.

3. Define the numerical statistics. At the bottom of the default chart there are two tabs. The active tab is the Chart tab; the inactive tab is the Sheet tab. Click the Sheet tab to enter your data. This process is shown in Figure 53.3.

FIG. 53.2

The toolbar performs many chart-manipulating functions.

FIG. 53.3

Click the sheet tab to enter your data.

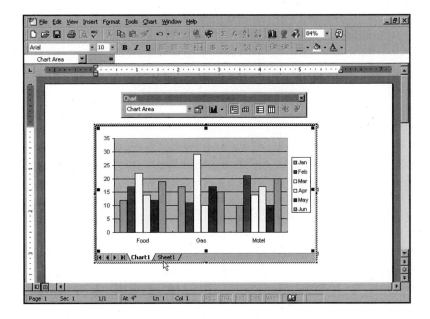

Using the Data Sheet

Entering the numerical data for your chart is very similar to entering data into any worksheet in Excel. The following steps aid you in entering your data.

1. Enter the Heading titles into the worksheet. The highlighted headings in Figure 53.4 illustrate this process. This particular example plots the amount of money spent on gasoline per month.

N O T E Don't worry about the positioning of your column headings to your row headings. You can change the information displayed under the X-axis by using the By Row or By Column buttons on the Chart Toolbar. ▨

2. Enter the data you want displayed on your chart under the appropriate columns.

3. Click the Chart tab and you see your data displayed on the chart. Figure 54.5 illustrates the data entered on a 3-D bar chart.

FIG. 53.4

Simply use the Tab key to move from cell to cell to enter your data.

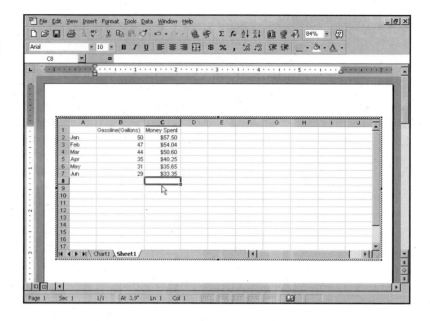

FIG. 53.5

Use the Chart toolbar to choose the chart that best identifies your data.

Customizing Your Chart

Once you have entered all of your data, you might want to customize the chart output in order to optimize your statistical representation. The Chart toolbar allows you to change the characteristics of your chart with a click of the mouse.

N O T E In order to make changes of any sort to your chart, you must activate the Edit Box surrounding the chart. This can be done by double-clicking your chart. The Chart Toolbar then appears in order to edit your chart. ■

In the next section, you'll see just a few of the customizing options that are available.

■ *Change the Color of the Graphing Medium.* To change the color of your graphing medium, which could be a section of a pie graph or a bar of a bar chart, just click the section until the edit box appears; then click the Format Data Series from the Chart Toolbar, select the Patterns tab, and choose a color.

 You can eliminate having to use the Chart Toolbar by double-clicking the section you would like to edit. The dialog box appears for that particular section.

■ *Changing Chart Type.* To change the chart type, click the chart type button on the Chart Toolbar and choose which type of chart you would like to use. Figure 53.6 shows you the types of charts you can choose from.

FIG. 53.6

There are several different charts to choose from.

■ *Changing X-Axis Titles.* If you would like to switch the data heading information on the X-axis, click the By Row or By Column button from the Chart Toolbar. This will change the output of your graph.

The Chart Toolbar and its buttons are shown in the following table:

Button	Name	Description
Chart Area	Chart Objects	This drop-down box allows you to select the area of the chart you would like to change. If you would like to change or remove the Legend, click the down arrow, then click legend. The edit box will appear around the legend of your chart.
	Format Selected Object	This button allows you to make a series of changes to the cosmetics of your chart by using 7 different tabs. For instance, if you wanted to change the order in which your statistical headings were displayed on the chart, you would choose the "Series Order" tab, then arrange the axis headings as you like.
	Chart Type Chart Type	This button allows you to choose which type of chart you would like to represent your data through. There are 18 different chart styles to choose from. Choose the chart that best represents your data, not the one that looks the best.

Part

VIII

Ch

53

continues

continued

Button	Name	Description
	Legend	This button allows you to delete or create a legend.
	Data Table	Allows you to create a table that shows the actual numeric value in accordance with the graph. This will definitely enhance whatever data presentation you are creation. It allows for comparison and validation of data.
	By Row	This button allows you to arrange your data by row. For instance, if you choose to represent your data by row, the row headings you have created will appear on the X-axis of the chart.
	By Column	This button allows you to arrange your data by column. If you choose to display your data in this way, the column headings you create will appear on the X-axis.
	Angle Text Downward	This button allows you to create a label for the specific graphing element such as a bar or a section of a pie chart. The label will be angled downward.
	Angle Text Upward	This button creates the same label as mentioned above, but the label is angled upward.

 TIP You can also manipulate your chart by clicking the area you would like to change. For instance, if you would like to change the color of one set of the graphing sections, just double-click the left mouse button over the section you would like to change and the Format Dialog box for that particular section appears.

Using Microsoft Equation 3.0

Office 97 empowers the user to create complex mathematical equations through the use of Microsoft Equation 3.0. Microsoft Equation 3.0 is an application that enables someone to display an equation by using a wide range of mathematical symbols.

While its use is limited to the display of complex equations, theorems, and the like, it's practical in the fact that it lists nearly all of the possible character elements that are used to create an equation. Suppose you constructed a theory upon which you would like to give a lecture—you aren't able to use a standard keyboard to type in the required mathematical symbols used in your formula. Microsoft Equation 3.0 enables you to build a mathematical presentation through defined mathematical symbols and templates. Microsoft Equation 3.0 can be used in Excel, Word, and PowerPoint.

N O T E Microsoft Equation 3.0 does not actually perform mathematical equations. It allows you to display them in conjunction with text and numerical characters. ▪

Using the Microsoft Equation Toolbar

Before you construct your equation, you should familiarize yourself with the Equation Toolbar and its many functions. The toolbar is comprised of both mathematical symbol lists and mathematical templates that aid you in creating an equation. The upper row on the Equation Toolbar consists of only mathematical symbols while the bottom row consists of the templates.

To open Microsoft Equation 3.0 choose Insert, Object, Microsoft Equation 3.0. You will notice a small edit box as shown in Figure 53.7. Figure 53.8 shows the Equation toolbar.

FIG. 53.7

The edit box can be sized by placing the pointer on the border then dragged to the desired shape.

The Equation Toolbar and its buttons perform the following functions:

FIG. 53.8

The Equation Toolbar and its 19 function buttons.

Button name	Description
Upper Row, Mathematical Symbols	
Relational Symbols	This button allows you to choose from 11 different relational symbols. A relational symbol expresses a shared relationship between two quantities. Most numerical relationships are equivalence, equality, and inequality.

continues

Part
VIII

Ch
53

continued

Button name	Description
Upper Row, Mathematical Symbols	
Spaces and Ellipses	This button allows you to choose from alignment symbols, different types of ellipses, and several different spacing symbols.
Embellishments	When you use mathematical variables to define a complex equation, chances are the variables will include bars, hats, primes, or dots attached to them in order to define a further mathematical function for that variable. This button allows you to insert some of these symbols.
Operator Symbols	This button allows you to choose from 12 different types of operator symbols. Operator symbols define a deeper mathematical operation.
Arrow Symbols	This button allows you to choose from 14 different arrow styles. Arrows can illustrate many mathematical functions. Some are yield, convergence, or a mapping.
Logical Symbols	This button allows you to choose from 8 different logical symbols. Some logical symbols represent "since," "therefore," "and," or "for all."
Set Theory Symbols	This button allows you to choose from 12 different set theory symbols. An example would be the union and intersection of two mathematical variables.
Miscellaneous	This button allows you to choose from 18 common mathematical symbols. Some symbols available are Planck's constant, perpendicular symbol, and partial derivative symbol.
Greek Characters (Lowercase)	This button allows you to choose from 28 lowercase Greek characters.
Greek Characters (Uppercase)	This button allows you to choose from 28 uppercase Greek characters.
Lower Row, Mathematical Templates	
Fence Templates	This button allows you insert a fence template to your document. An example of this would be enclosing similar expressions between an a pair of coexisting symbols. Some of these would include brackets, parentheses, and brackets used in quantum physics.

Button name	Description
Lower Row, Mathematical Templates	
Fraction and Radical Templates	This button allows you to choose from 10 different template styles that are used to create long division layouts, radicals, and fractions.
Subscripts and Superscripts	This button allows you to choose from 15 different templates that help you create subscripts and superscripts. These templates also allow you to position expressions above or beneath defined points.
Summation Template	Thisbutton allows you to choose from 5 different templates that create various types of sums. You are able to create repeated sum definitions.
Integral Templates	This button allows you to choose from 21 different types of integrals. Some of these include line integrals, triple integrals, and so on.
Underbar and Overbar Templates	This button allows you to create expressions by using bars. You can place the bars above or beneath the selected character or characters.
Labeled Arrow Templates	This button allows you to choose from 6 different arrow types. This function could be used to define a yield function in a chemistry formula.
Products and Set Theory Templates	This button allows you to choose from 20 products, coproducts, or intersection and union (set theoretic).
Matrix Templates	This button allows you to choose from 12 different templates that allow you to build determinants, matrices, and so on.

N O T E   A template in Microsoft Equation Editor 3.0 is used as a predetermined set of symbols and unfilled *spots*. You can build equations and expressions by filling these templates. After choosing a template, the insertion point will move to the "slot" that is commonly filled first. ■

Creating an Equation

Microsoft Equation 3.0 aids you in building equations by allowing you to choose templates and symbols from the Equation Toolbar. Upon choosing a template fill, you are able to fill in the slots. Equation Editor then adjusts spacing, formatting, and so on to adhere with typical mathematical layout.

Follow these steps to create an equation:

1. Choose where within your document, worksheet, or presentation you would like your equation placed.

Part
VIII

Ch
53

2. Choose Insert, Object, then Microsoft Equation 3.0. At this time you notice a small edit box along with the aforementioned Equation Toolbar.

3. Depending on the size and complexity of your equation, choose symbols or templates to complete the equation. Figure 53:9 shows the completion of the Fibonacci Number (Generalized) *w.*

N O T E You shouldn't try to manipulate the equation, such as text color, size, and the like, until you have documented the entire equation. If you do try to manipulate the equation you can distort the proper mathematical style. ▪

FIG. 53.9

The Fibonacci Number displayed within a Word Document.

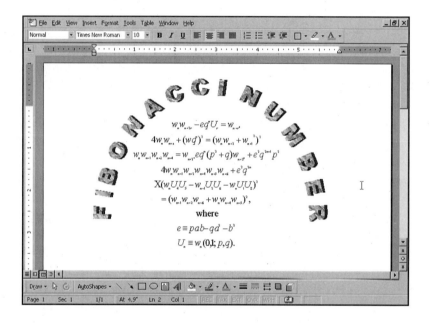

TIP When the edit box surrounds the equation you are working on you can use Microsoft Equation's standard Toolbar at the top to perform typical corrections or changes. Some of these procedures include text size, text style, bold, italic, and so on. Perform these tasks just as you would in a basic Word, Excel, or PowerPoint document.

Microsoft Organization Chart 2.0

Microsoft Organization Chart 2.0 enables you to set up data in a hierarchy-type manner in order to show the flow of a topic.

This application has many practical purposes. It can be used to show the flow chart of a company's organization method. With the president at the top of the hierarchy the chart will flow downward, displaying the positions occupied by others below the president. You could use this application to better understand the production of a certain product, such as a computer. You would be able to visually pinpoint at what station the manufacturer inserts the hard drive or from whom they purchase their software packages. With the increase of subscribers to the Internet many people would find this tool helpful in mapping out a Web Site. You can make these charts infinitely complex or as simple as you want. Microsoft Organization Chart 2.0 can be used in Excel, Word, or PowerPoint.

Perform the following steps to produce an organization chart:

1. Move your pointer to the area in which you would like your chart to be displayed.
2. Choose <u>I</u>nsert, <u>O</u>bject, then Microsoft Organization Chart 2.0. At this point you notice that the Microsoft Organization dialog box appears on the screen. The default chart setting can be seen in Figure 53.10.

FIG. 53.10
The center box is the hierarchy's main subject.

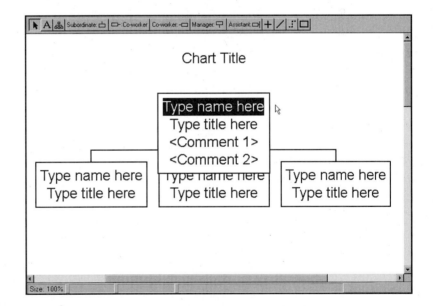

Part
VIII

Ch
53

N O T E In order to open Microsoft Organization chart in PowerPoint you must choose Insert, Picture, and Microsoft Organization Chart 2.0. To open this application in Excel you choose Insert, Object, then double-click Microsoft Organization Chart 2.0. ■

3. Begin creating your chart by adjusting the title name from default to your desired title. You notice that double-clicking the box creates a drop box that enables you to enter additional comments. Complete this process until you feel you have entered enough information.
4. Continue entering text within the remaining two boxes.

Now that you have created the beginning of your chart, you have to customize your chart's layout depending on your information's characteristics. You now have to arrange and edit your chart to fit accordingly with your information. Using the Microsoft Organization Toolbar makes this procedure very simple (see Figure 53.11). Figure 53.12 displays the Organization Chart Toolbar.

FIG. 53.11

Continue pressing Enter to add to the box.

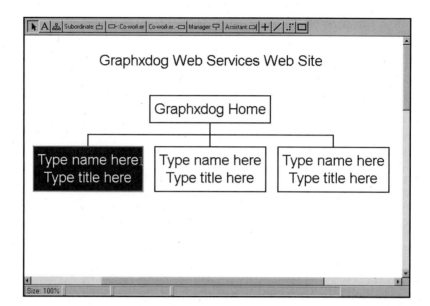

FIG. 53.12

Customize the layout of your chart with this toolbar.

Organization toolbar

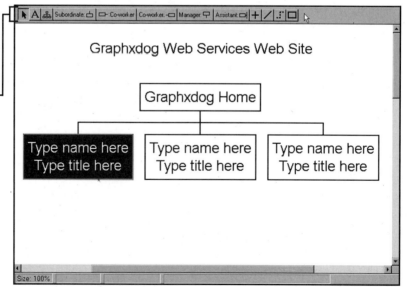

The Organization Chart Toolbar performs the following functions:

Button name	Description
Select	This button enables you to select which box of the organization chart you would like to work with.
Enter Text	This enables you to enter text within the chart area or background.
Zoom	This enables you to zoom in on a certain part of your chart. You might want to single out a certain section of your chart in order to correctly position your titles. This will enable you to do that.
Subordinate	This enables you to place an additional box beneath a box you select. In a chart, if you wanted the floor manager to be positioned beneath the division manager you would click Subordinate then click the box titled "division manager."
Co-Worker(Left)	This enables you to place a chart box to the left of a selected box.
Co-Worker(Right)	This enables you to place a chart box to the right of a selected box.
Manager	This button enables you to place a box directly above the selected box.
Assistant	This button will enable you to place a box beneath and to the left or the right of the selected box.

Changing Chart Attributes

Along with being able to organize your chart to your specifications, you are able to change certain attributes within your chart. These functions can be done by using the menu bar.

The menu bar performs the following tasks:

View Menu. The View menu enables you to size the window to actual size, 200% of actual size, or 50% of actual size. It also enables you to show or hide the drawing tools, including creating horizontal or vertical lines, diagonal lines, auxiliary lines, or rectangles.

Styles Menu. The Styles menu enables you to choose from eight different chart styles. These can act as a template for quicker information input.

Text Menu. This enables you to change the font characteristics. It can change text color, alignment, style, and size.

Boxes Menu. The Boxes menu enables you to change the characteristics of the boxes within your chart. It can change the color, add a drop shadow, change border style, border color, and line style.

Lines Menu. The Lines menu enables you to change the characteristics of your lines such as thickness, style, and color.

Chart Menu. The Chart menu changes your chart's background color.

TIP All of the previous menu options can be performed by right-clicking the area you would like to change. For instance, if you would like to change the background color of a chart, right-click the background. A menu box appears with a list of options. Choose color, then pick a color from the color dialog box. This process can be seen in Figure 53.13.

FIG. 53.13
Choose which attribute you would like to alter.

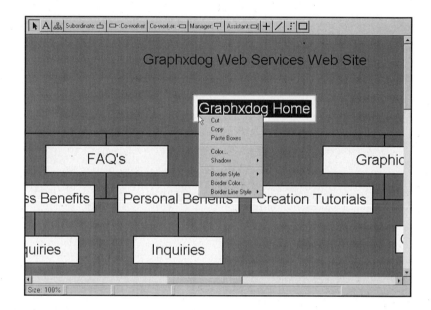

Part IX: Applying Office 97 in a Network or Workgroup

CHAPTER 54

Sharing and Securing Resources

by Nancy Warner

Resources on a network can be scarce. Only so much storage space is available, and it can disappear quickly. By sharing resources (such as files and printers) on your computer, you and other users can increase the capacity of your network.

When you share resources on your computer, you keep more control of them than you would if you had put them on a network storage device. You can control who can access the resources and what they can do with those resources. ∎

Share resources

You can make Office documents available to other users by sharing resources. Shared resources may need to be secured, so that only certain people can use them.

Use two levels of security

You can protect shared resources so that only authorized users can access them. Depending on your network, you may be able to choose between share-level and user-level security.

Understand the password cache

The number of passwords that a user needs to remember can quickly become overwhelming. The password cache can help you manage all your passwords.

Share and secure Office documents

Office documents are shared in basically the same way that all files are, but some special considerations exist.

Share Access databases

You have unique challenges and opportunities in sharing the data that Access databases contain.

Using Resource Sharing and Security

Mainframe computers were the original networks, with their many workstations continually sending and receiving information. While a user was initiating the work from the workstation, the mainframe did all the work—it had to because it had all the resources. All the processing power, storage devices, and printers were connected to the mainframe. This arrangement made security easy to set up, because all requests to use resources had to go through a single location.

The growth of the PC resulted in a new type of network, in which workstations could perform tasks without making a request of a central computer. The PC has all the resources that the mainframe once had a monopoly on—namely, processing power and storage capability. Although the PC became a valuable tool, it could not replace the mainframe; it still had to use the mainframe's resources. Eventually, the PC was created with many of the same capabilities as the mainframe, which resulted in the creation of client-server networks.

In a client-server network, one or more PCs (or a mainframe) acts as a server that controls access to network resources. PCs that are being used as workstations are called *clients*. Clients request the use of resources from servers. The final step in the evolution of the network (called peer-to-peer networking) allowed workstations to use resources located on other workstations. Although a server normally handles security, peer-to-peer networking also gives the client the capability to control access to its own resources. Figure 54.1 shows the different elements that a modern network can contain.

FIG. 54.1
Modern networks must integrate the new technology with the old.

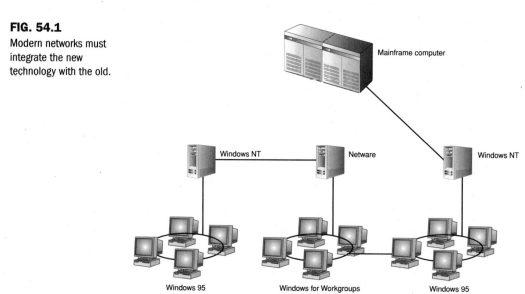

You can use peer-to-peer networking to share files created in any of the Office applications. The following two sections discuss how to share resources and which types of security you can use.

Sharing Peer Resources

A network is normally made up of many workstations and several servers. Files that many users need to use are usually stored on a server, but in some situations, files are stored on a workstation. Resources that are stored on a workstation instead of on a server are called *peer resources* because they are shared by means of peer-to-peer networking. Peer-resource sharing is a networking service that must be installed before you can take advantage of it. Open the Control Panel and double-click the Network option to see whether peer-resource sharing is installed. Figure 54.2 shows a Network properties dialog box for a workstation with peer-resource sharing installed for Microsoft Networks—File and print sharing for Microsoft Networks.

FIG. 54.2

You can share files and printers by using peer-resource sharing.

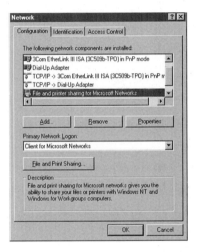

Part

IX

Ch

54

CAUTION

Peer resources can be shared for either Microsoft Networks or NetWare Networks, but they cannot be shared for both. Use the sharing method that gives the most users access to your resources, using the desired security method.

If peer resource sharing isn't installed, you have to install it before you can give other users access to documents on your computer. To install peer-resource sharing, follow these steps:

N O T E   For information about how to perform this procedure in Windows NT Workstation, see your Windows NT Workstation documentation. ▨

1. Open the Control Panel.
2. Double-click the Network option.
3. Click the Add button in the Configuration page of the Network properties dialog box to open the Select Network Component Type dialog box, shown in Figure 54.3.

FIG. 54.3

Use Select Network Component Type dialog box to select network components.

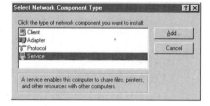

4. Choose the Service option.

5. Click the <u>A</u>dd button to open the Select Network Service dialog box, shown in Figure 54.4.

FIG. 54.4

Use the Select Network Service dialog box to install the proper services.

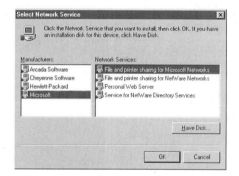

6. Select Microsoft in the Manufacturers list.

7. Select File and Print Sharing for Microsoft Networks in the Network Services list.

   If your computer is on a NetWare network, select File and Print Sharing for NetWare Networks instead.

8. Click the OK button.

N O T E To use file and print sharing for Microsoft Networks, you must have the Client for Microsoft Network installed. To install that client, follow the steps that you use to install peer-resource sharing, but choose Client and Client for Microsoft Networks in place of Service and File and Print Sharing for Microsoft Networks. ▉

When peer-resource sharing is installed, you can share files and printers with other users on your network. If you want to, you can share only files or only printers by choosing the Network option in the Control Panel and then clicking the File and Print Sharing button. The File and Print Sharing dialog box, shown in Figure 54.5, opens, allowing you to specify which types of resources can be shared on your computer.

A consideration that you must make before sharing resources on your computer is how to protect them from unwelcome users. Two types of security are available to protect shared resources; the following section covers both of them.

FIG. 54.5

Use this dialog box to select the resources to be shared.

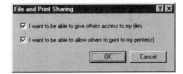

Securing Shared Resources

You can use Windows 95 security to limit the availability of shared resources on a network. The type of network and the type of established security measures determine the type of security that you can use on your network. Depending on those factors, several elements become important in securing shared resources:

- Windows 95 logon
- Share-level security for peer-resource sharing
- User-level security for peer-resource sharing
- Password cache

The Windows 95 logon becomes a key security feature if computers on a network must be logged onto a Windows NT domain or NetWare server. Windows cannot be started if a proper logon does not occur. In this case, network resources are protected, because all access to the network is denied. Remember that this feature prevents a user from starting Windows only when your network is using a Windows NT domain or NetWare server.

Forcing a computer to log onto a network before it can access the resources of that network protects the network resources. However, a user could still access the files on a computer without logging on to the network. A user could access files by using one of two methods:

- Starting the computer in safe mode
- Using a boot disk to start the computer

If these security problems are unacceptable, you should look into installing Windows NT Workstation on your computer.

Users can connect to shared folders and printers on Windows 95 computers that are using file and printer sharing services. You can protect these shared peer resources by using either share-level or user-level security. Both types of security require a user to supply a password to use a shared resource.

Share-level security (which is discussed further in "Using Share-Level Security" later in this chapter) is the simpler of the two types of security for peer-resource sharing. All the security and password validation is done on the computer that has the shared resource. Figure 54.6 shows the communication that takes place if a computer accesses a shared resource that uses share-level security.

FIG. 54.6

For share-level security, each computer handles the security of its own resources.

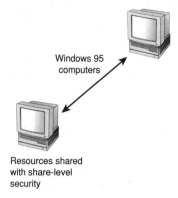

Windows 95 computers

Resources shared with share-level security

You can use share-level security to share resources as read-only, full access (read, write, or delete), or a combination. When using share-level security, you can specify how resources can be used when a password is supplied, but you cannot specify how specific users can use those resources. In other words, anyone who supplies the proper password can use the resource. You can supply a different password to be used for read-only and full access, however.

 TIP A resource can be shared more than once. If you need some users to have access to a resource for only a week and other users to have access for a month, share the resource twice and use a different password each time.

User-level security is a more complex type of security that uses the power of your network's built-in security. Instead of the security mechanism that resides on the machine that has the shared resources, user-level security checks users and their passwords against the network server. This type of security is referred to as *pass-through security* because the user name and password are passed through to the network server for authentication. Figure 54.7 shows the communication that takes place if a computer accesses a shared resource that uses user-level security.

FIG. 54.7

User-level security uses the network server to limit access to resources on other computers.

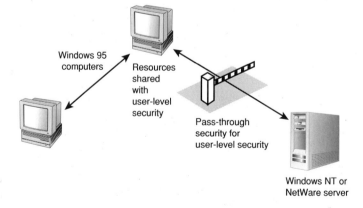

Windows 95 computers

Resources shared with user-level security

Pass-through security for user-level security

Windows NT or NetWare server

You can use user-level security to share resources as read-only, full access, or custom. (Custom sharing is discussed further in "Using User-Level Security" later in this chapter.) You don't have to supply any passwords—only users or groups of users. All user names and password information are maintained on the network server. Figure 54.8 shows the process that occurs when a user asks to use a resource shared with user-level security. The process goes as follows:

1. A computer requests a shared resource.
2. The computer with the shared resource asks the server if the user name and password supplied with the request are valid.
3. The server tells the computer with the shared resource if the user name and password are valid or invalid.
4. The computer with the shared resource either gives the requesting computer access to the resource that was requested or refuses it access, depending on the outcome of step 3.

When you designate which users can use the shared resource, you also designate how they can use it: read, write, delete, and so on.

FIG. 54.8
The network server decides whether a user can use a shared resource.

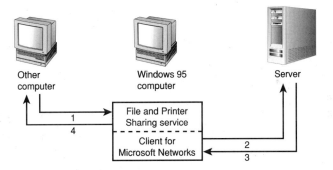

> **CAUTION**
> Groups of users are designated on a network server. A group named Accounting, for example, might include all the users in the accounting department. If a shared resource is made available to a group, everyone in the group is added, so be sure that is what you want.

Using Share-Level Security

To use share-level security, you must specify in your network properties. To verify the security that your computer is using, open the Network properties dialog box by choosing the Network option in the Control Panel. Click the Access Control tab. Figure 54.9 shows the Network Properties dialog box for a computer that is using share-level access control.

FIG. 54.9

Access control security is specified in the Network properties dialog box.

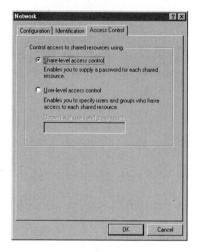

Share-level security puts the burden of limiting the access to shared resources on the computer that contains the shared resource. These resources can be folders or printers.

To share a folder by using share-level security, follow these steps:

N O T E Share-level security cannot be used on NetWare networks. ▪

1. Open a Windows Explorer window.
2. Right-click the Program Files folder.
3. Choose Sharing from the shortcut menu that appears. Figure 54.10 shows the Sharing dialog box that opens.

FIG. 54.10

The Sharing page indicates when a resource is not shared.

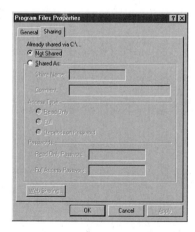

4. Click the Shared As button to share the folder.

The shared resource is given a default share name: the first 12 letters of the folder's name. The share name is what other users see when they use Network Neighborhood to locate the resource on your computer.

5. Change the share name to **Share Test.**

6. Add the comment **This is a test.**

 You can hide a shared resource from users who are browsing the Network Neighborhood by placing a dollar sign (**$**) at the end of the share name (**INVISIBLE$**, for example). The resource is still shared; users just can't find it by using Network Neighborhood.

---

7. Choose Depends on Password Access Type. When you choose this option, the type of access that users have depends on the passwords that they provide.

8. Type **read** in the Read-Only Password text box.

9. Type **full** in the Full Access Password text box.

Figure 54.11 shows what the Sharing dialog box should look like now. Users who enter **read** as the password have the capability only to read files in this folder, but users who enter **full** have full access to the folder. Entering passwords is covered in "Understanding the Password Cache" later in this chapter.

FIG. 54.11

The share name can be different from the resource's actual name.

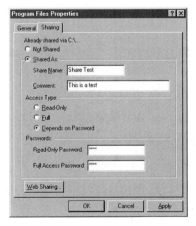

N O T E For security purposes, typed passwords appear on-screen as asterisks (*).

 If you leave the password text box blank, users do not have to supply a password when they use that resource.

---

10. Click the OK or Apply button to force your changes to take effect.

11. Retype your password choice(s) and click the OK button.

N O T E Click the Web Sharing button in the Sharing dialog box to share a resource by using the Internet's HTTP or FTP standards. ■

▶ **See** "Browsing Office Documents with Internet Explorer 3," **p. 890**

▶ **See** "Creating Web Pages with Word," **p. 910**

Using User-Level Security

You must specify that you want to use user-level security. This property is listed in the Network properties dialog box, which you open by choosing the Network option in the Control Panel and clicking the Access Control tab. Figure 54.12 shows the Network properties dialog box for a computer that is using user-level access control.

FIG. 54.12

You must specify the location of valid users and groups when you set up user-level security.

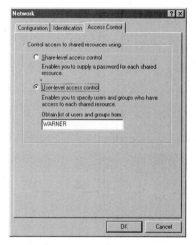

In addition to choosing user-level access control, you must provide the location of the users, groups of users, and their passwords. Those lists are used to enforce the security measures that you define for your shared resources. If you have to make this change in your network properties, you must restart the computer before the change takes effect.

N O T E If you are using file and print sharing for Microsoft Networks, a Windows NT domain or workstation must be your security provider. If you are using file and print sharing for NetWare, a NetWare server must be your security provider. ■

User-level security passes the job of limiting the access to shared resources to the computer that maintains security for the entire network. To share a folder by using user-level security, follow these steps:

1. Open a Windows Explorer window.

2. Right-click the Program Files folder.

3. Choose Sharing from the shortcut menu that appears. Figure 54.13 shows the Sharing dialog box that opens.

FIG. 54.13

You use the Sharing dialog box to give users access to shared resources.

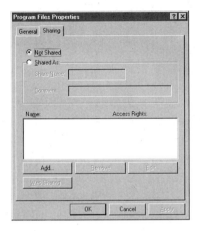

4. Click the Shared As button to share the folder.

   The shared resource is given a default share name: the first 12 letters of the folder's name. The share name is what other users see when they use Network Neighborhood to locate the resource on your computer.

5. Change the share name to **User** Test.

6. Add the comment **This is a test**.

N O T E To stop a resource from being shared, open the Sharing dialog box and click the Not Shared option button. ▨

That's all there is to sharing a resource when you use user-level security, but you still need to specify which users or groups of users can use the shared resource. As mentioned earlier in this chapter, you can specify what rights each user has to the shared resource. Follow these steps to allow users to access a shared resource:

7. Click the Add button to open the Add Users dialog box, which is shown in Figure 54.14. The list on the left is the list of users and groups obtained from the network server that will enforce security. On the right side is a list of the types of rights that can be given to a user: Read Only, Full Access, and Custom.

8. Choose The World (which basically means anyone) in the user list and click the Read Only button. Now anyone can have read-only access to the shared resource.

Part

IX

Ch

54

FIG. 54.14

User lists are obtained from the network server.

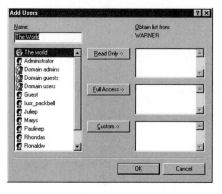

9. Choose the user Administrator and click the Full Access button to give that user full access to the shared resource. A single person in an icon represents a single user.

10. Select a group of users (indicated by an icon with two people) and click the Custom button.

11. Click the OK button and define the custom set of rights for the group you added in the previous step. Figure 54.15 shows the Change Access Rights dialog box that you use to customize users' access rights.

FIG. 54.15

Use this dialog box to customize rights for users who need only particular types of access.

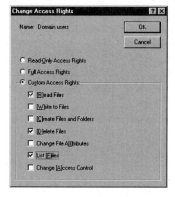

12. Select the rights that you want the user or group to have.

13. Click the OK button.

You can give custom rights to users or groups that need only a certain type of access. For example, you may want to give a user who performs backups or data entry more than read-only access but less than full access.

Figure 54.16 shows the Sharing page after the preceding changes.

FIG. 54.16

You can modify the user list for a shared resource in the Sharing page.

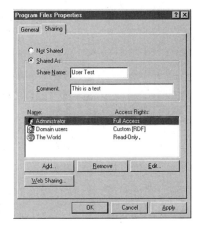

14. Click the OK or Apply button to force your changes to take effect.

 T I P   Use Net Watcher to see who is accessing your shared resources. Start Net Watcher by choosing it in the System Tools subfolder of the Accessories folder.

Understanding the Password Cache

When a network has many resources, the number of passwords needed to use all of them can become overwhelming. You could write all the passwords on a piece of paper and keep them near your computer, but that would nearly defeat the purpose. The password cache solves the problem of remembering multiple passwords; it stores your passwords in a password-list file, which has the extension .PWL. Password list files are encrypted, and unencrypted passwords are never sent over a network. This file can store passwords for the following network resources:

■ Windows 95 shared resources that are protected by share-level security

■ Password-protected applications that are written to the Master Password API

■ Windows NT computers

■ NetWare servers

> **CAUTION**
>
> You need to re-enter all your passwords if you delete the password-list file. Keep the passwords written down and stored somewhere safe, such as in your wallet or at home.

The password list is loaded when you log on to Windows 95. If the proper password isn't supplied to the Windows 95 logon or if you click the Cancel button, the password list is not loaded, and you have to enter a password for each password-protected resource.

Part

IX

Ch

54

When you try to access a password-protected resource, you see the Enter Network Password dialog box. You enter the password and click the OK button to use the resource. If the check box at the bottom of the dialog box is checked, the password is stored in the password cache.

TIP Use the password-list editor (PWLEDIT.EXE) to remove passwords from your password list. If the password-list editor not in your Windows directory, you can locate it on your Windows 95 disk(s), in the Admin\Apptools\Pwledit directory.

Now that you know how to share resources, you can apply that knowledge to sharing your Office documents. The following section discusses sharing Office documents.

Sharing Office Documents

Before you can share your documents, you need to know where they're saved. In Word, choose Tools, Options to open the Options dialog box. Then click the File Locations tab. Figure 54.17 shows the Options dialog box open to the File Locations page.

FIG. 54.17

Different types of files can be saved in different locations.

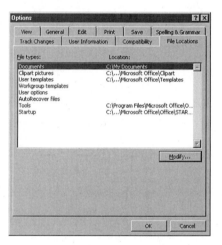

NOTE While Each Office application has a setting for file locations in the Options dialog box, the location of this option in the Options dialog box varies from one application to another. ▓

File types are listed on the left side of the File types/Location list, and the location of those types of files is listed on the right. Clip art, for example, is saved in the C:\Program files\Microsoft Office\Clipart directory. Documents normally are saved in the C:\My Documents directory. If that is where you save most of your files, you may not want to share that directory. You can change the Documents location by clicking the Modify button and choosing a new folder as the new default location for saving documents.

Create different folders for different users or groups and share each folder for the user or group that it was created for. You can make the shared folders subfolders in the directory in which you save your documents by default. Then you just have to double-click a shared folder when you save a document that needs to be shared.

Place all the documents that you want to share in a folder that you also want to share. Then use the sharing method that matches the security being used on your network.

You may have also noticed the two types of templates that can be saved. *Templates* are skeleton documents that are used to create new documents; they use the .DOT file extension. Two factors determine which templates are available and which tab templates are displayed with when you choose File, New:

- The file-location setting
- The folder in which the template is stored

Figure 54.18 shows the New dialog box that opens when you create a new document.

FIG. 54.18
Templates for new documents can be categorized.

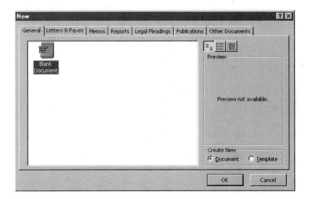

N O T E Any document (.DOC) file that you save in a Templates folder or one of its subfolders also acts as a template.

Templates are saved in the location specified in the File Locations section of the Options dialog box. Only templates in the specified folder(s) or its subfolders appear in the New dialog box. User templates appear in the General tab; templates in subfolders of the Templates folder appear in tabs that have the same names as the subfolders. Workgroup templates also appear in the General tab of the New dialog box.

Save any new templates that you create in the appropriate subfolder of your Templates folder, such as the Reports folder. Template (.DOT) files that you save in the Templates folder or any of its subfolders appear in the New dialog box.

TIP Generally, workgroup templates are those templates that all use. These templates should be stored in a folder that is shared by means of read-only access. Have your network administrator store workgroup templates on a network server for maximum protection, so that you or other users won't accidentally change them.

▶ **See** "Creating and Using Templates," **p. 91**

Sharing Access Databases

Access databases are unique among files that can be created by Office applications. Most Office applications create files that are then distributed to users, although several users can create them in a collaborative effort. Access databases, however, change continually throughout their existence.

The continual change of Access databases occurs because users add and modify data. Also, other users periodically generate reports from that data. This interactive process makes Access databases valuable.

> **N O T E** If you don't need any extra security for your Access database files, share them just as you would any other file. ▪

The type of security available through sharing isn't capable of handling Access files because of the unique nature of database files. Parts of a database file should be read-only; some parts should allow users to delete, add, and modify data; and other parts should allow users to add data but not delete or modify it. For these reasons, Access has its own system for securing data.

Applying Database Security in Access

The degree of security needed in an Access database can vary greatly. Access has several tools that allow you to customize the security of your database. The main security tools available to you in Access are the following:

- Passwords
- Encryption and decryption
- User accounts and groups
- Permissions

One of these security measures (or a combination) should fit your needs. These methods are discussed further in the following four sections.

Using Passwords   The simplest way to secure your database files is to set a password. Passwords are encrypted so that a user can't read them by reading the database file's contents. Each time that a password-protected Access file is opened, a dialog box requests a password from the user. If the user supplies the correct password, the file opens. Otherwise, the user is not allowed to open the file.

Passwords only limit who can open a database. Unless user-level security (described in "Using Accounts and Groups" and "Using Permissions") has been defined, a user can do anything to a database when it's open. If the database is being shared among a small group of users, setting a password is an ideal way to protect data without spending a great deal of time setting up a more advanced security scheme.

> **CAUTION**
>
> Replicated databases can't be synchronized if database passwords are defined. For more information see the section "Using Replication in Access."

▶ **See** "Using Replication in Access," **p. 1096**

Before you can set a password for a database, all users (including you) must close the file. You should also make a backup copy and store it in a secure location. To protect a database by adding a password, follow these steps:

1. Choose File, Open Database to display the Open dialog box.
2. Click the Exclusive check box.
3. Select a database and click the Open button or double-click the database to open it. The database is opened for exclusive use, so no other users can open it.
4. Choose Tools, Security, Set Database Password to open the Set Database Password dialog box, shown in Figure 54.19.

FIG. 54.19
Use this dialog box to set your database password.

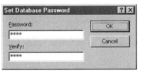

Part

IX

Ch

54

5. Type the password (passwords are case-sensitive) in the Password and Verify text boxes.
6. Click the OK button.

If you lose or forget your password, you cannot open the database.

> **CAUTION**
>
> If a database links to a table in a password-protected database, the password is cached (unencrypted) when the link is established. This unencrypted cached password could compromise the security of your database.

The password is now set. The next time any user opens the database, he or she must supply the password. To remove the password from the database, open the database exclusively and choose Tools, Security, Unset Database Password. Enter the password in the Unset Database Password dialog box and click the OK button.

If a database password doesn't supply the right kind of security, you may want to look into user-level security for an Access database—not to be confused with user-level security for shared resources. "Using User-Level Security" earlier in this chapter covers that topic.

N O T E If user-level security is being used, you must have Administer permissions to set a database password. ▣

Encrypting and Decrypting Access Databases   Encrypting a database doesn't limit access by authorized users; it compacts the file so that a user can't view its data by using a word-processing or utility program. For this reason, you should use encryption in conjunction with a password or user-level security. If you are using user-level security and want to encrypt or decrypt a database, you must have Modify Design permissions for all tables.

Decrypting a database simply reverses the action of the encryption process. To encrypt or decrypt a database, follow these steps:

1. Start Access without opening a database, or close the current database, if it is to be encrypted.

N O T E A database can't be encrypted or decrypted if any user has it open. ▣

2. Choose Tools, Security, Encrypt/Decrypt Database to open the Encrypt/Decrypt Database dialog box, which is similar to an Open dialog box.
3. Select the database you want to encrypt or decrypt.
4. Click the OK button.
5. In the Encrypt/Decrypt Database As dialog box, specify the name and location of the encrypted or decrypted database.
6. Click the Save button.

   If you use the same name and location for the encrypted/decrypted file as the original file, the original file will only be overwritten if the entire operation is performed successfully.

CAUTION

You must have enough space on your hard drive to store both the original database and the encrypted/decrypted database or the operation fails.

Using Accounts and Groups   Accounts and groups are used for user-level security. User-level security is similar to the security used on a network. Users must supply an account name and password before they can use the database. Information about user accounts is maintained in the workgroup information file. These accounts are placed in groups. Although additional groups can be created, two groups are present by default:

■ Admins (for administrators)

■ Users (for users)

Permissions are granted to users and groups to control their use of the database. The Users group, for example, may be allowed to read and write data to a table used for recording customer orders but denied all access to a table that stores payroll information. The Admins group has full access to all objects in a database. You can create additional accounts and groups to customize security for your database.

Adding user-level security to a database is a complex procedure that involves many decisions. Review the procedure for adding user-level security before beginning your planning. To add user-level security to a database, follow these steps:

1. Join a secure workgroup or create a new workgroup information file. You must exit Access to change workgroups. If you are using Windows 95, create or join a new workgroup by running Wrkgadm.exe.

> **CAUTION**
>
> The default workgroup information file is created with the name and organization that you supplied while installing Office. This information is easy to find, and a user can use it to create a duplicate file easily. Then he or she can use the duplicate file to get around user-level security.

2. Open a database.

3. Choose Tools, Security, User and Group Accounts. Figure 54.20 shows the User and Group Accounts dialog box, which appears when you choose this command.

FIG. 54.20

You use this dialog box to change user and group accounts.

4. Verify that the Admin account is selected in the Users page.

5. Click the Change Logon Password tab.

6. Type the new password (which is case-sensitive) in the New Password and Verify text boxes, but don't type anything in the Old Password text box.

7. Click the OK button.

8. To create an administrator's user account, click the New button in the Users page to open the New User/Group dialog box, shown in Figure 54.21.

9. Type the user name in the Name text box.

FIG. 54.21

You use the user name and personal ID to create an encrypted account name.

10. Type a personal identification in the Personal ID text box. The personal ID is not a password; it is used to encrypt the user name.

11. Click the OK button to create the new account.

12. Choose Admins in the Available Groups list and click the Add button.

13. Click the OK button to create the new administrator account.

14. Exit Access and log on as the administrator, using the account that you just created.

15. Remove the Admin user from the Admins group by selecting the Admin user and clicking the Delete key in the User and Group Accounts dialog box.

N O T E   If you want a user other than the administrator to own the database and all the objects in it, log on as that user. At minimum, the user must have Read Data and Read Design permissions in the database that is being secured. ▪

16. Open the database that you want to secure.

17. Choose Tools, Security, User-Level Security Wizard.

18. Follow the directions in the wizard dialog boxes.

The User-Level Security Wizard creates a new encrypted database and copies the objects from the database that is being secured. Object types that are selected in the first wizard dialog box are made secure by revoking all rights to those objects for the Users group. No changes are made in the original database that was being secured.

N O T E   After you use the User-Level Security Wizard to secure a database, only members of the Admins group have access to secured objects. ▪

After securing a database, you want to establish users and assign them permissions for objects in the database. The following section, "Using Permissions," shows you how to assign permissions to users.

Using Permissions   Permissions are used to limit the user's capability to work with different database objects. A user must have an account before he or she can be assigned permissions. To assign permissions, follow these steps:

1. Open the database that contains the objects that you want to secure.

TIP If you have only your groups created, you can assign permissions to groups and add the users later.

2. Choose Tools, Security, User and Group Permissions to open the User and Group Permissions dialog box, shown in Figure 54.22.

FIG. 54.22

You can assign permissions to individual users or groups of users.

3. If you want to assign permissions to individual users, click the Users option button in the Permissions tab.

   If you want to assign permissions to a group of users, click the Group option button.

4. Click the name of the user or group to which you want to assign permissions.

5. Use the Object Type drop-down list box to select the type of objects to choose from.

6. Select the object you want to assign permissions for.

TIP Select multiple objects to assign permissions for more than one object at a time.

7. Use the check boxes in the Permissions section to assign permissions to the selected user/group for the select object(s).

   A checked box means that the permission is assigned, and an unchecked box means that the permission is not assigned. Selecting some permissions automatically selects related permissions.

8. Repeat steps 3 through 7 for as many users and objects as necessary.

9. Click the OK button.

CAUTION

Permissions assigned to forms, reports, or modules do not take effect until the database is closed and opened again.

▶ **See** "Using VBA in Access," **p. 705**

Part

IX

Ch

54

Using Replication in Access

Replication allows you to make a copy of a database that can be synchronized with the original database. Synchronization causes changes in data to be shared between the two databases and any design changes in the original database to be made in the replica. The original database is called the *design master*, and the copy is called the *replica*. You can create more than one replica. All the replicas and the design master together are called a *replica set*.

N O T E Any of the replicas in a replica set can be made the design master. Only one member of the replica set can be the design master at any time, however. ▪

You can use replication to simplify many complex tasks, such as the following:

- *Distribute software written in Access.* Keep a design master that has the current version of the software and synchronize it with the replicas to make software updates.

- *Distribute data to users who must travel.* A salesperson could take a replica of a sales database to work with while traveling. Periodically, he or she could synchronize the database replica with the master.

- *Balance the load placed on database servers.* Load balancing can be accomplished by creating several replicas of a database to be placed on different servers. Users can then be distributed among the different servers to balance the load that each server has to handle.

- *Back up databases.* Using Replication to perform backups allows the database to remain online. In other words, users can continue to make changes during the backup.

Creating a Replica Creating a replica makes a copy of a database design and the data contained in that database. You can use a replica for many purposes. To create a replica of a database, follow these steps:

1. Using the exclusive option, open the database that you want to make a replica of.

> **CAUTION**
>
> Make yourself aware of all the changes that are made in your database when it is replicated. AutoNumber fields, for example, generate unique random numbers instead of unique sequential numbers. The Access help file contains a complete list of the changes.

2. If the database is protected by a password, remove the password (as described in "Using Passwords" earlier in this chapter).

3. Choose Tools, Replication, Create Replica and click the Yes button in the dialog box that prompts you to close the database.

   If this replica is the first one that you are making for this database, you must first make it a design master. In this case, you are asked whether you want to make a backup copy of the database before making it a design master. You should always have a current backup.

4. Select the location for the replica in the Location Of New Replica dialog box.

5. Click the OK button.

After creating a replica, you eventually will want to synchronize the design master and its replica, as described in the following section.

Synchronizing an Access Database   Members of a replica set are synchronized to exchange all updates that have been made in database objects and data. After two members are synchronized, their database design and the data that they contain are identical. To synchronize, follow these steps:

1. Open the member of a replica set that you want to synchronize.

2. Choose Tools, Replication, Synchronize Now.

3. Enter the name and location of the replica set member that you want to synchronize with the current database.

4. Click the OK button.

 TIP Click the Make *Filename* Design Master check box to make the replica the design master.

5. Click the Yes button when you are asked whether you want to close and reopen the database.

Part
IX

Ch
54

CHAPTER 55

Document Collaboration

by Nancy Warner

Office applications can create documents for publication, spreadsheets to run a company, and presentations to promote ideas. A single person rarely does these things, so Office applications need to let multiple users work together.

The workgroup features in Word, Excel, and PowerPoint allow their files to be worked on or shared by multiple users. Some files can be edited by several users simultaneously and PowerPoint even lets you conduct a presentation on a network. ■

Use master documents

Master documents allow multiple users to work on a document simultaneously.

Review changes

Track Changes lets users review the changes made to a file, accepting or rejecting them as they go.

Combine different versions

Different versions of a document or workbook can be combined to create a single document or summarized workbook.

Route files

Files can be routed to recipients using a routing slip. The file can be sent to all recipients at once or to each one in succession.

Protect files

Entire files can be protected or just certain elements of files can be protected using passwords or warnings.

Collaborating in Word

Microsoft Word lets you create documents that incorporate text and graphics. You can create letters, memos, faxes, newsletters, catalogs, and many other types of documents. Many times, Word is used in a business environment with groups of users that need to work together.

To accommodate the need for users to create documents as a team, Word has workgroup collaboration features that make it easier to protect and track changes in documents. These features can be broken into two distinct categories:

- Workgroup Review Features
- Security Features

Workgroup reviewing tools allow several users to work on a document either simultaneously or in succession and security features help limit the changes that can be made to a document in a workgroup environment. Both of these features are discussed in the next two sections of this chapter.

Reviewing Documents in a Workgroup

Documents created by more than one person have special requirements. There could be many parts to a document, each the responsibility of a different user. Someone could be in charge of creating the documents and need some control over the process, perhaps the final say on changes. Word has several tools to address the needs of documents being created in a workgroup. Those tools include:

- Master Documents
- Versions
- Tracking Changes
- Routing
- Comments

Each of these tools can help with creating documents in a workgroup, but they don't all have to be used. Review the following sections to determine which can best be used in your situation.

Using Master Documents

Only one person at a time can edit a regular Word document. This limitation can make creating a document with many authors very challenging. Either only one person can work on the document at a time, or the revisions must be compiled into a single document every time you want to see the results of everyone's work.

Word provides a tool to allow more than one author to work on a single document at one time. Any changes made to a part of the document are instantly reflected in the entire document. The tool that makes this possible is called a *master document*. Master documents consist of one or more subdocuments. Each subdocument is treated as if it were a regular Word document that is separate from the master document, but the contents of the subdocuments are combined to create the master document. To create a new master document, follow these steps:

1. Start a new document by clicking the New button.
2. Choose <u>M</u>aster Document from the <u>V</u>iew menu.
3. Create an outline of the master document using the Outlining toolbar.
4. Select the headings and text that you want to become subdocuments.
5. Click the Create Subdocument button on the Master Document toolbar, which is shown in Figure 55.1.

FIG. 55.1
The Master Document toolbar can be docked or floating.

> **N O T E**   The subdocument will be created with the heading style and outline level of the cursor's position when it is created. ▪

6. Choose <u>F</u>ile, <u>S</u>ave to save the master document and its subdocuments.
7. After choosing a name and location for the master document, click the Save button.

> **N O T E**   Word, based on the subdocuments' headings, automatically names them and saves them in the same location as the master document. ▪

Now, each user can work on their section of the document by editing the subdocument assigned to that section. Changes saved to subdocuments are instantly displayed in the master document, even if someone is viewing or editing it. When the document is printed, Word combines the master document with all of the subdocuments and prints it as one large document. In addition, Word automatically numbers pages, lines, and footnotes in sequence.

 Choose <u>V</u>iew, <u>D</u>ocument Map to quickly browse very large documents by seeing its structure and content at the same time.

Tracking Changes

The Track Changes feature marks the revisions that are made to a document. Revision marks can be customized by specifying what color they are or how edited text is displayed—if displayed at all.

> **CAUTION**
>
> For the Track Changes feature to be effective, all users who edit a document must use it. If a user doesn't use the feature, other users will not know what edits were made to the document by that user.

To begin using Track Changes, follow these steps:

1. Open the document that you want to edit.

2. Choose Tools, Track Changes, Highlight Changes to open the Highlight Changes dialog box shown in Figure 55.2.

FIG. 55.2

Track Changes While
Editing activates the
Track Changes feature.

3. Click the Track Changes While Editing check box. This activates the Track Changes feature.

N O T E   When the Track Changes feature is inactive, the text TRK in the status bar is dimmed. The text TRK is not dimmed when the feature is tracking changes. ▮

4. ˙Select Highlight Changes on Screen to have the edits displayed on-screen.

5. Select Highlight Changes in Printed Document to have the edits printed when the document is printed.

6. Click the OK button after making your selections.

You can also activate the Track Changes feature by right-clicking the text TRK in the status bar and choosing Track Changes from the pop-up menu. This menu also gives you access to the other Track Changes dialog boxes.

After activating the Track Changes feature, edits that you make on the document will be indicated according to the options that you have chosen in the Track Changes page of the Options dialog box. In addition, the name and initials from the User Information page of the Options dialog box is recorded with the edits. Figure 55.3 shows the Track Changes page of the Options dialog box. Choose Tools, Options and click the Track Changes tab to view this information.

Choose By Author as the color for edits and Word automatically chooses a different color for each different author that edits the document. An author is identified by the name contained on the User Information page of the Options dialog box.

Eventually, you will want to review all of the edits and determine which to accept and which to reject. Changes are reversed if they are rejected and no longer tracked if they are accepted. To accept or reject changes follow these steps:

1. Open the document that you want to review.

FIG. 55.3

Different types of edits can be marked differently.

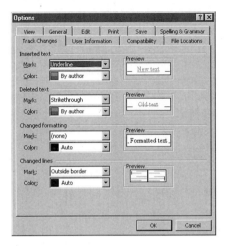

2. Choose Tools, Track Changes, Accept or Reject Changes from the to open dialog box shown in Figure 55.4.

FIG. 55.4

Detailed information about the edit, including the user, is displayed in the Accept or Reject Changes dialog box.

3. Click either of the Find buttons to move to the next or previous edit.

4. Click the Accept button to accept a change or the Reject button to reject it.

 Click the Accept All or Reject All button to immediately accept or reject all changes in a document.

This process can go on until a document is complete. When the process of editing and reviewing is done, you will have your finished document. In addition to the methods for tracking changes outlined in this section, the Reviewing Toolbar has buttons that can be used in the process. Figure 55.5 shows the buttons and what their purposes are.

FIG. 55.5

The Reviewing toolbar.

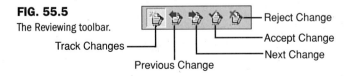

Track Changes

Previous Change

Next Change

Accept Change

Reject Change

Commenting on a Document When reviewing a handwritten or printed document, you probably write notes in the margin or near the text you are commenting on. This very common task can also be done in Word using the Comments feature (previously referred to as Annotations).

Comments can be used to either encourage a change or to explain why a change was made. For example, you could track changes in a document and comment on the edits that you make. Track Changes indicates the edits and Comments explains them. To use the Comments feature, follow these steps:

1. Place the cursor within or at the start of the word that you want to comment on.

N O T E You can also highlight selections of text containing more than one word. ▪

2. Choose Insert, Comment. The text is highlighted and the Comments pane is opened, as shown in Figure 55.6.

FIG. 55.6

The comments pane is contained within the document's window.

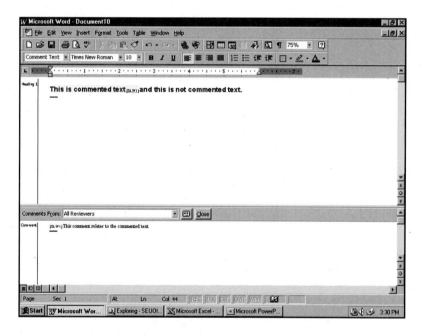

3. Type your comments, which will be identified by your initials and a unique number.

 T I P Click the Insert Sound Object button, which has a picture of a cassette tape on it, to record an audio message to be placed in the comment.

4. Click the Close button to close the Comments pane.

You or other users can view your comments by choosing Comments from the View menu. The Comments pane is displayed as in Figure 55.6. Select a user in the Comments From drop-down list to view only that user's comments.

As with the Track Changes feature, the Comments feature has command buttons on the Reviewing toolbar. Figure 55.7 shows the buttons and how they are used.

FIG. 55.7
The Comments feature buttons appear on the Reviewing toolbar.

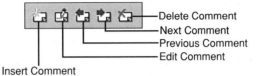

Delete Comment
Next Comment
Previous Comment
Edit Comment
Insert Comment

 T I P Rest the mouse pointer over commented text to view the comments and the initials of the user that entered them in a pop-up window.

Saving and Comparing Versions of Documents Word lets you create versions of a document. You can later compare versions of a document to determine if the changes made in it were necessary. There are two ways to save versions of a document:

- All versions in one file
- A separate file for each version

The next section discusses how to save versions of a document into a single file. After that, there are two sections on how to compare and merge documents.

Saving Document Versions

The ability to save multiple versions of a document in a single file is a new feature in Word 97. This feature, called *version control*, allows you to save a version of a document. After each edit, a new version can be saved until the document is completed. All of the versions are saved in the same file, but only one version of the document is active at a time. The user, the date and time, and any comments entered are saved with each version of a document. To save versions of a document, follow these steps:

1. After creating a new document, choose File, Versions.
2. Click the Save Now button in the Versions In Document dialog box shown in Figure 55.8.

Part
IX

Ch
55

FIG. 55.8
The Versions dialog box lists all the versions of a document.

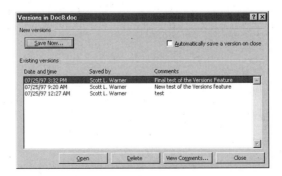

T I P Select the Automatically Save a Version on Close check box to save a new version each time the file is closed.

3. Enter any comments you have in the Save Version dialog box shown in Figure 55.9.

FIG. 55.9

Comments can help others understand the purpose of a document version.

4. Click the OK button to save the document and the version.

5. Enter the name and location for the document in the Save As dialog box and click the Save button.

Use the Versions dialog box to save future versions of the document. You can also use the Versions dialog box to open or delete a version of the document or view comments. After opening an older version of a document, you can save it as a different document in its own file.

N O T E   Word saves only the differences between the different versions to minimize the amount of storage space needed. ▪

Comparing Documents

After completing several versions of a document, it can become hard to remember what changes you have made. You also might have already accepted or rejected changes many times. In this case, you can use the Compare Documents tool to find the differences in the two documents. These are separate documents, not versions stored in a single file. To compare documents, follow these steps:

1. Open a document that you want to compare to another.

2. Choose Tools, Track Changes, Compare Documents.

3. Select the document that you want to compare to the current document and click the Open button.

 T I P If you want to use Compare Document on two versions of a document stored in the same file, use the Versions In Document dialog box to view the older version and save it as a separate document.

4. Accept or reject the changes that are indicated in the document.

The next section shows how to merge two different versions of a document when the versions are contained in different files.

Merging Documents

You can use the Merge Documents tool to combine the tracked changes from several different documents. The Merge Documents tool requires that the files used the Track Changes feature. If the files did not use this feature, you should use Compare Documents to review changes. To use Merge Documents, follow these steps:

1. Open the original copy of the document that you want to merge with the edited copies.

2. Choose Tools, Merge Documents.

3. Select the file to merge with current document and click the Open button.

4. Repeat steps 2 and 3 until you merge all of the edited copies.

5. Review the changes and accept or reject them.

Routing Documents with E-Mail

Now that you know how to use the workgroup review features, you should learn how to use routing slips to move documents around. This feature lets you send documents to other users that have e-mail. They can then make their edits and return the document to you. To use routing slips, follow these steps:

1. Choose File, Send To, Routing Recipient.

2. Select the profile to use in the Profile Name dialog box if you are asked to.

3. Click the Address button on the Routing Slip dialog box and select the recipients from your address book. Figure 55.10 shows the Routing Slip dialog box.

FIG. 55.10

The routing slip determines who should receive the document and in what order.

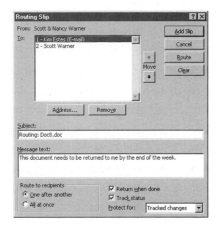

N O T E   Use the up and down arrow buttons to change the order of the recipients. ▪

4. In the Route to Recipients section of the Routing Slip dialog box, select the One After Another option button to have the document sent to each recipient in order. That way, each user reviewing the document can see the changes made by the previous recipient. Select the All at Once radio button to send the document to all recipients simultaneously.

5. In the Protect for drop-down list, the Tracked Changes option lets users make changes with the Track Changes feature activated. The Comments selection allows reviewers to enter comments, but they can't make any changes. Selecting Forms allows users to fill out a form, but they can't make changes to the form.

> **CAUTION**
>
> If you choose (None) in the Protect for drop-down list, no changes made by the reviewers are indicated in the document.

6. Select the Return When Done check box to have the document routed back to you after all of the recipients have reviewed it.

7. Type in any message text that you want and click the Add Slip button to save the routing slip information without sending the document. Click the Route button to save the routing slip information and send the document.

As each recipient receives the document, they can make their changes and send it on. After everyone has reviewed the document it will be sent back to you and you can review the changes, accepting or rejecting them.

N O T E   If you are sending the document to users with an older version of Word, be sure to save the document in a format that they can use. ▨

▶ **See** "File Compatibility and Conversion," **p. 1117**

Securing Documents

As a document is passed around a workgroup, there are opportunities for users to view or edit documents that they shouldn't. The Windows operating system and network operating systems have security measures to help prevent this, but they aren't always reliable. Word supplies some added protection for your documents by allowing you to protect an entire document or specific elements of a document. These security features are in addition to any other security provided for the computers in your network or workgroup.

Protecting a Document   Protecting a document is an option of the Save function. The author of the document controls this option. A document can be protected in three ways:

▨ The Read-Only Recommended feature displays a dialog box when the file is opened that suggests opening the document as read-only unless changes need to be made. This does not prevent the user from opening the file for editing. It is, as the title suggests, only a suggestion.

- The File Open Password feature requires the user to enter a password to open a document. If the correct password isn't supplied, the document cannot be opened.

- The File Modify Password requires that a user enter a password to make any changes to the document. When opening the document, you can choose to open it as read-only and you will not be prompted for the password.

Any of these methods can be used to protect a document or all three can be used at the same time. To use any of these protection features, follow these steps:

1. Choose File, Save As.

2. Click the Options button.

3. Select the Read-Only Recommended check box to activate that feature and enter the File Open password, the File Modify password, or both to activate those features. All of these fields are at the bottom of the Save dialog box shown in Figure 55.11.

FIG. 55.11

Use the Save dialog box to assign password protection to your document.

> **CAUTION**
>
> If you forget a password, your document can no longer be used, including any links that other documents have to it.

4. If you entered any passwords, you will be prompted to confirm them. Type them again and click the OK button.

5. Click the Save button.

Protecting Specific Elements of a Document   In addition to protecting an entire document, you can protect specific elements, including Tracked Changes, Comments, and Forms. To protect a specific element of a document, follow these steps:

1. Choose Tools, Protect Document.
2. Click the radio button of the element that you want to protect. Figure 55.12 shows the Protect Document dialog box.

FIG. 55.12

Use passwords to protect specific elements of a document.

3. Type a password and click the OK button.
4. Retype the password when you're prompted and click the OK button again.

Protecting the tracked changes prevents other users from turning the feature off or accepting or rejecting changes. Selecting Comments in the Protect Document dialog box only allows users to enter comments (no changes allowed). If the Forms option is selected, the user can fill out a form, but can't make any changes.

Collaborating in Excel

Excel workbooks can hold a variety of information coming from many different sources. Each source could submit information in a written or printed form for someone to consolidate the information into a single Excel workbook, but they would be very inefficient. Excel has two groups of features that allow workbooks to be shared by a workgroup:

■ Workgroup Sharing Features
■ Security Features

By using these features, Excel workbooks can edited directly by users who supply the information. There can still be a user who is in charge of overseeing the changes, but that user is now freed up to perform other tasks as well.

N O T E   Workbooks can be routed to a list of users. To learn how to route Office files using e-mail, see "Routing Documents with E-Mail" in this chapter. ■

Sharing Workbooks in a Workgroup

Excel has a sharing feature that allows multiple users to edit a workbook simultaneously or for several workbooks to be combined into a single workbook. To share a workbook, follow these steps:

1. Choose Tools, Share Workbook.

2. Select the Allow Changes by More Than One User at the Same Time check box to activate the sharing feature. This check box is on the Editing page of the Share Workbook dialog box shown in Figure 55.13.

FIG. 55.13

By activating this check box, you allow your Excel workbooks to be shared with other users.

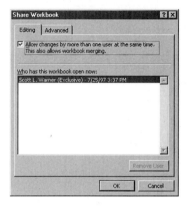

3. Click the Advanced tab.

4. In the Track Changes section, select how many days you want to keep a history of changes—if at all. You can also determine when to save changes and how conflicts should be resolved.

5. Click the OK button when you are finished.

After sharing a workbook, you can place it on a shared drive or a network drive so that others can edit it. Then, you can periodically review everyone's changes. To review changes to a document, follow these steps:

1. Choose Tools, Track Changes, Accept or Reject Changes.

2. Choose which changes you want to review in the Select Changes to Accept or Reject dialog box shown in Figure 55.14, and then click the OK button.

FIG. 55.14

By using the Accept or Reject Changes dialog box, you can limit the changes that you review.

3. Accept or reject the changes in the Accept or Reject Changes dialog box shown in Figure 55.15.

4. Click the Close button when you are finished.

FIG. 55.15

The change and the user who made it are listed in this dialog box.

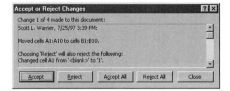

> **N O T E** Copies of shared workbooks can be merged, combining all changes for the two workbooks by choosing Tools, Merge Workbooks. Track Changes must be turned on for the workbooks and they must be versions of the same shared workbook. ▨

Using Comments in Workbooks

Comments can be used to explain the reason for a change or to explain the use of a cell in a workbook. Excel comments are denoted by a red triangle in the upper-right corner of a cell. To insert a comment, follow these steps:

1. Select the cell in which you want to place a comment.

2. Choose Insert, Comment.

 T I P   Right-click a cell and choose Insert Comment from the pop-up menu to add a comment to a cell.

3. Type your comments into the comment box that appears. Figure 55.16 shows the comment box.

FIG. 55.16

Comments look like sticky notes placed on the workbook.

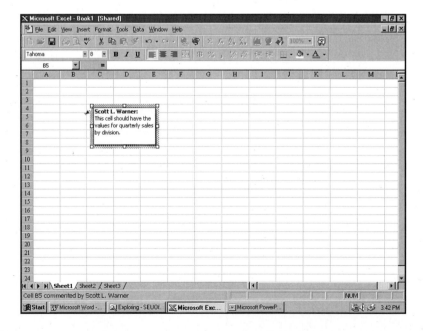

4. Press the Esc key once to stop editing the comment.

5. Use the arrow keys on your keyboard or the mouse to position the note where you would like it to appear.

 TIP If you have several comments very close to one another, position them so that they do not overlap if viewed simultaneously.

6. Press the Esc key to close the comment.

Users can tell that a cell has a comment by the red triangle. They can choose Comments from the View menu or rest their mouse over the cell to view the comment. If they switch to the Comments view, they will see all of the comments on the current view of the workbook. Figure 55.17 shows a workbook with several comments in Comments view.

FIG. 55.17

Comments can be moved and edited in Comments view.

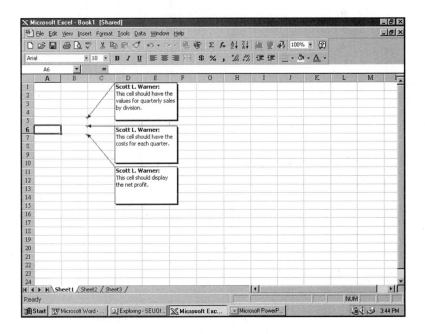

Comments can be used even if the workbook isn't being shared. They can make a workbook easier to read and understand, sometimes even to the author.

Consolidating Data

Data consolidation can be used to combine the data from workbooks or worksheets. It is not necessary to use Track Changes when using this tool. You can consolidate data in four ways:

- 3-D References
- By Position
- By Category
- PivotTable

Each of these methods has its advantages. For more information about each and how to decide which to use, consult the Excel help file for more information.

Securing Workbooks

Workbooks and individual worksheets can be secured. Choose Tools, Protection, Protect Sheet to open the Protect Sheet dialog box or choose Protect Workbook to open the Protect Workbook dialog box. Then, choose how you want to protect the workbook or worksheet and click the OK button.

N O T E Excel files can also be protected as a whole. See "Protecting a Document" in this chapter to see how Office documents can be protected using Save options. ■

To protect a workbook that you are going to share, choose Tools, Protection, Protect and Share Workbook. This is the only way that you can protect a shared workbook. After a workbook is shared, it can't be protected.

Collaborating in PowerPoint

PowerPoint has fewer collaboration features than other Office applications. There are no features that allow multiple users to work on presentations simultaneously, but there is a feature that lets many users participate in a PowerPoint presentation. To start a presentation conference, follow these steps:

N O T E The Meeting Minder, which is on the Tools menu, can be used to record note of a meeting. It can even add action items to individuals and schedule follow up meetings using Outlook. ■

1. Open a presentation.
2. Choose Presentation Conference from the Tools menu. Figure 55.18 shows the first dialog box in the Presentation Conference Wizard.

FIG. 55.18
The first dialog box of the Presentation Conference Wizard outlines the process.

3. Click the Next button to continue.

4. Choose to be the Presenter in the dialog box shown in Figure 55.19 and click the Next button to continue.

FIG. 55.19

The Presentation Conference Wizard makes joining a conference easy.

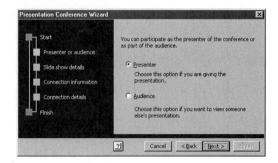

5. Click the Next button of the next wizard dialog box, which tells what slides will be shown.

N O T E Depending on your computer's configuration, your options might differ slightly. Click the question mark button at any time to receive help. ▪

6. Click the Next button of the next wizard dialog box, which gives information about the connection to be used for the conference.

7. Enter the names of the computers to participate in the conference or their Internet addresses and click the Next button.

8. Click the Finish button on the last dialog box, but be sure that the audience members click their Finish buttons first.

If you wanted to view a conference as an audience member, you would choose Audience in the second dialog box of the wizard, shown in Figure 55.19.

 T I P PowerPoint presentations can also be sent using a routing slip.

CAUTION

PowerPoint presentations can't be password protected using Save options.

Those are the ways that you can use your Office applications to collaborate on documents. While some features are common to all applications, each application has features that help take advantage of its strengths.

Part

IX

Ch

55

CHAPTER 56

File Compatibility and Conversion

by Nancy Warner

A lot of issues are involved when files from different versions of an application, and even files from different applications, need to be shared. Compatibility alone could dictate your actions, but there are many alternatives, as shown in this chapter.

There are many ways to share files among users with different versions of an application. Everyone could agree to use the oldest version in use or users with an older version could use a special viewer to work with newer files. The important thing is to define a strategy and educate all users how to use it. ▪

Develop compatibility strategy

Many options are available to make files work with Office and other applications. A good plan for sharing files makes file compatibility easier to deal with.

Convert files

Files can be converted into the current version of some Office applications.

Import files

Use files that were created in other applications, such as Lotus 1-2-3 or WordPerfect.

Export files

Save files in a format that others can use. You could save a file for a previous version of the Office application or for a different application.

Use backward compatibility

Around the world, over 40 million people use Office, and they don't all have the same version. The latest version of Office can use files from previous versions.

Understanding File Compatibility Issues

File compatibility is a very important issue. Your Office files are important and you want to be able to distribute them to others. However, other users may not have the same version of Office that you do or they may not have Office at all. To ensure that others can use the files that you create, you need to develop a strategy to make files compatible for as many users as possible. Some basic elements can be used as the basis for your strategy:

- Default Save
- File Converters
- File Viewers
- Dual File Formats

One of these features might resolve your compatibility issues, or you might have to use several of them in combination. The following sections discuss each.

Using Default Save

As you and other users upgrade your Office applications, there could be many different versions in use. The easiest way to share files in this situation is to always save files to the earliest version in use. This solution works very well for users who are outside of your company or location. However, this method has limitations, which are covered in the section "Understanding Backward Compatibility Issues in Office 97."

Default Save is a new feature in Office 97 that allows you to designate a particular format to use by default when saving a document. For example, you might always want to save documents in Word 2.0 format. Setting the Default Save option in each office application that uses it is covered in the following three sections.

N O T E The Default Save option can be used to save files in an earlier version of an Office application or to export the file to the file format for a different application.

Setting Default Save for Word

Before you can set the Default Save option in Word, you must have a document open. Otherwise, the menu choice used to set the option is unavailable. To set the Default Save option for Word, follow these steps:

1. Choose Options from the Tools menu.
2. Click the Save tab. Figure 56.1 shows the Options dialog box.
3. Select the file format you want to use in the Save Word Files As drop-down list box.

> **CAUTION**
>
> Make sure that you are aware of the limitations involved with saving your documents into an older or different format. Some features available in Word 97 are not present in other file formats.

FIG. 56.1

Use the Save tab in the Options dialog box to set your Default Save options.

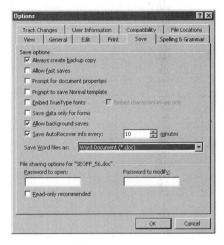

4. Click the OK button to save your changes.

Now when you save a document in Word, it will use the file format that you chose by default. You can then distribute your documents with confidence that others will be able to use them.

Setting Default Save for Excel

You must have a workbook open before you can set the Default Save option in Excel. To set the Default Save option for Excel, follow these steps:

1. Choose Options from the Tools menu.
2. Click the Transition tab. Figure 56.2 shows the Options dialog box.

FIG. 56.2

Using the Default Save option prevents you from saving Excel files in a format unusable by others.

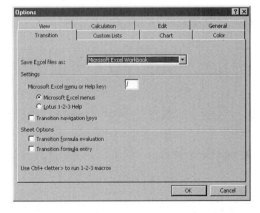

3. Select the file format you want to use in the Save Excel Files As drop-down list box.

Part

IX

Ch

56

 TIP Click the Transition navigation keys to use an alternate set of commands to perform tasks in Excel. This feature is for users who are new to Excel but proficient in another spreadsheet application, such as Lotus 1-2-3.

---

4. Click the OK button to save your changes.

Now when you save a workbook in Excel, it will use the file format that you chose by default. Others can then use the files even without the version of Excel that you are using.

Setting Default Save for PowerPoint

The Default Save option for PowerPoint can be set without opening a PowerPoint presentation. To set the Default Save option for PowerPoint, follow these steps:

1. Choose Options from the Tools menu.

2. Click the Save tab. Figure 56.3 shows the Options dialog box.

FIG. 56.3

Use the Save tab in the Options dialog box to set your Save options in PowerPoint.

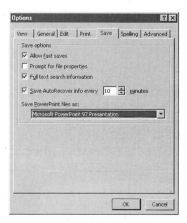

3. Select the file format you want to use in the Save PowerPoint Files As drop-down list box.

N O T E PowerPoint's Default Save option only lets you choose PowerPoint file formats, from the latest version back to version 3.0. ▪

4. Click the OK button to save your changes.

After determining the best file format to use, this method makes it easy to share PowerPoint presentation files. The next section discusses the use of file converters.

Using File Converters

File converters change the format in which a file is saved. The conversion can be from one version's file format to another, or from one application's file format to a different application's file format. Two types of file converters exist:

- Batch file converters
- Installable file converters

Batch file converters change entire directories of files. This type of converter would be used after upgrading all users. *Installable file converters* give users the ability to open files saved in a different format. There is an installable file converter for Word and PowerPoint.

A converter can also work in the other direction. For instance, when Word 97 users save a file for someone using Word 6.0/95, they must convert the file to the other users' file format.

N O T E   Word 6.0 and Word for Windows 95 use the same file format, so documents saved in either are interchangeable.

Originally, the conversion to Word 6.0/95 format was accomplished by saving the file in Rich Text Format (RTF), but this caused some confusion. In response, Microsoft has released a converter that allows Word 97 to save files in native Word 6.0/95 format, or Word 6.0/95 binary format. The Word 97 binary converter is available from Microsoft's Web site. To download the converter, follow these steps:

1. Connect to the Internet using a dial-up connection or your network connection.

2. Open a Web browser and go to the address **http://www.microsoft.com/word/**. You should see a page similar to the one shown in Figure 56.4, but it could be different because Web pages are updated frequently.

 T I P   Web pages for most Microsoft products can be viewed by adding a forward slash and the product name after Microsoft's Web address. For example, **http://www.microsoft.com/excel/** is the URL for the Excel Web page, while **http://www.microsoft.com/products/** will connect you to a page with hyperlinks to all Microsoft products.

3. Find the Word 6.0/95 Binary Converter for Word 97 and download the file. If needed, you can click the Search graphic at the top of the page to find the file. After you find the file, download it to your desktop or another location and install it by running the program file.

N O T E   The Word 97 binary converter is part of the Office 97 Service Release 1. If you have applied this service release, you already have the converter.

It is best to use converters when you have to share large documents that contain a lot of graphics or other embedded objects. The next section discusses the use of file viewers.

File Viewers

File viewers are programs that allow users to open and view files without having the software that created them. For example, the Word 97 viewer allows users to view Word 97 documents even if they don't have the full release of Word 97 installed on their computer. A PowerPoint

Part
IX

Ch
56

viewer has been available since its original release. All Microsoft viewers are freely distributable. With viewers, users who don't have Office can view documents created in Office. Viewers are available on Microsoft's Web site for Word, Excel, and PowerPoint.

 TIP WordPad is a word processor included with Windows 95. It is based on Microsoft Word and uses a file format very similar to Word 6.0/95. It can be used to view and edit Word 6.0/95 files, but some formatting might be lost in the process.

FIG. 56.4

Visit Microsoft's Word web page to download the Word 6.0/95 Binary Converter for Word 97.

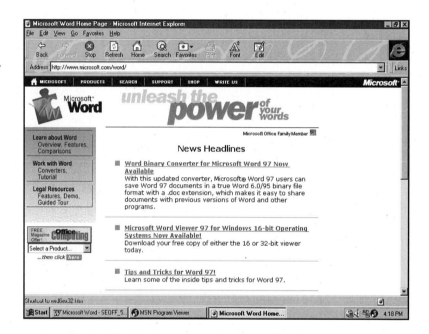

Dual File Formats

Dual file formats were created specifically for organizations that need to gradually upgrade their users to Office 97. It is available in Excel and PowerPoint. Files created in these applications can be saved as both the 97 version and the previous version (5.0/95 for both Excel and PowerPoint) using the Save As option of the File menu.

When a file is saved in a dual file format, a single file contains two sets of data. One set of data contains the file information that is common to both versions and the other contains the information specific to the new version.

NOTE When files saved using the dual file format are opened and edited by the previous version of the application, the formatting specific to the newer version is not affected. ■

Using Import/Export Filters

Users switching to Office 97 from other applications will be especially interested in the import and export filters. These filters allow Office applications to open files created in other applications and save files in the format of other applications. The filters available for the Office applications are covered in the next four sections.

N O T E Choosing a typical installation does not install all of the filters available for the Office Applications. ▨

Importing and Exporting Files in Word

Using an import filter is a fairly simple process. You save the file as you normally would, except that you choose a different format in the Save as type drop-down list box. Table 56.1 summarizes the filters that are included with Word.

Table 56.1   File Format Converters Supplied with Word

File Format	Description
HTML	Up to HTML 2.0.
WordPerfect for MS-DOS	5.x and 6.0, can't save to 6.0.
WordPerfect for Windows	5.x and 6.x, can't save to 6.0.
Microsoft Excel	2.x, 3.0, 4.0, 5.0, 95, Excel 97 (open only, can't save).
Microsoft Word	2.x, 6.0, and Word 95.
Word for the Macintosh	4.x, 5.x, Word 97.
Microsoft Works	3.0, 4.0 (for Windows 95).
Lotus 1-2-3	2.x, 3.x, 4.0. (open only, can't save).
Recover Text from Any File	Recovers text from damaged documents.
Text Only	Saves text in ANSI format.
DOS Text Only	Saves text in ASCII format.
Text Only w/ line breaks	Same as above with line breaks.
DOS Text Only w/ line breaks	Same as above with line breaks.
Text w/ Layout	Approximates formatting with spaces.
DOS Text w/ Layout	Approximates formatting with spaces.
Rich Text Format (RTF)	Saves all formatting using RTF standards.

Part

IX

Ch

56

NOTE Unless you have installed the Word 97 binary converter discussed in "Using File Converters," documents saved as Word 6.0/95 are actually saved in Rich Text Format. However, these files are treated as Word 6.0/95 documents because they use the .DOC extension. ■

The following steps are an example of saving (exporting) a Word document to WordPerfect 5.0 format:

1. Choose Save As from the File menu.
2. Select WordPerfect 5.0 in the Save as Type drop-down list box. Figure 56.5 shows the Save As dialog box ready to export a file.

CAUTION

Formatting can be lost or substituted when converting a file to a different format. You should make yourself aware of the consequences of exporting a file. Make backups of crucial documents before converting.

FIG. 56.5

Choose the file type from the drop-down menu in the Save As dialog box.

3. Click the Save button to complete the process.

To import a file of a different format into Word, simply select that file in the Open dialog box. Word performs the conversion automatically. The next section discusses the filters for Excel.

Importing and Exporting Files in Excel

By using the Open command in Excel, you can view files created in other programs or earlier versions of Excel. You can also save files to formats other than Excel 97 by using the Save As command. If files usually need to be saved in a format other than Excel 97, you can change the default save property as described in "Setting Default Save for Excel." Table 56.2 shows the import and export filters available for Excel.

Table 56.2   File Format Converters Supplied with Excel

File Format	Description
Microsoft Excel	2.x, 3.0, 4.0, 5.0/95, 5.0/95 and 97 (dual)
Lotus 1-2-3	1.x, 2.x, 3, 4
DBASE	DBF 2, DBF 3, DBF 4
SYLK	Symbolic Link
DIF	Data Interchange Format
CSV	Comma delimited
Text	Tab delimited
Formatted Text	Space delimited
Template	Excel template

The File Conversion Wizard can be used to convert multiple files to Excel 97 format in one action. To use the File Conversion Wizard, follow these steps:

1. Choose File Conversion from the Wizard submenu of the Tools menu.

2. Supply the location of the files that you want to convert and what format they are currently in, as shown in Figure 56.6. Click the Next button to continue.

FIG. 56.6

Use the Browse button to locate the files you want to convert.

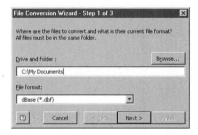

3. Select the files that you want to convert by clicking the box to the left of their name. A checked box means that the file will be converted. Figure 56.7 shows the second dialog box of the File Conversion Wizard. Click the Next button to continue.

 T I P   Click the Select All button to mark all of the files to be converted or the Unselect All button to make none of the files marked for conversion.

Part
IX

Ch

56

4. Select the location to save the converted files in using the wizard dialog box shown in Figure 56.8. Click the Finish button to start the conversion.

FIG. 56.7

Step 2 of the wizard
allows you to choose
the files to be
converted.

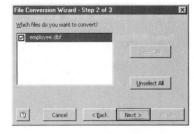

FIG. 56.8

Use the wizard's third
step to select the
destination to save your
converted file(s).

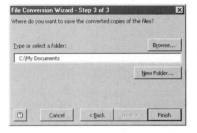

The formats that can be converted using this wizard translate well into Excel format. Other
formats do not convert as easily.

Opening a delimited text file is a task that deserves some explaining. Delimited text files contain data that is separated by commas or some other character. To open a delimited text file,
follow these steps:

1. Choose Open from the File menu.

2. Select the delimited text file in the Open dialog box and click the Open button.

3. The first dialog box of the Text Import Wizard, which is shown in Figure 56.9, opens.
   Select the options that describe your file. Usually, the default choices are correct. Click
   the Next button when you have finished.

FIG. 56.9

Use the Text Import
Wizard to open a
delimited text file.

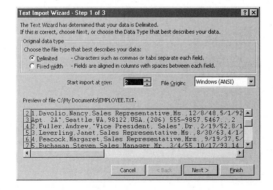

T I P The first row of many delimited text files contain headers that describe the columns of data. Select 2 in the Start Import at Row spin box to avoid importing the row of headers.

4. Select the delimiter used in the text file as shown in Figure 56.10. You also need to identify the text qualifier, which indicates the beginning and end of a text field. Text qualifiers are used so text fields can contain the character being used as the delimiter. Click the Next button to continue. Use the Other edit box if your delimiter is not one of the choices.

FIG. 56.10

Step 2 of the wizard allows you to select the delimiter.

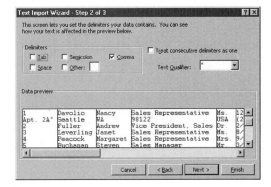

5. The final dialog box of the wizard, shown in Figure 56.11, allows you to specify the type of data that is contained in a column. Specifying a data type affects how the data is formatted after it is loaded into Excel. Click the Finish button when you are done.

FIG. 56.11

Use the final step to specify the type of data contained in the column.

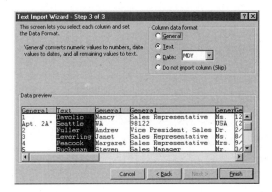

N O T E You can use the Back button to go back and change any of the choices that you made in the Table Import Wizard. ■

The next section discusses PowerPoint's filters for importing and exporting.

Importing and Exporting Files in PowerPoint

PowerPoint has a limited ability to export files into the formats of other applications. It can only save presentations to PowerPoint formats, although it can save it to any version's format. In addition, a presentation can be saved in Rich Text Format or parts of a presentation can be saved as graphics files.

While PowerPoint can't save files into other applications' file formats, it can import files created in other applications. Converters for Harvard Graphics and Lotus Freelance are included with PowerPoint.

> **CAUTION**
>
> Most of the formatting in Harvard Graphics and Lotus Freelance files is preserved, but there may be some things that don't translate easily.

Using one of several text or graphics file formats, you can still use presentations created in programs for which PowerPoint doesn't have a converter. Text formats preserve the text of the presentation and slides can be saved as graphic images. These files can then be used by PowerPoint or Word. The next four sections briefly discuss using other file formats with PowerPoint 97.

Converting Harvard Graphics Presentations to PowerPoint   PowerPoint's converter for Harvard Graphics automatically imports files for version 2.3 and DOS version 3.0. If the Harvard Graphics converter isn't installed, run the Office Setup program again, and choose to install it. To import a Harvard Graphics presentation, follow these steps:

1. Choose File, Open.
2. Select the version of Harvard Graphics files that you are searching for in the Files of Type drop-down list box.

 Saving newer Harvard Graphics files into an older version's file format allows you to use files from versions of Harvard Graphics that PowerPoint can't import.

3. Select the presentation that you want to convert.
4. Save the file to PowerPoint format after it's converted.

You can convert multiple files by opening them at the same time and then saving each one into PowerPoint format. The next section covers Lotus Freelance files.

Converting Lotus Freelance Presentations to PowerPoint   Files from Lotus Freelance versions 1.0, 2.0, and 4.0 for DOS are automatically imported by the PowerPoint converter. Again, the converter must be installed using the Office Setup program if it isn't present. To convert a Lotus Freelance presentation, follow these steps:

1. Choose File, Open.
2. Select the version of Lotus Freelance files that you are searching for in the Files of Type drop-down list.
3. Select the presentation that you want to convert.
4. Save the file to PowerPoint format after it's converted.

Sometimes, a file format can't be converted. In such cases, the text and the graphics could be saved and used to create a presentation in PowerPoint. The next section discusses how graphics and text from a presentation can be used.

Converting Presentation Graphics and Text to PowerPoint Graphics from presentations can be used even if the file format can't be converted into PowerPoint format. However, support for the specific graphic file format must be available. Table 56.3 shows the graphic file formats that are available in PowerPoint.

Table 56.3 Graphic File Formats Built-In to PowerPoint

File Format	Extension
JPEG	.JPG
Macintosh PICT	.PCT
Portable Network Graphics	.PNG
Windows Bitmap	.BMP
Windows Enhanced Metafile	.EMF
Windows Metafile	.WMF
AutoCAD	.DXF
CompuServe GIF	.GIF
Computer Graphics Metafile	.CGM
CorelDRAW 3.0, 4.0, 5.0, and 6.0	.CDR
Encapsulated PostScript	.EPS
Kodak Photo CD	.PCD
Micrografx Designer/Draw	.DRW
PC Paintbrush	.PCX
Tagged Image File Format (TIFF)	.TIF
Truevision Targa	.TGA
WordPerfect Graphics/DrawPerfect	.WPG

Part
IX

Ch
56

These graphics filters can help you use the graphics from a presentation. If you want to use the text for a presentation that PowerPoint doesn't have a converter for, you can save the presentation in a text file format (using its native application). The graphic elements of the presentations won't be saved, but the text can be used in PowerPoint or Word.

N O T E Graphics or text from a presentation can be used in any word processor or other application that can use the format that the text or graphics is saved in. ▪

The next section tells how to use the graphic design of a presentation that can't be converted.

Converting Presentations Using Graphics File Formats If you want to save the design of a presentation that can't be converted to PowerPoint, you can save the presentation into a graphic format. Saving a presentation in a graphics format converts each slide to a separate graphic image.

PowerPoint can then open the slides using the graphics filter. After all of the slides are imported, you can save the presentation into PowerPoint format. This or any of the previous methods can be used to import presentations into PowerPoint.

 T I P Although PowerPoint can't save files directly into another application's format, you can save slides as graphics files and import them into other applications.

Importing and Exporting Files in Access

Access can work with data that comes from many different data sources. Some are specific file formats and others work with Open Database Connectivity (ODBC). Table 56.4 lists the data sources that Access can use.

Table 56.4 Data Sources Supported by Access

Data Source	Versions Supported
Microsoft FoxPro	2.x, 3.0 (import only)
dBASE	III, III+, IV, 5
Paradox	3.x, 4.x, 5.0
Excel	3.0, 4.0, 5.0, 7.0/95, 8.0/97
Lotus 1-2-3	1.x, 2.x, 3, 4 (link is read-only)
Delimited Text Files	N/A
Fixed-Width Text Files	N/A
HTML	1.0, 2.0, 3.x
SQL Tables	ODBC-compliant data sources

N O T E The availability of drivers for ODBC data sources depends upon the cooperation of the companies that distribute those products. Drivers for databases such as Oracle and Sybase are available, but may cost extra to obtain.

Information stored in one of these data sources can be imported and exported by Access. There are two different types of imports that can be performed.

The data can be imported; the table's design and data are copied into an Access database. Another way to use other data sources from within Access is to link to a table. Linking to a table allows you to view and edit a table that is stored in a different file format, as well as a different file. While you can change the data contained in a linked table, you cannot change the table's design. To link to a table using Access, follow these steps:

1. Choose <u>L</u>ink Tables from the Get External <u>D</u>ata submenu of the <u>F</u>ile menu. You would have chosen Import to copy the table into the current Access database.

2. Select the data source that the table is contained in from the Files of <u>T</u>ype drop-down list box.

3. Select the table that you want linked.

N O T E You can import and link tables that are contained in other Access databases. ■

4. Click the Link button. A dialog box informs you when the process is completed.

T I P If you need data that is stored in a format that Access can't handle, save the data into one of the formats that it can handle and then import it.

The method for exporting data from an Access database is slightly different. Data can be exported to another Access database, as well as any of the data sources listed in Table 56.4. To export data from an Access database, follow these steps:

1. Select the table that you want to export.

2. Choose Save <u>A</u>s/Export from the <u>F</u>ile menu.

T I P You can also right-click the table you want to export and choose Save <u>A</u>s/Export from the pop-up menu. You can also copy the table to the current database.

3. Choose the To an External File or Database option in the Save As dialog box, shown in Figure 56.12.

4. Select the format to export the table into in the Save As Type drop-down list and then click the Export button.

The next section discusses some of the issues involved with saving files to an older version of the Office applications.

Part
IX

Ch
56

FIG. 56.12

Use the Save As dialog box in Access to choose where the table should be saved.

Understanding Backward Compatibility Issues in Office 97

While the latest versions of the Office applications can save their files in the format of their previous versions, there are certain features that have changed or didn't exist in the previous version. If you are using any of the affected features, it is important for you to know the consequences of saving a file in the older version. These issues are addressed for Word, Excel, and PowerPoint in the following three sections.

Understanding Backward Compatibility Issues in Word

Table 56.5 shows the results of saving a Word file into an older version. These issues won't affect most people. If you are experiencing a problem with files saved to an older version, check this table.

Table 56.5   Word 97 Features with Issues in Word 6.0/95 Format

Word 97 Feature	Results in Word 6.0/95 Format
Embedded Fonts	The embedded fonts are lost, Word 6.0 or 95 assigns the closest font available.
Vertical text in table cells	Vertical text is reformatted as horizontal text.
Vertically aligned text in table cells	Vertically aligned text is reformatted to align at the top of the cell.
Vertically merged table cells	Merged table cells are exploded into unmerged cells.
EMF, PNG, and JPEG graphics	Graphics are converted to WMF (Windows Metafile) or PICT (Macintosh) format, which does not support graphics compression. This increases file size of documents that contain graphics.
Office Art objects	Office Art objects are converted to the nearest available shape and tool.
Animated text (Animation tab)	Animated text formatting is lost.

Word 97 Feature	Results in Word 6.0/95 Format
Embossed and engraved characters (Font tab)	Embossed and engraved character formatting is lost. The text becomes formatted as white text. To change the color of the text, select the text, click Font (Format menu), and then click Auto or Black in the Color box.
Outline and heading numbered list (Outline Numbered tab)	Outline numbered lists and heading numbered lists are converted to regular text, but retain their appearance. In Word 6.0 and 95, you can use the Bullets and Numbering command (Format menu) to format the lists.
Multilevel bullets (Outline Numbered tab)	Multilevel bullets are converted to regular text, but retain their appearance. In Word 6.0 and 95, you can use the Bullets and Numbering command (Format menu) to format the lists.
Page borders (Page Border tab)	Page borders are not converted.
Character shading (Shading tab)	Character shading is lost.
Character borders (Borders tab)	Character borders are lost.
Paragraph borders (Borders tab)	New Word 97 paragraph borders are lost.
Floating pictures surrounded by wrapped text	Floating pictures are converted in frames to WMF (Windows Metafile) or PICT (Macintosh) format.
Floating OLE objects	Floating OLE objects are converted to OLE objects in frames.
Highlighting applied with the Highlight button (Formatting toolbar)	Highlighting is preserved in Word 95, but is lost in Word 6.0.
New document properties	New document properties are preserved in Word 95 but lost in Word 6.x. In Word, you can use the Properties command (File menu) to store information about the document, such as title, subject, author, manager, company, and so on.
HYPERLINK field (Insert menu)	The last value of the HYPERLINK field is retained as plain text, and the field itself is lost.

continues

Part

IX

Ch

56

Table 56.5   Continued

Word 97 Feature	Results in Word 6.0/95 Format
Password protection options in the Save As dialog box (File menu)	All document protection is lost. In Word 6.0 and 95, you can reapply document protection by clicking Save As (File menu), clicking Options, and then selecting the options you want on the Save tab.
Protect Document settings (Tools menu)	All document protection is lost. In Word 6.0 and 95, you can reapply document protection for tracked changes, comments, and forms by clicking Protect Document (Tools menu) and selecting the options you want. (In Word 6.0 and 95, tracked changes were called revisions, and comments were called annotations).
Tracked changes to paragraph numbers, and display fields (Tools menu)	Tracked changes to paragraph numbers, properties, and display fields properties are lost, but other tracked changes are retained and shown with revision marks.
DOCPROPERTY field	The DOCPROPERTY field is retained in Word 95. In Word 6.x, the field appears as Error! Bookmark not defined.
ActiveX controls on forms	ActiveX Controls can be used, but not modified.
Unicode characters (2 bytes per character)	May result in potential data loss. Unicode characters are mapped to corresponding ANSI (Windows) or 1 byte per character (Macintosh), or are converted to question marks (?) if no equivalent character is available. Foreign language characters are most likely to be affected.
Visual Basic macros	All macros created in Word 97 Visual Basic are lost.
Embedded fonts	Embedded fonts are lost, and Word 95 or Word 6.x assigns the closest font available.

Understanding Backward Compatibility Issues in Excel

Table 56.6 shows the results of saving an Excel file into an older version. Consult this table if you are experiencing problems while trying to save Excel files into an older version.

Table 56.6 Excel 97 Features with Issues in Excel 5.0/95 Format

Excel 97 Feature	Results in Excel 5.0/95 Format
Angled text	Angled text is reformatted to horizontal orientation.
Conditional formatting	Conditional formatting is lost, and cells are reformatted as normal text.
Data validation	Lost in the conversion.
Indenting within cells	Indentation within a cell is lost, and data remains left aligned.
Merge cells option on the Alignment tab in the Cells dialog box (Format menu)	Merged cells are unmerged.
New border styles	New border styles are converted to the nearest border style available in Microsoft Excel 5.0 or 95.
Partial page breaks	Partial page breaks are converted to full-page breaks.
Shrink to fit option on the Alignment tab in the Cells dialog box (Format menu)	Text and data retain the same point size they had before Shrink to fit was selected.
Defined labels	Lost in the conversion.
English language references in formulas	English language references are converted to A1 reference notations. However, names of named cells and ranges are preserved.
Calculated fields, calculated items, and formatting based on structure	These PivotTable features are preserved until the user makes changes to or refreshes the PivotTable data. Then they are lost.
PivotTable properties sheet	All new properties are lost. These include: Page field placement across columns or down rows, Alternate strings for NA and error cell display, Server-based page fields, AutoSort and AutoShow on fields, Multiselect on page fields, Persistent grouping and sorting, Data fields displayed as numbers.

continues

Part

IX

Ch

56

Table 56.6   Continued

Excel 97 Feature	Results in Excel 5.0/95 Format
Preserved formatting	Formatting is saved, but structured behavior is lost as soon as the user makes changes to or refreshes the PivotTable data.
3-D bar shapes (cylinder, pyramid, and cone)	3-D shapes are converted to 3-D column charts.
Angled text on axis and data labels	The text is formatted straight (0 degrees).
Bubble chart format	Bubble charts are converted to type 1 XY scatter charts.
Data tables on charts	Lost in the conversion.
Gradient fills	Gradient fills are converted to the nearest color and pattern.
Office Art objects	Office Art objects are converted to the nearest available shape and tool.
Pie-of-pie and bar-of-pie chart types	These charts are converted to type 1 pie charts.
Time series axis	Special scaling information is lost, and the axis is converted to a normal category axis.
Comments	Comments are converted to Cell Tips.
Hyperlink (Insert menu)	The HYPERLINK text and formatting is preserved, but the functionality is lost.
Multi-user workbooks	Sharing is disabled, and the change log is lost.
Revision marks and audit trail	Lost in the conversion; the change log is also lost.
Parameterized queries	Parameterized queries cannot be executed or edited.
Report templates	Lost in the conversion.
Shared queries (connections without a data source name, or DSN)	Files that contain connections without DSN are supported in Microsoft Excel 95 (with ODBC 2.0). In Microsoft Excel 5.0 (with ODBC 1.0) the user is prompted for connection information.

Excel 97 Feature	Results in Excel 5.0/95 Format
New Microsoft Excel objects, methods, and properties	Not all programming elements are 97 supported. For more information about compatibility, see Microsoft Office 97 Resource Kit and Microsoft Office Developer Web site.
ActiveX Controls (formerly OLE controls or OCX)	ActiveX Controls appear in the workbook but cannot be used.
User forms dialog controls	Lost in the conversion.
32,000 characters per cell	Characters beyond the 255th character are truncated.
65,536 rows per worksheet	Data in rows below row 16,384 are truncated.

Understanding Backward Compatibility Issues in PowerPoint

The look, or visual accuracy, of PowerPoint files is almost always preserved when saved to an older version. However, you may not be able to edit some objects that you otherwise could. Table 56.7 outlines the major issues for saving PowerPoint files to an older version's file format.

Table 56.7   PowerPoint 97 Features with Issues in PowerPoint 95 Format

PowerPoint 97 Feature	Results in PowerPoint 95 Format
Animated chart elements	Animated chart elements are displayed as static chart objects. PowerPoint 95 users must have Microsoft Graph to edit charts.
Custom shows	Slides appear in the presentation in the correct ordering, but Custom Show grouping information is lost.
Elevator effects	Elevator effects are converted to Wipe Up effects.
Native format movies and sounds	Movies and sounds are converted to Media Player and Sound Recorder objects.
Play options for CD tracking and movie looping	Play options are ignored.

continues

Table 56.7   Continued

PowerPoint 97 Feature	Results in PowerPoint 95 Format
Comments	Comments are converted to shapes with rich text format; cannot be turned on/off so hidden comments are displayed.
Hyperlinks that combine Play Sound with other action settings	Play Sound settings are lost.
Hyperlinks embedded within an object	The hyperlinks are lost.
Action settings embedded within an object	The action settings are lost.
3-D effects	3-D effects are converted as pictures.
AutoShapes	If there is no matching shape, AutoShapes are converted to freeform shapes.
Composite shapes	Composite shapes are converted to separate shapes and lines, which are grouped together.
Connectors	Connectors are converted as freeform lines, and lose their automatic connecting behavior.
Curves	Curves are approximated with connected line segments.
Gradient fills	Semi-transparency is lost on gradient fills.
Joins and endcaps of lines	On AutoShapes, these become mitered joins and round endcaps. On freeform shapes, they become round joins and round endcaps.
Objects that are linked or embedded	Brightness, contrast, and color transformation settings are lost.
Picture brightness, contrast, and color	These are rendered at current transformation PowerPoint 97 settings.
Picture fills	Picture fills are converted to picture objects.
Picture fills on shapes	The shape is converted as a picture object and is given a solid fill with the last applied foreground color.
Shadows, engraved	Engraved shadows take on embossed shadow effects.
Shadows, perspective	Perspective shadows are converted as shapes and grouped with the shape casting the shadow.

PowerPoint 97 Feature	Results in PowerPoint 95 Format
Shapes or arcs with attached text that are new in PowerPoint 97	These are converted to PowerPoint 95 freeform shapes or arcs and text boxes.
Text box margins block	Margins are averaged to center the text in the box.
Text effects	Text effects are converted as pictures.
Thick compound lines	Thick compound lines are converted as picture objects.
Charts	Users cannot edit charts unless they have Microsoft Graph.
Clip Gallery	The clip art is rendered as a picture object; double-clicking clip art does not launch ClipArt Gallery in PowerPoint 95.
PowerPoint macros	PowerPoint macros are not converted; there is no macro language in PowerPoint 95.
Unicode characters (2 bytes per character)	Unicode characters are mapped to corresponding ANSI. Foreign language characters are most likely to be affected.

Part X: Introduction to Developing Office Applications

CHAPTER 57

Creating Your Own Applications with VBA

by Keith MacKay

VBA is a tremendously versatile language that allows you to integrate elements from each Office application into one seamless system. To learn how to do so, there are some basic questions that must be answered and some technologies that must be understood. This chapter will outline these facets of application development and set you on the track to professional Office application development. ■

Understanding the development process

A little forethought and testing wrapped around your code development can make a world of difference.

Picking the base application

Each application has strengths and weaknesses. You'll need to pick a "home base" for your application.

Tools for expertise

Using the Object Browser and the Help system.

Learning the object models

The object model for each application is the key to understanding how to program it.

Using automation

Controlling one application from another is key to most complex application development. Here are the vital code snippets that enable control of each application.

Building an application

We put the pieces together and show how multiple applications can be used in conjunction with one another to solve problems.

Using a Good Development Process

Professional development proceeds in distinct phases to make sure that the resulting application is both fully conceived and adequately tested. Your own development should parallel this process to make sure that you have covered all your bases. The typical phases can take a variety of names, but typically consist of Design, Specification, Development, Testing, Documentation, and Release.

Design

The design phase really comes down to understanding the problem. What is the problem? You will sometimes be surprised at how difficult answering this question can be. You'll know in vague terms that you need something "better." Better than what? What's wrong with the current process or program? Speed? Efficiency? Waste? Lack of resources? Insufficient reporting? Vague reporting? No reporting? No paper trail? Too much paper generated?

Who's going to use your system? Just you? Others? Are their needs the same as yours? Does the current methodology work for them and not for you? Is the current methodology worse for them than it is for you?

Specification

Once you have actually defined the problem that needs to be solved, lay out exactly how you're going to solve it. Describe the process for each type of user of the system. Define the way the application will look, including all forms and reports. Define the fields necessary for each Access database or Excel table. Describe the handshake between applications. Which application will be in control?

Though this all sounds like a lot of work, it will invariably save you time in the long run. It is much more difficult to add a new feature later than to build it in at the beginning. In a professional environment, this serves as the blueprint for the project—the document in which both the client and developer agree on the scope of the project.

Development

Once you have your specifications (or *specs*) as a roadmap, begin development. Good specs can greatly speed development, because most of the difficult questions will have already been resolved. Am I using Excel or Access? What should this table look like? Good specs eliminate the tedious decisions of development, while still leaving all of the fun programming problems. (How do I make this most efficient? How do I make this element appear on a useful report?)

Testing

Someone other than the programmer should test the product once it has been built. The programmer is too familiar with the code, too close to the product. The programmer knows not to do silly things that will crash the product. An uninitiated tester, however, will be much more likely to break the product, providing indication of where the product is weak (or where the directions are not clear).

There is no shame in finding problems with your system at this stage—they are almost inevitable (the more complex the project, the more inevitable). As long as bugs are found during this testing phase, they can be fixed. Inadequate testing, however, will assure that there are problems with the final product. Better to over-test than under-test.

TIP When you get someone else to test your product, ask them to write down the specific steps (including menu options, which mouse button they clicked, where they were pointing, and so on) that cause any errors they find. If you are not able to reproduce their bug, you're going to have a very difficult time correcting it.

Documentation

Once you have completed the product and it is totally bug-free, it's time to document the product. Different types of documentation serve different purposes.

User documentation describes how to use the product and who to contact when there are problems. If you are the only person to use your program, user documentation is less important (though if you will only use this once in a blue moon, a record of the features and how to use them might prove useful as a reminder).

Code documentation consists of in-code comments and printouts of your code. This is vital to the success of any future code expansion or reuse of any of your code in other projects. You will be surprised how quickly you forget the specifics of the elegant coding solution that you designed. Without documentation describing the program flow for yourself, you will need to completely relearn the code—which can take almost as long as writing the code from scratch.

One final type of documentation is *installation documentation*. What files are necessary to use your product? Where must they be located? What versions of those files are required?

Release

Once the product is written, debugged, and documented, it's time to "roll it out." For distribution to others, prepare disk backups with descriptive labels, and make sure that the product is appropriately "initialized." Install the product, train users, collect feedback, and take notes on everything for the next version of the software. (You are going to rewrite it at some point, aren't you?)

Using Merit-Based Application Selection

Understanding which Office components to use for your application requires both familiarity with Office and an understanding of your problem. A little detective work may be required to determine which platform will serve best as the basis for your system. Here are some of the strengths and weaknesses of each application.

Access or Excel?

Most applications built around Office are based on either Access or Excel. When do you use each? Generally, Excel should be used whenever you need to do complicated (or iterative) calculations, while Access should be used to track and filter information. The distinction is less clear than it used to be—Excel provides a remarkable AutoFilter capability and can manipulate database tables using DAO. Sometimes the decision is easy—if you (or your users) have purchased one of the versions of Office that does not include Access, your development should happen in Excel. For more details on programming in Excel and Access, see Chapter 21, "Using VBA in Excel," and Chapter 35, "Using VBA in Access."

 DAO, Microsoft's Data Access Object library, provides generalized routines for manipulating databases.

Even if you do your development in Access, you will probably want to take advantage of Excel for special reporting options like pivot tables, goal seeking, trend forecasting, and fancy charting.

Binder

Binder provides a few built-in capabilities that are unavailable in any other platform: consistent headers and footers across sections (and therefore across different applications, because each section can contain a different application), and consecutive page numbering across sections (and therefore across different applications). If you need these capabilities in your reporting, you may want to build your application using Binder.

 Because Binder provides no facility for storing programming code, you will need to either store code within a Binder section or build a Binder on-the-fly using Automation. This latter approach tends to prove more robust for complex reporting.

Outlook

If your application needs to manage e-mail, contact information, or journal entries, consider incorporating Outlook. Outlook's built-in programming language (Visual Basic Scripting Edition, or VBScript) is a subset of VBA and is interpreted (hence slower). From a programming standpoint, it is typically better to control Outlook from an external application such as Word, Excel, or Access because their debugging environments are much more robust. For more information on programming Outlook, see Chapter 44, "Working with Forms," and Chapter 58, "Using VB Script."

PowerPoint

If you need to generate presentations, control of PowerPoint is the way to go. The PowerPoint VBA implementation in Office 97 is limited in some respects, though, so you might consider using a different application as the home application and just controlling PowerPoint through Automation. For more information on programming PowerPoint, see Chapter 26, "Using VBA in PowerPoint."

Word

Word is clearly the platform to use for text document manipulation. There are some other slick capabilities included in Word that you might want to use from Access or Excel, though.

For instance, case-switching operations and conversion of numbers to text (for spelling out on a check, perhaps?) are handled effortlessly by Word, but would need to be built up from pieces in Access or Excel. See the Word Automation examples later in this chapter for an example of how to take advantage of these lesser-used capabilities. For more information on programming Word, see Chapter 11, "Using VBA in Word."

Other Applications

Many of Microsoft's Shared Components are also available for use under code. These are not capable of hosting VBA, so applications cannot be built with them as the base. However, many of these components are ActiveX objects and therefore expose their object model. For more information on using ActiveX objects with Office 97 applications, see Chapter 48, "Using ActiveX Controls."

N O T E All ActiveX objects (including all of the applications described in this section) *expose* their object models. This means that their object model can be accessed by other programs via Automation. In theory, an application can also have an object model that is not exposed, but is only available when programming within the object itself—though there's little reason to do this from a programming point of view. The Binder object model is the other way around—it can only be accessed from Automation controlled by other applications. Its object model is exposed, but it has no facility to manipulate its own object model under code. ▪

Microsoft DataMap, MSGraph, and Internet Explorer are all good examples of components that can provide a great boost to your application when used under Automation.

N O T E Microsoft is not the only company to expose the object model in their products. Many vendors are adopting the COM (Component Object Model) standard. Microsoft licenses VBA for use in applications, too. This has been used to great advantage in Shapeware's Visio, a graphics tool used for things like floorplans, wiring diagrams, organizational charts, and other graphics composed of geometric shapes superimposed on an underlying grid. ▪

References and the Object Browser

Object models change as new versions are released, and new objects with exposed object models are released all the time. If you have installed an application on your system and you don't have adequate object model information, here are the tools to get the information you need.

Checking References

In the Visual Basic Editor (VBE), choose Tools, References. This will bring up the References dialog box (see Figure 57.1).

FIG. 57.1

The References dialog box from the Microsoft Word VBE.

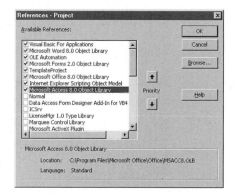

Every object that you wish to use under Automation must have a checked entry in this dialog box. You will probably find a large number of unchecked boxes in the References dialog box when you open it. This indicates that these items are installed on your system, but are not presently available for Automation from within the application you are using. To make them available, select the check box next to each item you wish to use. For instance, in our case we are adding the Access object model to our available object models.

Browsing an Object Library

Now that you have installed necessary references, let's open your object browser.

To start the Object Browser, select View, Object Browser, then click the Object Browser button on the toolbar or press F2 on the keyboard. This will display the Object Browser window as displayed in Figure 57.2.

The Object Browser has several key features. The Library drop-down list at the upper-left determines which ActiveX object library you are going to examine. You can also select All Libraries to view all objects that you have made available to your system in the References dialog box.

FIG. 57.2
The Object Browser, as displayed in Microsoft Word.

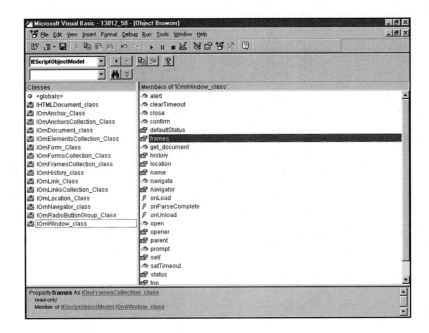

The Classes window at the left side of the Object Browser contains a list of all classes contained within the selected library. For all intents and purposes, each class corresponds to an object that can be manipulated under code. When you highlight a class with the mouse, its members (callable methods, readable and/or setable properties) appear in the Members window on the right.

The gray window at the bottom of the screen provides more details on the currently selected member (expected/optional arguments for methods, data type for properties, and so on). Though you can (with much work) get enough information to build an object model for a given library by viewing each class and member one at a time, for many applications there's an easier way.

Object Browser Help

By clicking with the right mouse button on any Class or Member name and clicking Help on the resulting (see Figure 57.3), you will be taken directly to the corresponding help topic (assuming the ActiveX object's creator provided a help file which includes a topic for that Class or Member). This is particularly useful when trying to chase down how to access an object under Automation in a brand-new application with limited available documentation.

FIG. 57.3

You can get help in the Object Browser for a specific Class item.

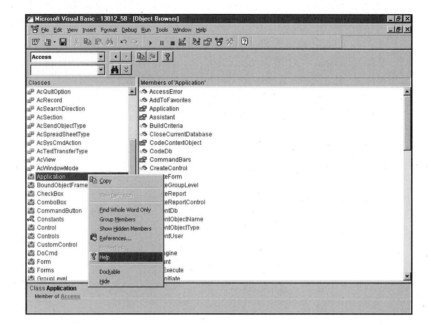

Learning the Object Models

The object model for each application defines which components of that application are available under program control. If you need a particular component of an application and it's not available in the object model, you may need to formulate a different approach or use a different application. Here are the top-level object models for Office.

 TIP You can find each of these object models by using the technique described earlier for obtaining help from within the Object Browser (select help for the Application Class). The help system can become confusing, though. If you launch Access help from within the Word VBE Object Browser, and then click the Help Topics button in the Help window, you will get the Contents for Word Visual Basic help, not Access help.

When you view an object model in the help system, you will notice that a color distinction is made between objects that are only objects and objects that are both objects and collections.

 TIP A *collection* is a series of like objects (just as the name implies). Collections can be stepped through, one element at a time, using the For Each statement (see the code examples at the end of this chapter for more information).

You will also notice that most object models require much more than a single screen to convey all necessary information. Click on the red hyperlinks on the help screens to jump down into the middle of an object model (see the Word object model later in this section for an example).

Access

The Access object model (see Figure 57.4) provides hooks to the major constructs in Access. Note that Microsoft also has DAO and Jet objects, which constitute Microsoft's database engine. These database engine constructs can be accessed under program control to manipulate databases in a variety of file formats under Automation (see the "Other Microsoft Shared Components" section later in this chapter for a DAO object model).

FIG. 57.4
The Microsoft Access object model.

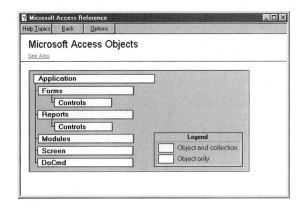

Binder

Microsoft Binder definitely has the simplest object model (see Figure 57.5). Dealing with the Binder under code, however, has some tricky nuances (see the Automation section later in this chapter for code examples).

FIG. 57.5
The Microsoft Binder object model.

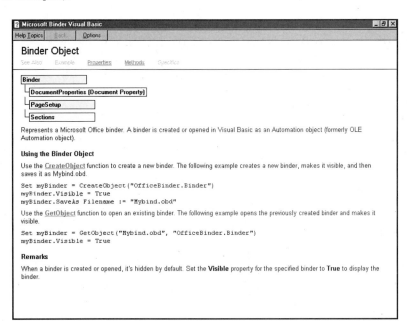

Excel

Microsoft Excel has one of the most developed and tested object models in Office (see Figure 57.6). VBA has been included in Excel since version 5.0, and millions of users have had a chance to test it. Look up the object model in Excel help to see the full picture.

FIG. 57.6

The Microsoft Excel object model.

Microsoft Excel Visual Basic

Help Topics | Back | Options

Microsoft Excel Objects

See Also

Application

- Workbooks [Workbook]
  - Worksheets [Worksheet] ▶
  - Charts [Chart] ▶
  - DocumentProperties [DocumentProperty]
  - VBProject
  - CustomViews [CustomView]
  - CommandBars [CommandBar]
  - PivotCaches [PivotCache]
  - Styles [Style]
    - Borders [Border]
    - Font
    - Interior
  - Windows [Window]
    - Panes [Pane]
  - Names [Name]
  - RoutingSlip
  - Mailer

- AddIns [AddIn]
- AutoCorrect
- Assistant
- Debug
- Dialogs [Dialog]
- CommandBars [CommandBar]
- Names [Name]
- Windows [Window]
  - Panes [Pane]
- WorksheetFunction
- RecentFiles [RecentFile]
- FileSearch
- FileFind
- VBE
- ODBCErrors [ODBCError]

▶ Click red arrow to expand chart

Legend
- ☐ Object and collection
- ☐ Object only

Outlook

The Outlook object model is structured somewhat differently from the rest of the Microsoft Office application object models. See Chapter 58, "Using VBScript," for more details on the Outlook object model and how to control it using VBScript.

PowerPoint

The PowerPoint object model (see Figure 57.7) is brand new in PowerPoint 97. Note that the event model has not been implemented in PowerPoint 97, and many user actions are not recorded by the Macro Recorder.

TIP You will likely have a great deal of difficulty trying to find the PowerPoint object model in the help system. In order to get to it, start your object browser in Word or Excel, and make sure that the PowerPoint object type library is checked under Tools, References. Select PowerPoint in the Library drop-down list, and right-click any of the Class names. Check the Show Hidden Members option (see Figure 57.8). A number of grayed-out Classes will appear. Right-click the Collection class entry, and click Help.

FIG. 57.7
The Microsoft
PowerPoint object
model.

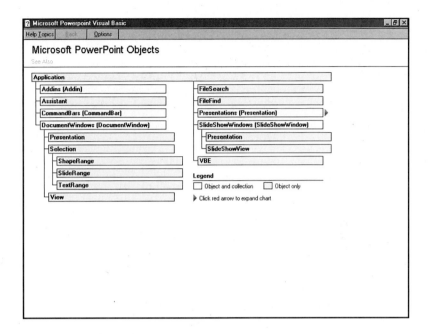

FIG. 57.8
Use Show Hidden
Members to reveal
other Class items and
Members in the Word
object model.

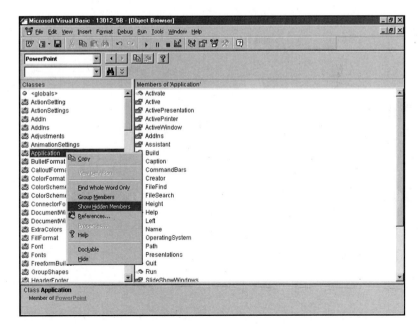

Word

The Word object model is brand new in Word 97 (see Figure 57.9). The WordBasic object (which was the only object in the Word 95 object model) still exists, sitting alongside the entire VBA object model implementation. This older facility is used by Word 97 to automatically convert Word 6.0/95 macros to Word 97. Each WordBasic call from Word 6.0 is merely changed into a call to WordBasic (for instance, a PageDown command in Word 6.0 is equivalent to WordBasic.PageDown in Word 97).

FIG. 57.9

The main Microsoft Word object model.

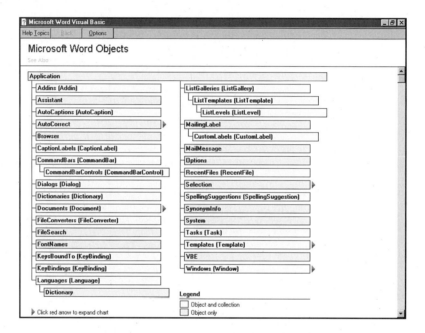

Now, if the help system hyperlink beside the Selection object is clicked, you will be taken down into the object model as shown in Figure 57.10.

Other Microsoft Shared Components

Many other of Microsoft's shared components are available through Automation. An object model for DAO when used with an ODBC-direct source is shown in Figure 57.11. An object model for the Office Assistant is shown in Figure 57.12. You can, in fact, control the crazed paper clip under code to some degree, but it's pretty limited. There are a number of canned actions for the Assistant which may be launched under code (see Listing 57.1). Note that some animations will only animate some Assistant characters while having no effect on others.

FIG. 57.10
Down in the middle of the Word 97 object model—starting from the Selection object.

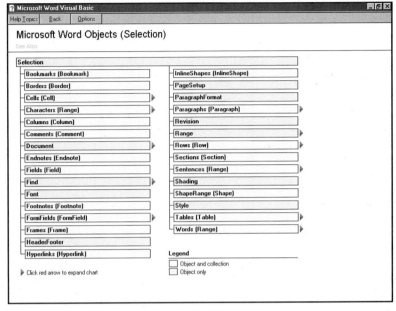

FIG. 57.11
The Microsoft DAO ODBC object model.

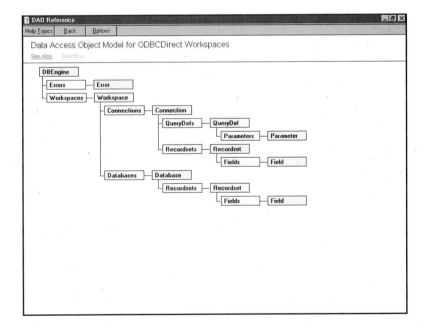

FIG. 57.12

The Office Assistant object model.

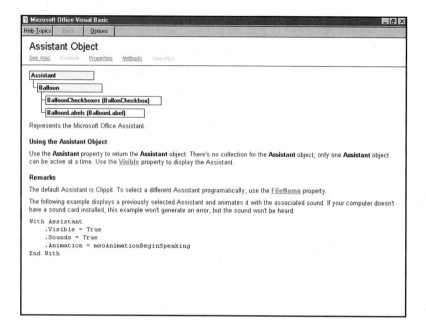

Here is a code snippet to place "Clippit" (or whichever other Assistant has been chosen) at a particular screen location, make it visible, and have it greet you:

Listing 57.1 Code Used to Place Clippit at a Certain Screen Location

```
With Assistant
    .Reduced = True
    .Move xLeft:= 300, yTop:= 200
    .Visible = True
    .Animation = msoAnimationGreeting
End With
```

For other assistant properties and animation options, search for Assistant Object and Animation Property in the Visual Basic Reference section of Microsoft Help.

Help

One of the greatest boons to development within Office is the Microsoft Help system. Learning your way around the help system is time well spent. Not only are the object models described, but also every VBA construct is covered in detail, including all available parameters for each and a variety of useful code examples.

As with any resource, the Help system has its limitations as well. You will often find that the exact example you need doesn't exist, or that a command you need is not cross-referenced as you might expect. Spending some time browsing the help system will help address these shortcomings to some degree. You should also check for additional help information from the Microsoft Web site (**www.microsoft.com**).

If you still can't find what you need, your bookstore is full of great Que books that might give you the exact example you need.

Automation

Automation (formerly called OLE Automation) is the technology by which applications can be controlled by one another under program control. The prerequisites for a system to use Automation are an application which can serve as an *Automation Client*, and an application which can serve as an *Automation Server*. An application can be neither, either or both a client and server. Automation Servers are synonymous with ActiveX components at the moment, because an ActiveX object is one which exposes its object model. Each of the major office applications can serve as an Automation Server, and most can serve as Automation Clients. Code examples to control each of the major office applications are included in the following sections.

Clients and Servers

In Table 57.1 you'll find a list indicating the Automation Client and Server status of the Office 97 applications. Office 97 has been a major step forward, allowing Automation between nearly every conceivable pair of Office applications.

Table 57.1   Client/Server Status of Office 97 Applications

Application	Client	Server
Access	yes	yes
Binder	no	yes
Excel	yes	yes
Outlook	yes	yes
PowerPoint	yes	yes
Word	yes	yes

To determine which ActiveX objects (Automation Servers) are installed on your system, from your Start button, select Run, type **regedit**, and then click OK. Choose Edit, Find and search for ProgId (see Figure 57.13).

FIG. 57.13

The Registry Editor displays a ProgId reference.

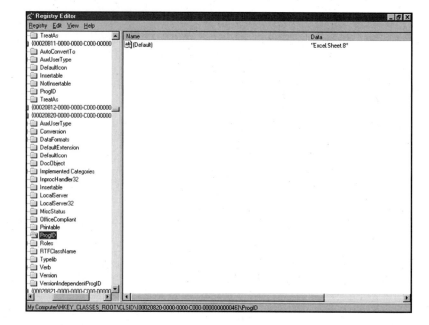

Every instance of ProgId indicates an object that is exposed. The name in the right-hand window that is associated with the ProgId is the correct name to use in your CreateObject or GetObject statement. To determine what functionality might be provided by the exposed object, use the Object Browser as described earlier in the chapter.

 The utility Regclean.exe, available from the Microsoft Web site (**www.microsoft.com**) will help to tidy up your registry. The registry stores configuration information so that Windows knows how to treat applications. When applications are deleted, however, their registry keys are not always removed. In some cases, mysterious system glitches can disappear simply by running REGCLEAN.EXE and following its recommendations.

Access

As mentioned earlier, each major office application is an Automation Server, and therefore available for use under code from other programs. For instance, use the following code in VBA under Excel, Word, or even PowerPoint to create an Access database.

```
Set objAccessApp = CreateObject("Access.Application")
```

The code in Listing 57.2 will grab an Access document that is already open, and print each form that is open. Note that the forms collection in Access only refers to forms that are open. Further code would be required to open a specific form before printing.

Listing 57.2   Grab an Open Access Document and Print All Open Forms

```
Sub DocumentForms()
    ' obtain particular Access object. Note: file must already be open.
    Set objAccessApp = GetObject("c:\My Documents\Sales4.mdb")
    ' set forms collection. Note: if no forms open, nothing will happen.
    Set frms = objAccessApp.forms
    ' step through open forms one at a time. Show name & print.
    For Each frm In frms
        MsgBox "Form name is " & frm.Name
        objAccessApp.DoCmd.PrintOut acPrintAll, , , acHigh, 1, True
    Next frm
    ' now clean up resources
    Set frms = Nothing
    Set objAccessApp = Nothing
End Sub
```

Binder

Binder, as a container object, provides a special case for Automation control. There is actually no VBE or other facility for storing code as part of a Binder object itself. Its object model is exposed, however, so it's possible to control a Binder's sections under code. For instance, Village Software Inc.'s FastPlan line of products (see Figure 57.14) make use of this capability. Each of the various sections consists of a Word document, Excel workbook, or PowerPoint slide show. By using Automation code that is hosted in one of the Excel sections, the user's information (entered once into a wizard) is copied as appropriate into any or all of the sections, regardless of the section's application type.

The trick to writing this type of code in Binder is to store all necessary code in a document that resides in a Section of the Binder. The Application object for Binder-compliant applications has a Container property that returns the particular Section instance within which the application lives. Getting the Parent property of this Section object will return the Binder that hosts the particular Section in question. Listing 57.3 shows an example that returns the Binder object when run from an Excel workbook in a Binder section:

Listing 57.3   Code in an Excel Section of a Binder to Return the Binder Object that Hosts the Section

```
' Get the workbook we're in
Set wb = ActiveWorkbook
' Get this workbook's particular Section
Set bdrSect = wb.Container
' Get the Binder object from the Section
Set bdrApp = bdrSect.Parent()
```

FIG. 57.14
Village Software's
FastPlan line of
products control
Microsoft's Binder under
code, allowing
integration of Word,
Excel, and PowerPoint
sections into a single
report.

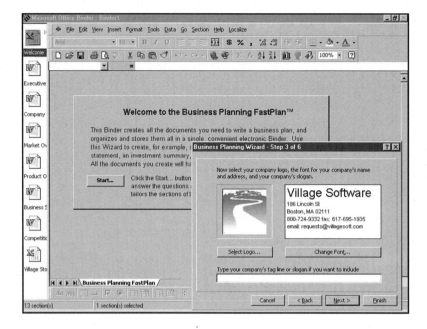

Note that what we're doing is essentially walking the tree backwards to find its top. Once we
have defined an object that references the base `Binder` object, we use a more standard walk-
the-model syntax to get down to the particular object we want, by way of the particular section
in which it lives. Note the use of the `Object` property of a `Section`—this is necessary to manipulate the object living in the section as an object (see Listing 57.4).

Listing 57.4   Code to Walk Up the Binder Tree to the Top, Then Down to an Excel Cell in the First Section

```
' Get Binder by walking backwards, as before
Set bdrApp = ActiveWorkbook.Container.Parent()
' Get the first section (this example assumes it's an Excel section)
Set invSect = bdrApp.Sections(1)
' Get the Excel object in the Section
Set objXL = invSect.Object
' Get the range we want
Set myRng = objXL.Range("A5")
```

Don't forget to Set all these object variables to `Nothing` at the end of your routine. See Listing
57.5 for the code sample for achieving this task.

Listing 57.5   Set Everything to *Nothing* at the End of Your Routines

```
Set myRng = Nothing
Set objXL = Nothing
Set invSect = Nothing
Set bdrApp = Nothing
```

> **T I P** For every object defined using a Set statement (for example, Set myWorkbook = Application.ActiveWorkbook), be sure to have a corresponding Set [object] = Nothing (Set myWorkbook = Nothing, in our example). This restores system resources used to store the object's information. It is easy to consume a lot of system resources by defining objects, especially when using Automation. If you have code like: Set xlApp = CreateObject (Excel.Application), the resources used to store that information are not restored *even when you close Excel*. You must explicitly set the object equal to Nothing to free the associate resources.

Excel

Automation in Excel is straightforward. To create an Excel workbook from an external application and drop information into a cell, you could use the in code Listing 57.6:

Listing 57.6   Creating an Instance of Excel and Dropping Information into It

```
' Create new Excel object
Set objExcelApp = CreateObject("Excel.Application")
' Make Excel visible to user. Created objects are invisible by default.
ObjExcelApp.Visible = True
' Get the active sheet of the workbook
Set objSheet = objExcelApp.ActiveSheet
' Get cell A1
Set objCell = objSheet.Range("A1")
' Put information into the cell
ObjCell.value = "information"
```

> **T I P** For some other examples of the sophisticated code behavior that can be achieved within Excel, see the free Village Software FastStart templates on the CD-ROM accompanying this book.

Outlook

Calling Outlook from Excel is described along with Outlook's object model in Chapter 58, "Using VBScript."

PowerPoint

PowerPoint 97 is the first version of PowerPoint that is officially supported as Automation-compatible. PowerPoint 95 had a "hidden" version of VBA that was not officially supported. PowerPoint 97 still is much weaker than Excel, Word, or Access in terms of VBA control. For example: many menu actions are not recorded by the Macro Recorder, there are no "Auto" macros, and it is not possible to dispatch code from a button or other Shape object unless a PowerPoint slideshow is running.

Here's how to grab the first object on an open PowerPoint Presentation (see Listing 57.7).

Listing 57.7   Grab the First Object in an Open PowerPoint Session

```
' Get the open PowerPoint object

Set objPptApp = GetObject(,"PowerPoint.Application")
' Get the first presentation in PPT
Set objPres = objPptApp.Presentations(1)
' Get the first slide in the presentation
Set objSlide = objPres.Slides(1)
' Get the first object on the slide
Set objOnSlide = objSlide.Objects(1)
```

Note that this coding technique is not very robust. If you have multiple PowerPoint Presentations open, you can't guarantee which one will be opened by the GetObject routine. Typically it's safer to include the file name in the GetObject statement.

Word

Word 97 is the first version of Word that can serve as an Automation Client using VBA (Word 95 only contained WordBasic, though it exposed the entire WordBasic language as the WordBasic object, and could thereby serve as an Automation Server).

Opening a new Word document can be done as in Listing 57.8:

Listing 57.8   Getting a Word Document

```
' Get Word App
Set wdApp = CreateObject("Word.Application")
' Make visible
wdApp.Visible = True
' Can open an existing document by using this command
wdApp.Documents.Open "c:\My Documents\letter.doc"
```

In general, for Automation the only real trick is to be able to set an object in your client application's code to equal the Application object of the desired server application. Once you've done that, you can write all of your code as if you are working in the server application, and just tack your representative object onto the beginning of the line.

Building an Application

All that's left now is to put the various techniques and tools that we have described together. As an example, here's a useful cross-application function that can serve as the basis for a check-writing application. When supplied with a number, the function will grab Word and use Word's text-conversion field operations to convert the digits into the appropriate spelled-out currency (see Listing 57.9). This function can be used from within Excel, PowerPoint, or Access.

Listing 57.9   Convert a Dollar Figure to Currency Text

```
Function ConvertCurrency(amt As Variant) As String
Dim wdObj As Object

  ' get Word
  Set wdObj = CreateObject("Word.Application")
  ' Create new document for field
  wdObj.Documents.Add
  ' insert the field to generate formatting
  wdObj.WordBasic.InsertField ("=" & amt & "\* dollartext \* MERGEFORMAT")
  ' Now grab the text
  wdObj.Selection.WholeStory
  ' Set function to be text value and clean up
  ConvertCurrency = wdObj.Selection
  Set wdObj = Nothing
End Function
```

Note that we've also made use of the WordBasic object to use the older InsertField function. To implement this routine using strict Word 97 VBA, you would need to use Field.Add, which requires more code setup.

We can test our function with the simple routine in Listing 57.10:

Listing 57.10   Routine to Test the Conversion Function

```
Sub testConvert()
    stDollar = ConvertCurrency(55.27)
    MsgBox stDollar, , "Amount in Dollars"
End Sub
```

Search for "fields, formatting field results," then "Format (*) field switches" in the Word help system for more information on formatting options that can be applied this way. ●

Using VBScript

by Keith MacKay

Just as VBA is adapted from Visual Basic, VBScript (Visual Basic Scripting Edition) is adapted from VBA. Microsoft Outlook is presently the only Office application that makes use of VBScript rather than VBA. VBScript is actually a strict subset of VBA, containing many of VBA's keywords and features and using them all in the same way. This chapter will describe what the differences are, as well as describe how to use VBScript within Outlook. ■

Using VBScript versus VBA

VBScript is a subset of VBA, and it's important to know what's there and what's not.

Adding VBScript code with Outlook

Outlook has the most limited development environment of all Office applications. We'll discuss how to use it.

Manipulating the Outlook object model with VBScript

Outlook has an object model unlike any other in Office. We'll discuss the details.

Debugging VBScript

Outlook's VBScript development environment is Spartan at best. We'll describe some techniques to compensate for the restrictions.

VBScript versus VBA

VBScript was designed to be a "light" version of VBA that would be safe and fast—the sort of thing that would be appropriate to programming a wide variety of applications from Web browsers to information managers. As a result of the design goals, many potentially dangerous functions have been omitted from the general VBScript definition (for example: declarations to external functions, file input/output, and Automation). Eliminating these features help to plug many security holes by default—if you cannot manipulate an external file, you can do less damage (intentional or accidental). To help stay small and fast, only Variant variables are used (there is no strict type declaration). The major specific differences between VBScript and VBA are described below.

Usage of Constants

One of the main differences in programming VBScript rather than VBA is the inability to use descriptive constant names as provided by the Outlook type library. Instead, the numeric values must be used when accessing these elements from within VBScript. For instance, Table 58.1 shows the constants and numeric values used to access Outlook's default folders.

Table 58.1   Microsoft Outlook's Default Folder Constants

Constant	Numeric value
olFolderDeletedItems	3
olFolderOutbox	4
olFolderSentMail	5
olFolderInbox	6
olFolderCalendar	9
olFolderContacts	10
olFolderJournal	11
olFolderNotes	12
olFolderTasks	13

To illustrate the difference in usage, here are two short code examples. Under VBA, you could use the code in Listing 58.1 to Access Outlook's default Tasks folder.

Listing 58.1   How to Access the Default Outlook Tasks Folder Using Automation from VBA

```
Set myOlApp = CreateObject("Outlook.Application")
Set myOlMAPI = myOlApp.GetNameSpace("MAPI")
Set myTasksFolder = myOlMAPI.GetDefaultFolder(olFolderTasks)
```

Under VBScript, you would use the code in Listing 58.2 to accomplish the same task.

Listing 58.2   How to Access the Default Outlook Tasks Folder using VBScript in Outlook

```
Set myOlMAPI = Application.GetNameSpace("MAPI")
Set myTasksFolder = myOlMAPI.GetDefaultFolder(13)
```

For a complete list of the constants included in the Outlook type library (and their numeric values), go to "Microsoft Outlook Constants" in Microsoft Outlook Visual Basic Help.

 T I P   Outlook Visual Basic Help is not installed during setup, though it is included in the ValuPack folder on the Office 97 CD-ROM. For more details, see the Microsoft Outlook Help topic "Getting Help for Visual Basic in Microsoft Outlook." Note, however, that the examples shown in Outlook Visual Basic Help are written in VBA, and not VBScript. They will work as shown when run under Automation from an external application (such as Microsoft Excel), but will need modification to run in VBScript. You can also download the help files (and other useful development examples) from the Microsoft Outlook Developer's Web site at **http://www.microsoft.com/outlookdev**.

Missing VBA Constructs in VBScript

VBScript, as defined, omits many VBA programming constructs. Even so, some of these constructs have been added back in to Outlook to provide adequate Office programmability (most notably, CreateObject has been included in Outlook's VBScript implementation, and Outlook contains some collections—though typical VBA collection management keywords are still omitted). Below we've included two useful tables: a conceptual table of VBA constructs omitted from VBScript and a list of specific VBA keywords omitted from VBScript.

Table 58.2 includes the general constructs that have been omitted from VBScript, along with their implications.

Table 58.2   Overview of VBA Constructs Omitted from VBScript

Omitted Construct	Note for VBScript Programming
Automation	No Automation functionality provided.
Collection support	Collection support not provided as in VBA. No Add, Count, Item, Remove. For Each…Next not supported.
Constants	No constants. No Const declarations, no type library constants.
DDE (Dynamic Data Exchange)	No DDE functionality provided.

continues

Table 58.2 Continued

Omitted Construct	Note for VBScript Programming
Error trapping	No error trapping or debugging capabilities provided.
File input/output	No file manipulation capabilities at all.
Financial functions	No financial functions.
Line tagging	No line numbers or labels. No GoTos, no On…GoTo, and so on.
Strict variable typing	All VBScript variables are Variant. No fixed length strings, no arrays, no type declarations or conversions. No VBA intrinsic data types.

Table 58.3 includes a list of VBA keywords omitted from VBScript, along with notes for the VBScript programmer.

Table 58.3 VBA Keywords Omitted from (or Changed in) VBScript

Keyword	Note for VBScript Programming
Add	Collections omitted.
Array	All VBScript variables are variant. No arrays.
CCur	All VBScript variables are variant. No conversion needed.
Clipboard	The Clipboard object is not supported.
Collection	Collections omitted.
#Const	VBScript interpreted; no conditional compilation facilities provided.
Const	No constants. See section on Outlook type library constants.
Count	Collections omitted.
CreateObject	Automation omitted.
CVar	All VBScript variables are variant. No conversion needed.
CVDate	All VBScript variables are variant. No conversion needed.
Date	Omitted.
Debug.Print	Debug functionality omitted.
Declare	No external declarations.
Def	No types.

Keyword	Note for VBScript Programming
DoEvents	Omitted.
End	Debug functionality omitted.
Erl	Debug functionality omitted.
Error	Debug functionality omitted.
For Each... Next	Collections omitted.
Format	All VBScript variables are variant. Not needed.
GetObject	Automation omitted.
GoSub...Return	Omitted.
GoTo	Omitted.
#If...Then...Else	VBScript interpreted; no conditional compilation facilities provided.
Item	Collections omitted.
Like	All VBScript variables are variant. Not needed.
LinkExecute	DDE functionality omitted.
LinkPoke	DDE functionality omitted.
LinkRequest	DDE functionality omitted.
LinkSend	DDE functionality omitted.
Lset	All VBScript variables are variant. Not needed.
Mid	Omitted.
New	Omitted.
On... GoSub	Omitted.
On...GoTo	Omitted.
On Error GoTo	Debug functionality omitted.
On Error...Resume	Debug functionality omitted.
Option Base	No arrays, hence no need to change array base.
Option Compare	All VBScript variables are variant. Not needed.
Option Private Module	Omitted.
Optional	Omitted.
ParamArray	Omitted.

continues

Table 58.3   Continued

Keyword	Note for VBScript Programming
Private	Scope of all procedures fixed.
Property Get	Omitted.
Property Let	Omitted.
Property Set	Omitted.
Public	Scope of all procedures/variables fixed.
Remove	Collections omitted.
Resume	Debug functionality omitted.
Resume Next	Debug functionality omitted.
Rset	All VBScript variables are variant. Not needed.
Static	Scope of procedures/variables fixed.
Stop	Debug functionality omitted.
Str	All VBScript variables are variant. Not needed.
StrConv	All VBScript variables are variant. Not needed.
Time	Omitted.
Timer	Omitted.
Type... End Type	No types.
TypeName	No types.
TypeOf	No types.
Val	All VBScript variables are variant. Not needed.
With...End With	Functionality omitted.

If you must have the functionality provided by some of these omitted keywords, you must leverage another application that does provide them. There are two ways to do this. You can either write all your code in the other application and only access Outlook using Automation, or you can write your code in VBScript in Outlook and access the necessary functionality from other applications via Automation from Outlook. For more information on controlling Outlook from external applications, see the debugging section below.

Using VBScript in Outlook

Outlook provides a number of built-in forms for each default Outlook folder. If these forms don't provide the functionality that your application requires, you can replace them with custom forms. On your custom forms, you can add functionality beyond that provided by default by using VBScript code.

Getting Into the Script Editor

You can get into the Outlook Script Editor from any form. As an example, we'll enter the Script Editor on a new form in the Contacts folder.

1. Open a contact so that the Contacts General form is displayed (see Figure 58.1)

FIG. 58.1

Display any form in the folder for which you wish to add code.

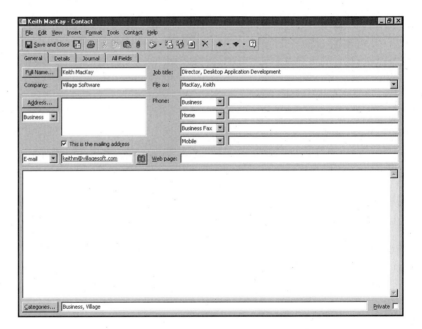

2. From the Tools menu, select Design Outlook Form (see Figure 58.2). This will bring up the general form in Design mode (see Figure 58.3).

Part

X

Ch

58

FIG. 58.2

From the Tools menu, choose Design Outlook Form to get into Form Design mode.

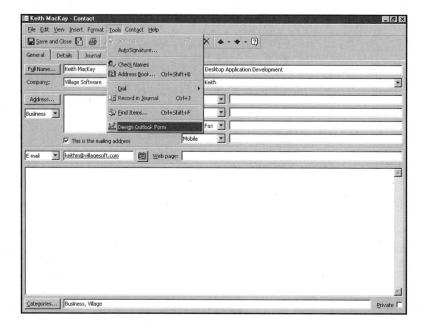

FIG. 58.3

The Contacts General form in Design mode.

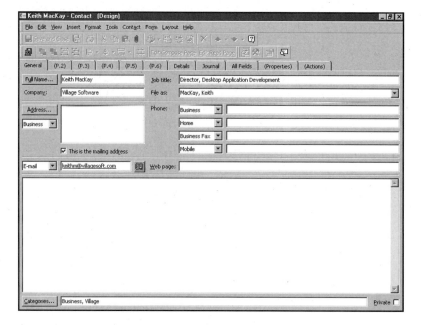

3. Click the (P.2) tab to get to a blank Contacts form (see Figure 58.4). Note that this step is only necessary if you wish to add buttons to a form or otherwise change its appearance. As far as Outlook is concerned, the same code will run in response to any form displayed in the current folder.

FIG. 58.4

An empty Contacts form, ready for customization.

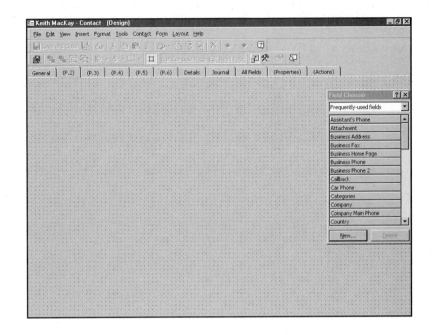

4. Choose Fo**r**m, **V**iew Code (see Figure 58.5) or click the View Code button on the toolbar (see Figure 58.6). This will display the Script Editor (see Figure 58.7).

FIG. 58.5

From the Fo**r**m menu, choose **V**iew Code.

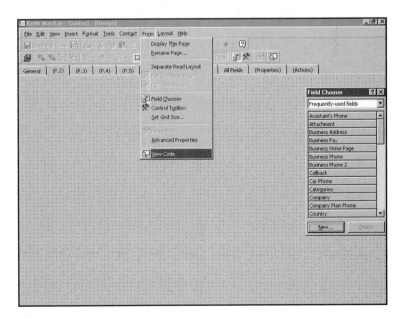

FIG. 58.6
Alternatively, you can
click the View Code
button on the toolbar.

FIG. 58.7
The Script Editor for this
form, ready to be filled
with VBScript.

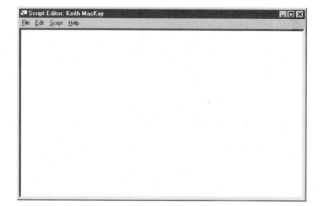

We'll add code into the Editor and describe how VBScript works in more detail in the next
section.

Adding Some VBScript Code to an Outlook Form

All VBScript code runs in response to one of twelve "events," listed below in Table 58.4.

Table 58.4 Outlook Events Available Under VBScript

Event	Occurrence
Click	When a Command Button Control is clicked
Open	When an Item is opened, before it's displayed
Close	Before an Item is closed
Read	When an Item is selected for editing
Write	Before an Item is written, when the user has tabbed off of it in a view
Send	Before an Item is sent, before the inspector is closed
Reply	When an Item is replied to
ReplyAll	When an Item receives an instruction to reply to all
Forward	When an Item is forwarded

Event	Occurrence
PropertyChange	When Standard Outlook Properties are changed
CustomPropertyChange	When Custom User Properties are changed
CustomAction	When an Item's custom action(s) is/are executed

For your code to operate in Outlook, it must be tied to one of these events. The only way to force code to happen at the user's discretion is by connecting it to the Click event of a Command Button Control inserted onto the form. Otherwise, all code must be tied directly to the standard events that are predefined by Outlook.

To add a Sub or Function for an event into your Script Editor, you can either type it in by hand, or you can drop a template in place and fill in the rest by hand. To drop a template into the Editor, choose Script, Event (see Figure 58.8).

FIG. 58.8

Select Script and then Event to drop a template VBScript routine into your Script Editor.

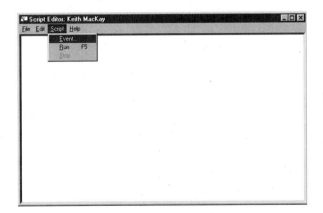

This will bring up the Events selection dialog box as shown in Figure 58.9. From this dialog box you can select any event (except Click) and it will be dropped automatically into your Script Editor.

FIG. 58.9

The Events selection dialog box. Note that a reminder of when the event will occur is provided for each event.

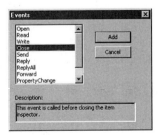

Figure 58.10 displays a code template for the Close event as it was dropped into the Script Editor.

FIG. 58.10

Code template for the Close event as generated from the Events selection dialog (from Script|Events).

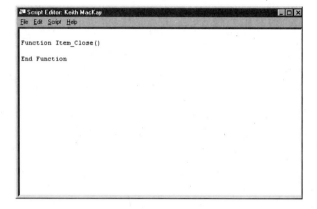

To complete our example, add the following line of code into the script editor.

Listing 58.3   Some Code That Will Operate Every Time an Item Is Closed

```
Function Item_Close()
   MsgBox "Now closing. Everything must go!"
End Function
```

Close the Script Editor, and publish this form to the Contacts folder: Select File, Publish Form As... (see Figure 58.11) or select the Publish Form As... button on the toolbar (see Figure 58.12).

Fill in the dialog box that appears (see Figure 58.13) with a name for your form and click the Publish button.

Choose Tools, Design Outlook Form again to toggle out of Design mode. Click the Save and Close button. When you do, the message will pop up (see Figure 58.14).

If you have some code that you do not want to run in response to an event, hold the Shift key down while the event occurs. For instance, holding Shift down while opening a form prevents any code linked to an Open event from running.

FIG. 58.11
Select File, Publish
Form As to save a
custom form into the
folder.

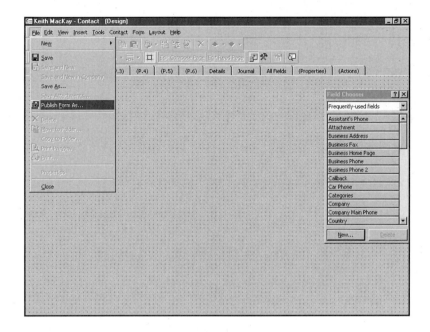

FIG. 58.12
The Publish Form As
button on the toolbar
performs the same
function.

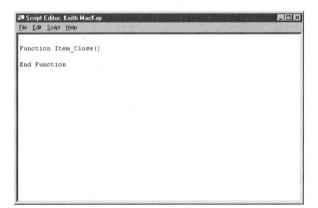

FIG. 58.13
Publish Form As dialog
box. Enter a name and
click Publish.

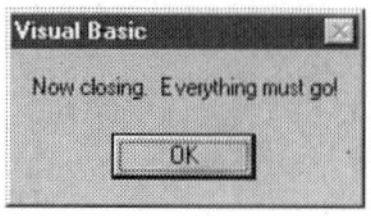

FIG. 58.14

A message popped up in response to the Close event.

Understanding the Outlook Object Model

Every Office application is programmed through accessing components of its object model.

N O T E An object model for an application is a definition of which components of that application are available for use in programming, and how those components are related to one another. ▪

Outlook Object Model Basics

Outlook's object model differs significantly from that of other Office applications (see Figure 58.15). The object model is not fixed, but can grow indefinitely as Outlook folders are added and nested one within another.

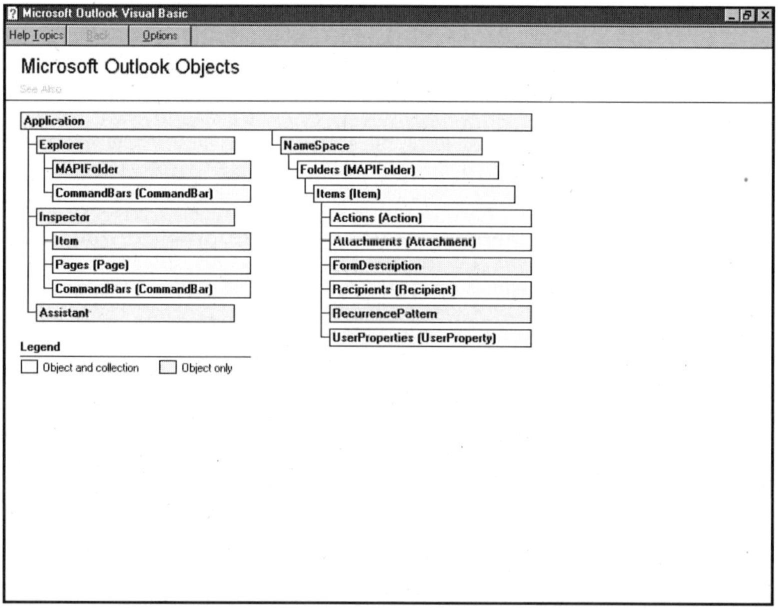

FIG. 58.15

The Outlook object model as found in Outlook Visual Basic Help.

Note that the Folders object in NameSpace is a collection of all folders contained in Outlook. Each of the folders in this collection may, in turn, have a folders item, which is a collection of subfolders for that folder. This can continue *ad infinitum*.

The main objects that you manipulate in Outlook are Folders and Items. Folders in the object model directly correspond to Outlook's folders as displayed by the Outlook Explorer window (see Figure 58.16) Items correspond to the eleven basic elements that are manipulated by Outlook. See the Outlook Items section later in this chapter for more details on Outlook Items and the objects that they can contain.

FIG. 58.16

The Outlook Explorer window displaying the Outlook folder hierarchy. Outlook's Folders collection always reflects the current tree structure.

Walking the Outlook Object Model

In general, object models are used to indicate the path that must be traversed in order to access a particular element of an application (this is sometimes referred to as "walking the object model"). For instance, to access a particular Outlook Item, you must start at the Application object, grab the appropriate NameSpace object, grab the appropriate MAPI Folder from the Folders collection, and then grab the appropriate Item from the Items collection within that particular MAPIFolder. To put the example into more concrete terms, Listing 58.4 contains VBScript code to grab a Contact Item within Outlook. Note how the object model is traversed.

Listing 58.4   Accessing a Contact Item Within Outlook

```
' Grab Contact Item.
' Note that Application refers to the Outlook application by default, when in
Outlook.
' Start by stepping from Application to NameSpace
Set myOlNameSpace = Application.GetNameSpace("MAPI")
' Now get default Contacts folder from Folders collection.
' Note that 10 is the Outlook constant that represents the Contacts folder.
Set myOlContactsFolder = myOlNameSpace.GetDefaultFolder(10)
' Now grab the Contact Items from the Contacts folder
Set myContactItems = myOlContactsFolder.Items
```

continues

Listing 58.4   Continued

```
' Now get the first Contact Item in the list (Item # 1)
Set myFirstContact = myContactItems(1)
```

N O T E   The NameSpace used by Outlook refers to that particular messaging system that Outlook is using. You will notice that GetNameSpace takes the argument "MAPI" in the example above. As of this writing, MAPI is the only NameSpace that is available to Outlook (MAPI is also the underlying messaging protocol used by Microsoft Exchange). Nevertheless, the Outlook object model was designed with expandability in mind, and as new messaging protocols are accepted by Microsoft, they will "drop" right into the object model without significant changes being required. ■

Although we traversed the object model one step at a time, we could have done it all in one step, as shown in Listing 58.5.

Listing 58.5   Accessing a Contact Item Within Outlook in One Step

```
Set myFirstContact =
Application.GetNameSpace("MAPI").GetDefaultFolder(10).Items(1)
```

Note that this compressed format is typically avoided. In general, the "interim" branches of the object model will be needed more than once in your code. It is faster to use an object variable that has already been defined than to re-walk the object model each time.

Outlook Items

There are eleven fundamental Items that Outlook manipulates (see Table 58.5), and seven objects that each of these Items can contain (see Table 58.6).

Table 58.5   Outlook Items

Item	Associated Folder	Description
AppointmentItem	Calendar	A unique appointment, one-time or recurring.
ContactItem	Contacts	A single contact.
JournalItem	Journal	A single journal entry.
MailItem	Inbox/mail folder	A mail message. Default Item object of Outlook.
NoteItem	Notes	A single note.
PostItem	public folder	A single post. Essentially a MailItem, but posted directly to target folder rather than mailed.

Item	Associated Folder	Description
RemoteItem	Inbox/mail folder	A truncated MailItem (header, 256 characters of body).
ReportItem	Inbox/mail folder	A report (typically error message) from mail system.
TaskItem	Tasks	A single task.
MeetingRequestItem	Calendar	Created by Outlook from AppointmentItem when MeetingStatus property set to olMeeting and sent to one or more users.
TaskRequestItem	Tasks	Created by Outlook from TaskItem when the Assign method is applied to it to delegate the task to a user.

Note that MeetingRequestItem and TaskRequestItem are created directly by Outlook in response to a particular event—they cannot be created directly under code unless the appropriate action is triggered on an AppointmentItem or TaskItem.

Table 58.6   Objects That All Outlook Items Contain

Object	Description
Actions	Particular action(s) appropriate to Item
Attachments	Linked/embedded object(s) in an Item.
FormDescription	Form properties for an Item.
Pages	Customized page(s) of an Item.
Recipients	Recipient(s) for an Item.
RecurrencePattern	The pattern of recurrence for AppointmentItem and TaskItem Items.
UserProperties	Custom field(s) added to Item (done during design time).

Note that objects in Table 58.6 that are plural indicate collections—there can be one or more of these objects connected with any particular Item.

Debugging Your VBScript Code

The VBScript Script Editor in Outlook is a Spartan development environment providing no robust debugging facilities. Though it will look and feel quite familiar to folks who programmed on the first personal computers fifteen years ago, it will likely prove frustrating in short order. Fortunately, there are a few things that can be done.

Debugging Within the Outlook Script Editor

VBScript provides no error-handling keywords, and Outlook's Script Editor provides no debugging tools, and very little in the way of text editing tools.

The tools that are provided consist of a menu option to run your code (performing a syntax check), and a menu option to move to a specific line of the script. To run your code, choose Script, Run. If an error is discovered, the particular line on which it occurred will be shown in the error message.

If you have received an error message which indicates a line number, choose Script, Goto to jump directly to the offending line of your script.

For find-and-replace operations, you will want to select all text in the Script Editor, cut it, and paste it into WordPad. After performing the replacement, select all text, copy it, and paste it back into Outlook's Script Editor.

If you run into problems, there are a few simple techniques that can be used to help give you insight into where your VBScript code is going wrong. The first is to always build your code up from small fragments that you know work correctly—if they work correctly when run separately, they will often work correctly when strung together. Another technique to use in the Script Editor is to make frequent use of MsgBox statements to print variable contents to the screen. While testing your code, this is an effective way to indicate where you are in the code and what's happening. For instance, one typical MsgBox technique would be along the lines of Listing 58.6, where strName is a variable that doesn't seem to work as it should.

Listing 58.6   MsgBox Debugging Technique for the Outlook Script Editor

```
MsgBox "Entering questionable code. Variable = " & strName
 'questionable code in here
MsgBox "Finished questionable code. Variable = " & strName
```

This way, we can just move the MsgBox statements around, and determine which part of the code is not performing as expected.

Using Internet Explorer for Generic Code Development

Internet Explorer provides a rudimentary debugging environment for VBScript development, including a single-step mechanism. Unfortunately for Outlook developers, Internet Explorer's VBScript environment does not provide Automation capability, so there is no way to control Outlook from within Internet Explorer. As a result, any Outlook-specific code development must be done either within Outlook's Script Editor or within another Office application via Automation, as described in the next section.

All the same, general program flow or utility routines that do not specifically refer to Outlook items can be written, tested, and debugged in Internet Explorer and then copied wholesale into Outlook.

Using Other Office Applications and Automation for Outlook-Specific Code Development

To get a more robust debugging environment, one useful technique is to write all your code in an application that provides better debugging facilities, and then transfer it back into Outlook once it works.

You will not be able to write any code that responds directly to Outlook events using this technique, because Outlook does not expose its event model. However, you will be able to write and test code that manipulates Outlook through Automation, and then copy it with minor changes into an event slot or button Click event.

As an example of the sorts of changes that must be performed, let's start with some code that walks through every Item in the Contacts folder and adds "Personal" to the Category if the home address is defined. Listing 58.7 displays how the code looks when run from Excel under Automation.

Listing 58.7 Excel Code to Update Outlook Categories Through Automation

```
Sub UpdateOutlookCategories()
    ' Define Outlook application object
    Set olApp = CreateObject("Outlook.Application")
    ' get namespace
    Set myNameSpace = olApp.GetNameSpace("MAPI")
    ' get contacts items
    Set myItems = myNameSpace.GetDefaultFolder(10).Items
    ' Now, loop thru contacts. Can't use For…Each in VBScript, so count 'em and
iterate
    numItems = myItems.Count
    For i = 1 To numItems
    Set ThisItem = myItems(i)
    If ThisItem.HomeTelephoneNumber <> "" Then
        ThisItem.Categories = ThisItem.Categories & ", Personal"
    End If
    Next i
End Sub
```

In order to copy this routine into Outlook, only one change really needs to be made. The definition of the Application object needs to be changed to be implicitly assumed, rather than generating an Outlook object with CreateObject. The net result is removal of one line of code and a slight change to a second line of code. The resulting Outlook-based code is displayed in Listing 58.8.

Listing 58.8 Code to Perform Our Task from Within Outlook, Rather Than from Excel

```
Sub UpdateOutlookCategories()
    ' Outlook application object defined by default. Get NameSpace.    '***
changed
    Set myNameSpace = Application.GetNameSpace("MAPI")         '*** changed
' get contacts items
    Set myItems = myNameSpace.GetDefaultFolder(10).Items
    ' Now, loop thru contacts. Can't use For…Each in VBScript, so count 'em and
iterate
    numItems = myItems.Count
    For i = 1 To numItems
    Set ThisItem = myItems(i)
    If ThisItem.HomeTelephoneNumber <> "" Then
        ThisItem.Categories = ThisItem.Categories & ", Personal"
    End If
    Next i
End Sub
```

When developing in this fashion, give the equivalent Subs the same name in both Excel and Outlook to help preserve maintainability and readability. In Outlook, you can then use the Call statement to run the code, as demonstrated in Listing 58.9. Note that you also should include the file location of this portable code inside the Sub itself, as a comment. This makes revamping the code easier.

Listing 58.9 Using the Call Statement Under VBScript in Outlook

```
Function Item_Open()
  Call myRoutine()
End Function
Sub myRoutine()
    ' this routine was written in Excel, and is named myRoutine in Excel, too.
    ' stored in Excel workbook c:\myWork\myStuff.xls
    ' do cool programming stuff in here
End Sub
```

TIP It is often easiest to store interim code or to move code back and forth between applications using NotePad or WordPad. For instance, while in the Script Editor in Outlook, choose Edit, Select All (or Ctrl+A) to select all text in the editor. Copy that text (Edit, Copy or Ctrl+C), open Notepad, and Edit, Paste (or Ctrl+V). This way, you can save multiple VBScript fragments (even from multiple forms) in a single, easily navigable document. Some programmers tend to use Notepad rather than an Excel or Word module for this sort of quick'n'dirty code storage, because Notepad is such a small application that it launches very quickly.

Appendixes

SE Using Office 97 CD

The contents of the CD-ROM are easily viewed and navigated through with any Web browser. If you do not have a browser, you can use Internet Explorer 3.02, which is provided. The contents of the CD are organized into the following categories:

- Electronic Books
- Software
- Business Sites on the Web
- Source Code and samples from the book

Detailed instructions on CD use and operation can be found in the Readme.doc file on the CD-ROM. ■

Electronic Books

This CD is packed with several electronic (Web-based) versions of Que's leading titles. Some of these titles include:

Office 97 Quick References

- *Office 97*
- *Word 97*
- *Excel 97*
- *Access 97*

Operating Systems

- *Platinum Edition Windows 5*
- *Special Edition Using Windows NT Workstation 4.0*

Internet

- *Special Edition Using Internet Explorer 3.0*
- *Special Edition Using FrontPage 97*

Software

The CD-ROM includes many full as well as trial-version software products and utilities to make your Office 97 computing experience more productive and exciting. All of the software can be installed directly from the CD-ROM.

Office 97 Add-Ins and Tools

Village Software FastStart Sampler Excel Solutions   The Village Software FastStart Sampler includes twelve ready-made Excel templates to provide spreadsheet solutions for common business and personal needs. These templates were hand-selected as a special sample package from Village Software's FastStarts product line.

ActiveOffice   ActiveOffice, the "Essential Graphics Companion to Microsoft Office," instantly transforms text and numbers into compelling graphics that effectively communicate the key ideas, trends, and relationships in all of your documents, spreadsheets, and presentations.

ActivePresenter   ActivePresenter gives you all of the tools you need to deliver high-impact, low-cost presentations on the Web. ActivePresenter—which features SPC's revolutionary Intelligent Formatting technology—includes everything you need to create, publish, and present in one powerful, simple-to-use solution.

Office Toys 97   Office Toys 97 is an add-in for Microsoft Word 97, which creates a toolbar filled with many great Word utilities. These utilities provide you with a quicker and smarter way to use Word 97 and the files you create. Some of the powerful utilities and functions include the following: Office Navigator, Project Manager, More Proofing Tools!, Formatting tools!, Auto-backup, Virus Alert!, Smart printing tools!, Style Management!, and much more.

Microsoft Office 97 Viewers   Microsoft provides distributable viewers for three of their Office products. These viewers enable you to share Word, Excel, and PowerPoint documents with individuals who have not installed Microsoft Office applications on their computer systems.

Business and Professional

Pagis Pro97   Pagis Pro97 is a fully featured scanning application that allows you to scan documents (one or multiple pages) into your Windows 95/NT 4.0 desktop. With a color, grayscale or binary scanner, you can easily scan documents into your PC and then file, copy, print, send or use them with your favorite application by simply "dragging and dropping" them onto the application icon.

GoldMine   GoldMine is the number one Workgroup Contact Manager. It is designed to automate business professionals—whether they work remotely in the field, alone on a desktop PC, or with others in networked offices. It combines contact management, day and time planning, sales automation, and mail list management with group calendaring, database design, data synchronization, and e-mail messaging.

WinFax Pro   WinFax Pro gives you hassle-free faxing anywhere, anytime. Why waste time printing documents and feeding a fax machine? Fax right from your computer. WinFax PRO is easy to install and use—step-by-step wizards show you exactly what to do.

Paint Shop Pro   Paint Shop Pro—a powerful and easy-to-use image viewing, editing, and conversion program—supports more than 30 image formats. With numerous drawing and painting tools, this might be the only graphics program you will ever need!

Internet

EarthLink Total Access   Total Access offers a quick-start tool for connecting to the Internet. EarthLink Network specializes in providing inexpensive Internet access throughout the United States.

Microsoft Internet Explorer 3.02   Microsoft Internet Explorer is a must-have application for Web viewing. With the explosion of the Web, many companies, organizations, and individuals are generating Web-based documents. In order to view these documents, you need a Web Browser. Even if you already have Netscape installed on your computer, many sites optimize their Web pages for Internet Explorer. The version that is provided runs on both Windows 95 and NT.

Adobe Acrobat Reader with Search 3.01   The free Adobe Acrobat Reader enables you to view, navigate, and print PDF files across all major computing platforms. Adobe has created two flavors of Acrobat Reader 3.01, Acrobat Reader and Acrobat Reader with Search. Reader with Search includes additions that allow the user to search within a collection of PDF files on a hard disk, CD, or local-area network (for which an index file has been created withthe Acrobat Catalog tool).

CuteFTP   CuteFTP is a Windows-based Internet application that allows you to use the capabilities of FTP without having to know all the details about the protocol itself. It simplifies FTP by offering a user-friendly, graphical interface instead of a cumbersome command-line utility.

WinZip   WinZip brings the convenience of Windows to the use of Zip files. It requires neither PKZIP nor PKUNZIP. The new WinZip Wizard makes unzipping easier than ever. WinZip features built-in support for popular Internet file formats, including TAR, gzip, UNIX compress, UUEncode, BinHex, and MIME. ARJ, LZH, and ARC files are supported via external programs. WinZip interfaces to most virus scanners.

WebPrinter 4-Pack   WebPrinter instantly turns your valuable Internet, CD-ROM, and Windows data into attractive booklets with WebPrinter. With only two clicks, sports stats, custom travel itineraries, financial how-to guides, product literature, maps, and even photos are transformed into convenient, double-sided booklets.

PointCast Network   Through personal news profiles, viewers are enabled to customize the information they receive. Viewers specify news topics of interest and the PointCast Network delivers current news to their desktops. They can modify personal news profiles at any time.

Business Sites on the Web

The CD includes a hyperlinked version of the Business Sites on the Web appendix from the book. To take advantage of Web publishing, click the hyperlink of any business site and go directly to their Web site.

Business Sites
on the Web

This appendix is a listing of business resources you can
find on the Internet. Whether you're just in the planning
and startup phase of your business, involved in international trade, need legal or accounting assistance, or interested in the latest trade shows and conferences, you'll find
a Web site that can help you find answers. ■

Business Startup and Planning

America's Brightest

http://www.americasbrightest.com/

This Santa Monica-based organization describes itself as the "one-stop shop" for small businesses and working professionals. A subscription-based service with a one-month free trial, America's Brightest offers giveaways and a wide range of discussion groups.

Big Dreams

http://vanbc.wimsey.com/~duncans/

Big Dreams is an online newsletter dedicated to individuals starting their own businesses. Visit the site and play the Business Game to ask yourself key questions about your new business, or take a look through current and archived issues for topical articles.

BizTalk

http://www.biztalk.com/

BizTalk is an electronic magazine devoted to small business. Departments include news, finance, law, politics, technology, and more. *BizTalk* runs contests to provide seed money for startup.

Business Plan Resource File

http://www.aifr.com/startup.html

Sponsored by the American Institute for Financial Research, this site is designed to help emerging businesses with their first business plan. A full compendium of general advice is offered in addition to having information on interactive business plan software.

Business Research Lab

http://spider.netropolis.net/brl/brl1.htm

This site is dedicated to the development of market research, an essential element for start-ups. Filled with tips and articles on conducting surveys and focus groups, the site also has a large number of sample surveys on file.

BuyersZone

http://www.buyerszone.com/index.html

BuyersZone is an online buyer's guide for businesses. It includes articles on what to look for in everything from 401(k) plans to voice mail systems. Also featured is The Inside Scoop, which offers the latest tips and stories of "buying disasters."

CCH Business Owner's Toolkit

http://www.toolkit.cch.com/

CCH (Commerce Clearing House) features articles on Small Office, Home Office (SOHO) guides to everyday business, coupled with a comprehensive listing of business tools, including model business forms, financial templates, and checklists.

Education, Training, and Development Resource Center for Business and Industry

http://www.tasl.com/tasl/home.html

This page, sponsored by Training and Seminar Locators Inc., offers help in finding business education resources. An index of qualified training providers and information about products and services is included.

Internal Revenue Service

http://www.irs.ustreas.gov/

An important step in planning your business is to establish your tax status and potential responsibilities. The new IRS site has a special "Tax Info for Business" section with many helpful tax guides, including the Tax Calendar to keep track of special deadlines; a Business Tax Kit, a downloadable package of forms and publications; and the interactive Tax Trails for Business.

LinkExchange

http://www.linkexchange.com/

LinkExchange is an online advertising network that claims more than 100,000 members. If you have a Web site to promote, you can join for free; you then display ads for other members, and they display ads for you. There are also low-cost paid services.

Marketing Resource Center

http://www.marketingsource.com/

A free service of Concept Marketing Group, Inc., the Marketing Resource Center has an extensive articles library on planning your business, marketing tools and contacts, a database of industry associations, and links to online business magazines.

Marketshares

http://www.marketshares.com/

Marketshares tracks the best commercial and corporate Web sites. You can use their built-in search engine or browse their categories including Arts & Entertainment, Business & Technology, Finance & Money, and Travel & Transportation. Most links include a paragraph describing the site.

PRONET

http://www.pronett.com/

PRONET is a multilingual interactive business centre: The corporate philosophy is to help small- to medium-sized businesses grow by helping them use the Internet as a natural extension of their communications and marketing programs.

Occupational Safety and Health Administration

http://www.osha.gov/

Aside from a wealth of information on health and safety regulations and statistics, the OSHA site features software advisors that you can download on confined space standards, and asbestos regulations to help you figure out your requirements.

Small Business Advisor

http://www.isquare.com/

A terrific collection of articles for the new businessperson forms the core of this site. Example titles include "Don't Make these Business Mistakes," "Getting Paid," and "Government Small Business Resources." You'll also find tax advice and a glossary of business terms.

Small Business Workshop

http://www.sb.gov.bc.ca:80/smallbus/workshop/workshop.html

Sponsored by the Canadian government, this site has a host of articles for any business around the world. Areas include Starting Your Business, Marketing Basics, Planning Fundamentals, Financing Your Business, and Basic Regulations.

Tax Planning

http://www.hooked.net/cpa/plan/index.html

"An ounce of prevention" is certainly worth more than a pound when it comes to taxes. This site specializes in information on tax planning—for individuals, businesses, and even an IRS audit. Take the tax challenge to find out how much you don't know about taxes.

Tax Prophet

http://www.taxprophet.com/

Hosted by Robert Sommers, the tax columnist for the *San Francisco Examiner*, the Tax Prophet has a number of FAQ files on tax issues and tax information for foreigners living in the U.S. The Interactive Tax Applications is very informative; try the Independent Contractor versus Employee Flowchart to check your job status.

U.S. Small Business Administration

http://www.sbaonline.sba.gov/

SBA Online is your online resource to government assistance for the small businessman. The site is organized into special areas on Starting, Financing, and Expanding Your Business, as well as other information on SCORE, PRONET, and local SBA links.

Business Financing

Angel Capital Electronic Network

http://www.sbaonline.sba.gov/ADVO/acenet.html

Angel Capital Electronic Network (ACE-Net), the Internet-based network, is sponsored by the SBA's Office of Advocacy. The site gives new options for small companies seeking investments in the range of $250,000 to $5 million.

America Business Funding Directory

http://www.businessfinance.com/

America Business Funding Directory is the first search engine dedicated to finding business capital. You can search categories ranging from venture capital to equipment lending to real estate, as well as a private capital network of accredited investors.

Bankruptcy FAQs

http://site206125.primehost.com/faqs.html

Sponsored by Gold & Stanley, P.C., commercial bankruptcy lawyers, this site answers many basic questions about the ins-and-outs of bankruptcy from all perspectives. Topics include "How to Recover Money" and "10 Things to Do when a Bankruptcy is Filed."

Closing Bell

http://www.merc.com/cb/cgi/cb_merc.cgi

Closing Bell provides a daily e-mail message containing closing prices and news for a personalized portfolio of market indices, mutual funds, and securities from the three major U.S. exchanges. Visitors can also sign up for news alerts during the day for followed companies.

Computer Loan Network

http://www.clnet.com/

Borrowers can use this Web site to add a loan Request for Proposal (RFP) directly to the CLN MortgageNet mortgage multiple listing service. Mortgage brokers, lenders, banks, and secondary marketers will search the system, locate your RFP, and then find ways to offer you a lower note rate than your currently quoted rate, if possible.

App B

Currency Converter

http://www.oanda.com/cgi-bin/ncc

An interactive Web page designed to allow you to see current conversions for 164 currencies. Convert your U.S. dollars to everything from the Albanian lek ($1 = 155 leks) to the Zambian kwacha ($1 = 1,310 kwacha). You can also check the previous day's rates or download a customizable currency converter.

EDGAR Database

http://www.sec.gov/edgarhp.htm

EDGAR, the Electronic Data Gathering, Analysis, and Retrieval system, performs automated collection, validation, indexing, acceptance, and forwarding of submissions by companies and others who are required by law to file forms with the U.S. Securities and Exchange Commission (SEC). Its primary purpose is to increase the efficiency and fairness of the securities market for the benefit of investors, corporations, and the economy. EDGAR is also a great resource of filing examples.

Export-Import Bank of the U.S.

http://www.exim.gov/

The Export-Import Bank offers programs on loans and guarantees, working capital, and export credit insurance. All the necessary application forms can be found online here with additional literature on importing from and exporting to various countries around the world.

FinanceNet

http://www.financenet.gov/

FinanceNet was established by Vice President Al Gore's National Performance Review in Washington, D.C. in 1994 and is operated by the National Science Foundation. This site features a listing of government asset sales including a subscription to daily sales.

Financial Women International

http://www.fwi.org/

Founded in 1921, Financial Women International serves women in the financial services industry who seek to expand their personal and professional capabilities through self-directed growth in a supportive environment. FWI's vision is to empower women in the financial services industry to attain their professional, economic, and personal goals, and to influence the future shape of the industry.

National Credit Counseling Service

http://www.nccs.org/

The National Credit Counseling Service's Web site features news about its Debt Management Program for businesses and individuals, as well a full range of information on credit, budgeting, and financial planning.

Prospect Street

http://www.prospectstreet.com/

Prospect Street is a venture capital firm specializing in resources for high-tech entrepreneurs: information technology, software, the Internet, and wireless communications. Its site has links to investment, stock, and technical research sources.

Securities and Exchange Commission

http://www.sec.gov/smbus1.htm

This page of the SEC site opens its small business area where you can find information on taking your small business public. In addition to a complete Q&A, you'll also find current and pending initiatives of interest.

U.S. Tax Code On-Line

http://www.fourmilab.ch/ustax/ustax.html

This Web page allows access to the complete text of the U.S. Internal Revenue Title 26 of the Code (26 U.S.C.). To make cross-referencing easy, hyperlinks are embedded throughout the text.

International Business and Trade

Asia-Pacific Economic Cooperation

http://www.apecsec.org.sg/

Based in Singapore, this organization's Web site carries information on the 18-member countries' economies, information on intellectual property rights overseas, and a financial procedures guidebook with government procurement outlines.

Bureau of Export Administration

http://www.bxa.doc.gov/

A key element of this site is the EAR Marketplace, a one-stop source for timely Export Administration Regulations data, including a current, searchable copy of the Export Administration Regulations online. You can also find current information on U.S. encryption policy here.

Central and Eastern Europe Business Information Center

http://www.itaiep.doc.gov/eebic/ceebic.html

CEEBIC is a primary information source for doing business in the emerging markets of central and eastern Europe. Each country has a full profile that includes market research and business and trade opportunities. A recently added page features tax and VAT rates for the area.

Contact! The Canadian Management Network

http://strategis.ic.gc.ca/sc_mangb/contact/engdoc/homepage.html

This bilingual (English and French) site features links to more than 1,500 Canadian small business support organizations. Here you'll also find a small business handbook on doing business in Canada and information on cross-cultural business strategies.

The Electronic Embassy

http://www.embassy.org/

The Electronic Embassy provides information on embassies for every country with special attention to those on the Internet. There is also an International Business Center that spotlights commercial and nonprofit organizations providing goods, services, or opportunities to international markets.

ExporTutor

http://web.miep.org/tutor/index.html

Is your business export-ready? Follow this site's 10-Step Road Map to Success in Foreign Markets, developed by Michigan State University's International Business Center, to find out. There's also a Quick Consultant with valuable information on everything from Accounting to Value Chain Analysis.

India Market Place

http://www.indiaintl.com/

Here you'll find in-depth information on doing business in India, Indian business news updated every business day, extensive information about trade shows being held in India, and links to India-based business management resources, directories and databases, and associations.

TrADE-Net Italy

http://www.tradenet.it/

Italy is filled with small- to medium-sized companies known for their quality and desire to export. TrADE-Net Italy has a searchable industry directory organized by category—perfect for finding your company just the right import item.

Venture Web—Japan

http://www.venture-web.or.jp/

Searching for a Japanese connection? Whether you're looking for a partner in Japan or marketing your availability to the Japanese market, you can submit your request for posting on the site. Other site areas shave information on export/import regulations and human resource links.

Web of Culture

http://www.worldculture.com/index.html

The Web of Culture is a wonderful site to visit before working with or going to a new country. The site includes information on business, religion, resources, and holidays. There's even a very visual page about gestures and their meanings in different countries.

Job Opportunities and Labor Resources

AFL-CIO

http://www.aflcio.org/

The AFL-CIO Web site focuses its information on unionization and other labor-related issues. New sections include an Executive Pay Watch, Ergonomics, Working Women, and Summer Jobs for Seniors.

America's Job Bank

http://www.ajb.dni.us/

A multi-state project of the public Employment Service, America's Job Bank is for both employers and employees. A section on Occupational Employment trends offers an interactive outlook handbook and answers to many surveys such as, "What's the fastest growing occupation?"

Computer Register

http://www.computerregister.com/

If you're in the market for computer consultants or related services, check out these extensive advertisements, including employment. Classifieds are provided for both job seekers and employers.

CareerPath.com

http://www.careerpath.com/

CareerPath.com posts more than 400,000 new jobs on the Internet every month, and is updated daily by newspapers across the U.S. You can search their help wanted database by category, newspaper, and keyword.

Department of Labor

http://www.dol.gov/

The government site has information on minimum wage regulations, labor protections, welfare reform, and small business retirement solutions. Visitors can access "America's Job Bank" as well as for such regulatory and statutory information.

Ernst & Young's Virtual HR Office

http://www.idirect.com/hroffice/

This site is a resource center for the human resource professional which includes a chat room, bulletin board, newsletter, and links to other HR sites in both the U.S. and Canada.

E-Span

http://www.espan.com/

Connecting the right person with the right job is what E-Span is all about. Visitors can access a résumé database, a reference and resource library, and information on career fairs.

JobWeb

http://www.jobweb.org/

Run by the National Associations of Colleges and Employers, JobWeb lists jobs, employer profiles, and career planning resources. One resource, the Catapult, offers a variety of career assessment tools.

National Center for Employee Ownership

http://www.nceo.org/

The National Center for Employee Ownership (NCEO) is a private, nonprofit organization. The NCEO site is a leading source of information on employee stock ownership plans (ESOPs), stock options, and other forms of employee ownership.

Telecommuting, Teleworking, and Alternative Officing

http://www.gilgordon.com/

This site features telecommuting information from around the world, and from many different perspectives, on the subjects of telecommuting, teleworking, the virtual office, and related topics. Includes a FAQ section and listing of upcoming events.

Legal and Regulatory

American Law Source Online (ALSO)

http://www.lawsource.com/also/

This site is notable because it has links to all American online legal systems, including the Federal judiciary and all 50 states and territories. ALSO has equally far-reaching coverage of Canadian and Mexican law.

Business Law Site

http://members.aol.com/bmethven/index.html

Sponsored by Methven & Associates, the Business Law Site covers federal and state statutes, and legal research sites for both business and high-tech law. You can also find a full compendium of tax forms, information on international law, and a listing of legal research sites.

Corporate Counselor

http://www.ljx.com/corpcounselor/index.html

The Corporate Counselor has resources including daily news, columns, and articles on employment law, securities, antitrust, and other business issues.

Department of Labor Poster Page

http://www.dol.gov/dol/osbp/public/sbrefa/poster.htm

A fixture in every American workplace finds its online equivalent: the Department of Labor mandatory notices. So far, you can download posters for the minimum wage requirements, OSHA, the Family Leave Act, and the Equal Opportunity Act. All posters are in PDF format; you'll need a PDF reader like Adobe Acrobat (**http://www.adobe.com**).

International Trade Law

http://itl.irv.uit.no/trade_law/

Sponsored by the Law Department at Norway's University of Tromsø, you can search this site for virtually any subject related to international trade law. Typical topics include Dispute Resolution, Customs, Protection of Intellectual Property, GATT, and other free trade treaties.

The Legal Information Institute

http://www.law.cornell.edu/

Sponsored by Cornell University, the Legal Information Institute Web site houses its collection of recent and historic Supreme Court decisions, hypertext versions of the full U.S. Code, U.S. Constitution, Federal Rules of Evidence and Civil Procedure, and recent opinions of the New York Court of Appeals complete with commentary. Fully indexed and searchable.

QuickForms Online

http://www.quickforms.com/

QuickForms is an easy-to-use interactive system that drafts sophisticated agreements automatically weighted in your favor. Answer a few questions online and you have your draft agreement in 10 minutes. A wide range of contracts is available.

Magazines Online

Advertising Age

http://www.adage.com/

All the information you could ever need about the movers and shakers of advertising. The site features a section called NetMarketing, on getting the most out of your Web site as well as the DataPlace, featuring industry reports and statistics.

Barron's Online

http://www.barrons.com/

In addition to complete contents of their weekly publication, *Barron's Online* features the ability to examine most companies mentioned in their articles through the Barron Dossiers. *Barron's Online* requires a free registration.

BusinessWeek

http://www.businessweek.com/

BusinessWeek's online-only content includes Maven, the interactive computer shopper, and BW Plus with listings of the best business schools, business book reviews, and articles on the computer industry and the Information Age. You can also access BW Radio, hourly market reports in RealAudio format.

Disgruntled

http://www.disgruntled.com/

Describing itself as "The Business Magazine for People Who Work for a Living," *Disgruntled* provides an irreverent look at being employed. There's even a Boss Button on every page, which takes you to a proper-looking spreadsheet when the boss is looking over your shoulder.

Entrepreneurial Edge Online

http://www.edgeonline.com/

Articles aimed at the innovative entrepreneur fill this site. You also find a Pointers from the Pros section, SmallBizNet (with a full digital library), and the Interactive Toolbox, a series of self-calculating worksheets and benchmarking and assessment tools.

Fast Company

http://www.fastcompany.com/

A new edge business magazine with a host of "how-to" articles: how to make a group decision like a tribe, how to deal with the issues of dating and sexual harassment on the job, how to choose a career counselor, how to disagree (without being disagreeable), and more.

Financial Times

http://www.usa.ft.com/

The online edition of the *Financial Times* is divided into three sections: News & Comment, with "tastes" of articles from the newspaper, as well as stock market information updated every 30 minutes; Themes & Topics, for categorized articles; and Connect & Respond, where online visitors can find services such as recruitment advertising and a library of annual reports.

Forbes Digital Tool

http://www.forbes.com/

In addition to current and archived articles from *Forbes*, this Web site features the Toolbox, a collection of reports and indices; ASAP, *Forbes'* supplement on the Information Age; Angles, a section on media and politics; and access to a free Investment Monitor.

Fortune

http://www.pathfinder.com/fortune/

Can't wait to see if you made the 500 this year? Check out the digital version of the famous survey as well as online areas dedicated to the stock market, mobile computing, managing your money, and information technology. You'll also find a special Fortune Forum for exchanging views on investing and related matters.

Hispanic Business Magazine

http://www.hispanstar.com/

This site covers information for business owners and professionals with a Hispanic interest. There is also a national résumé referral service, a market research area focusing on the U.S. Hispanic economic market, and a special events department that provides a calendar of events.

Inc. Online

http://www.inc.com/

Self-described as the "Web site for Growing Companies," *Inc. Online* is actually several minisites, including *Inc.* itself, with articles and archives; Business & Technology, with statistics to benchmark your business; and Local Business News, where you can choose from more than 25 U.S. cities for local business news and resources.

MoneyWorld Online

http://www.money-world.net/

MoneyWorld Online features investing information and tips on the most promising investment opportunities. *MoneyWorld* offers "hot-pick" IPOs, a series of long and short picks, and growth industry surveys.

Red Herring

http://www.herring.com/mag/home.html

Red Herring provides business information for the technology and entertainment industries with a special focus on emerging markets. Their online site features an Entrepreneurs Resource Center with workshops on the unique challenges facing business startups.

Success Magazine

http://www.SuccessMagazine.com/

The *Success* site includes a searchable archive of past articles, a survey of the best 100 franchises (with links), and the Source, a compendium of business-related links organized by subject.

The Wall Street Journal—Small Business Suite

http://update.wsj.com/public/current/summaries/small.htm

Although the interactive *Wall Street Journal* is a subscription service ($49 per year), this service is free. Articles of interest to small businesses are the primary feature here, along with a series of discussion groups, Web resources, and a business locator.

Marketing and Market Research

American Demographics/Marketing Tools

http://www.marketingtools.com/

At the American Demographics/Marketing Tools Web site, you can check out consumer trends, tactics and techniques for information marketers, or access *Forecast*, a newsletter of demographic trends and market forecasts.

American Marketing Association

http://www.ama.org/

AMA is a national organization of marketing professionals. Their Web site features a special section on Internet marketing ethics as well as a calendar of events, publications, and information on regional chapters.

Business Intelligence Center

http://future.sri.com/

What type of person is your customer? The Values and Lifestyles (VALS) program at SRI Consulting, hosts of this site, studies consumers by asking questions about their attitudes and values. You can answer an online questionnaire to determine your VALS type—and see how you fit with other consumers.

Business Wire

http://www.businesswire.com/

Business Wire is a leading source of news on major U.S. corporations, including Fortune 1000 and NASDAQ companies. You can look up a company, category, keyword, or region and find all the pertinent business news. You can sign up for their service online.

Commando Guide to Unconventional Marketing and Advertising Tactics

http://199.44.114.223/mktg/

This online reference covers such topics as how to market survey your competition, doing your own professional marketing and business plan, referral systems, barter exchanges, print advetorials, and telemarketing.

First Steps: Marketing and Design Daily

http://www.interbiznet.com/nomad.html

Developed by the Internet Business Network, First Steps contains a rich source of articles on market research and industry analysis regarding business to business transactions. Much of the marketing and design work is Internet-oriented.

International Public Relations

http://www.iprex.com/

IPREX specializes in international public relations. Its areas of expertise include business-to-business, crisis management, energy and environment, and technology. Its news section has valuable information on public relation trends.

Market Facts and Statistics

http://www.mightymall.com/sevenseas/facts.html

This 1996 survey covers the countries of the world's population, gross national product, and growth rate. Each country has a small paragraph on its economy and markets. The information is organized by major regions: Asia, Western Europe, Central Europe, Middle East, Atlantic, and West Indies.

Marketing Resource Center

http://www.marketingsource.com/

Sponsored by the Concept Marketing Group, the Marketing Resource Center maintains an articles archive with more than 250 business-related articles. Its Tools of the Trade section links to an association database and software for general business and project management.

Retail Futures

http://e1.com/RF/

Sponsored by the Institute for Retail and Merchandising Innovation, this site carries information on tracking customer preferences, category and brand management, regional marketing, and store and product design issues.

Sales Leads USA

http://www.abii.com/

This site is run by American Business Information, Inc., which specializes in generating company profiles. Free services include searching for businesses or people by name with American Directory Assistance or searching by type of business with American Yellow Pages.

Selling.com

http://www.selling.com/

This site is dedicated to salespeople and their needs. Here, you'll find a collection of selling concepts and exercises written by salespeople, for salespeople.

Sharrow Advertising & Marketing Resource Center

http://www.dnai.com/~sharrow/register.html

You have to register at first to visit this site, but it's well worth it; The Advertising Parody section is worth the time by itself. The BizInfo Resource Center has an overview of database marketing, a direct mail profit spreadsheet, and information on approaches to integrated marketing.

Top Marketing Tips, Tricks, and Techniques

http://www.disclosure.com/marketing/toptricks.html

What's the inside scoop? Check out this site, sponsored by Disclosure, Inc., for all the skinny on advertising, direct marketing, marketing law, marketing management, promotions, public relations, trade shows, and telemarketing.

U.S. Census Bureau

http://www.census.gov/

The Census Bureau is a great site to gather social, demographic, and economic information. The site has more than 1,000 Census Bureau publications featuring statistical information on such topics as the nation's population, housing, business and manufacturing activity, international trade, farming, and state and local governments.

World Business Solution

http://thesolution.com/

The World Business Solution is a free marketing manual available from TheSolution.com. There's also a section devoted to downloadable or lined handy forms and reference.

Nonprofit Information

Charity Village

http://www.charityvillage.com/cvhome.html

Hundreds of pages of news, jobs, resources, and links for the Canadian nonprofit community. Sponsored by Hilborn Interactive, Inc., this site is updated daily in both French ("Rue Principale") and English ("Main Street").

Council on Foundations

http://www.cof.org/index.html

The Council on Foundations is an association of foundations and corporations gathered to promote responsible and effective philanthropy. You'll find information on the various types of foundations as well as a Community Foundation Locator service.

The George Lucas Educational Foundation

http://glef.org/welcome.html

The George Lucas Educational Foundation, a tax-exempt, charitable organization based in Nicasio, California, was established to facilitate the innovative uses of multimedia technologies to enhance teaching and learning. The site has frequently updated information about innovative efforts to change education.

The Gen-X Group

http://www.globalserve.net/~genxgrp/

Gen-X Group is a not-for-profit Christian organization promoting charities and nonprofit organizations on the Internet. The site features a short course on how and why nonprofit organizations can get on the Web.

The Grantsmanship Center

http://www.tgci.com/

The Grantsmanship Center specializes in training for grant-writing and fundraising. Much of the site is designed to support their courses around the country. The site also contains a cross-referenced database of state and federal funding.

IdeaList

http://www.contact.org/

This site features a global directory of nonprofits with links to more than 10,000 sites in 110 countries. There is also an online library of tools for nonprofits, with information about fundraising and volunteering, accounting and management, legal issues, and nonprofit support organizations.

Nonprofit Resources Catalog

http://www.clark.net/pub/pwalker/

A personal project by the head of United Way Online, this site features meta-links (links to pages of links) dedicated to Interlink sites that benefit nonprofits. Categories include Fundraising and Giving, General Nonprofit Resources, and United Ways on the Internet.

Patents, Trademarks, and Copyrights

Basic Patent Information

http://www.fplc.edu/tfield/ipbasics.htm

Sponsored by the Franklin Law Center, this compendium of resources offers beginning information for artists, independent inventors, Internet authors and artists, programmers, and small business owners, including information on how to avoid being burned by fraudulent invention promotion schemes.

Copyright Clearance Center

http://www.copyright.com/

Copyright Clearance Center (CCC) is a not-for-profit organization created at the suggestion of Congress to help organizations comply with U.S. copyright law. CCC offers a number of catalogs that you can search to see if a work is registered.

Copyright Website

http://www.benedict.com/index.html

This lively site provides real-world, practical, and relevant copyright information, including a look at famous copyright infringement cases, copyright fundamentals, and distribution of copyright information over the Web.

Intellectual Property Center

http://www.ipcenter.com/

News and information on intellectual property issues dominate this site. Government statutes and decisions are highlighted, along with memos from law firms on intellectual property issues.

Nerd World: Copyrights & Patents

http://www.nerdworld.com/users/dstein/nw427.html

This site provides a resource of links to many patent attorneys and intellectual property law firms from around the world. A recent survey showed many contacts in the U.S., Canada, and Japan.

Patent Application Drafting

http://w3.gwis.com/~sarbar/patapp01.htm

This Web site gives an overview of the steps necessary for writing a patent application, section by section. Aside from covering the statutory legal requirements, Intellectual Property Attorney R. Lawrence Sahr gives insightful comments on the target audience for your patent: the patent office itself.

Patent Pending Resource

http://silkpresence.com/patents/

Sponsored by the patent law firm of Ogram & Teplitz, this site covers new patent laws, and a FAQ on provisional patent application that allows the "Patent Pending" label to be used. There are also online forms that ask a patent attorney's questions before you schedule a visit.

U.S. Patent Office

http://www.uspto.gov/

The home page for the U.S. Patent Office gives you access to downloadable patent application forms and searchable databases. These include both the U.S. Patent Bibliographic Database (U.S. patents issued from January 1, 1976 to July 8, 1997), and the AIDS Patent Database (full text and images of AIDS-related patents issued by the U.S., Japanese, and European patent offices).

Procurement and Contracting

Acquisition Reform Network

http://www-far.npr.gov/

The Acquisition Reform Network (ARNet) provides services to members of the government acquisition community, both public and private sector. Its resource center, the Federal Acquisition Virtual Library, provides links to numerous other federal acquisition resources on the World Wide Web. Numerous opportunities are also listed.

BidCast

http://www.bidcast.com/

BidCast is a subscription service that allows you to browse and search thousands of U.S. federal government bids. You can sign up on the e-mail service for personal notification. There is a free trial section that allows you to look at Commerce Business Daily listings.

Business Information and Development Services (BIDS)

http://www.bidservices.com/newindex.html

BIDS is an electronic publishing and consulting firm which informs small businesses about upcoming government contract opportunities and provides assistance in the procurement process. Their site offers information from both the Commerce Business Daily (U.S.) and Supply and Services Open Bidding Service (Canada).

Commerce Business Daily

http://www.govcon.com/public/CBD/

A sophisticated search engine for finding government procurement opportunities. You can search for a procurement or award under a specific category, by contract value, or by a search phrase. You can even specify the level of "fuzzyness" the engine uses to find items bearing a close similarity to your search criteria.

Electronic Commerce Program Office (ECPO)

http://www.arnet.gov/ecapmo/

The Electronic Commerce Program Office (ECPO) is a multi-agency group assembled under the co-leadership of the General Services Administration and the Department of Defense to implement Electronic Commerce/Electronic Data Interchange (EC/EDI) for the federal acquisition programs. An online tutorial can help you get started.

Electronic Commerce Resource Center

http://www.ecrc.ctc.com/

The ECRC Program promotes awareness and implementation of Electronic Commerce and related technologies into the U.S.-integrated civil-military industrial base. Downloadable products can be found in the Electronic Commerce Testbed.

Environmental Protection Agency Procurement

http://www.epa.gov/epahome/Contracts.html

Visit this site for a full listing of business opportunities and EPA acquisition resources. In addition to covering policy and procedure, you can also find an acquisition forecast and a special section devoted to small business opportunities.

FAA Acquisition Center

http://www.faa.gov/asu/asu100/acq-reform/acq_home.htm

After you've checked out the FAQ page on supplying to the Federal Aviation Administration, visit FAST, the FAA Acquisition System Toolset. FAST is an interactive databank designed to guide users through the FAA's new Acquisition Management System (AMS); it contains examples, templates, instructions, tips, policy documents, and other automated tools.

Federal Acquisition Institute

http://www.gsa.gov/fai/

Trying to find your way through the maze of federal acquisition? Pay a visit to the Federal Acquisition Institute, a one-stop acquisition training shop. Here you can sign-up for the FAI Online University or download a Contract Pricing Reference Guide.

General Services Agency

http://www.gsa.gov/

The GSA's mission is to provide expertly managed space, supplies, services, and solutions at the best value to Federal employees. In addition to full information on buying practices, you can also visit its online shopping service, GAO Advantage.

Government Accounting Office

http://www.gao.gov/

The U.S. General Accounting Office (GAO) is a nonpartisan agency that conducts audits, surveys, investigations, and evaluations of federal programs. You can sign up for daily reports through the GAO Daybook service or visit the GAO FraudNET for allegations of fraud, waste, abuse, or mismanagement of federal funds.

Government Contractors Glossary

http://www.kcilink.com/govcon/contractor/gcterms.html

An excellent resource for finding your way through the verbiage of government contracts. A special Acronym Table appears at the end of this guide to enable you to identify the full meaning of the most common government acronyms.

National Technology Transfer Center

http://www.nttc.edu/

The National Technology Transfer Center's task is to take technologies off laboratory shelves and put them to work in U.S. businesses and industries where taxpayers get even more benefits from their investments. Full database services, a training center, and links to other business assistance sites are hallmarks of this Web site.

State and Local Procurement Jumpstation

http://www.fedmarket.com/statejump.html

This invaluable Web page gives you links to procurement sources for all 50 states, not to mention Washington, D.C. and Guam. Most states also have some local listings for specific cities as well as economic development links supplying market data.

U.S. Business Center

http://www.business.gov/

This one-stop shop is designed to streamline interactions between businesses and the government. Common questions and answers are organized by subject, and an expert tool area gives you forms and guidance in everything from Disaster Assistance to Finding a Zip Code.

U.S. Post Office

http://www.usps.gov/business/

The post office wants to give you the business! This Web site provides an overview of doing business with the USPS and even tells you how to submit an unsolicited bid. You can download the Procurement Manual, as well as check out business opportunities.

U.S. Veteran Affairs

http://www.va.gov/osdbu/

The online Department of Veteran Affairs site promotes increased use of small and disadvantaged businesses, including acquisition opportunities. A focus of this site is the VA's 1997 Forecast which supplies marketing information useful to the small business person in selling their goods and services, both to the VA and to the VA's large prime contractors.

Small Office/Home Office

America's Small Business Finance Center

http://www.netearnings.com/

Sponsored by Net Earnings, Inc., this one-stop shop offers business advice on insurance policies and prices, and on applying for loans and credit cards. You can also sign up for online payroll service here.

American Express Small Business Exchange

http://www.americanexpress.com/smallbusiness/

The American Express Small Business Exchange offers online classifieds (buying and selling); expert advice where you can ask a specific question, browse the categories, or check out the tip of the month; and business planning and resources with information on starting, managing, or expanding your business.

Bathrobe 'til 10

http://www.slip.net/~sfwave/

This guide for the home professional offers articles and information for the solo self-employed. Concerned about word use? Pay a visit to the Grammar Queen to clear up those business correspondence blues.

Biz$hop

http://www.bizshop.com/

Biz$hop is a virtual company specializing in helping entrepreneurs achieve success in their own businesses. There are numerous reports and free business resources available—be sure to download the free "First 25 Business Decisions" report.

BizResource.com

http://www.bizresource.com/

Dedicated to encouraging small businesses and entrepreneurs, BizResource offers an ongoing series of business tips (both via e-mail and archived online), a business chat area, and a series of audio, video, and computer resources.

Business@Home

http://www.gohome.com/

An electronic magazine dedicated to the working-from-home community, *Business@Home* includes articles on opportunity, marketing, and technology. Its Cool Tools department reviews recent hardware and software important to the general home office worker, while the Consultant's Corner focuses on the consultants work experience.

Business Resource Center

http://www.morebusiness.com/

This site hosts an excellent four-part primer with advice and activities to get you thinking about your business, its customers, development, and marketing. In addition, you can find templates and worksheets for press releases and business plans.

Business Start Page

http://www.wp.com/fredfish/

Here's a great place to start your business day. This site offers a virtual desktop where you can find everything at your fingertips: Yellow, Blue, and International Page telephone directories, links to shipping companies, a reference library, and a series of tips and tricks.

Center for Family Business

http://199.103.128.199/fambiznc/cntprovs/orgs/necfb/

Run by Northeastern University, this site features an ongoing series of articles on running a family business (both home and office- or store-based). You'll find lots of information here on family business issues including generational change, sibling rivalries, and how to balance family and business priorities.

EGOPHER—The Entrepreneur Gopher

http://www.slu.edu/eweb/egopher.html

Sponsored by St. Louis University, EGOPHER is designed for people and organizations interested in new, small, or entrepreneurial businesses. A variety of Top 10 lists for entrepreneurs is available along with topical business resources and access to core research journal in entrepreneurship.

Electronic Money Tree

http://www.soos.com/$tree/

Aimed at the Internet-savvy (or those who want to be) entrepreneurs, the Electronic Money Tree consists primarily of a digest of articles. Sample articles include "Can SOHO Really Compete?," "Biz Tips," "Better Press Releases," and "Time Management."

Entrepreneur's Bookstore

http://kwicsys.com/books/

There are more than 600 information reports offered at this site, most from $1 to $2 each. The reports are categorized. Sample topic areas include Mail Order, Multilevel Marketing, Legal, and Direct Response TV.

Entrepreneur Magazine's BizSquare

http://www.entrepreneurmag.com/

This site is chock-full of information for the SOHO businessperson. Visit the Resource Center to check out the online Franchise 500 and Business Opportunity 500 lists. Then go to the SOHO Mall for all your business-related software, books, magazines, and audio or video-cassettes.

EntreWorld

http://www.entreworld.org/

The EntreWorld site is organized by business level. Visit the Starting Your Business area for information on business planning, finding the right people, or creating products that win loyalty. Running Your Business is devoted to later-stage companies with information on expanding your customer base and exit strategies.

FranInfo

http://www.frannet.com/

Thinking about franchising? Visit FranInfo's site to find information on buying a franchise or franchising your own business. The site has several self-tests to determine if you're ready for franchising, as well as a listing of franchises for sale.

Guide to the Small Business Administration

http://www.geocities.com/WallStreet/2172/

Before you dive into the SBA bureaucracy, you might want to visit this site first. There are lots of details covering the various SBA programs available with information to help you find just the right one for your business.

Heath's Computer and Telecommunication Acronym Reference

http://www.sbri.com/acro2.htm

Visit this site before your next cocktail party where you want to impress others with statements like, "My GOSIP is about to go LUNI on Harv's LANE." Or, maybe when you just want to find out what all those jargonese initials mean.

Home Office Association of America

http://www.hoaa.com/

There's power in numbers—even if you're working alone. The Home Office Association of America offers group health insurance, a long-distance calling plan, a debt collection service, home business and equipment insurance, and more. Be sure to visit their 50 Great Home Office Startup Ideas page.

Home Office Links

http://www.ro.com/small_business/homebased.html

A full compendium of Web links for small and home-based offices including franchises, business opportunities, reference material, newsgroups, searching tools, and services for small business. Links to just about anything related to small- and home-based business can be found here.

Home Office Mall

http://www.the-office.com/

A centralized location for products and services catering to the home office professional. Find everything from computers for rent to computer furniture, to networks for female executives.

Home Realtors Information Network

http://www.realtors.com/

About the only thing all home businesses have in common is the home. This Web site, sponsored by the National Association of Realtors, has almost 900,000 listings of homes around the country—and, of course, a search engine to help you find your dream office.

NetMarquee Family Business NetCenter

http://nmq.com/

This site supplies news and information for owners and executives in family-owned businesses. There is a calendar of events, weekly articles, and a listserve for ongoing discussion related to family businesses.

Offshore Entrepreneur

http://www.au.com/offshore/

With the motto, "Neither profit, nor opportunity, have any borders," the Offshore Entrepreneur takes you through the promise, pitfalls, and profit of basing your business in another country. The site offers abundant information on tax-planning and forming an offshore corporation.

Opportunities for Women in Small Business

http://www.mindspring.com/~higley/project.htm

One path around the glass ceiling is to open your own business. This site is dedicated to helping women choose and run a business. There are profiles of successful women as well as financial and legal advice and tips on how to avoid failure.

Resource Center for Home-Based Businesses

http://www.masseypub.com/

Learn from someone who made the home-based business dream come true. Featuring information on self-published brochures, this site offers a FAQ section, details on seminars, and an area devoted to mail order scams.

Retail Business Resource Center

http://www.retailadvz.com/

Looking for a site where you can learn from the experts? The Retail Business Resource Center offers theme-oriented live business chats, live workshops, and even a business therapist offering real-world solutions to real-world problems.

Small Business Innovative Research

http://www.sbir.dsu.edu/

Small Business Innovative Research is a federally supported program aimed at funding small businesses with money from Federal agency and department's R&D divisions. This site assists small companies in applying for that funding by answering questions and providing online tests.

SOHO America

http://www.soho.org/

SOHO America is a small business benefits association. In addition to news of interest to the small office/home office market, this site offers a comprehensive list of health benefits, business tools, and personal discounts available to members.

Your Small Office

http://www.smalloffice.com/

This site is the online presence of *Small Office Computing* and *Home Office Computing* magazines and features articles from those magazines. The Web site visitor will find a great number of reviews of network, computer, and office equipment as well as a full "How To" department covering everything from Startup to Sales and Marketing.

U.S. Chamber of Commerce Small Business Institute

http://www.uschamber.org/programs/sbi/index.html

The U.S. Chamber of Commerce runs a Small Business Institute with a variety of resources both for free and for sale. There are self-study programs on Mastering Your Business on the Internet and the Small Business Institute Series, as well as information on the SOHO Conference.

App
B

Travel and Transportation

Airlines of the Web

http://w2.itn.net/airlines/

Where can you find a listing of *all* the airlines, both passenger and cargo? At the Airlines of the Web site, of course. Passenger airlines are categorized by region, and you can also find airline-related information like 800 numbers and a link to a real-time reservation service.

American Airlines

http://www.americanair.com/aa_home.htm

The American Access Web site takes a full-service approach. Here, you can plan your travel, check out Advantage frequent flier miles, take advantage of the NetSaver fares, and download Personal Access, American's Windows-based software program that brings you dedicated AAdvantage information, travel planning, and up-to-the-minute information and specials.

American Movers Conference

http://www.amconf.org/

The American Movers Conference is an association of 3,000 professional moving companies in the U.S. Their site has information on how to prepare your move, how much a "self-haul" might cost, and listings of movers across the country.

Continental Airlines

http://www.flycontinental.com:80/index.html

Continental On-Line's main claim to fame is its C.O.O.L. Travel Assistant, which can be used to schedule and book airline travel on Continental, Continental Express, and Continental Micronesia, as well as more than 40 rental car companies and 26,000 hotels around the world.

FedEx

http://www.fedex.com/

Not only can you now track your overnight package online, but you can also use their interactive rate finder, and even ship packages via the Internet to more than 160 countries from the U.S. and Canada. There's also a searchable database of drop-off locations and downloadable software for managing your shipping, including the airbill printing.

HomeBuyer's Fair

http://www.homefair.com/home/

While most of this site is dedicated to helping you buy or sell your home, the HomeBuyer's Fair has some amazing interactive tools in its Popular Exhibits area. There's a Salary

Calculator for comparing the cost of living in hundreds of U.S. and international cities, a Moving Calculator for figuring the cost of a move, and a Relocation Crime Lab for comparing crime statistics.

InterKnowledge Travel Network

http://www.interknowledge.com/

When your business takes you to an exotic locale—meaning you've never been there before—stop by the InterKnowledge Travel Network site first. The site is characterized by beautiful images and full details on geography, culture, and climate.

Northwest Airlines

http://www.nwa.com/

This Northwest Airlines site has information on CyberSavers, their online low-cost tickets, as well as regular travel and frequent flier information. A full slate of vacation packages rounds out the site.

U.S. Air

http://www.usair.com/

Tune into the U.S. Air Web site to schedule and book a flight or check your frequent flyer miles. An extensive area of the site is devoted to its U.S. Airways Cargo service where you can use the software to track shipments with real-time information from airport drop-off to pickup.

United Parcel Service

http://www.ups.com/

Interactive functions featured at the UPS site include package tracking, cost-estimating, a drop-off locator, and pick-up scheduling. UPS also makes available free software for all of these functions, as well as up-to-the-minute zone and rate charts.

Trade Shows and Conferences

EXPOguide

http://www.expoguide.com/

If you're thinking about selling your product through a trade show, stop by this site first. It has a full listing of trade shows, conferences, and exhibitions, as well as comprehensive coverage of show services and associations. Although primarily intended for trade show managers, there's still plenty of information here for exhibiting companies.

CD Information

http://www.cd-info.com/CDIC/Industry/TradeShows.html

Today, much of computing and information storage and retrieval revolves around the CD-ROM. This site is CD-centric and lists many upcoming exhibitions, conferences, seminars, and workshops in a month-by-month format.

Guide to Unique Meeting Facilities

http://www.theguide.com/

A terrific resource for meeting planners, The Guide to Unique Meeting Facilities covers colleges and universities, retreat centers, camps and lodges, and cultural and historical venues, as well as traditional conference centers. There is also a Hot Date/Cool Rate area to highlight facilities with open, economical dates.

Major Trade Shows in Asia

http://www.tdb.gov.sg/trshow/tr_menu.html

You can start your search for Asian trade shows here, either by country, industry, or date. Fourteen countries, including Brunei, China, Japan, South Korea, and Vietnam, and more than 25 different industries are covered.

Trade Show Central

http://www.tscentral.com/

Sponsored by the International Association for Exhibition Management, Trade Show Central gives you easy access to information on more than 30,000 trade shows. Its searchable database links to an e-mail notification service where you can request more information. Its AudioNet connection broadcasts and archives keynote speeches from major events.

Wall Street Directory

http://www.wsdinc.com/index.html

Wall Street Directory offers a wide range of information for traders and investors. To see its up-to-the-minute conference information, select the Seminars-Shows-Conventions category and click the Search by Category button.

Small Business Administration Upcoming Events

http://www.sbaonline.sba.gov/gc/events.html

Organized on a monthly basis, the SBA keeps a listing of many business-related seminars and conferences. Although not hot-linked, all conferences have telephone contact information. Free seminars are prominently noted.

EventWeb

http://www.eventweb.com/

A free mailing list service for meeting, conference, and trade show promoters. Sample articles include "How to Exhibit at a Virtual Trade Show," "Expanding Educational Horizons in the Online World," and "Promote Your Speakers—Inexpensively!"

Tradeshow News Network

http://www.tsnn.com/

The Tradeshow News Network allows you to search for a trade show in the U.S. by location, date, or industry. Its Trade Show Education department offers tips on both exhibiting and attending, as well as an Ask the Expert section.

Virtual Online Trade Show

http://www.volts.com/

This site promotes the Virtual Trade Show concept, and is aimed at both exhibition managers and exhibitors. Exhibitors can see how they can save money, broaden their exposure, and communicate with their customers. ●

Index

Symbols

Web toolbar, 19, 886-887

WebPrinter (CD-ROM), 1190

what-if scenarios (worksheets), 414-415

While You Were Out forms (Outlook), 874

Widow/Orphan control, 104

Window menu commands

Check out Que® Books on the World Wide Web
http://www.quecorp.com

As the biggest software release in computer history, Windows 95 continues to redefine the computer industry. Click here for the latest info on our Windows 95 books

Make computing quick and easy with these products designed exclusively for new and casual users

Examine the latest releases in word processing, spreadsheets, operating systems, and suites

The Internet, The World Wide Web, CompuServe®, America Online®, Prodigy®—it's a world of ever-changing information. Don't get left behind!

Find out about new additions to our site, new bestsellers and hot topics

In-depth information on high-end topics: find the best reference books for databases, programming, networking, and client/server technologies

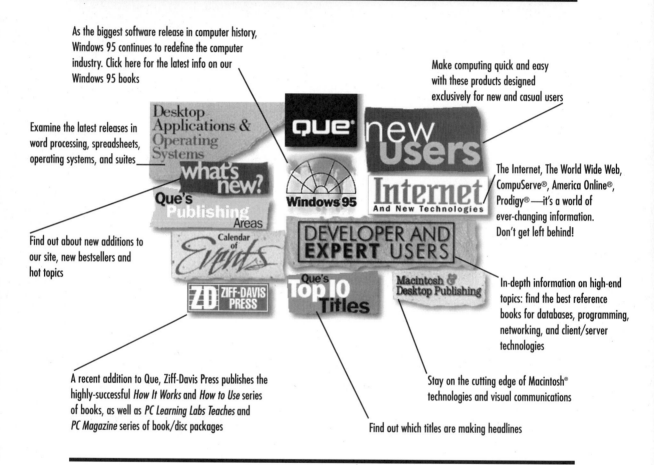

A recent addition to Que, Ziff-Davis Press publishes the highly-successful *How It Works* and *How to Use* series of books, as well as *PC Learning Labs Teaches* and *PC Magazine* series of book/disc packages

Stay on the cutting edge of Macintosh® technologies and visual communications

Find out which titles are making headlines

With 6 separate publishing groups, Que develops products for many specific market segments and areas of computer technology. Explore our Web Site and you'll find information on best-selling titles, newly published titles, upcoming products, authors, and much more.

- Stay informed on the latest industry trends and products available
- Visit our online bookstore for the latest information and editions
- Download software from Que's library of the best shareware and freeware

Complete and Return this Card
for a *FREE* Computer Book Catalog

Thank you for purchasing this book! You have purchased a superior computer book written expressly for your needs. To continue to provide the kind of up-to-date, pertinent coverage you've come to expect from us, we need to hear from you. Please take a minute to complete and return this self-addressed, postage-paid form. In return, we'll send you a free catalog of all our computer books on topics ranging from word processing to programming and the internet.

Mr. ☐   Mrs. ☐   Ms. ☐   Dr. ☐

Name (first) ☐☐☐☐☐☐☐☐☐☐☐   (M.I.) ☐   (last) ☐☐☐☐☐☐☐☐☐☐☐☐☐☐

Address ☐☐☐☐☐☐☐☐☐☐☐☐☐☐☐☐☐☐☐☐☐☐☐☐☐☐

City ☐☐☐☐☐☐☐☐☐☐   State ☐☐   Zip ☐☐☐☐☐ ☐☐☐☐

Phone ☐☐☐ ☐☐☐ ☐☐☐☐   Fax ☐☐☐ ☐☐☐ ☐☐☐☐

Company Name ☐☐☐☐☐☐☐☐☐☐☐☐☐☐☐☐☐☐☐☐☐☐☐

E-mail address ☐☐☐☐☐☐☐☐☐☐☐☐☐☐☐☐☐☐☐☐☐☐☐☐

1. Please check at least (3) influencing factors for purchasing this book.

Front or back cover information on book .... ☐
Special approach to the content .... ☐
Completeness of content... ☐
Author's reputation .... ☐
Publisher's reputation .... ☐
Book cover design or layout .... ☐
Index or table of contents of book .... ☐
Price of book.. ☐
Special effects, graphics, illustrations .... ☐
Other (Please specify): _____ ☐

2. How did you first learn about this book?

Saw in Macmillan Computer Publishing catalog .... ☐
Recommended by store personnel .... ☐
Saw the book on bookshelf at store .... ☐
Recommended by a friend .... ☐
Received advertisement in the mail .... ☐
Saw an advertisement in: _____ ☐
Read book review in: _____ ☐
Other (Please specify): _____ ☐

3. How many computer books have you purchased in the last six months?

This book only .... ☐   3 to 5 books .... ☐
2 books.................. ☐   More than 5 .... ☐

4. Where did you purchase this book?

Bookstore .... ☐
Computer Store .... ☐
Consumer Electronics Store .... ☐
Department Store .... ☐
Office Club .... ☐
Warehouse Club .... ☐
Mail Order .... ☐
Direct from Publisher .... ☐
Internet site .... ☐
Other (Please specify): _____ ☐

5. How long have you been using a computer?

☐ Less than 6 months   ☐ 6 months to a year
☐ 1 to 3 years   ☐ More than 3 years

6. What is your level of experience with personal computers and with the subject of this book?

	With PCs	With subject of book
New	☐	☐
Casual	☐	☐
Accomplished	☐	☐
Expert	☐	☐

Source Code ISBN: 0-7897-1396-9

7. Which of the following best describes your job title?

Administrative Assistant .... ☐
Coordinator .... ☐
Manager/Supervisor .... ☐
Director .... ☐
Vice President .... ☐
President/CEO/COO .... ☐
Lawyer/Doctor/Medical Professional .... ☐
Teacher/Educator/Trainer .... ☐
Engineer/Technician .... ☐
Consultant .... ☐
Not employed/Student/Retired .... ☐
Other (Please specify): _____ ☐

8. Which of the following best describes the area of the company your job title falls under?

Accounting .... ☐
Engineering .... ☐
Manufacturing .... ☐
Operations .... ☐
Marketing .... ☐
Sales .... ☐
Other (Please specify): _____ ☐

9. What is your age?

Under 20 .... ☐
21-29 .... ☐
30-39 .... ☐
40-49 .... ☐
50-59 .... ☐
60-over .... ☐

10. Are you:

Male .... ☐
Female .... ☐

11. Which computer publications do you read regularly? (Please list)

_____
_____
_____
_____
_____
_____
_____
_____
_____
_____
_____

Comments: _____
_____
_____

Fold here and scotch-tape to mail.

SOLVE YOUR BUSINESS PROBLEMS

If you need the right tool for your business task, go to the experts Microsoft chose to create their sample Excel applications. And it's not just Excel expertise--Village Software has authored Que book sections covering VBA (and VBScript) development across the rest of Office, too. Village Software's pre-built Business Solutions unlock the value of Microsoft Office for your company. For some free Village Software FastStart products, see the CD-ROM accompanying this book. For other great Village Software products, visit our website.

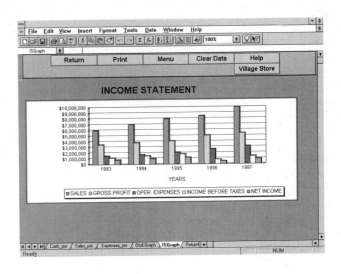

Our products are Microsoft Office Compatible, so you know they'll behave reliably. Our network of business experts also provides the in-depth knowledge necessary to create tools that will work for *your* business.

CUSTOM PROGRAMMING FROM INDUSTRY EXPERTS

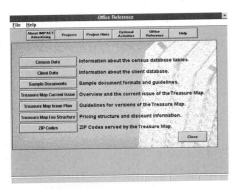

Village Software also provides custom development services. Our clients range from Fortune 500 clients to small businesses, and include projects such as automated intranet-based sales reporting for world-wide enterprises, financial systems in Excel and Access, and automated contact management in Outlook. To request a quote for a custom job, visit Village Software's customization website at www.villagesoft.com/custom.

Special prices for Que book readers!

VILLAGE SOFTWARE®

HTTP://WWW.VILLAGESOFT.COM/QUE

Licensing Agreement

By opening this package, you are agreeing to be bound by the following: